Fodor's 99

Caribbean

The complete guide, thoroughly up-to-date

Packed with details that will make your trip

The must-see sights, off and on the beaten path

What to see, what to skip

Beach strolls, countryside adventures, and town tours

Smart lodging and dining options

Essential local do's and taboos

Transportation tips, distances and directions

Key contacts, savvy travel tips

When to go, what to pack

Clear, accurate, easy-to-use maps

Fodor's Travel Publications, Inc.
New York • Toronto • London • Sydney • Auckland
www.fodors.com

Fodor's Caribbean

Editor: Laura M. Kidder

Editorial Contributors: Pamela Acheson, Carla Amour Hutchinson, Carol Bareuther, John Bigley, David Brown, Caroline V. Haberfeld, Anto Howard, David H. Jones, Christina Knight, Lynda Lohr, Karl Luntta, JoAnn Milivojevic, Paris Permenter, Eileen Robinson-Smith, Helayne Schiff, M. T. Schwartzman (Gold Guide editor), Jordan Simon, Jane E. Zarem

Editorial Production: Stacey Kulig

Maps: David Lindroth, *cartographer;* Steven Amsterdam and Robert Blake, *map editors*

Design: Fabrizio La Rocca, *creative director;* Guido Caroti, *associate art director;* Jolie Novak, *photo editor*

Production/Manufacturing: Mike Costa

Cover Photograph: Peter Guttman

Copyright

Special Sales

Fodor's Travel Publications are available at special discounts for bulk purchases for sales promotions or premiums. Special editions, including personalized covers, excerpts of existing guides, and corporate imprints, can be created in large quantities for special needs. For more information, contact your local bookseller or write to Special Markets, Fodor's Travel Publications, 201 East 50th Street, New York, NY 10022. Inquiries from Canada should be directed to your local Canadian bookseller or sent to Random House of Canada, Ltd., Marketing Department, 2775 Matheson Boulevard East, Mississauga, Ontario L4W 4P7. Inquiries from the United Kingdom should be sent to Fodor's Travel Publications, 20 Vauxhall Bridge Road, London SW1V 2SA, England.

PRINTED IN THE UNITED STATES OF AMERICA

10 9 8 7 6 5 4 3 2 1

CONTENTS

On the Road with Fodor's vi

About Our Writers *vi*
Connections *vii*
How to Use This Book *vii*
Don't Forget to Write *viii*

The Gold Guide xii

1 Destination: Caribbean 1

The Many Faces of the Islands *2*
New and Noteworthy *3*
What's Where *6*
Pleasures and Pastimes *6*
Fodor's Choice *10*

2 Anguilla 13

3 Antigua 34

4 Aruba 62

5 Barbados 89

6 Bonaire 124

7 British Virgin Islands 148

8 Cayman Islands 188

9 Curaçao 214

10 Dominica 239

11 Dominican Republic 264

12 Grenada 302

13 Guadeloupe 332

14 Jamaica 362

15 Martinique 404

16 Puerto Rico 434

17   Saba   473

18   St. Barthélemy   487

19   St. Eustatius   509

20   St. Kitts and Nevis   521

21   St. Lucia   556

22   St. Martin/St. Maarten   589

23   St. Vincent and the Grenadines   616

24   Trinidad and Tobago   654

25   Turks and Caicos Islands   686

26   U.S. Virgin Islands   706

     Index   786

Maps and Plans

The Caribbean x–xi
Island Finder 4–5
Anguilla 16–17
Antigua (and Barbuda) 36–37
Aruba 64–65
Barbados 92–93
Bridgetown 114
Bonaire 126–127
British Virgin Islands 150–151
Tortola 154–155
Virgin Gorda 170–171
Grand Cayman 190
Cayman Brac and Little Cayman 191
Curaçao 218–219
Willemstad 231
Dominica 242–243
Dominican Republic 268–269
Santo Domingo 289
Grenada (and Carriacou) 306–307
Guadeloupe 336–337
Jamaica 366–367
Montego Bay Dining and Lodging 370

Martinique 406–407
San Juan Exploring, Dining, and Lodging 437
Puerto Rico 442–443
Old San Juan Exploring 459
Saba 476–477
St. Barthélemy 490–491
St. Eustatius 512–513
St. Kitts 524–525
Nevis 540–541
St. Lucia 560–561
St. Martin/St. Maarten 592–593
St. Vincent 620–621
The Grenadines 634–635
Trinidad 656–657
Tobago 670–671
Turks and Caicos Islands 690–691
U.S. Virgin Islands 708–709
St. Thomas 714–715
Charlotte Amalie 735
St. Croix 742–743
St. John 762–763

ON THE ROAD WITH FODOR'S

WHEN I PLAN A VACATION, the first thing I do is cast around among my friends and colleagues to find someone who's just been where I'm going. That's because there's no substitute for a recommendation from a good friend who knows your tastes, your budget, and your circumstances, someone who's just been there. Unfortunately, such friends are few and far between. So it's nice to know that there's *Fodor's Caribbean*.

In the first place, this book won't stay home when you hit the road. It will accompany you every step of the way, steering you away from wrong turns and wrong choices and never expecting a thing in return. It includes a wonderful, full-color map from Rand McNally, the world's largest commercial mapmaker. Most important of all, it's written and assiduously updated by the kind of people you *would* hit up for travel tips if you knew them. They're as choosy as your pickiest friend, except they've probably seen a lot more of the Caribbean. In these pages, they don't send you chasing down every town and sight on the islands but have instead selected the best sights, the ones that are worthy of your time and money. Choosing an island is one of the first decisions you'll make, and to help you we've developed an "Island Finder" chart that gives you at-a-glance destination details. Will this be the vacation of your dreams? We hope so.

About Our Writers

Our success in achieving our goals—and in helping to make your trip the best of all possible vacations—is a credit to the hard work of our extraordinary writers.

Pamela Acheson spent 18 years in New York City as a publishing executive before heading south to divide her time between Florida and the Caribbean. She writes extensively about both areas and is a regular contributor to *Travel & Leisure, Caribbean Travel and Life, Florida Travel and Life, Fodor's Florida,* and *Fodor's Virgin Islands*. She is the author of *The Best of the British Virgin Islands* and *The Best of St. Thomas* and is currently working on *The Best of the Bahamas* and several Florida guides.

A native Dominican, **Carla Amour Hutchinson** has worked in the island's tourism industry for 25 years and has traveled throughout the Caribbean. A natural artist, Carla studied at the Parsons School of Design and is one of Dominica's foremost painters and writers. She runs her own art gallery and is the president of the island's Society for Historic Architectural Preservation and Enhancement and vice president of the Dominica Writers' Guild. She hopes that her work on the Dominica chapter will enable you to have an authentic island experience should you visit the slice of paradise that she calls home.

St. Thomas–based writer and dietitian **Carol M. Bareuther** publishes two weekly columns on food, cooking, and nutrition in the *Virgin Islands Daily News* and serves as the USVI stringer for the Reuters News Service International. She also writes about sports and travel for *Islands' Nautical Scene, Caribbean Week, Tropic Times,* the *Virgin Islands Business Journal,* and other publications. She's the author of two books, *Sports Fishing in the Virgin Islands* and *Virgin Islands Cooking.*

David H. Jones has lived and worked in the United States, Canada, South America, France, Japan, and Hong Kong. In previous professional lives, he has been President/CEO of the New Orleans Chamber of Commerce, Director of the Louisiana Film Commission, and a writer/producer for the Fox Network in Los Angeles. You can currently find him in New Orleans, where he edits the magazine, *Offbeat.*

Lynda Lohr spent the last 14 years as a St. John resident, much of it swimming at her favorite Hawksnest Beach. She's a veteran mainland and U.S. Virgin Islands journalist who works regularly for local, regional, and national publications. She lives with her cat and her boyfriend in a tiny cottage overlooking Cruz Bay.

Before settling back home in Cape Cod, **Karl Luntta** spent 12 years living and working in Africa, the South Pacific, and the Caribbean. Now a full-time travel writer, he's the author of *Jamaica Handbook, Caribbean Handbook,* and *Virgin Islands Handbook,* and *Caribbean: The Lesser Antilles.* He has contributed many articles and photographs to publications such as *Caribbean Travel and Life, Cape Cod Life,* and the *Boston Globe.* He has also published fiction and is a humor columnist with the *Cape Cod Times.*

JoAnn Milivojevic is a freelance writer and video producer based in Illinois, whose love affair with the Caribbean began 10 years ago while scuba diving in the Turks and Caicos Islands. She has produced video programs on the Cayman Islands and St. Kitts and Nevis; her articles on the Caribbean have appeared in publications nationwide. She travels regularly to the islands to "wine her waist" to *soca* music, collect folktales, and dive the salty blue.

After honeymooning in Jamaica a dozen years ago, **Paris Permenter** and **John Bigley** decided to specialize in writing about and photographing the Caribbean region. They're authors of *Caribbean with Kids, Caribbean for Lovers, Adventure Guide to the Cayman Islands,* and *Adventure Guide to the Leeward Islands.* Their work has appeared in publications nationwide. From their home base in Texas, they've also contributed to Fodor's *The Southwest's Best Bed and Breakfasts.*

Hurricane Marilyn blew **Eileen Robinson-Smith** out of the Caribbean and back to her lakeside home in Charleston, South Carolina. For the previous two years she lived in St. John and wrote the travel section and chef's column for *The Virgin Island Journal.* Before that she lived in St. Thomas, St. Croix, and Tortola, where she was the features editor of *The Virgin Islander.* As a travel editor, she has visited many other Caribbean islands, and her articles on food and travel have appeared in local, regional, and national publications including *Caribbean Travel & Life.*

Jordan Simon has visited nearly every speck of land in the Caribbean for Fodor's, *Caribbean Travel & Life, Modern Bride, Physicians Travel & Meeting Guide, Travel*

& Leisure, and *Travelage.* He is the author of *Fodor's Colorado, Fodor's Branson,* and the *USA Today Ski Atlas,* among others.

Jane Zarem is a freelance writer from Connecticut who travels frequently to the Caribbean. Among the score of islands she has explored, she finds it difficult to pick a favorite—she loves them all. She is a member of the New York Travel Writers' Association and the International Food, Wine & Travel Writers' Association, and has contributed to numerous Fodor's guides, among them *New England, USA, Cape Cod, Bahamas,* and *Great American Sports and Adventure Vacations.*

Connections

We're pleased that the American Society of Travel Agents continues to endorse Fodor's as its guidebook of choice. ASTA is the world's largest and most influential travel trade association, operating in more than 170 countries, with 27,000 members pledged to adhere to a strict code of ethics reflecting the Society's motto, "Integrity in Travel." ASTA shares Fodor's devotion to providing smart, honest travel information and advice to travelers, and we've long recommended that our readers—even those who have guidebooks and traveling friends—consult ASTA member agents for the experience and professionalism they bring to your vacation planning.

On Fodor's Web site (www.fodors.com), check out the new Resource Center, an online companion to the Gold Guide section of this book, complete with useful hot links to related sites. In our forums, you can also get lively advice from other travelers and more great tips from Fodor's experts worldwide.

How to Use This Book

Organization

Up front is the **Gold Guide,** an easy-to-use section divided alphabetically by topic. Under each listing you'll find tips, addresses, and phone numbers of organizations and companies that offer destination-related services and detailed information and publications.

The first chapter in the guide, **Destination: Caribbean,** helps get you in the mood for your trip. New and Noteworthy cues you in on trends and happenings, What's Where gets you oriented, Pleasures and Pastimes describes the activities and sights that really make the Caribbean unique, an Island Finder chart helps you compare qualities of all the islands, and Fodor's Choice showcases our top picks.

Chapters in this book are listed alphabetically by island; each island's section covers lodging, dining, beaches, outdoor activities and sports, shopping, nightlife and the arts, exploring, and ends with a section called A to Z, which tells you how to get there and get around and gives you important local addresses and phone numbers.

Icons and Symbols

★   Our special recommendations
✕   Restaurant
🏨   Lodging establishment
⚑   Campgrounds
🐥   Good for kids (rubber duckie)
☞   Sends you to another section for more information (in a hotel or restaurant review, it often refers you to a review elsewhere in the dining or lodging sections)
✉   Address
☎   Telephone number
🕐   Opening and closing times
💰   Admission prices (those we give apply to adults; substantially reduced fees are almost always available for children, students, and senior citizens)

Hotel Facilities

We always list the facilities that are available—but we don't specify whether they cost extra: When pricing accommodations, always ask what's included. In addition, assume that all rooms have private baths unless otherwise noted.

At the end of each review, we list the meal plans the hotel offers: **All-inclusive** (all meals and most activities), **Breakfast Plan** (BP, with a full breakfast daily), **Continental Plan** (CP, with a Continental breakfast daily), **European Plan** (EP, with no meals), **Full American Plan** (FAP, with all meals), or **Modified American Plan** (MAP, with breakfast and dinner daily). The FAP may be ideal if you're on a budget, but if you enjoy a different dining experience each night, it's better to book rooms on the EP. Since some hotels insist on the MAP, particularly in high season, find out whether you can exchange dinner for lunch or for meals at neighboring hotels.

Caribbean Addresses

"Whimsical" might best describe Caribbean addresses. Streets change name for no apparent reason, maps and signage aren't always reliable, and many buildings have no numbers. We've tried to supply cross streets, landmarks, and other directionals throughout. But to find your destination, you may have to ask a local—and be prepared for such directions as "Take a right at the fish market, then a left where you see the cow pasture." For information on writing to establishments on the islands, *see* Telephones and Mail *in* the A to Z section at the end of each chapter.

Restaurant Reservations and Dress Codes

Reservations are always a good idea; we note only when they're essential or when they're not accepted. Book as far ahead as you can, and be sure to reconfirm. Unless otherwise noted, the restaurants listed are open daily for lunch and dinner. We mention dress only when men must wear a jacket or a jacket and tie. Look for an overview in the What to Wear sections of the dining introductions for each island.

Credit Cards

The following abbreviations are used: **AE,** American Express; **D,** Discover; **DC,** Diners Club; **MC,** MasterCard; and **V,** Visa.

Don't Forget to Write

You can use this book in the confidence that all prices and opening times are based on information supplied to us at press time; Fodor's cannot accept responsibility for any errors. Time inevitably brings changes, so always confirm information when it matters—especially if you're making a detour to visit a specific place.

Were the restaurants we recommended as described? Did our hotel picks exceed your expectations? Did you find a museum we recommended a waste of time? Keeping a travel guide fresh and up-to-date is a big job, and we welcome your feedback, positive *and* negative. If you have complaints, we'll look into them and revise our entries when the facts warrant it. If you've discovered a special place that we haven't included, we'll pass the information along to our correspondents and have them check it out. So send us your thoughts via e-mail at editors@fodors.com (specifying the name of the book on the subject line) or on paper in care of the Caribbean editor at Fodor's, 201 East 50th Street, New York, NY 10022. In the meantime, have a wonderful trip!

Karen Cure
Editorial Director

The Caribbean

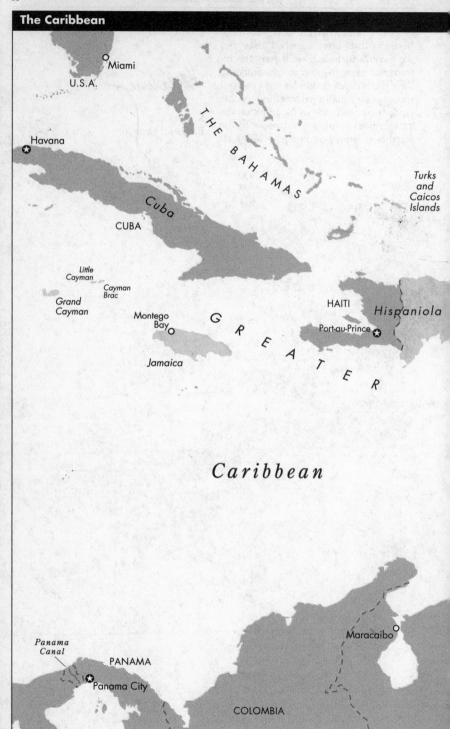

Miami
U.S.A.

Havana

THE BAHAMAS

Turks and Caicos Islands

Cuba

CUBA

Little Cayman

Cayman Brac

Grand Cayman

Montego Bay

GREATER

HAITI

Hispaniola

Port-au-Prince

Jamaica

Caribbean

Panama Canal

PANAMA

Panama City

COLOMBIA

Maracaibo

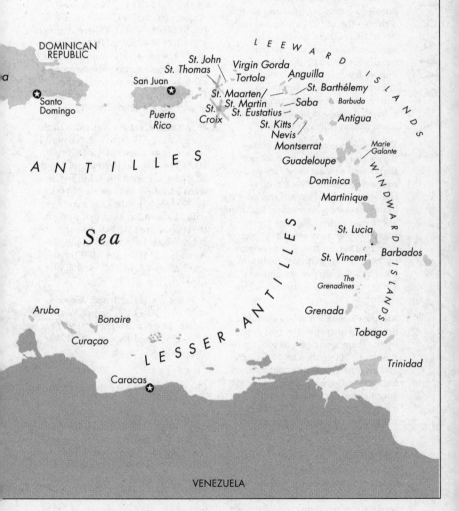

0   200 miles
0   300 km

N

ATLANTIC OCEAN

DOMINICAN
REPUBLIC

Santo
Domingo

San Juan

St. John
St. Thomas   Virgin Gorda
             Tortola   Anguilla
                                St. Barthélemy
St. Maarten/   Saba   Barbuda
St. Martin
St. Croix   St. Eustatius   Antigua
             St. Kitts
Puerto   Nevis
Rico   Montserrat
                              Marie
Guadeloupe   Galante

A N T I L L E S

Dominica

Martinique

Sea

St. Lucia

St. Vincent   Barbados

The
Grenadines

Aruba   Grenada
       Bonaire
Curaçao   Tobago

L E S S E R   A N T I L L E S   Trinidad

Caracas

L E E W A R D   I S L A N D S

W I N D W A R D   I S L A N D S

VENEZUELA

SMART TRAVEL TIPS A TO Z

*Basic Information on Traveling in the Caribbean,
Savvy Tips to Make Your Trip a Breeze, and
Companies and Organizations to Contact*

AIR TRAVEL

BOOKING YOUR FLIGHT

Price is just one factor to consider when booking a flight: frequency of service and even a carrier's safety record are often just as important. Major airlines offer the greatest number of departures. Smaller airlines—including regional and no-frills airlines—usually have a limited number of flights daily. On the other hand, so-called low-cost airlines usually are cheaper, and their fares impose fewer restrictions, such as advance-purchase requirements. Safety-wise, low-cost carriers as a group have a good history—about equal to that of major carriers.

When you book, **look for nonstop flights** and **remember that "direct" flights stop at least once.** Try to **avoid connecting flights,** which require a change of plane. Two airlines may jointly operate a connecting flight, so ask if your airline operates every segment—you may find that your preferred carrier flies you only part of the way. International flights on a country's flag carrier are almost always nonstop; U.S. airlines often fly direct.

Ask your airline if it offers electronic ticketing, which eliminates all paperwork. There's no ticket to pick up or misplace. You go directly to the gate and give the agent your confirmation number—a real blessing if you've lost your ticket or made last-minute changes in travel plans. There's no worry about waiting on line at the airport while precious minutes tick by.

CARRIERS

When flying internationally, you must usually choose between a domestic carrier, the national flag carrier of the country you're visiting, and a foreign carrier from a third country. National flag carriers have the greatest number

of nonstops. Domestic carriers may have better connections to your home town and serve a greater number of gateway cities. Third-party carriers may have a price advantage.

➤ MAJOR AIRLINES: **American Airlines** (☎ 800/433–7300), **Continental** (☎ 800/231–0856), **Delta** (☎ 800/241–4141), **Northwest Airlines** (☎ 800/447–4747), **TWA** (☎ 800/892–4141), **United Airlines** (☎ 800/538–2929), **US Airways** (☎ 800/842–5374). For island-specific information on and phone numbers for major airlines that serve the Caribbean, *see* the A to Z sections *in* individual island chapters.

➤ SMALLER AIRLINES: **American Eagle** (☎ 800/433–7300) to most islands via San Juan. **Carnival Air Lines** (☎ 800/824–7386) to Dominican Republic, Nassau, Puerto Rico. **LIAT** (Leeward Island Air Transport, ☎ 800/468–0482) to all the Lesser Antilles, with San Juan, St. Maarten, Antigua, St. Thomas, and Barbados its major hubs. **Winair** (Windward Island Airways, ☎ 800–634–4907) is a smaller, but still reliable version of LIAT.

➤ FROM THE U.K.: **British Airways** (☎ 0345/222–111). **British West Indian Airways** (BWIA; ☎ 0181/570–5552). **Caledonian** (☎ 01293/567–100).

CHARTERS

Charters usually have the lowest fares but are the least dependable. Departures are infrequent and seldom on time, flights can be delayed for up to 48 hours or can be canceled for any reason up to 10 days before you're scheduled to leave. Itineraries and prices can change after you've booked your flight.

In the U.S., the Department of Transportation's (DOT's) Aviation Consumer Protection Division has jurisdiction over charters and provides some protection. The DOT requires that money paid to charter operators be held in escrow, so if you can't pay with a credit card, **always make your check payable to a charter carrier's escrow account.** The name of the bank should be in the charter contract. If you have any problems with a charter operator, contact the DOT (☞ Airline Complaints, *below*). If you buy a charter package that includes both air and land arrangements, remember that the escrow requirement applies only to the air component.

CONSOLIDATORS

Consolidators buy tickets for scheduled international flights at reduced rates from the airlines, then sell them at prices that beat the best fare available directly from the airlines, usually without restrictions. Sometimes you can even get your money back if you need to return the ticket. Carefully read the fine print detailing penalties for changes and cancellations, and **confirm your consolidator reservation with the airline.**

➤ CONSOLIDATORS: **Cheap Tickets** (☎ 800/377–1000). **Up & Away Travel** (☎ 212/889–2345). **Discount Travel Network** (☎ 800/576–1600). **Unitravel** (☎ 800/325–2222). **World Travel Network** (☎ 800/409–6753).

COURIERS

When you fly as a courier, you trade your checked-luggage space for a ticket deeply subsidized by a courier service. It's all perfectly legitimate, but there are restrictions: You can usually book your flight only a week or two in advance, your length of stay may be set for a certain number of days, and you probably won't be able to book a companion on the same flight.

CUTTING COSTS

The least-expensive airfares to the Caribbean are priced for round-trip travel and usually must be purchased in advance. It's smart to **call a number of airlines, and when you're quoted a good price, book it on the spot**—the same fare may not be available the next day. Airlines gener-

ally allow you to change your return date for a fee. If you don't use your ticket, you can apply the cost toward the purchase of a new ticket, again for a small charge. However, most low-fare tickets are nonrefundable. To get the lowest airfare, **check different routings.** Compare prices of flights to and from different airports if your destination or home city has more than one gateway. Also price off-peak flights, which may be significantly less expensive.

Travel agents, especially those who specialize in finding the lowest fares (☞ Discounts & Deals, *below*), can be especially helpful when booking a plane ticket. When you're quoted a price, **ask your agent if the price is likely to get any lower.** Good agents know the seasonal fluctuations of airfares and can usually anticipate a sale or fare war. However, waiting can be risky: The fare could go *up* as seats become scarce, and you may wait so long that your preferred flight sells out. A wait-and-see strategy works best if your plans are flexible. If you must arrive and depart on certain dates, don't delay.

DISCOUNT PASSES

Regional airlines such as **LIAT** (☞ Carriers, *above*) have, in the past, offered special deals on flights between islands; inquire about them when you make reservations. Recently, **Air Jamaica** (☎ 800/523–5585) instituted an island-hopping program: If you stay over in Jamaica, you can fly to a second or even a third destination for free.

CHECK IN & BOARDING

Be sure to **reconfirm your flights on interisland carriers.** Passengers are often subject to their whim: If there are no other passengers on your flight, you may be requested (actually, ordered) to take a more convenient departure for the airline, or your plane may make unscheduled stops to pick up more clients or cargo. There are usually weight restrictions; if you don't travel light, you could be subject to outrageous surcharges. It's all part of the excitement—and unpredictability—of Caribbean travel.

THE GOLD GUIDE / SMART TRAVEL TIPS

Airlines routinely overbook planes, assuming that not everyone with a ticket will show up, but sometimes everyone does. When that happens, airlines ask for volunteers to give up their seats. In return these volunteers usually get a certificate for a free flight and are rebooked on the next flight out. If there aren't enough volunteers, the airline must choose who will be denied boarding. The first to get bumped are passengers who checked in late and those flying on discounted tickets, so **get to the gate, and check in as early as possible,** especially during peak periods.

Although the trend on international flights is to drop reconfirmation requirements, many airlines still ask you to reconfirm each leg of your international itinerary. Failure to do so may result in your reservation being canceled.

Always **bring a government-issued photo ID to the airport.** You may be asked to show it before you are allowed to check in.

ENJOYING THE FLIGHT

For more legroom, **request an emergency-aisle seat.** Don't sit in the row in front of the emergency aisle or in front of a bulkhead, where seats may not recline.

If you don't like airline food, **ask for special meals when booking.** These can be vegetarian, low-cholesterol, or kosher, for example.

When flying internationally, try to maintain a normal routine, to help fight jet-lag. At night, **get some sleep. By day, eat light meals, drink water (not alcohol), and move around the cabin** to stretch your legs.

Many carriers have prohibited smoking on all of their international flights; others allow smoking only on certain routes or certain departures, so **contact your carrier regarding its smoking policy.**

FLYING TIMES

The flying time from New York to San Juan, Puerto Rico, is 3½–4 hours; from Miami to San Juan it's 1½ hours. To Kingston or MoBay, Jamaica, flights from New York last about 3½ hours; those from Miami, about 1 hour. There are a few nonstop flights from London to Antigua and Barbados and from Paris to Guadeloupe, Martinique, and St. Martin—flying times are about 5–7 hours. Once you've arrived in the Caribbean, flight times between the islands range from 20 minutes to 2 hours.

HOW TO COMPLAIN

If your baggage goes astray or your flight goes awry, complain right away. Most carriers require that you **file a claim immediately.**

➤ AIRLINE COMPLAINTS: DOT Aviation Consumer Protection Division (✉ C-75, Room 4107, Washington, DC 20590, ☎ 202/366–2220). **Federal Aviation Administration (FAA) Consumer Hotline** (☎ 800/322–7873).

AIRPORTS

For information on airports, *see* the A to Z sections *in* individual island chapters.

BIKES IN FLIGHT

Most airlines will accommodate bikes as luggage, provided they're dismantled and put into a box. Call to see if your airline sells bike boxes (about $5; bike bags are at least $100) although you can often pick them up free at bike shops. International travelers can sometimes substitute a bike for a piece of checked luggage for free; otherwise, it will cost about $100. Domestic and Canadian airlines charge a $25–$50 fee.

CAMERAS & COMPUTERS

EQUIPMENT PRECAUTIONS

Always **keep your film, tape, or computer disks out of the sun.** Carry an extra supply of batteries, and **be prepared to turn on your camera, camcorder, or laptop** to prove to security personnel that the device is real. Always **ask for hand inspection of film,** which becomes clouded after successive exposure to airport X-ray machines, and **keep videotapes and computer disks away from metal detectors.**

TRAVEL PHOTOGRAPHY

Capturing frothy waves and palm-lined crescents on film is relatively easy if you keep a few thoughts in mind. **Don't let the brightness of the sun on sand and water fool your light meter.** You'll need to compensate or else work early or late in the day when the light isn't as harsh and contrast isn't such a problem. Try to **capture expansive views;** use a wide-angle lens, and look for vistas where the sea draws your eye into a scene. Consider shooting down onto the shore from a clearing on a hillside or from a rock on the beach.

➤ PHOTO HELP: **Kodak Information Center** (☎ 800/242–2424). **Kodak Guide to Shooting Great Travel Pictures,** available in bookstores or from Fodor's Travel Publications (☎ 800/ 533–6478; $16.50 plus $4 shipping).

CAR RENTAL

For information on car-rental agencies and costs in the Caribbean, see the A to Z sections in individual island chapters.

CUTTING COSTS

To get the best deal, **book through a travel agent who is willing to shop around.**

Also **ask your travel agent about a company's customer-service record.** How has the company responded to late plane arrivals and vehicle mishaps? Are there often lines at the rental counter? If you're traveling during a holiday period, does a confirmed reservation guarantee you a car?

Be sure to **look into wholesalers,** companies that do not own fleets but rent in bulk from those that do and often offer better rates than traditional car-rental operations. Prices are best during off-peak periods. Rentals booked through wholesalers must be paid for before you leave the United States.

➤ RENTAL WHOLESALERS: **Auto Europe** (☎ 207/842–2000 or 800/223–5555, FAX 800–235–6321). **Kemwel Holiday Autos** (☎ 914/835–5555 or 800/678–0678, FAX 914/835–5126).

INSURANCE

When driving a rented car you're generally responsible for any damage to or loss of the vehicle. You also are liable for any property damage or personal injury that you may cause while driving. Before you rent, **see what coverage you already have** under the terms of your personal auto-insurance policy and credit cards.

REQUIREMENTS

A standard U.S., Canadian, or British license is usually sufficient. For specific driving requirements, see the A to Z sections in individual island chapters.

SURCHARGES

Before you pick up a car in one city and leave it in another, **ask about drop-off charges or one-way service fees,** which can be substantial. Note, too, that some rental agencies charge extra if you return the car before the time specified in your contract. To avoid a hefty refueling fee, **fill the tank just before you turn in the car,** but be aware that gas stations near the rental outlet may overcharge.

CHILDREN & TRAVEL

CHILDREN IN THE CARIBBEAN

Caribbean islands and their resorts are increasingly sensitive to families' needs. Many now have children's programs. Baby food is easy to find, but outside major hotels you may not find such items as high chairs and cribs. When choosing a destination, **consider whether or not English is spoken widely;** the language barrier can frustrate children.

Be sure to plan ahead and **involve your youngsters** as you outline your trip. When packing, include things to keep them busy en route. On sightseeing days try to schedule activities of special interest to your children. If you're renting a car don't forget to **arrange for a car seat** when you reserve.

FLYING

If your children are two or older, **ask about children's airfares.** As a rule, infants under two not occupying a seat fly at greatly reduced fares or even for free.

In general the adult baggage allowance applies to children paying half or more of the adult fare. When booking, **ask about carry-on allowances for those traveling with infants.** In general, for babies charged 10% of the adult fare you're allowed one carry-on bag and a collapsible stroller, which may have to be checked; you may be limited to less if the flight is full.

Experts agree that it's a good idea to use safety seats aloft for children weighing less than 40 pounds. Airlines, however, can set their own policies: U.S. carriers allow FAA-approved models but usually require that you buy a ticket, even if your child would otherwise ride free, since the seats must be strapped into regular seats. Airline rules vary, so it's important to **check your airline's policy about using safety seats during takeoff and landing.** Safety seats cannot obstruct the movement of other passengers in the row, so get an appropriate seat assignment as early as possible.

When making your reservation, **request children's meals or a free-standing bassinet** if you need them; the latter are available only to those seated at the bulkhead, where there's enough legroom. Remember, however, that bulkhead seats may not have their own overhead bins, and there's no storage space in front of you—a major inconvenience.

GROUP TRAVEL

When planning to take your kids on a tour, look for companies that specialize in family travel.

➤ FAMILY-FRIENDLY TOUR OPERATORS: **Families Welcome!** (⊠ 92 N. Main St., Ashland, OR 97520, ☎ 541/482–6121 or 800/326–0724, FAX 541/482–0660). **Rascals in Paradise** (⊠ 650 5th St., Suite 505, San Francisco, CA 94107, ☎ 415/978–9800 or 800/872–7225, FAX 415/442–0289).

LODGING

Children are welcome in all except the most exclusive resorts; many hotels allow children under 12 or 16 to stay free in their parents' room (be sure to **ask the cutoff age** when booking). In addition, several hotel chains have children's programs, and many hotels and resorts arrange for baby-sitting. Do your research before going. While "kiddie camps" have become the norm in major resorts, some offer far more facilities than others. Most will remind you of kindergarten, with Disney videos, building blocks, brightly colored walls, milk and cookies, and little else. But more innovative programs will include island jaunts, ecological awareness studies, and fun, informative classes in local culture and cuisine (hair-braiding, reggae, folktales, and how to cook jerk on Jamaica, for example). Also **consider apartment and villa rentals** (☞ Lodging, *below*). When you book, be sure to **ask about the availability of baby-sitters, housekeepers, and medical facilities.** *See* Fodor's Choice, Hotels for Families, *in* Chapter 1 for specific recommendations.

CONSUMER PROTECTION

Whenever possible, **pay with a major credit card** so you can cancel payment or get reimbursed if there's a problem, provided that you can provide documentation. This is the best way to pay, whether you're buying travel arrangements before your trip or shopping at your destination.

If you're doing business with a particular company for the first time, **contact your local Better Business Bureau and the attorney general's offices** in your state and the company's home state, as well. Have any complaints been filed?

Finally, if you're buying a package or tour, always **consider travel insurance** that includes default coverage (☞ Insurance, *below*).

➤ LOCAL BBBs: **Council of Better Business Bureaus** (⊠ 4200 Wilson Blvd., Suite 800, Arlington, VA 22203, ☎ 703/276–0100, FAX 703/525–8277).

CRUISE TRAVEL

Cruising the Caribbean is perhaps the most relaxed and convenient way to tour this beautiful part of the world: You get all of the amenities of a Stateside hotel and enough activities to guarantee fun, even on rainy days.

Cruising through the islands is an entirely different experience from staying on one island.

Cruise ships usually call at several Caribbean ports on a single voyage but are at each port for only one night. Thus, although you may be exposed to several islands, you don't get much of a feel for any one of them.

As a vacation, a cruise offers total peace of mind. All important decisions are made long before boarding. The itinerary is set, and the total cost of your vacation is known almost to the penny. For details, see *Best Cruises '99*; the Cruise Primer chapter is particularly helpful if you're cruising for the first time.

To get the best deal on a cruise, **consult a cruise-only travel agency.**

➤ ORGANIZATIONS: To find out which ships are sailing where and when they depart, contact the **Caribbean Tourism Organization** (✉ 20 E. 46th St., 4th floor, New York, NY 10017, ☎ 212/682–0435). The **Cruise Lines International Association** (CLIA) publishes a useful pamphlet titled "Cruising Answers to Your Questions"; to order a copy send a self-addressed business-size envelope with 52¢ postage to CLIA (✉ 500 5th Ave., Suite 1407, New York, NY 10110).

➤ CRUISE LINES: **American Canadian Caribbean Line** (✉ Box 368, Warren, RI 02885, ☎ 401/247–0955 or 800/556–7450). **Carnival Cruise Lines** (✉ Carnival Pl., 3655 N.W. 87th Ave., Miami, FL 33178, ☎ 305/599–2600). **Celebrity Cruises** (✉ 5200 Blue Lagoon Dr., Miami, FL 33126, ☎ 800/437–3111). **Clipper Cruise Line** (✉ 7711 Bonhomme Ave., St. Louis, MO 63105, ☎ 800/325–0010). **Club Med** (✉ 40 W. 57th St., New York, NY 10019, ☎ 800/258–2633). **Commodore Cruise Line** (✉ 800 Douglas Rd., Coral Gables, FL 33134, ☎ 305/529–3000). **Costa Cruise Lines** (✉ World Trade Center, 80 S.W. 8th St., Miami, FL 33130, ☎ 800/462–6782). **Crystal Cruises** (✉ 2121 Ave. of the Stars, Los Angeles, CA 90067, ☎ 800/446–6620). **Cunard Line** (✉ 555 5th Ave., New York, NY 10017, ☎ 800/221–4770). **Dolphin/Majesty Cruise Lines** (✉ 901 South American Way,

Miami, FL 33132, ☎ 800/532–7788). **Holland America Line** (✉ 300 Elliott Ave. W, Seattle, WA 98119, ☎ 800/426–0327). **Norwegian Cruise Line** (✉ 95 Merrick Way, Coral Gables, FL 33134, ☎ 800/327–7030). **Premier Cruise Line** (✉ Box 517, Cape Canaveral, FL 32920, ☎ 800/473–3262). **Princess Cruises** (✉ 10100 Santa Monica Blvd., Los Angeles, CA 90067, ☎ 310/553–1770). **Radisson Seven Seas Cruises** (✉ 600 Corporate Dr., Suite 410, Fort Lauderdale, FL 33334, ☎ 800/333–3333). **Renaissance Cruises** (✉ 1800 Eller Dr., Suite 300, Box 350307, Fort Lauderdale, FL 33335, ☎ 800/525–2450). **Royal Caribbean Cruise Line** (✉ 1050 Caribbean Way, Miami, FL 33132, ☎ 800/327–6700). **Royal Olympic Cruises** (✉ 1 Rockefeller Plaza, Suite 315, New York, NY 10020, ☎ 800/872–6400). **Seabourn Cruise Line** (✉ 55 Francisco St., San Francisco, CA 94133, ☎ 800/351–9595). **Seawind Cruise Line** (✉ 1750 Coral Way, Miami, FL 33145, ☎ 800/258–8006). **Silversea Cruises** (✉ 110 E. Broward Blvd., Fort Lauderdale, FL 33301, ☎ 305/522–4477 or 800/722–6655). **Special Expeditions** (✉ 720 5th Ave., New York, NY 10019, ☎ 800/762–0003). **Star Clippers** (✉ 4101 Salzedo Ave., Coral Gables, FL 33146, ☎ 800/442–0551). **Windjammer Barefoot Cruises** (✉ 1759 Bay Rd., Miami Beach, FL 33139, ☎ 800/327–2602). **Windstar Cruises** (✉ 300 Elliott Ave. W, Seattle, WA 98119, ☎ 800/258–7245).

CUSTOMS & DUTIES

When shopping, **keep receipts** for all of your purchases. Upon reentering the country, **be ready to show customs officials what you've bought.** If you feel a duty is incorrect, appeal the assessment. If you object to the way your clearance was handled, get the inspector's badge number. In either case, first ask to see a supervisor, then write to the appropriate authorities, beginning with the port director at your point of entry.

IN THE CARIBBEAN

Most islands wave tourists through immigration and customs. Exceptions include major hubs within the

Caribbean, such as Jamaica and Antigua; to allay their concerns about smuggling or drug-running, they inspect most baggage at customs. If you're yachting through the islands—either bare-boat or charter—note that harbor customs are often thorough as well. Generally, similar rules apply throughout the Caribbean: You shouldn't bring more than 2 liters of alcohol, 2 cartons of cigarettes, or an inordinate amount of duty-free goods into any country. Just as in re-entering the United States, they might be confiscated or you'll be asked to pay a hefty import tax.

IN AUSTRALIA

Australia residents who are 18 or older may bring back $A400 worth of souvenirs and gifts (including jewelry), 250 cigarettes or 250 grams of tobacco, and 1,125 ml of alcohol (including wine, beer, and spirits). Residents under 18 may bring back $A200 worth of goods.

➤ INFORMATION: **Australian Customs Service** (Regional Director, ✉ Box 8, Sydney, NSW 2001, ☎ 02/9213–2000, FAX 02/9213–4000).

IN CANADA

Canadian residents who have been out of Canada for at least 7 days may bring in C$500 worth of goods dutyfree. If you've been away less than 7 days but more than 48 hours, the duty-free allowance drops to C$200; if your trip lasts 24–48 hours, the allowance is C$50. You may not pool allowances with family members. Goods claimed under the C$500 exemption may follow you by mail; those claimed under the lesser exemptions must accompany you. Alcohol and tobacco products may be included in the 7-day and 48-hour exemptions but not in the 24-hour exemption. If you meet the age requirements of the province or territory through which you reenter Canada, you may bring in, duty-free, 1.14 liters (40 imperial ounces) of wine or liquor *or* 24 12-ounce cans or bottles of beer or ale. If you're 16 or older you may bring in, duty-free, 200 cigarettes and 50 cigars.

You may send an unlimited number of gifts worth up to C$60 each dutyfree to Canada. Label the package UNSOLICITED GIFT—VALUE UNDER $60. Alcohol and tobacco are excluded.

➤ INFORMATION: **Revenue Canada** (✉ 2265 St. Laurent Blvd. S, Ottawa, Ontario K1G 4K3, ☎ 613/993–0534, 800/461–9999 in Canada).

IN NEW ZEALAND

Although greeted with a "Haere Mai" ("Welcome to New Zealand"), homeward-bound residents with goods to declare must present themselves for inspection. If you're 17 or older, you may bring back $700 worth of souvenirs and gifts. Your duty-free allowance also includes 4.5 liters of wine or beer; one 1,125-ml bottle of spirits; and either 200 cigarettes, 250 grams of tobacco, 50 cigars, or a combo of all three up to 250 grams.

➤ INFORMATION: **New Zealand Customs** (✉ Custom House, ✉ 50 Anzac Ave., Box 29, Auckland, New Zealand, ☎ 09/359–6655, ☎ 09/309–2978).

IN THE U.K.

From countries outside the EU, including those covered in this book, you may import, duty-free, 200 cigarettes or 50 cigars; 1 liter of spirits or 2 liters of fortified or sparkling wine or liqueurs; 2 liters of still table wine; 60 milliliters of perfume; 250 milliliters of toilet water; plus £136 worth of other goods, including gifts and souvenirs.

➤ INFORMATION: **HM Customs and Excise** (✉ Dorset House, ✉ Stamford St., London SE1 9NG, ☎ 0171/202–4227).

IN THE U.S.

U.S. residents may bring home $600 worth of foreign goods duty-free if they've been out of the country for at least 48 hours and haven't used the $600 allowance or any part of it in the past 30 days. This allowance, higher than the standard $400 exemption, applies to two dozen countries included in the Caribbean Basin Initiative (CBI). If you visit a CBI country and a non-CBI country, such as Martinique, you may still bring in

$600 worth of goods duty-free, but no more than $400 may be from the non-CBI country. If you're returning from the U.S. Virgin Islands (USVI), the duty-free allowance is $1,200. If your travel included the USVI and another country—say, the Dominican Republic—the $1,200 allowance still applies, but at least $600 worth of goods must be from the USVI.

U.S. residents 21 and older may bring back 1 liter of alcohol duty-free. In addition, regardless of your age, you're allowed 200 cigarettes and 100 non-Cuban cigars. Antiques, which the U.S. Customs Service defines as objects more than 100 years old, enter duty-free, as do original works of art done entirely by hand, including paintings, drawings, and sculptures.

You may also send packages home duty-free: up to $200 worth of goods for personal use, with a limit of one parcel per addressee per day (and no alcohol or tobacco products or perfume worth more than $5); label the package PERSONAL USE, and attach a list of its contents and their retail value. *Do not* label the package UNSOLICITED GIFT, or your duty-free exemption will drop to $100. Mailed items do not affect your duty-free allowance on your return.

➤ INFORMATION: **U.S. Customs Service** (Inquiries, ⊠ Box 7407, Washington, DC 20044, ☎ 202/927–6724; complaints, Office of Regulations and Rulings, ⊠ 1301 Constitution Ave. NW, Washington, DC 20229; registration of equipment, Resource Management, ⊠ 1301 Constitution Ave. NW, Washington DC 20229, ☎ 202/927–0540).

DISABILITIES & ACCESSIBILITY

ACCESS IN THE CARIBBEAN

In the Caribbean very few attractions and sights are equipped with ramps, elevators, or wheelchair-accessible rest rooms (except for those in Puerto Rico and the USVI, which have to abide by the Americans with Disabilities Act). However, major new properties are planning with the needs of travelers with disabilities in mind. Wherever possible in our lodging listings, we indicate whether special facilities are available.

LODGING

➤ BEST CHOICES: **Divi Hotels** (☎ 800/367–3484), which has six properties in the Caribbean, runs one of the best dive programs for people with disabilities at its resort in Bonaire.

MAKING RESERVATIONS

When discussing accessibility with an operator or reservations agent, **ask hard questions.** Are there any stairs, inside *or* out? Are there grab bars next to the toilet *and* in the shower/tub? How wide is the doorway to the room? To the bathroom? For the most extensive facilities meeting the latest legal specifications, **opt for newer accommodations,** which are more likely to have been designed with access in mind. Older buildings or ships may have more limited facilities. Be sure to **discuss your needs before booking.**

➤ COMPLAINTS: **Disability Rights Section** (⊠ U.S. Department of Justice, Civil Rights Division, ⊠ Box 66738, Washington, DC 20035–6738, ☎ 202/514–0301 or 800/514–0301, TTY 202/514–0383 or 800/514–0383, FAX 202/307–1198) for general complaints. **Aviation Consumer Protection Division** (☞ Air Travel, *above*) for airline-related problems. **Civil Rights Office** (⊠ DOT, Departmental Office of Civil Rights, S-30, ⊠ 400 7th St. SW, Room 10215, Washington, DC, 20590, ☎ 202/366–4648, FAX 202/366–9371) for problems with surface transportation.

TRAVEL AGENCIES & TOUR OPERATORS

As a whole, the travel industry has become more aware of the needs of travelers with disabilities. In the United States, the Americans with Disabilities Act requires that travel firms serve the needs of all travelers. Note, though, that some agencies and operators specialize in making travel arrangements for individuals and groups with disabilities.

➤ TRAVELERS WITH MOBILITY PROBLEMS: **Access Adventures** (⊠ 206

SMART TRAVEL TIPS / THE GOLD GUIDE

Chestnut Ridge Rd., Rochester, NY 14624, ☎ 716/889–9096), run by a former physical-rehabilitation counselor. **Accessible Journeys** (✉ 35 W. Sellers Ave., Ridley Park, PA 19078, ☎ 610/521–0339 or 800/846–4537, FAX 610/521–6959), for escorted tours exclusively for travelers with mobility impairments. **CareVacations** (✉ 5019 49th Ave., Suite 102, Leduc, Alberta T9E 6T5, ☎ 403/986–6404, 800/648–1116 in Canada) has group tours and is especially helpful with cruise vacations. **Flying Wheels Travel** (✉ 143 W. Bridge St., Box 382, Owatonna, MN 55060, ☎ 507/451–5005 or 800/535–6790, FAX 507/451–1685), a travel agency specializing in customized tours and itineraries worldwide. **Hinsdale Travel Service** (✉ 201 E. Ogden Ave., Suite 100, Hinsdale, IL 60521, ☎ 630/325–1335), a travel agency that benefits from the advice of wheelchair traveler Janice Perkins. **Tomorrow's Level of Care** (✉ Box 470299, Brooklyn, NY 11247, ☎ 718/756–0794 or 800/932–2012), for nursing services and medical equipment.

➤ TRAVELERS WITH DEVELOPMENTAL DISABILITIES: **Sprout** (✉ 893 Amsterdam Ave., New York, NY 10025, ☎ 212/222–9575 or 888/222–9575, FAX 212/222–9768).

DISCOUNTS & DEALS

Be a smart shopper and **compare all your options** before making any choice. A plane ticket bought with a promotional coupon may not be cheaper than the least expensive fare from a discount ticket agency. For high-price travel purchases, such as packages or tours, keep in mind that what you get is just as important as what you save. Just because something is cheap doesn't mean it's a bargain.

Consider visiting during the off-season, when prices usually plummet at even the glitziest resorts; you'll realize savings of up to 50% between April 15 and December 15. Moreover, you'll usually find fewer tourists, it's easier to rent a car, the water tends to be calmer and clearer, and you might stumble onto local festivals. Besides the region's traditional low season,

the Caribbean has other small "windows" during high season, when hotels that face sharp drops in occupancy quietly lower their rates for a week or so. A common window occurs in early-to-mid January, just after the Christmas rush and before the February surge of visitors. Remember that a certain budget, say $250 per day, goes much further on some islands (Dominica or Saba, for example) than on ritzy St. Bart's or Anguilla. And more developed islands (St. Thomas, St. Martin/Maarten, Aruba, Puerto Rico, Jamaica, Grand Cayman) tend to be more competitive and creative in their package deal pricing. All-inclusives aren't always the bargain they seem, especially if you're not a big drinker. Motorized water sports and scuba diving are rarely included, and island tours are occasionally extra as well. And if you're looking for a tranquil vacation, definitely avoid all-inclusives, many of which have "hospitality" staffers who all but drag you off your beach chair to play water volleyball.

CLUBS & COUPONS

Many companies sell discounts in the form of travel clubs and coupon books, but these cost money. You must use participating advertisers to get a deal, and only after you recoup the initial membership cost or book price do you begin to save. If you plan to use the club or coupons frequently, you may save considerably. Before signing up, find out what discounts you get for free.

➤ DISCOUNT CLUBS: **Entertainment Travel Editions** (✉ 2125 Butterfield Rd., Troy, MI 48084, ☎ 800/445–4137; $20–$51, depending on destination). **Great American Traveler** (✉ Box 27965, Salt Lake City, UT 84127, ☎ 801/974–3033 or 800/548–2812; $49.95 per year). **Moment's Notice Discount Travel Club** (✉ 7301 New Utrecht Ave., Brooklyn, NY 11204, ☎ 718/234–6295; $25 per year, single or family). **Privilege Card International** (✉ 237 E. Front St., Youngstown, OH 44503, ☎ 330/746–5211 or 800/236–9732; $74.95 per year). **Sears's Mature Outlook** (✉ Box 9390, Des Moines, IA 50306, ☎ 800/336–6330; $19.95

per year). **Travelers Advantage**
(✉ CUC Travel Service, ✉ 3033 S.
Parker Rd., Suite 1000, Aurora, CO
80014, ☎ 800/548–1116 or 800/
648–4037; $59.95 per year, single or
family). **Worldwide Discount Travel
Club** (✉ 1674 Meridian Ave., Miami
Beach, FL 33139, ☎ 305/534–2082;
$50 per year family, $40 single).

CREDIT-CARD BENEFITS

When you use your credit card to
make travel purchases you may get
free travel-accident insurance, colli-
sion-damage insurance, and medical
or legal assistance, depending on the
card and the bank that issued it.
American Express, MasterCard, and
Visa provide one or more of these
services, so **get a copy of your credit
card's travel-benefits policy.** If you're
a member of an auto club, always **ask
hotel and car-rental reservations
agents about auto-club discounts.**
Some clubs offer additional discounts
on tours, cruises, and admission to
attractions.

DISCOUNT RESERVATIONS

To save money, **look into discount-
reservations services** with toll-free
numbers, which use their buying
power to get a better price on hotels,
airline tickets, even car rentals. When
booking a room, always **call the
hotel's local toll-free number** (if one is
available) rather than the central
reservations number—you'll often get
a better price. Always ask about
special packages or corporate rates.

When shopping for the best deal on
hotels and car rentals, **look for guaranteed exchange rates,** which protect
you against a falling dollar. With your
rate locked in, you won't pay more,
even if the price goes up in the local
currency.

➤ AIRLINE TICKETS: ☎ **800/FLY–4–
LESS.**

➤ HOTEL ROOMS: **Steigenberger Reservation Service** (☎ 800/223–5652).

PACKAGE DEALS

Packages and guided tours can save
you money, but don't confuse the
two. When you buy a package, your
travel remains independent, just as
though you had planned and booked

the trip yourself. Fly/drive packages,
which combine airfare and car rental,
are often a good deal.

DIVING

The Caribbean offers some of the best
scuba diving in the world. For a list
of training facilities where you can
earn your diving certification card,
write to **PADI** (✉ Professional Association of Diving Instructors, 1251 E.
Dyer Rd., #100, Santa Ana, CA
92705). For more information, *see*
Water Sports *under* Pleasures and
Pastimes *in* Chapter 1.

DIVERS' ALERT

**Do not fly within 24 hours after scuba
diving.**

ECOTOURISM

Island governments are becoming
increasingly aware of their natural
resources. Many islands have established national parks, bird sanctuaries, and marine preserves. Bonaire,
Dominica, Guadeloupe, Saba, and
St. Lucia are among the leaders in
Caribbean environmental awareness.
These and other islands have special
programs, hikes, and tours that
promote a better understanding of
and a deeper appreciation for nature.
For more information *see* the Exploring, Outdoor Activities and Sports,
and A to Z sections *in* individual
island chapters.

ELECTRICITY

The general rule in the Caribbean is
110 and 120 volts AC, and the outlets take the same two-prong plugs
found in the United States, but there
are exceptions, particularly on the
French islands and those with a
British heritage. (For more information, *see* the A to Z sections *in* the
individual island chapters.) Be sure to
check with your hotel when making
reservations. If you're traveling to an
island that uses a foreign system,
bring a converter and an adapter.

If your appliances are dual-voltage,
you'll need only an adapter. Don't use
110-volt outlets, marked FOR SHAVERS
ONLY, for high-wattage appliances
such as blow-dryers. Most laptops
operate equally well on 110 and 220
volts and so require only an adapter.

THE GOLD GUIDE / SMART TRAVEL TIPS

FURTHER READING

Caribbean Style (Crown Publishers) is a coffee-table book with magnificent photographs of the interiors and exteriors of homes and buildings in the Caribbean. Short stories—some dark, some full of laughs—about life in the southern Caribbean made *Easy in the Islands,* by Bob Schacochis, a National Book Award winner. Schacochis has an ear for local patois and an eye for the absurd. In *Coming About: A Family Passage at Sea* author Susan Tyler Hitchcock details the adventure of a lifetime—one in which she and her family sail for nine months and 3,500 mi in the Bahamas and the Caribbean. The book offers an intimate look at the islands and is also a wonderful meditation on marriage and family. To familiarize yourself with the sights, smells, and sounds of the West Indies, pick up Jamaica Kincaid's *Annie John,* a richly textured coming-of-age novel about a girl growing up on Antigua. The short stories in *At the Bottom of the River,* also by Kincaid, depict island mysteries and manners. *Omeros* is Nobel Prize–winning Trinidadian poet Derek Walcott's imaginative Caribbean retelling of the *Odyssey.* Anthony C. Winkler's novels, *The Great Yacht Race, The Lunatic,* and *The Painted Canoe,* provide scathingly witty glimpses into Jamaica's class structure. Another notable chronicle of Caribbean life and customs is the provocative, imaginative novel *Wide Sargasso Sea,* by Jean Rhys. James Michener depicted the islands' diversity in his novel *Caribbean.* To probe island cultures more deeply, read V. S. Naipaul, particularly his *Guerrillas, The Loss of El Dorado* and *The Enigma of Arrival*; Eric William's *From Columbus to Castro*; and Michael Paiewonsky's *Conquest of Eden.* Though it was written more than 30 years ago, Herman Wouk's hilarious *Don't Stop the Carnival,* remains as fresh as ever in its depiction of the trials and tribulations of running a small Caribbean hotel. If you're keen on specific subjects such as history, cuisine, folklore, birdwatching, or diving, you'll find wonderful little locally written "books" on each island.

GAY & LESBIAN TRAVEL

The Caribbean is not one of the world's gay/lesbian-friendliest destinations. The Cayman Islands made headlines in January 1998 when they denied admittance to a gay-chartered cruise ship. And there have been isolated incidents of gay-bashing, including the murder of theater actor George Rose a few years ago, on the Dominican Republic. But it's unfair to single out these islands. To a certain extent, nearly every island frowns upon same-sex couples strolling hand-in-hand down a beach or street. That said, San Juan is a gay mecca, with numerous bars and guest houses. St. Thomas has a couple of gay bars and discos, while the West End of St. Croix has quietly become very gay-and-lesbian friendly. In general, the French Islands are the most tolerant, if not encouraging of gay and lesbian travelers. Couples may want to request a king-size bed in advance to avoid misunderstandings.

➤ GAY- AND LESBIAN-FRIENDLY TOUR OPERATORS: **Olivia** (✉ 4400 Market St., Oakland, CA 94608, ☎ 510/655–0364 or 800/631–6277, FAX 510/655–4334), for cruises and resort vacations for lesbians. **Atlantis Events** (✉ 9060 Santa Monica Blvd., Suite 310, West Hollywood, CA 90069, ☎ 310/281–5450 or 800/628–5268, FAX 310/281–5455), for mixed gay and lesbian travel. **Toto Tours** (✉ 1326 W. Albion Ave., Suite 3W, Chicago, IL 60626, ☎ 773/274–8686 or 800/565–1241, FAX 773/274–8695), for groups.

➤ GAY- AND LESBIAN-FRIENDLY TRAVEL AGENCIES: **Corniche Travel** (✉ 8721 Sunset Blvd., Suite 200, West Hollywood, CA 90069, ☎ 310/854–6000 or 800/429–8747, FAX 310/659–7441). **Islanders Kennedy Travel** (✉ 183 W. 10th St., New York, NY 10014, ☎ 212/242–3222 or 800/988–1181, FAX 212/929–8530). **Now Voyager** (✉ 4406 18th St., San Francisco, CA 94114, ☎ 415/626–1169 or 800/255–6951, FAX 415/626–8626). **Yellowbrick Road** (✉ 1500 W. Balmoral Ave., Chicago, IL 60640, ☎ 773/561–1800 or 800/642–2488, FAX 773/561–4497). **Skylink Travel and Tour** (✉ 3577 Moorland Ave.,

Santa Rosa, CA 95407, ☎ 707/585–8355 or 800/225–5759, FAX 707/584–5637) serves lesbian travelers.

HEALTH

There are few real hazards. The small lizards that seem to have overrun the islands are harmless, and poisonous snakes are hard to find, although you should exercise caution while bird-watching in Trinidad. Obviously, don't eat unfamiliar berries or leaves, unless you're on a nature walk with an experienced guide, and **beware of the manchineel tree,** whose apple-fruit is poisonous, and whose bark and leaves burn the skin. The worst problem may well be the tiny sand flies known as no-see-ums, which tend to appear after a rain, near wet or swampy ground, and around sunset, and the mosquitoes, which on some islands are particularly present from November to March. You may want to **bring along a good repellent.**

Sunburn or sunstroke can be serious. A long-sleeve shirt, a hat, and long pants or a beach wrap are essential on a boat, for midday at the beach, and whenever you go out sightseeing. **Use sunscreen** with an SPF (sun protection factor) of at least 15—especially if you're fair—and apply it liberally on nose, ears, and other sensitive areas. **Make sure the sunscreen is waterproof** if you're engaging in water sports, **limit your sun time** for the first few days, and be sure to **drink enough liquids,** monitoring intake of caffeine and alcohol, which hasten the dehydration process. A reminder: Even experienced swimmers should **exercise caution in waters on the windward (Atlantic) sides of the islands.** The unseen currents, powerful waves, strong undertows, and rocky bottoms can be extremely dangerous. Since health standards vary from island to island, **inquire about local conditions before you go.** No special shots are required for Caribbean destinations. (For more information, *see* the A to Z sections *in* individual chapters.)

MEDICAL PLANS

No one plans to get sick while traveling, but it happens, so **consider signing up with a medical-assistance company.** Members get doctor refer-

rals, emergency evacuation or repatriation, 24-hour telephone hot lines for medical consultation, cash for emergencies, and other personal and legal assistance. Coverage varies by plan, so **review the benefits of each carefully.**

➤ MEDICAL-ASSISTANCE COMPANIES: **International SOS Assistance** (✉ 8 Neshaminy Interplex, Suite 207, Trevose, PA 19053, ☎ 215/245–4707 or 800/523–6586, FAX 215/244–9617; ✉ 12 Chemin Riant-bosson, 1217 Meyrin 1, Geneva, Switzerland, ☎ 4122/785–6464, FAX 4122/785–6424; ✉ 10 Anson Rd., 14-07/08 International Plaza, Singapore, 079903, ☎ 65/226–3936, FAX 65/226–3937).

INSURANCE

Travel insurance is the best way to **protect yourself against financial loss.** The most useful plan is a comprehensive policy that includes coverage for trip cancellation and interruption, default, trip delay, and medical expenses (with a waiver for preexisting conditions).

Without insurance, you will lose all or most of your money if you cancel your trip, regardless of the reason. Default insurance covers you if your tour operator, airline, or cruise line goes out of business. Trip-delay covers unforeseen expenses that you may incur due to bad weather or mechanical delays. It's important to compare the fine print regarding trip-delay coverage when comparing policies.

For overseas travel, one of the most important components of travel insurance is its medical coverage. Supplemental health insurance will pick up the cost of your medical bills should you get sick or injured while traveling. U.S. residents should note that Medicare generally does not cover health-care costs outside the United States, nor do many privately issued policies. Residents of the United Kingdom can buy an annual travel-insurance policy valid for most vacations taken during the year in which the coverage is purchased. If you are pregnant or have a preexisting condition, make sure you're covered. British citizens should buy extra medical coverage when traveling overseas, according to the Association of British Insurers. Australian travelers should buy travel insurance, including extra medical coverage, whenever they go abroad, according to the Insurance Council of Australia.

Always **buy travel insurance directly from the insurance company**; if you buy it from a cruise line, airline, or tour operator that goes out of business you probably won't be covered for the agency or operator's default, a major risk. Before you make any purchase, **review your existing health and home-owner's policies** to find out whether they cover expenses incurred while traveling.

➤ TRAVEL INSURERS: In the U.S., **Access America** (✉ 6600 W. Broad St., Richmond, VA 23230, ☎ 804/285–3300 or 800/284–8300). **Travel Guard International** (✉ 1145 Clark St., Stevens Point, WI 54481, ☎ 715/345–0505 or 800/826–1300). In Canada, **Mutual of Omaha** (✉ Travel Division, ✉ 500 University Ave., Toronto, Ontario M5G 1V8, ☎ 416/598–4083, 800/268–8825 in Canada).

➤ INSURANCE INFORMATION: In the U.K., **Association of British Insurers** (✉ 51 Gresham St., London EC2V 7HQ, ☎ 0171/600–3333). In Australia, the **Insurance Council of Australia** (☎ 613/9614–1077, ℻ 613/9614–7924).

LANGUAGE

The fact that the history of the Caribbean is linked with that of several European and African countries is most obvious when you consider all the languages that are spoken on the islands. As for "official" languages, English is well-represented (14 island/island groups), followed by Dutch (5 islands, though, on many English is widely spoken), French (3 islands), and Spanish (2 islands). St. Maarten/St. Martin is split geographically, culturally, and linguistically— Dutch is spoken on one side, and French on the other.

Throughout the islands, you'll also find a variety of idiomatic expres-

sions, West Indian lilts and patois, and French Creole dialects that transform the official language into something else entirely. On Dominica, for example, English is the recognized tongue, but many locals speak a patois that mixes English, French, and African languages; on French-speaking St. Barts, some people use the Norman dialect of their ancestors; and on the Dutch islands, you'll encounter perhaps the most worldly tongue of all, Papiamento—a mixture of African languages as well as Dutch, English, French, Portuguese, *and* Spanish. There are also pockets where early Irish and Scottish settlers affected the island accent, as well as places where more recent East Indian arrivals have contributed to culture, food, and terminology. For specific details on what's spoken where (and how), *see* the A to Z sections *in* individual island chapters.

LODGING

Plan ahead and **reserve a room well before you travel to the Caribbean.** If you have reservations but expect to arrive later than 5 PM or 6 PM, tell the management in advance. Unless so advised, some places won't hold your reservations after 6 PM. Also, be sure to **find out what the quoted rate includes**—use of sports facilities and equipment, airport transfers, and the like—and whether the property operates on the European Plan (EP, with no meals), Continental Plan (CP, with Continental breakfast), Breakfast Plan (BP, with full breakfast), Modified American Plan (MAP, with two meals), or Full American Plan (FAP, with three meals), or is all-inclusive (including three meals, all facilities, and drinks unless otherwise noted). Be sure to **bring your deposit receipt** with you in case questions arise.

Decide whether you want a hotel on the leeward side of the island (with calm water, good for snorkeling) or the windward (with waves, good for surfing). Decide, too, whether you want to pay the extra price for a room overlooking the ocean or pool. At slightly less expensive properties, the difference may be as little as $10–$20 per room; at luxury resorts on pricey islands, however, it could be as much as $100 per room. Also **find out how close the property is to a beach;** at some hotels you can walk barefoot from your room onto the sand; others are across a road or a 10-minute drive away.

Nighttime entertainment is often alfresco in the Caribbean, so if you go to sleep early or are a light sleeper, ask for a room away from the dance floor.

Air-conditioning is not a necessity on all islands, many of which are cooled by trade winds, but it can be a plus if you enjoy an afternoon snooze. Breezes are best in second-floor rooms, particularly corner rooms. If you like to sleep without air-conditioning, make sure that windows can be opened and have screens. If you're staying away from the water, make sure the room has a ceiling fan, and that it works.

In this book, we categorize properties by price. Prices are intended as a guideline only. Larger hotels with more extensive facilities cost more, but the Caribbean is full of smaller places with charm, individuality, and prices that make up for their lack of activities—which are generally available on a pay-per-use basis everywhere. For more details, *see* the introductions to Lodging sections *in* individual island chapters.

APARTMENT & VILLA RENTALS

If you want a home base that's roomy enough for a family and comes with cooking facilities, **consider a furnished rental.** These can save you money, especially if you're traveling with a large group of people. Home-exchange directories list rentals (often second homes owned by prospective house swappers), and some services search for a house or apartment for you (even a castle if that's your fancy) and handle the paperwork. Some send an illustrated catalog; others send photographs only of specific properties, sometimes at a charge. Up-front registration fees may apply.

➤ RENTAL AGENTS: **At Home Abroad** (✉ 405 E. 56th St., Suite 6H, New York, NY 10022, ☎ 212/421–9165,

FAX 212/752–1591). **Europa-Let/ Tropical Inn-Let** (✉ 92 N. Main St., Ashland, OR 97520, ☎ 541/482–5806 or 800/462–4486, FAX 541/482–0660). **Hometours International** (✉ Box 11503, Knoxville, TN 37939, ☎ 423/690–8484 or 800/367–4668). **Property Rentals International** (✉ 1008 Mansfield Crossing Rd., Richmond, VA 23236, ☎ 804/378–6054 or 800/220–3332, FAX 804/379–2073). **Rental Directories International** (✉ 2044 Rittenhouse Sq., Philadelphia, PA 19103, ☎ 215/985–4001, FAX 215/985–0323). **Vacation Home Rentals Worldwide** (✉ 235 Kensington Ave., Norwood, NJ 07648, ☎ 201/767–9393 or 800/633–3284, FAX 201/767–5510). **Villas and Apartments Abroad** (✉ 420 Madison Ave., Suite 1003, New York, NY 10017, ☎ 212/759–1025 or 800/433–3020, FAX 212/755–8316). **Villas International** (✉ 950 Northgate Dr., Suite 206, San Rafael, CA 94903, ☎ 415/499–9490 or 800/221–2260, FAX 415/499–9491). **Hideaways International** (✉ 767 Islington St., Portsmouth, NH 03801, ☎ 603/430–4433 or 800/843–4433, FAX 603/430–4444; membership $99) is a club for travelers who arrange rentals among themselves. **Unusual Villa & Island Rentals** (✉ 409F North Hamilton St., Richmond, VA 23221, ☎ 804/288–2823, FAX 804/342–9016).

HOME EXCHANGES

If you would like to exchange your home for someone else's, **join a home-exchange organization,** which will send you its updated listings of available exchanges for a year and will include your own listing in at least one of them. It's up to you to make specific arrangements.

➤ EXCHANGE CLUBS: **HomeLink International** (✉ Box 650, Key West, FL 33041, ☎ 305/294–7766 or 800/638–3841, FAX 305/294–1148; $83 per year).

HOSTELS

No matter what your age, you can **save on lodging costs by staying at hostels.** In some 5,000 locations in more than 70 countries around the world, Hostelling International (HI), the umbrella group for a number of national youth hostel associations, offers single-sex, dorm-style beds and, at many hostels, "couples" rooms and family accommodations. Membership in any HI national hostel association, open to travelers of all ages, allows you to stay in HI-affiliated hostels at member rates (one-year membership is about $25 for adults; hostels run about $10–$25 per night). Members also have priority if the hostel is full; they're eligible for discounts around the world, even on rail and bus travel in some countries.

➤ HOSTEL ORGANIZATIONS: **Hostelling International—American Youth Hostels** (✉ 733 15th St. NW, Suite 840, Washington, DC 20005, ☎ 202/783–6161, ℻ 202/783–6171). **Hostelling International—Canada** (✉ 400-205 Catherine St., Ottawa, Ontario K2P 1C3, ☎ 613/237–7884, ℻ 613/237–7868). **Youth Hostel Association of England and Wales** (✉ Trevelyan House, ✉ 8 St. Stephen's Hill, St. Albans, Hertfordshire AL1 2DY, ☎ 01727/855215 or 01727/845047, ℻ 01727/844126); membership in the U.S. $25, in Canada C$26.75, in the U.K. £9.30).

MONEY

For information on currency, service charges, taxes, and tipping in the Caribbean, *see* the A to Z sections *in* individual island chapters.

CREDIT & DEBIT CARDS

Should you use a credit card or a debit card when traveling? Both have benefits. A credit card allows you to delay payment and gives you certain rights as a consumer (☞ Consumer Protection, *above*). A debit card, also known as a check card, deducts funds directly from your checking account and helps you stay within your budget. When you want to rent a car, though, you may still need an old-fashioned credit card. Although you can always *pay* for your car with a debit card, some agencies will not allow you to *reserve* a car with a debit card.

Otherwise, the two types of plastic are virtually the same. Both will get you cash advances at ATMs worldwide if your card is properly programmed

with your personal identification number (PIN). Both offer excellent, wholesale exchange rates. And both protect you against unauthorized use if the card is lost or stolen. Your liability is limited to $50, as long as you report the card missing.

➤ ATM LOCATIONS: **Cirrus** (☎ 800/424–7787). **Plus** (☎ 800/843–7587) for locations in the U.S. and Canada, or visit your local bank.

EXCHANGING MONEY

For the most favorable rates, **change money through banks.** Although fees charged for ATM transactions may be higher abroad than at home, Cirrus and Plus exchange rates are excellent, because they are based on wholesale rates offered only by major banks. You won't do as well at exchange booths in airports or rail and bus stations, in hotels, in restaurants, or in stores, although you may find their hours more convenient. To avoid lines at airport exchange booths, **get a bit of local currency before you leave home.**

➤ EXCHANGE SERVICES: **Chase *Currency To Go*** (☎ 800/935–9935; 935–9935 in NY, NJ, and CT). **International Currency Express** (☎ 888/842–0880 on the East Coast, 888/278–6628 on the West Coast). **Thomas Cook Currency Services** (☎ 800/287–7362 for telephone orders and retail locations).

TRAVELER'S CHECKS

Do you need traveler's checks? It depends on where you're headed. If you're going to rural areas and small towns, go with cash; traveler's checks are best used in cities. Lost or stolen checks can usually be replaced within 24 hours. To ensure a speedy refund, buy your own traveler's checks— don't let someone else pay for them: irregularities like this can cause delays. The person who bought the checks should make the call to request a refund.

PACKING

LUGGAGE

How many carry-on bags you can bring with you is up to the airline. Most allow two, but the limit is often reduced to one on certain flights. Gate agents will take excess baggage—including bags they deem oversize—from you as you board and add it to checked luggage. To avoid this situation, make sure that everything you carry aboard will fit under your seat. Also, get to the gate early, and request a seat at the back of the plane; you'll probably board first, while the overhead bins are still empty. Since big, bulky baggage attracts the attention of gate agents and flight attendants on a busy flight, make sure your carry-on is really a carry-on. Finally, a carry-on that's long and narrow is more likely to remain unnoticed than one that's wide and squarish.

If you are flying internationally, note that baggage allowances may be determined not by piece but by weight—generally 88 pounds (40 kilograms) in first class, 66 pounds (30 kilograms) in business class, and 44 pounds (20 kilograms) in economy.

Airline liability for baggage is limited to $1,250 per person on flights within the United States. On international flights it amounts to $9.07 per pound or $20 per kilogram for checked baggage (roughly $640 per 70-pound bag) and $400 per passenger for unchecked baggage. You can buy additional coverage at check-in for about $10 per $1,000 of coverage, but it excludes a rather extensive list of items, shown on your airline ticket.

Before departure, **itemize your bags' contents** and their worth, and label the bags with your name, address, and phone number. (If you use your home address, cover it so that potential thieves can't see it readily.) Inside each bag, **pack a copy of your itinerary.** At check-in, **make sure that each bag is correctly tagged** with the destination airport's three-letter code. If your bags arrive damaged or fail to arrive at all, file a written report with the airline before leaving the airport.

PACKING LIST

Dress on the islands is light and casual. Bring loose-fitting clothes made of natural fabrics to see you through days of heat and humidity. Take a cover-up for the beaches, not only to protect you from the sun but also to wear to and from your hotel room. Bathing suits and immodest attire are frowned upon off the beach on many islands. A sun hat is advisable, but you don't have to pack one—inexpensive straw hats are available everywhere. For shopping and sightseeing, bring walking shorts, jeans, T-shirts, long-sleeve cotton shirts, slacks, and sundresses. You'll need a light sweater for protection from the trade winds, and at higher altitudes. Evenings are casual, but "casual" can range from really informal to casually elegant, depending on the establishment. A tie is rarely required, but jackets are sometimes de rigueur in fancier restaurants and casinos.

In your carry-on luggage **bring an extra pair of eyeglasses or contact lenses and enough of any medication** to last the entire trip. You may also want your doctor to write a spare prescription using the drug's generic name, since brand names may vary from country to country. **Never put prescription drugs or valuables in luggage to be checked.** To avoid customs delays, carry medications in their original packaging. And don't forget to copy down and carry addresses of offices that handle refunds of lost traveler's checks.

PASSPORTS & VISAS

When traveling internationally, **carry a passport even if you don't need one** (it's always the best form of ID), and make **two photocopies of the data page** (one for someone at home and another for you, carried separately from your passport). If you lose your passport, promptly call the nearest embassy or consulate and the local police.

ENTERING THE CARIBBEAN

See the A to Z sections *in* individual island chapters for specific requirements.

PASSPORT OFFICES

The best time to apply for a passport or to renew is during the fall and winter. Before any trip, be sure to check your passport's expiration date and, if necessary, renew it as soon as

THE GOLD GUIDE / SMART TRAVEL TIPS

THE GOLD GUIDE / SMART TRAVEL TIPS

possible. (Some countries won't allow you to enter on a passport that's due to expire in six months or less.)

➤ AUSTRALIAN CITIZENS: **Australian Passport Office** (☎ 131–232).

➤ CANADIAN CITIZENS: **Passport Office** (☎ 819/994–3500 or 800/567–6868).

➤ NEW ZEALAND CITIZENS: **New Zealand Passport Office** (☎ 04/494–0700 for information on how to apply, 0800/727–776 for information on applications already submitted).

➤ U.K. CITIZENS: **London Passport Office** (☎ 0990/21010), for fees and documentation requirements and to request an emergency passport.

➤ U.S. CITIZENS: **National Passport Information Center** (☎ 900/225–5674; calls are charged at 35¢ per minute for automated service, $1.05 per minute for operator service).

SENIOR-CITIZEN TRAVEL

To qualify for age-related discounts, **mention your senior-citizen status up front** when booking hotel reservations (not when checking out) and before you're seated in restaurants (not when paying the bill). Note that discounts may be limited to certain menus, days, or hours. When renting a car, **ask about promotional car-rental discounts,** which can be cheaper than senior-citizen rates.

➤ EDUCATIONAL PROGRAMS: **Elderhostel** (✉ 75 Federal St., 3rd floor, Boston, MA 02110, ☎ 617/426–8056). **Interhostel** (✉ University of New Hampshire, ✉ 6 Garrison Ave., Durham, NH 03824, ☎ 603/862–1147 or 800/733–9753, FAX 603/862–1113).

STUDENT TRAVEL

The Caribbean is not as far out of a student's budget as you might expect. All but the toniest islands, such as St. Barthélemy, have camping facilities, inexpensive guest houses, or small no-frills hotels. You're most likely to meet students from other countries in the French and Dutch West Indies, where many go on holiday or sabbatical. Puerto Rico, Jamaica, Grenada, and Dominica, among others, have

large resident international student populations at their universities. In many cases, your student ID card may provide access to their facilities, from library to cafeteria.

TRAVEL AGENCIES

To save money, **look into deals available through student-oriented travel agencies.** To qualify you'll need a bona fide student ID card. Members of international student groups are also eligible.

➤ STUDENT IDs & SERVICES: **Council on International Educational Exchange** (✉ CIEE, ✉ 205 E. 42nd St., 14th floor, New York, NY 10017, ☎ 212/822–2600 or 888/268–6245, FAX 212/822–2699), for mail orders only, in the United States. **Travel Cuts** (✉ 187 College St., Toronto, Ontario M5T 1P7, ☎ 416/979–2406 or 800/667–2887) in Canada.

TELEPHONES

COUNTRY CODES

For specific details on making calls to, on, and from the islands, *see* the A to Z sections *in* individual island chapters.

INTERNATIONAL CALLS

AT&T, MCI, and Sprint international access codes make calling the United States relatively convenient, but you may find the local access number blocked in many hotel rooms. First ask the hotel operator to connect you. If the hotel operator balks, ask for an international operator, or dial the international operator yourself. One way to improve your odds of getting connected to your long-distance carrier is to travel with more than one company's calling card (a hotel may block Sprint, for example, but not MCI). If all else fails, call from a pay phone in the hotel lobby. Call your long-distance carrier for a list of access codes on the islands you plan to visit.

➤ ACCESS CODES: **AT&T Direct** (☎ 800/435–0812). **MCI WorldPhone** (☎ 800/444–4141). **Sprint International Access** (☎ 800/877–4646).

TOUR OPERATORS

Buying a prepackaged tour or independent vacation can make your trip to the Caribbean less expensive and more hassle-free. Because everything is prearranged, you'll spend less time planning.

Operators that handle several hundred thousand travelers per year can use their purchasing power to give you a good price. Their high volume may also indicate financial stability. But some small companies provide more personalized service; because they tend to specialize, they may also be more knowledgeable about a given area.

BOOKING WITH AN AGENT

Travel agents are excellent resources. In fact, large operators accept bookings made only through travel agents. But it's a good idea to **collect brochures from several agencies,** because some agents' suggestions may be influenced by relationships with tour and package firms that reward them for volume sales. If you have a special interest, **find an agent with expertise in that area**; the American Society of Travel Agents (☞ Travel Agencies, *below*) has a database of specialists worldwide.

Make sure your travel agent knows the accommodations and other services. Ask about the hotel's location, room size, beds, and whether it has a pool, room service, or programs for children, if you care about these. Has your agent been there in person or sent others you can contact?

Do some homework on your own, too: Local tourism boards can provide information about lesser-known and small-niche operators, some of which may sell only direct.

BUYER BEWARE

Each year consumers are stranded or lose their money when tour operators—even very large ones with excellent reputations—go out of business. So **check out the operator.** Find out how long the company has been in business, and ask several travel agents about its reputation. If the package or tour you are considering is priced lower than in your wildest dreams, **be skeptical.** Try to **book with a company that has a consumer-protection program.** If the

operator has such a program, you'll find information about it in the company's brochure. If the operator you are considering does not offer some kind of consumer protection, then ask for references from satisfied customers.

In the United States, members of the National Tour Association and United States Tour Operators Association are required to set aside funds to cover your payments and travel arrangements in case the company defaults. It's also a good idea to choose a company that participates in the American Society of Travel Agent's Tour Operator Program (TOP). This gives you a forum if there are any disputes between you and your tour operator; ASTA will act as mediator.

➤ TOUR-OPERATOR RECOMMENDATIONS: **American Society of Travel Agents** (☞ Travel Agencies, *below*). **National Tour Association** (✉ NTA, ✉ 546 E. Main St., Lexington, KY 40508, ☎ 606/226–4444 or 800/ 755–8687). **United States Tour Operators Association** (✉ USTOA, ✉ 342 Madison Ave., Suite 1522, New York, NY 10173, ☎ 212/599– 6599 or 800/468–7862, FAX 212/ 599–6744).

COSTS

The more your package or tour includes, the better you can predict the ultimate cost of your vacation. Make sure you know exactly what is covered, and **beware of hidden costs.** Are taxes, tips, and service charges included? Transfers and baggage handling? Entertainment and excursions? These can add up.

Prices for packages and tours are usually quoted per person, based on two sharing a room. If traveling solo, you may be required to pay the full double-occupancy rate. Some operators eliminate this surcharge if you agree to be matched with a roommate of the same sex, even if one is not found by departure time.

GROUP TOURS

Among companies that sell tours to the Caribbean, the following have a proven reputation and offer plenty of options. The classifications used below represent different price categories, and you'll probably encounter these terms when talking to a travel agent or tour operator. The key difference is usually in accommodations, which run from budget to better, and better-yet to best.

➤ DELUXE: **Globus** (✉ 5301 S. Federal Circle, Littleton, CO 80123-2980, ☎ 303/797–2800 or 800/221–0090, FAX 303/347–2080).

PACKAGES

Like group tours, independent vacation packages are available from major tour operators and airlines. The companies listed below offer vacation packages in a broad price range.

➤ AIR/HOTEL: **American Airlines Vacations** (☎ 800/321–2121). **Certified Vacations** (☎ 954/522–1440 or 800/233–7260). **Continental Airlines Vacations** (☎ 800/634–5555). **Delta Vacations** (☎ 800/872–7786). **US Airways Vacations** (☎ 800/455–0123). Puerto Rico only: **TWA Getaway Vacations** (☎ 800/438–2929). **United Vacations** (☎ 800/328–6877).

➤ FROM THE U.K.: **Caribbean Connection** (✉ Concorde House, Forest St., Chester CH1 1QR, ☎ 01244/341–131). **Caribtours** (✉ 161 Fulham Rd., London SW3 6SN, ☎ 0171/581–3517). **Hayes and Jarvis** (✉ Hayes House, 152 King St., London W6 0QA, ☎ 0181/748–0088). **Kuoni Travel** (✉ Kuoni House, Dorking, Surrey RH5 4AZ, ☎ 01306/740–888).

THEME TRIPS

➤ ADVENTURE: **American Wilderness Experience** (✉ Box 1486, Boulder, CO 80306, ☎ 303/444–2622 or 800/444–0099, FAX 303/444–3999).**NatureQuest** (✉ 934 Acapulco St., Laguna Beach, CA 92651, ☎ 714/499–9561 or 800/369–3033, FAX 714/499–0812).

➤ GOLF: **Stine's Golftrips** (✉ Box 2314, Winter Haven, FL 33883-2314, ☎ 407/933–0032 or 800/428–1940, FAX 407/933–8857).

➤ LEARNING: **Earthwatch** (✉ Box 9104, 680 Mount Auburn St., Watertown, MA 02272, ☎ 617/926–8200 or 800/776–0188, FAX 617/926–8532) for research expeditions. **National Audubon Society** (✉ 700 Broadway, New York, NY 10003, ☎ 212/979–3066, FAX 212/353–0190). **Natural Habitat Adventures** (✉ 2945 Center Green Court, Boulder, CO 80301, ☎ 303/449–3711 or 800/543–8917, FAX 303/449–3712). **Oceanic Society Expeditions** (✉ Fort Mason Center, Bldg. E, San Francisco, CA 94123-1394, ☎ 415/441–1106 or 800/326–7491, FAX 415/474–3395). **Smithsonian Study Tours and Seminars** (✉ 1100 Jefferson Dr. SW, Room 3045, MRC 702, Washington, DC 20560, ☎ 202/357–4700, FAX 202/633–9250).

➤ SAILING SCHOOLS: **Annapolis Sailing School** (✉ Box 3334, 601 6th St., Annapolis, MD 21403, ☎ 410/267–7205 or 800/638–9192). **Offshore Sailing School** (✉ 16731-110 McGregor Blvd., Ft. Myers, FL 33908, ☎ 941/454–1700 or 800/221–4326, FAX 941/454–1191).

➤ SPAS: **Spa-Finders** (✉ 91 5th Ave., #301, New York, NY 10003-3039, ☎ 212/924–6800 or 800/255–7727).

➤ SCUBA DIVING: **Rothschild Dive Safaris** (✉ 900 West End Ave., #1B, New York, NY 10025-3525, ☎ 212/662–4858 or 800/359–0747, FAX 212/749–6172). **Tropical Adventures** (✉ 111 2nd Ave. N, Seattle, WA 98109, ☎ 206/441–3483 or 800/247–3483, FAX 206/441–5431).

➤ YACHT CHARTERS: **Alden Yacht Charters** (✉ 1909 Alden Landing, Portsmouth, RI 02871, ☎ 401/683–4200 or 800/253–3654, FAX 401/683–3668). **Cat Ppalu Cruises** (✉ Box 661091, Miami, FL 33266, ☎ 305/888–1226 or 800/327–9600, FAX 305/884–4214). **Huntley Yacht Vacations** (✉ 210 Preston Rd., Wernersville, PA 19565, ☎ 610/678–2628 or 800/322–9224, FAX 610/670–1767). **Lynn Jachney Charters** (✉ Box 302, Marblehead, MA 01945, ☎ 617/639–0787 or 800/223–2050, FAX 617/639–0216). **The Moorings** (✉ 19345 U.S. Hwy. 19 N, 4th floor, Clearwater, FL 33764, ☎ 813/530–5424 or 800/535–7289, FAX 813/530–9747).

Nicholson Yacht Charters (✉ 29 Sherman St., Cambridge, MA 02138, ☎ 617/661–0555 or 800/662–6066, FAX 617/661–0554). **Ocean Voyages** (✉ 1709 Bridgeway, Sausalito, CA 94965, ☎ 415/332–4681, FAX 415/332–7460). **Russell Yacht Charters** (✉ 404 Hulls Hwy., #175, Southport, CT 06490, ☎ 203/255–2783 or 800/635–8895). **SailAway Yacht Charter Consultants** (✉ 15605 S.W. 92nd Ave., Miami, FL 33157-1972, ☎ 305/253–7245 or 800/724–5292, FAX 305/251–4408).

TRAVEL AGENCIES

A good travel agent puts your needs first. Look for an agency that has been in business at least five years, emphasizes customer service, and has someone on staff who specializes in your destination. In addition, **make sure the agency belongs to a professional trade organization,** such as the American Society of Travel Agents in the United States. If your travel agency is also acting as your tour operator, *see* Buyer Beware *in* Tour Operators, *above*).

➤ LOCAL AGENT REFERRALS: **American Society of Travel Agents** (ASTA, ☎ 800/965–2782 24-hr hot line, FAX 703/684–8319). **Association of Canadian Travel Agents** (✉ Suite 201, 1729 Bank St., Ottawa, Ontario K1V 7Z5, ☎ 613/521–0474, FAX 613/521–0805). **Association of British Travel Agents** (✉ 55–57 Newman St., London W1P 4AH, ☎ 0171/637–2444, FAX 0171/637–0713). **Australian Federation of Travel Agents** (☎ 02/9264–3299). **Travel Agents' Association of New Zealand** (☎ 04/499–0104).

TRAVEL GEAR

Travel catalogs specialize in useful items, such as compact alarm clocks and travel irons, that can **save space when packing.** They also offer dual-voltage appliances, currency converters, and foreign-language phrase books.

➤ CATALOGS: **Magellan's** (☎ 800/962–4943, FAX 805/568–5406). **Orvis Travel** (☎ 800/541–3541, FAX 540/343–7053). **TravelSmith** (☎ 800/950–1600, FAX 800/950–1656).

VISITOR INFORMATION

Most islands have a U.S.–based tourist board, listed with its name and address in the A to Z section of each island chapter; they can be good sources of general information, up-to-date calendars of events, and listings of hotels, restaurants, sights, and shops. The Caribbean Tourism Organization is another resource, especially for information on the islands that have very limited representation in the United States.

➤ CARIBBEAN-WIDE INFORMATION: **Caribbean Tourism Organization** (✉ 20 E. 46th St., New York, NY 10017-2452, ☎ 212/682–0435, FAX 212/697–4258; ✉ Vigilant House, 120 Wilton Rd., London SW1V 1JZ, England, ☎ 0171/233–8382).

U.S. GOVERNMENT

Government agencies can be an excellent source of inexpensive travel information. When planning your trip, **find out what government materials are available.**

➤ PAMPHLETS: **Consumer Information Center** (✉ Consumer Information Catalogue, Pueblo, CO 81009, ☎ 719/948–3334 or 888/878–3256) for a free catalog that includes travel titles.

WHEN TO GO

The Caribbean high season has traditionally been winter, usually extending from December 15 to April 14. This is when northern weather is at its worst, not necessarily when Caribbean weather is at its best. In fact, winter is when the Caribbean is at its windiest. It's also the most fashionable, the most expensive, and the most popular time to visit—and most hotels are heavily booked. You have to make your reservations at least two or three months in advance for the very best places (and sometimes a year in advance for the most exclusive spots). Hotel prices drop 20%–50% for summer (after April 15); cruise prices also fall. Saving money isn't the only reason to visit the Caribbean during the off-season. Temperatures are only a few degrees warmer, and more and more hotels and restaurants are staying open year-round, so things aren't as dead-quiet as they used to be. Late August, September, October, and early November are least crowded, but hotel facilities can be limited and some restaurants may be closed. Singles in search of partners should visit in high season or in summer, or choose a resort with a high year-round occupancy rate.

In summer the flamboyant trees are at their peak, as are most of the flowers and shrubs of the West Indies. The water is clearer for snorkeling and smoother for sailing in the Virgin Islands and the Grenadines, in May, June, and July. Generally speaking, there's more planned entertainment in winter. The peak of local excitement on many islands, most notably Trinidad, St. Vincent, and the French West Indies, is Carnival.

CLIMATE

The Caribbean climate is fairly constant. The average year-round temperatures for the region are 78°F–88°F. The extremes of temperature are 65°F low, 95°F high, but as everyone knows, it's the humidity, not the heat, that makes you suffer, especially when the two go hand in hand. You can count on downtown shopping areas being hot at midday any time of the year, but air-conditioning provides

some respite. Stay near beaches, where water and trade winds can keep you cool, and shop early or late in the day.

As part of the fall's rainy season, hurricanes occasionally sweep through the Caribbean. Check the news daily, and keep abreast of brewing tropical storms by reading Stateside papers if you can get them. The rainy season consists mostly of brief showers interspersed with sunshine. You can watch the clouds come over, feel the rain, and remain on your lounge chair for the sun to dry you off. A spell of overcast days is "unusual," as everyone will tell you.

High places can be cool, particularly when the Christmas winds hit Caribbean peaks (they come in late November and last through January). Since most Caribbean islands are mountainous or at least hilly (notable exceptions being the Caymans, Anguilla, Aruba, Bonaire, and Curaçao), the altitude always offers an escape from the latitude. Kingston (Jamaica), Port-of-Spain (Trinidad), and Fort-de-France (Martinique) swelter in summer; climb 1,000 ft or so and everything is fine.

➤ FORECASTS: **Weather Channel Connection** (☎ 900/932–8437), 95¢ per minute from a Touch-Tone phone.

1 Destination: Caribbean

THE MANY FACES OF THE ISLANDS

F YOU HAVE SEEN ONE ISLAND you have by no means seen them all. Tiny 5-square-mi Saba has less in common with the vast 19,000-square-mi Dominican Republic than Butte, Montana, has with Biloxi, Mississippi. Butte and Biloxi, however different in terrain and traits, sit in the same country and the citizenry speak more or less the same language. Saba, which is Dutch, and the Dominican Republic, whose roots are in Spain, simply sit in the same sea.

The Caribbean has towering volcanic islands, such as Saba; islands with lush rain forests, such as Dominica, St. Lucia, Martinique, and Guadeloupe; and some islands, notably Puerto Rico, that have both jungles and deserts. You'll find glittering discos, casinos, and dazzling nightlife on such islands as Aruba and the Dominican Republic, and throughout the region there are isolated cays with only sand, sea, sun, lizards, and mosquitoes. Some islands— Puerto Rico and St. Kitts among them— have ancient forts to view, while Barbados and the Caicos Islands have caverns and caves to explore. There are also places like Grand Turk and Little Cayman, where the only notable sights to see are beneath the translucent sea.

Different though they are in many ways, the islands are stylistically similar. The style setter is the tropical climate. Year-round summertime temperatures and a plethora of beaches produce a pace that's known as "island time." Only the trade winds move swiftly. Operating on island time means, "I'll get to it when the spirit moves me."

Similarities are also attributable to the history of the region. The agrarian Arawaks paddled up from South America and populated the islands more than 1,000 years ago. In the early 14th century, the mighty Caribs, who gave the area its name, arrived, probably from Brazil or Venezuela, gradually pushing the Arawaks up the spine of the Caribbean. (The original name of the Caribs was Galibi, a word the Spanish corrupted to *Canibal*—the origin of the word "cannibal.") Both tribes (as well as the peaceful Taino people of Puerto Rico, Hispaniola, Cuba, and Jamaica) had remarkably sophisticated cultures and elaborate sociological systems.

Christopher Columbus made four voyages through the region between 1492 and 1504, christening the islands while dodging the Carib arrows. He landed on or sailed past all of the Greater Antilles and virtually all of the eastern Caribbean islands. From the 16th century until the early 19th century, the Dutch, Danes, Swedes, English, French, Irish, and Spanish fought bitterly for control of the islands. Some islands have almost as many battle sites as sand flies. After gaining control of the islands and annihilating the remaining Arawaks (mostly through diseases brought from Europe) and Caribs (mostly by sword and musket), the Europeans established vast sugar plantations and brought in Africans to work the fields. With the abolition of slavery in the mid-19th century, Asians were imported as indentured laborers. Today, the Caribbean population is a rich gumbo of nationalities, including Americans and Canadians who have retired to and invested in the islands. Although little remains of the indigenous populations (there's a Carib reservation on Dominica and a community of Caribs on St. Vincent, as well as tantalizing, if sparse, archaeological remains), each colonial power left its own cultural imprint on the Caribbean.

It must be remembered that the Caribbean, like the European continent, is made up of individual countries, each with customs, immigration officials, and, in some instances, political difficulties. Most of the islands have opted for independence; others retain their ties to the mother country. They are developing nations, and many have severe economic and unemployment problems. Virtually all of the islands depend upon tourism. And, human nature being what it is, many islanders resent their dependency on tourist dollars. Like as not, the person who serves you has stood in a long line, vying with other anxious applicants for the few available jobs. After serving your meals or cleaning your luxurious room, he or she returns to a tiny shack knowing full well that in less than a week you will have shelled out more than an islander makes in a month.

Some visitors object to encountering resentment when all they seek is a pleasant vacation and they've paid dearly for it. Some feel rather keenly that they'd always like hot water—or at least *some* water—when they turn on the shower; in even the most luxurious resorts there are times when things simply don't work; it's a fact of Caribbean life. No matter how diligent the upkeep, humidity and salt air take their toll, and cracked tiles and chipped paint are common everywhere. Many first-time visitors also forget that they're in the tropics, and find it hard to get used to some of the fauna (a lizard scurrying away at the opening of a door is a common sight). Still other visitors simply have no patience with island time. There are those, however, who travel to the Caribbean year after year. Some return to the same hotel on the same beach on the same island, while others try to sample as much as this smorgasbord has to offer.

NEW AND NOTEWORTHY

Airline service to and from the Caribbean continues to expand. **Air Jamaica** is currently the most aggressive carrier, adding several flights daily from 10 North American gateways to Montego Bay, as well as jet service from that hub to such islands as Barbados, Antigua, St. Lucia, Grand Cayman, and Turks and Caicos. The airline has also instituted island-hopping at no extra charge: stay over in Jamaica and continue to a second or even third destination at no extra cost.

In the **Dominican Republic,** major plans are afoot to beautify and preserve Santo Domingo's 16th-century Colonial Zone. In addition to offering incentives that will enable more people to buy and renovate 500-year-old buildings in the zone, some of the ambitious projects underway include installing replicas of colonial gaslights, repairing ancient water pipes, repaving roads and sidewalks, and cleaning and restoring the collection of artifacts and tapestries in the castle of Don Diego Colon.

On July 18, 1995 **Montserrat's Soufrière Volcano** shook itself awake, violently changing the course of the island's history and ripping its culture apart. The destruction has been appalling. Plymouth, the capital, has been buried in ash. Boulders the size of houses have mashed everything in their path. Deep layers of ash now cover the southern half of the island, transforming the landscape into a monochromatic dull gray.

Evacuation began slowly, but as eruptions continued, more and more of the island was closed, more and more people forced to leave. Many went to Antigua and Britain, and others to the United States; some, however, have stayed. For an island with only 11,000 people before the evacuations, this upheaval has been particularly wrenching. No one knows when the volcano will slip back into dormancy, and everyone thinks of a future when the island will be able to welcome returning residents and visitors. Until then, the people of Montserrat need all the help they can get; donations can be made through your local branch of the Red Cross.

On **Puerto Rico**'s 100th anniversary of becoming a U.S. territory, plans were set in motion that may give the people of the island a say about whether or not it should become a state. On March 4, 1998 the U.S. House of Representatives narrowly approved a bill (the United States–Puerto Rico Political Status Act) that would allow the island to hold a referendum. Puerto Rico has voted in referendums in 1967, 1981, and 1993, with the goal of deciding whether it should become a state, remain a commonwealth, or become an independent nation. At press time, the bill for yet another referendum was pending in the U.S. Senate.

All over the world, as telecommunications boom, phone companies have come up with creative ways to accommodate the need for **new phone numbers.** It has even reached the Caribbean. This year, most of the islands have new area codes in effect. *See* Telephones and Mail *in* the A to Z section that ends each island's chapter for the latest information.

Island Finder

Island	Cost of Island	Number of rooms*	Nonstop flights	Cruise ship port	U.S. dollars accepted	Historic sites	Natural beauty	Lush	Arid	Mountainous	Rain forest	Beautiful beaches	Good roads	
Anguilla	$$$	978			•				•			•		
Antigua & Barbuda	$$$$	3,317	•	•	•	•	•		•			•	•	
Aruba	$$	6,150	•	•	•		•		•			•	•	
Barbados	$$$	6,000	•	•	•	•	•					•	•	
Bonaire	$$	803	•		•							•		
British Virgin Islands	$$$	1,224		•	•	•	•	•	•	•	•	•		
Cayman Islands	$$$$	3,453	•	•	•				•					
Curaçao	$$	2,200	•	•	•	•						•		
Dominica	$	757		•			•	•		•	•			
Dominican Republic	$	37,000	•			•	•	•		•	•	•		
The Grenadines	$$$	500					•			•		•		
Grenada	$$$	1,670		•	•	•	•	•		•	•	•		
Guadeloupe	$$	7,798		•			•	•		•	•		•	
Jamaica	$$$	16,103	•	•	•		•	•		•	•	•	•	
Martinique	$$$	6,960	•	•			•	•		•	•	•		
Nevis	$$$	400		•	•	•	•	•		•		•		
Puerto Rico	$	11,800	•	•	•	•	•	•		•	•	•	•	
Saba	$	96		•			•			•				
St. Barthélemy	$$$$	715		•	•					•		•	•	
St. Eustatius	$	95		•		•				•	•			
St. Kitts	$$	1,200		•	•		•	•		•	•	•	•	
St. Lucia	$$$	2,919	•	•	•	•	•	•		•	•	•	•	
St. Martin/St. Maarten	$$$	5,638	•	•	•			•		•		•	•	
St. Vincent	$$	730			•	•	•	•		•	•			
Trinidad	$	1,462	•								•			
Tobago	$$	1,500	•						•			•		
Turks and Caicos	$$$	1,300	•		•				•			•		
U.S. Virgin Islands:														
St. Croix	$$	1,104		•	•	•	•	•		•	•		•	
St. John	$$	713		•	•	•	•	•		•		•		
St. Thomas	$$	4,696	•	•	•					•		•	•	

* Figures based on 1997 estimates

Public transportation	Fine dining	Local cuisine	Shopping	Music	Casinos	Nightlife	Diving and Snorkeling	Sailing	Golfing	Hiking	Ecotourism	Villa rentals	All-inclusives	Campgrounds	Luxury resorts	Secluded getaway	Good for families	Romantic hideaway
	●	●	●	●			●					●	●		●	●		●
●	●	●	●		●	●	●	●	●				●		●		●	
●	●	●	●	●		●	●			●					●		●	●
●	●	●	●	●		●	●		●	●		●			●		●	
					●		●	●		●	●				●			
	●	●	●	●		●	●		●		●		●		●		●	
	●		●			●	●		●			●	●		●		●	
●	●	●	●		●	●	●	●		●							●	
●		●					●			●	●				●			●
●		●				●	●					●	●		●			●
		●					●	●	●		●	●			●	●	●	●
●	●	●	●	●		●	●	●	●	●	●				●	●		
●	●	●	●		●	●	●	●		●	●	●		●	●	●		
●	●	●	●	●		●	●	●	●	●	●	●	●		●		●	●
●	●	●	●			●	●	●	●	●	●	●		●				
	●	●		●		●	●	●		●	●				●	●		●
●	●	●	●	●		●	●					●			●	●		
	●						●			●	●	●			●	●		●
		●	●	●		●	●	●				●			●	●		●
		●					●			●	●					●		
	●	●	●	●	●	●	●	●	●	●	●		●		●	●	●	●
●	●	●	●		●	●	●	●	●	●	●	●	●		●	●	●	●
●	●	●	●		●	●	●	●				●	●		●	●	●	●
●	●	●	●		●	●	●			●	●				●	●	●	●
●		●		●		●	●		●						●	●		●
		●		●		●	●		●							●		
				●		●	●	●	●	●	●				●	●		●
●	●	●	●	●		●	●	●	●	●	●				●		●	
●	●	●	●				●	●		●	●	●		●	●	●	●	●
●	●	●	●			●	●				●	●			●		●	

WHAT'S WHERE

Finding Your Own
Place in the Sun

The Caribbean Sea, an area of more than a million square miles, stretches south of Florida down to the coast of Venezuela. The **Greater Antilles**—the islands closest to the United States—are composed of Cuba, Jamaica, Hispaniola (divided into Haiti and the Dominican Republic), and Puerto Rico. (Haiti and Cuba are not included in this book.) The **Cayman Islands** lie south of Cuba, while the **Turks and Caicos Islands,** in the Atlantic Ocean north of Hispaniola and technically part of the Bahamas, are included in this book because of their proximity to and affinity with the Caribbean islands. The **Lesser Antilles**—greater in number but smaller in size than the Greater Antilles—are divided into three groups: the **Leewards** and the **Windwards** in the eastern Caribbean, and the islands in the **southern Caribbean.** Islands in the Leeward chain are the U.S. Virgin Islands (USVI), the British Virgin Islands (BVI), Anguilla, St. Martin/St. Maarten, St. Barthélemy, Saba, St. Eustatius, St. Kitts, Nevis, Barbuda, Antigua, Montserrat, and Guadeloupe; the Windwards are composed of Dominica, Martinique, St. Lucia, St. Vincent and the Grenadines, and Grenada. Barbados is just east of this group. In the southern Caribbean, off the coast of Venezuela, Trinidad and Tobago are anchored in the east, while Aruba, Bonaire, and Curaçao (known as the ABC Islands) bathe in western waters.

PLEASURES
AND PASTIMES

Arts and Nightlife

CASINOS➤ You can flirt with Lady Luck until the wee hours on several islands. San Juan, **Puerto Rico,** arguably offers the most elegant, Old World–style casinos, in the suave Bondian tradition, followed by Santo Domingo, **Dominican Republic. Aruba** and **St. Maarten** have equally spacious casinos, but the ambience is distinctly more American (and, yes, that does mean tour groups at the one-armed ban-

dits). **Curaçao,** a quieter island in general, has a few more-restrained casinos, while **Antigua** offers perhaps the gaudiest establishment—King's Casino—as well as three small hotel casinos and a few tiny slots saloons.

MUSIC➤ Calypso was born in **Trinidad,** its catchy rhythms veiling the barbed working-class satire of many of the lyrics. **Jamaica** is the home of reggae, the Rastafarian sound that has racial, political, and religious undertones; its annual Sunsplash Festival (mid-July–August) is worldrenowned. The wild, pulsating merengue, born in the **Dominican Republic,** is exuberantly danced everywhere on the island. On Puerto Rico, you'll find the slightly less frenzied salsa, whose range encompasses unabashed hip-swiveling tunes and wailing ballads lamenting lost love. Both **Martinique** and **Guadeloupe** claim to be the cradle of the sinuous beguine, whose lilting rhythm sways like the palm trees. The music that animates **Barbados** ranges from *soca* (a mix of soul and calypso) and calypso to the hottest jazz. **St. Lucia** is also proud of its annual Jazz Festival (held each May). On many islands *zouk* (a syncopated beat, almost akin to Caribbean house) is now the rage.

NIGHTLIFE➤ Steel drums, limbo dancers, and jump-ups are ubiquitous in the Caribbean. Jump-up? Simple. You hear the music, jump up, and dance. Or just indulge the art of "liming" (we call it "hanging out"), which can mean anything from playing pool or dominoes to engaging in heated political debate to dancing. Bridgetown in **Barbados, Jamaica**'s Kingston, and **Trinidad**'s Port-of-Spain are loaded with lively night places, and San Juan's glittering Vegas-style floor shows are legendary. But each island also takes great pride in its rich heritage. Many major resorts host local floor shows, a riot of song, dance, and color, incorporating such uniquely Caribbean folkloric traditions as *mocko jumbies* (evil spirits) on stilts and re-creations of Carnival costumes and masks. San Juan, Puerto Rico's yearround Le Lai Lo Festival is perhaps the most successful attempt to introduce visitors to local music and dance.

Cuisine

Caribbean food is a complex blend of indigenous, African, and colonial influences. The Arawaks, Caribs, and Taino contributed native tubers (also called "provisions" in the islands) such as yuca (also known as cassava) and *tania* (also known as taro), leafy vegetables like callaloo (similar to spinach—though slightly bitter—it also doubles as the name of the soup made from it throughout the Lesser Antilles), and such spices as cilantro and *achiote*. From Africa came plantains, yams, green pigeon peas, and assorted peppers. The Spaniards brought rice, while the British imported such plants as breadfruit from the Pacific.

Don't shy away from such classic dishes as goat water (**Dominica,** among others), pepper pot (**Grenada, St. Lucia,** and most of the Windwards), and *sancocho* (the **Dominican Republic** and **Puerto Rico**), all thick sultry stews made with various meats and vegetables. Sample johnnycakes (Caribbean muffins) with breakfast, *fungi* (cornmeal) at lunch, local vegetables like christophene with dinner. Then try tangy soursop ice cream or passion fruit sorbet for dessert.

The national dish of **Jamaica** is salt fish and ackee: salted cod and a plant that, when boiled, tastes remarkably like scrambled eggs. You can still find such exotica as *crapaud* or "mountain chicken" (actually enormous frogs' legs) or agouti (a large rodent delicious when roasted or smoked) on Dominica. And you must try flying fish, the national dish of **Barbados. Grenada,** the spice island (it produces much of the world's supply of nutmeg and cloves), has an abundance of seafood and an incredible variety of fruits and vegetables. On **St. Lucia,** where countless banana plantations cover the mountainsides, you'll find many varieties of banana prepared in dozens of ways. The cuisine on **Martinique** and **Guadeloupe** is a marvelous marriage of Creole cooking and classic French dishes; you'll find much of the same on the other French islands of **St. Martin** and **St. Barts.** You'll also find a fine selection of French wines in the French West Indies. Anegada, in the **British West Indies,** is, arguably, where you'll find the Caribbean's best lobster. You can even find *roti* (a pancake stuffed with chicken or pork and rice) and curries, East Indian legacies that have gradually spread north from **Trinidad.**

Foreign Culture and History

AFRICAN➤ **Trinidad** moves with the rhythm of calypso and is the stomping ground of a flat-out, freewheeling Carnival that rivals the pre-Lenten celebrations in Rio de Janeiro and New Orleans. The Trinidadians have built up one of the most prosperous commercial centers in the Caribbean. Haiti was once another option. (It's now politically volatile and is not covered in this book.)

BRITISH➤ It was from **St. Kitts,** known as the Mother Colony of the West Indies, that British colonists were dispatched in the 17th century to settle Antigua, Barbuda, Tortola, and Montserrat. If you're a history buff, you won't want to miss the beautifully restored Nelson's Dockyard (as in Horatio, Lord) at **Antigua**'s English Harbour; Port Royal, outside Kingston, **Jamaica,** a pirates' stronghold until an earthquake shook things up in 1692; or the hunkering fortress of Brimstone Hill on St. Kitts. Sports fans who understand the intricacies of cricket can watch matches between **Nevis** and St. Kitts teams. And the waters around Antigua and the **BVI** are a mecca for serious sailors. **Barbados,** with its lovely trade winds, has cricket, horse racing at Garrison Savannah, and rugby.

DUTCH➤ **Saba, St. Eustatius, St. Maarten, Bonaire,** and **Curaçao** all fly the Dutch flag, but there the similarity ends. Saba is a tiny volcanic island known for its beauty, its friendly inhabitants, and its gingerbread-trimmed houses. Curaçao's colorful waterfront shops and restaurants are reminiscent of Amsterdam. Quiet St. Eustatius—affectionately called Statia—has well-preserved historical sites and is famed for being the first foreign nation to salute the new American flag in 1776. The main streets of Philipsburg, the capital of St. Maarten, are lined with colorful Dutch colonial buildings replete with fretwork and verandas. Bonaire is best known for its excellent scuba diving.

FRENCH➤ **Martinique, Guadeloupe, St. Martin,** and **St. Barthélemy** (often called St. Barts or St. Barth's) compose the French West Indies. The language, the currency, the culture, and the style are très French. St. Barts is the quietest (and chicest), Martinique the liveliest, St. Martin the friendliest, and Guadeloupe the lushest.

SPANISH➤ In the **Dominican Republic,** which occupies the eastern two-thirds of the island of Hispaniola, the language and culture are decidedly Spanish. The Colonial Zone of Santo Domingo is the site of the oldest city in the Western Hemisphere; its restored buildings reflect the 15th-century Columbus period. One also gets a sense of the past in **Puerto Rico**'s Old San Juan, with its narrow cobblestone streets and filigreed iron balconies.

Getting Away from It All

If you're looking to back out of the fast lane, you can park at a secluded, spartan mountain lodge on **Dominica,** a ruggedly beautiful island laced with rivers and waterfalls and embroidered with untamed vegetation. **Puerto Rico**'s luxuriant 28,000-acre El Yunque is the only rain forest in the U.S. Forestry system. Or opt for the quiet grandeur of a renovated sugar plantation on **Nevis** or **St. Kitts,** where you can feast in an elegant dining room or enjoy a barbecue on the beach. Tranquil **Anguilla,** with soft white beaches nudged by incredibly clear water, offers posh resorts as well as small, inexpensive, locally owned lodgings. From the low-key **Turks and Caicos Islands,** which lie in stunning blue-green waters, you can boat to more than a score of cays so isolated that even the term "low-key" would imply too fast a pace.

On tiny **Saba** there's little to do but tuck into a small guest house, admire the lush beauty of the island (hiking the aptly named Mt. Scenery), and chat with the friendly Sabans. Nearby **St. Eustatius,** where adventurers can crawl down into a jungle cradled within a crater, is another friendly, laid-back island. On **St. Lucia,** you can drive right into a volcano. **St. Vincent and the Grenadines** offer three tiny, private-island luxury resorts: Young Island, Palm Island, and Petit St. Vincent. Or you can opt for sleepy islands off islands, such as Vieques and Culebra (off **Puerto Rico**), or Marie Galante, Les Saintes, and La Désirade (off **Guadeloupe**)—all with practically deserted pristine beaches, true local color, and charming guest houses. Guadeloupe also has a 74,000-acre nature park with dramatic waterfalls, cool pools, and miles of hiking trails. Majestic Mount Pelée, a not entirely dormant volcano, towers over **Martinique**'s rain forest.

Golf

According to those who have played it, the course at Casa de Campo on the **Dominican Republic** is one of the best in the Caribbean. The course at the Four Seasons Resort on **Nevis** is also challenging (and breathtaking). Golfers on St. Thomas, **USVI** play the Mahogany Run. There are superb courses in **Puerto Rico,** including four shared by the Hyatt Dorado Beach and the Hyatt Regency Cerromar Beach. Among the courses on **Jamaica** are the top-rated Tryall near Montego Bay, and the new Negril Hills Golf Club. Golf is second only to cricket in **Barbados;** the Royal Westmoreland Golf Club opened its first 18 holes for the 1996 season; another 9 holes are under way. The **Cayman Islands** have an 18-hole championship course, the Links at Safehaven, and **Aruba** has the 18-hole, Robert Trent Jones–designed Tierra del Sol.

Water Sports

BOATING AND SAILING➤ Whether you charter a boat with a crew or captain a vessel yourself, the waters of the Caribbean are excellent for boating and sailing, and the many secluded bays and inlets provide ideal spots to drop anchor and picnic or explore. The marinas on Tortola in the **BVI** at Rodney Bay and Marigot in **St. Lucia,** throughout **St. Vincent and the Grenadines,** St. Thomas in the **USVI** and Port la Royale and Oyster Pond in **St. Martin** are the starting points for some of the Caribbean's finest sailing. Yachtspeople also favor the waters around **Antigua** and put in regularly at Nelson's Dockyard, which hosts a colorful regatta in late April or early May.

DIVING➤ Although **scuba** (the word is derived from what was once an acronym for "self-contained underwater breathing apparatus") diving is surprisingly simple, *call your physician before your vacation, and make sure that you have no condition that should prevent you from diving!* A full checkup is an excellent idea, especially if you're over 30. Since it can be dangerous to travel on a plane after diving, you should schedule both your diving courses and travel plans accordingly.

Learning to dive with a reputable instructor is a must. In addition to teaching you how to resurface properly, a qualified instructor can train you to read "dive tables," the charts that calculate how long you can safely stay at certain depths. Many resorts offer courses consisting of two to three hours of instruction on land and time in a swimming pool or waist-deep water to get used to the mouthpiece and hose (the regulator) and the mask. A shallow (20-ft), supervised dive from a boat or beach follows.

Successful completion of an introductory course may prompt you to earn a certification card—often called a C-card—from an accredited diving organization: NAUI (National Association of Underwater Instructors), CMAS (Confederation Mondiale des Activités Subaquatiques, which translates into World Underwater Activities Federation), NASE (National Association of Scuba Educators), or PADI (Professional Association of Diving Instructors). PADI offers a free list of training facilities (☞ Diving *in* the Gold Guide).

Jacques Cousteau named Pigeon Island, off the west coast of **Guadeloupe,** one of the 10 best dive sites in the world. The Wall off Grand Turk in the **Turks and Caicos Islands** is a sheer drop of 7,000 ft; more than 200 mi of reef surround the chain. The eruption of **Martinique**'s Mt. Pelée at 8 AM on May 8, 1902, resulted in the sinking of several ships that are now great sites. **St. Eustatius** also has an undersea "supermarket" of ships, as well as entire 18th-century warehouses below the surface of Oranjestad Bay. The waters surrounding all three of the **Cayman Islands** are acclaimed by experts; even novices adore Stingray City on Grand Cayman, where dozens of unusually tame stingrays swim and twist around divers in the shallow waters. **Bonaire**'s 86 spectacular sites, all protected as part of the Bonaire Marine Park, make that island a diving mecca. **Tortola** is famous in diving circles for the wreck of the RMS *Rhone,* a mail ship sunk by a hurricane in 1867. **Tobago** has a great array of unspoiled coral reefs, and it's the only place in the Caribbean where divers regularly see huge manta rays. **Saba** has some of the best advanced diving with its marine park and deep dive sites. **Dominica** offers dramatic underwater walls and sudden drops, as well as unusual volcanic vents (like diving in warm champagne), off Scott's Head.

SNORKELING➤ Snorkeling requires no special skills, and many establishments that rent equipment have a staff member to teach you the basics. As with any water sport, it's never a good idea to snorkel alone. You don't have to be a great swimmer to snorkel, but occasionally currents come up that require stamina. Time seems to slow down underwater, so wear a water-resis-

tant watch and let someone on land know when to expect you back. Remember that taking souvenirs—shells, pieces of coral, interesting rocks—is forbidden. Many reefs are legally protected marine parks, where removal of living shells is prohibited because it upsets the ecology.

WATERSKIING➤ Some large hotels have their own concessions, with special boats, equipment, and instructors. Many beaches (especially those in Barbados), however, are patrolled by individuals who own boats and several sizes of skis; they offer their services through a hotel or directly to you or can be hailed like taxis. Ask your hotel staff or other guests about their experiences with these entrepreneurs. Be *sure* they provide life vests and at least two people in the boat: one to drive and one to watch the skier at all times.

WINDSURFING➤ Windsurfing is as strenuous as it is exciting, so it may not be the sport to try on your first day out, unless you're already in excellent shape. Always windsurf with someone else around who can go for help if necessary.

Weddings

More and more couples are tying the knot in the sunny Caribbean. Recognizing this trend, many islands have relaxed their marriage requirements with shortened (or no) residency periods and simplified paperwork. In addition, many no longer require blood tests. To marry on most islands, you must submit the necessary paperwork before your stay. Ship your documents by courier or, if acceptable, fax them. Keep copies of all papers, and carry them with you on your trip. If this isn't your first marriage, you'll need to present a certified divorce decree or, if you're widowed, the death certificate of your previous spouse. (If this documentation is not in the island's official language, you may be required to supply a certified translation of it.) You'll also need to provide proof of your identity and citizenship (documentation requirements for this vary slightly). Wedding fees range from about $40 to $200, including a marriage license.

The easiest and most efficient way to arrange an island wedding is through a resort. Many of them not only have wedding packages but also staff members who can help you with all the pre-wedding paperwork as well as with the ceremony itself. (Some resorts, such as SuperClubs, even offer free weddings—including paperwork and a marriage official.) As soon as your reservations are confirmed, speak with the hotel's wedding coordinator.

FODOR'S CHOICE

Beaches

★ **Shoal Bay, Anguilla.** This 2-mi, L-shape beach of talcum-powder-soft white sand may get crowded, but that's only because it's one of the prettiest in the Caribbean.

★ **Seven Mile Beach, Grand Cayman, Cayman Islands.** It's actually 5½ mi of powdery white sand, litter- and peddler-free, and headquarters for the island's water sports concessions.

★ **Grande Anse Beach, Grenada.** Gentle surf laps the gleaming sand of this 2-mi beach. To the north, you can see the narrow mouth of St. George's Harbour and the pastel houses, with their fish-scale tile rooftops, that climb the surrounding hills.

★ **Seven Mile Beach, Jamaica.** Although it's no longer untouched by development, Negril's stretch of sand (truly 7 mi) is still a beachcomber's Eden. Nude-beach areas are found along several sections.

★ **Anse du Gouverneur, St. Barthélemy.** This beautiful, secluded spot offers good snorkeling and views of St. Kitts, Saba, and St. Eustatius.

★ **Orient Beach, St. Martin.** This lively strand, with lots of beach bars, is best known as the Caribbean's premier "clothing optional" beach—the sight of cruise ship passengers gawking is alone worth a visit.

★ **Macaroni Beach, Mustique, St. Vincent and the Grenadines.** Surfy swimming (be careful!), powdery white sand, a few palm huts and picnic tables, and very few people are the draws here.

★ **Trunk Bay, St. John, USVI.** You'll find sensational snorkeling on this perfect scimitar, one of many such sandy stretches on an island that's 70% protected national park.

Hotels

★ **Cap Juluca, Anguilla.** This spectacular 179-acre resort wraps around the edge of Maunday's Bay and almost 2 mi of sugary white-sand beach. (☞ also, Hotels for Families, below). $$$$

★ **Curtain Bluff, Antigua.** The setting is breathtaking—high on a bluff between the wild Atlantic and calm Caribbean. The ambience is pure country-club elegance. $$$$

★ **Hyatt Regency Aruba Resort & Casino, Aruba.** With central public areas styled after a Spanish grandee's villa, this is the island's top-flight luxury resort. $$$$

★ **Biras Creek, Virgin Gorda, BVI.** A former guest bought this resort and completely renovated it, from building a new kitchen to lining the beach with palm trees; it's now a spectacular hideaway. $$$$

★ **Spice Island Beach Resort, Grenada.** The spacious suites, fabulous bathrooms, and private plunge pools or in-room whirlpools are great, but it's the location on beautiful Grande Anse Beach that steals the show. $$$$

★ **Grand Lido Sans Souci, Jamaica.** As if the decorative luxury of this pastel cliffside palace weren't enough, a free spa session is also offered. $$$$

★ **Habitation Lagrange, Martinique.** Experience the Old World charms of Martinique's plantation-house society at this beautiful 19th-century manor. $$$$

★ **Four Seasons Resort, Nevis.** This model chain property strikes just the right balance between posh and casual; it also has a superb Robert Trent Jones Jr.–designed championship golf course and the sensuous Pinney's Beach at your doorstep. $$$$

★ **Horned Dorset Primavera, Puerto Rico.** The emphasis here is on privacy and relaxation. The pounding of the surf and the squawk of the resident parrot are the only sounds you'll hear as you lounge on the beach. $$$$

★ **Golden Lemon, St. Kitts.** St. Kitts and its sister island are beloved by Caribbean aficionados for their impeccably restored plantation inns (and their often eccentric owners); Arthur Leaman, a former design editor of *House and Garden,* has fashioned a jewel with an eclectic, international, and refined decor and clientele. $$$$

★ **Anse Chastanet Hotel, St. Lucia.** Rooms were designed to meld into the mountainside; louvered wooden walls open to stunning Piton and Caribbean vistas or to the deep-green forest. $$$–$$$$

★ **Cotton House, Mustique, St. Vincent and the Grenadines.** Whoever coined the term "lap of luxury" must have had in mind this exquisite resort on Mustique. Hobnob with the rich and famous on their private-island playground. $$$$

★ **Young Island Resort, Young Island, St. Vincent and the Grenadines.** On its own private island a stone's throw from St. Vincent's shore, these luxury cottages are halfway between Swiss Family Robinson's tree house and the Ritz. $$$$

★ **Grace Bay Club, Providenciales, Turks and Caicos.** Enjoy the views from your suite of Grace Bay's stunning turquoise waters, and take advantage of the expertly pampering service. $$$

★ **Caneel Bay Resort, St. John, USVI.** With seven beaches spread out over 170 acres, this open-air resort is a sun worshiper's paradise. Numerous tennis courts, myriad water sports, and good restaurants make it hard to stir from this luxury property. $$$$

★ **Ritz-Carlton, St. Thomas, USVI.** Built like a palatial Italian villa, there's elegance everywhere, from the marbled-floor reception area to a pool that seems to flow right into the sea. $$$$

Hotels for Families

★ **Cap Juluca, Anguilla.** In peak season, Cap Juluca Kids participants learn through activities such as trips to an island cave to hunt for fossils and crystals, and visits with the island's traditional boat builders. $$$$

★ **La Cabana All Suite Beach Resort & Casino, Aruba.** This Eagle Beach property offers Club Cabana Nana for children 5–12 with activities from sandcastle building to Papiamento lessons. Teens can join up with others their age to enjoy windsurfing, snorkeling, billiards, beach disco parties, and more. $$–$$$$

★ **Almond Beach Village, Barbados.** The Village gives kids not just their own recreation center but a whole section of the property with guest rooms set aside for families, as well as a family pool, a playground, an ice cream shop, a pizza parlor, and a restaurant with a kids' menu. $$$$

★ **Sonesta Beach Hotel & Casino, Curaçao.** This elegant hotel keeps young vacationers busy in the Just Us Kids program with treasure hunts along the beach, arts and crafts sessions, and sandcastle building. Children's menus are available at all the resort's restaurants. $$$–$$$$

★ **Boscobel Beach, Jamaica.** At "The Country Club by the Sea," the emphasis is on family fun, starting with top-notch children's programs. Four children's centers are designed to provide age-appropriate activities. $$$$

★ **Franklyn D. Resort (FDR), Jamaica.** On arrival, each family is assigned a girl Friday, who works with the children throughout their stay. The children's miniclub includes computer training, a satellite TV room, video games, donkey rides, picnics, arts and crafts, children's slides and pools, and a kiddies' disco. $$$$

★ **Renaissance Jamaica Grande, Jamaica.** Kids can romp in a replica of Dunn's River Falls or take part in Club Mongoose activities: cricket classes, an ecology awareness plan, and even a pen-pal program that teams up young guests with local kids. $$$$

★ **Hyatt Regency Cerromar Beach, Puerto Rico.** Activities at Cerromar center around what is billed as the world's longest freshwater swimming pool. You can ride floats down the pool's 900-ft length or plummet into the waters from a high-rise slide; Camp Hyatt entertains children with supervised activities when parents want time alone. $$$$

★ **Beaches, Providenciales, Turks and Caicos.** A nursery is available for infants and toddlers while the Cuda Kids Club keeps older children happy at the children's pool, kids' gazebo, playground, table tennis and pool table facilities, and at classes in everything from sandcastle building to reggae. Video game buffs will love the state-of-the-art games (all complimentary). Teens also have special activities including disco nights, movie nights, and sports tournaments. $$$$

⭐ **Renaissance Grand Beach Resort, St. Thomas, USVI.** The Kids Club features daily, year-round fun with magic tricks, a pirate hunt, limbo lessons, nature walks, and swimming instruction for ages two and up. *$$$$*

⭐ **Sapphire Beach Resort and Marina, St. Thomas, USVI.** On one of the island's most beautiful stretches of sand, and offering excellent snorkeling in calm, shallow waters, this resort also has a program for children ages 4–12 with sandcastle building, arts and crafts, storytelling, sing-alongs, and more. *$$$$*

Restaurants

⭐ **Malliouhana, Anguilla.** Exquisite service and a romantic open-air setting are the perfect match for this restaurant's exceptional haute French cuisine and wine cellar with nearly 20,000 bottles. *$$$$*

⭐ **Julian's, Antigua.** Everything about this eatery is stylish, from the simple yet striking decor to the chef's sophisticated takes on traditional dishes. *$$*

⭐ **Gasparito Restaurant, Aruba.** Tasty local cuisine is served in the refined gallery atmosphere of an authentic country house. *$–$$*

⭐ **Hemingway's, Grand Cayman, Cayman Islands.** Enjoy the breezes on Seven Mile Beach while sipping a Seven Mile Meltdown (dark rum, peach schnapps, pineapple juice, and fresh coconut) and savoring grouper stuffed with sweet corn and crab. *$$–$$$*

⭐ **Casa del Río, Dominican Republic.** At this re-creation of a 16th-century castle, master chef Phillipe Mongereau fuses Caribbean, French, and Asian cuisines to create his exquisite dishes. *$$–$$$*

⭐ **Château de Feuilles, Guadeloupe.** It's a bit of a trip, but velvety sea urchin pâté, kingfish fillet with vanilla, and pineapple flan are worth every mile. *$$–$$$$*

⭐ **Le Fromager, Martinique.** From its perch above St-Pierre, this beautiful restaurant offers views of the town's red roofs and the sea beyond, as well as delectable crayfish *colomobo* (curry) and sole *sauce pêcheur* (in a Creole sauce). *$–$$*

⭐ **Carl Gustaf, St. Barthélemy.** Sweeping views of Gustavia harbor and delectable French cuisine with an island accent are the draws here. *$$$–$$$$*

⭐ **Chez Martine, St. Martin.** The outstanding French cuisine and the intimate waterside setting have earned this restaurant a loyal following. *$$$–$$$$*

⭐ **Veni Mange, Trinidad.** Allyson Hennessey, a Cordon Bleu–trained chef with a local TV talk show, cooks up the best Creole lunches in town. *$$*

⭐ **Anacaona, Providenciales, Turks and Caicos.** This is a true gourmet dining experience, minus the attitude. Traditional French recipes are combined with Caribbean fruits, vegetables, and spices. *$$–$$$*

⭐ **Top Hat, St. Croix, USVI.** Both the wonderful Danish menu and the Danish owners are reminders of St. Croix's colonial past. Try the *frikadeller* (meatballs in a tangy sauce) and fried Camembert with lingonberries. *$$$–$$$$*

⭐ **Virgilio's, St. Thomas, USVI.** Come here for some of the best northern Italian cuisine in the islands, and don't leave without having a Virgilio's cappuccino, a chocolate-and-coffee drink so rich, it's dessert. *$$$$*

2 Anguilla

Updated by
Pamela
Acheson

"**B**ut I arranged for lobster in advance," snarled the man at the beachfront table. "That was the whole point of coming here." The waitress tried to soothe him: "I'm sorry, we ran out of lobsters, but it's really no problem; I've talked to the manager." But her gracious assurances and charming West Indian accent had no effect. The man's face reddened until it seemed he would explode. Just then, a handsome, wiry, Anguillan man approached from the beach, a bag over his shoulder. "Ah, yes. Here is the manager with fresh lobster, now," said the waitress with a smile. "I told you it was no problem."

Peace, pampering, fine dining, and beaches are among the star attractions on Anguilla (pronounced ang-gwill-a). If you're a beach lover, you may become giddy when you first spot the island from the air; its blindingly white sand and lustrous blue and aquamarine waters are intoxicating sights. If you don't like the sand, you won't find a lot to do here. There are no glittering casinos or nightclubs, no duty-free shops stuffed with irresistible buys (although you're only about 30 watery minutes from St. Martin/St. Maarten's bustling resorts and casinos). Sophisticated cuisine is the norm here, and there are numerous beachfront restaurants that have a casual atmosphere, yet serve up the latest culinary trends.

This dry, limestone isle is the most northerly of the Leeward Islands, lying between the Caribbean Sea and the Atlantic Ocean. It stretches, from northeast to southwest, about 16 mi and is only 3 mi across at its widest point. The highest spot is 213 ft above sea level, and there are neither streams nor rivers, only saline ponds used for salt production. The island's name, a reflection of its shape, is most likely a derivative of *anguille,* which means "eel" in French. (French explorer Pierre

Laudonnaire is credited with having given the island this name when he sailed by it in 1556.)

In 1631 the Dutch built a fort here, but no one has been able to locate its site. English settlers from St. Kitts colonized the island in 1650, and, except for a brief period of independence with St. Kitts–Nevis in the 1960s, Anguilla has remained a British colony ever since.

From the early 1800s, various island units and federations were formed and disbanded, with Anguilla all the while simmering over its subordinate status and enforced union with St. Kitts. Anguillans twice petitioned for direct rule from Britain and twice were ignored. In 1967, when St. Kitts, Nevis, and Anguilla became an associated state, the mouse roared, kicked St. Kitts policemen off the island, held a self-rule referendum, and for two years conducted its own affairs. A British "peacekeeping force" then parachuted down to the island, squelching Anguilla's designs for autonomy but helping a team of royal engineers stationed there to improve the port and build roads and schools. Today Anguilla elects a House of Assembly and its own leader to handle internal affairs, while a British governor is responsible for public service, the police, and judiciary and external affairs.

The territory of Anguilla includes a few islets or cays, such as Scrub Island to the east, Dog Island, Prickly Pear Cays, Sandy Island, and Sombrero Island. The island's population numbers about 8,000, predominantly of African descent but also including descendants of Europeans, especially the Irish, large numbers of whom came over from St. Kitts in the 1600s. Historically, because the limestone land was hardly fit for agriculture, attempts at enslavement and colonization never lasted long; consequently, Anguilla doesn't bear the scars of slavery found on so many other Caribbean islands. Because the island couldn't be farmed successfully (although cotton was produced here for a while), Anguillans became experts at making a living from the sea and are known for their boatbuilding and fishing skills. Tourism is the growth industry of the island's stable economy, but the government is determined to keep expansion at a slow and cautious pace to protect the island's natural resources and beauty. New hotels are being kept small, select, and definitely casino-free. The island has chosen to emphasize its high-quality service, serene surroundings, and friendly people.

Lodging

Anguilla has a wide range of accommodations. There are grand and sumptuous resorts, apartments and villas from the deluxe to the simple, and small, cozy, locally owned guest houses. Because Anguilla has so many beautiful and uncrowded beaches, it is not necessary (the way it is on some other islands) for beach lovers to choose a particular property because of its beach. If calling to reserve a room in a resort, inquire about special packages and the various meal plans available.

CATEGORY	COST*
$$$$	over $400
$$$	$275–$400
$$	$150–$275
$	under $150

All prices are for a standard double room, excluding 8% tax and 10% service charge and meal plan.

Hotels

$$$$ ☒ **Cap Juluca.** This spectacular 179-acre resort wraps around the edge
★   of Maunday's Bay, encompassing almost 2 mi of sugary-sand beach. Within its white, Moorish-style, two-story villas are very luxurious,

very spacious accommodations. Rooms are elegantly but comfortably decorated with Moroccan fabrics, Brazilian hardwood, and built-in seating areas that have the plumpest of cushions. The immense bathrooms vary in design, but many have two-person soaking tubs and look out to porches or gardens. George's, the resort's casual beachfront grill, is open for lunch and dinner and serves Creole-inspired seafood dishes, as well as lobster, local fish, steaks, and hamburgers right off the grill. Dinner is also served at the elegant adjoining restaurant, ☞ **Eclipse.** A romantic wedding gazebo surrounded by gardens is a lovely spot to tie the knot. Parents take note: An appealing activity program—with water sports, crafts, lessons on island culture, and visits to local boat builders—for children ages 4–12 is offered during July and August. ⊠ *Maunday's Bay (Box 240),* ☎ *264/497–6666 or 800/323–0139,* FAX *264/497–6617. 98 units, 18 private villas. 2 restaurants, bar, room service, pool, golf privileges, putting green, 3 tennis courts, croquet, health club, windsurfing, boating, shop, library, laundry service, babysitting, children's programs. AE, V. EP, FAP, MAP.*

$$$$ 🏨 **Malliouhana.** Anguilla's classiest resort—which has a remarkable 70%
★ rate of repeat guests—sits on 25 lush tropical acres on a promontory between two exquisite beaches. The lobby, boutique, restaurants, and bar are in a grand, multitiered, open-air building with tile floors and mahogany walls. A staff of over 200 awaits your every need. Rooms are in the main house and also in white Moorish-style buildings set along a bluff and in gardens. Units are sleekly decorated, with white walls and tile floors, rattan furniture with fat, white cotton cushions, and Haitian prints; marble bathrooms have oversize tubs. The ☞ **Malliouhana** restaurant is the most elegant on the island. Children will like the small beachfront playground with handsome wooden slides, swings, and games. A villa with three suites and its own pool is great for family get-togethers. ⊠ *Meads Bay (Box 173),* ☎ *264/497–6111 or 800/372–1323,* FAX *264/497–6011. 20 doubles, 15 junior suites, 15 1-bedroom suites, 4 2-bedroom suites, 1 3-bedroom villa. Restaurant, bar, 2 pools, beauty salon, massage, 4 tennis courts, exercise room, windsurfing, boating, waterskiing, playground. No credit cards. EP, MAP.*

$$$–$$$$ 🏨 **Frangipani Beach Club.** The splashy, inviting Frangipani consists of
★ pink, Spanish Mediterranean–style buildings with archways, stone balustrades, wrought-iron railings, and red-clay-tile roofs. Grounds are lushly landscaped with colorful tropical flowers. Each one-, two-, or three-bedroom suite has arched windows and exposed beam ceilings and is tastefully decorated with blond rattan furniture and colorful fabrics. All units have marble and tiled bathrooms and doors that open onto spacious terraces or balconies; many have full kitchens. The restaurant overlooks the ocean and has a French-influenced menu. ⊠ *Meads Bay (Box 328),* ☎ *264/497–6442 or 800/892–4564,* FAX *264/497–6440. 24 units. Restaurant, 2 bars, windsurfing. AE. EP.*

$$$–$$$$ 🏨 **Sonesta Beach Resort Anguilla.** This pink-and-green Moorish fantasia is right on the beach, and many rooms have grand views of St. Martin. Everywhere you look lush tropical plants peek through arches and surround fountains. The route to reception, the restaurants, and the 1,200-square-ft pool may take your breath away: You pass through a long, open-air arcade with authentic Moroccan mosaics and by a long reflecting pool. The rooms are done in pastel green-and-pink prints and have Moroccan throw rugs hither and yon; marble bathrooms have spacious tubs. The restaurant, ☞ **Casablanca,** is one of the best on the island. ⊠ *Rendezvous Bay West (Box 444),* ☎ *264/497–6999 or 800/766–3782 (reservations service),* FAX *264/497–6899. 80 rooms, 10 suites. 2 restaurants, bar, piano bar, pool, 2 tennis courts, exercise room, windsurfing, bicycles, shops, library. AE, D, MC, V. CP, EP, MAP.*

## 16

Anguilla

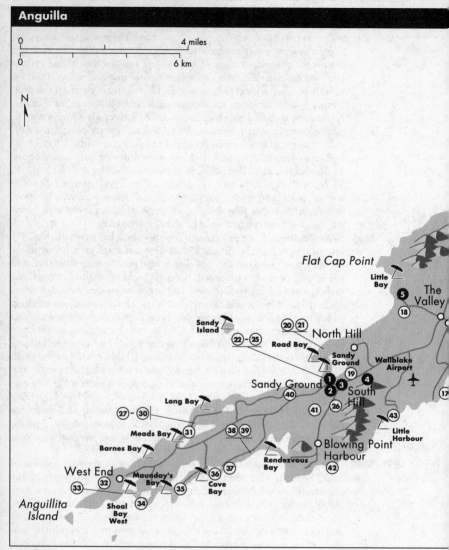

0 ————— 4 miles
0 ————— 6 km

N

Flat Cap Point

Little Bay

5

The Valley

18

20 **21**

North Hill

Road Bay

Sandy Island

22–**25**

Sandy Ground

1

3

19

Wallblake Airport

4

Sandy Ground

40

2

South Hill

26

41

43

Little Harbour

Long Bay

27–**30**

31

38 **39**

Meads Bay

Blowing Point Harbour

Barnes Bay

42

Rendezvous Bay

West End

33

32

Maunday's Bay

36 **37**

Cove Bay

34

35

17

Anguillita Island

Shoal Bay West

Exploring
Amerindian Mini-Museum, **8**
Bethel Methodist Church, **4**
Crocus Hill Prison, **5**
Heritage Collection, **9**
Island Harbour, **7**

Old Factory, **2**
Sandy Ground, **1**
Wallblake House, **3**
Warden's Place, **6**

Dining
Aquarium, **40**
Arlo's, **26**
Blanchard's, **27**
Cafe at Covecastles, **33**
Casablanca, **37**
Eclipse, **35**
Ferryboat Inn, **42**
La Fontana, **12**

Hibernia, **10**
Johnno's Beach Stop, **23**
Koal Keel, **16**
Leduc's, **32**
Lucy's Harbour View Restaurant, **41**
Malliouhana, **30**
Old House, **19**
Palm Court, **43**

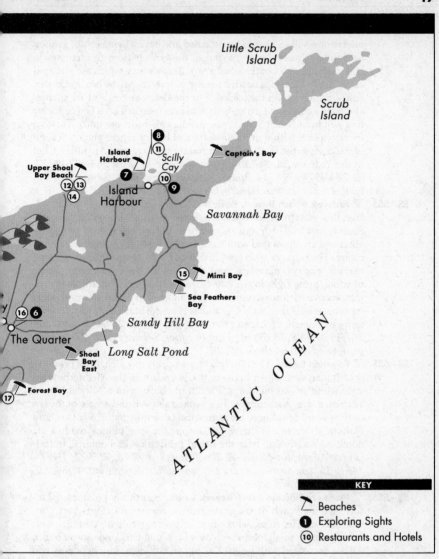

Little Scrub
Island

Scrub
Island

8

11

Island
Harbour

Scilly
Cay

Captain's Bay

Upper Shoal
Bay Beach

12 13

7

10

14

9

Island
Harbour

Savannah Bay

15 Mimi Bay

Sea Feathers
Bay

16 6

Sandy Hill Bay

The Quarter

Long Salt Pond

Shoal
Bay
East

ATLANTIC OCEAN

17 Forest Bay

KEY

Beaches

1 Exploring Sights

10 Restaurants and Hotels

Le Petit Pattissier, **16**
Riviera Bar &
Restaurant, **22**
Roy's, **18**
Straw Hat, **17**
Top of the Palms, **29**
Zara's, **14**

Lodging
Allamanda Beach
Club, **14**
Anguilla Great House
Beach Resort, **38**
Arawak Beach
Resort, **11**
Blue Waters, **34**
Cap Juluca, **35**
Carimar Beach Club, **28**

Cinnamon Reef Beach
Club, **43**
Covecastles Villa
Resort, **33**
Easy Corner Villas, **21**
Ferryboat Inn, **42**
Fountain Beach, **12**
Frangipani Beach
Club, **31**
Malliouhana, **30**
Mariners Cliffside
Beach Resort, **24**

Paradise Cove, **36**
Rainbow Reef, **15**
Rendezvous Bay
Hotel, **39**
Shoal Bay Villas, **13**
La Sirena, **29**
Skiffles Villas, **20**
Sonesta Beach
Resort Anguilla, **37**
Syd-an's, **25**

$$$ 🖼 **Cinnamon Reef Beach Club.** Low-key luxury sets the tone at this small,
★ appealing place. There are three types of casually decorated accommodations. Villa Suites are unattached and have a living room, a raised bedroom, a dressing room, a sunken shower, a patio with a hammock, and stunning views of the Caribbean. Beach Suites, which are also spacious, are in buildings nestled among palm trees on the beach. Garden Suites, which are on the backside of the Beach Suites, and are smaller and have a combined living-bedroom area (you can get a Garden Suite that adjoins a Beach Suite if you need a two-bedroom unit). This is a friendly place with a gracious staff and lots of repeat guests. Several of the chefs at the ☞ **Palm Court** restaurant have won Anguilla's Chef of the Year award. ⊠ *Little Harbour (Box 141),* ☎ *264/497–2727,* FAX *264/497–3727. 14 studios, 8 1-bedroom suites. Restaurant, bar, pool, 2 tennis courts, windsurfing. AE, MC, V. CP, MAP.*

$$–$$$ 🖼 **Arawak Beach Resort.** Built on the site of an ancient Arawak village, this waterfront resort showcases the region's Amerindian heritage. Studios and one-bedroom suites are in breezy, hexagonal, two-story villas and are decorated with hand-carved replicas of Amerindian furniture. The restaurant serves Caribbean and Amerindian dishes, using cassava, papaya, plantains, and other traditional island crops, some of which grow right in the courtyard. A small museum displays artifacts uncovered during construction. In addition to the usual water sports, canoeing is available. Scilly Cay and its beautiful beaches are just a minute away by launch. ⊠ *Island Harbour (Box 98),* ☎ *264/497–4888,* FAX *264/497–4898. 13 rooms, 3 junior suites, 1 luxury suite. Restaurant, pool, windsurfing, shop. AE. EP.*

$$–$$$ 🖼 **Fountain Beach.** The family who owns this tiny, delightful property
★ is of Italian descent—a heritage that's evident in the Mediterranean-style white stucco buildings. Each unit comes with a fully equipped kitchen, a large bathroom with a sunken shower, and a view of the sea or the pool. Furnishings are rattan and colorfully painted wicker, and Haitian art decorates the walls. Despite the long bumpy road to the hotel, guests from all over the island head to ☞ **La Fontana,** an Italian restaurant, for dinner. ⊠ *Shoal Bay (Box 474),* ☎ FAX *264/497–3491. 10 1-bedroom suites, 2 junior suites. Restaurant, pool. AE, MC, V. EP. Closed Sept.*

$$–$$$ 🖼 **Mariners Cliffside Beach Resort.** Cottages at this popular, casual resort face the beach or tropical gardens. Accommodations vary considerably in size, from deluxe two-bedroom, two-bath cottages with full kitchens to small rooms with twin beds, minibars, and shower baths. All are decorated with bright Caribbean fabrics. A stay here puts you at the far end of Anguilla's busiest stretch of sand and just a short stroll from beach bars and restaurants. Charter the resort's Boston whaler for picnics, snorkeling, and fishing trips. Local musicians perform at the on-site Carnivals restaurant, which is decorated with colorful Carnival costumes and paintings depicting life on the island. ⊠ *Sandy Ground (Box 139),* ☎ *264/497–2671,* FAX *264/497–2901. 32 1-bedroom suites, 35 studios. 2 restaurants, 2 bars, pool, hot tub, tennis court, windsurfing, boating, shop, laundry service. AE, MC, V. EP.*

$$ 🖼 **Anguilla Great House Beach Resort.** Rooms here are in white, West Indian–style bungalows strung along the bay and one of Anguilla's longest (2½ mi) beaches. From a chaise on your charming veranda, the view of the ocean is framed by vine-covered trellises and gingerbread trim. Most bungalows have five rooms, and each room has mahogany furnishings, hand-embroidered linens, a huge tile shower, and ceiling fans. The restaurant serves Continental and Caribbean cuisine. ⊠ *Rendezvous Bay (Box 157),* ☎ *264/497–6061, 800/583–9247, or 800/223–0079 (reservations service);* FAX *264/497–6019. 27 rooms. Restaurant, pool, exercise room, windsurfing. AE, MC, V. EP.*

$$ ⛢ **La Sirena.** At this small, well-run, good-value resort, you can stay in one of five spacious villas or one of 20 guest rooms. The complex's white-stucco buildings—all set amid tropical greenery—have red-tile roofs and lots of balconies and terraces. The interior decor is typical Caribbean—rattan furniture, pastel-print fabrics, and, of course, ceiling fans. The second-floor ☞ **Top of the Palms** restaurant serves Italian, Mexican, vegetarian, and Caribbean items—if the smells from the kitchen don't get you, the scent of the sea on a breeze will. ⊠ *Meads Bay (Box 200),* ☎ *264/497–6827 or 800/331–9358,* ⅏ *264/497–6829. 20 rooms, 3 2-bedroom villas, 2 3-bedroom villas. Restaurant, bar, 2 pools, snorkeling, car rental. AE, MC, V. EP, MAP.*

$$ ⛢ **Rendezvous Bay Hotel.** Opened in 1972, Anguilla's first resort sits amid 60 acres of coconut groves on the fine white sand of Rendezvous Bay, just 1 mi from the ferry dock. The lounge is the owner's showcase for his elaborate electric train set, complete with tunnels and multiple tracks. The original guest rooms are 100 yards from the beach and are quite spare, with one double and one single bed, a private shower-bath, Haitian art on the walls, and ceiling fans. Much newer two-story villas along the shore contain spacious, air-conditioned, one-bedroom suites with refrigerators or kitchenettes. These are decorated with natural wicker and pastel prints and can be joined to form larger suites. There's a wide beach and a rocky stretch of coast that's great for snorkeling. ⊠ *Rendezvous Bay (Box 31),* ☎ *264/497–6549, 908/738–0246, 800/274–4893 in the U.S., 800/468–0023 in Canada;* ⅏ *264/497–6026. 20 rooms, 24 1-bedroom villa suites. Restaurant, lounge, 2 tennis courts, windsurfing, recreation room. AE, MC, V. EP, MAP.*

$$ ⛢ **Shoal Bay Villas.** This small condominium hotel is tucked in a grove of palm trees on 2 mi of splendid sand. Units are in 13 villas and brightly decorated in pink and blue, with painted rattan furniture and fully equipped kitchens. There's no air-conditioning, but all rooms have ceiling fans. Le Beach Restaurant and Bar is an informal open-air spot that's open for breakfast, lunch, and dinner. All water sports can be arranged. ⊠ *Shoal Bay (Box 51),* ☎ *264/497–2051 or 800/497–2011,* ⅏ *264/497–3631. 2 studios, 2 2-bedroom units, 9 1-bedroom units, 2 doubles. Restaurant, bar, pool. AE, D, MC, V. EP.*

$–$$ ⛢ **Ferryboat Inn.** The spacious apartments at this small family-run complex are a bargain. Each is simply decorated with white or pastel fabrics and has a full kitchen, a dining area, cable TV, and ceiling fans. It's on a small beach and just a short walk from the ferry dock. The two-bedroom beach house is air-conditioned. All rooms and the open-air restaurant look out across the water toward hilly, more-populated St. Martin—a gorgeous view at night. The restaurant, ☞ **Ferryboat Inn,** is a romantic spot open to the ocean breezes. ⊠ *Blowing Point (Box 189),* ☎ *264/497–6613,* ⅏ *264/497–3309. 6 1- and 2-bedroom apartments, 1 beach house. Restaurant, bar, windsurfing. AE, MC, V. EP.*

$ ⛢ **Syd-an's.** These very basic efficiencies are a true bargain. Each has a kitchenette and a shower-bath and is comfortably furnished. Road Bay, with all its bustling activity, is just across the street. ⊠ *Sandy Ground,* ☎ *264/497–3180,* ⅏ *264/497–2332. 6 studios. Kitchenettes, shop. AE, MC, V. EP.*

Villas and Condominiums

The tourist office (☞ Visitor Information *in* Anguilla A to Z, *below*) has a complete listing of the plentiful vacation apartment rentals. You can also contact **Sunshine Villas** (⊠ Box 142, Blowing Point, ☎ 264/497–6149, ⅏ 264/497–6021), the **Anguilla Connection** (⊠ Island Harbour, ☎ 264/497–4403, ⅏ 264/497–4402), or **Select Villas of Anguilla** (⊠ Box 256, George Hill, ☎ 264/497–5810, ⅏ 264/497–5811).

$$$$ ⊞ **Covecastles Villa Resort.** What look like glistening, white pieces of
★ modern sculpture are actually elegant, comfortable, and very private
apartments. Each is decorated with custom-made wicker furniture,
raw-silk cushions, and hand-embroidered linens. Balconies are wide and
secluded, kitchens are state-of-the-art, and you can't beat the location
on one of Anguilla's prettiest beaches. The "supervilla" here is super-
luxurious, with a grand atrium entrance, a contemporary kitchen, and
a 75-ft veranda looking out to the ocean. The ☞ **Cafe at Covecastles**
is an elegant, intimate eatery. ⊠ *Shoal Bay West (Box 248),* ☎ *264/
497–6801, 800/348–4716, or 800/468–0023 in Canada;* FAX *264/
497–6051. 4 3-bedroom villas, 8 2-bedroom villas, 1 4-bedroom villa.
Restaurant, tennis court, shop. AE, MC, V.*

$$ ⊞ **Allamanda Beach Club.** Enjoy a view of the ocean from your bal-
cony at this casual resort. One-bedroom suites and studios fill the three-
story, white-stucco buildings just off the beach. Views are better from
the higher floors. All units have tile floors, full kitchens, and tropical-
print decor. The restaurant, ☞ **Zara's,** is a popular draw. ⊠ *Upper
Shoal Bay Beach (Box 662),* ☎ *264/497–5217,* FAX *264/497–5216. 16
units. Pool. MC, V.*

$$ ⊞ **Blue Waters.** These Moorish-style buildings sit at one end of a spec-
★ tacular ½-mi-long beach and are within walking distance of excellent
restaurants. Sunny one- and two-bedroom units are well-decorated with
pastel fabrics and have white tile floors, separate dining areas, full
kitchens, and comfortable balconies or terraces. ⊠ *Shoal Bay West (Box
69),* ☎ *264/497–6292,* FAX *264/497–3309. 9 apartments. AE, MC, V.*

$$ ⊞ **Easy Corner Villas.** The location, on a bluff overlooking Road Bay,
means you have to walk five minutes to the beach, but the price is right
at these modest two- and three-bedroom villas. All are adequately fur-
nished and have well-equipped kitchens with microwaves. ⊠ *South Hill
(Box 65),* ☎ *264/497–6433 or 264/497–6541,* FAX *264/497–6410. 10
units. Kitchenettes. AE, MC, V.*

$$ ⊞ **Paradise Cove.** The luxury one- or two- bedroom apartments here
are in two-story buildings rimmed with balconies and patios and set
amid beautiful tropical landscaping. Each spacious unit overlooks a
courtyard (which has two Jacuzzis and a large pool) and has rattan
and wicker furniture and colorful tropical-print fabrics, a fully equipped
kitchen, and private laundry facilities. Maid service and private cooks
are available. Quiet Cove Beach is just a short walk away. ⊠ *Cove Beach
(Box 135),* ☎ *264/497–2259,* FAX *264/497–2149. 14 units. Restaurant, bar, pool, shop, playground, laundry service. AE, MC, V.*

$$ ⊞ **Rainbow Reef.** Three seaside acres provide a dramatic setting for
this tiny group of villas. Each little white house has two bedrooms, a
fully equipped kitchen, a spacious dining-living area, and a large gallery
overlooking the sea. A gazebo and barbecue facilities is perched right
above the beach. ⊠ *Sea Feather Bay (Box 130),* ☎ *264/497–2817 or
708/325–2299,* FAX *264/497–3116. 4 villas. No credit cards.*

$$ ⊞ **Skiffles Villas.** These self-catering villas, perched on a hill overlooking
★ Road Bay, are usually booked a year in advance. The one-, two-, and
three-bedroom apartments have fully equipped kitchens, floor-to-ceiling windows, and pleasant porches. ⊠ *Lower South Hill (Box 82),* ☎
264/497–6619, 219/642–4855, or 219/642–4445; FAX *264/495–6110.
5 units. Pool. No credit cards.*

$–$$ ⊞ **Carimar Beach Club.** Right on the beach at beautiful Mead's Bay,
you'll find six two-story buildings that are capped by orange-tile roofs
and are full of archways. Two are close to the water's edge, but all have
ocean views. Bright white apartments have one or two bedrooms, a
living-dining area, and fully equipped kitchens. All units have a patio
or balcony that looks over the water. There's no restaurant, but sev-

eral are within walking distance. ✉ *Meads Bay (Box 327),* ☎ *264/ 497–6881,* 𝔽𝔸𝕏 *264/497–6071. 23 rooms. 2 tennis courts. AE, MC, V.*

Dining

Anguilla has an extraordinary number of excellent restaurants—from truly elegant establishments to down-home seaside shacks. Most restaurants are open to the breezes, and many have terraces where you can dine under the stars. Call ahead—in the winter to make a reservation, and in the late summer and fall to confirm if the place you've chosen is open. Restaurants not affiliated with a hotel often tack on an additional 5% to the service charge if you pay by credit card.

What to Wear

During the day, casual clothes are widely accepted: Shorts will be fine, but bathing suits and cover-ups won't. In the evening, shorts are okay at the extremely casual eateries. Elsewhere, women should wear sundresses or nice casual slacks; men will be fine in shirtsleeves and casual pants. Some hotel restaurants are more formal and may have a jacket requirement in high season; ask when you make your reservation.

CATEGORY	COST*
$$$$	over $45
$$$	$35–$45
$$	$25–$35
$	under $25

*per person for a three-course meal, excluding drinks and 8% sales tax

West End

CONTEMPORARY

$$$–$$$$ ✕ **Eclipse.** At the end of 1996, Belgian Bernard Erpicum, owner of the trendy celebrity hot spot Eclipse in Los Angeles, took over this restaurant at the ☞ **Cap Juluca** resort. "Cuisine of the Sun" is the theme of the California-inspired menu, and selections include roasted local wahoo with an almond-orange crust and flash-grilled ahi tuna with herbs and salsa. Risottos (including one with lobster), several pastas, and sashimi are also available. The setting at the water's edge on a half-moon bay is open to soft evening breezes. ✉ *Maunday's Bay,* ☎ *264/ 497–6666. Reservations essential. AE, MC, V.*

ECLECTIC

$$$$ ✕ **Malliouhana.** Sparkling crystal and fine china, exquisite service, ★ and a spectacularly romantic, candlelit, open-air setting complement exceptional haute French cuisine at this restaurant in the ☞ **Malliouhana** resort. Consulting chef Michel Rostang, renowned for his Paris boîte, and chef Alain Laurent create a new menu each season. Past choices have included conch chowder with fennel, grilled snapper with pumpkin, lobster medallions with seasoned polenta, and chicken breasts from Bresse stuffed with asparagus. Don't pass up desserts here. The wine cellar contains nearly 25,000 bottles. ✉ *Meads Bay,* ☎ *264/497– 6111. Reservations essential. AE, MC, V. Closed Sept.–Oct.*

$$$–$$$$ ✕ **Cafe at Covecastles.** Elegant, intimate dinners are served here amid a garden overlooking beautiful Shoal Bay. Each season a new menu of excellent dishes combines the best of Caribbean and French cooking. Past favorites include West Indian chicken stew, lobster medallions with ginger sauce, roasted vegetable lasagna, balsamic-marinated tuna with sautéed spinach and veal chops in truffle cream sauce. There are only seven tables here, and ☞ **Covecastles Villa Resort** guests have priority, so call for reservations well in advance. ✉ *Shoal Bay West,* ☎ *264/ 497–6801. Reservations essential. AE. Closed Sept.–Nov. No lunch.*

$$$ ✕ **Blanchard's.** Bob and Melinda Blanchard's popular waterfront spot
★   has floor-to-ceiling doors that fold back to let in the breezes. The
eclectic menu includes Cajun, Caribbean, and Asian dishes: green-
chili corn cakes, wild mushroom ragout, and Indonesian beef satay for
starters; swordfish stuffed with leeks and fontina cheese or red snap-
per brushed with a balsamic mango glaze for entrées. Fish is the spe-
cialty, and if you hanker for more straightforward fare, you can order
a Black Angus hand-cut steak, a free-range chicken, or one of the
daily pastas. Desserts are tempting, especially the cappuccino brown-
ies and the remarkable gingerbread box filled with warm bananas and
cinnamon cream. There's also a 2,000-bottle wine cellar and a selec-
tion of fine Armagnacs and cognacs. ⊠ *Meads Bay,* ☎ *264/497–
6100. Reservations essential. AE, MC, V. Closed Sun. No lunch.*

$$$ ✕ **Leduc's.** Chef Maurice Leduc, owner of the well-known Autre Chose
in Boston, brings his culinary skills to his new West End open-air
restaurant. Folk art murals decorate the dining terrace, and the menu
is an inspired blend of French, contemporary, and Caribbean cuisines.
Stop here for tasty fish cakes with tropical salsa; fresh loin of tuna grilled
with a sesame and cilantro pesto; veal marsala; grilled duck with fresh
fig sauce; and spaghettini tossed with caramelized onion, eggplant, and
goat cheese. ⊠ *West End Bay,* ☎ *264/496–6393. AE, MC, V. No lunch.*

$$ ✕ **Top of the Palms.** The atmosphere may be casual at this indoor-out-
door eatery in ☞ **La Sirena** hotel but the chefs are definitely on their
toes. Anguillan fish soup or crispy conch fritters are good starters. Then
move on to seafood quesadillas, tagliatelle with fresh garden vegeta-
bles, steamed grouper on a bed of lemongrass, or thyme-crusted fillet
of snapper. ⊠ *Mead's Bay,* ☎ *264–497–6827. AE, MC, V.*

Sandy Ground, South Hill, and Rendezvous Bay

CARIBBEAN/CREOLE

$$ ✕ **Lucy's Harbour View Restaurant.** At this terrace restaurant, sweeping sea views and Lucy's delicious whole red snapper are the special-
ties. You could also try curried and Creole dishes, such as conch and
goat. Be sure to order the sautéed potatoes (but be very conservative
with the tableside hot sauce). A reggae band plays on Wednesday and
Friday nights. ⊠ *South Hill,* ☎ *264/497–6253. MC, V. Closed Sun.*

$ ✕ **Johnno's Beach Stop.** Performances by the island band Dumpa and
the AnVibes make this *the* place to be on Sunday afternoon, but the
grilled or barbecued lobster, kingfish, snapper (all of which Johnno
catches himself), and chicken are good any time. This is a classic
Caribbean beach bar, attracting a funky eclectic mix, from locals to
movie stars. ⊠ *Sandy Ground,* ☎ *264/497–2728. MC, V.*

ECLECTIC

$$$–$$$$ ✕ **Casablanca.** Multiarched ceilings with Moroccan mosaics and night-
time views of St. Maarten's twinkling lights lend a dramatic air to this
favored dining spot in the ☞ **Sonesta Beach Resort Anguilla.** Appe-
tizers include fresh lobster spring roll, island pumpkin soup, and
chunky fish chowder. Grilled tuna with sesame soy glaze, potato crusted
Atlantic salmon, shellfish pepper pot, and beef tenderloin with béar-
naise sauce are a few of the entrées found on a menu that hints at
Caribbean, Pacific Rim, and South American flavors. The mascar-
pone pumpkin cheesecake may sound unorthodox, but it's the hit of
the dessert list. ⊠ *Rendezvous Bay,* ☎ *264/497–6999. AE, MC, V.*

$$–$$$$ ✕ **Riviera Bar & Restaurant.** The menu here has a mix of French, Creole, and Asian offerings—French cheeses, homemade pâté, sushi,
sashimi, oysters sautéed in soy sauce and sake, and conch in a spicy
Creole sauce. The grilled lobster and fish soup Provençale and the
sumptuous chocolate mousse are highly recommended. Crowds
gather here Saturday evening for special paella or couscous dinners.

The beachside setting is informal, and tables are on a huge deck overlooking the water. There's a very happy happy hour from 6 to 7 daily. Live bands play here in season. ⊠ *Sandy Ground,* ☎ *264/497–2833. AE, MC, V.*

$$ ✕ **Ferryboat Inn.** This charming waterside restaurant in the ☞ Ferryboat Inn is a short walk from the ferry dock at Blowing Point. Tables
★ are open to the breezes, and the nighttime view of St. Martin makes it even more romantic. The French onion and black-bean soups, grilled lobster, lobster thermidor (the specialty), and *entrecôte du vin au poivre* (a version of steak au poivre with a red wine sauce) are all delicious. There are also veal and chicken dishes, hamburgers, and omelets. ⊠ *Cul de Sac Rd., Blowing Point,* ☎ *264/497–6613. AE, MC, V. No lunch Sun.*

$ ✕ **Aquarium.** A popular local hangout, this upstairs terrace eatery is gussied up with gingerbread trim, bright blue walls, and red tablecloths. For lunch, there are sandwiches and burgers. Stewed lobster, curried chicken, barbecued chicken, and mutton stew are offered at night. ⊠ *South Hill,* ☎ *264/497–2720. No credit cards. Closed Tues., Sun.*

ITALIAN

$–$$ ✕ **Arlo's.** This popular Italian restaurant, with its expansive dining terrace, sits on a hilltop overlooking the sea. It has just been taken over
★ by Frenchman Phillipe Kim, and his menu has lots of new selections. The pizza is still the best on the island; if you don't want it as a main course, consider sharing one as an appetizer. Then choose from a list of entrées that includes seafood fettuccine, *farfalle* (bow-tie pasta) with salmon in a dill sauce, chicken stuffed with mushrooms and spinach in a lobster sauce, spaghetti carbonara, and veal marsala. There's always a nightly appetizer and entrée special. ⊠ *South Hill,* ☎ *264/497–6810. MC, V. Closed Sun. and Sept.–Oct. No lunch.*

The Valley, George Hill, and The Forest

CAFÉ

$ ✕ **Le Petit Patissier.** This café is above the well-known ☞ Koal Keel restaurant. Freshly brewed teas, espresso, and cappuccino plus just-baked pastries, breads, and cakes are served from morning to night indoors or on the small balcony. ⊠ *The Valley,* ☎ *264/497–2930. AE, MC, V. Closed Sept.–mid-Oct.*

CARIBBEAN/CREOLE

$–$$ ✕ **Old House.** Guests enjoy the relaxing atmosphere and the local cuisine at this lovely restaurant on a hill near the airport. Tables are dec-
★ orated with fresh flowers, even at breakfast, when regulars know to order the island fruit pancakes. For lunch or dinner try the conch simmered in lime juice and wine, curried local lamb with pigeon peas and rice, or Anguillan pot fish cooked in a sauce of limes, garlic, and tomatoes. ⊠ *George Hill,* ☎ *264/497–2228. MC, V.*

CONTEMPORARY

$$$ ✕ **Palm Court.** This stylish eatery in the ☞ Cinnamon Reef Beach Club
★ is a long palm-lined corridor with terra-cotta tile floors, Haitian furniture, a beautiful mural of local fish, and arched picture windows that frame the Caribbean. Frenchman Didier Rochat and Anguillan Vernon Hughes collaborate to create an exciting nouvelle Caribbean menu. Char-grilled tuna atop papaya with red-onion salsa, diced lobster and fresh vegetables served in the shell with basmati rice and baby leeks, spicy jumbo shrimp with Thai chilies and coconut milk, roast duck in a port wine and raisin sauce, and rack of lamb roasted with island sage are house specialties. The mango puffs in caramel sauce are famous. ⊠ *Little Harbour,* ☎ *264/497–2727. AE, MC, V. Closed mid-Sept.–mid-Oct.*

ECLECTIC

$$$–$$$$ ✕ **Koal Keel.** This restaurant, in a restored 18th-century great house
★   that was once part of a sugar and cotton plantation, is a nice alternative to the island's beachfront eateries. The dining room has period furniture, and the original handwrought stone walls are broken by window-size open spaces, creating a cool, breezy atmosphere. A replica rock oven is used to bake fresh breads and to roast chickens and racks of lamb. The cuisine here is "Euro-Carib," and Chef Smoke makes abundant use of local ingredients. Try the pea soup, a smooth blend of pigeon peas and Caribbean sweet potatoes, then move on to the succulent goatfish with snow peas and ginger, the lobster ravioli, or the smoked grouper on a bed of leeks. Save room for the chocolate fondant. More than 20,000 bottles of wine are stored in the wine cellar here. For lighter fare, try ☞ **Le Petit Patissier** upstairs. ⊠ *The Valley,* ☎ *264/497–2930. Reservations essential. AE, MC, V. Closed Sept.–mid-Oct.*

$$–$$$ ✕ **Straw Hat.** If you pick a table along the edge of this remarkable restaurant, you can peer right into the sea: the hexagonal, open-air structure is built over the water and gentle waves roll in beneath it. The menu combines French and Caribbean ingredients and cooking styles. For appetizers, start with Caribbean fish chowder, pork with chestnut dumplings, or sautéed shrimp. Grilled New York strip steak, conch cakes, Jamaican jerk pork or chicken, and grouper with citrus sauce are specialties. ⊠ *Forest Bay,* ☎ *264/497–8300. AE, MC, V. No lunch.*

ENGLISH

$ ✕ **Roy's.** The dainty pink-and-white-covered deck belies the rowdy reputation of Roy and Mandy Bosson's pub, an Anguillan mainstay with some of the island's best buys. The menu's most popular items are Roy's fish-and-chips, cold English beer, pork fricassee, and a wonderful chocolate rum cake. Sunday's lunch special is roast beef and Yorkshire pudding. A faithful clientele gathers in the lively bar. ⊠ *Crocus Bay,* ☎ *264/497–2470. MC, V. Closed Mon. No lunch Sat.*

East End

ECLECTIC

$$–$$$$ ✕ **Hibernia.** Some of the island's most creative dishes are served in this wood-beamed cottage restaurant. Unorthodox yet delectable culinary pairings—inspired by the chef's continued travels from France to the Far East—include Peking chicken pancakes, duck breast with grilled almonds and passion-fruit sauce, fricassee of lobster in mustard cinnamon sauce, spicy lobster soufflé, and an unusual Thai-inspired bouillabaisse of assorted local seafood. For dessert, try the talked-about prunes in Armagnac chocolate sauce with homemade chestnut ice cream. ⊠ *Island Harbour,* ☎ *264/497–4290. AE, MC, V. Closed Mon.*

$$–$$$ ✕ **Zara's.** Award-winning island chef Shamash presides at this cozy indoor restaurant at the ☞ **Allamanda Beach Club,** where the cuisine is a mix of Italian and Caribbean. Try the lobster pasta in a white wine sauce, the garlic-crusted snapper, or the very popular seafood platter, which has a bit of everything from conch to calamari. Grilled chicken, steaks, and veal are also available. ⊠ *Upper Shoal Bay,* ☎ *264/497–3229. AE, MC, V.*

ITALIAN

$$ ✕ **La Fontana.** At this small restaurant in the ☞ **Fountain Beach** hotel Northern Italian dishes have spicy island touches, thanks to the Rastafarian chef. Possibilities include fettuccine *al limone* (with a sauce of black olives, lemon, Parmesan, and butter), pasta with lobster and fresh herbs, and a daily Rasta pasta special. Also on the menu are grilled duck, steak, fish, and chicken, as well as a fantastic lobster dish cooked

with black olives, capers, and tomatoes. ⊠ *Shoal Bay,* ☎ *264/497–3492. AE, MC, V. Closed Wed. and Sept.*

Beaches

Renowned for their beauty, the dazzling white-sand beaches are the best reason to come to Anguilla, and each one is different. You'll find long stretches that are great for walking, deserted sands, and beaches lined with bars and restaurants—all accompanied by surf that ranges from wild to super calm.

NORTHEAST COAST

If you make the grueling, four-wheel-drive-only trip along the inhospitable dirt road that leads to the northeastern end of the island toward Junk's Hole, **Captain's Bay** will reward you with peaceful isolation. The surf here slaps the sands with a vengeance, and the undertow is strong—wading is the safest water sport.

The mostly calm waters of **Island Harbour** are surrounded by a long, slender beach. For centuries Anguillans have ventured from these sands in colorful, handmade fishing boats to seek the day's catch. There are several beach bars and restaurants, and this is the departure point for the three-minute boat ride to **Scilly Cay.** A beach bar on the cay serves drinks and grilled seafood.

NORTHWEST COAST

Barnes Bay is a superb for windsurfing and snorkeling. In high season this beach can get a bit crowded with day-trippers from St. Martin.

At **Little Bay,** sheer cliffs embroidered with agave and creeping vines rise behind a small gray-sand beach, usually accessible only by water (it's a favored spot for snorkeling and night dives). Virtually assured of total privacy, the hale and hearty can also clamber down the cliffs by rope to explore the caves and surrounding reef.

The clear blue waters of **Road Bay** beach are usually dotted with yachts. The Mariners Cliffside Beach Resort, several restaurants, a water-sports center, and lots of windsurfing and waterskiing activity make this area (often referred to as Sandy Ground) an active and commercial one. It's a typical Caribbean scene as fishermen set out in their boats and goats ramble the littoral at will. The snorkeling isn't very good here, but the sunset vistas are glorious.

From a distance, **Sandy Island,** nestled in coral reefs about 2 mi from Road Bay, appears to be no more than a tiny speck of sand and a few spindly palm trees. It has the look of a classic deserted island, but it's got the modern-day comforts of a beach boutique, beach bar, and restaurant. Use of snorkeling gear and underwater cameras is free. A ferry heads there every hour from Sandy Ground.

SOUTHEAST COAST

Mimi Bay is a difficult-to-reach, isolated, ½-mi-long beach east of Sea Feathers Bay. The trip is worth it. When the surf is not too rough, the barrier reef makes for great snorkeling.

Not far from Sea Feathers Bay is **Sandy Hill,** a base for fishermen. Here you can buy fish and lobster right off the boats and snorkel in the warm waters. Don't plan to sunbathe—the beach is quite narrow here.

Unfortunately, it's no longer a secret that **Shoal Bay East**—Shoal Bay, via Shoal Bay Road—is one of the prettiest beaches in the Caribbean. But this 2-mi L-shape strip of talcum-powder-soft white sand is still worth a visit. There are beach chairs, umbrellas, and a backdrop of sea-grape and coconut trees. For seafood and tropical drinks there's

Trader Vic's, Uncle Ernie, and the Round Rock. Shops that sell T-shirts, sunscreen, and the like abound. There's good snorkeling in the offshore coral reefs, and the water-sports center here can arrange diving, sailing, and fishing trips.

SOUTHWEST COAST

Cove Bay, lined with coconut palms, is one of the quieter beaches on Anguilla. There's a little beach bar and a place you can rent floats, umbrellas, and mats.

One of the most popular beaches, wide, mile-long **Maunday's Bay** is known for good swimming and snorkeling; you can rent water-sports gear at Tropical Watersports (☞ Boating and Sailing *in* Outdoor Activities and Sports, *below*).

Rendezvous Bay is 1½ mi of pearl-white sand. The water is calm, and there's a great view of St. Martin. The Anguilla Great House Beach Resort's (☞ Lodging, *above*) open-air beach bar is handy for snacks and frosty island drinks.

Adjacent to Maunday's Bay is **Shoal Bay West,** a dazzling beach with several striking villa complexes, including the sculpturelike Cove Castles. Beachcombers may find lovely conch shells here.

Outdoor Activities and Sports

BOATING AND SAILING

Anguilla is the perfect place to try all kinds of boating and sailing activities, from lazing about in a paddleboat to energetically managing a Windsurfer. The major resorts offer complimentary Windsurfers, paddleboats, and water skis to their guests. If your hotel has no water-sports facilities, you can get in gear at the **Dive Shop** (⊠ Sandy Ground, ☎ 264/497–2020) or charter its *Sundancer,* a 30-ft powerboat. **Tropical Watersports** (⊠ Sandy Ground, ☎ 264/497–6666) rents Sunfish and Hobie Cats. You can rent sailboats and speedboats from **Sandy Island Enterprises** (⊠ Sandy Ground, ☎ 264/497–6395).

CYCLING

There are plenty of flat stretches on Anguilla, making wheeling pretty easy. **Multiscenic Tours** (☎ 264/497–5810) rents mountain bikes at George Hill and the Blowing Point Ferry Terminal.

FISHING

Albacore and kingfish are among the sea creatures angled after off Anguilla's shores. Arrange trips through **Sandy Island Deep Sea Fishing** in Sandy Ground (☎ 264/497–6395).

HORSEBACK RIDING

Scenic nature trails and miles of beaches are the perfect places to horseback ride, even if you're the novice. Ride English or Western at **El Rancho–Del Blues** (☎ 264/497–6164). Rides are scheduled daily, and end with an afternoon swim at a beach.

SCUBA DIVING

Seven sunken wrecks and a long barrier reef and exceptionally clear water offer excellent diving opportunities. The **Dive Shop** (☞ Boating and Sailing, *above*) is a full-service dive operator with a PADI 5-Star Training Center.

SEA EXCURSIONS

There are several tiny islands just offshore that you can easily reach by boat. Picnic, swimming, and diving excursions to Prickly Pear, Sandy Island, and Scilly Cay are available through **Sandy Island Enterprises** (⊠ Sandy Ground, ☎ 264/497–6395). **Anguilla Sails Ltd.** (⊠

Sandy Ground, ☎ 264/497–2253) offers day sails, sunset sails, and moonlight cruises. *Chocolat* (✉ Sandy Ground, ☎ 264/497–3394) is a 35-ft catamaran that is available for private charter and also has scheduled day, sunset, and evening excursions to nearby cays. **BING!** (✉ Sandy Ground, ☎ 264/497–6395) specializes in day, evening, and overnight trips for two to four people in a 37-ft sailboat.

TENNIS

There are a number of tennis courts (some lighted) and several tennis pros at resorts on Anguilla. If you're not staying at a resort but wish to use its courts, simply call in advance and make a reservation. Peter Burwash International, highly respected for its tennis programs, manages those at the **Malliouhana** (☎ 264/497–6111), which has four Laykold hard courts, and at **Cap Juluca** (☎ 264/497–6666) with three hard courts. Two Deco Turf tournament courts are at **Cinnamon Reef Beach Club** (☎ 264/497–2727). **Carimar** (☎ 264/497–6881) has one hard court. You'll find two hard courts at the **Fountain Beach and Tennis Club** (☎ 264/497–6395). There are two Laykold hard courts at the **Sonesta Beach Resort Anguilla** (☎ 264/497–6999). **Rendezvous Bay** (☎ 264/497–6549) has two hard courts. There's one Deco Turf hard court at **Cove Castles** (☎ 264/497–6801). The **Mariners Cliffside Beach Resort** (☎ 264/497–2671) has one hard court.

Shopping

The free publications *Anguilla Life* and *What We Do in Anguilla,* which are available at the airport and in shops and hotel lobbies, are full of shopping tips. There are a number of outstanding local artists who sell their work in galleries. For upscale European designer sportswear, check out the little clothing boutiques (most of which are branches of far larger stores in Marigot on St. Martin). For a better selection, catch the ferry to St. Martin and spend the day in chic boutiques showcasing the latest in Italian and French fashions.

CLOTHES

Azemmour Boutique (✉ Cap Juluca resort, Maunday's Bay, ☎ 264/497–6666) specializes in European swimwear and also carries coverups, sandals, beach bags, and fine jewelry.

Beach Stuff (✉ Back St., South Hill, ☎ 264/497–6814), in its brightly painted building, attracts the younger crowd with bathing suits and cover-ups, sunglasses, T-shirts, and other sportswear.

Boutique at Malliouhana (✉ Meads Bay, ☎ 264/497–6111) is the most upscale shop on Anguilla, selling such designer specialties as jewelry by Oro De Sol, Gottex swimwear, Go Silk resort wear, and Robert LaRoche sunglasses.

Caribbean Fancy (✉ George Hill Rd., ☎ 264/497–3133) features Ta-Tee's line of cool, crinkle-cotton resort wear and also sells books, coffees and spices, and gift items.

Caribbean Silkscreen (✉ South Hill, ☎ 264/497–2272) creates designs and prints them on golf shirts, hats, sweatshirts, and jackets.

Java Wraps (✉ George Hill Rd., ☎ 264/497–5497), a small outpost of the Caribbean chain, has superb batik clothing for the whole family.

La Romana (✉ Meads Bay, ☎ 264/497–6181), a miniversion of the well-known international specialty boutique, is the place to go for swimwear, Fendi fashions, and fine luggage.

La Sirena Boutique (✉ Meads Bay, ☎ 264/467–6827) is bursting with colorful dresses, slacks, belts, and other accessories.

Objets D'Art Collectibles (✉ Warden's Place, The Valley, ☎ 264/497–2787) is a gallery that also sells "wearable art," sandals, jewelry, and fabrics.

Oluwakemi's Afrocentric Boutique (⊠ Lansome Rd., The Valley, ☎ 264/497–5411) sells books, sandals, umbrellas, jewelry, T-shirts, hats, and a variety of other garments. You can also choose from an array of fabrics and have virtually any item of apparel custom-made.

Sunshine Shop (⊠ South Hill, ☎ 264/497–6964) stocks cotton *pareos* (sarong-like beach cover-ups), silk-screen items, cotton resort wear, and hand-painted Haitian wood items.

Valley Gap (⊠ Shoal Bay Beach, ☎ 264/497–2754) sells a selection of local crafts, plus T-shirts and swimwear.

Vanhelle Boutique (⊠ Sandy Ground, ☎ 264/497–2965) is a little shop with an appealing selection of gift items, as well as Brazilian swimsuits for men and women.

Whispers (⊠ Cap Juluca, ☎ 264/497–6666) carries Caribbean handicrafts and stylish resort wear for men and women.

FOODSTUFFS

Fat Cat Gourmet. If you plan to picnic (on the beach or in your room), try this place for escargots to go, as well as take-out quiche, soups, chili, chicken, and conch dishes. (⊠ *George Hill,* ☎ *264/497–2307).*

Amy's Bakery (⊠ Blowing Point, ☎ 264/497–6775) turns out homemade pies, cakes, tarts, cookies, and breads.

HANDICRAFTS

Alicea's Place (⊠ The Quarter, ☎ 264/497–3540), a small boutique, sells locally made ceramics and pottery and lifelike wooden flowers from Bali.

Anguilla Arts & Crafts Center (⊠ The Valley, ☎ 264/497–2200) carries a wide selection of island crafts.

Cheddie's Carving Studios (⊠ The Cove, ☎ 264/497–6027) showcases Cheddie's own fanciful creatures crafted out of textured woods, including mahogany, walnut, and driftwood. Even the whimsically carved desk and balustrade in his studio testify to his vivid imagination.

Devonish Art Gallery (⊠ George Hill Landing, ☎ 264/497–2949) purveys the wood, stone, and clay creations of Courtney Devonish, an internationally known potter and sculptor, as well as works by other prominent local artists.

Michele R. Lavalette Art Studio (⊠ North Hill, ☎ 264/497–5668) displays the appealing watercolors and oil paintings of Michele Lavalette, a French artist who has lived on Anguilla since 1985. Stop in and you'll often get a chance to meet the artist herself.

Mother Weme (⊠ The Valley, ☎ 264/497–4504) is an internationally known artist who paints charming montages of Anguillan and general Caribbean life, incorporating homes, churches, marketplaces, and people. Call for an appointment.

New World Gallery (⊠ The Valley, ☎ 264/407–5950) has frequent exhibits of local art and also sells jewelry, textiles, and antiquities.

Savannah Gallery (⊠ The Valley, ☎ 264/497–2263) specializes in Caribbean art, including watercolors, oil paintings, and brightly painted metal work.

Scruples Gift Shop (⊠ Social Security Bldg., The Island, ☎ 264/497–2800) offers simple gift items, such as shells, handmade baskets, wooden dolls, hand-crocheted mats, lace tablecloths, and bedspreads.

Nightlife and The Arts

Nightlife

A Calypso combo plays most nights in season at **Cinnamon Reef Beach Club** (⊠ Little Harbour, ☎ 264/497–2727). The **Dune Preserve** (⊠ Rendezvous Bay, ☎ no phone) is the home of Bankie Banx, Anguilla's most popular recording star, who performs here weekends and during the full

moon. During high season, **Eclipse** (⊠ Cap Juluca, ☎ 264/497–6666)
entertains with live music at dinner. Things are pretty loose and lively
at **Johnno's Beach Stop** (⊠ Sandy Ground, ☎ 264/497–2728), a beach
bar that has live music and alfresco dancing nightly and also on Sunday afternoons, when it feels as if the entire island population is in at-
tendance. **Raffie's Back Street** (⊠ Sandy Ground, ☎ 264/497–3918)
is the spot to go for late-night—even all-night on weekends—food, music,
and dance. For soft dance music after a meal, go to **Lucy's Palm Palm**
(⊠ Sandy Ground☎ 264/497–2253); there is usually a live band on
Tuesday and Friday evenings. **Uncle Ernie's** (⊠ Shoal Bay, ☎ no phone)
often has music, and a lively crowd heads here almost every night. At
Smitty's (⊠ Island Harbour, ☎ 264/497–4300) the crowd swings all
day and well into the night. There's live music nightly in season at the
Malliouhana (⊠ Meads Bay, ☎ 264/497–6111) during cocktail hours.

The Arts

The **Mayoumba Folkloric Theater,** a group made up of the best performers
in the Anguilla Choral Circle, performs song-and-dance skits depicting Antillean and Caribbean culture with African drums and a string
band. They appear every Thursday night at **La Sirena Hotel** (⊠ Meads
Bay, ☎ 264/497–6827).

Exploring Anguilla

Exploring on Anguilla is mostly about checking out the spectacular
beaches and classy resorts. Though the island has only a few roads,
some are in bad condition and none of them is marked, so you may
get lost your first time out. Although locals are more than happy to
provide directions, having a map—and checking it frequently against
passing landmarks—is the best strategy. If you didn't get a map at the
airport, the ferry dock, or your hotel, head to the tourist office in the
Valley (☞ Visitor Information *in* Anguilla A to Z, *below*).

*Numbers in the margin correspond to points of interest on the Anguilla
map.*

SIGHTS TO SEE

❽ Amerindian Mini-Museum. A small display of objects used by the
Arawak Indians that inhabited Anguilla centuries ago is showcased here.
There's also a 4- × 8-ft oil painting that shows what Big Springs, a nearby
ceremonial ground, might have looked like when Amerindians lived
there. ⊠ *Arawak Beach Resort, Island Harbour,* ☎ *264/497–4888.*
▭ *Free.* ☉ *Mon.–Sat. 9–4:30.*

❹ Bethel Methodist Church. Not far from Sandy Ground, at South Hill,
this charming little church provides an excellent example of skillful island stonework. It also has some colorful stained-glass windows. ⊠
South Hill, ☎ *no phone.*

❺ Crocus Hill Prison. On the highest point in Anguilla—213 ft above sea
level—the historical prison is pretty much in ruin, but the view is outstanding. ⊠ *Valley Rd. at Crocus Hill.*

❾ Heritage Collection. Anguillan artifacts, old photographs, and records
trace the island's history from the days of the Arawaks to the present
at this inviting museum. You can see examples of ancient pottery
shards and stone tools along with fascinating photographs of the island in the early 20th century, including many that depict the heaping
and exporting of salt and the christening of schooners. Also on display is a complete set of beautiful postage stamps issued by Anguilla
since 1967. ⊠ *East End at Pond Ground,* ☎ *264/497–4440.* ▭ *Free.*
☉ *Mon.–Sat. 10–4:30.*

❼ Island Harbour. Anguillans have been fishing for centuries in the brightly painted, simple, handcrafted fishing boats that line the shore of the harbor. It's hard to believe, but skillful pilots take these little boats out to sea as far as 50 or 60 mi. Late afternoon is the best time to see the day's catch—piles of lobsters and wriggling local fish. ⊠ *Island Harbour, at northwest end of island, facing Island Harbour Bay.*

❷ Old Factory. For many years the cotton that was grown on Anguilla and imported to England was ginned in this beautiful historic building. Some of the original ginning machinery is intact and on display here, and this is also the home of the **Anguilla Tourist Board** (☞ Visitor Information *in* Anguilla A to Z, *below*). ⊠ *The Valley,* ☎ *264/497–2759.* 🎟 *Free.* ☉ *Weekdays 10–noon, 1–4.*

❶ Sandy Ground. This is by far the most active and most developed of the island's beaches, and almost everyone who comes to Anguilla stops by here at least one afternoon or evening. Little open-air bars and restaurants line the shore, and there are several little boutiques, a dive shop, and a small commercial pier. This is where you catch the ferry for tiny Sandy Island, just 2 mi offshore.

❸ Wallblake House. On Wallblake Road, just north of the roundabout, is a plantation house with spacious rooms and handsome woodwork that was built in 1787 by Will Blake (Wallblake is probably a corruption of his name). The place is associated with many a tale involving murder, high living, and the French invasion in 1796. Its days of debauchery are over, though; today it's owned and actively used by the Catholic Church. On the grounds are an ancient vaulted stone cistern and an outbuilding called the Bakery (which wasn't used for making bread at all but for baking turkeys and hams). Call Father John (☎ 264/497–2405) to make an appointment to tour the plantation. ⊠ *Wallblake Rd., The Valley.*

❻ Warden's Place. This former sugar-plantation great house was built in the 1790s and is a fine example of island stone work. It's now the site of the Koal Keel restaurant (☞ Dining, *above*), but for many years it served as the residence of the island's chief administrator, who also doubled as the only medical practitioner. ⊠ *The Valley.*

Anguilla A to Z

Arriving and Departing
BY AIRPLANE

American Airlines (☎ 264/497–3131) is the major airline with non-stop flights from the continental United States to its hub in San Juan, from which the airline's **American Eagle** flies three times daily (twice daily off-season) to Anguilla's Wallblake Airport (☎ 264/497–2719). **Windward Islands Airways** (☎ 264/775–0183) wings in daily from St. Thomas and at least three times a day from St. Maarten's Juliana Airport. **LIAT** (☎ 264/465–2286) comes in from Antigua, Nevis, St. Kitts, St. Maarten, and St. Thomas. **Air Anguilla** (☎ 264/497–2643) offers several flights daily from St. Maarten and the U.S. Virgin Islands and provides air-taxi service on request from neighboring islands. **Tyden Air** (☎ 264/497–2719) has scheduled flights four times a week to both St. Thomas and St. Kitts from Anguilla and offers charter day trips to many neighboring islands.

From the Airport: You'll find taxis lined up at the airport to meet the planes. A trip from the airport to Sandy Ground will cost about $8; to West End resorts, it costs between $15 and $20.

BY BOAT

Two firms run ferryboats frequently between Anguilla and St. Martin. Boats leave from Blowing Point on Anguilla every ½ hour from 7:30 to 5 and from Marigot on St. Martin every ½ hour from 8 to 5:30. There are also evening ferries that leave from Blowing Point at 6 and 9:15 and from Marigot at 7 and 10:45. You pay a $2 departure tax before boarding and the $9 one-way fare ($11 evenings) on board. Don't buy a round-trip ticket, because it restricts you to the boat for which it is purchased. On very windy days the 20-minute trip can be bouncy, and if you suffer from motion sickness, you may want medication. An information booth outside the customs shed in Blowing Point is usually open daily from 8:30 to 5, but sometimes the attendant wanders off.

From the Docks: Taxis are always waiting to pick passengers up at the Blowing Point landing. It costs $12 to get to the Malliouhana hotel, $15 to the Cap Juluca hotel, and $18 to most hotels that are farther afield.

Electricity

The current is 110 volts, exactly what you find in the U.S. Your standard two-prong plugs will work just fine.

Emergencies

Ambulance: ☏ 264/497–2551. **Hospital:** There's a 24-hour emergency room at the **Princess Alexandra Hospital** (✉ Stoney Ground, ☏ 264/497–2551). **Pharmacies:** The Government Pharmacy (✉ The Valley, ☏ 264/497–2551), in Princess Alexandra Hospital, is open daily from 8:30–8:30. The **Paramount Pharmacy** (✉ Waterswamp, ☏ 264/497–2366) is open Monday–Saturday 8:30–8:30 and has a 24-hour emergency service. **Police and fire:** ☏ 911, or 264/497–2333 for nonemergencies.

Festivals and Seasonal Events

In February the **National Cultural & Educational Festival** celebrates traditional Anguillas cultures with a variety of programs involving dance, storytelling, games, and music. March brings **Moonsplash,** a three-day music festival that showcases local talent and begins on the night of the full moon. August is **Carnival** time; during the first two weeks of the month, there are parades with colorful floats, street dancing, boat racing at Sandy Ground, and lots of general merrymaking.

Getting Around

CAR RENTALS

This is your best bet for maximum mobility if you're comfortable driving on the left and don't mind some jostling. Anguilla's roads are generally paved (in a manner of speaking), but those that are not (some even leading to a fancy hotel) can be incredibly rutted. Observe the 30 mph speed limit, and watch out for livestock that amble across the road. To rent a car you'll need a valid driver's license and a local license, which you can obtain for $6 at any of the car-rental agencies.

Avis (✉ Airport Rd., ☏ 264/497–6221) rents sedans and four-wheel-drive vehicles. **Budget** (✉ Airport Rd., ☏ 264/497–2217) has many four-wheel-drive vehicles and sedans to choose from. **Connors (National)** (✉ Blowing Point, ☏ 264/497–6433) rents four-wheel-drive vehicles and air-conditioned sedans. Head to **Island Car Rental** (✉ Airport Rd., ☏ 264/497–2723) for car rentals, including four-wheel-drive vehicles. Count on $45 to $55 per day's rental, plus insurance. Motorcycles and scooters are available for about $35 per day from **R & M Cycle** (✉ Sandy Ground, ☏ 264/497–2430).

TAXIS

Taxi rates are regulated by the government, and there are fixed fares from point to point (they should be listed in brochures the drivers carry). Posted rates are for one or two people; each additional passenger adds $3 to the total. Tipping (about 10% of the total fare) is welcome.

Guided Tours

A round-the-island tour by taxi will take about 2½ hours and will cost $40 for one or two people, $5 for each additional passenger.

Bennie's Tours (✉ Blowing Point, ☎ 264/497–2788) and **Malliouhana Travel and Tours** (✉ The Valley, ☎ 264/497–2431) put together personalized package tours of the island.

Language

English, with a strong West Indian lilt, is spoken here.

Money Matters

CURRENCY

Though the legal tender here is the Eastern Caribbean (E.C.) dollar, U.S. dollars are widely accepted. (You'll often get change in E.C. dollars.) The E.C. dollar is fairly stable relative to the U.S. dollar, hovering between EC$2.60 and $2.70 to the U.S. dollar. Credit cards are not always accepted, and it's hard to predict where you'll need cash. Some resorts will only settle in cash; a few will also accept personal checks. Some restaurants add on a small charge if you pay with a credit card. Be sure to carry lots of small bills; change for a $20 is often difficult to obtain. Note: Prices quoted throughout this chapter are in U.S. dollars unless indicated otherwise.

SERVICE CHARGES, TAXES, AND TIPPING

A 10% service charge is added to all hotel bills; sometimes it covers all staff members, and sometimes it doesn't. If you're unsure whether or not to tip hotel staff, ask the hotel management about its policies. There's an 8% tax on accommodations. A 10% service charge is added to most restaurant bills. Ask if you're not sure, and if you're particularly pleased with the service, you can certainly leave a little extra above and beyond the service charge. Tip taxi drivers 10% of the fare. The departure tax is $10 at the airport, $2 if you leave by boat.

Opening and Closing Times

Banks are open Monday–Thursday 8–3 and Friday 8–5. No two shops seem to have the same hours, but many are open between 10 and 4 on weekdays. Call the shop, ask at the tourist office for opening and closing times, or adopt the island way of doing things: If it's not open when you stop by, stop by again.

HOLIDAYS

New Year's Day, Easter (Apr. 4), Labour Day (May 1), Anguilla Day (May 29), Whit Monday (May 25), August Monday (Aug. 2), Constitution Day (Aug. 8), Separation Day (Dec. 19), Christmas, Boxing Day (Dec. 26).

Passports

U.S. and Canadian citizens need proof of identity. A passport is preferred (even one that has expired within the last five years). Also acceptable is a photo ID, such as a driver's license, *along with* a birth certificate (with raised seal) or naturalization papers. All visitors must also have a return or ongoing ticket. Visitor's passes are valid for stays of up to three months. British citizens must have a passport.

Precautions

The manchineel tree, which resembles an apple tree, shades many beaches. The tree bears poisonous fruit, and the sap from the tree causes painful blisters. Avoid sitting beneath the tree, because even dew or raindrops falling from the leaves can blister your skin. Be *sure* to take along insect repellent—mosquitoes can be pesky in the late afternoon.

Anguilla is a quiet, relatively safe island, but there's no point in tempting fate by leaving your valuables unattended in your hotel room, on the beach, or in your car.

Telephones and Mail

To call Anguilla from the United States, dial area code 264 + 497 + the local four-digit number. (The area code was recently changed from 809.) International direct dial is available on the island. To make a local call on the island, just dial the seven-digit number.

Cable & Wireless (⊠ Wallblake Rd., ☎ 264/497–3100) is open weekdays 8–6, Saturday 9–1, Sunday 10–2 and sells Caribbean Phone Cards ($5, $10, $20 denominations) for use in specially marked phone booths. The card can be used for local calls and those to other islands.

You can also use the card to call the United States and, in this case, bill the call to MasterCard or Visa. Inside the departure lounge at the Blowing Point ferry dock and at the airport, there's an AT&T USADirect access telephone for collect or credit-card calls to the United States.

Airmail letters to the United States and Canada cost EC60¢; postcards, EC25¢. When writing to the island, you don't need a postal code; just include the name of the establishment, address (location or post-office box), and Anguilla.

Visitor Information

In the United Kingdom, contact the **Anguilla Tourist Office** (⊠ 3 Epirus Rd., London SW6 7UJ, ☎ 0171/937–7725).

On Anguilla, the **Anguilla Tourist Office** (⊠ Social Security Bldg., The Valley, ☎ 264/497–2759 or 800/553–4939, FAX 264/497–2710) is open weekdays 8–noon and 1–4.

3 Antigua

Updated by
Jordan Simon

I t's Antigua Sailing Week, the island's version of the Henley Regatta. Seasoned sea salts claim prized seats on the flagstone terrace of the 18th-century Admiral's Inn in English Harbour. Some of the boats are docked so close by that you can almost eavesdrop from shore. Competitors trade stories (tall and otherwise) of sailing—and drinking—two sheets to the wind, while eyeing the yachts. Blazered bluebloods mingle with lobster-hued tourists; it's Cannes on water.

Antigua (an-*tee*-ga), the largest of the British Leeward Islands (108 square mi), is renowned among sailors for its incomparable air of nautical history: Lord Horatio Nelson headquartered his fleet here during colonial times, and English Harbour, in the southeast of the island, is steeped in that era's history. At its center, Nelson's Dockyard, now a national park, is Antigua's answer to Williamsburg, Virginia—a carefully restored gem of British Georgian architecture. For Anglophiles and history buffs, English Harbour and the surrounding villages and sights will be immensely rewarding. Antigua seduces landlubbers and sailors alike with its sensuous beaches, 366 in all, one for every day of the year and one left over, as locals like to boast. All of them are public, some are absolutely deserted, and others lined with resorts offering sailing, diving, windsurfing, and snorkeling.

The original inhabitants of Antigua were the Ciboney. They lived here 4,000 years ago and disappeared mysteriously, leaving the island unpopulated for about 1,000 years. When Columbus arrived in 1493, the Arawaks had set up housekeeping. The English took up residence in 1632. After 30-odd years of bloody battles involving the Caribs, the Dutch, the French, and the English, the French ceded the island to the English in 1667. Unlike many other Caribbean islands, which spent centuries being reflagged by various nations, Antigua remained under English control until achieving full independence, with its sister island

Barbuda (26 mi to the north), which holds a mere 1,200 of the country's 80,000 inhabitants, on November 1, 1981.

Those in search of beaches, nightlife, shopping, and restaurants will want to head to the northwestern end of the island, where resorts and hotels are scattered from Five Islands Harbour, south of St. John, to Dickenson Bay and points north. One of the least-developed parts of the island is in the southwest, in the shadow of Antigua's highest mountain, Boggy Peak. Fry's Bay and Darkwood Beach hold long, unspoiled scimitars of sand.

With so much to offer, tourism is clearly the leading industry here, and building (and after Hurricanes Luis and Marilyn, rebuilding) has been rampant in the last decade. But Antigua maintains a strong sense of national identity to match its rich historic inheritance. Its cricketers, like the legendary Viv Richards (arguably the greatest batsman the game has ever seen), are famous throughout the Caribbean. Its people are known for their sharp commercial spirit (a typically revealing—and disarming—sign reads DIANE'S BOUTIQUE AND CAR PARTS); their wit; and, unfortunately at the government level, their corruption.

Lodging

Scattered along Antigua's sandy beaches and tropical hillsides are exclusive, elegant hideaways; romantic restored inns; casual, go-barefoot-everywhere places; and all-inclusive hot spots for couples. Choose accommodations near St. John's—anywhere between Dickenson Bay and Five Islands Harbour—if you want to be close to the action. English Harbour, far from St. John's, has the best inns and several excellent restaurants, and it is the hangout for the yachting crowd. The resorts elsewhere on the island cater more to guests who want to stay put or are seeking seclusion. Many of the smaller resorts have have become all-inclusive to survive the fierce competition, but you can usually work out EP rates if you'd rather sample the island's restaurants. Many properties sustained some damage during the 1995 hurricanes, but most have been renovated and, in many cases, improved. Unconfirmed rumor has it that the legendary deluxe enclave Jumby Bay, located on its own private island, which closed after squabbling amongst its super-wealthy villa owners, may reopen in 1999. The drive to reopen it as a resort is being spearheaded by none less than Robin Leach. The price categories below reflect the room cost during high season.

CATEGORY	COST*
$$$$	over $400
$$$	$275–$400
$$	$150–$275
$	under $150

All prices are for a standard double room, excluding 8½% tax and 10% service charge.

$$$$ ★ ⊡ **Curtain Bluff.** Howard Hulford built this resort more than 30 years ago, and he's still very active in its management. You're likely to see him puttering around his beloved gardens (Antigua's lushest and as impeccably manicured as the clientele) or tasting a new wine for his legendary cellar of over 20,000 bottles. The resort is spectacularly set on a bluff bordered on one side by the wild Atlantic and on the other by the calm Caribbean. Standard rooms with stylish, soothing fabrics, wicker furnishings, and terraces or balconies are in two-story beachfront buildings facing the Caribbean. Suites—huge split-level apartments with two balconies, a large living room, and, up a flight of steps, a spacious bedroom—zigzag up the bluff. Swiss chef Reudi Portmann has ruled

36

Exploring
Barbuda, **15**
Betty's Hope, **13**
Curtain Bluff, **5**
Devil's Bridge, **12**
English Harbour, **8**
Falmouth, **7**
Fig Tree Drive, **4**
Ft. George, **6**
Ft. James, **2**
Harmony Hall, **10**
Indian Town, **11**
Megaliths of
Greencastle Hill, **3**
Parham, **14**
St. John's, **1**
Shirley Heights, **9**

Dining
Admiral's Inn, **45**
Al Porto, **36**
Alberto's, **47**
Averill's, **42**
Big Banana–Pizzas on
the Quay, **25**
Calypso, **26**
Chez Pascal, **32**
Coco's, **35**
Coconut Grove, **19**
Commissioner's
Grill, **27**
Julian's, **28**
Le Bistro, **17**
Lobster Pot, **23**
Redcliffe Tavern, **29**
Russell's, **24**
Southern Cross, **43**
Wardroom
Restaurant, **46**

Lodging
Admiral's Inn, **45**
Carlisle Bay Club, **39**
Catamaran Hotel, **41**
Colonna Beach
Hotel, **18**
Copper and Lumber
Store Hotel, **46**
Curtain Bluff, **38**
Dickenson Bay
Cottages, **21**
Falmouth Beach
Apartments, **40**
Galley Bay, **33**
Hawksbill Beach
Hotel, **34**
Inn at English
Harbour, **44**
Jolly Harbour Beach
Resort Marina and
Golf Club, **36**
K Club, **50**

Antigua (and Barbuda)

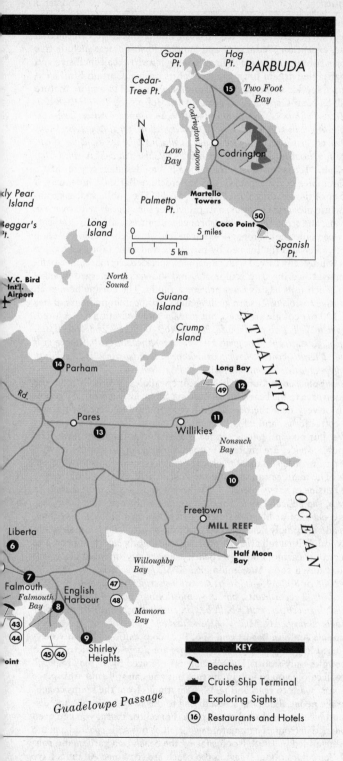

Lord Nelson Beach
Hotel, **16**

Pineapple Beach
Club, **49**

Rex Blue Heron, **37**

Rex Halcyon Cove
Beach Resort, **22**

Royal Antiguan
Resort, **31**

St. James's Club, **48**

Sandals Antigua
Resort and Spa, **20**

Siboney Beach
Club, **19**

Yepton Beach
Resort, **30**

the kitchen of the greenery-filled open-air restaurant since the resort opened. Jacket and tie are required for dinner of classic Continental cuisine, except on Wednesday and Sunday. Resort extras include free deep-sea fishing and scuba diving, making it a virtual all-inclusive and a remarkable bargain for a property of its caliber. Curtain Bluff's exceptional service and country-club ambience appeal to a more mature crowd. ⊠ *Near Carlisle Bay (Box 288), St. John's,* ☎ *268/462–8400, 212/289–8888 in NY,* ℻ *268/462–8409. 54 rooms, 7 suites. 2 restaurants, lounge, in-room safes, pool, beauty salon, putting green, 4 tennis courts, croquet, exercise room, squash, 2 beaches, dive shop, snorkeling, boating, fishing, shop. AE. FAP. Closed mid-May–mid-Oct.*

$$$$ ⚿ **K Club.** "K" is for Krizia, the famed Italian designer; her dramatic ★ style animates every aspect of this superdeluxe Barbuda hideaway, a member of the Leading Hotels of the World. The public spaces gleam with white tiles and columns, natural wicker furnishings with oversize cushions, and striking cloth-and-bronze sculptures. All rooms and cottages open onto the champagne-color beach. The decor is chic and cool: white wicker and tile livened by turquoise and mint fabrics, wooden chairs whimsically carved with pineapples, speckled ceramic lamps, bamboo mats, towering fruit sculptures, and showers submerged in vegetation. Each unit has its own private veranda. The cuisine here is an innovative fusion of Tuscan grilling and Caribbean ingredients. Rates of $1,100 per couple are steep, but privacy and discretion are assured. ⊠ *Spanish Wells Point, Barbuda,* ☎ *268/460–0300,* ℻ *268/460–0305. 39 units. Restaurant, bar, grill, kitchenettes, pool, hot tub, 9-hole golf course, 2 tennis courts, beach, snorkeling, windsurfing, waterskiing, fishing, recreation room. AE, MC, V. FAP, MAP.*

$$$$ ⚿ **Pineapple Beach Club.** A broad stone walk leads directly from the reception area to the beach of this bustling, all-inclusive resort. All rooms are on or very near the beach and have redwood louvered windows, terra-cotta floors, and bright Caribbean colors. There are no phones or TVs, but fax and phone service is available at the front desk. The new public spaces are impressive: open, flowing, in stone and tile, with wicker furnishings, handsome local paintings, and enormous potted plants. The main restaurant and the Pelican grill serve well-above-average cuisine, a savvy blend of Caribbean and Continental dishes; of the two, the Pelican offers a more intimate ambience. The Outhouse Bar is a classic Caribbean hangout, perched atop a hill with sweeping views and seemingly held together by business cards, license plates, and driftwood. With a full array of water sports, nightly entertainment, and an electronic casino, Pineapple Beach is an activity-oriented place, but it quiets down soon after midnight. ⊠ *St. John's (Box 54),* ☎ *268/ 463–2006 or 800/345–0356 (reservations service),* ℻ *268/465–2452. 125 rooms. 2 restaurants, bar, air-conditioning, pool, 4 tennis courts, croquet, horseshoes, volleyball, beach, snorkeling, windsurfing, boating, waterskiing. AE, MC, V. All-inclusive.*

$$$$ ⚿ **Sandals Antigua Resort and Spa.** Pool competitions, beach volley- ★ ball, aerobics, and evening social events are a few of the activities at this couples-only resort. The schedule is organized by a "play maker," who will cajole you to join in the fun, but you can still enjoy this place if you just want to read and relax. Everything, from the tennis coaching to the pedal boats, the scuba diving to the swim-up pool-bars, discos, and meals, is included in the price. For a little extra, you can even get married in front of a miniature waterfall. A full-scale spa and a piano bar were added in 1998. Rooms facing the beach or a garden and rondavels (circular cottages) facing the beach are spacious. All units have coffeemakers, TVs, patios, and hair dryers. Many have four-poster beds, and all are light and fresh in pastels and/or bright floral fabrics. Four restaurants prepare Continental, Italian, Japanese, and South-

western-steak-house fare. Public areas are handsome, especially the beachfront restaurant, with its yellow-and-white awnings and painted ceiling. The open-air reception area, with stone arches, stained glass, and marble floors, opens onto a courtyard with painted tile stairways and an unimpeded view to the sea. ✉ *St. John's (Box 147)*, ☎ *268/ 462–0267 or 800/726–3257 in the U.S. (reservations service)*, ℻ *268/462–4135. 191 units. 4 restaurants, 4 bars, air-conditioning, in-room safes, 5 pools, 5 hot tubs, spa, 2 tennis courts, exercise room, beach, dive shop, snorkeling, windsurfing, boating, waterskiing, shop, nightclub. AE, D, DC, MC, V. All-inclusive.*

$$$–$$$$ ⌂ **Galley Bay.** This legendary small resort, virtually leveled by the one-two punch of Hurricanes Luis and Marilyn, has been completely restored. It's now a much livelier, younger (and therefore less exclusive), all-inclusive retreat, with double the number of rooms and showy features like a waterfall and man-made grotto in the pool. A beach of ravishing champagne-color sand, a blue lagoon, manicured gardens, even a bird sanctuary (complete with trails) surround the enclave. The new owners are faithful to the unique combination of West Indian and Tahitian elements that made the original so charming. Hence, there's a thatched-roof reception area filled with African carvings and Caribbean art naïf, as well as the Gauguin Village, a series of wattle-and-daub thatched double cottages. Enlivened by sinuous Gaudi-esque stucco walls and colorful Haitian artworks, they can be a little claustrophobic. The beachfront rooms are airy, with terra-cotta tiles, local and Haitian art, and custom-made rattan and bamboo furnishings. All include bathrobes, coffeemakers, and hair dryers in addition to the expected amenities. All in all, this is a model re-creation of a classic. ✉ *Five Islands (Box 305, St. John's)*, ☎ *268/462–0302 or 800/345–0356 (reservations service)*, ℻ *268/462–4551. 61 rooms. Restaurant, bar, grill, lounge, air-conditioning, in-room safes, refrigerators, pool, tennis court, exercise room, beach, snorkeling, windsurfing, boating, bicycles. AE, D, DC, MC, V. All-inclusive, EP.*

$$$–$$$$ ⌂ **St. James's Club.** This out-of-the-way hotel is on the 100-acre spit of land that helps form Mamora Bay. Rooms and one-bedroom suites in the main buildings at the water's edge are painted in pastel colors; some have romantic canopy beds. You enter past the "villa village," a tight cluster of two-bedroom units atop the hills that spill down toward the main hotel. Although well decorated, these villas include views of your neighbor's roof. You can dine at the three restaurants: the Rainbow Garden, an elegant spot for a seafood dinner; the more casual, alfresco Docksider Cafe for island cuisine; or the Poolside Reef Deck, a breakfast and lunch spot. Fortunately, the same management team behind ☞ **Galley Bay** and ☞ **Pineapple Beach Club** took over in 1997, and are making long overdue improvements. They've already converted the casino into a swanky nightclub and have created a sleek, more restrained gambling den next door. Rooms have been given fresher, more vibrant color schemes, though years of neglect still show in soiled hall carpets and the like. Overall, the St. James tends to live off its *renommée* (it had been affiliated with other like-named properties in London and Paris) rather than what it delivers. That said, the beaches and extensive sports facilities—and such amenities as a hotel helicopter that can be chartered for sightseeing—make this a fine, if overpriced, resort. ✉ *Mamora Bay (Box 54, St. John's)*, ☎ *268/463–2006 or 800/ 274–0008 (reservations service)*, ℻ *268/463–2452. 178 units. 4 restaurants, 4 bars, deli, air-conditioning, fans, room service, 3 pools, beauty salon, hot tub, massage, golf privileges, 7 tennis courts, croquet, exercise room, horseback riding, 2 beaches, dive shop, dock, snorkeling, windsurfing, boating, waterskiing, shops, casino, nightclub, playground, helipad. AE, D, DC, MC, V. All-inclusive, EP.*

$$$ ⊞ **Hawksbill Beach Hotel.** Thirty-seven acres of the bucolic Five Islands peninsula, including five beaches (you can bathe in the buff at one), make up the grounds of this resort. The main building, the reception area, and the dining room rest on a small bluff that commands a view of the sea and Montserrat beyond, set off by the restored ruins of a sugar mill in the foreground. Gingerbread-trimmed cottages surrounded by lawns and facing the sea hold deluxe rooms with wicker furnishings, tile floors, and floral pastels. Less expensive rooms are in garden-view cottages, most of which have restricted beach views and are the same size as the pricier beachfront units. All bedrooms are small, and there's no air-conditioning, TV, or phone. The classiest accommodations are in the three-bedroom West Indian Great House, a colonial-style building with king-size beds and kitchenettes. Fourteen secluded beachfront rooms, elevated on a minibluff with the finest vistas of all, were added in 1997. They have powder blue walls, gleaming white tile floors, light rattan furnishings, hand-painted bathroom tiles, and vaulted ceilings. The most astonishing views are from Units 138–142. Men are requested not to wear short sleeves in the dining room after 7 PM. Though children are more welcome than they used to be, Hawksbill is more a place for young couples and singles. Breakfast and most water sports are free. ⊠ *St. John's (Box 108)*, ☎ *268/462–0301 or 800/223–6510 (reservations service), 416/622–8813 in Canada;* ℻ *268/462–1515. 113 rooms. 2 restaurants, 2 bars, fans, pool, tennis court, 5 beaches, snorkeling, windsurfing, boating, shop. AE, DC, MC, V. BP, MAP.*

$$$ ⊞ **Inn at English Harbour.** The reception area, bar and dining room, and six of the guest rooms of this inn sit atop a hill with views of English Harbour. The bar, with its green leather chairs, wooden floors, stone walls, and maritime prints, is one of the most pleasant on the island, and the flagstone-terrace dining room offers an unparalleled romantic ambience and dependable Continental fare. Off to the side of the main house are the hilltop rooms, in individual, cottage-style units nestled amid typical English gardens. Down the steep hill, right on the beach, are 22 rooms in two-story wooden buildings surrounded by hibiscus and bougainvillea. All rooms have phones, wall safes, refrigerators, and hair dryers and are attractively furnished with rattan furniture and tropical or floral fabrics. Also on the beach is a second bar-restaurant that stays open until 6 PM. A shuttle bus runs guests up and down the hill. The beach, like all those in English Harbour, is not the best. ⊠ *St. John's (Box 187)*, ☎ *268/460–1014 or 800/223–6510; 800/424–5500 in Canada (reservations service);* ℻ *268/460–1603. 28 rooms. Restaurant, 2 bars, grill, in-room safes, refrigerators, beach, snorkeling, windsurfing, boating. AE, MC, V. CP, MAP.*

$$–$$$ ⊞ **Copper and Lumber Store Hotel.** Overlooking the marina at English Harbour, this former supply store for Nelson's Caribbean fleet and fine example of Georgian British architecture has been beautifully transformed into a gracious inn. Warm brick, hardwood floors, timbered ceilings, old sailing prints and nautical maps, and burgundy-leather armchairs and sofas lend the property an Old World charm unique in the West Indies. Antique washstands, secretaries, four-poster canopy beds, and other Georgian furnishings decorate the suites; additional touches in many include wrought-iron chandeliers, mahogany steamer trunks, brass sinks, and faux gas lamps. All suites have showers, and though they lack air-conditioning, ceiling fans create nice breezes. Unfortunately, many rooms have become frayed around the edges and could use a facelift. The beautifully restored ☞ **Wardroom Restaurant** offers top-class Continental cuisine. A ferry service shuttles guests to a beach on the other side of English Harbour. Be warned that the hotel sits inside a national park and visitors stream through the area during the day. ⊠

St. John's (Box 184), ☎ 268/460–1058, ⅻ 268/460–1529. 14 suites. Restaurant, pub, fans. AE, MC, V. EP, MAP.

$$–$$$ ⊞ **Dickenson Bay Cottages.** There are only 13 units at this small development on Marble Hill, just above Dickenson Bay. The two-story villa-style buildings are surrounded by gardens and furnished with high-quality painted rattan, blond woods, and soft pastel and floral fabrics. Downstairs is a well-equipped kitchen and a large living room area with a TV. The bedroom and bathroom are up a flight of stairs. Larger units have two bedrooms upstairs and a large veranda overlooking the ocean. One annoyance is the lack of a cross breeze, which obliges you to keep the air-conditioner on. Guests have beach privileges at the excellent but busy beach at Halcyon Cove, just a five-minute walk away, and you can use the tennis and water-sports facilities there at a 20% discount. Entertainment and restaurants are available at nearby resorts. ⊠ St. John's (Box 1379), ☎ 268/462–4940, ⅻ 268/462–4941. 13 units. Air-conditioning, kitchenettes, pool. AE, DC, MC, V. EP.

$$–$$$ ⊞ **Rex Blue Heron.** When Rex Hotels purchased this faded little resort on one of the island's loveliest beaches, management gave it a complete overhaul. The seemingly endless tiled reception area, filled with potted plants, polished-wood rafters, and oversize rattan furnishings with brilliantly hued cushions, is perhaps its most imposing aspect. Everything else is on a smaller scale, from the cozy pool to even cozier rooms. Don't be misled by the mousy faux stucco buildings. Each room has hardwood or gleaming white tile floors, powder-blue and tropical-print fabrics, stylish ceramic lamps, a patio or a terrace, and a hair dryer. All but the standard ones have air-conditioning, satellite TV, and dazzling ocean views. It's extremely difficult to get a reservation, since discerning European tour operators keep it booked throughout the year. The low prices, intimacy, and seclusion lure a young, hip clientele. ⊠ Johnson's Point (Box 1715), ☎ 268/462–8565 or 800/255–5859 (reservations service), ⅻ 268/462–8005. 64 rooms. Restaurant, bar, air-conditioning, pool, snorkeling, windsurfing, boating, shop. AE, D, MC, V. All-inclusive, EP.

$$–$$$ ⊞ **Rex Halcyon Cove Beach Resort.** Many European and American tour groups patronize this large, somewhat impersonal hotel on beautiful Dickenson Bay, so it's typically crowded and your neighbor may be paying a third of what you are. Accommodations are in two- and three-story flat-roof buildings scattered around the courtyard or along the beach. They have white tile floors and are decorated with blond wood and mint fabrics. All have a private balcony or patio, but only higher-grade accommodations have a full bath, a TV, and a refrigerator. A water-sports center on the busy beach offers excursions on a glass-bottom boat and waterskiing, in addition to the usual activities. The Warri Pier restaurant, set on stilts over the ocean, serves fine seafood and grilled items all day long. ⊠ St. John's (Box 251), ☎ 268/462–0256 (reservations service), ⅻ 268/462–0271. 194 rooms, 16 1-bedroom suites. 2 restaurants, 4 bars, ice cream parlor, air-conditioning, pool, beauty salon, 4 tennis courts, beach, dive shop, windsurfing, boating, waterskiing, shops, car rental. AE, D, DC, MC, V. EP, MAP.

$$–$$$ ⊞ **Royal Antiguan Resort.** This nine-story high-rise hotel, possibly the island's ugliest, is set on the waterside a few miles south of St. John's. The hotel caters to groups and conventions and is by far the most "stateside-like" hotel on Antigua; though sterile, it has all the amenities and facilities of a moderate American chain. Rooms and suites have minibars and TVs; higher categories have VCRs and marble vanities. Among the facilities here are a huge ballroom used for meetings and cocktail parties, a shopping arcade, and 130 slot machines. An ongoing several-million-dollar renovation

has brightened the hotel's interior, and the grounds and facade have received a much-needed face-lift—royal blue awnings now shade the terraces, the tennis courts have been resurfaced, and the gardens are immaculately tended. Fancier shops now line the arcade, and the cuisine, a sophisticated fusion of island ingredients and nouvelle preparations, has been greatly improved. ⊠ *Deep Bay (Box 1322, St. John's),* ☎ *268/462–3733 or 800/228–9898 (reservations service),* FAX *268/462–3732. 300 rooms. 3 restaurants, 4 bars, air-conditioning, minibars, pool, beauty salon, golf privileges, 8 tennis courts, exercise room, beach, dive shop, snorkeling, windsurfing, boating, waterskiing, fishing, shops, casino. AE, D, MC, V. All-inclusive, EP, MAP.*

$$–$$$ 🏨 **Siboney Beach Club.** When Tony Johnson arrived in Antigua in the
★   late '50s, he planned to stay just a few weeks. Instead, he ended up building or refurbishing some of the island's finest resorts and eventually opened his own small gem set in a garden on Dickenson Bay. Each suite has a small bedroom, a cleverly designed Pullman kitchen, a modestly furnished living room, and a plant-filled patio or balcony that looks out to greenery. Their decor varies slightly, but all rooms feature rattan and rich tropical fabrics, as well as knickknacks from Tony's travels; most units are air-conditioned. Room 9 is for those who revel in sea views, but the soothing sound of the surf permeates even those with partial views. A few yards away is an excellent, although often busy, calm-water beach and the ☞ **Coconut Grove,** where you can enjoy great breakfasts and lunches as well as candlelight dinners at the water's edge. The staff is very friendly, and Tony is always available to offer advice and good cheer. ⊠ *St. John's (Box 222),* ☎ *268/462–0806 or 800/533–0234,* FAX *268/462–3356. 12 suites. Restaurant, bar, kitchenettes, beach. AE, MC, V. EP, MAP.*

$$ 🏨 **Carlisle Bay Club.** Don't be deceived by the rather flamboyant lobby filled with the whimsical jumble of the owner's travels: elephant tusk chairs, Greco-Roman nudes, Oriental rugs, and a grand piano, which should all clash, yet somehow blend harmoniously. This is a pleasantly low-key retreat set amid lavish gardens on a handsome, ecru crescent of sand. The enormous, individually owned duplex villas, which sleep four comfortably, are decorated differently, but each has an oceanview patio, sizable bath, full kitchen (rather superfluous now that the property has become all-inclusive), rattan furnishings, and washed-out pastel fabrics. It's an astonishing bargain for families and for those who want nothing more than a tranquil beach vacation. ⊠ *Carlisle Bay (Box 1515, St. John's),* ☎ *268/462–1377,* FAX *268/462–1365. 30 units. Restaurant, bar, grill, air-conditioning, fans, kitchenettes, 10 tennis courts, beach, snorkeling, windsurfing, boating. AE, MC, V. All-inclusive.*

$$ 🏨 **Colonna Beach Hotel.** The architecture here is an appealing blend of Caribbean and Mediterranean: Red-tile and stucco buildings with terra-cotta floors surround a faux sugar mill. The most magnificent touch is the free-form pool, said to be the largest in the Lesser Antilles. Units, all with TVs, hair dryers, and patios or balconies, run the gamut from standard hotel rooms to two- and three-bedroom villas (some of which were poorly designed and don't catch a cross breeze). The fresh interiors have immaculate tile floors, wicker and rattan furnishings, and imported Italian fabrics with designs that range from bold stripes to seashell pastels. The public spaces look a tad dilapidated, but the rooms are well maintained and even so-called garden-view units have at least a partial sea view. The junior suites, a good value, have two patios and a sofa bed. The artificial beaches are among this resort's drawbacks, along with the constant threat of bankruptcy. But the staff is generally engaging and helpful, the location between the airport and St. John's is central, and the two restaurants (one or the other of which

is often closed) serve fine Italian food. ✉ *St. John's (Box 591)*, ☎ *268/ 462–6263*, FAX *268/462–6430. 117 units. 2 restaurants, 3 bars, air-conditioning, in-room safes, minibars, pool, 2 beaches, snorkeling, wind-surfing, boating, casino. AE, D, MC, V. EP, MAP.*

$$ 🏨 **Yepton Beach Resort.** This Swiss-designed, full-service, all-suites resort is set on Hog John Bay on the Five Islands peninsula, not far from St. John's. The Mediterranean-style white-stucco buildings are situated so that rooms have views of both the resort's attractive beach and a lagoon dotted with pelicans and egrets. Two-room suites hold a bedroom and a large living room with a kitchenette, and studios have a Murphy bed and a kitchenette. The units are carefully maintained, though typically bland in dark rattan and glass furnishings, with pastel fabrics and island prints. Many packages are available. ✉ *St. John's (Box 1427)*, ☎ *268/462–2520 or 800/361–4621*, FAX *268/462–3240. 38 units. Restaurant, air-conditioning, kitchenettes, pool, 2 tennis courts, beach, snorkeling, boating. AE, MC, V. All-inclusive, EP, MAP.*

$ 🏨 **Admiral's Inn.** This lovingly restored 18th-century Georgian inn is
★ the centerpiece of the magnificent Nelson's Dockyard complex. Once the engineers' office and warehouse (its bricks were originally used as ballast for British ships), the Admiral's Inn reverberates with history. The best rooms, upstairs in the main building, have the original timbered ceilings, complete with iron braces, hardwood floors, and massive whitewashed brick walls. Straw floor mats from Dominica, four-poster beds in most rooms, and views through wispy Australian pines to the sunny harbor beyond complete the effect. The rooms in the garden annex are smaller and somewhat airless. The Loft, which used to be the dockyard's joinery, has two big bedrooms, an enormous kitchen, and a magnificent view from the timbered living room onto the busy harbor. Be aware that this inn sits smack in the middle of a bustling daytime tourist attraction, although there's a complimentary beach shuttle and use of water sports at Falmouth Beach Apartments. The ☞ **Admiral's Inn** restaurant is very popular with locals. ✉ *St. John's (Box 713)*, ☎ *268/460–1027 or 800/223–5695 (reservations service)*, FAX *268/460–1534. 14 rooms, 1 2-bedroom apartment. Restaurant, pub, air-conditioning, fans. AE, MC, V. EP, MAP.*

$ 🏨 **Catamaran Hotel.** This plantation-style house, with a wraparound veranda supported by classical-style pediments, sits on a minuscule Falmouth Harbour beach lined with palm and almond trees. The best rooms are the eight first-floor suites, with four-poster beds, full baths, kitchenettes, and private balconies. Even the spartan, less expensive rooms has nice touches like faux Victorian gas or straw lamps and darkwood beds. None of the rooms has air-conditioning, a TV, or a telephone. Yet for those who want a low-key, low-priced, tranquil resort, this property 2 mi from English Harbour offers excellent value. ✉ *Falmouth (Box 958)*, ☎ *268/460–1036*, FAX *268/460–1506. 16 rooms. Restaurant, bar, beach, dock, shops. AE, D, MC, V. EP.*

$ 🏨 **Falmouth Beach Apartments.** The best accommodations at this sister hotel to the ☞ **Admiral's Inn** are in a colonial-style house on the property's small, palm-lined beach. These quiet, simple units are basically one large room—a bedroom–living-room–kitchenette combination—and a bathroom with a shower. All open onto a wraparound veranda with views of the water and the hilly peninsula opposite. Units have no air-conditioning (those upstairs catch the breezes better), and no telephones or TVs. Accommodations in four modern buildings perched on the hillside have separate kitchens, bedrooms with twin beds, and bathrooms with showers. Old maps or striking artwork jazz up the standard rattan-and-beige-tile decor. All apartments have daily maid service. The sheltered beach is perfect for toddlers and small children who are learning to swim. ✉ *Falmouth Harbour (Box 713)*, ☎

268/460–1094 or 800/223–5695 (reservations service), FAX *268/460–
1534. 28 rooms. Kitchenettes, beach, boating. AE, MC, V. EP.*

$ ▣ **Jolly Harbour Beach Resort Marina and Golf Club.** This is more a
vacation-home compound than a mere resort. Although the main activity area strives to re-create a Mediterranean village with red-tile roofs
and pale-mustard arches and columns, the 500-acre development generally lacks style. That said, its villas—cookie-cutter duplex units that
seem straight from the Sunbelt—are perhaps the best bargain on Antigua. All look out onto the beach or marina and have kitchens, ceiling fans (only 40 units currently have air-conditioning), two bedrooms,
and full baths. The units are individually decorated, but most have wicker
furnishings, off-white tile floors, and pastel colors. Jolly Harbour is
ideal for families on a budget or those who want everything at their
fingertips: Guests also have use of the facilities at the all-inclusive
Club Antigua next door. The golf course is scheduled for an expansion from 9 to 18 holes in late 1998. The ☞ **Al Porto** is a top quality
Italian eatery. ✉ *Jolly Harbour (Box 1793),* ☎ *268/462–6166,* FAX *268/
462–6167. 502 villas (approximately 220 in rental pool at any given
time). 4 restaurants, 2 bars, fans, kitchenettes, pool, 9-hole golf course,
4 tennis courts, squash, 2 beaches, dive shop, dock, windsurfing, boating, waterskiing, shops. AE, MC, V. EP.*

$ ▣ **Lord Nelson Beach Hotel.** If you don't mind a bit of chipped paint
and organized chaos, you'll love this funky, laid-back resort run for
decades by the Fuller family, who can regale you with stories about
the time Eugene Fodor himself stayed here. The best rooms are in a
two-story, apricot-color building looking directly onto the horseshoe-
shape beach. Each unit is a hodgepodge of design elements: One room
has beautiful tile floors and an ornately carved high-standing bed from
Dominica, and several others have four-poster beds, antique armoires,
and vivid local still lifes. The newer units are lacking in style. Guests
eat in the timbered dining room, dominated by a replica of the boat
in which Captain Bligh was cast off from the *Bounty*; expect hearty
dishes such as stuffed pork chops, wahoo, and snapper. Because the
resort is fairly isolated (5 mi from St. John's), budget an extra EC$25
for cab fare to any meal you have elsewhere. An extensive collection
of windsurfing boards, easy access to the water, and a dedicated pro
have made the Lord Nelson a mecca for windsurfers. ✉ *St. John's (Box
155),* ☎ *268/462–3094,* FAX *268/462–0751. 16 rooms. Restaurant, bar,
beach, dive shop, windsurfing. AE, MC, V. EP, FAP, MAP. Closed Sept.*

Dining

Antigua's restaurants prepare a range of cuisines, and you can find excellent food whether you feel like dressing up or dressing down. It's
impossible not to find fresh seafood, and virtually every chef incorporates
local ingredients and elements of West Indian and Creole cuisine. Alas,
the food is often overcooked, even in the tonier establishments.

Most menus list prices in E.C. dollars, but you should make sure
which currency you're dealing with. It's also a good to ask if credit
cards are accepted. Dinner reservations are needed during high season.

What to Wear

Perhaps because of the island's British heritage, Antiguans tend to
dress more formally for dinner than is the custom on many of the other
Caribbean islands. A few places, which will be noted, require a jacket.
Wraps and shorts (no beach attire) are de rigueur for lunch, except at
local hangouts.

CATEGORY	COST*
$$$	over $30
$$	$20–$30
$	under $20

per person for a three-course meal, excluding drinks, service, and 7% sales tax

AMERICAN

$–$$ ✕ **Averill's** This place practically defines the casual marina eatery. It has all the right elements: sleek yachts moored at the deck, fresh sea breezes, exuberant boating barflies, and simple yet scrumptious food. Fresh fish daily might include wahoo in caper, butter, and lemon sauce or dolphinfish in shrimp sauce. Excellent starters include fried calamari, cumin-crusted shrimp, and sesame chicken. The ambience is fun and raucous on Mondays (Roast Pork barbecue) and Fridays (Prime Rib night). Averill knows her clientele: as she says, "I'll do a burger or a burrito if I have to!" ⊠ *Catamaran Marina, Falmouth Harbour,* ☎ *268/463–8866. AE, MC, V. Closed June–Sept.*

CARIBBEAN/CREOLE

$–$$ ✕ **Coco's.** Perched on a hill overlooking a lovely bay, Coco's could be recommended simply for the most ravishing sunsets on Antigua, followed by the moon dappling the water with a thousand pieces of light. But it's also an uncommonly handsome place, replicating an old chattel house, with cheerful aquamarine trim, bleached wood deck, gingerbread fretwork, and blue tile tables. Reggae and calypso play softly in the background. Local fare is presented with European flair, from the conch fritters and spicy crab cakes to the grilled lobster. ⊠ *Mt. Prospect, Jolly Bay,* ☎ *268/462–9700. AE, MC, V. Closed Mon.*

$ ✕ **Calypso.** The St. John's professional set frequents this cheerful outdoor spot. At lunchtime it is packed with smartly dressed lawyers and government functionaries smoking cigars and chatting over traditional Caribbean food. Tables are under green umbrellas on a sunny trellised patio dominated by the remains of a brick kiln. Specials change every day, but you can usually count on stewed lamb, grilled lobster, and baked chicken served with rice, dumplings, and *fungi,* (a pastalike vegetable dish made of cornmeal and okra). ⊠ *Redcliff St., St. John's,* ☎ *268/ 462–1965. AE, MC, V. Closed Sun. No dinner Sat.–Thurs.*

$ ✕ **Commissioner's Grill.** The gaudy exterior—in raspberry, mango, blueberry, and lavender—of this 19th-century tamarind warehouse seems edible itself. The interior is more restrained, with white tile floors, powder-blue chairs, floral tablecloths, and local touches like wind chimes, Antiguan pottery, conch shells, and historic maps. Specials might include whelks in garlic butter, snapper in lobster sauce, marinated conch, or shrimp Creole. Local seafood is the obvious choice, although beef and poultry are also reliable. ⊠ *Commissioner Alley and Redcliffe St., St. John's,* ☎ *268/462–1883. AE, DC, MC, V.*

$ ✕ **Russell's.** Vivacious owner Russell Hodge had the brilliant idea of restoring a part of Ft. St. James, with its gorgeous views of the bay and headlands, and converting it into an open-air restaurant. Potted plants and faux-Victorian gas lamps lend a romantic aura to the cool stone-and-wood terrace. The menu features delectable local specialties with an emphasis on seafood. You might start with conch fritters or whelks in garlic butter, then try an excellent snapper Creole. Live jazz is a lure Thursday nights and there's merengue on Sundays. Russell's sister Valerie owns the estimable Shirley Heights Lookout (☞ Nightlife, below), and sister Patsy runs the delightful Pumpkin Runner, a fast-food van dispensing savory local dishes every night in St. John's. The Hodges might well be Antigua's first family of food. ⊠ *Fort James,* ☎ *268/ 462–5479. AE, DC.*

CONTINENTAL

$$–$$$ ✕ **Coconut Grove.** Coconut palms grow up through the roof of this
   ★   open-air thatched restaurant, candles flicker gently in lanterns illumi-
       nating colorful local artwork, and waves lap the white-coral sand a
       few feet away. For a romantic evening, head here when there's a full
       moon and reserve Table 1, closest to the water and under the stars.
       The place is part of the ☞ **Siboney Beach Resort.** The new chef hails
       from Lyon, France, and the menu at last matches the sublime setting.
       The signature dish has long been beer-battered shrimp with coconut
       cream and chili sauces. But be adventuresome and try the chilled lob-
       ster farfalle (bow-tie pasta), tossed in light shrimp oil with grapefruit
       and mango, the salmon stuffed with seafood mousse in cilantro sauce,
       or the unimpeachable rack of lamb. Add to all this warm service with-
       out a spot of pretention and you have the makings of the classic beach
       restaurant. ⊠ *Dickenson Bay,* ☎ *268/462–1538. AE, MC, V.*

   $$ ✕ **Julian's.** You enter this restaurant—Antigua's finest—through a
   ★   lovely historic courtyard, where a jazz combo serenades diners on
       weekends. The intimate dining room (only eight tables) has olive straw-
       and-rattan chairs, lime-green rafters and shutters, and black-and-white
       napery. Chef and co-owner Julian Waterer is daringly unconventional,
       brilliantly counterpointing flavors and colors; even his lentil soup is
       perfectly textured. Other choices on the rotating menu might include
       blackened Brie with grapefruit, asparagus, and honey; wild mush-
       room, leek, and feta strudel in onion marmalade; rosettes of salmon
       and leeks steamed with dill, swimming in ginger-scented beurre blanc;
       or peppered veal sweetbreads pan-seared with bacon. You can order
       some excellent wines by the glass off the well-considered list. The de-
       lightful upstairs lounge is perfect for an aperitif or a cordial, with just
       the right British touch, including a dartboard and a fine single-malt
       selection. ⊠ *Corn Alley and Church La., St. John's,* ☎ *268/462–4766.
       AE, D, MC, V. Closed Mon. No lunch Sun.*

 $–$$ ✕ **Lobster Pot.** A fishing boat sits in the center of this romantic beach-
   ★   front restaurant's flagstone dining room, and sea breezes sweep in
       through the open gallery. The best seats are right on the water. The di-
       verse menu is a mix of fresh seafood, pasta, and Creole- and Caribbean-
       style dishes. Starters include the lobster and pineapple phyllo with tamari
       and chili dips, and the grilled baby eggplant stuffed with cheese and
       herbs. Follow these with coconut-milk curry shrimp; baked breast of
       chicken stuffed with goat cheese, broccoli, and sun-dried tomatoes; herb-
       encrusted swordfish in tomato sauce; or succulent lobster. The wine
       list is well considered and very fairly priced, with most selections in
       the $20 range. ⊠ *Runaway Bay,* ☎ *268/462–2856. D, MC, V.*

 $–$$ ✕ **Redcliffe Tavern.** Every item on the tavern's northern Italian–Con-
       tinental–Creole menu is wonderfully fresh. The dinner menu includes
       pastas, grilled chicken, fresh local lobster, spicy Creole crab puffs, and
       a smoked salmon and shellfish terrine in lime mousseline. The lunch
       menu also lists salads, sandwiches, and burgers. The dining room is
       on the second floor of a colonial warehouse set amid the courtyards
       of Redcliffe Quay. Brick and stone walls are decorated with antique
       water-pumping equipment still bearing the original English maker's crests.
       Salvaged from all over the island, the old machines, with their flywheels
       and pistons, have been imaginatively integrated—one supports the
       buffet bar. You can also dine on the treetop-level terrace. ⊠ *Redcliffe
       Quay, St. John's,* ☎ *268/461–4557. AE, MC, V.*

 $–$$ ✕ **Wardroom Restaurant.** An atmosphere of Olde England pervades
       this restaurant on the ground floor of the beautifully restored ☞ **Cop-
       per and Lumber Store Hotel.** The dining room, with massive brick walls
       and stained wood beams, opens out to a courtyard hung with bougainvil-
       lea and to views of the floodlit battlements of English Harbour. The

menu is international, mixing dishes such as West African peanut soup with lobster in puff pastry, a good selection of local fish dishes, and even lamb cutlets. ⊠ *Nelson's Dockyard,* ☎ *268/460–1058. AE, DC, MC, V. Closed Wed. No lunch.*

$ ★ ✕ **Admiral's Inn.** Known as the Ad to yachtspeople, this historic English Harbour tavern in the ☞ **Admiral's Inn** hotel is a must for Anglophiles and mariners. At the bar inside, you can sit and soak up the centuries under dark, timbered wood (the bar top even has the names of sailors from Nelson's fleet carved into it), but most guests tend to sit on the terrace under shady Australian gums to enjoy the views of the harbor complex and Clarence House opposite. Specialties include curried conch, fresh snapper with equally fresh limes, and lobster thermidor. The pumpkin soup is not to be missed. ⊠ *Nelson's Dockyard,* ☎ *268/460–1027. Reservations essential. AE, MC, V.*

FRENCH

$$$ ★ ✕ **Chez Pascal.** Pascal and Florence Milliat built this charmer atop a hill themselves. The terrace overlooks a lit-up pool, and the dining room is tastefully decorated with dark rattan furnishings and tropical upholstery, jade tablecloths, ceramics, local paintings, and copper pots. Pascal's classic Lyonnaise cuisine with tropical touches will put you in an even more romantic mood. He has a remarkably deft hand with delicate sauces. Witness the chicken liver mousse with *gourgettes* (tiny goat-cheese pastries) in lemon sauce, impossibly light and fluffy, or lobster medallions in basil cream. Finish off with a heavenly flourless chocolate cake or classic tart Tatin. If you're too sated to go home, Pascal has just constructed four enormous rooms with cathedral ceilings, wicker furniture, stunning sea views, baby blue accents, and whirlpool tubs; all for $100–$130 a night! The only drawback is its comparatively remote location: you'll need a car or taxi. ⊠ *Galley Bay Hill,* ☎ *268/462–3232. Reservations essential. AE, D, MC, V. Closed Aug.*

$$ ✕ **Le Bistro.** This Antiguan institution, run by husband-and-wife team Raffaele and Phillippa Esposito, is remarkably consistent in every aspect, starting with a casually elegant decor, with accents of peach and pistachio that perfectly match the napery, brick tile work, jade chairs, and even the painted lighting fixtures. Trellises cannily divide the large space into intimate sections, with tables staggered just the right distance apart. The chefs, who all hail from France, delight in blending their regional fare with indigenous ingredients. You might start with fresh seafood roulade in calypso dill sauce or shrimp stuffed with seafood mousse laced with saffron sauce. Sterling entrées include a roast duck in mango sauce and medallions of lobster in wine and pumpkin sauce. As for dessert, Le Bistro's version of Death by Chocolate is a lingering, exquisite torture to the taste buds. ⊠ *Hodges Bay,* ☎ *268/462–3881. Reservations essential. AE, MC, V. Closed Mon. No lunch.*

ITALIAN

$$–$$$ ✕ **Southern Cross.** This exceptional Italian eatery is owned by Flavio Scala, who has been a helmsman on several Italian entries to the Americas Cup. No surprise then that's it's popular with the yachting set. The brick-and-mahogany bar, scrap metal artwork, vaulted ceilings, stonework, driftwood chandeliers, and director chairs set the smart tone. The menu follows through with a blend of classic and inventive Italian food, from veal marsala to gnocchi with white truffles. ⊠ *English Harbour Yacht Club Marina,* ☎ *268/460–1797. Reservations essential. AE, MC, V. No lunch Sun.*

$–$$ ★ ✕ **Alberto's.** Above Willoughby Bay on Antigua's southeast side, this superior Italian restaurant is a bit out of the way but popular nevertheless. The ebullient owner, Alberto, taught his culinary secrets to his English wife, Vanessa, and the two turn out delicious seafood. Try island lobster (perhaps grilled with basil and garlic); cockles Alberto; the chef's creation of the evening (you're in luck if it's baked grouper in pine-nut crust or snapper *marechiaro,* in a tomato, olive, and caper sauce); or more traditional dishes such as eggplant parmigiana, osso buco, or linguine with clams. The ravioli in creamy walnut sauce and breadfruit in garlic parsley butter are sheer heaven. Tables line a balcony open to the breezes and hung with bougainvillea, and painted china graces the walls (check out the octopuses and squids on the plates by the bar). ⊠ *Willoughby Bay,* ☎ *268/460–3007 or via VHF 68. Reservations essential. AE, D, MC, V. Closed Mon. and July–Oct. No lunch.*

$–$$ ✕ **Al Porto.** This unassuming spot at ☞ Jolly Harbour Beach Resort, looks like the kind of place where pasta would be overcooked and flailing in canned tomato sauce. Instead, you'll receive dazzling antipasti (yummy eggplant parmigiana), creative pizzas (try the seafood), and lovingly prepared northern Italian fare. Specials might be bacon-wrapped shrimp in white wine sauce, chicken *valdostana* (grilled with mushrooms, tomatoes, onions), or tagliatelle with cèpes. You can even select and grill your own fillet. The interior is dark and cramped with unusual, almost disturbingly hallucinogenic paintings; the simple, sunny terrace overlooks the marina. ⊠ *Jolly Harbour,* ☎ *268/462–6166. AE, MC, V.*

$ ✕ **Big Banana-Pizzas on the Quay.** This tiny, often crowded spot is
★   tucked into one side of a restored warehouse with broad plank floors and stone archways. It serves some of the island's best pizza and tasty specials like conch salad. There's live entertainment some nights. ⊠ *Redcliffe Quay, St. John's,* ☎ *268/462–2621. AE, MC, V.*

Beaches

All of Antigua's beaches are public, and many are dotted with resorts that provide water-sports-equipment rentals and a place to grab a cool drink. Sunbathing topless or in the buff is strictly illegal except on one of the small beaches at Hawksbill Beach Hotel. Beware that on the one or two days a week that cruise ships dock in St. John's, buses drop off loads of cruise-ship passengers on virtually all the west-coast beaches. Choose this day to tour the island by car, visit one of the more remote east-end beaches, or take a day trip to Barbuda.

ANTIGUA

Carlisle Bay has a large coconut grove and two long, snow-white beaches over which the estimable Curtain Bluff resort sits. Standing on the bluff of this peninsula, you can see the almost-blinding blue waters of the Atlantic Ocean drifting into the Caribbean Sea.

Dickenson Bay has a lengthy stretch of powder-soft white sand and exceptionally calm water. Here you'll find small and large hotels, super-casual beach bars, and beachfront restaurants. Water-sports equipment can be rented at the Halcyon Cove.

Driftwood Beach is a delightful taupe ribbon on the southwest coast that's anchored by a lively beach bar, which serves terrific local food, including fresh lobster, for lunch.

Five Islands Peninsula has four secluded beaches (including one for bathing in the buff) of fine tan sand and coral reefs for snorkeling. The Hawksbill Beach Hotel is here.

Half Moon Bay, a ¾-mi crescent of sand, is a prime area for snorkeling and windsurfing. On the Atlantic side of the island, the water can be quite rough at times.

Johnson's Point is a deliciously deserted beach of bleached white sand on the southwest coast.

Long Bay, on the far eastern coast, has coral reefs in water so shallow that you can actually walk out to them. Along the beach are the Long Bay Hotel and the rambling Pineapple Beach Club.

Pigeon Point, near English Harbour, is a fine white-sand beach with calm water. Several restaurants and bars are nearby.

Runaway Beach is home to the Barrymore Beach Hotel and the Runaway Beach Hotel, so its stretch of white sand can get crowded.

BARBUDA

Coco Point on Barbuda is an uncrowded 8-mi stretch of white sand. Barbuda, encircled by reefs and shipwrecks, is great for scuba diving.

Outdoor Activities and Sports

Participant Sports

BICYCLING

Bicycling isn't terribly arduous on Antigua, except in the most southern region, where the roads soar, dip, and corkscrew. Try **Sun Cycles** (⊠ Nelson Dr., Hodges Bay, ☎ 268/461–0324) for rentals.

BOATING

Needless to say, the surrounding waters are delightful for cruising, whether in a skiff or a schooner. Experienced boaters will particularly enjoy the east coast, which is far more rugged, with several offshore islets; be sure to get a good nautical map as there are numerous minireefs that can prove treacherous. If you're just looking for a couple of hours of wave hopping, stick to the Dickenson Bay/Runaway area.

Halcyon Cove Watersports (⊠ Dickenson Bay, ☎ 268/462–0256) offers waterskiing and other water rides and rents small boats. **Nicholson Yacht Charters** (☎ 800/662–6066) are real professionals. A long-established island family, they can charter you anything from a 20-ft ketch to a giant schooner. **Sea Sports** (⊠ Dickenson Bay, ☎ 268/462–3355) rents Jet Skis and Sunfish and offers parasailing and waterskiing trips. The atmosphere here can be hectic.

FISHING

The waters surrounding Antigua teem with game fish like marlin, wahoo, and tuna, although the selection isn't world-class like it is around Trinidad, the Dominican Republic, and the Bahamas. **Nimrod** (☎ 268/463–8744) is a 50-ft cruiser whose captain, Terry Bowen, is extremely knowledgeable. Sunset cruises and island circumnavigations are also offered. The 45-ft Hatteras Sportfisherman **Obsession** (☎ 268/462–2824) has top-of-the-line equipment, including an international standard fighting chair, outriggers, and handcrafted rods.

FITNESS CENTERS

Fitness Shack (⊠ Dickenson Bay, ☎ 268/462–5223) has extensive fitness equipment and aerobics classes as well as an adjacent spa. **Get Physical** (⊠ Woods Centre, St. John's, ☎ 268/462–9541) is open late (10 PM). It has a full complement of weight training and cardiovascular equipment, as well as regular aerobics and step classes. **National Fitness Centre** (⊠ Campsite, St. John's, ☎ 268/462–3682) offers a good selection of StairMasters, weight machines, and aerobics classes.

GOLF

Cedar Valley Golf Club (⊠ Friar's Hill, northeast of St. John's, ☎ 268/462–0161) has a 6100-ft, 18-hole course. The terrain is bland, fairly easy, and not terribly well-maintained.

HORSEBACK RIDING

Comparatively dry Antigua is best for beach rides, though you won't find anything wildly romantic and deserted à la *The Black Stallion*. **Spring**

Hill Riding Stables (✉ Falmouth, ☎ 268/460–1333) offers trail rides on the beach or through the bush. **St. James Stables** (✉ Mamora Bay, ☎ 268/463–2006) offers a variety of trail rides, mostly on the beach, on some magnificent animals. They offer lessons as well.

SCUBA DIVING

With all the wrecks and reefs, there are lots of undersea sights to explore. Among the favorites are Green Island, Cades Reef, and Bird Island (a national park). There are several varieties of coral, with brain and elk predominating, canyons, pillars, underwater caverns, and sheer walls. There's also a parade of marine life from gargantuan groupers to gliding manta rays, sensuously waving gorgonians to colorful sea anemone, and the usual gatherings of parrotfish, sergeant majors, and triggerfish.

Big John's Dive Antigua (✉ Rex Halcyon Cove, Dickenson Bay, ☎ 268/462–3483) offers certification courses and day and night dives from Rex Halcyon Cove. **Dockyard Divers** (✉ Nelson's Dockyard, English Harbour, ☎ 268/464–8591, FAX 268/460–1179), owned by British ex-merchant seaman Captain A. G. Fincham, is one of the oldest-established outfits on the island and offers diving and snorkeling trips, PADI courses, and dive packages with accommodations.

TENNIS

The **Temo Sports Complex** (✉ Falmouth Bay, ☎ 268/463–1781) has two floodlit tennis courts, three glass-backed squash courts, showers, a sports shop, and snack bars.

Many of the larger resorts have their own tennis courts. Guests have top priority; for nonguests, court fees are about $30 an hour. The **St. James's Club** (✉ Mamora Bay, ☎ 268/460–5000) has seven (five lighted for night play); **Sandals** (✉ Dickenson Bay, ☎ 268/462–0267), two; **Rex Halcyon Cove Beach Resort** (✉ Dickenson Bay, ☎ 268/462–0256), four (lighted); and **Curtain Bluff** (✉ Curtain Bluff, ☎ 268/462–8400), four Har-Tru and a grass court.

WATERSKIING

Halcyon Cove Watersports (☎ 268/462–0256) and **Sea Sports** (☎ 268/462–3355), both at Dickenson Bay, will take you waterskiing.

WINDSURFING

Most major hotels offer windsurfing equipment. The best area is the northern coast, which is slightly less protected and sees a challenging juxtaposition of sudden calms and gusts. **Halcyon Cove Watersports** (✉ Rex Halcyon Cove Beach Resort, Dickenson Bay, ☎ 268/462–0256) offers rentals and instruction. **Windsurfing Antigua** (✉ Lord Nelson Beach Hotel, ☎ 268/462–3094 or 268/462–9463), run by expert Patrick Scales, is the spot for serious board sailors. Rates are $25 per hour to rent, $60 per hour for a private beginner's lesson.

Spectator Sports

For information about sports events, contact **Antigua Sports and Games** (☎ 268/462–1925).

CRICKET

Practically the only thing most Americans know about this game is that there's something called a sticky wicket. Here, as in Britain and all the West Indies, the game is a national passion. Youngsters play on makeshift pitches, which are comparable to sandlots, and international matches are usually fought out in the stadium on Independence Avenue in St. John's. For information on top matches and their venues, call the **Antigua Cricket Association** (✉ Newgate St., St. John's, ☎ 268/462–9090) or the **Antigua Cricket Board** (☎ 268/462–5462).

Shopping

Antigua's duty-free shops are at Heritage Quay; they're the reason so many cruise ships call here. Bargains can be found on perfumes, liqueurs and liquor (including, of course, Antiguan rum), jewelry, china, and crystal. As for local items, look for straw hats, baskets, batik, pottery, and hand-printed cotton clothing.

Areas

Redcliffe Quay, on the waterfront at the south edge of St. John's, is by far the most appealing shopping area. Several restaurants and more than 30 boutiques, many with one-of-a-kind items, are set around landscaped courtyards shaded by colorful trees. **Heritage Quay,** also in St. John's, has 35 shops—including many that are duty-free—that cater to the cruise-ship crowd that docks almost at its doorstep. Outlets here include Benetton, the Body Shop, Polo, Gucci, and Oshkosh B'Gosh. The main tourist shops in St. John's are along **St. Mary's, High,** and **Long streets.**

Specialty Items

ART

Harmony Hall (⊠ At Brown's Bay Mill, near Freetown, ☎ 268/460–4120) is the sister to the original Jamaica location. In addition to "Annabella Boxes," books, and cards, there are pottery and ceramic pieces, carved wooden birds, and ever-changing exhibits. **Island Arts Galleries** (⊠ Alton Pl., Sandy La., behind Hodges Bay Club, ☎ 268/461–3332; ⊠ Heritage Quay, ☎ 268/462–2787; ⊠ St. James's Club, ☎ 268/460–5000), run by artist-filmmaker Nick Maley and his wife, Gloria, is a melting pot for Caribbean artists, with prices ranging from $10 to $15,000; some of the art naïf pieces are stunning, and the genre paintings of local life often have a raw elemental power.

Seahorse Studios (⊠ Falmouth Harbour, ☎ 268/460–1417), opened by John and Katie Shears, presents the works of good artists, primarily land and seascapes in seashell colors. They also carry the exquisite pottery of Nancy Nicholson, in unusual shapes with vibrant sea colors and motifs like dolphins and fish.

BOOKS AND MAGAZINES

Map Shop (⊠ St. Mary's St., St. John's, ☎ 268/462–3993) has a "must" buy for those interested in Antiguan life: the paperback *To Shoot Hard Labour: The Life and Times of Samuel Smith, an Antiguan Workingman*. Also check out any of the books of Jamaica Kincaid, whose works on her native Antigua have won international, albeit controversial, acclaim. The shop also offers a fine assortment of books on Caribbean cuisine, flora, fauna, and history.

CIGARS, LIQUOR, AND LIQUEURS

La Casa Habana (⊠ Heritage Quay, ☎ 268/462–2677) sells Cuban cigars, but remember that it's illegal to bring them back to the United States. **Manuel Diaz Liquor Store** (⊠ Long and Market Sts., St. John's, ☎ 268/462–0440) has a wide selection of Caribbean rums and liqueurs. **Quin Farara** (⊠ Heritage Quay, ☎ 268/462–1737; ⊠ Long St., ☎ 268/462–0463; ⊠ Jolly Harbour, ☎ 268/462–6245) offers some of the best bargains on both hard liquor and wines.

CLOTHING

Base (⊠ Redcliffe Quay, ☎ 268/460–2500) is the brainchild of English designer Steven Giles, whose striped or monochrome cotton-and-Lycra resort wear remains all the rage on the island. The hand-dyed clothing and scarves of the famed **Caribelle Batik** (⊠ St. Mary's St., St. John's, ☎ 268/462–2972) duplicate the festive colors of a Caribbean

Carnival. **CoCo Shop** (⊠ St. Mary's St., St. John's, ☏ 268/462–1128) is a favorite source for Sea Island cotton designs, Daks clothing, and Liberty of London fabrics, along with the shop's own designs for the country-club set. **Galley Boutiques** (⊠ Main shop in English Harbour, ☏ 268/460–1525; ⊠ St. James's Club, ☏ 268/460–1333) is where Janie Easton sells her original designs at reasonable prices.

Jacaranda (⊠ Redcliffe Quay, ☏ 268/462–1888) sells batiks, sarongs, and swimwear. **Noreen Phillips** (⊠ Redcliffe Quay, ☏ 268/462–3127) creates glitzy appliquéd and beaded evening wear inspired by the colors of the sea and sunset, in sensuous fabrics ranging from chiffon and silk shantung to Italian lace and Indian brocade. **A Thousand Flowers** (⊠ Redcliffe Quay, ☏ 268/462–4264) carries resort wear made of comfortable silks, linens, and batiks from all over the world.

DUTY-FREE GOODS

Little Switzerland (⊠ Heritage Quay, ☏ 268/462–3108) sells pricey items from Belleek china to Bijan fragrances in a luxurious, air-conditioned setting. **Norma's Duty-Free Shop** (⊠ Heritage Quay Shopping Center and the Halcyon Cove, ☏ 268/462–0172) has bargains in jewelry, perfumes, and china ranging from Lladro to Limoges. **Specialty Shoppe** (⊠ St. Mary's St., ☏ 268/462–1198) has wares—from local carvings to imported china and cosmetics—that make impressive gifts.

HANDICRAFTS

You can see original slave shackles in the overgrown courtyard of **Coates Cottage** (⊠ Lower Nevis St., ☏ 268/462–3636), a peeling, 18th-century gingerbread that holds superb local artworks and crafts; an added bonus is that artists and artisans often utilize the space as a temporary studio. **Craft Originals Studio** (⊠ Coast Rd., near the airport, ☏ 268/463–2519) is where Trinidadian Natalie White sells her sculptured cushions and wall hangings, all hand-painted on silk and signed. **Dalila** (⊠ Redcliffe Quay, ☏ 268/462–3625) displays colorful hand-painted wooden carvings of animals and banana trees, as well as charming bonnets and sundresses. **Isis** (⊠ Redcliffe Quay, ☏ 268/462–4602) sells a range of island and international bric-a-brac, such as antique jewelry, hand-carved walking sticks, and glazed pottery.

Kate Designs (⊠ Redcliffe Quay, ☏ 268/460–5971) sells acclaimed artist Kate Spencer's distinctive work from neighboring St. Kitts: lovely silk-screened scarves and sarongs, as well as vividly colored place mats, paintings, prints, even note cards, and Dale Isaac's whimsical hats. **Mimosa** (⊠ Heritage Quay, ☏ 268/462–2923) sells hand-painted wind chimes and porcelain clowns in island dress. **The New Pottery** (⊠ Cedar Grove, ☏ 268/461–3085) features the work of gifted potter Sarah Fuller, whose cobalt blue glazes are truly striking. In addition to the usual mugs, vases, and plates, she also fashions ceramic fish and mobiles.

JEWELRY

Colombian Emeralds (⊠ Heritage Quay, ☏ 268/462–2086) is the largest retailer of Colombian emeralds in the world. The **Goldsmitty** (⊠ Redcliffe Quay, ☏ 268/462–4601) is Hans Smit, an expert goldsmith who turns gold, black coral, and precious and semiprecious stones into one-of-a-kind works of art. (Be aware that environmental groups discourage tourists from purchasing corals that are designated as endangered species, because the reefs are often harvested carelessly.)

PERFUMES

Little Switzerland (⊠ Heritage Quay, ☏ 268/462–3108) has an extensive selection of European scents for men and women. **La Parfumerie** (⊠ Heritage Quay, ☏ 268/462–2601) imports high-priced scents. **Scent**

Shop (⊠ High St., ☎ 268/462–0303) in downtown St. John's offers scent-sational buys in perfumes and cosmetics.

Nightlife and the Arts

Most of Antigua's evening entertainment centers on the resort hotels, which present calypso singers, steel bands, limbo dancers, and folkloric groups on a regular basis. Check with the tourist office (☞ Visitor information *in* Antigua A to Z, *below*) for up-to-date information.

Nightlife

BARS

The **Bay House** (⊠ Tradewinds Hotel, Marble Hill, ☎ 268/462–1223) is in a small hilltop hotel perpetually booked by British Airways flight attendants, who have made the bar a lively, gossipy hangout—and perhaps the closest thing Antigua has to a stylish singles bar. There is live piano music (often drowned out by boisterous singing). Don't come for the overpriced food, which runs from clichéd to creative, but for the company, who lounge at the bar or by the pool as if this were a hip, rich uncle's country estate. **Big Banana** (⊠ Redcliffe Quay, ☎ 268/462–2621) presents live dance bands well into the night on Tuesday and Thursday.

Colombo's (⊠ Galleon Beach Club, English Harbour, ☎ 268/460–1452) is the place to be on Wednesday night for live reggae. It's also a huge yachtie hangout, with pennants of various boats hanging from the rafters (along with the clientele on rowdier nights). Beware: The once fine Italian fare is now overrated. The down-home **Crazy Horse Saloon** (⊠ Redcliffe Quay, ☎ 268/462–7936) corrals tourists and locals for everything from pool tournaments to Mexican and country-and-western bands to happy-hour specials like two-for-one margaritas (ladies drink free) on Mondays. Sports fans also gravitate here for its five, huge stereo TVs broadcasting games from around the world via satellite. The **Jolly Roger** (⊠ Dickenson Bay, ☎ 268/462–2064) lures a boisterous group for its four-hour Saturday-night booze cruises. Sail under the stars for a barbecue with an open bar, and dance to live island music.

The Mad Mongoose (⊠ Falmouth Harbour, ☎ 268/463–7900) is a wildly popular yachtie joint, splashed in vivid Rasta colors, with a game room and satellite TV: major singles action here. **Millers by the Sea** (⊠ Runaway Beach, ☎ 268/462–9414) draws a crowd that spills over onto the beach for its ever-popular happy hour and live nightly entertainment. Dance on the beach way into the night (or to mingle with cruise-ship passengers on heavy-traffic days). **Russell's** (⊠ Fort James, ☎ 268/462–5479) presents live jazz combos on Thursday nights and merengue bands from the Dominican Republic, attracting an enthusiastic crowd that shakes and shimmies with wild abandon, on Sunday evenings. **Shirley Heights Lookout** (⊠ Shirley Heights, ☎ 268/463–1785) hosts Sunday-afternoon barbecues that continue into the night with music and dancing. It's the place to be Sunday afternoons and Thursday evenings, when residents, visitors, and the yachting crowd gather for boisterous fun, the latest gossip, and great sunsets.

CASINOS

There are four major casinos on Antigua, as well as several holes-in-the-wall that feature mainly one-armed bandits. Hours depend on the season, so it's best to inquire upon your arrival to the island. The "world's largest slot machine" and gaming tables are at the **King's Casino** (⊠ Heritage Quay, ☎ 268/462–1727). The **St. James's Club** (⊠ Mamora Bay, ☎ 268/463–1113) has a flamboyant casino with a European ambience. The casino at the **Royal Antiguan Resort** (⊠ Deep Bay, ☎ 268/462–3733) is a model of those in Atlantic City, New Jersey.

Ribbit (⌧ Donovans, Green Bay, ☎ 268/462–7996) hosts a lively mix of locals and tourists who dance (no shorts allowed) under a strobing laser light system that could provoke a headache if the beers and blaring sound system don't. It's open Wednesday–Saturday from 10:30 PM. Admission is EC$10 Fridays, EC$20 Saturdays, when there's usually a live band. Semiformal attire (really no jeans or halter tops) is rather pretentiously requested on weekends. Guards and metal detectors ensure a safe party atmosphere. The **Web** (⌧ Old Parham Rd., St. John's, ☎ 268/462–3186) attracts a somewhat rowdier, more local crowd and spins more ethnic sounds such as reggae, soca, and salsa.

The Arts

ISLAND CULTURE

Forget the fun but hokey folkloric shows offered by the big hotels. There are two enterprising organizations dedicated to keeping Antiguan traditions alive (of course, to earn a living, many performers participate in the more touristy shows as well). The truly versatile **Antigua Community Players** (call the president, Mrs. Edie Hill-Thibou, for information on events and venues, ☎ 268/460–5625) specializes in performing the haunting rhythms of Benna (indigenous Antiguan/African music), as well as fierce gospel concerts, and even creditable Gilbert and Sullivan productions. Original plays in rapid-fire patois are difficult to understand. **Antigua Dance Theater** (call the director, Gilbert Laudat, at ☎ 268/461–9519 for information) performs at special island business functions, but occasionally gives dazzling shows for the general public. The drum and percussion music is simple, derived from age-old African rhythms, the dancers incredibly lithe and graceful.

Exploring Antigua

Before you start exploring, study a map (major hotels provide free maps and island brochures). Road names are not posted, so you need to have a sense of direction before heading off. The easiest way to get to anything is to see if a popular restaurant is near it, since easy-to-spot signs leading the way to restaurants are posted all over the island. Don't hesitate to ask anyone you see for directions. Bear in mind that locals generally give directions in terms of landmarks that may not seem much like landmarks to you (turn left at the yellow house, or right at the big tree). If you happen to be in St. John's, stop in at the tourist bureau, at the corner of Long and Thames streets (☞ Visitor Information *in* Antigua A to Z, *below*). It's a good idea to wear a swimsuit under your clothes while you're sightseeing—one of the sights to strike your fancy may be a secluded beach.

Numbers in the margin correspond to points of interest on the Antigua (and Barbuda) map.

SIGHTS TO SEE

⑬ **Betty's Hope.** Just outside the village of Pares, a marked dirt road leads to the village of Betty's Hope, Antigua's first sugar plantation, founded in 1650. You can tour the twin windmills and view exhibits on the island's sugar era in the visitor center. The village isn't much now, but the private trust overseeing its restoration has ambitious plans. ⌧ *Pares,* ☎ *268/462–1469.* 🎫 *Free.* ⊙ *Tues.–Sat. 10–4*

⑤ **Curtain Bluff.** At the tip of a tiny outcropping of land, between Carlisle Bay and Morris Bay, Curtain Bluff offers dramatic views of the color contrasts where waters of the Atlantic Ocean meet those of the Caribbean Sea. From here, the main road skirts the southwest coast, dancing in and out of hardwood trees and offering tantalizing glimpses of lovely beaches and spectacular views. The road then veers away from the water and goes through the villages of Bolans and Jennings.

⑫ Devil's Bridge. This natural formation, sculpted by the crashing breakers of the Atlantic at Indian Creek, is a national park. Blowholes have been carved by the hissing, spitting surf. They may be hard to spot at first, but just wait until a wave bursts through!

⑧ English Harbour. The most famous of Antigua's attractions lies on the coast, just south of Falmouth. In 1671 the governor of the Leeward Islands wrote to the Council for Foreign Plantations in London, pointing out the advantages of this landlocked harbor. By 1704 English Harbour was in regular use as a garrisoned station.

In 1784, 26-year-old Horatio Nelson sailed in on HMS *Boreas* to serve as captain and second-in-command of the Leeward Island Station. Under his command was the captain of HMS *Pegasus,* Prince William Henry, Duke of Clarence, who was to ascend the throne of England as William IV. The prince was Nelson's close friend and acted as best man when Nelson married Fannie Nisbet on Nevis in 1787.

When the Royal Navy abandoned the station at English Harbour in 1889, it fell into a state of decay. The Society of the Friends of English Harbour began restoring it in 1951, and on Dockyard Day, November 14, 1961, **Nelson's Dockyard** was opened with much fanfare.

The dockyard is reminiscent, albeit on a much smaller scale, of Williamsburg, Virginia. Within the compound there are crafts shops, hotels, and restaurants. It is a hub for oceangoing yachts and serves as headquarters for the annual Sailing Week Regatta. A community of mariners keeps the area active in season. Beach lovers tend to stay elsewhere on the island, but visitors who enjoy history and who are part of (or like being around) the nautical scene often choose one of the nearby hotels. If you'd like to get a look at the area from the water, board the *Horatio Nelson* for a 20-minute guided cruise (☞ Guided Tours *in* Antigua A to Z, *below*).

The **Admiral's House Museum** displays ship models, a model of English Harbour, silver trophies, maps, prints, and Nelson's very own telescope and tea caddy. ⌧ *English Harbour,* ☎ *268/463–1053 or 268/463–1379.* ⌧ *$2.* ☉ *Daily 8–6.*

⑦ Falmouth. This town sits on a lovely bay backed by former sugar plantations and sugar mills. **St. Paul's Church** was rebuilt on the site of a church once used by troops during the Nelson period.

④ Fig Tree Drive. This road takes you through the rain forest, which is rich in mangoes, pineapples, and banana trees (*fig* is the Antiguan word for banana). The rain-forest area is the hilliest part of the island—**Boggy Peak,** to the west, is the highest point, rising to 1,319 ft.

⑥ Ft. George. East of **Liberta,** one of the first settlements founded by freed slaves, on Monk's Hill, this fort was built from 1689 to 1720. It wouldn't be of much help to anybody these days, but among the ruins you can make out the sites for its 32 cannons, its water cisterns, the base of the old flagstaff, and some of the original buildings.

② Ft. James. Named after King James II, this fort was constructed between 1704 and 1739 as a lookout point for the city and St. John's Harbour. The ramparts overlooking the small islands in the bay are in ruins, but 10 cannons still point out to sea.

⑩ Harmony Hall. Northeast of Freetown (follow the signs) is this interesting art gallery. A sister to the Jamaican gallery near Ocho Rios, Jamaica, Harmony Hall is built on the foundation of a 17th-century sugar-plantation great house. Artists Graham Davis and Peter and Annabella Proudlock, who founded the Jamaican gallery, teamed up with local entrepreneur Geoffrey Pidduck to create an Antiguan art gallery specializing in high-quality West Indian art. A large gallery is used for one-man shows, and another exhibition hall displays watercolors. A small bar and an outside restaurant under the trees are open in season. There's even a pool, and boat rides can be organized to nearby islets, making this a potential day trip. ⊠ *Brown's Mill Bay,* ☎ *268/463–2057 or 268/460–4120.* ⏾ *Daily 10–6.*

⑪ Indian Town. Archaeological digs at this national park have revealed evidence of Carib occupation. This is one of the prettier parts of the island.

❸ Megaliths of Greencastle Hill. It's an arduous but rewarding climb to these eerie rock slabs. Some say the megaliths were set up by humans for the worship of the sun and moon; others believe they are nothing more than unusual geological formations.

⑭ Parham. This tiny village is a splendid, sleepy example of a traditional colonial settlement. **St. Peter's Church,** built in 1840 by Thomas Weekes, an English architect, is an octagonal Italianate building whose facade was once richly decorated with stucco, key-stone work, and a majestic ribbed ceiling, though it suffered considerable damage during the earthquake of 1843.

❶ St. John's. Antigua's capital, home to some 40,000 people (approximately half the island's population), lies at sea level at the inland end of a sheltered bay on the northwest coast of the island. The city has seen better days, but it is undergoing a face-lift, and there are some notable historic sights, pleasant shopping areas, and good restaurants. Although much of the city looks shabby, it is definitely worth a visit. Most of the gift stores and restaurants are near the waterfront. Up the hill is Antigua's downtown, with stores carrying major appliances, plumbing supplies, and other goods unlikely to be of interest to tourists.

Signs at the **Museum of Antigua and Barbuda** say PLEASE TOUCH, encouraging visitors to explore Antigua's past. Try your hand at the educational video games or squeeze a cassava through a *matapi* (a grass sieve). Exhibits interpret the history of the nation from its geological birth to its political independence in 1981. There are fossil and coral remains from some 34 million years ago, a life-size replica of an Arawak house, models of a sugar plantation and a wattle-and-daub house, and a minishop with handicrafts, books, historical prints, and paintings. The colonial building that houses the museum is the former courthouse, which dates from 1750. ⊠ *Church and Market Sts.,* ☎ *268/462–1469.* ⊠ *Free.* ⏾ *Weekdays 8:30–4, Sat. 10–1.*

At the south gate of the **Anglican Cathedral of St. John the Divine,** there are figures of St. John the Baptist and St. John the Divine said to have been taken from one of Napoléon's ships and brought to Antigua. The original church was built in 1681, replaced by a stone building in 1745, and destroyed by an earthquake in 1843. The present building dates from 1845. With an eye to future earthquakes, the parishioners had the interior completely encased in pitch pine, hoping to forestall heavy damage. The church was elevated to the status of cathedral in 1848. ⊠ *Between Long and Newgate Sts.,* ☎ *268/461–0082.*

Shopaholics head directly for **Heritage Quay,** a continually expanding multimillion-dollar shopping complex. Two-story buildings showcase stores specializing in duty-free goods, sportswear, T-shirts, imports from down-island (paintings, T-shirts, straw baskets), and local crafts, plus several restaurants and a casino. Cruise-ship passengers disembark here from the 500-ft-long pier. ⊠ *High and Thames Sts.*

Redcliffe Quay, set at the water's edge just south of Heritage Quay, is the most appealing part of St. John's. Attractively restored buildings in a riot of cotton-candy colors house shops, restaurants, and boutiques and are linked by courtyards and landscaped walkways. This is the shopping area favored by residents and return guests. There are no duty-free shops, but there are many other interesting choices. There are also cafés where you can sit and ponder the scene of two centuries ago, when slaves were held here prior to being sold.

At the far south end of town, where Market Street forks into Valley Road and All Saints Road, a whole lot of haggling goes on every Friday and Saturday, when locals jam the public **marketplace** to buy and sell fruits, vegetables, fish, and spices. Be sure to ask before you aim a camera; expect your subject to ask for a tip. This is shopping the old-time Caribbean way, a jambalaya of sights, sounds, and smells.

⑨ Shirley Heights. This bluff affords a spectacular view of English Harbour. The heights are named for Sir Thomas Shirley, the governor who fortified the harbor in 1787. You can stop in at **Shirley Heights Lookout,** a restaurant built into the remnants of the 18th-century fortifications. Most notable for its boisterous Thursday and Sunday barbecues (☞ Nightlife, *above*), it serves dependable burgers, pumpkin soup, grilled items, and rum punches.

Not far from Shirley Heights is the **Dows Hill Interpretation Centre,** where observation platforms provide still more sensational vistas of the whole English Harbour area. There's a multimedia sound-and-light presentation on the island's history and culture, from the days of the Amerindians to the present. *For information, call National Parks Authority at* ☎ *268/460–2777.* ☑ *EC$15.* ☉ *Daily 9–5.*

⑮ Barbuda

Twenty-six miles north of Antigua is Barbuda—a flat, 62-square-mi coral atoll with 17 mi of pinkish white-sand beaches. Almost all the island's 1,200 people live in **Codrington.** Barbuda's 8-mi **Coco Point Beach** lures beachcombers, and the island is ringed by wrecks and reef, making it a great draw for divers and snorkelers. Ornithologists and bird lovers come here, too. The **Bird Sanctuary,** a wide mangrove-filled lagoon, is home to an estimated 170 species of birds, including frigate birds with 8-ft wingspans.

The sole historic ruin here is **Martello Tower,** which is believed to have been a lighthouse built by the Spaniards before the English occupied the island. LIAT (☞ Arriving and Departing *in* Antigua A to Z, *below*) has regularly scheduled daily flights from Antigua to Barbuda (with departure times just right for day-trippers); air and boat charters are also available. Those wishing to overnight here can choose from two superluxury resorts and several guest houses (contact the department of tourism and the hotel association for details on charters and overnight stays; ☞ Visitor Information *in* Antigua A to Z, *below*).

Antigua A to Z

Arriving and Departing

BY AIRPLANE

American Airlines (☎ 268/462–0950) has daily direct service from New York and Miami, as well as several flights from San Juan that connect with flights from more than 100 U.S. cities. **Air Canada** (☎ 268/462–

1147) has nonstop service from Toronto. **Air France** (☎ 268/462–1763) has nonstop service from Paris. **British Airways** (☎ 268/462–3219) has nonstop service from London. **BWIA** (☎ 268/462–3101) has nonstop service from New York, Miami, and Toronto. **LIAT** (☎ 268/480–5600) has daily flights from Antigua to Barbuda, as well as to and from many other Caribbean islands. **V. C. Bird International Airport** is a major hub for traffic between Caribbean islands; it is always busy with tiny planes taking off and landing.

From the Airport: Taxis meet every flight, and drivers will offer to guide you around the island. The taxis are unmetered, but rates are posted at the airport and drivers are required to carry a rate card with them. The fixed rate from the airport to St. John's is $12 (although drivers have been known to *quote* E.C. dollars) and from the airport to English Harbour, $21.

Electricity

Antigua runs on 110 volts, allowing the use of most small U.S. appliances. Outlets are both two- and three-pronged, so bring an adaptor; ask your hotel if a converter is required for laptop computers.

Emergencies

Ambulance: ☎ 268/462–0251. **Fire:** ☎ 268/462–0044. **Hospital:** Holberton Hospital (✉ Hospital Rd., St. John's, ☎ 268/462–0251) has a 24-hour emergency room. **Pharmacies:** Medical and other supplies are available at **City Pharmacy** (✉ St. Mary's St., St. John's, ☎ 268/462–1363) and **Health Pharmacy** (✉ Redcliffe St., St. John's, ☎ 268/462–1255). **Police:** ☎ 268/462–0125.

Festivals and Seasonal Events

Antigua Sailing Week takes place at the end of April and early May, and draws more than 300 extraordinary yachts for a series of races in several boat classes. The salt air crackles with excitement like a nautical Kentucky Derby. **Antigua Tennis Week,** usually held the second week of May, features exhibitions by such masters as Billie Jean King, Fred Stolle, and Bob Lutz, plus a pro-am tournament. **Carnival,** which runs from the end of July to early August, is one of the Caribbean's more elaborate, with eye-catching costumes, fiercely competitive bands, and the only Caribbean Queen show (a.k.a. the Miss Antigua Contest).

Getting Around

BUSES

You'll see two bus stations in St. John's, near the Botanical Gardens and near Central Market, but don't expect to see many buses. Bus schedules here epitomize what is called "island time," which is to say they roll when the spirit (infrequently) moves them.

CAR RENTALS

To rent a car, you'll need a valid driver's license and a temporary permit ($20), which is available through the rental agent. Rentals average about $50 per day in season, with unlimited mileage. You'll probably get a better daily rate if you rent for several days. Most agencies rent automatic, stick-shift, and right- and left-hand-drive vehicles, as well as four-wheel-drive vehicles ($55 per day). Although these four-wheel-drive vehicles will get you more places and are refreshingly open, beware that the roads are full of potholes (though the government is finally repaving the more heavily trafficked routes), and a day in such a vehicle can leave you feeling as if you've been through a paint-mixing machine! Remember to drive on the left (pay particular attention getting in and out of rotaries and making turns), and know that virtually all roads are unmarked. Fortunately, there are no incredibly steep curves as on so many other Caribbean islands.

Among the agencies are **Avis** (⊠ Airport, ☎ 268/462–2840; ⊠ St. James Club, Mamora Bay, ☎ 268/462–5000), **Budget** (⊠ Airport, ☎ 268/462–3009 or 800/472–3325), **Hertz** (⊠ Airport, ☎ 268/462–6450; ⊠ All Saints Rd., St. John's, ☎ 268/462–4114; ⊠ Jolly Harbour, ☎ 268/462–6268), **Dollar** (⊠ Nevis St., St. John's, ☎ 268/462–0362), **National** (⊠ Coolidge St., St. John's, ☎ 268/462–2113 or 800/328–4567), and **Thrifty** (⊠ Airport, ☎ 268/462–0976).

You can rent Honda or Yamaha motorcycles for $35 per day ($150 per week) at **Shipwreck** (⊠ English Harbour, ☎ 268/460–2711). Scooters run $25 per day, $85 per week.

TAXIS

If you're uncomfortable about driving on the left or are prone to getting lost, a taxi is your best bet, although fares mount up quickly. Taxis are unmetered, but rates are fixed from here to there, and drivers are required to carry a rate card at all times. They'll even take you from the St. John's area to English Harbour and wait for a "reasonable" amount of time (about a half hour) while you look around, for about $40. You can always call a taxi from the stand in St. John's (☎ 268/462–0711, or 268/462–5190 after 6 PM).

Guided Tours

Virtually all taxi drivers double as guides, and you can arrange an island tour with one for about $20 an hour. Every major hotel has a cabbie on call and may be able to negotiate a discount, particularly off-season.

BOAT

Jolly Roger (☎ 268/462–2064) cruises, on a true-to-life replica of a pirate ship, come complete with "pirate" crew, limbo dancing, plank walking, and other pranks. **Kokomo Cats** (☎ 268/462–7245) runs several cruises, including one to deserted beaches, one to English Harbour, and one to sunset-gazing spots. The glass-bottom **Shorty's** (☎ 268/462–6326) offers various snorkeling trips to Bird Island, as well as sunset cruises and lobster picnics. Board the glass-bottom **Splish Splash** (☎ 268/462–3483) for two-hour snorkeling trips to Paradise Reef. **Titi I** (☎ 268/460–1452), a 34-ft motorboat powered with twin 300 Evinrudes, will take you to nearby islets, remote beaches, or out for specially tailored snorkeling trips.

Miguel's Holiday Adventures (☎ 268/460–6885) leaves every Tuesday, Thursday, and Saturday morning at 10 AM from the Hodges Bay jetty for snorkeling at Prickley Pear Island. Miguel and his wife Josephine also prepare a scrumptious lunch, including barbecued lobster and curried conch, treating the day like an extended family excursion. You can hike to the other side of the island where you'll discover blowholes and, in spring, nesting turtles. Miguel even brings along fishing rods: snapper, barracuda, and mackerel teem in the surrounding waters. **Wadadli Cats** (☎ 268/462–4792) operates various cruises, including a circumnavigation of the island, on its three sleek catamarans.

ORIENTATION

Antours (⊠ St. John's, ☎ 268/462–4788), by far the most professional outfit on Antigua, gives half- and full-day tours of the island, focusing on obvious highlights such as Shirley Heights and English Harbour. Antours is also the American Express representative on the island.

SPECIAL-INTEREST

Estate Safari Adventure (☎ 268/462–4713) operates tours to the "wilds" of Antigua's interior, where there are few marked trails and roads are rough. You'll see deserted plantation houses, rain-forest trails, and ruined sugar mills and forts. The luxuriant tropical forest around the island's highest point, Boggy Peak, is especially worth seeing. The cost of the tour (about $60 per person) includes lunch and snorkeling at a secluded beach. **Horatio Nelson** (⊠ Dockyard Divers, ☎ 268/464–8591) provides a good view of English Harbour from the water; hop on board for the 20-minute guided cruise. The tour costs $6 per person. **Tropikelly** (☎ 268/461–0383) offers an off-road adventure in a four-wheel-drive vehicle, allowing participants to appreciate the island's topography. Hiking is involved, though it's not strenuous. The tour visits the island's plantation houses, forts, and rain forests.

Language
Antigua's official language is English, and it's often spoken with a heavy West Indian lilt.

Money Matters
CURRENCY

Local currency is the Eastern Caribbean dollar (EC$), which is tied to the U.S. dollar and fluctuates only slightly. At hotels, the rate is EC$2.60 to US$1; at banks, it's about EC$2.70. American dollars are readily accepted, although you will usually receive change in E.C. dollars. Most places quote prices in E.C. dollars and most hotels, restaurants, and duty-free shops take major credit cards; all accept traveler's checks. It's a good idea to inquire at the tourist office or your hotel about the current credit-card policy. Note: Prices quoted throughout this chapter are in U.S. dollars unless indicated otherwise.

SERVICE CHARGES, TAXES, AND TIPPING

Hotels usually add a 10% service charge to your bill. In restaurants, a 10% service charge is usually added to your bill, and it is customary to leave another 5% if you are pleased with the service. Hotels collect an 8.5% government room tax; some restaurants will add a 7% tax. The departure tax is $14.

Taxi drivers expect a 10% tip, porters and bellmen about $1 per bag. Maids are rarely tipped, but if you think the service exemplary, figure $2–$3 per night. Staff at all-inclusives are not supposed to be tipped unless they've truly gone out of their way.

Opening and Closing Times
Although some **stores** still follow the tradition of closing for lunch, most shops, especially in season, are open Monday–Saturday 9–5; if a cruise ship is in, shops in Heritage and Redcliffe Quays are likely to open Sunday. **Banks** have varying hours but are generally open Monday–Thursday 8–2 and Friday 8–4. **Post offices** are open Monday–Saturday 9–4.

HOLIDAYS

New Year's Day, Good Friday (Apr. 2), Easter Sunday and Monday (Apr. 4–5), Labour Day (1st Mon. in May), Independence Day (Nov. 1), Christmas, and Boxing Day (Dec. 26).

Passports
U.S. and Canadian citizens need proof of identity. A valid passport is most desirable, but a birth certificate is acceptable provided it has a raised or embossed seal and has been issued by a county or state (not a hospital) and provided that you also have some type of photo identification, such as a driver's license. A driver's license by itself is not sufficient. British citizens need a passport. All visitors must present a return or ongoing ticket.

Precautions

Some beaches are shaded by manchineel trees, whose leaves and applelike fruit are poisonous to touch. Most of the trees are posted with
warning signs; even raindrops falling from them can cause painful blisters. If you come in contact with one, rinse the affected area and contact a doctor. Throughout the Caribbean, incidents of petty theft are
increasing. Leave your valuables in the hotel safe-deposit box; don't
leave them unattended in your room or on the beach. Also, the streets
of St. John's are fairly deserted at night, so it's not a good idea to wander out alone.

Telephones and Mail

To call Antigua from the United States, dial 1, then area code 268, then
the local seven-digit number. Few hotels have direct-dial telephones,
but connections are easily made through the switchboard. The Caribbean
Phone Card, available in $5, $10, and $20 amounts, can be used for
local and long-distance calls and for access to AT&T USA Direct lines.
Phone-card phones work much better than the regular pay phones. You
can purchase the card from most hotels or a post office. Some phone-
card booths can now access Sprint and MCI. In addition, there are several Boatphones scattered throughout the island at major tourist sights;
simply pick up the receiver and the operator will take your credit-card
number (any major card) and assign you a PIN (personal identification number). Calls using your PIN are then charged to that credit card.

To place a call to the United States, dial 1, the appropriate area code,
and the seven-digit number, or use the phone card or one of the AT&T
USA Direct phones, which are available at several locations, including the airport departure lounge, the cruise terminal at St. John's, and
the English Harbour Marina. To place an interisland call, dial the
local seven-digit number.

Airmail letters to North America cost EC90¢; postcards, EC45¢. Letters to the United Kingdom cost EC1.20; postcards are EC60¢. The
post office is at the foot of High Street in St. John's.

Visitor Information

Before you go, contact the **Antigua and Barbuda Tourist Offices** in the
United States (⊠ 610 5th Ave., Suite 311, New York, NY 10020, ☎
212/541–4117, www.antigua-barbuda.org; ⊠ 25 S.E. 2nd Ave., Suite
300, Miami, FL 33131, ☎ 305/381–6762; a new toll-free information number [888/268–4227] has live operators standing by weekdays
9–5), in Canada (⊠ 60 St. Clair Ave. E, Suite 304, Toronto, Ontario
M4T 1N5, ☎ 416/961–3085), and in the United Kingdom (⊠ Antigua House, 15 Thayer St., London W1M 5LD, ☎ 0171/486–7073).

Once on Antigua, visit the **Antigua and Barbuda Department of Tourism**
(⊠ Thames and Long Sts., St. John's, ☎ 268/462–0480), open Monday–Thursday 8–4:30, Friday 8–3. There is also a tourist-informa-
tion desk at the airport, just beyond the immigration checkpoint. The
tourist office gives limited information. You may have more success
with the **Antigua Hotels and Tourist Association** (⊠ Lower St. Mary's
St., St. John's, ☎ 268/462–0374).

4 Aruba

Updated by
Jordan Simon

A natural coral limestone bridge, burnished beige in the golden sun, straddles a perfect crescent of ecru sand and sapphire surf. Terns and snowy egrets dive-bomb for their lunch. To one side, towering cacti and rock formations and boulders, like jagged Henry Moore sculptures, stretch as far as the eye can see. To the other side . . . a parking lot with safari vans, a sea of wildly colored T-shirts (with even wilder slogans), and a ramshackle building advertised in big hand-painted letters as the THIRST AID STATION. *Welcome to Aruba—an uneasy truce between natural beauty and tourism.*

That delicate balance is the key to Aruba's undeniable success. Most of the island gleams with a fierce, extraterrestrial beauty, its battered coast defying development. But balmy sunshine, silky sand, aquamarine waters, and constant trade winds (so strong they've bent Aruba's trademark divi-divi tree at a surreal 45-degree angle) have made the calmer southwest coast a tourist mecca. Most of its 29 hotels sit side by side down a single strip of shore, with restaurants, exotic boutiques, fiery floor shows, and glitzy casinos on the premises. Nearly every night there are theme parties, treasure hunts, beachside barbecues, and fish fries with steel bands and limbo or Carnival dancers. Surround all this with warm blue-green waters whose visibility extends up to 100 ft, and you've got the perfect destination for anyone who wants sun salted with lots of activities.

The "A" in the ABC Islands (the other two being Bonaire and Curaçao), Aruba is small—only 19½ mi long and 6 mi across at its widest point. Once a member of the Netherlands Antilles, Aruba became an independent entity within the Netherlands in 1986, with its own royally appointed governor, and a 21-member elected parliament. With education, housing, and health care financed by an economy based on tourism, the island's population of 89,000 recognizes visitors as valued guests. The national anthem proclaims, "The greatness of our people is their great cordiality," and this is no exaggeration. Waiters serve you with smiles, English is spoken everywhere, and hotel hospitality directors appear delighted to serve your special needs.

The island's distinctive beauty lies in its countryside—full of rocky deserts, divi-divi trees, cactus jungles alive with the chattering of wild parakeets, secluded coves, and blue vistas with crashing waves. With its low humidity and average temperature of 82°F, Aruba has the climate of a paradise. Sun, cooling trade winds, friendly and courteous service, modern and efficient amenities, golf and tennis clubs, modern casinos, glorious beaches, duty-free shopping, and remarkably varied cuisine help fill Aruba's more than 7,000 hotel rooms.

Lodging

Hotels are fairly expensive in Aruba. To save money, take advantage of the many airline and hotel packages, which are plentiful and considerably less expensive than the one-night rate. Or go during low season (summer), when rates are discounted by as much as 40%.

Most of the hotels are west of Oranjestad along L. G. Smith and J. E. Irausquin boulevards and are miniresort complexes, with—get ready—their own drugstores, boutiques, fitness centers, beauty parlors, casinos, restaurants, gourmet delis, water-sports centers, and car-rental and travel desks. Meeting rooms, room service, laundry and dry cleaning services, in-room safe and minibar or refrigerator, and baby-sitting are standard amenities at all but the smallest properties, and daily activities (beach bingo, volleyball, aerobics, craft classes, Papiamento—a mix of Spanish, Dutch, English, and Portuguese—lessons, supervised children's activities, etc.) are usually part of the package. Children often get free accommodation in their parents' room; check for age qualifications. Hotel restaurants and clubs are open to all guests on the island, so you can visit other properties no matter where you're staying. Most hotels, unless specified, do not include meals in their room rates. One property, not listed, that bears watching, is the Radisson, Aruba's first high-rise hotel and one of Liz Taylor's favorite haunts when she was married to Eddie Fisher. The hotel planned to close for several months in 1998 for a complete $35 million renovation.

CATEGORY	COST*
$$$$	over $325
$$$	$240–$325
$$	$175–$240
$	under $175

All prices are for a standard double room during high season, excluding 6% government tax and 11% service charge.

$$$$ **Aruba Marriott Resort and Stellaris Casino.** Aruba's most expensive luxury high-rise resort is on the far end of Palm Beach, close to the Tierra del Sol golf course. The ziggurat atrium is functional, giving no hint of the classy interior. You'll hear the sound of water everywhere, whether it's the trickling of streams and waterfalls in the elegant marble lobby and around the tropically landscaped free-form pool or the beating of the surf. Rooms are spacious and attractively appointed (crisp green-on-white decor softened by floral bedspreads and pastel watercolor paintings), and all have an ocean view and a balcony, as well as such extras as true walk-in closets, hair dryers, robes, and irons. The hotel's pricey gourmet restaurant, Tuscany, offers superlative Italian

Aruba

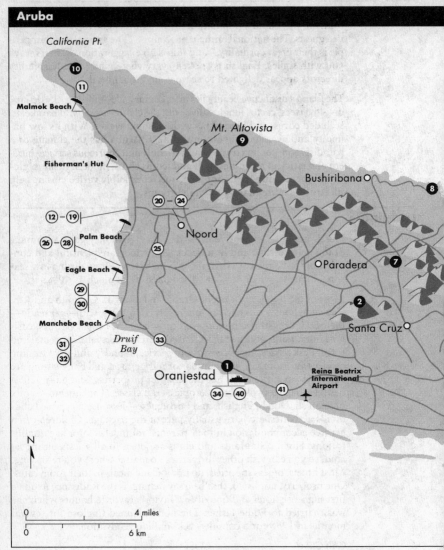

California Pt.

⑩
⑪

Malmok Beach

Mt. Altovista
⑨

Fisherman's Hut

Bushiribana ○

⑧

② — ②
⑳ — ㉔

⑫ — ⑲

○ Noord

㉖ — ㉘ Palm Beach

㉕

○ Paradera

Eagle Beach

⑦

㉙
㉚

②

Manchebo Beach

Santa Cruz ○

㉛
㉜

Druif
Bay

㉝

①
Oranjestad

Reina Beatrix
International
Airport

㉞ — ㊵

㊶

N

0   4 miles
0   6 km

Exploring

Alto Vista Chapel, **9**
California
Lighthouse, **10**
Caves (Guadirikiri
and Fontein), **6**
Frenchman's Pass, **3**
Hooiberg (Haystack
Hill), **2**
Natural Bridge, **8**

Oranjestad, **1**
Rock Formations
(Ayo and Casibari), **7**
San Nicolas, **4**
Seroe Colorado, **5**

Dining

Boonoonoonoos, **35**
Brisas del Mar, **42**
Buccaneer
Restaurant, **20**
Charlie's Restaurant
& Bar, **43**
Chez Mathilde, **36**
Frankie's Prime
Grill, **37**
Gasparito Restaurant
and Art Gallery, **21**

Kowloon, **38**
Mi Cuchina, **26**
Old Cunucu
House, **15**
The Paddock, **39**
La Paloma, **22**
Papiamento, **23**
Le Petit Café, **40**
Valentino's, **24**
Ventanas del Mar, **11**

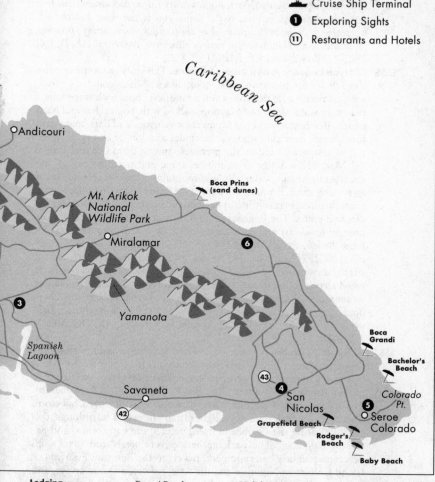

KEY
↗ Beaches
🚢 Cruise Ship Terminal
❶ Exploring Sights
⑪ Restaurants and Hotels

Caribbean Sea

○ Andicouri

Boca Prins
(sand dunes)

Mt. Arikok
National
Wildlife Park

○ Miralamar

❻

③

Yamanota

*Spanish
Lagoon*

Boca
Grandi

Bachelor's
Beach

㊸
❹
San
Nicolas

⑤ ○ Seroe
Colorado

*Colorado
Pt.*

Grapefield Beach

Savaneta ○

㊷

Rodger's
Beach

Baby Beach

Lodging
Allegro Resort &
Casino, **16**
Amsterdam
Manor Beach
Resort, **27**
Aruba Marriott
Resort and Stellaris
Casino, **12**
Aruba Palm Beach
Hotel & Casino, **18**

Bucuti Beach
Resort, **29**
Bushiri Beach
Resort, **33**
La Cabana All Suite
Beach Resort &
Casino, **28**
Divi Aruba Beach
Resort, **31**

Holiday Inn Aruba
Beach Resort &
Casino, **13**
Hyatt Regency Aruba
Resort & Casino, **14**
Manchebo Beach
Resort, **30**
Mill Resort, **25**
Sonesta Resorts at
Seaport Village, **34**

Stauffer Hotel
Aruba, **17**
Tamarijn Aruba, **32**
Vistalmar, **41**
Wyndham Aruba
Beach Resort and
Casino, **19**

cuisine and smart service, but a library hush prevails. A linked adjacent time-share property has been under construction seemingly forever. ✉ *L. G. Smith Blvd. 101, Palm Beach,* ☎ *297/8–69000 or 800/ 223–6388 (reservations service),* FAX *297/8–60649. 413 rooms, 18 suites. 3 restaurants, 5 bars, café, air-conditioning, in-room safes, minibars, no-smoking floors, pool, beauty salon, indoor and outdoor hot tubs, massage, saunas, spa, 3 tennis courts, aerobics, health club, horseshoes, volleyball, beach, dive shop, dock, windsuring, boating, jet skiing, waterskiing, shops, casino, concierge, car rental. AE, D, DC, MC, V. All-inclusive, EP, FAP, MAP.*

$$$$ 🏨 **Hyatt Regency Aruba Resort & Casino.** This truly romantic resort—
★   a top choice for honeymooners—looks like a Spanish grandee's palace, with art deco–style flourishes and a multilevel pool with waterfalls, a two-story water slide, and a lagoon stocked with tropical fish and black swans. Rooms, done in gemstone color schemes and dark mahogany furnishings, have tiny step-out balconies and lots of extras. Four excellent restaurants are on the premises, among them Olé and Ruinas del Mar. Their design is exquisite: stone and marble "ruins" surrounded by moats, waterfalls, and fountains. The lush grounds invite an evening stroll. Families will appreciate Camp Hyatt, a children's program that imaginatively incorporates Aruban storytelling, cooking, and arts and crafts. The Regency Club floor has extras such as free Continental breakfast and concierge service. ✉ *J. E. Irausquin Blvd. 85, Palm Beach,* ☎ *297/8–61234 or 800/554–9288 (reservations service),* FAX *297/8–61682. 342 rooms, 18 suites. 4 restaurants, 5 bars, snack bar, air-conditioning, in-room safes, minibars, no-smoking floor, room service, pool, beauty salon, 2 outdoor hot tubs, massage, sauna, steam rooms, 2 tennis courts, health club, volleyball, beach, dive shop, dock, snorkeling, windsurfing, boating, jet skiing, waterskiing, fishing, shops, casino, children's program, playground. AE, DC, MC, V. EP, MAP.*

$$$$ 🏨 **Tamarijn Aruba.** A series of low-rise buildings stretches along the property of this all-inclusive resort. The lobby is a tropical color-wheel in dizzying mango, lilac, periwinkle, tangerine, slate blue, and flamingo pink; a lovely mural states *"Bon Bini"* ("Welcome" in Papiamento). The spacious oceanfront rooms have a casual feel, with woven, but worn, fiber mats on dark tile floors, light rattan and wood furnishings, colors duplicating the Caribbean itself, painted tile bathrooms, and patios or balconies. The package here covers meals and snacks, all beverages, nightly entertainment, tickets to the Bon Bini Festival (☞ Island Culture *in* Nightlife and the Arts, *below*), a sunset cruise, and an array of outdoor activities. It's a low-key, active place that caters to couples and families. The only price you'll pay is that service here could stand some improvement. ✉ *J. E. Irausquin Blvd. 41, Bravo Beach,* ☎ *297/8–24150 or 800/554–2008 (reservations service),* FAX *297/8– 31940. 236 rooms. 3 restaurants, 3 bars, snack bar, 2 pools, barbershop, 2 tennis courts, Ping-Pong, shuffleboard, volleyball, beach, snorkeling, windsurfing, boating, waterskiing, fishing, mountain bikes, shops, car rental. AE, D, DC, MC, V. All-inclusive.*

$$$–$$$$ 🏨 **Allegro Resort & Casino.** Teeming activity surrounds the clover-leaf-shape pool with a waterfall and two whirlpool tubs at the heart of this large resort. The buzz is indicative of the atmosphere in general: A social director is always cajoling you to participate in everything from beer-drinking contests to bikini shows. Rooms are done in rich shades of aquamarine, purple, green, and yellow and furnished in light rattan. This resort is not as luxurious as others in its price range. White-tiled bathrooms are a bit tight, and balconies are no more than narrow step-outs. However, it remains popular with American and Canadian tour groups. ✉ *J. E. Irausquin Blvd. 83, Palm Beach,* ☎ *297/8–*

64500 or 800/447–7462, FAX 297/8–23191. *419 rooms. 2 restaurants, 4 bars, air-conditioning, pool, 2 outdoor hot tubs, 2 tennis courts, exercise room, Ping-Pong, volleyball, beach, snorkeling, windsurfing, boating, waterskiing, shops, casino. AE, D, DC, MC, V. All-inclusive, EP.*

$$$–$$$$ 🏨 **Bushiri Beach Resort.** Two long, low buildings—constructed around three hot tubs and situated on a wide expanse of beach—make up Aruba's first all-inclusive resort. A fresh paint job (in sea colors, no less) has gone a ways toward sprucing up the otherwise nondescript structures, though recently renovated rooms remain fairly plain. But do you need great architecture and decor when you can have an enthusiastic staff (this is a hotel-training school) and comprehensive activities programs (for children and adults)? Included in the package here are island tours, casino trips, three meals a day (beverages, too), a poolside barbecue, a glass-bottom-boat expedition, Papiamento lessons, and a midnight buffet. You'll be hard-pressed to find a better deal. ✉ *L. G. Smith Blvd. 35, Oranjestad,* ☎ *297/8–25216, 800/462–6867, or 800/462–6868;* FAX *297/8–26789. 150 rooms, 4 suites. Restaurant, 2 bars, grill, air-conditioning, in-room safes, refrigerators, 2 pools, wading pool, beauty salon, outdoor hot tubs, 2 tennis courts, exercise room, Ping-Pong, beach, snorkeling, windsurfing, boating, fishing, shop, children's program, airport shuttle. AE, DC, MC, V. All-inclusive.*

$$$–$$$$ 🏨 **Sonesta Resorts at Seaport Village.** For those who enjoy being in
★ the thick of things, this sprawling downtown property is surrounded by shops, restaurants, and casinos galore. The resort includes a newer hotel with roomy suites set near a small man-made beach, and the original high-rise with compact but attractive rooms above the Seaport Mall (pick the quieter garden-view rooms here). In the lobby, which is connected to the mall, parrots fly free in a tropical garden atrium, and you can board a motor skiff for a day trip to the resort's 40-acre private island. The gourmet restaurant, L'Escale, is one of Aruba's most creative—and expensive. This lively property is a top choice for singles, but it has plenty for families, too. It also offers such incentives as discount rates for senior citizens and "A Taste of Seaport Village" program that lets you dine at various restaurants in the adjacent malls. ✉ *L. G. Smith Blvd. 9, Oranjestad,* ☎ *297/8–36000 or 800/766–3782 (reservations service),* FAX *297/8–34389. Sonesta Resort & Casino: 285 rooms, 15 suites; Sonesta Suites & Casino: 250 suites. 4 restaurants, 4 bars, kitchenettes, no-smoking floor, 2 pools, massage, tennis court, aerobics, exercise room, volleyball, beach, shops, 2 casinos, nightclub, playground, coin laundry, concierge, convention center. AE, DC, MC, V. All-inclusive, EP, FAP, MAP.*

$$$–$$$$ 🏨 **Wyndham Aruba Beach Resort and Casino.** The grand public areas are cavernous enough to accommodate conventioneers and big groups, which make up a good portion of the clientele. While impressive—with marble, stonework, terra-cotta floors, cathedral ceilings, and abstract paintings—these areas are soulless; you can practically hear your footsteps echo. The property has been plagued since its opening by financial woes, explaining why it was first a Concorde, then a Hilton. Still, if bustle and nonstop activity make your day, you'll be right at home here. Rooms, average in size and oddly configured, are pretty in dusty rose, peach, taupe, and sea-foam green and equipped with coffeemaker, iron and ironing board, refrigerator, hair dryer, and ocean-view balcony. Fountains splash playfully into the large free-form pool, and the Casablanca Casino has Rick's Place in mind. The new Polynesian Pago Pago restaurant is like a restrained, contemporary Trader Vic's. A full-service spa, extensive activities for the kids, and a Red Sail water sports facility on the beach are pluses. There's a fee for use of the health club. ✉ *J. E. Irausquin Blvd. 77, Palm Beach,* ☎ *297/8–64466 or 800/ 996–3426 (reservations service),* FAX *297/8–68217. 378 rooms, 66*

suites. 5 restaurants, 6 bars, deli, air-conditioning, in-room safes, pool, wading pool, beauty salon, massage, sauna, steam room, tennis court, health club, Ping-Pong, shuffleboard, volleyball, beach, dive shop, dock, snorkeling, windsurfing, boating, jet skiing, waterskiing, shops, casino, playground, concierge, convention center. AE, D, DC, MC, V. CP, EP, FAP, MAP.

$$–$$$$ 🏨 **La Cabana All Suite Beach Resort & Casino.** At the top end of Eagle
★   Beach, across the busy road from the sand, is Aruba's largest time-share complex, a completely self-contained, well-maintained village. The original four-story building faces the beach and forms a horseshoe around a huge free-form pool with a water slide, poolside bar, café, and water-sports center. One-third of the rooms have a full sea view. All rooms—studio suites and one-bedroom suites—are comfortable and have a fully equipped kitchenette, a small balcony, and a whirlpool for two. Pricier suites and villas are separated from the main building by a parking lot, making them more secluded and quieter. Shuttle buses run you over to the upscale casino, where the hotel has a theme restaurant and the Tropicana showroom. ✉ *J. E. Irausquin Blvd. 250, Eagle Beach,* ☎ *297/8–39000, 212/251–1710 in NY, or 800/835–7193;* 𝗙𝗔𝗫 *297/8–37208. 803 suites. 4 restaurants, 3 bars, grocery, ice cream parlor, air-conditioning, in-room safes, 3 pools, 3 outdoor hot tubs, massage, sauna, aerobics, basketball, health club, 5 tennis courts, racquetball, shuffle-board, squash, volleyball, beach, dive shop, dock, snorkeling, wind-surfing, boating, jet skiing, waterskiing, shops, casino, theater, video games, children's program, playground, coin laundry, chapel, car rental. AE, DC, MC, V. All-inclusive, EP, FAP, MAP.*

$$–$$$ 🏨 **Aruba Palm Beach Hotel & Casino.** Dotting the drive leading up to this pink, eight-story Moorish palazzo are pink-swaddled palm trees; the pink motif is continued throughout the public spaces. Tiki huts line the large, well-manicured tropical garden, which is home to a pair of vociferous parrots. The oversize guest rooms are cheerfully decorated in plaids, pastels, and tropical prints; each has a large walk-in closet and a postage-stamp-size balcony that overlooks the ocean, the pool, or the garden. Organized activities keep things hopping here. Still, the atmosphere remains low-key, and the staff treats you like family, which may explain the high repeat business. For a peaceful meal, eat alfresco in the rock-garden setting of the Seawatch Restaurant. For live music, try the Players Club lounge. A limbo and steel-band show is scheduled one night a week. ✉ *J. E. Irausquin Blvd. 79, Palm Beach,* ☎ *297/8–63900 or 800/345–2782 (reservations service),* 𝗙𝗔𝗫 *297/8–61941. 186 rooms. 2 restaurants, 2 bars, deli, air-conditioning, refrigerators, room service, pool, wading pool, 2 tennis courts, volleyball, beach, dive shop, snorkeling, windsurfing, boating, waterskiing, shops, casino. AE, D, DC, MC, V. EP, MAP.*

$$–$$$ 🏨 **Bucuti Beach Resort.** The intimate, European-style Bucuti is re-
★   freshingly peaceful. When you're seated and handed a cool towel in the lobby, it's clear that the gracious staff understands hospitality. Ha-cienda-style buildings house enormous, sunny rooms that have bright floral decor, handsome blond-wood furnishings, sparkling tile floors, and a terrace or balcony with an ocean view. Room extras include hair dryers and irons. The grounds are lushly landscaped, and the resort has an enviable location on the widest, most secluded section of Eagle Beach. The oceanfront restaurant, which looks like a beached galleon, is known islandwide for its theme dinners. ✉ *J. E. Irausquin Blvd. 55-B, Eagle Beach,* ☎ *297/8–36141 or 800/528–1234,* 𝗙𝗔𝗫 *297/8–25272. 63 rooms. Restaurant, bar, grocery, air-conditioning, refrigerators, pool, exercise room, volleyball, beach, bicycles, shop, coin laundry, business services. AE, D, DC, MC, V. CP, MAP.*

$$–$$$ ☷ **Divi Aruba Beach Resort.** The motto at this popular, Mediterranean-style low-rise is "barefoot elegance," which means you can streak through the busy lobby in your bikini. The main section of the resort has standard guest rooms, beachfront lanai rooms, and casitas (garden bungalows) that look out onto individual courtyards and are, for the most part, only steps from the beach. Remodeled bathrooms, white-tile floors, light-wood furniture, and soothing new mint and jade hues have improved this property tremendously, but the churlish service could use a thorough overhaul. There are daily activity programs and nightly theme dinners; the Red Parrot restaurant offers romantic beachside dining. *L. G. Smith Blvd. 93, Divi Beach, Oranjestad,* ☎ *297/8–23300 or 800/554–2008 (reservations service),* FAX *297/8–31940. 203 rooms. 2 restaurants, 2 bars, air-conditioning, refrigerators, 2 pools, outdoor hot tub, tennis court, shuffleboard, volleyball, beach, dive shop, snorkeling, windsurfing, boating, waterskiing, mountain bikes, shops. AE, D, DC, MC, V. All-inclusive, EP, FAP, MAP.*

$$ ☷ **Holiday Inn Aruba Beach Resort & Casino.** This is one of the larger properties on Palm Beach, but its size is cleverly camouflaged. Three seven-story buildings are set apart from each other along a sugary, palm-dotted beach. Rooms are clean, spacious, and attractive in shades of pale green and rose. The pool's cascading waterfalls and sundeck draw as large a crowd as the wide beach—this area is the site of organized activities. This friendly, reasonably priced resort is a reliable choice for families; as many as two children stay free with their parents, and the resort has created a complimentary Little Rascals Club for kids 5–12. Reasonable all-inclusive packages are available. ⊠ *J. E. Irausquin Blvd. 230, Palm Beach,* ☎ *297/8–63600 or 800/465–4329 (reservations service),* FAX *297/8–65165. 600 rooms. 3 restaurants, 3 bars, air-conditioning, no-smoking rooms, refrigerators, 2 pools, massage, 6 tennis courts, exercise room, Ping-Pong, beach, dive shop, dock, snorkeling, windsurfing, boating, waterskiing, shops, casino, children's program, concierge. AE, DC, MC, V. All-inclusive, EP, FAP, MAP.*

$$ ☷ **Manchebo Beach Resort.** As they say in the hotel industry, this motel has "location, location, location." It's set on one of the prettiest stretches of Eagle Beach amid 100 acres of gardens—with everything from bougainvillea to cacti—just five minutes from town and right across from the Alhambra complex of shops, restaurants, and a casino. The atmosphere is wonderfully mellow, with an international clientele that appreciates a bargain (children under 16 stay free with their parents). Rooms are good-sized, with wicker and blond-wood furnishings, bright florals, and such welcome amenities as irons and coffeemakers. The French Steakhouse is renowned for its *churrasco* (Argentinian mixed grill), and there's nightly entertainment at the semi-alfresco Bistro. The affable staff is as laid-back as the resort, but everyone is still helpful. ⊠ *J. E. Irausquin Blvd. 55 , Eagle Beach,* ☎ *297/8–23444 or 800/528–1234 (reservations service),* FAX *297/8–33667 or 297/8–32446. 71. 2 restaurants, 2 bars, snack bar, air-conditioning, fans, in-room safes, refrigerators, pool, beach, dive shop, snorkeling, shop, car rental. EP, MAP. AE, D, DC, MC, V.*

$–$$ ☷ **Amsterdam Manor Beach Resort.** This mustard-color hotel—all gables and turrets—looks like part of a Dutch colonial village. It's a cozy enclave that surrounds a lovely pool with waterfall, and though the peace is interrupted slightly by traffic noise from the boulevard, glorious Eagle Beach is just across the street. Rooms are furnished in either Dutch modern or provincial style and range from small studios with a balcony and a whirlpool bathtub to two-bedroom suites with peaked ceilings, a whirlpool bathtub and shower, and a full kitchen. Free diving lessons are available twice a week; there aren't many other activities, so the property stays fairly calm. ⊠ *J. E. Irausquin Blvd. 252,*

Eagle Beach, ☎ *297/8–71492 or 800/766–6016,* FAX *297/8–71463.*
72 units. Restaurant, bar, air-conditioning, fans, in-room safes, kitchens,
pool, snorkeling, playground, coin laundry, car rental. AE, MC, V. EP.

$–$$ ⊞ **Mill Resort.** Two-story, whitewashed, red-roof buildings flank the
open-air common areas of this small condo hotel. The architecture is
striking: clean geometric lines, skylights, wood-beam ceilings over
walkways. Request one of the rooms renovated in 1996; their blond-
wood and rattan furnishings and cool powder-blue color schemes are
appealing. Junior suites have a king-size bed, a sitting area, and a
kitchenette. Studios have a full kitchen but, alas, only a queen-size con-
vertible sofa bed, a tiny bathroom, and no balcony. This moderately
priced resort draws couples seeking a quiet getaway (no organized activities or casino here) and families with small children. The beach is
only a five-minute walk away (though there's a shuttle), a morning coffee hour and a weekly scuba lesson are among the on-site amenities,
and the Wyndham's facilities are yours to use. The Mill Resort took
over the venerable Old Mill (De Olde Molen) restaurant next door in
1998. The menu was being changed at press time, but word has it that
you'll find such Continental dishes as beef Stroganoff and Wiener
schnitzel. ⊠ *J. E. Irausquin Blvd. 330, Noord,* ☎ *297/8–67700,* FAX
297/8–67271. 200 units. Restaurant, bar, grill, grocery, air-condi-
tioning, in-room safes, kitchenettes, 2 pools, wading pool, beauty
salon, massage, saunas, 2 tennis courts, exercise room, shop, coin
laundry, car rental. AE, DC, MC, V. EP.

$ ⊞ **Stauffer Hotel Aruba.** Of the hotels in the high-rise zone, the four-
story Stauffer offers the best deal. There are no grand sea views or
sparkling pool here, but $100 a night gets you a terrific location across
from Palm Beach and the facilities of the Aruba Palm Beach Resort (which
you can use as a Stauffer guest). The motel-style rooms are snug and
modern—if slightly musty and dimly lit—with blond-wood furnishings and olive and light floral decor. There's complimentary coffee or
tea service in the morning, and the nearby bus stop makes a rental car
unnecessary unless you want to explore farther afield. ⊠ *J. E. Irausquin*
Blvd. 370, Palm Beach, ☎ *297/8–60855,* FAX *297/8–60856. 181*
rooms. Air-conditioning, in-room safes, shop. AE, D, DC, MC, V. EP.

$ ⊞ **Vistalmar.** There's no beach here, but the sea and a swimming pier
are just across the street. The simply furnished, one-bedroom apartments have a full kitchen, a living-dining room, and a broad sun-
porch. The friendly owners provide snorkel gear and stock the
refrigerator with breakfast fixings. A drawback is the distance from
town, but a rental car is included in the rate. ⊠ *A. O. Yarzagaray, Bu-*
cutiweg 28, Noord, ☎ *297/8–28579,* FAX *297/8–22200. 8 rooms. Air-*
conditioning, kitchens, coin laundry. No credit cards. CP.

Dining

Aruba grabbed the gold in the 1996 Caribbean Culinary Competition
and the silver in 1997, so you can expect many outstanding meals during your visit. Although most resorts offer better-than-average dining,
don't be afraid to try one of the many excellent, reasonably priced, independent restaurants. Although you'll find a variety of cuisines, many
menus are designed to please American palates; if you're not adventurous, you can get fresh surf and New York turf almost anywhere,
and fast-food chains abound. It's worth experimenting with Aruban
specialties—*pan bati* is a mildly sweet beaten bread that resembles a
pancake, and *keshi yena* is a marvelous baked concoction of Gouda
cheese, spices, and meat or seafood in a rich brown sauce.

On Sunday, you may have a hard time finding a restaurant outside of
a hotel that's open for lunch, and many restaurants are closed for din-

ner on Sunday or Monday. Good hotel dining options are the extensive buffet at the Holiday Inn or the wonderful champagne brunch at the Hyatt. Reservations are essential for dinner during high season.

What to Wear

Even the finest restaurants require at the most only a jacket for men and a sundress for women. And anytime you plan to eat in the open air, remember to douse yourself from head to toe with insect repellent—the mosquitoes can get unruly.

CATEGORY	COST*
$$$	over $25
$$	$15–$25
$	under $15

per person for a three-course meal, excluding drinks, 10%–15% service charge, and tax

ASIAN

$–$$ ✕ **Kowloon.** In addition to many Chinese provinces, Indonesia is also represented on the menu here. Try the *bami goreng*, a noodle dish with shreds of shrimp, pork, vegetables, and an Indonesian blend of herbs and spices. *Saté* (grilled strips of beef or chicken in a spicy peanut sauce), curried dishes, and steak prepared in a variety of ways are also available. The modern Asian decor blends well with the island's palms and sands. ⊠ *Emmastraat 11, Oranjestad,* ☎ *297/8–24950. AE, MC, V.*

CARIBBEAN/CREOLE

$$ ✕ **Boonoonoonoos.** The name—say it just as it looks!—means "extraordinary" in Papiamento, a bit of hyperbole for this Austrian-owned Caribbean bistro in the heart of Oranjestad. The specialty here is Pan-Caribbean cuisine. The decor is pleasing with festive fiesta colors, ceramic lamps, and palm thatching. The tasty food is accompanied by hearty portions of peas, rice, and plantains. The roast chicken Barbados is marinated in a piña colada sauce—sweet and tangy. The Jamaican jerk ribs (a 300-year-old recipe) are tiny but spicy, and the satin-smooth hot pumpkin soup drizzled with cheese and served in a pumpkin shell may as well be dessert. Avoid the place when it's crowded, since the service and the quality of the food deteriorate. ⊠ *Wilhelminastraat 18A, Oranjestad,* ☎ *297/8–31888. AE, MC, V. No lunch Sun.*

$–$$ ✕ **Brisas del Mar.** This friendly, 16-table place overlooking the sea makes you feel as if you're dining in an Aruban home. Old family recipes use indigenous ingredients like the aromatic *yerbiholé* leaf (it has something of a minty basil flavor) and the sizzling Mme. Jeanette pepper. Try the smashing steamy fish soup, *keri keri* (shredded fish kissed with annatto seed), or some of the best pan bati on the island. The catch of the day cooked Aruban-style (panfried and covered in a tangy Creole sauce, or panfried in garlic butter on request) has drawn a crowd for more than 20 years. The terrace is inviting on a breezy night. ⊠ *Savaneta 222A, Savaneta,* ☎ *297/8–47718. AE, MC, V. No lunch Mon.*

$–$$ ✕ **Gasparito Restaurant and Art Gallery.** As the name implies, this charm-
★ ing restaurant is also a gallery that showcases the works of local artists on softly lit white walls. It's set in an authentic *cunucu* (country house)—in Noord not far from the hotel strip— with lovely highback hardwood chairs and steel cunucu lamps. The Aruban specialties—pan bati, keshi yena, fish croquettes, conch stew, stewed chicken, Creole-style fish fillet—are a feast for both the eye and the palate, so it comes as no surprise that Gasparito's chefs walk away with top awards in Caribbean culinary competitions. The standout dish is poached barracuda topped with shrimp mousse on herb pasta in mustard saffron sauce, a triumph of delicate flavors and textures; barracuda ravioli is

another fine choice. Service is discreet and very accommodating (they'll stay open if you come for a late dinner). ✉ *Gasparito 3, Noord,* ☎ *297/8–67044. AE, D, MC, V. Closed Sun. No lunch.*

$–$$ ✕ **Mi Cushina.** The restaurant's name is Papiamento for "my kitchen," and couldn't be more appropriate. Owner-chef Wyjkie Maduro's family has lived on Aruba since 1754, and he has made the preparation and promotion of Aruban cuisine his life's work. The dining room is a re-creation of an old farmhouse, with antique tools, grandfather clocks, family photos, even coffee bags for decoration. The authentic fare includes hard-to-find *kreeft stoba* (lobster stew), *concomber stoba* (a thick sultry stew made with small wild cucumbers, goat meat, sweet potatoes, pumpkin, and salt pork) and a definitive keshi yena. Mr. Maduro also prepares specialties from various forms of offal; ask him to describe *soppi di mondongo,* which includes goat stomach and hooves. He'll make it sound remarkably appetizing—and it is. ✉ *L. G. Smith Blvd. 228,* ☎ *297/8–72222. AE, MC, V. Closed Mon.*

CONTINENTAL

$$–$$$ ✕ **Chez Mathilde.** This elegant restaurant occupies one of the last sur-
★   viving 19th-century houses on Aruba. Ask to sit in the swooningly romantic Pavilion Room, which has an eclectic mix of turn-of-the-century Italian and French decor, heavy damask drapes, brass gas lamps, ivy-covered walls, and private nooks and crannies. The back room greenhouse atrium is an appealing second choice. The outstanding French-style menu is constantly re-created by the Dutch chef, who has a deft touch with sauces. Feast on artfully presented baked escargots with herbs and garlic, honey duck with chestnut puree and roasted onions, quail stuffed with calf's sweetbreads in a bell pepper sauce, braised monkfish in a watercress and vermouth sauce, or filet mignon in a signature pepper sauce prepared table-side. The crêpes suzette and profiteroles will also please your taste buds. ✉ *Havenstraat 23, Oranjestad,* ☎ *297/ 8–34968. Reservations essential. AE, DC, MC, V. No lunch Sun.*

ECLECTIC

$$–$$$ ✕ **Old Cunucu House.** On a small estate in a residential area three minutes from the high-rise hotels, you'll find this restaurant in a 76-year-old white-stucco structure with slanting roofs. The decor is charming: wood-beam ceilings, ceramic wall hangings, crisp green napery that complements the many potted plants, and a terra-cotta courtyard filled with bougainvillea. Dine on red snapper (or whatever fish happens to be fresh that day), almond-fried shrimp with lobster sauce, Cornish hen, New York sirloin, or beef fondue à deux. On Friday, you're serenaded by an Aruban trio; on Saturday by a mariachi band. ✉ *Palm Beach 150, Noord,* ☎ *297/8–61666. AE, MC, V. Closed Sun. No lunch.*

$$–$$$ ✕ **Papiamento.** Longtime restaurateurs Lenie and Eduardo Ellis de-
★   cided Aruba needed a bistro that was elegant, intimate, and always romantic. So they converted their 130-year-old home into just such a spot. You can feast sumptuously indoors surrounded by antiques, or outdoors in a patio garden decorated with enormous ceramics (designed by Lenie) and filled with ficus and palm trees adorned with lights. The chef utilizes flavors from both Continental and Caribbean cuisines to produce favorites that include seafood and meat dishes. Try the Dover sole, the Caribbean lobster, shrimp and red snapper cooked table-side on a hot marble stone, or the "claypot" for two—a seafood medley prepared in a sealed clay pot. ✉ *Washington 61, Noord,* ☎ *297/8– 64544. Reservations essential. AE, MC, V. Closed Mon. No lunch.*

$$–$$$ ✕ **Ventanas del Mar.** The floor-to-ceiling windows of this elegant restaurant look out across the back 9 holes of a golf course and beyond to rolling sand dunes and the sea off the island's western tip. Dining on the intimate terrace amid flickering candlelight is very romantic.

Sandwiches, salads, conch fritters, nachos, and quesadillas fill the midday menu; at night the emphasis is on seafood (roasted red snapper, crab cakes, coconut and almond shrimp in orange ginger sauce, spicy seared tuna with apple and mint) and meat (prime rib, veal chop in rosemary demi-glace, herbed half chicken). ⊠ *Tierra del Sol Golf Course, Malmokweg,* ☎ *297/8–67800. AE, MC, V.*

$–$$$ ✕ **Buccaneer Restaurant.** Imagine you're in a sunken ship with fishnets hanging from the ceiling and sharks, barracudas, and groupers swimming past portholes. That's the Buccaneer, a virtual underwater grotto—with a fantastic 5,000-gallon saltwater aquarium and 12 porthole-size tanks—snug in an old stone building flanked by heavy black chains. The surf-and-turf dishes are prepared by the chef-owners with European élan. Order the catch of the day or shrimp with Pernod or smoked pork cutlets with sausage, sauerkraut, and potatoes. Go early (around 5:45 PM) to get a booth next to the aquariums. ⊠ *Gasparito 11-C, Noord,* ☎ *297/8–66172. AE, MC, V. Closed Sun. No lunch.*

$–$$$ ✕ **Frankie's Prime Grill.** In the splashy Royal Plaza Mall, Frankie's
★ (owned by the same family who operates the successful ☞ Le Petit Café) specializes in Argentine prime beef and grilled seafood. You can eat on the palm-filled wraparound terrace or in the more refined, air-conditioned interior. You might start with the garlicky escargots, seafood crepe, or Caesar salad (big enough for two). Prime churrasco (here, a thick slab of beef prepared Argentine-style) and *scampi los barquitos* (jumbo shrimp sautéed in butter and garlic) are the most popular entrées; just try to leave room for *tres lechi* (a Cuban cake made with three different types of milk). ⊠ *Royal Plaza 135, Oranjestad,* ☎ *297/ 8–38471 or 297/8–38473. AE, DC, MC, V.*

$–$$ ✕ **Charlie's Restaurant & Bar.** Charlie's has been a San Nicolas hangout for more than 50 years. During the oil-refinery days, it drew all kinds of roughs and scruffs. Now tourists flock here to gawk at the decor: The walls and ceiling are *covered* with license plates, hard hats, sombreros, life preservers, baseball pennants, intimate apparel, credit cards, you name it. Decent but somewhat overpriced house specialties are Argentine tenderloin and "shrimps—jumbo and dumbo" (dumb because they were caught). And don't leave before trying Charlie's special "honeymoon sauce" (so called because it's really hot). Folks come here more for the nonstop party feel—an oddly endearing hybrid of a frathouse and a beach bar—than the food, though. ⊠ *Zeppenfeldstraat 56, San Nicolas,* ☎ *297/8–45086. No credit cards. Closed Sun.*

$–$$ ✕ **Le Petit Café.** The motto here is "Romancing the Stone"—referring to tasty cuisine cooked on hot stones. Alfresco dining in a bustling square lets you keep an eye on things, but fumes from nearby traffic might spoil your meal. Jumbo shrimp, sandwiches, ice cream, and fresh fruit dishes are light choices. ⊠ *Emmastraat 1, Oranjestad,* ☎ *297/8– 26577;* ⊠ *American Hotel, J. E. Irausquin Blvd. 83,* ☎ *297/8–64368. AE, DC, MC, V. No lunch Sun.*

$–$$ ✕ **The Paddock.** This typical Dutch *eet-café* (a café that serves full meals) is a casual open-air terrace overlooking the pier and whichever cruise ships happen to be in port (it's a favorite with the crews and sailors from around the world). French bread with Brie, fried eggs, bami goreng, saté, and fresh seafood salads are among the offerings. All-you-can-eat spareribs ($10) are the specials on Wednesday. Service isn't included in the bill, so remember to tip the jean-clad staff. ⊠ *L. G. Smith Blvd. 13, Oranjestad,* ☎ *297/8–32334. MC, V.*

ITALIAN

$–$$ ✕ **La Paloma.** "The Dove" is a no-frills, low-key Italian eatery tightly packed with tables that are usually full. Top seller on the international and Italian menu is veal *paisano* (layered veal, mozzarella, ricotta, and spinach, baked to bubbling). Caesar salad and minestrone soup are house specialties. Drop by for the lively family atmosphere, the simple food, and the reasonable prices. ⊠ *Noord 39, Noord,* ☎ *297/8–62770. AE, MC, V. Closed Tues. No lunch.*

$–$$ ✕ **Valentino's.** The tables in this airy two-level dining room are placed comfortably far apart, and the service is attentive. The Italian menu has knockouts such as the Caribbean lobster on a bed of linguine with marinara sauce and fettuccine in smoked-salmon cream sauce. Unfortunately, the attached time-share resort has begun offering free meals in exchange for a hard-sell tour, diminishing the otherwise elegant ambience. Still, the restaurant has long been a favorite with locals celebrating special occasions, which gives it a congenial party atmosphere, and the staff is so enthusiastic you half expect them to break out into a Puccini aria. ⊠ *Caribbean Palm Village, Noord 43E, Noord,* ☎ *297/8–62700. Reservations essential. AE, DC, MC, V. Closed Sun. No lunch.*

Beaches

Beaches in Aruba are legendary: white sand, turquoise waters, and virtually no garbage—everyone takes the NO TIRA SUSHI (NO LITTERING) signs very seriously, especially with an Afl500 ($280) fine. The major beaches, which back up to the hotels along the southwestern strip, are public and crowded. You can make the two-hour hike from the Holiday Inn to the Bushiri Beach Hotel without ever leaving sand. Make sure you are well protected from the sun—it scorches fast, and the trade winds can make it deceptively cool. Luckily, there's at least one covered bar (and often an ice cream stand) at virtually every hotel you pass. If you stroll at night, you can hotel-hop for dinner, dancing, gambling, and late-night entertainment. On the northern side of the island, heavy trade winds make the waters too choppy for swimming, but the vistas are great, and the terrain is wonderful for sunbathing and geological exploration.

Baby Beach. On the island's eastern tip, this semicircular beach borders a bay that's as placid as a wading pool and only 4–5 ft deep—perfect for tots and terrible swimmers. Thatched shaded areas are good for cooling off. You may occasionally find topless sunbathers here.

Boca Grandi. Toward the island's eastern tip (near the Seagrape Grove and the Aruba Golf Club), Boca Grandi is excellent for wave jumping and windsurfing. Strong swimming skills are a must here.

Boca Prins. You'll need a four-wheel-drive vehicle to make the trek here. Near the Fontein Cave and Blue Lagoon, this beach is about as large as a Brazilian bikini, but with two rocky cliffs and tumultuously crashing waves, it's as romantic as you get in Aruba. Boca Prins is famous for its backdrop of enormous vanilla sand dunes. This is not a swimming beach, however. Bring a picnic, a beach blanket, and sturdy sneakers.

Eagle Beach. Across the highway from what is quickly becoming known as Time-Share Lane is Eagle Beach on the southern coast. Not long ago, it was a nearly deserted stretch of pristine sands dotted with the occasional thatched picnic hut. Now that the time-share resorts are completed, this beach hops.

Fisherman's Hut. Next to the Holiday Inn, this beach is a windsurfer's haven. Take a picnic lunch (tables are available) and watch the elegant purple, aqua, and orange sails struggle in the wind.

Grapefield Beach. To the north of San Nicolas, this sweep of blinding white sand in the shadow of cliffs and boulders is perfect for advanced windsurfing.

Malmok Beach. On the northwestern shore, this small, nondescript beach (where some of Aruba's wealthiest families have built tony residences), also known as Boca Catalina, borders shallow waters that stretch 300 yards from shore. It's the perfect place to learn to windsurf. Right off the coast here is a favorite haunt for divers and snorkelers—the wreck of the German ship *Antilla,* scuttled in 1940.

Manchebo Beach (formerly Punta Brabo Beach). In front of the Manchebo Beach Resort, this impressively wide stretch of white powder is where officials turn a blind eye to topless sunbathers.

Palm Beach. Once called one of the 10 best beaches in the world by the *Miami Herald,* this is the stretch behind the Allegro Resort and Casino, Aruba Hilton Hotel and Casino, Aruba Palm Beach, and Holiday Inn hotels. It's the center of Aruban tourism, offering the best in swimming, sailing, and fishing. During high season, however, it's a sardine can.

Rodger's Beach. Next to Baby Beach on the eastern tip of the island, this is a beautiful curving stretch of sand only slightly marred by the view of the oil refinery at the far side of the bay.

Outdoor Activities and Sports

On Aruba you can participate in every conceivable water sport as well as play tennis and golf or go on a fine hike through Arikok National Park. An up-and-coming sport popular with locals is bouldering. It's similar to mountain climbing and rappelling, only up and down the boulders of the Ayo rock formations (☞ Exploring Aruba, *below*) or the cliffs at the island's eastern tip, which are more porous and can be dangerous. Gear isn't available for rental as yet, but the Hyatt Regency (☞ Lodging, *above*) can make arrangements for large groups to be guided by sergeants of the Royal Dutch Marines, no less! Another favorite local pastime—which requires only heavy-duty jeans and a strong seat, thighs, and stomach—is climbing the dunes at Boca Prins (☞ Beaches, *above*) and sliding down.

BOWLING

The **Eagle Bowling Palace** (⊠ Pos Abou, ☎ 297/8–35038) has 12 lanes, a cocktail lounge, and a snack bar; it's open 10 AM to 2 AM. Games run $5.75–$11.20, depending on the time you play.

FISHING

With catches including barracuda, kingfish, bonito, and black and yellow tuna, deep-sea fishing is great sport on Aruba. Many charter boats are available for a half- or full-day sail.

De Palm Tours (⊠ L. G. Smith Blvd. 142, ☎ 297/8–24400 or 800/766–6016) can arrange trips for up to six people, in a variety of boat sizes and styles. Half-day tours, including all equipment, soft drinks, and a box lunch, are around $250 for up to four people; full-day tours run about $500. **Pelican Tours** (⊠ J. E. Irausquin Blvd. 230, ☎ 297/8–31228 or 297/8–24739) and **Red Sail Sports** (⊠ L. G. Smith Blvd. 83, ☎ 297/8–61603) also arrange deep-sea-fishing charters.

GOLF

Golf may seem incongruous on an arid island like Aruba, yet there are two golf courses; the constant trade winds and occasional stray goat add unexpected hazards.

Aruba Golf Club (⊠ Golfweg 82, near San Nicolas, ☎ 297/8–42006) has a 9-hole course with 20 sand and 5 water traps, roaming goats, and lots of cacti. There are 11 AstroTurf greens, making 18-hole tournaments a possibility. The clubhouse contains a bar and men's and women's locker rooms. The course's official U.S. Golf Association rating is 67; greens fees are $7.50 for 9 holes, $10 for 18 holes. Caddies and club rentals are available.

Two elevated 18-hole minigolf courses surrounded by a moat are available at **Joe Mendez Adventure Golf** (⊠ Sasakiweg, ☎ 297/8–76625). There are also paddleboats and bumper boats, a bar, and a snack stand. A round of minigolf is $6.50 per 18 holes, and you can play between noon and 11:30 PM.

The **Tierra del Sol** (⊠ Malmokweg, ☎ 297/8–67800) is on the northwest coast near the California Lighthouse. Designed by Robert Trent Jones Jr., this 18-hole, par-71, 6,811-yard championship course combines Aruba's native beauty, such as the flora, cacti, and rock formations, with the lush greens of the world's best courses. The three knockout holes are 5, with a saltwater marsh inhabited by wild egrets; 12, perched on a cliff overlooking the sea; and 15, whose fairway rolls along dunes. The $120 greens fee includes a golf cart. Club rentals are $25–$45. Half-day "No Embarrassment" golf clinics, a bargain at $50, include lunch in the clubhouse. The pro shop is one of the Caribbean's most elegant, with an extremely attentive staff.

HIKING

Hiking, whether alone or in a guided group, is generally not too strenuous, although you should exercise caution with the strong sun—bring plenty of water and a sun hat or visor. Sturdy, cleated shoes are a must to grip the granular, occasionally steep terrain.

There are no marked trails through the **Arikok National Wildlife Park,** but that doesn't mean you can't blaze your own. Watch for snakes in this arid landscape, as well as the omnipresent thorny cacti. Wild donkeys, goats, rabbits, parakeets, and a plethora of lizards (even the occasional iguana) will be your companions. The park is crowned by 577-ft Mt. Arikok, so climbing is also a possibility.

De Palm Tours (☞ Fishing, *above*) offers a guided three-hour trip to remote sites of unusual natural beauty accessible only on foot. The fee is $25 per person, including refreshments and transportation; a minimum of four people is required.

HORSEBACK RIDING

Three ranches offer short jaunts along the beach or a longer trail ride through countryside flanked by cacti, divi-divi trees, and aloe vera plants. Be sure to request a stop-off at the natural pool, which is reputed to have restorative powers (most tour operators refuse to drive their vehicles down the pitted dirt road for insurance reasons).

De Palm Tours (☞ Fishing, *above*) books all the riding tours for all three of the islands ranches; rates run about $25 for hour-long trips through countryside, $35 for a two-hour beach tour. Remember to wear a hat and take lots of sunscreen.

PARASAILING

Motorboats from Eagle and Palm beaches tow people up and over the water for about 12 minutes ($45 for a single seater, $75 for a tandem). Note that there's really no official center where you can make arrangements, just independent operators stationed on the beaches.

SCUBA DIVING AND SNORKELING

With visibility of up to 90 ft, Aruban waters are excellent for snorkeling and diving. Certified divers can go wall diving or reef diving—or explore wrecks sunk during World War II. The *Antilla* shipwreck—a German freighter sunk off the northwest coast of Aruba near Palm Beach—is popular with both divers and snorkelers. Other top sites include Malmok Reef, Kantil Reef, Mangel Halto Reef, Mike Reef, the Jane Sea Wreck, and Tugboat Wreck. All have several varieties of coral, fish ranging in size from grunts to groupers, sensuously waving sea fans, giant sponge tubes, gliding manta rays, sea turtles, lobsters, octopuses, and green moray eels.

Expect snorkel gear to rent for about $15 per day, and snorkel trips to cost around $25. Scuba rates are not much more at around $30 for a one-tank reef or wreck dive, $45 for a two-tank dive, $35 for a night dive. Resort courses (introduction to scuba diving) average $70; complete open-water certification costs around $300.

Among the top operators in Aruba are **Aruba Pro Dive** (✉ Ponton 88, ☎ 297/8–25520), **Charlie's S.E.A. Scuba** (✉ San Nicolas, ☎ 297/8–45086), **Scuba Aruba** (✉ Seaport Mall, ☎ 297/8–34142), and **Mermaid Sports Divers** (✉ Manchebo Beach Resort, ☎ 297/8–35546). **De Palm Tours** (☞ Fishing, *above*) offers daily snorkeling and scuba-diving trips. However, its rates ($30–$45) are the most expensive on the island. **Pelican Watersports** (☞ Fishing, *above*) offers snorkeling and scuba diving, as well as scuba instruction and certification. It also offers wreck and night dives at reasonable rates. **Red Sail Sports** (☞ Fishing, *above*) offers scuba packages, resort courses, PADI-certification courses, night diving, and underwater camera rental.

TENNIS

Aruba's winds make tennis a challenge even if you have the best of swings, but world-class tennis has just arrived, at the **Aruba Racquet Club** (✉ Rooisanto 21, ☎ 297/8–60215). The $1.4 million club was designed by Stan Smith Design International and is near the Aruba Marriott. There are eight tennis courts (six lighted), as well as a swimming pool, an aerobics center, and a restaurant. Court fees are $10 per hour; a lesson with a pro costs $20 for ½ hour, $35 for 1 hour.

WINDSURFING

The tranquil waters of the southwestern coast make it ideal for both beginners and intermediates, as the winds are steady but sudden gusts rare. Experts will find the Atlantic coast, especially around Grapefield and Boca Grandi beaches, more challenging; winds are fierce and unpredictable, often shifting course without warning. Most operators also offer complete vacation packages for windsurfers.

Fisherman's Huts Windsurf Center (✉ Aruba Marriott Resort, L. G. Smith Blvd. 101, ☎ 297/8–69000) rents Mistrals and Fanatic boards for $60 per day ($40 for two hours). Beginner lessons are $45, including rental; private lessons are $75. **Pelican Watersports** (☞ Fishing, *above*) rents equipment and offers classes with a certified Mistral instructor. Stock and custom boards rent for $40 per two hours, $60 per day. **Red Sail Sports** (☞ Fishing, *above*) offers two-hour beginner lessons for $45 ($60 for two people). It also rents Fanatic boards and regular windsurfing boards by the hour, day, and week.

Windsurfing instruction and board rental are also available through **De Palm Tours** (☞ Fishing, *above*), **Roger's Windsurf Place** (✉ L. G. Smith Blvd. 472, ☎ 297/8–61918), and **Sailboard Vacation** (✉ L. G. Smith Blvd. 462, ☎ 297/8–61072).

Shopping

Duty-free is a magic word here. Major credit cards are welcome virtually everywhere, U.S. dollars are accepted almost as often as local currency, and traveler's checks can be cashed with proof of identity.

Aruba's souvenir and crafts stores are full of Dutch porcelains and figurines, as befits the island's Netherlands heritage. Dutch cheese is a good buy (you are allowed to bring up to 1 pound of hard cheese through U.S. customs), as are hand-embroidered linens and any products made from the native aloe vera plant—sunburn cream, face masks, and skin refreshers. Local arts and crafts are generally undistinguished, running toward wood carvings and earthenware emblazoned with "Aruba: One Happy Island" and the like. Since there's no sales tax, the price you see on the tag is the price you pay. (Note that although all larger stores in town and at hotels are duty free, in tiny shops and studios, you may have to pay the ABB, or value-added tax of 6.5%.) Don't try to bargain. Arubans consider it rude to haggle, despite what you may hear to the contrary.

Areas and Malls

Oranjestad's **Caya G. F. Betico Croes** is Aruba's chief shopping street, lined with several duty-free boutiques and jewelry stores noted for the aggressiveness of their vendors on cruise ship days. Most of the malls are in Oranjestad and are attractive gabled, pastel-hued re-creations of Dutch colonial architecture.

For late-night shopping, head to the **Alhambra Casino Shopping Arcade** (⊠ L. G. Smith Blvd. 47, ☎ 297/8–35000), open 5 PM–midnight. Souvenir shops, art boutiques, and fast-food outlets fill the arcade attached to the busy casino. The **Aquarius Mall** (⊠ Elleboogstraat 1) is small but relatively upscale, with shops such as Boolchand's Jewelers. The **Holland Aruba Mall** (⊠ Havenstraat 6) houses a collection of smart shops and eateries.

Newest on the bustling shopping scene is **Royal Plaza Mall** (⊠ L. G. Smith Blvd. 94), across from the cruise-ship terminal. Here you'll find cafés, a post office branch (open Monday–Saturday 7–5), and such stores as Nautica, Benetton, Tommy Hilfiger, and Gandelman Jewelers. There's also the Internet Café, where you can send E-mail home and get your caffeine fix all in one stop. **Port of Call Marketplace** (⊠ L. G. Smith Blvd. 17, ☎ 297/8–36706) features fine jewelry, perfumes, duty-free liquors, batiks, crystal, leather goods, and fashionable clothing.

Seaport Village Mall (⊠ L. G. Smith Blvd. across from the harbor, ☎ 297/8–36000), five minutes from the cruise terminal, is the site of the Crystal Casino and more than 120 stores, boutiques, and perfumeries, with merchandise to meet every taste and budget. The **Seaport Cinema** (☎ 297/8–36000) in Seaport Market Place (across from Seaport Village) has six theaters showing the latest U.S. movies in English. The **Strada I and Strada II** (⊠ Corner of Klipstraat and Rifstraat) are two complexes of shops in tall Dutch buildings painted in pastels. Strada II is home to Fendi, whose Etrusco striped vinyl luggage is available at a 45% discount.

Specialty Items

CLOTHES

Confetti (⊠ Seaport Village Mall, ☎ 297/8–37454) sells the hottest European and American swimsuits, cover-ups, beach hats, and other beach essentials. **J. L. Penha & Son's** (⊠ Caya G. F. Betico Croes 11, ☎ 297/8–24161), another venerated name in Aruban merchandising, also sells clothes, perfumes, and cosmetics and features Boucheron, Lanvin, Dior, and Cartier for women and Givenchy and Pierre Cardin for men. **La Difference** (⊠ Seaport Village Mall, ☎ 297/8–22547) traffics in glitzy, ritzy resort apparel, including beaded or sequined blouses and hats. **Les Accessoires** (⊠ Seaport Village Mall, ☎ 297/8–36000) sells purses made in Florence and exclusive leather designs, with prices ranging from $85 to $600. Their Venezuelan *pareos* (sarong-like wraps) come in handy as pool cover-ups. **Wulfsen & Wulfsen** (⊠ Caya G. F. Betico Croes 52, ☎ 297/8–23823), one of the highest-rated stores in the Netherlands Antilles for 25 years—and for much longer in Holland—sells Italian, French, German, and Dutch unisex fashions. The Dutch line, Mexx, is a favorite of hip teens; Betty Barkley and Mondo are popular with women. Men's clothes range from the conservative to the wild.

DUTY-FREE GOODS

For leather goods (including Bally shoes), perfumes, and cosmetics, stop in at **Aruba Trading Company** (⊠ Caya G. F. Betico Croes 12, ☎ 297/8–22602), whose name is synonymous with old-fashioned reliability. ATC offers internationally known brand names at discounts, but you have to hunt for them. **Little Switzerland** (⊠ Caya G. F. Betico Croes 14; also locations in several hotel shopping arcades and in the new Royal Plaza Mall, ☎ 297/8–21192), the St. Thomas–based giant, has china, crystal, and fine tableware, and offers good buys on Omega and Rado watches, Swarovski silver, Baccarat crystal, and Lladro figurines.

HANDICRAFTS

Art and Tradition Handicrafts (⊠ Caya G. F. Betico Croes 30, ☎ 297/8–36534) sells intriguing items that look hand-painted but aren't. Buds from the mopa mopa tree are boiled to form a resin, to which artists add vegetable colors. This resin is then stretched by hand and mouth. Tiny pieces are cut and layered to form intricate designs on wooden shapes—truly unusual gifts. At **Artesania Aruba** (⊠ L. G. Smith Blvd. 178, ☎ 297/8–37494) you'll find charming Aruban home-crafted pottery, silk-screened T-shirts and wall hangings, and folklore objects. There's a kiosk in the shopping district on Betico Croes as well. The **Artistic Boutique** (⊠ Caya G. F. Betico Croes 25, ☎ 297/8–23142; ⊠ Aruba Hilton, ☎ 297/8–64466 ext. 3508; ⊠ Seaport Village Mall, ☎ 297/8–32567; ⊠ Holiday Inn, ☎ 297/8–33383) sells Aruban hand-embroidered linens, gold and silver jewelry, Persian carpets and dhurries, porcelain and pottery from Spain, and lots of antiques. **Creative Hands** (⊠ Socotorolaan 5, Oranjestad, ☎ 297/8–35665) sells porcelain and ceramic cunucu houses and divi-divi trees, but the store's real draw is its exquisite Japanese dolls. **Trudy's Pottery** (⊠ Sun Plaza Matt, ☎ 297/8–22744) fashions striking earthenware, as well as glazed over or overglazed vases and pots that are unusually shaped.

JEWELRY

If green fire is your passion, **Colombian Emeralds** (⊠ Seaport Village Mall, ☎ 297/8–36238 or 203/325–9786 customer service office in CT) has a dazzling array, as well as watches by Breitling, Raymond Weil, Seiko, Tissot, and more. **Gandelman Jewelers** (⊠ Caya G. F. Betico Croes 5-A, ☎ 297/8–34433) sells Gucci and Swatch watches at reasonable prices, gold bracelets, pink and red coral, and a full line of Gucci accessories, from key chains to handbags. **Kenro Jewelers** (⊠ Sonesta Seaport Mall, ☎ 297/8–34847 or 297/9–33171) has two stores in the same mall, attesting to the huge selection of merchandise, including Mikimoto pearls, the Ramon leopard collection, and various watches.

Nightlife and the Arts

Nightlife

Unlike on many islands, nightlife isn't confined to the touristic folklorico shows at the hotels. Arubans like to party, and the more the merrier. For information on specific events—as well as shopping, sightseeing, sports, and dining recommendations (and a few coupons)—check out the free magazines *Aruba Nights, Aruba Events, Experience Aruba,* and *Aruba Holiday,* all available at the airport and at hotels.

BARS

Mambo Jambos (✉ Royal Plaza Mall, L. G. Smith Blvd. 94, ☎ no phone) is daubed in tropical drink, uh, sunset colors, with parrots painted on the ceiling. It offers several house-specialty libations. **Iguana Joe's** (✉ Royal Plaza Mall, L. G. Smith Blvd. 94, ☎ no phone) is giving Mambo Jambos a run for its money with a creative reptilian-theme decor in inoffensive planter's punch colors like lime and grape. A uniquely Aruban institution is the ***chiva parranda*** (☎ 297/8–37643) which literally translates to "bus out on the town." The bus in question is a psychedelically hand-painted 1947 Ford. Every Tuesday and Thursday at 6:30 as many as 40 passengers board ready to carouse at a carousel of five typically local bars, including a humble rum shop, with a refueling stop for dinner. The cost is $49.50, including being picked up (and poured off) at your hotel. As your affable host will likely remark, "I finally learned how to cash in on being a party animal."

CASINOS

Casinos are all the rage in Aruba, offering something for high rollers and low-stakes types, as well as live entertainment in their lounges nightly. The crowds seem to flock to the newest of the new.

Marriott's **Stellaris Casino** (✉ L. G. Smith Blvd. 101, ☎ 297/8–69000) is the latest dazzler on the high-roller scene. Sonesta's 24-hour **Crystal Casino** (✉ L. G. Smith Blvd. 82, ☎ 297/8–36000) enjoyed the business until the Hyatt Regency expanded the ultramodern **Copacabana Casino** (✉ J. E. Irausquin Blvd. 85, ☎ 297/8–61234), an enormous complex with a Carnival in Rio theme and live entertainment. Then it was the wildly popular **Royal Cabana Casino**—largest in the Caribbean—in La Cabana All Suite Beach Hotel (✉ J. E. Irausquin Blvd. 250, ☎ 297/8–79000) with its sleek interior, multitheme three-in-one restaurant, and showcase Tropicana nightclub.

You'll always find some action in the **Alhambra Casino** (✉ L. G. Smith Blvd. 47, Oranjestad, ☎ 297/8–35000), where a "Moorish slave" gives every gambler a hearty handshake upon entering. The **Aruba Palm Beach Hotel Casino** (✉ J. E. Irausquin Blvd. 79, ☎ 297/8–63900) opens at 10 AM for slots, 6 PM for all games. The **Grand Holiday Casino** (✉ Holiday Inn Beach Resort, J. E. Irausquin Blvd. 230, ☎ 297/8–67777) has sports betting in addition to the usual slots and table games. The **Royal Palm Casino** (✉ J. E. Irausquin Blvd. 83, ☎ 297/8–64500) opens daily at 1 PM for slots, 5 PM for all games. Low-key gambling can be found at the waterside **Seaport Casino** (✉ L. G. Smith Blvd. 9, ☎ 297/8–35027). Smart money is on the **Wyndham Casablanca Casino,** quietly elegant with a Bogart theme (✉ J. E. Irausquin Blvd. 77, ☎ 297/8–64466).

DANCE AND MUSIC CLUBS

Arubans usually start partying late, and action doesn't pick up till around midnight, mostly on the weekends. At the **Cellar** (✉ Klipstraat 2, ☎ 297/8–26490), live bands perform Monday, Wednesday, Friday, and Saturday; it may be blues, jazz, funk, reggae, or rock. For fresh air, head to the **Penthouse** bar area and dance floor on the roof. Another popular nightclub is **Cheers Café Bistro** (✉ L. G. Smith Blvd. 17, ☎ 297/8–30838) in the Port of Call Marketplace near the pier. The dance floor is usually so packed that you can barely wiggle, and the party typically spills out onto the side porch.

New on the dancing scene is the **Cobalt Club** (☎ 297/8–38381) atop the Royal Plaza Mall downtown, where merengue, salsa, *soca* (up-tempo calypso), and other Latin and Caribbean tunes, state-of-the-art laser and sound systems, and indoor and outdoor bars keep the party moving. There are even a twinkling, "star-lit" ceiling and beach murals for character. Also new is **City One** (✉ Italiastraat 42, ☎ 297/8–33888), the island's largest disco, with a cavernous dance floor, two bars, and big-screen TVs that flash music videos and recent release films.

The **Guana Lounge** (✉ Royal Cabana Casino, J. E. Irausquin Blvd. 250, ☎ 297/8–79000) has soft soothing jazz with background accompaniment of pinging one-armed bandits.

THEME NIGHTS

One of the unique things about Aruba's nightlife is the number of specialty theme nights offered by the hotels: at last count there were more than 30. Each "party" features a buffet dinner, entertainment (usually of the limbo, steel-band, stilt-walking variety), and dancing. Best bets are **Aruban Folkloric** on Friday at the Manchebo Beach Hotel, **Pirates Night** on Sunday at the Bucuti Beach Resort, **Brazilian Jungle Night** on Saturday at the Bushiri Beach Resort, and **Caribbean Carnival Royale** on Monday at the Costa Linda. The top show groups tend to rotate among the resorts, so there's bound to be something going on every night of the week. For a complete list, contact the Aruba Tourism Authority (☞ Visitor Information *in* Aruba A to Z, *below*).

The Arts

ISLAND CULTURE

An Aruban must is the **Bon Bini Festival,** held every Tuesday from 6:30 PM to 8:30 PM in the outdoor courtyard of the Ft. Zoutman Museum. *Bon Bini* is Papiamento for "welcome," and this tourist event is the Aruba Institute of Culture and Education's way of introducing you to all things Aruban. Stroll by the stands of Aruban foods, drinks, and crafts, or watch entertainers perform Antillean music and folkloric dancing. ✉ *Oranjestraat, look for clock tower,* ☎ *297/8–22185.* 💵 *$3.*

Check with your hotel to find out if the **Cultural Center,** or *Cas di Cultura* (✉ Vondellaan 2, Oranjestad, ☎ 297/8–21010), has booked local folkloric troupes and singers.

THEATER

The term is used advisedly, referring primarily to glitzy Vegas-style revues and "everybody rumba-type" audience participation cabarets. **Tropicana** (✉ J. E. Irausquin Blvd. 250, ☎ 297/8–69806), La Cabana All Suite's cabaret theater and nightclub, features first-class, flashy Las Vegas–style revues, usually showcasing female impersonators, and a special comedy series every weekend. The theater in the **Wyndham Aruba** (✉ J. E. Irausquin Blvd. 77, ☎ 297/8–64466) has an entertaining Cuban review (with a bit of flesh) from 8 to 10 PM Tuesday–Saturday.

Twinklebone's House of Roast Beef (✉ Noord 124, ☎ 297/8–26780) does serve succulent prime rib and the like. But it's best known for the fun, impromptu cabaret of Carnival music put on by the staff every night but Sunday. Some customers find it hokey; others eat it up.

Exploring Aruba

Oranjestad, the capital of Aruba, is good for shopping by day and dining by night, but the "real Aruba"—what's left of a wild, untamed beauty—can be found only in the countryside. Rent a car, take a sightseeing tour, or hire a cab for $25 an hour (for up to four people). The main highways are well paved, but on the island's windward side some roads are still a mixture of compacted dirt and stones. Although a car is fine, a four-wheel-drive vehicle will allow you to explore the unpaved interior. Traffic is sparse, and you can't get lost. If you do lose your way, just follow the divi-divi trees (because of the direction of the trade winds, the trees are bent toward the leeward side of the island, where all the hotels are). Signs leading to sights of interest are often small and hand-lettered (though this is slowly changing as the government puts up official road signs), so watch closely.

Few beaches outside the hotel strip have refreshment stands, so take your own food and drink. And one more caution: Note that there are *no* public bathrooms—anywhere—once you leave Oranjestad, except in the infrequent restaurant.

Numbers in the margin correspond to points of interest on the Aruba map.

SIGHTS TO SEE

⑨ Alto Vista Chapel. Alone near the northwest corner of the island sits the scenic little Alto Vista Chapel. The wind whistles through the simple mustard-color walls, eerie boulders, and looming cacti. Along the side of the road back to civilization are miniature crosses painted with depictions of the Stations of the Cross and hand-lettered signs exhorting PRAY FOR US, SINNERS, and the like—a primitive yet powerful evocation of faith. To get here, follow the rough, winding dirt road that loops around the island's northern tip, or, from the hotel strip, take Palm Beach Road through three intersections and watch for the asphalt road to the left just past the Alto Vista Rum Shop.

⑩ California Lighthouse. At the far northern end of the island stands the closed lighthouse. It's surrounded by huge boulders that look like extraterrestrial monsters and sand dunes embroidered with scrub that resemble tawny undulating sea serpents. In this stark landscape, you'll feel as though you've just landed on the moon. Next to the trattoria, there's a placard explaining the history of the lighthouse and the wreck of the German ship, the *California* (just off the tip of the island here).

⑥ Caves. Anyone looking for geological exotica should head for the northern coast, driving northwest from San Nicolas. Stop at the two old Indian caves **Guadirikiri** and **Fontein**. Both were used by the native Indians centuries ago (notice the fire mark in the ceiling above); sadly, the walls are marred by modern graffiti. You may enter the caves, but there are no guides available, and bats are known to make appearances (not to worry—they won't bother you). Wear sneakers and take a flashlight or rent one from the soda vendor who has set up shop here. Locals don't like to advertise it, but some of the petroglyphs look suspiciously new; rumor has it that they were added for greater authenticity by a European film crew shooting commercials in the 1970s. Just before the Fontein and Guadirikiri caves lies the **Tunnel of Love** (also known as Huiliba), a heart-shape tunnel containing naturally sculpted rocks that look just like the Madonna, Abe Lincoln, even a jaguar. The climb through the tunnel is strenuous and shouldn't be attempted by anyone not in good physical condition (children might also find it difficult). Remember, admission is free to all three caves—don't be deterred by the occasionally pushy vendors.

③ Frenchman's Pass. A bit of history can be found along this dark, luscious stretch of road arbored by overhanging trees and bordered by towering cacti. Local legend claims that the French and native Indians warred here during the 17th century for control of the island. To reach the pass, drive east on L. G. Smith Boulevard past a shimmering vista of blue-green sea toward San Nicolas, on what is known as the sunrise side of the island. Turn left where you see the drive-in theater (a popular hangout for Arubans), drive to the first intersection, turn right, and follow the curve to the right. Gold was discovered on Aruba in 1824, and nearby you'll find the massive cement-and-limestone ruins of the **Balashi Gold Smelter** (take the dirt road that veers to the right)—a lovely place to picnic and listen to the parakeets. A magnificent, gnarled divi-divi tree guards the entrance.

2 **Hooiberg.** Haystack Hill, as this 541-ft peak is known in English, is inland just past the airport. If you have the energy, climb the 562 steps to the top for an impressive view of the city. To get here from Oranjestad, turn onto Caya C. F. Croes (shown on island maps as 7A) toward Santa Cruz; the peak will be on your right.

3 **Natural Bridge.** This bridge, in the center of the windward coast, was sculpted out of coral rock by centuries of raging wind and sea. To reach it, follow the main road inland (Hospitalstraat) and then signs that lead the way. Just before you reach the natural bridge, you'll pass the massive, intriguing stone ruins of the **Bushiribana Gold Smelter,** which resembles a crumbling fortress, and a section of surf-pounded coastline called Boca Mahose. Near the natural bridge is a café overlooking the water and a souvenir shop stuffed with trinkets and T-shirts.

1 **Oranjestad.** Aruba's charming Dutch capital is best explored on foot. There are many shopping malls with boutiques and shops. The palm-lined thoroughfare in the center of town runs between pastel-painted buildings, old and new, of typical Dutch design.

At the **Archaeology Museum** you'll find two rooms chock-full of fascinating Indian artifacts, farm and domestic utensils, and skeletons. Across the street you'll see the handsome Protestant church. ✉ *Zoutmanstraat 1,* ☎ *297/8–28979.* ✇ *Free.* ⊙ *Weekdays 8–noon and 1:30–4:30.*

One of the island's oldest buildings, **Ft. Zoutman** was built in 1796 and used as a major fortress in the skirmishes between British and Curaçao troops. The Willem III Tower, named for the Dutch monarch of that time, was added in 1868. The fort's museum displays centuries' worth of Aruban relics and artifacts in an 18th-century Aruban house. ✉ *Zoutmanstraat,* ☎ *297/8–26099.* ✇ *$1.15.* ⊙ *Weekdays 9–noon and 1:30–4:30.*

The tiny **Numismatic Museum,** next to St. Francis Roman Catholic Church, displays coins and paper money from more than 100 countries. ✉ *Zuidstraat 7,* ☎ *297/8–28831.* ✇ *Free.* ⊙ *Weekdays 7:30–noon and 1–4:30.*

7 **Rock Formations.** The massive boulders at **Ayo** and **Casibari** are said to be a mystery since they don't match the geological makeup of the island. Whether they're a mystery or not, you can climb to the top for fine views of Aruba's arid countryside or snapshots of brown or blue lizards as you hike among the towering cactus. Climbing is not recommended for children or those not in the best of shape—there are no handrails on the way up, and you must move through tunnels and on narrow steps and ledges to reach the top. At Ayo you'll find ancient pictographs in a small cave (the entrance is protected by iron bars so that the artifacts are protected from vandalism). Access to Casibari is via the Tanki Highway 4A and to Ayo is via Highway 6A; watch carefully for the turnoff signs near the center of the island on the way to the windward side. Ayo's smooth surfaces are luring curious local boulder climbers (☞ Outdoor Activities and Sports, *above*).

4 **San Nicolas.** During the heyday of the Exxon refineries, Aruba's oldest village was a bustling port; now it's dedicated to tourism, with the main-street promenade full of interesting kiosks. The entire San Nicolas district is undergoing a massive revitalization project that will in-

troduce parks, a cultural center, a central market, and an arts promenade, but it's hard to say what will be finished when. The **China Clipper Bar** on Main Street used to be a famous "red-light" bar frequented
by sailors docked in port. Another institution is **Charlie's Bar,** a San
Nicolas hangout for more than 50 years (☞ Dining, *above*). Stop in
for a drink and advice on what to do on this section of the island.

❺ Seroe Colorado. Just east of San Nicolas (follow the signs out of town
past the incongruous refinery), this residential community, built to house
oil workers, is an eery oasis of calm, with an intriguing 1939 chapel.
The site is surreal: towering organ pipe cacti nearly as tall as the belching smokestacks of the oil refinery form the backdrop for sedate whitewashed cottages.But the real reason to come here is the second, "secret"
natural bridge. Keep bearing east past the community, continuing uphill until you run out of road. You can then hike down (it's not too
strenuous, but watch your footing) into one of the few pristine, isolated spots on Aruba. While the cathedralesque formation isn't as
spectacular as its celebrated sister, the raw elemental power of the sea
that created it, replete with hissing blow holes, certainly is.

Aruba A to Z

Arriving and Departing
BY AIRPLANE
Aruba is 2½ hours away from Miami and 4 hours from New York.
Flights leave daily to Aruba's Reina Beatrix International Airport (☎
297/8–24800) from New York area airports and Miami International
Airport with easy connections from most American cities.

Air Aruba (☎ 297/8–23151), the island's official airline, flies nonstop
to Aruba daily from Miami and Newark. Twice-weekly service has begun
from Baltimore. **ALM** (☎ 297/8–23546), the major airline of the Dutch
Caribbean islands, flies six days a week nonstop from Miami and
twice weekly from Fort Lauderdale to Aruba. **American Airlines** (☎
297/8–22006) offers daily nonstop service from both Miami and New
York. **Continental** (☎ 800/231–0856) has twice-weekly nonstop service from Houston. Air Aruba and ALM also have connecting flights
to Caracas, Bonaire, Curaçao, St. Maarten, and other islands. ALM
also offers a "Visit Caribbean Pass" for interisland travel. From Toronto
and Montréal, you can fly to Aruba on American Airlines via San Juan.

Electricity
Aruba runs on a 110-volt cycle, same as in the United States; outlets
are usually the two-prong variety. Total blackouts are rare, and most
of the large hotels have reliable backup generators.

Emergencies
Ambulance and Fire: ☎ 115. **Hospital:** Horacio Oduber Hospital,✉
L. G. Smith Blvd., ☎ 74300. **Pharmacy:** the Botica del Pueblo (✉ G.
F. Betico Croes Blvd. 48, ☎ 297/8–22154) is open Monday–Satur-
day from 8 to noon and 2:30 to 5. **Police:** ☎ 11000.

Festivals and Seasonals Events
February or March witnesses a spectacular **Carnival,** a riot of whirling
color dancing to the tune of steel bands, culminating in a Grand Parade where some of the floats rival Mardi Gras at the Big Easy for sheer
extravagance. Held May–October, **One Cool Summer** is a series of culinary, athletic, musical, cultural, and other events. Check with your hotel
for specifics.

Getting Around

Remember, the island's winding roads are poorly marked, if at all (though this is slowly changing as the government installs new road signs and more clearly marked sights of interest). The major attractions are fairly easy to find; others you'll happen upon only by sheer luck (or with an Aruban friend). International traffic signs and Dutch-style traffic signals (with an extra light for a turning lane) can be misleading if you're not used to them; use extreme caution, especially at intersections, until you grasp the rules of the road. Speed limits are rarely posted, but are usually 80 kph (50 mph). Gas prices average $1 a liter (roughly ⅓ gallon), which is fairly reasonable by Caribbean standards.

BICYCLES, MOPEDS, AND MOTORCYCLES

Rental rates vary according to the make of the vehicle; expect to pay around $20 a day for an 80cc to $40 for a 250cc. For Yamaha scooters, contact **George's Cycle Center** (✉ L. G. Smith Blvd. 136D, ☏ 297/8–25975). Other moped, scooter, and motorcycle rental companies are **Nelson Motorcycle Rental** (✉ Gasparito 10A, ☏ 297/8–66801), **Ron's Motorcycle Rental** (✉ Bakval 17A, ☏ 297/8–62090), and **Semver Cycle Rental** (✉ Noord 22, ☏ 297/8–66851). **Pablito's Bike Rental** (✉ L. G. Smith Blvd. 234, ☏ 297/8–78655) rents mountain bikes for $10 per day.

BUSES

Buses run hourly trips between the beach hotels and Oranjestad. One-way fare is $1, and exact change is preferred. Buses also run down the coast from Oranjestad to San Nicolas for the same fare. Contact the Aruba Tourism Authority (☞ Visitor Information, *below*) for a bus schedule, or inquire at the front desk of your hotel.

CAR RENTALS

You'll need a valid driver's license to rent a car, and you must meet the minimum age requirements of each rental service (Budget, for example, requires drivers to be over 25; Avis between the ages of 23 and 70; and Hertz, over 21). A deposit of $500 (or a signed credit-card slip) is required. Rates are between $50 and $65 a day. Insurance is available starting at $10 per day, and all companies offer unlimited mileage. Local car-rental companies generally have lower rates. If possible, make reservations before arriving, and opt for a four-wheel-drive vehicle if you plan to explore the island's natural sights.

Avis (✉ Kolibristraat 14, ☏ 297/8–28787; ✉ airport, ☏ 297/8–25496), **Budget Rent-a-Car** (✉ Kolibristraat 1, ☏ 297/8–2860 or 800/472–3325), **Dollar Rent-a-Car** (✉ Grendeaweg 15, ☏ 297/8–22783; ✉ airport, ☏ 297/8–25651; ✉ Manchebo, ☏ 297/8–26696), **Hedwina Car Rental** (✉ Bubali 93A, ☏ 297/8–76442; ✉ airport, ☏ 297/8–30880), **Hertz, De Palm Car Rental** (✉ L. G. Smith Blvd. 142, ☏ 297/8–24545; ✉ airport, ☏ 297/8–24886), **National** (✉ Tanki Leendert 170, ☏ 297/8–21967; ✉ airport, ☏ 297/8–25451), and **Thrifty** (✉ Balashi 65, ☏ 297/8–55300; ✉ airport, ☏ 297/8–35335).

TAXIS

There is a dispatch office at the airport (☏ 297/8–22116); you can also flag down taxis on the street. Rates are fixed (i.e., there are no meters) and you and the driver should agree on the fare before your ride begins. Add $1 to the fare after midnight and on holidays. All Aruba's taxi drivers have participated in the government's Tourism Awareness Programs and have received their Tourism Guide Certificate. An hour's tour of the island by taxi will run you about $25, with from one to four people in the car. A taxi from the airport to most hotels will run $12–$17; from major hotels into town, $6–$7.

Guided Tours

BOAT

If you try a cruise around the island, know that on choppy waters stirred up by trade winds, trimarans are much smoother than monohulls. Sucking on a peppermint or lemon candy may help a queasy stomach; avoid going with an empty or overly full stomach. Moonlight cruises cost about $25 per person. (Be prepared to sail with a lot of honeymooners.) There are also a variety of snorkeling, dinner and dancing, and sunset party cruises to choose from, priced from $25 to $60 per person. Many of the smaller operators work out of their homes; they often offer to pick you up (and drop you off) at your hotel or meet you at particular hotel pier.

Contact **De Palm Tours** (✉ L. G. Smith Blvd. 142, ☎ 297/8–24400 or 800/766–6016), **Red Sail Sports** (✉ Seaport Village Mall, Oranjestad, ☎ 297/8–24500), **Pelican Watersports** (✉ J. E. Irausquin Blvd. 230, ☎ 297/8–31228), **Pirate Cruises** (☎ 297/8–24554), or **Wave Dancer** (☎ 297/8–25520).

One favorite is the four-hour snorkel, sail, open-bar, and lunch cruise aboard the *Mi Dushi,* (☎ 297/8–28919), a beautifully restored 1925 Swedish sailboat. This two-masted wooden vessel is captained by Mario Maduro and a fun crew who act as lifeguards, snorkel instructors, bartenders, galley staff, deckhands, and storytellers. Two stops are made for snorkeling; save your energy for the second one at the wreck of the *Antilla;* the cost is $45. You can get tattooed on the lethal $1 drinks served on **Tattoo Party Cruises** (☎ 297/8–23513). Don't be surprised if you end up essaying the wild Tattoo rope swing, coaxed into performing the sexiest dance, or even being threatened with walking the plank. It's a favorite among both singles and honeymooners.

ORIENTATION

You can see the sights in a day. Although most highways are in excellent condition, signs and directions are haphazard, making a guided tour your best option for exploring if you have only a short time.

De Palm Tours (☞ *above*) has a near monopoly on the Aruban sightseeing business; reservations may be made through its general office or at hotel tour-desk branches. The basic 3½-hour tour hits the high spots of the island, including Santa Anna Church, Casibari Rock Formation, the Natural Bridge, and the Gold Smelter Ruins. Wear tennis or hiking shoes (there will be optional climbing) and note that the air-conditioned bus can get cold. The tour, which begins at 9:30 AM, picks you up in your lobby and costs $20 per person. There's also a fun full-day Jeep Adventure tour ($45 per person) that hits some popular spots that are difficult to find on your own. Take a bandanna to cover your mouth, as the ride on rocky dirt roads can get dusty. De Palm also offers full-day tours of Caracas, Venezuela ($240, passport required), and Curaçao ($200). Prices include round-trip airfare, transfers, sightseeing, and lunch; there's free time for shopping. **Aruba Friendly Tours** (✉ Cumana 20, Oranjestad, ☎ 297/8–23230, ℻ 297/8–33074) also takes you to Aruba's main sights.

SPECIAL-INTEREST

For a tour of prehistoric Indian cultures, volcanic formations, and natural wildlife, contact archaeologist Egbert Boerstra of **Marlin Booster Tracking, Inc.,** at Charlie's Bar (☎ 297/8–41513). The fee for a four-hour tour is $50 per person, including a cold picnic lunch and beverages. Tours are available in English, Dutch, German, Spanish, and French.

You can now explore an underwater reef teeming with marine life without getting wet. **Atlantis Submarines** (✉ Seaport Village Marina, ☎

297/8–36090) operates a 65-ft, air-conditioned sub that takes 46 passengers 95–150 ft below the surface along Barcadera Reef. The two-hour trip (including boat transfer to the submarine platform and 50-minute plunge) costs $68 for adults, $34 for children 4–16. Another option is the **Seaworld Explorer** (☎ 297/8–62807), a semisubmersible that allows you to sit and view Aruba's marine habitat from 5 ft below the surface. The cost is $33 ($19 for children 2–12) for a 1½-hour tour.

Romantic **horse-drawn-carriage rides** through the city streets of Oranjestad run $30 for a 30-minute tour; hours of operation are 7–11 PM and rides depart from the clock tower at the Royal Plaza Mall.

Language

Everyone on the island speaks English, but the official language is Dutch. Most locals, however, speak Papiamento—a fascinating, rapid-fire mix of Spanish, Dutch, English, and Portuguese—in normal conversation. Here are a few helpful phrases: *bon dia* (good day), *bon nochi* (good night), *masha danki* (thank you very much).

Money Matters

CURRENCY

Arubans happily accept U.S. dollars virtually everywhere, so there's no real need to exchange money, except for necessary pocket change (for soda machines or pay phones). The currency used, however, is the Aruban florin (AFl), which, at press time, exchanged to the U.S. dollar at AFl1.77 for cash, AFl1.79 for traveler's checks, and to the Canadian dollar at AFl1.51. The Dutch Antillean florin (used in Bonaire and Curaçao) is not accepted in Aruba. If you need fast cash, you'll find ATMs that accept international cards at the major malls, Caribbean Mercantile Bank, and Amro Bank. Major credit cards and traveler's checks are widely accepted (with ID). Prices quoted throughout this chapter are in U.S. dollars unless otherwise noted.

SERVICE CHARGES, TAXES, AND TIPPING

Hotels usually add an 11% service charge to the bill and collect a 6% government tax. You will sometimes see a $3-per-day energy surcharge tacked on also. Restaurants usually include a 10%–15% service charge on the bill; when in doubt, ask. If service isn't included, a 10% tip is standard; if it is included it's still customary to add something extra, usually small change, at your discretion. For purchases, you'll pay a 6.5% ABB tax (a value-added tax) in all but the duty-free shops. Taxi drivers expect a 10%–15% tip, but it isn't mandatory. Porters and bellmen should receive about $1 per bag; chamber maids about $1 a day. The airport departure tax is $20.

Opening and Closing Times

Banks have hours weekdays 8–noon and 1:30–4. The Aruba Bank at the airport is open Saturday 9–4 and Sunday 9–1. Shops are generally open between 8 AM and noon and 2 PM and 6 PM, Monday–Saturday. Some stores stay open through the lunch hour, noon–2 PM, and many open when cruise ships are in port on Sundays and holidays. Nighttime shopping at the Alhambra Bazaar runs 5 PM–midnight.

HOLIDAYS

New Year's Day, Betico Croes Birthday (politician who aided Aruba's transition to semi-independence; Jan. 25), Carnival Monday (Feb. 15), National Anthem and Flag Day (Mar. 18), Good Friday (Apr. 2), Easter Monday (Apr. 5), Queen's Birthday (Apr. 30), Labor Day (May 1), Ascension Day (May 14), Christmas (Dec. 25–26).

Passports

U.S. and Canadian citizens need a valid passport or a birth certificate with a raised seal and a government-issued photo ID. All other nationalities must have a valid passport.

Precautions

Arubans are very friendly, so you needn't be afraid to stop and ask anyone for directions. It's a relatively safe island, but common-sense rules still apply. Don't leave things in a rental car, and lock the car when you leave it. Leave valuables in your hotel safe, and don't leave bags unattended in the airport, on the beach, or on tour transports.

Mosquitoes can be bothersome during the rainy season (November–March), so pack some repellent. The strong trade winds are a relief in the subtropical climate, but don't hang your bathing suit on a balcony—it will probably blow away. Help Arubans conserve water and energy: Turn off air-conditioning when you leave your room, and keep your faucets turned off.

Telephones and Mail

To call Aruba direct from the United States, dial 011–297–8, followed by the number in Aruba. Local and international calls in Aruba can be made via hotel operators or from the Government Long Distance Telephone, Telegraph, and Radio Office (SETAR), in the post office building in Oranjestad. When making calls on Aruba, simply dial the five-digit number. To reach the United States, dial 001, then the area code and number. Local calls from a pay phone cost AFl.25.

You can send an airmail letter from Aruba to the United States and Canada for AFl1.40 and a postcard for AFl.60; to a letter to Europe is AFl1.50, a postcard AFl.70. When addressing letters to Aruba, don't worry about the lack of "formal" addresses (in some places) or postal codes; the island's postal service knows where to go.

Visitor Information

Contact the **Aruba Tourism Authority** (☎ 800/862–7822, www.arubatourism.com) at one of its many offices (✉ 1 Financial Plaza, Suite 136, Fort Lauderdale, FL 33394, ☎ 954/767–6477; ✉ 199 14th St. NE, Suite 2008, Atlanta, GA 30309-3688, ☎ 404/892–7822; ✉ 1000 Harbor Blvd., Ground Level, Weehawken, NJ 07087, ☎ 201/330–0800; ✉ 12707 North Freeway, Suite 138, Houston, TX 77060-1234, ☎ 713/872–7822; ✉ 86 Bloor St. W, Suite 204, Toronto, Ontario, M5S 1M5, ☎ 416/975–1950 or 800/268–3042).

In Aruba, the **Aruba Tourism Authority** (✉ L. G. Smith Blvd. 172, Eagle Beach, ☎ 297/8–23777) has free brochures and information officers who are ready to answer any questions.

5 Barbados

Updated by
Jane E. Zarem

Head wrapped neatly in a kerchief and her skirt just sweeping the sand, the doll lady trudges along the beach to the shade of a mahogany tree and settles in for the day. Her bag is full of unfinished poppets and bits of cloth. Today, she's making eyes. Cutting deftly with oversize shears, one tip broken off, white and black snippets give expression to blank faces. She beckons to passersby: "Doll, lady?" In a sea of luxury, the doll lady and her work are cultural anchors.

Barbadians (Bajans) are a warm, friendly, and hospitable people who are genuinely proud of their country and culture and welcome visitors as privileged guests. The business community is sophisticated, and the government is stable, so life here continues after the tourists pack up their sun oils and return home. Most of the 260,000 Bajans live in the area around the capital city of Bridgetown, on the southwest coast, or along the west coast as far as Speightstown in the north and Oistins in the south. Others reside in tiny hamlets in the island's 11 parishes.

Barbados lies partially in the Atlantic Ocean and partially in the Caribbean Sea, 100 mi east of the Lesser Antilles chain that arcs from the Virgin Islands to Trinidad. The island is 21 mi long, 14 mi wide, and relatively flat; the highest point, Mt. Hillaby, is in the north and has an elevation of 1,115 ft. Impenetrable acres of sugarcane cover the hills and valleys in the interior, punctuated by the sugar factories and plantation great houses the crop has sustained for centuries. While many Caribbean islands are the peaks of a volcanic mountain range, Barbados is the top of a single coral and limestone mountain, which provided the building blocks for many of those plantation manors.

Besides picturesque rolling hills, a perimeter of white-sand beaches, a central flatland for planting, and even deposits of oil underground, Barbados's unique geology has created one of the most popular tourist attractions, Harrisons Cave. This natural phenomenon has bubbling streams, cascading waterfalls, and stalactites and stalagmites created by the constant drip of calcite-laden water. Barbados is the only island in the West Indies to have underground reservoirs for fresh water; elsewhere, people must catch rainwater, desalinate seawater, or both.

It was during a search for fresh water that Barbados was "discovered" by the Portuguese in 1536. They didn't stay long, but did give the island its name, (Los) Barbados, "the bearded ones," after its native fig trees with beardlike roots. The British landed, by accident, a century later in what is now Holetown, in the parish of St. James. The first British settlement was established two years later, in 1627. Unlike the European custody fights experienced by neighboring islands, British rule remained uninterrupted for 340 years, until 1966, when Barbados became independent. The island has since had an elected Prime-Minister and membership in the Commonwealth of Nations.

Tourist facilities in Barbados are top-notch. Beaches along the tranquil west coast, facing the Caribbean, are backed by posh resorts and private residences that are virtually enveloped in lush foliage and a quiet atmosphere. This luxurious area is appropriately called the "Platinum Coast," and it's a favorite destination of British and Canadian vacationers. Americans tend to prefer the hotels and resorts stretched along the beaches of the much busier south coast, which has shopping opportunities, countless restaurants, and an active nightlife. Bajans like to spend their holidays along the rugged east coast where the Atlantic surf pounds against gigantic boulders.

Barbados retains a noticeable British atmosphere: Most Bajans are members of the Anglican church, afternoon tea is a ritual, cricket is the national sport and passion (Barbados produces some of the world's top cricketers), and polo, "the sport of kings," is played all winter. The tradition of dressing for dinner is firmly entrenched, yet the island's atmosphere is hardly stuffy. You can dine by candlelight facing the sea, in festive company at a sumptuous Bajan buffet, or casually with a burger at the beach. This is still the Caribbean, after all.

Lodging

Most visitors to Barbados choose to stay on either the fashionable west coast north of Bridgetown, or the action-packed south coast. The west coast beachfront resorts in the parishes of St. Peter, St. James, and St. Michael are mostly self-contained. Highway 1, a two-lane road with considerable traffic, runs past these resorts, which makes strolling to a bar or restaurant difficult. Along the south coast, in Christ Church parish, many hotels are clustered near or along the busy strip known as St. Lawrence Gap, where dozens of small restaurants, bars, and nightclubs are close by. On the much more remote east coast, a couple of inns offer oceanfront views and a get-away-from-it-all tranquility.

Accommodations range from elegant resorts and private villas to modest but comfortable small hotels and inns. Another popular option is a time-share condominium, or an apartment or home rental. Hotels usually operate on the EP plan (no meals included) but also offer CP (Continental breakfast) or MAP (breakfast and dinner) if you wish; some require MAP in the winter season, and a few are all-inclusive. The hotels below all have TVs and radios unless otherwise noted.

CATEGORY	COST*
$$$$	over $400
$$$	$275–$400
$$	$150–$275
$	under $150

All prices are for a standard double room, excluding 7½% government tax and 10% service charge.

Hotels

BRIDGETOWN AREA

$$ 🏨 **Barbados Hilton.** On a small peninsula within walking distance of Bridgetown and separated from an oil tankfield by thick trees and foliage, this large resort bustles with activity and people attending seminars and conferences. An array of services and facilities are available to business travelers, who appear to be the hotel's target market. An atrium lobby greets you when you arrive, and there's a 1,000-ft-wide, sandy beach with full water sports and lots of shops to keep you busy. All rooms have balconies and telephones with voice mail and data ports. ⊠ *Needham's Point, St. Michael (Box 510, Bridgetown),* ☎ *246/426–0200 or 800/ HILTONS (reservations service),* ℻ *246/436–8946. 182 rooms, 2 suites. Restaurant, 2 bars, lobby lounge, air-conditioning, minibars, pool, 4 tennis courts, health club, beach, windsurfing, shops, business services, meeting rooms. AE, DC, MC, V. CP, EP, FAP, MAP .*

$$ 🏨 **Grand Barbados Beach Resort.** A mile south of Bridgetown on Carlisle Bay, this beachfront high-rise has roomy, well-equipped rooms and suites, each with a large, private balcony. The Aquatic Club executive floor rates include Continental breakfast and secretarial services. Despite the oil refinery nearby, the white-sand beach is lapped by a surprisingly clear sea. There are plenty of water sports, including the on-site Mistral Windsurfing School and a boat rental facility. Nightly live music, a dance floor, and a 260-ft-long pier that's perfect for romantic walks extend activities into the evening. ⊠ *Aquatic Gap, St. Michael (Box 639, Bridgetown),* ☎ *246/426–4000 or 800/742–4276, 800/ 223–9815 (reservations services),* ℻ *246/429–2400. 128 rooms, 5 suites. 2 restaurants, 2 bars, air-conditioning, minibars, pool, barbershop, beauty salon, hot tub, sauna, tennis court, exercise room, beach, dive shop, snorkeling, windsurfing, boating, shops, concierge floor, business services, meeting rooms. AE, DC, MC, V. CP, EP, FAP, MAP.*

EAST COAST

$ 🏨 **Atlantis Hotel.** The Atlantis provides a congenial atmosphere in a quiet area of the majestically rocky Atlantic coast, where the views out to the open sea are mesmerizing. The lodging has evolved from a modest family guest house into a small hotel, and the more modern facility has not altered the warmth the Atlantis staff has bestowed on its guests for over a century. Rooms are modest and have no TVs—although some have balconies overlooking that great view. The daily Bajan buffet in the ☞ **Atlantis Hotel** restaurant makes it a very popular luncheon spot. There is a beachfront, but Bathsheba beach is right next door and a safer place to swim and surf. ⊠ *Bathsheba, St. Joseph,* ☎ *246/433– 9445. 8 rooms. Restaurant, bar, beach. AE. EP, MAP.*

$ ★ 🏨 **Edgewater Inn.** This rather secluded hideaway is perched on a cliff overlooking the pounding surf and unusual rock formations at Bathsheba Beach. Despite its proximity to the sea, the Edgewater resembles a mountain lodge in both appearance and ambience. Bounded by Joe's River, a national park, and a 9-mi strip of sand, the property also backs up to an 85-acre rain forest. Yoga classes, nature walks, and guided hikes are available to guests. All rooms and the ☞ **Edgewater Inn** dining room have an ocean view and hand-hewn local mahogany doors, moldings, and furniture. A shuttle will meet your plane or take you shopping,

Exploring

Andromeda Gardens, **21**

Animal Flower Cave, **26**

Barbados Wildlife Reserve, **24**

Barclays Park, **22**

Bridgetown, **1**

Codrington Theological College, **20**

Emancipation Memorial, **12**

Farley Hill, **23**

Flower Forest, **29**

Folkestone Marine Park & Visitor Centre, **28**

Francia Plantation House, **14**

George Washington House, **10**

Gun Hill Signal Station, **15**

Harrison's Cave, **31**

Mount Gay Rum Visitors Centre, **32**

Oistins, **13**

Ragged Point Lighthouse, **19**

Rum Factory and Heritage Park, **17**

St. Nicholas Abbey, **25**

Sam Lord's Castle, **18**

Six Men's Bay, **27**

Sunbury Plantation House & Museum, **16**

Tyrol Cot Heritage Village, **11**

Welchman Hall Gully, **30**

Dining

Atlantis Hotel, **51**

Bagatelle Great House, **71**

Bonito Beach Bar & Restaurant, **53**

Brown Sugar, **35**

Carambola, **65**

The Cliff, **70**

David's Place, **41**

Edgewater Inn, **52**

Fathoms, **69**

Josef's, **47**

La Maison, **60**

Olives Bar & Bistro, **63**

Palm Terrace, **59**

Pisces, **46**

Plantation Restaurant and Garden Theater, **43**

Ragamuffins, **64**

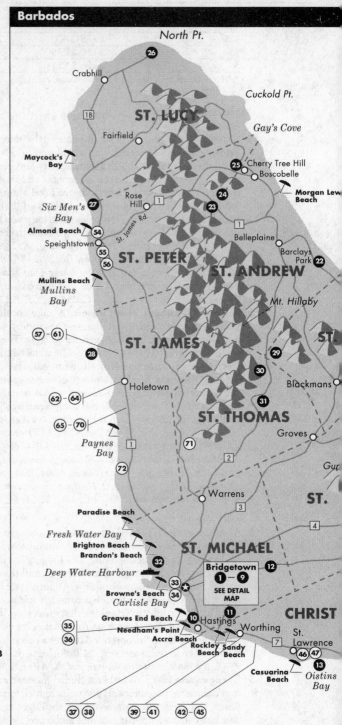

Barbados

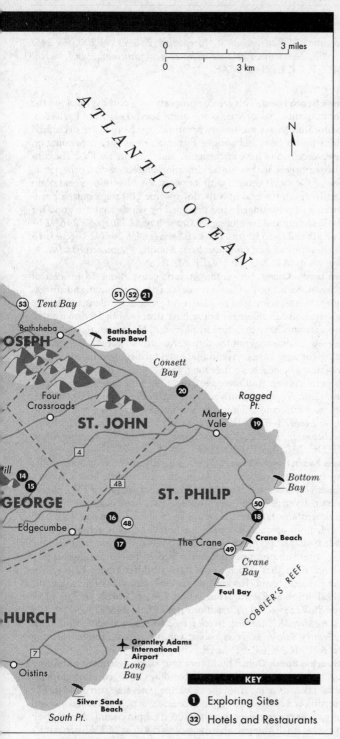

Rose and Crown, **72**
Sunbury Plantation
House, **48**
Waterfront Cafe, **33**

Lodging
Accra Beach Hotel &
Resort, **38**
Almond Beach
Club, **67**
Almond Beach
Village, **54**
Atlantis Hotel, **51**
Barbados Hilton, **36**
Casuarina Beach
Club, **45**
Club Rockley
Barbados, **37**
Cobblers Cove
Hotel, **55**
Coconut Creek
Club, **66**
Coral Reef Club, **57**
Crane Beach Hotel, **49**
Discovery Bay
Hotel, **61**
Divi Southwinds
Beach Resort, **43**
Edgewater Inn, **52**
Glitter Bay, **58**
Grand Barbados
Beach Resort, **34**
Little Bay Hotel, **42**
Mango Bay Hotel &
Beach Club, **62**
Oasis Hotel, **40**
Royal Pavilion, **59**
Sam Lord's Castle, **50**
Sandridge Beach
Hotel, **56**
Sandy Beach Island
Resort, **39**
Southern Palms Beach
Club & Hotel, **44**
Treasure Beach, **68**

snorkeling, or pub crawling. But overall, you must be content with watching the birds and butterflies, taking a hike, or surfing Soup Bowl most of the time. ⊠ *Bathsheba, St. Joseph;* ☎ *246/433–9900,* FAX *246/433–9902. 24 rooms. Restaurant, bar, air-conditioning, pool, beach. AE, MC, V. CP, EP, FAP, MAP.*

SOUTH COAST

$$$ ⊞ **Crane Beach Hotel.** This remote property on a cliff overlooking the dramatic Atlantic coast remains one of the special places of Barbados. The panoramic views are simply breathtaking. Rooms are decorated with four-poster beds and antique furniture; rates vary depending on the view, some rooms have kitchenettes, and there are no TVs. The constant ocean breeze makes air-conditioning unnecessary. Corner Suite 1 is one of the nicest rooms, with its two walls of windows and patio terrace. To reach the beach, walk down some 200 steps onto a beautiful stretch of pink-tinged sand thumped by waves that are good for both bodysurfing and swimming. ⊠ *Crane Bay, St. Philip,* ☎ *246/423–6220 or 800/223–6510 (reservations service),* FAX *246/423–5343. 18 rooms. Restaurant, bar, fans, minibars, 2 pools, 4 tennis courts, beach, meeting room. AE, DC, MC, V. EP, MAP.*

$$$ ⊞ **Sam Lord's Castle.** Set on the Atlantic coast about 14 mi east of Bridgetown, Sam Lord's Castle is not a castle with moat and towers but a great house surrounded by 72 acres of grounds, gardens, and beach. The seven rooms in the main house have canopied beds; downstairs, the public rooms have furniture by Sheraton, Hepplewhite, and Chippendale—for admiring, not for sitting. Additional guest rooms in surrounding cottages have conventional hotel furnishings and some have kitchenettes. The beach is a mile long, the Wanderer Restaurant offers Continental cuisine, and there are even a few slot machines, as befits a pirate's lair. A special tennis package includes unlimited court time, airport transfers, and a Thursday Shipwreck party. ⊠ *Long Bay, St. Philip,* ☎ *246/423–7350,* FAX *246/423–5918. 248 rooms. 3 restaurants, air-conditioning, 3 pools, 7 tennis courts, beach, shops, meeting room. AE, D, DC, MC, V. EP, FAP, MAP.*

$$–$$$ ⊞ **Accra Beach Hotel & Resort.** The beautifully appointed rooms in the four-story Accra have balconies facing the sandy white beach. Rooms are attractively decorated in soft pastel colors and each has a TV, a phone, and a hair dryer. Six duplex penthouse suites have oceanview sitting rooms downstairs, refrigerators, and a spacious bedroom and huge bath with whirlpool upstairs. Between the hotel and its beach are a large clover-leaf-shaped pool, snack bar, and poolside bar for drinks. In the evening, after sumptuous dining in the Sirocco restaurant, take a turn on a dance floor that's open to the stars. Children under 12 stay free in their parents' room. Rooms and facilities are accessible to people with disabilities. ⊠ *Rockley (Box 73W), Christ Church,* ☎ *246/435–8920 or 800/223–6510 (reservations service),* FAX *246/435–6794. 122 rooms, 6 suites. Restaurant, snack bar, 2 bars, air-conditioning, fans, pool, beauty salon, exercise room, squash, beach, shops, meeting rooms. AE, MC, V. CP, EP, MAP.*

$$–$$$ ⊞ **Casuarina Beach Club.** This luxury four-story apartment hotel consists of five clusters of Spanish-style buildings in 7½ acres of gardens. The hotel takes its name from the casuarina pines that surround it. The quiet setting is a rarity among south coast resorts. The restaurant and one of two bars are on the beach—900 ft of pink sand. A reception area includes small lounges where you can get a dose of TV (there aren't any in the rooms). All rooms and one- or two-bedroom suites have kitchenettes and large balconies. Scuba diving, golf, and other activities can be arranged. The Casuarina Beach is popular with those who prefer self-catering holidays in a secluded setting yet want to be close to the

action. It's 20 minutes from Bridgetown and within walking distance of restaurants, nightlife, and shopping. All facilities are handicapped accessible. ✉ *St. Lawrence Gap, Christ Church,* ☎ *246/428–3600; 800/742–4276 or 800/223–9815 (reservations services),* FAX *246/428– 1970. 124 rooms, 34 suites. Restaurant, 2 bars, air-conditioning, fans, kitchenettes, pool, 2 tennis courts, squash, beach, shops, children's program, meeting room. AE, D, MC, V. CP, EP.*

$$–$$$ 🏨 **Club Rockley Barbados.** On 65 acres near one of the most popular beach areas in Barbados, this all-inclusive resort offers extensive amenities and an excellent location for golf and tennis. The resort's 9-hole, par 36 golf course—the only one on the south coast—is challenging, attractive, and open to the public. The one- and two-bedroom accommodations are made out of former time-share condominiums, and the remaining time-shares are set apart from the hotel facility. Each room has a balcony or patio. There's free shuttle service to the beach, just five minutes away. ✉ *Golf Club Rd., Hastings, Christ Church,* ☎ *246/ 435–7880 or 800/777–1250 (reservations service),* FAX *246/435–8015. 150 rooms. 2 restaurants, 3 bars, air-conditioning, kitchenettes, 7 pools, beauty salon, 9-hole golf course, 5 tennis courts, squash, shops, children's program. AE, DC, MC, V. All-inclusive.*

$$ 🏨 **Divi Southwinds Beach Resort.** In this resort on 20 lush acres, the toss-up is whether to take one of the larger rooms, with a kitchenette and a balcony that overlooks the gardens and pool, or one of the smaller, older rooms just steps from the sandy white beach. Though all rooms are pleasant, the buildings themselves are plain. Guests come for action, and that includes making full use of the water-sports facilities. ✉ *St. Lawrence Gap, Christ Church,* ☎ *246/428–7181 or 800/367– 3484 (reservations service),* FAX *246/428–4674. 155 rooms. 2 restaurants, 2 bars, air-conditioning, kitchenettes, 2 pools, beauty shop, putting green, 2 lighted tennis courts, basketball, volleyball, beach, dive shop, shops, meeting rooms. AE, DC, MC, V. CP, EP, FAP, MAP.*

$$ 🏨 **Oasis Hotel.** The Oasis is a real find just minutes from the city. More attractive inside than it appears from the road, it's a comfortable all-suite hotel. All units have one bedroom, kitchenettes, and balconies or patios. An on-site convenience store, the Mini-Cube, sells grocery items. Scuba lessons are given in the pool. It's a three-minute walk to the beach, where you can snorkel, kayak, sail, and ride the surf on boogie boards. ✉ *Worthing (Box 39 W), Christ Church,* ☎ *246/435–7930 or 800/223–9815,* FAX *246/435–8232. 23 suites. Restaurant, bar, air-conditioning, in-room safes, kitchenettes, pool, snorkeling, boating, shop, meeting room. AE, DC, MC, V. All-inclusive.*

$$ 🏨 **Southern Palms Beach Club & Hotel.** A plantation-style hotel on a 1,000-ft stretch of pink sand near the Dover Convention Center, this is a convenient businessperson's hotel and a good choice for energetic guests wanting to be near the St. Lawrence Gap's shops and restaurants. You can choose from standard rooms, deluxe oceanfront suites with kitchenettes, and a four-bedroom penthouse. Each wing of the hotel has its own small pool. ✉ *St. Lawrence Gap, Christ Church,* ☎ *246/428–7171,* FAX *246/428–7175. 71 rooms, 20 suites, 1 penthouse. Dining room, bar, air-conditioning, in-room safes, refrigerators, 2 pools, miniature golf, tennis court, shuffleboard, beach, snorkeling, shop, business services, meeting room. AE, DC, MC, V. CP EP, FAP, MAP.*

$–$$ 🏨 **Sandy Beach Island Resort.** On a wide, sparkling-white beach, this comfortable hotel has modern rooms done in tropical colors, and one- and two-bedroom suites with full kitchens and dining areas. The Beachfront Restaurant serves a West Indian buffet Tuesday and Saturday nights, and there's also a boardwalk gazebo, a roof garden, and a free-form pool with a poolside bar. Scuba-diving certification, deep-sea fishing, harbor cruises, and catamaran sailing can be arranged. It's a convenient walk to St. Lawrence Gap. ☒ *Worthing, Christ Church;* ☎ *246/435–8000 or 800/742–4276, 800/448–8355, 800/223–9815, or 800/GO–BAJAN (reservations services);* ⅃ℵX *246/435–8053. 41 rooms, 87 suites. Restaurant, 2 bars, air-conditioning, kitchenettes, pool, beach, snorkeling, windsurfing, boating, shops, meeting room. AE, DC, MC, V. CP, EP, FAP, MAP.*

$ 🏨 **Little Bay Hotel.** This small hotel is a find for anyone who wants to go easy on the wallet and yet sleep to the sounds of the sea. Each room has a private balcony, small lounge, and kitchenette. TVs are available or, you can catch up on the news and sports in the small lounge next to the popular restaurant, Southern Accents. ☒ *St. Lawrence Gap, Christ Church,* ☎ *246/435–7246,* ⅃ℵX *246/435–8574. 10 rooms. Restaurant, bar, air-conditioning, fans, kitchenettes, beach. AE, MC, V. EP.*

WEST COAST

$$$$ 🏨 **Almond Beach Club.** This west coast resort is perfect for couples, honeymooners, and singles who want luxurious surroundings and no extra expenses. In addition to food, beverages, and sporting activities, the price of a room here gets you shopping excursions to Bridgetown, privileges at ☞ **Almond Beach Village** (which has a golf course), and transportation to the airport. All rooms have coffeemakers, hair dryers, and views of the ocean or the pool and gardens; junior suites have balconies. Meals are excellent, from the lavish breakfast buffets and four-course lunches to the afternoon teas and intimate dinners. There's also Enid's, a colorful, West Indian, on-site restaurant. If you need still more meal variety, you can try area restaurants that are part of the dine-around program (for guests staying seven days or more). Many duty-free stores and boutiques are within strolling distance; there's even a branch of Cave Shepard, the Bridgetown department store, in a small shopping center across the street. ☒ *Vauxhall, St. James,* ☎ *246/432–7840 or 800/425–6663 (reservations service),* ⅃ℵX *246/432–2115. 133 rooms, 28 junior suites. 2 restaurants, 4 bars, air-conditioning, in-room safes, 3 pools, sauna, tennis court, squash, beach, snorkeling, windsurfing, boating, waterskiing, airport shuttle. AE, MC, V. All-inclusive.*

$$$$ 🏨 **Almond Beach Village.** At the ☞ **Almond Beach Club**'s sister re-
★   sort, on 30 landscaped acres near Speightstown, there's plenty to keep everyone in the family busy: a mile-long beach; an executive, three-par golf course; nine pools; restaurants that serve Continental, Italian, and local cuisine; and such activities as shopping excursions, island tours, Caribbean cooking classes, and a dine-around program. The family section has junior and one-bedroom suites, a nursery, a play area, a wading pool, and a supervised Kid's Klub with extensive (and separate) programs for infants–age 12. A historic sugar mill on the property is a lovely spot for wedding ceremonies. If all this isn't enough, you can hop the shuttle to the Club and use the facilities there. Seven low-rise buildings house the large, comfortable, attractive guest rooms; each has a coffeemaker and a hair dryer. All meals (including all beverages), activities, and departure transfers are included in the rates. ☒ *Heywoods, Hwy. 1, St. Peter,* ☎ *246/422–4900 or 800/425–6663,* ⅃ℵX *246/422–0617. 288 rooms. 4 restaurants, 5 bars, air-conditioning, in-room safes, 9 pools, wading pool, 9-hole golf course, 5 tennis courts, health club, racquetball, squash, beach, snorkeling, windsurfing, boating, waterskiing, fishing, shops, dance club, children's program, meeting room, airport shuttle. AE, MC, V. All-inclusive.*

$$$$ 🏨 **Cobblers Cove Hotel.** This intimate all-suite resort, 12 mi up the west
★   coast from Bridgetown, combines comfort and informal elegance in an English-style country house. The pink-and-white building and 3 acres of tropical gardens are bordered on three sides by stone walls, giving the property self-contained privacy. Suites are in 10 two-story, shin-

gle-roof cottages arranged in a V-shape around the great house. Each has a sitting room with wet bar, louvered shutters that open onto a large patio or hardwood balcony, and bleached wood furniture with upholstered cushions in soft tropical colors. Bedrooms are air-conditioned. There's an excellent restaurant, a sociable bar, and a clublike lounge-library. For all-out luxury, stay in the Colleton Suite or Camelot Suite. Upstairs in the great house, each of these spacious, stylish suites has a king-size four-poster bed, whirlpool bath, and a large sitting room with spiral staircase leading to a secluded rooftop sundeck and private plunge pool. Guests enjoy special rates and guaranteed tee times at the nearby Royal Westmoreland Golf Club. From January to March, this hotel has a primarily adults-only atmosphere. ⊠ *Road View, Speightstown, St. Peter,* ☎ *246/422–2291 or 800/890–6060 (reservations service),* FAX *246/422–1460. 40 suites. Restaurant, bar, snack bar, air-conditioning, in-room safes, minibars, pool, golf privileges, tennis court, beach, snorkeling, windsurfing, boating, waterskiing, library, babysitting, meeting room. MC, V. CP, EP, FAP, MAP.*

$$$$ ▦ **Glitter Bay.** On this estate in the 1930s, Sir Edward Cunard of the English shipping family built a great house and a beach house that resembled his palazzo in Venice. Cunard's parties in honor of visiting aristocrats and celebrities gave Glitter Bay an early reputation for grandeur and style. Today, newer buildings angled back from the beach contain one- and two-bedroom suites and duplex penthouses, all with king or two twin beds, and private balconies or terraces; some have full kitchens. The beach house is now five garden suites. Manicured gardens separate the reception area and a large, comfortable tea lounge from an alfresco dining room (where evening entertainment is held), the pools with waterfall and footbridge, and a half mile of beach. Glitter Bay is more casual and family-oriented than its next-door sister property, the ☞ **Royal Pavilion,** but the resorts share facilities, including water sports, and dining privileges. Guests also enjoy golf privileges at Royal Westmoreland Golf Club (with complimentary transportation).⊠ *Porters, St. James,* ☎ *246/422–5555 or 800/223–1818 (reservations service),* FAX *246/422–3940. 83 suites. Restaurant, air-conditioning, fans, in-room safes, minibars, room service, 2 pools, beauty salon, massage, golf privileges, 2 lighted tennis courts, exercise room, beach, snorkeling, windsurfing, boating, waterskiing, shops, babysitting, children's program, laundry service, concierge, meeting room. AE, D, DC, MC, V. EP, MAP.*

$$$$ ▦ **Royal Pavilion.** Of the 75 suites here, 72 are oceanfront; the remaining ★ three are nestled in a two-story garden villa. Ground-floor rooms allow guests simply to step through sliding doors, cross their private patio, and walk onto the sand. Second- and third-floor suites have king or two twin beds and such amenities as hair dryers. Breakfast and lunch are served alfresco along the edge of the beach. Afternoon tea and dinner are in the ☞ **Palm Terrace.** The Royal Pavilion attracts sophisticated guests who want serenity (it's best to leave the kids at home). Recreational facilities and dining privileges are shared with the adjoining and more informal sister hotel, ☞ **Glitter Bay.** ⊠ *Porters, St. James,* ☎ *246/422–4444 or 800/223–1818 (reservations service),* FAX *246/422–3940. 75 suites. 2 restaurants, 2 bars, air-conditioning, room service, pool, beauty salon, golf privileges, 2 tennis courts, beach, snorkeling, windsurfing, boating, waterskiing, shops, laundry service, concierge, meeting room. AE, D, DC, MC, V. EP, MAP.*

$$$–$$$$ ▦ **Coconut Creek Club.** The atmosphere is casual at this luxury resort, set on handsomely landscaped grounds overlooking the ocean. From a low bluff, steps lead down to two secluded coves and a small, private beach. Some rooms have ocean views; others overlook the garden or pool; TVs are available for a small fee. Entertainment and dancing takes place at the bar pavilion. ⊠ *Hwy. 1, Derricks, St. James (Box 249, Bridgetown);* ☎ *246/432–0803;* ℻ *246/432–0272. 53 rooms. Dining room, bar, air-conditioning, pool, beach, snorkeling, boating, baby-sitting. AE, DC, MC, V. All-inclusive.*

$$$–$$$$ 🏨 **Coral Reef Club.** Guests at this small, family-owned and -managed resort spend their days relaxing on the white-sand beach or around the pool, taking time out for the hotel's superb afternoon tea. The public areas ramble along the beach and face the Caribbean Sea, and small coral-stone cottages are scattered over the surrounding 12 flower-filled acres. (The cottages farthest from the beach are a bit of a hike to the main house.) Accommodations are spacious and graced with fresh flowers. Each room has a small patio, and amenities such as radios and hair dryers. Junior suites have a sitting area and large private balcony or patio; cottage-style suites have an additional single bed and dressing room. TV is available by request only and carries an extra charge. The restaurant is noted for its tantalizing cuisine; Bajan chef Graham Licorish adds European flair to local seafood and produce (children's meals are available). Guests on MAP have dining and golf privileges at Royal Westmoreland Golf Club. The Folkestown Underwater Marine Park is adjacent to the hotel, offering great snorkeling opportunities. Another convenience is the free weekday shuttle into Bridgetown. ⊠ *Holetown, St. James,* ☎ *246/422–2372 or 800/525–4800 (reservations service),* ℻ *246/422–1776. 34 rooms, 30 suites. Restaurant, bar, air-conditioning, fans, in-room safes, refrigerators, room service, 2 pools, beauty salon, massage, golf privileges, 3 tennis courts, exercise room, beach, snorkeling, windsurfing, boating, waterskiing, shops, billiards, baby-sitting, children's program, business services, meeting room. AE, MC, V. EP, MAP.*

$$$–$$$$ 🏨 **Mango Bay Hotel & Beach Club.** In central Holetown and within walking distance of shops and historical sites, Mango Bay's whitewashed buildings face the beach and are surrounded by tropical gardens. Each room has a private terrace or balcony and a picturesque view of the garden, pool, or beach (which determines the rate), and all are decorated in bright Caribbean colors with lightly colored wicker furniture. The all-inclusive price extends to beverages and a dine-around program for guests staying a week or more. Activities include water sports (and scuba instruction), aquacise, a catamaran cruise, glass-bottom boat rides, snorkeling trips, walking tours, and a shopping trip to Bridgetown. In the evening, there's always entertainment after dinner and nightcaps at the piano bar. Children three years and under stay free. ⊠ *2nd St., Holetown, St. James,* ☎ *246/432–1384 or 800/GO–BAJAN (reservations services),* ℻ *246/432–5297. 64 rooms. Restaurant, bar, piano bar, air-conditioning, in-room safe, 2 pools, beach, snorkeling, windsurfing, boating, waterskiing. AE, MC, V. All-inclusive.*

$$$–$$$$ 🏨 **Treasure Beach.** The atmosphere here is quiet and pleasant. Guests, particularly British vacationers, often stay two or three weeks, giving the hotel an almost residential quality. Most of the one-bedroom suites create a horseshoe around a small garden and pool, others have sea views, but all are just steps from the beach. Suites are spacious, with large kitchenettes. Sitting rooms have comfortable chairs and sofas, small tables, and a few books; full-length shutters open onto large patios or verandas. The restaurant's reputation for gourmet meals and fine service attracts an outside clientele as well as hotel guests. ⊠ *Paynes Bay, St. James,* ☎ *246/432–1346; 800/742–4276 or 800/223–6510 (reservations services),* ℻ *246/432–1094. 29 1-bedroom suites, 1 2-bedroom penthouse suite. Restaurant, bar, air-conditioning, fans, kitchenettes, pool, beach, snorkeling. AE, DC, MC, V. CP, EP, MAP.*

$$–$$$ 🏨 **Discovery Bay Hotel.** In historic Holetown this quiet hotel—with a grand, white-columned, plantation-style entrance—is surrounded by 4½ acres of tropical gardens and bordered by a broad strand of St. James beach. It's perfect for both couples and families. Deluxe rooms have ocean views; others open onto a central lawn and pool area. The hotel's location provides easy access to local shops and restaurants, as well as the public bus. A shuttle to Bridgetown, 8 mi south, is available to guests on weekdays. ⊠ *Hwy. 1, Holetown, St. James,* ☎ *246/432–1301; 800/742–4276 or 800/223–6510 (reservations services),* FAX *246/432–2553. 88 rooms. Restaurant, lobby lounge, air-conditioning, kitchenettes, minibars, pool, Ping-Pong, beach, boating, shop, meeting room. AE, MC, V. CP, MAP.*

$–$$ 🏨 **Sandridge Beach Hotel.** The rooms and suites at this fashionable beachfront property near Speightstown are styled in bright colors and tropical furnishings. Choose to stay in a basic hotel room, a studio with kitchenette, or a one-bedroom suite with kitchenette. Ground-floor rooms have wide doors and ramps, allowing easy access for guests with disabilities. Among the water activities is a glass-bottom boat ride where you can glimpse undersea life without getting wet. One of the two pools has a dramatic waterfall and deck of coral stone. ⊠ *Road View, St. Peter,* ☎ *246/422–2361,* FAX *246/422–1965. 28 rooms, 30 suites. 2 restaurants, 2 bars, air-conditioning, kitchenettes, 2 pools, beach, snorkeling, windsurfing, boating, baby-sitting, meeting room. AE, DC, MC, V. EP, CP, MAP, FAP.*

Villas and Condominiums

Villas, private homes, and condos are available south of Bridgetown in the Hastings-Worthing area, and along the west coast in St. James and in St. Peter. Two- to three-bedroom condos near the beach start at $800–$1,000 per week in the summer—double that in winter. Most include maid service, and a cook can be arranged through the owner or manager. Rentals are also available through Barbados realtors; among them are **Alleyne, Aguilar & Altman** (⊠ Derricks, St. James, ☎ 246/432–0840), **Bajan Services** (⊠ Gibbs Beach, St. Peter, ☎ 246/422–2618), **John M. Bladon & Co., Ltd.** (⊠ Hastings, Christ Church, ☎ 246/426–4640), and **Ronald Stoute & Sons Ltd.** (⊠ Sam Lord's Castle, St. Philip, ☎ 246/423–6800). The **Barbados Tourism Authority** (☎ 246/427–2623, FAX 246/426–4080) has a listing of apartments and rates. In the United States, contact **At Home Abroad** (☎ 212/421–9165).

Dining

To keep their sophisticated international clientele happy, many of the best hotels and restaurants employ chefs who were trained in New York and Europe. Most menus include seafood: dolphinfish, kingfish, snapper, and flying fish are prepared every way imaginable. Flying fish is so popular a delicacy that it has become a national symbol. Shellfish abounds; on the other hand, so does steak. Gourmet dining here usually involves dishes served with finely blended sauces.

West Indian cuisine offers an entirely different dining experience. The African heritage brings to the table rice, peas, beans, and okra—the staples that make a perfect base for slowly cooked meat and fish dishes. Many side dishes are cooked in oil (the pumpkin fritters can be addictive). And be cautious at first with the West Indian condiments; like the sun, they're hotter than you think.

Buljol is a cold salad of marinated, raw codfish, tomatoes, onions, sweet peppers, and celery. Callaloo soup is made from the spinachlike vegetable that gives the dish its name, crabmeat, and seasonings.

Christophenes (squashlike vegetables) are served as a side dish or pureed into steaming hot soup. *Conkies* are cornmeal, coconut, pumpkin, raisins, sweet potatoes, and spices, mixed together, wrapped in a banana leaf, and steamed. *Cou-cou* is a mixture of cornmeal and okra, topped with a spicy Creole sauce made from tomatoes, onions, and sweet peppers, and often served with steamed flying fish. To make a pepper-pot stew Bajan style, you need a hearty mix of oxtail, beef chunks, and "any other meat you may have," simmered overnight and flavored with *cassareep*, an ancient preservative and seasoning that gives the stew its dark, rich color.

For breakfast and dessert you'll find a cornucopia of fresh tropical fruit: mangoes, soursop, papaya (pawpaw), and, in season, softball-size "mammy apples," a sweet, thick-skinned fruit with giant seeds. In addition to the local and omnipresent Banks beer and Mount Gay rum, Bajan liquid refreshments include *falernum* (a liqueur concocted of rum, sugar, lime juice, and almond essence) and *mauby* (a nonalcoholic drink made by boiling bitter bark and spices, straining the mixture, and sweetening it).

What to Wear
Barbados's British heritage keeps the dress code conservative and, on occasion, formal. This can mean a jacket and tie for gentlemen and a cocktail dress for ladies in some restaurants, particularly in winter. Other places are more casual, although jeans and shorts are always frowned upon at dinner. Beach attire should only be worn at the beach.

CATEGORY	COST*
$$$	over $40
$$	$20–$40
$	under $20

per person for a three-course meal, excluding drinks and 10% service charge

Bridgetown Area
CARIBBEAN/CREOLE

$$–$$$ ✕ **Brown Sugar.** A special-occasion atmosphere prevails inside this restored West Indian wooden house across from the Grand Barbados Beach Resort. Dozens of ferns and hanging plants decorate the breezy multilevel restaurant. An extensive and authentic Sugar Planter's Buffet Luncheon (noon to 2:30)—from cou-cou to pepper-pot stew—is popular with local businesspeople. Dinner entrées include local black-bellied lamb, Creole orange chicken, and homemade desserts, such as angelfood chocolate mousse cake, passion-fruit or nutmeg ice cream, and lime cheesecake. ✉ *Aquatic Gap, Bay St., St. Michael,* ☎ *246/426–7684. AE, DC, MC, V. No lunch Sat.*

$–$$ ✕ **Waterfront Cafe.** Facing the busy harbor in Bridgetown, this friendly bistro is the perfect place to enjoy a drink, snack, or meal—and people-watch. Locals and tourists gather at outdoor café tables for sandwiches, salads, fish, pasta, pepper-pot stew, and tasty Bajan snacks such as buljol, fish cakes, or plantation pork (plantains stuffed with spicy minced pork). The panfried flying-fish sandwich is especially popular. In the evening, from the brick and mirrored interior, you can gaze through the arched windows while you savor '90s-style Creole cuisine, enjoy cool trade winds, and listen to live music. ✉ *The Careenage, Bridgetown, St. Michael,* ☎ *246/427–0093. AE, DC, MC, V. Closed Sun.*

East Coast
CARIBBEAN/CREOLE

$ ✕ **Atlantis Hotel.** The seemingly endless luncheon buffet and magnificent ocean view make this restaurant in the ☞ **Atlantis Hotel** a real find. Under the direction of owner-chef Enid Maxwell, the staff serves up an enormous Bajan buffet daily, with pumpkin fritters, spinach cake, pickled breadfruit, fried flying fish, roast chicken, pepper-pot stew, and okra and eggplant. Homemade coconut pie tops the dessert list. All that for $12.50 per person, except on Sunday, when a few dishes are added to the groaning board and the price rises to $17.50. ⊠ *Atlantis Hotel, Bathsheba, St. Joseph,* ☎ *246/433–9445. AE.*

$ ✕ **Bonito Beach Bar & Restaurant.** When you tour the rugged east coast, plan to lunch here on Mrs. Enid Worrell's wholesome West Indian home-cooking. The view of the Atlantic from the second-floor dining room is the most striking aspect of this otherwise plain restaurant. Lunch might be a choice of fried fish, baked chicken, or beef stew, accompanied by vegetables and salads fresh from the family garden. If your timing is right, Mrs. Worrell might have homemade cheesecake for dessert. Be sure to try the fresh fruit punch—with or without rum. The Bajan luncheon buffet, on Wednesday and Sunday from 1 to 3, is popular. ⊠ *Coast Rd., Bathsheba, St. Joseph,* ☎ *246/433–9034. No credit cards.*

ECLECTIC

$ ✕ **Edgewater Inn.** You'll be nearly surrounded by 85-acres of rain forest when dining at the ☞ **Edgewater Inn**'s restaurant, yet still overlook the famed Soup Bowl beach. Enjoy a cool drink and the wonderful view while sitting at hand-carved mahogany tables and chairs; then choose from sandwiches, salads, French-bread pizzas, or traditional Bajan dishes for a filling lunch. The best treat at the dessert buffet is a help-yourself frozen-yogurt machine. Dinners are also served here, but it's mostly lodgers who partake. ⊠ *Bathsheba, St. Joseph,* ☎ *246/433–9900. AE, MC, V.*

South Coast

CARIBBEAN/CREOLE

$$$ ✕ **Plantation Restaurant and Garden Theater.** The Bajan buffet and entertainment on Wednesday and Friday are big attractions here (☞ Nightlife and the Arts, *below*). The Plantation is in a renovated Barbadian residence surrounded by spacious grounds above the Southwinds Resort. Dinner is served either indoors or on the terrace. ⊠ *St. Lawrence Rd., Christ Church,* ☎ *246/428–5048. AE, MC, V. No lunch.*

$$ ✕ **David's Place.** Come here for first-rate Barbadian food in a first-rate location—a black-and-white Bajan cottage overlooking St. Lawrence Bay. Waves slap against the pilings of the open-air deck—a rhythmic accompaniment to the soft classical music playing. The specialties—local flying fish, pepper-pot stew, curried shrimp—and other entrées, including a vegetarian platter, come with homemade cheese bread. Dessert might be banana pudding, carrot cake with rum sauce, or a cakelike dessert called *cassava pone*. David's has an extensive wine list. ⊠ *St. Lawrence Main Rd., Worthing, Christ Church,* ☎ *246/435–9755. AE, MC, V. Closed Mon.*

$–$$ ✕ **Sunbury Plantation House.** In the Courtyard Restaurant, on a patio
★ surrounded by beautiful gardens, luncheon is served to visitors as part of the house tour (☞ Exploring, *below*). The Bajan buffet includes chicken and fish, salads, rice and peas, and steamed local vegetables. Sandwiches and other à la carte items are available, too. Trifle, pastries, and ice cream are dessert choices. A special mood is created in the evening, when groups of no more than 20 people dine on a five-course dinner, with wine and liqueurs, in the elegant plantation-house. ⊠ *St. Philip,* ☎ *246/423–6270. Reservations essential. AE, MC, V.*

ECLECTIC

$$–$$$ ✕ **Josef's.** Swede Nils Ryman successfully creates a menu from the unusual combination of Caribbean and Scandinavian fare. That means great fresh seafood, including lobster from the rocky east coast, and

toast Skagen, made from diced shrimp blended with mayonnaise and fresh dill. Red meats include pepper steak and rack of lamb. Stroll around the garden before moving to the alfresco downstairs dining room or to an upstairs table with a sea view. ⊠ *Waverly House, St. Lawrence Gap, Christ Church,* ☎ *246/435–6541. AE, MC, V.*

SEAFOOD

$$–$$$ ✕ **Pisces.** Here flying fish, dolphinfish, kingfish, crab, shrimp, prawns,
★ and lobster are prepared any way from charbroiled to sautéed. Specialties include conch strips in tempura, tropical gazpacho, panfried fillets of flying fish with a toasted almond crust and light mango-citrus sauce, and pepper-encrusted tuna with fresh papaya and balsamic vinaigrette. There are also some chicken and beef dishes. Whatever your selection, the herbs that flavor it and the vegetables that accompany it will have come from the chef's own garden. Homemade rum raisin ice cream is a delicious dessert. Enjoy your meal in a contemporary setting filled with hanging tropical plants and twinkling white lights that reflect on the water. ⊠ *St. Lawrence Gap, Christ Church,* ☎ *246/ 435–6564. AE, DC, MC, V. No lunch.*

West Coast

CONTEMPORARY

$$$ ✕ **The Cliff.** Chef Paul Owens and manager Manuel Ward have cre-
★ ated one of the finest dining establishments in Barbados. Imaginative art accents the tiered dining terrace, and every candlelit table has a view of the sea. The artistry extends to the innovative menu, which offers excellent cuts of meat and fresh fish, creatively presented with nouvelle accents and accompanied by the freshest of local vegetables. Don't skip dessert, which falls in the "sinful" category. ⊠ *Derricks, St. James,* ☎ *246/432–1922. AE, DC, MC, V. No lunch.*

$$$ ✕ **Palm Terrace.** Within the ☞ **Royal Pavilion** hotel, the Palm's French executive chef and his team apply their talents to an international à la carte menu that combines Barbadian produce with top-quality imports. The result is modern European creations, such as mille-feuille of home-smoked chicken with tomato, chives, and carrots in a light mustard cream sauce. Fresh mint accents New Zealand rack of lamb, and pan-fried crab becomes a stuffing for the breast of chicken entrée. Each evening there is a roast from the carvery. Widely spaced tables, comfortable chairs, and palms swaying under floor-to-ceiling arches create a formal yet relaxed ambience as you dine facing the Caribbean Sea. ⊠ *Royal Pavilion, Porters, St. James,* ☎ *246/422–4444. AE, DC, MC, V. Closed Sun. No lunch.*

ECLECTIC

$$$ ✕ **Carambola.** Dramatic lighting, alfresco dining, and a cliffside set-
★ ting overlooking the Caribbean make this restaurant one of the island's most romantic. It also serves some of the best food. The menu is a mix of classic French and Caribbean cuisines—with Asian touches thrown in for good measure. Start with a spicy crab tart, served with hollandaise sauce on a bed of sweet pepper coulis. For an entrée, try fillet of mahimahi broiled with Dijon mustard sauce, or sliced duck breast with a wild mushroom fumet served with stuffed tomatoes and *gratin dauphinoise* (potatoes au gratin). When you think you can't eat another bite, the *citron gâteau* (lime mousse on a bed of lemon coulis) is a wonderfully light finish. ⊠ *Derricks, St. James,* ☎ *246/432–0832. Reservations essential. AE, MC, V. Closed Sun. No lunch.*

$$–$$$ ✕ **Bagatelle Great House.** This restaurant, one of Barbados's oldest, is in a restored plantation house (circa 1645) that has been designated a "house of architectural and historical interest" by the Barbados National Trust. Its name derives from a 19th-century poker game during which Lord Willoughby, first governor of Barbados and then owner of the property, staked his house. "A mere bagatelle," he shrugged, upon losing the bet. The ambience is romantic and still very much like a private Colonial home. An international mix of French and Caribbean cuisine is served for light lunches and elegant dinners. Try the always-special Caribbean lobster or, perhaps, fresh-caught dorado grilled on a traditional coal pot; delicious parsley crepes filled with fresh vegetables and daubed with a rich Creole sauce will please any vegetarian. The garden terrace offers intimacy with tables for two. Upstairs, reached by an impressive double Palladian staircase, is a gallery of Caribbean art, a craft showroom, and a gift shop. ⊠ *Hwy. 2A, St. Thomas,* ☎ *246/421–6767. Reservations essential. AE, MC, V.*

$$–$$$ ✕ **Olives Bar & Bistro.** Owner-chef Larry Rogers and his wife Michelle have turned a colorful old Bajan-style house into a delightfully casual restaurant. Mediterranean and Caribbean flavors enliven gourmet pizzas and salads; special dishes on the bistro-style menu might include tasty Swiss-style *rösti* potatoes (shredded and fried like a pancake) with smoked salmon and sour cream, and fresh seafood, such as seared yellow fin tuna with ratatouille. Dine inside or in the courtyard; the upstairs bar is a popular gathering spot where you can mingle over coffee, refreshing drinks, or snacks (pizza, pastas, salads). ⊠ *2nd St., Holetown, St. James,* ☎ *246/432–2112. AE, MC, V. No lunch.*

$$ ✕ **Ragamuffins.** The only restaurant on Barbados within an authentic chattel house, Ragamuffins is funky, lively, and affordable. The menu offers seafood, perfectly broiled T-bone steaks, and vegetarian dishes like Bajan stir-fried vegetables with noodles. The kitchen is within sight of the bar—which is a popular meeting spot most evenings. It's informal, fun for the family, and the food is delicious. ⊠ *1st St., Holetown, St. James,* ☎ *246/432–1295. AE, MC, V. No lunch.*

FRENCH

$$$ ✕ **La Maison.** This restaurant in Balmore House, a coral-stone man-
★ sion on St. James Bay, exudes elegance and romance. English country furnishings and a wood-paneled bar open onto the beachfront dining terrace. The mood is set for the terrific gourmet cuisine. A French chef, direct from the Loire Valley, creates seafood specials, including a flying-fish parfait appetizer and classic salmon in cream sauce. Chocolate soufflé is a dessert special. ⊠ *Holetown, St. James,* ☎ *246/ 432–1156. Reservations essential. AE, DC, MC, V. Closed Mon..*

SEAFOOD

$$–$$$ ✕ **Rose and Crown.** A variety of fresh seafood is served in this casual eatery, but it's the local lobster that's high on diners' lists. Meat eaters can sink their teeth into perfectly broiled U. S.-choice steak or one of several chicken dishes. Indoors is a paneled bar; outdoors are tables on a wraparound porch. Although the restaurant has been an institution for two decades, the new chef/owner Dennis Newton (formerly with the Royal Pavilion hotel) brings excellent credentials to the kitchen. ⊠ *Prospect, St. James,* ☎ *246/425–1074. AE, MC, V. Closed Sat. No lunch.*

$$ ✕ **Fathoms.** Veteran restaurateurs Stephen and Sandra Toppin open this beach restaurant seven days a week for lunch and dinner. Fathoms is casual by day, candlit by night, and its 22 well-dressed tables are scattered from the inside dining rooms to the patio's ocean edge. Seafood is the focus here—from straightforward grilled lobster and jumbo baked shrimp to cashew-crusted kingfish. The upstairs bar has a pool table. ⊠ *Paynes Bay, St. James,* ☎ *246/432–2568. AE, MC, V.*

Beaches

Barbados beaches have fine white sand and are all open to the public. Most beaches have access from the road so nonguest bathers do not have to pass through hotel property. On east coast beaches, the Atlantic Ocean surf can be rough with a strong undertow, so swimming and surfing are dangerous there. South coast beaches, dotted with tall palms, have medium-to-high surf; the waves get bigger the farther southeast you go. Gentle Caribbean waves lap the west coast and its beaches are shaded by leafy mahogany trees.

EAST COAST

With long stretches of open beach and crashing ocean waves, rocky cliffs, and verdant hills, the windward side of Barbados won't disappoint anyone who seeks dramatic views. This is also where Barbadians have second homes and spend holidays. But be cautioned: Swimming at east coast beaches is treacherous even for strong swimmers and *not* recommended. The waves are high, the bottom tends to be rocky, and the currents are unpredictable.

The rolling waves at **Bathsheba Soup Bowl** are popular among surfers (and daydreamers). You'll see local people catching a wave on any given day; it is also the location of the Caribbean Surfing Championships, which are held each November.

A worthwhile, little-visited beach for those who don't mind trekking about a mile off the beaten path is **Morgan Lewis Beach.** It's east of Morgan Lewis Mill, the oldest intact windmill on the island. Turn east on the small road that goes to the town of Boscobelle (between Cherry Tree Hill and Morgan Lewis Mill); but instead of going to town, take the even less-traveled road (unmarked on most maps; you will have to ask for directions) that goes down the cliff to the beach. What awaits is more than 2 mi of unspoiled, virtually uninhabited white sand and sweeping views of the Atlantic coast.

SOUTH COAST

South coast beaches in Christ Church are much busier than those on the west coast and generally draw a young, energetic crowd. The quality of the beaches is consistently good; the reef-protected waters are safe for swimming and snorkeling.

Accra Beach, in Rockley, is very popular. There are lots of people, lots of activity, food and drink nearby, and rental equipment for snorkeling and other water sports. There's a parking lot at the beach. **Casuarina Beach,** at the Casuarina Beach Club in the St. Lawrence Gap area, is a beach with lots of breeze and a fair amount of surf. Public access is from Maxwell Coast Road. **Greaves End Beach,** south of Bridgetown at Aquatic Gap, between the Grand Barbados Beach Resort and the Barbados Hilton in St. Michael, is a good spot for swimming. **Needham's Point,** with its lighthouse, is one of Barbados's best beaches. It's crowded with local people on weekends and holidays. In Worthing, next to the Sandy Beach Island Resort, **Sandy Beach** has shallow, calm waters and a picturesque lagoon. It's an ideal location for families, with beach activities on weekends. There's parking on the main road and plenty of places nearby to buy food or drink.

Farther east, closer to where the Caribbean meets the Atlantic, the surf becomes stronger and the winds higher, making it the island's premier windsurfing venue.

The cove at **Bottom Bay,** north of Sam Lord's Castle, is lovely. Follow the steps down the cliff to a strip of white sand lined by coconut palms and faced by an aquamarine sea. There's even a cave to explore. It's out of the way and not near restaurants, so bring a picnic lunch. **Crane Beach** is popular but can be rough water; swimming is not encouraged except for the very experienced. **Foul Bay** is ruggedly attractive and perfect for alfresco lunches (pack your own picnic), but swimming is dangerous for all but very good swimmers. **Silver Sands Beach,** close to the southernmost point of the island, has a beautiful expanse of white sand beach, with a stiff breeze that appeals to windsurfers.

WEST COAST

The west coast has the stunning coves and white-sand beaches that are dear to postcard publishers—plus calm, clear water for snorkeling, scuba diving, and swimming. West coast beaches continue almost unbroken from Almond Beach Village in the north down to Bridgetown. Elegant private homes and luxury hotels take up most of the beachfront property in this area, which is why this stretch of sandy shoreline is called Barbados's Gold Coast.

Although west coast beaches are seldom crowded, they are not the place to find isolation. Vendors stroll by, selling handmade baskets, hats, dolls, jewelry, and even watercolors; owners of private boats offer waterskiing, parasailing, and snorkel cruises. There are no concession stands, but hotels welcome nonguests for terrace lunches (wear a cover-up). Picnic items and necessities can be bought at the Sunset Crest shopping center in Holetown.

Brighton Beach, just north of Bridgetown, is not far from the port and is a favorite of locals. It's a large beach and has a beach bar. **Mullins Beach,** south of Speightstown at Mullins Bay, is a good place for a swim and is safe for snorkeling. There's easy parking on the main road; and when you want a break from the sun, Mullins Beach Bar has snacks and drinks. **Paynes Bay,** south of Holetown, is the site of a number of luxury hotels. It's a very pretty area, with plenty of beach to go around. Parking areas and access are available opposite the Coach House Pub. Grab a bite to eat at Bomba's Beach Bar.

Outdoor Activities and Sports

Participant Sports

FISHING

Half- or full-day fishing charter trips are available for serious deep-sea fishers looking for billfish. For those who prefer angling in calm, coastal waters where wahoo, barracuda, and other small fish reside.

Billfisher II (⊠ Bridge House, The Careenage, Bridgetown, ☎ 246/431–0741) is a 40-ft Pacemaker; trips accommodate up to six people and include drinks and transportation to and from the boat. Full-day charters include a full lunch and guaranteed fish! *Blue Jay* (⊠ St. James, ☎ 246/422–2098) is a 45-ft, fully equipped fishing boat, with a crew that knows the waters where blue marlin, sailfish, barracuda, and kingfish play. Four people can be accommodated; each is guaranteed his or her own rod and chair and can invite, free of charge, a spouse or guest. Drinks and snacks are provided.

GOLF

Barbadians love golf, and golfers love Barbados. Greens fees range from $22.50 for 9 holes at Club Rockley to $145 for 18 holes at Royal Westmoreland Golf Club.

Almond Beach Village (⊠ St. Peter, ☎ 246/422–4900), on the northwest corner of the island, has a 9-hole, par-3, executive course for guest use only; clubs are provided. **Club Rockley Barbados** (⊠ Rockley, Christ Church, ☎ 246/435–7873), on the south coast, has a challenging

9-hole course that can be played as 18 from varying tee positions; trolleys and clubs can be rented. The **Royal Westmoreland Golf Club** (⊠ St. James, ☎ 246/422–4653) has a world-class Robert Trent Jones Jr. 18-hole championship course that meanders through the 500-acre Westmoreland Sugar Estate past million-dollar villas, and overlooks the scenic west coast. Nine additional holes are under way. Greens fees include use of an electric cart; equipment rental is available. To play here, you must stay at a hotel with access privileges (of the hotels reviewed herein, Cobblers Cove, Coral Reef Club, Glitter Bay, Royal Pavilion have privileges). The prestigious **Sandy Lane Golf Club** (⊠ St. James, ☎ 246/432–4563) will be open while the Sandy Lane Hotel is undergoing renovations.

HIKING

Hilly but not mountainous, the northern interior and east coast of Barbados is ideal for hiking. The **Barbados National Trust** (⊠ Wildey House, Wildey, St. Michael, ☎ 246/426–2421) sponsors free 5-mi walks year-round on Sunday, from 6 AM to about 9:30 AM and from 3:30 PM to 5:30 PM, as well as moonlight hikes when the heavens permit. Newspapers announce the time and meeting place (or you can call the Trust).

HORSEBACK RIDING

Horseback riding through the hilly north country of Barbados or along the beach is an exhilarating way to explore the island—sort of like driving with the top down. Equestrian tours can accommodate any level of experience. Advance reservations are recommended. The **Caribbean International Riding Center** (⊠ Auburn, St. Joseph, ☎ 246/433–1453 or 246/420–1246) offers one- and two-hour rides through the countryside of the Scotland District and longer treks that continue on to Morgan Lewis beach on the Atlantic coast. Prices range from $40 for a one-hour trail ride to $82.50 for a 2½ hour trek; transportation to and from your hotel is included. On the west coast, **Brighton Stables** (⊠ Black Rock, St. Michael, ☎ 246/425–9381) offers one-hour rides along beaches and palm groves for $27.50, including transportation.

PARASAILING

Parasailing is available, wind conditions permitting, on the beaches of St. James and Christ Church. The chute is attached to a custom-crafted 32-ft speedboat with an attached launching and landing platform, and a hydraulic winch system for hauling you in simply and safely—even for children or the physically challenged. **Skyrider Parasail** (☎ 246/435–0570) operates from Bay Street in Bridgetown, but the boat does pickups all along the west coast. Just flag down the boat, though the operator may find you first. Rates are $45 per flight—and they even take credit cards (MasterCard and Visa).

SCUBA DIVING AND SNORKELING

Dive sites are concentrated along the west coast, between Bridgetown and Maycocks Bay, St. Lucy. Certified divers can explore barrier reefs and sunken wrecks, sea fans and corals, and more than 50 varieties of fish. Underwater visibility is generally 80–90 ft. Not to be missed is the *Stavronikita,* a 356-ft Greek freighter that was deliberately sunk at about 135 ft; hundreds of butterfly fish hang out around its mast, and the thin rays of sunlight filtering down through the water make exploring the huge ship a wonderfully eerie experience. Virtually every part of the ship is accessible.

Dive shops provide instruction in scuba diving—a three-hour beginner's "resort" course (about $75) or a weeklong certification course (about $350), followed by a shallow dive—usually on Dottin's Reef, off Holetown. Once certified, a one-tank dive runs about $40–$45; a two-tank is $50–$55. Gear for snorkeling can be rented for a small charge from most hotels. Snorkelers can usually accompany dive trips for about $20 for a two-hour trip.

Dive Boat Safari (⊠ Barbados Hilton, St. Michael, ☎ 246/427–4350) offers full diving and instruction services. The **Dive Shop, Ltd.** (⊠ Aquatic Gap, near Grand Barbados Beach Resort, St. Michael, ☎ 246/426–9947 or 800/693–3483) is the oldest established dive shop on Barbados; it has one- and two-tank dive trips, or you can purchase a six-dive package. **Exploresub Barbados** (⊠ St. Lawrence Gap, Christ Church, ☎ 246/435–6542) is a PADI five-star training facility that offers a full range of daily dives. **Hightide** (⊠ Sandy Lane Hotel, St. James, ☎ 246/432–0931) offers one- and two-tank dives, night reef/wreck/drift dives, the full range of PADI instruction, and free transportation.

SEA EXCURSIONS

Minisubmarine voyages are enormously popular with families and those who enjoy watching fish but are unable to snorkel or dive.The 48-passenger *Atlantis III* turns the Caribbean into a giant aquarium. The 45-minute trip aboard the Canadian-built, 50-ft submarine takes you to wrecks and reefs as deep as 150 ft below the surface for a look at what even sport divers rarely see. The nighttime dives, using high-power searchlights, are spectacular. Classical music plays while an oceanography specialist informs during both day and night dives, either of which last about 90 minutes. ⊠ *Bridgetown Harbour, Spring Garden Hwy.,* ☎ 246/436–8929. ➋ $70.

Children will love the *Atlantis SEATREC* (Sea Tracking and Reef Exploration Craft), which allows passengers to "snorkel without getting wet!" The 46-passenger vessel has large viewing windows 6 ft below the surface where you can stay dry and still view the underwater marine life on a near-shore reef. ⊠ *Bridgetown Harbour, Spring Garden Hwy.,* ☎ 246/436–8929. ➋ $29.50.

Party boats depart from the Careenage or Bridgetown Harbour area. For around $55, lunchtime snorkeling and cocktail-hour sunset catamaran cruises are available on **Limbo Lady** (☎ 246/420–5418) and on **Irish Mist, Spirit of Barbados, Tiami II,** and **Tropical Dreamer** (☎ 246/427–7245). **Secret Love** (☎ 246/432–1972), a 41-ft Morgan sailboat, offers daily lunchtime or evening snorkel cruises.

The red-sailed *Jolly Roger* "pirate" party ship runs lunch-and-snorkeling cruises, with complimentary drinks, along the west coast for $52.50. **Bajan Queen**, under the same management as the *Jolly Roger,* also sails Saturday evenings (⊠ Fun Cruises, Shallow Draught Harbour, Bridgetown, ☎ 246/436–6424). A motor vessel rather than a sailboat, the 100-ft M/V *Harbour Master* has four decks, fun and games, food and drink, and an adventurous spirit. It can land on beaches to access many hotels; you can view the briny deep from its on-board 34-seat semisubmersible. It leaves Bridgetown for four- and five-hour cruises along the west coast, stopping in Holetown and at beaches along the way. ☎ 246/430–0900. ➋ $50. ☺ Tues. and Thurs.–Sat.

SURFING

The best surfing is on the east coast, and most wave riders congregate at the Soup Bowl, near Bathsheba. An annual international competition is held on Barbados every November, when the surf is at its peak.

TENNIS AND SQUASH

Most hotels have tennis courts that can be reserved day and night. Be sure to pack your whites, as appropriate dress is expected on the courts. On the west coast, public tennis courts are available for free on a first-come, first-serve basis at **Folkestone Park** (✉ Holetown, ☎ 246/422–2314). On the south coast, **National Tennis Centre** (✉ Sir Garfield Sobers Sports Complex, Wildey, St. Michael, ☎ 246/437–6010) charges $12 per hour and requires reservations.

On the south coast, **Accra Beach Hotel and Resort** (✉ Rockley, Christ Church, ☎ 246/435–8920) offers squash to its guests only. At **Club Rockley Barbados** (✉ Rockley, Christ Church, ☎ 246/435–7880) nonguests can reserve courts for $10 per hour. At the **Barbados Squash Club** (✉ Marine House, Christ Church, ☎ 246/427–7913), courts can be reserved at the rate of $9 for 45 minutes. On the west coast, the **Almond Beach Village** (✉ Speightstown, St. Peter, ☎ 246/422–4900) has a squash court for its guests and anyone staying at its sister resort, **Almond Beach Club** in St. James.

WATERSKIING

Many hotels on both the west and south coasts offer waterskiing. If your hotel doesn't, or if you're on the east coast try **Blue Reef Watersports** at the Royal Pavilion Hotel in St. James (☎ 246/422–4444), which offers waterskiing to nonguests of the hotel. Private speedboat owners troll for business along the waterfront in St. James and Christ Church, but keep in mind that with these independent operators, you water-ski at your own risk.

WINDSURFING

Barbados ranks as one of the best locations in the world for windsurfing and is part of the World Cup Windsurfing Circuit. Windsurfing is best between November and April, when the winds are strongest, and along the southeast coast of the island, where the Barbados Windsurfing Championships are held mid-January. Boards and equipment are often guest amenities at the larger hotels and can usually be rented by nonguests.

Mistral Windsurfing School is at Grand Barbados Hotel in Carlisle Bay, south of Bridgetown (☎ 246/426–4000); **Silver Rock Windsurfing Club,** is at Silver Rock Hotel, Silver Sands Beach (☎ 246/428–2866); and **Windsurf Village Barbados** (✉ Maxwell Main Rd., Christ Church, ☎ 246/428–9095) is a hotel that caters to windsurfing aficionados.

Spectator Sports

CRICKET

The island is mad for cricket, and you can sample a match at almost any time of year. Although the season is from May to late December, international test matches are usually played from January to April. The newspapers give the details of time and place. Tickets to cricket matches at Kensington Oval, Bridgetown, range from $5 to $25.

HORSE RACING

Horse racing takes place on alternate Saturdays, from January to March, and May to December, at the **Garrison Savannah** in Christ Church, about 3 mi south of Bridgetown. The annual Cockspur Cup is run in early March. ✉ Christ Church, ☎ 246/426–3980. ⬜ $5. ☉ 1:30 on race days.

POLO

If you've never experienced a polo match, here's a great opportunity. And if you're an old hand, you'll be in enthusiastic company watching a match in Barbados. Polo matches are inexpensive (about $2.50) and are played at the **Barbados Polo Club** in Holders Hill, St. James (☎ 246/427–0022), on Wednesday and Saturday from October–April. The Mercedes-Benz Crystal Trophy Tournament takes place in late February. Hang around the club room after the match. That's where the lies, the legends, and the invitations happen.

RUGBY

The rough-and-tumble game of rugby is played at the Garrison Savannah, and touring teams are always welcome to visit the clubhouse and join in the customary social activity; schedules are available from the **Barbados Rugby Club.** (✉ Garrison Savannah, Box 365, Bridgetown, ☎ 246/435–6543).

SOCCER

The "football," or soccer, season runs January–June at National Stadium. For game information contact the **Barbados Football Association** (✉ Box 1362, Belleville, St. Michael, ☎ 246/228–1707 or 246/228–0149).

Shopping

Areas and Malls

Bridgetown's **Broad Street** is the main thoroughfare and primary shopping area in the capital. Downtown merchants are well-known for their high-quality merchandise, good service, and excellent value. **Cave Shepard** and **Harrison's** are the largest department stores, with huge selections of duty-free merchandise; branches of these two stores are at the Cruise Ship Terminal, the airport, and in large hotels. **DaCosta's Mall,** also on Broad Street, has 35 shops that sell everything from Piaget to postcards; **Mall 34,** Broad Street, has 22 shops where you can buy duty-free goods, souvenirs, or a snack. At the **Cruise Ship Terminal** shopping arcade, cruise-ship passengers can buy both duty-free goods and Barbadian-made merchandise at 19 duty-free shops, 13 boutiques, and a dozen vendor carts and stalls. Shopping hours in Bridgetown are generally weekdays 8:30–4:30 and Saturday 8:30–1.

There are two **Chattel House Village** complexes: one in Holetown, on the west coast; another in St. Lawrence Gap, on the south coast. Each village is a cluster of brightly colored chattel houses, which are actually shops selling local products, rums and liqueurs, hand-designed clothing, beachwear, and souvenirs. **DaCosta's West Mall** is a small, modern shopping center in Holetown, with high-quality shops that sell duty-free goods, island wear, groceries, and services; **Sunset Crest,** also in Holetown, has a branch of the Cave Shepard department store and several smaller shops. The **Quayside Shopping Center,** in Rockley, Christ Church, has a small group of exclusive shops.

ANTIQUES

Many of the antiques you'll find in Barbados originated in Britain, although there are also wonderful local pieces from days gone by—particularly mahogany furniture, such as planters' chairs and the classic Barbadian rocking chair, as well as old prints and paintings.

Antiquaria (✉ Spring Garden Hwy., St. Michael's Row, Bridgetown, ☎ 246/426–0635), a pink Victorian house next to the Anglican cathedral, sells antique silver, brassware, mahogany furniture, and maps and engravings of Barbados. A branch is in Holetown, St. James (☎ 246/432–2647), opposite Sandpiper Inn. Both shops are open every day but Sunday. Barbadian and British antiques and fine memorabilia are the stock of **Greenwich House Antiques** (✉ Greenwich Village, Trents Hill, St. James, ☎ 246/432–1169). It's a whole plantation house full of antique Barbadian mahogany furniture, crystal, silver, china, and pictures and is open daily from 10:30 AM to 6 PM.

CLOTHES

Whether in a boutique, gift shop, or department store, shopping for dresses and resort wear handmade in Barbados from hand-printed fabrics is a distinct pleasure.

Bagshaw's (⊠ Chattel Village, Holetown, ☎ 246/432–4929) sells clothing and household accessories created from fabrics silk-screened by hand in vibrant Caribbean colors and prints. **Coconut Junction & Lazy Days** (⊠ Quayside Shopping Center, Rockley, Christ Church, ☎ 246/435–8115), actually two shops in one, have top-quality beachwear, beach accessories, and beach equipment—including surf and boogie boards.

Try **Origins—Colours of the Caribbean** (⊠ The Careenage, Bridgetown, ☎ 246/436–8522), where original hand-painted and batik clothing, imported cottons, linens and silks for day and evening, and handmade jewelry and accessories are the order of the day; the hand-painted T-shirt dresses, priced at about $100, are fabulous. At **Sunny Shoes Inc.** (⊠ Cave Shepherd, Broad St., Bridgetown, ☎ 246/431–2121) concessionaire DeCourcey Clarke will make a pair of women's strap sandals while you wait—in any color(s) you wish—for about $30.

DUTY-FREE GOODS

Duty-free values on luxury goods—such as fine bone china, crystal, cameras, porcelain, leather, stereo and video equipment, jewelry, perfume, and clothing—are mostly found in Bridgetown's Broad Street stores. Prices for many items are often 30%–50% less than those back home. In order to purchase items duty-free, visitors must show out-going travel tickets and a passport at the time of purchase—or you can have your purchases delivered free to the airport or harbor for pickup. Duty-free alcohol, tobacco products, and some electronics equipment *must* be delivered to you at the airport or harbor.

Cave Shepherd (☎ 246/431–2121), the island's largest department store, offers a wide selection of tax-free luxury goods at five locations, including Broad Street, DaCosta's West Mall in Holetown, the airport, and the Cruise Ship Terminal. **Correia's** (⊠ Prince William Henry St., Bridgetown, ☎ 246/429–5985), just off Broad Street, sells gold, diamond, and gemstone jewelry and watches—at 30% less than U.S. retail—under the watchful eye of Maurice and Marcelle Correia, certified gemologists. **De Lima's** (⊠ 20 Broad St., Bridgetown, ☎ 246/426–4644) is the centerpiece of its own small mall and stocks high-quality imports. Among the specialty shops here are several jewelry stores and a few crafts stores. **Harrison's** is a large specialty retailer with 11 locations on the island, including two large stores on Broad Street in Bridgetown. Luxury name-brand goods from the fashion corners of the world are available at duty-free prices. **Little Switzerland** is the anchor shop at DaCosta's Mall on Broad Street (☎ 246/431–0030), and has a branch at the Cruise Ship Terminal. You'll find perfume, jewelry and fine watches, cameras and audio equipment, Swarovski and Waterford crystal, and Wedgwood china. **The Royal Shop** (⊠ 32–34 Broad St., Bridgetown, ☎ 246/429–7072) carries fine watches and jewelry fashioned in Italian gold, Caribbean silver, diamonds, and other gems.

HANDICRAFTS

Typical island crafts are pottery, woven mats and place mats, hand-printed fabrics, dolls, needlecraft, shellwork, wood carvings, baskets and straw items, and artwork. These kinds of items can be found in stores year-round, at the Barbados Museum Annual Craft Fair held each December, and at major festivals (Crop Over, Oistins Fish Festival, Holetown Festival, etc.).

Best 'n the Bunch (⊠ St. Lawrence Gap, Christ Church, ☎ 246/428–2474) is in a brightly painted building at the Chattel House Village. Look here for jewelry designed and crafted by Bajan David Trottman. The **Best of Barbados** shops (⊠ Mall 34, Broad St., Bridgetown, ☎ 246/436–1416, and 13 other locations) offer the highest-quality artwork and crafts, in both "native style" and modern designs; everything is made or designed in Barbados. Local artist Jill Walker sells her cheerful watercolors and prints here. **Earthworks** (⊠ Edgehill Heights, No. 2, St. Thomas, ☎ 246/425–0223) is a family-owned and-operated pottery where you can purchase anything from a complete dinner service to a one-of-a-kind clay art piece.

At family-operated **Fairfield Pottery & Gallery** (⊠ North of Bridgetown, St. Michael, ☎ 246/424–3800), located in an old syrup boiling house, each original piece is handcrafted using local clays and individually painted; call for a tour of the works—items can be purchased on-site or in island gift shops. **Pelican Village** (⊠ Harbour Rd., between Cheapside Market and Bridgetown Harbour, ☎ 246/426–4391) offers bargains from local craftspeople. In a cluster of open-air, conical shops, you can watch as goods are crafted. Locally made handbags and leather goods, coconut-shell accessories, mahogany items, and grass rugs and mats are good buys. For artwork from Barbados and elsewhere in the Caribbean, visit the **Verandah Art Gallery** (⊠ Broad St., Bridgetown, ☎ 246/426–2605). At **Women's Self Help** (⊠ Broad St., next to Nelson's Statue, Bridgetown, ☎ 246/426–2570), you can find homemade embroidery and crochet work, shell art, baskets, children's clothes, jams and jellies, and candy.

Nightlife and the Arts

Nightlife

When the sun goes down, the musicians come out and folks go limin' in Barbados (anything from hanging out to a chat-up or jump-up). Competitions among reggae groups, steel bands, and calypso singers are major events, and tickets can be hard to come by—but give it a try. Most of the large resorts have weekend shows for visitors.

For the adventurous party-lover, a late-night (after 11) excursion to **Baxter Road**, "the street that never sleeps," is de rigueur for midnight Bajan street snacks, local rum, great gossip, and good storytelling. Enid & Livy's and Collins are just two of the long-standing favorite haunts. On weekends, the popular **Oistins Fish Fry** is a serious rival to Baxter Road; the south coast fishing village becomes an outdoor street fair, with barbecued chicken and flying fish, drinks, music, camaraderie and other festivities.

BARS

Barbados supports the rum industry in more than 1,600 "rum shops," simple bars where people (mostly men) congregate to discuss the world's ills, and in more sophisticated inns, where you'll find world-class rum drinks made with the island's renowned Mount Gay and Cockspur rums.

Bert's Bar at the Abbeville Hotel (⊠ Worthing Main Rd., Christ Church, ☎ 246/435–7924) serves the best daiquiris in town . . . any town. **The Boatyard** (⊠ Bay St., Bridgetown, ☎ 246/436–2622) has a pub atmosphere, with both DJ and live band music; it stays open until the wee hours and is popular with both locals and visitors. **Bubba's Sports Bar** (⊠ Rockley Main Rd., Christ Church, ☎ 246/435–6217) has two satellite dishes, a 10-ft video screen, and 12 additional TVs playing live sports action while you sip a Banks or enjoy a Bubba burger, or both. **Champers** (⊠ Hastings, Christ Church, ☎ 246/435–6644) is a waterfront wine bar, where folks gather for good conversation, a great view, snacks, and a selection from the extensive wine list. **Coach House** (⊠ Paynes Bay, St. James, ☎ 246/432–1163) is the only west coast nightspot with live entertainment Tuesday–Saturday nights. On

Thursday, stop in for an evening of mellow jazz at **Cobbler's Cove** (⊠ Hwy. 1, St. Peter, ☎ 246/422–2291).

The **Ship Inn** (⊠ St. Lawrence Gap, Christ Church, ☎ 246/435–6961) is a friendly pub with live band music.

DANCE CLUBS

The most popular club is still **After Dark** (⊠ St. Lawrence Gap, Christ Church, ☎ 246/435–6547), with the longest bar on the island, a jazz-club annex, and an outdoor area where reggae, soca, and calypso headliners appear live. **Harbour Lights** (⊠ Marine Villa, Bay St., Bridgetown, St. Michael, ☎ 246/436–7225), in a typical old Bajan home, has an open-air beachfront location. It claims to be the "home of the party animal" and, most any night, features dancing under the stars to live reggae and soca music. **Le Mirage** (⊠ The Careenage, Bridgetown, ☎ 246/228–8115) is an innovative disco, with a sophisticated sound system, brilliant lightshow, a slide down to the dance floor, caged dancers, and a big-screen video; open nightly, the scene ranges from alternative and Euro-disco to oldies or Caribbean party nights with live bands. **Waterfront Cafe** (⊠ The Careenage, Bridgetown, ☎ 246/427–0093) has sophisticated live jazz music in the evening, with a small dance floor for dancing. Tuesday and Wednesday, it's steel pan; Thursday, Dixieland; Friday, Latin jazz; Saturday, contemporary jazz. The location alongside the wharf adds to the atmosphere.

THEME NIGHTS

On Wednesday and Friday evenings at **Plantation Restaurant and Garden Theater,** the "Barbados Tropical Spectacular" calypso cabaret features dancing, fire-eating, limbo, steel-band music, and the award-winning sounds of Spice & Company. The cost for a Barbadian cuisine dinner, unlimited drinks, transportation, and the show is $52.50; for the show and drinks only, you pay $25. ⊠ *St. Lawrence Rd., Christ Church,* ☎ *246/428–5048. AE, MC, V.*

Arts

GALLERIES

Barbados Arts Council (⊠ Pelican Village, Harbour Rd., Bridgetown, ☎ 246/426–4385) exhibits drawings, paintings, and other art, with a new show about every two weeks. **Barbados Gallery of Art** (⊠ The Garrison, Bush Hill, St. Michael, ☎ 246/228–0149) has a permanent collection of 20th-century Barbadian and Caribbean fine art and also changing exhibitions. The gallery is closed on Sunday and Monday and there is a small entrance fee. **Queen's Park Art Gallery** (⊠ Queen's Park, Bridgetown, ☎ 246/427–2345), the island's largest gallery, is managed by the National Culture Foundation and presents monthly exhibits. The **Studio Art Gallery** (⊠ Fairchild St., Bridgetown, ☎ 246/427–5463) exhibits and sells local work (particularly that of Rachael Altman) and will frame purchases. **The Verandah Art Gallery** (⊠ Broad St., Bridgetown, ☎ 246/426–2605) has a wide selection of original paintings and carvings by Bajan artists and sculptors, along with some Haitian pieces, batiks, ceramics, jewelry, and prints for sale.

OPERA

Three weeks of opera and Shakespeare plays are presented by the **Holder's Season** each March. The open-air theater seats 600 and has won acclaim for its productions, which have included headliner Luciano Pavarotti, an 18th-century opera set in Barbados, and a commissioned work for a steel drum orchestra. ⊠ *Holder's House, Holder's Hill, St. James,* ☎ *246/432–6385.*

THEATER

Barbados has a number of talented theater and dance troupes that perform throughout the year. For details about current productions, contact **Barbados Activities Hub** (☎ 246/431–2094 or 246/431–2121).

The show *1627 and All That* has a 17th-century Barbados theme and is performed by the energetic dancers of the Pinelands Creative Workshop, dressed in period costumes and accompanied by lively steel band music. ✉ *Barbados Museum, Hwy. 7, Garrison, St. Michael,* ☎ 246/428–1627. 🖾 *$25.*

Exploring Barbados

The island is divided into 11 parishes. The terrain and vegetation change dramatically as you wander from one to the other and so do the pace and ambience. Bridgetown, the capital, is a rather modern and sophisticated city. Platinum Coast (west coast) resorts and private homes ooze luxury, whereas the small villages and vast sugar plantations found throughout central Barbados mark the island's history. The heavy surf of the Atlantic Ocean has designed the cliffs of the remote east coast, and the northeast is called Scotland, because that's what its hilly landscape resembles. And along the lively south coast, there's an energy that continues day and night.

The Barbados National Trust (✉ Wildey House, Wildey, St. Michael, ☎ 246/426–2421), has designed the **Heritage Passport,** a 50% discounted admission to Barbados's most popular attractions and historic sites. A Full Passport includes 16 sites and costs $35; a Mini-Passport includes five sites and costs $18. Children under 12 are admitted free if accompanied by a Passport holder (maximum two children per passport). Passports can be purchased at hotels, Trust headquarters, or at the sites.

❶ Bridgetown

This bustling city is a major duty-free port. The principal thoroughfare is Broad Street, which leads west from Trafalgar Square. The busy capital is complete with rush hours and traffic congestion. Sightseeing should take only a half-day or so, and the shopping area is compact.

SIGHTS TO SEE

Numbers in the margin correspond to points of interest on the Bridgetown map.

❾ **Barbados Museum.** This intriguing museum, in the former Military Prison, has artifacts from Arawak days (around 400 BC) and mementos of military history and everyday life in the 19th century. You'll see cane-harvesting tools, wedding dresses, ancient (and frightening) dentistry instruments, and slave sale accounts kept in a spidery copperplate handwriting. Wildlife and natural history exhibits, a gift shop, and a good café are also here. ✉ *Hwy. 7, Garrison Savannah,* ☎ 246/427–0201. 🖾 *$5.* ☉ *Mon.–Sat. 9–5, Sun. 2–6.*

❷ **Barbados Synagogue.** This synagogue represents the oldest Jewish congregation in the western hemisphere; it began with Jews who left Brazil in the early 1620s and introduced sugarcane to Barbados. The adjoining Jewish Cemetery has tombstones dating back to the 1630s. The original house of worship, built in 1654, was destroyed in a hurricane in 1831. The building was rebuilt in 1833 and restored by the Barbados National Trust in 1992. Services are again being held, and the building is open to the public for viewing. ✉ *Synagogue La.,* ☎ 246/426–5792. 🖾 *Donation requested.* ☉ *Weekdays 9–4.*

❽ **The Careenage.** The finger of sea that made early Bridgetown a natural harbor and gathering place is where working schooners were ca-

Barbados Museum, **9**

Barbados Synagogue, **2**

The Careenage, **8**

Harry Bayley Observatory, **5**

Parliament Buildings, **6**

Queen's Park, **3**

St. Michael's Cathedral, **4**

Trafalgar Square, **7**

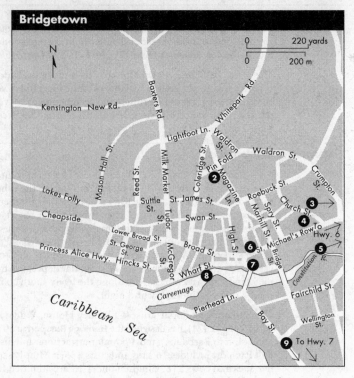

Bridgetown

reened (turned on their sides) to be scraped of barnacles and repainted. Today the Careenage serves mainly as a marina for pleasure yachts and excursion boats. The two bridges over the Careenage are the Chamberlain Bridge and the Charles O'Neal Bridge.

⑤ Harry Bayley Observatory. Built in 1963, this is the headquarters of the Barbados Astronomical Society. The observatory, equipped with a 14-inch reflector telescope, is rather unique in the Caribbean. ⊠ *Off Hwy. 6, Clapham,* ☎ *246/426–1317 or 246/422–2394.* ⚑ *$4.* ☼ *Fri. 8:30 AM–11:30 PM.*

⑥ Parliament Buildings. Built around 1870, these buildings, adjacent to Trafalgar Square, house the third-oldest Parliament of the British Commonwealth. A series of stained-glass windows depicting British monarchs from James I to Queen Victoria adorn these Victorian government buildings. Like so many smaller buildings in Bridgetown, they stand beside a growing number of modern offices.

③ Queen's Park. Northeast of Bridgetown, Queen's Park has one of the largest trees in Barbados, an immense baobab more than 10 centuries old. The historic Queen's Park House, former home of the commander of the British troops, has been converted into a theater, with an exhibition room on the lower floor and a restaurant. ⊠ *Constitution Rd., St. Michael,* ⚑ *Free.* ☼ *Daily 9–5.*

④ St. Michael's Cathedral. Although no one has proved it conclusively, George Washington, on his only visit outside the United States, is said to have worshiped at St. Michael's Cathedral. The original structure was nearly a century old when Washington visited in 1751. Destroyed twice by hurricanes, it was rebuilt in 1784 and again in 1831. ⊠ *Spry St., east of Trafalgar Sq.*

❼ **Trafalgar Square.** In the center of town, across from the Parliament Buildings and the Careenage, its monument to Lord Horatio Nelson predates Nelson's Column in London's Trafalgar Square by 27 years. (Nelson was based here as a 19-year-old lieutenant in 1777.) Also here are a war memorial, and a fountain that commemorates the advent of running water in Barbados in 1865.

West Coast and the North

Holetown is the center of the Gold Coast resort area and the place where Captain John Powell landed in 1625 and claimed the island in the name of King James. The port city of Speightstown is more characteristically West Indian with its 19th-century architecture, quaint shops, and restaurants. Many of the downtown buildings have been restored or are undergoing restoration.

The northern reaches of the island, St. Peter and St. Lucy parishes, provide a range of terrain. Between the tiny fishing towns along the northwestern coast and the sweeping views out to the Atlantic Ocean on the northeastern coast are forest and farm, moor and mountain. Most guides include this loop on a daylong island tour—it's a beautiful drive.

Numbers in the margin correspond to points of interest on the Barbados map.

SIGHTS TO SEE

🐚 ㉖ 🐚 **Animal Flower Cave.** Small sea anemones, or sea worms, resemble jewel-like flowers when they open their tiny tentacles. They live in small pools—some large enough to swim in—in a cave at the very northern tip of Barbados. The view from inside the cavern as waves break just outside is magnificent. ✉ *North Point, St. Lucy,* ☎ *246/439–8797.* 🎫 *$1.50.* ⊙ *Daily 9–4.*

🐚 ㉔ **Barbados Wildlife Reserve.** The reserve is home to herons, land turtles, a kangaroo, screeching peacocks, innumerable green monkeys, geese, brilliantly colored parrots, and a friendly otter. The fauna are not in cages, so step carefully and keep your hands to yourself. The preserve has been much improved in recent years with the addition of a giant walk-in aviary and natural-history exhibits. ✉ *Farley Hill, St. Peter,* ☎ *246/422–8826.* 🎫 *$10.* ⊙ *Daily 10–5.*

㉓ **Farley Hill.** At this national park in northern St. Peter, across the road from the Barbados Wildlife Reserve, the imposing ruins of a plantation great house are surrounded by gardens, lawns, an avenue of towering royal palms, and gigantic mahogany, whitewood, and casuarina trees. Partially rebuilt for the filming of *Island in the Sun,* the classic 1957 film starring Harry Belafonte and Dorothy Dandridge, the structure was later destroyed by fire. Behind the estate, there's a sweeping view of the part of Barbados called Scotland for its rugged landscape. ✉ *St. Peter.* 🎫 *$1.50 per car; walkers free.* ⊙ *Daily 8:30–6.*

🐚 ㉘ **Folkestone Marine Park & Visitor Centre.** At this park, north of Holetown, there's a lot for the whole family to enjoy—both on land and offshore. A museum illuminates some of the island's marine life; and for some firsthand viewing, there's an underwater snorkeling trail around Dottin's Reef (glass-bottom boats are available for nonswimmers). A dredge barge sunk in shallow water is home to myriad fish, and it and the reef are popular with scuba divers. Also keep your eyes out for huge sea fans, soft coral, and the occasional giant turtle. ✉ *Holetown, St. James,* ☎ *246/422–2314.* 🎫 *60¢.* ⊙ *Weekdays 9–5.*

㉜ **Mount Gay Rum Visitors Centre.** Take a 45-minute tour to learn the colorful story behind the world's oldest rum and about the rum-making process. The tour concludes with a tasting, and rum can be purchased at the gift shop. You can stay on for lunch if you wish. The center is just five minutes north of the port and downtown Bridgetown. ✉ *Spring Garden Hwy.,* ☎ *246/425–8757.* ☜ *$6.* ☉ *Weekdays 9–3:45.*

㉕   St. Nicholas Abbey. This property was named for a former owner, a prominent farmer with no religious connection to St. Nicholas. It is the oldest (circa 1650) great house in Barbados and is worth visiting for its stone-and-wood architecture—one of only three original Jacobean-style houses still standing in the Western Hemisphere. It has Dutch gables, finials of coral stone, and an herb garden in a medieval design. Fascinating home movies by the present owner's father record Bajan town and plantation life in the 1930s. ✉ *Near Cherry Tree Hill, St. Lucy,* ☎ *246/422–8725.* ☜ *$2.50.* ☉ *Weekdays 10–3:30.*

㉗   Six Men's Bay. On the northwest coast, on Highway 1 beyond Speightstown, a winding road takes you through tiny fishing and boatbuilding villages in what is truly picture-postcard Barbados—a far cry from the tourist areas.

East Coast and Central Barbados

The Atlantic Ocean crashes dramatically against the east coast of Barbados, where, over eons, the waves have eroded the shoreline into caves, arches, cliffs, and sea rocks that look like giant mushrooms. Narrow roads weave among the ridges, and small villages cling to hillsides that slide into the sea. Locals come to the coastal areas of Bathsheba and Cattlewash to spend weekends and holidays. The geological and natural history of central Barbados is represented by fascinating caves, a mile-long gully, and tropical vegetation covering the hilly terrain.

SIGHTS TO SEE

★ **㉑   Andromeda Gardens.** A fascinating collection of unusual and beautiful plant specimens from around the world are cultivated in 6 acres of gardens nestled among streams, ponds, and rocky outcroppings overlooking the sea above the Bathsheba coastline. The gardens were created in 1954 with flowering plants collected by the late horticulturist Iris Bannochie. They are now administered by the Barbados National Trust. The Hibiscus Café serves snacks and drinks, and there's a Best of Barbados gift shop on the property. ✉ *Bathsheba, St. Joseph,* ☎ *246/433–9384.* ☜ *$5.* ☉ *Daily 9–5.*

㉒   Barclays Park. Just north of Bathsheba, this park was given to the people of Barbados by Barclays Bank. It offers a gorgeous view of the ocean, picnic facilities, and a popular bar-restaurant. At the nearby **Chalky Mount Potteries,** potters make and sell their wares.

㉔   Codrington Theological College. The coral-stone buildings and serene grounds of Codrington College, an Anglican seminary founded in 1745, stand on a cliff overlooking Consett Bay. You're welcome to tour the buildings and grounds, including a well-laid-out nature trail. Keep in mind, though, that this is a theological college; beachwear isn't appropriate. ✉ *St. John,* ☎ *246/433–1274.* ☜ *$2.50.* ☉ *Daily 10–4.*

⑫   Emancipation Memorial. This larger-than-life statue of a slave—with raised hands, evoking both contempt and victory, and broken chains hanging from each wrist—is commonly referred to as the "Bussa Statue." Bussa was the man who, in the early part of the 19th century, led the first slave rebellion in Barbados. The statue's location at the St. Barnabas Roundabout (intersection of the ABC Highway and Highway 5, St. Michael), just outside Bridgetown, overlooks a broad expanse of cane field, making the monument all the more poignant.

㉙   Flower Forest. Treat yourself to a meander through 8 acres of fragrant flowering bushes, canna and ginger lilies, puffball trees, and more than a hundred other species of flora in a tranquil setting. There's also a beautiful view of Mt. Hillaby from here. ⊠ *Richmond Plantation, Hwy. 2, St. Joseph,* ☎ *246/433–8152.* ☜ *$6.* ☼ *Daily 9–5.*

⑭ Francia Plantation House. Owned and occupied by descendants of the original owner, the house was built in 1913 in a style that blends European and Caribbean influences. You can tour the house and gardens. ⊠ *St. George,* ☎ *246/429–0474.* ☜ *$1.50.* ☼ *Weekdays 10–4.*

⑮ Gun Hill Signal Station. The view from Gun Hill is so pretty it seems almost unreal. Shades of green and gold cover the fields all the way to the horizon, the picturesque gun tower is surrounded by brilliant flowers, and the white limestone lion behind the garrison is a famous landmark. Military invalids were once sent here to convalesce. ⊠ *St. George,* ☎ *246/429–1358.* ☜ *$4.* ☼ *Mon.–Sat. 9–5.*

☙ **㉛ Harrison's Cave.** This pale-gold limestone cavern, complete with stalactites, stalagmites, subterranean streams, and a 40-ft waterfall, is a rare find in the Caribbean, and is one of Barbados's most popular attractions. The one-hour tours are made by electric tram and fill up fast. Reserve a spot ahead of time (hard hats are provided, but all that may fall on you is a little dripping water). ⊠ *Hwy. 2, St. Thomas,* ☎ *246/ 438–6640.* ☜ *$7.50.* ☼ *Daily 9–6; last tour at 4.*

⑲ Ragged Point Lighthouse. Appropriately named, this is where the sun first shines on Barbados and its dramatic Atlantic seascape. You can see the entire east coast from the lighthouse—a particularly fascinating view on a stormy day.

㉚ Welchman Hall Gully. Part of the National Trust in St. Thomas parish, here's another chance to commune with nature in peace and quiet. Acres of labeled flowers and trees stretch along in a mile-long natural gully, with the occasional green monkey showing itself. ⊠ *St. Thomas,* ☎ *246/438–6671.* ☜ *$5.* ☼ *Daily 9–5.*

South Coast and Southeast Barbados

In Christ Church, on the heavily traveled south coast, you'll find the St. Lawrence Gap, condos, high-rise hotels, beach parks, many places to eat, drink, and shop, and the traffic (including public transportation) that serves them. This area is much more built up and congested than St. James Parish, on the west coast.

In contrast, the broad, flat terrain in the southeast is comprised of acre upon acre of sugarcane fields, interrupted only by an occasional oil well and a few tiny villages hugging crossroads. Along the byways are colorful chattel houses, the property of tenant farmers. Historically, these typically Barbadian, ever-expandable houses were built to be dismantled and moved as required.

SIGHTS TO SEE

⑩ George Washington House. In 1751, long before the American Revolution, George Washington brought his brother Lawrence to Barbados to recover from tuberculosis. At this house atop Bush Hill, in the historic Garrison area south of Bridgetown, the brothers spent seven weeks, during which time poor George contracted smallpox. The gray, two-story T-shaped house with adjacent watermill is now owned by Barbados Light & Power Co. and has been converted to offices.

⑬ Oistins. Boats in this major fishing village leave before dawn each morning and return to the waterfront fish market with their catches. The annual Oistins Fish Festival, held at the end of March, is a weekend of celebration, arts and crafts, boat racing, dancing, and singing.

⑰ **Rum Factory and Heritage Park.** A long entrance through the cane fields brings you to the first rum distillery to be built in Barbados in this century. Opened in late 1996 on a 350-year-old molasses and sugar plantation, the spotless, high-tech distillery produces ESA Field white rum and its premium Alleyne Arthur varieties. Adjacent is the 7-acre Heritage Park, which showcases Bajan skills and talents in its Art Foundry and Cane Pit Amphitheatre, along with an array of shops and carts filled exclusively with local products, crafts, and foods. ⊠ *Foursquare Plantation, St. Philip,* ☎ *246/423–6669.* ☞ *$12.* ☼ *Sun.–Thurs. 9–5, Fri.–Sat. 9–9.*

⑱ **Sam Lord's Castle.** The Regency house built by the buccaneer Sam Lord is considered by many to be the finest mansion in Barbados. Built in 1820 and now part of a resort (☞ Lodging, *above*), the opulent estate features double verandas on all sides and magnificent plaster ceilings created by Charles Rutter, who crafted the ceilings in England's Windsor Castle. Most of the rooms are furnished with fine mahogany furniture and gilt mirrors. Sam Lord is reputed to have acquired these from passing ships that he lured onto treacherous reefs by hanging lanterns in palm trees to simulate harbor lights. ⊠ *Long Bay, St. Philip,* ☎ *246/423–7350.* ☞ *$5; hotel guests free.* ☼ *Daily 10–4.*

⑯ **Sunbury Plantation House & Museum.** Lovingly rebuilt after a 1995 fire destroyed everything but the thick flint-and-stone walls of this 300-year-old plantation house, Sunbury is once again an elegant representation of life on a Barbadian sugar estate in the 18th and 19th centuries. Period furniture has been donated to lend an air of authenticity. Come for lunch (☞ Dining, *above*). ⊠ *St. Philip,* ☎ *246/423–6270.* ☞ *$5 tour only; $12.50 with buffet lunch.* ☼ *Daily 10–5.*

⑪ **Tyrol Cot Heritage Village.** This interesting coral-stone cottage just south of Bridgetown was constructed in 1854 and has been preserved as an example of period architecture. In 1929, it became home to Sir Grantley Adams, the first premier of Barbados and the only prime minister of the short-lived West Indies Federation. Part of the National Trust, the cottage is now filled with antiques and memorabilia belonging to Sir Grantley and Lady Adams and is the centerpiece of an outdoor "living" museum of colorful chattel houses, each with a traditional artisan or craftsman at work inside. The crafts are for sale, and refreshments are available at the "rum shop." ⊠ *Rte. 2, St. Michael,* ☎ *246/424–2074 or 246/436–9033.* ☞ *$5.* ☼ *Mon.–Fri. 9–5.*

Barbados A to Z

Arriving and Departing

BY AIRPLANE

American Airlines (246/428–4170) and **BWIA** (☎ 246/426–2111) both have nonstop flights from New York to Grantley Adams International Airport and direct flights from Miami. American Eagle, American's regional partner, serves Barbados from other U.S. cities with connecting flights through San Juan. **Air Jamaica** (☎ 246/420–1956 or 800/523–5585) has daily nonstop service from New York. From Canada, **Air Canada** (☎ 246/428–5077) flies nonstop from Toronto. From London, **British Airways** (☎ 246/436–6413 or 800/247–9297) has nonstop service and BWIA connects through Trinidad.

Inter-island service is scheduled on **LIAT** (☎ 246/495–1187), **Air Martinique** (☎ 246/431–0540), and **BWIA** (☎ 246/426–2111); **Air St. Vincent/Air Mustique** (☎ 246/428–1638) links Barbados with St. Vincent and the Grenadines.

From the Airport: Note that **Airport taxis** aren't metered. A large sign at the airport announces the fixed rate to each hotel or parish, stated in both Barbados and U.S. dollars (about $28 to Speightstown, $20 to west coast hotels, $10–$13 to south coast ones). The Adams-Barrow-Cummins (ABC) Highway bypasses Bridgetown, which saves time getting to the west coast.

BY BOAT

Barbados is a popular cruise port—half the annual visitors to the island are cruise passengers. Bridgetown's Deep Water Harbour is on the northwest side of Carlisle Bay and up to eight cruise ships can dock at one time at the snazzy **Cruise Ship Terminal.** Passengers can browse in 19 duty-free shops and 13 local retail stores in the terminal's attractive shopping arcade; a dozen vendors display their handicrafts in colorful reproductions of chattel houses just outside the building. Downtown Bridgetown is a ½-mi walk from the pier; a taxi costs about $3 each way.

Electricity

Electric current on Barbados is 110 volts/50 cycles, U.S. standard. For travelers from the UK or other countries that operate on 220-volt current, hotels have adapters/transformers for guest use.

Emergencies

Ambulance: ☎ 115. **Fire:** ☎ 113. **Hospitals:** Bayview Hospital (⊠ St. Paul's Ave., Bayville, St. Michael, ☎ 246/436–5446). Queen Elizabeth Hospital (⊠ Martindales Rd., St. Michael, ☎ 246/436–6450). **Police:** ☎ 112. **Scuba-diving accidents:** Divers' Alert Network (DAN) (☎ 246/684–8111 or 246/684–2948). 24-hour decompression chamber (⊠ Coast Guard Defence Force, St. Ann's Fort, Garrison, St. Michael, ☎ 246/436–6185).

Festivals and Seasonal Events

In mid-January, the **Barbados "Paint it Jazz" Festival** is one of the Caribbean's premier jazz events, a weekend jammed with performances by international artists, jazz legends, and local talent. In February, the week-long **Holetown Festival** is held at the fairgrounds in Holetown to commemorate the date in 1627 when the first European settlers arrived in Barbados; food, hymns, carnival rides, the Royal Barbados Police Force band and mounted troops add to the enjoyment. **Holder's Opera Season** is a three-week run of opera, music, and theater performances at the end of March.

Around the Easter weekend in April, **Oistins Fish Festival** celebrates the rich history of this south coast fishing village; events include fishing, boat racing, fish-boning competitions, food, arts and crafts, dancing, and road racing. Dubbed the "World's Greatest Street Party," **De Congaline Carnival** is a festive celebration of music, dance, and local arts and crafts; held at the end of April, the highlight is the Caribbean's longest conga line! **Gospelfest** is held the last weekend in May and features performances by Gospel headliners from around the world. Dating back to the 19th century, the **Crop Over Festival** celebrates the end of the sugar cane harvest with competitions, music and dancing, Bajan food, and arts and crafts; a six-week event beginning at the end of June, the grand finale is a huge carnival parade on **Kadooment Day,** August 2 (the first Monday in August) is the culmination of Crop Over. It is a national holiday and the biggest party day of the year. Visitors are welcome to participate.

Getting Around

BUSES

Buses and maxitaxis provide a great opportunity to experience local color, and your fellow passengers will be eager to share their knowledge. Blue buses with a yellow stripe are public, yellow buses with a blue stripe are private, and private maxitaxis may be any color. ZR vans, white with a burgundy stripe, are also private. All travel constantly along Highway 1 (St. James Road) and Highway 7 (South Coast Main Road) and are inexpensive (a little less than $1 for any destination; exact change required on public buses, appreciated on private ones). They pass along main roads about every 20 minutes and are usually packed. Bus stops are marked by small signs on roadside poles that say TO CITY or OUT OF CITY, meaning the direction relative to Bridgetown. Flag down the bus with your hand, even if you're standing at the stop; they don't always stop automatically.

CAR RENTALS

It's a pleasure to explore Barbados by car. Take time to study a map—although small signs tacked to trees and poles at intersections in the island's interior point the way to most attractions. The remote roads are in good repair, yet few are well lighted at night—and night falls quickly at about 6 PM year-round. Even in full daylight, the tall sugarcane fields lining the road in interior sections can make visibility difficult. Use caution: Pedestrians often walk in the roads. And remember: Drive on the left, and be especially careful negotiating roundabouts (traffic circles).

To rent a car you must have an international driver's license or Barbados driving permit, obtainable at the airport, police stations, and major car-rental firms for $5 with a valid driver's license. Nearly 30 offices rent cars or minimokes (open-air vehicles) for $75–$85 a day (or about $225 a week), usually with a three- or four-day minimum; rental cars with air-conditioning are $85–$90 a day, or approximately $275–$285 a week. The fee generally includes insurance and a local driver's license. All rental companies provide pickup and delivery service, offer unlimited mileage, and accept major credit cards. Gas costs nearly $4 an Imperial gallon (approximately 5 quarts). The speed limit, in keeping with the pace of life, is 30 mph in the country, 20 mph in town. And in and around Bridgetown, Bajans actually have a rush hour: 7:30–8:30 AM and 4:30–5:30 PM.

Among the agencies are **Corbins Car Rentals** (✉ St. Michael), ☎ 246/427–0531 or 246/426–8336), **Courtesy Rent-A-Car** (✉ Grantley Adams International Airport, ☎ 246/431–4160), **Dear's Garage** (✉ Christ Church, ☎ 246/429–9277 or 246/427–7853), **National Car Rentals** (✉ Bush Hall, St. Michael, ☎ 246/426–0603), **P&S Car Rentals** (✉ St. Michael, ☎ 246/424–2052), **Sunny Isle Motors** (✉ Worthing, ☎ 246/435–7979), and **Sunset Crest Rentals** (✉ St. James, ☎ 246/432–1482).

TAXIS

Taxis aren't metered but operate according to fixed rates set by the government. They carry up to five passengers, and the fare may be shared. For short trips, the rate per mile (or part thereof) should not exceed $1.50. Taxi drivers are courteous and knowledgeable, and most will narrate a tour at a fixed hourly rate of $17.50 for up to three people. Be sure to settle the rate before you start off, and agree on whether it's in U.S. or Barbados dollars.

Guided Tours

Barbados has a lot to see. A half- or full-day bus or taxi tour is a good way to get your bearings and can be arranged by your hotel. The price varies according to the number of attractions included; an average full-day tour (five–six hours) costs about $30–$50 per person and generally includes lunch and admissions.

HELICOPTER

Bajan Helicopters (⊠ Bridgetown Heliport, ☎ 246/431–0069) offers an eagle's-eye view of Barbados. Price per person ranges from $65 for a 20- to 25-minute "Discover Barbados" flightseeing tour to $115 for a 30- to 35-minute full "Island Tour" that makes a full circuit of the coastline.

ORIENTATION

Sally Shearn operates **VIP Tour Services** (⊠ Hillcrest Villa, Upton, St. Michael, ☎ 246/429–4617) and personalizes tours to suit your taste. Bajan-born Ms. Shearn knows her island well and provides a choice of tours (coastal, inland, cultural, naturalist, architectural, or customized), with refreshment stops. She picks up her clients in an air-conditioned Mercedes-Benz and charges $40 per hour for four people, with a minimum of four hours.

L. E. Williams Tour Co. (☎ 246/427–1043) offers a 6½-hour, 80-mi island tour for about $50 per person. A bus picks you up between 8:30 and 9:30 AM and takes you through Bridgetown, the St. James beach area, past the Animal Flower Cave, Farley Hill, Cherry Tree Hill, Morgan Lewis Mill, the east coast, St. John's Church, Sam Lord's Castle, and Oistin's fishing village, and to the parish of St. Michael, with drinks along the way and a West Indian lunch at the Atlantis Hotel in Bathsheba.

SPECIAL-INTEREST

Every Wednesday afternoon from mid-January through mid-April, the **Barbados National Trust** (☎ 246/426–2421) offers a bus tour of historical great houses and modern private homes open for public viewing, including Tyrol Cot Heritage Village (St. Michael); St. Nicholas Abbey (St. Peter), Francia Plantation, Drax Hall, and Brighton Great House (St. George), Villa Nova (St. John), Sam Lord's Castle and Sunbury Plantation House (St. Philip). The cost is $18 per person, which includes transportation to and from your hotel. (If you wish to visit the homes on your own, they're open on those Wednesday afternoons from 2:30–5:30; entrance fees at each range from $1.25–$5.)

Highland Outdoor Tours (⊠ Canefield, St. Thomas, ☎ 246/438–8069) specializes in special-interest adventure trips to the island's seldom-seen natural wonders. Visitors have the option of half-day or full-day horseback treks (including a bareback ride in the surf), scenic hiking expeditions, and tractor-drawn jitney rides through some of Barbados's great plantations. Prices range from $25 per person for a short, two-hour plantation tour by open jitney to $100 per person for the 7-mi Horseback Trek. A 5-mi Scenic Safari Hike is $70. All tours include refreshments and transportation to and from your hotel.

Take a rum distillery tour to learn about rum-making on the island where rum was born. From the **Malibu Visitor Centre**, you can take a full tour of their West Indies distillery and a visit to the sampling room; other options include lunch and a full day of water sports and beach activities. ⊠ *Brighton, Black Rock, St. Michael,* ☎ *246/425–9393.* ☞ *$5; $22.50 with lunch; $37.50 day pass.* ☉ *Weekdays 9–5.*

On the 45-minute tour at the **Mount Gay Rum Visitors Centre,** learn the colorful story behind the world's oldest rum. The tour concludes with a tasting, and rum can be purchased at the gift shop. ⊠ *Spring Garden Hwy, Bridgetown.,* ☎ *246/425–8757.* ☞ *$5.* ☉ *Weekdays 9–4.*

Language
English is the official language and is spoken by everyone, everywhere. There is a Bajan dialect, however, which is based on African rhythms

but has an almost Irish or Scottish lilt. You'll notice the "R" sound is much more pronounced, for example, than in British English. Further, the letter "Z" is referred to as "Zed," as it is in Great Britain and most of Canada. As for the African influence, you'll notice it in names for typically Bajan foods, such as cou-cou and buljol.

Money Matters

CURRENCY

The **Barbados dollar** (BD$1) is tied to the U.S. dollar at the rate of BD$1.98 to $1. Either currency, major credit cards, and travelers checks are accepted island-wide. Be sure you know which currency is being quoted when making a purchase. Prices quoted throughout this chapter are in U.S. dollars unless otherwise noted.

SERVICE CHARGES, TAXES, AND TIPPING

A 7½% government tax is added to all hotel bills. A 10% service charge is usually added to hotel bills and restaurant checks in lieu of tipping (tip beyond the charge to recognize extraordinary service). If no service charge is added, tip waiters 10%-15% and maids $1 per room per day. Bellhops and airport porters should be tipped $1 per bag. Taxi drivers expect a 10% tip.

A 15% VAT is imposed on restaurant meals, some food items bought at the supermarket, admissions to attractions, and merchandise sales (other than duty-free); prices are often tax-inclusive; if not, the VAT will be added to your bill. At the airport you must pay a departure tax of $12.50 in either currency before leaving Barbados; there is no charge for children 12 and under.

Opening and Closing Times

Bridgetown **offices** and **stores** are open weekdays 8:30–4:30, Saturday 8:30–1. Out-of-town locations may stay open later. Some supermarkets are open daily 8–6 or later. **Banks** are open Monday–Thursday 8–3, Friday 8–5; at the airport, the Barbados National Bank is open from 8 AM until the last plane leaves or arrives, seven days a week (including holidays).

HOLIDAYS

New Year's Day, Errol Barrow Day (Jan. 21), Good Friday (Apr. 2), Easter Monday (Apr. 5), Labour Day (May 1), Whit Monday (May 24), Kadooment Day (Aug. 2), United Nations Day (Oct. 7), Independence Day (Nov. 30), Bank Holiday (Dec. 1), Christmas, and Boxing Day (Dec. 26).

Passports

U.S. and Canadian citizens can enter for up to three months with proof of citizenship and a return or ongoing ticket. Acceptable proof is a valid passport or an original birth certificate and a government authorized photo ID; a voter registration card or baptismal certificate is not acceptable. British citizens need a valid passport.

Precautions

Crime is not a major problem, but take normal precautions. Don't tempt people by leaving valuables unattended on the beach or in plain sight in your room, and don't pick up hitchhikers. If you're driving a rental car and looking for parking in Bridgetown, be wary of friendly Bajans who offer to "find you a park" for a fee; it may be an illegal parking spot.

Insects aren't much of a problem, but if you plan to hike or spend time on secluded beaches in late afternoon, it's wise to use insect repellent. Beware of the little green apples that fall from the large branches of the manchineel tree—they may look tempting, but they are poisonous to eat and toxic to the touch. Even taking shelter under the tree when it rains can give you blisters. Most manchineels are identified with signs. If you do come in contact with one, immediately wash yourself off with water, go to the nearest hotel, and have someone there phone for a physician. The water on the island is plentiful and pure. It is naturally filtered through 1,000 ft of pervious coral and safe to drink from the tap.

Telephones and Mail

The area code for Barbados is 246. Except for emergency numbers (☞ Emergencies, *above*) all phone numbers have seven digits and begin with 22, 23, 42, or 43. Direct-dialing to the U.S., Canada, and the UK is efficient and relatively inexpensive, but always check with your hotel to see if they add a surcharge.To charge international calls to a major credit card at direct-dialing rates, dial ☎ 800/877−8000.

An airmail letter from Barbados to the United States or Canada costs BD90¢ per half ounce; an airmail postcard costs BD65¢. Letters to the United Kingdom are BD$1.10; postcards are BD70¢. The main post office, in Cheapside, Bridgetown, is open weekdays 7:30−5; the Sherbourne Conference Center branch is open weekdays 8:15−4:30; branches in each parish are open weekdays 8−3:15. When sending mail to Barbados, be sure to include the parish name in the address.

Visitor Information

For information before you go, contact the **Barbados Tourism Authority.** In the United States: ⊠ 800 2nd Ave., 2nd floor, New York, NY 10017, ☎ 212/986−6516 or 800/221−9831, ☒ 212/573−9850; ⊠ 150 Alhambra Circle, Suite 1270, Coral Gables, FL 33134 , ☎ 305/442−7471, ☒ 305/567−2844; ⊠ 2442 Hinge St., Troy, MI 48083, ☎ 810/740−7835, ☒ 810/740−9434; ⊠ 3440 Wilshire Blvd., Suite 1215, Los Angeles, CA 90010, ☎ 213/380−2198, ☒ 213/384−2763. In Canada: ⊠ 105 Adelaide St., Suite 1010, Toronto, Ontario M5H−1P9, ☎ 416/214−9880, ☒ 416/214−9882. In the United Kingdom: ⊠ 263 Tottenham Court Rd., London W1P OLA, ☎ 0171/636−9448, ☒ 0171/637−1496. For information on the **Internet,** the official Web site of the Barbados Tourism Authority is www.barbados.org.

In Barbados, the **Barbados Tourism Authority** is on Harbour Road in Bridgetown (☎ 246/427−2623, ☒ 246/426−4080). Hours are 8:30−4:30 weekdays. Information booths, staffed by Tourism Authority representatives, are located at Grantley Adams International Airport (☎ 246/428−5570, ☒ 246/428−0937) and at Bridgetown's Cruise Ship Terminal (☎ 246/426−1718).

6 Bonaire

Updated by
Jordan Simon

T*he tranquil, otherworldly landscape resembles a Dalí canvas, its colors so primary
they seem artificial. Joshua trees pierce an
azure sky like cathedral spires. On one side, a salt
pond, the delicate hue of Cristal Rosé champagne,
shimmers. On the other, psychedelically green parrotfish glide through ocean shallows practically to
the sand, where tangles of tortured driftwood,
bleached stark white, rise like the earth's bones.
Just a hint of rose signals the arrival of dusk; a flock
of pink flamingos darkens the sky like an eclipse,
blends into the deepening blush of the setting sun,
and then disappears.*

For years, Bonaire was regarded simply as a diving mecca, with most
visitors practically oblivious to the equally rich beauty on land. But
the government embarked on an ambitious program to expand its eco-
tourism base without succumbing to overdevelopment. Now there are
facilities and tours geared toward snorkelers, hikers, bikers, kayakers.
There are also new luxury resorts that offer pampering, fine dining,
and solitude—solitude that will be preserved with a moratorium on
further building until at least 2000.

Bonaire, on land, is a stark desert island, perfect for those who are turned
off by the overcommercialized high life of the other Antillean islands.
There's an array of exotic wildlife—from fowl to flowers—that will
keep you awestruck for days. It's the kind of place where you'll want
to rent a four-wheel-drive vehicle and go off in search of flamingos,
iguanas, or the yellow-winged parrot named the Bonairian lora.

Divers still come to Bonaire as pilgrims to a holy land. Here, diving is
learned and perfected. Even Bonaire license plates tout the island as
"A Diver's Paradise." But the residents have worked hard to preserve

this paradise (any diver with a reckless streak should go elsewhere). Way back in 1979—when green was just becoming a color to be dealt with—the government made all the waters surrounding Bonaire part of a marine park. The underwater park includes, roughly, the entire coastline—from the high-water tidemark to a depth of 200 ft—all of it protected by such strict regulations as mandatory warm-up dives with a local instructor and bans on spearfishing and coral collecting.

With just over 14,000 inhabitants, this little (112-square-mi) island has the feeling of a small community with a gentle pace. As the locals say, folks simply come here to dive, eat, dive, sleep, and dive. But, they also come to kayak, mountain bike, hike, snorkel, and simply soak in the sunshine and natural beauty of the island.

Lodging

Hotels on Bonaire, with the exception of Harbour Village and Plaza Resort Bonaire, cater primarily to avid divers who spend their days underwater and come up for air only for evening festivities. Hence, hotel facilities tend to be modest, with clean but unadorned rooms, small swimming pools, a restaurant, and perhaps a bar. Services are often limited to laundry, baby-sitting, car rental, and travel services; unless noted below, room service is not typically available. Groomed sandy beaches are not a requisite for a hotel, but an efficient dive shop is. Many resort accommodations have fully equipped kitchens and in-room safes. Although the larger hotels offer a variety of meal plans, most are on the EP; and, as a rule, hotel restaurants are more expensive than restaurants in town. Many properties offer all-inclusive packages for an extra per-day charge.

Rental apartments are available through **Black Durgon Inn Properties** (☎ 599/7–5736, 800/526–2370 in the U.S.; FAX 599/6–8846), **Bonaire Sunset Villas** (☎ 800/223–9815, FAX 599/7–8118), **Club Laman Caribe** (☎ 599/7–6840, FAX 599/7–7741), **Sunset Oceanfront Apartments** (☎ 800/223–9815, FAX 599/7–8865), and **T.L.C. Inns of Bonaire** (☎ 599/7–5516, 800/748–8733 in the U.S.; FAX 599/7–5517).

CATEGORY	COST*
$$$$	over $225
$$$	$150–$225
$$	$100–$150
$	under $100

All prices are for a standard double room in high season, excluding a $6.50-per-person, per-night, government room tax; 6% VAT; and 10%–15% service charge.

$$$$ ★ 🏨 **Harbour Village Beach Resort.** This well-run, upscale resort on a lovely palm tree–lined beach has it all, for divers and nondivers. Wide walkways bordered by lush foliage and blooming tropical flowers separate nine low-rise, Mediterranean-style buildings, with Moorish arches, mustard stucco walls, and red barrel-tile roofs. Pleasant rooms and suites are done in dusty rose and aqua with white tile floors, straw mats, and natural wood furniture and have French doors leading to a terrace or patio overlooking either the sea or the marina. A full-service European spa and fitness center offers an array of body treatments and physical activities. There's also a water-sports center with a dive shop, a marina replete with bustling pubs full of yachties, some fine restaurants (including the ☞ **Admiral's Tavern**), a tennis program, and a 9-hole golf course and small casino that are poised to open in late 1998. ⊠ *Kaya Gobernador Debrot (Box 312),* ☎ *599/7–7500 or 800/ 424–0004 (reservations service),* FAX *599/7–7507. 64 rooms, 8 suites,*

Bonaire

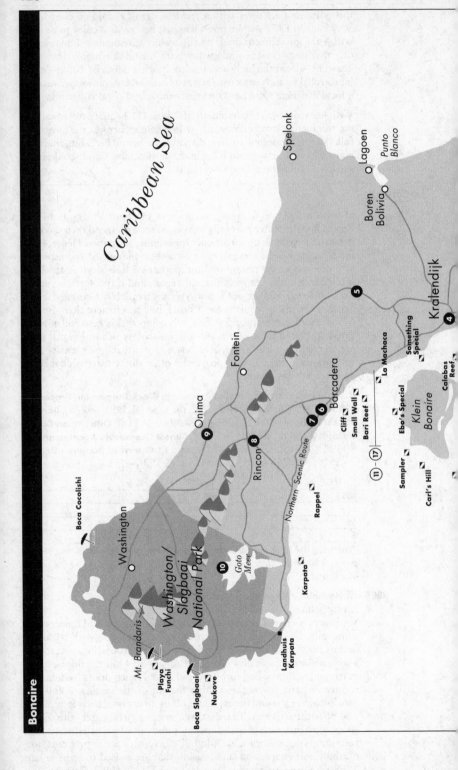

Caribbean Sea

Spelonk

Lagoen
Punto Blanco
Boren
Bolivia

Kralendijk

4

Something Special

La Machaca

5

Barcadera

Celabas Reef

7 6

Cliff
Small Wall
Bari Reef

Ebo's Special

Klein Bonaire

Fontein

Onima

9

Rincon

8

Sampler

Carl's Hill

Northern Scenic Route

Rappel

11 – 17

Karpata

Boca Cocolishi

Washington

Washington/ Slagbaai National Park

10

Goto Meer

Mt. Brandaris

Playa Funchi

Boca Slagbaai

Nukove

Landhuis Karpata

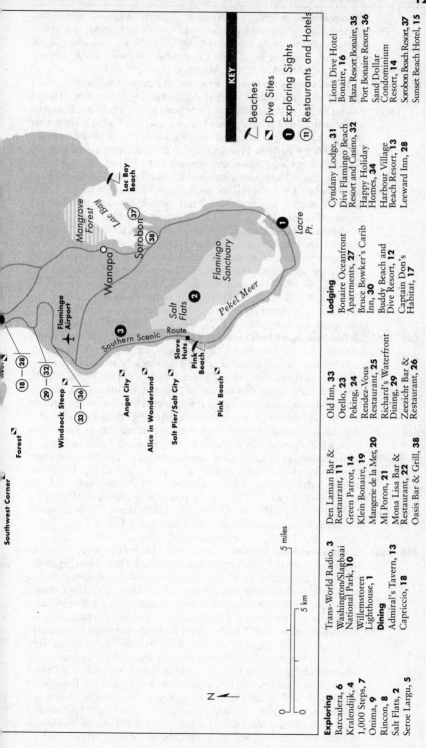

KEY

⚡ Beaches

⚡ Dive Sites

❶ Exploring Sights

⑪ Restaurants and Hotels

Lions Dive Hotel
Bonaire, **16**
Plaza Resort Bonaire, **35**
Port Bonaire Resort, **36**
Sand Dollar
Condominium
Resort, **14**
Sorobon Beach Resort, **37**
Sunset Beach Hotel, **15**

Cyndany Lodge, **31**
Divi Flamingo Beach
Resort and Casino, **32**
Happy Holiday
Homes, **34**
Harbour Village
Beach Resort, **13**
Leeward Inn, **28**

Lodging
Bonaire Oceanfront
Apartments, **27**
Bruce Bowker's Carib
Inn, **30**
Buddy Beach and
Dive Resort, **12**
Captain Don's
Habitat, **17**

Old Inn, **33**
Otello, **23**
Peking, **24**
Rendez-Vous
Restaurant, **25**
Richard's Waterfront
Dining, **29**
Zeezicht Bar &
Restaurant, **26**

Den Laman Bar &
Restaurant, **11**
Green Parrot, **14**
Klein Bonaire, **19**
Mangerie de la Mer, **20**
Mi Poron, **21**
Mona Lisa Bar &
Restaurant, **22**
Oasis Bar & Grill, **38**

Exploring
Barcadera, **6**
Kralendijk, **4**
1,000 Steps, **7**
Onima, **8**
Rincon, **9**
Salt Flats, **2**
Seroe Largu, **5**

Trans-World Radio, **3**
Washington/Slagbaai
National Park, **10**
Willemstoren
Lighthouse, **1**
Dining
Admiral's Tavern, **13**
Capriccio, **18**

70 *condominium units. 5 restaurants, 3 bars, café, air-conditioning, refrigerators, room service, pool, outdoor hot tub, sauna, spa, steam room, 4 tennis courts, aerobics, health club, beach, dive shop, dock, snorkeling, windsurfing, boating, waterskiing, bicycles, shops, library. AE, D, DC, MC, V. EP, FAP, MAP.*

$$$–$$$$ ★ **Captain Don's Habitat.** Once a sort of extended home of Captain Don Stewart, the island's wildest sharp-shooting personality, Habitat can no longer pass itself off as a mere guest house for divers. Stewart's Curaçaoan partners have poured money into this resort, adding a set of upscale rooms (junior suites) and then a long row of Mediterranean-style private villas (the Hamlet section) that rank among the island's best: All are spacious, with ocean-view verandas, full kitchens, and stylish appointments. The updated original 11 Antillean-style cottages have fully stocked kitchens, wicker furnishings, and garden views. Unexpectedly elegant touches throughout include Haitian artwork, intriguingly textured fabric wall hangings, and mahogany trim. Another 10 deluxe cottages are planned for construction in 1998. The atmosphere at the Habitat is laid-back and easygoing (no rooms have TVs), with the emphasis on round-the-clock diving, although the delightful terrace bar sees plenty of partying. ⊠ *Kaya Gobernador Debrot 103 (Box 88),* ☎ *599/7–8290 or 800/327–6709 (reservations service),* FAX *599/7–8240. 21 cottages, 11 villas, 24 suites. Restaurant, 2 bars, air-conditioning, fans, in-room safes, kitchenettes, pool, volleyball, beach, dive shop, dock, bicycles. AE, D, DC, MC, V. EP, FAP, MAP.*

$$$–$$$$ **Divi Flamingo Beach Resort and Casino.** This plantation-style resort consists of a hotel and the Club Flamingo studio apartments, which have the newest and nicest rooms. It's the oldest hotel on the island—a former internment camp for German POWs during World War II, and even those rooms that have been "renovated" still cry out for new furnishings and another coat of fresh paint. However, the handsome dark-wood furnishings, tropical prints, charming original wood beams, and spectacular ocean views from deluxe-room terraces and balconies draw a fair share of repeat guests. Its highly regarded dive facility and upbeat activities programs are other attractions. The dive operation even has specially trained masters who teach scuba diving to individuals with disabilities and dive with them. ⊠ *J. A. Abraham Blvd. 40,* ☎ *599/7–8285 or 800/367–3484 (reservations service),* FAX *599/7–8238. 105 rooms, 40 time-share units. 2 restaurants, 2 bars, air-conditioning, 2 pools, outdoor hot tub, tennis court, beach, 2 dive shops, casino. AE, D, MC, V. All-inclusive, EP, MAP.*

$$$–$$$$ **Lions Dive Hotel Bonaire.** The successful Lions Dive group from Curaçao took over this condominium resort in mid-1996. Then began the process of upgrading the 31 studios and one- and two-bedroom suites in the coral-pink and pale yellow two-story buildings. For privacy, rooms on the second floor are more desirable than those on the first because the rooms are set around a quadrangle containing a small pool and sunbathing area—there's no beach for lounging (plans are afoot to create a man-made strand by the end of 1998). The studio apartments have a kitchenette, while the suites have a spacious living room with sofa bed, a large balcony looking out to sea, and a full kitchen. All units are ideal for families. The new decor scheme is typical but fresh, with light florals and pastels, wicker furnishings, and sparkling white tile floors. The plain but clean bedrooms are small, but their marble-tiled bathrooms (with shower only) are large. ⊠ *Kaya Gobernador Debrot 90 (Box 380),* ☎ *599/7–5580 or 888/546–6734 (reservations service),* FAX *599/7–5680. 31 units. Restaurant, bar, air-conditioning, fans, kitchenettes, pool, dive shop, dock. AE, DC, MC, V. CP, FAP, MAP.*

$$$–$$$$ **Plaza Resort Bonaire.** This flagship property of the Dutch Van der Valk hotel chain features lush tropical grounds winding around a man-

made lagoon with bridges, a gorgeous stretch of beach, loads of resort amenities, an activities program, and the largest guest rooms on the island. Great expense and care have been lavished on the resort. But for all its facilities, it's just too big (even the staff get lost!) and cold for cozy little Bonaire, with precious little island flavor other than a few dazzling underwater and bird photos in the vast, antiseptic lobby. Each room has terra-cotta tile floors, spartan green rattan furnishings, and pastel floral bedspreads. Bathrooms are enormous and have deep bathtubs, double marble vanities, and bidets. One- and two-bedroom villas include full kitchens. ⊠ *J. A. Abraham Blvd. 80,* ☎ *599/7–2500 or 800/766–6016 (reservations service),* FAX *599/7–7133. 174 units. 3 restaurants, 4 bars, café, air-conditioning, fans, in-room safes, refrigerators, room service, pool, wading pool, beauty salon, 4 tennis courts, aerobics, beach, dive shop, dock, windsurfing, boating, bicycles, shops, casino. AE, D, DC, MC, V. EP, FAP, MAP.*

$$$–$$$$ ▥ **Port Bonaire Resort.** Opened adjacent to the airport in late 1994, Port Bonaire is a group of luxury apartments and penthouses with seaview patios or balconies (though there's no beach). The overall design, with tile roofs and pastel exteriors, is called Dutch Mediterranean. Florals and powder blue predominate the color scheme, with cream tiles and blond-wood furnishings. Families will find the fully equipped kitchens handy; they even have microwaves, dishwashers, and clotheswashing machines. Daily maid service is a welcome convenience. There are no on-site facilities, but you can use those at the new ☞ **Plaza Resort Bonaire** (you'll need a car to get there and into town). ⊠ *c/o Plaza Resort Bonaire, J. A. Abraham Blvd. 80,* ☎ *599/7–2500 or 800/766–6016 (reservations service),* FAX *599/7–7133. 26 units. Kitchenettes, pool. AE, D, DC, MC, V. EP.*

$$$–$$$$ ▥ **Sand Dollar Condominium Resort.** These spacious time-share apartments combine a European design with a tropical rattan decor, though this varies according to the individual owner's taste. Each has cable TV, a full kitchen, a large bathroom, a queen-size sofa bed, and a patio or terrace that looks out to the sea (views from the ground-floor units are obstructed by foliage). This American enclave is popular with serious divers and their families and is booked months in advance. There's a beach, but it's minuscule and disappears at high tide. The resort's ☞ **Green Parrot** restaurant serves breakfast, lunch, and dinner; there's a grocery store for those who prefer to cook. ⊠ *Kaya Gobernador Debrot 79,* ☎ *599/7–8738 or 800/228–4773 (reservations service),* FAX *599/7–8760. 85 units. Restaurant, bar, grocery, ice cream parlor, air-conditioning, kitchenettes, pool, 2 tennis courts, beach, dive shop. AE, D, DC, MC, V. EP, FAP, MAP.*

$$–$$$$ ▥ **Buddy Beach and Dive Resort.** Very reasonable rates and cozy, well-equipped accommodations keep guests coming back to enjoy this growing complex on a small beach that offers superb shore snorkeling. The original 10 apartments, given a face-lift and air-conditioning in 1995, are small (bordering on claustrophobic) and oddly configured, but clean, with kitchenette, tile floors, twin beds, sofa bed, and shower-only bathroom. Those facing northwest have million-dollar views of the ocean beyond the streams that wind through the resort's central garden and charming minilagoon. There are also four three-story buildings with studios, one-, two-, and three-bedroom apartments to choose from. Buildings 2 and 6 offer more limited ocean views; request units in Buildings 1 and 7, which were renovated most recently. ⊠ *Kaya Gobernador Debrot 85 (Box 231),* ☎ *599/7–5080 or 800/786–3483 (reservations service),* FAX *599/7–8647. 40 units. Restaurant, air-conditioning, kitchenettes, 2 pools, beach, dive shop. AE, D, MC, V. EP.*

$$$ ▥ **Sorobon Beach Resort.** The Sorobon is a secluded cluster of chalet-style cottages on a lovely private sandy beach at Lac Bay, on the south-

east shore. This unpretentious small resort caters to "naturalists" who take its "clothing-optional" motto literally. Each chalet consists of two small one-bedroom units, with simple light-wood Scandinavian furnishings, a kitchen, and a shower-only bath. New owners added a swimming pool and several more modern chalets in the past couple of years, and expansion projects continue through 1998. In keeping with the get-away-from-it-all concept, you won't find air-conditioning, TVs, phones, or radios in the rooms. A daily shuttle will take you to town. ⊠ *Lac Bay (Box 14),* ☎ *599/7–8080 or 800/828–9356 (reservations service),* 𝔽𝔸𝕏 *599/7–5363. 30 units. Restaurant, bar, fans, in-room safes, kitchenettes, beach, snorkeling, boating, library, laundry service, airport shuttle. AE, MC, V. EP.*

$$–$$$ 🏨 **Bonaire Oceanfront Apartments.** These simply furnished but immaculate one- and two-bedroom apartments are just a three-minute walk from central Kralendijk. Though small, they're fully equipped with every conceivable amenity, including balcony or patio opening right onto smashing views of the bay and Klein Bonaire. ⊠ *Kaya Grandi, Kralendijk,* ☎ *599/7–4000 or 800/748–8733 (reservations service),* 𝔽𝔸𝕏 *599/7–2211. 12 units. Air-conditioning, fans, in-room safes, kitchenettes, pool. MC, V. EP.*

$$–$$$ 🏨 **Sunset Beach Hotel.** This 12-acre resort encompasses one of the island's better hotel beaches (though all rooms are set back from the beach, and even the best have only a garden view). There's also a water-sports concession and a thatched-roof seaside restaurant where the popular Bonairian Theme Night takes place on Saturday nights. Request one of the renovated rooms, which were gutted in 1996, replacing old wooden floors, funky-color furniture, and plumbing fixtures with tidy white tile floors, rattan furnishings, tropical-print curtains and bedspreads, and all new plumbing. ⊠ *Kaya Gobernador Debrot 75 (Box 333),* ☎ *599/7–8448 or 800/344–4439 (reservations service),* 𝔽𝔸𝕏 *599/7–8118. 142 rooms, 3 1-bedroom suites. 2 restaurants, air-conditioning, in-room safes, refrigerators, pool, 3 outdoor hot tubs, 2 tennis courts, Ping-Pong, shuffleboard, volleyball, beach, dive shop, snorkeling, windsurfing, boating, laundry service and dry cleaning, travel services, car rental. AE, D, DC, MC, V. EP, FAP, MAP.*

$–$$ 🏨 **Bruce Bowker's Carib Inn.** American diver Bruce Bowker started his ★   small diving lodge out of a private home about a mile from the airport, continually adding on to and refurbishing the place. Rattan furnishings, cable TVs, completely renovated kitchens (in all but the standard rooms), and a family-style atmosphere have turned his homey hostelry into one of the island's best bets, albeit one that gets booked far in advance by repeat guests. Bowker knows everybody by name and loves to fill special requests. Novice divers will enjoy Bowker's small scuba classes (one or two people); PADI (Professional Association of Diving Instructors) certification is available. The beach is just a sliver but is fine for shore entries. ⊠ *On main road just outside Kralendijk (Box 68),* ☎ *599/7–8819,* 𝔽𝔸𝕏 *599/7–5295. 10 units. Air-conditioning, refrigerators, pool, beach, dive shop. AE, MC, V. EP.*

$ 🏨 **Cyndany Lodge.** If a plump wallet is more important to you than fancy beachfront accommodations, consider Cyndany Lodge, a small complex of basic motel-style rooms in a quiet residential area within walking distance of the beach and dive shop at the ☞ **Divi Flamingo Beach Resort and Casino.** The tiled rooms are basic but clean and air-conditioned and outfitted with a refrigerator and wet bar. Inexpensive breakfast and lunch items are available at the small, open-air café in the courtyard. ⊠ *Kaya Inglatera 12,* ☎ *599/7–5516 or 800/748–8733 (reservations service),* 𝔽𝔸𝕏 *599/7–5517. 12 rooms. Café, air-conditioning, minibars, refrigerators. AE, MC, V. EP.*

$ ⌂ **Happy Holiday Homes.** In a quiet residential area not far from the airport, this small complex of bungalows across the street from the ocean is an ideal budget option. The comfortable accommodations are spic-and-span clean, with wood ceilings, gleaming white tile floors, and colorful pillows and throw rugs; each has a barbecue and deck furniture on the sun terrace or garden patio, fully equipped kitchen, living-dining area, air-conditioned bedrooms, and cable TV, all for under $100 per night. The friendly owners, Louise and Val Villanueva, go all out for their guests, from grocery shopping to arranging car rental or diving and windsurfing packages. ⌂ *Punt Vierkant 9,* ☎ *599/7–8405,* FAX *599/7–8605. 12 1- and 2-bedroom bungalows. Air-conditioning, in-room safes, kitchenettes, coin laundry, airport shuttle. MC, V. EP.*

$ ⌂ **Leeward Inn.** American owners Don and Ditta Balstra have restored this 80-year-old guest house and modernized its six rooms. Those who eschew luxury in favor of basic amenities and budget rates come for the friendly service and the inexpensive meals at the on-site Harthouse Café, which has wonderful dive photos, magnificent local murals, and yummy pizzas. The pastel-painted rooms have light tile floors, twin beds, mix-and-match, "garage-sale" furniture, and modern bathrooms (shower only, except for one room). Television, refrigerator, and air-conditioning have been added to a few rooms (ceiling fans and breezes keep things cool in other rooms); Don and Ditta expect every room to be fully outfitted by late 1998. The inn is a block from the sea and a 10-minute walk to the Divi Flamingo beach. ⌂ *Kaya Grandi 60, Kralendijk,* ☎ *599/7–5516 or 800/748–8733 (reservations service),* FAX *599/7–5517. 5 rooms, 1 suite. Restaurant. AE, MC, V. EP.*

Dining

Menus cover everything from French, Continental, Mexican, Indonesian, and Chinese to Italian fare, and in just about every restaurant you'll have a fresh seafood choice brought in from the surrounding waters. In season, try the snapper, wahoo, or dorado (a mild white fish). Meat lovers will appreciate the Argentinian beef popping up on menus around the island, while vegetarians will be pleased with dishes prepared from the fresh fruits and vegetables shipped in from Venezuela. The other good news is that dining on Bonaire is far less expensive than on neighboring islands.

What to Wear

Dress on the island is casual but conservative. Most places don't allow beachwear; even casual poolside restaurants prefer a cover-up.

CATEGORY	COST*
$$$	over $25
$$	$15–$25
$	under $15

*per person for a three-course meal, excluding drinks, 6% VAT, and 10%–15% service charge

ASIAN

$ ✕ **Peking.** Of the half dozen Chinese restaurants on the island, locals prefer Peking. The air-conditioned room is not fancy: It's packed with round dining tables topped by lazy Susans, but you'll be glad they're there to give you easy access to the huge servings of delicious food. Chicken in black bean sauce, fried rice dishes, and other Cantonese standards are available, as are steaks, local seafood, and Indonesian dishes such as *nasi goreng* (Indonesian fried rice). Take-out is also an option. ⌂ *Kaya Korona,* ☎ *599/7–7170. AE, DC, MC, V. Closed Wed.*

CARIBBEAN/CREOLE

$–$$ ✕ **Mi Poron.** Set in the breezy courtyard of a traditional Bonairian home, Mi Poron serves up the true flavor of the island, from stewed conch or goat to fried fish. As you pass through the house to the courtyard, take a moment to look at the decor and furnishings typical of Bonairian homes in the not-so-distant past. ⊠ *Kaya Caracas 1,* ☎ *599/7–5199. MC, V. Closed Mon. No lunch Sun.*

$–$$ ✕ **Zeezicht Bar & Restaurant.** Zeezicht (pronounced *zay-zeekt* and meaning sea view) is open for three meals a day. At breakfast and lunch you'll get basic American fare with an Antillean touch, such as a fish omelet. Dinner is either on the terrace overlooking the harbor or in the homey, rough-hewn main room, which sports a nautical theme replete with fishnets, pirate murals, and mermaids carved into the wood beam columns. Locals are dedicated to this hangout, especially for the seviche, conch sandwiches, and the Zeezicht special soup with conch, fish, shrimp, and oysters. ⊠ *Kaya Corsow 10, across from Karel's Beach Bar,* ☎ *599/7–8434. AE, MC, V.*

CONTINENTAL

$–$$ ✕ **Admiral's Tavern.** This marina tapas bar, part of the ☞ **Harbour Village** complex, is a delightful addition to Bonaire's dining scene. The ambience is soothing: A rough-wood terrace overlooks the twinkling lights of the boats in the marina (so close you can spy on their occupants), while the interior room is draped with fishnets, buoys, and ships' steering wheels and is dominated by a gorgeous carved Venezuelan mahogany bar. Three or four tapas (those delectable Spanish appetizer-size treats) make a fine meal: Choose from such dishes as tuna empanadas, shrimp in garlic sauce, tortillas, and more filling pastas, such as penne with scallops swimming in saffron cream sauce. ⊠ *Kaya Gobernador Debrot,* ☎ *599/7–7500. AE, D, DC, MC, V.*

$–$$ ✕ **Rendez-Vous Restaurant.** The terrace of this café, with a canopy of electric stars, is the perfect place to watch the world of Bonaire go by as you fill up on warm, fresh French bread with garlic butter, hearty homemade soups, seafood, steaks, and vegetarian specialties. The Dutch pea soup, sautéed veggies baked in puff pastry, scallops Provençale in phyllo, beer batter shrimp, and sautéed squid, shrimp, or conch are the favorites. All-you-can-eat pork ribs draw a crowd on Wednesday. ⊠ *3 Kaya L. D. Gerharts,* ☎ *599/7–8454. AE, MC, V. Closed Sun.*

ECLECTIC

$–$$ ✕ **Green Parrot.** This family-run restaurant, on the dock of the ☞ **Sand Dollar Condominium Resort,** serves the biggest hamburgers and the best strawberry margaritas on the island. Char-grilled steaks, Creole fish, and barbecued chicken and ribs go perfectly with the crispy onion loaf. Transplanted Englishman Kirk Gosden, who manages the place, has added theme dinner nights; Monday dine on Italian, Saturday come for the barbecue buffet. This is where you'll find both the American expatriates and tourists hanging out. ⊠ *Kaya Gobernador Debrot 79,* ☎ *599/7–5454. AE, MC, V.*

$–$$ ✕ **Klein Bonaire.** From this relaxed, café-style terrace, you can watch
★   the people strolling the quiet waterfront across the street. It's wonderfully atmospheric, with terra-cotta floors, hardwood and natural wicker chairs, stained glass, a fishing boat, and local arts and crafts, including painted Creole houses and tulips as napkin holders. You can have a drink at the lovely semicircular bar while waiting for your meal, or even take in a game of billiards. There's an à la carte menu, imaginatively blending Caribbean influences with Continental standards such as dorado fillet with Brie in a light mustard sauce or chicken stuffed with Gorgonzola in dill sauce. At lunch, the *pannekoeken,* or Dutch pancakes, are enormous crepes filled with ham, green peppers, onions, and mush-

rooms, or apples and raisins. A separate bar menu features smaller portions and lighter fare, including *saté* (grilled beef or chicken with peanut sauce). Save room for Klein Bonaire's signature chocolate mousse, served chilled. Look for the landmark red British phone booth that sits outside the door. ⊠ *Kaya C. E. B. Hellmund 5,* ☎ *599/7– 8617. AE, MC, V. Closed Mon. No lunch.*

$–$$ ✕ **Mangerie de la Mer.** Owner Ed de Vuyst and owner-chef Joop van der Ligt have created Bonaire's most playful restaurant: a Riviera bistro gone tropical. It's a riot of delicious colors: mint, peach, and banana. The old structure retains the original wood ceilings but Ed and Joop have added unique touches, ranging from the traditional (faux-Tiffany lamps, floral arrangements) to marvelously absurd (porcelain busts of Charlie Chaplin and Marilyn Monroe and a wood painting of Laurel and Hardy). The food is just as fun and eclectic with the menu changing completely every six weeks. Joop might start you off with smoked chicken salad with pine nuts drizzled with raspberry dressing or a classic carpaccio. For a main dish try pork tenderloin in amaretto cream sauce, and finish with a towering *coupe* Mont Blanc (the sundae to end all sundaes). Be sure to chatter with Gabber and Goofie, the majestic blue and yellow macaws in back. ⊠ *Kaya Bonaire 4C,* ☎ *599/7–2888. MC, V. Closed Sun.*

$–$$ ✕ **Mona Lisa Bar & Restaurant.** Here you'll find Continental fare, along with a few authentic Dutch and Indonesian dishes. The most popular plate is the pork tenderloin drizzled with peanut sauce, although other reliable choices include grouper in papaya sauce and a terrine of smoked chicken with mustard dressing and pineapple. This is also a late-night hangout for local schmoozing and light snacks or fresh catch of the day, served until about 2 AM in the colorful bar adorned with various baseball-style caps. The intimate stucco-and-brick dining room, presided over by a copy of the famous painting of the smiling lady, is decorated with brick-and-iron grillwork, hurricane lamps, gloomy Rembrandt imitations, lace curtains, and whirring ceiling fans. ⊠ *Kaya Grandi 15,* ☎ *599/7–8718. AE, MC, V. Closed weekends.*

$–$$ ✕ **Oasis Bar & Grill.** Near the far southern end of the island, the Oasis presents a harmonious blend of terra-cotta tile floors and comfortable rattan furnishings surrounding a half-moon bar. There's also an area for alfresco dining on the brick terrace. Caesar and Greek salad, popcorn shrimp, steak strips, burgers, smoked marlin, and a variety of chicken preparations fill out the grill menu. This casual eatery is a favorite of those headed to Lac Bay for windsurfing. ⊠ *Kaminda Sorobon 64, Lac Bay,* ☎ *599/7–8198. AE, MC, V. Closed Mon.*

$–$$ ✕ **Old Inn.** Potted plants surround the wicker chairs of this friendly restaurant across the street from the Plaza Resort Bonaire. The food is equally eclectic: French, barbecue, or Indonesian. Try the snails in garlic sauce, the nasi goreng, or the pork medallions in mushroom sauce. The real specialty is rijstaffel or "rice table," a sumptuous buffet of over 20 sweet or moderately spicy Indonesian dishes. ⊠ *J. A. Abraham Blvd., Kralendijk,* ☎ *599/7–6666. MC, V. No lunch.*

ITALIAN

$–$$ ✕ **Capriccio.** Classic Italian finally made its way to Bonaire with the
★ opening of this wonderful Italian-run eatery. The pastas are handmade daily, and there's a true climate-controlled wine cellar. You'll have a choice of casual à la carte dining on the terrace or a romantic, candlelit dinner in the tonier, air-conditioned dining room with lace curtains, candles, and floral sprays. If your appetite is hearty, go for the six-course, prix-fixe "tour of the menu." Otherwise, sure bets are the smoked fish appetizer, prosciutto with hearts-of-palm salad, pumpkin ravioli with sage and Parmesan, gnocchi al pesto, lamb with arti-

chokes, penne with lobster cream sauce, and (surprisingly) turkey breast in sweet-and-sour sauce with stewed cabbage. Pizza, calzone, and other standards are, of course, available. ⊠ *Kaya Isla Riba 1,* ☎ *599/7–7230. AE, MC, V. Closed Tues. No lunch Sun.*

$–$$ ✕ **Otello.** This unpretentious Italian restaurant resides in an orange octagonal building a block off the main street downtown. The exterior belies the charming Mediterranean decor and romantic candlelit tables inside. Tagliatelle with creamy Parmesan and ground meat sauce is the signature pasta. There's also lobster or meat lasagna, shrimp in balsamic vinegar, and filet mignon with green peppers. An array of wines, cappuccino, and espresso helps round out the meal. ⊠ *Kaya Prinses Marie 4,* ☎ *599/7–4449. MC, V. Closed Mon.*

SEAFOOD

$–$$ ✕ **Den Laman Bar & Restaurant.** A 6,000-square-ft aquarium provides the backdrop to this casual, nautically decorated restaurant. Eat indoors next to the glass-enclosed "ocean show" (request a table in advance) or outdoors on the noisier patio overlooking the sea. Pick a fresh Caribbean lobster from the tank or order red snapper Creole, a hands-down winner. Another winner is Liz Rijna, whose concoctions knocked the island bartending competition for a loop. Homemade cheesecake is a draw, as is the live entertainment each Saturday night. ⊠ *Kaya Gobernador Debrot 77,* ☎ *599/7–8955. AE, MC, V. Closed Tues. No lunch.*

$–$$ ✕ **Richard's Waterfront Dining.** Animated and congenial owner Richard
★   Beady's alfresco eatery on the water is casually romantic and has become the most recommended restaurant on the island—a reputation that's well deserved. Richard, originally from Boston, sets the tone by personally checking on every table. The fresh daily menu is listed on large blackboards, and the food is consistently excellent, catering to American palates with flavorful, not spicy, preparations. Among the best dishes are conch *alajillo* (fillet of conch with garlic and butter), shrimp primavera, and grilled wahoo. Filet mignon béarnaise satisfies those seeking something other than creatures from the deep. ⊠ *J. A. Abraham Blvd. 60,* ☎ *599/7–5263. MC, V. Closed Mon. No lunch.*

Beaches

Don't come expecting Aruba-length stretches of glorious white sand. The island's beaches are smaller, and though the water is indeed blue (several shades of it, in fact), the sand is not always white. You can have your pick of beaches in Bonaire according to color: pink, black, or white. The best hotel beaches are found at Harbour Village, Sunset Beach, and Sorobon (the only clothing-optional beach on the island, reserved for the exclusive use of hotel guests).

Boca Cocolishi. Hermit crabs can be found along the shore of this black-sand beach in Washington/Slagbaai National Park on the northeast coast. This beach gives new meaning to the term "windswept": Cooling breezes whip the water into a frenzy as the color of the sea changes from midnight blue to aquamarine. The water is too rough for anything more than wading; however, the spot is perfect for an intimate picnic à deux. To get there, take the Northern Scenic Route to the park, and then ask for directions at the gate.

Boca Slagbaai. Inside Washington/Slagbaai Park is this beach of coral fossils and rocks with interesting coral gardens that are good for snorkeling just offshore. Bring scuba boots or canvas sandals to walk into the water, because the coral "beach" is rough on bare feet. The gentle surf makes it an ideal place for picnicking or swimming. The exquisite ocher-and-russet building here houses a restaurant serving fine lunches Thursday–Sunday.

Lac Bay Beach. Adjacent to the Sorobon Resort Beach, Lac Bay is *the* windsurfing beach. You'll find a restaurant-bar at the far end near the bay entrance, and a couple of windsurfing outfitters.

Pink Beach. As the name suggests, the sand here has a pinkish tint that takes on a magical shimmer in the late-afternoon sun. The water is suitable for swimming, snorkeling, and scuba diving. Take the Southern Scenic Route on the western side of the island, past the Trans-World Radio station, close to the slave huts. A favorite hangout for Bonairians on the weekend, it is virtually deserted during the week.

Playa Funchi. This Washington Park beach is notable for the lagoon on one side, where flamingos nest, and the superb snorkeling on the other, where iridescent green parrotfish swim right up to shore.

Outdoor Activities and Sports

CYCLING

Twenty-one-speed mountain bikes are the perfect way to travel Bonaire's more than 180 mi of unpaved roads (as well as the many paved roads). Rentals (which include trail maps, water bottles, helmet, lock, repair, and first-aid kits) and half-day and full-day guided excursions ($40 and $65, respectively, in addition to bike rental) are available from **Cycle Bonaire** (✉ Kaya L. D. Gerharts 11D, ☎ 599/7–7558).

FISHING

Bonaire's waters teem with big game fish, from marlin to tuna to sailfish. Captain Cornelis of **Big Game Sportfishing** (✉ Kaya Warawara 3, ☎ 599/7–6500, FAX 599/7–5517) offers deep-sea charters for those in search of wahoo, marlin, tuna, swordfish, and sailfish. His rates, which cover bait, tackle, and refreshments, average $350 for a half day, $500 for a full day for up to four people. **Piscatur Charters** (✉ Kaya H. J. Pop 4, ☎ 599/7–8774) offers light-tackle angler reef fishing for jacks, barracudas, and snappers from a 15-ft skiff. Rates are $200 for a half day, $300 for a full day. The 42-ft sportfisherman *Piscatur* is available for charter at $350 for a half day, $500 for a full day, and carries up to six passengers. Bonefishing runs $200 for a half day.

HORSEBACK RIDING

Hour-long trail rides ($20) at the 166-acre **Kunuku Warahama Ranch** (☎ 599/7–7324) take riders through groves of cactus where iguanas, wild goats, donkeys, and flamingos reside. Reserve one of the gentle pintos and palominos a day in advance, and try to go earlier in the morning, when it's a bit cooler. There's an alfresco restaurant, a golf driving range, and two playgrounds for the kids to help fill the warmer afternoon hours.

PARASAILING

Parasailing, that 10-minute sensation of floating dozens of feet above the water, is now available on Bonaire. Excursions are available from **Karel's Watersports** (☎ 599/7–4434).

SCUBA DIVING

Bonaire has some of the best reef diving this side of Australia's Great Barrier Reef. It takes only 5–25 minutes to reach many sites, the current is usually mild, and although some reefs have very sudden, steep drops, most begin just offshore and slope gently downward at a 45-degree angle. General visibility runs 60 to 100 ft, except during surges in October and November. You can see an enormous range of coral: from knobby-brain and giant-brain coral to elkhorn, staghorn, mountainous star, gorgonian, and black coral. You'll also encounter schools of parrotfish, surgeonfish, angelfish, eels, snapper, and grouper. Beach diving is excellent just about everywhere on the island's leeward side, so night diving is popular. There are sites here suitable for every skill level; they're clearly marked by yellow stones on the roadside.

In the well-policed Bonaire Marine Park, which encompasses the entire coastline around Bonaire and Klein Bonaire, visitors take the rules seriously. Don't even think about (1) spearfishing; (2) dropping anchor; or (3) touching, stepping on, or collecting coral. You must pay an admission charge of $10 (fees are used to maintain the park), for which you receive a colored plastic tag (to attach to an item of scuba gear) entitling you to one calendar year of unlimited diving in the park. Tags are available at all scuba facilities and from the park headquarters in the Barcadera (☎ 599/7–8444). Check-out dives—diving first with a master before going out on your own—are required on the island, and you can arrange them through any dive shop. All Bonaire dive operations offer free-buoyancy-control, advanced-buoyancy-control, and photographic-buoyancy-control classes.

The *Guide to the Bonaire Marine Park* lists 44 of the more than 80 dive sites that have been identified and marked by moorings. Another fine reference book is the *Diving and Snorkeling Guide to Bonaire* by Jerry Schnabel and Suzi Swygert. Guides associated with the various dive centers can give you more complete directions. It's difficult to recommend one site over another because all have lush coral formations, fairly mild currents, and an array of fascinating marine life. The following are a few popular sites to whet your appetite; these and other sites are pinpointed on the Bonaire map.

Angel City. Take the trail down to the shore adjacent to the Trans-World Radio station; dive in and swim south to Angel City, one of the shallowest and most popular sites in a two-reef complex that includes Alice in Wonderland. The boulder-size green-and-tan coral heads are home to black margates, Spanish hogfish, gray snappers, and large purple tube sponges.

Bari Reef. Go to the free slide show on Tuesday at the Sand Dollar Condominium Resort to catch a glimpse of the elkhorn and fire coral, queen angelfish, and other wonders of Bari Reef, just off the resort's pier.

Calabas Reef. Off the Divi Flamingo Beach Resort, this is the island's busiest dive site. All divers using the hotel's facilities make their warm-up dive here, where they can inspect the wreck sunk for just this purpose. The site is replete with Christmas-tree worms, sponges, and fire coral adhering to the ship's hull. Fish life is frenzied, with the occasional octopus putting in an appearance.

Forest. You'll need to catch a boat to reach Forest, a dive site off the coast of Klein Bonaire, so named for the abundant black-coral forest found there. This site gets a lot of fish action, including a resident spotted eel that lives in a cave.

Rappel. This is one of the most spectacular dives, near the Karpata Ecological Center. The shore is a sheer cliff, and the lush coral growth is home to an unusual variety of marine life, including occasional orange sea horses, squid, spiny lobsters, and spotted trunkfish.

Small Wall. One of Bonaire's three complete vertical wall dives, Small Wall is off the Black Durgon Inn and is one of the most popular night-diving spots. Access is made by boat (Black Durgon guests can access it from shore). The 60-ft wall is frequented by squid, turtles, tarpon, and barracudas and has dense hard and soft coral formations; it also allows for excellent snorkeling.

Something Special. Just south of the entrance of the marina, this spot is famous for its garden eels, which wave about from the relatively shallow sand terrace looking like long grass in a breeze.

Windsock Steep. In front of the small beach opposite the airport runway, this makes an excellent shore dive (from 20 to 80 ft) and is a popular place for snorkeling close to town. The current is moderate, the elkhorn coral profuse; you may also see angelfish and rays.

Habitat Dive Center (⊠ Captain Don's Habitat, Kaya Gobernador Debrot 103, ☎ 599/7–8290), **Peter Hughes Dive Bonaire** (⊠ Divi Flamingo Beach Resort, ☎ 599/7–8285 or 800/367–3484), and **Sand Dollar Dive and Photo** (⊠ Sand Dollar Condominium Resort, Kaya Gobernador Debrot 79, ☎ 599/7–5252 or 800/288–4773), are all PADI dive facilities qualified to offer both PADI and NAUI (National Association of Underwater Instructors) certification courses as well as IDD (the primary European certification program). Sand Dollar Dive and Photo is also qualified to certify dive instructors and offers an array of underwater photography and videography courses as well.

Other centers include **Bonaire Scuba Center** (⊠ Black Durgon Inn, 599/7–5736; in the U.S.: ⊠ Box 775, Morgan, NJ 08879, ☎ 908/566–8866 or 800/526–2370), **Bon Bini Divers** (⊠ Lions Dive Resort Bonaire, Kaya Gobernador Debrot 90, ☎ 599/7–5580 or 800/327–5425), **Bruce Bowker's Carib Inn Dive Center** (⊠ Bruce Bowker's Carib Inn, Airport Rd., ☎ 599/7–8819, FAX 599/7–5295), **Buddy Dive Resort** (⊠ Kaya Gobernador Debrot 85, ☎ 599/7–5080), **Dive Inn** (⊠ Close to South Pier, Kaya C. E. B. Hellmund, ☎ 599/7–8761), **Great Adventures at Harbour Village** (⊠ Harbour Village Beach Resort, Kaya Gobernador Debrot, ☎ 599/7–7500 or 800/424–0004), and **Toucan Diving** (⊠ Plaza Resort Bonaire, J. A. Abraham Blvd. 80, ☎ 599/7–2500).

Americans Jerry Schnabel and Suzi Swygert of **Photo Tours N.V.** (⊠ Captain Don's Habitat, Kaya Gobernador Debrot 103, ☎ 599/7–5390, FAX 599/7–4089) specialize in teaching and guiding novice through professional underwater photographers. They also offer land-excursion tours of Bonaire's birds, wildlife, and vegetation. **Dee Scarr's Touch the Sea** (⊠ Box 369, ☎ 599/7–8529) is a personalized (two to four people at a time) diving program that provides interaction with marine life; it is available to certified divers.

SEA KAYAKING

Sea kayaking has taken off in a big way in Bonaire, especially among divers and snorkelers, who use the kayak to reach new and different dive sites and simply tow the craft along during their dive. Nondivers use kayaks to explore the flora and fauna of the island's rich mangroves (use plenty of insect repellent before touring a mangrove). Guided trips and kayak rentals are available from **Sand Dollar Dive and Photo** (☞ Scuba Diving, *above*) and **Jibe City** (⊠ Lac Bay, ☎ 599/7–4455). Kayaks go for $10 (single) and $15 (double) per hour; $25 and $35, respectively, per half day.

SNORKELING

Don't consider snorkeling the cowardly diver's sport; in Bonaire the experience can be anything but elementary because the surface water tends to be choppy due to the trade winds. The better spots for snorkeling are on the leeward side of the island, where you have shore access to the reefs, and along the west side of Klein Bonaire, where the reef is better developed.

Bonaire, in conjunction with *Skin Diver Magazine,* developed the world's first **Guided Snorkeling Program** in 1996. The highly educational and entertaining program begins with a slide show presenting a variety of topics, from a beginner's look at reef fish, coral, and sponges to advanced fish identification, mangroves, and night snorkeling. Participants also preview the site they will visit with a certified snorkel guide. There are 12 sites, providing something suitable for all skill levels. Guided snorkeling can be arranged through most resort dive shops (☞ Lodging, *above*); the cost is $25 (discounts available for more than one session) and includes slide presentations, transportation to the site, and a guided tour of the site. Snorkel gear is an additional $9 per 24-hour period.

TENNIS

Tennis is not a common activity on tiny Bonaire, but you do have a few options to volley about. At the following resorts, court prices generally run about $20 per hour for nonguests (free for guests), but pros aren't available. **Plaza Resort Bonaire, Sunset Beach Hotel, Divi Flamingo Beach Resort,** and the **Sand Dollar Condominium Resort** (☞ Lodging, *above*). Plan to play in the early morning or evening hours to avoid the worst of the day's heat.

WATERSKIING

To water-ski—from lessons on how to stay above the water to showing off for your friends, **Club Nautico** (☒ Kaya Jan N. E. Craane 24, ☎ 599/7–5800) and **Great Adventures at Harbour Village** (☒ Kaya Gobernador Debrot, ☎ 599/7–7500) can make arrangements for you. The cost is around $20 for 15 minutes of skiing.

WINDSURFING

Lac Bay, a protected cove on the east coast, is ideal for windsurfing. Novices will find it especially comforting since there's no way to be blown out to sea. The **Bonaire Windsurf Place** (☒ Amboina 18, ☎ 599/7–2288 or 800/225–0102), commonly referred to as the Place, set up shop on Sorobon Beach in 1996. They rent the latest Mistral and Naish equipment for $35–$60 per hour. A two-hour lesson priced at $35 includes equipment rental; private lessons are $45 per hour without equipment, and the three-day-lesson package is a real bargain at $150. **Windsurfing Bonaire,** known locally as Jibe City (☒ Lac Bay, ☎ FAX 599/7–5363, ☎ 800/748–8733 for a U.S. representative), offers lessons for $30–$40; board rentals start at $20 an hour, $40 for a half day. There are pickups at all the hotels at 9 AM and 1 PM; ask your hotel to make arrangements.

Shopping

You can get to know all the shops in Kralendijk in an hour or so. But sometimes there's no better way to enjoy some time out of the sun and sea than to go shopping (particularly if your companion is a dive fanatic and you're not). Almost all the shops are on the Kaya Grandi or on adjacent streets and in tiny malls. The most distinctive local crafts are fanciful painted pieces of driftwood and hand-painted *cunucu,* or little wilderness houses. One word of caution: Buy as many flamingo T-shirts as you want, but don't take home items made of goatskin or tortoiseshell; they are not allowed into the United States.

Specialty Items

CLOTHES

Benetton (☒ Kaya Grandi 49, ☎ 599/7–5107) has added Bonaire to its list of franchises in the Caribbean and makes the claim that prices here are 30% less than in New York. **Best Buddies** (☒ Kaya Grandi 32, ☎ 599/7–7570) stocks a selection of Indonesian batik shirts and *pareos* (beach wraps), bathing suits, and Bonaire T-shirts. Colorful cotton resort wear is available at **Bye-Bye Bonaire** (☒ Harbourside Mall, ☎ 599/7–7578).

Cigar smokers will find friends at **Little Holland** (✉ Harborside Mall, ☏ 599/7–5670) as they breathe in the smoky splendor of Havanas. Montecristo, H. Upmann, Romeo & Juliet, and Cohiba are all here. Far from being banished to the porch, smokers are welcomed into the acclimatized Cedar Cigar Room. **Sparky's** (✉ Harborside Mall, ☏ 599/7–5288) sells perfumes and makeup from Lancôme, Estée Lauder, Chanel, and Ralph Lauren, to name a few.

HANDICRAFTS

The **Bonaire Art Gallery** (✉ Kaya L. D. Gerharts 10, ☏ 599/7–7120) showcases the works (paintings, etchings, driftwood sculptures, funky "found objects," unusual wind chimes, and jewelry) of local artists, as well as imported goods from Africa and Latin America. **Donzie** (✉ Kaya Bonaire adjacent to Zeezicht Bar and Restaurant, ☏ 599/7–7642) offers unique jewelry created from island odds and ends (shiny beads, sun-bleached bones, and sea-polished colored glass) as well as local art, secondhand clothing, and antiques. Be forewarned: Owner Donna Dovale closes the store after lunch and on Sunday. A government-funded crafts center, **Fundashon Arte Industri Bonairiano** (✉ J. A. Abraham Blvd., Kralendijk, catercorner to post office, ☏ no phone) sells locally made necklaces of black coral, hand-painted shirts and dresses, and the "fresh craft of the day." **Littman Gifts** (✉ Kaya Grandi 35, ☏ 599/7–6767) is the place for batik cloth by the yard, European costume jewelry, T-shirts, framed underwater pictures, and glass flamingos. **Things Bonaire** (✉ Kaya Grandi 38C, ☏ 599/7–8423) sells T-shirts, earrings, batik dresses, souvenirs, and guidebooks.

Nightlife and the Arts

Nightlife

Most divers are exhausted after they finish their third, fourth, or fifth dive of the day, which probably explains why there are so few discos in Bonaire. Indeed, their idea of nightlife is looking for the famed elusive "green flash" just before sunset, a harbinger of luck (some swear it exists, others that it can only be seen after several daiquiris), or night-diving in a truly surreal world. This is also the kind of island where events like full-moon snorkeling and windsurfing are popular but you should be an experienced hand to join the lunatic locals!

Check out the list of weekly events at the tourist information office (☞ Visitor Information *in* Bonaire A to Z, *below*) or inquire about activities at your hotel's front desk. You'll also find information in the free magazines *Bonaire Holiday, Bonaire Affair,* and *Bonaire Nights.*

BARS

Happy hours are very popular on the island, especially at **Captain Don's Habitat** (✉ Kaya Gobernador Debrot 103, ☏ 599/7–8290) on Thursday night. **City Cafe** (✉ Kaya Isla Riba 3, ☏ no phone) is a wacky hangout splashed in magenta, banana, and electric blue, offering such cocktails as Alabama Slammers (amaretto, gin, Southern Comfort, lemon) and snack food like chicken pies and satés. The popular bar **Karel's** (✉ Kaya J. N. E. Craane 12, ☏ 599/7–8434), on the waterfront across from the Zeezicht Bar and Restaurant, sits on stilts above the sea and is *the* place for mingling with islanders, dive pros, and tourists, especially Friday and Saturday nights, when there's live island and pop music. **Klein Bonaire** (✉ Kaya C. E. B. Hellmund 5, ☏ 599/7–8617) offers live jazz weekends. The **Plaza Resort Bonaire** (✉ J. A. Abraham Blvd. 80, ☏ 599/7–2500) has its happy hour on Friday night. The music is live, and the drink specials keep coming.

CASINOS

For years the island had only one casino, the **Divi Flamingo Beach Casino** (✉ J. A. Abraham Blvd. 40, ☎ 599/7–8285), which opens at 8 PM and is closed Sunday. A newer and fancier casino opened at the **Plaza Resort Bonaire** (✉ J. A. Abraham Blvd. 80, ☎ 599/7–2500) in late 1995. At press time, the **Harbour Village Beach Resort** (☞ Lodging, *above*) was talking of opening a small but fancy casino sometime in 1998.

DANCE CLUBS

Fantasy Disco (✉ Kaya L. D. Gerharts 11, ☎ 599/7–6345) is the island's main dance spot. It's spacious, features big-screen TVs and taped merengue, jazz, rock, reggae, and occasional live performances. Lady's Night on Wednesday is very popular.

MOVIES

The **Bonaire Twin Cinema** (✉ Kaya Prinses Marie, Kralendijk, ☎ 599/7–2400) opened in downtown Kralendijk in 1996. There are four to six showings a day of recent-release movies (primarily American hits, but occasionally there are films from Europe and Latin America). Tickets are Naf10.

The Arts

Nature's artistry is given top billing on Bonaire. Slide shows of underwater and above-water scenes fascinate both divers and nondivers. Dee Scarr, a dive guide, presents the fascinating "Touch the Sea" show Monday night at 8:45, November–June, at **Captain Don's Habitat** (☞ Bars, *above*). Check with the Habitat for other shows (Bonaire Above and Below, Sea Turtles, Adventures of Captain Don, etc.) throughout the week. **Sunset Beach Hotel** (✉ Kaya Gobernador Debrot 75, ☎ 599/7–8448) offers slide shows on identifying sea critters Tuesday night at 8:45 and on the island's flora and fauna Thursday night at 8:15. Flora and fauna of the Caribbean are the focus of the slide show presented by naturalist Jerry Ligon Thursday night at 8:15 at the **Sand Dollar Condominium Resort** (✉ Kaya Gobernador Debrot 79, ☎ 599/7–8738).

ISLAND CULTURE

Top performers on the island, including guitarist Cai-Cai Cecelia, the Kunuku Band, and Duo Flamingo, migrate among the island's top resorts to entertain throughout the week. Don't miss the Bonairian folklore nights, with live island music and dancing, along with typical local foods, Tuesday night at 8 at **Captain Don's Habitat** (☞ Bars, *above*) and the **Sunset Beach Hotel** (✉ Kaya Gobernador Debrot 75, ☎ 599/7–8448) on Saturday at 7:30.

Exploring Bonaire

Two routes, north and south from Kralendijk, the island's small capital, are possible on the 24-mi-long island; either one will take from a few hours to a full day, depending upon whether you stop to snorkel, swim, dive, or lounge.

Numbers in the margin correspond to points of interest on the Bonaire map.

❹ Kralendijk

Bonaire's capital city (population 2,500) is five minutes from the airport and a short walk from Bruce Bowker's Carib Inn and the Divi Flamingo Beach Resort. There's not much to explore here, but there are a few sights worth noting in this small, tidy city.

Kralendijk has one main drag, J. A. Abraham Boulevard, which turns into **Kaya Grandi** in the center of town. Along it are most of the island's major stores, boutiques, restaurants, duty-free shops, and jewelry stores. Across Kaya Grandi, opposite the Littman jewelry store, is Kaya L. D. Gerharts, with several small supermarkets, the ALM office, a handful of snack shops, and some of the better restaurants. Walk down the narrow waterfront avenue called Kaya C. E. B. Hellmund, which leads straight to the **North and South piers.** In the center of town, the Harbourside Mall has chic boutiques. Along this route is **Fort Oranje,** with cannons pointing to the sea. From December through April, cruise ships dock in the harbor once or twice a week. The elegant white structure that looks like a tiny Greek temple is the **Fish Market**; local fishermen no longer bring their catches here (they sell out of their homes these days), but you'll find plenty of fresh produce.

South Bonaire

The trail south from Kralendijk is chock-full of icons—both natural and man-made—that tell the minisaga of Bonaire. Rent a four-wheel-drive vehicle (a car will do, but during the rainy months the roads can become muddy, making traction difficult) and head south along the Southern Scenic Route. The roads wind through otherworldly desert terrain, full of organ-pipe cacti and spiny-trunk mangroves—huge stumps of saltwater trees that rise out of the marshes like witches. Watch for long-haired goats and lizards of all sizes.

SIGHTS TO SEE

2 **Salt Flats.** When touring the southern section of the island, you can't miss the salt flats, voluptuous white drifts that look something like huge mounds of vanilla ice cream. Harvested once a year, the "ponds" are owned by the Akzo Nobel Salt Company, which has reactivated the 19th-century salt industry with great success. (One reason for that success is that the ocean on this part of the island is higher than the land—which makes irrigation a snap.) Keep a lookout for the three 30-ft obelisks—white, blue, and red—that were used to guide the trade boats coming to pick up the salt. Look also in the distance across the pans to the abandoned solar salt works that is now a designated **flamingo sanctuary.** With the naked eye, you might be able to make out a pink-orange haze just on the horizon; with binoculars you will see a sea of bobbing pink bodies. The sanctuary is completely protected, and no entrance is allowed (flamingos are extremely sensitive to disturbances of any kind), but if luck is on your side, somewhere along the far southern route you'll find some flamingos close enough to the road to hear and see more clearly.

Slave Huts. The gritty history of the salt industry is revealed in Rode Pan, the site of two groups of tiny slave huts. The white grouping is on the right side of the road opposite the Akzo Nobel Salt Works; the second grouping, called the red slave huts (though they appear yellow), stretches across the road a bit farther on toward the southern tip of the island. During the 19th century, the salt workers, imported slaves from Africa, worked the fields by day, then crawled into these huts at night to sleep. Each Friday afternoon, they walked seven hours to Rincon to weekend with their families, returning each Sunday to the salt pans. In recent years, the government has restored the huts to their original simplicity. Only very small people will be able to go inside, but take a walk around and poke your head in for a look.

3 **Trans-World Radio.** The first landmark you'll come to on the Southern Scenic Route is an unexpected symbol of modernism—the towering 500-ft antennas of one of the most powerful stations in Christian broadcasting. From here, evangelical programs and gospel music are transmitted daily in five languages to all of North, South, and Central America, as well as the entire Caribbean.

① Willemstoren Lighthouse. At the southern tip of the island, Bonaire's first lighthouse was built in 1837 and is now automated (but closed to visitors). Take some time to explore the beach and notice how the waves, driven by the trade winds, play a crashing symphony against the rocks. Locals make a habit of stopping here to collect pieces of driftwood in spectacular shapes and to build fanciful pyramids from found objects washed ashore.

North Bonaire

The Northern Scenic Route takes you right into the heart of Bonaire's natural wonders—desert gardens of towering cacti (*kadushi,* used to prepare soup, and the thornier *yatu,* used to build cactus fencing), tiny coastal coves, dramatically shaped coral grottoes, and plenty of fantastic panoramas. The road also weaves through spectacular eroded pink-and-black limestone walls and eerie rock formations with fanciful names like the Devil's Mouth and Iguana Head (you'll need a vivid imagination and sharp eye to recognize them).

A snappy excursion with the requisite photo stops will take about 2½ hours, but if you pack your swimsuit and a hefty picnic basket (forget about finding a Burger King), you could spend the entire day exploring this northern sector, including a few hours snorkeling in Washington/Slagbaai Park. Head out from Kralendijk on the Kaya Gobernador N. Debrot until it turns into the Northern Scenic Route. Note that once you pass the Radio Nederland radio towers, you cannot turn back to Kralendijk. The narrow road becomes one-way until you get to Landhuis Karpata, and you will have to follow the cross-island road to Rincon and return via the main road through the center of the island.

SIGHTS TO SEE

⑥ Barcadera. Once used to trap goats, this cave is one of the oldest in Bonaire; there's even a tunnel that looks intriguingly spooky. It's the first sight along the northern route; watch closely for a yellow marker on your left before you reach the towering Radio Nederland antennas. Pull off across from the entrance to the Bonaire Caribbean Club, and you'll discover some stone steps that lead down into a cave full of stalactites and vegetation.

Goto Meer. This saltwater lagoon near the northern end of the island is a popular flamingo hangout. Bonaire is one of the few places in the world where pink flamingos nest. The spindly legged creatures—affectionately called "pink clouds"—at first look like swizzle sticks. But they're magnificent birds to observe—and there are about 15,000 of them in Bonaire. The best time to catch them at home is January–June, when they tend to their gray-plumed young. For the best view of these shy birds, take the newly paved access road running alongside the lagoon through the jungle of cacti to the parking and observation area on the rise overlooking the lagoon and Washington/Slagbaai Park beyond.

Landhuis Karpata. This mustard-color building was the land house of an aloe plantation over a hundred years ago. Notice the rounded outdoor oven where aloe was boiled down before exporting the juice. At press time, the Bonairian government was considering making Karpata a rest stop and drink stand, since there is nothing of the sort in this section of the island. We can only hope!

⑦ 1,000 Steps. Once you've passed the Radio Nederland towers on the main road headed to the north end of the island, watch closely for a short yellow marker on the opposite side of the road to locate 1,000 Steps, a limestone staircase carved right out of the cliff. If you take the trek down them, you'll discover a lovely coral beach and protected cove where you can snorkel and scuba dive. Actually, you'll climb only 67 steps, but it feels like 1,000 when you walk up carrying scuba gear.

⑨ Onima. Small signposts direct the way to the Indian inscriptions found on a 3-ft limestone ledge that juts out like a partially formed cave entrance. Look up to see the red-stained designs and symbols inscribed on the limestone, said to have been the handiwork of the Arawak Indians when they inhabited the island centuries ago. The pictographs were recently dated—they're at least 500 years old—and new descriptive placards were being erected at press time. To reach Onima, pass through Rincon on the road that heads back to Kralendijk, but take the left-hand turn before Fontein.

⑧ Rincon. The original Spanish settlement on the island, Rincon became home to the slaves brought from Africa to work on the plantations and salt fields. Superstition and voodoo lore still have a powerful impact here, more so than in Kralendijk, where the townspeople work hard at suppressing the old ways. Rincon is now a well-kept cluster of pastel cottages and century-old buildings that constitute Bonaire's oldest village. Watch your driving here—both goats and dogs often sit right in the middle of the main drag. There are a couple of local eateries, but the real temptation is **Prisca's Ice Cream** (☎ 599/7–6334), to be found at her house on Kaya Komkomber (watch for the hand-lettered road sign).

⑤ Seroe Largu. Just off the main road, this spot, at 394 ft, is one of the highest on the island. A paved but narrow, twisting road leads to a magnificent daytime view of Kralendijk's rooftops and the island of Klein Bonaire; at night, the city lights below make this a romantic stop.

☝ ⑩ Washington/Slagbaai National Park. Once a plantation producing divi-divi trees (whose pods were used for tanning animal skins), aloe (used for medicinal lotions), charcoal, and goats, the park is now a model of conservation, designed to maintain fauna, flora, and geological treasures in their natural state. The 13,500-acre tropical desert terrain can easily be toured by the dirt roads. As befits a wilderness sanctuary, the well-marked, rugged roads force you to drive slowly enough to appreciate the animal life and the terrain. A four-wheel-drive vehicle is a must. (Think twice about coming here if it rained the day before—the mud you may encounter will be more than inconvenient.) If you are planning to hike, bring a picnic lunch, camera, sunscreen, and plenty of water. There are two different routes: The long one, 22 mi (about 2½ hours), is marked by yellow arrows; the short one, 15 mi (about 1½ hours), is marked by green arrows. Goats and donkeys may dart across the road, and if you keep your eyes peeled, you may catch sight of large iguanas, camouflaged in the shrubbery.

Bird-watchers are really in their element here. Right inside the park's gate, flamingos roost on the salt pad known as **Salina Mathijs,** and exotic parakeets dot the foot of **Mt. Brandaris,** Bonaire's highest peak, at 784 ft. Some 130 species of colorful birds fly in and out of the shrubbery in the park. Keep your eyes open and your binoculars at hand. (For choice beach sites in the park, *see* Beaches, *above.*) Swimming, snorkeling, and scuba diving are permitted, but visitors are requested not to frighten the animals or remove anything from the grounds. There is absolutely no hunting, fishing, or camping allowed. A useful guidebook to the park is available at the entrance for about $6. ☎ 599/7–8444. ✎ $5. ☉ *Daily 8–5, but you must enter before 3.*

Bonaire A to Z

Arriving and Departing

BY AIRPLANE

ALM (☎ 599/7–7400) and **Air Aruba** (☎ 599/7–8300) will get you to Bonaire. ALM has two nonstop flights a week from Miami, daily flights via Curaçao from Miami, and two flights a week from Atlanta tied in with United. ALM flies to Aruba, Curaçao, Jamaica, and St. Maarten, as well as other Caribbean islands, using Curaçao as its Caribbean hub. It also offers a Visit Caribbean Pass, which allows easy interisland travel. Air Aruba flies three days a week from Newark and daily from Miami to Aruba with connecting service to Bonaire. **United Airlines** (☎ 800/241–6522) offers connecting service with **Antillean Air** (☎ 599/7–8500) from Miami twice a week.

From the Airport: Bonaire's **Flamingo Airport** (☎ 599/7–3800) is tiny, but you'll appreciate its welcoming ambience. The customs check is perfunctory if you are arriving from another Dutch isle; otherwise you will have to show proof of citizenship (☞ Passports, *below*), plus a return or ongoing ticket. Rental cars and taxis are available at the airport, but try to arrange the pickup through your hotel. A taxi will run between $8 and $12 (for up to four people) to most hotels.

Electricity

Bonaire runs on 120 AC/50 cycles. A transformer and occasionally a two-prong adapter is required.

Emergencies

Ambulance: ☎ 599/7–8900. **Emergency assistance:** ☎ 599/7–8000. **Hospital:** St. Franciscus Hospital (⊠ Kaya Soeur Bartola 2, Kralendijk, ☎ 599/7–8900). **Pharmacy:** Botika Bonaire (⊠ Kaya Grandi 27, by Harbourside Mall, ☎ 599/7–8905) is open Monday–Saturday 8–7. **Police and Fire:** ☎ 108 or 110. **Scuba-diving emergencies:** There's a hyperbaric decompression chamber next to the hospital in Kralendijk (☎ 599/7–8187).

Festivals and Special Events

Carnival, generally held the second week of February, is the usual nonstop parade of glitter, steel bands, floats, and wild costumes, albeit on a much smaller scale than other islands. It culminates in the ceremonial burning in effigy of King Momo, representing the spirit of debauchery. An **International Fishing Tournament** is held toward the end of March. Early October sees the well-attended—and competitive— **International Sailing Regatta.**

Getting Around

You can zip about the island in a car or a four-wheel-drive vehicle. Scooters and bicycles are less practical but can be fun, too. Just remember that there are miles of unpaved road (though several leading to sights of interest on the northern end of the island were paved in late 1995); the roller-coaster hills at the national park require a strong stomach; and during the rainy season (July–October), mud—called Bonairian snow—can be difficult to navigate. All traffic stays to the right, and, delightfully, there has yet to be a single traffic light. Signs or green arrows are usually posted to leading attractions; if you stick to the paved roads and marked turnoffs, you won't get lost.

BICYCLES AND SCOOTERS

Bonaire Bicycle & Motorbike Rental (☎ 599/7–8226), **Harbour Village Beach Resort** (⊠ Kaya Gobernador Debrot, ☎ 599/7–7500), and **Hot Shot Rentals** (⊠ Kaya Bonaire 4, ☎ 599/7–7166) rent regular, hybrid, and Dutch touring bikes. The first two also rent scooters; single seaters cost around $26 per day or $130 per week, while double seaters run about $32 per day or $175 per week. For mountain bikes, try **Captain Don's Habitat** (⊠ Kaya Gobernador Debrot 130, ☎ 599/7–8290 or 599/7–8913) or **Cycle Bonaire** (⊠ Kaya L. D. Gerharts 11, ☎ 599/7–7558). Rates average around $15–$20 per day, and a credit-card or cash deposit is usually required.

CAR RENTALS

You'll need a valid U.S., Canadian, or International Driver's license to rent a car, and you must meet the minimum and maximum age requirements (usually 25 and 70) of each rental company. There's a government tax of $3.50 per day per car rental; gas costs about $2.50–$3 per gallon. **Budget** (☎ 599/7–7424) rents cars, Suzuki minivans, and four-wheel-drive vehicles at its six locations, but reservations can be made only through the head office. Pickups are at the airport (☎ 599/7–8315) and at several hotels. It's always a good idea to make advance reservations (☎ 800/472–3325 in the U.S., FAX 599/7–8865). Prices range from $40 a day for a Suzuki minivan or Nissan Sentra to $60 a day for an automatic, air-conditioned, four-door sedan. Remember, there are always substantial savings if you rent by the week.

Other agencies are **Avis** (⊠ Flamingo Airport, ☎ 599/7–5795, FAX 599/7–5793), **Dollar Rent-a-Car** (⊠ Flamingo Airport, ☎ 599/7–8888, 599/7–5588 at the airport, FAX 599/7–7788), **Flamingo Car Rental** (⊠ Kaya Grandi 86, ☎ 599/7–8888 or 599/7–5588 at the airport, FAX 599/7–7788), and **Island Rentals** (⊠ Kaya Industria 31, ☎ 599/7—2100, FAX 599/7–8745), which rents soft-top Jeeps for $40 a day.

TAXIS

Taxis are unmetered; they have fixed rates controlled by the government. A trip from the airport to your hotel will cost between $10 and $15 for up to four passengers. A taxi from most hotels into town costs between $5 and $8. Fares increase from 7 PM to midnight by 25% and from midnight to 6 AM by 50%. Taxi drivers are usually knowledgeable enough about the island to conduct half-day tours; they charge about $30 for up to four passengers for half-day northern- or southern-route tours. Call **Taxi Central Dispatch** (☎ 599/7–8100 or dial 10), or inquire at your hotel.

Guided Tours

BOAT TOURS AND CRUISES

The Siamese sailing junk **Samur** (☎ 599/7–5433), the 56-ft privateer's ketch **Mistress** (☎ 599/7–8330), the sailing yacht **Lady Curzon** (☎ 599/7–2050), the 56-ft ketch **Sea Witch** (☎ 599/7–5433), and the trimaran **Woodwind** (☎ 599/7–8285) offer a variety of cruises for snorkeling, picnicking, and watching the sunset. Prices range from $25 to $50 per person. A private day's cruise on the sailboat **Oscarina** (☎ 599/7–8290 or 599/7–8988) is $350 for a party of four. A three-day Curaçao cruise aboard the *Sea Witch* runs $250 per person. The *Samur* features a seven-course Thai dinner cruise once each week; even at $90 per head, it always sells out well in advance. For those who prefer to skipper their own vessel, charter sailboats are available from **Club Nautico** (⊠ Kaya Jan N. E. Craane 24, ☎ 599/7–5800). Glass-bottom-boat trips are offered on the **Bonaire Dream** (⊠ Harbour Village Marina, Kaya Gobernador Debrot, ☎ 599/7–8239 or 599/7–4514). The 1½-hour trip costs $23 and leaves twice daily, except Sunday, from the Harbour Village Marina. You can also buy tickets at most hotels.

ORIENTATION

If you don't like to drive, **Bonaire Sightseeing Tours** (☎ 599/7–8778, FAX 599/7–4890) will chauffeur you around the island on various tours, among them a two-hour Northern Island Tour ($20), which visits the 1,000 Steps; Goto Lake; Rincon, the oldest settlement on the island; and Indian inscriptions at Onima; and a two-hour Southern Island Tour ($20), which covers Akzo Nobel Salt Company, a modern salt-manufacturing facility where flamingos gather; Lac Bay; and the oldest lighthouse on the island. A half-day city-and-country tour ($25) visits sights in both the north and south. **Baranka Tours** (☎ 599/7–2200, FAX 599/7–2211) offers similar tours at slightly less cost. **Achie's Tours** (✉ Kaya Nikiboko Noord 33, ☎ 599/7–8630, FAX 599/7–4430) also offer several half- and full-day island tours.

SPECIAL-INTEREST

Bonaire Nature Tours (☎ 599/7–7714) offers full-day natural-history tours of Bonaire's Washington/Slagbaai National Park. 13,500 acres of majestic scenery, wildlife, unspoiled beaches, and tropical flora. The price is $50 and includes the park entrance fee and guided snorkeling. Half-day cave and swamp tours are also available.

Language

The official language is Dutch, but few speak it, and even then only on official occasions. The street language is Papiamento, a mixture of Spanish, Portuguese, Dutch, English, African, and French—full of colorful Bonairian idioms that even Curaçaoans sometimes don't get. You'll light up your waiter's eyes, though, if you can remember to say *masha danki* (thank you) and *pasa un bon dia* (have a nice day). English is spoken by most people working at the hotels, restaurants, and tourist shops, but a Spanish phrase book may come in handy.

Money Matters

CURRENCY

The great thing about Bonaire is that you don't need to convert your American dollars into the local currency, the NAf guilder. U.S. currency and traveler's checks are accepted everywhere, and the difference in exchange rates is negligible. Banks accept U.S. dollar banknotes at the official rate of NAf1.78 to the U.S. dollar, traveler's checks at NAf1.80. This rate is practically fixed. The rate of exchange at shops and hotels ranges from NAf1.75 to NAf1.80. The guilder is divided into 100 cents. Note: Prices quoted here are in U.S. dollars unless indicated otherwise.

SERVICE CHARGES, TAXES, AND TIPPING

Hotels charge a room tax of $6.50 per person, per night. A VAT (Value Added Tax) of 6% is tacked on to dining and lodging costs. There's no sales tax on purchases in Bonaire. Departure tax when going to Curaçao is $5.75. For all other destinations it's $10. Many hotels (not all) add a 10%–15% maid service charge to your bill. Most restaurants add a 10%–12% service charge to your bill. Taxi drivers expect a 10% tip, but it isn't mandatory (unless you can't stand to be glared at). Bellhops should receive $1 per bag.

Opening and Closing Times

Stores in the Kralendijk area are generally open Monday–Saturday 8–noon and 2–6 PM. On Sundays and holidays, and when cruise ships arrive, most shops open for a few extra hours. Most **restaurants** are open for lunch and dinner, but few not affiliated with hotels are open for breakfast. **Banks** are open Monday–Friday 8–4.

HOLIDAYS

New Year's Day, Good Friday (Apr. 2), Easter (Apr. 4), Queen's Birthday (Apr. 30), Labor Day (May 1), Bonaire Day (Sept. 6), Christmas and the day after (Dec. 25–26).

Passports

U.S. and Canadian citizens need only proof of identity (a valid passport or a birth certificate with a raised seal along with a photo ID). British subjects may carry a British Visitor's Passport, available from any post office; all other visitors must carry valid passports. In addition, all visitors must have a return or ongoing ticket and is advised to confirm that reservation 48 hours before departure.

Precautions

Because of violent trade winds pounding against the rocks, the windward (eastern) side of Bonaire is much too rough for diving. The *Guide to the Bonaire Marine Park* (available at dive shops around the island) specifies the level of diving skill required for 44 sites, and knows what it's talking about. No matter how beautiful a beach may look, heed all warning signs regarding the rough undertow. Also get an orientation on what stings underwater and what doesn't.

During Bonaire's "rainy season" (November–April), the mosquitoes can be fierce. Smart, happy people douse themselves with repellent and also spray their hotel room before going to bed. Open-air restaurants usually have a can of repellent handy. Bonaire has a reputation for being friendly and safe, but lately, even residents are locking their car doors. Don't leave your camera in an open car, and leave your money, credit cards, jewelry, and other valuables in your hotel's safety-deposit box.

Telephones and Mail

It's difficult for visitors to Bonaire to get involved in dramatic, heart-wrenching phone conversations or *any* phone discussions requiring a degree of privacy: Only about one-third of the major hotels have phones in their rooms, so calls must be made from hotel front desks or from the central telephone-company office in Kralendijk. Telephone connections have improved, but static is still common. To call Bonaire from the United States, dial 011–599–7 + the local four-digit number. When making interisland calls, dial the local four-digit number. Local phone calls cost NAf25¢. Forget about trying to use your phone cards; it's theoretically possible, but utterly maddening trying to get connected to the right operator. You can try AT&T by dialing 001–800/872–2881 from public phones, but there are no guarantees.

At press time, airmail postage rates to the United States and Canada were NAf1.75 for letters and NAf90¢ for postcards; to Britain, NAf2.50 for letters and NAf1.25 for postcards.

Visitor Information

Contact the **Bonaire Government Tourist Office** (✉ 10 Rockefeller Plaza, Suite 900, New York, NY 10020, ☎ 212/956–5912 or 800/266–2473, FAX 212/956–5913, www.bonaire.org) for advice and information on planning your trip. Ask about diving packages, either including accommodations or not. In Bonaire, stop by the **Bonaire Tourist Board** (✉ Kaya Simon Bolivar 12, ☎ 599/7–8322 or 599/7–8649, FAX 599/7–8408) office for a map and list of weekly events.

7 British Virgin Islands

Updated by
Pamela
Acheson

*T*he eight-seater Cessna took off smoothly and on schedule for the 20-minute flight from St. Thomas. As it flew up the Sir Francis Drake Channel to the Beef Island/Tortola Airport, the passengers gazed out at stunning views of island and channel. Suddenly, everyone turned from the windows and looked at each other quizzically. They sat in stunned silence as the plane flew right past the airport and headed to the little runway on nearby Virgin Gorda. After this unscheduled landing, the pilot turned around nervously, and said, "Sorry, I'm late for my wedding," he said. "Nelson, my copilot, will fly you back to Tortola."

The British Virgin Islands consist of about 50 islands, islets, and cays that are serene, seductive, spectacularly beautiful, and still remarkably laid-back. At some points they lie only a mile or so from the U.S. Virgin Islands, but they remain unique and have managed to retain their quiet, friendly, and very casual character. Although the past five years have seen a huge increase in the number of automobiles and the construction of a cruise-ship dock, and this past year a four-lane highway—complete with stoplights—in Road Town, for the most part, the BVI still remain happily free of the runaway development that has detracted from the charm of so many West Indian islands.

The pleasures here are understated: sailing around the multitude of tiny, nearby islands; diving to the wreck of the RMS *Rhone*, sunk off Salt Island in 1867; snorkeling in one of hundreds of wonderful spots; walking empty beaches; taking in spectacular views from the islands' peaks; and settling in on a breeze-swept terrace to admire the sunset.

Several factors have enabled the BVI to retain the endearing qualities of yesteryear's Caribbean: no building can rise higher than the surrounding palms—two stories is the limit, and there are no direct flights from the mainland United States, thus holding back the tourism tide to some extent. Many visitors travel here by water, either aboard their own ketches and yawls or on one of the convenient ferryboats that cross the turquoise waters between St. Thomas and Tortola. Such a passage is a fine prelude to a stay in these unhurried tropical havens.

Tortola, about 10 square mi, is the largest and most populated of the islands; Virgin Gorda, with 8 square mi, ranks second. The islands scattered around them include Jost Van Dyke, Great Camanoe, Norman, Peter, Salt, Cooper, Ginger, Dead Chest, and Anegada. Tortola has the most hotels, restaurants, and shops. Virgin Gorda offers a limited number of restaurants and shops, and many of its resorts are self-contained. Jost Van Dyke is a major charter boat anchorage, and while little bars line the beach at Great Harbour, there are few places to stay. The other islands are either uninhabited or have a single hotel or resort. Many of these, such as Peter Island, offer excellent anchorages, and their bays and harbors are very popular with overnighting boaters.

Sailing has always been a popular activity in the BVI. The first arrivals here were a romantic seafaring tribe, the Ciboney Indians. They were followed (circa AD 900) by the Arawak Indians, who sailed from South America, established settlements here, and farmed and fished. Still later came the mighty Caribs.

In 1493 Christopher Columbus was the first European to visit. Impressed by the number of islands dotting the horizon, he named them *Las Once Mil Virgines*—The 11,000 Virgins—in honor of the 11,000 virgin-companions of Saint Ursula, martyred in the 4th century. In the ensuing years, the Spaniards passed through these waters fruitlessly seeking gold. Then came the pirates, who found the islands' hidden coves and treacherous reefs ideal bases from which to prey on passing galleons crammed with Mexican and Peruvian gold, silver, and spices. Among the most notorious of these fellows were Blackbeard Teach, Bluebeard, Captain Kidd, and Sir Francis Drake, who lent his name to the channel that sweeps through the two main clusters of the BVI.

In the 17th century, the colorful cutthroats were replaced by the Dutch who, in turn, were sent packing by the British. It was the British who established a plantation economy, and for the next 150 years developed the sugar industry through the labor of African slaves. When slavery was abolished in 1838, the plantation economy quickly faltered, and the majority of the white population left for Europe.

The islands dozed, a forgotten corner of the British empire, until the early 1960s. In 1966 a new constitution granting greater autonomy to the islands was approved. While the governor is still appointed by the Queen of England, his or her limited powers concentrate on external affairs and local security. The Legislative Council, which consists of representatives from nine island districts, administers other matters. General elections are held every four years. The arrangement seems to suit the British Virgin Islanders just fine: The political mood is serene, with none of the occasional political turmoil found on other islands.

In the 1960s Laurance Rockefeller and American-expatriate Charlie Cary brought the beginnings of tourism to the BVI. In 1965 Rockefeller set about creating the Little Dix resort on Virgin Gorda. Dedicated to preserving the natural beauty of the island while providing its guests with unpretentious yet elegant surroundings, Little Dix set the standard that still prevails in the BVI. A few years later, Cary and his wife, Ginny, established the Moorings marina complex on Tortola, and sailing in the area burgeoned.

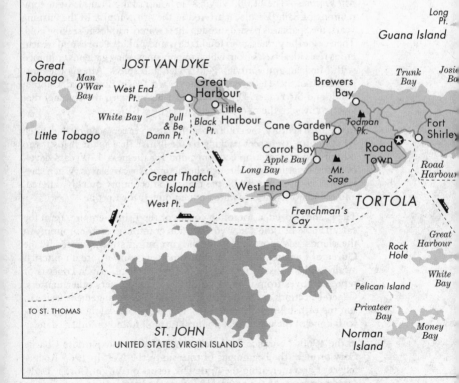

A T L A N T I C

Long
Pt.
Guana Island

*Great
Tobago*

JOST VAN DYKE

Man
O'War
Bay

West End
Pt.

Great
Harbour

Little
Harbour

White Bay

Pull
& Be
Damn Pt.

Black
Pt.

Trunk
Bay

Josie
Ba

Brewers
Bay

Cane Garden
Bay

Todman
Pk.

Fort
Shirley

Little Tobago

Carrot Bay

Apple Bay

Mt.
Sage

Road
Town

Road
Harbour

Great Thatch
Island

Long Bay

West End

West Pt.

Frenchman's
Cay

TORTOLA

*Great
Harbour*

Rock
Hole

*White
Bay*

Pelican Island

Privateer
Bay

*Money
Bay*

TO ST. THOMAS

ST. JOHN
UNITED STATES VIRGIN ISLANDS

**Norman
Island**

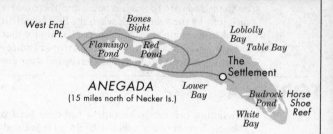

West End
Pt.

Bones
Bight

Loblolly
Bay

Table Bay

Flamingo
Pond

Red
Pond

The
Settlement

ANEGADA
(15 miles north of Necker Is.)

Lower
Bay

Budrock
Pond

Horse
Shoe
Reef

White
Bay

O C E A N

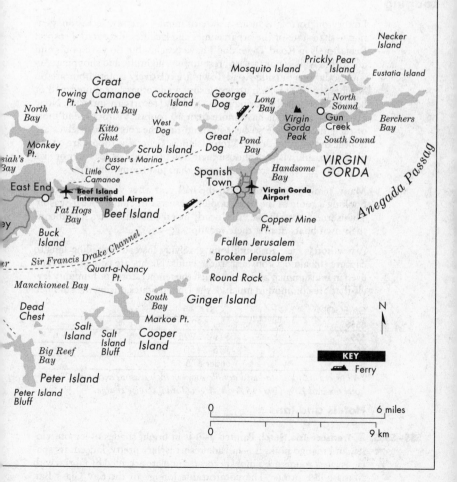

Necker
Island

Prickly Pear
Island

Mosquito Island

Eustatia Island

*Great
Camanoe*

Towing
Pt.

Cockroach
Island

George
Dog

Long
Bay

North
Sound

*North
Bay*

North Bay

West
Dog

Virgin
Gorda
Peak

Gun
Creek

Berchers
Bay

Kitto
Ghut

Great
Dog

Pond
Bay

South Sound

*Monkey
Pt.*

Scrub Island

*VIRGIN
GORDA*

siah's
Bay

Pusser's Marina

Little
Camanoe

Spanish
Town

Handsome
Bay

East End

**Beef Island
International Airport**

Virgin Gorda
Airport

Anegada Passag

Fat Hogs
Bay

Beef Island

Copper Mine
Pt.

Buck
Island

Sir Francis Drake Channel

Fallen Jerusalem

Broken Jerusalem

Quart-a-Nancy
Pt.

Manchioneel Bay

Round Rock

Dead
Chest

South
Bay

Ginger Island

Markoe Pt.

Salt
Island

Salt
Island
Bluff

*Cooper
Island*

*Big Reef
Bay*

N

Peter Island

Peter Island
Bluff

KEY
Ferry

0   6 miles

0   9 km

Although offshore banking is currently the BVI's number-one industry, tourism has been a major source of income. The majority of jobs on the islands are tourism-related, and there may well be even more such jobs by the year 2003, when the Beef Island airport expansion is slated to be completed. Still, there is no doubt that British Virgin Islanders—who so love their unspoiled tropical home—will maintain its easygoing charms for both themselves and their guests.

TORTOLA

Unwinding can easily become a full-time occupation on Tortola. Though Tortola offers a wealth of things to see and do, many visitors prefer just to loll about on a deserted beach or linger over lunch at one of the island's many delightful restaurants. Beaches are never more than a few minutes away, and the steeply sloping green hills that form Tortola's spine are continuously fanned by gentle trade winds. The neighboring islands glimmer like emeralds in a sea of sapphire. It's a world far removed from the hustle of modern life.

Lodging

Luxury on Tortola is more a state of mind—serenity, seclusion, gentility—than state-of-the-art amenities and facilities. Except for Prospect Reef, hotels in Road Town don't have beaches but do have pools and are within walking distance of restaurants, nightlife, and shopping. Accommodations outside Road Town are relatively isolated but are on beaches, some of which are exquisite, while others are quite small or have been enlarged by bringing in sand. BVI resorts are intimate: None are large—only four have more than 50 rooms. Visitors spend most of their time outside so bear in mind that the rooms themselves are not the draw in the British Virgin Islands. Generally, rooms are on the plain side, and visitors choose their hotel because of location or size or price. Guests are treated as more than just room numbers.

Many, many visitors return to the BVI year after year, often making booking a room at the more popular resorts difficult, even off-season. This is true despite the fact that nearly half the island visitors stay aboard their own boats during their vacations.

A few hotels lack air-conditioning, relying instead on ceiling fans to capture the almost constant trade winds. Nights are cool and breezy, even in midsummer, and never reach the temperatures or humidity levels that are common in much of the United States during the summer.

CATEGORY	COST*
$$$$	over $225
$$$	$150–$225
$$	$75–$150
$	under $75

All prices are for a standard double room in high season, excluding 7% hotel tax and 10% (5%–15% on Virgin Gorda) service charge.

Hotels and Inns
ROAD TOWN

$$$–$$$$ ★ 🏨 **Treasure Isle Hotel.** Painted as it is in bright shades of lemon, violet, and mango pink, this hillside resort is very pretty, indeed. Its spacious guest rooms are simply decorated and are accented by fabrics with Matisse-like prints. The comfortable lounge of the Spy Glass Bar, which is open to the breezes and the heady aroma of tropical flowers, is the perfect place to contemplate the harbor and distant islands. Dinner at the ☞ **Lime 'n' Mango** restaurant is romantic. Road Town's shops

and marinas are nearby, and there's transportation to Cane Garden Bay, Brewers Bay, and Cooper Island on different days each week. ⌧ *Waterfront Dr. (Box 68),* ☎ *284/494–2501,* FAX *284/494–2507. 40 rooms. Restaurant, 2 bars, pool, shop. AE, MC, V. EP.*

$$$ 🏨 **Moorings-Mariner Inn.** This inn is also the headquarters for the Moorings Charter operation. It's popular with both yachting folk—who find its facilities convenient and the companionship of fellow "boaties" congenial—and landlubbers who want to be within walking distance of town. The atmosphere is laid-back *and* lively. There are four full-size suites, but even standard rooms are on the large side, and all accommodations are comfortable. The pale-peach decor is picked up in the peach floor tiles, and bright, tropical-print fabrics add splashes of contrasting color. All rooms have a small kitchenette and a balcony, and you'll face the water in all but the eight rooms that overlook the pool or the tennis court. ⌧ *Waterfront Dr. (Box 139),* ☎ *284/494–2332,* FAX *284/494–2226. 38 rooms, 2 suites. Restaurant, bar, kitchenettes, pool, tennis court, volleyball, dive shop, shop. AE, MC, V. EP.*

$$–$$$$ 🏨 **Prospect Reef Resort.** This complex of brightly painted buildings sits on 7 sprawling acres laced with rock paths and a network of lagoons. The 11 units include small rooms; larger rooms with kitchenettes; and two-story, two-bedroom apartments with private interior courtyards. All have a balcony or a patio. There's plenty to do here, with a camp for the kids, six lighted tennis courts, and a rather rustic pitch-and-putt golf course. Cool off in the 25-meter swimming pool, the separate diving pool, or one of the two saltwater swimming areas at the edge of a narrow, artificial beach. The resort has its own harbor, and sailboats are available for daylong—or longer—adventures. If all this isn't enough, take a complimentary trip to Cooper Island, Marina Cay, or Cane Garden Bay. Relax with locals and guests in the intimate ☞ **Callaloo** restaurant. ⌧ *Waterfront Dr. (Box 104),* ☎ *284/494–3311,* FAX *284/494–5595. 130 rooms. 2 restaurants, 2 bars, 2 pools, 2 saltwater pools, beauty salon, 6 tennis courts, shops, children's program, convention center. AE, MC, V. EP.*

$$–$$$ 🏨 **Fort Burt Hotel.** Originally a fort built by the Dutch in the 17th century, this hillside landmark is at the edge of town and—like all good Caribbean forts and hotels—overlooks the harbor. The owners have expanded the hotel with care, and much of the original stonework exterior remains. New rooms and suites have been added, and older ones have been completely overhauled. Although room furnishings are still somewhat modest, you get a private balcony with terrific harbor views. You could also go all out and book one of the two suites that have private pools. ⌧ *Waterfront Dr. (Box 3380),* ☎ *284/494–2587,* FAX *284/ 494–2002. 17 rooms. Restaurant, bar, pool. AE, MC, V. EP.*

$$–$$$ 🏨 **Maria's Hotel by the Sea.** Perched on the edge of Road Harbour, next to the large government building and the cruise-ship dock, this simple hotel is an easy walk from restaurants in town. The small rooms are minimally decorated with white rattan furniture, floral-print bedspreads, and murals painted by local artists. All rooms have balconies, some of which have harbor views. A freshwater pool is available for cooling dips. ⌧ *Waterfront Dr. (Box 206),* ☎ *284/494–2595. 20 rooms. Restaurant, bar, kitchenettes, pool. AE, MC, V. EP.*

$$–$$$ 🏨 **Village Cay Resort.** This pleasant, compact hotel looks out on Road Harbour and several marinas. It's popular with yachters and those who love to shop and dine (you're not far from town here). Rooms are nicely decorated in rattan furniture and tropical prints. Some units have cathedral ceilings and harbor views; the rooms in back are quite small. After trotting to town and back, you can have a swim and then head

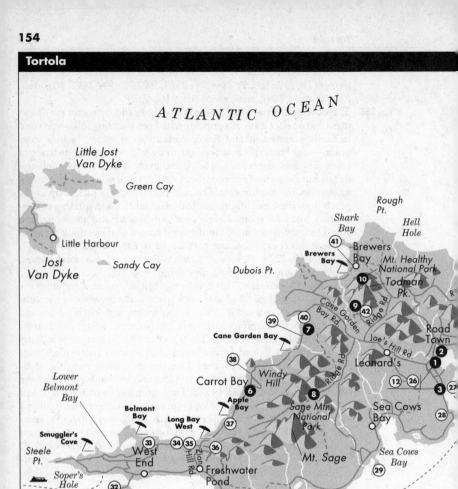

ATLANTIC OCEAN

Little Jost
Van Dyke

Green Cay

Little Harbour

Jost
Van Dyke

Sandy Cay

Dubois Pt.

Rough
Pt.

Shark
Bay

Hell
Hole

Brewers
Bay

Brewers Bay

Mt. Healthy
National Park

Todman
Pk.

Cane Garden
Bay Rd.

Road
Town

Cane Garden Bay

Joe's Hill Rd

Leonard's

Ridge Rd.

Lower
Belmont
Bay

Carrot Bay

Windy
Hill

Sea Cows
Bay

Belmont
Bay

Smuggler's
Cove

Apple
Bay

Sage Mtn.
National
Park

Steele
Pt.

Long Bay
West

Soper's
Hole

West
End

Zion Hill Rd.

Freshwater
Pond

Mt. Sage

Sea Cows
Bay

Little Thatch
Island

Frenchman's
Cay

TO ST. THOMAS

ST. JOHN

Exploring
Cane Garden Bay, **7**
Ft. Burt, **2**
Ft. Recovery, **4**
Frenchman's Cay, **5**
J.R. O'Neal Botanic
Gardens, **3**
Mt. Healthy
National Park, **10**
North Shore Shell
Museum, **6**

RMS *Rhone*, **11**
Road Town, **1**
Sage Mountain
National Park, **8**
Skyworld, **9**

Dining
The Apple, **36**
Brandywine Bay, **46**
C and F
Restaurant, **20**
Cafesito, **25**
Callaloo, **28**
Capriccio di Mare, **16**
Conch Shell Point, **44**
The Fishtrap, **12**
Garden
Restaurant, **33**

The Last Resort, **45**
Lime 'n' Mango, **24**
Mrs. Scatliffe's, **38**
Myett's, **39**
The Pub, **21**
Pusser's Landing, **32**
Pusser's Pub, **15**
Quito's Gazebo, **40**
Skyworld, **42**
Spaghetti
Junction, **18**

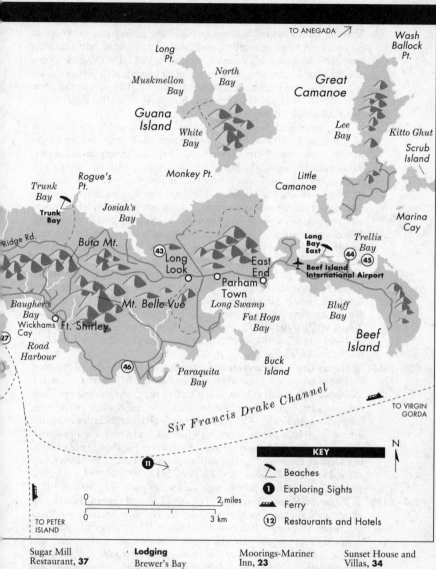

TO ANEGADA

Wash
Ballock
Pt.

Long
Pt.

North
Bay

Great
Camanoe

Muskmellon
Bay

Guana
Island

White
Bay

Lee
Bay

Kitto Ghut

Scrub
Island

Rogue's
Pt.

Monkey Pt.

Little
Camanoe

Marina
Cay

Trunk
Bay

**Trunk
Bay**

Josiah's
Bay

Ridge Rd.

Buta Mt.

(43)

Long
Look

East
End

Long Bay
East

Trellis
Bay

(44)

(45)

Beef Island
International Airport

Parham
Town

Baugher's
Bay

Mt. Belle-Vue

Long Swamp

Bluff
Bay

Wickhams
Cay

Ft. Shirley

Fat Hogs
Bay

Beef
Island

(27)

Road
Harbour

(46)

Paraquita
Bay

Buck
Island

Sir Francis Drake Channel

TO VIRGIN
GORDA

(11)

KEY

N

Beaches

Exploring Sights

Ferry

Restaurants and Hotels

0   2 miles
0   3 km

TO PETER
ISLAND

Sugar Mill
Restaurant, **37**
Tavern in the
Town, **19**
Virgin Queen, **13**

Lodging
Brewer's Bay
Campground, **41**
Fort Burt Hotel, **27**
Frenchman's Cay
Hotel, **31**
Hotel Castle
Maria, **22**
Long Bay Beach
Resort, **33**
Maria's Hotel
by the Sea, **17**

Moorings-Mariner
Inn, **23**
Mount Sage Villas, **26**
Nanny Cay Resort
and Marina, **29**
Ole Works Inn, **44**
Prospect Reef
Resort, **28**
Sebastian's on the
Beach, **35**
Sugar Mill Hotel, **37**

Sunset House and
Villas, **34**
Tamarind Club
Hotel and Villas, **43**
Treasure Isle
Hotel, **24**
Village Cay
Resort, **14**
The Villas at Fort
Recovery Estates, **30**

for the bar. ⊠ *Wickham's Cay (Box 145),* ☎ *284/494–2771,* FAX *284/ 494–2773. 18 rooms. Restaurant, bar, pool. AE, MC, V. EP.*

$$ 🏨 **Hotel Castle Maria.** You can spend all the money you save here at the nearby in-town attractions. And these very simple accommodations have everything most folks need: a refrigerator and cable TV; some rooms also have full kitchenettes, balconies, and air-conditioning. Refresh yourself either in the bar or the freshwater pool. ⊠ *Waterfront Dr. (Box 206),* ☎ *284/494–2553. 30 rooms. Bar, pool. AE, MC, V. EP.*

OUTSIDE ROAD TOWN

$$$–$$$$ 🏨 **Long Bay Beach Resort.** Spectacularly set on a gentle mile-long arc
★   of white sand, this hotel is one of the best on Tortola, thanks to the fine management of James Hawkins. There's a variety of accommodations, including 32 deluxe beachfront rooms, with two queen-size beds or one king-size four-poster bed, marble-top wet bars, showers with Italian tiles, and balconies. There are also smaller beach cabanas: 10 tropical hideaways set on stilts at the water's edge. Hillside choices all have balconies and lovely views and range from small rooms with Jacuzzis to studios with comfortable seating areas to roomy one- and two-bedroom villas with full kitchens. Floral prints and rattan furniture are used throughout. The casual Beach restaurant offers all-day dining inside and around the beachside pool, and the ☞ **Garden Restaurant** serves gourmet dinners in a romantic, candlelit setting. Peter Burwash runs the tennis program. A rustic 9-hole, par-3, pitch-and-putt golf course complete the complex. ⊠ *Long Bay (Box 433), Road Town,* ☎ *284/495–4252 or 800/729–9599 (reservations service),* FAX *284/495–4677. 62 rooms, 20 villas. 2 restaurants, 2 bars, 2 pools, 3 tennis courts, beach, shop. AE, MC, V. EP.*

$$$–$$$$ 🏨 **Nanny Cay Resort and Marina.** With its pastel, gingerbread-trimmed buildings clustered amid overgrown gardens, this hotel exudes the ambience of a small village, albeit one in need of sprucing up. Each room has a patio or balcony, kitchenettes, air-conditioning, ceiling fans, telephones, and cable TV. Typically tropical decor includes cane furniture, floral bedspreads, shuttered windows, and a pastel color scheme. There's a nice-size swimming pool, a saltwater pool made out of large boulders at the water's edge, and an artificial beach. ⊠ *Nanny Cay (Box 281), Road Town,* ☎ *284/494–2512,* FAX *284/494–0555. 42 rooms. 2 restaurants, 2 bars, pool, saltwater pool. AE, MC, V. EP.*

$$$–$$$$ 🏨 **Sugar Mill Hotel.** The owners of this small, out-of-the-way hotel know what they're doing—they were food and travel writers before they opened the Sugar Mill more than two decades ago. Their savvy has paid off: many visitors return year after year. The reception area, bar, and restaurant are in the ruins of a centuries-old sugar mill, and the walls throughout are hung with bright Haitian artwork. Guest houses are scattered up a hill; the rooms are simply decorated in soft pastels and have rattan furnishings. There's a small circular swimming pool set into the hillside and a tiny beach where lunch is served, in season, on a shady terrace. The ☞ **Sugar Mill Restaurant** is well known on the island. ⊠ *Apple Bay (Box 425)Road Town,* ☎ *284/495–4355,* FAX *284/495–4696. 21 rooms. 2 restaurants, 2 bars, pool, beach. AE, MC, V. EP.*

$$$–$$$$ 🏨 **The Villas at Fort Recovery Estates.** This very remote complex has
★   all the ingredients for a good Caribbean vacation: grounds full of tropical flowers; a somewhat remote, beachside setting in and around the remnants of a Dutch fort; friendly, helpful management; and many amenities. All the one- to four-bedroom villas and apartments have excellent views (sliding glass doors open onto patios or balconies that face Drake Channel) and fully equipped kitchens. Living rooms (not air-conditioned) can be used as a bedroom for one child. A gourmet kitchen provides room-service dinners, which are served course by course

and accompanied by candlelight. There's exercise and yoga classes, massages, VCRs and videos for rent, and baby-sitting services; arrangements can be made for car rental, guided land and water tours, and more. ⊠ *Waterfront Dr. (Box 239), Road Town,* ☎ *284/495–4354,* FAX *284/495–4036. 17 units. Room service, pool, massage, beach, snorkeling, baby-sitting. AE, MC, V. EP.*

$$$ ⊞ **Frenchman's Cay Hotel.** This small, casual collection of one- and two-bedroom condos overlooks Drake's Channel. Each unit includes a full kitchen, a dining area, and a sitting room—ideal for families or couples. Rooms are done in neutral colors, with cream-color curtains and bedspreads and tile floors. Ceiling fans and pleasant breezes keep things cool. There's a small pool and a modest-size artificial beach that's sandy to the water's edge but rocky offshore (snorkelers will enjoy the reef here). The alfresco bar and dining room are breeze-swept and offer simple fare. ⊠ *Frenchman's Cay (Box 1054), West End,* ☎ *284/495– 4844,* FAX *284/495–4056. 9 units. Restaurant, bar, fans, pool, tennis court, beach. AE, MC, V. EP.*

$$–$$$ ⊞ **Ole Works Inn.** Nestled in the hillside across the road from one of Tortola's most beautiful beaches is this rustic but appealing inn— owned by local recording star Quito Rhymer. A steeply pitched roof, wood, and island stonework add a contemporary flair to what was once an old sugar mill. Simply decorated rooms have ceiling fans, air-conditioning, and refrigerators. The Honeymoon Suite has an indoor swing for two. ⊠ *Cane Garden Bay (Box 560), Road Town,* ☎ *284/ 495–4837,* FAX *284/495–9618. 15 rooms, 3 suites. MC, V. EP.*

$$–$$$ ⊞ **Sebastian's on the Beach.** The best rooms here are the eight small ones that open right onto the beach. They're airy and white, simply decorated with floral-print curtains and bedspreads, and have either terraces or balconies and great water breezes and views (the ocean lulls you to sleep). Bathrooms have only stall showers, and ceiling fans and louvered windows keep the rooms cool. The other 18 rooms are very simple, lack views, and can be noisy. Some of these are across the street and are considerably cheaper than the beach rooms. The casual restaurant looks out over the water; at lunch you can order fresh salads, grilled vegetables, and a variety of soups and sandwiches; for dinner, the menu includes grilled fish, lobster, and steak. ⊠ *Apple Bay (Box 441), Road Town,* ☎ *284/495–4212,* FAX *284/495–4466. 26 rooms. Restaurant, bar, snack bar, fans, beach. AE. EP.*

$$–$$$ ⊞ **Tamarind Club Hotel and Villas.** This small, out-of-the-way resort on the northeastern side of the island is charming and intimate. It's tucked into a valley not too far from East End and about a half-mile inland from the beach at Josiah's Bay. The nine rooms are built around a courtyard and a pool that has a swim-up bar. All rooms have ceiling fans; some are air-conditioned. The largest, the Honeymoon Suite, has it's own private patio. There are also three two-bedroom villas. ⊠ *Josiah's Bay (Box 441), Road Town,* ☎ *284/495–2477 or 888/744–3376,* FAX *284/495–2858. 9 rooms, 3 2-bedroom villas. Restaurant, bar, fans, pool. MC, V. EP.*

Private Homes and Villas

Areana Villas (⊠ Box 263, Road Town, ☎ 284/494–5864, FAX 284/ 494–7626) represents the island's top-of-the-line properties. Homes offer accommodations for 2 to 10 people in one- to five-bedroom villas, decorated in soothing pastels. Many have swimming pools, Jacuzzis, and glazed terra-cotta courtyards. On Long Bay, Areana works with **Sunset House and Villas,** an exquisite hideaway whose first guest was Britain's Princess Alexandra (but you needn't be royalty to receive the royal treatment here). The company also works with Equinox House, also on Long Bay, a handsome three-bedroom estate set among lavish tumbling gardens. Rates vary but range from expensive ($$$) to very expensive ($$$$) in season. **Mount Sage Villas** (⊠ Sage Mountain Rd. (Box 821) Road Town, ☎ 284/495–9567), near the highest peak on Tortola, is a bit of a drive down to the beaches, but views and breezes are spectacular.

Campgrounds

$ ⚠ **Brewers Bay Campground.** Both prepared and bare sites are on Brewers Bay, one of Tortola's prime snorkeling spots. Check out the ruins of the distillery that gave the bay its name. There are public bathrooms but no showers. ⊠ *Brewers Bay (Box 185), Road Town, ☎ 284/494–3463. 10 prepared and 18 bare sites. Restaurant, bar, beach, windsurfing, baby-sitting. No credit cards.*

Dining

On Tortola, seafood is plentiful, and although other fresh ingredients are scarce, the island's chefs are an adaptable lot, who apply creative genius to whatever the weekly supply boat delivers. (Unfortunately, some restaurants have found it cheaper to serve fish imported frozen from Miami than local fresh fish.) Contemporary American dishes prepared with a Caribbean influence are very popular. The fancier, more expensive restaurants have dress codes: long pants and collared shirts for men, and elegant, casual resort wear for women.

CATEGORY	COST*
$$$$	over $35
$$$	$25–$35
$$	$15–$25
$	under $15

per person for a three-course meal, excluding drinks and service; there is no sales tax in the BVI

Road Town

AMERICAN/CASUAL

$$–$$$$ ✕ **The Pub.** At this lively waterfront spot, tables are arranged along a terrace facing a small marina and Road Town harbor. Hamburgers, salads, and sandwiches are typical lunch offerings. In the evening you can also choose grilled fish, steak, chicken, sautéed conch, or barbecued ribs. There's entertainment here weekends and almost always a spirited dart game. ⊠ *Waterfront Dr., ☎ 284/494–2608. Reservations not accepted. AE, MC, V. Closed Sun.*

$–$$ ✕ **Pusser's Pub.** Almost everyone who visits Tortola stops here at least once to have a bite to eat and to sample the famous Pusser's Rum Painkiller. The menu includes cheesy pizza, such pub grub as shepherd's pie, and such local specialties as Road Town Rice and chicken *rotis* (flatbread wrapped around a curry of chicken and vegetables). ⊠ *Waterfront Dr., ☎ 284/494–3897. AE, MC, V.*

CARIBBEAN

$$$–$$$$ ✕ **Callaloo.** Windows open to the breezes at this romantic second-floor
★   restaurant that overlooks a small marina at the ☞ **Prospect Reef Resort.** The extensive West Indian–influenced menu includes cracked jerk conch and pumpkin crepes for appetizers, as well as spicy callaloo pepper pot and sweet potato soups. For the main course, try Caribbean beef Wellington (wrapped in sweet potatoes and spinach), grilled shrimp over linguine, or blackened swordfish with a mango salsa. Rum cheesecake and Tia Maria tiramisu are dessert specialties. ⊠ *Waterfront Dr., ☎ 284/494–3311. Reservations essential. AE, MC, V.*

$$–$$$$ ✕ **C and F Restaurant.** Crowds head to this casual spot for the best
★   barbecue in town (chicken, fish, and ribs), fresh local fish prepared your

way, and excellent curries. Sometimes there's a wait for a table, but it's worth it. The restaurant is just outside Road Town, on a side street past the Moorings and just past Riteway. ⊠ *Purcell Estate,* ☎ *284/ 494–4941. Reservations not accepted. AE, MC, V. No lunch.*

ENGLISH

$–$$$$ ✕ **Virgin Queen.** The sailing and rugby crowd and locals gather here to play darts, drink beer, and eat Queen's Pizza, which some say is the best pizza in the Caribbean. Also on the menu is excellent West Indian and English fare: salt fish, barbecued ribs with beans and rice, bangers and mash, shepherd's pie, and chili. ⊠ *Fleming St.,* ☎ *284/494–2310. Reservations not accepted. No credit cards. Closed Sun.*

$–$$ ✕ **Tavern in the Town.** Birds and bougainvillea brighten the garden setting of this English-style pub. Aside from mixed grills and fish-and-chips, you can also order such entrées as duck in orange and rum sauce and garlic shrimp, as well as hamburgers. There's cozy indoor dining, too. ⊠ *Waterfront Dr.,* ☎ *284/494–2790. MC, V. Closed Sat.*

ITALIAN

$$–$$$$ ✕ **Spaghetti Junction.** This cozy indoor spot is popular with the boating crowd. Penne with a spicy tomato sauce, spinach-mushroom lasagna, and capellini with shellfish are house specialties here, but the menu also includes more traditional Italian fare (veal or chicken parmigiana, pasta, etc.). The sun-dried tomatoes in the Caesar salad are a nice twist. Check out the gorilla in the rest room. ⊠ *Waterfront Dr.,* ☎ *284/494–4880. MC, V. Closed Sept. and holidays. No lunch.*

$–$$ ✕ **Capriccio di Mare.** The owners of the well-known Brandywine Bay ★ restaurant also run this authentic Italian outdoor café. People stop by in the morning for an espresso and a fresh pastry, and all day long for a cappuccino or a tiramisu, delicious toast Italiano (grilled ham and Swiss cheese sandwiches), fresh salads, bowls of perfectly cooked linguine or penne with a variety of sauces, and crispy tomato and mozzarella pizzas. Drink specialties include the Mango Bellini, an adaptation of the famous Bellini cocktail served by Harry's Bar in Venice. ⊠ *Waterfront Dr.,* ☎ *284/494–5369. Reservations not accepted. No credit cards. Closed Sun. Closes at 9:30 PM Mon.–Sat.*

MEXICAN

$$–$$$$ ✕ **Lime 'n' Mango.** A long open-air veranda is the romantic setting for this popular restaurant at the ☞ **Treasure Isle Hotel.** The menu features local specialties and, surprisingly, authentic Mexican cuisine. Try the conch fritters, salt fish cakes, or Jamaican calamari for an appetizer. The fajitas—chicken, beef, or vegetarian—are the best Mexican entrée; they arrive at your table sizzling in a hot iron frying pan, with a side basket of warm tortillas. The coconut shrimp is also popular, and the Anegada lobster is always fresh. There's a West Indian barbecue here Saturday night. ⊠ *Waterfront Dr.,* ☎ *284/494–2501. AE, MC, V.*

SEAFOOD

$$–$$$$ ✕ **The Fishtrap.** Dine alfresco at this laid-back restaurant, which serves grilled local lobster, several local catches-of-the-day, plus steaks, and chicken. The lunch menu includes burgers and salads as well as a few Mexican items. ⊠ *Columbus Centre, Wickham's Cay,* ☎ *284/494– 3626. AE, MC, V. No lunch Sun.*

SPANISH

$$–$$$$ ✕ **Cafesito.** Folks stop by this open-air eatery for pitchers of sangria and an assortment of tapas (Spanish appetizers), such as potato croquettes, roasted garlic and Brie wrapped in phyllo dough, and grilled shrimp. Many make a meal out of tapas while others save room for

the spicy chorizo and chicken paella, or the roasted pork loin and garlic wrapped in apple-smoked bacon. ⊠ *Romasco Pl., Wickham's Cay,* ☎ *284/494–7412. AE, MC, V.*

Outside Road Town

AMERICAN/CASUAL

$$–$$$ ✕ **Pusser's Landing.** Yachters flock to the two-story home of this popular waterfront restaurant. Downstairs belly up to the large, outdoor mahogany bar or choose a waterside table for drinks, sandwiches, and light dinners. Head upstairs for quieter alfresco dining and a delightfully eclectic menu that includes homemade black bean soup, freshly grilled local fish, pasta, and such pub favorites as shepherd's pie. The air-conditioned Dinner Theater, with its 15-ft movie screen, features prix-fixe, three-course meal-and-movie combos and sports events. ⊠ *Soper's Hole,* ☎ *284/495–4554. AE, MC, V.*

CARIBBEAN

$$–$$$$ ✕ **The Apple.** This small, inviting restaurant is in a little West Indian house. Soft candlelight creates a relaxed atmosphere in which to partake of fish steamed in lime butter, conch or whelks in garlic sauce, or other local seafood dishes. There's a traditional West Indian barbecue and buffet every Sunday evening from 7 until 9, and coconut chips and conch fritters are served at happy hour weekdays from 5 until 7. The excellent lunch menu includes sandwiches, meat and vegetarian lasagna, lobster quiche, seafood crepes, and croissants with ham and Swiss or spinach and feta. ⊠ *Little Apple Bay,* ☎ *284/495–4437. AE, MC, V.*

$$–$$$ ✕ **Mrs. Scatliffe's.** The best West Indian cooking on the island is here, according to many knowledgeable Tortolans (though some bemoan, "She's gone Continental"). Meals are served on the upstairs terrace of Mrs. Scatliffe's home. The food is freshly prepared (vegetables come from the family garden); the baked chicken in coconut is meltingly tender. After dinner, live entertainment is provided by family members. ⊠ *Carrot Bay,* ☎ *284/495–4556. Reservations essential. No credit cards.*

$$–$$$ ✕ **Myett's.** Right in the middle of Cane Garden Bay Beach, this two-
★   level restaurant and bar is hopping day and night. Chowder made with fresh Anegada lobsters is the house specialty. The menu includes everything from hamburgers to fruit platters and vegetarian dishes to grilled shrimp, lobster, steak, and tuna. Sunday there's an all-day barbecue buffet and a live reggae band. ⊠ *Cane Garden Bay,* ☎ *284/495–9543. Reservations not accepted. MC, V.*

$$–$$$ ✕ **Quito's Gazebo.** This rustic beachside bar and restaurant is owned and operated by Quito Rhymer, a multitalented BVI recording star who plays the guitar and sings Calypso ballads and love songs Tuesday, Thursday, Friday, and Sunday; a reggae band performs Saturday. The menu is Caribbean with an emphasis on fresh fish. Try the conch stew or the curried chicken. A Caribbean buffet is featured on Sunday night, and Friday is fish-fry night. The atmosphere is so convivial that by the time you finish dinner here you are likely to find yourself swapping yarns with some colorful local personalities. ⊠ *Cane Garden Bay,* ☎ *284/ 495–4837. MC, V. Closed Mon.*

CONTEMPORARY

$$$–$$$$ ✕ **Garden Restaurant.** Relax over dinner in this dimly lit, intimate, open-air restaurant at ☞ **Long Bay Beach Resort.** The extensive menu changes daily: appetizers might include escargot and Portobello mushrooms in pastry or Caesar salad with passion-fruit croutons; and the list of entrées might feature broiled swordfish steak with pecan-lime butter, duck breast with Grand Marnier sauce, or beef tenderloin with red pepper salsa. Pecan pie and rum cheesecake are among the dessert specialties. ⊠ *Long Bay,* ☎ *284/495–4252. AE, MC, V.*

$$$–$$$$ ✕ **Skyworld.** The longtime owner-chef of the well-known Upstairs
★ restaurant took over this mountaintop aerie several years ago, bring-
ing his superb menu with him. Come at sunset and watch the western
horizon go ablaze with color, then settle back in the casually elegant
dining room to feast. The superbly cooked filet mignon with peaches
and port wine sauce is truly exceptional. Other specialties include a
delicious lobster au gratin appetizer, grilled local fish, roast duck, and
key lime pie. This is also a special place for lunch. Be sure to walk up
to the Skyworld Observatory for a terrific view of neighboring is-
lands. ✉ *Ridge Rd.,* ☎ *284/494–3567. AE, MC, V.*

$$$–$$$$ ✕ **Sugar Mill Restaurant.** Candles gleam, and the background music
is peaceful in this well-known, romantic restaurant. Within a 360-year-
old mill that's part of their ☞ **Sugar Mill Hotel,** owners Jeff and Jinx
Morgan never disappoint. Well-prepared selections on the à la carte
menu, which changes nightly, include pasta and vegetarian entrées.
Smoked salmon corncakes or Caribbean sweet potato soup are good
starters. House favorite entrées include the roasted pepper stuffed
pork tenderloin, the regimental beef curry with *poppadoms* (Indian
popovers), marinated roast duck, and fresh local fish with Creole
sauce. ✉ *Apple Bay,* ☎ *284/495–4355. AE, MC, V.*

ENGLISH

$$–$$$ ✕ **The Last Resort.** Actually on Bellamy Cay just off Beef Island (free
ferry service provided to and from Trellis Bay/Beef Island), this spot
features an English buffet, complete with pumpkin soup, prime rib and
Yorkshire pudding, and vegetarian selections—as well as the inimitable
cabaret humor and ribald ditties of owner Tony Snell, the BVI's an-
swer to Benny Hill. ✉ *Bellamy Cay,* ☎ *284/495–2520. AE, MC, V.*

ITALIAN

$$$–$$$$ ✕ **Brandywine Bay.** For the best in romantic dining, don't miss this
★ hillside gem. Candlelit, outdoor tables have a sweeping view of neigh-
boring islands. Owner-chef Davide Pugliese prepares foods the Tuscan
way: grilled with lots of fresh herbs. The remarkable menu can include
homemade mozzarella, foie gras, grilled local wahoo, and grilled veal
chop with ricotta and sun-dried tomatoes; it always includes duck with
an exotic fruit sauce. The wine list is excellent, and the lemon tart and
the tiramisu are irresistible. ✉ *Sir Francis Drake Hwy., east of Road
Town,* ☎ *284/495–2301. Reservations essential. AE, MC, V. Closed
Sun. No lunch.*

SEAFOOD

$$$–$$$$ ✕ **Conch Shell Point.** This peaceful, alfresco restaurant sits on a point
★ overlooking boat-studded Trellis Bay on Beef Island, just off Tortola's
east end. The menu features fish fresh out of the local waters. Tender
swordfish steaks, mahimahi, and grouper filets are popular choices and
can be prepared grilled, blackened, or panfried with a variety of light
sauces. Duck, chicken, and steaks are also available. ✉ *Beef Island,
East End, just past airport,* ☎ *284/495–2285. AE, MC, V. Closed Mon.*

Beaches

Beaches in the BVI have less development than those on St. Thomas
or St. Croix—and fewer people. Try to get out on a dive-snorkeling
boat or a day-trip sailing vessel at least one day during your stay. This
is often the best way to reach the most virgin Virgin beaches (some of
which have no road access) on the less-populated islands.

Tortola's north side has a number of perfect, palm-fringed white sand
beaches that curl around turquoise bays and coves. Nearly all are ac-
cessible by car (preferably one with four-wheel-drive), albeit down bumpy

roads that corkscrew precipitously. Facilities run the gamut, from absolutely none to a number of beachside bars and restaurants plus water-sport equipment rentals.

If you want to surf, the area of **Apple Bay** (⊠ North Shore Rd.), which includes **Little Apple Bay** and **Capoon's Bay**, is the spot—although the beach itself is pretty narrow. Sebastian's, the very casual hotel here, caters to those in search of the perfect wave. Good waves are never a sure thing, but you're more apt to catch one in January and February.

The water at **Brewers Bay** (⊠ Brewers Bay Rd. W or Brewers Bay Rd. E) is good for snorkeling and there's a campground and beach bar here. The beach and its old sugar mill and rum-distillery ruins are just north of Cane Garden Bay (up and over a steep hill), just past Luck Hill. There's another entrance just east of Skyworld.

Cane Garden Bay (⊠ Cane Garden Bay Rd.) rivals St. Thomas's Magens Bay in beauty and is Tortola's most popular beach. It's the closest one to Road Town—one steep uphill and downhill drive—and is also one of the BVI's best-known anchorages. You can rent sailboards and such, and nosh or sip at a variety of places, including Quito's Gazebo, where local recording star Quito Rhymer sings four nights a week. For true romance, nothing beats stargazing from the bow of a boat, listening to Quito's love songs drift across the bay.

Elizabeth Beach (⊠ Ridge Rd.) is a wide sandy stretch lined with palm trees, accessible by walking down a private road. The undertow can be severe here in winter.

Josiah's Bay (⊠ Ridge Rd.) is another favored place to hang ten, although in winter the undertow is often strong. The wide and oft-deserted beach is a nice place for a quiet picnic.

The scenery at **Long Bay East** (⊠ Beef Island Rd.) on Beef Island draws superlatives: You can catch a glimpse of Little Camanoe and Great Camanoe islands, and if you walk around the bend to the right, you can see little Marina Cay and Scrub Island. Long Bay is also a good place to find interesting seashells. Take the Queen Elizabeth II Bridge to Beef Island and watch for a small dirt turnoff on the left before the airport. Follow the road that curves along the east side of the dried-up marsh flat; don't drive directly across the flat as you can damage it.

Long Bay West (⊠ Long Bay Rd.) is a stunning, mile-long stretch of white sand. Have your camera ready for snapping the breathtaking approach. Although Long Bay Resort sprawls along part of it, the entire beach is open to the public. The water is not as calm here as at Cane Garden or Brewers Bay, but it's still swimmable.

After bouncing your way to the beautiful **Smuggler's Cove** (⊠ Belmont Rd.), you'll really feel as if you've found a hidden piece of the island, although you probably won't be alone on weekends. There's a fine view of the island of Jost Van Dyke, and the snorkeling is good.

About the only thing you'll find moving at **Trunk Bay** (⊠ Ridge Rd.) is the surf. It's directly north of Road Town, midway between Cane Garden Bay and Beef Island, and to reach it you have to hike down a *ghut* (gully) from the high Ridge Road.

Outdoor Activities and Sports

Participant Sports

HORSEBACK RIDING

If you've ever wanted to ride a horse along a deserted beach, now's your chance. Or you can head up to Tortola's ridges for scenic views.

Call **Shadow Stables** (✉ Ridge Rd., ☎ 284/494–2262), which offers small group rides down onto the shore or up into the hills. The **Ellis Thomas Riding School** (✉ Sea Cows Bay, ☎ 284/494–4442) teaches riding and also has trips through scenic hills and along sandy beaches.

SAILING

The BVI are a popular sailing destination. The islands are close together and are surrounded by calm waters, so it's fairly easy to sail from one anchorage to the next. If you know how to sail, you can charter a bareboat (perhaps for your entire vacation); if you're unschooled, you can hire a boat with a captain or take lessons. **Full Sailing School** (✉ Maya Cove, ☎ 284/494–0512), offers beginner and advanced sailing lessons.

SCUBA DIVING AND SNORKELING

Clear waters and numerous reefs mean that the BVI have some of the best scuba diving and snorkeling opportunities in the Caribbean. The wreck of the *Rhone,* which sank a century ago in a devastating hurricane, is popular with snorkelers and divers.

Baskin' in the Sun (✉ Prospect Reef, ☎ 284/494–2858) has beginner and advanced diving courses and daily trips. **Underwater Safaris** (✉ The Moorings, ☎ 284/494–3235), offers resort and advanced diving courses and scheduled day and night dives.

SPORTFISHING

The deep-sea fishing is so good here that several tournaments draw competitors from around the world for the largest bluefish, wahoo, and shark. You can bring your own catch back to your hotel's restaurant, and the staff will prepare it for you for dinner. For a few hours of reel fun, try **Pelican Charters Ltd.** (✉ Prospect Reef, ☎ 284/496–7386).

TENNIS

Tortola's tennis facilities range from simple, untended, concrete courts to professionally maintained surfaces where organized tournaments and socials are hosted. Listed below are facilities available to the public; some have restrictions for nonguests.

Frenchman's Cay. Here you'll find an artificial-grass court with a pretty view of Sir Francis Drake Channel. Those who patronize the hotel or restaurant can use the court free of charge; for others, there's an hourly charge. Although the court is lighted, there's no pro available to be your guiding light, so to speak. ✉ *West End,* ☎ *284/495–4844.*

Moorings-Mariner Inn. Hotel, marina, and Treasure Isle Hotel guests have free access to the one all-weather hard court here. But the lack of lights and a pro staffer may leave you in the dark. ✉ *Road Town,* ☎ *284/494–2331.*

Prospect Reef Resort. Hotel guests can play free by day (there's a fee for lights) on any of six hard-surface courts; nonguests pay by the hour. You can make an appointment with the island's most famous pro, Mike Adamson. ✉ *Road Town,* ☎ *284/494–3311.*

WINDSURFING

The winds are so steady here that some locals use sailboards to get from island to island. One of the best spots for sailboarding is at Trellis Bay on Beef Island. **Boardsailing BVI** (✉ Trellis Bay, Beef Island, ☎ 284/495–2447) offers private and group lessons and rentals.

Spectator Sports

BASKETBALL

The NBA games are a national passion and folks also play pretty good basketball here. Die-hard fans can catch games at the New Recreation Grounds on Monday, Wednesday, Friday, or Saturday between May and August. For information, contact the BVI Tourist Board (☎ 284/494–3134).

Fans of this sport are fiercely loyal and are an exuberant crowd at cricket matches. They're held at the New Recreation Grounds, next to the J. R. O'Neal Botanic Gardens, weekends February–April.

SOFTBALL

If you enjoy watching softball, you can catch local games on weekend evenings at the Old Recreation Grounds between Long Bush Road and Lower Estate Road. The season runs February–August.

Shopping

The BVI are a shopper's delight, but you can find some interesting items, particularly artwork. Don't be put off by an informal shop entrance. Some of the best finds in the BVI lie behind shopworn doors.

Areas
Most of the shops and boutiques on Tortola are clustered on and off Road Town's Main Street and at **Wickham's Cay** shopping area adjacent to the marina. There's also an ever-growing number of art and clothing stores at **Soper's Hole** on the island's West End.

Specialty Stores
ART

Caribbean Fine Arts Ltd. (✉ Main St., Road Town, ☎ 284/494–4240) has a wide range of Caribbean art, including original watercolors, oils, and acrylics, as well as signed prints, limited-edition serigraphs, and turn-of-the-century sepia photographs.

Collector's Corner (✉ Columbus Centre, Wickham's Cay, ☎ 284/494–3550) carries prints of antique maps, watercolors by local artists, gold and silver jewelry, coral, and Larimar—a pale blue Caribbean gemstone.

Islands Treasures (✉ Soper's Hole, ☎ 284/495–4787) sells elaborate model ships; coffee-table books on the Caribbean; maps and prints; and watercolors, paintings, pottery, and sculpture by island artists.

Sunny Caribbee Art Gallery (✉ Main St., Road Town, ☎ 284/494–2178) has one of the largest displays in the Caribbean of paintings, prints, and watercolors by artists from all of the Caribbean islands.

CLOTHES AND TEXTILES

Arawak (✉ On the dock at Nanny Cay, ☎ 284/494–5240) carries gifts, batik sundresses, sportswear and resort wear for men and women, accessories, and children's clothing.

Caribbean Handprints (✉ Main St., Road Town, ☎ 284/494–3717) creates Caribbean-themed silk-screened fabric and sells it by the yard or in all forms of clothing and beach bags.

Domino (✉ Main St., Road Town, ☎ 284/494–5879) sells a colorful array of comfortable, light cotton clothing, including selections from Indonesia, plus island jewelry and gift items.

The Pusser's Company Store (✉ Main St. and Waterfront Rd., Road Town, ☎ 284/494–2467; ✉ Soper's Hole Marina, ☎ 284/495–4603) features nautical memorabilia, ship models, marine paintings, an entire line of clothes and gift items bearing the Pusser's logo, handsome decorator bottles of Pusser's rum, and numerous Caribbean books.

Sea Urchin (✉ Columbus Centre, Road Town, ☎ 284/494–3129 or 284/494–2044; ✉ Soper's Hole Marina, ☎ 284/495–4850) has a good selection of island-living designs: print shirts and shorts, slinky swimsuits, cover-ups, sandals, and T-shirts.

Turtle Dove Boutique (⊠ Flemming St., Road Town, ☏ 284/494–3611) is one of the best shops on the BVI for international swimwear and silk and linen dresses, as well as gifts and accessories for the home.
Violet's (⊠ Wickham's Cay I, ☏ 284/494–6398) features a collection of beautiful silk lingerie and a small line of designer dresses.
Zenaida's of West End (⊠ Frenchman's Cay, ☏ 284/495–4867) displays the fabric finds of Argentine Vivian Jenik Helm, who travels through South America, Africa, and India in search of batiks, hand-painted and hand-blocked fabrics, and interesting weaves that can be made into *pareos* (women's wraps) or wall hangings. The shop also sells unusual bags, belts, sarongs, scarves, and ethnic jewelry.

FOODSTUFFS

Ample Hamper (⊠ Village Cay Marina, Wickham's Cay, ☏ 284/494–2494; ⊠ Soper's Hole Marina, ☏ 284/495–4684) has a good selection of cheeses, wines, fresh fruits, and canned goods from the United Kingdom and the United States. You can have the management here provision your yacht or rental villa.
Fort Wine Gourmet (⊠ Main St., Road Town, ☏ 284/494–3036), a café-cum-store, carries a remarkably sophisticated variety of gourmet items and fine wines and champagnes, including Petrossian caviar and Hediard goods from France.
Gourmet Galley (⊠ Wickham's Cay II, Road Town, ☏ 284/494–6999) sells wines, cheeses, fresh fruits and vegetables, and provides full provisioning for yachtspeople and villa renters.

GIFTS

Buccaneer's Bounty (⊠ Main St., Road Town, ☏ 284/494–7510) carries a delightful assortment of greeting cards, nautical and tropical artwork, books on seashells, and books on the islands.
Caribbean Corner Spice House (⊠ Main St., Road Town, ☏ 284/494–5564; ⊠ Soper's Hole, ☏ 284/495–4498) makes and sells exotic herbs and spices, jams, jellies, hot sauces, and natural soaps. You'll find Cuban cigars here, too.
J. R. O'Neal, Ltd. (⊠ Main St., Road Town, ☏ 284/494–2292) stocks the shelves of its somewhat hidden shop with fine crystal, Royal Worcester china, a wonderful selection of hand-painted Italian dishes, handblown Mexican glassware, ceramic housewares from Spain, and woven rugs and tablecloths from India.
The Sunny Caribbee Herb and Spice Company (⊠ Main St., Road Town, ☏ 284/494–2178), in a brightly painted West Indian house, packages its own herbs, teas, coffees, herb vinegars, hot sauces, natural soaps, skin and suntan lotions, and exotic concoctions—Arawak Love Potion and Island Hangover Cure, for example. You'll also find Caribbean books and art and hand-painted decorative accessories.

JEWELRY

Felix Gold and Silver Ltd. (⊠ Main St., Road Town, ☏ 284/494–2406) may have an unimpressive site, but the handcrafted jewelry made in the workshop here is exceptional. Choose from island or nautical themes or have something custom-made out of sterling silver or 14-karat gold.
Samarkand (⊠ Main St., Road Town, ☏ 284/494–6415) sells handmade gold and silver pendants, earrings, bracelets, and pins—many with an island theme—plus genuine Spanish pieces of eight (coins—old Spanish pesos of eight *reals*—commonly found in sunken galleons).

PERFUMES AND COSMETICS

Flamboyance (⊠ Main St., Road Town, ☏ 284/494–4099; ⊠ Soper's Hole Marina, ☏ 284/495–5946) carries a wide selection of designer fragrances and upscale cosmetics.

Nightlife and the Arts

Nightlife

Like any good sailing destination, Tortola has a number of watering holes that are popular with salty and not-so-salty dogs alike. Many offer entertainment; check the weekly *Limin' Times* for current schedules. The local beverage is a Painkiller, an innocent-tasting mixture of fruit juices and rums. It goes down smoothly but packs quite a punch, so give yourself a moment before you order another!

Bing's Drop In Bar. This rollicking local hangout has a DJ nightly in season. ⊠ *Fat Hog's Bay, East End,* ☎ *284/495–2627.*

Bomba's Surfside Shack. By day, this little shack—covered with everything from crepe paper leis to license plates to colorful graffiti—looks like a pile of junk; by night, it's one of Tortola's liveliest spots and one of the Caribbean's most famous beach bars. Sunday at 4 there's always some sort of live music, and Wednesday at 8 the locally famous Blue Haze Combo shows up to play everything from reggae to top 40 tunes. Every full moon bands play all night long and people flock here from all over Tortola and from other islands. ⊠ *Apple Bay,* ☎ *284/495–4148.*

Jolly Roger. An ever-changing array of local, American, and down-island bands play everything from rhythm and blues to reggae to country to good old rock and roll Friday and Saturday starting at 8. ⊠ *West End,* ☎ *284/495–4559.*

Myett's. Bands play here Friday and Saturday evenings and Sunday afternoons, and there's usually a lively dance crowd. ⊠ *Cane Garden Bay,* ☎ *284/495–9543.*

The Pub. Here you'll find an all-day happy hour on Friday, guitarist Reuben Chinnery on Friday and Saturday, and late-night local bands on occasion. ⊠ *Waterfront St., Road Town,* ☎ *284/494–2608.*

The Pusser's Deli. Thursday is nickel-beer night, and crowds gather here for courage (John Courage, that is) by the pint. Other nights try Pusser's famous mixed drinks—Painkillers—and snack on the excellent pizza. ⊠ *Waterfront St., Road Town,* ☎ *284/494–4199.*

Pusser's Landing. The schedule at Pusser's varies nightly, but you can usually count on some kind of live music (it could be reggae, rock, or a steel band) on Friday and Saturday evenings and Sunday afternoon. ⊠ *Soper's Hole, West End,* ☎ *284/495–4554.*

Quito's Gazebo. BVI recording star Quito Rhymer sings island ballads and love songs, accompanied by the guitar at this rustic beachside bar-restaurant. Solo shows are on Sunday, Tuesday, and Thursday nights at 8:30; Friday and Saturday, Quito and the band The Edge pump out a variety of tunes. ⊠ *Cane Garden Bay,* ☎ *284/495–4837.*

Sebastian's. There's often live music here on Saturday and Sunday, and you can dance under the stars. ⊠ *Apple Bay,* ☎ *809/495–4214.*

Stanley's Welcome Bar. It gets rowdy when crews stop by to drink and indulge in time-honored, fraternity-type high jinks, such as piling up on the tire swing outside. ⊠ *Cane Garden Bay,* ☎ *284/495–4520.*

The Arts

Classics in the Atrium. Musical artists from around the world perform here October–February each year. Past artists have included Britain's premier a cappella group, Black Voices; New Orleans jazz pianist Ellis Marsalis; and Keith Lockhart and the Serenac Quartet (from the Boston Pops Symphony). ⊠ *The Atrium at the H. Lavity Stoutt Community College, Paraquita Bay,* ☎ *284/494–4994.*

Exploring Tortola

Tortola does not have many historical sites to visit, but it does have lots of beautiful natural scenery. Although you could explore the island's 10 square mi in a few hours, opting for such a whirlwind tour would be a mistake. Life in the fast lane has no place among some of the Caribbean's most breathtaking panoramas and prettiest beaches. Also, the roads aren't that good, making driving less than pleasant. The best strategy is to explore a bit of the island at a time. For example, you might try Road Town one morning, West End the next afternoon.

Numbers in the margin correspond to points of interest on the Tortola and Virgin Gorda maps.

Sights to See

❼ Cane Garden Bay. Exceptionally calm crystalline waters and a silky stretch of sand make this enticing beach one of Tortola's most popular getaways. Its existence is no secret, however, and it can get crowded, especially when cruise ships are in Road Harbour.

❷ Ft. Burt. The most intact historic ruin on Tortola was built by the Dutch in the early 17th century to safeguard Road Harbour. It sits on a hill on the western edge of Road Town and is now the site of a small hotel and restaurant. The foundations and magazine remain, and the structure offers a commanding view of the harbor. ⊠ *Waterfront Dr.,* ☎ *no phone.* ✆ *Free.* ☉ *Daily dawn–dusk.*

❹ Ft. Recovery. The unrestored ruins of the 17th-century Dutch fort, 30 ft in diameter, sit amid a profusion of tropical greenery on the Villas at Fort Recovery Estates grounds. There are no guided tours, but the public is welcome. ⊠ *Waterfront Dr.,* ☎ *284/485–4467.* ✆ *Free.*

❺ Frenchman's Cay. On this little island connected by a causeway to Tortola's West End, there's a marina and a captivating complex of pastel West Indian–style buildings with shady balconies, colonnaded arcades, shuttered windows, and gingerbread trim that house art galleries, boutiques, and restaurants. **Pusser's Landing** is a lively place where you can stop for a cold drink (many are made with Pusser's famous rum) and a sandwich and watch the boats come and go from the harbor.

❸ J. R. O'Neal Botanic Gardens. Take a walk through this 2¾-acre showcase of lush tropical plant life. There are sections devoted to prickly cacti and succulents, hothouses for ferns and orchids, gardens of medicinal herbs, and plants and trees indigenous to the seashore. From the tourist board office, cross Waterfront Drive and walk one block over to Main Street and turn right. Keep walking until you see the BVI High School. The gardens are on your left. ⊠ *Botanic Station,* ☎ *284/494–4997.* ✆ *Free.* ☉ *Mon.–Sat. 9–4:30.*

❿ Mt. Healthy National Park. The remains of an 18th-century sugar plantation are here. The windmill structure has been restored, and you can see the ruins of a mill round, a factory with boiling houses, storage, stables, hospital, and many dwellings. This is a nice place to picnic. ⊠ *Ridge Rd.,* ☎ *no phone.* ✆ *Free.* ☉ *Daily dawn–dusk.*

❻ North Shore Shell Museum. On Tortola's north shore, this casual museum has a very informal exhibit of shells, unusually shaped driftwood, fish traps, and traditional wooden boats. ⊠ *North Shore Rd.,* ☎ *no phone.* ✆ *Free.* ☉ *Daily dawn–dusk.*

⓫ RMS *Rhone*. Get yourself some snorkeling gear and hop a dive boat to this wreck, off Salt Island (just across the channel from Road Town) and part of the BVI National Parks Trust. This is your chance to float on crystal-clear water over or near one of the world's best wrecks: a royal mail steamer 310 ft long that sank here in a hurricane in 1867 and was later used in the movie *The Deep*. Its four parts are at various depths from 30 to 80 ft. Nearby Rhone Reef is only 20–50 ft down. Every dive outfit in the BVI (☞ Scuba Diving and Snorkeling *in* Outdoor Activities and Sports, *above*) runs superlative scuba and snorkel tours here. For timid snorkelers, simple and safe flotation devices are available, and the scuba supervisors will keep an eye on you.

❶ Road Town. The laid-back capital of the BVI is on the south side of Tortola and looks out over Road Harbour. It takes only an hour or so to stroll down Main Street and along the waterfront, checking out the traditional pastel-painted West Indian buildings with high-pitched, corrugated tin roofs, bright shutters, and delicate fretwork trim.

Choose a seat on one of the benches in **Sir Olva Georges Square,** and watch the people come and go from the ferry dock and customs office across the street. Also keep an eye out for the clock on the post office, which borders the other side of the square. Its hands permanently pointed to 10 minutes to 5 until last year, when they mysteriously started pointing to 5 minutes to 12. ⊠ *Waterfront Dr.*

For hotel and sightseeing brochures and the latest information on everything from taxi rates to ferry boat schedules, stop in the **BVI Tourist Board** office in downtown Road Town. ⊠ *Wickham's Cay I,* ☎ *284/ 494–3134.* ⊙ *Weekdays 9–5.*

❽ Sage Mountain National Park. At 1,716 ft, Sage Mountain is the highest peak in the BVI. From the parking area, a trail will lead you in a loop not only to the peak itself (and extraordinary views) but also to the island's small rain forest, sometimes shrouded in mist. Most of the forest was cut down over the centuries to clear land for sugarcane, cotton, and other crops, as well as pastureland and timber; in 1964 this park was established to preserve what rain forest remained. Up here you can see mahogany trees, white cedars, mountain guavas, elephant-ear vines, mamey trees, and giant bulletwoods, to say nothing of such birds as mountain doves and thrushes. Take a taxi from Road Town or drive up Joe's Hill Road and make a left onto Ridge Road toward Chalwell and Doty villages. The road dead-ends at the park. ⊠ *Ridge Rd.,* ☎ *no phone (contact tourist office for information).* ⊠ *Free.*

❾ Skyworld. Drive up here and climb the observation tower for a stunning, 360 degree view of numerous islands and cays. On a clear day, you can even see St. Croix (40 mi away) and Anegada (20 mi away). ⊠ *Ridge Rd.,* ☎ *no phone.* ⊠ *Free.*

VIRGIN GORDA

Virgin Gorda, with its mountainous central portion connected by skinny necks of land to southern and northern appendages—on a map it looks like the slightest breeze would cause the whole island to splinter apart—is quite different from Tortola. The pace is even slower here, and Virgin Gorda receives less rain, so some areas are more arid and home to scrub brush and cactus. Goats and cattle own the right of way, and the unpretentious friendliness of the people is winning.

Lodging

Virgin Gorda's charming hostelries appeal to a select, appreciative clientele. Repeat business is extremely high here. Visitors who prefer Sheratons, Marriotts, and the like may feel they get more for their money

on other islands. But the peace and pampering offered on Virgin Gorda
are priceless to the discriminating traveler. For price categories, *see* the
chart *under* Lodging *in* Tortola, *above*.

Hotels and Inns

$$$$ ☒ **Biras Creek Hotel.** A longtime guest purchased Biras Creek several
★ years ago and turned it into one of the classiest resorts in the Caribbean.
Units are in cottages and each has a bedroom and a living room area
decorated in soft Caribbean colors and fabrics, and floors of terra-cotta
tiles. Off the bath is an enclosed, garden shower that's open to the sky.
Although entrances are discreetly hidden among the trees, many of the
cottages are just feet from the water's edge. Bike paths and trails lead
to the beaches and the ☞ **Biras Creek** restaurant (one of the best in
the BVI). The general manager, Jamie Holmes, brings his special touch
and years of Caribbean hotel experience to this 140-acre hideaway. The
hilltop open-air bar and restaurant area is made of stonework and has
stunning views of North Sound. A "Sailaway" package includes two
nights on a private yacht. ☒ *North Sound (Box 54),* ☎ *284/494–3555
or 800/223–1108,* ℻ *284/494–3557. 32 suites. Restaurant, bar, pool,
air-conditioning, 2 tennis courts, hiking, beach, snorkeling, windsurfing, boating, bicycles, shop.AE, MC, V. FAP.*

$$$$ ☒ **Bitter End Yacht Club and Marina.** This family-oriented, convivial
★ resort-cum-marina stretches along the coastline of North Sound and
is accessible only by boat. Accommodations range from comfortable
hillside or beachfront villas to live-aboard yachts. The BEYC extends
a friendly welcome to all its guests, and your day can include as many
or as few activities as you wish. There are daily snorkeling and diving
trips to nearby reefs, cruises, windsurfing lessons, excursions to local
attractions, and lessons at the Nick Trotter Sailing School. Regarded
as the best sailing instruction in the Caribbean, the school helps both
seasoned salts and beginners sharpen their nautical skills. When the
sun goes down, the festivities continue at the Clubhouse, an open-air
restaurant overlooking the Sound. ☒ *North Sound (Box 46),* ☎ *284/
494–2746,* ℻ *284/494–4756. 100 rooms. Restaurant, bar, pool,
beach, dive shop, snorkeling, windsurfing. AE, MC, V. FAP.*

$$$$ ☒ **Little Dix Bay.** Relaxed elegance is the hallmark at this outstanding
★ resort. It sits among the mangroves, along the edge of a sandy beach.
Duplexes with hexagonal units and quadraplex cottages are tucked
among the trees and on a little hillside. Interiors have handsome fieldstone walls and are decorated in Caribbean prints. About half the rooms
are air-conditioned. The spacious open-air library offers stateside daily
newspapers and CNN. Lawns are beautifully manicured; the reef-protected beach is long and silken; and the candlelight dining in an open
peak-roof pavilion is a memorable experience. Families are made to
feel welcome here, and the outstanding children's program includes treasure hunts to nature walks to tennis games. This resort is also popular with honeymooners and older couples who have been coming for
years. The ☞ **Little Dix Bay Pavilion** is an unforgettable setting for
any meal. ☒ *Little Dix Bay (Box 70),* ☎ *284/495–5555,* ℻ *284/495–
5661. 98 rooms. 3 restaurants, 2 bars, 7 tennis courts, beach, snorkeling, windsurfing, library, children's programs. AE, MC, V. EP, MAP.*

$$$ ☒ **Olde Yard Inn.** Owners Charlie Williams and Carol Kaufman have
★ cultivated a friendly, refreshing atmosphere at this quiet retreat just out-
side Spanish Town. Classical music plays in the bar; books line the walls
of the octagonal library cottage. The ☞ **Olde Yard Inn** restaurant's
French-accented dinners are lovingly prepared and served with style
in the alfresco dining areas. The lunch restaurant, ☞ **Sip and Dip Grill,**
overlooks the pool. Guest rooms are cozy and very simply furnished
(in warmer months, request a room with air-conditioning). You can

Mountain
Pt.

George
Dog

Cockroach
Island
6

Long Bay

Great
Dog

West
Dog

Mahoe
Bay **19**

18

17

Pond
Bay

Sir Francis Drake Channel

Little Dix
Bay

Savannah
Bay

Colison Pt.

16

St. Thomas
Bay

13 **14**

15

Handsome
Bay

TO TORTOLA

Virgin Gorda
Airport

Spanish Town
Fort Pt.

11

2 **1**

12

10

Valley Trunk
Bay

Little Trunk
Bay

The
Valley

Copper Mine
Bay

The Crawl

Spring Bay

7

Devil's Bay

3 **8**

9

4

Copper Mine
Pt.

Crook's
Bay

Stoney
Bay

Fallen
Jerusalem

6

Exploring
The Baths, **3**
Coastal Islands, **6**
Copper Mine Point, **4**
Little Fort
National Park, **2**
Spanish Town, **1**
Virgin Gorda Peak
National Park, **5**

Dining
The Bath and Turtle, **11**
Biras Creek, **22**
Chez Bamboo, **12**
The Clubhouse, **23**
The Crab Hole, **13**
The Flying Iguana, **10**
Giorgio's Italian
Restaurant, **17**

Little Dix Bay
Pavilion, **16**
Mad Dog's, **9**
Olde Yard Inn, **15**
Pusser's at Leverick
Bay, **20**
Sip and Dip Grill, **15**
Teacher's Ilma's, **14**
Top of the Baths, **8**

Lodging
Biras Creek Hotel, **22**
Bitter End Yacht Club
and Marina, **23**
Guavaberry Spring Bay
Vacation Homes, **7**
Leverick Bay
Hotel, **20**
Little Dix Bay, **16**

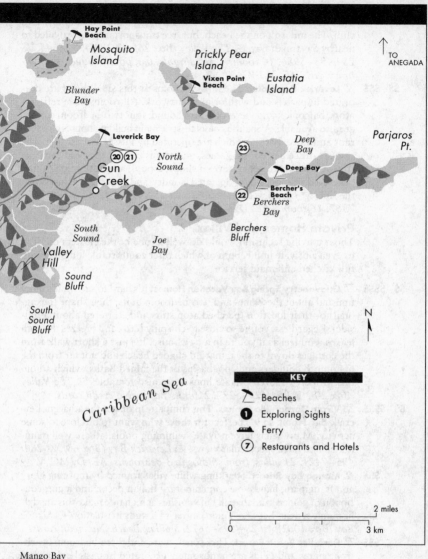

Hay Point
Beach

*Mosquito
Island*

*Prickly Pear
Island*

*Vixen Point
Beach*

*Eustatia
Island*

↑ TO
ANEGADA

*Blunder
Bay*

Leverick Bay

*Deep
Bay*

*Parjaros
Pt.*

⑳ ㉑

*North
Sound*

㉓

Deep Bay

Gun
Creek

㉒

Bercher's
Beach

*Berchers
Bay*

*South
Sound*

*Joe
Bay*

*Berchers
Bluff*

*Valley
Hill*

*Sound
Bluff*

*South
Sound
Bluff*

Caribbean Sea

N

KEY	
⟍	Beaches
❶	Exploring Sights
⛴	Ferry
⑦	Restaurants and Hotels

0		2 miles
0		3 km

Mango Bay
Resort, **18**
Olde Yard Inn, **15**
Paradise Beach
Resort, **19**
Virgin Gorda
Villa Rentals, **21**

make arrangements for day-sails and scuba diving excursions, and you can swim in the large pool and work out or get a massage in the health club. The inn isn't on the beach, but free transportation is provided to nearby Savannah Bay. ⊠ *The Valley (Box 26)*, ☎ *284/495–5544*, FAX *284/495–5986. 14 rooms. 2 restaurants, bar, pool, croquet, shop, library. AE, MC, V. EP.*

$$–$$$ 🖭 **Leverick Bay Hotel.** The hillside rooms at this small hotel are decorated in pastels and with original artwork. All rooms have refrigerators, balconies, and views of North Sound; four two-bedroom condos are also available. A Spanish colonial–style main building houses a restaurant and store, both of which are operated by Pusser's of Tortola. The resort's office has books, games, and tennis rackets that you can borrow. A restaurant, a bar, several shops, a pool, a beauty salon, a tiny beach, a dive shop, a coin-operated laundry, and a market are just down the hill. ⊠ *Leverick Bay (Box 63)*, ☎ *284/495–7421*, FAX *284/495–7367. 16 rooms. AE, D, MC, V. EP.*

Private Homes and Villas

Those craving seclusion would do well at one of the clusters of villas or even a private home, both of which offer comfortable lodgings with full kitchen and maid service.

$$–$$$$ 🖭 **Guavaberry Spring Bay Vacation Homes.** It's hard to say what's more unusual about these one- and two-bedroom units: their shape (hexagonal) or their location (perched atop stilts and scattered about a hillside). Regardless, you're so close to chirping birds and breezes through leaves, you feel as if you're in a tree house. It's just a short walk from the cottages down to the tamarind-shaded beach and not far from the mammoth boulders and cool basins of the famed Baths, which adjoin this property. Eleven private houses are also rentable. ⊠ *The Valley (Box 20)*, ☎ *284/495–5227. 21 units.Beach. No credit cards.*

$$–$$$$ 🖭 **Virgin Gorda Villa Rentals.** This company manages the adjacent Leverick Bay Hotel, so it's perfect for those who want to be close to some activity. Many villas have private swimming pools; all are well maintained and have spectacular views. ⊠ *Leverick Bay (Box 63)*, ☎ *284/495–7421. 21 villas, from studios to 3-bedrooms. AE, D, MC, V.*

$$$ 🖭 **Mango Bay Resort.** Sparkling white villas framed by morning glory and frangipani, handsome contemporary Italian decor, and a gorgeous ribbon of golden sand that all but vanishes at high tide make this an idyllic family retreat. Even for Virgin Gorda it's a study in isolation. ⊠ *Mahoe Bay (Box 1062)*, ☎ *284/495–5672. 5 villas. Beach. No credit cards.*

$$$ 🖭 **Paradise Beach Resort.** These one-, two-, and three-bedroom beachfront suites and villas are handsomely decorated in pastel colors and Caribbean style and feature outdoor showers. Four-wheel-drive vehicles are included in the daily rate. ⊠ *Mahoe Bay (Box 534)*, ☎ *284/495–5871. 9 units. Beach. No credit cards.*

Dining

There is a wide variety of restaurants on Virgin Gorda, from simple to elegant. Hotels that are accessible only by boat will arrange transport in advance upon request for nonguests who wish to dine at their restaurants. It is wise to make dinner reservations almost everywhere. The fancier, more expensive restaurants have dress codes: long pants and collared shirts for men and elegant casual resort wear for women. For price categories, *see* the chart *under* Dining *in* Tortola, *above.*

AMERICAN/CASUAL

$$–$$$ ✕ **Pusser's at Leverick Bay.** This two-level restaurant at the ☞ Leverick Bay Hotel looks out over picturesque North Sound. The upstairs is slightly more formal, and the menu is a combination of steak house

and English pub. Below, the Beach Bar offers light fare all day, including hamburgers, salads, and pizzas, and a nightly theme menu. Tuesday is pizza-and-beer night. Thursday is $1 Heineken night. ⊠ *Leverick Bay,* ☎ *284/495–7369. AE, MC, V.*

$$–$$$ ✕ **Top of the Baths.** At the entrance to the Baths, this open-air restaurant serves food all day long, starting at 8 AM. Hamburgers, salads, and sandwiches are offered at lunch. Conch seviche and lentil soup are among the dinner appetizers. Entrées include Cornish hen with wild rice and grilled swordfish with fresh rosemary sauce. For dessert, you can choose from such delectables as lemon cheesecake and pecan pie. ⊠ *The Valley,* ☎ *284/495–5497. AE, MC, V.*

$$ ✕ **The Bath and Turtle.** You can really sit back and relax at this infor-
★ mal patio tavern with a friendly staff. Burgers, well-stuffed sandwiches, pizzas, pasta dishes, and daily specials round out the casual menu. Live entertainers perform on Wednesday and Sunday nights. ⊠ *Virgin Gorda Yacht Harbour,* ☎ *284/495–5239. MC, V.*

$$ ✕ **The Flying Iguana.** Lifelike iguanas perch in the plants of the comfortable lounge at this charming restaurant. The open-air dining room looks out over Virgin Gorda's tiny airport to the sea. Sandwiches and thick, juicy hamburgers are served for lunch. The dinner menu includes a pasta special, grilled chicken, and steaks. ⊠ *At the airport,* ☎ *284/ 495–5277. AE, MC, V.*

$–$$ ✕ **Sip and Dip Grill.** The pool at the ☞ **Olde Yard Inn** is the setting
★ for this pleasant, informal lunch spot. Come here for grilled fish, pasta salads, chilled soups, and ice cream. Sunday evening it has a barbecue and live entertainment. ⊠ *The Valley,* ☎ *284/495–5544. Reservations not accepted. AE, MC, V. No dinner Mon.–Sat.*

$ ✕ **Mad Dog's.** Piña coladas are *the* thing at this breezy bar just outside of The Baths. The all-day menu includes BLTs, hot dogs, and burgers. ⊠ *The Valley,* ☎ *284/495–5830. Reservations not accepted. MC, V. No dinner.*

CAJUN/CREOLE

$$–$$$ **Chez Bamboo.** This pleasant little hideaway isn't really that hard to find: just look for the building with the purple and green latticework. Candles on the dining room tables and the patio create a mellow atmosphere in which to enjoy such dishes as conch gumbo, Chez B's bouillabaisse, and leg of lamb *pistou* (baked with a crust of pistachio nuts). Stop by on Sunday for some live jazz. ⊠ *Across from, and a little north of, Virgin Gorda Yacht Harbour,* ☎ *284/495–5752. Reservations not accepted. AE, MC, V. Closed Mon. No lunch.*

CARIBBEAN/CREOLE

$$–$$$$ ✕ **Teacher's Ilma's.** Delightful local atmosphere and delicious native-style family dinners—including local goat, fresh grouper or snapper, pork, and chicken—are givens at the restaurant in this small house. ⊠ *The Valley,* ☎ *284/495–5355. Reservations essential. No credit cards. No lunch.*

$–$$ ✕ **The Crab Hole.** This homey hangout serves West Indian specialties such as callaloo soup, salt fish, stewed goat, curried chicken roti, rice and peas, and green bananas. ⊠ *The Valley,* ☎ *284/495–5307. No credit cards.*

CONTEMPORARY

$$$$ ✕ **Biras Creek.** This hilltop restaurant at the ☞ **Biras Creek Hotel** is
★ built of island stonework and has a signature turret roof. The setting is stunning: Broad steps lead up to an open-air lounge and restaurant with beautiful views of North Sound. The gourmet menu changes daily to accommodate resort guests. Appetizers might be chilled yellow pepper soup, conch fritters with papaya sauce, or avocado and lob-

ster salad. Roast duck breast with plum sauce, grilled swordfish with bacon and caper sauce, pan-seared snapper with a ginger beurre blanc, and a roast breast of pheasant are some of the enticing entrées offered. Delightful desserts include key lime pie with raspberry sauce, a warm treacle tart, and a rich chocolate brownie with chocolate sauce. Dinner ends with Biras Creeks' signature offering of stilton and port. ⊠ *North Sound,* ☎ *284/494–3555. Reservations essential. AE, MC, V.*

$$$$ ✕ **Little Dix Bay Pavilion.** For an elegant evening, at the ☞ **Little Dix**
★   **Bay** resort, you can't do better than this—the candlelight in the main open-air pavilion is enchanting, the menu sophisticated, the service attentive. The dinner menu changes daily, but there's always a fine selection of superbly prepared seafood, meat, and vegetarian entrées, including gingered duck breast with Pacific Rim vegetables, black Angus rib eye with horseradish and mustard sauce, pan-seared snapper with christophene ratatouille. The breakfast and lunch buffets here shine. ⊠ *Spanish Town,* ☎ *284/495–5555, ext. 174. AE, MC, V.*

$$–$$$$ ✕ **Olde Yard Inn.** Dinner at the ☞ **Olde Yarde Inn** is a charming, civilized affair. The intimate dining room is suffused with gentle classical melodies and the scent of herbs; a cedar roof covers the breezy, open-air room, which is decorated with old-style Caribbean charm. The French-accented cuisine includes lamb chops with mango chutney, chicken breast in a rum cream sauce, garlic shrimp, grilled local fish, steaks, and lobster. Chocolate mousse, cheesecake, and key lime pie are sweet endings. ⊠ *The Valley, north of the marina,* ☎ *284/495–5544. AE, MC, V.*

ITALIAN

$$$–$$$$ ✕ **Giorgio's Italian Restaurant.** Gaze out at the stars and listen to the water lap against the shore while dining on veal scaloppine, filet mignon with mushrooms, or fresh local fish. Lunch fare at this pleasant, casual establishment includes pizzas and sandwiches. ⊠ *Mango Bay, 10 mins north of Yacht Harbour,* ☎ *284/495–5684. MC, V.*

SEAFOOD

$$$ ✕ **The Clubhouse.** The Bitter End's open-air, waterfront restaurant is a favorite rendezvous for the sailing set—busy day and night. At the lavish buffets you also get your choice of an entrée for breakfast, lunch, and dinner. Dinner selections include grilled swordfish or tuna, chopped sirloin, scallops, and shrimp. ⊠ *Bitter End Yacht Club, North Sound,* ☎ *284/494–2746. AE, MC, V.*

Beaches

The best beaches are most easily reached by water, although they are also accessible on foot, usually after a moderately strenuous hike of 10 to 15 minutes. Either way, your persistence is amply rewarded.

Anybody going to Virgin Gorda must experience swimming or snorkeling among its **unique boulder formations** (⊠ Lee Rd.). But why go to **The Baths,** which is usually crowded, when you can catch some rays just north at **Spring Bay Beach,** which is a gem, and, a little farther north, at the **Crawl?** Both are easily reached from The Baths on foot via Lee Road, or by swimming.

From Biras Creek or Bitter End on the north shore, you can walk to **Bercher's Beach** and along the windswept surf.

Footpaths from Bitter End and foot and bike paths from Biras Creek lead to **Deep Bay,** a calm, well-protected swimming beach.

Mosquito Island's **Hay Point Beach** is a broad band of white sand accessible only by boat or by a path from the dock at Drake's Anchorage resort.

Leverick Bay (⊠ Leverick Bay Rd.) is a small, busy beach-cum-marina that fronts a resort restaurant and pool. Don't come here to be alone, but do come if you want a lively little place and a break from the island's noble quiet. The view of Prickly Pear Island is also a plus, and there's a dive facility right here to motor you out to beautiful Eustatia Reef just across North Sound.

It's worth going out to **Long Bay** (⊠ Plum Tree Bay Rd., near Virgin Gorda's northern tip, past the Diamond Beach Club), for the snorkeling (Little Dix Bay resort has outings here). The drive takes about a half hour after the turnoff from North Sound Road, and a dirt road makes up part of the route.

For a wonderfully private beach close to Spanish Town, try **Savannah Bay** (⊠ North Sound Rd.). It may not always be completely deserted, but it's a lovely long stretch of white sand.

Prickly Pear Island has a calm swimming beach at **Vixen Point Beach.**

Outdoor Activities and Sports

Participant Sports

FISHING

Sportfishing is so good here that anglers from around the world fly here for annual tournaments. **Captain Dale** (⊠ Biras Creek, North Sound, ☎ 284/495–7248) takes people out on *Classic,* his 38-ft Bertram.

SAILING

BVI waters are calm and are a terrific place to learn to sail. The **Nick Trotter Sailing School** (⊠ Bitter End Yacht Club, North Sound, ☎ 800/872–2392). Both beginner and advanced courses are offered here.

SCUBA DIVING AND SNORKELING

The North Sound has some terrific snorkeling spots. The **Bitter End Yacht Club** (⊠ Bitter End Yacht Club, North Sound, ☎ 800/872–2392) offers a number of snorkeling trips.

WINDSURFING

The North Sound is a good place to learn to windsurf: it's protected, so you can't be easily blown out to sea! The **Bitter End Yacht Club** (⊠ Bitter End Yacht Club, North Sound, ☎ 800/872–2392) gives lessons and rents equipment.

Spectator Sport

CRICKET

Cricket matches can be seen at the **Recreation Grounds** in Spanish Town February–April. Contact the tourist office (☎ 284/494–3134) for specific information on game dates and times.

Shopping

On Virgin Gorda most boutiques are within hotel complexes. One of the best is in Little Dix Bay. Other properties—Biras Creek, the Bitter End, Leverick Bay, and nearby Mosquito Island's Drake's Anchorage—have small but equally select boutiques, and there's a more than respectable and diverse scattering of shops in the mini-mall adjacent to the bustling yacht harbor in Spanish Town.

ART

Olde Yard Inn Boutique (⊠ The Valley, ☎ 284/495–5544) carries locally crafted sculptures, pottery, jewelry, and paintings; books on the islands; and some clothing and gift items.

Thee Artistic Gallery (⊠ Virgin Gorda Yacht Harbour, ☎ 284/495–5761) features Caribbean jewelry, 14-karat-gold nautical jewelry, maps, collectible coins, and some crystal.

CLOTHING

DIVE BVI (⊠ Virgin Gorda Yacht Harbour, ☎ 284/495–5513) sells books about the islands as well as men's and women's sportswear, sunglasses, and beach bags.

Island Silhouette in Flax Plaza (⊠ Near Fischer's Cove Beach Hotel, ☎ no phone) is the place to go for resort wear hand-painted by Virgin Gorda artists, and locally made tie-dyed T-shirts.

Next Wave (⊠ Virgin Gorda Yacht Harbour, ☎ 284/495–5623) sells bathing suits, T-shirts, and canvas tote bags.

Pavilion Gift Shop (⊠ Little Dix Bay Hotel, ☎ 284/495–5555) has the latest in resort wear for men and women, as well as jewelry, books, and expensive T-shirts.

Pelican's Pouch Boutique (⊠ Virgin Gorda Yacht Harbour, ☎ 284/495–5599) is where you'll find a large selection of swimsuits plus cover-ups, T-shirts, and accessories.

Pusser's Company Store (⊠ Leverick Bay, ☎ 284/495–7369) has a trademark line of rum products, gift items, and sportswear.

Tropical Gift Collections (⊠ The Baths, ☎ 284/495–5380) specializes in locally made handicrafts, including hats, bags, and pottery. Island spices are also for sale.

FOODSTUFFS

Bitter End's Emporium (⊠ North Sound, ☎ 284/494–2745) is the place for such edible treats as local fruits, cheeses, and bakery goods.

Commissary and Ship Store (⊠ The Valley, ☎ 284/495–5555) offers daily specials prepared by Little Dix Resort chefs as well as assorted cheeses, canned goods, wines, and gourmet items.

Wine Cellar and Bakery (⊠ Virgin Gorda Yacht Harbour, ☎ no phone) bakes bread, rolls, muffins, and cookies and has sandwiches and sodas to go.

GIFTS

Palm Tree Gallery (⊠ Leverick Bay, ☎ 284/495–7421) sells attractive handcrafted jewelry, paintings, and one-of-a-kind gift items, as well as games and books about the Caribbean.

The Reeftique (⊠ Bitter End, North Sound, ☎ 284/494–2745) carries a variety of gift items, including island crafts and jewelry, clothing, and nautical odds and ends with the Bitter End logo.

HANDICRAFTS

Virgin Gorda Craft Shop (⊠ Virgin Gorda Yacht Harbour, ☎ 284/495–5137) features the work of island artisans, and carries West Indian jewelry and crafts styled in straw, shells, and other local materials. It also stocks clothing and paintings by Caribbean artists.

Nightlife

The Bath and Turtle (⊠ Virgin Gorda Yacht Harbour, ☎ 284/495–5239) is a good spot to rub elbows with local music aficionados as well as boaters. One of the liveliest spots on Virgin Gorda, this informal pub hosts island bands on Wednesday and Sunday from 8 PM until midnight.

Bitter End Yacht Club (⊠ North Sound, ☎ 284/494–2746) features local bands several nights a week in season. Call for schedules.

Chez Bamboo (⊠ Across from Virgin Gorda Yacht Harbour, ☎ 284/495–5752) is the place to go to listen to jazz Saturday nights.

Little Dix Bay (✉ Little Dix Bay, ☎ 284/495–5555) presents elegant live entertainment several nights a week in season.

Pirate's Pub at Andy's Chateau (✉ The Valley, ☎ 284/495–5252) offers live music and the closest thing to a disco here Friday, Saturday, and Sunday nights.

Pusser's at Leverick Bay (✉ Leverick Bay, ☎ 284/495–7370) has live bands on Saturday night and Sunday afternoon.

Sip and Dip Grill (✉ Olde Yard Inn, ☎ 284/495–5544) has a live local band at their Sunday night barbecue.

Exploring Virgin Gorda

One of the most effective ways to see Virgin Gorda is by sailboat. Paved roads are few and far between, alternative routes are limited, and most byways don't follow the scalloped shoreline. The main road also sticks resolutely to the center of the island, linking The Baths at the tip of the southern extremity with Gun Creek and Leverick Bay in the north and providing exhilarating views from its higher points. The panorama of a craggy shoreline, scissored with grottoes and fringed by palms and the island's trademark boulders, possesses a primitive beauty. If you choose to drive, that you can hit all of the sights in one day. The best plan of attack is to explore the area near your hotel (either The Valley or North Sound) first, and then and take one day to drive to the other end of the island. En route, stop to climb Gorda Peak, which is in the center of the island. One road runs between The Valley and North Sound.

Sights to See

❸ **The Baths.** It's well worth your time to visit Virgin Gorda's most celebrated site. Giant boulders, brought to the surface eons ago by a vast volcanic eruption, are scattered about the beach and in the water. Some are almost as large as small houses and form remarkable grottoes. Climb between these rocks to swim in the many pools. Early morning and late afternoon are the best times to visit, since The Baths and the beach here are usually crowded with cruise-ship passengers and day-trippers from Tortola. (If it's privacy you crave, follow the shore north for a few hundred yards to reach several quieter bays—**Spring**, the **Crawl**, **Little Trunk**, and **Valley Trunk**—or head south along the trail to **Devil's Bay**. These beaches have the same giant boulders as those found at The Baths.) ✉ *Lee Rd.,* ☎ *no phone.* 🎟 *Free.*

❻ **Coastal Islands.** You can easily reach the quaintly named islands of **Fallen Jerusalem** and the **Dog Islands** by boat. They are all part of the BVI National Parks Trust, and their seductive beaches and unparalleled snorkeling opportunities display the BVI at their beachcombing, hedonistic best. Contact **DIVE BVI** (✉ Virgin Gorda Yacht Harbour, ☎ 284/495–5513) for expert diving instruction, certification, and day trips. ☎ *No phone.* 🎟 *Free.*

❹ **Copper Mine Point.** Here you'll see a tall, stone shaft silhouetted against the sky and a small stone structure that overlooks the sea. These are the ruins of a copper mine established here 400 years ago and worked first by the Spanish, then by the English until the early 20th century. ✉ *Copper Mine Rd.,* ☎ *no phone.* 🎟 *Free.*

❷ **Little Fort National Park.** A 36-acre wildlife sanctuary and the ruins of an old fort can be found here. Piles of giant boulders similar to those found at The Baths are scattered throughout the park. ✉ *Spanish Town Rd.,* ☎ *no phone.* 🎟 *Free.*

❶ **Spanish Town.** Virgin Gorda's main settlement, on the island's southern wing, is a peaceful village so tiny that it barely qualifies as a town at all. Also known as the Valley, Spanish Town is home to a marina, a small cluster of shops, and a couple of car-rental agencies. Just north of town is the ferry slip. At the **Virgin Gorda Yacht Harbour** you can enjoy a stroll along the dockfront and maybe do a little shopping.

⑤ **Virgin Gorda Peak National Park.** There are two trails, and small signs on North Sound Road mark both entrances to the 265-acre park and the island's summit at 1,359 ft. Sometimes the signs are missing, so keep your eyes open for a set of stairs that disappears into the trees. It's about a 15-minute hike, from either entrance, up to a small clearing, where you can climb a ladder to the platform of a wooden observation tower. If you're keen for some woodsy exercise or just want to stretch your legs, go for it. Unfortunately, the view at the top is somewhat tree-obstructed. ⊠ *North Sound Rd.,* ☎ *no phone.* 🎟 *Free.*

JOST VAN DYKE

Named after an early Dutch settler, Jost Van Dyke is a small island northwest of Tortola and is *truly* a place to get away from it all. Mountainous and lush, the 4-mi-long island—home to only about 140 people—has one tiny resort, some rental houses, a campground, and fewer than a dozen informal eateries. With only a handful of cars and a single road, the island makes you feel as if you've stepped back in time. This is one of the most popular anchorages in the Caribbean, and there is a disproportionately large number of informal bars and restaurants, which have helped earn Jost its reputation as the "party island" of the BVI.

Lodging

For price categories, *see* the chart *under* Lodging *in* Tortola, *above.*

$$$ 🏨 **Sandcastle.** This six-cottage hideaway is on a ½-mi stretch of white-sand beach on remote White Bay. There's "nothing" to do here, except relax in a hammock, read, walk, swim, and enjoy sophisticated cuisine by candlelight in the ☞ **Sandcastle** restaurant. You can also make arrangements for diving, sailing, and sportfishing trips. ⊠ *White Bay,* ☎ *284/495–9888,* 𝔽𝔸𝕏 *284/495–9999. 6 cottages. Restaurant, bar, beach. MC, V. EP.*

$$$ 🏨 **Sandy Ground Estates.** This collection of eight privately owned one- and two-bedroom houses is tucked into the foliage along the edge of a beach at the east end of Jost Van Dyke. Each one is architecturally different, and interiors range from spartan to stylish. The fully equipped kitchens can be prestocked if you supply a list of groceries (this is a good idea as supplies are limited on the island), and there are four very casual restaurants on the other side of the hill—a long walk away. ⊠ *Sandy Ground,* ☎ *284/495–3391. 8 houses. Beach. No credit cards.*

$ ⛺ **White Bay Campground.** On remote White Bay beach, this simple campground has bare sites, equipped tent sites (tents with electricity and one lamp), and screened cabins. The owners will take you on nature walks and can arrange island tours and sailing and diving trips. ⊠ *White Bay,* ☎ *284/495–9312. 8 bare sites, 4 prepared sites, 4 cabins. Restaurant, bar, beach. No credit cards.*

Dining

Restaurants on Jost Van Dyke are very informal (some serve meals family style at long tables) but charming. The island is a favorite charter stop, and you're bound to hear people exchanging stories about the previous night's anchoring adventures. Most restaurants don't take reservations, and in all cases, dress is informal. For price categories, *see* the chart *under* Dining *in* Tortola, *above.*

$$$ ✕ **Sandcastle.** Candlelit dinners in the tiny beachfront dining room of the ☞ **Sandcastle** cottage complex are four-course, prix-fixe affairs. The menu changes but can include a West Indian pumpkin or a curried apple soup, curried shrimp or three-mustard chicken, and, for dessert, rum bananas or key lime pie. Reservations are requested by 4 PM. Sandwiches are served at lunch at the Soggy Dollar Bar, famous for allegedly being the birthplace of the lethal Painkiller drink. ✉ *White Bay,* ☎ *284/495–9888. MC, V.*

$$–$$$ ✕ **Abe's Little Harbour.** Specialties at this informal, popular spot include fresh lobster, conch, and spare ribs. During most of the winter season, there's a pig roast every Wednesday night. ✉ *Little Harbour,* ☎ *no phone (boaters can use VHF Channel 16). No credit cards.*

$$–$$$ ✕ **Rudy's Mariner Rendezvous.** This simple eatery at the western end of the beach specializes in lobster and other seafood dishes and has live entertainment several nights a week. ✉ *Great Harbour,* ☎ *284/ 495–9282. No credit cards.*

$–$$$ ✕ **Club Paradise.** The dinner menu at this casual beachfront establishment includes grilled local fish such as mahimahi, red snapper, and grouper; grilled steak; and barbecued chicken and ribs. Hamburgers, West Indian conch stew, and curried chicken are the luncheon fare. Be sure to try the excellent black bean soup. ✉ *Great Harbour,* ☎ *284/ 495–9267. No credit cards.*

$–$$$ ✕ **Foxy's Tamarind.** One of the true hot spots in the BVI—and a "must
★ stop" for yachters from the world over—Foxy's hosts the madcap Wooden Boat Race every August or September and throws big parties on New Year's Eve, April Fools' Day, and Halloween. This lively place serves local dishes and the best barbecue, and it makes a rum punch that's all its own. Foxy himself plays the guitar and delights in creating calypso ditties about his guests. Next door is Foxy's Store, which sells clothing, sundries, souvenirs, and cassettes of Foxy performing. ✉ *Great Harbour,* ☎ *284/495–9258. AE, MC, V. No lunch.*

$–$$$ ✕ **Harris' Place.** Owner Harris Jones is famous for his Monday, Thursday, and Saturday pig-roast buffets and Monday night's Lobstermania. Harris' Place is a great spot to rub elbows with locals and the charter-boat crowd. There's live reggae music Thursday and Saturday. ✉ *Little Harbour,* ☎ *284/495–9302. AE, MC, V.*

$–$$$ ✕ **Sydney's Peace and Love.** Here you'll find great lobster, barbecue, and a sensational (for the BVI) jukebox. The cognoscenti sail here for dinner since there's no beach—meaning no sand fleas, which are especially irksome in the evening. ✉ *Little Harbour,* ☎ *284/495–9271. No credit cards.*

$ ✕ **Happy Laurry's Snack Bar.** A great choice for a quick meal—snacks, fritters, fish, chicken, and chips. ✉ *Great Harbour,* ☎ *no phone (boaters can use VHF Channel 16). No credit cards.*

Beaches

White Bay, on the south shore, west of Great Harbour, has a long stretch of white sand. Just offshore, the little islet known as **Sandy Cay** is a gleaming scimitar of white sand, with marvelous snorkeling.

PETER ISLAND

A dramatic, hilly island with wonderful anchorages and beautiful beaches, Peter Island is about 5 mi directly south across the Sir Francis Drake Channel from Road Town, Tortola. Set amid the string of small islands that stream from the southern tip of Virgin Gorda, the island is an idyllic hideaway replete with white sand beaches, stunning views, and the Peter Island Resort. You can sail here on your own craft or take a launch from the Peter Island dock just east of Road Town, Tortola ($15 each way or free if you're coming for dinner; just mention that you have a reservation).

Lodging

For price categories, *see* the chart *under* Lodging *in* Tortola, *above.*

$$$$
★ 🏨 **Peter Island Resort and Yacht Harbour.** This resort, which is owned and run by the Amway Corporation, closed down for the last half of 1997 to redo rooms, to enlarge the ☞ **Tradewinds Restaurant** and the gift shop, and to expand the dock and marina area that's so popular with charterers. Rooms have been retiled and elegant French doors now lead to private balconies. New, colorful, print bedspreads and draperies have lightened and brightened the rooms. There's lots to do here: Facilities include (but truly are not limited to) a tennis program run by Peter Burwash, a water-sports center, mountain bicycles, a 20-station fitness trail, and a 5-star PADI dive facility. The 50 guest rooms, in four-unit cottages tucked among beds of radiant tropical flowers, are either on the beach or near the pool. Beachfront units are beautiful stone-and-wood structures that open onto a lovely stretch of sand. The less expensive ocean-view and garden-view rooms look across the pool toward the hills and Tortola. A spectacular hilltop villa, the Crow's Nest, has four bedrooms, a living room, a state-of-the-art kitchen, a dining room, a terrace, an inner courtyard, an entertainment system, domestic help, vehicles, and a private swimming pool. Those seeking seclusion take note: The resort's beaches are on bays that are popular charter-boat anchorages and Amway regularly schedules incentive trips here for its distributors. ✉ *Sprat Bay (Box 211), Road Town, Tortola,* ☎ *284/495–2000 or 800/346–4451,* 𝖥𝖠𝖷 *284/495–2500. 50 rooms, 2 villas. 2 restaurants, 2 bars, pool, 4 tennis courts, basketball, exercise room, beach, dive shop, windsurfing, mountain bikes, laundry service, helipad. AE, MC, V. FAP.*

Dining

For price categories, *see* the chart *under* Dining *in* Tortola, *above.*

ECLECTIC
$$$$
✕ **Tradewinds Restaurant.** The ☞ Peter Island Resort's open-air dining room overlooks the Sir Francis Drake Channel and is an enchanting setting for dinner. The à la carte menu offers mostly Continental selections, with subtle Caribbean touches; Saturday night is buffet night. After dinner, dance under the stars to soft, rhythmic tunes performed by local musicians three or four nights a week in season. ☎ *284/495–2000. Reservations essential. AE, MC, V. No lunch.*

$$$–$$$$
✕ **Deadman's Bay Bar and Grill.** The resort's casual grill on the beach serves lunches of ribs, burgers, grilled fish, and a bountiful salad bar. Sunday lunch features a lavish West Indian buffet and a steel band. A dinner with a choice of grilled local fish, steak, or chicken is served most evenings. Try one of the many delicious frozen tropical drinks. ☎ *284/495–2000. Reservations essential. AE, MC, V.*

Beaches

Palm-fringed **Dead Man's Bay,** called one of the world's 10 most romantic beaches, is just a short hike from the dock. Snorkeling is good at both ends of the beach, and you'll find a bar and restaurant for lunch.

If you feel like taking a hike instead of heading down to Dead Man's Bay, follow the road up, and when it levels off bear right and head down to the other side of the island and secluded **White Bay.**

ANEGADA

Anegada lies low on the horizon about 14 mi north of Virgin Gorda. Unlike the other hilly volcanic islands in the chain, this is a flat coral and limestone atoll. Nine miles long and 2 mi wide, the island rises no more than 28 ft above sea level. In fact, by the time you're able to see it, you may have run your boat onto a reef. (More than 300 captains, unfamiliar with the waters, have done so since exploration days; note that bareboat charters don't allow their vessels to head here without a trained skipper.) Although the reefs are a sailor's nightmare, they (and the shipwrecks they've caused) are a scuba diver's dream. Snorkeling, especially in the translucent waters around Loblolly Bay on the north shore, is also a transcendent experience. You can float in shallow, calm, totally reef-protected water just a few feet from shore and see one coral formation after another, each shimmering with a rainbow of colorful fish. Such watery pleasures are complemented by ever-so-fine, ever-so-white sand (the northern and western shores have long stretches of the stuff) and the occasional beach bar (stop in for burgers, Anegada lobster, or a frosty beer). The island's population of about 150 lives primarily in a small, south-side village called the Settlement. Many local fisherfolk are happy to take visitors out bonefishing.

Lodging

For price categories, *see* the chart *under* Lodging *in* Tortola, *above.*

$$$$ 🏨 **Anegada Reef Hotel.** If you favor laid-back living (meaning, among other things, absolutely no schedules), this is the spot for you. Pack a bathing suit and a few warmer garments for the evening, and you're good to go. The hotel's 16 simply furnished rooms are laid out in motel fashion. It has its own narrow strip of beach, but beach lovers will want to spend their days on the deserted beaches at the other side of the island; you can be dropped off with a picnic lunch or be picked up and returned to the hotel for lunch. Snorkeling and diving are also popular activities as are deep-sea fishing or bonefishing in the flats. Cool down with a drink in the outdoor bar or sample the island's famous lobster and munch on a cold salad in the ☞ **Anegada Reef** restaurant. ⊠ *Setting Point,* ☎ *284/495–8002,* 🖷 *284/495–9362. 16 rooms. Restaurant, bar, beach. No credit cards. FAP.*

$$ 🏨 **Neptune's Treasure.** In addition to double and single rooms that are very basically furnished and have private baths, this little guest house also offers tents with foam mattresses and linens. There's a restaurant, ☞ Neptune's Treasure, and a little gift shop on the premises. ⊠ *Between Pomato and Saltheap points,* ☎ *284/495–9439. 4 rooms, 6 tents. Restaurant, beach. AE, MC, V.*

$ ⛺ **Anegada Beach Campground.** The tents (8 × 10 ft or 10 × 12 ft) here are pitched in a marvelously serene setting. Sites cost $7 per person, per night. ⊠ *The Settlement,* ☎ *284/495–8038. Restaurant, bar, beach. No credit cards.*

Dining

There are between three and eight restaurants open at any one time, depending on the season and also on whim. Check when you're on the island. For price categories, *see* the chart *under* Dining *in* Tortola, *above.*

SEAFOOD

$$$ ✕ **Anegada Reef Hotel.** Seasoned yachters gather nightly at the ☞ **Anegada Reef Hotel**'s bar-restaurant to converse and dine with the hotel guests. Dinner is by candlelight and always includes famous Anegada lobster, steaks, and chicken—all prepared on the large grill by the little open-air bar. ⊠ *Anegada Reef Hotel,* ☎ *284/495–8002. Reservations essential. No credit cards.*

$$–$$$ ✕ **Neptune's Treasure.** The owners catch, cook, and serve the seafood (lobster is a specialty) at this casual bar and restaurant in the ☞ Neptune's Treasure guest house. ⊠ *Between Pomato and Saltheap points,* ☎ *284/495–9439. AE.*

$$–$$$ ✕ **Pomato Point.** This relaxed restaurant-bar is on a narrow beach, a short walk from the Anegada Reef Hotel. Entrées include steak, chicken, lobster, and fresh-caught seafood. Owner Wilfred Creque displays various island artifacts, including shards of Arawak pottery and 17th-century coins, cannonballs, and bottles. ⊠ *Pomato Point,* ☎ *284/495–8038. Reservations essential. No credit cards.*

$–$$$ ✕ **Big Bamboo.** Ice-cold beer, island drinks, burgers, and grilled Anegada lobster entice a steady stream of barefoot diners to this beach bar. ⊠ *Loblolly Bay,* ☎ *no phone (boaters can use VHF Channel 16). AE.*

Shopping

Pat's Pottery (⊠ The Settlement, ☎ 284/495–8031) sells bowls, plates, cups, candlestick holders, original watercolors, and more. **Anegada Reef Hotel Boutique** (⊠ Setting Point, ☎ 284/495–8002) has a bit of everything: resort wear, hand-painted T-shirts, locally made jewelry, books, and one-of-a-kind gifts.

OTHER BRITISH VIRGIN ISLANDS

Cooper Island

This small hilly island on the south side of the Sir Francis Drake Channel, about 8 mi from Road Town, Tortola, is popular with the charter-boat crowd. There are no roads (which doesn't really matter because there aren't any cars), but you will find a beach restaurant, a casual little hotel, a few privately owned houses (some of which are available for rent), and great snorkeling at the south end of Manchioneel Bay.

Lodging

For price categories on this and the islands discussed below, *see* the chart *under* Lodging *in* Tortola, *above.*

$$–$$$ 🏨 **Cooper Island Beach Club.** Two West Indian–style cottages—set back from the beach among the palm trees—house 12 no-frills units with a living area, a small but complete kitchen, and a balcony. A stay here takes you back to the basics: You use rainwater that has been collected in a cistern, and you can't use any appliances because electricity is so limited (who needs pressed clothes and blow-dried hair anyway?). There's plenty of "civilization," however, at the on-site bar, which fills nightly with groups of boaters. ⊠ *Machioneel Bay (Box 859), Road Town, Tortola,* ☎ *413/659–2602 or 800/542–4624. 12 rooms. Restaurant, beach, dive shop. MC, V. EP.*

Dining

For price categories on this and the islands discussed below, *see* the chart *under* Dining *in* Tortola, *above.*

$$–$$$ ✕ **Cooper Island Restaurant.** Ferry service from Road Town is available only to guests of ☞ **Cooper Island Beach Club,** but this restaurant is a popular stop for boaters. Come here for great ratatouille (it's a main course at lunch, an appetizer at dinner); grilled fish, chicken, and steak; and conch Creole. For lunch, there are also hamburgers, conch fritters, and pasta salad. ⊠ *Machioneel Bay,* ☎ *no phone (boaters can use VHF Channel 16). Reservations essential. AE, MC, V.*

Guana Island

Guana Island is very quiet and, because the whole thing is owned by a hotel, *very* private. There are *no* public amenities, and access is limited (the hotel sends a private launch to pick its guests up on Beef Island). If you arrive on your own boat, the only place you're allowed is on the beach.

Dining and Lodging

$$$$ ✕🏨 **Guana Island.** The hotel complex is atop a hill, a 10-minute walk from the beach, and the views of neighboring islands are stunning. Fifteen comfortable guest rooms are spread among seven houses that are scattered throughout the grounds. The houses are decorated in Caribbean style, with rattan furniture, and each has its own porch. You can observe more than 50 species of bird on this island, and the terrain is a verdant collection of tropical plants ringed by six deserted beaches. Guests mingle during cocktail hour, and often choose to dine together at several large tables in the main house, but there are small tables if you prefer a more intimate meal. ✉ *Hilltop (Box 32), Road Town, Tortola,* ☎ *284/494–2354,* 🖷 *914/967–8048. 15 rooms. Restaurant, ceiling fans, tennis court, croquet, hiking. No credit cards. FAP.*

Necker Island

Necker Island is a private island just north of Virgin Gorda. Accommodations here are luxurious, but you can only stay if you rent the whole island.

Lodging

$$$$ 🏨 **Necker Island.** You and as many as 23 friends can lease the whole island, including its five beaches, many walks, tennis court, luxurious villa with 10 spacious guest rooms, and two Balinese cottages. A chef prepares gourmet meals for you in the state-of-the-art kitchen; a full staff takes care of everything else. ☎ *284/494–2757. Pool, beaches, boating. AE, MC, V.*

Marina Cay

Beautiful little Marina Cay is in Trellis Bay, not far from Beef Island. Sometimes you can see it and its large J-shape coral reefs—a most dramatic sight—from the air during the approach to the airport on Beef Island. With only 6 acres, this islet is considered small even by BVI standards. There's a restaurant, Pusser's Store, and a six-unit hotel here. Ferry service is free from the dock on Beef Island.

Lodging

$$–$$$ 🏨 **Marina Cay Hotel and Restaurant.** The tiny island's only hotel has four double rooms and two suites, all with lovely views of the water and neighboring islands. Each has its own porch. Ferry service is free from the dock on Beef Island. Call for ferry times, which vary with the season. ✉ *West side of Marina Cay (Box 76), Road Town, Tortola,* ☎ *284/494–2174,* 🖷 *284/494–4775. 6 units. Restaurant, bar, beach. AE, D, DC, MC, V. EP.*

Dining

$$–$$$ ✕ **Marina Cay Restaurant.** Ferry service is available from Beef Island dock to this beachfront restaurant on a tiny islet. The dinner menu ranges from fish and lobster to steak, chicken, and barbecued ribs. Pusser's Painkiller Punch is the house specialty. ✉ *Pusser's Marina Cay,* ☎ *284/ 494–2174. AE, MC, V.*

BRITISH VIRGIN ISLANDS A TO Z

Arriving and Departing
BY AIRPLANE

There's no nonstop service from the continental United States to the BVI; connections are usually made through San Juan, Puerto Rico, or St. Thomas, USVI. Airlines serving both San Juan and St. Thomas include **American** (☎ 340/774–6464), **Continental** (☎ 340/777–8190), and **Delta** (☎ 340/774–9300). **American Eagle** (☎ 340/776–2560) flies from San Juan to Tortola. **Air St. Thomas** (☎ 284/495–5935) flies between St. Thomas and Virgin Gorda. Regularly scheduled flights between the BVI and most other Caribbean islands are provided by **LIAT** (☎ 284/495–1187). Many Caribbean islands can also be reached through **Gorda Aero Service** (✉ Tortola, ☎ 284/495–1571), a charter service.

Both the Beef Island/Tortola and Virgin Gorda airports are classic Caribbean—always sleepy. Sometimes the Beef Island gets crowded before departures, and lines at service desks move slowly when this happens; give yourself at least an hour.

From the Airport: Most hotels provide transport, but you must make such arrangements prior to arrival. At the Beef Island/Tortola airport, taxi drivers usually hover at the exit from customs. Fares are officially set; they're not negotiable and are lower per person for more than one person. Figure about $15 for up to three people and $5 for each additional passenger for the 20-minute ride to Road Town, and about $20–$30 for the 45-minute ride to West End. Expect to share your taxi, and be patient if your driver searches for people to fill his cab—only a few flights land each day, and this could be your driver's only run.

You can also call the **BVI Taxi Association** (☎ 284/495–2378). On Virgin Gorda call **Mahogany Taxi Service** (☎ 284/495–5469). If you're staying anywhere on the North Sound in Virgin Gorda, you can fly to Beef Island/Tortola and catch the nearby North Sound Express (☞ Getting Around, *below*), or you can fly to Virgin Gorda and take a taxi to North Sound. From there a hotel launch will meet you, but you must have made arrangements with your hotel before your arrival. Don't get nervous if your land taxi leaves you by yourself on a deserted dock and tells you to wait for your skipper—someone *will* show up. If your destination is Leverick Bay, your land taxi will take you there directly.

By Boat

Ferries connect St. Thomas, USVI, with Tortola and Virgin Gorda. **Native Son, Inc.** (☎ 284/495–4617) operates three ferries (*Native Son, Oriole,* and *Voyager Eagle*) and has daily service between St. Thomas and Tortola (West End and Road Town). **Smiths Ferry Services** (☎ 284/495–4495 or 284/494–2355) operates between downtown St. Thomas and Road Town and West End daily. **Speedy's Ferries** (☎ 284/495–5240) runs between Virgin Gorda, Tortola, and St. Thomas on Tuesday, Thursday, and Saturday. **Inter-Island Boat Services'** *Sundance II* (☎ 284/495–4166) connects St. John and West End, Tortola, daily.

Electricity

Electricity is 110 volts, the same as it is in the United States. The electricity is quite reliable.

Emergencies

Clinics: On Virgin Gorda, there is a clinic in Spanish Town, or the Valley (☎ 284/495–5337). There is also a clinic on Virgin Gorda at North Sound (284/495–7310). **Hospital:** Peebles Hospital (☎ 284/494–

3497) is in Road Town. **Emergencies:** The general emergency number is ☎ 999. **Pharmacies:** In Road Town, try **J. R. O'Neal Drug Store** (☎ 284/494–2292) or **Lagoon Plaza Drug Store** (☎ 284/494–2498). The Spanish Town pharmacy is **Medicure** (☎ 284/495–5479).

Festivals and Seasonal Events

In March, catch the breathtaking displays of local foliage at the **Horticultural Society Show** at the Botanical Gardens (☎ 284/494–4557). Also in March, join in the fun at the **Virgin Gorda Festival,** which culminates with a parade on Easter Sunday. In April, glimpse the colorful spinnakers as sailing enthusiasts from around the world gather for the internationally known **BVI Spring Regatta.** May is the time for partying at **Foxy's Wooden Boat Regatta** on Jost Van Dyke. In August, try your hand at sportfishing as anglers from around the globe compete to land the largest catch at the **BVI Sportfishing Tournament.** Also in August, you can participate in two weeks of joyful revelry during the **BVI Summer Festival** on Tortola. If you've always wanted to escape to the islands and live on a boat, then the November **BVI Boat Show** is for you. If you want to compete in sailing races and games, drop in on Virgin Gorda's North Sound during the last six weeks of the year for the **Bitter End Yacht Club's Competition Series,** including the Invitational Regatta. For the best in local *fungi* bands (bands that makes music using household items—washboards, spoons, and the like—as instruments), stop by the **Scratch/Fungi Band Fiesta** in December (☎ 284/494–2629).

Getting Around

AIRPLANES

Gorda Aero Service (✉ Tortola/Beef Island Airport, ☎ 284/495–1571) flies between Tortola and Anegada on Monday, Wednesday, and Friday and offers charter flights between Tortola, Virgin Gorda, and Anegada as well as to other Caribbean islands.

BUSES

There's bus service on Tortola. For information about rates and schedules, call **Scato's Bus Service** (☎ 284/494–2365). Taking the bus is a great way to meet locals, albeit at a bumpy snail's pace. Look for an eight-passenger van with Scato's name on the front, and wave your hand when you see it. The fare ranges from $2 to $10, depending on where you are going. Rates are determined by the driver, and there's no set rate, since the bus can pick you up anywhere and drop you anywhere.

CAR RENTALS

Driving in Tortola is on the left side of the road. Main roads are, for the most part, well paved, but there are exceptionally steep hills and sharp curves; driving demands your complete attention. Basically, a main road encircles the island and several roads cross the island. Speed limits (rarely enforced) are 20 mph in town and 30 mph outside town. Gas costs about $2 a gallon.

On Tortola, **Avis** (☎ 284/494–3322) rents four-wheel-drive vehicles and cars in Road Town. **Budget** has two offices (✉ Wickham's Cay I, Road Town, ☎ 284/494–2639; ✉ Wickham's Cay II, Road Town, ☎ 284/494–5150) and rents both cars and four-wheel-drive vehicles. **Hertz** (✉ West End☎ 284/495–4405) also rents four-wheel-drive vehicles and cars.

On Virgin Gorda, **Mahogany Rentals and Taxi Service** (✉ Spanish Town, ☎ 284/495–5469) rents four-wheel-drive vehicles and compact cars. **Speedy's** (✉ Spanish Town, ☎ 284/495–5240) provides four-wheel-drive vehicles and compact cars.

FERRIES

Speedy's Fantasy (☎ 284/495–5240) makes the run between Road Town, Tortola, and Spanish Town, Virgin Gorda, daily. **North Sound Express** (☎ 284/494–2746) boats run daily between Virgin Gorda's North Sound and Beef Island/Tortola. The **Peter Island Ferry** (☎ 284/495–2000) runs daily between Peter Island's private dock on Tortola (just east of Road Town) and Peter Island. **Jost Van Dyke Ferry Service** (☎ 284/494–2997) makes the Jost Van Dyke–Tortola run several times daily.

TAXIS

Your hotel staff will be happy to summon a taxi for you. Rates aren't published so you should negotiate the fare with your driver before you start your trip. The taxi number is also the license plate number. If you would like the same taxi to pick you up for the return trip, ask your driver. There's a **BVI Taxi Association** stand in Road Town near the ferry dock (☎ 284/494–2875), at Wickham's Cay I (☎ 284/494–2322), and at the Beef Island/Tortola airport (☎ 284/495–2378). You can also usually find a taxi at the ferry dock at Soper's Hole, West End, where ferries arrive from St. Thomas. **Mahogany Rentals and Taxi Service** (✉ The Valley, ☎ 284/495–5469) provides taxi service all over Virgin Gorda. **Andy's Taxi and Jeep Rental** (✉ The Valley, ☎ 284/495–5252 or 284/495–5353) offers taxi service from one end of Virgin Gorda to the other.

Guided Tours

To do some chauffeured sightseeing on Tortola, get in touch with the **BVI Taxi Association** (☞ Getting Around, *above*); the minimum is three persons. **Travel Plan Tours** (☎ 284/494–2872) can arrange island tours, boat tours, and yacht charters from it's Tortola base. To arrange tours on Virgin Gorda, contact **Andy's Taxi and Jeep Rental** (☎ 284/495–5252 or 284/495–5353) and **Mahogany Rentals and Taxi Service** (☎ 284/495–5469).

Language

English is the official language, and it's often spoken with a West Indian accent.

Money Matters

CURRENCY

The currency is the U.S. dollar. Any other currency must be exchanged at a bank.

SERVICE CHARGES, TAXES, AND TIPPING

There's a 7% government tax on hotel rooms, and the service charge ranges from 12% to 15%. Tip porters and bellhops $1 per bag. Sometimes a service charge (10%) is included on restaurant bills; it's customary to leave an additional 5% if you really liked the service. If no charge is added, 15% is the norm. Cabbies normally aren't tipped because most own their cabs; add 10%–15% if they exceed their duties. There is no sales tax in the BVI. The departure tax is $10 by plane and $5 by boat.

Opening and Closing Times

Banks usually have hours Monday–Thursday 9–2:30 and Friday 9–2:30 and 4:30–6. Stores are generally open Monday–Saturday 9–5.

HOLIDAYS

New Year's Day, Commonwealth Day (Mar. 10), Good Friday (Apr. 2), Easter Monday (Apr. 5), Whit Monday (May 24), Sovereign's Birthday (June 14), Territory Day (July 1), BVI August Festival Days

(Aug. 2–4), St. Ursula's Day (Oct. 19), Birthday of Heir to the Throne (Nov. 12), Christmas, Boxing Day (Dec. 26).

Passports

U.S. and Canadian citizens need a valid passport or a birth certificate with a raised seal along with a government-issued photo ID. Visitors from all other countries need a valid passport.

Precautions

Although crime is almost nonexistent, use common sense: don't leave your camera on the beach while you take a dip or your wallet on a hotel dresser when you go for a walk.

Telephones and Mail

The area code for the BVI is 284; when you make calls from the United States and Canada, you need only dial the area code and the number (there's no country code). From the United Kingdom, you must dial 001 and then the area code and the number. To call anywhere in the BVI once you've arrived, dial all seven digits. A local call from a public pay phone costs 25¢, but pay phones are frequently on the blink. An alternative is a Caribbean phone card, available in $5, $10, and $20 denominations. It's sold at most major hotels and many stores and can be used to call all over the Caribbean and to access USADirect from special phone-card telephones.

For credit card or collect long-distance calls to the United States, use a phone-card telephone or look for special **USADirect** phones, which are linked directly to an AT&T operator. For access dial 800/872–2881, or dial 111 from a pay phone and charge the call to your MasterCard or Visa. USADirect and pay phones can be found at most hotels and in towns.

There are post offices in Road Town on Tortola and in Spanish Town on Virgin Gorda. (Note that postal service in the BVI isn't very efficient.) Postage for a first-class letter to the United States, Canada, and the United Kingdom is 35¢; for a postcard, 20¢. For a small fee, **Rush It** in Road Town (☎ 284/494–4421) and in Spanish Town (☎ 284/495–5821) offer most U.S. mail and UPS services (via St. Thomas the next day). If you wish to write to an establishment on the BVI, include the specific island in the address; there are no postal codes.

Visitor Information

Information about the BVI is available through the **British Virgin Islands Tourist Board** (✉ 370 Lexington Ave., Suite 313, New York, NY 10017, ☎ 212/696–0400 or 800/835–8530) or the **British Virgin Islands Information Offices** in San Francisco (✉ 1804 Union St., Suite 305, San Francisco, CA 94123, ☎ 415/775–0344 or 800/232–7770 nationwide). British travelers can write or visit the **BVI Information Office** (✉ 110 St. Martin's La., London WC2N 4DY, ☎ 0171/240–4259).

On Tortola there's a **BVI Tourist Board Office** at the center of Road Town near the ferry dock, just south of Wickham's Cay I (✉ Box 134, Road Town, Tortola, ☎ 284/494–3134). The Virgin Gorda **BVI Tourist Board** is in Virgin Gorda Yacht Harbour, Spanish Town (☎ 284/495–5182).

For all kinds of useful information about these islands, including rates and phone numbers, get a free copy of *The Welcome Tourist Guide*, available at hotels, restaurants, and stores.

8 Cayman Islands

Updated by
JoAnn
Milivojevic

*S ee that white ring?" asks the fisherman point-
ing to a murky band of white near Little
Cayman's shore, "There's bonefish there,
digging into the bottom searching for crabs." The
man wades into the warm water. The noon sun
doesn't seem to affect him: he wears no sunglasses,
no hat, and not a trickle of sweat is evident. A gallon water jug with its top cut off serves as a bucket;
he reaches in, grabs some minnows, and flicks
them into the water. They break the surface like
raindrops. Distant thunder rolls, and a few cigar-
shape clouds linger overhead. The fisherman casts
his line and waits, content to be in pure aqua,
pure peace.*

Fisherfolk aren't the only ones drawn to the Cayman Islands. This British
colony, which consists of Grand Cayman and the two smaller Cayman
Brac and Little Cayman islands, is one of the Caribbean's hottest destinations for scuba diving, windsurfing, golf, shopping, eating, dancing—you name it. If you want a little hustle and bustle with your rest
and relaxation, Grand Cayman won't let you down. If it's pure R&R
you seek, you'll find pockets of sweet seclusion, especially on Cayman
Brac and Little Cayman.

Columbus is said to have sighted the islands in 1503, but he didn't stop
off to explore. He did note that the surrounding sea was alive with turtles, so the islands were named Las Tortugas. The name was later
changed to Cayman. Until the late 1600s, when England took these
islands and Jamaica over from Spain under the Treaty of Madrid, the
Caymans remained largely uninhabited. After that point, however,
people came from many countries—England, Holland, Spain, France—
and for many reasons. Some were refugees from the Spanish Inquisi-

tion or deserters from Oliver Cromwell's army in Jamaica. Others were brought by the seas. The Caymans' caves and coves were perfect hideouts for the likes of Blackbeard, Sir Henry Morgan, and other pirates out to plunder Spanish galleons. And many's the ship that fell afoul of the reefs surrounding the islands, often with the help of Caymanians, who lured vessels to shore with beacon fires (more than one pioneer's home was built using the remnants of such ships).

The legend of one wreck in particular—the Wreck of the Ten Sails—has remained popular with the Caymanians through the years. In 1794 a convoy of 10 Jamaican ships bound for England foundered on the reefs. In this instance, the islanders made valiant rescue attempts. They saved everyone, including, it was said, a few members of royalty. The tale has it that a grateful King George III decreed that Caymanians would forever be exempt from conscription and would never have to pay taxes. And though Caymanians don't pay taxes, research completed in 1994 shows this tale to be purely fictional. This British colony has a governor, who appoints three official members to the Legislative Assembly and has to accept the advice of the Executive Council in all matters except foreign affairs, defense, internal security, and civil-service appointments. Though the governor is appointed from England, locally elected Caymanians greatly influence how their islands are run.

Today's Caymans may be seasoned with suburban prosperity, particularly Grand Cayman (residents joke that the national flower is the satellite dish), and stuffed with crowds (the hotels that line the famed Seven Mile beach are often full, even in the slow summer season), but the 31,000 Cayman Islanders—most of whom live on Grand Cayman—add considerable flavor with their renowned courtesy and civility. The cost of living may be about 20% higher here than in the United States (one U.S. dollar is only worth about 80 Cayman cents), but you will not be hassled by panhandlers or feel afraid to walk around on a dark evening (the crime rate is very low). Add political and economic stability to the mix, and you have a fine island recipe indeed.

GRAND CAYMAN

Grand Cayman is world-renowned for two offshore activities: banking and scuba diving. The former pays dividends in the manicured capital of George Town, bulging as it does with some 554 banks. The latter offers its rewards in translucent waters that are full of colorful and varied life—much of it protected by a marine parks system. While about a third of Grand Cayman's visitors come for the diving, a growing number are young honeymooners. The island offers many pleasures from shopping for jewelry to fine dining to simply strolling hand-in-hand on a powder-soft beach.

Lodging

In the off season (summer), it's easy to find lodgings, even on short notice, but for peak season and holiday visits, book well in advance. Note that most hotels require a 7- or 14-day minimum stay at Christmastime, though condominiums will let you book on a day-to-day basis for stays of any length you like.

Brace yourself for resort prices—there are few accommodations in the economy range. Most of the larger hotels along Seven Mile Beach don't offer meal plans. Smaller properties that are farther from restaurants usually offer MAP or FAP (to estimate rates for hotels offering MAP or FAP, add about $40 per person per day to the average price ranges below). More than half the rooms are rental condos and villas; all are

Grand Cayman

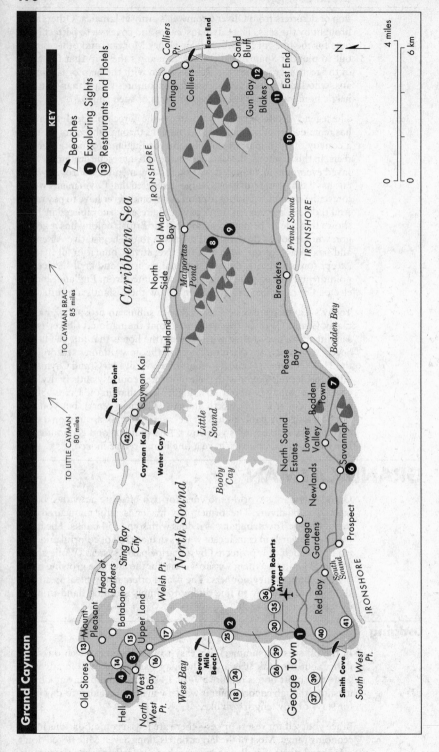

KEY

Beaches

① Exploring Sights

⑬ Restaurants and Hotels

Caribbean Sea

TO CAYMAN BRAC
85 miles

TO LITTLE CAYMAN
80 miles

North Sound

IRONSHORE

Old Man Bay

North Side

Hutland

Malportas Pond

⑧

⑨

Breakers

Frank Sound

IRONSHORE

Pease Bay

Bodden Bay

⑦ Bodden Town

Lower Valley

Savannah

⑥

Newlands

North Sound Estates

Little Sound

Booby Cay

Rum Point

Cayman Kai

⑫

Water Cay

Welsh Pt.

Sting Ray City

Head of Barkers

Batabano

Mount Pleasant

⑬

⑭

③

⑮ Upper Land

⑯

⑰

Old Stores

Hell ⑤

North West Pt.

④

West Bay

Seven Mile Beach

⑱ – ㉔

㉕

②

㉖ ㉙

㉗ ㉚

⑩

Colliers Pt.

East End

Tortuga

Colliers

Sand Bluff

East End

Gun Bay ⑫

Blakes ⑪

⑩

Omega Gardens

Red Bay

⑳ – ㉙

Owen Roberts Airport

㊱

㉟

㉚

George Town

①

㊵

㊶

㊲ – ㊴

Smith Cove

South West Pt.

Prospect

South Sound

IRONSHORE

㊷ Cayman Kai

4 miles

6 km

0

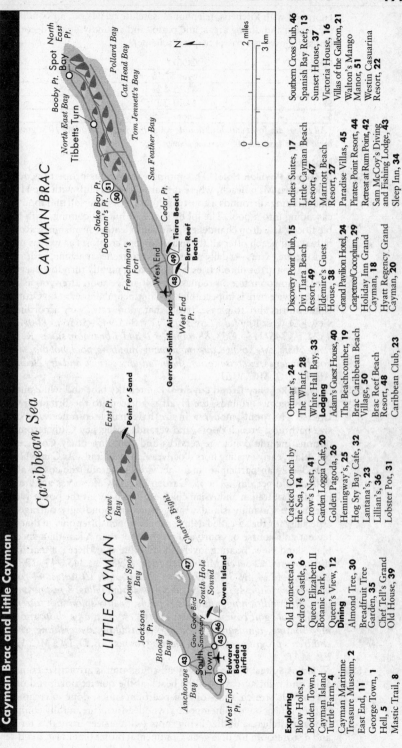

Exploring
Blow Holes, **10**
Bodden Town, **7**
Cayman Island
Turtle Farm, **4**
Cayman Maritime
Treasure Museum, **2**
East End, **11**
George Town, **1**
Hell, **5**
Mastic Trail, **8**
Old Homestead, **3**
Pedro's Castle, **6**
Queen Elizabeth II
Botanic Park, **9**

Dining
Almond Tree, **30**
Breadfruit Tree
Garden, **35**
Chef Tell's Grand
Old House, **39**
Cracked Conch by
the Sea, **14**
Crow's Nest, **41**
Garden Loggia Cafe, **20**
Golden Pagoda, **26**
Hemingway's, **25**
Hog Sty Bay Cafe, **32**
Lantana's, **23**
Lillian's, **36**
Lobster Pot, **31**
Ottmar's, **24**
The Wharf, **28**
White Hall Bay, **33**

Lodging
Adam's Guest House, **40**
The Beachcomber, **19**
Brac Caribbean Beach
Village, **50**
Brac Reef Beach
Resort, **48**
Caribbean Club, **23**
Discovery Point Club, **15**
Divi Tiara Beach
Resort, **49**
Eldemire's Guest
House, **38**
Grand Pavilion Hotel, **24**
Grapetree/Cocoplum, **29**
Holiday Inn Grand
Cayman, **18**
Hyatt Regency Grand
Cayman, **20**
Indies Suites, **17**
Little Cayman Beach
Resort, **47**
Marriott Beach
Resort, **27**
Paradise Villas, **45**
Pirates Point Resort, **44**
Retreat at Rum Point, **42**
Sam McCoy's Diving
and Fishing Lodge, **43**
Sleep Inn, **34**
Southern Cross Club, **46**
Spanish Bay Reef, **13**
Sunset House, **37**
Victoria House, **16**
Villas of the Galleon, **21**
Walton's Mango
Manor, **51**
Westin Casuarina
Resort, **22**

equipped with kitchens, telephones, satellite television, air-conditioning, living and dining areas, and patios and are individually decorated
(most following a pastel tropical scheme).

CATEGORY	COST*
$$$$	over $275
$$$	$225–$275
$$	$150–$225
$	under $150

*All prices are for a standard double room in winter, excluding 10% govern-
ment room tax and 10% service charge.*

Hotels

$$$$ 🏨 **Grand Pavilion Hotel.** This intimate, luxurious property is across
★ from Seven Mile Beach, where it shares a beach club with the Hyatt.
The building surrounds a courtyard that has a waterfall and fountains
cascading into a pool. The lobby is august but welcoming, with marble floors, teardrop chandeliers, and plush leather furnishings. Rooms
in teal and peach offer all the usual modern comforts as well as many
considerate extras—a daily newspaper, a coffee/tea machine, bathrobes,
an amazing array of toiletries, a pants press, nightly turndown service,
even an in-room fax on request (it will arrive soon after you ask for
it; the service here is impeccable). A Continental dinner at ☞ **Ottmar's**
restaurant is sure to please. (Note that room rates vary according to
view.) ⬚ *West Bay Rd. (Box 30117),* ☎ *345/945–5656 or 800/437–
4824,* 𝔽𝔸𝕏 *345/945–5353. 88 rooms, 5 2- and 3-bedroom suites. Restaurant, 2 bars, café, lounge, air-conditioning, minibars, pool, hot tub, sauna,
golf privileges, exercise room, shop, laundry service and dry cleaning.
AE, D, DC, MC, V. EP.*

$$$$ 🏨 **Hyatt Regency Grand Cayman.** Painted sky blue and white and set
★ amid gorgeous grounds, the Hyatt is adjacent to the Britannia Golf
Course. The rooms, moderate in size, have marble entranceways, oversize bathtubs, French doors, and verandas. Regency Club accommodations include concierge services and complimentary Continental
breakfast, early evening hors d'oeuvres, and cocktails. At Camp Hyatt,
kids 3–12 can participate in an activities program (the cost is about
$50 a child per day). The ☞ **Garden Loggia Café** serves an interest-
ing blend of Italian and Asian cuisines. This is by far the poshest lodging in the Cayman Islands; rates are correspondingly outrageous,
especially for the so-called deluxe rooms, which differ only in that they
have a golf-course or courtyard view rather than a less-than-spectac-
ular island view. Boating lovers should note that there's a marina on
the property. ⬚ *Seven Mile Beach (Box 1698),* ☎ *345/949–1234 or
800/233–1234,* 𝔽𝔸𝕏 *345/947–5336. 225 rooms, 10 suites; 44 rooms
in Regency Club; 35 1-, 2-, 3-, and 4-bedroom villas. 3 restaurants, 4
bars, air-conditioning, minibars, 4 pools, beauty salon, hot tub, massage, 9-hole golf course, 4 tennis courts, croquet, dive shop, snorkeling, boating, windsurfing, boating, parasailing, waterskiing, shops,
children's program, car rental, meeting rooms. AE, D, DC, MC, V. CP,
EP, MAP.*

$$$$ 🏨 **Indies Suites.** Cayman's only all-suite hotel is attractive, comfort-
★ able, and right across from the beach at the quieter north end of the
Seven Mile stretch. One- or two-bedroom suites, done in cream and
burnt orange, have contemporary wooden furniture, a fully equipped
modern kitchen, a dining-living room (with a sleeper sofa), a terrace,
and a storeroom for dive gear. Continental buffet breakfast, maid service, a free sunset cruise once a week, and a live band that entertains
in the lushly landscaped courtyard twice a week are nice extras. The
lobby is spectacular, with vintage 1930s Fords on display. ⬚ *Seven Mile
Beach (Box 2070 GT),* ☎ *345/947–5025 or 800/654–3130,* 𝔽𝔸𝕏 *345/*

947–5024. *38 suites. Bar, snack bar, grocery, air-conditioning, pool, hot tub, dive shop, snorkeling, coin laundry. AE, MC, V. CP.*

$$$$ 🏨 **Spanish Bay Reef.** Flowering trees and bushes surround pale pink, two-story, stucco units at Grand Cayman's only all-inclusive resort, which is on a small sandy beach at the northwest tip of the island. Boardwalks connect the simple but comfortable guest rooms, which have bright Caribbean print spreads and curtains. The outdoor bar-dining area surrounds the pool and has views of the ocean; the indoor bar-dining area is spacious and made of coral-stone. Spanish Bay Reef itself is a deep drop-off, which means superior diving and snorkeling; instruction in both is offered. Rates include round-trip transfers, taxes and gratuities, shore diving, boat dives, and use of bicycles (not in mint condition). Fishing charters are also available. ⊠ *West Bay (Box 903),* ☎ *345/949–3765 or 800/482–3483 (reservations service),* FAX *345/949–1842. 50 units. Restaurant, bar, pool, hot tub, dive shop. AE, D, MC, V. All-inclusive.*

$$$–$$$$ 🏨 **Marriott Beach Resort** This five-story luxury property is just 1 mi
★ from George Town. Designed in colonial style with arched doorways, the airy, marble lobby opens onto a plant-filled courtyard. Families like the large adjoining rooms done in bright tropical colors; all have balconies. Price varies according to the view, which is either of the ocean or the garden courtyard. There's a snorkeling reef 50 ft from shore, a beach bar near the pool, a dive shop with equipment for every possible water sport, and a full-service spa. The Marriott has the island's largest conference center, so it's predictably popular for conventions. ⊠ *Seven Mile Beach (Box 30371),* ☎ *345/949–0088 or 800/228–9290,* FAX *345/949–0288. 315 rooms, 4 suites. Restaurant, bar, snack bar, air-conditioning, pool, beauty salon, hot tub, spa, beach, dive shop, snorkeling, windsurfing, shops, laundry services and dry cleaning, meeting rooms, car rental. AE, D, DC, MC, V. EP.*

$$$–$$$$ 🏨 **Westin Casuarina Resort.** The Casuarina is on the beach, so its choice rooms have at least partial ocean views (standards have an "island" view, which translates into the parking lot and main drag). The lobby spills out onto the waterfront, where tall royal palms shade the elegant walkway. Rooms have bleached white-wood furniture and stucco ceilings, and the color schemes range from subdued mountain colors and desert pastels to brighter jades and ultramarines. The suites aren't much different from one-bedroom lodgings, so they're hardly worth the extra money. ⊠ *Box 30620,* ☎ *345/945–3800 or 800/228–3000,* FAX *345/949–5825. 351 rooms, 5 suites. 2 restaurants, 2 bars, grill, pool, beauty salon, 2 hot tubs, 2 tennis courts, exercise room, beach, dive shop, shops. AE, D, MC, V. EP.*

$$–$$$ 🏨 **Holiday Inn Grand Cayman.** This sprawling modern hotel is as unpretentious as it is cheerful (the bright tropical colors in the spacious public rooms will lift even the weariest traveler's spirits), and it's set on a wide, picturesque stretch of sand. Guest rooms are standard: comfortable, if not luxurious, with pool or ocean views. The huge breakfast buffet is a good value, and don't miss Barefoot Man; he's something of a local celebrity who plays reggae on the patio piano four nights a week. As many as four people can stay in a room without additional charge, making this economical for families. ⊠ *Seven Mile Beach (Box 904),* ☎ *345/945–4444 or 800/421–9999,* FAX *345/945–4213. 215 rooms. 3 restaurants, 2 bars, ice cream parlor, air-conditioning, pool, dive shop, nightclub, coin laundry, laundry service, business services, meeting rooms, car rental. AE, DC, MC, V. CP, EP, MAP.*

$$ 🏨 **Sleep Inn.** This two-story Choice Hotels affiliate is a quick stroll
★ from Seven Mile Beach, close to the airport, and just a mile from George Town's shops—how's that for convenient location? Rooms are motel-modern, with peaches-and-cream pastels and contemporary

wood furnishings. The Dive Inn dive shop is here, as are tour agencies and car and motorcycle rental offices. ✉ *Box 30111,* ☎ *345/949–9111 or 800/753–3746,* FAX *345/949–6699. 124 rooms. Bar, grill, air-conditioning, pool, hot tub, dive shop, shop, laundry service and dry cleaning, meeting room, car rental. AE, D, MC, V. EP.*

$ 🏨 **Sunset House.** Low-key and laid-back describe this resort with sparse, motel-style rooms on the ironshore (very sharp, hard, calcified black coral) south of George Town, 4 mi from Seven Mile Beach. A congenial staff, a happening bar, and a seafood restaurant are pluses, but the diving (and the dive packages) attract most guests. Full dive services include free waterside lockers, two- and three-tank dives at the better reefs around the island, and Cathy Church's U/W Photo Centre. It's a five-minute walk to a sandy beach, 10 minutes to George Town. ✉ *S. Church St. (Box 479),* ☎ *345/949–7111 or 800/854–4767,* FAX *345/949–7101. 59 rooms. Restaurant, bar, air-conditioning, 2 pools, hot tub, dive shop. AE, D, MC, V. CP, EP, MAP.*

Guest Houses

They may be some distance from the beach and short on style and facilities, but these lodgings offer rock-bottom prices (all fall well below the $ category), a friendly atmosphere, and your best shot at getting to know the locals. Rooms are clean and simple, often with cooking facilities, and most have private bathrooms. Many establishments also have outdoor grills and picnic tables that you can use. A rental car is recommended. These establishments do not accept personal checks or credit cards but do take reservations through the **Cayman Islands Reservation Service** (✉ 6100 Blue Lagoon Dr., Suite 150, Miami, FL 33126; ☎ 800/327–8777).

Adam's Guest House (✉ Melnac Ave. near the Seaview Hotel (Box 312), ☎ 345/949–2512, ☎ FAX 345/949–0919), 1 mi south of George Town and 4 mi from the beach, has five rooms, all with kitchenette. **Eldemire's Guest House** (✉ S. Church St. (Box 482), ☎ 345/949–5387, FAX 345/949–6987), Grand Cayman's first guest house, has seven rooms and is a 15-minute drive to Seven Mile Beach, but less than a mile south of pretty Smith Cove Bay.

Villas and Condominiums

Cayman Islands Reservation Service (☞ *see* Guest Houses, *above*) and can describe and book most condominiums and villas on the islands. **Cayman Villas** (✉ Box 681, ☎ 345/947–4144 or 800/235–5888, FAX 345/949–7471), and **Hospitality World Ltd.** (✉ Box 30123, ☎ 345/949–3458 or 800/232–1034, FAX 345/949–7054) are local agencies that can also make reservations.

Cayman Islands Department of Tourism provides a complete list of condominiums and small rental apartments in the $$ range. Many of these are multibedroom units that become affordable when shared by two or more couples. Rates are higher in winter, and there may be a three- or seven-night minimum. The following complexes bear a marked similarity to one another: All have fully equipped kitchens, telephones, satellite TV, air-conditioning, living and dining areas, and patios. Differences arise in property amenities and proximity to town. All are well-maintained and directly on the beach, though you'll need a car for grocery shopping.

$$$$ 🏨 **The Beachcomber.** Each of the simply furnished two-bedroom apartments in this older condo community has a view of the ocean from a private, screened patio. When the sun gets too warm, you can retreat to the shade of the palabas on Seven Mile Beach or go snorkeling in the reef just offshore. There's a grocery store across the street and count-

less shopping and dining outlets within walking distance, so you don't really need a car. ⊠ *Seven Mile Beach (Box 1799),* ☎ *345/945–4470 or 800/327–8777,* FAX *345/945–5019. 23 units. Grills, air-conditioning, pool, beach, coin laundry. AE, MC, V.*

$$$$ ⚓ **Discovery Point Club.** This secluded complex, which is at the far north end of Seven Mile Beach in West Bay (6 mi from George Town), has a lovely beach and great snorkeling in the protected waters of nearby Cemetery Reef. Tennis courts, a hot tub, and a pool add to the appeal here. Kids 12 and under stay free April–December. ⊠ *West Bay (Box 439),* ☎ *345/945–4724 or 800/327–8777 (reservations service),* FAX *345/945–5051. 45 units. Grills, pool, hot tub, 2 tennis courts, beach, coin laundry. AE, MC, V.*

$$$$ ⚓ **Villas of the Galleon.** The exteriors of these deluxe stucco cottages look shabby, but the interiors are attractive and beautifully maintained, and their location—on the widest section of Seven Mile Beach, just across from the Jack Nicklaus–designed Links Golf Club—couldn't be better. Each duplex one- or two-bedroom unit has a full kitchen, a terrace, and enormous closets (a big plus for families); decor varies, though such tasteful touches as eggshell tile floors, pastel finishes, and rattan furnishings are not uncommon. ⊠ *Seven Mile Beach (Box 1797),* ☎ *345/945–4433,* FAX *345/945–4705. 74 units. Grills, air-conditioning, beach, coin laundry. AE, MC, V.*

$$$–$$$$ ⚓ **Caribbean Club.** Eighteen one- and two-bedroom villas (six on the beach) make up this quiet condominium getaway. Although these units are not necessarily deluxe, they are secluded and have tidy tiled baths and simple wicker furniture. There's also maid service—always a plus. ⊠ *Seven Mile Beach (Box 30499),* ☎ *345/945–4099 or 800/327–8777 (reservations service),* FAX *345/945–4443. 18 villas. Restaurant, bar, air-conditioning, tennis court, beach, coin laundry, laundry service and dry cleaning. AE, MC, V. EP, MAP.*

$$$ ⚓ **Grapetree/Cocoplum.** A half mile from George Town on Seven Mile Beach, these sister condos are adjacent to one another. Grapetree's two-bedroom, two-bath units are carpeted, and have traditional wicker furnishings and a beige and brown decor. Cocoplum's units are similar, though they're decorated with Caribbean pastel prints, and their grounds have more plants and trees. ⊠ *Seven Mile Beach (Box 1802),* ☎ *345/949–5640 or 800/635–4824,* FAX *345/949–0150. 51 units. Air-conditioning, 2 pools, tennis court, beach. AE, MC, V.*

$$$ ⚓ **Retreat at Rum Point.** The Retreat has its own narrow beach with casuarina trees, far from the madding crowd on the north-central tip of Grand Cayman. As many as six people can rent a two-bedroom villa here, and two or three people will be comfortable in a one-bedroom unit. The decor in these privately owned condos varies—for the most part, you'll find tropical motifs and wicker furniture. All units are spacious and have a washer and dryer. If you're a diver, take advantage of superb offshore diving (there are dive facilities nearby), including the famed North Wall. You'll be stranded without a car; it's a 35-minute drive to town or the airport. ⊠ *North Side (Box 46),* ☎ *345/945–9135,* FAX *345/945–9058. 23 units. Restaurant, bar, air-conditioning, pool, sauna, tennis court, exercise room, racquetball. MC, V.*

$$–$$$$ ⚓ **Victoria House.** The one-, two-, and three-bedroom units in this simple building have white walls and tile floors and are decorated with muted Caribbean prints and rattan furniture. You may choose from a range of activities including tennis and water sports. The Victoria is 3 mi north of town on a quiet stretch of Seven Mile Beach; if you're an early riser, you may catch a glimpse of giant sea turtles on the sand. ⊠ *Seven Mile Beach, near West Bay (Box 30571),* ☎ *345/945–4233,* FAX *345/945–5328. 25 units. Air-conditioning, tennis, scuba diving, beach, snorkeling, coin laundry. AE, MC, V.*

Dining

Grand Cayman's restaurants satisfy every palate and pocketbook. Big spenders will find gourmet cuisine, and those on a budget will appreciate the abundance of moderately priced ethnic eateries. Local hangouts that serve West Indian fare offer the most in flavor and in value.

Fish—including grouper, snapper, tuna, wahoo, and marlin—is served either simply (baked, broiled, steamed) or Cayman-style (with peppers, onions, and tomatoes). Conch, the meat of a large pink mollusk, is ubiquitous in stews and chowders and as fritters or panfried (cracked). Caribbean lobster is available but is often quite expensive, and other shellfish are in short supply in local waters. The only traditional culinary treat of the islands is turtle—served in soup or stew or as a steak—though fewer restaurants offer it these days.

All the restaurants reviewed are on Grand Cayman because there are few to none on the sister islands (visitors eat at the resorts and guest houses). Dining out here can be expensive, so replenish your billfold because some places do not accept plastic. Many restaurants add a 10%–15% service charge to the bill, so check before leaving a tip.

What to Wear

Smart casual wear (slacks and sundresses) is acceptable for dinner in all but a few places. The nicer resorts and more expensive restaurants may require a jacket, especially in high season; ask when making reservations. Shorts are usually acceptable during the day, but unless you're going to an ultracasual beach bar, beachwear (bathing suits, cover-ups, tank tops, etc.) is a no-no. Most restaurants have an alfresco dining section, and if you plan to dine under the stars, you may need a spritz of bug spray (mosquitoes can be pesky), which most places provide.

CATEGORY	COST*
$$$	over $30
$$	$20–$30
$	under $20

per person for a three-course meal, excluding drinks and service charge

ASIAN

$–$$ ✕ Golden Pagoda. Hakka-style cooking (similar to using a hibachi) is featured at this well-known Chinese restaurant. Among its specialties are butterfly shrimp and chicken in black-bean sauce. Takeout, or takie-outie, they call it, is now available, as are showy Japanese *teppanyaki* (grilled foods prepared before your eyes) dinners for two Tuesday–Saturday night. ⊠ *West Bay Rd.,* ☎ *345/949–5475. Reservations essential for Japanese dinner. AE, MC, V. No lunch weekends.*

CARIBBEAN/CREOLE

$$–$$$ ✕ Almond Tree. This eatery combines architecture from the South Seas isle of Yap with bones, skulls, and bric-a-brac from Africa, South America, and the Pacific. Good-value seafood entrées include turtle steak and fresh grouper, with "All-U-Can-Eat" entrées for CI$12 on Wednesday and Friday. ⊠ *N. Church St.,* ☎ *345/949–2893. AE, MC, V. Closed Sun.*

$$–$$$ ✕ Hemingway's. Sea views and breezes attract diners to this classy open-
★ air restaurant on Seven Mile Beach. In the evening (except Sunday), candlelight and a guitarist add even more romance to the place. Nouvelle Caribbean and seafood dishes include pumpkin-coated mahimahi with mango juice, macadamia-crusted pork loin, and grouper stuffed with crab and sweet corn in a jerk cream sauce. Portions are large, and service is superb. For a tropical drink, try the Seven Mile Meltdown, with dark rum, peach schnapps, pineapple juice, and fresh coconut.

✉ *West Bay Rd., across from the Hyatt,* ☎ *345/945–5700. AE, D, DC, MC, V. No dinner Sun.*

$–$$$ ✕ **Hog Sty Bay Cafe.** Lots of socializing goes on in the casual atmosphere of this English-style café on George Town's harbor. It's a classic Caribbean hangout, with hand-painted wooden fish hanging everywhere, an invigorating mix of zany residents, and curious tourists. A simple menu of Caribbean dishes as well as sandwiches and hamburgers will satisfy you for lunch or dinner. Many believe the conch fritters served here are the best in town. Come to watch the sun set from the seaside patio or to enjoy the weekday happy hour. ✉ *N. Church St.,* ☎ *345/949–6163. AE, MC, V.*

$–$$$ ✕ **White Hall Bay.** Locals love White Hall Bay, which occupies a charming, traditional waterfront home that's decorated with with gourds, straw bags, and black-and-white photos of old-timers. The food is equally traditional, from sultry turtle and pepper-pot stews (both seeming to have bubbled for years) to luscious yam cake and coconut cream pie. ✉ *N. Church St.,* ☎ *345/949–8670. AE, D, MC, V.*

$ ✕ **Breadfruit Tree Garden.** This is another spot that's favored by locals—as much for the delicious food as for the reasonable prices. The jerk chicken rivals any on the island. Also on the menu are curry chicken and stewed pork, oxtail, rice and beans, and homemade soups. Drinks include breadfruit, mango, passion fruit, and carrot juices. The interior is a little kitschy with silk roses, white porch swings, straw hats, empty birdcages, and fake ivy crawling along the ceiling. It's open until the wee hours, which makes it a good midnight munchie stop. ✉ *Eastern Ave., George Town,* ☎ *345/945–2124. No credit cards.*

CONTEMPORARY

$$–$$$ ✕ **Lantana's.** Alfred Schrock, longtime chef at the Wharf Restaurant, ★ now creates excellent American-Caribbean lunches and dinners here. Enjoy lobster quesadillas, homemade lamb sausage, or blackened king salmon over cilantro linguine with banana fritters and cranberry relish. If you come for nothing else, *don't* miss the incredible roasted garlic soup and the apple pie. The decor of the bilevel restaurant—potted plants, teak furniture, painted wooden fish—places you in the perfectly serene island state of mind. ✉ *Caribbean Club, West Bay Rd.,* ☎ *345/ 945–5595. AE, D, MC, V. No lunch weekends.*

CONTINENTAL

$$$ ✕ **Chef Tell's Grand Old House.** TV celebrity chef Tell Erhardt's menu consists of Continental entrées and a few local specialties. Among the spicier appetizers is fried coconut shrimp with mustard apricot sauce. On the milder side are entrées such as lobster served "The Chef's Way" (dipped in egg batter and sautéed with shallots, mushrooms, and white wine) and duck with fresh pear chutney. The oceanside gazebos, surrounded by palms and cooled by ceiling fans, are refreshing and lively; stellar service makes a meal here all the more enjoyable. ✉ *S. Church St.,* ☎ *345/949–9333. Dinner reservations essential. DC, MC, V. Closed Sun. No lunch Sat.*

$$$ ✕ **Ottmar's.** This quietly elegant restaurant in the ☞ **Grand Pavilion** ★ **Hotel** is styled after a West Indian great house. Jade carpeting, peach walls, mahogany furniture, glass chandeliers and a trickling fountain, create an attractive setting for the excellent service. Favorites on the international menu include bouillabaisse, chicken breast Oscar (topped with crab, asparagus, and hollandaise), and French pepper steak (flamed in cognac and doused with green peppercorn sauce and crème fraîche). ✉ *West Bay Rd.,* ☎ *345/945–5879 or 345/945–5882. Reservations essential. AE, D, DC, MC, V. No lunch.*

ECLECTIC

$$–$$$ ✕ **Garden Loggia Café.** At the ☞ Hyatt's café you can dine in a beautifully landscaped courtyard or inside surrounded by soothing pastels and the coolness of ceiling fans and marble-top tables. The café serves Italian and Asian cuisine and is open for dinner only during high season (mid-December–May). The Sunday champagne brunch, featuring everything from fresh seafood to waffles and custom-made omelets, draws a crowd. Reserve a seat as early as possible. ✉ *West Bay Rd.,* ☎ *345/949–1234. Reservations essential. AE, D, DC, MC, V.*

$$–$$$ ✕ **The Wharf.** Stylishly decorated in blue and white, the Wharf looks onto a veranda and the nearby sea. On the surf-and-turf menu are conch fritters, home-smoked salmon, "seafood a l'aneth" (lobster and scallops in dill sauce), veal scallopini, and steak fillet béarnaise; anything on the fresh daily menu is recommended. Live Paraguayan music entertains diners. The Ports of Call bar is a perfect spot from which to watch the sun set, and tarpon feeding off the deck is a nightly (9 PM) spectacle here. ✉ *West Bay Rd.,* ☎ *345/949–2231. AE, D, MC, V. No lunch weekends.*

$ ✕ **Lillian's.** Island and Spanish dishes are the specialties at this diner, which is always filled with locals during lunchtime. Daily specials include barbecue ribs, meat loaf, and fish rundown, a stew made with fish, plantain, cassava, sweet potato, and breadfruit in a white sauce (squirt a bit of lime on it and it's perfection). Lillian occasionally makes "Fish Tea," which is really a soup and is said to be an aphrodisiac. ✉ *Christian Plaza, near airport, on North Sound Rd.,* ☎ *345/ 949–2178. No credit cards. Closed Sun. No dinner.*

SEAFOOD

$$–$$$ ✕ **Lobster Pot.** The second-floor terrace of this cozy restaurant overlooks the bay downtown, so the sunsets are an extra attraction. The menu includes both Continental dishes and such Caribbean specialties as conch chowder, seafood curry, shrimp Diane, and, of course, lobster. This place is popular, and the constant turnover creates a rather frenzied atmosphere. If you can't make it for dinner, drop by the pub and have a frozen banana daiquiri. ✉ *N. Church St.,* ☎ *345/ 949–2736. AE, D, MC, V.*

$–$$$ ✕ **Cracked Conch by the Sea.** This island favorite provides patio din-
★   ers with a panoramic view of the sea. Specialties here include cracked (tenderized and panfried) conch, conch fritters, conch chowder, spicy Cayman-style snapper, and turtle steak. The Sunday buffet is a divine array of island-style curries and jerk meats; don't miss the cassava cake, a thick, sweet, spongy dessert. ✉ *West Bay Rd., near Turtle Bay Farm,* ☎ *345/945–5217. MC, V.*

$–$$ ✕ **Crow's Nest.** About a 15-minute drive south of George Town, this secluded restaurant is in a rustic West Indian Creole cottage set amid overgrown foliage and flowering shrubs right on the beach (diners often go snorkeling after lunch). For the best breezes, sit on the terrace, which is draped in fishnets. The shark du jour, herb-crusted dolphinfish with lobster sauce, swordfish with jerk mayo, and shrimp and conch dishes are excellent, as is the chocolate fudge rum cake. ✉ *South Sound Rd.,* ☎ *345/949–9366. AE, MC, V. No lunch Sun.*

Beaches

You may read or hear about the "dozens of beaches" on these islands, but that's more exaggeration than reality. Grand Cayman's west coast, the most developed area of the entire colony, is where you'll find the famous **Seven Mile Beach** (actually 5½ mi long) and its expanses of powdery white sand. The beach is litter-free and sans peddlers, so you can relax in an unspoiled, hassle-free (if somewhat crowded) atmosphere.

This is also Grand Cayman's busiest vacation center, and most of the island's accommodations, restaurants, and shopping centers are on this strip. You'll also find headquarters for the island's aquatic activities here (☞ Outdoor Activities and Sports, *below*).

Grand Cayman also has several smaller beaches—coves, really. **Smith Cove,** off South Church Street and south of the Grand Old House, is a popular local bathing spot on weekends. The best windsurfing is just off the beaches of **East End,** at Colliers, by Morritt's Tortuga Club. The beach can be lovely if it's kept clean of seaweed tossed ashore by trade winds, but the windsurfing is the real draw here. Seldom discovered by visitors unless they're staying here are the beautiful beach areas of **Cayman Kai** (which was undergoing some development at press time), **Rum Point,** and, even more isolated and unspoiled, **Water Cay.** These are favored hideaways for residents and popular Sunday picnic spots.

Outdoor Activities and Sports

Participant Sports

FISHING

If you enjoy action fishing, Cayman waters have plenty to offer—blue and white marlin, yellowfin tuna, sailfish, dolphinfish, and wahoo. Bonefish and tarpon are also plentiful off Little Cayman. Some 25 boats are available for charter, offering fishing options that include deep-sea, reef, bone, tarpon, light-tackle, and fly-fishing. Grand Cayman charter operators to contact are **Charter Boat Headquarters** (☎ 345/945–4340), **Crosby Ebanks** (☎ 345/945–4049), **Island Girl** (☎ 345/945–3029), and **Bayside Watersports** (☎ 345/949–3200).

GOLF

The **Grand Cayman–Britannia** golf course (☎ 345/949–8020), next to the Hyatt Regency, was designed by Jack Nicklaus. The course is really three in one—a 9-hole par-70 regulation course, an 18-hole par-57 executive course, and a Cayman course (played with a Cayman ball that goes about half the distance of a regulation ball). Greens fees range from $40 to $90. Golf carts ($15–$25) are mandatory.

Windier, and therefore more challenging, are the **Links at Safe Haven** (☎ 345/949–5988), Cayman's first 18-hole championship golf course, set amid a virtual botanical garden of indigenous trees, plants, and flowering shrubs. The Roy Case–designed par-71, 6,519-yard course also has an aqua driving range (the distance markers and balls float), a two-story clubhouse, locker rooms, a pro shop, a patio bar with live jazz happy hours on weekends, and a fine restaurant that serves Continental and Caribbean cuisine daily for lunch and dinner. Greens fees run to $60. Golf carts ($15–$20 per person) are mandatory.

HIKING

Nature trails abound on all three islands (on the sister islands, it's best to ask locals for directions—you'll probably be standing right next to the start of a trail without realizing it). Guided nature walks are available at the National Trust's **Mastic Trail** on Grand Cayman (✉ Off Frank Sound Rd., ☎ 345/949–1996 for reservations and information), a rugged 2-mi slash through pristine woodlands, mangrove swamps, and ancient rock formations. Tours are by appointment, daily 10–3, and cost $30 per person.

SCUBA DIVING AND SNORKELING

To call the Cayman Islands a scuba diver's paradise is not overstating the case. Jacques Cousteau named Bloody Bay (off Little Cayman) one of the world's top dives, and the famed Cayman Wall, off Grand Cayman, ranks up there as well. You'll find pristine water (visibility often exceeding 100 ft), breathtaking coral formations, and plentiful and exotic marine life. Many top-notch dive operations offer a variety of services, instruction, and equipment. A Grand Cayman must-see for adventurous souls is Stingray City, which has been called the best 12-ft dive (or snorkel) in the world. Here you'll find dozens of unusually tame stingrays—tame enough to suction squid from your outstretched palm and gracefully swim around you in the shallow waters.

The best shore-entry snorkeling spots are off the ironshore south of George Town, at Eden Rock and Parrot's Landing; north of town, at the reef just off the West Bay Cemetery on Grand Cayman's west coast; and in the reef-protected shallows of the island's north and south coasts, where coral and fish life are much more varied and abundant.

Divers are required to be certified and possess a "C" card or take a short resort or full certification course. A certification course, including classroom, pool, and boat sessions as well as checkout dives, takes four to six days and costs $350–$400. A short resort course usually lasts a day and costs about $80–$100. It introduces the novice to the sport and teaches the rudimentary skills needed to make a shallow, instructor-monitored dive.

All dive operations (where you can also rent snorkel gear) on Cayman are more than competent; among them are **Aquanauts** (☎ 345/945–1990 or 800/357–2212), **Bob Soto's** (☎ 345/949–2022 or 800/262–7686), **Don Foster's** (☎ 345/949–5679 or 800/833–4837), **Eden Rock** (☎ 345/949–7243), **Parrot's Landing** (☎ 345/949–7884 or 800/448–0428), **Red Sail Sports** (☎ 345/949–8745 or 800/255–6425), and **Sunset Divers** (☎ 345/949–7111 or 800/854–4767). **Turtle Reef Divers** (☎ 345/949–1700) is one of the first to offer Nitrox dives/certification (a diver's bottom time is extended). Their location next to the Turtle Farm is excellent for shore dives and is off the beaten path of other dive operators. The brand-new dive gear is another plus. You can get complete information on all operators from the Department of Tourism (☞ Visitor Information *in* Cayman Islands A to Z, *below*). A single-tank dive averages $45; a two-tank dive, about $55. Snorkel-equipment rental runs from $5 to $15 a day.

Most operations can rent all diving gear, including equipment for underwater photography; Bob Soto's, Don Foster's, and Cathy Church's U/W Photo Centre have facilities for film processing and underwater photo courses.

One-week live-aboard dive cruises are available on the 110-ft **Cayman Aggressor III** (☎ 800/348–2628) and the luxury yacht **Little Cayman Diver II** (☎ 800/458–2722).

SUBMARINING

Atlantis Submarines (☎ 345/949–7700 or 800/253-0493) takes you to undersea depths of 100 ft without getting wet. The air-conditioned cabin keeps you cool and comfortable as you glide past rich coral reefs and spectacular marine life. An expert narrates the journey.

The **Nautilus** (☎ 345/949–1355) is semi-submersible (part of the boat remains above water). You can sun on the deck or venture to the cabin below where windows allow you to see the reefs and marine life. Theme cruises (mystery theater, dinner at sunset, etc.) are also offered.

TENNIS

Most hotels and condo complexes have tennis courts (some lighted) for guests. If your hotel doesn't have a court, contact one that does (☞ Lodging, *above*) to see whether you can reserve play time or arrange lessons with a pro.

WINDSURFING

Sailboards Caribbean (✉ West Bay Rd., ☎ 345/949–1068) offers windsurfing rentals and lessons for everyone, whether you're a beginner or a veteran who loves those high winds. **Cayman Windsurf** (☎ 345/945–7492) also offers lessons and rentals on the east end of the island at Morritt's Tortuga Club and on North Sound by Safe Haven.

Spectator Sports

Rugby, football (soccer), and cricket are popular during their respective seasons. The upgraded Truman Bodden Sports Complex, behind the John Gray High School in George Town, can now host major sporting events. It has a professional quality track-and-field facility and a stadium that seats 3,000. Check the local paper for schedules.

Shopping

On Grand Cayman, the good news is that there's no sales tax *and* there's plenty of duty-free merchandise. The bad news is that prices on imported merchandise—English china, Swiss watches, French perfumes, and Japanese cameras and electronic goods—are not always lower than elsewhere. To make sure you get a bargain, price items before you leave home, and use it to comparison shop. Locally made items to watch for include woven mats and baskets as well as jewelry made of a marblesque stone called Caymanite—which comes from the cliffs of Cayman Brac—or of authentic sunken treasure and ancient coins. Relatively inexpensive rings and earrings made with semiprecious stones, coral, and seashells also abound. Cigar lovers take note: some shops carry such Cuban beauties as Cohiba and Partagas (enjoy them on the island as bringing them back to the United States is a no-no).

Although you'll find black coral products in Grand Cayman, they're controversial. Most of the coral used to make items sold here comes from Belize and Honduras, because Cayman Islands marine law prohibits the removal of live coral from its own sea. Black coral grows at a very slow rate (only about 3 inches every 10 years), it is often designated as an endangered species, and reefs are not always harvested carefully. Environmental groups generally discourage people from purchasing coral products. If you feel differently, there are a number of local craftsmen who use coral to create unique items.

Areas and Malls

The main shopping areas are **Elizabethan Square, Cardinal Avenue,** and the chic **Kirk Freeport Plaza,** known for its fine jewelry, plus duty-free china, crystal, Gucci items, perfumes, and fine cosmetics. The **Queen's Court Shopping Centre,** on Seven Mile Beach close to town, has shops that sell an array of souvenirs, crafts, and gifts. At the **West Shore Shopping Centre,** on Seven Mile Beach, you'll find good-quality island art, beachwear, and more.

Specialty Items

ART

Debbie van der Bol runs the arts-and-crafts shop **Pure Art** (☎ 345/949–9133) on South Church Street and at the Hyatt Regency (☎ 345/945–5633). She sells watercolors, wood carvings, and lacework by local artists, as well as her own sketches and cards. You'll find original prints, paintings, and sculpture with a tropical theme at **Island Art Gallery** (☎ 345/949–9861) in the Anchorage Shopping Centre in George Town. The **Kennedy Gallery** (☎ 345/949–8077), in West Shore Centre and on Fort Street in George Town, features primarily limited-edition pastel watercolors of Cayman scenes by Robert E. Kennedy.

CLOTHES

Calico Jack's (⌂ West Bay Rd., George Town, ☎ 345/949–4373) is a good source for local T-shirts, casual resort wear, and dive gear (truly self-contained, it also operates a dive shop and pub).

FOODSTUFFS

Tortuga Rum Company's (⌂ North Sound Road just on the outskirts of George Town, ☎ 345/949–7701, 345/949–7866, or 345/949–7867) has scrumptious rum cake (sealed fresh) that's sweet and moist and makes a great souvenir. You can find these cakes at a number of George Town shops and at the airport's duty-free shops.

HANDICRAFTS

The **Heritage Crafts Shop** (☎ 345/949–7093), near the harbor in George Town, sells local crafts and gifts. The coral creations of **Bernard Passman** (⌂ Fort St., George Town, ☎ 345/949–0123) have won the approval of the English royal family. **Carey Cayman Coral** (⌂ South Sound Rd., no phone) is a workshop run by Carey Hurlstone. Carey, a gentle bear of a man covered with tattoos, professes he was a biker with the Hell's Angels before coming home to Cayman to work as a craftsman. He makes black coral jewelry and figurines and carves glass. His workmanship is superb, and his prices are quite reasonable for the quality. You'll also find beautiful coral pieces at **Richard's Fine Jewelry** (⌂ Harbour Dr., George Town, ☎ 345/949–7156), where designers Richard and Rafaela Barile attract a share of celebrities.

Nightlife

The **Holiday Inn** (☎ 345/947–4444) offers something for everyone: At **Coconuts** (☎ 345/947–5757) young American stand-up comedians perform Wednesday–Sunday. Crowds also gather poolside, where island-famous Barefoot Man sings and plays the piano four nights a week. Dancing here is spontaneous and welcome; this is also a great spot to just people-watch.

Long John Silver's Nightclub (☎ 345/949–7777), at the Treasure Island Resort, is a spacious, tiered club that's usually filled to capacity when the island's top bands play. **Sharkey's** (⌂ Falls Shopping Centre, Seven Mile Beach, ☎ 345/947–5366) is a popular disco and bar filled with rock-and-roll paraphernalia of the 1950s. Latest to hit the hot-spot list is **Planet** (☎ 345/949–7169), with its nightly drink specials, live entertainment, and theme nights; the youngish crowd can get rowdy, and brawls aren't exactly out of the ordinary here.

Locals and visitors frequent the **Cracked Conch** (⌂ West Bay Rd., near Turtle Farm, ☎ 345/945–5217) for karaoke, classic dive films, and a great happy hour with hors d'oeuvres Tuesday–Friday evenings.

For current entertainment, look at the freebie magazine *What's Hot* or check the Friday edition of the *Caymanian Compass* for listings of music, movies, theater, and other entertainment possibilities.

Exploring Grand Cayman

The historic capital of George Town, which is at one end of Seven Mile Beach, is easy to explore on foot. If you're a shopper, you can spend days here, otherwise you can tour downtown in an hour. Simply stroll along Harbor Drive and weave up and down the store-lined streets. The portion of the island called West End is noted for its jumble of affluent colonial neighborhoods and rather tawdry tourist attractions. A drive along West Bay road will take you past the dense Seven Mile Beach area and into a less congested scene. It's about ½ hour to West

Bay from George Town. The less developed East End has natural attractions, from blow holes to botanical gardens, as well as the remains of the original settlements. Plan on at least 45 minutes for the drive out from George Town. You need a day to circle and explore the entire island—including a stop at a beach for a picnic or swim.

Numbers in the margin correspond to points of interest on the Grand Cayman and Cayman Brac and Little Cayman maps.

George Town

❶ **George Town.** Begin exploring the capital by strolling along the waterfront, Harbour Drive. The circular gazebo is where visitors from the cruise ships disembark. Diagonally across the street is the **Elmslie Memorial United Church,** named after Scotsman James Elmslie, the first Presbyterian missionary to serve in the Caymans. The church was the first concrete-block building built in the Cayman Islands. Its vaulted ceiling, wooden arches, and sedate nave reflect the quietly religious nature of island residents. Along your rambles, you'll come across **Fort Street,** a main shopping street where you'll also notice the small clock tower dedicated to Britain's King George V and the huge fig tree manicured into an umbrella shape. Here, too, is a statue (unveiled in 1994) of national hero James Bodden, the father of Cayman tourism. Across the street is the **Cayman Islands Legislative Assembly Building,** next door to the 1919 **Peace Memorial Building.** The fact that the Caymanians built a memorial to peace rather than war speaks to their character. The structure was planned as a dramatic building cited to terminate the vista down Edward Street. The increasing scale of newer buildings nearby, however, has diminished its scale somewhat.

On Edward Street, you'll find the charming **library,** built in 1939; it has English novels, current newspapers from the United States, and a small reference section. It's worth a visit just for the Old World atmosphere and a look at the shields that depict Britain's prominent institutions of learning; they decorate the ceiling beams. Across the street is the **courthouse.** Down the next block is the financial district, where banks from all over the world have offices.

Straight ahead is the **General Post Office,** also built in 1939, with its strands of decorative colored lights and some 2,000 private mailboxes on the outside. (Mail is not delivered on the island.) Behind the post office is **Elizabethan Square,** a shopping and office complex on Shedden Road with food, clothing, and souvenir establishments. The courtyard has benches placed around a garden and a fountain; it's a pleasant place to rest your feet.

Built in 1833, the **Cayman Islands National Museum** was used as a courthouse, a jail (now the gift shop), a post office, and a dance hall before reopening in 1990 as a museum. It's small but fascinating, with excellent displays and videos that illustrate local geology and the history of Cayman plant, animal, and human life. Pick up a walking-tour map of George Town at the museum gift shop before leaving. ⊠ *Harbour Dr.,* ☎ *345/949–8368.* 🖅 *$5.* ☉ *Weekdays 9–5, Sat. 10–4.*

GEORGE TOWN ENVIRONS

❷ **Cayman Maritime Treasure Museum.** At this "treasure" just outside George Town, you'll find dioramas that demonstrate how Caymanians became seafarers, boatbuilders, and turtle breeders. An animated figure of Blackbeard the pirate spins salty tales about the pirates and buccaneers who "worked" the Caribbean. Since the museum is owned by a professional treasure-salvaging firm, it's not surprising that there are a lot of artifacts from shipwrecks. ⊠ *West Bay Rd., near Hyatt Regency,* ☎ *345/945–5033.* 🖅 *$5.* ☉ *Mon.–Sat. 9–5.*

Around the Island

To see the rest of the island, rent a car or scooter, or take a guided tour (☞ Cayman Islands A to Z, *below*). A full-day guided tour (sufficient to see the major sights) is comparable in cost to a single day of car rental. The flat road that circles the island is in good condition, with clear signs. Venturing away from the Seven Mile Beach strip, you'll encounter the more down-home character of the island.

WEST END

④ Cayman Island Turtle Farm. Started in 1968 as both a conservation and a commercial enterprise, the farm has become the island's most popular attraction (some 200,000 visitors a year). You'll find turtles of all ages and sizes, from Ping Pong–ball-size eggs to elderly 600-pounders (some turtles live as long as 100 years). The farm releases about 5% of its stock out to sea every year, harvests turtles for local restaurants, and exports the byproducts. (Note: U.S. citizens cannot take home any turtle products because of a U.S. ban.) In the adjoining café, you can sample turtle soup or turtle sandwiches while viewing an exhibit about turtles. ⊠ *West Bay Rd.,* ☎ *345/949–3893.* ☞ *$5.* ☉ *Daily 8:30–5.*

⑤ Hell. This tiny village is little more than a patch of incredibly jagged rock formations called ironshore. The big attraction here is the small post office where you can get cards and letters postmarked from Hell (a postcard of bikini-clad beauties emblazoned with WHEN HELL FREEZES OVER gives you a picture of what this place is like). There are also lots T-shirt and souvenir shops. The town's theme is carried to the nearby nightclub—Club Inferno—which is run by the McDoom family.

③ Old Homestead. Formerly known as the West Bay Pink House, this is probably the most photographed home in Grand Cayman. The pink-and-white Caymanian cottage was built in 1912 of wattle and daub around an ironwood frame. Cheery Mac Bothwell, who grew up in the house, takes you on tours that present a nostalgic and touching look at life in Grand Cayman before the tourism and banking booms. ⊠ *West Bay Rd.,* ☎ *345/949–7639.* ☞ *$5.* ☉ *Mon.–Sat. 8–5.*

EAST END

⑩ Blow Holes. These make the ultimate photo opportunity as crashing waves force water into caverns and send geysers shooting up through the ironshore.

⑦ Bodden Town. In the island's original capital you'll find an old **cemetery** on the shore side of the road. Graves with A-frame structures are said to contain the remains of pirates. There are also the ruins of a **fort** and a wall erected by slaves in the 19th century. A curio shop serves as the entrance to what's called the **Pirate's Caves,** partially underground natural formations that are more hokey (decked out with fake treasure chests and mannequins in pirate garb) than spooky.

⑪ East End. The claim to fame of this area—besides being the island's first recorded settlement—is that it's home to renowned local musician Fiddle Man, a.k.a. Radley Gourzong, who occasionally performs his distinctive form of music (akin to Louisiana's zydeco) here with his band, the Happy Boys.

⑧ Mastic Trail. In the 1800s, this woodland trail was often used as a shortcut to and from the North Side. The low-lying area was full of hardwood trees, including mahogany, West Indian cedar, and the mastic that early settlers used to build their homes. Along the trail, you'll see an abundance of trees, birds, and plants unique to this old-growth forest. It's on National Trust territory, and you can call to book a guide. ⊠ *Frank Sound Rd.,* ☎ *345/949–0121.*

⑥ **Pedro's Castle.** Built in 1780, this modest burgher's home hardly qualifies for palatial status but lays claim to being the oldest structure on the island. Legends linked to it abound, but what is known is that the building was struck by lightning in 1877 and left in ruins until bought by a restaurateur in the 1960s. Gutted once again by fire in 1970, the building was purchased by the government in 1991 for restoration as a historic landmark. The site is due to open at press time. ⊠ *South Sound Rd., Savannah,* ☎ *no phone.* ⊒ *Free.*

⑨ **Queen Elizabeth II Botanic Park.** This 60-acre wilderness preserve showcases the variety of indigenous habitats and plants. Interpretive signs identify the flora along the walking trail. Halfway along the trail is a walled compound housing the rare blue iguana found only in remote sections of the Caymans. You will also see native orchids and, if you're lucky, the brilliant green Cayman parrot. ⊠ *Frank Sound Rd.,* ☎ *345/945–9462.* ⊒ *$3.* ⊙ *Daily 7:30–5:30.*

⑫ **Queen's View.** This functions as both a lookout point and a monument dedicated by Queen Elizabeth in 1994 to commemorate the legendary Wreck of the Ten Sails, which took place just offshore.

CAYMAN BRAC

Brac, the Gaelic word for "bluff," aptly identifies this island's most distinctive feature, a rugged limestone cliff that runs down the center of the 12-mi-long island and soars to 140 ft at the island's eastern end. Lying 89 mi northeast of Grand Cayman, Brac is accessible via Cayman Airways and Island Air. Only 1,200 people live on the island, in communities such as Watering Place and Spot Bay. Residents are very friendly, so it's easy to strike up conversation; in fact, you'll often have to be the one to end the chat if you expect to do anything else that day. Crime is practically unheard of—court is held here for a single day about once every three months.

Lodging

Hotels here are usually a better value than their prices indicate at first glance. Rates often include at least meals if not drinks and diving, too. In addition, lodgings here are much cozier and more intimate than their Grand Cayman counterparts, and hoteliers often treat guests like family. Most hotels give you the option of including all meals in your stay, but there are a few restaurants on the island. To reach them, however, you'll need a taxi or, if you're feeling up to it, you can go by bike (most hotels have bicycles for guest use). Restaurants serve island fare (stewed fish, conch fritters, curries), and portions are generally large.

For price categories, *see* the chart *under* Lodging *in* Grand Cayman, *above.*

Hotels

$$–$$$ 🖬 **Brac Reef Beach Resort.** Because of its all-inclusive dive package, this resort is popular with divers. With that said, it seems ironic that the main building is set back from the shore and that none of the rooms has a water view (though rooms on the ground floor have patios, and some on the second floor have balconies). The resort does have a pretty beach, however, and many amenities, including a pool, guest bicycles, a dive shop, and a two-story dock (its gazebo is glorious on a star-filled night, when you can see brilliantly hued fish darting about). The modest all-inclusive package rates include three buffet meals daily, all drinks, airport transfers, and taxes and service charges for two persons; dive packages costs a little more. There are also theme events such as English high tea as well as weekly cocktail parties. ⊠ *Stake Bay (Box 56),* ☎ *345/948–7323 or 800/327–3835; 813/323–8727 in FL (reservations service);* FAX *345/948–7207. 40 rooms. Restaurant, bar, air-conditioning, pool, hot tub, tennis court, dive shop, snorkeling, bicycles. AE, D, MC, V. All-inclusive, EP, FAP, MAP.*

$ 🏨 **Divi Tiara Beach Resort.** Most folks come here for the water sports: the diving facility is famous, and a resort shuttle will take you across the island to a great snorkeling spot. Rooms (which are a little rundown) have tile floors, bright tropical prints, rattan furniture, louvered windows, and balconies. Many also have ocean views (though standard rooms have neither a view nor a TV). The more expensive rooms have whirlpool bathtubs. Kids 16 and under stay free in their parents' room. ⊠ *Box 238,* ☎ *345/948–1553; 919/419–3484 or 800/367–3484 in the U.S.;* FAX *345/948–7316 or 919/419–2075 in the U.S. 70 rooms. Restaurant, bar, pool, tennis court, volleyball, dive shop, snorkeling, fishing, shop. AE, MC, V. All-inclusive, EP, FAP, MAP.*

$ 🏨 **Walton's Mango Manor.** This two-story, traditional West Indian home
★ has five rooms (with bath) and a tranquil setting. Throughout you'll find beautiful antique furnishings and architectural details such as the stairway handrail, which is a relic from an old ship. The nearby ironshore beach is the perfect place for a sunrise walk. The proprietors love to relate Brac history and help you make arrangements for game fishing trips, scuba diving excursions, and other activities. As only breakfast is included, you'll need a car so you can get out for other meals and explore the island. ⊠ *Stake Bay (Box 56),* ☎ FAX *345/948–0518. 5 rooms. Air-conditioning, fans. AE, MC, V. CP.*

Condominium

$ 🏨 **Brac Caribbean Beach Village.** This small complex is on the same
★ beach as some of the resorts, but instead of just a room you get a two-bedroom, 2½-bath fully furnished apartment right on the sand. The units are bright and airy with beige walls, rattan furniture, white tile floors, and pastel floral prints. With advance notice, the management company will stock your kitchen with groceries and arrange for dive packages, rental cars, and maid service (each at minimal additional cost). Kids 11 and under stay free with their parents. ⊠ *Stake Bay (Box 4),* ☎ *345/948–2265 or 800/791–7911,* FAX *345/948–2206. 16 rooms. Restaurant, bar, air-conditioning, pool, coin laundry. MC, V. EP.*

Beaches

The accommodations on the **southwest coast** have fine small beaches, better for sunning than for snorkeling because of the abundance of turtle grass in the water. Guests and nonguests are welcome on hotel beaches.

Outdoor Activities and Sports

SCUBA DIVING AND SNORKELING

The waters off Cayman Brac are more pristine than those off Grand Cayman, so you'll see more (and larger) critters. The snorkeling is excellent off the north coast. Many fish have taken to the Russian warship that was scuttled offshore from the now-defunct Buccaneer's Inn. (Look for the beautiful queen angel fish that makes its home between two of the guns.) All the ship's doors have been removed, so you can swim through it—not for the faint of heart as it's pitch black in some spaces.

Brac Aquatics (☎ 345/949–1429 or 800/544–2722) and **Divi Tiara** (☎ 345/948–1553 or 800/367–3484) offer scuba and snorkeling gear and courses.

Cayman Brac is a spelunker's paradise. There are several large caves (namely **Peter's, Great, Bat,** and **Rebeka's**), some of which are still used for hurricane protection. Wear sneakers (not, say, flip-flops); some of the paths to the caves are steep and rocky.

Exploring Cayman Brac

Cayman Brac Museum. In addition to displaying the implements used in the daily lives of Bracers in the '20s and '30s, this two-room museum exhibits a few oddities, such as a 4,000-year-old Viking ax. The variety of Brac flora on the property includes unusual orchids, mangoes, papaya, agave, and cacti. ⊠ *Old Government Administration Bldg., Stake Bay,,* ☎ *345/948–2622.* ☒ *Free.* ☉ *Weekdays 9–noon and 1–4, Sat. 9–noon..*

Parrot Preserve. The easiest place to spot the endangered Cayman Brac parrot is in this preserve on Major Donald Drive (also known as Lighthouse Road); this 6-mi dirt road also leads to ironshore cliffs that offer the best panoramic view of North East Point and the open ocean. Swimming is possible, but unlike at Seven Mile Beach, the bottom is rocky and clogged with turtle grass.

LITTLE CAYMAN

Only 7 mi from Cayman Brac, Little Cayman Island has a population of about 100 on its 12 square mi. This is a true hideaway: few phones, fewer shops, no man-made sights or nightlife to speak of—just spectacular diving, great fishing, fantastic bird-watching, placid beaches, and laid-back camaraderie.

Lodging

Accommodations are mostly in small lodges, many of which offer meal and dive packages. The meal packages are a good idea; the chefs in most places are impeccably trained.

Hotels

$$ ⊞ **Little Cayman Beach Resort.** This two-story property is considerably
★ less rustic than other Little Cayman resorts. Air-conditioned rooms have contemporary furnishings and tropical, jewel-tone color schemes. Numbers 115, 116, 215, and 216 have a water view—and you don't pay extra for it. The elegant (for Little Cayman) dining room overlooks a bar and seats 50 for family-style buffet meals. If you feel lazy, take advantage of one of the double hammocks that are hung hither and yon throughout the property. If you're the active type, the resort offers fishing and diving packages (it has a complete dive operation) and also caters to bird-watchers and soft-adventure eco-tourists. Paddleboating, sailing, kayaking, and exploring the island by bike are other ways to keep busy. All-inclusive packages (of both the dive and nondive variety) include three meals daily, all alcoholic and soft drinks, airport transfers, taxes, and gratuities. ⊠ *Blossom Village (Box 51),* ☎ *345/948–1033 or 800/327–3835,* ☒ *345/948–1045. 32 rooms. Restaurant, bar, pool, hot tub, tennis court, dive shop, fishing, bicycles, shop. AE, D, MC, V. All-inclusive, EP, FAP, MAP.*

$$ ⊞ **Pirates Point Resort.** The guest-house feel of this informal resort generates
★ almost instant camaraderie among those who stay here, and many people return year after year. Owner Gladys Howard is no doubt another reason for the repeat business. Her down-home welcome (she's originally from Texas) belies her upscale meals (she trained at Cordon Bleu with Julia Child, James Beard, and Jacques Pepin). Rooms, which

are showing signs of wear (window screens could use some patching, for example), have tiled floors, ceiling fans, and white rattan and wicker furnishings. "Relaxing" rates (for nondivers) include the mouth-watering meals and wine; all-inclusive rates include meals, alcoholic beverages, two daily boat dives, fishing, and picnics on uninhabited Owen Island. ✉ *Preston Bay (Box 43),* ☎ *345/948–1010,* FAX *345/948–1011. 10 rooms. Restaurant, bar, dive shop, fishing, bicycles, airport shuttle. MC, V. All-inclusive, FAP.*

$$ 🏠 **Sam McCoy's Diving and Fishing Lodge.** Stays here are ultracasual.
★ Bedrooms (all with bath) are simple but cheerful and are done in royal and powder blues. You eat at beachside barbecues or with Sam, the good natured owner, and his family in a thatched dining room that's decorated with fishing nets, diving artifacts, and guests' artwork. "Relaxing" rates (for nondivers) include three meals a day and airport transfers; all-inclusive rates also include beach and boat diving. Sam's son, Chip, is a *very* experienced fishing guide; his bonefishing trips cost around $25 an hour. ✉ *North Side (Box 12),* ☎ *800/626–0496,* ☎ FAX *345/948–0026. 6 rooms. Air-conditioning, fans, pool. AE, MC, V. All-inclusive, FAP.*

$$ 🏠 **Southern Cross Club.** Rooms here are in cottages on a pretty beach,
★ and all have fabulous views of the sparkling sea. Pastel color schemes and wicker furniture keep you comfortable while freshly tiled floors, air-conditioning, and ceiling fans keep you cool. Service and meals are impeccable, though diving (including Nitox diving) and fishing (deep-sea, light-tackle, bottom, and bone) are the true draws here. ✉ *South Hole Sound (Box 44),* ☎ *345/948–1099 or 800/899–2582; 317/636–9501 in the U.S.;* FAX *317/636–9503. 10 rooms. Restaurant, bar, dive shop, snorkeling, fishing, bicycles, airport shuttle. AE, MC, V. FAP.*

Villas

$$ 🏠 **Paradise Villas.** The 12, cozy, one-bedroom units here have full kitchens, air-conditioning, and terraces that open onto the beach. Your quarters are simply but immaculately appointed with rattan furnishings and muted abstract fabrics. If you get tired of cooking for yourself, delicious island-style food (not to mention the island's only bar) is just steps away at the Hungry Iguana restaurant. ✉ *Southern Hole Sound (Box 48),* ☎ *345/948–0004. 12 units. Pool, dive shop. AE.*

Beaches

The beach at **Point o' Sand,** on the eastern tip of the island, is an isolated patch of powder and is worth every effort to reach by boat, car, or bike. **Owen Island,** which is rowboating distance (200 yards) from the south coast, has a sandy beach. You can pack a picnic lunch and spend the day.

Outdoor Activities and Sports

BIRD-WATCHING

Governor Gore Bird Sanctuary, established in 1994, is home to 5,000 pairs of red-footed boobies (the largest colony in the western hemisphere) and 1,000 magnificent frigate birds. You may catch black frigates and snowy egrets competing for lunch in dramatic dive-bombing battles. The sanctuary is near the airport.

FISHING

Bloody Bay, off the north coast, has spectacular fishing, which includes angling for tarpon and bonefish. **Sam McCoy's Fishing & Diving** (☎ 345/949–2891 or 800/626–0496) and **Southern Cross Club** (☎ 800/899–2582) offer deep-sea fishing. During Million Dollar Month (June) there are fishing competitions on all three islands; registered anglers can win cash and vacation prizes by landing record-breaking catches.

Five tournaments are held, each with its own rules, records, and entrance fees. For information and applications, write to the Million Dollar Month Committee (⊠ *Box 878 GT, Grand Cayman, Cayman Islands, BWI*).

SCUBA DIVING AND SNORKELING

Famed Bloody Bay Wall is just 15 minutes from Little Cayman by boat. The drop begins at a mere 18 ft and plunges to more than 1,000 ft, with visibility often reaching 150 ft—diving doesn't get much better than this. Most hotels have diving instructors and equipment; you can also contact **Paradise Divers** (☎ 345/948–0004 or 800/450–2084), **Reef Divers** (☎ 345/948–1033), **Sam McCoy's Fishing & Diving** (☎ 345/949–2891 or 800/626–0496), or the **Southern Cross Club** (☎ 800/899–2582).

CAYMAN ISLANDS A TO Z

Arriving and Departing

BY AIRPLANE

Flights land at Owen Roberts Airport (Grand Cayman), Gerrard-Smith Airport (Cayman Brac), or Edward Bodden Airfield (Little Cayman). For flight information, call Owen Roberts Airport (☎ 345/949–5252).

American Airlines (☎ 800/433–7300 or 345/949–8799) has daily nonstop flights from both Miami and Raleigh/Durham, North Carolina. **American Trans Air** (☎ 800/225–2995) is a charter service that offers direct weekly flights from Indianapolis and Cincinnati. **Cayman Airtours** (☎ 800/247–2966) offers package deals. **Cayman Airways** (☎ 800/422–9626 or 345/949–2311) flies nonstop to Grand Cayman from Miami two or three times daily, from Tampa four times a week, from Orlando three times a week, and from Houston and Atlanta three times a week. **Delta Airlines** (☎ 800/221–1212) has daily nonstops from Atlanta to Grand Cayman. **Northwest** (☎ 800/447–4747 or 345/949–2956) has regularly scheduled nonstop flights from Miami. **US Airways** (☎ 800/428–4322) flies daily nonstop from Tampa and three times a week from Pittsburgh and Charlotte, North Carolina.

Air service from Grand Cayman to Cayman Brac and Little Cayman is offered via **Cayman Airways** (☞ *above*) and **Island Air** (☎ 345/949–5152 or 800/922–9606).

From the Airport: Upon arrival, some hotels offer free pickup at the airport. Taxi service and car rentals (☞ Getting Around, *below*) are also available.

Electricity

Electricity is the same in the Caymans as it is in the United States (110-volt, 60 cycle); it's reliable throughout the islands.

Emergencies

Ambulance: ☎ 911 or 555. **Hospital/Recompression Chamber:** George Town Hospital has a two-man double-lock recompression chamber (⊠ Hospital Rd., George Town, ☎ 345/949–4234 or 555); it's manned on a 24-hour on-call basis by trained staff from the Cayman Islands Divers chapter of the British Sub Aqua Club, and it's supervised by a doctor trained in hyperbaric medicine. **Pharmacy:** Island Pharmacy (☎ 345/949–8987) is in West Shore Centre on Seven Mile Beach. **Police and Hospitals:** ☎ 911.

Festivals and Seasonal Events

During April's colorful **Batabano Carnival,** revellers dress up as dancing flowers and swimming stingrays. If you want to see an utterly British

Parade spiced with island-style panache, check out the **Queen's Birthday** bash in June. At the sportfishing competitions in **Million Dollar Month** (June), huge cash prizes are awarded, including one for a quarter of a million dollars that's given to the angler who breaks the existing Blue Marlin record. The end of October sees the carnival-like atmosphere of **Pirates Week** (which really lasts 10 days and includes a mock invasion of Hog Sty Bay by a mock Blackbeard and company). Visitors and locals dress up like pirates and wenches; music, fireworks, and a variety of competitions take place island-wide. Visitors and locals dress up like pirates and wenches; music, fireworks, and a variety of competitions take place island-wide.

Getting Around

If your accommodations are along Grand Cayman's Seven Mile Beach, you can walk or bike to the shopping centers, restaurants, and entertainment spots along West Bay Road. George Town is small enough to see on foot. If you're touring Grand Cayman by car, there's a well-maintained road that circles the island; it's hard to get lost. To get around on Cayman Brac or Little Cayman, you'll need to rent a car or a moped; your hotel can make the arrangements for you. Many resorts also offer bicycles for local sightseeing.

BICYCLES, MOTORCYCLES, AND SCOOTERS

When renting a motor scooter or bicycle, don't forget that you need sunblock and that driving is on the left. Bicycles ($10–$15 a day) and scooters ($25–$30 a day) can be rented from **Bicycles Cayman** (☎ 345/949–5572), **Cayman Cycle** (☎ 345/945–4021), **Eagles Nest** (☎ 345/949–4866) specializes in renting Harley Davidson motorcycles, and **Soto Scooters** (☎ 345/945–4652).

CAR RENTALS

Grand Cayman is relatively flat and fairly easy to negotiate if you're careful of the traffic. To rent a car, bring your current driver's license, and the car-rental firm will issue you a temporary permit ($5). Most firms have a range of models, from compacts to Jeeps to minibuses. Rates range from $35 to $55 a day. The major agencies have offices in a plaza across from the airport terminal, where you can pick up and drop off vehicles. Just remember, driving is on the left, so when pulling out into traffic, look to your right. Gas prices at press time were about $2.40 for an "imperial" gallon which is slightly more than a U.S. gallon.

Car-rental companies are **Ace Hertz** (☎ 345/949–2280 or 800/654–3131), **Budget** (☎ 345/949–5605 or 800/472–3325), **Cico Avis** (☎ 345/949–2468 or 800/331–1212), **Coconut** (☎ 345/949–4377 or 800/262–6687), **Economy** (☎ 345/949–9550), **Soto's 4X4** (☎ 345/945–2424), and **Thrifty** (☎ 345/949–6640 or 800/367–2277).

TAXIS

Taxis offer island-wide service. Fares are determined by an elaborate rate structure set by the government, and although it may seem pricey for a short ride (fare from Seven Mile Beach for four people to the airport ranges from $10 to $15), cabbies rarely try to rip off tourists. Ask to see the chart if you want to double-check the quoted fare.

A. A. Transportation (☎ 345/949–7222), **Cayman Cab Team** (☎ 345/945–1173), and **Holiday Inn Taxi Stand** (☎ 345/945–4491) offer 24-hour service.

Guided Tours

BOAT

The most impressive sights are underwater. On Grand Cayman, don't miss a trip on *Atlantis* submarine (☎ 345/949–7700), which takes 48 passengers, a driver, and a guide down along the Cayman Wall to depths of up to 100 ft. This $2.8-million vessel has entertained hundreds of thousands of passengers, has all sorts of safety features—including a monitoring boat that constantly circles on the surface—and is air-conditioned. Through its large windows, you can see huge barrel sponges, corals in extraterrestrial-like configurations, strange eels, and schools of beautiful and beastly fish. Night dives are especially dramatic; the artificial lights of the sub make the colors more vivid than they during daytime excursions. Costs range from around $60 to $80 per person for trips from an 1 hour to 1½ hours. The company also operates private trips on a research submersible that reaches depths of 800 ft. In the *Seaworld Explorer* (☎ 345/949–8534), you sit before windows in the hull of the boat just 5 ft below the surface, observing divers who swim around with food, attracting fish to the craft. The cost of this hour-long trip is $29.

Guided snorkeling trips usually include stops at Stingray City Sandbar, Coral Garden, and Conch Bed, the top snorkel sites. Trips are available through **Charter Boat Headquarters** (☎ 345/945–4340), **Captain Eugene's Watersports** (☎ 345/949–3099), and **Kirk Sea Tours** (☎ 345/949–6986)

Full-day trips include lunch prepared on the boat or onshore and cost under $40 per person; half-day trips average $25. Glass-bottom-boat trips also cost around $25 and are available through **Aqua Delights** (☎ 345/945–4786), **Cayman Mermaid** (☎ 345/949–8100), and **Kirk Sea Tours** (☎ 345/949–6986).

Sunset sails, dinner cruises, and other theme (dance, booze, pirate, etc.) cruises are available aboard the *Jolly Roger* (☎ 345/949–8534), a replica of a 17th-century Spanish galleon; *Blackbeard's Nancy* (☎ 345/949–8988), a 1912 topsail schooner; and the *Spirit of Ppalu* (☎ 345/949–1234), a 65-ft glass-bottom catamaran. Party cruises typically run $20–$50 per person.

HELICOPTER/AIRPLANE

Cayman Helicopter Tours (☎ 345/949–4400) operates a six-passenger, air-conditioned helicopter that makes quick work of taking in the geographical features of Grand Cayman. The waters around the island are so clear that you can see shipwrecks, stingrays, and shallow reefs from the air. Fares start at around $150 per person. **Seaborne Flightseeing Adventures** (☎ 345/949–6029) offers a 25-minute narrated "flightseeing" tour for $56 per person.

ORIENTATION/SPECIAL-INTEREST

Guided day tours of Grand Cayman can be arranged with **A. A. Transportation Services** (☎ 345/949–7222, ask for Burton Ebanks), **Majestic Tours** (☎ 345/949–7773), **Reids Premier Tours** (☎ 345/949–6531), **Rudy's Travellers Transport** (☎ 345/949–3208), and **Tropicana Tours** (☎ 345/949–0944). Half-day tours average $30–$50 a person and generally include a visit to the Turtle Farm and Hell in West Bay, drives along Seven Mile Beach and through George Town, and time for shopping downtown. In addition to those stops, full-day tours, which average $55–$75 per person and include lunch, also visit Bodden Town to see pirate caves and graves and the East End to see blowholes on the ironshore and the site of the famous Wreck of the Ten Sails.

Language

English is the official language, and it is spoken with a distinctive brogue that reflects Caymanians' Welsh, Scottish, and English heritage. For example, "three" is pronounced "tree"; "pepper" is "pep-ah"; and Cayman is "K-*man*." The number of Jamaican residents in the workforce means the Jamaican patois and heavier accent is also common. (Other Jamaican influences are tales about the *duppy*—pronounced like "puppy"—a scary night creature that haunts the Caymans.) You'll also hear first names preceeded by "Mr." or "Miss" (e.g., Mr. Sam)—these are terms of respect generally used for senior Caymanian citizens.

Money Matters

CURRENCY

Although the American dollar is accepted everywhere, you'll save money if you go to the bank and exchange U.S. dollars for Cayman Island (CI) dollars, worth about US$1.20 at press time. The Cayman dollar is divided into a hundred cents with coins of 1¢, 5¢, 10¢, and 25¢ and notes of $1, $5, $10, $25, $50, and $100. There is no $20 bill. Prices are often quoted in Cayman dollars, so it's best to ask. All prices quoted here are in U.S. dollars unless otherwise noted.

SERVICE CHARGES, TAXES, AND TIPPING

At large hotels, a service charge is generally included and can be any where from 6%–10%, smaller establishments and some villas and condos leave tipping up to you. There is a 10% government tax added at all accommodations and a departure tax of $10. Otherwise, there is no tax on goods or services. Tipping is customary at restaurants, note that some automatically include 15% on the bill—so check the tab carefully. Taxi drivers expect a 10%–15% tip.

Opening and Closing Times

Banks are generally open Monday–Thursday 9–2:30 and Friday 9–1 and 2:30–4:30. Shops are open weekdays 9–5, and Saturday in George Town from 10 to 2; in outer shopping plazas, they are open from 10 to 5. Shops are usually closed Sunday except in hotels.

HOLIDAYS

New Year's Day, Ash Wednesday (Feb. 17), Good Friday (Apr. 2), Easter Sunday (Apr. 4), Discovery Day (May 19), Queen's Birthday (June 16), Constitution Day (July 7), Christmas, and Boxing Day (Dec. 26).

Passports

U.S., U.K., and Canadian citizens should carry a valid passport but can also prove citizenship by showing a birth certificate with a raised seal along with a government-issued photo ID. All visitors must have a return ticket.

Precautions

Locals zealously conserve fresh water, so don't waste a precious commodity. Caymanians also strictly observe and enforce laws that prohibit collecting or disturbing endangered animal, marine, and plant life and historical artifacts found throughout the islands and surrounding marine parks; simply put, take only pictures and don't stand on reefs for that kills them.

Penalties for drug and firearms importation and possession of controlled substances include large fines and prison terms.

Theft is not widespread, but be smart: Lock up your room and car and secure valuables as you would at home. Outdoors, marauding blackbirds called ching chings have been known to carry off jewelry if it is left out in the open.

Poisonous plants on the island include the maiden plum, the lady hair, and the manchineel tree. If in doubt, don't touch. The leaves and applelike fruit of the manchineel are poisonous to touch and should be avoided; even raindrops falling from them can cause painful blisters.

Telephones and Mail

For international dialing to Cayman, the area code is 345 (recently changed from 809). To call outside, dial 0 + 1 + area code and number. You can call anywhere, anytime, through the cable and wireless system and local operators. To make local calls, dial the seven-digit number. To place credit-card calls, dial 110. AT&T USADirect (☎ 800/872–2881) and MCI Direct (☎ 800/624–1000) can be used from any public phone and most hotels.

Beautiful stamps are available at the main post office in downtown George Town and at the philatelic office in West Shore Plaza. Both are open weekdays from 8:30 to 3:30 and Saturday from 8:30 to 11:30. Sending a postcard to the United States, Canada, the Caribbean, or Central America costs CI20¢. An airmail letter is CI30¢ per half ounce. To Europe and South America, the rates are CI25¢ for a postcard and CI40¢ per half ounce for airmail letters. When addressing letters to the Cayman Islands be sure to include "BWI" (British West Indies) at the bottom of the envelope. Note that the islands don't use postal codes, but don't let this worry you; your letter should arrive fine without one.

Visitor Information

For the latest information on activities and lodging, write or call any of the offices of the **Cayman Islands Department of Tourism**: ✉ 6100 Blue Lagoon Dr., 6100 Waterford Bldg., Suite 150, Miami, FL 33126-2085, ☎ 305/266–2300; ✉ 2 Memorial City Plaza, 820 Gessner, Suite 170, Houston, TX 77024, ☎ 713/461–1317; ✉ 420 Lexington Ave., Suite 2733, New York, NY 10170, ☎ 212/682–5582; ✉ 9525 W. Bryn Mawr Ave., Suite 160, Rosemont, IL 60018, ☎ 847/678–6446; ✉ 3440 Wilshire Blvd., Suite 1202, Los Angeles, CA 90010, ☎ 213/738–1968; ✉ 234 Eglinton Ave. E, Suite 306, Toronto, Ontario M4P 1K5, ☎ 416/485–1550; and ✉ Trevor House, 100 Brompton Rd., Knightsbridge, London SW3 1EX, ☎ 0171/581–9960. You can also check out the department of tourism's Web site www.caymans.com.

The main office of the **Department of Tourism** is in the Pavilion (✉ Cricket Sq. and Elgin Ave., ☎ 345/949–0623). Information booths are at the airport (☎ 345/949–2635); in the George Town Craft Market, on Cardinal Avenue, open when cruise ships are in port (☎ 345/949–8342); and in the kiosk at the cruise-ship dock in George Town (no phone). There is also an islands-wide tourist hot line (☎ 345/949–8989). You can also contact the **Tourist Information and Activities Service** (☎ 345/949–6598, FAX 345/945–6222) day or night for complete tourist information and free assistance in booking island transportation, tours, charters, cruises, and other activities.

9 Curaçao

Updated by
Jordan Simon

*C*reaking, rickety boats line the waterfront;
all have made the improbable journey here
from Venezuela at the crack of dawn. Vendors cackle, assaulting passersby with pleas to buy
everything from fish to straw hats. Stout, uncon-
cerned matrons in hair curlers haggle in three languages. Tourists fumble for their cameras, trying
frantically to capture the moments on film. This
is Willemstad's famed Floating Market, as astonishing a parade of humanity as any in New York
or Cairo.

Despite such bustling, colorful, multiethnic sights as the Floating
Market, Curaçao—the largest island of the Netherlands Antilles (38
mi long and 2–7½ mi wide)—is also the most staunchly Dutch; from
its architecture, cuisine, and language (Dutch is spoken more often
than Papiamento, the language common to all the Netherlands Antilles) to the waves of blond tourists arriving daily from Amsterdam.
Its charming Dutch capital of Willemstad, underwater park, Seaquarium, floating market, and dozens of little cove beaches make it ideal
for exploring.

Thirty-five miles north of Venezuela and 42 mi east of Aruba, Curaçao
sits below the so-called hurricane belt. The sun smiles down on the island, but it's never stiflingly hot owing to gentle trade winds. Water
sports—including outstanding reef diving—attract enthusiasts from all
over the world. Though Curaçao claims 38 beaches, it doesn't have
long strips of silky sand; rather, they're rocky stretches of washed-up
coral that eventually breaks down into smooth white or pink sand. The
island is dominated by an arid countryside, rocky coves, and a sprawling capital built around a natural harbor. Until recently, the economy
was based not on tourism but on oil refining, and it catered to offshore
corporations seeking tax hedges. Although tourism has become a
major economic force in the past decade, with millions of dollars in-

vested in restoring old colonial landmarks and modernizing hotels, Curaçao's atmosphere remains comparatively low-key.

As seen from the Otrabanda of Willemstad by the first-time visitor, Curaçao's "face" will be a surprise—spiffy rows of pastel-color town houses that look transplanted from Holland. Although the gabled roofs and red tiles show a Dutch influence, the gay colors of the facades are peculiar to Curaçao. It is said that a popular governor suffered from migraines, a condition irritated by the color white, so all the houses were painted in colors. Government funding has allowed for a tremendous boost in restoration of these houses, so you'll notice bright new coats of paint. The dollhouse look of the land houses or *landhuizen* (plantation houses) makes a cheerful contrast to the stark cacti and the austere shrubbery that dot the countryside.

The history books still cannot agree on who discovered Curaçao—one school of thought believes it was Alonzo de Ojeda, while another says it was Amerigo Vespucci—but they agree that it was around 1499. The first Spanish settlers arrived in 1527. In 1634 the Dutch came via the Netherlands West India Company. They promptly shipped off the Spaniards and the few remaining Indians—survivors of the battles for ownership of the island, famine, and disease—to Venezuela. Eight years later, Peter Stuyvesant began his rule as governor, which lasted until he left for New York around 1645. Twelve Jewish families arrived from Amsterdam in 1651, and by 1732 there was a synagogue; the present structure is the oldest synagogue still in use in the Western Hemisphere. Over the years, the city built fortresses to defend against French and British invasions—many of those ramparts now house restaurants and hotels. The Dutch claim to Curaçao was recognized in 1815 by the Treaty of Paris. In 1954 Curaçao became an autonomous part of the Kingdom of the Netherlands, with a governor appointed by the queen, an elected parliament, and an island council.

Today Curaçao's population is derived from more than 50 nationalities in an exuberant mix of Latin, European, and African roots and a Babel of tongues, resulting in superb restaurants and an active cultural scene. The island, like its Dutch settlers, is known for its religious tolerance, and tourists are warmly welcomed.

Lodging

Curaçao offers an array of accommodations, from large beachfront resorts spread along the island's southern coast to budget and business-class hotels in downtown Willemstad. Beach hotels on the southwestern end of the island tend to be small, secluded, and peaceful but are a 30- to 45-minute drive from town. Those beach hotels just east and west of Willemstad proper tend to be large-scale, bustling luxury resorts. Most hotels provide either beach or shopping shuttles, baby-sitting, laundry service, car rental, and business and travel services. The larger hotels provide activity programs (for adults and for children) and allow children to stay in their parents' room for free or at a discounted rate. They also either include a Continental breakfast or offer a large buffet breakfast. Full American Plans are not popular because of the abundance of good restaurants. At press time, one of the island's oldest hotels, the Curaçao Caribbean, was undergoing a renovation as part of a conversion into a Sheraton Four Corners.

Rentals are popular with European visitors. Contact the **Curaçao Tourism Development Foundation** (✉ Box 3266, Curaçao, Netherlands Antilles, ☎ 5999/461–6000, FAX 5999/461–2305) at least two months in advance for a list of available properties.

CATEGORY	COST*
$$$	over $225
$$	$125–$225
$	under $125

All prices are for a standard double room, including 7% government tax and 12% service charge.

$$$ 🏨 **Kadushi Cliffs.** If you've brought the family for a week or more, you might want to rent a condo here, in the peaceful, lush, western part of the island. The modern two-bedroom villas are all attractively furnished and have fully equipped kitchens. A pool and a restaurant are the only real facilities (there's a tiny crushed coral beach), but this keeps the noise down. Regulars return year after year for the solitude and seclusion. The Cliff House restaurant arguably offers the most jaw-dropping sunset views on Curaçao, though the ordinary Continental fare is a letdown. You'll need a rental car to see anything else of the island or go to Willemstad for dining and shopping. ⊠ *Westpunt,* ☎ *5999/864–0200 or 800/448–8355 (reservations service),* ⅁ *5999/864–0282. 12 villas. Restaurant, bar, air-conditioning, in-room safes, kitchenettes, refrigerators, in-room VCRs, pool, tennis court, volleyball, beach, playground. AE, DC, MC, V. EP.*

$$$ 🏨 **Sonesta Beach Hotel & Casino.** Curaçao's most luxurious resort is a
★ sprawling, burnished-ocher low rise, built to blend in with the surrounding Dutch colonial–style architecture. The attention to authenticity was such that the casino's floor pattern was adapted from a land house, and public spaces are filled with striking contemporary and African-inspired artwork. The impressive approach leads you through lushly landscaped grounds brimming with oleander, hibiscus, and gently swaying palms; the beach is gorgeous. The tasteful, large accommodations have a muted pastel or delicate floral color scheme and a terrace or a balcony. Many suites have their own private solarium and whirlpool tub. Price is determined by view, though all rooms have at least a partial ocean vista. There's also an array of daily activities and nightly entertainment. The on-site ☞ **Emerald Steakhouse** does up fine USDA prime cuts.⊠ *Piscadera Bay (Box 6003),* ☎ *5999/736–8800 or 800/766–3782 (reservations service),* ⅁ *5999/462–7502. 212 rooms, 32 suites. 3 restaurants, 2 bars, air-conditioning, in-room safes, minibars, no-smoking rooms, room service, pool, wading pool, 2 outdoor hot tubs, massage, saunas, steam rooms, 2 tennis courts, aerobics, health club, volleyball, dive shop, dock, windsurfing, boating, shops, casino, children's program, concierge. AE, D, DC, MC, V. EP, FAP, MAP.*

$$–$$$ 🏨 **Princess Beach Resort and Casino.** You can't beat the location on one of the most beautiful beaches in Curaçao and right in front of the Underwater Marine Park. Guest rooms are spacious, if somewhat worn and musty smelling (except for those in the newer high-rise tower conveniently near all the activities), and roughly half have fine ocean views. The pathway to the rooms is through lush, tropical grounds; be forewarned, you may have quite a hike. This is a high-energy place, with lively happy hours, popular theme buffet dinners, and a slew of sports activities and nightly entertainment. It is also one of the few hotels on the island to offer no-smoking rooms. ⊠ *Martin Luther King Blvd. 8,* ☎ *5999/736–7888, 800/327–3286, or 800/992–2015 (reservations service);* ⅁ *5999/461–4131. 332 rooms, 9 suites. 3 restaurants, 4 bars, air-conditioning, in-room safes, no-smoking rooms, room service, 2 pools, exercise room, volleyball, beach, dive shop, dock, windsurfing, boating, shops, casino. AE, DC, MC, V. CP, EP, FAP, MAP.*

$–$$$ 🏨 **Avila Beach Hotel.** The royal family of Holland and its ministers stay
★ at this 200-year-old mansion overlooking the ocean for three good reasons: the privacy, the personal service, and the peace. The incompa-

rable Old World air begins in the lobby, with gilt mirrors, Oriental rugs, porcelain figurines, and old gas lamps. There is a room here for everyone, from the budget-priced, basic rooms in the original house to larger, more modern rooms in the moderately priced La Belle Alliance section to the luxurious rooms in the Blues Wing, built in late 1996 on a rocky peninsula. The restaurant has a unique outdoor dining area shaded by an enormous tree. A terrace with Adirondack chairs (referred to on the island as Avila chairs) overlooks the two crescent beaches and the pier bar where live jazz takes center stage Thursday and Saturday evenings. Many consider this quiet, family-owned-and-operated hotel the best buy on the island. ✉ *Penstraat 130134 (Box 791), Willemstad,* ☎ *5999/461–4377 or 800/448–8355 (reservations service),* ℻ *5999/461–1493. 107 rooms, 8 suites. 3 restaurants, 3 bars, air-conditioning, in-room safes, kitchenettes, refrigerators, tennis court, beach, conference center. AE, DC, MC, V. EP, MAP.*

$$ 🏨 **Habitat Curaçao.** The island's newest option is a casual dive resort 12 mi west of Willemstad on the beach at Rif St. Marie. It's a sprawling property with clusters of canary yellow, red-roofed buildings with cheerful turquoise trim surrounded by tropical foliage and connected by stairways and winding paths. The rooms, referred to as junior suites because of the spacious, furnished terrace or balcony attached to each, take their bright colors and decor from the coral reef just offshore; the marine-life fabrics were specially commissioned from top local artist Nena Sanchez. Each has a fully equipped kitchenette and roomy bathroom with shower, but no TV or phone. The raised pool next to the ocean affords grand vistas, and the top-notch dive facilities offer 24-hour diving. Be sure to request an ocean view, as the price is the same and only 40 rooms feature one. ✉ *Coral Estates, Rif St. Marie,* ☎ *5999/864–8800 or 800/327–6709 (reservations service),* ℻ *5999/864–8464. 56 suites, 20 2-bedroom cottages. Restaurant, bar, air-conditioning, pool, beach, dive shop, dock, shops, meeting room. AE, DC, MC, V. CP, EP.*

$$ 🏨 **Holiday Beach Hotel and Casino.** This former Holiday Inn is a four-story, U-shape, aquamarine-color building surrounding a pool. Rooms, which desperately need a face-lift, have a beige, khaki, aquamarine, and rose color scheme, with bleached wood and rattan furniture. The lobby is spacious to permit the assembly of tour groups, and one of the island's largest casinos, Casino Royale, is off the lobby. The crescent beach is quite large for Curaçao and dotted with palm trees. Although this is an older property, it's a fair choice for value on a budget. ✉ *Otrabanda, Pater Euwensweg 31 (Box 2178), Willemstad,* ☎ *5999/462–5400 or 800/444–5244 (reservations service),* ℻ *5999/462–4397. 200 rooms. 2 restaurants, 2 bars, room service, pool, 2 tennis courts, Ping-Pong, shuffleboard, volleyball, beach, dive shop, windsurfing, boating, casino, video games, playground. AE, DC, MC, V. EP.*

$$ 🏨 **Lions Dive Hotel Curaçao.** This yellow-and-blue caravansary is a hop, skip, and plunge away from the Seaquarium (complimentary admission is given to guests), on a quarter mile of private beach. Most of the guests are dive enthusiasts satisfied by the top-notch scuba center and the young staff, who are eager to please. Rooms are airy, modern, and light-filled, with tile floors, wicker furnishing, and large bathrooms (showers only). French doors lead out to a spacious balcony or terrace, and every room has a view of the sea. The Sunday-night happy hour is especially festive, with a merengue band playing poolside. By midnight, however, the only sound to be heard is the whir of your room's air-conditioner. Dive packages are offered with Underwater Curaçao. ✉ *Bapor Kibra,* ☎ *5999/461–8100 or 888/546–6734 (reservations service),* ℻ *5999/461–8200. 72 rooms. Restaurant, bar, air-conditioning,*

Curaçao

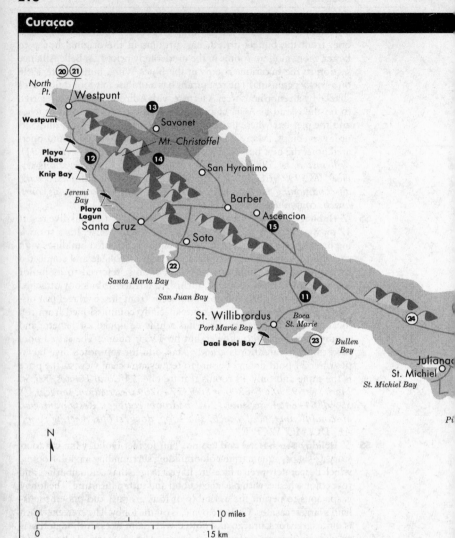

N

| 0 | | | | 10 miles |
| 0 | | | | 15 km |

Exploring
Boka Tabla, **13**
Christoffel Park, **14**
Country House
Museum, **15**
Curaçao
Seaquarium, **19**
Curaçao Underwater
Marine Park, **18**

Hato Caves, **16**
Landhuis
Brievengat, **17**
Landhuis Jan Kok, **11**
Landhuis Knip, **12**
Senior Curaçao
Liqueur Distillery, **10**

Dining
Bistro Le
Clochard, **27**
Cactus Club, **41**
Café du Port, **33**
Emerald
Steakhouse, **25**

Fort Nassau
Restaurant, **39**
Fort
Waakzaamheid
Tavern, **30**
Golden Star
Restaurant, **38**
Jaanchi's Restaurant, **20**
Mambo Beach, **36**

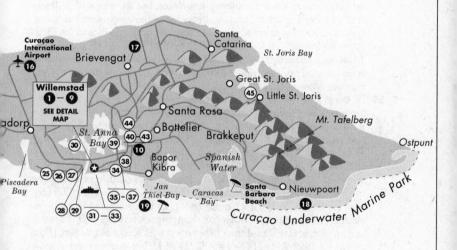

KEY

🏖 Beaches

🚢 Cruise Ship Terminal

1 Exploring Sights

20 Restaurants and Hotels

Caribbean Sea

Curaçao
International
Airport
16

Brievengat

17

Santa
Catarina

St. Joris Bay

Great St. Joris

45 Little St. Joris

Mt. Tafelberg

Willemstad
1 – **9**
SEE DETAIL
MAP

Santa Rosa

44
Bottelier
40 **43**
10
Brakkeput

Ostpunt

adorp

*St. Anna
Bay*
30 **39**

38
Bapor
Kibra

*Spanish
Water*

25 **26** **27**
34

*Piscadera
Bay*

35 – **37**
*Jan
Thiel Bay*

*Caracas
Bay*

Santa
Barbara
Beach

Nieuwpoort

18

28 **29**   **31** – **33**   **19**

Curaçao Underwater Marine Park

La Pergola, **32**
Rijstaffel Indonesia
Restaurant, **40**
De Taveerne, **44**
Tentaboka, **42**
Toscanini, **45**
Zeelandia, **43**

Lodging
Avila Beach Hotel, **34**
Coral Cliff Resort
and Beach Club, **22**
Habitat Curaçao, **23**
Holiday Beach Hotel
and Casino, **26**
Kadushi Cliffs, **21**

Landhaus Daniel, **24**
Lions Dive Hotel
Curaçao, **37**
Otrabanda Hotel &
Casino, **28**
Plaza Hotel and
Casino, **31**
Porto Paseo Hotel
and Casino, **29**

Princess Beach Resort
and Casino, **35**
Sonesta Beach Hotel
& Casino, **25**

ceiling fans, in-room safes, pool, exercise room, beach, dive shop, dock, windsurfing, boating. AE, DC, MC, V. EP.

$$ ☷ **Plaza Hotel and Casino.** PLEASE DON'T TOUCH THE PASSING SHIPS is the slogan at the island's first high-rise hotel and the only hotel in the world with marine-collision insurance. The ships do come close, since the structure is built right into the massive walls of a 17th-century fort at the entrance of Willemstad's harbor. You give up beachfront (you have beach privileges at Seaquarium and there's a beach shuttle) for walking access to the city's center. Consequently, it's a business traveler's oasis, but there are loads of activities to satisfy vacationers, too. The lobby is marble, with handsomely upholstered furniture, lazy ceiling fans, stuccoed arches, flamingo statues, antique grandfather clocks, and a winding lagoon and waterfall, all giving it the air of some elegant colonial outpost. Aging decor in the guest rooms is a letdown in comparison (many carpets, even bedspreads, have stains or cigarette burns), but is gradually being replaced by sterile, if clean, furnishings and color schemes. The recently reopened, rooftop restaurant offers overpriced Continental cuisine with a few Caribbean flourishes, but the views of Willemstad's harbor are utterly breathtaking, as are the lovely new murals of typical city and country scenes adorning the walls. ⊠ *Plaza Piar (Box 229), Willemstad,* ☎ *5999/461–2500,* FAX *5999/461–6543. 236 rooms, 18 suites. 2 restaurants, 3 bars, snack bar, air-conditioning, in-room safes, room service, pool, exercise room, dive shop, casino, business services, meeting rooms. AE, DC, MC, V. CP.*

$–$$ ☷ **Coral Cliff Resort and Beach Club.** Seclusion and rustic simplicity are everything here. Set on a pretty half-moon beach a 45-minute ride west of Willemstad, the resort, which seems to be perpetually under construction, is popular with Dutch tourists. Deluxe rooms are comfortable and attractive, with motel-modern furnishings, shower-only bathrooms, and small balconies. Romantics opt for the junior suites with whirlpool tub on the balcony. A pool with swim-up bar, a wading pool, and eight villas suitable for families were added in 1997; further expansion calls for 21 more rooms to be completed in 1998. A shuttle runs guests into town for shopping; otherwise, you'll need a car for sightseeing and dining off-property. ⊠ *Santa Marta Bay (Box 3782),* ☎ *5999/864–2666 or 800/223–9815 (reservations service),* FAX *5999/864–1781. 62 units. Restaurant, bar, pool, wading pool, miniature golf, tennis court, Ping-Pong, beach, dive shop, dock, billiards, casino, playground, coin laundry, meeting room. AE, D, DC, MC, V. CP, EP, FAP, MAP.*

$ ☷ **Landhaus Daniel.** Dating from 1711, this mustard plantation house with white colonnades and red tile roof was never a part of a farm but served as an inn for travelers going east or west on the island. The property, near the narrow center of the island, has a restaurant serving excellent French-inspired fare and a pool; a dive center was being added at press time. Rooms are tiny but clean, with basic furnishings. All have private bathrooms with showers; only two are air-conditioned (the rest have ceiling fans), but the trade winds usually take care of any excessive heat at night. You'll feel far more comfortable in the original land house; a row of claustrophobic rooms developed from the slave quarters have even less charm than a stateside motel and without the amenities, though they've cleverly attached the bathrooms to the outside of each unit. Nonetheless, this is a fine budget option providing the fun atmosphere of a youth hostel with its billiards, darts, and TV room. ⊠ *Wegnaar Westpunt,* ☎ *5999/864–8400. 7 rooms. Restaurant, bar, ceiling fans, pool, dive shop. AE, MC, V. EP, MAP.*

$ ⊞ **Otrabanda Hotel & Casino.** Built in 1990, this little city hotel—a superior value—is across the harbor from downtown Willemstad, in the historic Otrabanda section. Standard rooms are cramped but appealing, with terrific harbor views, rattan furnishings, and paintings of country scenes. The most attractive and roomiest are those tucked under the peaked roof. A swimming pool and large sun terrace were added in late 1996. ⊠ *Breedestraat, Otrabanda,* ☎ *5999/462–7400,* FAX *5999/462–7299. 42 rooms, 3 suites. Restaurant, bar, coffee shop, snack bar, air-conditioning, pool, casino. AE, MC, V. CP.*

$ ⊞ **Porto Paseo Hotel and Casino.** This charming property on the Otra-
★ banda side of the harbor recalls a typical land house, with tropical gardens, lamp-lit flagstone courtyard, rock walls, and mustard-color bungalow-style buildings with red-tile roofs. At its center is the hotel, a restored 17th-century building. It's a remarkably peaceful, private place amid the city's bustle. Squawking white cockatoos preside over the entrance to an open-air bar splashed with murals depicting island life and overlooking Santa Anna Bay. The unadorned but pleasant rooms, all with showers, shimmer in silver, mauve, and ecru. ⊠ *De Rou-villeweg 47, Willemstad,* ☎ *5999/462–7878,* FAX *5999/462–7969. 45 rooms, 4 suites. Restaurant, bar, air-conditioning, kitchenettes, pool, casino. AE, DC, MC, V. CP, EP.*

Dining

Dine under the boughs of magnificent old trees, in the romantic gloom of wine cellars in renovated land houses, or on the ramparts of 18th-century forts. Curaçaoans partake of some of the best Indonesian food in the Caribbean, and you'll also find fine French, Swiss, Dutch, and Swedish fare.

What to Wear

Dress in restaurants is almost always casual (though beachwear is generally not acceptable). Some of the resort dining rooms and nicer restaurants require that men wear jackets, especially in high season; ask when you make reservations.

CATEGORY	COST*
$$$$	over $40
$$$	$30–$40
$$	$15–$30
$	under $15

per person for a three-course meal, excluding drinks and service charge

AMERICAN

$ ✕ **Cactus Club.** A veritable grove of aloe and cacti greets you in the courtyard of this Caribbean version of Bennigan's. The inside is surprisingly subdued: faux Tiffany lamps, hanging plants, whirring ceiling fans. Food is cheap and filling, including fettuccine Alfredo, fajitas, buffalo wings, Cajun snapper, and burgers. It's predictably popular with both locals and homesick Americans. ⊠ *Van Staverenweg 6, Willemstad,* ☎ *5999/737–1600. DC, MC, V.*

ASIAN

$–$$ ✕ **Rijstaffel Indonesia Restaurant.** An antique rickshaw guarding the
★ entrance sets the mood in this tranquil spot. No steaks or chops served here, just exotic delicacies that make up the traditional Indonesian banquet called rijsttafel, where some 16 to 25 dishes are set buffet-style around you. Smaller appetites should opt for the *nasi rames,* a miniversion with only eight dishes. Vegetarians will be pleased that a 16-course vegetable rijsttafel is also available. An à la carte menu includes fried noodles, fresh jumbo shrimp in garlic, and combination meat-and-

fish platters. The walls are hung with batiks, *ikat* (a form of Indonesian fabric) tapestries, basketwork, copper pots, and beautiful Indonesian *wajang* dolls and shadow puppets ($25–$40) that make stunning gifts. ⊠ *Mercurriusstraat 13–15, Saliña,* ☎ *5999/461–2606. AE, DC, MC, V. No lunch Sun.*

CARIBBEAN/CREOLE

$-$$ ✕ **Tentaboka.** The most upscale local eatery on the island, Tentaboka
★   gleams with polished wood floors and ceilings, spackled walls plastered with ceramic plates, handsome photos, fishnets, and such local artworks as driftwood sculptures and painted wood land houses. But the food is wonderfully down-home: papaya stew with goatmeat, salted meat, pork tails, *keshi yena* (Gouda stuffed with chicken, capers, and raisins), oyster soup, savory fish patties, and shrimp creole. Everything is served with helpings of *funchi* (cornmeal), pumpkin fritters, and vegetables. If you can't decide, there are combination plates for two that could feed a family. ⊠ *Schottegatweg Oost 185, Saliña,* ☎ *5999/465–7678. AE, MC, V. Closed Sun.*

$ ✕ **Golden Star Restaurant.** This place looks and feels more like a friendly roadside diner, but the native food here is among the best in town. Owner Marie Burke turns out such Antillean specialties as *bestia chiki* (goat stew), shrimp Creole, and delicately seasoned grilled conch, with generous heaps of rice, fried plantains, and avocado. Steaks and chops can be had for the asking. ⊠ *Socratestraat 2, Klein Kwartier, Willemstad,* ☎ *5999/461–8828. AE, DC, MC, V. Closed Tues.*

$ ✕ **Jaanchi's Restaurant.** Tour buses stop regularly at this open-air restaurant for lunches of mouthwatering Curaçaoan dishes. The main-course specialty is a hefty platter of fresh-caught fish, conch, or shrimp with potatoes or funchi and vegetables on the side. Curaçaoans joke that Jaanchi's "iguana soup is so strong it could resurrect the dead"— truth is, it tastes just like chicken soup, only better. Jaanchi Jr. says, if you want iguana, you should order in advance "because we have to go out and catch them." He's not kidding. He usually closes at 6:30 PM but will stay open later if you call ahead to reserve a spot. If you can, call ahead to find out if they expect huge tour groups that day; the food and service can deteriorate dramatically. ⊠ *Westpunt 15, Westpunt,* ☎ *5999/864–0126. AE, DC, MC, V.*

CONTINENTAL

$$-$$$$ ✕ **De Taveerne.** From the intricate detail of its antiques and brickwork
★   to its impressive Continental menu, this restaurant is the most elegant, romantic spot on the island. The magnificently renovated, maroon-and-white octagonal land house was built in the 1800s by an exiled Venezuelan revolutionary. Upstairs is a gallery showcasing local artists. You'll dine in the wine cellar, whose stuccoed walls, brickwork, wood beams, wrought iron lamps, Dutch genre landscapes, farming implements, and antique gilt mirrors evoke the bygone plantation days. The best appetizer is the salmon carpaccio with laurel bay dressing en brioche. The entrées are rich and decadent: velvety lobster bisque finished with Armagnac, sautéed goose liver in plum sauce, smoked eel with horseradish. Finish with the unforgettable broiled pears, topped with vanilla ice cream and drenched with Curaçao chocolate liqueur. ⊠ *Landhuis Groot Davelaar, on Silena, near Promenade Shopping Center,* ☎ *5999/737–0669. AE, D, DC, MC, V. Closed Sun.*

$$-$$$ ✕ **Zeelandia.** The setting is hard to beat: a mustard-and-white land house with orange trim. It's a toss-up which is more romantic: dining in the old-fashioned dining room, with wood beams, crisp mint-and-white napery, and terra-cotta floors; or al fresco under the spreading branches of an ancient flamboyant tree. The specialties include rack of lamb in morel sauce, sesame-coated monkfish, and prawns in ginger sauce with deep-fried leeks. At $36, the elaborate four-course dinner is a tremendous value. ⊠ *Landhuis Zeelandia, Polarisweg 28, Saliña,* ☎ *5999/461–4688. AE, DC, MC, V. No lunch Sat. or Sun.*

$–$$ ✕ **Bistro Le Clochard.** This romantic gem is built into the 18th-century Rif Fort—an oasis of arched entryways, exposed brickwork, wood beams, and lace curtains. Cocktails and hors d'oeuvres are served on the Waterside Terrace, with its view of the floating bridge and harbor. The French and Swiss dishes, emphasizing game, are consistently well prepared, though pricey. Try the the cream of chestnut soup perfumed with gin and garnished with morels, the fresh-fish platters, the locally grown ostrich, the cutlet of wild boar or the veal in mushroom sauce. Savor the fondue and let yourself get carried away by the unusual setting; save room for the chocolate mousse. On weekends, an inexplicably corny duo plays, but you might enjoy the complimentary snacks of Friday's 5-to-7 Hungry Hour. ⊠ *On the Otrabanda, Rif Fort, Willemstad,* ☎ *5999/462–5666. AE, DC, MC, V. Closed Sun. No lunch Sat.*

$–$$ ✕ **Fort Nassau Restaurant.** This is *the* place to view twinkling Curaçao at night. On a hill above Willemstad, the restaurant is built into an 18th-century fort with a 360-degree view. Go for a drink in the breezy Battery Terrace bar or dine in air-conditioned comfort in front of huge bay windows. The variegated tile work throughout is absolutely stunning. The menu is diverse, from rabbit, duck, pigeon, and beef preparations to lightly broiled fish (ask the waiter what's fresh). Stay away from the enticing yet overly complex stabs at innovative cuisine: The simple selections are best here. Dinner seatings are at 7 and 9. ⊠ *Schottengatweg 82, near Juliana Bridge, Willemstad,* ☎ *5999/461–3450. Reservations essential. AE, D, DC, MC, V. No lunch weekends.*

ECLECTIC

$–$$ ✕ **Mambo Beach.** On the west end of Seaquarium Beach (and we do mean *on* the beach), Mambo Beach is a hip, open-air bar and grill spread over the sand that serves surprisingly good food for breakfast, lunch, and dinner. Baguettes dominate the lunch menu, while steaks, fresh seafood, and pasta fill the dinner menu. The half-order bowl of pasta is large enough to feed two. More creative offerings include smoked marlin with sun-dried tomatoes (rather tritely called Marlin Monroe), fettuccine with shrimp and saffron, or salmon fried in couscous. This is a fantastic place to watch the setting sun, but don't forget your insect repellent and apply it liberally. ⊠ *Seaquarium Beach,* ☎ *5999/461–8999. AE, MC, V.*

$–$$ ✕ **Fort Waakzaamheid Tavern.** High on a hill overlooking Willemstad and the harbor, this fort was captured by Captain Bligh of HMS *Bounty* two centuries ago. Now it is controlled by an Irishman, Tom Farrel, who operates an open-air restaurant and bar in the evening. The atmosphere is informal, and the food is primarily barbecued seafood and steaks decorated with your own makings from a salad bar. You will be equally well greeted if you go just for cocktails and snacks—and the sunsets are magnificent. ⊠ *Off main highway on Otrabanda side of suspension bridge, Seru Domi, Willemstad,* ☎ *5999/462–3633. AE, D, MC, V. Closed Tues. No lunch.*

$ ✕ **Café du Port.** This alfresco café serves a variety of crepes, baguette sandwiches—the salmon salad and pâté are good choices—burgers, and cold drinks (from shakes and sodas to fancier alcohol-infused libations). Egg dishes and ham and Dutch cheese are available for breakfast. It's a scenic spot to cool off with a drink when those feet get tired of walking; the view of the floating bridge is splendid. ⊠ *Handelskade 13, Punda, Willemstad,* ☎ *5999/465–0670. AE, MC, V.*

ITALIAN

$–$$ ✕ **La Pergola.** Built into the stuccoed walls of the Waterfort Arches, with huge picture windows fronting the rambunctious sea, copper pots hanging everywhere, and a pretty pink-and-white arbor wound with bunches of grapes, La Pergola offers creative variations on Italian standards and no fewer than 14 pastas. Try the smoked salmon drizzled with olive oil and studded with cloves or the grouper siciliana with capers, olives, anchovies, tomatoes, and garlic. Pizza reigns supreme (13 choices) on the terrace menu. The polenta and tiramisu are among the Caribbean's most authentic. ✉ *Waterfort Arches, Willemstad,* ☎ *5999/461–3482. AE, DC, MC, V. No lunch Sun.*

$–$$ ✕ **Toscanini.** The setting for this rather remote eatery is exquisite: The outdoor terrace (with brick floors underneath a raw wood canopy) overlooks Table Mountain and a spotlit windmill and garden. Huge potted plants, highback chairs, and hurricane lamps add a note of elegance. The delectable fare includes osso buco, *farfalle* (bow-tie pasta) with wild mushrooms and pancetta, and sardines in tomato vinaigrette. The enterprising owners, Hand and Chantal Wiggemans, grow their own organic fruits and vegetables which they use not only in restaurant preparations but in bottled gourmet delicacies for sale in the tiny adjoining shop, La Provence (the marinated eggplant, citrus marmalade, and brandied cherry preserves are standouts). ✉ *Juan Luis 87, West Groot St., Joris,* ☎ *5999/767–3603. AE, MC, V. Closed Sun.–Tues. No lunch.*

STEAK

$–$$ ✕ **Emerald Steakhouse.** Set in the ☞ **Sonesta Beach Hotel,** Emerald
★ is one of the most sophisticated settings. Candlelit tables, rich wood paneling, and a pianist playing through the meal make this a good choice for a special dinner. Start with Caesar salad à deux, prepared tableside. The beef dishes, featuring thick USDA prime cuts, are grilled and sauced to taste; there's also a vegetarian offering and some seafood on the menu. The bar offers the finest selection of single-malt scotches and brandies on the island. ✉ *Piscadera Bay,* ☎ *5999/736–8800. AE, D, DC, MC, V. No lunch.*

Beaches

Curaçao has some 38 beaches, but unfortunately some are rocky and litter-strewn. The best way to find "your" beach is to rent a Jeep, motor scooter, or heavy-treaded car. Ask your hotel to pack a picnic basket and go exploring. Curaçao doesn't have Aruba's long stretches of sand; instead, you'll discover the joy of inlets: tiny bay openings to the sea marked by craggy cliffs, exotic trees, and scads of pebbles. Imagine a beach that's just big enough for two. Beware of thorns and keep an eye out for flying fish. They propel their tails through the water until they reach a speed of 44 mph, then spread their fins and soar.

Hotels with the best beaches include the Sonesta Beach Hotel (impressively long); the Princess Beach (impressively sensuous); and the Lions Dive Beach Resort on the Seaquarium Beach (impressive for its amenities). No matter where you're staying, beach hopping to other hotels can be fun. Nonguests are supposed to pay the hotels a beach fee, but often there's no one to collect.

Daai Booi Bay. This sandy shore is dotted with thatched shelters. The road to this public beach (follow signs from the church of St. Willibrordus) is a small paved highway flanked by thick lush trees and huge organ-pipe cacti. The beach is curved, with shrubbery rooted into the side of the rocky cliffs—a great place for swimming.

Knip Bay. The beach has two parts: Big (Groot) Knip and Little (Kleine) Knip. Only Little Knip is shaded with trees, but these are manchineels (raindrops or dewdrops dripping off their leaves can cause blisters), so steer clear of them. Also beware of cutting your feet on beer-bottle caps. Both beaches have alluring white sand, but only Big Knip has changing facilities. Big Knip also has several tiki huts for shade and calm turquoise waters that are perfect for swimming and lounging. The protected cove, flanked by sheer cliffs, is usually a blast on Sunday, when there is occasionally live music. To get there, take the road to the Knip Land house, then turn right. Signs will direct you.

Playa Abao. Northwest of Knip Bay, Playa Abao has crystal-clear turquoise water and a small beach. Sunday afternoons are crowded and festive. There's a snack bar and public toilets.

Playa Lagun. This northwestern stretch is dotted with powder-blue camping huts and caught between towering gunmetal gray cliffs. Cognoscenti know this is one of the best places to snorkel—you may even go nose to nose with the resident giant squid.

Santa Barbara. To reach this popular family beach on the eastern tip you can drive through one of Curaçao's toniest neighborhoods, Spanish Water, where gleaming white yachts replace humble fishing fleets. The beach has changing facilities and a snack bar but charges a small admission fee, usually around $2.25 per person. Around the bend, **Caracas Bay** is a popular dive site, with a sunken ship so close to the surface that snorkelers can view it clearly.

Seaquarium's Beach. You'll pay a fee ($2.25 per person) to enter here but the array of amenities (rest rooms, showers, boutiques, watersports center, snack bar, restaurants with beach bars, thatched shelters and palm trees for shade, security patrols, even a calling station to call or fax home) on this 1,600-ft man-made beach and calm waters protected by a carefully placed breakwater are well worth it.

Westpunt. On the northwest tip of the island, Westpunt is shady in the morning. It doesn't have much sand, but you can sit on a shaded rock ledge. On Sunday, watch the divers jump from the high cliff.

Outdoor Activities and Sports

Participant Sports

BOATING AND SAILING

The constant trade winds make sailing a delightful challenge for experts, and a superlative place to learn all the ropes. **Sail Curaçao** (✉ Kima Kalki Marina, Brakkeput Ariba 62, Spanish Water, ☎ 5999/767–6003) offers day sails, sailing instruction, snorkeling trips, and windsurfing. **Coral Cliff Diving** (✉ Coral Cliff Hotel, Santa Martha Bay, ☎ 5999/864–2822) rents pedal boats and Hobie Cats, and underwater cameras. **Top Watersports Curaçao** (✉ Seaquarium Beach, ☎ 5999/461–7343) rents smaller craft like Sunfish, as well as water scooters, canoes, snorkel gear, and floating mats.

FISHING

There are surprisingly few charter boats available for deep-sea fishing, but the small 18-ft *Hemingway* (☎ 5999/888–8086) offers Penn International, senator, and spinning reels, and an experienced guide. It can accommodate no more than two people (one person $45, two $70), but can negotiate fairly deep water where shark, wahoo, tuna, barracuda, sailfish, and marlin are abundant. They'll pick up at your hotel.

FITNESS CENTERS

Body Beach (✉ Lions Dive Hotel, ☎ 5999/465–7969) is open to nonguests for a fee. It schedules exercise classes and is equipped with the latest fitness equipment. **Sundance Health & Fitness Center** (✉ John F. Kennedy Blvd. at Rif Recreation Area, ☎ 5999/462–7740) has all the gentle luxuries, including Turkish bath, sauna, whirlpool, massage, and beauty treatments. A professional medical staff is on hand.

GOLF

Curaçao Golf and Squash Club (⊠ Wilhelmenalaan, ☎ 5999/737–3590) welcomes visitors daily 8–8 in high season. The 9-hole course is a challenge because of the stiff trade winds and the sand greens. Greens fees are $20 for 18 holes.

HORSEBACK RIDING

Ashari's Ranch (⊠ Groot Piscadera, Kaya A23, ☎ 5999/869–0315) is the only stable to offer romps to the beach and through the countryside. It costs $30 for a 1½ hour ride. Trail rides are available at **Christoffel Park** (☎ 5999/864–0363), with prices ranging from $25 to $70 depending on the trail and length of time selected. Make reservations well in advance for a park tour on these gentle, smooth-gaited "paseo" horses.

RUNNING

Rif Recreation Area, locally known as the *corredor,* stretches from the water plant at Mundo Nobo to the Sonesta Beach Hotel. It consists of more than a mile of palm-lined beachfront, a wading pond, and a jogging track with an artificial surface, as well as a big playground. There is good security and street lighting along the entire length of the beach.

SCUBA DIVING AND SNORKELING

Curaçao has facilities for all kinds of water sports, thanks to the government-sponsored **Curaçao Underwater Marine Park,** which includes almost a third of the island's southern diving waters. Scuba divers and snorkelers can enjoy more than 12½ mi of protected reefs and shores, with normal visibility from 60 to 80 ft (up to 150 ft on good days). With water temperatures ranging from 75° to 82°F, wet suits are generally unnecessary. No coral collecting, spearfishing, or littering is allowed. An exciting wreck to explore is the SS *Oranje Nassau,* which ran aground more than 90 years ago and now hosts hundreds of exotic fish and unusually shaped coral.

Most hotels either offer their own program of water sports or will be happy to make arrangements for you. An introductory scuba resort course usually runs about $60–$75. Full certification courses average $200 for three days and $325 for the advanced five-day version. Single-tank dives are $33–$35, two-tank dives $55–$60 at virtually every operator. Snorkel gear commonly rents for $12–$15 per day.

Coral Cliff Diving (⊠ Coral Cliff Hotel, Santa Martha Bay, ☎ 5999/864–2822) offers an open-water certification course and a full schedule of dive and snorkeling trips to Curaçao's southwest coast. It also rents pedal boats, Hobie Cats, and underwater cameras. **Habitat Curaçao**'s (⊠ Coral Estates, Rif St. Marie, ☎ 5999/864–8800) dive center offers a full array of training, from a two-day, three-dive introductory course to underwater video and photography courses ($275–$400). **Princess Divers** (⊠ Princess Beach Resort, Dr. Martin Luther King Blvd. 8, ☎ 5999/965–8991) offers a variety of shore and boat dives and packages, as well as certified PADI instruction. **Underwater Curaçao** (⊠ Bapor Kibra, ☎ 5999/461–8100) offers complete vacation-dive packages in conjunction with the Lions Dive Hotel & Marina. Its fully stocked dive shop, between the Lions Dive Hotel and the Curaçao Seaquarium, rents and sells equipment. Personal instruction and group lessons are conducted on state-of-the-art dive boats.

TENNIS

Most hotels (including Sonesta Beach, Curaçao Caribbean, Princess Beach, and Holiday Beach) offer well-paved courts, illuminated for day and night games. These courts are usually occupied by guests of the hotels. Your best bet if you're not staying at one of these properties is the **Santa Catherina Sports Complex** (✉ Club Seru Coral, Koraal Partier 10, ☎ 5999/767–7028), where court time costs $20 an hour.

WINDSURFING

Top Watersports Curaçao (✉ Seaquarium Beach, ☎ 5999/461–7343) is the top windsurfing center on the island, offering both rentals and instruction. This section of coast tends to be calmer than most, making it ideal for beginners, although the breezes are sufficiently steady to keep experienced windsurfers on their toes.

Spectator Sports

Centro Deportivo Curaçao (✉ Bonamweg 49, ☎ 5999/737–6620), a modern and comfortable stadium about 10 minutes from town, holds soccer matches and baseball games March–October. It's open daily 9:30–12:30 and 1–6.

Shopping

Curaçao has long enjoyed the reputation of having some of the best shops in the Caribbean, with classier displays and a better variety than on many islands, but don't expect posh Madison Avenue boutiques. With a few exceptions (such as at Benetton, which recently moved into the Caribbean with a vengeance), the quality of women's fashions here lies along the lines of sales racks. Many shops are closed on Monday and virtually all lock up by 6 PM the remainder of the week. If you're looking for bargains on Swiss watches, cosmetics, cameras, crystal, perfumes, Nike or Reebok sneakers, or electronic equipment, do some comparison shopping back home and come armed with a list of prices. Willemstad is no longer a free port: there's now a tax and consequently prices are higher. Curaçao does offer a number of exciting buys, from Dutch classics like embroidered linens, blue delft china, even clogs to local crafts (you can find some marvelous ceramic work, from painted tiles to exact miniature replicas of land houses). There are also some fine local painters, most of whom work in the landscape mode.

Areas

Most of the shops are concentrated in **Willemstad**'s Punda within about a six-block area. The main shopping streets are Heerenstraat, Breedestraat, and Madurostraat. Heerenstraat and Gomezplein are pedestrian malls, closed to traffic, and their roadbeds have been raised to sidewalk level and covered with pink inlaid tiles.

Specialty Items

ART

Casa di Alma Blou (✉ 67–69 De Rouvilleweg, ☎ no phone) is set in a gorgeous 19th-century indigo town house and presents the top local artists; you'll find shimmering landscapes, dazzling local photographs, ceramics, even African-inspired Carnival masks.

CLOTHING

Benetton (✉ Madurostraat 4, ☎ 5999/461–4619, and other locations) has winter stock in July and summer stock in December; all of it is 20% off the retail price. **Boutique Aquarius** (✉ Breedestraat 9, ☎ 5999/461–2618) sells Fendi merchandise for 25% less than in the United States. Fendi fanatics can stock up on belts, shoes, pocketbooks, wallets, and even watches. **Boutique Liska** (✉ Schottegatweg Oost 191-A, ☎ 5999/461–3111) draws local residents shopping for smart women's fashions. **Clog Dance** (⊠ De Rouvilleweg 9B, ☎ 5999/462–3280) is where to go if you long for Dutch clogs, cheeses, tulips, delftware, Dutch fashions, or chocolate. **Crazy Look** (⊠ Madurostraat 32, ☎ 5999/461–1440) has French, Italian, and Dutch fashions with a hip European look, as well as trendy sweatshirts and baggy pants. For the latest European shoes to go with a funky new outfit, visit **Cinderella** (⊠ Haaranstraat 4, ☎ 5999/461–5000).

FOODSTUFFS

Toko Zuikertuintje (⊠ Zuikertuintjeweg, ☎ 5999/737–0188), a supermarket built on the original 17th-century Zuikertuintje Landhuis, is where most of the local elite shop for all sorts of European and Dutch delicacies. Shopping here for a picnic is a treat in itself.

GIFTS

Although Curaçao's shops are no longer duty-free, there are still numerous stores that offer the usual vast selection of electronics, china, crystal, perfumes, and jewelry at discounted prices. **Boolchand's** (⊠ Heerenstraat 4B, ☎ 5999/461–2262) handles an interesting variety of merchandise behind a facade of red-and-white-checked tiles. Stock up here on French perfumes, British cashmere sweaters, Italian silk ties, Dutch dolls, Swiss watches, and Japanese cameras. **Julius L. Penha & Sons** (⊠ Heerenstraat 1, ☎ 5999/461–2266), in front of the Pontoon Bridge, sells French perfumes, Hummel figurines, linen from Madeira, delftware, and handbags from Argentina, Italy, and Spain. The store also has an extensive cosmetics counter. **Little Switzerland** (⊠ Breedestraat 44, ☎ 5999/461–2111) is the place for bargain shopping; you'll find perfumes, jewelry, watches, crystal, china, and leather goods at significant savings.

HANDICRAFTS

Arawak Craft Factory (⊠ Cruise Terminal, Otrabanda, ☎ 5999/462–7249) has a factory showroom of native-made crafts. You can purchase a variety of tiles, plates, pots, and tiny replicas of land houses. A special walkway allows you to watch the artisans at work and even ask questions. **Bamali** (⊠ Breedestraat 2, ☎ 5999/461–2258) sells Indonesian batik clothing, leather bags, and charming handicrafts. **Black Koral** (⊠ Princess Beach Hotel, ☎ 5999/465–2122) is owned by Dutch-born artisan Bert Knubben, one of Curaçao's true characters. For the past 30 years, he has been designing and sculpting the most exciting black-coral jewelry in the Caribbean—and he even dives for the coral himself, with special permission from the government. Dolphin pendants and twiglike earrings finished in 14-karat gold are excellent buys. Call before you drop by. **Fundason Obra di Man** (⊠ Bargestraat 57, Punda, ☎ 5999/461–2413) stocks native crafts and curios. Particularly impressive are the posters of Curaçao's architecture.

Gallery 86 (⊠ Trompstraat, Punda, ☎ 5999/461–3417) features the works of local artists and occasionally those of South Americans and Africans. **Kas di Arte Kursou** (⊠ Breedestraat 126, Otrabanda, ☎ 5999/864–2516) carries a variety of handmade souvenirs. **Landhuis Groot Santa Martha** (⊠ Santa Martha, ☎ 5999/864–1559) is where artisans with disabilities fashion handicrafts of varying types. **Yaqui** (⊠ De Rouvilleweg 9A, ☎ 5999/462–7533) is something of an anomaly, selling Mayan and Incan artifacts of clay, obsidian, and onyx, as well as modern tribal paintings on bark and leather.

JEWELRY

Gandelman (⊠ Breedestraat 35, ☎ 5999/461–1854; ⊠ Sonesta Beach Hotel, ☎ 5999/462–8386) has watches by Cartier and Piaget, leather goods by Prima Classe and Baccarat, and Daum crystal. **La Zahav N.V.** (⊠ Curaçao International Airport, ☎ 5999/868–9594) is one of the best places to buy gold jewelry—with or without diamonds, rubies, and emeralds—at true discount prices. The shop is in the airport transit hall, just at the top of the staircase.

LINENS

New Amsterdam (⊠ Gomezplein 14, ☎ 5999/461–2469) is the place to price hand-embroidered tablecloths, napkins, and pillowcases. Tablecloths begin at $35, double bedspreads at $100.

PERFUMES AND COSMETICS

Sparky's (⊠ Braastraat 23, ☎ 5999/461–7462) carries all the major brands of cosmetics and perfume.

Nightlife

Friday is the big night out, with rollicking happy hours—most with live music—at several hotels, most notably the Holiday Beach and Avila Beach (☞ Lodging, *above*). The once-a-month open house at Landhuis Brievengat (☞ Exploring, *below*) is a great way to meet interesting locals—it usually offers a folkloric show, snacks, and local handicrafts. Every Friday night the land house holds a big party with two bands. Check with the tourist board for the schedule of folkloric shows (usually nothing spectacular, but a nice diversion on an island not noted for nightlife or spectacle) at various hotels.

BARS

Blues (⊠ Avila Beach Hotel, Penstraat 130, ☎ 5999/461–4377) focuses on live jazz Thursday and Saturday. The bar is at the end of the pier; magnificent sunset views are guaranteed. A well-lit indoor-outdoor bar, **Rum Runners** (⊠ Otrobanda Waterfront, De Rouvilleweg 9, ☎ 5999/462–3038) serves up tapas in a casual atmosphere that's reminiscent of a college fraternity hall. A second location of this popular club opened in 1997 at Habitat Curaçao (☎ 5999/864–8800). **Mambo Beach** (☎ 5999/461–8999), an open-air bar on Seaquarium Beach, draws a hip, young crowd; beach volleyball and a live bands are often featured during happy hour on Sunday.

Keizershof, a complex of renovated heritage buildings at the corner of Otrabanda's Hoogstraat and Rouvilleweg, has it all, with two restaurants and a café in addition to dancing under the stars at **Keizershof Terrace** (☎ 5999/462–3493) and sing-alongs at **Pianobar Kalimba** (☎ 5999/462–3583).

CASINOS

Gambling seems almost an afterthought on Curaçao, primarily designed to give the business people something to do before they retire. The following **hotels** all have casinos that are open daily 1 PM–4 AM (for more details, ☞ Lodging, *above*): The Sonesta Beach, Plaza Hotel, Holiday Beach, Otrabanda, Porto Paseo, and the Princess Beach. Of these, only the Sonesta and Princess Beach casinos approach even a small Vegas hotel in terms of variety of games and Bond-like elegance.

DANCE AND MUSIC CLUBS

The Saliña district is the spot for clubbing: you'll find everything from merengue to house. **Club Safari** (⊠ Lindbergweg, Saliña, ☎ 5999/465–5433) attracts the more mature crowd seeking late-night pleasures, with a line on Saturday night that stretches down the block. **Façade** (⊠ Lindbergweg 32, Saliña, ☎ 5999/461–4640) is a hip Curaçao dance spot and a great place to meet locals who favor the Latin flair of the music here. It's dark and cool, with huge bamboo chairs for lounging. The disco floor, complete with flashing lights, is often shared by a variety of intense live bands. The **Jail Club** (⊠ Keukenplein, ☎ 5999/465–

8610) comes complete with a warden, caged or chained dancers, graffiti lit by black light, and, on the mellower second floor, individual "cells" for private rendezvous.

Exploring Curaçao

Willemstad

In the southern half of the island, the capital city is cut in two by Santa Anna Bay. There are three ways to make the crossing: (1) drive or take a taxi over the Juliana Bridge, (2) traverse the Queen Emma Pontoon Bridge on foot, or (3) ride the free ferry, which runs when the Pontoon bridge is open for passing ships. All the major hotels outside of town offer free shuttle service to town once or twice daily. Shuttles coming from the Otrabanda side leave you at Rif Fort. From there it's a short walk north to the foot of the Pontoon Bridge. Shuttles coming from the Punda side leave you near the main entrance to Fort Amsterdam.

What does the capital of Curaçao have in common with New York City? Broadway, for one. Here it's called Breedestraat, but the origin is the same. Dutch settlers came here in the 1630s, the same period when they sailed through the Narrows to Manhattan, bringing with them original red-tile roofs, first used on the trade ships as ballast and later incorporated into the architecture of Willemstad.

Willemstad is a favorite cruise stop for two reasons: The shopping is considered among the best in the Caribbean, and a quick tour of most of the downtown sights can be managed within a six-block radius. Santa Anna Bay slices the city down the middle: On one side is the Punda, and on the other is the Otrabanda (literally, the "other side"). Think of the Punda as the side for tourists, crammed with shops, restaurants, monuments, and markets. Otrabanda is less touristy, with lots of narrow, winding streets full of private homes notable for their picturesque gables and Dutch-influenced designs.

Numbers in the margin correspond to points of interest on the Willemstad map.

SIGHTS TO SEE

❾ Curaçao Museum. Housed in a century-old former plantation house, this small museum is filled with artifacts, paintings, and antique furnishings that trace the island's history. This is also the venue for art exhibitions that visit the island. ⊠ *Leeuwenhoekstraat,* ☎ *5999/462–3873.* ☜ *$2.25.* ⊙ *Mon.–Sat. 9–noon and 2–5, Sun. 10–4.*

❻ Floating Market. Each morning dozens of Venezuelan schooners laden with tropical fruits and vegetables arrive at this bustling market on the Punda side of the city. Fresh mangoes, papayas, and exotic vegetables vie for space with freshly caught fish and herbs and spices. It's probably too much to ask a tourist to arrive by 6:30 AM, when the buying is best, but there's plenty of action to see throughout the afternoon. Any produce bought here, however, should be thoroughly washed or peeled before eating. ⊠ *Sha Caprileskade.*

❷ Ft. Amsterdam. Step through the archway and enter another century. The entire structure dates from the 1700s, when it was the center of the city and the most important fort on the island. Now it houses the governor's residence, the Fort Church, the ministry, and other government offices. Outside the entrance a series of majestic gnarled *wayaka* trees are fancifully carved with a dragon, a giant squid, and a mermaid—the work of noted local artist Mac Alberto, who can be seen strolling the streets impeccably garbed in blinding white suits, a courtly boutonniere in his lapel. ⊠ *Foot of Queen Emma Bridge.*

Curaçao
Museum, **9**

Floating
Market, **6**

Ft. Amsterdam, **2**

Mikveh Israel-
Emanuel
Synagogue, **3**

Old Market
(Marche), **4**

Plaza Piar, **1**

Queen Emma
Bridge, **5**

Queen Juliana
Bridge, **8**

Scharloo, **7**

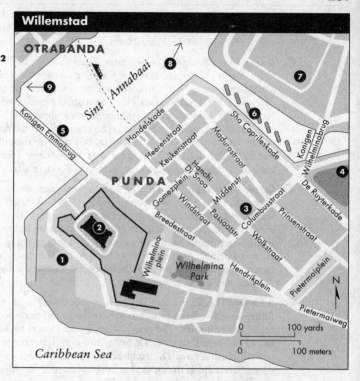

Willemstad

OTRABANDA

Sint Annabaai

PUNDA

Wilhelmina Park

Caribbean Sea

| 0 | | 100 yards |
| 0 | | 100 meters |

Konigen Emmabrug · Handelskade · Heerenstraat · Keukenstraat · D. Hanchi Di Snoa · Gomezplein · Windstraat · Breedestraat · Passaatstr. · Middenstr. · Madurostraat · Sha Caprileskade · Columbusstraat · Wolkstraat · Prinsenstraat · De Ruyterkade · Konigen Wilhelminabrug · Wilhelminaplein · Hendrikplein · Pietermaiplein · Pietermaiweg

③ Mikveh Israel-Emanuel Synagogue. This synagogue was dedicated in 1732 by the Jewish community that came from Amsterdam in 1651 to establish a new congregation. Jews from Portugal and Brazil, fleeing persecution, soon joined them, and by the early 1700s more than 2,000 Jews were in residence. This temple, the oldest still in use in the Western Hemisphere, is one of the most important sights in Curaçao and draws 20,000 visitors a year. Enter through the Spanish-tiled courtyard around the corner from Columbusstraat on Hanchi Di Snoa, and ask the front office to direct you to the guide on duty. A unique feature is the brilliant white sand covering the synagogue floor, a remembrance of Moses leading his people through the desert and of the Diaspora. The Hebrew letters on the four pillars signify the names of the Four Mothers of Israel: Sarah, Rebecca, Rachel, and Leah. The fascinating **Jewish Cultural Museum** (☎ 5999/461–1633) in the back displays Jewish antiques (including a set of circumcision instruments) and artifacts from Jewish families collected from all over the world. The gift shop has excellent postcards and commemorative medallions. English and Hebrew services are held Friday at 6:30 PM and Saturday at 10 AM. Men who attend should wear a jacket and tie. ⊠ *Hanchi Di Snoa 29,* ☎ *5999/461–1067.* ☜ *Small donation expected in synagogue; Jewish Cultural Museum $2.* ◔ *Weekdays 9–11:45 and 2:30–5 (closing time depends on schedule of services).*

④ Old Market (Marche). Behind the post office is where you'll find local women preparing hearty Antillean lunches at the Old Market. For $4–$6 you can enjoy such Curaçaoan specialties as funchi, keshi yena, goat stew, fried fish, peas and rice, and fried plantains. ⊠ *De Ruyterkade.*

① Plaza Piar. This plaza, next to Fort Amsterdam, was dedicated to Manuel Piar, a native Curaçaoan who fought for the independence of Venezuela under the liberator Simon Bolívar. On one side of the plaza is the **Waterfort,** a bastion dating from 1634. The original cannons are still positioned in the battlements. The foundation, however, now forms the walls of the Plaza Hotel.

❺ Queen Emma Bridge. This bridge is affectionately called the Swinging Old Lady by the natives. If you're standing on the Otrabanda side, take a few moments to scan Curaçao's multicolor "face" on the other side of Santa Anna Bay. If you wait long enough, the bridge will swing open (at least 30 times a day) to let the seagoing ships pass through. The original bridge, built in 1888, was the brainchild of the American consul Leonard Burlington Smith, who made a mint off the tolls he charged for the bridge. Initially, the charge was 2¢ per person for those wearing shoes, free to those crossing barefoot. Today it's free to everyone.

❽ Queen Juliana Bridge. This 1,625-ft-long bridge, to the north of the Queen Emma Bridge, was completed in 1974 and stands 200 ft above water—a great vantage point for photos of the city. It's the bridge you drive over to cross to the other side of the city, and although the route is time-consuming (and more expensive if you're going by taxi), the view is worth it. At every hour of the day, the sun casts a different tint over the city, creating an ever-changing panorama; the nighttime view, rivaling Rio's, is breathtaking.

❼ Scharloo. The Wilhelmina Drawbridge connects Punda with the once-flourishing district of Scharloo, where the early Jewish merchants first built stately homes. The end of the district closest to Kleine Werf is now a red-light district and is pretty run-down, but the rest of the area is well worth a visit. The architecture along Scharlooweg (much of it dating from the 17th century) is intriguing, and, happily, many of the structures that had become dilapidated have been meticulously renovated.

The Rest of the Island

The Weg Maar Santa Cruz road through the village of Soto winds to the northwest tip of the island through landscape that Georgia O'Keeffe might have painted—towering cacti, flamboyant dried shrubbery, and aluminum-roof houses. Throughout this *cunucu,* or countryside, you'll see fishermen hauling in nets, women pounding cornmeal, and an occasional donkey blocking traffic. Land houses, large plantation houses from centuries past, dot the countryside, though most are closed to the public. Their facades, however, can often be glimpsed from the road. To explore the island's eastern side, take the coastal road—Martin Luther King Boulevard—from Willemstad about 2 mi to Bapor Kibra. Here you'll find the Seaquarium and the Underwater Park.

Numbers in the margin correspond to points of interest on the Curaçao map.

SIGHTS TO SEE

⑬ Boka Tabla. At Boca Tabla, the sea has carved a magnificent grotto. Safely tucked in the back, you can watch and listen to the waves crashing ferociously against the rocks. Several of the surrounding minicaverns serve as nesting places; watch flocks of parakeets emerge in formation, magnificent hawks soar and dip, and gulls divebomb for lunch. ⊠ *Westpunt Hwy., just past village of Soto.*

★ **⑭ Christoffel Park.** This fantastic 4,450-acre garden and wildlife preserve centers on the towering Mt. Christoffel. The park consists of three former plantations with individual trails that take about 1 to 1½ hours each to traverse. You may drive your own car (if it has heavy-treaded wheels) or rent a four-wheel-drive vehicle with an accompanying guide (NAf150 for up to five passengers). Start out early (by 10 AM the park starts to feel like a sauna), and if you're going solo, first study the *Excursion Guide to Christoffel Park* sold at the front desk of the elegant, if dilapidated, Landhuis Savonet (the plantation house turned Natural History Museum); it outlines the various routes and identifies the flora and fauna found here. There is a 20-mi network of roads, and no matter what route you take, you'll be treated to views of hilly fields full of prickly-pear cacti, divi-divi trees, bushy-haired palms, and exotic flowers that bloom unpredictably after November showers. There are also caves—the strong at heart will revel in the rustling of bat wings and the sight of scuttling scorpion spiders (not poisonous)—and ancient Indian drawings.

As you drive through the park, watch for tiny deer, goats, and small wildlife that might dart in front of your car. The whip snakes and minute silver snakes you may encounter are not poisonous. White-tail hawks may be seen on the green route, white orchids and crownlike passionflowers on the yellow route. Climbing the 1,239-ft **Mt. Christoffel** on foot is an exhilarating experience and a definite challenge to anyone who hasn't grown up scaling the Alps. The park's guidebook claims the round-trip will take you one hour, and Curaçaoan adolescent boys do make a sport of racing up and down, but it's really more like two (sweaty) hours from the base of the mountain for a reasonably fit person who's not an expert hiker. And the last few feet are deadly. The view from the peak, however, *is* thrilling—a panorama of the island, including Santa Marta Bay and the tabletop mountain of St. Hironimus. On a clear day, you can even see the mountain ranges of Venezuela, Bonaire, and Aruba. ⊠ *Savonet,* ☎ *5999/864–0363.* ▧ *Park and museum NAf25 (approximately $13.50), museum only $3.* ☉ *Mon.–Sat. 8–4, Sun. 6–3; last admittance 1 hr before closing.*

ⓖ **Country House Museum.** This thatched-roof cottage is a living museum demonstrating country life as it was in the 19th century. It's filled with antique furniture, farm implements, and clothing typical of colonial life on the island. Out back is a minifarm with vegetable garden, penned donkeys, and caged parrots, eagles, and iguanas. Look closely at the fence—it's made of living cacti. There's also a snack bar. A festival featuring live music and local crafts takes place here on the first Sunday of each month. ⊠ *Dokterstuin 27,* ☎ *5999/864–2742.* ▧ *$1.50.* ☉ *Tues.–Fri. 9–4, weekends 9–5.*

ⓐ ⓙ **Curaçao Seaquarium.** The Seaquarium is *the* place to see the island's underwater treasures without getting your feet wet. It's the world's only public aquarium where sea creatures are raised and cultivated totally by natural methods. Where else can you hand-feed a shark (or watch a diver do it)? The **Animal Encounters** section consists of a broad, 12-ft-deep open-water enclosure that brings you face to face with a variety of jaws. Snorkelers and divers are welcome to swim freely with stingrays, tarpon, groupers, and such. Diving instruction and equipment are part of the package; it's a thrilling introduction to the sport in a controlled environment, and, in fact, up to 75% of participants have never tried diving before. The highlight for most is the variety of sharks in one section of the enclosure, safely divided off by mesh fencing and thick Plexiglas; divers and snorkelers can feed the sharks by hand in perfect safety through holes in the Plexiglas. If shark feeding isn't your cup of tea, there is an underwater observatory where you can watch. The cost is $55 for divers, $30 for snorkelers, which includes admission to the Seaquarium, training in snorkeling and scuba diving, use of equipment, and food for the fish, turtles, and sharks. Reservations for Animal Encounters must be made 24 hours in advance.

You can spend several hours mesmerized by the 46 freshwater tanks full of more than 400 varieties of exotic fish and vegetation found in the waters around Curaçao, including sharks, lobsters, turtles, corals, and sponges. Look out for the more than 5-ft-long mascot, Herbie the lugubrious jewfish. One outdoor enclosure houses a sea lion and a sea bear (yes, they're different, like a horse and a mule). There's a snack bar and restaurant on the grounds in case you get hungry. There are also glass-bottom-boat tours, fun feeding shows, and a viewing platform overlooking the wreck of the steamship SS *Oranje Nassau,* which sank in 1906 and now sits in 10 ft of water. A nearby 495-yard man-made beach is well suited to novice swimmers and children, and bathroom and shower facilities are available. A souvenir shop sells some of the best postcards and coral jewelry on the island. ⊠ *Bapor Kibra,* ☎ *5999/461–6666,* ℻ *5999/461–3671.* 🖃 *$13.25.* ⊙ *Daily 8:30–5:30.*

⑱ Curaçao Underwater Marine Park. About 12½ mi of untouched coral reefs off the southeast shore have been granted the status of national park. Mooring buoys placed at the most interesting dive sites on the reef provide safe anchoring and prevent damage to the reef. Several sunken ships lie awaiting visitors in the deep. The park stretches along the south shore from the Princess Beach Hotel in Willemstad to the eastern tip of the island.

⑯ Hato Caves. Hour-long guided tours wind down into various chambers to the water pools, voodoo chamber, wishing well, fruit bats' sleeping quarters, and Curaçao Falls, where a stream of silver joins with a stream of gold (they're colored by lights) and is guarded by a limestone "dragon" perched nearby. Hidden lights illuminate the limestone formations (use your imagination and you'll see such fantastic shapes as The Sleeping Giant, Madonna, and Woolly Mammoth) and gravel walkways. This is one of the better Caribbean caves open to the public, but keep in mind that there are 49 steep steps to reach the entrance, and the cave itself is dank and hot (though they've put electric fans in some areas to provide relief). There are also a few surrounding acres of untended gardens that make for pleasant strolling and picnicking. ⊠ *Head northwest toward airport, take right onto Gosieweg, follow loop right onto Schottegatweg, take another right onto Jan Norduyn-weg, a final right onto Rooseveltweg, and follow signs,* ☎ *5999/868– 0379.* 🖃 *$6.25.* ⊙ *Daily 10–5.*

⑰ Landhuis Brievengat. This mustard-color plantation house is a fine example of the island's past. You can see the original kitchen still intact, the 18-inch-thick walls, fine antiques, and the watch towers once used for lovers' trysts. The restaurant, open only on Wednesday and Friday, serves a fine rijstaffel. Friday night a party is held on the wide wraparound terrace, with bands and plenty to drink ($6 cover charge). On the last Sunday of the month (6–7:30 PM), this estate holds an open house with crafts demonstrations and folkloric shows. ⊠ *10-min drive northeast of Willemstad, near Centro Deportivo sports stadium,* ☎ *5999/ 737–8344.* 🖃 *$1.* ⊙ *Mon.–Sat. 9:15–12:15 and 3–6.*

⑪ Landhuis Jan Kok. For a splendid view, and some unusual island tales of ghosts, visit this mid-17th-century plantation house overlooking the salt pans. Since the hours are irregular, be sure to call ahead to arrange a tour of this reputedly haunted house, or stop by on Sunday mornings, when the proprietor occasionally opens the small restaurant behind her home and serves delicious Dutch pancakes. ⊠ *Weg Naar San Willibrordus,* ☎ *5999/864–8087.* 🖃 *$3.* ⊙ *Weekdays 11 AM–8 PM, but call ahead to arrange tour.*

⑫ **Landhuis Knip.** In terms of the number of slaves held, this was the largest plantation on the island in its prime. It therefore comes as no surprise that the slave revolt took place here in 1795. The renovated plantation house near the western tip of the island is filled with period furnishings, clothing, and other household goods. You can also walk around the extensive stables and barns used in the operation of this maize plantation. ⊠ *Weg Naar Santa Cruz,* ☎ *5999/864–0244.* ☒ *$2; free Sun.* ☉ *Sun.–Fri. 9–noon and 2–4.*

⑩ **Senior Curaçao Liqueur Distillery.** Located in the charming 17th century Landhuis Chobolobo (just outside Willemstad), this is where the famed Curaçao liqueur, made from the peels of the bitter Iranha orange, is produced. Don't expect a massive factory—it's just a small showroom in the open-air foyer. There are no guides, but delightful old handpainted posters explain the distilling process, and you'll be graciously offered several samples in assorted flavors. If you're interested in buying–the orange-flavored chocolate liqueur is delicious over ice cream— you can choose from a complete selection, which is bottled in a variety of fascinating shapes, including Dutch ceramic houses. ⊠ *Landhuis Chobolobo, Saliña Arriba,* ☎ *5999/461–3526.* ☒ *Free.* ☉ *Mon.–Fri. 8–noon and 1–5.*

Curaçao A to Z

Arriving and Departing

BY AIRPLANE

American Airlines (☎ 5999/869–5707) flies direct daily from Miami. **ALM** (☎ 5999/869–5533), Curaçao's national airline, maintains frequent service from Miami and Atlanta. For Atlanta departures, ALM has connecting services (through-fares) to most U.S. gateways with Delta. ALM also offers a **Visit Caribbean Pass**, allowing easy interisland travel. **Air Aruba** (☎ 5999/868–3777) has daily direct flights to Curaçao (flights make brief stops in Aruba) from both Miami and Newark airports. Air Aruba also has regularly scheduled service to Curaçao from Baltimore, and to Aruba and Bonaire. **Guayana Air** (☎ 5999/461–3033 or 5999/869–5533) now offers nonstop service from New York. **KLM** (☎ 5999/465–2747) flies direct from Amsterdam. **E Liner Airways** (☎ 5999/868–5099 or 5999/560–4773) has interisland service, including sightseeing and beach tours of Aruba and Bonaire.

Electricity

The current is 110–130 volts/50 cycles, which is compatible with small American appliances like electric razors and blow dryers. Ask your hotel whether an adaptor is necessary for laptop computers.

Emergencies

Ambulance: ☎ 112. **Hospital:** St. Elisabeth's Hospital (⊠ Breedestraat 193, ☎ 5999/462–4900 or 5999/462–5100); note that the hospital is equipped with a hyperbaric chamber. **Pharmacies:** The centrally located **Botica Popular** (⊠ Madurostraat 15, ☎ 5999/461–1269) is open daily from 8 AM–6 PM; you can also ask your hotel for the nearest one. After normal business hours, dial 2222 to see which pharmacy has the night rotation. **Police or fire:** ☎ 114.

Festivals and Seasonal Events

Carnival lasts longer on Curaçao than many islands, the revelries beginning at New Year's and continuing until midnight the day before Ash Wednesday. A more restrained, Dutch version than Trinidad's, it's still an explosion of color, with band competitions and costume balls. The highlight of Carnival is the **Tumba Festival** (dates vary), a fourday musical event featuring fierce competition between local musicians for the honor of having their piece selected as the official road march during parades. Another endearing local event is the Easter Monday **Seú Folklore Parade,** which features groups celebrating the harvest in traditional costumes. The two major **musical events** are the **Curaçao Salsa Festival,** held in June or July and the **Curaçao International Jazz Festival,** held October or November, both of which attract major international performers and enthusiastic audiences, including Grammy nominees/winners Celia Cruz, Tito Puente, Dee Dee Bridgewater, and Take Six.

Getting Around

CAR RENTALS

You can rent a car from **Budget** (☎ 5999/868–3466 or 800/472–3325), **Avis** (☎ 5999/461–1255 or 800/331–1212), **Dollar** (☎ 5999/461–3144), or **National Car Rental** (☎ 5999/868–3489 or 800/328–4567) at the airport or have one delivered free to your hotel. Rates typically range from about $60 a day for a Toyota Tercel to about $75 for a four-door sedan or four-wheel-drive vehicle; add 6% tax and required $10 daily insurance. If you're planning to do country driving or rough it through Christoffel Park, a four-wheel-drive vehicle is best. All you'll need is a valid U.S, Canadian, or British driver's license.

TAXIS

Taxi drivers have an official tariff chart, with fares from the airport vicinity to Willemstad and the nearby beach hotels running about $10–$15, $25–$40 to hotels in the west end of the island. Taxis tend to be moderately priced, but since there are no meters, you should confirm the fare with the driver before departure. There is an additional 25% surcharge after 11 PM. Taxis are readily available at hotels; in other cases, call **Central Dispatch** (☎ 5999/869–0747).

Guided Tours

BOAT TOURS

Seaworld Explorer (☎ 5999/462–8833), a semisubmersible, runs hour-long tours of the island's beautiful coral reefs ($30). Many sailboats and motorboats offer comparably priced sunset cruises ($30), snorkel trips ($25), and daylong snorkel and picnic trips to Klein Curaçao ($50), the "clothes optional" island between Curaçao and Bonaire. Top choices among the many boats for all-day snorkeling trips, including snacks or breakfast and barbecue are the 90-ft, turbo-driven *Waterworld* (☎ 5999/465–6042), the twin-masted sailboat *Vira Cocha* (☎ 5999/560–0292), the 120-ft Dutch sailing ketch *Insulinde* (☎ 5999/560–1340), and the 90-ft schooner *Bounty* (☎ 5999/560–1887). Prices run $50–$65.

ORIENTATION

Casper Tours (✉ Matiustraat 3, ☎ 5999/465–3010) has very personal, amiable service. For around $30 per person, you'll be escorted around the island in an air-conditioned van, with stops at the Juliana Bridge, the salt lakes, Knip Bay for a swim, the grotto at Boca Tabla, and Jaanchi's Restaurant (☞ Dining, *above*)—famous for its native cuisine—for lunch (not included in price). **Curven Tours** (✉ Nilda Pintostraat 39, ☎ 5999/737–9806) offers island tours and special packages to Venezuela. **Shorex** (no address, pick up at hotel, ☎ 5999/462–8833) books a variety of entertaining island tours, including Eastern Highlights, a five-hour tour that visits Curaçao Ostrich Farm, Fort Nassau, an herb garden, and Landhuis Jan Thiel ($27). **Taber Tours** (✉ Dokway z/n, ☎ 5999/737–6637) offers a three-hour East Tour ($13) that includes visits to the Curaçao Liqueur Factory at Landhuis Chobolobo, the Curaçao Museum, and the Bloempot shopping center. An array of countryside tours and day trips to Aruba ($175) and Bonaire ($145) are also available.

SPECIAL-INTEREST

For personalized history and nature tours, contact **Dornasol Tours** (✉ Ficusweg 9, ☎ 5999/868–2735); half-day tours run $25 and full-day tours are $40 per person. **Shorex** (☞ Orientation Tours, *above*) offers the Willemstad Trolley Train Tour, which passes all the major downtown sights in just over an hour. The tour commences at Fort Amsterdam, and includes such landmarks as the Floating Market, Mikveh Israel-Emanuel Synagogue, National Archives, and Scharloo District. The cost is $15.90. The **Ostrich Express** (☎ 5999/560–1276) is a true curiosity, visiting one of the largest ostrich farms outside Africa. The 60-minute guided tour explains their development from egg to mature bird. Kids particularly enjoy the tour, since they can hold an egg, stroke a fluffy day-old chick, even sit atop a fully grown ostrich for an unusual photo op. The price is $8.50 for adults, $5.60 for children 2–14, and they pick you up at your hotel. **Christoffel National Park** (☎ 5999/864–0363) offers several fascinating tours led by park rangers. Every Friday morning at 10, they lead a 2½-mi nature hike, discoursing on the indigenous flora and fauna. The fee ($8.50) includes an iguana presentation and soft drink. Jeep tours ($100 for one–five people) go off the beaten track, raising plenty of dust. Finally, 15-minute deer watching expeditions (with no more than eight people to prevent startling the skittish creatures) track the herd of 150–200 small white-tail deer in the park for $6 per person.

Language

Dutch is the official language, but the vernacular is Papiamento—a mixture of Dutch, African, French, Portuguese, Spanish, and English. Developed during the 18th century by Africans, Papiamento evolved as the mode of communication between landowners and their slaves. To guarantee a smile, wish someone *bon dia* (good day) or offer a warm *masha danki* (thank you) after someone has performed a service. These days, however, English as well as Spanish—and, of course, Dutch—are studied by schoolchildren. Anyone involved with tourism—shopkeepers, restaurateurs, and museum guides—speaks English.

Money Matters

CURRENCY

U.S. dollars—in cash or traveler's checks—are accepted nearly everywhere, so there's no need to worry about exchanging money. However, you may need small change for pay phones, cigarettes, or soda machines. The currency in the Netherlands Antilles is the guilder, or florin, as it is also called, indicated by an fl or Naf on price tags. The U.S. dollar is considered very stable; the official rate of exchange at press time was NAf1.77 to US$1. Note: Prices quoted here are in U.S. dollars unless indicated otherwise.

SERVICE CHARGES, TAXES, AND TIPPING

Hotels add a 12% service charge to the bill; restaurants add 10%–15%. Hotels collect a 7% government tax. Most shops and restaurants also tack on 6% ABB tax (a new value-added tax aimed specifically at tourists). The airport international departure tax is NAf22.50 (or $12.50), while the interisland departure tax is NAf10 (about $5.65).

As service is usually included, tipping at restaurants is not expected, though if you found the waitstaff exemplary, you can add another 5%–10% to the bill. Taxi drivers normally receive a 10% gratuity, but this is at your discretion. Tip porters and bellmen about $1 a bag, the hotel housekeeping staff $2–$3 per day.

Opening and Closing Times

Most **shops** are open Monday–Saturday 8–noon and 2–6. **Banks** are open weekdays 8–3:30 or 8–11:30 and 1:30–4.

HOLIDAYS

New Year's Day, Good Friday (Apr. 2), Easter Monday (Apr. 5), the Queen's Birthday (not Beatrix, but rather her mother, Juliana; Apr. 30), Labor Day (May 1), Curaçao Flag Day (July 2), and Christmas.

Passports

U.S. and Canadian citizens need either a valid passport or a birth certificate with a raised seal along with a government-authorized photo ID. British citizens must produce a passport. All visitors must show an ongoing or return ticket.

Precautions

Mosquitoes definitely exist on Curaçao, at least during the rainy season. The bad news is the rainy season falls between November and April, coinciding with the tourist high season. To be safe, keep perfume to a minimum, be prepared to use insect repellent before dining alfresco, and spray your hotel room at night—especially if you've opened a window. If you plan to go into the water, beware of long-spined sea urchins, which can be painful if you come in contact with them.

Do not eat any of the little green applelike fruits (they even smell like apples) of the manchineel tree: They're poisonous. In fact, steer clear of the trees altogether; raindrops or dewdrops dripping off the leaves can blister your skin. If contact does occur, rinse the affected area with water and, in extreme cases, get medical attention. Usually, the burning sensation won't last longer than two hours.

Crime is on the increase in Curaçao, so common-sense rules apply. Lock rental cars, use the theft deterrent device if provided by the rental firm, and do not leave valuables in the car. Use the in-room safe or leave valuables at the front desk of your hotel, and never leave bags unattended at the airport, on tours, or on the beach. Before eating any fruit you buy in a produce market, be sure to wash it thoroughly or peel it.

Telephones and Mail

Phone service through the hotel operators in Curaçao is slow, but direct-dial service, both on-island and to the United States, is fast and clear. Hotel operators will put the call through for you, but if you make a collect call, do check immediately that the hotel does not charge you as well. AT&T Direct service is available by calling 001/800–872–2881, which connects you with an AT&T International operator, but it's nearly impossible from pay phones, and you hotel will likely ask a surcharge. To call Curaçao direct from the United States, dial 011–5999 plus the number in Curaçao. To place a local call on the island, dial the seven-digit local number. An airmail letter to the United States, Canada, or the United Kingdom costs NAf2.25, a postcard NAf1.25.

Visitor Information

Contact the **Curaçao Tourist Board** (✉ 475 Park Ave. S, Suite 2000, New York, NY 10016, ☎ 212/683–7660 or 800/332–8266, FAX 212/683–9337, curacao@ix.netcom.com; ✉ 330 Biscayne Blvd., Suite 808, Miami, FL 33132, ☎ 305/374–5811 or 800/445–8266, FAX 305/374–6741 for information).

In Curaçao, the **Curaçao Tourism Development Foundation** has two offices on the island where multilingual guides are ready to answer questions. You can also pick up maps, brochures, and a copy of *Curaçao Holiday*. The main office is in Willemstad at Pietermaai No. 19 (☎ 5999/461–6000); the other is at the airport (☎ 5999/868–6789).

10 Dominica

Updated by
Carla Amour
Hutchinson

In the early hours of the morning—after the day's first rainfall has seemingly washed the whole world clean—the sun slides up into the sky over the mountains and under the arch of a faint rainbow. Aroused by the light, birds begin their wildly orchestrated chorus—nature's alarm clock. In breezes heavy with the scents of damp earth and lemongrass and not yet fully warmed by the sun, leaves quiver and sparkle with raindrops and dew and the promise of another beautiful day.

"Isle of beauty, Isle of splendor," rings the first line of the National Anthem of the Commonwealth of Dominica. Indeed, the intensity of the unspoiled beauty and splendor of this isle, dubbed "the Nature Island of the Caribbean," is truly inspiring as it turns and twists, towers to mountain crests, then tumbles to falls and valleys. The weather is equally dramatic: torrential rain, dazzling sunshine, and, above all, rainbows, are likely to greet you in the course of a single day.

They say that if Christopher Columbus were to come back today, Dominica (pronounced dom-in-*ee*-ka) would be the only island in the Caribbean that he would recognize. Much of the interior is still covered by luxuriant rain forest and remains inaccessible by road: a wild place straight out of Conan Doyle's *Lost World*. The Smithsonian has called Dominica a giant plant laboratory, unchanged for 10,000 years. The island's rugged northwest is home to the last survivors of the region's original inhabitants, the Caribs. Folklore and superstition have also survived. In the villages of the green interior, you'll still find people who believe in *souqouyans* and *loups-garous,* diabolical spirits that can purportedly fly. *Obeah,* a system of magic originating in Africa, still has some practitioners.

Wedged between two rich French islands, Guadeloupe to the north and Martinique to the south, Dominica has always been something of an anomaly. Its most famous sons have been daughters: Jean Rhys, the novelist, and Dame Eugenia Charles, "Iron Lady" of the Caribbean, who was the first woman to have headed a government in this part of the world (and she did it for 15 years). Dominica's official language is English, its roads are driven on the left, its family and place names are frequently French, and its religion predominantly Catholic. It's just 29 mi long and 16 mi wide and has a population of only about 72,000, but it's an independent commonwealth (its capital is Roseau, pronounced rose-*oh*) with a seat at the United Nations. Unusual for the Caribbean, its economy is still based on agriculture. Bananas, not tourist dollars, are the largest money-earner.

Historically, nature has been Dominica's greatest enemy. It had too many mountains to make the cultivation of sugar profitable. It had too many rivers to make an effective road network viable. It rained too much. It has been sorely tried by hurricanes: by David in 1979, by Hugo in 1989, and by Marilyn in 1995. But today nature is also Dominica's greatest asset. There may not be casinos or swim-up bars here, but if you want to take a leave of absence from the 20th century—to hike into virgin rain forest, scuba dive, watch whales, or explore waterfalls and volcanic lakes straight out of an Indiana Jones movie—this is the place to do it. Dominicans are realizing the island's vast potential, and tourism development is on the rise. Indeed, with the celebration of the island's 21st year as an independent commonwealth in 1999, Dominica is poised to become a trendsetter not only in agricultural and industrial diversification, but also in the area of eco-tourism. Mountain lodges are being built. Life is being breathed back into old plantation houses. If realized, the Waitikubuli Trail, a hiking trail that's slated to traverse the island from north to south, will be the most spectacular of its kind in the Caribbean. Yet despite the change, Dominica's people strive to retain their friendly and polite ways—how the Caribbean used to be and, on this island, how it still is.

Lodging

Places to stay are as varied as the island's landscapes; there are downtown hotels, mountain retreats, plantation great houses, and seaside cottages. More small family-owned properties are opening all the time. Prices are low (though they rise and fall with the seasons), and most properties offer packages with dives, hikes, and tours included; MAP is also a frequent option. You'll find all the usual amenities—on-site restaurants and bars and in-room phones, cable-equipped TVs, air-conditioning, and bathrooms. Just about anywhere you stay, friendly staffers will try to assist you with any request; but don't expect fast-paced big-city-style service—people here still operate on "island time."

CATEGORY	COST*
$$$	over $100
$$	$65–$100
$	under $65

All prices are for a standard double room, excluding 5% tax, 3% sales tax, and 10%–15% service charge.

Hotels

$$$ 🏨 **Anchorage Hotel.** Whatever your interest—hiking, scuba diving, whale-watching, fishing, bird-watching, cultural heritage—the friendly staffs at the Anchorage's on-site dive shop and tour company can create an itinerary for you. All of this family-run hotel's comfortably furnished rooms have phones, cable TV, and balconies. The 20 superior rooms have Caribbean views and two double beds; 12 smaller, standard rooms face the pool and the ocean and have two twin beds or

one double. Renovations in 1998 gave the property more of an island feel: there's an underwater theme in the restaurant and a tropical-garden atmosphere in the bar, both of which are perched above the Caribbean Sea. Squash players take note: This hotel has the only private court on the island; you can use it free if you're a guest, but it's best to bring your own racket. ⊠ *Castle Comfort (Box 34, Roseau),* ☎ *767/448–2638,* FAX *767/448–5680. 32 rooms. Restaurant, bar, airconditioning, pool, squash, dive shop. AE, D, MC, V. EP, FAP, MAP.*

$$$ 🏨 **Castaways Beach Hotel.** The closest beachfront hotel to the capital draws an eclectic crowd: Some people just want to lounge on the beach (perhaps near the beach bar), while others—many of them families—want to make good use of the on-site dive shop and sports center. Snorkeling and scuba diving, kayaking, Sunfish sailing, whale-watching, beach volleyball, and tennis are all options here. The spacious rooms have balconies, cable TV, and ceiling fans (six rooms have airconditioning); all are basically furnished but comfortable and cool. In the evening, guests gather in the terrace restaurant as much for the tropical, laid-back atmosphere as for the local cuisine. On Sunday there's a beach barbecue with live music. ⊠ *11 mi north of Roseau (Box 5, Roseau),* ☎ *767/449–6244,* FAX *767/449–6246. 26 rooms. Restaurant, 2 bars, fans, tennis court, volleyball, beach, dive shop, snorkeling, boating, fishing. MC, V. Closed early Sept.–mid-Oct. EP, MAP.*

$$$ 🏨 **Evergreen Hotel.** This small establishment, just 2 mi from downtown Roseau, is truly a family-run place. One of the owners' daughters, Jill, manages the hotel and its courteous staff; another daughter ensures that all the dishes prepared in the ☞ **Crystal Terrace Restaurant and Bar** are excellent; a son, Carl, is a noted artist whose paintings and wood carvings adorn public areas. Spacious rooms in the newer annex are painted in unexpected colors and decorated with bright floral prints and rattan furniture; all have such amenities as cable TV, large showers, and balconies with sea views. Rooms in the older building—a stone-and-wood structure with a red roof—have a quaint, cottage feel with less-exuberant color schemes, wooden furnishings, and needlepoint hangings on the walls. Though they don't have breathtaking sea views, they have modern facilities and are very comfortable. The grounds contain a garden—abloom with tropical flowers and full of fruit trees alongside towering evergreens—and a pool, near which is a staircase down to the sea. ⊠ *Castle Comfort (Box 309, Roseau),* ☎ *767/448–3288,* FAX *767/448–6800. 16 rooms. Restaurant, bar, air-conditioning, pool, meeting room. AE, D, MC, V. CP, MAP.*

$$$ 🏨 **Fort Young Hotel.** Once the island's main military installation, Fort
★ Young is now one of Roseau's top downtown hotels. The fort was built in the late 1700s, and decorative features from that era—cannons at the entrance, flagstone floors, and massive walls—convey a sense of history. In 1998 the hotel was expanded along the side of a dramatic cliff; 24 modern guest rooms rooms were added, as were a pool—complete with waterfalls and fountains—an exercise room, and a restaurant and bar. In addition, a new commercial center has stores that you can access via a boardwalk that's linked to the Roseau Bayfront. All rooms have modern furnishings and such amenities as private baths (shower-only tubs) cable TV, and balconies. Rooms in the original section are quieter and have dramatic sea views. The ☞ **Marquis de Bouille** restaurant is known for its Creole cuisine with a twist; its bar for its exotic cocktails. ⊠ *Victoria St. (Box 519, Roseau),* ☎ *767/448–5000,* FAX *767/448–5006. 57 rooms. 2 restaurants, 2 bars, air-conditioning, fans, 2 pools, exercise room. AE, MC, V. EP, FAP, MAP.*

$$$ 🏨 **Garraway Hotel.** Owner-managers Derek and Marilyn Garraway proudly compare their establishment to a Ramada or Marriott. It's an apt comparison except that this waterfront hotel is more elegant than

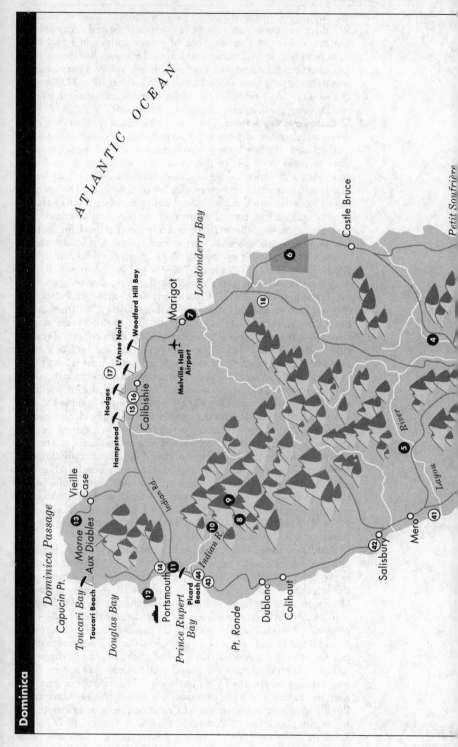

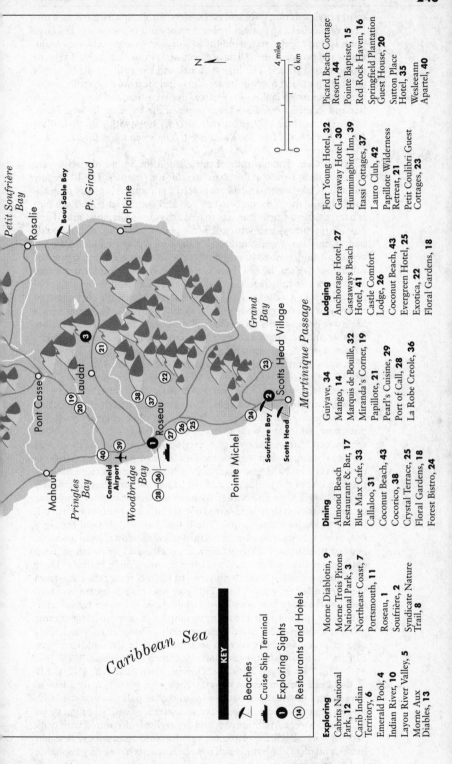

Exploring

Cabrits National
Park, **12**
Carib Indian
Territory, **6**
Emerald Pool, **4**
Indian River, **10**
Layou River Valley, **5**
Morne Aux
Diables, **13**

Morne Diablotin, **9**
Morne Trois Pitons
National Park, **3**
Northeast Coast, **7**
Portsmouth, **11**
Roseau, **1**
Soufrière, **2**
Syndicate Nature
Trail, **8**

Dining

Almond Beach
Restaurant & Bar, **17**
Blue Max Cafe, **33**
Callaloo, **31**
Coconut Beach, **43**
Cocorico, **38**
Crystal Terrace, **25**
Floral Gardens, **18**
Forest Bistro, **24**

Guiyave, **34**
Mango, **14**
Marquis de Bouille, **32**
Miranda's Corner, **19**
Papillote, **21**
Pearl's Cuisine, **29**
Port of Call, **28**
La Robe Creole, **36**

Lodging

Anchorage Hotel, **27**
Castaways Beach
Hotel, **41**
Castle Comfort
Lodge, **26**
Coconut Beach, **43**
Evergreen Hotel, **25**
Exotica, **22**
Floral Gardens, **18**

Fort Young Hotel, **32**
Garraway Hotel, **30**
Hummingbird Inn, **39**
Itassi Cottages, **37**
Lauro Club, **42**
Papillore Wilderness
Retreat, **21**
Petit Coulibri Guest
Cottages, **23**

Picard Beach Cottage
Resort, **44**
Pointe Baptiste, **15**
Red Rock Haven, **16**
Springfield Plantation
Guest House, **20**
Sutton Place
Hotel, **35**
Wesleeann
Apartel, **40**

KEY

Beaches
Cruise Ship Terminal
● Exploring Sights
⑭ Restaurants and Hotels

Caribbean Sea

Pringles Bay

Mahaut ○

Pont Casse ○

Woodbridge Bay

Canefield Airport ✈

Roseau ○ ① ⚓

Pointe Michel

Soufrière Bay Soufrière ②
Scotts Head *Scotts Head*

Scotts Head Village ○

Martinique Passage

Grand Bay

La Plaine ○

Laudat

③

Rosalie ○
Bout Sable Bay

Pt. Giraud

Petit Soufrière Bay

N

0   4 miles
0   6 km

most hotels catering to business travelers. Public spaces have such distinctive touches as paintings by local artists and vetiver mats. The large guest rooms are decorated mainly in soft, soothing pastels—sea foam, coral, and powder blue. All have direct-dial phones and cable TV; some have in-room faxes. The higher floors and the roof terrace survey a colorful jumble of rooftops that seems straight from a Chagall canvas. The restaurant specializes in creative Creole cuisine, and the downstairs bar and sidewalk café have great views of the bay and the west coast. ⊠ *Bayfront (Box 789, Roseau),* ☎ *767/449–8800,* FAX *767/449–8807. 20 rooms, 11 suites. Restaurant, bar, air-conditioning, fans, hot tub, meeting room. AE, DC, MC, V. EP.*

$$$ ★ 🏠 **Lauro Club.** The murmur of the sea and the sound of crickets are all you're likely to hear at this charming cliff-top complex. The 10 brightly painted, solar-powered villas are placed so that there's plenty of beautifully landscaped ground between you and your neighbors. Each unit is named after a Caribbean dance (e.g., the Quadrille, the Limbo) and has a large sitting area with a trundle bed, a bedroom with a double bed, ceiling fans, a well-equipped kitchenette, and a spacious hardwood veranda (though none has a phone or a TV). Six have sea views; the other four are up the hill a bit but still offer a glimpse of the water. Walkways wind through the property and to a small swimming pool and a Jacuzzi; a wooden stairway corkscrews down the cliff to a spot where you can swim among giant, volcanic boulders. The terrace bar's Saturday evening barbecue is very popular, and the staff members are amiable and accommodating. The resort is a little isolated (between Roseau and Portsmouth and about 13 mi from each), so if you stay here, consider renting a car. ⊠ *Grand Savanne (Box 483, Salisbury),* ☎ *767/449–6602,* FAX *767/449–6603. 10 units. Restaurant, bar, fans, kitchenettes, pool, hot tub, beach. AE, MC, V. EP, MAP.*

$$$ ★ 🏠 **Petit Coulibri Guest Cottages.** You need four-wheel-drive to reach this aerie above the village of Soufrière on an old plantation road. But once here, you won't want to come down. In one direction, you can see clear to Martinique (you may even spot whales); in the other, you look to the jungly slopes of Morne Fou. Everything here is solar-powered or runs on batteries; water comes from cisterns, a tree grows up through one of the buildings, and the mountain promises spectacular hikes. Owners Loye and Barney Barnard and their daughter Amy have ensured that each stone-and-wood cottage (the loft bedrooms have pillow-level sea views) is unique. You'll find hardwoods used throughout, as well as such touches as stained-glass windows, local artwork, beds swathed in mosquito netting, and ceramic-and-straw lamps. Each cottage has two bedrooms, a kitchenette, and a huge balcony. There are also two small studios, with views of foliage, rather than sea, from their verandas; they don't have kitchens, but this just means you take meals at the main house with the family. Loye is known for her culinary skills and has prepared many a sumptuous surprise using organic produce (cottage guests should reserve meals 24 hours in advance). She's also an artist, and her gallery represents a few of Dominica's artists. ⊠ *Petit Coulibri Estate, near Soufrière (Box 331, Roseau),* ☎ FAX *767/446–3150. 3 cottages, 2 studios. Dining room, pool. AE, MC, V. EP.*

$$$ ★ 🏠 **Red Rock Haven.** Set on red-clay cliffs, this place is truly a haven. Exotics and hybrids spill out of urns and over pathways on the landscaped grounds. The cottages have wide terraces with stunning views of the windswept Atlantic coast and are stylishly decorated with original artwork. Each has a phone, comfortable furnishings, designer linens, and plenty of large beach towels. Kitchens have every appliance and piece of crockery you could possibly need and, on request, the staff will fill up the pantry. Daily maid service is provided and, with a little notice and a little extra money, the maid will prepare meals for you as well. Stocked bookshelves are another bonus (you're encouraged to make a contribution when you leave). The white-sand beach, arguably the prettiest on the island, is a short trek down a path. Although the property is close to several points of interest, most aren't within walking distance, so you'll need to rent a car. ✉ *Pointe Baptiste, Calibishie (Box 71, Roseau),* ☎ *767/448–2181,* ℻ *767/448–5787. 3 cottages. Fans, kitchenettes, beach. AE, MC, V. EP.*

$$$ 🏨 **Wesleeann Apartel.** From the outside, this hotel looks like a French apartment block plunked down on the edge of the Caribbean. That said, the spacious one-, two-, and three-bedroom apartments are ideal for families or couples sharing. Each unit has a balcony with a sea view; cable TV; a phone; a breakfast room; and a kitchenette with a microwave oven, a refrigerator, and utensils. Room decor consists of white-tile floors, white rattan furniture, and floral-chintz fabrics. The top-floor restaurant serves Creole food; ask for a seat near the windows, so you can dine with the ocean as your backdrop. ✉ *8 9th St., Canefield (Box 1764, Roseau),* ☎ *767/449–0419,* ℻ *76/7449–2473. 12 apartments, 1 suite. Restaurant, bar, air-conditioning, kitchenettes, refrigerators, exercise room, meeting room. AE, MC, V. EP.*

$$–$$$ 🏨 **Papillote Wilderness Retreat.** Lush greenery abounds at this moun-
★ tain retreat: The nearby river and waterfall beckon you to take a dip, and 200-ft Trafalgar Falls is a short hike from your room. Owner Anne Jean-Baptiste's botanical garden is a mind-boggling collection of rare and indigenous plants and flowers—all planted around secluded mineral pools and stone sculptures. Anne's walking tours of the garden end at the bird-watching station at the top of the property. Although the rustic rooms are painstakingly decorated with such local handicrafts as quilts and pottery, they're somewhat dark and aren't as spectacular as their surroundings. Sadly, the island's main hydroelectric plant is only a short distance away, and in some rooms the hum of electricity is louder than the croaking of tree frogs. Yet Papillote remains a special place, imbued with the vitality and commitment of its owners and staffed by some of the island's friendliest people. The terrace-style ☞ Papillote restaurant, which has spectacular mountain and valley views, serves excellent local cuisine. ✉ *Trafalgar Falls Rd. (Box 2287, Roseau),* ☎ *767/448–2287,* ℻ *767/448–2285. 10 rooms. Restaurant, bar, shop. AE, DC, MC, V. EP, MAP.*

$$–$$$ 🏨 **Sutton Place Hotel.** The Harris family has sunk its life savings—and
★ then some—into transforming a historic 1890s residence in the heart of Roseau into a small beautifully refurbished hotel. Everything, from the wrought-iron gates at the entrance (bought in Trinidad) to the tauroniro wood floors (from South America), suggests that no expense has been spared. Steps lead from the street to a pleasant, antiques-filled reception area. Standard rooms on the second floor are attractively furnished with fabrics and fittings imported from New York. On this floor you and other guests share a lounge and a kitchenette where Continental breakfast is served. The three spacious top-floor suites have fully equipped kitchenettes, antique furnishings, teak louvered windows, and polished wood floors. Some of the structure's original stonework can still be seen in the large, ground-floor restaurant, which serves good Creole and East Indian food. Downstairs, Cecil Harris, one of the owners' sons, runs the Cellars bar—a popular local hangout. There's also a quaint courtyard where meals are sometimes served. ✉ *25 Old St., Roseau,* ☎ *767/448–8700,* ℻ *767/448–3045. 5 rooms, 3 suites. Restaurant, bar, air-conditioning, fans. AE, D, MC, V. CP, MAP.*

$$ 🏨 **Coconut Beach Hotel.** After being pounded by Hurricane Marilyn in 1995, rooms at this beachfront hotel were mostly occupied by students from the nearby medical college. With the completion of two chalet-style additions 50 ft from the beach, the hotel can once again welcome

visitors. Each of the 12 one-bedroom units has a living-dining room and a kitchen. Amenities include phones and satellite TVs; six upstairs rooms have small verandas. The ☞ **Coconut Beach** bar-restaurant, which specializes in seafood, is a hub of activity right on Picard Beach—a long stretch of golden sand. ⊠ *Picard Beach (Box 37, Roseau),* ☎ *767/445–5393,* ℻ *767/445–5693. 12 units. Restaurant, bar, air-conditioning, kitchenettes, beach. AE, D, MC, V. CP, EP, FAP, MAP.*

Guest Houses and Lodges

$$$ 🏨 **Castle Comfort Lodge.** This excellent dive lodge, run by enthusias-
★ tic locals Derek and Ginette Perryman, wins a loyal following for its first-rate dive shop and excellent-value dive packages. Rooms are in two buildings: one directly on the sea, the other at the back of the property. Each room has white rattan furnishings, fish-pattern fabrics, and a veranda. The back rooms are smaller but make up for this by offering cable TV and phone. As a bonus, the home-cooked meals—served on a large, airy terrace—are bountiful and delicious. The Perrymans can also arrange inland adventures and nature walks. Their MAP package, which includes five days of diving and a night dive, is one of the best deals on Dominica. ⊠ *1½ mi south of Roseau (Box 63, Roseau),* ☎ *767/448–2188,* ℻ *767/448–6088. 15 rooms. Restaurant, dive shop. AE, MC, V. MAP.*

$$$ 🏨 **Exotica.** Fae and Atherton Martin, a prominent local couple (he is
★ a former minister of agriculture and the current president of the Dominica Conservation Association), own this small, peaceful resort. Getting here is an adventure: The road corkscrews up the mountain—the vegetation becoming lusher with every turn—until you reach flower- and tree-filled grounds 1,600 ft above the ocean. The handsome wood-and-stone villas have red galvanized roofs with solar panels. The bright, cheerful interiors have rattan furnishings, floral-print fabrics, peaked ceilings, and tile floors. Each unit also has a phone, a TV, a kitchenette, a bedroom with two (extra-long) double beds, and a large living room with a trundle bed. If you don't want to cook, Fae serves delicious Creole food (produce often comes for her organic garden) at the on-site Sugar Apple café. A nearby river is a good spot for swimming. The property is a great place to bird-watch, and its grounds contain more than 50 varieties of flowers and 30 types of fruit trees. The views of the ocean in the distance are stunning, and there are great hiking opportunities on Morne Anglais. ⊠ *Gommier, southeast of Roseau (Box 109, Roseau),* ☎ *767/448–8839,* ℻ *767/448–8829. 8 villas. Restaurant, kitchenettes. AE, MC, V.*

$$$ 🏨 **Picard Beach Cottage Resort.** Here eight wooden cottages fringe Dominica's longest beach and are set on land that was once part of a coconut plantation. Upon arrival, the staff welcomes you with rum punch and makes sure that your one-bedroom cottage has a bouquet of fresh flowers. Each cottage can accommodate up to four people and has a kitchenette (stocked with coffee fixings and herbal tea), locally made furnishings, and a veranda. Another thoughtful touch is the basin of freshwater at the bottom of your veranda's stairs, so you can rinse the sand from your feet before entering after a day at the beach. Stone paths run from each cottage through the ground's profusion of flowering trees, shrubs, and palms. Le Flambeau Restaurant is next door, and the resort is a 15-minute walk to Portsmouth's stores and a 10- to 20-minute drive to many area sights. ⊠ *Prince Rupert Bay (Box 34, Roseau),* ☎ *767/445–5131,* ℻ *767/445–5599. 8 cottages. Restaurant, bar, kitchenette, beach. AE, MC, V. EP, MAP.*

$$–$$$ 🏨 **Hummingbird Inn.** The ambience of this simple hilltop retreat, just
★ a short drive from Roseau and Canefield Airport, is created by owner Jean James Finucane, an American-educated Dominican with an en-

dearing smile and a passion for hummingbirds. Two bungalows with outstanding Caribbean views hold 10 rooms. Interiors are simple—white walls, terra-cotta-tile floors, and peaked wooden ceilings. Varnished wooden hurricane windows can be left open all night to let in fresh breezes and the sounds of tree frogs and the ocean a few hundred yards below. There's no air-conditioning, TV, or phones. Instead, there are such tropical fixtures as ceiling fans, handmade quilts, hammocks, and tables fashioned out of gommier and red cedar wood. One large suite also has a stately, mahogany four-poster bed and kitchen. Jean is an expert on Creole cooking, and the Hummingbird's cook is perhaps the best of any guest house on Dominica. ☒ *Morne Daniel, 2 mi north of Roseau (Box 1901, Roseau),* ☎ ℻ *767/449–1042. 9 rooms, 1 suite. Restaurant, bar, fans. AE, MC, V. EP, MAP.*

$$–$$$ ★ 🏨 **Pointe Baptiste.** Alec Waugh wrote a book here, Noel Coward was a visitor, and Princess Margaret stayed during her honeymoon. It's easy to see why. This weathered plantation house exudes Old World charm. The setting, above a beautiful beach, is divine; the antiques-filled interior, patrician. There are three rooms in the main house, which also contains a superb library. A whitewashed cottage straight out of a Ralph Lauren catalog contains an additional room. Note that this is not a place for the smart set: it's an old house, with antiquated fittings, and guests are expected to "do" for themselves (though a local cook can be provided by arrangement). As the main house can be rented only in its entirety, and you will need a car to do anything, a stay here is not for all pocketbooks, either. For those wanting something more affordable, the family also runs D'Auchamps Apartments, an attractive property on the other side of the island, near Trafalgar Falls. ☒ *2 mi northwest of village of Calibishie (c/o Mrs. Geraldine Edwards, Calibishie Village),* ☎ ℻ *767/445–7322. 3 rooms, 1 cottage. D, MC, V.*

$$ 🏨 **Springfield Plantation Guest House.** The giant palms that mark your arrival here are enough to convey the age of this 19th-century plantation guest house on 200 lush acres. Although a bit gloomy and run-down, it's full of character and feels like something out of Jean Rhys's *Wide Sargasso Sea.* The wood-paneled dining room has antique furniture and a piano; pictures of clipper ships and a portrait of King George V hang on the wall. Rooms upstairs in the main house are done in real plantation style: four-poster beds, antiques, and floral linens. (Room 6 is especially imposing.) Other rooms are in a guest cottage and a long, wooden building across the courtyard. The restaurant (reservations are a must) serves true Dominican dishes, often with estate-grown organic vegetables. There are nature trails and good river swimming on the plantation, which is also home to SCEPTRE (Springfield Centre for Environmental Protection, Research and Education). ☒ *Box 456, Roseau,* ☎ *767/449–1401,* ℻ *767/449–2160. 7 rooms, 2 cottages. Restaurant, bar. AE, D, MC, V. CP, EP, FAP, MAP.*

$–$$ 🏨 **Floral Gardens.** It's a surprise to find a Swiss chalet–style hotel—complete with latticed windows and flower boxes—on the edge of a rain-forest reserve; owner O. J. Seraphin, a former prime minister and full-time human dynamo, and his driven wife, Lily, are probably the only people who could carry it off. As you may guess from the higgledy-piggledy layout, the hotel has grown bit by bit over the years. Hurricane Marilyn did considerable damage in 1995, but this merely gave the Seraphins an excuse to undertake further renovations and expansions. They've already added a botanical garden and pool with a waterfall, and at press time, O. J. was overseeing the building of a minimall with six boutiques (each one slated to showcase a different island craft or product) and a conference hall. The older guest rooms in the main building are decorated with island crafts and homey fabrics. Though they once had a slightly claustrophobic feel, recently enlarged verandas and windows have made them just as accommodating as the newer, larger units across the road and overlooking the Pagua River. An additional seven suites were added in 1998. The ☞ **Floral Gardens** restaurant is one of the best on the island. ✉ *Concord,* ☎ *767/445–7636,* FAX *767/445–7636. 15 rooms, 7 suites. Restaurant, shop, meeting rooms. AE, MC, V. EP, MAP.*

$–$$ ⊡ **Itassi Cottages.** Run by the same family that owns ☞ **Sutton Place**
★ **Hotel,** these three self-contained cottages pretty well live up to the promise in the brochure: ". . . for discerning travelers who are not necessarily loaded." Set on beautifully landscaped grounds, the two-bedroom, two-bath cottage can house as many as six people; the one-bedroom, one-bath cottage houses up to four people; and the studio cottage comfortably houses two people. Each cottage has a kitchen, ceiling fans, and cable TV, and there's a shared laundry facility. The decor is homey with a mix of antiques, straw mats, handmade floral bedspreads, calabash lamps. Wraparound porches have hammocks and sweeping views of Roseau, Scotts Head, and the Caribbean. ✉ *Morne Bruce, about 1 mi southeast of Roseau (Box 319, Roseau),* ☎ *767/448–7247,* FAX *767/448–3045. 3 cottages. Fans, kitchenettes, laundry service. AE, MC, V.*

Dining

Dominica may be only a few miles from Martinique and Guadeloupe, the Caribbean's culinary capitals, but don't expect gourmet dining or excellent wines. Look, instead, for Creole fare using the cornucopia of vegetables that grow in the fertile Dominican soil. Sweet green plantains, *kushkush* yams, breadfruit, dasheen (a tuber similar to the potato; called "taro" elsewhere), and other items are staples. You'll find fresh fish on virtually every menu (often cooked in *sancouche,* (a Creole method of cooking using coconut milk) and occasionally "mountain chicken"—a euphemism for a large frog called *crapaud.* Two rare delicacies for the intrepid diner are *manicou* (a small opossum) and the tender, gamey *agouti* (a large, indigenous rodent)—both are best smoked or stewed. The local drink is spiced rum—a cask rum steeped with herbs such as annisette (called "nanny") and *pweve* (lemongrass).

What to Wear
Dominica is not exactly the fashion hub of the Caribbean, but most Dominicans dress elegantly and practically when eating out—for dinner it's shirt and trousers for men and modest dresses for women. During the day, nice shorts are acceptable at most places; beach attire is almost always frowned upon.

CATEGORY	COST*
$$$	over $35
$$	$15–$35
$	under $15

per person for a three-course meal, excluding drinks, service charge, and 3% tax

CARIBBEAN/CREOLE

$$–$$$ ✕ **Coconut Beach.** This casual beachfront bar-restaurant at the ☞ Coconut Beach Hotel is popular with visiting yacht owners, expatriate students from the nearby medical school, and anyone interested in an afternoon on a stretch of golden-sand beach. Fresh tropical drinks and local seafood dishes are the specialty here; sandwiches and rotis are also served. ✉ *Picard Beach,* ☎ *767/445–5393. AE, D, MC, V.*

$$–$$$ ✕ **La Robe Creole.** In a pretty building near the cathedral, you can dine
★ on a meal selected from an eclectic à la carte menu. Callaloo and crab soup, made with dasheen and coconut, is a specialty. Other tasty options include lobster and conch crepes, charcoal-grilled fish and meats,

barbecued chicken, and a selection of salads. The dining room is a cozy place, with wood rafters, ladder-back chairs, and colorful madras tablecloths. The downstairs take-out annex, the Mouse Hole, is an inexpensive place to stock up for a picnic. The restaurant also makes its own delicious mango chutney, which you can buy in local shops. ⊠ *3 Victoria St., Roseau,* ☎ *767/448–2896. D, MC, V. Closed Sun.*

$$ ✕ **Floral Gardens.** You may feel as if you're dining in a private home
★ at this warm, welcoming restaurant of the ☞ **Floral Gardens** hotel, particularly if owner O. J. Seraphin is around. Wood paneling, rough-hewn timber beams, and vetiver mats create a rustic atmosphere. Tables are laid out in an L-shape in the main building, and there are more tables in a gallery-style building across the road, overlooking the river. The food is delectable; sample local specialties, such as crapaud, agouti, or crayfish caught by the local Carib Indians, whose reservation adjoins the property. There are also vegetarian dishes. ⊠ *Concord,* ☎ *767/ 445–7636. AE, MC, V.*

$$ ✕ **Papillote.** Just outside Anne Jean-Baptiste's stone-and-tile restaurant
★ at the ☞ **Papillote Wilderness Retreat,** you'll find botanical gardens and a bubbling hot-spring pool (just the spot to savor a lethal rum punch before or after dinner). This place is just as popular with birds and butterflies—and tour groups—as ever. Try the bracing callaloo soup, dasheen puffs, chicken rain forest (marinated with papaya and wrapped in banana leaves), and, if they're on the menu, the succulent *bouk* (tiny, delicate, river shrimp). ⊠ *Trafalgar Falls Rd., Roseau,* ☎ *767/448– 2287. Reservations essential. AE, D, MC, V.*

$–$$ ✕ **Almond Beach Restaurant & Bar.** If you're visiting one of the island's northeast beaches, stop here for a lunch of callaloo soup, lobster, or octopus. Select from tantalizing juices—guava, passion fruit, and soursop—or one of the spice rums. Try the pweve or *lapsenth,* a violet-scented pick-me-up and digestive. The genial owners, the Joseph family, are experts on local culture and customs and sometimes arrange traditional *belé* dance or *jing ping* (a type of folk music) performances on weekends. ⊠ *Calibishie,* ☎ *767/445–7783. AE, D, MC, V.*

$–$$ ✕ **Callaloo Restaurant.** Mrs. Marge Peters is the vivacious hostess of this small, informal eatery. She takes pride in age-old cooking traditions and uses only the freshest local produce. (What she does with breadfruit alone—roasted slabs, puffs, creamy velouté, juice, pie— could fill a cookbook.) Changing lunch and dinner specials might include pepper-pot soup, curried conch, or crab callaloo—fragrant with cumin, coconut cream, lime, clove, and garlic. Most everything here is homemade, including the juices (try the sea moss— it "puts lead in your pencil") and the ice cream (the soursop is marvelous). ⊠ *66 King George V St., Roseau,* ☎ *767/448–3386. AE, D, MC, V.*

$–$$ ✕ **Mango.** From 8 AM to 11 PM (till 1 AM on weekends) locals flock to this unassuming restaurant and bar in the heart of Portsmouth. Seating is either indoors or outdoors on a wooden veranda that encircles a huge mango tree. Folks come as much for the relaxing ambience as for Peter Pascal's solid home cooking. The *lambi* (conch) is tender as can be, the goat *colombo* (curry) has quite a kick, and the mountain chicken is succulent. This is one of the few places where you can find *breego,* a tiny flavorful conch. ⊠ *Bay St., Portsmouth,* ☎ *767/445– 3099. AE, D, MC, V.*

$–$$ ✕ **Miranda's Corner.** Driving toward Pont Casse beyond the Springfield Plantation, you'll begin to see the hills full of anthuriums, ginger lilies, and poinsettias, and plantations of tomatoes and cabbages. At the bend in the road there's a tree with a sign that reads: MIRANDA'S CORNER—a bar, rum shop, and diner all in one. Miranda Alfred and three of her children are at home here, serving every type of client, from Italian tourists to banana farmers. The specialties are numerous—

even the shrimp from her pond is prepared with a potion of passion
and a fistful of flavor. This joint is open for breakfast, lunch, and dinner, and if you want something specially prepared, just call ahead and
Miranda will help you out. ✉ *Mount Joy, Springfield,* ☎ *767/449–
2509. No credit cards.*

$–$$ ✗ **Pearl's Cuisine.** Inside a restored, green-and-white, Creole-style
house, Chef Pearl, with her robust and infectious character, prepares
some of the island's best local delicacies. She offers everything from
sousse (pickled pigs' feet) to mountain chicken and crayfish done in
typical Dominican style. Ask for a table on the open-air gallery that
looks out over the streets of Roseau. ✉ *50 King George V St., Roseau,*
☎ *767/448–8707. AE, D, MC, V.*

ECLECTIC

$$–$$$ ✗ **Marquis de Bouille.** The candlelit dining room at the historic ☞ **Fort**
★ **Young Hotel**—with its stone walls adorned with fine art and its wooden
ceiling—is one of the island's classier restaurants. The Jamaican chef
adds flourishes from his homeland to the Continental and Dominican
dishes. The menu includes callaloo and pumpkin soups, grilled lobster,
and blue marlin in a lime sauce. ✉ *Victoria St., Roseau,* ☎ *767/448–
5000. AE, MC, V.*

$$ ✗ **Crystal Terrace Restaurant and Bar.** At the restaurant-bar of the ☞
Evergreen Hotel you can enjoy a meal on a large airy terrace that over-
looks the sea or relax at the striking art deco–style bar with its crys-
tal chandeliers, and, of course, tropical cocktails. Delicious dinner
appetizers include a choice of soup and salad; entrées of chicken, fish,
and beef are served with local produce, such as kushkush and plan-
tains. For dessert, there's fresh fruit or homemade cake and ice cream.
✉ *Castle Comfort, Roseau,* ☎ *767/448–3288. AE, MC, V.*

$–$$ ✗ **Blue Max Cafe.** No prizes for guessing the former profession of
Mourad Zarkha, one of the owners of this popular bistro. The one-
time pilot has filled the few walls of this open balcony café with photos of fighter planes and airline posters. The decor—hand-painted
furnishings, faux-marble-top tables, a large bar, clay urns, and palm
and banana trees—is just as eclectic as the menu, which has Creole,
French, Italian, and Middle Eastern dishes. Stop by for lunch, dinner,
or happy hour; on weekends there's live music. ✉ *Corner of Old St.
and Kennedy Ave., Roseau,* ☎ *767/449–8907. MC, V. Closed Sun.*

$–$$ ✗ **Forest Bistro.** If you've been diving or driving in Soufrière, be sure
to stop by Andre and Joyce Charles's place—a naturalist's haven,
where the faint hum of a generator, turned on to milk the cows, is the
only hint of civilization. Set on what remains of the island's finest lime
orchards, with views of the lush mountains and distant sea, the small
bistro manages to be far more pleasant than the simple, open-sided concrete building with its galvanized roof suggests. The decor includes smart
green tables and striped director's chairs. Breakfasts of eggs, bacon,
and fried plantains and hearty lunches of kingfish, tuna, and mahimahi—
served with vegetables from the restaurant's own garden—are some
of the dishes on the menu. ✉ *Soufrière,* ☎ *767/448–7105. Reservations essential. No credit cards.*

$–$$ ✗ **Guiyave.** This popular lunchtime restaurant in the center of Roseau
is actually two businesses in one. Downstairs is a pastry shop, where
owner Hermina Astaphan makes chicken patties, spicy rotis, and a
scrumptious selection of pies, tarts, and cakes. These can also be ordered at the upstairs restaurant (run by her son), along with more elaborate fare, such as mountain chicken, steamed fish, and chicken in a
sweet-and-sour sauce. You may dine in the green-and-white wood-pan-
eled dining room, which has a bar at one end, or on the sunny balcony
perched above Roseau's colorful streets—the perfect spot to indulge

in one of the fresh-squeezed tropical juices. ⊠ *15 Cork St., Roseau,* ☏ *767/448–2930. AE, MC, V. No dinner.*

$–$$ ✕ **Port of Call Restaurant and Bar.** The newest addition to Roseau's restaurant scene is open daily from 8 AM to 11 PM, with furnishings and decor in grays and whites. Inside a beautifully restored town house—done in a gray-and-white color scheme—the management here is always ready to meet your desires, whether it's for a local cuisine, a hamburger with french fries, or an exotic cocktail from the bar. The downstairs lounge has a cozy atmosphere. ⊠ *3 Kennedy Ave., Roseau,* ☏ *767/449–9646 or 767/448–2910. AE, D, MC, V.*

FRENCH

$–$$ **Cocorico.** The brainchild of a young couple from Lille, this restaurant is a bit of France in downtown Roseau. In a pretty Creole-style dwelling, which they have decorated in blue and white, you can drink espresso and eat *baguettes au jambon* or beef *à la française* (ham or beef sandwiches on French bread). There's also a selection of French products, including chocolate from Martinique and (of all things) tripe from Brittany. ⊠ *58 King George V St., Roseau,* ☏ *no phone. No credit cards.*

Beaches

If you want to hang out on sugar-white beaches dotted with vendors and beach bars, there are plenty of better places to do it than Dominica. You'll find mostly black-sand beaches, evidence of the island's volcanic origins or secluded white- or brown-sand beaches along the northeast coast. Swimming off the rocky shores has its pleasures, too: the water is deeper and bluer, and the snorkeling is far more interesting. The best sand beaches are around Portsmouth or in the northeast of the island.

On the northeast coast, **Woodford Hill Bay, Hampstead, L'Anse Noir,** and **Hodges** are the island's most beautiful beaches. They're excellent for snorkeling and scuba diving, though their wind-tossed beauty can be dangerous; there are strong currents as well as whipped-cream waves. From these beaches you can see the island of Marie Galante, part of Guadeloupe.

Picard Beach, on the northwest coast, is the island's best beach. Great for windsurfing and snorkeling, it's a 2-mi stretch of brown sand fringed with coconut trees. The Picard Beach Cottage Resort and Coconut Beach Hotel (☞ Lodging, *above*) are along this beach.

In the southeast, near La Plaine, **Bout Sable Bay** is not much good for swimming, but the surroundings are stirringly elemental: towering red cliffs challenge the rollicking Atlantic.

The beaches of the southwest coast are mostly rocks and black sand, but the snorkeling and scuba diving are excellent because of the dramatic underwater walls, sudden drops, and very clear waters. At **Scotts Head** and **Soufrière Bay,** you will find some of the finest snorkeling and scuba diving in the world. At one spot volcanic vents puff steam into the sea; the experience has been described as "swimming in champagne," so the spot has come to be called "Champagne."

Outdoor Activities and Sports

BOATING AND SAILING

West coast waters are deep, and the coves there are numerous. Motorboat and sailing excursions include those to neighboring islands as well as to secluded spots on Dominica itself. You can arrange trips through **Dominica Tours** (☞ Guided Tours *in* Dominica A to Z, *below*) and the **Castaways Beach Hotel** (⊠ Mero, ☏ 767/449–6245).

Dominica's majestic mountains, clear rivers, and lush vegetation all combine to make rambling about a great pleasure. The island is, in fact, crisscrossed by ancient footpaths, some created by the Nègres Marrons, escaped slaves (including some Carib Indians) who established camps in the mountains. There are now ambitious plans afoot to incorporate these old trails into the Waitikibuli Trail, which would traverse the island from north to south. Existing trails range from easy-going to arduous. For the former, all you'll need are sturdy, rubber-soled shoes and an adventurous spirit; for the latter, sturdy hiking boots; and for both, plenty of insect repellent.

For the hike to Boiling Lake or the climb up Morne Diablotin, you will need hiking boots, a guide, and water. Guides will charge about $30–$35 per person and can be contacted through the **Dominica Tourist Office** (☞ Visitor Information *in* Dominica A to Z, *below*) or the **Dominica Forestry Division** (☎ 767/448–2401 or 767/448–2638). Most hotels and guest houses will also be able to assist you in contacting a certified and reputable guide.

"Amazing! Incredible! Fantastic!" These are some of the words people use when they surface after a dive in Dominica. Voted one of the top 10 dive destinations in the world by *Skin Diver* and *Rodale's Scuba Diving* magazines, Dominica is a paradise for divers and snorkelers alike. There are numerous excellent sites at points all along the west coast of the island, but highly reputed are those in the southwest—within and around the Soufrière Marine Park. This bay is the site of a submerged volcanic crater and is a designated Marine Reserve, with stringent regulations in force to prevent the degradation of the ecosystem. Within ½ mi of the shore, there are vertical drops from 800 ft to more than 1,500 ft. Visibility frequently extends to 100 ft. There are not so many large fish as on some other islands (they are not fed here), but marine life is abundant. Shoals of several thousand boga fish, Creole wrasse, or blue cromis are not uncommon, and you might even see a spotted moray eel or a honeycomb cowfish. Crinoids (rare elsewhere) are also abundant, as are giant barrel sponges. The opportunities for underwater photography, particularly macrophotography, are unparalleled. The going rate is about $60–$65 for a two-tank dive or $80–$90 for a resort course with two open-water dives. All scuba diving operators also offer snorkeling; equipment rents for $10–$20 a day.

Anchorage Dive Center (✉ Anchorage Hotel, Castle Comfort, ☎ 767/448–2638) has two dive boats that can take you out diving day and night. They also offer PADI instruction (all skill levels), snorkeling and whale-watching trips, and shore diving. **Dive Castaways** (✉ Castaway Beach Hotel, ☎ 767/449–6244), a PADI dive shop 11 mi north of Roseau, has two boats and offers diving and courses as well as other water (including snorkeling) and beach activities. **Dive Dominica** (✉ Castle Comfort Lodge, ☎ 767/448–2188, FAX 767/448–6088) has four boats and is one of the island's oldest dive shops on the island. They conduct NAUI, PADI, and SSI courses and offer diving, snorkeling, and whale-watching trips, primarily of the southwest coast. For the advanced set, there are dives in areas with drop-offs, walls, and pinnacles—by day or night. **Nature Island Dive** (✉ Soufrière, ☎ 767/449–8181) is run by three enthusiastic couples who share four nationalities (Canadian, British, American, and Dominican) among them. They have two boats, and some of the island's best dive sites are nearby. Full PADI courses and PADI-approved resort courses are offered.

SWIMMING

With 365 rivers—one for every day of the year—it's not surprising that river swimming is one of the most popular pastimes on Dominica. On the west coast, good bets include the Machoucherie and Picard rivers; on the east coast there's the White River—all are clean, and you can also sunbathe and picnic on their banks.

WHALE-WATCHING

There are few sights more thrilling than seeing a pod of sperm whales just yards ahead of your boat. Humpback whales, false killer whales, minke, and orcas are all occasionally seen, as are different species of dolphin. But the resident sperm whales (they calve in Dominica's 3,000-ft-deep waters) are truly the stars of the show. **The Anchorage Dive Center** and **Dive Dominica** (☞ Scuba Diving and Snorkeling, *above*) are two of the best whale-watching operators. During the expedition, you may be asked to assist in recording sightings, which aids these operators in collecting data that can be shared with local and international organizations.

WINDSURFING

Although windsurfing is not a very widely practiced sport in Dominica, there are a few individuals who will swear that the conditions are right for an exhilarating experience. Following are the places where information can be obtained on the best places to surf. Contact the **Anchorage Hotel** (☞ Scuba Diving, *above*), and the **Castaways Beach Hotel** (☞ Boating, *above*).

Shopping

The distinctive handicrafts of the Carib Indians include traditional baskets made of dyed *larouma* reeds and waterproofed with tightly woven *balizier* leaves. These crafts are sold at the reservation as well as in Roseau's shops. Dominica is also noted for its spices (especially saffron), hot peppers, bay rum, and coconut oil; its vetiver-grass mats are sold all over the world. Cafe Dominique, the local equivalent of Jamaican Blue Mountain coffee, is an excellent buy. Dominican rum is stronger, and rougher, than French brands—try Macoucherie. Proof that the old ways live on in Dominica can be found in the number of herbal remedies available. One stimulating memento of your visit is rum steeped with Bois Bandé (scientific name Richeria Grandis), a tree whose bark is reputed to have aphrodisiacal properties. Most of the major supermarkets will also stock most of these items—try **Whitchurch** (✉ Kennedy Ave., Roseau, ☎ 767/448–2181) or **Brizee's** (✉ Canefield, ☎ 767/448–2087).

Area

One of the easiest places to pick up a souvenir is the **Old Market Plaza,** just behind the Dominica Museum, in Roseau. Slaves were once sold here, but today it is the scene of happier trading: Handcrafted jewelry, T-shirts, spices, souvenirs, and batiks are available from a select group of entrepreneurs in open-air booths set up on the cobblestones. This is a favorite shopping stop for the cruise ship passengers who disembark onto the jetty across the street.

Specialty Items

ART

Gallery #4 (✉ 4 Hanover St., Roseau, ☎ 767/448–6900) is owned by Dominica's most prominent artist and houses pieces by local painters who work in a variety of mediums. Earl Ettienne will be happy to explain the processes involved in producing his own work as well as those of his fellow artists. Commissions are accepted and can often be completed in time for your departure.

CLOTHING

Ego Boutique (⊠ 9 Hillsborough St., Roseau, ☎ 767/448−2336) is run by Florence Green who proudly announces that the staff can communicate in Spanish, English, and French. The items for sale add to the international atmosphere: clothing, crafts, and home accessories from around the world with an emphasis on pieces from developing countries in the Caribbean, Latin America, and Africa.

GIFTS AND SOUVENIRS

Fadelle's (⊠ 28 Kennedy Ave., Roseau, ☎ 767/448−2686) sells fresh and dried floral arrangements, woven-straw items, and works done in wood. You'll also find soaps, perfumes, and sauces.

Rainforest Shop (⊠ 17 Old St., Roseau, ☎ 767/448−8834) sells everything from toucan-shape toothbrush holders to doorstops. The goods come from all over the Caribbean as well as Central and South America. All are brightly colored and hand-painted. One dollar from every sale goes toward protecting the rain forest.

HANDICRAFTS

Balisier's (⊠ 35 Great George St., Roseau, ☎ no phone) owner, Hilroy Fingol, is a young artist who specializes in airbrush painting. At his small outlet, you'll find some very creative and unique T-shirts and paintings. His mom and sister also stock the store with charming sunbonnets, Carnival dolls, and island jewelry.

Caribana (⊠ 31 Cork St., Roseau, ☎ 767/448−7340), one of the island's oldest crafts shops, specializes in Dominican arts and crafts. You will find unique pieces of furniture, home accessories, jewelry, wood carvings, baskets, books, condiments, and body potions. At the **Iris Dangleben Gallery**, at the rear of the store, you'll also find a selection of fine art by local and visiting artists. The gallery's intimate café, a popular gathering spot for the artistic community, serves the best cup of coffee in town.

Dominica Pottery (⊠ Bayfront St. and Kennedy Ave., Roseau, ☎ no phone) is run by a local priest, whose products are fashioned with various local clays and glazes. An assortment of handmade cards and other types of local crafts add to the refined selection of pottery.

Papillote Wilderness Retreat (⊠ Trafalgar Falls Rd., Trafalgar, ☎ 767/448−2287) has an intimate gift shop with an excellent selection of local handcrafted goods. The collection of wood carvings by Louis Desire is particularly outstanding.

Tropicrafts (⊠ Corner of Queen Mary St. and Turkey La., Roseau, ☎ 767/448−2747; ⊠ Bay St., Portsmouth, ☎ 767/445−5956) has a back room where you can watch the local ladies weave grass mats. You'll also find a variety of arts and crafts from around the Caribbean; local wood carvings; rum; hot sauces; perfumes; and traditional Carib baskets, hats, and woven mats.

Nightlife and the Arts

Although Dominica is not known for wild nightlife and casinos, the friendly and intimate atmosphere at its numerous bars and hangouts will keep you entertained for hours. If you're looking for jazz, calypso, reggae, steel band, *soca* (a variation of calypso), cadence/zouk, or jing ping—a type of folk music featuring the accordion, the *quage* (a kind of washboard instrument), drums, and a "boom boom" (a percussive instrument)—you're sure to feel the rhythm. Wednesday through Friday nights are really lively on Dominica, and during Carnival, Independence Day, and the summer celebrations, things are especially intense. Indeed, Carnival here is the most spontaneous Carnival in the Caribbean—locals and visitors alike "free-up themselves" in the midst of all the revelry. In addition, the annual World Creole Music Festival in late October is a three-day (and night) extravaganza. Throughout the year most of the larger hotels have live evening entertainment.

Nightlife

QClub (✉ Corner of High St. and Bath Rd., Roseau, ☎ 767/448–2995) is the hottest place to be on a Friday night. You can dance to local music and international hits until dawn—perhaps taking occasional breaks in the cocktail lounge—a respite from all the heart-thumping, foot-stomping rhythms. On your way out, stop at one of the trucks loaded with fresh produce and buy a coconut.

Symes Zee's (✉ 34 King George V St., Roseau, ☎ 767/448–2494) has a band that plays jazz, blues, and reggae. The crowd here often flows out into the street, particularly after 10 on Thursday night. Symes Zee, a gray-bearded blues man, owns this joint and likes to join in with the band to bring down the house in his own special way. There's no cover, and the food, drinks, and cigars sold here are reasonably priced.

Warehouse (✉ Outside Roseau, just past Canefield airport, ☎ 767/449–1303) is *the* place to dance to disco on Saturday nights. DJs are brought in from other islands to ensure that there's variety to all the vibrations. The dancing continues till dawn. Check it out!

The Arts

Arawak House of Culture (✉ Kennedy Ave. near the Government Headquarters, Roseau, ☎ 767/448–2401) is the Dominica's performing arts theater. A number of productions are staged here throughout the year, including plays, recitals, and dance performances.

Caribana's Iris Dangleben Gallery (✉ 31 Cork St., Roseau, ☎ 767/448–7340) is the site of the Dominica Writers' Guild's presentation, "Word, Sound & Power" on the first Wednesday of each month; during this event writers share their works with an audience in an informal and inspirational atmosphere. Don't forget to bring along some of your favorite works, as the audience is always invited to participate. Entrance is free, though donations are welcomed.

Exploring Dominica

Despite the small size of this almond-shape island, it can take a couple hours to travel between the many popular destinations. Many sights are isolated and difficult to find; you may be better off taking an escorted tour (☞ Guided Tours *in* Dominica A to Z, *below*). Note, however, that the divisions of forestry and tourism are working to improve the island's signage and make it easier for visitors to find their way around. If you do go it alone, drive carefully: The roads can be narrow and winding. Plan on eight hours to see the highlights; to fully experience the island, set aside a couple of days and work in some hikes.

Numbers in the margin correspond to points of interest on the Dominica map.

SIGHTS TO SEE

⑫ Cabrits National Park. Just north of the town of Portsmouth, this 250-acre park is—along with Brimstone Hill in St. Kitts, Shirley Heights in Antigua, and Fort Charlotte in St. Vincent—among the most significant historic sites in the Caribbean. The heart of the park is the **Ft. Shirley** military complex. Built by the British between 1770 and 1815, it once comprised 50 major structures, including storehouses that housed 500 men. With the help of the royal navy (which sends sailors ashore to work on the site each time a ship is in port) and local volunteers, historian Lennox Honychurch has restored the fort. On-site there's also a small museum that highlights the natural and historic aspects of the park; a marine park; and a cruise ship terminal, the only such berth in a national park. The cruise-ship facility offers a cooperative crafts shop, a continuously screened film about Ft. Shirley, and occasional live dance or music performances. The herbaceous swamps nearby are an important site for several species of rare birds and plants, including the white mangrove.

⑥ Carib Indian Territory. More than 500 years ago, when Europeans first set foot on Dominica, they were greeted by an indigenous Caribbean tribe who called themselves the Kalinago, but who the Europeans came to call the Caribs. In 1903, after centuries of conflict with other tribes and with European colonists, the Caribs were granted a portion of land (approximately 3,700 acres) on the island's northeast coast, to establish a reservation with their own chief. Today, it's known as Carib Territory. Here you'll find these generous, shy, proud people— who resemble native South Americans—living like most other people in rural Caribbean communities. Many are farmers and fishermen; others are entrepreneurs who have opened little shops, restaurants, and guest houses. Still others are craftspeople whose knowledge of basket weaving, wood carving, and canoe building has been passed down from one generation to the next for centuries.

You can buy exquisitely made Carib baskets at roadside stands in the territory as well as at numerous stores throughout the island. (Note that the prices are ridiculously low considering the high quality of the work; to bargain would be offensive.) The Caribs' long, elegant canoes are created from the trunk of a single gommier tree. If you're lucky, you may catch canoe builders at work. (Feel free to chat with these friendly craftspeople, but if you want to take photographs, it's respectful to ask first.) Be sure to stop by the reservation's Catholic church in Salibia to see its unique altar. It was designed by local historian-author-artist Lennox Honychurch, and was once a canoe.

Within the territory you'll also find **L'Escalier Tête Chien** (Snake's Staircase, with "Tête Chien" being the name of a snake that has a head resembling that of a dog)—a hardened lava flow formation that runs down into the Atlantic. The ocean here is particularly fierce and the shore is full of countless coves and inlets. According to Carib legend, at night the nearby Londonderry Islets metamorphose into grand canoes to take the spirits of the dead out to sea.

Though there's not currently much in the territory that demonstrates the Caribs' ancient culture and customs, plans for a museum showing early Carib life are in the works. In addition, the territory's Karifuna Cultural Group travels around Dominica, performing traditional dance and wearing traditional costumes—their bodies painted and adorned with feathers and beads.

④ Emerald Pool. To reach this spot in the Morne Trois Pitons National Park, you follow a trail that starts at the side of the road near the reception center (it's an easy, 20-minute walk). Along the way, you'll pass lookout points with views of the windward (Atlantic) coast and the forested interior before ending at a swirling basin into which a 50-ft waterfall splashes. If you don't want a crowd, before going find out whether there are cruise ships in port, as this spot is popular with cruise-ship tour groups.

⑩ Indian River. Indian River in Portsmouth was a Carib Indian settlement (hence the name) before the colonists drove them into the interior. Wildlife spotting from a rowboat on the mangrove-lined river is a great way to spend an afternoon. To arrange such a trip, stop by the visitor center at the mouth of the river and ask someone there to recommend a guide. The center is also the headquarters of the Portsmouth Indian River Tour Guides Association, whose president has been lobbying for government regulations that will preserve the area. (Don't allow anyone claiming to be a guide cajole you into taking a powerboat ride up and back down the river.) Most trips take you up as far as the jungle bar, which serves great punches and juices (it's customary to buy your guide a drink, though no guide would ever ask you to do so). Tours take from one to three hours and cost $15–$25.

⑤ Layou River Valley. Along the road west from the Pont Casse roundabout to the village of St. Joseph, there are plantations that grow almost every type of island produce and flower imaginable. At the bottom of a deep gorge—past all the lush terraces of bananas, cocoa, citrus fruits, and coconuts—is the Layou, the island's longest river. In November of 1997, a massive landslide deep in the interior deposited thousands of tons of earth into the Layou, causing a damn to form. Subsequent rains and slides have silted up the entire river and caused flooding in the Hillsbourough Estate area, along the mouth of the river at Layou Village. Scientists say it will take about 7–10 years before the Layou River returns to its original width. Although you can still visit the area, authorities say that it's no longer safe to swim in the river.

⑬ Morne Aux Diables. In the far north of Dominica, this peak soars 2,826 ft above sea level and slopes down to Toucari and Douglas bays and long stretches of dark-sand beach. To reach the mountain, take the road along the Caribbean coast. It twists by coconut, cocoa, and banana trees; past fern-festooned embankments; over rivers; and into villages where brightly painted shanties are almost as colorful as all the flowers.

⑨ Morne Diablotin. In the Northern Forest Reserve, which you can access from the west coast, is Dominica's highest summit (4,747 ft). It takes its name from a bird, known in English as the black-capped petrel, which was prized by hunters in the 18th-century. Though there aren't many of these birds left today, Dominica is still a birder's paradise: 135 species live or migrate here, including bananaquits, exotic flycatchers, and fluorescent hummingbirds. The five- to eight-hour hike up Morne Diablotin isn't for everyone. You need a guide, sturdy hiking shoes, warm clothing, and a backpack with refreshments and a change of clothes (including socks) that are wrapped in plastic to keep them dry. When he's not working as a forest ranger, bird expert Betrand Jno Baptiste takes people on hikes (☞ also Hiking *in* Outdoor Activities and Sports, *above*); if he's not available, ask him to recommend another guide.

③ Morne Trois Pitons National Park. Dedicated as a national park in 1975, and slated to become a United Nations' World Heritage Site, this 17,000-acre (covering 9% of Dominica) swath of lush, mountainous land in the south-central interior is the crown jewel of the Nature Island. Named after one of the highest (4,600 ft) mountains on the island, it contains the world's largest boiling lake, majestic waterfalls, and cool mountain lakes. There are four types of vegetation zones here. Ferns grow 30 ft tall and wild orchids sprout from trees, sunlight leaks through green canopies, and a gentle mist rises over the jungle floor. A system of trails has been developed in the park, but a shortage of funds, excessive rainfall, and the profusion of vegetation all make them hard to maintain. Access to the park is possible from most points of the compass, though the easiest approaches are via the small, mountaintop villages of Laudat (pronounced low-dah) and Cochrane.

About 5 mi out of Roseau, the Wotton Waven Road branches off toward **Sulphur Springs,** where you'll see the belching, sputtering, and gurgling releases of hot springs—evidence of the area's volcanic activity. At the base of Morne Micotrin, you'll find two crater lakes: the first, at 2,500 ft, is **Freshwater Lake.** According to a local legend, the lake is haunted by a vindictive mermaid and a monstrous serpent with a gemlike carbuncle on its forehead. Farther on is **Boeri Lake,** fringed with greenery and with purple hyacinths floating on its surface. But the undisputed highlight of the park is **Boiling Lake.** The world's largest boiling lake, it is a cauldron of gurgling gray-blue water, 70 yards wide and of unknown depth, with water temperatures from 180°F to 197°F. It's believed that the lake is not a volcanic crater but a flooded fumarole—a crack through which gases escape from the molten lava below. The two- to four-hour (one way) hike up to the lake is challenging (be prepared to slip and slide the whole way up). You'll need attire appropriate for a strenuous hike as well as a guide (☞ Hiking *in* Outdoor Activities and Sports, *above*). Most guided trips start early (no later than 8 AM) for this all-day, 7-mi (round-trip) trek. On your way to Boiling Lake, you'll pass through the **Valley of Desolation,** a sight that definitely lives up to its name. Harsh, sulfuric fumes have destroyed virtually all the vegetation in what must have once been a lush forested area. Small hot and cold streams with water of various colors—black, purple, red, orange—web the valley. Stay on the trail to avoid breaking through the crust that covers the hot lava. During this hike, you'll pass rivers where you can refresh yourself with a dip. At the beginning of the trail is the **TiTrou Gorge.** Here you can swim in the pool or relax in the hot water springs along one side. If you're a strong swimmer, you can head up the gorge to a cave (it's about a five-minute swim) that has a magnificent waterfall; a crack in the cave about 50 ft overhead lets in some sunlight.

Also in the National Park are some of the island's most spectacular waterfalls. The 45-minute hike to **Sari Sari Falls,** accessible through the east coast village of La Plaine, can be hair-raising. But the sight of water cascading some 150 ft into a large pool is awesome. So large are these falls that you feel the spray from hundreds of yards away. Just beyond the village of Trafalgar and up a short hill, there's a parking lot where guides are available to take you on a rain-forest trek to the twin **Trafalgar Falls.** If you like a little challenge, let your guide take you up the riverbed to the cool pools at the base of the falls. You need a guide for the arduous 75-minute hike to **Middleham Falls.** The turn-off for the trailhead is just before the village of Laudat. A 60-minute hike will take you to another spectacular waterfall, one where water cascades 100 ft over boulders and vegetation and then into an ice-cold pool (a swim here is absolutely exhilarating). Guides for these hikes are available at the trailheads; still, it's best to arrange a tour before even setting out (☞ Guided Tours *in* Dominica A to Z, *below*).

❼ Northeast Coast. The northeast coast has steep cliffs, dramatic reefs, and rivers that swirl down through forests of mangroves and fields of coconut. The road along the Atlantic, with its red cliffs and windswept trees, crosses the Hatton Garden River before entering the village of **Marigot,** the birthplace of Dominica's Prime Minister Edison James. In the northeastern region there are numerous estates—old family holdings planted with fruit trees. Beyond Marigot and the Melville Hall Airport is the beautiful **Londonderry Estate.** The beach here is inspiring, with driftwood strewn about its velvety black sands (swimming isn't advised owing to the strong currents). Farther along the coast, beyond the village of Wesley (which has a gas station and a shop that sells wonderful bread) and past Eden Estate, there are still more beautiful **beaches**

and coves. The snorkeling and swimming are excellent at Woodford Hill Bay, Hodges Beach, Hampstead Estate, and L'Anse Noir. A stop in the charming community of **Calibishie** is a must; here you'll find bars and restaurants right on the beach. At Bense, a village in the interior just past Calibishie, you can take a connector road to **Chaud dwe** (pronounced show-dweh), a beautiful bathing spot in a valley; the only crowd you're likely to encounter is a group of young villagers frolicking in the 15-ft-deep pool and diving off the 25-ft-high rocks.

⑪ Portsmouth. Portsmouth's past is more illustrious than its present. It was once intended to be the capital of Dominica, thanks to its superb harbor on **Prince Rupert Bay**. In its heyday, as many as 400 ships docked here at one time. In 1782 it was also the site of the decisive Battle of Les Saintes, a naval engagement between the French and the English. The English won that battle, but lost the much tougher fight against malaria-carrying mosquitoes that bred in the nearby swamps. As a result, Roseau, not Portsmouth, is today the capital. Maritime traditions are continued here by the yachting set, and a 2-mi stretch of sandy beaches fringed with coconut trees runs to the Picard Estate area.

❶ Roseau. Roseau is one of the smallest capital cities in the Caribbean. Its wood-and-stone houses, with their brightly painted shutters and roofs, and its bustling marketplace transport you back to an earlier time in the Caribbean. Although you could walk the entire town in about an hour, on a more leisurely stroll you'll get a much better feel of the place. Don't be intimidated by the locals' eagerness to make friends; Dominicans are reputed to be some of the friendliest folk in the Caribbean. Indeed, they're so helpful that, before you can finish asking for directions, they may start to shepherd you through the streets.

Over the past four years, the community has organized programs and projects to preserve the city's architectural heritage, and several interesting buildings have been restored. Of particular note are the **Lilac House** on Kennedy Avenue (it has three types of gingerbread fretwork, latticed veranda railings, and heavy hurricane shutters) and the **J. W. Edwards Building** (it has a stone base and a wooden second-floor gallery), which sits on one of the main corners of the French Quarter at Old and King George V Streets. This area was laid out by the French according to a radial (rather than a grid) plan, so streets such as Hanover, King George V, and Old radiate from one main section called the marketplace. South of the marketplace is the **Fort Young Hotel,** which was built as a British fort in the 18th century; the nearby **state house, public library,** and **Anglican cathedral** are also worth a visit.

The 40-acre **Botanical Gardens,** founded in 1891 as an annex of Kew Gardens, in London, is a great place to relax, stroll, or maybe watch a cricket match. In addition to the extensive collection of tropical plants and trees, there's also a parrot aviary. At the forestry division's office, which is also on the garden grounds, you'll find brochures and booklets on the island's flora, fauna, and national parks. One of the forestry officers, Arlington James, is particularly knowledgeable on these subjects. He or one of the other staff members can also recommend good hiking guides. ⊠ *Forestry Division,* ☎ *767/448–2401, ext. 3417,* ℻ *767/448–7999.* ☉ *Mon. 8–1 and 2–5, Tues.–Fri. 8–1 and 2–4.*

New developments at **Bayfront** on the Dame M. E. Charles Boulevard, have brightened up the waterfront. The old post office now houses the **Dominica Museum.** This labor of love by local writer and historian Lennox Honychurch contains furnishings, documents, prints, and maps that date back hundreds of years; you'll also find an entire Carib hut as well as Carib canoes, baskets, and equipment. The museum is

open Monday–Friday 9–4 and Saturday 9–noon, and admission is
$2. Dr. Honeywell's sister, Sarah, has her own labor of love: the
D'Auchamps Gardens, just outside Roseau en route to Trafalgar. Here
marked walkways pass exotic anthuriums, ferns, heliconias, and many
other plants. An "honesty box" at the information area has a sign re-
questing a $2 donation for your walk and another $1 for the pamphlet
that shows what's in the garden and where. Of course, Sarah herself
may be on hand to take you on a 1-hour tour ($10) followed by some
refreshments. The garden is open daily 9–4.

② **Soufrière.** This lazy, sunbaked village lies within the bay that's part of
the National Marine Park and is nestled at the base of the cliffs that
rise to the village of Galleon. First settled by French lumbermen in the
17th century, the Frenchness of Soufrière (the name comes from the
nearby sulfur springs) can still be heard and felt. Today Soufrière is
primarily a fishing village whose residents are very laid-back and just
as charming as the town itself. (The Catholic church, built of volcanic
stone and painted with red and blue trim, is one of the prettiest on the
island.) It's also the jumping-off point for some exceptional diving and
snorkeling sites within the marine park (☞ Scuba Diving and Snorkeling *in* Outdoor Activities and Sports, *above*). Scotts Head Peninsula,
referred to as Dominica's feet (its the very southern tip of the island)
juts into the bay, separating the Caribbean Sea from the Atlantic
Ocean, and offers wonderful views of Martinique; it's also a good lookout point for spotting sperm whales.

⑧ **Syndicate Nature Trail.** The bird on Dominica's flag, the green and purple Sisserou parrot, is found only on Dominica and is an endangered
species. At last count there were only 60 of these shy and beautiful birds
in the wild. The west coast road at the bend near Dublanc that leads
to the Syndicate Estate also leads to the 200-acre site of **Project Sisserou.**
This protected site, which includes the Syndicate Nature Trail, has been
set aside with the help of some 6,000 schoolchildren, each of whom donated 25¢ to help protect the habitat of the flying pride of Dominica,
as well as countless other species of bird and other types of wildlife.
The trail passes through three types of forest, and is a casual walk (just
bring a sweater and binoculars). Forestry division officials can advise
you on the best times to visit and on the dos and don'ts of visiting a
wildlife preserve.

Dominica A to Z

Arriving and Departing
BY AIRPLANE
American Eagle (☎ 767/448–2181) flies into Melville Hall Airport every
afternoon from San Juan. **Air Guadeloupe** (☎ 767/448–2181) flies from
Pointe-à-Pitre to Canefield Airport twice daily. **Cardinal Airlines** (☎
767/449–0600) flies from Antigua, Barbados, and St. Maarten into
Canefield Airport daily. **Helen Air** (☎ 767/448–2181) serves Dominica
from Barbados and St. Lucia and arrives twice daily at both Melville
Hall and Canefield airports. **LIAT** (☎ 767/448–2421) connects with
flights from the United States on Antigua, Barbados, Guadeloupe,
Martinique, St. Lucia, St. Maarten, and San Juan, arriving at Melville
Hall Airport.

From the Airport: Canefield Airport (✉ About 3 mi north of Roseau,
☎ 767/449–1199) handles only small aircraft and daytime flights; landing here can be a hair-raising experience for those uneasy about flying. Cab fare is about $15 to Roseau. Melville Hall Airport (✉ On
the northeast coast, ☎ 767/445–7100) handles larger planes; the 75-
minute drive to Roseau, which takes you through the island's Central

Forest Reserve, is a tour in itself. The trip costs about $50 by private taxi or $17 per person by co-op cab.

BY FERRY
Express des Isles (✉ c/o Whitchurch Shipping & Tours, ☎ 767/448–2181) has scheduled service Monday, Wednesday, and Friday–Sunday from Guadeloupe in the north to Martinique and St. Lucia in the south, with stops at Les Saintes and Dominica. The crossing, in a jet catamaran, costs $90–$120, takes approximately 90 minutes, and offers superb views of the other islands.

Electricity

Electric voltage is 220/240 AC, 50 cycles. American appliances require an adapter, however, some establishments offer dual voltage (110/120 volts) or may provide transformers and/or adapters.

Emergencies

Ambulance, fire, and police: ☎ 999. **Hospital:** Princess Margaret Hospital (✉ Federation Dr., Goodwill, ☎ 767/448–2231 or 767/448–2233). **Pharmacy:** Jolly's Pharmacy(✉ 12 King George V St., Roseau, ☎ 767/448–3388) is open during regular business hours but can be contacted 24 hours a day by phone.

Festivals and Seasonal Events

Dominica will celebrate its 21st anniversary of independence in 1999, and a special Millennium Commission has been set up to further develop all the island's festivities in 1999 and 2000. The January–February Carnival celebrations—**Mas Domnik**—are slated to be bigger and better than ever. April's **Gospel Festival**—which draws singers from throughout the region—will kick off the anniversary celebrations. Events will continue in August, with the **Dominica Festival of the Arts,** and in September and October with **Independence Day** celebrations. Festivities will culminate in late October with the **World Creole Music Festival,** a four-day music and cultural event that draws performers and Creole music enthusiasts from around the globe.

Getting Around

CAR RENTALS
Driving in Dominica is on the left side, though you can rent vehicles with a steering wheel on either the left or right side. The roads (some of the best in the Eastern Caribbean, barring the occasional pothole) can be narrow, and they meander around the coast and through mountainous terrain. Daily car-rental rates begin at $35 (weekly about $220), plus $7–$17 a day for collision damage insurance (optional). A deposit is usually required, and you'll need to buy a visitor's driving permit (EC$20) at the airports or at the traffic division office on High Street in Roseau.

Most companies offer daily rates, specials depending on the season, and weekly and monthly rates. Try **Avis** (✉ 4 High St., Roseau, ☎ 767/448–5819), **Best Deal Car Rental** (✉ 15 Hanover St., Roseau, ☎ 767/449–9204), **Valley Rent-a-Car** (✉ Goodwill Rd., Roseau, ☎ 767/448–3233), and **Wide Range Car Rentals** (✉ 79 Bath Rd., Roseau, ☎ 767/448–2198).

TAXIS
You can hail taxis at the airports and in Roseau. Rates are fixed by the government, but prices can usually be negotiated. You could also opt for a co-op, sharing a taxi (and the fare) with other clients going in the same direction. Drivers are also happy to offer their services as guides at the cost of $18 an hour, per car of four, with tip extra. It's good to get a recommendation from your hotel or the tourist board

(☞ Visitor Information, *below*) before selecting a driver. For more information and cab company phone numbers, contact **Dominica Taxi Association** (✉ Deep Water Harbour, Woodbridge Bay, ☎ 767/449–8533). Two of the better operators are **Mally's Tour & Taxi Service** (☎ 767/448–3114) and **Julius John's** (☎ 767/449–1968).

VANS

Vans are a cheap, though not always dependable, means of transportation. They cruise the island and, like taxis, stop when hailed. You can also catch a van in Roseau by the bridges over the Roseau River as well as at other designated bus stops. Vans leave regularly from about 6 AM to 8 PM and travel to most communities. They cost EC$1–EC$10.

Guided Tours

Caribana (✉ 31 Cork St., Roseau, ☎ 767/448–7340) conducts walking tours of Roseau that take you to artists' studios, craftspeoples' workshops, and galleries. They also offer architectural heritage tours. The cost of $15 per person includes a guide, maps, and refreshments. **Dominica Tours** (✉ Anchorage Hotel, Castle Comfort, ☎ 767/448–2638) offers a variety of tours (including those tailored to your interests) in sturdy four-wheel-drive, air-conditioned vehicles. Prices range from $25 to $50 per person. **Ken's Hinterland Adventure Tours & Taxi Service** (✉ 10a Old St., Roseau, ☎ 767/448–4850) offers excursions in four-wheel-drive vans (with air-conditioning and two-way radios) with knowledgeable guides. Their botanical and ornithological trips are good. Tours cost from $25 to $50 per person.

Language

The official language is English. Most Dominicans also speak a patois dialect that's a mixture of French, English, and African words.

Money Matters

CURRENCY

The official currency is the Eastern Caribbean dollar (EC$). Figure about EC$2.60 to the US$1. U.S. dollars are readily accepted, but you'll usually get change in EC dollars. Major credit cards are widely accepted, as are traveler's checks. Prices throughout this chapter are quoted in U.S. dollars unless indicated otherwise.

SERVICE CHARGES, TAXES, AND TIPPING

Hotels collect a 5% government hotel occupancy tax, restaurants a 3% government sales tax. The departure tax is US$12 or EC$30. Most hotels and restaurants add a 10% service charge to your bill. A 5% tip for exceptionally good service on top of the service charge is always welcomed; just be sure to check whether the service charge has actually been added and tip accordingly.

Opening and Closing Times

Businesses and **post offices** are open weekdays 8–1 and 2–4, Saturday 8–1. Some **stores** have longer hours, but you should call ahead to confirm them. **Banks** are open Monday–Thursday 8–3, Friday 8–5.

HOLIDAYS

New Year's (Jan. 1–2), Shrove Tuesday (Feb.17), Labour Day (May 1), Whit Monday (May 24), Emancipation Day (Aug. 2), Independence Day and Community Service Day (Nov. 3–4), Christmas, and Boxing Day (Dec. 26).

Passports

U.S. citizens need a valid passport or an original birth certificate along with a government-issued photo ID. U.K. and Canadian citizens must have a valid passport, and all visitors need a return or ongoing ticket.

Precautions

Bring insect repellent. If you're susceptible to motion sickness, be sure to bring along some medication—the roads twist and turn dramatically. If you plan to hike, pack good sneakers and/or rugged hiking boots (trail conditions vary), a backpack, and an extra set of hiking clothes. Unlike neighboring Martinique and Guadeloupe, topless bathing is not in vogue on Dominica. A note in the government tourist guide also states that swimsuits may not be worn in the street. As with all destinations in the world, crime has been known to rear its ugly head on Dominica. It's always wise to secure valuables in hotel safes and not carry too much money or many valuables around. Remember that if you rent a car to tour the island, you may have to park it in a remote area; it's wise not to leave valuables in your vehicle while you're off on a hike or a tour. It's best to visit Grandbay, in the southeast of the island, accompanied by a knowledgeable guide.

Telephones and Mail

To call Dominica from the United States, dial the area code, 767, and the local access code, 44, followed by the five-digit local number. On the island, you need to dial the seven-digit number that follows the area code. The island has a very advanced telecommunication system and, hence, efficient direct-dial international service. All pay phones are equipped for local and overseas dialing and accepting either EC coins or phone cards, which you can buy at many island stores and at the airports.

First-class letters to North America cost EC95¢; postcards cost EC50¢; to the United Kingdom letters cost EC90¢, postcards EC55¢. Dominica is often confused with the Dominican Republic so when addressing letters to the island, be sure to write: The Commonwealth of Dominica, Eastern Caribbean. Islands in this part of the Caribbean do not use postal codes.

Visitor Information

Before you go, contact the **Dominican Tourist Office** (✉ 10 E. 21st St., Suite 600, New York, NY 10010, ☎ 212/475–7542, ℻ 212/460–8287, www.dominica.dm; ✉ 12 Rue de Madrid, 75008 Paris, France, ☎ 33/ 01–53–42–41–15); or the **Office of the Dominica High Commission, London** (✉ 1 Collingham Gardens, London SW5 0HW, ☎ 0171/370– 5194, ℻ 0171/373–8743).

While on Dominica, contact the main office of the **Division of Tourism** (✉ National Development Corp., Valley Rd., Roseau, ☎ 767/448– 2045). The branch at the **post office** (✉ Bay St., ☎ no phone) is open weekdays 8–4, Saturday 9–1. The office at **Canefield Airport** (☎ 767/ 449–1242) is open weekdays 7 AM–6 PM. The one at **Melville Hall Airport** (☎ 767/445–7051) is open weekdays 7 AM–6 PM.

11 Dominican Republic

Updated
by Eileen
Robinson Smith

*I*t's Sunday—family day, party day. Dominicans love a fiesta. A family hosts guests at their
Barahona vacation home. The mountains are
carpeted with emerald rain forests and laced with
silvery streams that spill past fruit trees and flowers to sugary-sand beaches. The children shriek as
they duck into the icy water. A group of men
stands under a cascade, each man trying to endure
the cold shower longer than the next in a friendly
display of machismo. A merengue plays, and a husband dances sensually with his wife.

It's hard to say which is more likely to leave you breathless in the Dominican Republic (D.R.): the unspoiled scenery or the merengue—wonderful, sexy music that Dominicans seem to dance to 365 days a year.
Sprawling over two-thirds of the island of Hispaniola, which it shares
with Haiti, the D.R. is a delightful, almost magical, place. Its people
are friendly and hospitable by nature; if you return their courtesy, they
will do their best to ensure that your vacation is memorable. The D.R.
also happens to be one of the least expensive Caribbean destinations.

Hispaniola has had a stormy history replete with revolutions, military
coups, invasions, epidemics, and bankruptcy. Columbus happened
upon this island on December 5, 1492, and on Christmas Eve his ship,
the *Santa María,* was wrecked on its Atlantic shore. He named it La
Isla Española (The Spanish island), established a small colony, and sailed
back to Spain on the *Pinta.* Santo Domingo, which is on the south coast,
was founded in 1496 by Columbus's brother, Bartholomew Columbus, and Nicolás de Ovando, and during the first half of the 16th century it became the bustling New World hub of Spanish commerce and
culture. In the 17th century, the western third of the island was ceded
to France. A slave revolt there in 1804 resulted in the establishment
of Haiti—the first black republic. Dominicans and Haitians battled for

control of the island throughout the 19th century. The Dominicans declared themselves independent from Haiti in 1844 and from Spain in 1865. The country was, however, bankrupt by the turn of the century.

The United States helped to administer the island's finances, and U.S. Marines occupied the country from 1916 until 1924, when a new Dominican constitution was signed. Rafael Trujillo ruled the D.R. with an iron fist from 1930 until his assassination in 1961. A short-lived democracy was overthrown soon after, and U.S. Marines were sent down yet again in 1965. The country has been relatively stable since the early 1970s, and its government has been a staunch supporter of the United States. Indeed, American influence looms large in Dominican life. Major thoroughfares in the capital, Santo Domingo, are named after American presidents; many Dominicans speak at least rudimentary English and have relatives living in the States; and baseball is a national passion. Still, this is a vibrantly Latin country—at times cool, collected, and laid-back; at times fiery hot, frenetic, and chaotic.

Dominican towns and cities are generally not quaint, neat, or particularly pretty, and poverty is everywhere. However, the ever-increasing role of tourism in the economy is bringing about changes that benefit residents and visitors alike: major highways are being repaved; unsightly electrical lines are being replaced by underground cables; sidewalks, lighting, and signage in urban areas are being improved; and the banks are issuing low-interest loans to people who want to buy and restore colonial buildings. Plans are on the drawing board for still more projects. Clearly the D.R. is realizing more of its vast potential.

The country has several areas with all the attractions and amenities necessary for the perfect island vacation. Santo Domingo is the oldest continuously inhabited city in this half of the globe, and many visitors find it difficult to tear themselves away from its 16th-century Colonial Zone. Sun worshipers head to one of the many beach resorts: Punta Cana, Puerto Plata, Barahona, and Samaná—to name a few. The highest peak in the West Indies, Pico Duarte (10,370 ft), lures hikers to the central mountain range. Ancient sunken galleons and coral reefs divert divers and snorkelers. And everywhere there is the breathtaking scenery, the land ever turning and twisting and towering into mountains before tumbling into the sea.

Lodging

The D.R. has the largest hotel inventory (37,000 rooms and growing) in the Caribbean, and the options range from rustic country inns to some of the world's poshest resorts and Santo Domingo hotels. Puerto Plata alone has 12,500 rooms. The fierce competition translates into some of the best hotel buys in the Caribbean. Be sure to inquire about special packages when you call to reserve; arranging your hotel through a tour operator will cost considerably less, especially if airfare and transfers are included in the price.

Hotels in Santo Domingo generally base their tariffs on the EP (no meals or activities included) and maintain the same room rates throughout the year. In contrast, resorts have high winter and low summer rates—with prices reduced by as much as 50%. Along the north coast, you'll find many all-inclusive properties (three meals a day as well as all beverages, activities, and entertainment included). Those that aren't all-inclusive offer EP, MAP (breakfast and dinner included) and occasionally FAP (all meals). For FAP/MAP, add $20–$30 per person to the rates in the chart below; for all-inclusive plans, add $40–$45 per person.

CATEGORY	COST*
$$$$	over $175
$$$	$125–$175
$$	$75–$125
$	under $75

All prices are for a standard double room, in high season, excluding 10% service charge and 13% tax.

Boca Chica/Juan Dolio

$$$–$$$$ ★ ⊞ **Hamaca Beach Hotel.** A convenient location and plenty of activities are among the draws here. This large, all-inclusive Coral resort is a half hour east of Santo Domingo and close to Las Américas Airport. Its impressive reception area has terra-cotta floors, wicker furnishings, and huge floral arrangements. The stylish, spacious guest rooms have painted-rattan and dark-wood furnishings and floral linens that co-ordinate with pale-green tile floors. There's a lovely champagne-color beach with two huge thatched-roof bars; you'll also find a juice bar, Chinese and Italian restaurants, and a *palapa* (thatched-roof shelter) where live music plays each night. There's quite a bit of casino action here as well, and the disco is a lot of—if not too much—fun. ⊠ *Boca Chica Beach,* ☎ *809/523–4611,* ⅢX *809/566–2436. 465 rooms. 4 restaurants, 3 bars, grill, air-conditioning, 3 pools, 2 tennis courts, archery, horseback riding, bicycles, beach, dive shop, snorkeling, windsurfing, boating, casino, dance club, playground, laundry service, meeting rooms. AE, DC, MC, V. All-inclusive.*

$$$ ⊞ **Talanquera Country and Beach Resort.** At this relaxed family- and couples-oriented resort, guest quarters are in pink-stucco low-rise buildings on 1,260 lushly landscaped acres. You can explore the grounds—perhaps resting beside a stream, a fish pond, or a swimming pool (one has a waterfall)—on foot or on horseback along a riding trail. Rooms are comfortable, though they could use a face-lift. Those in the San Pedro wing are on the beach. At night, the staff puts on shows, and the beachside palapa becomes a disco (drinks are free till 2 AM), where you can move to hot pop-merengue sounds and then cool off at the water's edge. For a taste of fine contemporary Caribbean cuisine, a meal in ☞ L'Ecrevisse restaurant is a must. ⊠ *Juan Dolio Beach,* ☎ *809/526–1510 or 800/971–1467,* ⅢX *809/526–2408. 319 rooms. 4 restaurants, 5 bars, air-conditioning, 3 pools, 2 tennis courts, archery, exercise room, horseback riding, Ping-Pong, volleyball, beach, dive shop, snorkeling, windsurfing, bicycles, dance club, children's program. AE, DC, MC, V. All-inclusive.*

$$–$$$ ★ ⊞ **Capella Beach Resort.** Set on 17 acres punctuated with benches and manicured shrubbery, this grand resort is an eclectic mix of architectural styles—from Victorian to Moorish. Its yellow-stucco exterior is accented with white latticework and columns; coral stonework; and a peaked, red-tile roof. The large, quiet guest rooms have a civilized, almost British air; all have terraces or balconies, some with sea views. Chambermaids wear colorful Dominican costumes instead of standard uniforms, and the concierges speak four languages. The buffet area and the Pescador seafood restaurant are open-air with thatched roofs; the food in the Italian restaurant is laudable. There are often evening shows at the seaside pool—one night you might find a *folklorico* dance ensemble, another night a musical performance. Beginning dive classes and sea kayaking are available. ⊠ *Villas Del Mar (Box 4750, Santo Domingo),* ☎ *809/ 526–1080 or 800/924–5044,* ⅢX *809/526–1088. 283 rooms, 22 suites. 3 restaurants, 3 bars, air-conditioning, minibars, 2 pools, massage, sauna, 2 tennis courts, health club, beach, snorkeling, windsurfing, boating, shops, dance club, recreation room, children's programs, concierge floor, meeting rooms. AE, MC, V. All-inclusive, EP, MAP.*

The Amber Coast

$$$$ **Flamenco Beach Resort, Villas Doradas,** and **Playa Dorada.** Lined up along a mile-long white-sand beach, all three of these high-energy hotels have a variety of social and sports activities, but that's where their similarities end. Guest rooms and public areas at the older Playa Dorada are dowdy and in need of refurbishment. The Villas Doradas is a step up: rooms are attractively decorated and have abstract paintings hung on their walls; all have cable TV and safes. The Chinese restaurant here is surprisingly good, as is the beachside Brazilian eatery. Although busy and crowded, the newer Flamenco is definitely the best of the trio. The public spaces have cobblestone and Andalusian brick floors. The main free-form pool (with a swim-up bar) is designed to resemble a lake, complete with waterfall and lapping waves. Oversize rooms and suites have tasteful rattan furnishings, terra-cotta floors, bright floral upholstery, minibars, cable TV, and balconies or terraces. The Club Miguel Angel—almost a hotel within this hotel—offers premium concierge service. The only thing that's missing at the Flamenco is an ocean view. ✉ *Flamenco: Playa Dorada (Box 532, Puerto Plata),* ☎ *809/320–5084 or 800/545–8089,* FAX *809/320–6319. 582 units. 6 restaurants, 3 bars, air-conditioning, 2 pools, 2 tennis courts, beach, dive shop, snorkeling, windsurfing, boating, waterskiing, shops, concierge floor. AE, DC, MC, V. All-inclusive.* ✉ *Villas: Playa Dorada (Box 1370, Puerto Plata),* ☎ *809/320–3000 or 800/545–8089,* FAX *809/ 320–4790. 244 rooms. 5 restaurants, 2 bars, air-conditioning, in-room safes, pool, golf privileges, 3 tennis courts, beach, dive shop, snorkeling, windsurfing, car rental.* ✉ *Playa: Playa Dorada (Box 272, Puerto Plata),* ☎ *809/586–3988 or 800/545–8089,* FAX *809/320– 4448. 351 rooms, 1 suite. 4 restaurants, 2 bars, ice cream parlor, air-conditioning, pool, golf privileges, tennis court, horseback riding, jogging, beach, water sports, dive shop, snorkeling, windsurfing, bicycles, casino, dance club*

$$$$ ★   **Gran Ventana.** Set on 250 acres of creatively landscaped grounds, this hotel is characterized by style and pizzazz. The lobby is a show piece, with a central fountain, surrounded by wicker chairs, hand-hewn wooden tables, and commodious white sofas with striped pillows. The main buffet dining area is divided into three spaces set in Victorian-style gazebos. Rooms are in two handsome buildings with canopied entrances, ochre-stucco facades, and red-tile roofs. Most rooms have sea views obstructed only by a few palms and a picket fence that helps to keep the beach private and tranquil. During dinner in the Caracol restaurant, the moonlit waves will mesmerize you as you sample the pumpkin soup, the creative salads, and the barbecued meats and seafood. At press time, an addition of 140 spacious rooms was being built between the hotel and the shopping plaza. ✉ *Playa Dorado (Box 22, Puerto Plata),* ☎ *809/412–2525,* FAX *809/412–2526. 303 rooms, 31 suites. 3 restaurants, 3 bars, grocery, air-conditioning, 2 pools, beauty salon, sauna, 3 tennis courts, exercise room, bicycles, beach, snorkeling, windsurfing, boating, shops, dance club, recreation room, convention center, car rental. AE, DC, MC, V. All-inclusive.*

$$$$ **Paradise Beach Club and Casino.** Of all the hotels in Playa Dorada, this is one of the few that fronts the beach. Its low-rise buildings have a unique Victorian-Caribbean design with latticed balconies. Paths wind through palms, birds-of-paradise, and hibiscus from the reception area down to the beach. Rooms are decorated in a carefully chosen palette of pastel greens and blues. Standard rooms have one double or two twin beds; some of the one-bedroom suites have kitchens. In the center of the resort is a free-form pool, with a water channel that winds its way from the pool to the beach. Two of the resort's three restaurants are open-air and on the beach. ✉ *Playa Dorada (Box 337),* ☎

Dominican Republic

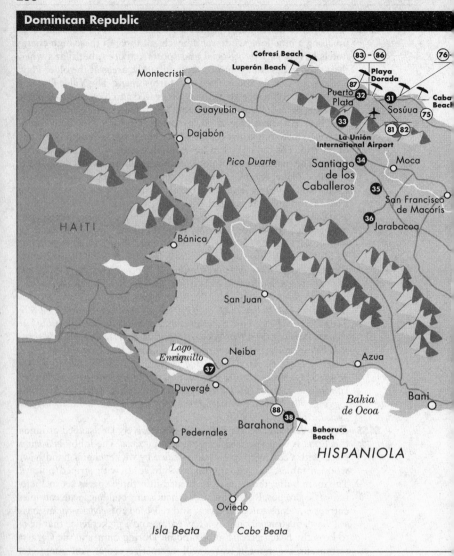

Exploring

Altos de Chavón, **27**
Barahona, **38**
Isla Saona, **28**
Jarabacoa, **36**
Lago Enriquillo, **37**
Laguna Grí-Grí, **30**
Mt. Isabel de Torres, **33**
Parque de los Tres Ojos, **25**
Puerto Plata, **32**

Samaná, **29**
San Pedro de Macorís, **26**
Santiago de los Caballeros, **34**
Sosua, **31**
La Vega Vieja, **35**

Dining

Acuarela, **86**
La Bahía, **44**
La Briciola, **55**

Café de France, **72**
Caribae, **78**
Casa del Río, **63**
Don Pepe, **50**
L'Ecrevisse, **61**
El Conuco, **52**
Fogarate, **41**
Fonda de la Atarazana, **43**
Guajiro's Caribbean Cafe, **76**
Hemingway's Cafe, **81**

Neptuno's Club, **60**
Pappalapasta, **54**
La Puntilla de Piergiorgio, **80**
Restaurant Reina de España, **42**
Restaurant Sully, **47**
Ristorante Sabatini, **79**
Scherezade, **53**
Spaghettissimo, **45**
Vesuvio, **46**
Villa Serena, **73**

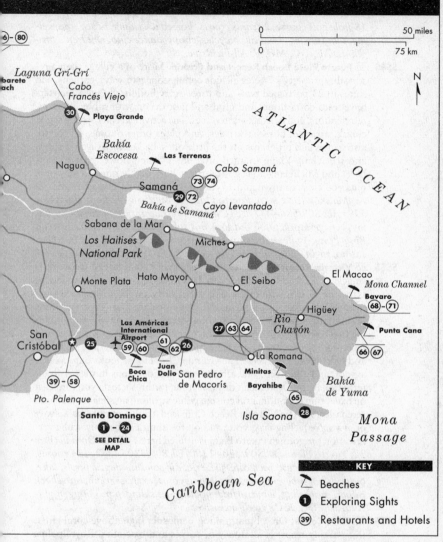

0 — 80

Laguna Grí-Grí
barete
ach
*Cabo
Francés Viejo*
30 ● **Playa Grande**

50 miles
0
0
75 km

N

A T L A N T I C   O C E A N

*Bahía
Escocesa*   **Las Terrenas**
Nagua
Cabo Samaná
Samaná 73 74
29 72
Bahía de Samaná *Cayo Levantado*
Sabana de la Mar
*Los Haitises
National Park* Miches
El Macao
Mona Channel
Monte Plata Hato Mayor El Seibo Higüey **Bavaro**
68 – 71
*Las Américas
International
Airport* 27 63 64 *Río
Chavón* **Punta Cana**
San
Cristóbal ★ 25 59 60 61 66 67
62 26
**Boca
Chica** **Juan
Dolio** San Pedro
de Macorís *La Romana*
39 – 58 **Minitas** *Bahía
de Yuma*
Bayahibe
Pto. Palenque 65
28
Isla Saona *Mona
Passage*

Santo Domingo
1 – 24
**SEE DETAIL
MAP**

Caribbean Sea

KEY
⌇ Beaches
① Exploring Sights
㊴ Restaurants and Hotels

Lodging

Bavaro Beach
Resort, **68**

Cabarete Beach
Hotel, **75**

Capella Beach
Resort, **62**

Caribbean Village
Bavaro, **71**

Casa Bonita, **88**

Casa de Campo, **64**

Casa del Mar, **65**

Flamenco Beach
Resort, Villas Doradas,
and Playa Dorada, **82**

Gran Hotel Lina
and Casino, **58**

Gran Ventana, **83**

Hamaca Beach
Hotel, **59**

Hotel El Embajador
and Casino, **49**

Hotel Gran Bahía, **74**

Hotel Hispaniola, **56**

Hotel Palacio, **57**

Hotel Santo
Domingo, **39**

Inter-Continental
Hotel V
Centenario, **51**

Jaragua Renaissance
Resort and Casino, **48**

Marco Polo Club, **79**

Melia Bavaro, **69**

Melia Santo
Domingo Hotel, **40**

Natura Park, **70**

Paradise Beach
Club and Casino, **85**

Paradisus Punta
Cana, **67**

Puerto Plata Beach
Resort and Casino, **87**

Punta Cana Beach
Resort, **66**

Sand Castle, **77**

Talanquera Country
and Beach Resort, **61**

Victoria Resort, **84**

Villa Serena, **73**

809/320–3663 or 800/752–9236 (reservations service), ℻ 809/320–4858. 436 rooms, 73 suites. 3 restaurants, 3 bars, air-conditioning, pool, 18-hole golf course, 2 tennis courts, horseback riding, beach, snorkeling, windsurfing, boating, bicycles, shops, dance club, children's programs. AE, DC, MC, V. All-inclusive.

$$$$ 🏨 **Puerto Plata Beach Resort and Casino.** More of a village than a resort, this property's 7 acres include cobblestone pathways, gardens, and suites in 23 porticoed two- and three-story buildings. Guest quarters have terra-cotta floors and mint and jade decor, with cable TV, mini-refrigerators, and balconies or terraces. The activities center sets up scuba clinics, arranges horseback rides, and plans other outings. There are also games and programs for the little ones. La Lechuza disco is glitzy, and the Ylang-Ylang (named after the evening flower that blooms here) and Michelangelo restaurants are both highly rated. A stay here puts you close to town and 15 minutes by car from Playa Dorada. ✉ Av. Malecón (Box 600), Puerto Plata, ☎ 809/586–4243 or 800/348–5395, ℻ 809/586–4377. 216 units. 4 restaurants, bar, air-conditioning, refrigerators, pool, outdoor hot tub, 4 tennis courts, basketball, Ping-Pong, volleyball, snorkeling, windsurfing, boating, bicycles, casino, nightclub, children's programs. AE, MC, V. All-inclusive.

$$$$ 🏨 **Victoria Resort.** This study in pastels and gingerbread fretwork is
★   smack in the middle of the Playa Dorada golf course with a view of Isabel de Torres Mountain. The open, airy public areas have such touches as wicker furniture, marble tile floors, and carnival masks hung on mint green walls. Deluxe accommodations—in a two-story building that's set apart form other structures in the complex for peace and quiet—are spacious and have plantation-style wicker furniture, tile floors, and balconies or terraces. The Grande Club House looks onto a lake, a pool, and a hot tub. The alfresco café has delicious buffets with international and Dominican dishes. At the Jardin Victoria you can feast on exceptional Continental cuisine while strolling musicians stroll and serenade you. The Victoria Beach Club is just a five-minute walk away or, if you're feeling lazy, you can hop the shuttle. The only scuba certification program in Puerto Plata is offered here. ✉ Playa Dorada (Box 22, Puerto Plata), ☎ 809/320–1200, ℻ 809/320–4862. 124 rooms, 66 suites. 2 restaurants, café, pizzeria, air-conditioning, 2 pools, lake, outdoor hot tub, golf privileges, tennis court, exercise room, horseback riding, snorkeling, windsurfing, boating, jet skiing, parasailing, nightclub. AE, DC, MC, V. All-inclusive.

$$–$$$ 🏨 **Sand Castle.** On a breathtaking peninsula high above coral cliffs, this striking resort is a fantasy of curves and balconies. Royal palms rise majestically from the beachside gardens. Accommodations are built around tempting shops and small eateries, all surrounded by artistically pruned trees and shrubs. Rooms and suites are spacious, and most have balconies with views of the bay and beach. The decor includes such appointments as attractive wall hangings and stained-glass windows. Shuttles carry you to Sosua Beach. You can also keep busy by participating in the organized activities or seeing the sights in the nearby village of Sosua. Or you can simply languish beside the cliffside pool. ✉ Puerto Chiquito, Sosua, ☎ 809/471–5111, ℻ 809/471–5112. 240 units. 2 restaurants, 7 bars, pizzeria, snack bar, air-conditioning, 2 pools, horseback riding, snorkeling, windsurfing, boating, bicycles, shops, dance club, convention center. AE, MC, V. All-inclusive.

$$ 🏨 **Marco Polo Club.** In an enclosed property with gardens and a lagoon, this Victorian-style complex has three stories of freshly painted and remodeled luxury apartments equipped with kitchens, tile baths with Jacuzzis, and balconies with French doors that open to the sea.

The decor is tasteful with ceramic-tile floors, tropical pastel color schemes, and high-quality rattan furnishings. Prices include Continental breakfast, though there's a $10 room-rate surcharge if you plan to share an apartment with three or more friends or family members. Even so, this hotel is a good deal, indeed. A meal in the French restaurant or the Italian ☞ **Ristorante Sabatini** is likely to be memorable. Note that Holland International sometimes books the whole place for its package tours, so reserve well in advance. At press time, construction had been halted on a 50-room waterfront addition, but do inquire about it when making a reservation. ⊠ *El Batey, Sosua,* ☎ *809/571–3128,* 𝖥𝖠𝖷 *809/571–3233. 8 apartments. 2 restaurants, bar, air-conditioning, kitchenettes, 2 pools, beach, dance club. AE, MC, V. CP.*

$-$$ ⊞ **Cabarete Beach Hotel.** Set on a tantalizing curve of golden sand, this
★ small delightful hotel is ideal for those who love to windsurf or swim (the surrounding reef protects the beach from fierce breakers). The highly recommended deluxe rooms have full ocean views and air-conditioning. Standard rooms (some with air-conditioning) are slightly smaller and noisier. All rooms are decorated with bright framed prints and blond-wood furnishings, including rocking chairs. The lovely terrace restaurant is known for its bountiful breakfast buffets of homemade breads, muffins, and pastries. The Tropical Bar—a riot of painted gourds and coconuts, colorful murals, and thatching—prides itself on its fresh fruit juices and more than 50 exotic libations. The hotel staff is unfailingly helpful and courteous, and the BIC Windsurf Center is right next door. ⊠ *Cabarete,* ☎ *809/571–0755,* 𝖥𝖠𝖷 *809/571–0831. 24 rooms. Restaurant, bar, beach, windsurfing. AE, MC, V. EP, MAP.*

Barahona

$-$$ ⊞ **Casa Bonita.** In the scenic southwest, this gentrified country inn is a charming alternative to the high-rise hotels and busy all-inclusive properties. Julio and Virginia Schiffino expanded their home and added 12 criollo-style cottages with roofs of thatched *cana,*(a type of palm) rough-hewn walls, and simple furnishings. Six have air-conditioning, and all face the sea or the verdant rain forest of the Sierra de Bahoruco and two mountain rivers. The open-air gallery, adjacent sitting areas, and restaurant overlook the pool area and are tastefully appointed with comfortable sofas and scads of colorful throw pillows. By 1999, the owners' nearby deluxe Bahoruco Beach Resort should be fully operational. ⊠ *In foothills, 8 mi from Barahona,* ☎ *809/696–0215,* 𝖥𝖠𝖷 *809/223–0548. Restaurant, bar, pool. AE, MC, V. EP, MAP.*

La Romana

$$$$ ⊞ **Casa del Mar.** This new deluxe resort, its whimsical gingerbread fretwork awash in Caribbean colors, is on an exceptional palm-fringed ribbon of white sand close to the airport and ☞ **Casa de Campo**. Most of the attractive guest rooms have views of the sea, the spectacular pools, or both. In one of the dining areas, buffets of fresh, tasty dishes are served beneath stunning chandeliers. (Be sure to check out the sundae bar, which has ice cream in such exotic flavors as coconut or corn). There's more fine dining to be found in the on-site Asian and Italian restaurants. ⊠ *Bayahibe Bay,* ☎ *809/221–8880 or 800/472–3985,* 𝖥𝖠𝖷 *809/221–8881. 600 rooms. 4 restaurants, bar, air-conditioning, 2 pools, 2 tennis courts, archery, volleyball, beach, dive shop, snorkeling, boating, windsurfing, dance club. AE, DC, MC, V. All-inclusive.*

$$$-$$$$ ⊞ **Casa de Campo.** "House in the Country" is an understated appel-
★ lation for this enormous complex. It sprawls over 7,000 acres and can accommodate some 3,000 guests (indeed, many wealthy Dominicans have luxurious second homes here). It includes 350 casitas (two-story buildings with large guest quarters) and 150 one-, two-, and three-bedroom villas with kitchens. D.R.-born Oscar de la Renta helped design

much of the resort, owns a villa here, and has a boutique in the on-site Altos de Chavón—a re-creation of a medieval Mediterranean village that is also an artist's colony. Also on-site are two 18-hole golf courses (one of them—called Teeth of the Dog—has seven holes that skirt the sea and is rated one of the top courses in the Caribbean), 13 tennis courts, horseback riding trails, polo grounds, an archery area, a trap shooting area, a 5,000 seat amphitheater at which such big-name entertainers as Julio Iglesias perform, and La Romana Airport. Minibuses provide free transportation around the resort and to tiny Minetas Beach. You can also rent golf carts (they're included in the price of the villas), scooters, and bicycles. Excellent children's programs—including "Kid's Night Out," when children spend a supervised evening at a center with games and videos—make this complex perfect for families. About the only disadvantage is that most accommodations don't even have a glimpse of the sea. ⊠ *5 min cab ride from La Romana (Box 140, La Romana),* ☎ *809/523–3333 or 800/877–3643 (reservations service),* ℻ *809/523–8548. 500 units. 9 restaurants, 8 bars, air-conditioning, 14 pools, hot tub, sauna, 2 18-hole golf courses, 13 tennis courts, archery, health club, horseback riding, dive shop, snorkeling, windsurfing, boating, fishing, bicycles, shops, theater, children's programs. AE, DC, MC, V. All-inclusive, EP, MAP.*

Punta Cana

$$$$ 🏨 **Caribbean Village Bavaro.** This well-managed, sprawling property—a member of the Allegro family—has a glorious white-sand beach. (To reach it, you pass through an impressive palapa entrance.) All rooms have balconies; waterfront rooms are both minimalistic and tastefully decorated with pastel color schemes and many potted plants. Though most of the activity seems to center around the pool, there are plenty of beachside water sports (motorized activities like jet skiing cost extra). The resort's buffet meals are elaborate affairs, with such touches as a carving station and a pasta bar with bottles of flavored oil. ⊠ *Cabeza de Toro (Box 68), Bavaro,* ☎ *809/221–3139; 305/460–8961 or 800/ 858–2258 (reservations services);* ℻ *305/460–8964. 540 rooms. 3 restaurants, 3 bars, air-conditioning, pool, 4 tennis courts, beach, snorkeling, windsurfing, boating. All-inclusive. AE, MC, V.*

$$$$ 🏨 **Paradisus Punta Cana.** Billed as the "all-inclusive exclusive beach resort," the Paradise, like its sister property the ☞ **Melia Bavaro,** has an open-air lobby of lagoons and rock gardens. Trilingual concierges stand ready to handle your every request. Rooms are luxurious, with tropical motifs and furnishings. The path to the elegant casino (players dress accordingly) is punctuated by sculptures. From the simple grilled seafood and meats at the beach palapas to the sophisticated international fare at the à la carte Romantico restaurant, the cuisine here is outstanding. You can work off all the calories by participating in one of many activities—everything from archery to windsurfing. Weddings here are blissful, and the honeymoon packages are exceptional deals. ⊠ *Bavaro Beach,* ☎ *809/687–9923 or 800/33–MELIA (reservations service),* ℻ *809/687–0752. 434 suites. 6 restaurants, 3 bars, air-conditioning, 4 tennis courts, beauty salon, archery, health club, windsurfing, children's programs. AE, DC, MC, V. All-inclusive.*

$$$–$$$$ 🏨 **Melia Bavaro.** A long, tropically landscaped drive leads to the Melia's huge, open-air lobby, with a dramatic lagoon. Walkways traverse the property's lush gardens and mangrove forest. The main hotel overlooks a pool that's as peaceful as an afternoon siesta, and another pool with a swim-up bar is alongside a white-sand beach. For the best quarters, ask for a suite in one of the bungalows that dot the grounds. The Licey restaurant is on a pond and has a standout gourmet menu. After a buffet dinner, lights are dimmed, candles are lit, and the Bel-

grade Symphony Quartet plays while gliding around the pond in a small boat. You can finish up the evening at the Coco disco-pub or take the shuttle bus to the casino at the Melia's sister hotel, the ☞ **Paradisus Punta Cana.** A new shopping center, Plaza, is just next to the resort. ✉ *Bavaro Beach,* ☎ *809/221–2311 or 800/33–MELIA (reservations service),* ⨳ *809/686–5427. 772 suites. 7 restaurants, 2 bars, air-conditioning, 2 pools, beauty salon, hot tub, archery, health club, horseback riding, beach, snorkeling, windsurfing, boating. AE, DC, MC, V. EP, FAP, MAP.*

$$$–$$$$ ▦ **Natura Park.** Here's a new concept: an eco-sensitive all-inclusive. At this squeaky clean, environmentally correct establishment, meals are made from wholesome, all-natural ingredients, and furniture is handcrafted from the coco palms that were cut down to make room for the property's gardens, walkways, and man-made lakes. The grounds also have what remains of a coconut plantation as well as a mangrove forest and a natural lake. Guest rooms are in 12 buildings that put stone, wood, and cane to very good use. The outdoor à la carte restaurant looks onto a spectacular pool (with a swim-up bar) and beyond to Bavaro Beach. In addition to the usual resort-type activities, here you can learn to dance the merengue, take cooking classes, or enjoy a full hour of horseback riding each day. ✉ *Bavaro Beach,* ☎ *809/221–2626 or 888/ 628–8727,* ⨳ *809/221–6060. 523 rooms, 6 suites. 3 restaurants, 4 bars, 2 pools, hot tub, 4 tennis courts, horseback riding, beach, windsurfing, boating, children's programs. AE, MC, V. All-inclusive.*

$$–$$$$ ▦ **Bavaro Beach Resort.** On a divine, 20-mi stretch of Bavaro Beach,
★ you'll find this huge complex of five low-rise luxury hotels. Each room has a private balcony or terrace, cable TV, and a refrigerator. Rooms in the Bavaro Beach Hotel are the largest and are decorated with furnishings made of wood and hemp and with bright, striped upholstery. Rooms in the Bavaro Gardens Hotel are done in vivid primary colors. The Bavaro Casino Hotel has several duplex suites that are ideal for families. The Bavaro Golf Hotel has suites with kitchenettes. The Bavaro Palace is the most refined and subdued of the five hotels. A social director coordinates a wide variety of daily activities, and there's nightly entertainment at each hotel. The complex also has a casino, a nightclub with Las Vegas–style reviews that showcase island culture, and two discos. Most important, the staff is friendly, and the beach is fabulous. ✉ *Higüey,* ☎ *809/686–5797,* ⨳ *809/686–5680. 1,953 units. 9 restaurants, 14 bars, air-conditioning, 7 pools, beauty salon, 18-hole golf course, 6 tennis courts, archery, horseback riding, beach, dive shop, snorkeling, windsurfing, boating, waterskiing, bicycles, shops, casino, 2 dance clubs, nightclub. AE, MC, V. FAP, MAP.*

$$–$$$$ ▦ **Punta Cana Beach Resort.** Several coral-and-aquamarine buildings dot the lush grounds here. The eclectically decorated lobby has Dominican crafts, birdcages, and lots of plants. Rooms are spare, and though some need a little work, most are pleasant in shades of jade, coral, and cream with wicker furnishings. Opt for one of the 54 new deluxe rooms, each with a balcony and a kitchenette, in the Cocotal building. The lagoonlike pool has a swim-up bar, and you can look beyond it to the gorgeous beach and the huge entertainment palapa. Among the many activities are guided nature walks on a marked trail through a mahogany forest (where you'll find several natural freshwater pools) and nightly musical entertainment. Nearby there's an 18-hole golf course. ✉ *7 mi from Punta Cana International Airport (Box 1083, Santo Domingo),* ☎ *809/221–2262 or 800/972–2139,* ⨳ *809/687–8745. 395 units. 5 restaurants, 3 bars, grocery, air-conditioning, pool, beauty salon, golf privileges, 4 tennis courts, beach, dive shop, snorkeling, windsurfing, boating, waterskiing, dance club, baby-sitting, children's programs, playground. AE, DC, MC, V. EP, MAP.*

Samaná

$$$$ ⊞ **Hotel Gran Bahía.** Overdevelopment has not yet reached the water's
★ edge near this small hotel. This Victorian-style building is all turrets,
gables, and fretwork; it also has graceful verandas that overlook the
pool and the sea beyond (in winter, you may see whales offshore). Guest
rooms are very large and have cheerful floral prints, tiled floors, and
pastel watercolor paintings. The grand yet welcoming reception area
and three-story, white, colonnaded, atrium surround a spectacular
fountain flanked by cozy nooks—perfect places to sip a cocktail, read,
or both. The superb views make breakfast on your private balcony a
treat. Dining in the alfresco restaurant is pleasant, or you can try a meal
in the pastel-pretty indoor eatery. In the pool area, which looks like a
Mexican town square, you may be serenaded by musicians playing Spanish ballads. ⊠ *10 min from Samaná (Box 2024, Santo Domingo),* ☎
809/538–3111, FAX *809/538–2764. 110 rooms. 2 restaurants, bar, air-
conditioning, pool, beauty salon, golf privileges, 2 tennis courts,
archery, exercise room, horseback riding. AE, MC, V. All-inclusive.*

$$ ⊞ **Villa Serena.** This little-known gem is down the beach from the fish-
★ ing village of Las Galeras and at the end of the long, scenic road from
Puerto Plata. Croatian expats Natasha Despotovic and Kresimir Zovko
have worked hard to make this an intimate place. Each room is indi-
vidually decorated and has a lanai that overlooks the Bahía de Rincón.
The more expensive rooms have air-conditioning; the rest have ceiling
fans. Prices include breakfast, and the ☞ **Villa Serena** restaurant serves
some of the best food on the peninsula. The large veranda is an ex-
cellent spot for a cocktail. The hotel has a private beach in front, as
well as a small, free-form pool. ⊠ *Las Galeras (Box 51–1),* ☎ *809/
696–0065,* FAX *809/538–2545. 11 rooms. Restaurant, bar, pool, horse-
back riding, beach, dive shop, snorkeling, bicycles. AE, MC, V. CP.*

Santo Domingo

$$$$ ⊞ **Inter-Continental Hotel V Centenario.** Well-heeled travelers have
★ made this spot on the Malecón their top choice. Marble floors and pil-
lars give the reception area a polished look. Rooms are decorated in
earth tones—a refreshing touch in a part of the world so in love with
pastels—Dominican handicrafts, and burnished rattan furnishings.
Each has a mini-refrigerator, cable TV, and a safe. You can try your
luck at the casino or relax in an easy chair in the lounge. The casual
coffee shop looks out over the Caribbean, and the bar and alfresco
seafood restaurant share a seaview terrace with the small pool. ⊠ *Av.
George Washington 218,* ☎ *809/221–0000,* FAX *809/221–2020. 200
rooms, 26 suites. 3 restaurants, 2 bars, air-conditioning, in-room safes,
refrigerators, pool, sauna, tennis court, squash, shops, casino, free
parking. AE, MC, V. EP, FAP, MAP.*

$$$ ⊞ **Hotel El Embajador and Casino.** Although this landmark hotel and
casino isn't on the Malecón, it's in a safe, quiet, residential neighbor-
hood close by. At press time the hotel was closed for a top-to-toe renovation—one that's expected to make it as spectacular today as it was
in its prime, when Trujillo reigned. The spacious lobby will remain a
social hub, and near its fountain, orchestras will still perform. Rooms
will be completely redone; those on the fifth and sixth floors will be
transformed into executive rooms with extra amenities. The large pool
will remain open to the public and will no doubt continue as a popular weekend gathering place. A new Continental restaurant will have
a Florentine theme. ⊠ *Av. Sarasota 65,* ☎ *809/221–2131 or 800/843–
3311 (reservations service),* FAX *809/532–4494. 304 rooms, 12 suites.
2 restaurants, 2 bars, air-conditioning, minibars, pool, 4 tennis courts,
exercise room, shops, casino, concierge floor, business services. AE, DC,
MC, V. CP, MAP.*

$$$ ⊞ **Hotel Santo Domingo.** Surrounded by walled gardens and over-
★ looking the Caribbean, this in-town getaway is favored by business-
people and diplomats (many VIPs check into one of the Excel Club's
eight rooms, which have king-size beds and offices with speaker phones,
printers, and modem lines). Oscar de la Renta helped to design the in-
teriors of the guest rooms, all of which have balconies. The elegant Cafe-
tel restaurant serves buffet lunches and hosts an Italian night, merengue
combos draw locals to Las Palmas for dancing, and the Marrakesh Café
& Bar attracts a sophisticated after-work crowd. Its Casablanca-style
decor complements that of the lobby with its red-enameled pagoda chairs
and potted palms. A trellised arcade leads to a pool surrounded by green-
ery. ⊠ *Avs. Independencia and Abraham Lincoln (Box 2112),* ☎ *809/
221–7111 or 800/877–3643,* FAX *809/221–1511. 220 rooms. 2 restau-
rants, 2 bars, air-conditioning, pool, beauty salon, sauna, 3 tennis
courts, meeting rooms, car rental, helipad. AE, MC, V. CP.*

$$–$$$ ⊞ **Melia Santo Domingo Hotel.** In 1997 the Spanish hotel company,
Sol Melia, signed the management contract for this 11-story high-rise
on the Malecón. (At press time, the hotel's owners were planning $5
million dollars' worth of renovations.) The hotel has many business
amenities, including secretarial services and cellular phone rentals. For
those in search of leisure activities, there are tennis courts, a gym, and
a glorious rooftop pool; an excellent piano bar, El Yarey; and a casino,
where the usual drinks and cigarettes are on the house, and hostesses
dish out a rich, flavorful soup to help gamblers to keep up their
strength. ⊠ *Av. George Washington 365 (Box 8326),* ☎ *809/686–6666
or 800/33–MELIA (reservations service),* FAX *809/687–8150. 242
rooms, 16 suites. 3 restaurants, 2 bars, piano bar, air-conditioning, mini-
bars, no-smoking rooms, pool, beauty salon, 2 tennis courts, health
club, shops, casino, dance club, business services, travel services. AE,
DC, MC, V. EP, FAP, MAP.*

$$ ⊞ **Gran Hotel Lina and Casino.** Freshly painted in bold Caribbean colors (from mango to hot pink), the exterior of this hotel now dazzles
just as much as its interior. In public areas, marble floors gleam, mirrored brass colonnades sparkle and shine, and modern artwork intrigues.
Guest rooms (done in surprisingly staid shades of dusky rose) have minibars and huge marble baths. In the Lina restaurant, Santo Domingo's
elite dine on Continental and Dominican fare (often made using the
same secret recipes once used to prepare meals for Trujillo himself),
while a pianist tickles the ivories. In a palm-studded courtyard at the
rear of the hotel, you'll find a large pool, a children's pool, a gym, a
whirlpool, and a sauna. The hotel staff is helpful and very efficient. ⊠
Av. Máximo Gomez (Box 1915), ☎ *809/563–5000,* FAX *809/686–5521.
214 rooms, 4 suites. Restaurant, coffee shop, piano bar, air-conditioning,
minibars, 2 pools, hot tub, sauna, 2 tennis courts, health club, casino,
nightclub, business services. AE, DC, MC, V. EP, FAP, MAP.*

$$ ⊞ **Hotel Hispaniola.** This place draws a young, fun crowd including
many Italian visitors. The Spanish-style lobby is connected to a casino
that's full of striking paintings, stained-glass details, and towering flo-
ral arrangements. A small arcade of shops leads to a bar-café and one
of the hotel's restaurants, which serves a Sunday buffet. Guest rooms
were refurbished in 1997, and have wicker and handcrafted pine fur-
nishings, new carpeting, cable TV, and balconies. Flanking the well-
manicured pool area are 13 garden rooms; some of those on the second
floor have terraces with sea views. The gracious staff deserves very high
marks. Note that a stay here gets you privileges at the ☞ **Hotel Santo
Domingo** across the street. ⊠ *Avs. Independencia and Abraham Lin-
coln (Box 2112),* ☎ *809/221–1511 or 800/877–3643,* FAX *809/535–
4050. 165 rooms. 2 restaurants, bar, air-conditioning, minibars, pool,
casino, dance club, meeting rooms. AE, MC, V. CP.*

$$ ⊞ **Jaragua Renaissance Resort and Casino.** Fourteen acres of gar-
★ dens, waterfalls, and fountains surround this pink, contemporary com-
plex—a true oasis in the midst of the bustling city. Glamour and luxury
abound, from the penthouses to the 20,000-square-ft casino. Local and
big-name entertainers perform in the 800-seat La Fiesta Showroom.
The new Renaissance Club—29 rooms on executive, concierge floors—
often sells out on weeknights. Twelve cabanas surround the Olympic-
size free-form pool. Rates are based on the view: garden, pool, or ocean.
Rooms in the garden building have recently been renovated. The cour-
teous, professional staff always makes you feel welcome. ⊠ *Av. George
Washington 367,* ☎ *809/221–2222, 800/331–3542, or 800/468–
3571 (reservations service);* FAX *809/686–0528. 292 rooms, 8 suites. 3
restaurants, 4 bars, air-conditioning, minibars, pool, hot tubs, saunas,
spa, golf privileges, 4 tennis courts, casino, dance club, recreation
room, concierge floors. AE, MC, V. EP, FAP, MAP.*

$ **Hotel Palacio.** An 18th century building, once the residence of former
president Buenaventura Baez, houses this unique hotel in the heart of
the Colonial Zone. It looks like a museum: antique lights illuminate
the bar, and the public spaces are enhanced with Spanish colonial an-
tiques, reproductions, and just enough artwork to give it a gallery ef-
fect. Rooms are small and *very* simple; a few have kitchenettes. On the
roof you'll find a gym and whirlpool, and although there is no on-site
restaurant, there is a patio bar. Businesspeople gravitate to this hotel,
not only because of its affordable rates, but also because of its many
business amenities—secretarial services, Internet facilities, and pro-
fessional guides. Note that the area around the hotel is poorly lit and
deserted at night; be sure to take a cab in your evening comings and
goings. ⊠ *106 Calle Duarte,* ☎ *809/682–4730,* FAX *809/687–5535.
16 rooms, 2 suites. Bar, in-room safes, minibars, hot tub, exercise room,
business services. AE, MC, V. EP.*

Dining

The island's culinary repertoire includes Spanish, Latin American, Ital-
ian, Middle Eastern, Japanese, and Chinese cuisines—not to mention
a considerable number of American fast-food options. Every year,
there are more establishments that serve contemporary Caribbean
dishes as well as places that offer *nueva cocina* (new kitchen) Dominicana.
Regardless of the type of restaurant, if seafood is on the menu, it's bound
to be fresh.

Among the best Dominican specialties are *sancocho* (a thick stew usu-
ally made with five different meats and served with rice and avocado
slices), *arroz con pollo* (rice with chicken), and *plátanos* (plantains) in
all their tasty varieties. Many meals are finished with *majarete,* a corn-
meal custard. Shacks and stands that serve cheap eats are an integral
part of the culture and landscape. They might offer johnnycakes (fried
dough stuffed with everything from chicken to seafood) or pork sand-
wiches laden with onions, tomatoes, pickles, and seasonings. Presidente
is the best local beer; Barceló *anejo* (aged) rum is as smooth as cognac,
though Brugal is the most popular local brand.

What to Wear
In resort areas, shorts and bathing suits under beach wraps are usu-
ally (but not always) acceptable at breakfast and lunch. For dinner, long
pants, skirts, and collared shirts are the norm. Restaurants tends to be
more formal in Santo Domingo, both at lunch and at dinner, with long
pants required for men and dresses suggested for women. Ties are not
required anywhere but jackets are (even at the midday meal) in some
of the finer establishments.

CATEGORY	COST*
$$$	over $30
$$	$15–$30
$	under $15

per person for a three-course meal, excluding drinks, 10% service charge, and 13% sales tax

Boca Chica

SEAFOOD

$–$$ ✕ **Neptuno's Club.** This breezy seaside eatery is little more than a shack perched above the water and seemingly held together by the barnacles of marine memorabilia (from giant turtle shells to driftwood). The best tables are at the far end of the dock. Stay with the simple, fresh fish dishes: paella, grilled sea bass and grouper, lobster, and the sautéed squid served sizzling in the pan. True gourmet this isn't, but the lively crowd and gin-clear waters make it memorable. ⊠ *Boca Chica Beach,* ☎ *809/523–4703. MC, V. Closed Mon.*

La Romana

ECLECTIC

$$–$$$ ✕ **Casa del Río.** You can look out over the Río Chavón while you dine
★ in the candlelit stone cellar at this re-creation of a 16th-century castle. The imaginative decor is a mere backdrop for the creative cuisine of chef Philippe Mongereau. He blends classical French methodology with indigenous ingredients; after a recent trip to Japan, he has added a few Asian touches as well. The sautéed salmon is served on a bed of leeks and shiitaki mushrooms—all topped with a picante cassis sauce. The marinated-squid-and-arugula salad has a sesame oil dressing, and the steamed sea scallops are wrapped in cabbage leaves and served with pureed caviar in a Japanese vinaigrette. The warm, sugar-encrusted chocolate-pudding cake is divine. ⊠ *Altos de Chavón,* ☎ *809/523–3333, ext. 2345. Reservations essential. AE, DC, MC, V. No lunch.*

The Amber Coast

CARIBBEAN/CREOLE

$–$$ ✕ **Guajiro's Caribbean Cafe.** Thatching, nautical paraphernalia dangling from the rafters, and rough-hewn wood tables and chairs give this casual eatery a rustic feel. Try the green plantain soup or *yuca* (an island tuber) in *mojo* (a lime, garlic, and olive oil marinade) to start, then *pollo à la merengue* (sweet and spicy coriander chicken) or *filetillo saltado* (catch of the day, usually in *sofrito*, a savory sauce of garlic, green pepper, and tomato). The Cuban sandwiches burst with roast pork, ham, cheese, and pickles. Latin jazz nights are scheduled regularly and draw a rollicking crowd. ⊠ *Calle Pedro Clisande, El Batey, Sosua,* ☎ *809/571–2161. Reservations not accepted. AE, MC, V.*

CONTEMPORARY

$$ ✕ **Acuarela.** Named after a fragrant, white, tropical flower, this café is set in a 120-year-old home surrounded by a garden. It's a hip, contemporary place with some very creative cuisine. The clientele—well-heeled expats and Dominicans—is partial to such appetizers as fried Camembert wrapped in prosciutto and served with guava-orange sauce. For entrées, you might try the curried goat; the grilled lamb with rosemary, rum, and a tomato-onion chutney; or the slow-cooked, fat-free duck. ⊠ *Certad 3 at Presidente Vasquez, Puerto Plata,* ☎ *809/586–5314. AE, MC, V. Closed Mon.*

ECLECTIC

$–$$ ✕ **Hemingway's Cafe.** As much a restaurant as a memorial to the great
★ writer, this place is full of old photos that chronicle his life and dishes with names that bring to mind his work. Everyone, from long-haired

expats to government VIPs, comes to savor the Pamplona burgers (with cheese, bacon, sautéed onions) or the world-class fajitas For Whom the Bell Tolls (in chicken, shrimp, or beef versions). Sangria, with lots of fresh fruit, is the house drink. The café cranks out food continuously from 11 AM till 2 AM, which is about when the rock and reggae bands that play here finish their last set. ⊠ *Playa Dorada Plaza,* ☎ *809/320–2230. AE, MC, V.*

ITALIAN

$$–$$$ ✕ **La Puntilla de Piergiorgio.** Here, atop a cliff, you're pampered by
★   waiters as you sit overlooking the precipice. Cascades of pink bougainvillea rustle about you in the cooling sea breeze. The food is exceptional and straightforward: gnocchi with a tomato-basil cream sauce, shrimp-laced fettuccine, or a simple grilled lobster are among the choices. Live bands often play in the bandstand, and if you don't have a car, the restaurant will pick you up and drop you off in a festive horse-drawn wagon. At press time, Piergiorgio's was working on its 51-room inn, which will no doubt have the same charm and style as the restaurant. ⊠ *Calle La Puntilla 1, El Batey, Sosua,* ☎ *809/571–2215. AE, DC, MC, V.*

$$–$$$ ✕ **Ristorante Sabatini.** Potted palms and overhead fans add to the sultry tropical ambience of this waterfront restaurant adjacent to ☞ **Marco Polo Club** apartment hotel. Tuscan cuisine is a specialty, though the menu has dishes from throughout Italy. You can head for the antipasto buffet before selecting such pasta dishes as tortellini with fresh seafood in a cream sauce. Ask to be seated at table No. 4, which is in a Victorian-style gazebo that overlooks the sea. ⊠ *El Batey, Sosua,* ☎ *809/571–3128. AE, MC, V.*

SEAFOOD

$–$$ ✕ **Caribae.** Aquariums teeming with sea creatures decorate the dining room of this warm, unassuming spot. You can choose your own lobster, shrimp, or oysters for the barbecue. The restaurant grows its own vegetables and has its own shrimp farm, and this helps to keep the prices reasonable. For $20, you can take a guided kayak tour of the shrimp farm and have lunch on the terrace overlooking the swimming pool. Bring a bathing suit. ⊠ *Camino Libre 70, Sosua,* ☎ *809/571–3138. AE, MC, V.*

Juan Dolio

CONTEMPORARY

$–$$ ✕ **L'Ecrevisse.** The intimate dining room of the ☞ **Talanquera Coun-**
★   **try and Beach Resort,** is one of the country's strongholds of innovative contemporary Caribbean cuisine. It's also one of the few restaurants in the world to have earned two Awards of Excellence from *Wine Spectator* magazine for its wine list, which has some 475 selections. Among the excellent appetizers is the cold lobster with avocado and calypso sauce (a crab reduction). Mango sorbet with guavaberry sauce clears your palate for such entrées as the fillet Sir Francis Drake—a perfect tenderloin wrapped in phyllo and served with a tangy tamarind sauce—or the sea bass with shrimp, fine herbs, and island fruits. A soufflé and a glass of dessert wine make a fabulous finish. The decor is formal and romantic, and the service is white glove, but the atmosphere is relaxed. ⊠ *Juan Dolio Beach,* ☎ *809/526–1510. AE, DC, MC, V.*

Samaná

ECLECTIC

$–$$ ✕ **Café de France.** Local aficionados swear the beef here is the best in the D.R.—try the fillet in a mushroom or a peppercorn sauce. Seafood here is also dependable: one standout is shrimp (or grouper) in garlic-coconut sauce. The small bistro is on the waterfront and is simply decorated, with white stucco walls and red tablecloths. An even more casual annex serves knockout pizzas. ⊠ *Malecón,* ☎ *no phone. MC, V.*

SEAFOOD

$$
★ ✕ **Villa Serena.** At the very end of the long road from Puerto Plata is this spot in the small ☞ **Villa Serena** hotel. On the beach and the Bahía del Rincón, the open-air restaurant faces the tradewinds. Specialties include fresh fish and delicious homemade desserts. ⊠ *Las Galeras,* ☎ *809/696–0065. MC, V.*

Santo Domingo
CARIBBEAN/CREOLE

$
★ ✕ **El Conuco.** The name means "the countryside," and it *is* hard to believe that this thatched-roof patio—alive with hanging plants, hibiscus, and frangipani—is smack in the center of Santo Domingo. The Dominican dishes here are superb, from *la bandera* (white rice, kidney beans, and stewed beef duplicating the colors of the flag) to a magnificent, delicately flaky *bacalao de la comai* (cod in white cream sauce with garlic and onions). The ambience is always celebratory; waiters dance with you or take to makeshift drum sets—all in in time with the taped merengue music that plays in the background. ⊠ *152 Casimiro de Moya,* ☎ *809/686–0129 or 809/689–4290. MC, V.*

$ ✕ **Fogarate.** This Dominican-themed buffet restaurant is full of color: in the picket fence painted in primary hues, in the striped tablecloths, and in the long floral skirts worn by waitresses. *Typico* decorations include bright carnival masks and models of local buses. The buffet, which is open for lunch and dinner (service till 1 AM), is quite a spread, with such local favorites as sancocho, flat bread, red beans, rice, yuca, creamed potatoes, savory pork, and beef. Dessert is coconut cream or flan. Don't be surprised if a merengue dancer pulls you from your seat. ⊠ *Av. George Washington 517,* ☎ *809/688–0044. AE, MC, V.*

ITALIAN

$$–$$$ ✕ **La Briciola.** The owners did an exemplary job of modernizing the interiors of these adjoining, 16th-century colonial buildings while preserving their architectural integrity. The arch-ceiling, stone-and-brick main dining room and the more casual piano bar overlook a courtyard whose trees are lit romantically at night. A vocalist serenades. Mahogany furnishings, wooden chandeliers, and Italian tile work create an elegant atmosphere. Excellent fresh pastas include velvety gnocchi *fume* (with Scamorze cheese, ham, and cream). The classic Italian and seafood dishes are deftly prepared: try the osso buco or the grouper *al limone* (with lemon). Have the paternal owner, Franco Ricobono, help you select from the extensive, all-Italian wine list. His son Alexandro can help you choose a grappa to complement the delicious tiramisu. ⊠ *Calle Arzobispo Merino 152-A at Padre Bellini,* ☎ *809/688–5055. Jacket required. AE, DC, MC, V. Closed Sun.*

$$–$$$
★ ✕ **Pappalapasta.** Delicious food and a location around the corner from the Presidential Palace make this restaurant popular with politicians, diplomats, and those who seek their favor. A series of intimate dining rooms is handsomely decorated with rattan and polished hardwood furnishings, abstract artwork, Tiffany-style lamps, and cut-glass windows. Start with a classic selection of antipasto—carpaccio, eggplant Parmesan, or tuna with capers. Pumpkin ravioli in almond butter and gnocchi al pesto are pasta standouts. You may also opt for the sublime sea bass meunière or snapper *chiaro di mare* (with olives, capers, garlic, tomato, and peppers). The service, although attentive, is surprisingly leisurely; maybe they're waiting discreetly for your deal to be closed. ⊠ *Calle Dr. Baez 23,* ☎ *809/689–4849. Jacket required. AE, MC, V. Closed Mon.*

$$–$$$ ✕ **Spaghettissimo.** This contemporary Italian spot deserves the word-
★ of-mouth fame it enjoys. Owner Frederic Gollong will charm you with
his dry wit and welcoming ways. The canopied entrance leads first to
the bar and then to the buffet dining room. From the carpaccio of swordfish to such delicacies as the meringue confection aptly named The Cloud,
the quality and freshness of the food are apparent. Savor Frederic's own
smooth foie gras and the roasted red and yellow peppers in olive oil.
For a pasta course, try the penne with artichokes, mushrooms, sun-
dried tomatoes, and olive oil. Consider the specials of the week, such
as lamb with eggplant in red sauce. On Wednesday night, live jazz on
the candlelit patio captures a devoted crowd. ⊠ *13 Paseo de Los
Locubres,* ☎ *809/565–3708 or 809/547–2650. AE, DC, MC, V.*

$$–$$$ ✕ **Vesuvio.** Businessmen "do lunch" here on weekdays, celebrities
★ such as Julio Iglesias pop in from time to time, and Dominican families make the atmosphere lively on Sunday. This place has been an institution for 42 years, and although the decor could use an update, the
food and service are superb. Almost everything on the menu is either
freshly caught, homemade, or homegrown. Start with any of the an-
tipasti, then segue into the squid-ink linguine with squid and shrimp
or the risotto with sun-dried tomatoes, mozzarella, and basil. The
boiled lobster with tomato, onion, and olive oil is simple but memorable. The elaborate pastry cart will tempt you, as will the wine list
(the admirable cellar has 200 selections). ⊠ *Av. George Washington
521,* ☎ *809/221–3333. Reservations not accepted. AE, DC, MC, V.*

MIDDLE EASTERN

$$–$$$ ✕ **Scherezade.** The exotic decor—Moorish arches, tile work, a terrace
with orchids—is just one of the things that has made this new restaurant so popular. The excellent service is provided by waiters who wear
embroidered vests and fez hats. Hummus, not butter, comes with the
pita bread. For a starter, you might try the velvety cream of asparagus
and watercress or the tabbouleh. Superb entrées include the Madagascar
shrimp in green pepper and spinach sauce or the Arabian lobster,
grilled simply with oil, garlic, and lemon. Desserts include baklava,
orange soufflé, or ginger flan. ⊠ *Av. Roberto Pastoriza,* ☎ *809/227–
2323,* FAX *809/540–3030. AE, DC, MC. Closed Mon.*

SEAFOOD

$–$$ ✕ **La Bahía.** The catch of the day is always tops at this unpretentious
spot. Try the kingfish in coconut sauce. The conch, which appears in
a variety of dishes, is also good. For starters, try the *sopa palúdica,* a
thick soup made with fish, shrimp, and lobster and served with tangy
garlic bread. The decor strikes a nautical note, with fishing nets and
seashells. ⊠ *Av. George Washington 1,* ☎ *809/682–4022. Reservations not accepted. AE, MC, V.*

SPANISH

$$–$$$ ✕ **Don Pepe.** This may sound like a Mexican fast-food joint, but it was
once the home of one of Santo Domingo's old families, the Guerreros.
With its pink-stucco, arched interiors, it still looks like an elegant residence. Demi-pillars, chandeliers, and European tiles add to the effect.
The owner, Pepe, serves traditional Spanish fare made with high-quality ingredients. Soups are particularly flavorful, such as the *sopa de ajo*
(garlic soup) and black bean. Poultry and game, are good choices, as
are the paella and the *mariscos* (shellfish). Finish with flan and a *teja,*
a thin, dark cookie in the shape of a roof tile. ⊠ *Calle Santiago at Av.
Pasteur,* ☎ *809/689–7612. AE, DC, MC, V.*

$–$$$ ✕ **Restaurant Reina de España.** Here, classic Spanish food is served in
an elegant setting. Stone walls and mahogany details are warmed by
light from crystal chandeliers. In the foyer, a waterfall cascades down

the stone work. If your Spanish is rusty, you can just point at what you want—up to the rafters for tapas of the aging hams and cheeses that hang down there or over to a table laden with lobster, sea bass, red snapper, and prawns. The very fresh seafood is delicately prepared, from the squid in its own ink to the paella. The rabbit in garlic sauce and the grilled sweetbreads are also standouts. The chocolate soufflé or home-made nougat ice cream are happy endings, indeed. ⊠ *Cervantes 103, Gazcue,* ☎ *809/685–2588 or 687-5029. AE, DC, MC.*

$–$$ ✕ **Fonda de la Atarazana.** Here, dinner and dancing on the brick patio of a 17th-century building in the Colonial Zone make for a *very* romantic evening. The place is known more for its atmosphere than its food, though. ⊠ *La Atarazana 5,* ☎ *809/689–2900. AE, MC, V.*

$–$$ ✕ **Restaurant Sully.** Sully (pronounced *sue*-lee) is the name of the own-ers of this Spanish-Dominican restaurant, run with great family pride. Patrons have confidence in the quality of the food and, notably, the freshness of the seafood: It's the big draw here, and visitors have been known to take a 15-minute cab ride from the Malecón to sample it. The dishes are served steaming hot, from the Spanish bouillabaisse to mussels in a puréed marinara sauce. Several variations of paella are offered, from the traditional Valenciana to the more daring *negra,* black from the ink of the squid. Lobster here is prepared 10 ways; it's divine served with a brandy sauce. ⊠ *Av. Charles Sumner 19 at Calle Las Caobas,* ☎ *809/682–2169. AE, DC, MC, V.*

Beaches

The Dominican Republic has more than 1,000 mi of beaches, includ-ing the Caribbean's longest strip of white sand: Punta Cana/Bavaro. Many beaches are accessible to the public and may tempt you to stop for a swim. That's part of the uninhibited joy of this country. Do be careful, though: Some have dangerously strong currents.

Boca Chica is the beach closest to Santo Domingo (2 mi east of Las Américas Airport, 21 mi from the capital), and it's crowded with city folks on weekends. This beach was once an immaculate stretch of fine white sand. "Progress" has since cluttered it with plastic beach tables, chaise longues, pizza stands, and beach cottages for rent. But the sand is still fine, and you can walk far out into clear blue water, which is protected by coral reefs.

Cabarete Beach, on the north coast, has ideal wind and surf conditions. It's an integral part of the international windsurfing circuit.

Juan Dolio is a narrow beach of fine white sand about 20 minutes by car east of Boca Chica. Here you'll find many resorts—the Metro Hotel and Marina, the Decameron, the Capella, the Talenquera, and the Diamond Coral Costa Caribe, to name a few. Within the Diamond, the first new casino to open in seven years is giving customers the VIP treatment. Says owner, John Dades, "What makes us different than most on the island is that we smile if you win!" Sol Melia, a Spanish hotel company, has just opened the Melia Juan Dolio Resort, Spa, and Casino here, as well.

Luperón Beach, about an hour's drive west of Puerto Plata, is a wide white-sand beach fit for snorkeling, windsurfing, and scuba diving. The Luperón Beach Resort is handy for rentals and refreshments.

Playa Grande, on the north coast, is a long stretch of powdery sand that's slated for development (the Playa Grande Hotel has already dis-turbed the solitude). For now, however, the entire northeast coast still seems like one unbroken golden stretch, littered only with kelp, drift-wood, and the occasional beer bottle. If you don't mind the lack of fa-cilities, you have your pick of deserted beaches here.

Puerto Plata, on the north's "Amber Coast" (so called because of its unusual—and large—deposits of amber), is still being developed, especially the Playa Dorada area. The beaches are of soft beige or white sand, with lots of reefs for snorkeling. The Atlantic waters are great for windsurfing, waterskiing, and fishing expeditions.

Punta Cana, the gem of the Caribbean, is a 20-mi strand of pearl-white sand shaded by coconut palms. It's on the easternmost coast, which includes Bavaro Beach, and it is the home of several top resorts.

La Romana is the home of the 7,000-acre Casa de Campo resort, so you're not likely to find any private place in the sun here. The miniature **Minitas Beach** and lagoon are in this area.

Sosua has a lovely beach where calm waters gently lap a shore of soft white sand. Unfortunately the backdrop here is a string of tents where hawkers push cheap souvenirs. You can, however, get snacks and rent water-sports equipment from the vendors.

Las Terrenas, on the north coast of the Samaná Peninsula, looks like something from *Robinson Crusoe*: tall palms list toward the sea; the beach is narrow but sandy; and there's plenty of color—vivid blues, greens, and yellows. Two hotels are right on the beach at Punta Bonita.

Outdoor Activities and Sports

Although there's hardly a shortage of activities here, the resorts have virtually cornered the market on sports, including every conceivable water sport. In some cases, facilities may be available only to guests. You can check with the hotels or the tourist office (☞ Visitor Information *in* the Dominican Republic A to Z, *below*) for more details.

Participant Sports

BICYCLING

Pedaling is easy on pancake-flat beaches, but there are also some steep hills in the D.R. Bikes are available at **Dorado Naco** (✉ Dorado Beach, ☎ 809/320–2019), **Hotel Cofresi** (✉ Puerto Plata, ☎ 809/586–2898), **Jack Tar Village** (✉ Puerto Plata, ☎ 809/586–3800), and **Villas Doradas** (✉ Playa Dorada, Puerto Plata, ☎ 809/320–3000).

BOATING

Sailing conditions on the gin-clear waters are ideal, with a constant tradewind. Favorite excursions include day trips to Catalina Island and sunset cruises on the Caribbean. Prices for crewed sailboats of 26 ft and longer with a capacity of 4 to 12 people range from $120 to $700. Hobie Cats and pedal boats are available at **Heavens** (✉ Playa Dorada, ☎ 809/586–5250). The private marina at **Casa de Campo** (✉ La Romana, ☎ 809/523–3333) has charter sailing vessels. Also check with **Club Med** (✉ Punta Cana, ☎ 809/567–5228).

FISHING

Marlin and wahoo are among the fish that folks angle for here. (Note that fishing is best between January and June.) Costs to charter a boat—with a crew, refreshments, bait, and tackle—range $300–$500 for a half day or $400–$700 for a full day. You can arrange trips through **Actividas Acuaticás** (✉ Playa Dorada, ☎ 809/586–3988) or the marina at **Casa de Campo** (☞ Boating, *above*).

GOLF

Casa de Campo (☎ 809/523–3333) has two 18-hole Pete Dye courses that are open to the public (a third course is open to villa owners only). These courses are known to dedicated golfers everywhere, and *Golf* magazine has called this "the finest golf resort in the world." Greens fees range from $85–$125; if you're an avid golfer, though, inquire about the resorts multiday passes and golf packages. The **Bavaro Beach**

resort's 18-hole course is open to its own guests and those of other hotels. The greens fee for those not staying at Bavaro is $32; golf carts rent for $50. **Playa Dorada**'s 18-hole Robert Trent Jones–designed course is open to guests staying at all the hotels in the complex. Greens fees range from $15 (9 holes) to $27. Guests in Santo Domingo hotels are usually allowed to use the 18-hole course at the **Santo Domingo Country Club** (☎ 809/530–6606) on weekdays—*after* members have teed off—for $35 (9 or 18 holes). The **Metro Country Club** (☎ 809/526–3315), east of Santo Domingo on the road to La Romana, has an 18-hole public course designed by Charles Ankrom. Greens fees will run $35–$50, and a cart (required on weekends) costs $16–$20.

HIKING

At 10,370 ft, **Pico Duarte** is the highest peak in the West Indies and a favorite for serious hikers and mountain climbers. Hire a guide in La Ciénaga, one hour and 8½ mi west of Jarabacoa, if you are prepared and equipped for an arduous 12-mi, two-day climb; you can also rent a mule there. The park service (☎ 809/472–4204) can assist you with obtaining a guide.

HORSEBACK RIDING

The 250-acre Equestrian Center at **Casa de Campo** (☎ 809/523–3333) has something for both Western and English riders—a dude ranch, a rodeo arena, guided trail rides, and jumping and riding lessons. Guided rides run about $20 an hour; lessons cost $40 an hour. **Gran Chaparral** (✉ Puerto Plata, ☎ 809/320–4450) is a ranch that offers beach rides of varying lengths and costs on its well-trained, gaited horses. **Rancho Isabella** (✉ East of Playa Dorada, ☎ 809/707–3627) gives delightful, six-hour trail rides in the country and on the beach; a Dominican buffet lunch is included in the cost of $45.

SCUBA DIVING

Ancient sunken galleons, undersea gardens, and offshore reefs are the lures here. Most resorts have dive shops on the premises or can arrange trips for you. Be sure to ask when making reservations.

TENNIS

There must be a million nets around the island, and most of them can be found at the large resorts. **La Terraza Tennis Club** (☎ 809/523–8548 ask for the tennis office) at the Casa de Campo resort has been called the "Wimbledon of the Caribbean." This 12-acre facility, perched on a hill with sea views, has 13 Har-Tru courts. Nonguests are welcome (just call in advance); court time costs $20 an hour; lessons are $40 an hour. The **Playa Naco Golf & Tennis Resort** (☎ 809/320–6226 ext. 2568) in Playa Dorada allows nonguests to play on its four clay courts for $4 an hour—day or night. Lessons from a pro cost $14 an hour.

WINDSURFING

Between June and October, **Cabarete Beach** has what many consider to be optimal windsurfing conditions: wind speeds at 20–25 knots and 3- to 15-ft waves. The Professional Boardsurfers Association has included Cabarete in its international windsurfing slalom competition. The novice is also welcome to learn and train on modified boards stabilized by flotation devices. **Carib BIC Center** (✉ Cabarete Beach, ☎ 809/571–0640, ℻ 809/571–0649) offers equipment and instruction. Lessons are generally $30–$35 an hour; boards rent for $20 an hour.

Spectator Sports

BASEBALL

Baseball is the national pastime and passion. The 1997 World Series put Dominican players and their island in the limelight. A handful of Dominicans on the Miami Marlins, including heavy hitter Moises

Alou, helped the team beat the Cleveland Indians. In addition, D.R. hero, pitcher Pedro Martinez, has made headlines several times. He won the Cy Young Award and was voted the most valuable player in the National League, though he was a veritable newcomer with only three years' experiences under his glove. In November 1997, Martinez's biggest score made international headlines: he accepted a six-year contract, offered by the Boston Red Sox, for $75 million. With some of those dollars, Martinez is building a church in his small home town near the capital.

Triple-A-level Dominican and Puerto Rican players and some American major leaguers hone their skills in the D.R.'s Professional Winter League, which plays October–January. As many as 20,000 fans often crowd the **Liga de de Béisbol** stadium (☎ 809/567–6371) in Santo Domingo. If your Spanish is good, you can call the stadium or consult local newspaper listings for details on the five teams and game schedules; otherwise, you may want to ask staff at your hotel to arrange tickets for you. Games are also played in the Tetelo Vargas Stadium in the town of San Pedro de Macorís (☞ Eploring, *below*).

HORSE RACING

There are races (flats) year-round at the **Hipódromo V Centenario.** ⊠ *Av. Las Américas, Santo Domingo,* ☎ *809/687–6060.* ☜ *Free.* ☉ *Daily 8 AM–2:45 PM.*

POLO

Casa de Campo is the key place in the Caribbean to play or watch the fabled sport of kings. The resort has always prided itself on the polo traditions it has kept alive since its opening some 20 years ago. (For many years a nephew of the Maharajah of Jodhpur, Jaber Singh, was an instructor. His pupils included Ramfis Trujillo, son of the former dictator.) Matches are scheduled from October to June, with high goal players flying in from France and Argentina. Private polo lessons and clinics are there for those who always wanted to give it a shot.

The ponies pound down the field at **Sierra Prieta** (Santo Domingo) and at **Casa de Campo** (La Romana). The season runs November–May. For information about matches, call ☎ 809/565–6880.

Shopping

The hottest items right now are cigars. Many exquisite hand-wrapped smokes come from the island's rich Ciabo Valley, and Fuente cigars, handmade in Santiago, are highly prized. Dominican rum and coffee are also good buys. The D.R. is the homeland of designer Oscar de la Renta, and you may want to stop at the chic shops that carry his creations. Hand-carved, wooden rocking chairs are big sellers, and you can buy them boxed and unassembled for easy transport. La Vega is famous for its *diablos cajuelos* (devil masks), which are worn during Carnival. Look also for the delicate, ceramic lime figurines that symbolize the Dominican culture; without faces, these dolls represent the D.R.'s mixture of cultures.

Though locally crafted products are often of a high caliber (and often very affordable), expect to pay hundreds of dollars for designer jewelry made of amber and larimar. Larimar—a semiprecious stone that's the color of the Caribbean sea—is found on the D.R.'s south coast. Prices vary according to the stone's hue; the rarest and most expensive gems have a milky haze, and the less-expensive are solid blue. Amber has been mined extensively between Puerto Plata and Santiago. A fossilization of resin from a prehistoric pine tree, it often encases ancient animal and plant life from leaves to spiders to tiny lizards. Beware of fakes, which are especially prevalent in street stalls. Visit a reputable dealer or store and ask how to tell the difference between real larimar and amber and imitations.

Bargaining is both a game and a social activity in the D.R., especially with street vendors and at the stalls in El Mercado Modelo. Vendors are disappointed and perplexed if you don't haggle. They're also tenacious, so unless you really plan to buy, don't even stop to look.

Shopping Districts

SANTO DOMINGO

El Mercado Modelo, a covered market, borders Calle Mella in the Colonial Zone. Vendors here sell a dizzying selection of Dominican crafts. The restored buildings of **La Atarazana** (⊠ Across from Alcazar in the Colonial Zone) are filled with shops, art galleries, restaurants, and bars. One of the main shopping streets in the Colonial Zone is **Calle El Conde,** which has been transformed into a pedestrian thoroughfare. Some of the best shops on **Calle Duarte,** are north of the Colonial Zone, between Calle Mella and Avenida de Las Américas. **Plaza Criolla** (⊠ Av. Maximo Gomez) is filled with shops that sell everything from scents to nonsense. Two major malls are **Unicentro** (⊠ 406 Av. Abraham Lincoln) and **Plaza Central** (⊠ Avs. Winston Churchill and 27 de Febrero), which include top international boutiques.

PUERTO PLATA

The seven showrooms of the **Tourist Bazaar** (⊠ Calle Duarte 61) are in an old mansion with a patio bar. **Playa Dorada Plaza** (⊠ Calle Duarte at Av. 30 de Marzo) is a shopping center in the American tradition. Stores here sell everything from cigars, rum, coffee, and herbal remedies to ceramics, hand-carved wooden items, and T-shirts. A popular shopping street for costume jewelry and souvenirs is **Calle Beller.**

ALTOS DE CHAVÓN

In this re-creation of a Mediterranean village on the grounds of the Casa de Campo resort, you'll find art galleries, boutiques, and souvenir shops are grouped around a cobbled square. Extra special are: El Club de Cigaro, Casa de la Perla, for expensive European lingerie and women's clothing, and the rotating art exhibits displayed at the Museo Arqueológico Regional.

Specialty Items

CLOTHING

Check out the Dominican fashions at **Jenny Polanco's** boutiques in the Melia Santo Domingo hotel, (⊠ Av. George Washington 365, Santo Domingo, ☎ 809/686–6666, ext. 2270), **Plaza Central** (⊠ Avs. Winston Churchill and 27 de Febrero, Santo Domingo, ☎ 809/541–5929), and the **Paradise Beach Club and Casino** (⊠ Playa Dorada, ☎ 809/ 586–3663, ext. 314).

DUTY-FREE ITEMS

Duty-free shops selling liquor, cameras, and the like are at the **Centro de los Héroes** (⊠ Av. George Washington, Santo Domingo), the **Hotel El Embajador** (⊠ Av. Sarasota 65, Santo Domingo), and **Las Américas Airport** (☎ 809/549–0450).

HANDICRAFTS

Ambar Tres (⊠ La Atarazana 3, Santo Domingo, ☎ 809/688–0474) carries a wide selection of items made with this Dominican gem. **Arawak Gallery** (⊠ Av. Pasteur 104, Santo Domingo, ☎ 809/685– 1661) specializes in pre-Columbian artifacts and contemporary pottery and paintings.

Artesanía Lime (⊠ Autopista Duarte, km 2½, Santiago, ☎ 809/582–3754) is worth a visit for its mahogany carvings and Carnival masks.

Collector's Corner Gallery and Gift Shop (⊠ Plaza Shopping Center, Calle Duarte at Av. 30 de Marzo, Puerto Plata, ☎ no phone) offers a wide range of souvenirs, including those made of amber.

El Conde Gift Shop (⊠ Calle El Conde 153, Santo Domingo, ☎ 809/682–5909) is a terrific spot for exquisite mahogany carvings.

Galería de Arte Mariano Eckert (⊠ At Av. Winston Churchill and Calle Luis F. Tomen, 3rd floor, Santo Domingo, ☎ 809/541–7109) focuses on the work of Eckert, an older Dominican artist who is know for his still lifes.

Galería de Arte Nader (⊠ Rafael Augusto Sanchez 22, Ensanche Pianttini and Plaza Andalucia II, Santo Domingo, ☎ 809/687–6674 or 809/544–0878) showcases top Dominican artists in a variety of media. The gallery staff is well known in Miami and New York and works with Sotheby's.

Lyle O. Reitzel Art Contemporaneo (⊠ Plaza Andalucia II, Santo Domingo, ☎ 809/227–8361) specializes in very contemporary art, such as that of José Garcia Cordero, a Dominican living in Paris.

Novo Atarazana (⊠ Atarazana 21, Santo Domingo, ☎ 809/685–0582) has an assortment of local artwork.

TOBACCO

Santo Domingo Cigar Club (⊠ Av. George Washington 367, ☎ 809/221–1483), in the lobby of the Jaragua Renaissance Hotel, is a great place to find yourself a good smoke.

Nightlife

Get a copy of the magazine *Vacation Guide* and the newspaper *Touring*—both available free at the tourist office and at hotels—to find out what's happening around the island. Also look in the *Santo Domingo News* and the *Puerto Plata News* for listings of events. The monthly *Dominican Fiesta* also provides up-to-date information.

CAFÉS

Café Atlántico is responsible for bringing happy hour and Tex-Mex dishes to the Dominican Republic. Usually young, very lively, and very friendly, the late-afternoon yuppie crowd comes for the music, the food, the exotic drinks, the big-name Dominican singers, and the energetic atmosphere. Monday, interestingly enough, and Friday, are the best nights. ⊠ *Av. J. A. Aybar 152 at Av. Abraham Lincoln, Santo Domingo,* ☎ *809/565–1841.*

Museo del Jamón is a casual boîte. The best times to come are Thursday and Sunday evenings (after 10 PM) for the folkloric and Spanish dance shows. The brilliantly lit Alcazar provides a thrilling backdrop. If you must order food here, stick with the cold tapas, the air-dried ham, and the aged Spanish cheese. ⊠ *La Atarazana 9, Santo Domingo,* ☎ *809/688–9644.*

CASINOS

Gambling here is more a sideline than a raison d'être as in, say, Las Vegas. Although most casinos are in the larger hotels of Santo Domingo, there are others here and there. All offer blackjack, craps, and roulette and are generally open daily 3 PM–4 AM. Free buffets are sometimes set up at midnight, when some of the name entertainers come on. You must be 18 to enter, and jackets are required.

In Santo Domingo, the most popular casinos are in the **Embajador** (⊠ Av. Sarasota, ☎ 809/533–2131), the **Hotel Gran Lina** (⊠ Av. Máximo Gómez, ☎ 809/563–5000), the **Hispaniola** (⊠ Av. Independencia, ☎

809/221–7111), and the **Jaragua Renaissance** (⊠ Av. George Washington 367, ☎ 809/686–2222).

DANCE CLUBS

Santo Domingo has its share of hot spots, and just about every resort in Puerto Plata has live entertainment, dancing, or both. You'll soon discover that there's no such thing as "last call" in the D.R. Customers usually decide when closing time will be.

Andromeda (⊠ Puerto Plata, ☎ 809/586–5250) is a dance club and video bar that gets going in the wee hours (after 1 AM).

La Aurora (⊠ Av. Hermanos Deligne, Santo Domingo, ☎ 809/685–6590) is the after hours supper club where *capitaleños* (natives of Santo Domingo) head when all the other partying is over. Savor typical dishes—even sancocho—mingle with other revelers, and hang with the musicians who entertained everybody earlier. This is the spot of choice for Santo Domingo's hottest bands.

Bachata Rosa (⊠ La Atarazana 9, Zona Colonia, Santo Domingo, ☎ 809/688–0969 or 809/682–7726), named after a popular song by the Dominican merengue megastar Juan Luís Guerra (he's part-owner), is *the* Santo Domingo disco. It has three floors and includes a stage, a dance floor, and a Caribbean restaurant. There's live music on many nights. Guerra has his videos going on three wide screens. Free transportation is available to all hotels.

Bottoms (⊠ Av. Tiradentes, Santo Domingo, ☎ 809/541–6226), on the 12th floor of the Plaza Hotel, has a great view. The multilevel, mirrored, and metal space also hosts a variety of special events, from lingerie fashion shows to performances by the latest bands.

Crazy Moon (⊠ Paradise Beach Club and Casino, Puerto Plata, ☎ 809/320–3663) is a lively disco where Latin music is mixed with American and Euro tunes.

Disco Free (⊠ Av. Ortega y Gaset, Santo Domingo, ☎ 809/565–8100), Santo Domingo's gay dance club, is open Thursday–Sunday. The music is a mix of merengue, salsa, and New York house.

Guácara Taína (⊠ Av. Rómulo Betancourt 655, Santo Domingo, ☎ 809/530–2666), a cultural center–disco set in a cave, hosts folkloric dances during the early evening and later is transformed into one of the city's hottest nightspots. It has two dance floors, three bars, and lots of nooks and crannies.

Las Palmas (⊠ Hotel Santo Domingo, Avs. Independencia and Abraham Lincoln, Santo Domingo, ☎ 809/221–7111) has a happy hour (6 PM to 8 PM) that's made joyous, indeed, thanks to two-for-one drinks and energetic bands.

Pyramide (⊠ Corner of Avs. Pedro Clisante and Dr. Rosen, Sosua, ☎ no phone) in the heart of El Batey, is a disco with the best sound and lights in town.

Exploring the Dominican Republic

Santo Domingo

Spanish civilization in the New World began in the 12-block area of Santo Domingo called the Colonial Zone. This historical area is now a bustling, noisy district with narrow cobbled streets, shops, restaurants, and residents. It's easy to imagine this old city as it was when the likes of Columbus, Cortés, Ponce de León, and pirates sailed in and out and colonists were settling themselves in the New World. Tourist brochures tout that "history comes alive here"—a surprisingly truthful statement.

A quick taxi tour of the old section takes about an hour, but if you're interested in history, you'll want to spend a day or two exploring the many old "firsts," and you'll want to do it in the most comfortable shoes you own. Wearing shorts, miniskirts, and halter tops in churches is considered inappropriate. Men in Santo Domingo never wear shorts. (Note: Hours and admission charges are erratic.)

Parque Independencia separates the old city from the new. Avenidas 30 de Marzo, Bolívar, and Independencia traverse the park and mingle with avenues named for George Washington, John F. Kennedy, and Abraham Lincoln. Modern Santo Domingo is a sprawling, noisy city with a population of close to 2 million.

Numbers in the margin correspond to points of interest on the Santo Domingo map.

SIGHTS TO SEE

☝ ㉓ **Acuario Nacional.** The largest aquarium in the Caribbean has an impressive collection of tropical fish and dolphins, though its construction was a controversial public expenditure. ⊠ *In Sans Souci district, Av. de las Américas,* ☎ *809/592–1509.* ☜ *Free.* ⊙ *Weekdays 8–5, Sat. 8–4, Sun. 9–12:30.*

☝ ❺ **Alcazar de Colón.** The castle of Don Diego Colón, built in 1514, was painstakingly reconstructed and restored in 1957. Forty-inch-thick coral limestone walls were patched and shored with blocks from the original quarry. The Renaissance-style structure, with its balustrade and double row of arches, has strong Moorish, Gothic, and Isabelline influences. There are 22 rooms, furnished in a style to which the viceroy of the island would have been accustomed—right down to the dishes and the viceregal shaving mug. Many of the period paintings, statues, tapestries, and furnishings were donated by the University of Madrid. ⊠ *On Plaza de España (just off Calle Emiliano Tejera at foot of Calle Las Damas),* ☎ *809/687–5361.* ☜ *RD$10.* ⊙ *Mon. and Wed.–Fri. 9–5, Sat. 9–4, Sun. 9–1.*

❷ **La Atarazana.** The Royal Mooring Docks made up the colonial commercial district, where naval supplies were stored. There are eight restored buildings, the oldest of which dates from 1507. It now houses crafts shops, restaurants, and art galleries. ⊠ *Calle La Atarazana.*

⓫ **Calle Las Damas.** The New World's oldest street, the "Street of the Ladies" was named after the elegant ladies of the court who, in the Spanish tradition, promenaded in the evening. Here you'll see a sundial dating from 1753 and the **Casa de los Jesuitas,** which houses a fine research library for colonial history as well as the Institute for Hispanic Culture. ☜ *Free.* ⊙ *Weekdays 8–4:30.*

❼ **Capilla de los Remedios.** The Chapel of Our Lady of Remedies was originally built in the 17th century as a private chapel for the family of Francisco de Dávila. Early colonists also worshiped here before the completion of the cathedral. Its architectural details, particularly the lateral arches, are evocative of the Castilian Romanesque style. ⊠ *Calle Las Damas, at foot of Calle de Las Mercedes,* ☎ *no phone.* ☜ *Free.* ⊙ *Mon.–Sat. 9–6; Sun. masses begin at 6 AM.*

⓬ **Casa de Bastidas.** There's a lovely inner courtyard here with tropical plants and temporary-exhibit galleries. ⊠ *Calle Las Damas, just off Calle El Conde,* ☎ *no phone.* ☜ *Free.* ⊙ *Tues.–Sun. 9–5.*

❹ **Casa del Cordón.** This structure, built in 1503, is the Western Hemisphere's oldest surviving stone house. It's recognizable by the sash of the Franciscan order carved in stone over the arched entrance. Columbus's son Diego Colón, viceroy of the colony, and his wife lived here until the Alcazar was finished. It was in this house, too, that Sir Fran-

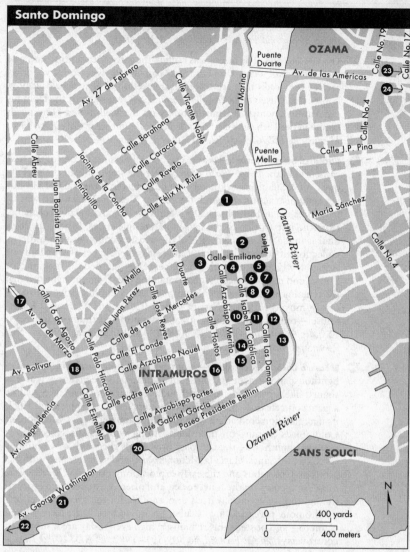

Santo Domingo

Acuario Nacional, **23**
Alcazar de Colón, **5**
La Atarazana, **2**
Calle Las Damas, **11**
Capilla de los
Remedios, **7**
Casa de Bastidas, **12**
Casa del Cordón, **4**
Casa de Tostado, **15**
Catedral Santa María
la Menor, **14**

El Faro a Colón, **24**
Hostal Palacio
Nicolás de Ovando, **9**
Iglesia y Convento
Domínico, **16**
Iglesia Santa
Bárbara, **1**
Jardín Botánico
Nacional Dr. Rafael
M. Moscoso, **17**
El Malecón, **21**

Monestario de San
Francisco, **3**
Montesinos, **20**
Museo de las
Casas Reales, **6**
Pantheon Nacional, **8**
Parque Colón, **10**
Parque
Independencia, **18**
Plaza de la
Cultura, **22**

Puerta de la
Misericordia, **19**
Torre del
Homenaje, **13**

cis Drake was paid a ransom to prevent him from totally destroying the city. ☒ *Corner of Calle Emiliano Tejera and Calle Isabel la Católica,* ☎ *no phone.* 🎟 *Free.* ◷ *Weekdays 8:30–4:30.*

⑮ Casa de Tostado. The house was built in the early 16th century and was the residence of writer Don Francisco Tostado. Its twin Gothic windows are the only ones that are still in existence in the New World. It now houses the **Museo de la Familia Dominicana** (Museum of the Dominican Family), which features exhibits on the well-heeled Dominican family in the 19th century. ☒ *Calle Padre Bellini, near Calle Arzobispo Meriño,* ☎ *809/689–5057.* 🎟 *RD$10.* ◷ *Thurs.–Tues. 9–2.*

⑭ Catedral Santa María la Menor. The coral limestone facade of the first cathedral in the New World towers over the south side of the ☞ **Parque Colón.** Spanish workmen began building the cathedral in 1514 but left off construction to search for gold in Mexico. The church was finally finished in 1540. Its facade is composed of architectural elements from the late Gothic to the lavish plateresque styles. Inside, the high altar is made of beaten silver, and the treasury contains a magnificent collection of gold and silver. Of interest is the **Chapel of Our Lady of Antigua,** which for more than four centuries guarded the magnificent bronze and marble sarcophagus containing (say Dominican historians) the remains of Christopher Columbus. The sarcophagus was most recently moved to ☞ **El Faro a Colón** (Columbus Memorial Lighthouse)—only the latest in the great navigator's posthumous journeys. ☒ *Calle Arzobispo Meriño,* ☎ *809/689–1920.* 🎟 *Free.* ◷ *Mon.–Sat. 9–4; Sun. masses begin at 6 AM.*

⟳ ㉔ El Faro a Colón. This striking—if not exactly architecturally significant—lighthouse monument and museum dedicated to the great navigator is shaped like a pyramid cross (although from ground level it looks like a giant concrete casket). The lighthouse complex was completed in 1992, its inauguration coinciding with the 500th anniversary of Christopher Columbus's landing on the island. Along with its showpiece laser-powered lighthouse, the complex now holds the tomb of Columbus (☞ Catedral Santa María la Menor, *above*) and six museums with exhibits on Columbus and the early exploration of the New World. One museum focuses on the long, rocky, and often controversial history of the lighthouse memorial itself and another on the great navigator's posthumous peregrinations (Cuba, Spain, and the D.R. have all laid claim to—and hosted—his remains, which even today are a subject of controversy). ☒ *Av. España,* ☎ *809/591–1492.* 🎟 *RD$10.* ◷ *Tues.–Sun. 10–5.*

⑨ Hostal Palacio Nicolás de Ovando. This was once the residence of Nicolás de Ovando, one of the principal organizers of the colonial city. Overlooking the water, it was transformed into a hotel, which has since closed. (At press time, it was undergoing a multimillion dollar restoration and was slated to reopen as a 108-room Sofitel hotel.) ☒ *Calle Las Damas 44,* ☎ *809/687–3101.*

⑯ Iglesia y Convento Domínico. This graceful building with the rose window is the Dominican Church and Convent, founded in 1510. In 1538 Pope Paul III visited here and was so impressed with the lectures on theology that he granted the church and convent the title of university, making it the oldest institution of higher learning in the New World. ☒ *Calle Padre Bellini and Av. Duarte,* ☎ *809/682–3780.* 🎟 *Free.* ◷ *Tues.–Sun. 9–6.*

❶ Iglesia Santa Bárbara. This combination church and fortress, the only one of its kind in Santo Domingo, was completed in 1562. ☒ *Av. Mella,* *between Calle Isabel la Católica and Calle Arzobispo Meriño,* ☏ *no phone.* 🎫 *Free.* ☉ *Weekdays 8–noon; Sun. masses begin at 6 AM.*

⑰ Jardín Botánico Nacional Dr. Rafael M. Moscoso. The Dr. Rafael M. Moscoso National Botanical Garden, the largest garden in the Caribbean, is north of town in the Arroyo Hondo district. Its 445 acres include a Japanese garden, a great ravine, a glen, a gorgeous display of orchids, and an enormous floral clock. You can tour the gardens by train, boat, or horse-drawn carriage. ✉ *Av. República de Colombia at Av. de los Proceres,* ☏ *809/687–6211.* 🎫 *RD$10.* ☉ *Tues.–Sun. 9–5.*

In the 320-acre **Parque Zoológico Nacional** (National Zoological Park), not far from the botanical gardens, animals roam free in natural habitats. There's an African plain, a children's zoo, and what the zoo claims is the world's largest birdcage. ✉ *Av. Máximo Gómez at Av. de los Proceres,* ☏ *809/562–2080.* 🎫 *RD$5.* ☉ *Tues.–Sun. 9–6.*

㉑ El Malecón. Avenida George Washington, better known as the Malecón, which is lined with tall palms and Las Vegas–style tourist hotels, breezes along the Caribbean Sea. The Parque Litoral de Sur borders the avenue from the colonial city to the Hotel Santo Domingo, a distance of about 3 mi. The seaside park, with its cafés and places to relax, is a popular spot, but beware of pickpockets.

❸ Monasterio de San Francisco. Constructed between 1512 and 1544, the San Francisco Monastery contained the church, chapel, and convent of the Franciscan order. Sir Francis Drake's demolition squad significantly damaged the building in 1586, and in 1673 an earthquake nearly finished the job, but when it's floodlit at night, the ruins are indeed dramatic. ✉ *Calle Hostos at Calle Emiliano.*

⑳ Montesinos. One of the first things you'll see as you approach the Colonial Zone is this statue, only slightly smaller than the Colossus of Rhodes, staring out over the Caribbean. Montesinos was the Spanish priest who came to the Dominican Republic in the 16th century to appeal for human rights for Indians.

❻ Museo de las Casas Reales. The Museum of the Royal Houses has collections displayed in two early 16th-century palaces that have been altered many times. Exhibits cover everything from antique coins to replicas of the *Niña,* the *Pinta,* and the *Santa María.* There are statue and cartography galleries, coats of armor and coats of arms, coaches and a royal court room, gilded furnishings, and Indian artifacts. The first room of the former governor's residence has a wall-size map marking the routes sailed by Columbus's ships on expeditions beginning in 1492. ✉ *Calle Las Damas at Calle de Las Mercedes,* ☏ *809/682–4202.* 🎫 *RD$10.* ☉ *Tues.–Sat. 9–4:45, Sun. 10–1.*

❽ Pantheon Nacional. The National Pantheon, which dates from 1714, was once a Jesuit monastery and later a theater. Trujillo had it restored in 1955 with an eye toward being buried there. (He is buried instead at Père Lachaise in Paris.) An allegorical mural of his assassination is painted on the ceiling above the altar, where an eternal flame burns. The impressive chandelier was a gift from Spain's Generalissimo Franco. ✉ *Calle Las Damas, near corner of Calle de Las Mercedes,* ☏ *no phone.* 🎫 *Free.* ☉ *Mon.–Sat. 10–5.*

❿ Parque Colón. The huge statue of Columbus here dates from 1897 and is the work of French sculptor Gilbert. On the west side of the square is the **old town hall** and, on the east, the **Palacio de Borgella,** residence of the governor during the Haitian occupation of 1822–44 and presently the seat of the Permanent Dominican Commission for the Fifth Centennial of the Discovery and Evangelization of the Americas. Gallery spaces house architectural and archaeological exhibits pertaining to the fifth centennial.

⑱ Parque Independencia. Independence Park, on the far western border of the Colonial Zone, is a big city park dominated by the marble and concrete **Altar de la Patria.** The impressive mausoleum was built in 1976 to honor the founding fathers of the country (Duarte, Sánchez, and Mella).

㉒ Plaza de la Cultura. Landscaped lawns, modern sculptures, and sleek buildings make up the Plaza de la Cultura. Among the buildings are the **Teatro Nacional** (National Theater; ☎ 809/687–3191), which stages performances in Spanish; the **Biblioteca Nacional** (National Library; ☎ 809/688–4086), in which the written word is Spanish; and museums and art galleries, whose notations are also in Spanish. The **Museo del Hombre Dominicano** (Museum of Dominican Man; ☎ 809/687–3623) traces the migrations of Indians from South America through the Caribbean islands. The **Museo de Historia Natural** (Museum of Natural History; ☎ 809/689–0106) examines the flora and fauna of the island. In the **Museo de Arte Moderno** (Museum of Modern Art; ☎ 809/682–8260), the works of 20th-century Dominican and foreign artists are displayed. Native sons include Elvis Aviles, an abstract painter whose works have a lot of texture. His art has obvious Spanish influences with Dominican symbols, such as those from the Taino Indians. Tony Capellan is one of the most well-known, representing the D.R. in major international exhibitions such as a recent one in South Africa. ⌑ *Museums RD$10 each.* ☉ *Tues.–Sat. 10–5.*

⑲ Puerta de la Misericordia. The "Gate of Mercy" is part of the old city wall. It was here on the plaza, on February 27, 1844, that Ramón Mata Mella, one of the country's founding fathers, fired the shot that began the struggle for independence from Haiti. ⌖ *Calle Palo Hincado at Calle Arzobispo Portes.*

⑬ Torre del Homenaje. You won't have any trouble spotting the Tower of Homage in Ft. Ozama. The fort sprawls two blocks south of the Casa de Bastidas, with a brooding crenellated tower that still guards the Ozama River. Built in 1503 to protect the eastern border of the city, the sinister tower was the last home of many a condemned prisoner. ⌖ *Paseo Presidente Bellini, overlooking Río Ozama,* ☎ *no phone.* ⌑ *RD$10.* ☉ *Tues.–Sun. 8–7.*

The East Coast

Las Américas Highway (built by the dictator Trujillo as a place for his son to race his sports cars) runs east along the coast from Santo Domingo to La Romana—about a two-hour drive. All along the highway are small resorts where you can find refreshments or stay overnight. East of La Romana are Punta Cana and Bavaro, glorious beaches on the sunrise side of the island. Along the way is Higüey, an undistinguished collection of ramshackle buildings notable only for its controversial church and shrine (someone apparently had a vision of the Virgin Mary here), consecrated by Pope John Paul II in 1984, which resembles a pinched, concrete McDonald's arch.

Numbers in the margin correspond to points of interest on the Dominican Republic map.

SIGHTS TO SEE

㉗ Altos de Chavón. Cattle and sugarcane used to be the two big mainstays around La Romana. That was before Gulf & Western created (and subsequently sold) the Casa de Campo resort, which is a very big business, indeed. Altos de Chavón, a re-creation of a 16th-century Mediterranean village and artist's colony, is on the resort grounds. It sits on a bluff overlooking the Río Chavón, about 3 mi east of the main facility of Casa de Campo. You can drive there easily enough, or you can take one of the free shuttle buses. There are cobblestone streets lined with lanterns, wrought-iron balconies and wooden shutters, and courtyards swathed with bougainvillea. More than a museum piece, this village, fashioned after a Tuscan hill town, is a place where artists live, work, and play. Dominican and international painters, sculptors, and artisans come here on a rotating basis, to teach sculpture, pottery, silk-screen printing, weaving, dance, and music at the art school, which is affiliated with New York's Parsons School of Design. They work in their studios and crafts shops and sell their finished wares. The village, which looks like it has stood for centuries, also houses a disco; an archaeological museum; five restaurants; and a 5,000-seat outdoor amphitheater where the likes of Frank Sinatra and Julio Iglesias have entertained. The focal point of the village is **Iglesia St. Stanislaus,** which is named after the patron saint of Poland in tribute to the Polish pope John Paul II, who visited the Dominican Republic in 1979 and left some of the ashes of St. Stanislaus behind. The charmed chapel is the romantic setting of many a wedding, with honeymoons following at the resort.

㉘ Isla Saona. Just off the east coast of Hispaniola lies this island, now a national park inhabited by sea turtles, pigeons, and other wildlife. Caves here were once used by Indians. The beaches are beautiful, and legend has it that Columbus once strayed ashore here.

㉕ Parque de los Tres Ojos. About 1½ mi outside the capital is the Park of the Three Eyes. The "eyes" are cool blue pools peering out of deep limestone caves, and it's actually a four-eyed park. If you've a mind to, you can look into the eyes more closely by climbing down into the caves.

㉖ San Pedro de Macorís. The national sport and the national drink are both well represented in this city, an hour or so east of Santo Domingo. Some of the country's best baseball games are played in **Tetelo Vargas Stadium.** Many major-league players in the States have roots here. The grander homes in the area most likely belong to Dominican baseball stars like George Bell and Tony Fernandez. The **Macorís Rum distillery** is on the eastern edge of the city. Outside town is **Juan Dolio,** a beach and resort area popular with capitaleños and foreign visitors.

The Southwest

㉚ Barahona. The latest area to be developed in the D.R. is still wild and pristine. Here mountains carpeted with rain forests and laced with streams slope down into white stretches of sand. You can bathe in the cascades of icy mountain rivers or in hot thermal springs surrounded by dense foliage, llanai vines, and fruit trees. Barahona is a tropical Garden of Eden. Be tempted to come while you and yours can still have it all to yourself.

㉗ Lago Enriquillo. The largest lake in the Antilles is near the Haitian border. The salt lake is also the lowest point in the Antilles: 114 ft below sea level. It encircles wild, arid, and thorny islands that serve as sanctuary to such exotic birds and reptiles as the flamingo, the iguana, and the caiman—the indigenous crocodile. The area is targeted by the government for improvements and infrastructure designed for eco-tourists.

The Cibao Valley

The heavily trafficked road north from Santo Domingo, known as the Autopista Duarte (at press time, it was slated to be opened as a four-lane divided highway), cuts through the lush banana plantations, rice and tobacco fields, and royal poinciana trees of the Cibao Valley. All along the road there are stands where, for a few centavos, you can buy ripe pineapples, mangoes, avocados, *chicharrones* (either fried pork rinds or chicken pieces), and fresh fruit drinks.

㊱ **Jarabacoa.** Nature lovers should consider a trip to Jarabacoa, in the mountainous region known rather wistfully as the Dominican Alps. There's little to do in the town itself but eat and rest up for excursions on foot, horseback, or by motorbike taxi to the surrounding waterfalls and forests—quite incongruous in such a tropical country. Accommodations in the area are rustic but comfortable. Recommended are **Alpes Dominicanos** (☏ 809/581–1462), which offers both hotel rooms with kitchenettes and individual self-service cottages, and the hacienda-style motel **Pinar Dorado** (☏ 809/574–2820).

㉟ **La Vega Vieja.** In the heart of the Cibao is La Vega. Founded in 1495 by Columbus, it's the site of one of the oldest settlements in the New World. The inquisitive will find the tour of the ruins of the original settlement, the Old La Vega, a rewarding experience. About 3 mi north of La Vega is **Santo Cerro** (Holy Mount), site of a miraculous apparition of the Virgin and therefore many local pilgrimages. The **Convent of La Merced** is here, and the views of the Cibao Valley are breathtaking. The new town boasts a remarkable church of its own, **Concepción de la Vega,** constructed in 1992 to commemorate the 500th anniversary of the discovery (and evangelization) of America. The unusual modern Gothic style—all curvaceous concrete columns, arches, and buttresses—is striking indeed.

La Vega is also celebrated for its Carnival, featuring the haunting devil masks. These papier-mâché creations are intricate, fanciful gargoyles painted in surreal colors; spiked horns and real cow's teeth lend an eerie authenticity. Several artisans work in dark, cramped studios throughout the area; their skills have been passed down for generations. The studio closest to downtown is that of José Luís Gomez. Ask any local (tip 10–20 pesos) to guide you to his atelier (no phone). José speaks no English but will show you the stages of mask development. He sells the masks, which make extraordinary wall hangings, for $50–$60, a great buy, considering the craftsmanship.

㉞ **Santiago de los Caballeros.** The second city of the D.R., where many past presidents were born, sits about 90 mi northwest of Santo Domingo. This industrial center has a surprisingly charming, provincial ambience. A massive monument honoring the restoration of the republic guards the entrance to the city. Traditional yet progressive, Santiago is relatively new to the tourist scene, but try to set aside a day or two to explore this city, which dates from the 1500s. Architecturally diverse, there are colonial-style buildings with wrought-iron details and tiled porticos as well as many homes reflecting a Victorian influence with the requisite gingerbread latticework and fanciful colors. Santiago is a center for processing tobacco leaf. You can gain an appreciation of the art and skill of Dominican (similar to Cuban) cigar making with a colorful tour of **E. Leon Jiménez Tabacalera** (☏ 809/563–1111 or 809/535–5555).The best hotel in town is the **Gran Almirante** (☏ 809/580–1992, FAX 809/241–1492).

The Amber Coast

The Autopista Duarte ultimately leads (in three to four hours from Santo Domingo) to the Amber Coast, so called because of its large, rich, and unique deposits of amber. The coastal area around Puerto Plata is a region of splashy resorts and mega-developments like Costambar and Playa Dorada. The north coast boasts more than 70 mi of beaches, with condominiums and villas going up fast. The farther east from Puerto

Plata and its little sister, Sosua, you get, the prettier and less spoiled the scenery becomes. The autopista runs past Cabarete, a neat village that's a popular windsurfing haunt, and Playa Grande. The white-sand beach is miraculously undisturbed and unspoiled.

SIGHTS TO SEE

③⓪ Laguna Grí-Grí. This swampland, which looks as if it's smack out of the Louisiana bayou country, has the added attraction of a cool blue grotto that almost outdoes the Blue Grotto of Capri. Laguna Grí-Grí is only about 90 minutes west of Puerto Plata, in Río San Juan (ask your hotel concierge for directions off the autopista).

③③ Mt. Isabel de Torres. Southwest of Puerto Plata, this mountain soars 2,600 ft above sea level. On the mountain there's a botanical garden, a huge statue of Christ, and a spectacular view. At press time, the government was replacing the cable so that cable cars could, once again, take sightseers to the top. ⊠ *Follow signs from autopista,* ☎ *no phone.* ⌨ *RD$20 round-trip.* ☉ *Cable car slated to operate Mon.–Tues. and Thurs.–Sun. 9–5.*

③② Puerto Plata. Although now quiet and almost sleepy, this was a dynamic city in its heyday. You can get a feeling for this past in the magnificent Victorian gazebo in the central **Parque Independencia.** Next to the park, the **Catedral de San Felipe** recalls a simpler, colonial past. On Puerto Plata's own Malecón, the **Fortaleza de San Felipe** protected the city from many a pirate attack and was later used as a political prison. The fort is most dramatic at night.

Puerto Plata is also the home of the **Museo de Ambar Dominicano,** (Dominican Amber Museum), which is in a lovely galleried mansion. The museum displays and sells the D.R.'s national stone. Semiprecious, translucent amber is actually fossilized pine resin that dates from about 50 million years ago, give or take a few millennia. Shops on the first floor of the museum sell amber, souvenirs, and ceramics. ⊠ *Calle Duarte 61,* ☎ *809/586–2848.* ⌨ *RD$15.* ☉ *Mon.–Sat. 9–5.*

②⑨ Samaná. Back in 1824, a sailing vessel called the *Turtle Dove,* carrying several hundred escaped American slaves from the Freeman Sisters' underground railway, was blown ashore in Samaná. The escapees settled and prospered, and today their descendants number several thousand. The churches here are Protestant; the worshipers live in villages called Bethesda, Northeast, and Philadelphia; and the language spoken is an odd 19th-century form of English—although you're more likely to hear Spanish.

The marine life in the surrounding waters is attracting more people. Sportfishing at Samaná is considered to be among the best in the world. In addition, about 3,000 humpback whales winter off the coast of Samaná from December to March. Major whale-watching expeditions are being organized and should boost the region's economy without scaring away the world's largest mammals.

Samaná makes a fine base for exploring the area's natural splendors. Most hotels on the peninsula arrange tours to **Los Haitises National Park,** a remote, unspoiled rain forest with limestone knolls, crystal lakes, mangrove swamps teeming with aquatic birds, and caves stippled with Taino petroglyphs. **Las Terrenas,** a remote stretch of beautiful, nearly deserted beaches on the north coast of the Samaná peninsula attracts surfers and windsurfers. There are several modest seafood restaurants (the best is **Boca Fina,** ☎ no phone), a dusty main street in the town of Las Terrenas, a small airfield, the comparatively grand all-inclusive **El Portillo Beach Club** (☎ 809/688–5785), and several congenial hotels right on the beach at Punta Bonita. If you're happy just hanging out drinking beer and soaking up the sun, this is the place for you. The road from Samaná, even though it's longer and not paved, is a lot less strenuous than the route over the hills from Sanchez.

㉛ Sosua. This small community was settled during World War II by 600 Austrian and German Jews. After the war, many of them returned to Europe or went to the United States, and most of those who remained married Dominicans. Only a few Jewish families reside in the community today, and there's only one small one-room synagogue. The flavor of the town is decidedly Spanish. (Note: The roads off the autopista have been repaved and repaired.)

Sosua, called Puerto Plata's little sister, has become one of the country's most popular destinations. Hotels and condos are going up at breakneck speed. It actually consists of two communities, **El Batey**, the modern hotel development, and **Los Charamicos,** the old quarter, separated by a cove and one of the island's prettiest beaches. The sand is soft and white; the water, crystal clear and calm. The walkway above the beach is packed with tents filled with souvenirs, pizzas, and even clothing for sale—a jarring note in this otherwise idyllic setting.

Dominican Republic A to Z

Arriving and Departing

BY AIRPLANE

International flights generally arrive at **Las Américas International Airport** (☎ 809/549–0450), about 20 mi outside Santo Domingo, and **La Unión International Airport** (☎ 809/586–0107 or 809/586–0219), about 15 mi east of Puerto Plata on the north coast. There's also **La Romana International Airport** (☎ 809/556–5565) at the Casa de Campo resort (☞ Lodging, *above*). Anticipate long lines and allow 1½ to two hours for checking in for an international flight. Do confirm your flight two days in advance. Keep a sharp eye on your luggage. If you fly out of a U.S. airport such as Miami, where a shrink-wrap service is offered, avail yourself of it. (Plastic-wrap your bag like meat in a supermarket and no one is likely to tamper with it.) Be prepared for a daunting experience as you leave customs. There will be a frenzy of waiting friends, relatives, drivers, and *buscones* (porters).

American Airlines (☎ 809/542–5151) has the most extensive service to the D.R. It flies nonstop from New York and Miami to Santo Domingo, Puerto Plata, and La Romana and offers connections to both Santo Domingo and Puerto Plata from San Juan, Puerto Rico. From San Juan, **American Eagle** (☎ 809/542–5151) has a six daily flights to Santo Domingo, two daily flights to La Romana, two flights daily to Santiago, and several flights weekly to Punta Cana. **Continental** (☎ 809/562–6688) flies nonstop from Newark to Puerto Plata and Santo Domingo. **TWA** (☎ 809/689–6073) has nonstop service to Santo Domingo from New York's Kennedy Airport.

Several regional carriers serve neighboring islands. **ALM** (☎ 809/687–4569) connects Santo Domingo to St. Maarten and Curaçao. Domestic service is now available on **Air Santo Domingo** (☎ 809/683–8020) from Herrera Airport (☎ 809/567–3900) in Santo Domingo to other airfields in La Romana, Samaná, and Santiago.

From the Airport: Taxis are available at the airports, and the 25-minute ride into Santo Domingo averages about RD$250. Fares from the Puerto Plata airport average RD$200 to Playa Dorada. Some order has been imposed outside the airport—taxis line up and, for the most part, charge the official established rates. If you've arranged for a hotel transfer, which is a good idea, a representative should be waiting for you in the immigration hall.

Electricity

The current is 110 volts, 60 cycles—just like in the United States. You'll hear much talk about electrical blackouts, but they occur less and less and tend to last only one to two minutes. (When they're over, everyone claps.) Hotels and most restaurants have back-up generators.

Emergencies

Hospitals: Santo Domingo emergency rooms that are open 24 hours are **Centro Médico Sosua** (✉ Av. Martinez, Sosua, ☎ 809/571–3949), **Centro Médico Universidad Central del Este** (UCE; ✉ Av. Máximo Gómez 68, Santo Domingo, ☎ 809/221–0171), **Clínica Abreu** (✉ Calle Beller 42, Santo Domingo, ☎ 809/688–4411), **Clínica Dr. Brugal** (✉ Calle José del Carmen Ariza 15, Puerto Plata, ☎ 809/586–2519), and **Clínica Gómez Patino** (✉ Av. Independencia 701, Santo Domingo, ☎ 809/685–9131).

Pharmacies: Pharmacies that are open 24 hours a day include **Farmacia Deleyte** (✉ Av. John F. Kennedy 89, Puerto Plata, ☎ 809/586–2583) and **San Judas Tadeo** (✉ Av. Independencia 57, Santo Domingo, ☎ 809/689–6664). **Police:** ☎ 711 in **Santo Domingo;** ☎ 809/586–2804 in **Puerto Plata;** ☎ 809/571–2233 in **Sosua.**

Festivals and Seasonal Events

Santo Domingo hosts a **Carnival** in late February. The renowned **Festival del Merengue** is held in late July and early August in Santo Domingo, and showcases name entertainers, bands, and orchestras. During the last week in August, the island's top restaurants compete in the capital city's **Gastronomic Festival.** In October, the **Puerto Plata Festival** transforms the Amber Coast into one giant fiesta.

Getting Around

AIRPLANES

Air Santo Domingo (☞ Arriving and Departing by Airplane, *above*) offers airline service between Santo Domingo and Puerto Plata, Punta Cana, La Romana, El Portillo, and Santiago. As a rule, each hop is about $50 (you can keep costs down by avoiding stopovers). For surprisingly reasonable rates, you can also charter a small plane for trips around the island or to neighboring islands. Contact Jimmy or Irene Butler at **Air Taxi** (✉ Núñez de Cáceres 2, Santo Domingo, ☎ 809/227–8333 or 809/567–1555).

BUSES

Traditionally, *públicos* or *conchos* are small blue-and-white or blue-and-red cars that run regular routes, stopping to let passengers on and off. But now everyone is getting into the act. Anyone who owns a car can operate it as a *público* and after 5 PM many do, considering it as their second job. The fare is RD$2. Competing with the públicos are the *colectivos* (privately owned buses), whose drivers coast around the major thoroughfares, leaning out of the window or jumping out to try to persuade you to climb aboard. It's a colorful, if cramped, way to get around town. The fare is about RD$1.

Privately owned, air-conditioned buses make regular runs to Santiago, Puerto Plata, and other destinations. You should make reservations by calling **Metro Buses** (☎ 809/566–7126 in Santo Domingo, 809/586–6062 in Puerto Plata, or 809/587–4711 in Santiago) or **Caribe Tours** (☎ 809/221–4422). One-way bus fare from Santo Domingo to Puerto Plata is RD$80 (about US$6), and it takes four hours. Metro's buses have more of an upscale clientele. Although the coffee, water, and cookies are complimentary, there are no movies. Caribe, which shows bilingual movies, is favored by the locals; buses are often filled to capacity, especially on weekends.

Frequent service from Santo Domingo to the town of La Romana is provided by **Express Bus.** Buses depart from Revelos Street in front of Enriquillo Park, every hour on the hour, from 5 AM to 9 PM; the schedule is exactly the same from Romana. The office of this bus line is now closed, so there's no phone. But a ticket-taker will take your 40 pesos (US$2.90) just before departure. Travel time is about 1¾ hours, and if luck is with you, you will get the larger bus, which will show a first-rate American movie. Once in town you can take a taxi from the bus stop to Casa de Campo ($7) or Casa del Mar ($10).

Voladoras (fliers) are vans that run from Puerto Plata's Central Park to Sosua and Cabarete a couple of times each hour for RD$10. They have a reliable schedule and aren't always labeled with their destination.

CAR RENTALS

You'll need a valid driver's license from your own country and a major credit card and/or cash deposit. Rates average US$70 and up per day. Ask around, as some local agencies give better rates. Try the following local and international companies: **Avis** (☎ 809/535–7191), **Budget** (☎ 809/562–6812), **Hertz** (☎ 809/221–5333), **McBeal** (☎ 809/688–6518), **National** (☎ 809/562–1444), and **Nelly Rent-a-Car** (☎ 809/544–1800, 800/526–6684 in the U.S.).

Driving is on the right. Many Dominicans drive recklessly, and their cars are often in bad shape (missing headlights, taillights, etc.). It's strongly suggested that you don't drive outside the major cities at night. If you must, use extreme caution, especially on the narrow, unlighted mountain roads. Whenever you drive, watch out for pedestrians, bicycles, motorbikes, and the occasional stray cow or goat.

Traffic and directional signs are less than adequate; before setting out, consult with your hotel concierge about routes and buy a good road map. Also, fill up—and keep an eye on—the tank; gas stations are few and far between in rural areas. (At press time, gas was about $1.76 to $2.20 a gallon.) Although some roads are still full of potholes, others have been greatly improved: The route between Santo Domingo and Santiago is now a four-lane divided highway, and the road between Santiago and Puerto Plata now has a smooth new blacktop. Surprisingly, many of the scenic secondary roads are in good shape.

The 80 kph (50 mph) speed limit is strictly enforced. Note that outside Santiago, you might be pulled over for speeding, even if you weren't. You'll be expected to pay a bribe of about RD$40 (about US$3). Pay it, smile, and moan about it later. The hassles just aren't worth it if you don't. The police count on these payoffs to augment their meager incomes. Upon taking office, the new president allegedly doubled the policemen's salaries and is hoping to increase them even more—perhaps eliminating the need for such "moonlighting."

MOTORBIKE TAXIS

Motoconchos are a popular and inexpensive way to get around such tourist areas as Puerto Plata, Sosua, and Jarabacoa. You can flag one of these bikes down alongside rural roads and in town; rates vary from RD$3 to RD$20 per person, depending upon distance. Be careful: No helmets are provided, and the Dominicans drive like maniacs!

TAXIS

Taxis, which are government regulated, line up outside hotels and restaurants. They're unmetered, and the minimum fare within Santo

Domingo is about RD$50 (US$4), but you can bargain for less if you order a taxi away from the major hotels. Some taxis aren't allowed to pick up from hotels, so they hang out on the street in front of them. (Note: Avoid unmarked street taxis, particularly in Santo Domingo—they're a little risky, and there have been incidents of robberies.) On the average, they're $1 cheaper per ride.

Hiring a taxi by the hour—with unlimited stops—is RD$125 (US$10) per hour with a minimum of two hours. Be sure to establish the time that you start; drivers like to advance the time a little. Always carry small denominations, like 5-, 10-, and 20-peso notes, because drivers rarely seem to have change. Taxis can also drive you to destinations outside the city. Rates are posted in hotels and at the airport. Sample fares from Santo Domingo are RD$1,000 (US$80) to La Romana and RD$1,900 (US$150) to Puerto Plata. If you're negotiating, the going rate is RD$5 per kilometer. Round-trips are considerably less than twice the one-way fare. Two good cab companies are **El Conde Taxi** (☎ 809/563–6131) and **Tecni-Taxi** (☎ 809/567–2010 in Santo Domingo, 809/320–7621 in Puerto Plata).

Radio taxis are not only convenient but also a wise choice if you don't speak Spanish. The fare is negotiated over the phone when you make the appointment. The most reliable company is **Apolo Taxi** (☎ 809/541–9595). The standard charge is RD$100 per hour during the day and RD$120 at night, no minimum, and with as many stops as you like. Another option is to go in high-Dominican style and hire a limo, even if it's just for a night. Call the **Limousine Connection** (☎ 809/540–5304 or 809/567–3435), whose rates run around $49 per hour.

Guided Tours

Apolo Tours (☎ 809/586–5329) offers a full-day tour of Playa Grande and tours to Santiago (including a casino tour) and Sosua. It will also arrange transfers between your hotel and the airport, day trips, and custom and small-group tours along the north coast, which include stops for swimming and an overnight stay at Samaná. **Cabemba Tours** (☎ 809/586–2177) runs various tours of the Cibao Valley and the Amber Coast, including Puerto Plata, Sosua, and Río San Juan. **Caribbean Jeep Safaris** (☎ 809/571–1924) is an English-speaking outfit that runs Jeep tours in the mountains behind Puerto Plata and Sosua, ending up at the Cabarete Adventure Park, where you can swim in an underground pool and explore caves with Taino rock paintings. Buffet lunch and unlimited drinks are included in the RD$600 price.

Ecoturisa (☎ 809/221–4104) arranges ecological tours and cultural and scientific expeditions, many of them tailored to the clients' needs. **Go Dominican Tours** (☎ 809/586–5969) has tours to Jarabacoa for $85, which include lunch, drinks, and 3½ hours of river rafting; jumping off cliffs is optional. Jeep safaris trek to flower, fruit, and coffee plantations. Horseback riding in the Puerto Plata area is another option. **Iguana Mamma, Mountain Bike and Hiking** (☎ 800/571–0908) offers adventure tours with an ecological conscience: 20% of their profits are donated to local environmental projects and education. **Prieto Tours** (☎ 809/685–0102), which operates Gray Line of the D.R., has half-day bus tours of Santo Domingo, nightclub tours, beach tours, trips to Cibao Valley and the Amber Coast, and a variety of other excursions. **Turinter** (☎ 809/685–4020) tours include dinner and a show or casino visit, a full-day tour of Samaná, and specialty trips (museum, shopping, fishing). Before leaving home, you can also make arrangements with **Winchester Tours** (☎ 800/391–2473), a Massachusetts-based company that specializes in wildlife and bird-watching tours of Barahona for groups of 6–10 nature lovers. Fred Sladen, president, also acts as tour leader.

Having lived in the Caribbean for 15 years, he's a recognized authority on tropical birds and ecosystems and is a very personable host as well. He, too, donates to conservation organizations in the D.R.

Language

Before you travel to the D.R., it might not be a bad idea to rent Spanish audiotapes from the library or study a quick guide to "travel Spanish" and take it with you. Staff at major tourist attractions and front-desk personnel in the major hotels speak a fascinating form of English, and you may have difficulty making yourself understood. Outside the popular tourist establishments restaurant menus are in Spanish as are traffic signs everywhere. Using smiles and gestures will help, and though you can manage with just English, people are even more courteous if you try to speak their language.

Money Matters

CURRENCY

The coin of the realm is the Dominican peso, which is divided into 100 centavos. It is written RD$ and fluctuates relative to the U.S. dollar. At press time, RD$14 was equivalent to US$1. Always make certain you know in which currency any transaction is taking place. Do yourself a favor and carry a pocket calculator to make conversions easier. Prices quoted in this chapter are in U.S. dollars unless noted otherwise.

SERVICE CHARGES, TAXES, AND TIPPING

A 10% service charge is added to restaurant checks and hotel bills as is a 13% government tax. The D.R. also has a $10 departure tax. If you found the service to your liking tip an extra 5%–10%. It's customary to leave a dollar per day for the hotel maid. Taxi drivers expect a 10% tip, especially if they've had to lift luggage or to wait for you. Skycaps and hotel porters expect at least RD$5 per bag.

Opening and Closing Times

Offices and **shops** are open weekdays 8–noon and 2–6, Saturday 8–noon. About 50% of the stores stay open all day, no longer closing for a midday siesta. **Government offices,** including post offices, have hours weekdays 7:30–2:30. **Banks** are open weekdays 8:30–4:30.

HOLIDAYS

New Year's Day, Our Lady of La Altagracia Day (Jan. 21), Duarte's Birthday (Jan. 26), Independence Day (Feb. 27) Good Friday (Apr. 2), Labor Day (May 1), Corpus Christi (June 3), Restoration Day (Aug. 16), Our Lady of Las Mercedes Day (Sept. 24), Columbus Day (Oct. 26), Discovery of Hispaniola Day (Dec. 5), and Christmas.

Passports

U.S. and Canadian citizens must have either a valid passport or proof of citizenship, such as an original (not photocopied) birth certificate. Legal residents of the United States must have an alien registration card (green card) and a valid passport. British citizens need a valid passport. Upon arrival at the airport, all visitors must purchase a $10 tourist card. Keep the bottom half of the card in a safe place, because you'll need to present it to immigration authorities when you leave. All foreign visitors must pay a $10 departure tax, as well. Both it and the tourist card must be paid for in U.S. dollars (cash not traveler's checks), so allow for it.

Precautions

Though it's reasonably safe to drink water from the tap (especially in the better resorts), you're better off playing it safe by drinking bottled water. Try to arrive at the very start of a buffet meal, before the food has sat out for a while in the tropical heat.

In Santo Domingo, as in any other big city, be conscious of your wallet or pocketbook, especially around the Malecón (waterfront boulevard), where pickpockets are a problem. Note that at night you may see men in civvies with shoulder rifles standing outside businesses or homes. Do not be unnerved by this. These men are the Dominican equivalents of private security guards. In general, the island is very safe, and you don't hear about violent crime against tourists. If you rent a car, don't drink and drive. Always lock your car and never leave valuables in it even if it is locked. Getting behind the wheel here makes the streets of Rome or Paris seem like peaceful, country lanes. Be alert and aware, and drive with caution.

Telephones and Mail

To call the D.R. from the United States, dial 1 and then the area code 809 and the local number. From the D.R., there's direct-dial service to the United States; just dial 1, followed by the area code and number.

Airmail postage to North America for a letter or postcard costs RD$2, to Europe RD$4, and may take up to three weeks to reach the destination. Or you can pay almost US$1.45 to buy a pale green stamp for "fast mail" in a gift shop (post offices are not easy to find); supposedly it will take a card only three days to get to the States.

Visitor Information

Before you go, contact the **Dominican Republic Tourist Office** (✉ 136 E. 57th St., Suite 803, New York, NY 10022, ☎ 212/575–4966 or 888/374–6361, www.dr1.com; ✉ 2355 Salzedo Ave., Suite 307, Coral Gables, FL 33134, ☎ 305/444–4592 or 888/358–9594; ✉ 1464 Crescent St., Montréal, Québec, H3A 2B6, ☎ 514/933–6126).

In the Dominican Republic, the **Secretary of Tourism** (✉ Officinas Guberbamentales Bldg. D, ☎ 809/221–4660) is in Santo Domingo in a complex of government offices at the corner of Avenida Mexico and Avenida 30 de Marzo. Unless you are seeking special assistance, it's not worth making the trek here for the limited material offered to tourists. Another source of information is the **Ministry of Tourism** (✉ Av. Mexico, ☎ 809/221–4660) in Santo Domingo. At press time, the tourist office was planning to set up information kiosks along the Malecón in Santo Domingo and in other tourist areas. In Puerto Plata, the **tourist office** (✉ Playa Long Beach, ☎ 809/586–3676) is open weekdays 9–2:30.

12 Grenada

By Jane E.
Zarem

It's cool, dark, and pungent inside the nutmeg co-op. In loose floral skirts and cotton shirts, bandanas around their heads, the ladies of Gouyave work hard for their money. Perched on stools, facing huge wooden chutes, they handle nutmegs all day. Fingers move like lightning, sorting thousands per hour. When sunlight briefly brightens the room, the chute wall reveals someone's handwritten message: GOD LOOKED AT MY WORK AND WAS PLEASED. THEN HE LOOKED AT MY SALARY, BOWED HIS HEAD, AND SADLY WALKED AWAY.

Grenada, a jewel of an island 21 mi long and 12 mi wide, is bordered by 45 beaches and countless secluded coves, crisscrossed by nature trails, and filled with spice plantations, tropical forests, and select hotels that cling to hillsides and overlook the sea. Grenada's sweetly naive spirit and eye-popping natural beauty juxtapose with top facilities and sensible development. St. George's is one of the most charming capital cities in the Caribbean; Grand Anse, one of the finest beaches.

If the Irish hadn't beaten them to the name, Grenadians might very well have called their land the Emerald Isle, for the lush rain forests and the thick vegetation on the hillsides give it a rich, green beauty that few places can match. Grenada lies in the eastern Caribbean, 12 degrees north of the equator, and is the most southerly of the Windward Islands. The nation of Grenada really consists of three inhabited islands: Grenada is the largest, with 120 square mi and a population of about 96,000 people; Carriacou (pronounced *car*-ree-a-coo), 23 mi north of Grenada, has 13 square mi and a population of about 5,000; and Petit Martinique, 2 mi northeast of Carriacou, has just 486 acres and a population of 700. Although Carriacou and Petit Martinique are popular for day trips or fishing and snorkeling excursions, most of the tourist activity is on Grenada, as is the capital St. George's and it's eponymous picturesque harbor.

Nicknamed the Isle of Spice, Grenada is a major producer of nutmeg, cinnamon, mace, cocoa, and other common spices. The pleasant aroma of spices fills the air: in markets, in restaurants, and in pubs (where nutmeg is sprinkled on rum punches).

Although he never set foot on Grenada, Columbus sighted the island in 1498 and named it Concepción. Spanish sailors following in his wake renamed it Granada, after the Andalusian city in the hills of their homeland. Adapted to Grenade by French colonists, the transformation to Grenada was completed by the British in the 18th century.

European settlement was a long, difficult process. Throughout the 17th century, Grenada was the scene of many bloody battles between Carib Indians and the French. Upon losing their last battle in 1651, the surviving Caribs committed mass suicide by leaping off a cliff rather than surrendering. The French ultimately were overwhelmed by the British in 1762, thus beginning a seesaw of power between the two nations. By the Treaty of Versailles in 1783, Grenada was granted to the British and, almost immediately, African slaves were brought in to work the sugar plantations. Slavery continued for 50 years until it was abolished in 1834.

In 1974 Grenada was granted total independence within the British Commonwealth. The New Jewel Movement (NJM) seized power in 1979, formed the People's Revolutionary Government, and named as prime minister Maurice Bishop, who established controversial ties with Cuba. A 1983 coup d'état led to his execution and that of many of his supporters. NJM Deputy Prime Minister Bernard Coard and Army Commander Hudson Austin took over the government. At the request of Grenada's Governor General, U.S. troops intervened on October 25, 1983, and evacuated American students who were attending St. George's University Medical School. Coard and Austin were arrested, and resistance to the intervention was quickly quelled.

The late Herbert A. Blaize was elected prime minister in December 1984. With millions of dollars in U.S. and Canadian aid, his government reorganized Grenada's economy to emphasize agriculture, light manufacturing, and tourism. The country rebuilt roads and installed a direct-dial telephone system. Grenada's modern Point Salines International Airport, which opened in 1984, enabled jets to land day or night.

The peaceful progress of this island nation continues. Grenada's popularity as a vacation destination increases each year as travelers seek new and exotic islands. Hotels have expanded, and new ones are on the drawing board; but any expansion of the tourism industry is carefully controlled. No building can stand taller than a coconut palm, and construction on the beaches must be at least 165 ft from the high-water mark. Hotels, resorts, and restaurants remain, for the most part, comparatively small and family-owned, run by people who get to know their guests and pride themselves on personalized service. They're typical of the islanders as a whole—friendly, hospitable, and hardworking.

Lodging

Grenada's lodgings are in the southwest, primarily on or near Grand Anse Beach. They range from simply furnished kitchenette apartments to suites of Caribbean-style elegance. Many hotels are owned by Grenadians; others are run by British or American expatriates who thrive on the simplicity of life here. The hotels tend to be small and intimate, with friendly managers and owners and attentive staff. Families should note that some resorts may not welcome children during the winter season (December 15–April 15); call ahead. Prices during the summer may be discounted by up to 40%.

CATEGORY	COST*
$$$$	over $275
$$$	$200–$275
$$	$125–$200
$	under $125

All prices are for a standard double room in high season, excluding 8% government tax and 10% service charge.

Grenada

HOTELS

$$$$ 🏨 **Calabash Hotel.** Suites in this very elegant, comfortable, hotel on the L'Anse aux Epines peninsula are in two-story cottages scattered over 8 acres of tropical gardens that hug the curved beach and a yacht harbor on Prickly Bay. The cottages are framed by fragrant frangipani and colorful hibiscus, bougainvillea, and oleander blossoms. Twenty-two suites have whirlpool baths; eight have private plunge pools. Each suite has a spacious bedroom and sitting area, as well as a veranda where breakfast is delivered. Rooms have rattan and wicker furniture and are decorated in soothing pastels and island-print fabrics. Fans dangle from whitewashed ceilings. Bathrooms are equipped with hair dryers and lighted makeup mirrors. Calabash has a loyal following of British guests, who return year after year. At ☞ **Cicely's**, the hotel's award-winning restaurant, a well-trained staff serves excellent food. ✉ *L'Anse aux Epines (Box 382), St. George's,* ☎ *473/444–4234; 800/223–6510, 800/223–9815, or 800/742–4276 (reservation services),* FAX *473/444–5050. 30 suites . Restaurant, 2 bars, air-conditioning, room service, pool, tennis court, exercise room, shuffleboard, beach, snorkeling, boating, shop, billiards, library, baby-sitting, dry cleaning, laundry service, concierge. AE, MC, V. CP, MAP.*

$$$$ 🏨 **LaSOURCE.** Minutes from the airport (but away from the flight path), this all-inclusive resort and spa unfolds on 40 acres facing Pink Gin Beach. The complex is reminiscent of a 19th-century West Indian colonial village, with the gracious main building resembling a governor's residence. Its grand reception hall leads to a breezy courtyard, around which are the spa-treatment rooms, a restaurant with a colonnaded dining terrace, a piano bar, and a two-level swimming pool. Guest quarters are in four-story buildings, all facing the beach. (Be prepared for lots of stairs; there are no elevators.) Bedrooms have Persian rugs on Italian marble floors; Jamaican mahogany furniture and woodwork; four-poster king-size beds; high ceilings; balconies overlooking the sea; and marble bathrooms. Junior suites have a comfortable sitting area with a bay window. You can experiment with the chef's light spa cuisine or choose richer menu selections. In addition to the usual resort sports, yoga and fencing are offered. Rates include *everything*—even spa treatments (aromatherapy, wraps, rubs, massages, and facials)—and tipping isn't allowed. ✉ *Pink Gin Beach (Box 852), St. George's,* ☎ *473/444–2556 or 800/544–2883 (reservations service),* FAX *473/444–2561. 100 rooms. 2 restaurants, piano bar, air-conditioning, fans, minibars, pool, beauty salon, hot tub, sauna, spa, 9-hole golf course, 2 tennis courts, aerobics, archery, health club, jogging, Ping-Pong, volleyball, beach, dive shop, snorkeling, windsurfing, boating, waterskiing, shop, cabaret, airport shuttle. AE, MC, V. All-inclusive.*

$$$$ 🏨 **Spice Island Beach Resort.** You won't find a better location in
★   Grenada than this classic beach resort. In some suites you can step from your room right onto Grand Anse Beach. Other suites have terraces that overlook garden, sea, or sunset. The luxurious rooms are spacious, stylishly decorated in sand and coral tones, with vast mirrored closets

and extra-large, skylighted bathrooms with whirlpool tubs, hair dryers, and plenty of plush towels. Thirteen private plunge pool suites are just 50 ft from the beach; 39 whirlpool suites are in either beachfront or garden locations. Four Royal Suites, each 1,473 square ft, are the ultimate luxury, with a 16- × 20-ft pool, a garden, a sitting room, a sundeck, and an in-room fitness area with exercise bike and sauna. There's a TV in the library and in each Royal Suite. You can dine at ☞ Spice Island Beach Resort's beachside restaurant (several times a week in season, there's also entertainment) or at ☞ Blue Horizons Cottage Hotel's restaurant, ☞ La Belle Creole. You also have free use of Sunfish, pedal boats, kayaks, and snorkel gear for an hour per day. ⊠ *Grand Anse (Box 6), St. George's,* ☎ *473/444–4258; 800/223–6510, 800/223–9815, or 800/742–4276 (reservations services),* FAX *473/444–4807. 56 suites. Restaurant, bar, air-conditioning, fans, minibars, room service, tennis court, exercise room, beach, snorkeling, boating, bicycles, shop, library, laundry service, concierge, meeting room. AE, D, DC, MC, V. All-inclusive, CP, MAP.*

$$$ 🏨 **Mahogany Run.** Just over the hill from Grand Anse Beach, this colony of Mediterranean-style buildings slopes down to Morne Rouge Beach. Sixteen deluxe suites are stacked on six levels. Each has a living room, kitchen, bedroom, and luxurious bath (with bathrobes, too). All have either a covered veranda or patio and dramatic views of the bay. Some are air-conditioned (at an extra charge). You can walk down to the beach or take the free water shuttle to Dr. Groom's Beach Club for water sports, beach volleyball, and a café. Rates include airport transfers, housekeeping, and breakfast cooked and served in your suite. ⊠ *Morne Rouge (Box 730), St. George's,* ☎ *473/444–3171,* FAX *473/444–3172. 16 suites. Restaurant, bar, in-room safes, minibars, beach, snorkeling, laundry service, airport shuttle. AE, MC, V. CP, EP.*

$$$ 🏨 **Mariposa Beach Resort.** Like its adjacent sister property, ☞ Mahogany Run, Mariposa's rooms are piled atop one another in buildings on the hillside. Each room has a water view, a covered veranda or garden, a TV, and a bathroom decorated with Italian tiles. It's a short walk downhill to Morne Rouge Beach or a water taxi ride to the beach club. The restaurant specializes in seafood and international dishes. Rates remain the same year-round. ⊠ *Morne Rouge (Box 730), St. George's,* ☎ *473/444–3839,* FAX *473/444–3172. 32 rooms. Restaurant, bar, air-conditioning, in-room safes, room service, pool, beach, laundry service. AE, MC, V. MAP.*

$$$ 🏨 **Secret Harbour Resort.** On a cliff above Mount Hartman Bay (and away from the throng on the south coast), this cliffside resort primarily attracts a yachting crowd. The on-site Moorings' Club Mariner Watersports Centre has a fleet of small sailboats and yachts available for day or long-term charters. The resort has 20 private suites, each beautifully decorated with two antique, four-poster full-size beds and an Italian-tile bath. If you stay here, you have free use of water-sports equipment, including Windsurfers, Sunfish, and sailboats. Just offshore, Calvigny Island is a 10-minute ride by speedboat; bring a picnic and spend the afternoon on your own deserted isle. ⊠ *L'Anse aux Epines (Box 11), St. George's,* ☎ *473/444–4439,* FAX *473/444–4819. 20 suites. 2 restaurants, bar, air-conditioning, pool, tennis court, beach, dive shop, dock, windsurfing, boating. AE, D, DC, MC, V. EP, MAP.*

$$–$$$ 🏨 **Allamanda Beach Resort and Spa.** The newest addition to the Grand Anse hotel scene is this 50-room resort directly on the beach, adjacent to Camerhogne Park. Some rooms have adjoining doors, a good choice for families; others have whirlpool baths and beautiful views of beach and sea. All rooms are freshly appointed with modern tropical decor and tile floors, cable TV, and a balcony or patio; some are wheelchair-accessible. Bathrooms have hair dryers. The spa offers aerobics classes,

Exploring
Annandale Falls, **6**
Bay Gardens, **3**
Belair, **19**
Carib's Leap, **13**
Concord Falls, **8**
Dougaldston Spice
Estate, **9**
Fisherman's Museum, **11**
Gouyave Nutmeg
Cooperative, **10**
Grand Anse, **2**
Grand Etang
National Park, **7**
Grenville, **16**
Historical Museum, **17**
Laura Herb and Spice
Garden, **5**
Levera Nat'l. Park, **14**
Mt. Rodney Estate, **12**
River Antoine Rum
Distillery, **15**
St. George's, **1**
Sandy Island, **18**
Tyrrel Bay, **20**
Westerhall, **4**

Dining
Aquarium, **41**
La Belle Creole, **34**
The Boatyard, **46**
La Boulangerie, **31**
Callaloo, **52**
Canboulay, **33**
Cicely's, **45**
Coconut Beach, **24**
Cot Bam, **27**
La Dolce Vita, **36**
Joe's Steak House, **32**
Mama's, **21**
The Nutmeg, **22**
Le Petit Conch Shell, **50**
Red Crab, **48**
Rudolf's, **23**
La Sagesse, **49**
Scraper's, **51**
Spice Island, **29**
Tabanca at Journey's End, **30**

Lodging
Allamanda Beach
Resort and Spa, **26**
Blue Horizons
Cottage Hotel, **34**
Calabash Hotel, **45**
Caribbee Inn, **54**
Coyaba Beach, **28**
Flamboyant Hotel and
Cottages, **35**
LaSOURCE, **40**
Mahogany Run, **37**
Mariposa Beach Resort, **38**
Renaissance Grenada
Resort, **25**
Rex Grenadian, **39**
La Sagesse, **49**
Secret Harbour Resort, **44**
Silver Beach Resort, **53**
Spice Island, **29**
True Blue Inn, **43**
Twelve Degrees North, **47**
Wave Crest, **42**

Grenada (and Carriacou)

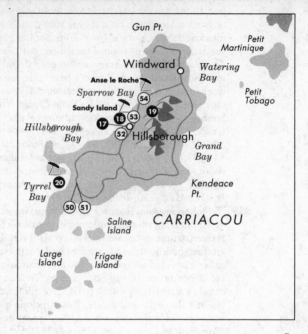

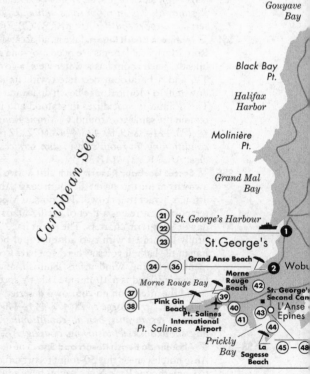

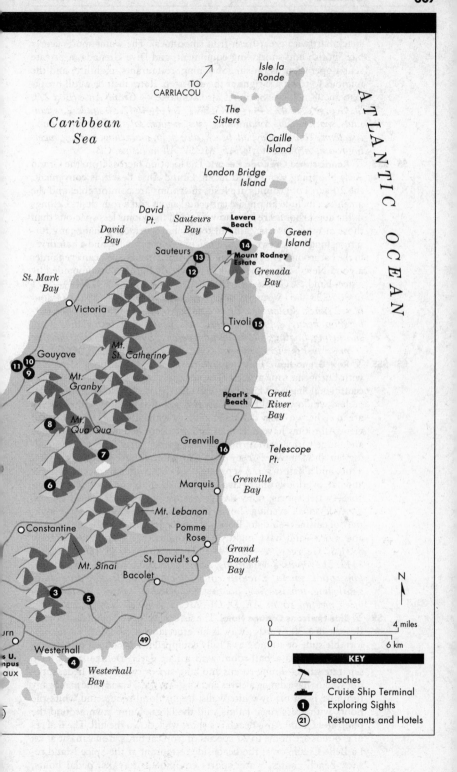

Caribbean Sea

ATLANTIC OCEAN

TO CARRIACOU

Isle la Ronde

The Sisters

Caille Island

London Bridge Island

David Pt.

David Bay

Sauteurs Bay

Levera Beach

Green Island

14

■ **Mount Rodney Estate**

Sauteurs

Grenada Bay

13

12

St. Mark Bay

○ Victoria

○ Tivoli **15**

Mt. St. Catherine

Gouyave ○

11 **10**
9

Mt. Granby

Pearl's Beach

Great River Bay

8 *Mt. Qua Qua*

7

Grenville ○
16

Telescope Pt.

6

Marquis ○

Grenville Bay

Mt. Lebanon

○ Constantine

Pomme Rose ○

Grand Bacolet Bay

Mt. Sinai

St. David's ○

Bacolet ○

3 **5**

49

urn

Westerhall ○

s U.
npus
aux

4

Westerhall Bay

N

| 0 | | 4 miles |
| 0 | | 6 km |

KEY

⛱ Beaches

🚢 Cruise Ship Terminal

① Exploring Sights

㉑ Restaurants and Hotels

tai chi, and massage and beauty treatments. Two dining rooms serve a choice of international cuisine or spa food, and there's a poolside snack bar (with great fresh-fruit smoothies). The water-sports center has Sunfish and snorkeling equipment, and Dive Grenada, a private scuba operation, is on-site. Shopping, restaurants, nightlife, and the minibus to town are right at the doorstep. Rates include a full breakfast; an all-inclusive option is also available. ⊠ *Grand Anse (Box 27), St. George's,* ☎ *473/444–4645,* ℻ *473/444–4647. 50 suites. 2 restaurants, snack bar, air-conditioning, fans, in-room safes, refrigerators, pool, spa, tennis court, volleyball, beach, dive shop, snorkeling, boating, meeting room, airport shuttle. AE, MC, V. All-inclusive, CP.*

$$–$$$ 🖬 **Renaissance Grenada Resort.** The location (across from the Grand Anse Shopping Center and facing Grand Anse Beach) is convenient, the 20 acres of grounds are lush, the rooms are comfortable, and the amenities include an on-site car-rental agent and a tour desk. Ceilings in the guest rooms are low, however, and the rooms less spacious than those at other resorts. Still, all rooms have attractive mahogany furniture, king-size or twin beds, a balcony or patio, a TV, and a hair dryer in the bathroom. The restaurant has a varied menu—you can even order a good New York–style steak. The weekly buffet is accompanied by a steel-band. ⊠ *Grand Anse (Box 441), St. George's,* ☎ *473/444–4371 or 800/223–9815 (reservations service),* ℻ *473/444–4800. 184 doubles, 2 suites. Restaurant, 2 bars, snack bar, air-conditioning, pool, barbershop, beauty salon, 2 tennis courts, health club, beach, dive shop, snorkeling, boating, shops, laundry service, business services, meeting room, travel services, car rental. AE, DC, MC, V. CP, EP, MAP.*

$$–$$$ 🖬 **Rex Grenadian.** This massive resort near the airport is popular with European tour groups. The snazziest rooms are adjacent to the central building—a white, faux-Palladian palace with lofty ceilings, vast arched windows, trellised walkways, and tiled terraces. Other rooms are in eight two-story cliffside buildings with either a garden or ocean view. All rooms have balconies and are decorated in robin's-egg blue and taupe with rattan furniture. Basic garden-view rooms have a ceiling fan and shower. For an extra $25 you can have air-conditioning, a tub, and a hair dryer. A separate pool area, with a terrace restaurant and bar, overlooks one of two beaches. All kinds of activities are available—water sports, rainy-day programs (bingo, local-dialect classes, dance lessons), evening shows, happy hours. Restaurants serve a variety of cuisines—Indian, British, Chinese, Italian, Caribbean, seafood, and more—and have nightly entertainment. ⊠ *Point Salines (Box 893), St. George's,* ☎ *473/444–3333 or 800/255–5859,* ℻ *473/444–1111. 212 rooms. 8 restaurants, 2 bars, café, piano bar, air-conditioning, fans, pool, sauna, 2 tennis courts, health club, beach, dive shop, snorkeling, windsurfing, boating, waterskiing, cabaret, business services, meeting room. AE, D, DC, MC, V. All-inclusive, CP, EP, MAP.*

$$
★   🖬 **Blue Horizons Cottage Hotel.** The sister hotel of ☞ Spice Island Beach Resort, just 300 yards away, is an especially good value. Each comfortable suite or studio has a fully equipped kitchenette, a private terrace, a TV, and a bathroom with a hair dryer. Deluxe suites have separate sitting-dining rooms and king-size or two double beds; superior studios have dining alcoves and king-size beds. Handsome mahogany furniture is set off by white walls, bright floral prints, and white-tile floors with grass rugs. Palms stud the large, sunny lawn around the pool, and Grand Anse Beach is a short walk down the hill. The 6 acres of grounds are home to 21 species of tropical birds. You can eat at ☞ La Belle Creole or at the beachside restaurant at the Spice Island resort. Beach chairs, water-sports equipment (kayaks, pedal boats, snorkeling gear, Sunfish), a Jacuzzi, and tennis and fitness facilities (at Spice Island) are free for guests at either hotel. Children under 12 stay

free in winter; under 18 are free off-season. ⊠ *Grand Anse (Box 41), St. George's,* ☎ *473/444–4316 or 473/444–4592; 800/223–9815 or 800/742–4276 (reservations services),* FAX *473/444–2815. 26 suites, 6 studios. Restaurant, 2 bars, air-conditioning, fans, kitchenettes, pool, baby-sitting, children's programs, laundry service, meeting room, car rental. AE, MC, V. CP, EP, MAP.*

$$ ▦ **Coyaba Beach Resort.** Coyaba means "heaven" in the Arawak In-
★ dian language. Right on Grand Anse Beach—certainly a heavenly spot—
Coyaba is a comfortable, good-value hotel. A loyal clientele returns again
and again, giving Coyaba a consistently high occupancy rate. You'll find
complimentary non-motorized, water-sports equipment; tennis; vol-
leyball; a pool with Grenada's only swim-up bar; and dining in a bam-
boo-walled restaurant or on the terrace. Rooms, decorated with natural
wood and Arawak-inspired folk art, are in several peach-pink, two-story
buildings that surround 5½ acres of beautifully landscaped lawns and
gardens; the beach is just beyond the gardens. Each room has a king-
size or two double beds, a balcony or patio, a TV, and a bathroom with
a hair dryer. Three rooms are wheelchair-accessible. Most rooms have
a water view. There's musical entertainment several nights a week.⊠
Grand Anse (Box 336), St. George's, ☎ *473/444–4129; 800/223–9815
or 800/742–4276 (reservations services),* FAX *473/444–4808. 70 rooms.
2 restaurants, 2 bars, air-conditioning, pool, tennis court, shuffleboard,
volleyball, beach, dive shop, snorkeling, shop, laundry service, meet-
ing room. AE, D, DC, MC, V. CP, EP, FAP, MAP.*

$$ ▦ **Flamboyant Hotel and Cottages.** The rooms and suites of this Grena-
dian-owned hotel/self-catering resort have views that sweep over the
entire Grand Anse Bay to St. George's. All quarters are simply furnished,
and each has a balcony. One-bedroom suites and two-bedroom/two-
bath cottages, each with a kitchen and lounge, make this a good spot
for families. Be prepared to climb stairs: the rooms are built into a rather
steep hill, and the stairway to Grand Anse Beach is at least 100 steps.
But don't worry: Halfway down you can stop for a dip in the pool,
grab a bite at the Beachside Terrace restaurant (West Indian and Continental cuisine), or pull up a chair at the cabana bar. ⊠ *Grand Anse
(Box 214), St. George's,* ☎ *473/444–4247; 800/223–9815 or 800/
742–4276 (reservations services),* FAX *473/444–1234. 37 rooms, 20
suites, 2 cottages. Restaurant, bar, air-conditioning, kitchenettes, minibars, pool, beach, snorkeling, shop, cabaret, laundry service, meeting
room. AE, D, MC, V. CP, EP, MAP.*

$$ ▦ **True Blue Inn.** Although the "blue" in the inn's name is a nod to the
fact that this area was once the site of an indigo plantation, it could
just as easily reflect the beautiful color of the adjacent bay. Tony and
Gillian Potter built their small hotel in 1990 on 2 acres of lawns and
gardens that slope down to the waterfront. Four spacious one-bedroom
apartments are perched cliffside, among the trees; each has a veranda
that overlooks the sea. Three private two-bedroom cottages are nes-
tled in the gardens near the pool. Each apartment and cottage has a
dining area, a living room with a sofa bed, a fully equipped kitchen,
air-conditioned bedrooms with king-size or twin-size beds, ceiling fans,
cable TV, and daily maid/laundry service. Sunsets are spectacular from
Indigo's restaurant. Light meals, barbecues, and cocktails are served
dockside at the Landing, where boaters frequently tie up at the private
dock to enjoy a meal. The inn is a five-minute drive to Grand Anse
Beach, but you can swim in True Blue bay. You can also get free dive
instruction in the pool from Scuba Express, the on-site dive operation,
or arrange scuba or snorkeling trips and yacht charters at the dock.
⊠ *Old Mill Ave., True Blue Bay (Box 308), St. George's,* ☎ *473/444–
2000 or 800/742–4276 (reservations service),* FAX *473/444–1247. 7 units.*

2 restaurants, bar, air-conditioning, fans, kitchenettes, pool, dive shop, dock, boating, laundry service. AE, MC, V. EP.

$ ☷ **La Sagesse.** This secluded hideaway is in a nature reserve on a lovely bay 10 mi east (25 mins by car) of Point Salines International Airport. The grounds include a salt-pond bird sanctuary, thick mangroves, and several nature trails. The main guest house has two suites with kitchenettes and high ceilings. There's also a two-bedroom beach cottage, with a wraparound veranda, and two budget-priced rooms behind the ☞ La Sagesse patio restaurant. All rooms are just 30 ft from the beach and have screened-in patios and ceiling fans. The only TV is in the bar. Plan on renting a car if you stay this far out, although Mike Meranski, the cheerful American owner, will run you into town for groceries. ✉ *La Sagesse Nature Center (Box 44), St. David's,* ☎ *473/444–6458 or 800/322–1753,* FAX *473/444–6458. 6 rooms. Restaurant, bar, fans, kitchenettes, beach, snorkeling, laundry service. MC, V. EP.*

APARTMENT HOTELS

These fully equipped units can be very affordable lodging options. Contact the tourist office (☞ Visitor Information *in* Grenada A to Z, *below*) for additional establishments.

$$ ☷ **Twelve Degrees North.** Eight top-of-the-line one- and two-bedroom apartments come with private beach, pool, tennis, and maid service (includes cooking and laundering). You have free use of Sunfish, Windsurfers, and ocean kayaks; fishing, scuba diving, and day sails can be arranged. A minimum stay of one week is required during peak season. ✉ *L'Anse aux Epines (Box 241), St. George's,* ☎ *473/444–4580 or 800/322–1753,* FAX *473/444–4580. 8 apartments. Pool, massage, tennis court, beach, snorkeling, boating, laundry service. AE, V. EP.*

$ ☷ **Wave Crest Holiday Apartments.** Owner-manager Joyce DaBreo runs a tight ship. She and her husband take great pains to keep all their sunny one- and two-bedroom self-catering apartments spotless. Each unit has a kitchen, a dining-living room, a phone, cable TV, and a veranda. Restaurants, the Grand Anse shopping center, and the beach are a five-minute walk away. ✉ *Grand Anse (Box 278), St. George's,* ☎ *473/444–4116,* FAX *473/444–4847. 14 1-bedroom apartments, 6 2-bedroom apartments. Breakfast room, air-conditioning, kitchenettes, babysitting. AE, D, MC, V. EP.*

VILLA AND PRIVATE-HOME RENTALS

Several local agencies handle rentals of villas and private homes: The most reliable is **Villas of Grenada** (✉ Box 218, St. George's, ☎ 473/440–1896, FAX 473/444–4529). In-season rates range from about $600 a week for a two-bedroom home with a pool to about $3,500 for a six-bedroom home on the beach.

Carriacou

$$ ☷ **Caribbee Inn.** This rambling country house is high on a promontory over the sea—the perfect place for a honeymoon. The panoramas are magnificent, particularly at sunset. Hillside suites are themed (Colonial, South American, West Indian) and have four-poster beds draped with netting, soft pastel color schemes, and Italian-tile floors. One suite has a step-up shower with an open-air view of the bay; another has its own beach. Breakfast and dinner (French Creole cuisine) are served in the dining room—and don't be surprised if owner Wendy Cooper's low-flying macaw joins you. The inn is somewhat isolated and not suitable for children, but it offers great opportunities for nature walks meditation, and total relaxation. There's an airport courtesy car, but you may want to rent a car for exploring. ✉ *Prospect,* ☎ *473/443–7380,* FAX *473/443–8142. 6 rooms, 3 suites. Dining room, bar, beach, library, laundry service, airport shuttle. No credit cards. CP, EP, MAP.*

$ ☒ **Silver Beach Resort.** This laid-back beachfront resort is a short walk from the jetty in Hillsborough. Choose between a room or self-catering cottage with sitting room and kitchenette. All quarters are comfortably furnished and have a patio or balcony; most have an ocean view. There's a full-service scuba-diving facility on-site, and certification courses are available for beginners and experts. You can also arrange spearfishing excursions or fishing trips on the resort's 30-ft Chris Craft. From the dock you can see Sandy Island, a deserted islet a stone's throw from shore where you can picnic, snorkel, or play Robinson Crusoe. Silver Beach's open-air restaurant serves hearty breakfasts and Caribbean and seafood dinners. MAP guests may dine around at other restaurants. Children under 12 stay free in the room with their parents.⊠ *Silver Beach, Beausejour Bay,* ☎ *473/443–7337; 800/742–4276 or 800/223–9815 (reservations services),* FAX *473/443–7165. 10 rooms, 6 cottages. Restaurant, bar, fans, kitchenettes, tennis court, dive shop, dock, snorkeling, windsurfing, boating, shop, laundry service, travel service, airport shuttle, car rental. AE, D, MC, V. CP, EP, MAP.*

Dining

Grenada grows everything from cabbages and tomatoes to bananas, mangoes, papaya (called *pawpaw*), plantains, melons, *callaloo* (similar to spinach), breadfruit, oranges, tangerines, limes, christophenes (similar to squash), avocados—the list is endless. And all dishes are enhanced by the wide range of spices grown here. Be sure to try one of the exotic ice creams made from guava or nutmeg.

Fresh seafood of all kinds, including lobster and oysters, is also plentiful. Conch, known here as *lambi,* is popular and appears on most menus in some form, often curried or in a stew. Almost all Grenadian restaurants serve seafood and at least some native dishes.

Rum punches are served everywhere, and although no two places make them exactly alike, they're always served with grated nutmeg on top. Carib, the locally brewed beer, is also very popular and quite good.

What to Wear

Dining in Grenada is a casual experience. Collared shirts and long pants for gentlemen and casual sundresses for ladies are apropos; even the fanciest restaurants don't require gentlemen to wear a jacket. Beachwear should be reserved for the beach.

CATEGORY	COST*
$$$	over $35
$$	$20–$35
$	under $20

per person for a three-course meal, excluding drinks, service, and 8% government tax

Grenada

CAFÉ

$ ✕ **La Boulangerie.** This French bakery and coffee shop, convenient to the Grand Anse hotels, is a great place for breakfast or a light meal. You can order a French croissant, a baguette, and other special breads and pastries. You'll also find espresso, juices, sandwiches, pizza, roasted chicken, and homemade gelati. It's open Monday–Saturday 8 AM–8:30 PM and Sunday 9 AM–2 PM. There's also free delivery. ⊠ *Le Marquis Shopping Complex, Grand Anse,* ☎ *473/444–1131. AE, MC, V.*

CARIBBEAN/CREOLE

$$$ ✕ **Spice Island Beach Resort.** Diners tend to dress for the five-course,
★ fixed-price evening meal at the ☞ **Spice Island Beach Resort's** open-

air dining room, separated from Grand Anse Beach by the narrowest of paths. Roast beef or grilled pork are as likely to appear on the menu as such local fare as chicken stuffed with breadnuts or grapefruit consommé. Entrées are flavored with local spices and accompanied by locally grown vegetables. A dessert table may be loaded with pineapple pie, homemade nutmeg or mango ice cream, and chocolate truffle torte. Wednesday is Grenadian Night, when crab back, sea egg, roast suckling pig, and all the trimmings are on the buffet, followed by dancing under the stars. Come Friday, an equally festive barbecue is accompanied by steel-band music. ⊠ *Grand Anse,* ☎ *473/444–4258 or 473/444–4423. Reservations essential. AE, D, DC, MC, V.*

$$–$$$ ✕ **La Belle Creole.** Creative West Indian cuisine and a wraparound view
★ of Grand Anse are the claims to fame of the romantic hillside restaurant at the ☞ **Blue Horizons Cottage Hotel.** The lunch and fixed-price dinner menus are always changing but are based on original recipes of the owner's mother, a pioneer in incorporating local products into "foreign" cuisines. Favorite dishes include Grenadian caviar (roe of the white sea urchin), soursop mousse, lobster-egg flan, and callaloo quiche, as well as entrées of lobster à la Creole and spice ginger pork chops. The expert service and graciousness of the staff is bound to impress even the most jaded traveler. On Sunday, a local band plays at the lunchtime poolside barbecue. ⊠ *Grand Anse,* ☎ *473/444–4316 or 473/444–4592. Reservations essential. AE, D, MC, V.*

$$ ✕ **Coconut Beach, the French Creole Restaurant.** Take local seafood,
★ add butter, wine, and Grenadian herbs, and you have excellent French Creole cuisine. Throw in a beautiful setting at the northern end of Grand Anse Beach, and this West Indian cottage becomes an even more delightful spot. Lobster is a specialty and may be wrapped in a crepe, dipped in garlic butter, or added to spaghetti. There's also the seafood platter, Caribbean chicken, lambi Calypso, and T-bone steak. Homemade coconut pie is a winner for dessert. Coconut's is casual enough that you can wander down the beach and stop by for an alfresco lunch. In season, there's a beach barbecue with live music each Wednesday, Friday, and Sunday night. Free transportation can be arranged. ⊠ *Grand Anse Beach,* ☎ *473/444–4644. AE, D, MC, V. Closed Tues.*

$ ✕ **Cot Bam.** An acronym for "Club on the Beach at Morne Rouge," Cot Bam is actually on Grand Anse Beach, next to the Coyaba Beach Resort and within walking distance of all the Grand Anse hotels. There's a casual atmosphere at this bar-restaurant-nightclub, with its tin roof and tile floor, and it's open for breakfast, lunch, and dinner. Stroll from the beach onto the outdoor terrace for a Carib beer and a chicken *roti* (a turnover filled with curried meat, potatoes, and beans) with coleslaw. Or come in the evening for the special lambi curry or other native dishes, served inside, and eat, dance, or chat the night away. ⊠ *Grand Anse Beach,* ☎ *473/444–2050. AE.*

$ ✕ **Mama's.** Mama's has been a fixture for years. Following the tradition of her late mother, one of Mama's daughters will set generous helpings of local specialties before you—roast turtle, lobster salad, callaloo soup, christophene salad, or fried plantain, as well as such exotica as *tatou* (armadillo), *manicou* (opossum), and sea urchin. There's no menu. Up to 25 native dishes are served family-style at a fixed EC$45 per person. You will not leave hungry. ⊠ *Lagoon Rd., Belmont, St. George's,* ☎ *473/440–1459. Reservations essential. No credit cards.*

$ ✕ **The Nutmeg.** Fresh seafood, homemade West Indian dishes, great hamburgers, and the view make this a favorite with locals and visitors alike. It's upstairs on the Carenage (over Sea Change Book Store), with large open windows from which you can watch the harbor traffic as you eat. Try the great callaloo soup, curried lambi, lobster, or shrimp, or just stop by for a rum punch and a roti. ⊠ *The Carenage, St. George's,* ☎ *473/440–2539. AE, D, MC, V.*

CONTEMPORARY

$$–$$$ ✕ **Cicely's.** The small, open-air restaurant at the ☞ Calabash Hotel,
★ named for award-winning chef Cicely Roberts, is surrounded by palms, tropical flowers, and twinkling lights. Cicely's culinary skills are complemented by those of Graham Newbould, former chef to the British royal family; the result is Continental cuisine with a Caribbean flair. The five-course, prix-fixe dinner is a good bet; past menus have included chilled lobster mousse, lovely cream of tannia (like potato) soup or christophene vichyssoise, baked stuffed rainbow runner or charcoal-grilled pork fillet with piquant guava-garlic-ginger sauce. Choose fresh-fruit sorbet or cheese and English-style biscuits to top off your meal. Soft piano music accompanies dinner. ⊠ *L'Anse aux Epines,* ☎ *473/ 444–4334. Reservations essential. AE, MC, V.*

ECLECTIC

$–$$ ✕ **The Boatyard.** Set in the middle of a marina, this lively place is usually full of boaters as well as expatriates. Burgers, fish-and-chips, and deep-fried shrimp are served at lunchtime. At dinner you might order club steaks, lobster, and grilled meat or seafood brochettes. The menu always includes pasta, a vegetarian plate, and some West Indian dishes—and even some Mexican snacks. In season, there's music and dancing on weekend nights. ⊠ *Spice Island Marina, L'Anse aux Epines,* ☎ *473/444–4662. MC, V. Closed Mon.*

$$–$$$ ✕ **Canboulay.** Owners Erik and Gina-Lee Johnson put Canboulay on
★ the map by reconfiguring local cuisine to reflect their Caribbean-African-Asian-European cultural backgrounds. The menu changes often, but typical selections include crab crepes with a puree of callaloo, breadfruit vichyssoise, African *bobotie* (spiced, raisin-studded ground beef topped with a baked custard), five-star versions of roti and *parang poulet* (chicken breasts stuffed with zesty sweet potatoes) with citrus caramel sauce. The frozen chocolate-mocha cheesecake is a show-stopper. Wednesday is seafood night; Thursday is cabaret night in season. Canboulay is high on a hill overlooking Grand Anse, and the dining room's shutters open to hilltop breezes and a grand view that's especially mezmerizing at lunchtime. ⊠ *Morne Rouge,* ☎ *473/444–4401. Reservations essential. AE, MC, V. No lunch Sat. Closed Sun.*

$ ✕ **Rudolf's.** This busy, English-style waterfront pub offers fine West Indian fare, as well as fish-and-chips, sandwiches, and burgers. Skip the attempts at international haute cuisine and enjoy the crab back, lambi, steak, and delectable nutmeg ice cream. This is *the* place for eaves-dropping on local gossip. The rum punches are lethal—even for Grenada. It's open from 10 AM to midnight for lunch and dinner. ⊠ *The Carenage, St. George's,* ☎ *473/440–2241. MC, V. Closed Sun.*

ITALIAN

$$$ ✕ **La Dolce Vita.** Just a five-minute walk from Grand Anse Beach, this is the place to come for fine dining and, at the same time, to satisfy your Italian taste buds. The chef is noted for his homemade pasta, prepared fresh daily. Start with a selection of cold and hot antipasti, then try lobster spaghetti, gnocchi, or fresh seafood. The attractive dining room has large, arched openings along the front wall, allowing a magnificent view of Grand Anse, the twinkling lights of St. George's, and the Caribbean Sea. ⊠ *Cinnamon Hill Hotel, Grand Anse,* ☎ *473/444– 4301. Reservations essential. D, MC, V. Closed Mon. No lunch.*

SEAFOOD

$–$$ ✕ **Aquarium Beach Club and Restaurant.** The club rents ocean kayaks and snorkeling equipment. When you come up for air, enjoy fresh seafood or luncheon salads and a cool drink at the restaurant. Happy hour is from 5:30 PM to 7 PM, then dinner is served. Besides fresh fish and lobster, the menu might include callaloo cannelloni or pepper steak. Saturday is volleyball day; on Sunday, there's a lobster barbecue with all the fixings. The atmosphere here is very congenial. ⊠ *Point Salines,* ☎ *473/444–1410. Dinner reservations essential. AE, MC, V.*

$–$$ ✕ **La Sagesse.** A perfect spot to soothe a frazzled soul, ☞ La Sagesse resort's open-air, mostly seafood restaurant, and beach bar is on a secluded cove in a nature preserve 20 minutes from Grand Anse. You can combine your meal with a swim or hike. Select from sandwiches, salads, or lobster for lunch. Lambi, smoked marlin, dolphinfish, fillet of grouper, and tuna steak are joined on the dinner menu by chicken francaise and a daily vegetarian special. Wash down your meal with a cold beer or a delicious fresh fruit smoothie. Transportation to and from your hotel is provided. ⊠ *La Sagesse Nature Center, St. David's,* ☎ *473/444–6458. Dinner reservations essential. AE, MC, V.*

$–$$ ✕ **Red Crab.** Locals and expats love to gather at this pub, especially on Saturday night. The curried lambi and garlic shrimp keep the regulars coming back. Seafood, particularly lobster, and steak are staples of the menu; hot garlic bread comes with all orders. You can eat inside or under the stars. There's live music Monday and Friday in season. ⊠ *L'Anse aux Epines (near the Calabash),* ☎ *473/444–4424. AE, MC, V. Closed Sun.*

$–$$ ✕ **Tabanca at Journey's End.** Evening dining on a terrace at the edge
★   of the sea, with the twinkling lights of the Grand Anse waterfront and St. George's Harbour in the distance, is the lure for those who want a touch of romance as well as a terrific seafood dinner. The fillet of kingfish topped with a poached egg wins raves, as does the fresh broiled grouper. Carib beer is on tap, and the special rum punch hits the spot—all evening long. ⊠ *Grand Anse Beach,* ☎ *473/444–1300. AE, D, DC, MC, V. Closed Tues. No lunch.*

STEAK

$–$$ ✕ **Joe's Steak House.** Need a break from West Indian cuisine and want an all-American steak? Just a five-minute walk from the Grand Anse hotels, you'll find eight different cuts of charcoal-broiled USDA-certified steaks done to your liking, as well as ribs, lobster, chicken, fish, and more. It's a family restaurant, and kids can pick from their own menu. Joe's can get crowded. ⊠ *Le Marquis Complex, Grand Anse,* ☎ *473/444–4020 or 473/444–4379. AE, MC, V. Closed Mon. No lunch.*

Carriacou
CARIBBEAN/CREOLE

$ ✕ **Callaloo Restaurant & Bar.** Right on Main Street, this quaint second-floor restaurant has extraordinary views of Sandy Island and Hillsborough Bay. Excellent seafood dishes, including lobster thermidor, are reasonably priced. The callaloo soup is outstanding. ⊠ *Hillsborough,* ☎ *473/443–8004. AE, MC, V. Closed Sept.*

$ ✕ **Le Petit Conch Shell.** At this tiny, open-air restaurant, bar, and grill just one block from Tyrrel Bay in Harvey Vale, you can have an inexpensive lunch of fried chicken 'n' chips, burgers, or roti. Top your meal off with rum raisin ice cream. At dinner, the cook prepares lobster, lambi, grilled steak, fish, chicken, mutton, pork or lamb chops—each served with rice 'n' peas and local vegetables. This is a good place to stop for a quick bite while touring or when coming ashore from your yacht. ⊠ *Tyrrel Bay,* ☎ *473/443–6174. No credit cards.*

SEAFOOD

$ ✕ **Scraper's.** Scraper's serves up lobster, conch, and fresh catches, along with a simple spirit and decor seasoned with occasional calypsonian serenades (by owner Steven Gay "Scraper," who's a pro). Order a rum punch and exercise your right to do nothing but enjoy yourself. ✉ *Tyrrel Bay*, ☎ *473/443–7403. AE, D, MC, V.*

Beaches

Grenada

Grenada has some 80 mi of coastline, 65 bays, and 45 white-sand beaches—many in secluded little coves—and all are public. Most of the best beaches are on the Caribbean, south of St. George's in the Grand Anse and L'Anse aux Epines areas where the resort hotels are also clustered. Virtually every hotel, apartment complex, and residential area has easy access to a beach or tiny cove.

Grand Anse Beach, about a 10-minute ride from St. George's, is the loveliest and most popular beach on Grenada. It's a gleaming, 2-mi semicircle of white sand lapped by clear, gentle surf. Brilliant rainbows frequently spill a spectrum of color into the aquamarine sea from the high green mountains that frame St. George's Harbour, visible to the north. Mature sea-grape trees and coconut palms provide shady areas to escape the midday sun. At the **Vendors Market** at about the midpoint of the beach, you can buy spices and palm hats and baskets, T-shirts, and coral jewelry—you can even get your hair braided. **La Sagesse Beach,** at La Sagesse Nature Center on Grenada's southern coast is a lovely, quiet refuge with a strip of powdery white sand. Plan a full day with nature walks and a delicious lunch at the small inn adjacent to the beach. **Levera Beach,** part of Levera National Park, is another beautiful beach. The park is at the extreme north of the island, about a 90-minute drive from St. George's. A natural reef protects swimmers from the rough Atlantic surf. Changing rooms are available. **Morne Rouge Beach** is on the Caribbean, about 1 mi south of Grand Anse Bay and 3 mi south of St. George's Harbour. The beach forms a ½-mi-long crescent and has a gentle surf that is excellent for swimming. A small café serves light meals during the day. **Pearl's Beach,** north of Grenville on the island's Atlantic coast, has miles of light gray sand fringed with palm trees. The beach is usually deserted, and the surf can be high. Near the beach is Grenada's old (pre-1984) airport runway. **Pink Gin Beach** is at Point Salines, near the airport. Besides Grenada's two mega-resorts, Rex Grenadian and LaSOURCE, you'll also find the Aquarium Beach Club with open-air dining, bar, reef snorkeling, and kayak rentals. Consider spending time here before an afternoon flight.

Carriacou

Anse La Roche is about a 15-minute hike from the village of Prospect, in the north. Like all the beaches on Carriacou, this one has pure white sand, sparkling clear water, and abundant marine life for snorkelers to view. It's never crowded here. In **Hillsborough,** day-trippers with swimming gear can take a dip at the beach adjacent to the jetty. The beach stretches for quite a distance, so you needn't swim too close to the boat traffic. **Sandy Island** is a truly deserted island off Hillsborough—just a strip of white sand, with a ridge of palm trees, surrounded by a reef and crystal-clear waters. Anyone hanging around the jetty with a motorboat will provide transportation for a few dollars. At **Tyrrel Bay,** a swath of sandy beach follows the coastline. There's a lot of boating activity here, but the bay is large enough to find a quiet spot.

Outdoor Activities and Sports

BOATING AND SAILING

As the "Gateway to the Grenadines," Grenada attracts significant numbers of seasoned sailors to its waters. Large marinas are in the lagoon area of St. George's and at Prickly Bay on the south coast of Grenada and at Tyrrel Bay in Carriacou. You can charter a yacht, with or without crew, for weeklong sailing vacations through the Grenadines or along the coast of Venezuela. Scenic day sails along Grenada's coast or between Grenada and Carriacou are also options.

On Grenada: **Moorings "Club Mariner" Watersports Center** (☎ 473/444–4439 or 473/444–4549), at the Secret Harbour Hotel, L'Anse aux Epines, has half- and full-day skippered charters, small rental sailboats, and a range of sailing programs for beginning and experienced sailors. **Footloose Yacht Charters** (☎ 473/440–7949) has both sailing or motoring yachts available for day trips around Grenada or longer charters to the Grenadines. **Seabreeze Yacht Charters** (☎ 473/444–4924) at the Spice Island Marine Centre on Prickly Bay rents sailing or power yachts, with or without crew, by day or week. **Starwind Enterprise** (☎ 473/440–3678) offers day, half-day, and sunset sailing trips along Grenada's southwest coast aboard *Starwind I,* a 36-ft sailing yacht, or *Starwind II,* a 43-footer.

On Carriacou: **Carriacou Yacht Charters** (☎ 473/443–8599) has a 76-ft ketch, *Suvetar,* which specializes in cruising the Grenadines for either long- or short-term charters or for day trips.

CAMPING

Camping is allowed in Grenada's Grand Etang National Forest Reserve and on school and church grounds on Carriacou, but there are no camping facilities anywhere.

CYCLING

Level ground is rare in Grenada, but that doesn't stop the aerobically primed. And besides, renting a mountain bike is much less expensive than renting a four-wheel-drive vehicle. Roads are narrow and winding, however, and sharing lanes with fast-moving vehicles can be hazardous. You can rent bikes at **Ride Grenada** (✉ L'Anse aux Epines, ☎ 473/444–1157).

FISHING

Deep-sea fishing around Grenada is excellent, with marlin, sailfish, yellowfin tuna, and dolphinfish topping the list of good catches. You can arrange half- or full-day fishing trips with **Bezo Charters** (☎ 473/443–5477 or 473/443–5021), which has a 32-ft Bowen Pirogue, *Bezo*; **Evans Chartering Services** (☎ 473/444–4422 or 473/444–4217) with its 35-ft Bertram Sport Fisherman, *Xiphias Seeker*; **Mermaid Charters**(☎ 473/444–2848) which takes you about on its 28-ft Cuddy Cabin power boat, *Nice Vice*; and **Starwind Enterprises** (☎ 473/440–3678), which has a 33-ft Chris Craft, *Nansea B.*

GOLF

The lay of the land in Grenada doesn't really lend itself to championship golfing, although there is a course in St. George's determined golfers might want to try. The 9-hole **Grenada Golf and Country Club** (☎ 473/444–4128), near Grand Anse, is open to visitors. Greens fees are EC$7. Club rental and instruction are available. Your hotel can make arrangements for you. In addition, *see* Lodging, *above.* **LaSOURCE** has a short 9-hole course for the use of guests.

HIKING

Mountain trails wind through **Grand Etang National Park and Forest Preserve** (☎ 473/440–6160), and if you're lucky, you may get a glimpse of a monkey or some exotic birds on your hike. There are trails for all levels—from a self-guided nature trail around Crater Lake to a demanding one through the bush to the peak of Mount Qua Qua (2,300 ft) to an extremely tough one up Mount St. Catherine (2,757 ft). Pants and hiking shoes are recommended. The cost is $25 per person for a 4-hour guided hike up Mount Qua Qua, $20 each for two or more, or $15 each for three or more; the Mount St. Catherine hike starts at $35. For guides contact **Arnold's Tours** (☎ 473/440–0531), **Telfor Bedeau Hiking Tours**(☎ 473/442–62001), or **Henry's Safari Tours**(☎ 473/ 444–5313).

RUNNING

At 4 PM on alternate Saturdays throughout the year, the **Hash House Harriers** (☎ 473/440–3343) welcomes not-so-serious runners and walkers for exercise and fun in the countryside.

SCUBA DIVING AND SNORKELING

Diving in this area is excellent, with visibility up to 200 ft. Hundreds of varieties of fish and more than 40 species of coral await you at more than a dozen sites off Grenada's southwest coast and another 20 or so around Carriacou's reefs and neighboring islets. A superb spot for diving is *Bianca C,* a 600-ft cruise ship that caught fire and sank in 1961, settled in waters more than 100 ft deep, and is now home to giant turtles, spotted eagle rays with 15-ft wingspans, and a 350-pound grouper that lives in the ship's smokestack. Kick-em Jenny, a small island off Carriacou, is another favorite destination.

The best **snorkeling** in Grenada is at Molinère Point, north of St. George's, and at Sandy Island, a few hundred yards off Carriacou's coast. Most dive operators take snorkelers along on dive trips or have special snorkeling adventures.

These PADI-certified dive operators offer both scuba and snorkeling trips to reefs and wrecks, including night dives and special excursions to the *Bianca C.* They also offer resort courses for beginning divers and certification instruction for experienced divers. Prices run about $35–$45 for a one-tank dive, $50–$60 for *Bianca C.,* and $55–$65 for night dives. Discounted 5- and 10-dive packages are also offered. Resort courses cost about $60, snorkeling trips about $20.

In Grenada: **Dive Grenada** (✉ Allamanda Beach Resort, Grand Anse Beach, ☎ 473/444–1092); **Grand Anse Aquatics** (✉ Coyaba Beach Resort, Grand Anse Beach, ☎ 473/444–1046 or 473/444–4808); **Sanvics Scuba Watersports** (✉ Renaissance Grenada Resort, Grand Anse Beach, ☎ 473/444–4371, ext. 638); **Scuba Express** (✉ True Blue Inn, True Blue, ☎ 473/444–2133), which also offers trips to Atlantic Ocean sites; **SCUBA World** (✉ Rex Grenadian Resort, Point Salines, ☎ 473/444–3333, ext. 584 and ✉ Secret Harbour Resort, L'Anse aux Epines, ☎ 473/444–4504).

On Carriacou: **Carriacou Silver Diving** (✉ Main St., Hillsborough, ☎ 473/443–7882) and **Tanki's Watersport Paradise** (✉ L'Esterre Bay, ☎ 473/443–8406).

TENNIS

Several hotels have tennis courts for guests. Visitors who are not staying at one of these hotels may play on public courts in Grand Anse and in Tanteen, St. George's.

Calabash (☎ 473/444–4234), **Coral Cove** (☎ 473/444–4217), **Coyaba Beach Resort** (☎ 473/444–4129), **Grand Anse Beach Resort** (☎ 473/444–4645). **LaSOURCE**(☎ 473/444–2556), **Renaissance Grenada** (☎ 473/444–4371), **Rex Grenadian** (☎ 473/444–3333), **Secret Harbour** (☎ 473/444–4548), **Island Beach Resort** (☎ 473/444–4258), and **Twelve Degrees North** (☎ 473/444–4580).

Shopping

The best souvenirs of Grenada are little spice baskets filled with cinnamon, nutmeg, mace, bay leaves, cloves, turmeric, and ginger. You can buy them for as little as $2 in practically every shop, at the open-air market, or at the vendors markets near the pier and on Grand Anse Beach. Vendors also sell inexpensive handmade fabric dolls, T-shirts, coral jewelry, seashells, and hats and baskets handwoven from green palm fronds. Bargaining isn't customary with vendors (although sometimes you might strike a deal); it's certainly not expected in the shops.

Areas and Malls

A short walk from the resorts in Grand Anse is the **Grand Anse Shopping Centre,** which includes a supermarket-liquor store, a clothing store, a bank, a fast-food restaurant, a pharmacy, an art gallery, and several small gift shops. **Le Marquis Complex,** diagonally across the street, has restaurants, shops, an art gallery, and tourist services.

In St. George's vendor stalls and small souvenir shops along the **Carenage** are particularly convenient for cruise-ship passengers. On the north side of the harbor, **Young Street** is a main (though narrow) shopping thoroughfare; it rises steeply from the Carenage, then descends just as steeply to the market area.

Specialty Items

DUTY-FREE GOODS

Duty-free shops at the airport sell liquor at discounts of up to 50%, as well as a few gift and craft items. Duty-free purchases can be collected over the counter, even at the in-town shops, but you must show your passport and ticket to get the duty-free price.

Bon Voyage (☎ 473/440–4217 or 473/444–4165) sells crystal, jewelry, and china at the airport and in a shop on the Carenage in St. George's. **Gift Shop** (✉ Grand Anse Shopping Centre, ☎ 473/444–4408) is an outlet for such imported luxury items as watches, leather goods, fine jewelry, crystal, and china. **Gitten's** (☎ 473/444–2549) carries perfume and cosmetics at its shop on the Carenage and also has a branch in the airport departure lounge.

FOODSTUFFS

Marketing & National Importing Board (✉ Young St., St. George's, ☎ 473/440–1791) stocks fresh fruits and vegetables, spices, hot sauces, molasses, nutmeg, and other local products. Prices are much less expensive than in gift shops. The **open-air market** (✉ Market Sq., St. George's, ☎ no phone) is open weekday mornings, but Saturday morning is the best—and busiest—time to go. Vendors sell fruits and vegetables from their own gardens, coconut water, and spices. It's a feast for the eyes as well as for the stomach. This is the place to stock up on fresh spices to bring home—at a significant savings. You'll also find clothing, leather sandals, and handcrafted items for sale.

GIFTS AND SOUVENIRS

Arawak Islands (✉ Upper Belmont Rd., St. George's, ☎ 473/444–3577) produces exotic island perfumes, colognes, body oils, soaps, herbal teas, and potpourris—all packaged for gift-giving. Their workshop is on site. No credit cards are accepted. **Gifts Remembered** (✉ Cross St., St. George's, ☎ 473/440–2482; ✉ Coyaba Beach Resort, Grand Anse, ☎ 473/444–4129) is crammed with wonderful, inexpensive stuff, including T-shirts, hammocks, scrimshaw, spices, sundries, and hand-painted masks made from calabash halves. **Spice Island Perfumes** (✉ The Carenage, St. George's, ☎ 473/440–2006) offers an olfactory extravaganza of fragrances, body oils, and natural extracts of locally grown spices and herbs. Best of all are its tiny wooden pots of solid perfume, including bitter orange, jasmine, or spice for around $8. They also have colorful island sportswear and *pareos* (sarong-like beach wraps).

HANDICRAFTS

Art Fabrik (⊠ Young St., St. George's, ☎ 473/440–0568) is a batik studio, where you can watch artisans create batik by painting fabric with hot wax and dyeing it in colorful tropical colors before turning it into clothing or accessories. The dyeing room is on the first floor; as likely as not, you'll see lengths of batik hanging out to dry in the courtyard. You can buy batik by the yard ($22–$27, depending on the width) or fashioned into dresses, shirts, shorts, hats, scarves, and more. **Grenada Craft Centre**(⊠ Lagoon Rd., St. George's, ☎ 473/440–9512 or 473/440–9514) is both a workshop and store. You can watch craftsmen as they create jewelry, pottery, batik, wood carvings, baskets, silk-screen-printed T-shirts, and woven items that are all sold in the shop next door. **Imagine** (⊠ Grand Anse Shopping Centre and Rex Grenadian Hotel, ☎ 473/444–4028) specialize in island handicrafts, including straw work, ceramics, island fashions, and batik fabrics. **Mas' Arts and Crafts,** (⊠ Le Marquis Complex, Grand Anse, ☎ no phone) is a small, family-owned shop; three grown children create products and Mom tends the store. One child (an architect) creates tiny, colorful Caribbean stilt-houses, another hand-paints stylish designs on T-shirts. There are also little painted fishing boats, jewelry, pottery, and knickknacks. The quality is excellent, and prices are very reasonable. **Tikal** (⊠ Young St., St. George's, ☎ 473/440–2310), a long-established boutique, is well known for its exquisite baskets, artwork, jewelry, batik items, and fashions, both locally made and imported from Africa and Latin America. **White Cane Industries** (⊠ The Carenage, near the public library, St. George's, ☎ 473/444–2014) stocks bargain baskets, hats, and spectacularly colored rag rugs, all handwoven locally by sight-impaired craftspeople. Credit cards are not accepted.

RECORDS

Turbo Charge Records & Tapes (⊠ St. John's St., St. George's, ☎ 473/440–0586) is where to buy the latest reggae, calypso, *soca* (soul calypso; has an up-tempo calypso beat), and steel-band music.

Nightlife and the Arts

Nightlife

Grenada's nightlife is focused on the resort hotels. During the winter season, Spice Island Beach Resort, Calabash, Coyaba, Rex Grenadian, and Renaissance Grenada hotels have a steel band or other local entertainment several nights of each week (☞ Lodging, *above*). Your hotel or the tourist office (☞ Visitor Information *in* Grenada A to Z *below*) will have information about where bands are performing on a given night. You can also pick up a copy of *The Barnacle*, a free weekly newspaper that's available at the airport and most hotels.

BARS

Beachside Terrace (⊠ Flamboyant Hotel, Grand Anse, ☎ 473/444–4247) is casual and unpretentious and draws a crowd for crab racing on Monday night, a live steel band on Wednesday, and a beach barbecue with calypso music on Friday. **Boatyard** (⊠ L'Anse aux Epines, ☎ 473/444–4662), at the marina, is the place to be on Wednesday, when there's a live band, and on Friday from 11 PM till sunup, when there's a steel band and international discs are spun by a smooth-talkin' local DJ. **Brown Sugar** (⊠ above South Winds Cottages, Grand Anse, ☎ 473/444–2374) has steel-pan music Friday starting at 6 PM. **Casablanca** (⊠ Grand Anse, ☎ 473/444–1631) is a sports bar where you can play chess, backgammon, cards, dominoes, darts, pool or snooker, and watch games on a big-screen TV while having a drink and a snack. It's open Monday–Saturday 11 AM–3 AM and Sunday 6 PM–1 AM. **Village Hotel** (✉ Grand Anse, ☎ 473/444–4097) presents live jazz on Wednesday 8:30–midnight.

DANCE CLUBS

Cot Bam (✉ Grand Anse Beach, ☎ 473/444–2050) hits the spot for visitors who want something simple, lively, and friendly for little money. Dancing, dining, and socializing take place nightly. The place is open until 3 AM on Friday and Saturday. **Dynamite Disco** (✉ The Limes, Grand Anse ☎ 473/444–4056) has a party atmosphere every weekend, with disco, reggae, and calypso music. At **Fantazia 2001** (✉ Morne Rouge Beach, ☎ 473/444–4224 or 473/444–1189), a popular disco, soca, reggae, and international tunes are played from 9:30 PM until the wee hours on Friday and Saturday night. There's also a folkloric show on Friday evening, and Wednesday is always "golden oldies" night. It's dark and loud and fun, with a mix of locals and tourists. There's a small cover charge (EC$5) on weekends. **Island View** (✉ Woburn, St. George's, ☎ 473/444–1878 has Caribbean music and dancing on Friday and Saturday nights. **Le Sucrier** (✉ Sugar Mill, Grand Anse Roundabout, ☎ 473/444–1068) is open Wednesday–Saturday 9 PM–3 AM. Wednesday is "oldies" night, there's live jazz on Thursday, and a mostly young crowd gathers for dancing to the latest tunes on Friday and Saturday.

THEME NIGHTS

Rhum Runner (✉ The Carenage, St. George's, ☎ 473/440–2198), a 60-ft twin-deck catamaran, leaves from the jetty at 7:30 PM each Friday and Saturday for a moonlight cruise in the waters around St. George's and Grand Anse, returning about midnight. Tickets are $7.50 (EC$20), and reservations are recommended. On Wednesday from 6 to 9 , there's a sunset dinner cruise for $40 per person; reservations must be made by 4:30 the day before. **Rhum Runner II**, a 72-ft sister ship, operates monthly moonlight cruises the Friday and Saturday nights nearest the full moon for $11 (EC$30) per person (add EC$6 for a barbecue dinner).

The Arts

ISLAND CULTURE

Marryshow Folk Theatre (✉ Herbert Blaize St., St. George's, ☎ 473/440–2451) presents concerts, plays, and special cultural events. Call for a schedule.

GALLERIES

Art Grenada (✉ No. 7, upstairs in Grand Anse Shopping Centre, ☎ 473/444–2317) is a fine-arts gallery that displays and sells works exclusively by Grenadian artists. Exhibits change monthly, and shipping of purchases can be easily arranged. **United Artists Art Gallery** (✉ No. 15, Le Marquis Complex, Grand Anse, ☎ 473/444–5022) displays and sells a unique collection of top-quality original artwork. You'll find wood and stone carvings, painted masks, paintings, furniture, and other objets d'art created by artists from Grenada, Carriacou, and Petit Martinique. **Yellow Poui Art Gallery** (✉ Cross St., St. George's, ☎ 473/440–3001) displays and sells original artwork—paintings, sculpture, photography, lithographs, and antique engravings—by artists from Grenada and elsewhere in the Caribbean.

On Carriacou, in the village of L'Esterre, hand-painted signs announce THIS WAY TO THE GREAT ARTIST, **CANUTE CALLISTE**. If you get lost, one of his many grandchildren will lead the way. Works by Calliste, colorful watercolors of island scenes, are also available at the Carriacou Museum and at Yellow Poui Art Gallery in St. George's, Grenada.

Exploring Grenada (and Carriacou)

Numbers in the margin correspond to points of interest on the Grenada (and Carriacou) map.

Grenada

It may be hard to pull yourself away from the beach to see the rest of this lovely island, but a day or more of exploring is worth the effort: the scenery is stunning, and the scent of nutmeg fills the air. St. George's is a capital city, with a busy harbor, interesting shops, and several historic sites. A trip into the countryside and a visit to a spice plantation and a nutmeg processing plant will help you see what makes Grenada tick. Along the scenic west coast road, you're likely to come across a group of strapping young fishermen pulling in an enormous seine-fishing net in a tug-of-war with the sea; it's an all-day job, and a share of the catch is the reward. Passing through tiny villages, you'll receive waves from folks relaxing on the verandas of their colorful cottages while children play in the yard, and women doing laundry by the riverside and walking with baskets of clothes on their heads. If you're a little adventurous, take guided hikes into the thick of the rain forest, up a mountainside, or to hidden waterfalls in Eden-like surroundings.

SIGHTS TO SEE

❻ Annandale Falls and Visitors Centre. A mountain stream cascades 50 ft into a pool surrounded by exotic tropical vines, such as liana and elephant ears. This is a lovely spot for swimming and picnicking. ⊠ *Main interior road, 15 mins northeast of St. George's,* ☎ *473/440–2452.* ☜ *$1.* ⊙ *Daily 9–5.*

❸ Bay Gardens. Just 15 minutes from St. George's is a private horticultural paradise. On what was once a sugar plantation, some 450 species of island flowers and plants are cultivated in patterns mimicking their growth in the wild. Eight acres of paths are open to visitors. ⊠ *Mt. Airy, St. Paul's.* ☎ *473/440–5338.* ☜ *$1.* ⊙ *Daily 9–4.*

⓭ Carib's Leap. At Sauteurs (the French word for leapers), on the northernmost tip of the island, Carib's Leap (also called Leapers Hill) is the 100-ft vertical, seaside cliff from which Carib Indians flung themselves in 1651, denying surrender to their French captors.

❽ Concord Falls. The west coast road winds past soaring mountains and valleys covered with palms and bamboo, mango and breadfruit trees, banana plants and tropical flowers. Just off the road, about 8 mi north of St. George's, are the Concord Falls—three waterfalls with a small visitor center, a viewing platform, some vendors selling local products, and a changing room for donning a bathing suit. The first waterfall is accessible from the road, and during the dry months (January to May), when the currents aren't too strong, you can take a dip under the cascade. Reaching the other waterfalls requires an hour's hike through the rain forest. The third one is the most spectacular, thundering down 65 ft over huge boulders and creating a small pool (no swimming permitted at the upper falls). It's smart to hire a guide. The path is clear, but slippery boulders near the end can be treacherous without a guide's assistance. ⊠ *Coast Rd.* ☜ *$1 for changing room.*

❾ Dougaldston Spice Estate. Just south of Gouyave, this historic plantation still grows and processes spices the old-fashioned way. You can see cocoa, nutmeg, mace, cloves, cinnamon, and other spices laid out on giant racks to dry in the sun. A worker will be glad to explain the process (and will appreciate a small donation). You can purchase spices for about $2 a bag. ⊠ *Gouyave,* ☎ *no phone.* 🔊 *$1.* ⊙ *Weekdays 9–4.*

⓫ Fisherman's Museum. On the outskirts of Gouyave in a place called Mabouya, Anthony Joseph operates a small roadside museum dedicated to the island's fishermen. The collections, assembled over the past 20 years, touch on fishing equipment, the resources of the sea, the forest's impact, the life of the beach, and the social life of the fishermen. Mr. Joseph is your tour guide, and his narrative is enchanting. ⊠ *Western Main Rd., Gouyave,* ☎ *no phone.* 🔊 *75¢.* ⊙ *Daily 9–4.*

☙ ❿ Gouyave Nutmeg Processing Cooperative. Gouyave is the center of Grenada's nutmeg industry. A tour of the Nutmeg Processing Cooperative in the center of town makes a fragrant, fascinating ½ hour. Workers in the three-story plant, which turns out 3 million pounds per year of Grenada's most famous export, sort nutmegs by hand and pack them in burlap bags for shipping worldwide. ⊠ *Gouyave,* ☎ *473/444–8337.* 🔊 *$1.* ⊙ *Weekdays 10–1 and 2–4.*

❷ Grand Anse. Grand Anse, a residential and commercial area about 5 mi south of downtown St. George's, is named for the world-renowned beach it surrounds. Most of Grenada's tourist facilities—resorts, restaurants, some shopping, and nightlife—are in or near Grand Anse.

Grand Anse Beach is a 2-mi crescent of sand, shaded by coconut palms and sea-grape trees, with gentle turquoise surf. A handful of resort hotels line the beachfront, and there's a public entrance at Camerhogne Park, just a few steps from the main road. **St. George's University Medical School,** which for years held classes in their enviable beachfront location in Grand Anse, has consolidated most of its facility in True Blue, a nearby residential area. The school still owns the Grand Anse property, but it's currently used only for administrative offices.

☙ ❼ Grand Etang National Park. Deep in the interior of lush, mountainous Grenada is a bird sanctuary and forest reserve, with miles of hiking trails, lookouts, and fishing streams. **Crater Lake** is a 30-acre expanse of glassy, cobalt-blue water that fills the crater of an extinct volcano 1,740 ft above sea level. Although claims are made that it's bottomless, maximum soundings are recorded at 18 ft. The informative **Grand Etang Forest Center** has displays on the local wildlife and vegetation. A forest manager is on hand to answer questions. There's a small snack bar and souvenir stand nearby. ⊠ *Main interior road, between Grenville and St. George's,* ☎ *473/440–6160.* 🔊 *$1.* ⊙ *Daily 8:30–4.*

⓰ Grenville. The island's second-largest city retains its historical identity as a French Colonial market town. Saturday is market day, and the town fills with people doing their weekly shopping. The local spice-processing factory, **Grenville Cooperative Nutmeg Association** (☎ 473/442–7241), the largest on the island, is open to the public for guided tours. Near Grenville is defunct **Pearls Airport,** which was replaced in October 1984 by Point Salines International Airport; a deteriorating Cuban plane sits at the end of what used to be the runway. There's a good view north to the Grenadines and a nice beach nearby.

☙ ❺ Laura Herb and Spice Garden. The 6½-acre gardens are part of an old plantation in the village of Laura, in St. David's, just 6 mi east of Grand Anse. It belongs to the Minor Spices Cooperative and is funded by the European Union. You can see and learn about medicinal spices and herbs, including cocoa, clove, nutmeg, pimiento, cinnamon, turmeric, and tonka beans (vanilla). A 45-minute tour of the spice-processing plant includes explanations of the medicinal benefits of the various products. ⊠ *Laura,* ☎ *473/443–2604.* 🔊 *$2.* ⊙ *Weekdays 8–4.*

⑭ Levera National Park and Bird Sanctuary. This portion of Grenada's protected parkland encompasses 450 acres at the northeastern tip of the island, where the Caribbean Sea meets the Atlantic Ocean. Facilities include a visitor center, changing rooms, a small amphitheater, and a gift shop. There's a beautiful beach with a natural reef barrier that protects swimmers from the rough Atlantic surf. Thick mangroves provide food and protection for nesting seabirds and seldom-seen tropical parrots. Some fine Arawak ruins and petroglyphs can be seen, and the first islet of the Grenadines is visible in the distance.

⑫ Mt. Rodney Estate. When touring the island, plan lunch in Sauteurs. A road winds up a mountainside to an 1880s plantation house, lovingly restored by Lin and Norris Nelson. Sugar, coffee, and cocoa grew on the plantation in its heyday and the fabulous views north to the Grenadines remain. Buffet luncheon is served from noon to 2 PM on the dining terrace. Quench your thirst with rum punch or lemonade, then dig into the pumpkin soup, flying fish, ginger chicken, callaloo, breadfruit salad, rice 'n' peas, and *cou-cou* (cornmeal mixture). Lin will be happy to show you around the house. (This lunch stop is often included on a guided island tour; or, call 473/442–9420 for reservations.)

⑮ River Antoine Rum Distillery. At this rustic operation, kept open primarily as a museum, rum is produced by the same methods used since the distillery opened in the mid-1700s. The process begins with the crushing of sugarcane from adjacent fields in the River Antoine Estate. The result is a potent overproof rum that will knock your socks off. ⊠ *River Antoine Estate, St. Patrick's,* ☎ *473/442–7109.* ⊡ *$1.* ☉ *Guided tours daily 9–4.*

❶ St. George's. Grenada's capital city and major port is one of the most picturesque and still-authentic West Indian towns in the Caribbean. Narrow streets lined with shops wind up, down, and across steep hills. Pastel-painted warehouses with roofs covered in orange-tiles (brought over as ballast in 18th-century ships) cling to the waterfront. Small, rainbow-hued houses rise from the waterfront and disappear into steep green hills.

St. George's Harbour is the center of town. Schooners, ferries, and tour boats tie up along the seawall or at the small dinghy dock. Cruise ships dock at the large pier at the harbor entrance or anchor just outside and transport passengers ashore by tender. On weekends, a windjammer is likely to be anchored in the middle of the harbor, giving the scene a 19th-century appearance.

The **Carenage**, the roadway and walkway around horseshoe-shape St. George's Harbour, is the capital's main thoroughfare. Warehouses, small shops, and restaurants face the water. At the center of the Carenage, on the pedestrian plaza, sits the *Christ of the Deep* statue. It was presented to Grenada by Costa Cruise Line in remembrance of their ship *Bianca C,* which burned and sank in the harbor in 1961 and is now a favorite dive site(☞ Outdoor Activities and Sports, *above*). Near the Cruise-ship Welcome Center, at the south end of the Carenage, the Grenada Board of Tourism has its offices and, nearby, you can buy inexpensive spices and crafts at a row of vendor stalls.

The **Grenada National Museum** (⊠ Young and Monckton Sts., ☎ 473/440–3725), a couple of blocks off the Carenage, is set in the foundation of a French army barracks and prison that was built in 1704. The small museum has exhibits of news items, photos, and proclamations regarding the 1983 intervention, along with memorabilia from earlier historical periods. The museum is open weekdays 9–4:30 and Saturday 10–2; admission is $1.

An engineering feat for its time, the 340-ft long **Sendall Tunnel** was built in 1895 and named for an early governor. It separates the harborside of St. George's from the Esplanade on the bay side of town, where the open-air meat and fish markets are. The Esplanade is also the terminus of the minibus route.

Don't miss picturesque **Market Square,** a block from the Esplanade at Granby Street. It's open every weekday morning but really comes alive on Saturday from 8 AM to noon. Vendors sell baskets, spices, brooms, clothing, knickknacks, coconut water, and fresh produce. Market Square is also where parades and political rallies take place—and the beginning of the minibus routes to outer areas of the island.

St. Andrew's Presbyterian Church, built in 1830, is at the intersection of Halifax and Church streets. Also known as Scots' Kirk, it was constructed with the help of the Freemasons. Built in 1826, the beautiful stone and pink-stucco **St. George's Anglican Church,** on Gore Street, is filled with statues and plaques depicting Grenada in the 18th and 19th centuries. **St. George's Methodist Church,** on Green Street near Tyrrel Street, was built in 1820 and is the oldest original church in the city. The Gothic tower of **St. George's Roman Catholic Church** dates from 1818, but the current structure was built in 1884; the tower is the most visible landmark in the city.

On Church Street, **York House,** (1801), is home to Grenada's Houses of Parliament and Supreme Court. It, the neighboring Registry building (1780), and Government House (1802) are fine examples of early Georgian architecture.

Marryshow House (✉ Herbert Blaize St., ☎ 473/440–2451), built in 1917, combines Victorian and West Indian architecture. The former home of T. A. Marryshow, political promoter of one West Indian nation, it's now the local center of the University of the West Indies and home to the Marryshow Folk Theatre, Grenada's first cultural center. Plays, West Indian dance and music, and poetry readings are occasionally presented here. (☞ Nightlife and the Arts, *above*).The house is open weekdays 8:30–4:30 and Saturday 9–1; admission is free.

Ft. George is high on the hill at the southern tip of Church Street. The fort, which rises above the entrance to St. George's Harbour, is Grenada's oldest. It was built by the French in 1705 to protect the harbor. No shots were ever fired until October 1983, when Prime Minister Bishop and some of his followers were assassinated in the courtyard. The fort now houses police headquarters but is open to the public daily during daylight hours; admission is free. The 360-degree view of the capital city and St. George's Harbour is spectacular.

On Richmond Hill, high above the city of St. George's and the harbor, historic **Ft. Frederick** provides a magnificent panoramic view. The fort was completed in 1791; it was the headquarters of the People's Revolutionary Government during the infamous intervention of 1983. Today, you can get a bird's-eye view of the prison, on top of an adjacent hill, where the perpetrators of that event are incarcerated for life.

In St. Paul's, five minutes outside St. George's, **de la Grenade Industries** (☎ 473/440–3241) is a spice-processing plant that manufactures award-winning products made from nutmeg and other homegrown fruits and spices: syrups, jams and jellies, and liqueurs. It began in 1960 as a cottage industry. You're welcome to watch the process and purchase gift items from the retail operation on site. The plant is open weekdays 8–5 and Saturday 9–12:30; admission is free.

④ Westerhall. This residential area about 5 mi southeast of St. George's is known for its beautiful villas, gardens, and vistas. Pricy development is happening here: European and North American retirees and local businesspeople are building elegant homes with sight lines to the sea.

Carriacou

Carriacou, the land of many reefs, is a hilly island and (unlike it's lush sister island of Grenada) has neither lakes nor rivers—only rain water, caught in cisterns and purified with bleach. It gets pretty arid during the dry season (January–May). Nevertheless, plenty of fruit is grown here, and the climate seems to suit the mahogany trees used locally for furniture-making and the white cedar critical to the boatbuilding that has made Carriacou famous.

This little island (13 square mi) packs a lot of punch—rum punch, that is. With more than a hundred rum shops and only one gas station, Carriacou brings the fastest metabolism down to a quiet purr and exudes the hallmark friendliness and peace of a Caribbean retreat. Simplicity is the pleasure here, not luxury.

Hillsborough is the main town. Rolling hills cut a wide swath through the island's center, from Gun Point, in the north, to Tyrrel Bay, in the south. The small town of Windward, on the east coast, is a boatbuilding community. You'll likely encounter half-finished hulls on the roadside. Originally constructed for interisland commerce, the boats are now built for fishing and pleasure sailing. If you're lucky, you may catch the launching of a new boat, which is cause for great celebration.

SIGHTS TO SEE

⑲ Belair. For a wonderful bird's-eye view of Carriacou's west coast, drive to Belair, 700-ft above sea level, in the north-central part of the island. On the way, you'll pass the photogenic ruins of an old sugar mill. The Belair lookout is adjacent to **Princess Royal Hospital**. The view of Hillsborough, the harbor, and endless sea is restorative itself.

⑰ Historical Museum. The only museum in the eastern Caribbean that is owned by the people, not the government, is housed in an old cotton ginnery a block from the waterfront. The museum has exhibits of Amerindian, European, and African artifacts; a collection of watercolors by local artist Canute Caliste; and a gift shop loaded with local items.⊠ *Paterson St., Hillsborough.* ⌨ *$2.* ⊙ *Weekdays 9:30–4, Sat. 10–4.*

⑱ Sandy Island. Just off the west coast of Carriacou and visible from Silver Beach Resort, tiny Sandy Island is a gorgeous sand bar, lapped by crystal-clear water, with nothing more on it than some palm trees. For a few dollars, a local fellow with a motorboat will transport you back and forth. Bring your snorkeling gear and, if you wish, a picnic—and leave all your cares behind. This is truly paradise.

⑳ Tyrrel Bay. Picturesque Tyrrel Bay is a large protected harbor in the southwest of Carriacou. The bay is almost always full of sailboats, power boats, and working boats—coming, going, or bobbing at their moorings. Edging the bay is a beach, with pure white sand; bars, restaurants, a guest house, and a few shops are along the waterfront.

Grenada A to Z

Arriving and Departing

BY AIRPLANE

American Airlines (☎ 473/444–2222) has daily flights into Grenada's Point Salines International Airport from major U.S. and Canadian cities via its San Juan hub. **BWIA** (☎ 473/444–4134) flies direct from

New York and Miami. **British Airways** (☎ 473/440–2796) flies from London twice a week.

LIAT (☎ 473/440–2796 or 473/440–4121) has scheduled service between Grenada and neighboring Caribbean islands. Between Grenada and Carriacou's Lauriston Airport, scheduled service is available on **Region Air** (☎ 473/444–1117), **Airlines of Carriacou** (☎ 473/444–3549 or 473/444–1475), and **HelenAir** (☎ 473/444–2266 or 473/444–4101, ext. 2090; on Carriacou, 473/443–8260).

From the Airport: No bus service is available between the Point Salines airport and hotels, but taxis are always available. Fares to St. George's are $12; to the hotels of Grand Anse and L'Anse aux Epines, $10. Rides taken between 6 PM and 6 AM incur a $4 surcharge. From Carriacou's Lauriston Airport to Hillsborough, the fare is $4.

Electricity

Electric current on Grenada is 220 volts/50 cycles. Appliances rated at 110 volts (U.S. standard) will work only with a transformer and adapter plug. For dual-voltage computers or appliances, you'll still need an adapter plug; some hotels will loan adapters (and even transformers) to guests. Most hotels have 110 outlets for shavers; very few have 110 lines in guest rooms.

Emergencies

Ambulance: In St. George's, Grand Anse, and L'Anse aux Epines, ☎ 434. In St. Andrew's, ☎ 724. On Carriacou, ☎ 774. **Coast Guard:** ☎ 399.

Hospitals: St. George's Hospital (☎ 473/440–2051); **St. Andrew's Hospital**, Mirabeau (on the east coast) (☎ 473/442–7251); **Carriacou Hospital** (☎ 473/443–7400).

Pharmacies: Gitten's (✉ Halifax St., St. George's, ☎ 473/440–2165 or 473/440–2340 after hrs) is open weekdays 8–6 and Saturday 8–3. **Gitten's Drugmart** (✉ Main Rd., Grand Anse, ☎ 473/444–4954 or 473/440–2340 after hrs) is open Monday–Saturday 9–8, Sunday and holidays 9–noon. **Parris' Pharmacy Ltd.** (✉ Victoria St., Grenville, ☎ 473/442–7330), on the windward side of the island, is open Monday–Wednesday and Friday 9–4:30, Thursday 9–1, and Saturday 9–7. On Carriacou, try **Vena Bullen** (✉ Hillsborough ☎ 473/443–7468. **Police and fire:** ☎ 911.

Festivals

GRENADA

In late January, the **Spice Island Game Fishing Tournament** is held. Sportfishermen are invited to vie for cash prizes for the biggest billfish (marlin, sailfish, yellowfin tuna).

The last weekend in January, triathletes from around the world compete in the annual **Grenada International Triathlon.** The two-day competition starts and finishes at Grand Anse Beach. Participants swim 1½-km, cycle 25-km, and run 5-km on the first day. A three-person relay takes place on the second day. Teams must include at least one female and have a combined age of at least 100 years.

February 7 is **Independence Day.** A highlight is a military parade at Queen's Park, on the north side of St. George's. Beginning around March 17 and lasting a week, the **St. Patrick's Day Fiesta** is celebrated in Sauteurs (St. Patrick's Parish), in the north of Grenada. There are arts and crafts, agricultural exhibits, food and drink, and a cultural extravaganza with music and dancing. Each June 29, the **Fisherman's Birthday Celebration** is held in villages on Grenada's west coast, particularly in Gouyave. There's a blessing of the boats, boat racing, fishing contests, and a lot of music and dancing in the street—sort of a mini-Carnival. In early August, the annual **Rainbow City Festival** is held in Grenville. More of an agricultural fair, with local arts and crafts and livestock, there's also food, drink, and music. During the second week of August, a month of calypso road shows culminates in the **Grenada Carnival.** There's a beauty pageant, a soca monarch competition, continuous steel-pan and calypso music, a final Monday night jump-up, and a huge Parade of the Bands on the last Tuesday.

Yacht races are held often during the year. The **Grenada Sailing Festival** is an annual event organized by the Grenada Yacht Club and held the first week of February. In early August, the **Grenada to Carriacou Yacht Race** is a highlight of the Carriacou Regatta (☞ *below*).

CARRIACOU

A highlight of most festivals and events on Carriacou is the **Big Drum Dance,** unique to this island (and neighboring Union Island). To the rhythmic beat of drums, costumed dancers recreate their French and African heritage in celebration of the harvest of land and sea.

The island's biggest event of the year is the four-day **Carriacou Carnival,** held the second week of February. Revelers participate in parades, calypso contests, music and dancing, and general frivolity.

During the first weekend in August, the **Carriacou Regatta** is a test of skills for the designers and sailors of Carriacou's workboats and schooners. It's the largest sailing event in the Grenadines, attracting yachts and sailboats from throughout the Caribbean for three days of rowboat, sailboat, workboat, longboat, and model boat races. Festivities also include road relays, fashion shows, donkey rides, and greasy pole contests—and music and partying galore.

In December, the week before Christmas, the **Carriacou Parang Festival** is a cultural celebration derived from the Spanish word for ad-libbing. Costumed singers travel from village to village, creating spontaneous songs based on local gossip and accompanied by guitar, violin, and drum.

Getting Around

BUSES

Privately owned 15-passenger minivans ply the winding road between St. George's and Grand Anse. Hail one anywhere along the way, pay EC$1, and hold on to your hat. They pass by frequently from about 6 AM to 8 PM daily except Sunday and holidays. You can get just about anywhere else on the island via these minivans, too, but be prepared for packed vehicles, unpredictable schedules, loud music, and some hairraising maneuvers. The one-way fare between St. George's and Grand Etang is EC$3; La Sagesse, EC$2.50; Sauteurs, EC$5.

On Carriacou, the minibus fare between Hillsborough and Harvey Vale or Windward is EC$2; from Harvey Vale to Windward, EC$4.

CAR RENTALS

Most of the 650 mi of paved roads are in good condition—but are steep and winding beyond the Grand Anse area. Driving is on the left.

To rent a car, you will need a valid driver's license with which you may obtain a local permit from the traffic department (at the Central Police Station, on the Carenage) or some car-rental firms at a cost of EC$30. Rental cars (including four-wheel-drive vehicles) cost $45–$60 a day or $220–$285 a week with unlimited mileage. In high season, there may be a 3-day minimum rental. Gas costs about $2.60 per gallon.

Avis (☎ 473/440–3936 or 473/440–2624; 473/444–4563 after hours) is at Spice Island Rental on Paddock and Lagoon roads in St. George's. **David's** (☎ 473/444–3399 or 473/444–3038) has offices at Point Salines International Airport, Grenada Renaissance Resort, Rex Grenadian Hotel, and the Limes in Grand Anse. **Dollar Rent-a-Car** (☎ 473/444–4786) is at Point Salines Airport. In the True Blue area, call **McIntyre Bros. Ltd.** (☎ 473/444–3944 or 473/443–5319 after hrs). On Carriacou, **Barba's Auto Rentals** (☎ 473/443–7454) will meet you at the airport.

FERRIES

Osprey Express, a semi-hovercraft, makes the round-trip voyage between Grenada, Carriacou, and Petit Martinique every day except Wednesday, taking about 2 hours each way. The per-person fare is $15 one-way, $28 round-trip.

Schooners ***Alexia II, Alexia III and Adelaide B*** leave from Grenada's St. George's Harbour mornings (except Monday and Thursday), ferrying both cargo and passengers on the 4-hour voyage to Carriacou; they return from Carriacou to Grenada daily (except Tuesday and Friday). *Adelaide B* continues on from Carriacou to Petit Martinique (about a 1½-hour trip) on Wednesday and Saturday afternoons, returning early on Monday and Thursday mornings. The fare between Grenada and Carriacou is $7.50 one-way, $12 round-trip; between Carriacou and Petit Martinique, it's about $5 each way.

The mailboat between Carriacou and Petit Martinique makes one round-trip on Monday, Wednesday, and Friday, leaving Petit Martinique at 8 AM and returning from Windward, Carriacou, at noon. The fare is about $5 each way.

TAXIS

Taxis are plentiful and rates are set by the government. The trip between Grand Anse and St. George's costs about $8. A $4 surcharge is added for rides taken between 6 PM and 6 AM. Taxis often wait for fares at hotels, at the cruise-passenger welcome center, and on the Carenage. They can be hired at an hourly rate of $15.

Water taxis—a lovely way to get around on a warm day—are available along the Carenage. For EC$1.50, you can be hand-rowed from one side of harbor to the other; for EC$5, a motorized boat will deliver you to your Grand Anse–area hotel.

Guided Tours

Guided tours generally cover St. George's, Grand Etang National Park, spice plantations in Gouyave, rain-forest hikes, and day trips to Carriacou.

For a special treat, take part in Grenada's **People-to-People Program.** With a little notice, you can meet local people with similar interests and foster an intercultural friendship—play a round of golf, attend a church service, have lunch, or simply sightsee with your island host. For details, contact Edyth Leonard at New Trends Tours (✉ Grand Anse, Box 797, St. George's, ☎ 473/444–1236, FAX 473/444–4836).

TOUR OPERATORS

Amerindian Tours (☎ 473/440–9686) offers innovative tours of waterfalls, spice plantations, old forts, and historic sites. **Arnold's Tours** (☎ 473/440–0531 or 473/440–2213, FAX 473/440–4118) offers land, sea, and "Lan-Sea" combination tours. Prices range from $25 for an island tour, hiking trip, or sunset cruise to $140 for an all-day cruise to Carriacou. Dennis Henry of **Henry's Safari Tours** (☎ 473/444–5313,

FAX 473/444–4847) knows Grenada like the back of his hand. He leads adventurous hikes and four-wheel-drive vehicle safaris, or you can design your own tour. Depending on the size of the group, a full-day island tour, including lunch, costs $40–$55 per person; a six-hour hike to Concord Falls is $30–$45 per person. **Spiceland Tours** (☎ 473/440–5127 or 473/440–5180) has several five- and seven-hour island tours, from an "Urban/Suburban" tour of St. George's and the South Coast to an "Emerald Forest Tour" highlighting Grenada's natural beauty.

Other reputable operators that offer similar guided tours are **Sunshine Tours** (☎ 473/444–2831), **Sunsation Tours** (☎ 473/444–1594), and **Caribbean Horizon Tours** (☎ 473/444–3944).

Carriacou minibus drivers will take you on a four-hour island tour for about $60 (EC$150).

Language

English—spoken with a fetching, musical lilt—is the official language here. You'll hear a slight British influence; for example, "it is" is often run together as "'tis" (as in "'Tis a nice day"). Creole patois isn't commonly heard except, perhaps, among older folks in the countryside.

When you're buying spices, you may be offered "saffron" and "vanilla." The saffron is really turmeric, a ground yellow root, rather than the fragile pistils of crocus flowers; the vanilla is an essence made from locally grown tonka beans, a close substitute, but not the real thing. No one is trying to pull the wool over your eyes; these are common local names.

If you want a refreshing drink of coconut water at the market, for EC$1 or so, the "jelly man" will hack off the top of a fresh green "jelly" (coconut) for you with one swipe of his machete. And if someone offers you a candy, you'll be asked if you'd like a "sweetie."

A Grenadian will always greet you with a friendly "good morning," "good afternoon," or "good evening," and, quite frankly, will be disappointed if the courtesy isn't returned. That's true whether it's a perfect stranger or someone you've seen before. Though such greetings are common throughout the Caribbean, in Grenada they will often be followed by, "Are you enjoyin' it?"

Money Matters

CURRENCY

Grenada uses the Eastern Caribbean (EC) dollar. The official exchange rate is fixed at EC$2.67 to US$1; cabs, shops and hotels sometimes have slightly lower rates (EC$2.50–EC$2.60). You can exchange money at banks and hotels, but U.S. currency, traveler's checks, and major credit cards are widely accepted. Although prices are usually quoted in EC dollars, be sure to ask which currency is referred to when you make purchases and business transactions. Hotels are not permitted to give foreign currency in change or on departure. (Throughout this chapter, prices are quoted in U.S. dollars unless otherwise indicated.)

SERVICE CHARGES, TAXES, AND TIPPING

Many hotels and restaurants add a 10% service charge to your bill. If a service charge is not included in your hotel or restaurant bill, a 10% gratuity should be added. Additional tipping is unnecessary except for extraordinary service. An 8% government tax is added to all hotel and restaurant bills. The departure tax is $14 for adults and $7.50 for children ages 5–11, payable in either currency. Children under five are exempt. A surcharge of $4 is levied when departing Carriacou.

Opening and Closing Times

Stores are generally open weekdays 8 AM–4 or 4:30 PM and Saturday 8–1; some close from 12–1. Most are closed Sunday, although tourist shops usually open if a cruise ship is in port. Banks are open Monday–Thursday 8–3, Friday 8–5. The main post office, on Lagoon Road, by the Port in St. George's, is open weekdays 8–3:30. Each town or village has a post office branch.

HOLIDAYS

Public holidays when banks and shops are closed are: New Year's Day, Independence Day (Feb. 7), Good Friday (Apr. 2), Easter Monday (Apr. 5), Labour Day (May 1), Whit Monday (May 24), Corpus Christi (June 3), Emancipation Holidays (1st Mon. and Tues. in Aug.), Carnival (2nd Mon. in Aug.), Thanksgiving Day (Oct. 25), Christmas, and Boxing Day (Dec. 26).

Passports

U.S., Canadian, or British citizens must provide a valid passport and a return or ongoing ticket.

Precautions

Crime is not a big problem in Grenada, but it's a good idea to secure your valuables in the hotel safe and not leave items unattended on the beach. Regarding flora and fauna, be aware that removing bark from trees, taking wildlife from the forest and removing coral from the sea are all forbidden. Also, be careful when walking late at night in Grand Anse; it's dark enough to bump into one of the cows that graze silently by the roadside or trip in a hole dug by a land crab! Insects are only a nuisance after heavy rains, when mosquitoes emerge, and on the beach after 4 PM, when tiny sand flies begin to bite. It's a good idea to bring repellent when hiking in the rain forest. Taking photos of market vendors, private citizens, or their homes is not appreciated without first asking permission and offering a gratuity for the favor. Water from hotel taps is perfectly safe to drink.

Telephones and Mail

Grenada has a fully digital telecommunications service and can be dialed directly from the United States and Canada. The area code is 473. From Grenada, you can place direct-dial calls to anywhere in the world from pay phones, card phones, and most hotel room phones. For international calls using a major credit card, dial 111; there's no surcharge.

Airmail rates for letters to the United States, Canada, and the United Kingdom are EC75¢ for a ½-ounce letter and EC35¢ for a postcard. When addressing a letter to Grenada, there's no postal code to include; simply write "Grenada, West Indies" after the local address.

Visitor Information

The **Grenada Board of Tourism** (☏ 473/440–2001 or 473/440–2279, FAX 473/440–6637), on the south side of the Carenage, in St. George's, distributes maps, brochures, and information on accommodations, tours, and other services. You'll want to pick up a copy of *Greeting,* the official publication of the board of tourism and the Grenada Hotel Association. It's available free in most hotels.

For information before leaving home, contact the **Grenada Board of Tourism** in the United States (✉ 800 2nd Ave., Suite 400K, New York, NY 10017, ☏ 212/687–9554 or 800/927–9554, FAX 212/573–9731); in Canada (✉ 439 University Ave., Suite 820, Toronto, Ontario M5G 1Y8, ☏ 416/595–1339, FAX 416/595–8278); or in the United Kingdom (✉ 1 Collingham Gardens, Earl's Court, London SW5 0HW, ☎ 0171/370–5164 or 0171/370–5165, FAX 0171/370–7040). For information on the Internet, the Grenada Board of Tourism Web site address is www.grenada.org.

You can make hotel reservations at any of the hotels that are members of the **Grenada Hotel Association** by calling the association (☎ 473/444–1353 or 800/322–1753 in the United States and Canada, FAX 473/444–4847).

13 Guadeloupe

Updated by
David H. Jones

The narrow road to the fishing village of St-François on Grande-Terre often runs precipitously close to the Caribbean. Beyond the town center and down near the beach, it passes men cleaning exotic fish or fashioning langouste traps from chicken wire and tree branches. The beach bustles with swimmers, sunbathers, and boats sailing out to sea—or perhaps just down the coast to a resort. At a nearby open-air restaurant, a machete-wielding chef deftly halves a lobster and then throws it on a hot grill. Not far away, women sell vegetables, spices, and fruit. Guadeloupe is alive around you.

Sprawling and changing by the mile—from jungle highlands to seaside resorts, from mall shopping to rustic dining—Guadeloupe is varied, rich, and alive. It looks like a giant (629-square-mi) butterfly resting on the sea between Antigua and Dominica. Its wings—Basse-Terre and Grande-Terre—are the two largest islands in the Guadeloupe archipelago. The Rivière Salée, a 4-mi seawater channel flowing between the Caribbean and the Atlantic, forms the "spine" of the butterfly. Smaller, flatter Grande-Terre (218 square mi) is dry, flat, and sandy. It has Guadeloupe's best beaches, restaurants, casinos, resorts, and clubs. Basse-Terre ("low land") is wild, wet, and mountainous. It once lagged behind Grande-Terre, but today is popular with those who love hiking, whale-watching, diving, or deep-sea fishing. Its lush, precipitous west coast is as beautiful as any other place in the Caribbean. On Les Saintes, La Désirade, Marie-Galante, and the other islands of the archipelago, you'll find places that have remained largely untouched by the world.

Guadeloupe was annexed by France in 1674. During the French Revolution, battles broke out between royalists and revolutionaries on the island. In 1794 Britain aided Guadeloupe royalists, and that same year France dispatched Victor Hugues to sort things out. (In virtually every town and village you'll run across a "Victor Hugues" street, boulevard, or park.) After his troops banished the British, Hugues abolished slavery and guillotined recalcitrant planters. Those who managed to keep their heads fled to Louisiana or hid in the hills of Grande-Terre, where their descendants now live. Hugues—"the Robespierre of the Isles"—was soon relieved of his command, slavery was reestablished by Napoléon, and the French and English continued to battle over the island. The 1815 Treaty of Paris restored Guadeloupe to France, and in 1848, due largely to the efforts of Alsatian Victor Schoelcher, slavery was abolished. The island was made a *département* of France in 1946, and in 1974 it was elevated to a *région,* administered by a prefect appointed from Paris. With Martinique, St. Barts, and St. Martin, it is part of *les Antilles Françaises,* or French West Indies.

An old saying of the French Caribbean refers to *"les grands seigneurs de la Martinique et les bonnes gens de la Guadeloupe"* (the lords of Martinique and the bourgeoisie of Guadeloupe). And though there are few aristocrats left on Martinique, the saying still holds some truth in Guadeloupe. Middle-class French tourists come (most on package tours) to swim and sunbathe, scuba dive, or hike. But sugar, not tourism, is still Guadeloupe's primary source of income. Only about 10% of the workforce is employed in the tourism industry. At harvest time in January, the fields teem with workers cutting cane, and the roads are clogged with trucks taking the harvest to factories or distilleries.

Everything about Guadeloupe—from the *franglais* (*le topless, le weekend, le snack-bar*) to the zippy little cars and ubiquitous *vendeuses de la plage* (women who model bathing suits on *le beach* and do a striptease show in the process)—is French. And whether in hotel corridors or on the beach, at breakfast or on a dive boat, cigarette smoke is as much a part of the ambience as the tropical breeze. The prices are Parisian, and unlike on St. Martin and St. Barts, there are stiff taxes on most goods. To really feel at home here, some *français* is indispensable, though you may receive a bewildering response in Creole patois. Still you'll always be made to feel welcome in this land of volcanoes, French food, and 'ti punch (white rum, sugarcane syrup, and a squeeze of lime).

Lodging

On Guadeloupe, you can opt for a splashy hotel with a full complement of resort activities or choose a small *relais* (inn). If French is not your forte, you'll fare better in the large hotels. Gosier and Bas-du-Fort are generally considered resort areas, but the places around Ste-Anne and St-François have their fair share of resorts. There are also small hotels on Iles des Saintes and Marie-Galante. More, and better, hotels are also opening on Basse-Terre. Most hotels include buffet breakfast in their rates. Prices decline 25%–40% in the off-season.

CATEGORY	COST*
$$$$	over $300
$$$	$225–$300
$$	$150–$225
$	under $150

All prices are for a standard double room, excluding taxe de séjour, which varies from hotel to hotel, and 10%–15% service charge.

Hotels

GRANDE-TERRE

$$$$ ★ 🏨 **La Cocoteraie.** This very private annex to ☞ **Le Méridien** consists of suites housed in smart, blue and white, colonial-style buildings. Twenty

are directly on the beach, the rest have views of either the marina or the extravagantly large pool surrounded by Chinese vases. Each suite has a large living room, a veranda, and two bathrooms. The decor is a handsome blend of bright pastels, dark mahogany furnishings, and madras upholstery. The Robert Trent Jones–designed golf course is just across the road, and you also have full use of the facilities of Le Méridien. Under the energetic leadership of the on-site manager, Fidel Montana, the resort is focusing more and more on the American market. The staff all speak English, and the restaurant's international cuisine caters to lighter tastes. ✉ *Av. de l'Europe, St-François 97118,* ☎ *590/ 88–79–81 or 800/543–4300 (reservations service),* FAX *590/88–78– 33. 52 suites. Restaurant, in-room safes, minibars, pool, 2 tennis courts, exercise room, beach. AE, DC, MC, V. CP, MAP.*

$$$–$$$$
★ ▥ **Auberge de la Vieille Tour.** The raised lobby, with its magnificent view of Iles des Saintes, is just one of the many touches that make this such a fine resort. Another is the staff's quiet efficiency, and still another is the clever landscaping that masks the three, large, apartment-style buildings containing the lowest-priced rooms. With their cheerful, blue-and-white nautical decor and tiled floors—not to mention their sea views—these rooms are an excellent value. The 32 deluxe, cliff-top suites each have a split-level bedroom–living room (with a trundle bed) and glass-walled bathrooms (with spectacular ocean views). The resort's social hub is the handsome bar–gourmet restaurant. Built around massive, 200-year-old stone walls a sugar mill, it serves fine French food and has an extensive wine list. Breakfast, lunch, and barbecue fare are served at the poolside *ajoupa,* an open-sided structure. As on most of Guadeloupe, the beach is rather *petit.* ✉ *Rte. de Montauban, Gosier 97190,* ☎ *590/84–23–23 or 800/322–2223 (reservation service),* FAX *590/84–33–43. 148 rooms, 32 suites. 2 restaurants, bar, pool, 2 tennis courts, beach, shops. AE, DC, MC, V. BP, MAP.*

$$$–$$$$
▥ **Club Méditerranée La Caravelle.** This version of the well-known chain has air-conditioned twin-bed rooms, some with balconies, and 50 secluded acres at the western end of a magnificent white-sand beach. Nice extras include a volleyball court, calisthenics classes, and a language lab where you can take French classes. The property draws a fun-loving, younger crowd, most of whom are from France, and serves as the home port for Club Med's sailing cruises. ✉ *Quart Carvelle Ste-Anne 97180,* ☎ *590/85–49–50 or 800/258–2633 (reservations service),* FAX *590/85–49–70. 310 rooms. Restaurant, pub, air-conditioning, pool, 6 tennis courts, aerobics, volleyball, beach, snorkeling, boating. AE, MC, V. All-inclusive.*

$$$–$$$$
▥ **La Créole Beach Hotel.** Ten acres of tropical greenery and two beaches are the lush setting for this comfortable hotel. Although its maze-like corridors and pathways can be somewhat confusing, its rooms are spacious and have sliding glass doors that open onto balconies. The decor is dominated by vivid jungle-print fabrics. The water sports center offers excursions to Ilet du Gosier. The restaurant, Le Zawag, serves excellent lobster and is very popular at night. ✉ *Pointe de la Verdure (Box 19), Gosier 97190,* ☎ *590/90–46–46 or 800/755– 9313 (reservations service),* FAX *590/90–46–66. 156 rooms, 6 duplexes. 2 restaurants, bar, air-conditioning, pool, 2 tennis courts, snorkeling, boating, car rental. AE, DC, MC, V. CP, EP, MAP.*

$$$–$$$$
▥ **Le Méridien St-François.** You couldn't pack more activity into one vacation than is offered by this hotel, which is adjacent to ☞ **La Cocoteraie** hotel. The 150-acre resort puts out its own *A to Z Leisure Guide* and broadcasts from Télé Méridien to let you know what's going on. The activities director organizes everything from boccie to book lending. The beach hut is a busy place even off-season. Standard rooms

are modest, and wear and tear has taken its toll, but all have small balconies, about half of which face the sea. Odd-numbered rooms have the best views. Decor is standard to the Méridien chain, right down to the mint-and-orange fabrics and boxy configurations. This one at least has a few individual touches, such as flowerpots on the balconies. ⊠ *Ave. de I Europe, St-François 97118, ☎ 590/88–51–00 or 800/ 543–4300 (reservations service), ℻ 590/88–40–71. 267 rooms, 10 suites. 2 restaurants, 2 bars, air-conditioning, pool, spa, 2 tennis courts, beach, snorkeling, boating, shops, dance club, car rental. AE, D, MC, V. CP, MAP.*

$$–$$$ ▨ **Anchorage.** The 27 acres of this resort are spread along the coast a few miles from St-François. Indeed, the complex is so large that one trek to the man-made beach at one end may prompt you to rent a car. Rooms are either in Creole-style buildings or in 34 villas that climb the rise behind them. All rooms have terra-cotta floors, rich russet-patterned bedspreads, ceramic lamps, and such original touches as antique radios. The formal restaurant offers à la carte dining, but most evenings, guests attend the theme buffet at the Blanc Mangé restaurant; performers entertain on its large piazza, across from which is an open-sided disco. The Anchorage may not have the best beach on the island, but it does have the largest swimming pool. ⊠ *Anse des Rochers, St-François 97118, ☎ 590/93–90–00, ℻ 590/93–91–00. 356 rooms. 2 restaurants, grocery, snack bar, pool, 2 tennis courts, archery, beach, shop, dance club, meeting rooms, car rental. MC, V. EP, MAP.*

$$–$$$ ▨ **Canella Beach Residence.** In this resort built to resemble a Creole village, you have a choice of single-level or duplex studios and junior or duplex suites. Each unit has its own terrace or balcony (units on the top floor have the best views). The decor is a refreshing departure from the usual Caribbean pastels: earth tones complement white-tile floors and rattan furnishings. The complex has its own semiprivate cove, a beach bar, and free water sports. At the Verandah restaurant you can dine indoors in air-conditioning or enjoy the sea breezes outdoors. But, if you choose the latter and leave your breakfast unattended, even for a moment, the birds will have a field day with your croissants. The nighttime menu includes Creole and French dishes. ⊠ *Pointe de la Verdure, Gosier 97190, ☎ 590/90–44–00; 800/223–9815 or 212/251– 1800 in NY (reservations services); ℻ 590/90–44–44. 146 rooms. Restaurant, bar, kitchenettes, pool, 4 tennis courts, beach, snorkeling, windsurfing, boating, waterskiing, fishing. AE, DC, MC, V. EP, MAP.*

$$–$$$ ▨ **Fleur d'Epée Novotel/Marissol.** "If you can't beat them, join them" could be the motto for the merger of these two hotels on a cove near Bas-du-Fort. Tour groups from France are still the primary clientele, and when both hotels are full, the narrow strip of sand they share can get rather crowded. Rooms at the Fleur d'Epée are rather cramped, but the powder-blue fabrics and white tiles give them a pleasant, fresh look; those at Marissol are equally pleasant. All rooms have terraces, most with sea views. ⊠ *Gosier 97190, ☎ 590/90–40–00, ℻ 590/90–99– 07. 400 rooms. 4 restaurants, bar, air-conditioning, minibars, pool, beach, snorkeling, boating. AE, D, DC, MC, V. CP, MAP.*

$$–$$$ ▨ **Golf Marine Club Hotel.** This small, moderately priced establishment is close to St-François's shops and restaurants. But the hotel's name overpromises: It isn't a club, the municipal golf course is across the street, and it has neither marina nor beach (the nearest public beach is two blocks away). All the rooms have balconies, but those facing the street tend to be noisy. A third of the rooms have loft bedrooms and a roll-out couch in the lounge. There are also 15 bungalows on the premises. The relaxed, informal restaurant is on the patio terrace. ⊠ *Av. de l'Europe (Box 204), St-François 97118, ☎ 590/88–60–60, ℻ 590/88–68– 98. 88 units. Restaurant, pool, 2 tennis courts. AE, MC, V. CP, MAP.*

336

Exploring

Allée du Manoir, **36**

Anse Bertrand, **13**

Bas-du-Fort, **2**

Basse-Terre, **32**

Bouillante, **27**

Cascade aux
Ecrevisses, **23**

Chutes du Carbet, **35**

La Désirade, **39**

Edgar-Clerc Archaeo-
logical Museum, **10**

Etang As de Pique, **31**

Gosier, **4**

Guadeloupe Aquarium, **3**

Les Mamelles, **21**

Marie-Galante, **38**

Matouba, **29**

Morne-à-l'Eau, **15**

Le Moule, **9**

Parc Archéologique
des Roches Gravées, **34**

Parc National de la
Guadeloupe, **19**

Parc Tropical de
Bras-David, **22**

Petit-Bourg, **25**

Pigeon Island, **26**

Pointe des Châteaux, **7**

La Pointe de la
Grande Vigie, **12**

Pointe-Noire, **18**

Pointe-à-Pitre, **1**

Porte d'Enfer, **11**

Port Louis, **14**

Ravine Chaude, **16**

Ste-Anne, **5**

St-Claude, **30**

St-François, **6**

Ste-Rose, **17**

Terre-de-Haute, **37**

Vernou, **24**

Vieux Fort, **33**

Vieux-Habitants, **28**

Zévalos, **8**

Zoological Park and
Botanical Gardens, **20**

Dining

Auberge de la
Vieille Tour, **61**

Auberge de
St-François, **78**

L'Auberge les
Petits Saints aux
Anacardies, **55**

Le Bananier, **62**

Le Baobob, **74**

Château de Feuilles, **85**

Chez Clara, **40**

Chez Jackye, **45**

Chez Violetta-
La Creole, **63**

Le Corsaire, **69**

El Dorado, **53**

Guadeloupe

Guadeloupe Passage

Anse Laborde

Anse Bertrand, **13** **86**
N8

Souffleur
N6

Port Louis **14**
Beauport
N6

Anse du
Vieux Fort
Pte. Allègre
Ilet à Fajou
Petit-Canal

Anse du Canal

La Grande
-Anse **42**
40
41 **17** Ste-Rose

Vieux-Bourg
N5

Grand
Cul-de-Sac
Marin
Jabrun
du Sud

44 **43**
Deshaies
Lamentin
Abyn

La Raizet
International
Airport

45
N2
46
18
Pointe-
Noire
19
PARC NATIONAL
DE LA GUADELOUPE
16 **59**
Destrelan
N1
Pointe-
à-Pitre
1

Anse
Caraïbe
20
Bas-du-Fort
2 **3**

La Traversée
Mahaut **21**
D23
Petit
Cul-de-Sac
Marin
60 **61**

22 **23**
24
Vernou
25
58
Petit-
Bourg

BASSE-TERRE
Goyave

Malendure
Pigeon
Island **47**
26 **48**
27
Bouillante
N2
Ste-Marie
N1

Marigot
La Soufrière
Ste-Marie

Vieux-
Habitants **28**
Matouba
29
Capesterre-
Belle-Eau

Plage de
Rocroy
St-Claude
35 **36**

30
D11
49
Carbet
St-Sauveur
Bananier

Basse-Terre
Gourbeyre
N1
Trois-Rivières

Caribbean
Sea
32
D6
31
34 **50**

Anse Turlet
33
D6
51

Vieux Fort

KEY

Cruise Ship Terminal

Ferry

1 Exploring Sights

40 Restaurants and Hotels

Iles des Saintes (Les Saint

37 Terre-de-Haut
Place Crawen

Terre-
de-Bas
52 **57**

La Coche
Grand Ilet

Le Flibustier, **72**

Folie Plage, **86**

Les Gommiers, **46**

Le Jardin Créole, **54**

Le Karacoli, **42**

La Louisiane, **82**

Nilce's Bar, **57**

Les Oiseaux, **76**

La Plantation
Ste-Marthe, **82**

Le Rocher de
Malendure, **48**

Rosini, **71**

La Saladerie, **52**

La Table Creole, **68**

Le Touloulou, **87**

Lodging

Anchorage, **77**

Auberge de l'Arbes
à Pain, **91**

Auberge de la
Distillerie, **58**

Auberge de la
Vieille Tour, **61**

L'Auberge les Petits
Saints aux Anacardies, **55**

Bois Joli, **56**

Canella Beach
Residence, **67**

Cap Sud Caraïbes, **66**

Club Méditerranée
La Caravelle, **73**

La Cocoteraie, **79**

La Créole Beach
Hotel, **64**

Domaine de
Petite-Anse, **47**

Fleur d'Epée
Novotel/Marissol, **60**

Fort Royal
Touring Club, **43**

Golf Marine Club
Hotel, **81**

Grande Anse Hotel, **51**

Hôtel le Clipper, **70**

Hôtel St. Georges, **49**

Hôtel Hajo, **88**

Le Jardin Malanga, **50**

Le Méridien
St-François, **80**

Le Mirage, **92**

L'Oasis, **93**

L'Orchidée, **65**

La Plantation
Ste-Marthe, **82**

Relais du Moulin, **75**

Relais des Sources, **59**

Résidence de la Pointe
Batterie, **44**

Résidence Soleil Le
Vant, **89**

La Sucrerie du Comté, **41**

Tropical Club Hotel, **84**

Au Village du Ménard, **90**

$$–$$$ ⊞ **La Plantation Ste-Marthe.** You're a few miles inland here, among
★ gently rolling hills and fields, but the grounds are lovely (bits of old
sugar-refinery machinery are cleverly incorporated into the landscaping), you can see the ocean from some guest rooms, and there's shuttle service to the beach. The whole place is also sumptuous: the august,
almost baroque reception area has columns of pale blue and mango;
vast murals; a winding double staircase of polished wood; and marble floors. The large, elegant rooms are in four three-story Creole-style
buildings, with spacious terraces that overlook the large pool. The duplex suites have loft-style bedrooms above salons. Throughout the hotel,
furnishings are unique modern adaptations (they incorporate cane
work) of French period pieces. Mahogany beds and aquamarine and
coral tile work contribute to the refined aura. Next to the free-form
pool, which was designed to resemble a lake, you'll find the outstanding ☞ La Plantation Ste-Marthe restaurant. ⊠ *St-François 97118,*
☎ *590/93–11–11 or 800/333–1970 (reservation service),* ℻ *590/88–*
72–47. 96 rooms, 24 duplexes. Restaurant, bar, air-conditioning, in-
room safes, minibars, pool, meeting rooms. AE, MC, V. EP, MAP.

$–$$$ ⊞ **Hôtel le Clipper.** Looking much like a beached ocean liner, this aptly
named hotel is, in fact, on the edge of a large, palm-shaded beach.
(Though the beach is private, it's shared by the Clipper's neighboring
sister establishment, the Hotel Salako.) This whitewashed high-rise's
rooms have private baths and balconies that face the sea. Four miles
from Pointe-à-Pitre and 6 mi from the airport, this hotel joins a thicket
of accommodations that are clustered near the Casino de Gosier. Any
annoyance the bustle may cause is more than offset by the convenience
of having plenty of car rental agencies and several restaurants within
easy walking distance. ⊠ *Pointe de la Verdure 97190,* ☎ *590/84–01–*
75, ℻ *590/84–38–15. 88 rooms. Restaurant, bar, air-conditioning,*
pool, beach, snorkeling, boating. AE, DC, MC, V. CP, MAP.

$–$$ ⊞ **Cap Sud Caraïbes.** This tiny relais is on a country road between Gosier
and Ste-Anne and just a five-minute walk from a quiet beach. It's
homey and simple, but it's a good value for the money and the staff
does its best to make you feel comfortable. Each individually decorated
room has a balcony and either a shower or an enormous bathtub. ⊠
Gosier 97190, ☎ *590/85–96–02,* ℻ *590/85–80–39. 12 rooms. Bar,*
air-conditioning, pool, snorkeling, dry cleaning, laundry service, air-
port shuttle. MC, V. CP.

$–$$ ⊞ **L'Orchidée.** Though it doesn't have a beach or all the facilities of a
large resort, this hotel has a lot to offer. Its spotless studios have dark-
wood furnishings, teal fabrics, sparkling white-tile floors, and balconies.
A stay here gets you a free membership to the local recreation center,
which has a pool. On the ground floor a small shop serves morning
coffee, and the hotel's English-speaking owner-manager Madame
Karine Chenaf will help you plan your day. ⊠ *32 bd. Général de*
Gaulle, Gosier 97190, ☎ *590/84–54–20,* ℻ *590/84–54–90. 18 stu-*
dios. Dining room, air-conditioning, kitchenettes. MC, V. EP.

$–$$ ⊞ **Relais du Moulin.** A restored windmill serves as the reception room
for this relais. A spiral staircase leads up to a TV-reading room, from
which there's a view of the countryside. Rooms, which are all housed
in bungalows, are immaculate but claustrophobic, somehow managing to pack in twin beds, small terraces, and kitchenettes. The restaurant overlooks the windmill. Try the house specialty: grouper and
lobster served with Creole sauce or stuffed with fresh pâté. The seven-
course, 220F *menu dégustation* (tasting menu) is a good way to sample Creole cooking. The beach is a 10-minute hike away. ⊠ *Châteaubrun,*
Ste-Anne 97180, ☎ *590/88–23–96 or 800/223–9815,* ℻ *590/88–*
03–92. 40 rooms. Restaurant, bar, air-conditioning, kitchenettes, pool,
tennis court, archery, bicycles. AE, DC, MC, V. CP, MAP.

$–$$ 🏨 **Tropical Club Hotel.** Great windsurfing and swimming at a strip of golden sand are big draws for this hotel on the northeastern coast of Grande-Terre. The almond-shape pool is next to an open-sided dining room that serves French and Creole fare. The guest rooms are in three buildings on a rise. Each room has a double bed and two bunk beds, which are tucked in an annex and are ideal for children (those under 21 stay free). Each room also has a private balcony, a kitchenette, and a sea view. There are three tennis courts nearby. ⊠ *Plage Autre Bord, Le Moule 97160,* ☎ *590/93–97–97,* ℻ *590/93–97–00. 72 rooms. Restaurant, bar, air-conditioning, fans, kitchenettes, pool, boccie, exercise room, beach, windsurfing, shop. AE, MC, V. CP, MAP.*

BASSE-TERRE

$$$–$$$$ 🏨 **Auberge de la Distillerie.** Not only is this country inn homey, but
★ it also has a great location close to the Parc National de la Guadeloupe. In the 19th-century main house, each of the 12 guest rooms has a unique decor that incorporates wicker furnishings, tile floors, wood beams, ceramic lamps, and local artwork. Each also has a terrace; some have a refrigerator. There are also slightly larger bungalows (that have slightly larger terraces) and a rustic wood chalet that sleeps two to four people. The restaurant, noted for its delectable Creole cuisine, is built around the pool. You can swim in or take a boat trip on the Lézarde River. ⊠ *Tabanon, Petit Bourg 97170,* ☎ *590/94–25–91 or 800/322–2223,* ℻ *590/94–11–91. 12 rooms, 2 bungalows, 1 chalet. Restaurant, bar, patisserie, air-conditioning, pool. AE, MC, V. CP, MAP.*

$$$–$$$$ 🏨 **Le Jardin Malanga.** Alfresco lunches of grilled dorado—served with
★ vegetables grown on the property—a cliffside swimming pool, and a flower-filled garden are just some of the delights here. Accommodations are in the antiques-filled main house (circa 1927) and in three simply but pleasantly furnished cottages. Each room's white-tile bathroom gleams; next to its tub is a one-way picture window that looks out on the lush surroundings. Guadeloupe's national park is not far away. ⊠ *Hermitage, Trois-Rivières 97114,* ☎ *590/92–67–57,* ℻ *590/92–67–58. 12 rooms. Air-conditioning, pool. AE, MC, V. CP.*

$–$$$ 🏨 **Résidence de la Pointe Batterie.** Opened in 1997, this resort is
★ neatly camouflaged in the foothills above Deshaies Bay and on the site of the old Pointe Batterie cannons. The villas are strategically sited up the side of a particularly steep hill. Most will comfortably accommodate from two to six people. Two have amenities for people with disabilities, and the seven *villas deluxe* have private decks and swimming pools. The property's hub is the reception area, and near it you'll find a communal pool and an open-air game room. The multilevel restaurant is at the bay's edge. Make no mistake: You have to hike around this complex, but the privacy of the accommodations and the singular rustic-yet-ritzy atmosphere make all the trekking worthwhile. ⊠ *Point Batterie, Deshaies 97126,* ☎ *590/28–57–03,* ℻ *590/28–57–28. 24 villas. Restaurant, bar, air-conditioning, in-room safes, kitchenettes, pool, recreation room. AE, MC, V. CP, MAP.*

$$ 🏨 **Fort Royal Touring Club.** This modern white structure overlooks two pristine beaches. Each spacious room has a terrace or balcony with a sea view, tile floors, handsome wicker and rattan furnishings, and mahogany beds. You can also choose the solitude of the 78 bungalows nestled on the grounds and by the beach. All rooms are air-conditioned and have either two twin beds or one double bed. The hotel offers tours into the national park and plenty of other activities, most of them beach related. ⊠ *Pointe du Petit Bas-Vent, Deshaies 97126,* ☎ *590/25–50–00,* ℻ *590/25–50–01. 107 rooms, 78 bungalows, 2 suites. Restaurant, bar, air-conditioning, 2 pools, miniature golf, 4 tennis courts, hiking, 2 beaches, dive shop, snorkeling, boating. AE, MC, V. CP, EP, MAP.*

$–$$ ⊞ **Hôtel St. Georges.** The large rooms of this hillside hotel are in three-story buildings that look like Richard Rogers versions of Creole houses. They're decorated with bright fabrics and teak and rattan reproduction furniture. All have spacious bathrooms and small verandas. Views are of the pool, which, though large and unusual, does not make as spectacular a vista as the charming village of St-Claude, the ocean, or the mountains—all nearby. The bar here is ultrahip. ⊠ *Rue Gratien Parize, St-Claude 97120,* ☎ *590/80–10–10,* ℻ *590/80–30–50. 38 rooms, 2 suites. Restaurant, bar, air-conditioning, pool, exercise room, squash, billiards, shop. D, MC, V. CP, EP, MAP.*

$ ⊞ **Domaine de Petite-Anse.** The ocher, red-roofed buildings of this complex spill down lushly landscaped hills above the ocean. Accommodations are either in simple and small—though well-equipped—rooms (ask for one with a sea view, which costs the same as one without) or bungalows with full baths, kitchenettes, and terraces. The decor consists of dark rattan furniture lightened by bright floral fabrics. The staff is friendly, but most speak only a little English. The resort, which is noted for its dive shop and nature tours of the national park, is very popular with young French couples and families. ⊠ *Plage de Petite-Anse, Monchy, Bouillante 97125,* ☎ *590/98–78–78 or 800/322–2223,* ℻ *590/98–80–28. 135 rooms, 40 bungalows. Restaurant, bar, air-conditioning, in-room safes, refrigerators, pool, archery, hiking, volleyball, dive shop, snorkeling, boating, shop. AE, DC, MC, V. EP.*

$ ⊞ **Grande-Anse Hotel.** Less than a mile from a black-sand beach and offering spectacular mountain views, this relais is a good choice for nature lovers. (It's also near the ferry to Iles des Saintes.) Accommodations are in bungalows that have small balconies. The heavy, polished wood furnishings should achieve antique status in a few years. The staff can help you arrange water sports and nature hikes. ⊠ *Trois-Rivières 97114,* ☎ *590/92–90–47,* ℻ *590/92–93–69. 16 bungalows. Restaurant, bar, air-conditioning, refrigerators, pool. MC, V. CP, MAP.*

$ ⊞ **Relais des Sources.** This relais is set in the foothills of Grosse Montagne, only a few hundred yards from the Ravine Chaude thermal baths and in a landscape of sugarcane fields and sleepy villages. There are five (rather dark) rooms in the main building and 10 bungalows scattered about the shady property. The bungalows are equipped with kitchenettes, phones, and TVs. The (extremely young) staff will take care of your every need—from baby-sitting to airport transfers. On the downside, you might mistake the swimming pool for a birdbath, and the nearest beach is 9 mi away. ⊠ *Lamentin 91729,* ☎ *590/25–31–04,* ℻ *590/25–30–63. 5 rooms, 10 bungalows. Restaurant, bar, air-conditioning, pool, shop. AE, MC, V. CP, MAP.*

$ ⊞ **La Sucrerie du Comté.** The ruins and rusting equipment of a 19th-century sugar factory punctuate the lawns and gardens. In fact, it is the historically significant grounds, along with the attractive public areas, that are this resort's main attractions. The interiors of the fine restaurant and bar re-create plantation living, with wood beams, stone walls, and towering floral arrangements. Twenty-six bungalows duplicate the gingerbread architecture of the turn of the century, with small but pretty rooms. The nearest beach is a 10-minute stroll through a tangle of greenery. ⊠ *Comté de Lohéac, Ste-Rose 97115,* ☎ *590/28–60–17,* ℻ *590/28–65–63. 50 rooms. Restaurant, bar, air-conditioning, pool, tennis court. AE, DC, MC, V. CP, MAP.*

ILES DES SAINTES

$–$$ ⊞ **L'Auberge les Petits Saints aux Anacardies.** This distinctive inn is
★   trimmed with trellises and topped by dormers. A glorious clutter greets you in the reception area: It's crammed with antiques and objets d'art collected by owners Jean-Paul Colas and Didier Spindler. If you see some-

thing you like, you can take it away for a price. Room furnishings are a similarly odd assortment of antiques. Eight rooms have queen-size beds and two have twin beds; all have private baths. There's also a one-bedroom bungalow. Throughout the inn, windows open to a view of gardens, hills, and the bay (Room 2 has an extraordinary vista). The outstanding restaurant, ☞ **L'Auberge les Petits Saints aux Anacardies**, only serves lunch on weekends, but a prix-fixe (150F) menu is available nightly. ⊠ *La Savane, Terre-de-Haut 97137,* ☎ *590/99–50–99,* ℻ *590/99–54–51. 10 rooms, 1 bungalow. Restaurant, bar, air-conditioning, pool, sauna. AE, MC, V. CP, MAP.*

$–$$ 🏨 **Bois Joli.** A beautiful setting, right on the bay, is the attraction here. Most of the rooms, either in the inn or one of the bungalows, are air-conditioned but rather drab. The restaurant serves wonderful clams in Creole sauce on a terrace that overlooks the sea. Water sports can be arranged, and the Anse Crawen nudist beach is a five-minute walk away. ⊠ *Terre-de-Haut 97137,* ☎ *590/99–50–38 or 800/223–9815,* ℻ *590/99–55–05. 21 rooms, 8 bungalows. Restaurant, bar, pool, airport shuttle. MC, V. CP, MAP.*

MARIE-GALANTE
There are several small lodgings on Marie-Gallante. **Auberge de l'Arbre à Pain** (7 rooms, ☎ 590/97–73–69) in Grand Bourg, **Hôtel Hajo** (6 rooms, ☎ 590/97–32–76) in Capesterre, **Résidence Soleil Le Vant** (10 rooms, ☎ 590/97–31–55, ℻ 590/97–41–65), also in Capesterre, and **Au Village de Ménard** (5 bungalows, ☎ 590/97–09–4502, ℻ 590/97–15–40) in St-Louis.

LA DÉSIRADE
An even more remote island than Marie-Galante, La Désirade offers only a few lodging options. In Grande-Anse, there's a 10-room hotel called **L'Oasis** (☎ 590/20–02–12). Its restaurant isn't fancy, but it serves excellent seafood. There's also **Le Mirage,** a tiny 8-room establishment (☎ 590/20–01–08 ℻ 590/20–07–45).

Villas

For information about villas, apartments, and private rooms in modest houses, contact **Gîtes de France** (⊠ 5 Square de la Banque, Pointe-a-Pitre 97171, ☎ 590/91–64–33, ℻ 590/91–45–40) or the **Association des Villas et Meublés de Tourisme** (⊠ 12 Faubourg Alexandre Issac, Pointe-a-Pitre 97171, ☎ 590/82–02–62, ℻ 590/82–56–65).

Dining

Guadeloupe's fine Creole dishes feature local seafood and vegetables, such as christophenes and plantains. Favorite appetizers are *accras* (codfish fritters), *boudin* (highly seasoned pork sausage), and *crabes farcis* (stuffed land crabs). *Blaff* is a spicy fish stew. *Langouste* (lobster) and *lambi* (conch) are widely available, as is *souchy,* a Tahitian version of sushi. The island has more than 700 restaurants—including those that serve French, Italian, African, Indian, Vietnamese, and South American food—but they aren't cheap. The local libation is 'ti punch—a heady concoction of rum, lime juice, and sugarcane syrup. This innocent-sounding little drink packs a wallop.

What to Wear
Dining is casual at lunch, but beach attire is a no-no. Except at the more laid-back marina and beach eateries, dinner is slightly more formal. Long pants, collared shirts, and skirts or dresses are appreciated, although not required.

CATEGORY	COST*
$$$$	over $60
$$$	$45–$60
$$	$30–$45
$	under $30

*per person for a three-course meal, excluding drinks and service

Grande-Terre

CARIBBEAN/CREOLE

$$–$$$$ ✕ **Le Bananier.** *"Nouvelle cuisine Créole"* (creatively prepared dishes that use local produce) is the specialty at this well-established Gosier restaurant. Try the stuffed rockfish or the poultry supreme with conch. The dining room, with its beamed ceiling and lush plants, is a cheery space, and Jean Clarus is one of the most experienced chefs on the island. A wide selection of wines is available. ⊠ *Montauban, Gosier,* ☎ *590/84–34–85. MC, V.*

$–$$ ✕ **Chez Violetta–La Creole.** The late Violetta Chaville established this restaurant's à la carte Creole menu when she was head of Guadeloupe's association of *cuisinières* (female chefs). Her brother has carried on her cooking traditions, dishing up specials such as red snapper in *belle doudou* sauce, a Creole mix of onions, tomatoes, peppers, and spices. The food, although still good, has been eclipsed by other island kitchens, but the restaurant remains a stop on many visitors' itineraries. ⊠ *Eastern outskirts of Gosier village,* ☎ *590/84–10–34. AE, MC, V.*

$ ✕ **Folie Plage.** This lovely spot, north of Anse-Bertrand, is especially popular with families on weekends. Prudence Marcelin prepares reliable Creole food; superb *court bouillon* (fish broth) and imaginative curried dishes are among the specialties. There is a children's wading pool here. ⊠ *Anse Laborde,* ☎ *590/22–11–17. No credit cards.*

$ ✕ **La Table Creole.** Carmélite Jeanne rules the kitchen of this little terrace eatery, and she turns out dazzling, deceptively mild Creole cuisine
★   that can heat you up like the noonday sun. Sea urchin gratin, succulent kingfish, snapper blaff (a West Indian version of bouillabaisse), and goat *colombo* (curry) are among her memorable specialties. Fresh flowers are everywhere, and Madame Jeanne usually dresses colorfully to match. ⊠ *St-Félix,* ☎ *590/84–28–28. MC, V. No dinner Sun.*

CONTEMPORARY

$$–$$$$ ✕ **Château de Feuilles.** This restaurant is 9 mi from Le Moule—on the
★   Campêche road between Gros-Cap and Campêche—and it's worth a special trip. You'll be hard pressed to find a finer luncheon than that served by Martine and Jean-Pierre Dubost. The country setting is relaxed and stylish. While waiting for your meal you can take a dip in the pool or stroll around the 2-acre farm. For an aperitif, you can choose from about 20 different punch concoctions. The changing menu may include goose rillettes (pâté), velvety sea urchin pâté, kingfish fillet with vanilla, swordfish with sorrel, or the deep-sea fish *capitan* grilled with lime and green pepper. For dessert, try the pineapple flan. ⊠ *Rte. Campêche,* ☎ *590/22–30–30. MC, V. Closed Mon. No dinner (except for groups of 10 or more by reservation).*

$$$ ✕ **Auberge de la Vieille Tour.** Tables here are grouped around a his-
★   toric, whitewashed sugar mill; the conservatory-style extension has views up into lighted trees. It's hard to choose from chef Claude Davin's changing menu; entrées have included smoked swordfish with a two-pepper mousse and blinis, noisettes of lamb in honey and lime, and sea bream kissed with passion-fruit vinegar. For a sampling of Davin's work, opt for the menu dégustation. There's an extensive (and expensive) wine list. A band plays cool jazz Wednesday–Saturday evening. ⊠ *Gosier,* ☎ *590/84–23–23. AE, DC, MC, V.*

$–$$$ ✕ **Les Oiseaux.** In a stucco-and-stone house set in a tangle of gardens
★ that overlook the sea, owner-chefs Claudette and Arthur Rolle prepare
such dishes as *entrecôte Roquefort* (shark steak with coconut) and *marmite de* Robinson (a stew of dorado, kingfish, tuna, shrimp, and vegetables). Ask Claudette to show you her book of local remedies. If your
French is *very* good she might even prepare a special infusion for your
particular complaint. If English is your only language, perhaps simply
having a homemade *digestif* (after-dinner liqueur) will be enough to
cure what ails you. ⊠ *Anse des Rochers,* ☎ *590/88–56–92. Reservations essential. AE, MC, V. Closed Oct. No lunch Mon.–Wed.*

ECLECTIC

$$–$$$$ ✕ **Le Flibustier.** The name is French for "the buccaneer," and this rustic hilltop farmhouse plays on the theme for all it's worth. Waiters dress
like extras from *Hook.* Roasting sides of meat are the backdrop for
lots of piratical carrying-on. It's particularly lively after 8 PM, when
staffers from the neighboring Club Med come in to hold court, smoke
up a storm, and serenade attractive guests with ribald ditties. You can
order a complete dinner—mixed salad, grilled lobster, coconut ice
cream, 'ti punch, and half a pitcher of wine—or à la carte off the blackboard menu. ⊠ *La Coline, Fonds Thézan (between Ste-Anne and St-Félix),* ☎ *590/88–23–36. No credit cards. Closed Mon. No lunch Sun.*

$$–$$$$ ✕ **La Louisiane.** The owner, chef Daniel Hugon, who hails from the
★ Carlton in Cannes, prepares such traditional favorites as duck-liver confit with raspberry vinaigrette or smoked fish as starters, then crayfish
flambé, fillet of beef in green pepper sauce, or roast rack of lamb. The
Creole menu (120F) is a fine buy. The dozen tables of this small restaurant are on a terrace decorated with paintings and flower-filled hanging pots. The restaurant is on the road to Ste-Marthe, about 2 mi from
St-François, and Monsieur Hugon will send a car for you upon request.
You'll receive far better service if you speak adequate French. ⊠ *St-François,* ☎ *590/88–44–34. MC, V. Closed Mon. and Sept.*

$ ✕ **Le Corsaire.** Le Corsaire rates highly among the many restaurants
on Gosier's main drag. The waitstaff affects a piratical look with ponytails, earrings, and goatees. A *vivier* (lobster tank) and a flamboyant
mural of a buccaneer and his ship dominate the decor. Maman is a
sweetie, singing out *"C'est bon?"* from the kitchen and nodding approvingly as you eat. For 99F you get a set menu, which might start
with a conch tart or stuffed crab, then segue into beef brochette, octopus fricassee, or chicken colombo. The King Creole menu at 120F
nets you a large lobster. You can also order pizzas for 40F–52F. ⊠ *Rte.
des Hôtels, Gosier,* ☎ *590/84–17–39. AE, MC, V. No lunch Mon.*

FRENCH

$$–$$$$ ✕ **La Plantation Ste-Marthe.** Housed in the ritzy ☞ La Plantation Ste-
★ Marthe resort, this restaurant (under new chef Bruno Brazier) changes
its menu every two months and serves exceptionally good French food.
For starters, try the *salade auchoise,* a green salad with duck, or the
carpaccio *de filet de boeuf,* thin slices of raw beef with aromatic herbs.
Then move on to a bouillabaisse Creole or *noisettes* (small round
steaks cut from the rib or loin) of lamb with thyme. The three-chocolate mousse for dessert is a killer. The wine list is extensive. ⊠ *St-François,* ☎ *590/93–11–11. AE, MC, V.*

ITALIAN

$$–$$$ ✕ **Rosini.** This well-established restaurant in Gosier offers some of the
best Italian food on the island. Be sure to ask for a table on the upper
level; the downstairs section is drab and impersonal. A specialty here
is the homemade ravioli (try the mixed ravioli, which includes artichoke,
salmon, and shrimp). Most of the other Italian classics, like osso buco

or saltimbocca, are also offered. Some of the more complex dishes, such as the homemade gnocchi, must be ordered 24 hours in advance. ⊠ *La Porte des Caraïbes, Gosier,* ☎ *590/90–87–81. AE, D, MC, V.*

SEAFOOD

$$–$$$$ ✕ **Auberge de St-François.** Claude Simon's country home is set in an orchard, and his tables are set with Royal Doulton china and fine crystal. Dining is indoors or on one of the flower-filled patios, with a superb view of Marie-Galante and Pointe des Châteaux. The house specialty is crayfish prepared in several ways (the unusual fricassee with bacon and scallops is a standout). The brochette of smoked shark with a pepper sauce and the conch dishes are also good. A *menu touriste* (180F) of three courses, each with a choice of three dishes, is an affordable alternative to the à la carte offerings. Monsieur Simon has a superior cellar of vintage wine and champagne to complement his cuisine. ⊠ *St-François,* ☎ *590/88–51–71. MC, V. Closed Sun.–Mon.*

$$–$$$$ ✕ **Le Baobab.** Perched atop a cliff at the Hôtel La Toubana, this airy, open-sided restaurant is *the* place to go for lobster. Choose your own from the large vivier and then retire to the veranda with a 'ti punch to enjoy the spectacular view of the ocean. There's a basic lobster menu for 195F. For more exotic creations, expect to pay 350F. If you want to stay, the hotel has a cluster of simple but pleasant bungalows. There is also a swimming pool, and a small, private beach at the bottom of the cliff. A steel band plays in the evening. ⊠ *Durivage, Ste-Anne,* ☎ *590/88–25–57 or 800/322–2223. AE, MC, V.*

Basse-Terre

CARIBBEAN/CREOLE

$–$$$ ✕ **Le Karacoli.** With her flowing white dress and flamboyant style, Lu-
★ cienne Salcede, the owner of this pleasant seaside restaurant, looks as though she walked off the set of *Showboat.* The restaurant's entrance, along a rather scruffy lane by a campground, doesn't bode well, but this restaurant is outstanding. There are two dining areas: inside, at dark, wood tables, or outside, on the terrace, where all you hear are the splash of the waves and the rustling of coconut palms. The food is solid Creole fare: goat colombo, boudin, court bouillon. For dessert, try the banana flambé, heavily perfumed with rum, followed by a homemade digestif. By then, you'll be ready to stretch out on the chaise longues that Lucienne sets out just for that purpose. When you wake up, she'll even lend you a beach towel for a swim. ⊠ *La Grande-Anse, north of Deshaies,* ☎ *590/28–41–17. MC, V. No dinner.*

$–$$ ✕ **Chez Clara.** Clara Lasueur, who gave up a jazz-dancing career in Paris
★ to run her family's seaside restaurant with her mother, dishes out delicious Creole meals. Seating is on the inviting terrace of a gorgeous Creole house with lacy gingerbread trim. Clara takes the orders (her English is excellent), and the place is often so crowded with her friends and fans that you may have to wait at the octagonal wooden bar before being seated. The food is worth the wait, however—check the daily specials listed on the blackboard, for example, the succulent octopus or sublime ginger carambola (star fruit) sorbet. ⊠ *Ste-Rose,* ☎ *590/ 28–72–99. MC, V. Closed Wed. and Oct. No dinner Sun.*

ECLECTIC

$ ✕ **Chez Jackye.** Jacqueline Cabrion serves Creole and African dishes in her cheerful, plant-filled seaside restaurant. Creole boudin is a house specialty, as are lobster (grilled, vinaigrette, or fricassee), fried crayfish, clam blaff, and goat in port sauce. There's also a wide selection of omelets, sandwiches, and salads. For dessert, try the peach Melba or banana flambé. The 120F menu will have you waddling out happily. ⊠ *Anse Guyonneau, rue de la Bataille, Pointe-Noire,* ☎ *590/98– 06–98. DC, MC, V. Closed Sun.*

$ ✕ **Les Gommiers.** A changing menu here may list crayfish soup, octopus fricassee, pork chops with banana, goat colombo, seafood paella, and grilled entrecôte. Banana splits and profiteroles are on the dessert list. For lunch, salade Niçoise and other light dishes are offered. Fixed menus at 70F and 100F are sensational values. Lovely peacock chairs grace the bar, and polished wood furnishings and potted plants fill the dining room. ⊠ *Rue Baudot, Pointe-Noire,* ☎ *590/98–01–79. MC, V. No dinner Sun.–Tues.*

SEAFOOD

$–$$ ✕ **Le Rocher de Malendure.** You know the seafood is fresh here be-
★ cause the owner's husband, Francky, catches it himself. Tables are laid out on a series of airy, wooden verandas built up around the rock that gives the restaurant its name. The specialty is the *menu de la mer,* a pungent medley of souchy and smoked fish. The dorado, swordfish, conch, and lobster from the restaurant's own vivier are all excellent. If you want to catch fish, owner Ghiselaine Nouy will be happy to arrange a deep-sea fishing trip with Captain Francky. ⊠ *Bouillante,* ☎ *590/98–70–84. DC, MC. Closed 1st half of Sept. No dinner Sun.*

Iles des Saintes

ECLECTIC

$–$$$ ✕ **Le Jardin Créole.** License plates from around the world adorn the walls of this small combination restaurant-bar near the docks of Terre-de-Haut. Owners Michele and Marie Barrabes whip up a variety of rum drinks for those waiting for the ferry. In addition, the restaurant produces moderately priced dishes ranging from goat with curry to the freshest fish of the day. ⊠ *Pl. du Débarcadère, Terre-de-Haut,* ☎ *590/ 99–55–08. AE, MC, V. Closed Sept. and the last 2 wks in June.*

$–$$ ✕ **L'Auberge les Petits Saints aux Anacardies.** Guests and nonguests
★ alike enjoy dining in the veranda restaurant of ☞ **L'Auberge les Petits Saints aux Anacardies.** Proprietor Jean Paul Colas laughingly likes to say about his set *tableau de jour* menu that, "It's like eating at your grandmother's house. You don't like the food, you can go somewhere else." But chances are you won't, with choices such as mahimahi in a passion-fruit sauce, steak au poivre, smoked local fish, and a devilishly delicious chocolate cake. The wine list is excellent. Reservations are strongly recommended, and if you're not a guest of the hotel, you can only get lunch here on weekends (though dinner is never a problem). ⊠ *La Savane, Terre-de-Haut,* ☎ *590/99–50–99. AE, MC, V.*

$–$$ ✕ **El Dorado.** This plant-filled, Creole-style house with a double veranda—on Bourg's delightful main square—is the setting for tasty Creole fare. There's a three-course menu for 75F. The pizza, which is served only at night, is made on the premises, the beef for the barbecue steaks is imported from France, and the wine list is decent. ⊠ *Bourg, Terre-de-Haut,* ☎ *590/99–54–31. MC. Closed Sun.*

$–$$ ✕ **Nilce's Bar.** This piano bar and restaurant is in a large Creole-style house right on the waterfront and is *the* place for Terre-de-Haut's barefoot crowd. Owner Ghyslain Laps serves breakfast, lunch, and dinner, as well as a wide selection of ice creams in the upstairs dining room. Downstairs, local musicians (including Laps's wife, Nilce), perform Brazilian, French, and Creole music. Dogs and children wander about— it's very casual and informal. The later it gets, the raunchier it gets. ⊠ *Bourg, Terre-de-Haut,* ☎ *590/99–56–80. AE, MC, V.*

$ ✕ **La Saladerie.** This delightful seaside terrace restaurant serves a so-
★ phisticated mélange of Creole and Continental dishes. You might begin with a warm crepe filled with lobster, conch, octopus, and fish. Entrée specialties include an assortment of smoked fish served cold and stuffed

fish fillet in a white-wine sauce. The wine list is pleasantly varied. ⊠ *Anse Mirre, Terre-de-Haut,* ☎ *590/99–53–43. MC, V.*

Marie-Galante
SEAFOOD

$–$$ ✕ **Le Touloulou.** On the curve of Petite-Anse beach, this ultracasual eatery serves sumptuous seafood at down-to-earth prices. Chef Patrice Pillet's standouts include conch *feuilleté* (in puff pastry) with yams and the very local *bébélé* (tripe with breadfruit, plantains, and dumplings). There are set menus for 60F, 90F, and 140F. ⊠ *Petite-Anse,* ☎ *590/ 97–32–63. MC, V. Closed Mon. and mid-Sept.–mid-Oct.*

Beaches

Guadeloupe's beaches are generally narrow (particularly since the hurricanes of 1995) and tend to be cluttered with cafés and cars (when the parking spots fill up, folks create impromptu lots in the sand). But all beaches are free and open to the public; for a small fee, hotels allow nonguests to use changing facilities, towels, and beach chairs. On the southern coast of Grande-Terre, from Ste-Anne to Pointe des Châteaux, you'll find stretches of soft white sand. Along the western shore of Basse-Terre, you'll see signposts to many small beaches. The sand starts turning gray as you reach Pigeon Island; it becomes volcanic black farther south. There are several nudist beaches (noted below), and topless bathing is common. Note that the Atlantic waters on the northeast coast of Grande-Terre are too rough for swimming.

Anse de la Gourde is a beautiful stretch of sand that becomes very popular on weekends. It's between St-François and Pointe des Châteaux. **Plage Caravelle,** just outside Ste-Anne, is one of the longest and (the occasional dilapidated shack aside) prettiest stretches of sand on Grande-Terre. Protected by reefs, it's also a fine snorkeling spot. Club Med occupies one end of this beach. **Ilet du Gosier** is a little speck off the shore of Gosier where you can bathe in the buff. Take along a picnic for an all-day outing. The beach is closed on weekends. **Pointe Tarare,** a secluded sandy strip just before the tip of Pointe des Châteaux, is one of the most popular nudist beaches on Grande-Terre. There's a small bar-café in the parking area—a four-minute walk away. **Souffleur,** on the west coast of Grande-Terre and north of Port-Louis, has brilliant flamboyant trees that bloom in the summer. There are no facilities on the beach, but you can buy picnic supplies from nearby shops.

La Grande-Anse, just outside Deshaies on the northwest coast of Basse-Terre, is a secluded beach of soft beige sand that's sheltered by palms. There's a large parking area but no facilities other than those at a nearby restaurant. **Malendure** beach lies on the west coast of Basse-Terre, across from Pigeon Island. Several scuba operations are based here (☞ Outdoor Activities and Sports, *below*). There are also glass-bottom-boat trips for those who prefer to keep their heads above water.

Place Crawen, a secluded beach for skinny-dipping (but not on Sunday, as many local families come here), is a ½-mi stretch of white sand on Terre-de-Haut. **Les Pompierres,** a palm-fringed stretch of tawny sand, is a popular Les Saintes beach on Terre-de-Haut. **Petite-Anse,** on Marie-Galante, is a long gold-sand beach crowded with locals on weekends. The only facilities are at the little seafood restaurant nearby.

Outdoor Activities and Sports
BICYCLING

The French are mad about *le cyclisme,* so if you want to feel like a native, take to two wheels. Pedal fever hits the island in August every year, when hundreds of cyclists converge on the island for the 10-day Tour de Guadeloupe which covers more than 800 mi. On Grande-Terre, you can rent bikes in Pointe-à-Pitre at **Vélon Tout Terrain** (☎ 590/97–85–40), which also offers mountain-bike tours in Basse-Terre and Marie-Galante. In St-François you can rent from **Espace VTT** (☎ 590/88–79–91). On Terre-de-Haut, try **Iguana Electric Bike** ☎ 590/99–58–34.

BOATING AND SAILING

If you plan to sail these waters, you should be aware that the winds and currents of Guadeloupe tend to be strong. There are excellent, well-equipped marinas in Pointe-à-Pitre, Bas-du-Fort, Deshaies, St-François, and Gourbeyre. Many beachfront hotels lease Hobie Cats, Sunfish, pedal boats, motorboats, and water skis. You can make arrangements to rent a yacht (bareboat or crewed) in Bas-du-Fort at **Dufour** (☎ 590/90–74–43), **Moorings** (☎ 590/90–81–81), **Star Voyages Antilles** (☎ 590/90–86–26), and **Stardust** (☎ 590/90–92–02).

FISHING

In Guadaloupe's waters you can fish for bonito, dolphinfish, captain fish, barracuda, kingfish, marlin, and tuna. Expect to pay about 3,500F for a half-day's boat charter and 4,500F for a full day. The best skipper on the island is Captain Francky at **Le Rocher de Malendure** (✉ Pigeon Island, ☎ 590/98–70–84). **Caraïbe Pêche** (✉ Marina, Bas-du-Fort, ☎ 590/90–97–51) also does trips.

FLYING

ULMs (Ultra Léger Motorisés) are extremely ultralight seaplanes that soar along the coast at approximately 100 ft. The cost is 210F for 10 minutes. Go for a ride at **Holywind** (✉ Canella Beach Residence, Pointe de la Verdure, Gosier, Grande-Terre, ☎ 590/90–44–00) or **Le Méridien** (✉ St-François, ☎ 590/88–51–00).

GOLF

Golf Municipal St-François (✉ St-François, ☎ 590/88–41–87) has an 18-hole Robert Trent Jones course, an English-speaking pro, a clubhouse, a pro shop, and electric carts for rental. The greens fee is 250F.

HIKING

With hundreds of trails and countless rivers and waterfalls, the **Parc National de la Guadeloupe,** on Basse-Terre, is a hiker's paradise. Some of the trails should be attempted only with an experienced guide. All tend to be muddy, so wear a good pair of boots. Trips for as many as 12 people are arranged by **Organisation des Guides de Montagnes de la Caraïbe** (✉ Maison Forestière, Matouba, ☎ 590/94–29–11). A half-day guided tour costs $80; a full day, $150. The acknowledged pros in the private sector are at **Parfum d'Aventure** (✉ Roche Blonval, St-François, Grande-Terre, ☎ 590/88–47–62), who offer everything from hiking to four-wheel-drive safaris, sea kayaking, and white-water canoeing.

HORSEBACK RIDING

You can arrange lessons, beach rides, or trips with a picnic lunch through **Le Criolo** (✉ St-Félix, Gosier, Grande-Terre, ☎ 590/84–04–06). More exciting are the half- or full-day excursions offered by **La Manade** (✉ St-Claude, Basse-Terre, ☎ 590/81–52–21). Trails lead through the rain forest.

SCUBA DIVING

The main diving area, at the Cousteau Underwater Park just off Basse-Terre near Pidgeon Island, offers routine dives to 60 ft. But the numerous glass-bottom boats and day-trippers make the site feel like a crowded marine car-park. That said, the underwater sights are spectacular.

Guides and instructors here are certified under the French CMAS rather than PADI or NAUI. The atmosphere on the dive boats is not as friendly as on many islands (and everyone smokes!).

Leading operations include **Caraïbes Plongées** (⊠ Gosier, Grande-Terre, ☎ 509/90–44–90), **Chez Guy et Christian** (⊠ Plage de Malendure, Basse-Terre, ☎ 590/98–82–43), **Les Heures Saines** (⊠ Plage de Malendure, Basse-Terre, ☎ 590/98–86–63), and **Marine Anse Plongée** (⊠ Bouillante, Basse-Terre, ☎ 590/98–78–78).

On Iles des Saintes, the **Centre Nautique des Saintes** (⊠ Plage de la Coline, Terre-de-Haut, ☎ 590/99–54–25) and **Espace Plongé Caraïbes** (⊠ Bourg, Terre-de-Haut, ☎ 590/99–51–84) arrange dives.

SNORKELING AND SEA EXCURSIONS

Most hotels rent snorkeling gear and post information about trips. The *King Papyrus* (⊠ Marina, Bas-du-Fort, Grande-Terre, ☎ 590/90–92–98) is a catamaran that's available for full-day snorkeling outings replete with rum, dances, and games; a moonlight sail is also a possibility. **Nautilus Club** (⊠ Plage de Malendure, Basse-Terre, ☎ 590/98–89–08) offers (rather crowded) glass-bottom-boat tours and snorkeling.

TENNIS

Courts (most lighted for evening play) are at many hotels, including **Auberge de la Vieille Tour** (⊠ Rte. de Montauban, Grande Terre, ☎ 590/84–23–23; two courts), **Caravelle/Club Med** (⊠ Quart Carvelle, Grande Terre, ☎ 590/85–49–50; six courts), **La Créole Beach** (⊠ Pointe de la Verdure, Gosier, ☎ 590/90–46–46; two courts), **Golf Marine Club Hotel** (⊠ Ave. de l'Europe, St. Francois, ☎ 590/88–60–60; two courts), **Hamak** (⊠ St. Francois, ☎ 590/88–59–99; one court), **Le Manganao** (⊠ St. Francois, ☎ 590/88–80–00; four courts), **Le Méridien St-François** (⊠ Avenue de l'Europe, St-Françcois, ☎ 590/88–51–00; two courts), and **Relais du Moulin** (⊠ Châteaubrun St. Anne, ☎ 590/88–23–96; one court).

On Grande-Terre, you can also play at the **Marina Club** (☎ 590/90–84–08) in Pointe-à-Pitre and at the **Tennis League of Guadeloupe** (☎ 590/90–90–97) at the Centre Lamby-Lambert Stadium in Gosier.

WINDSURFING

Most beachfront hotels can help you arrange lessons and rentals. Windsurfing buffs congregate at the **UCPA Hotel Club** (☎ 590/88–64–80) in St-François on Grande-Terre. You can also rent a *planche-à-voile* (Windsurfer) through **Callinago** (⊠ Gosier, Grande-Terre, ☎ 590/84–25–25).

Shopping

You can find good buys on anything French—perfume, crystal, china, cosmetics, fashions, scarves. Many stores offer a 20% discount on luxury items purchased with traveler's checks or, in some cases, major credit cards. As for local handicrafts, you'll see a lot of junk, but you can also find fine wood carvings, madras table linens, island dolls dressed in madras, woven straw baskets and hats, and *salako* hats made of split bamboo. Of course there's the favorite Guadeloupean souvenir—rum.

Areas and Malls

Grande-Terre's newest and largest shopping mall, Destrelland, has more than 70 stores and is just minutes away from the airport, which, with its duty-free stores, is a shopping destination in its own right. In **Pointe-à-Pitre** you may enjoy browsing in the street stalls around the harbor quay and at the two markets (the best is the Marché de Frébault). The town's main shopping streets are rue Schoelcher, rue de Nozières, and the lively rue Frébault. At the St-John Perse Cruise Terminal there's an attractive mall with about two dozen shops. **Bas-du-Fort**'s two shopping areas are the Cora Shopping Center and the marina, where there are 20 or so boutiques and quite a few restaurants. In **St-François** there are several shops surrounding the marina.

Specialty Items

CHINA, CRYSTAL, AND SILVER

Rosebleu (⊠ 5 rue Frébault, Pointe-à-Pitre, Grande-Terre, ☎ 590/82–93–43; also at airport) sells china, crystal, and silver by top manufacturers, including Christoffle.

COSMETICS AND LINGERIE

Soph't (⊠ 41 Immeuble Lesseps, Centre St-John Perse, Pointe-à-Pitre, Grande-Terre, ☎ 590/83–07–73) is the place to buy delicate, fanciful, and very French lingerie. **Vendome** (⊠ 8–10 rue Frébault, Pointe-à-Pitre, Grande-Terre, ☎ 590/83–42–84) is Guadeloupe's exclusive purveyor of Stendhal and Germaine Monteil cosmetics.

HANDICRAFTS

Boutique de la Plage (⊠ Bd. Général de Gaulle, Gosier, ☎ 590/84–52–51) offers a mind-boggling jumble of items ranging from tacky tchotchkes ("fertility" sculptures, for example), to sublime art naïf canvases for as little as $20. The **Centre d'Art Haitien** (⊠ 65 Montauban, Gosier, ☎ 590/84–32–60) is the place to buy imaginative art.

La Case à Soie (⊠ Ste-Anne, ☎ 590/88–11–31) sells flowing silk dresses and scarves in Caribbean colors. The **Centre Artisanat,** also in Ste-Anne, offers a wide selection of local crafts.

Brigitte Boesch, a German-born painter who has exhibited all over the world, is now living in St-François (☎ 590/88–48–94); her studio is worth a visit. **Joel Nankin** (☎ 590/23–28–24), a Guadeloupean painter, specializes in masks and acrylic and sand paintings.

On Basse-Terre, the **Centre de Broderie** (⊠ Vieux Fort, ☎ 590/92–04–14) is renowned for its traditional lacework. The center is built into the ruins of Fort L'Olive, and you can watch local ladies tat intricate tablecloths, napkins, and place mats. This kind of lacework is rare, so prices are *très cher* ($30 for a doily).

On the Iles des Saintes, head for **José Beaujour** (⊠ Terre-de-Bas, ☎ 590/99–80–20) for an authentic salako hat. **Mahogany Artisanat** (⊠ Bourg, Terre-de-Haut, ☎ 590/99–50–12) sells Yves Cohen's batik and hand-painted T-shirts in luminescent seashell shades. **Pascal Foy** (⊠ Rte. à Pompierres, Bourg, Terre-de-Bas, ☎ 590/99–52–29) produces stunning homages to traditional Creole architecture: paintings of houses that incorporate collage and make marvelous wall hangings. Prices begin at $90.

LIQUOR AND TOBACCO

Le Raizet International Airport (☎ 590/21–14–66) has a good selection of island rums and tobacco. **Délice Shop** (⊠ 45 rue Achille René-Boisneuf, Pointe-à-Pitre, Grande-Terre, ☎ 590/82–98–24) is the spot for island rums and items from France—from cheese to chocolate.

PERFUMES

L'Artisan Parfumeur (⊠ Centre St-John Perse, Pointe-à-Pitre, Grande-Terre, ☎ 590/83–80–25) sells top French and American brands as well as tropical scents. **Au Bonheur des Dames** (⊠ 49 rue Frébault, Pointe-à-Pitre, Grande-Terre, ☎ 590/82–00–30) offers an array of cosmetics and skin-care products, in addition to its perfumes. **Phoenicia** (⊠ Bas-du-Fort, ☎ 590/90–85–56; ⊠ 8 rue Frébault, Pointe-à-Pitre,

Grande-Terre, ☎ 590/83–50–36; ⊠ 121 bis rue Frébault, Pointe-à-Pitre, Grande-Terre, ☎ 590/82–25–75) sells various perfumes.

Nightlife

Cole Porter notwithstanding, Guadeloupeans maintain that the beguine began here (the Martinicans and St. Lucians make the same claim for their islands). Discos come, discos go, and the current music craze is zouk (music with an African-influenced Caribbean rhythm), but the beat of the beguine remains steady. Many of the resorts have dinner dancing, as well as entertainment by steel bands and folk groups.

BARS AND NIGHTCLUBS

Le Figuier Vert (⊠ Mare Galliard, Gosier, Grande-Terre, ☎ 590/85–85–51) offers live jazz Friday and Saturday nights. **Le Jardin Brésilien** (⊠ Bas-du-Fort, Grande-Terre, ☎ 590/90–99–31), at the marina, has live music. So does **Jungle Café** (☎ 590/90–99–31). **Lele Bar** (⊠ Le Méridien, St-François, ☎ 590/88–51–00) draws locals and tourists alike. If you're on Les Saintes, check out **Café de la Marina** (⊠ Terre-de-Bas, ☎ 590/99–53–78). Locals congregate here after the day-trippers leave; there's always someone playing the Saintois version of a bagpipe. Sultry Brazilian chanteuse Nilce Laps holds sway nightly at **Nilce's Bar** (⊠ Terre-de-Haut, ☎ 590/99–56–80) at the pier in Bourg.

CASINOS

There are two casinos on the island. Both are on Grande-Terre and both have American-style roulette, blackjack, and chemin de fer. Admission is $10. The legal age is 21, and you'll need a photo ID. Jacket and tie are not required, but "proper attire" means no shorts. **Casino de Gosier** (⊠ Gosier, ☎ 590/84–18–33) has a bar and restaurant and is open Monday–Saturday 9 PM–dawn. Slot machines open at 10 AM. **Casino de St-François** (⊠ Marina, St-François, ☎ 590/88–41–31) has a snack bar and nightclub and is open Tuesday–Sunday 9 PM–3 AM.

DISCOS

Night owls should note that carousing is not cheap. Most discos charge a cover of at least $8, which includes one drink (drinks cost about $5 each). On Grande-Terre, **Caraïbes 2** (⊠ Carrefour de Blanchard, Bas-du-Fort, ☎ 590/90–97–16) features Brazilian dancing. In Gosier, try **New Land** (⊠ Rte. de la Riviera, ☎ 590/84–34–91) and **Zenith** (⊠ Rte. de la Riviera, ☎ 590/90–72–04). Outside Gosier, there's **Shiva 1** in Le Moule (☎ 590/23–53–59). On Basse-Terre, try **La Plantation** (⊠ Gourbeyre, ☎ 590/81–23–37) and **Chez Vaneau** (⊠ Mahaut, ☎ 590/98–25–72).

Exploring Guadeloupe

To see each "wing" of the butterfly, you'll need to budget at least one day. Grande-Terre, which has better roads and is much easier to negotiate, has pretty villages all along its south coast; don't miss the spectacular Pointe des Châteaux. You can see the main sights in Pointe-à-Pitre, in about a half a day. Touring the rugged, mountainous Basse-Terre is a challenge; getting about takes much longer. If time is a problem, head straight to the spectacular west coast; you could easily spend a day traveling its length, stopping for a bit of sightseeing, lunch, and a swim. For the outlying islands, budget more time and more money, as you will probably have to stay overnight.

Numbers in the margin correspond to points of interest on the Guadeloupe map.

Grande-Terre

SIGHTS TO SEE

⑬ Anse Bertrand. The northernmost village in Guadeloupe lies 4 mi south of La Pointe de la Grande Vigie. It was the Caribs' last refuge and was prosperous in the days of sugar. Most of the excitement takes place in the St-Jacques Hippodrome, where horse races and cockfights are held. The beach at nearby Anse Laborde is good for swimming.

② Bas-du-Fort. The main attraction in this town is the **Fort Fleur d'Epée**, an 18th-century fortress that hunkers down on a hillside behind a deep moat and was the scene of hard-fought battles between the French and the English in 1794. You can explore its well-preserved dungeons and battlements and, on a clear day, take in a sweeping view of Iles des Saintes and Marie-Galante.

⑩ Edgar-Clerc Archaeological Museum. This museum contains Amerindian artifacts from the personal collection of Edgar-Clerc, a well-known archaeologist and historian. There are several rooms with displays pertaining to the Carib and Arawak civilizations. ⊠ *La Rosette,* ☎ *590/ 23–57–57.* ⊒ *Free.* ⊘ *Thurs.–Tues. 9–12:30 and 2–5.*

④ Gosier. This pretty village, with red-roofed villas perched above the sea could be a small town on the Côte d'Azur. People stroll about with baguettes under their arms or sit at sidewalk cafés reading *Le Monde* and drinking *planteurs,* the local rum punch. It's the island's major tourist center, with hotels and inns, nightclubs, shops, a casino and a long stretch of sand.

③ Guadeloupe Aquarium. The Caribbean's largest aquarium is a good place to spend an hour or two. The small but well-thought-out facility is on a harbor near Pointe-a-Pitre. ⊠ *Pl. Créole, off Rte. N4,* ☎ *590/90–92–38.* ⊒ *35F.* ⊘ *Daily 9–7.*

⑮ Morne-à-l'Eau. This agricultural city of about 16,000 people is home to an amphitheater-shape cemetery, with black-and-white checkerboard tombs, elaborate epitaphs, and multicolor (plastic) flowers. On All Saints' Day (November 1) it's the scene of a moving (and photogenic) candlelight service.

⑨ Le Moule. Once the capital city of Guadeloupe, this port city of about 17,000 has had more than its fair share of troubles: It was bombarded by the British in 1794 and 1809 and by a hurricane in 1928. Canopies of flamboyant trees hang over its narrow streets, where colorful vegetable and fish markets do a brisk business. The town hall, with graceful balustrades, and a small 19th-century neoclassical church are on the main square. Le Moule also has a beach protected by a reef, making it perfect for windsurfing.

⑦ Pointe des Châteaux. The island's easternmost point, this is where the Atlantic and the Caribbean both crash against huge rocks, carving them into pyramidlike shapes. The majestic cliffs are reminiscent of the headlands of Brittany. The only human contribution to this elemental scene is a massive concrete cross. From this point there are spectacular views of Guadeloupe's south and east coasts and the island of La Désirade. A poem by Nobel Prize–winner Alexis Léger (better known as St-John Perse), inscribed on a panoramic map of the area, conjures the magic of the place. On weekends, locals come in large numbers to walk their dogs, surf, or look for romance.

⑫ La Pointe de la Grande Vigie. At the northernmost tip of the island, you can park your car and walk along paths that lead right out to the edge. There's a splendid view of the watery inlet of Porte d'Enfer from here. On a clear day you can also see Antigua, 35 mi away.

① Pointe-à-Pitre. This city of some 100,000 people in the southwest of Grande-Terre is not the capital (that honor goes to the much smaller Basse-Terre city), but it is the island's commercial and industrial hub. It's bustling, noisy, and hot—a place of honking horns and traffic jams. By day, its pulse is fast, but at night its streets are almost deserted.

The city has suffered severe damage over the years from earthquakes, fires, and hurricanes. The most recent damage was done by Hurricanes Frederick (1979), David (1980), and Hugo (1989). On one side of rue Frébault, you can see the remaining French colonial structures; on the other, the modern city. The downtown area has been rejuvenated. Completion of the Centre St-John Perse has transformed old warehouses into a cruise-terminal complex that consists of the Hotel St-John, restaurants, shops, and the port authority headquarters.

The heart of the old city is **Place de la Victoire,** surrounded by wood buildings with balconies and shutters and many sidewalk cafés. At the southern edge, you can watch the busy harbor life. Place de la Victoire was named in honor of Victor Hugues's 1794 victory over the British. The sandbox trees in the park are said to have been planted by Hugues the day after the victory. During the French Revolution, Hugues ordered the guillotine to be set up in the square so that the public could witness the bloody end of 300 recalcitrant royalists. Today the palm-shaded park is a popular gathering place, with stalls that sell everything from clothes to kitchen utensils.

Even more colorful is the bustling **marketplace,** between rues St-John Perse, Frébault, Schoelcher, and Peynier. It's a cacophonous place, where housewives bargain for papayas, breadfruits, christophenes, tomatoes, and a bright assortment of other produce.

Anyone with an interest in French literature and culture won't want to miss the **Musée St-John Perse.** It's dedicated to Guadeloupe's most famous son and one of the giants of world literature, Alexis Léger, better known as St-John Perse, winner of the Nobel Prize for Literature in 1960. Some of his finest poems are inspired by the history and landscape—particularly the sea—of his beloved Guadeloupe. The museum contains a complete collection of his poetry, as well as some of his personal belongings. There are also works written about him and various mementos, documents, and photographs. Before you go, look for his birthplace at No. 54 rue Achille René-Boisneuf. ✉ *Corner of rues Noizières and Achille René-Boisneuf,* ☎ *590/90–07–92.* 🖃 *10F.* ☉ *Thurs.– Tues. 8:30–12:30 and 2:30–5:30.*

Guadeloupe's other famous son is celebrated at the **Musée Schoelcher.** Victor Schoelcher, a high-minded abolitionist from Alsace, fought against slavery in the French West Indies during the 19th century. The museum contains many of his personal effects, and exhibits trace his life and work. ✉ *24 rue Peynier,* ☎ *590/82–08–04.* 🖃 *10F.* ☉ *Weekdays 8:30–11:30 and 2–5.*

For fans of French ecclesiastical architecture, there's the imposing **Cathédrale de St-Pierre et St-Paul,** on rue Alexandre Isaac. Built in 1807, it has been terribly battered by hurricanes and is now reinforced with iron pillars and ribs that look like leftovers from the Eiffel Tower. But the fine stained-glass windows and Creole-style upper balconies still make it worth a look.

⑪ Porte d'Enfer. The Gate of Hell, 1½ mi north of Campêche, marks a dramatic point on the coast where two jagged cliffs are stormed by the wild Atlantic waters. One legend has it that a Madame Coco strolled out across the waves carrying a parasol and vanished without a trace.

⑭ Port Louis. This fishing village of about 7,000 is best known for the Souffleur beach. It was once one of the island's prettiest, but it has become a little shabby. Still, the sand is fringed by flamboyant trees, and though the beach is crowded on weekends, it's blissfully quiet during the week. There are also spectacular views of Basse-Terre.

❺ Ste-Anne. In the 18th century, this town, 8 mi east of Gosier, was a sugar-exporting center. Sand has replaced sugar as the town's most valuable asset. La Caravelle and the other soft white-sand beaches here are among the best in Guadeloupe. On a more spiritual note, Ste-Anne has a lovely cemetery with stark-white above-ground tombs.

❻ St-François. This was once a simple little village primarily involved with fishing and harvesting tomatoes. The fish and tomatoes are still here, but so are some of the island's ritziest hotels. Avenue de l'Europe runs between the well-groomed 18-hole Robert Trent Jones–designed municipal golf course and the marina. On the marina side, a string of shops, hotels, and restaurants cater to tourists.

❽ Zévalos. Four miles north of St-François on Route 4 is this handsome colonial mansion that was once the manor house of the island's largest sugar plantation. (It's not open to the public.)

Basse-Terre

Yellow butterflies—clouds of them—are the first thing you see when you arrive on Basse-Terre. Rugged, green, and mysterious, this half of Guadeloupe is all mountain trails, lakes, waterfalls, and hot springs. It's the home of La Soufrière volcano, as well as of the capital city, also called Basse-Terre. The northwest coast, between Bouillante and Grande-Anse, is magnificent; the road through here twists and turns up steep hills smothered in vegetation and then drops down and skirts deep blue bays and colorful seaside towns. Constantly changing light, towering clouds, and frequent rainbows only add to the beauty. The Parc National is crisscrossed by numerous trails, many of them following the old *traces*, routes that porters once took across the mountains.

SIGHTS TO SEE

㊱ Allée du Manoir. There's no sign of the manor house, but a fantastic tunnel of century-old royal palms, near the village of Capesterre, is still here. Soaring to as much as 100 ft, the palms have survived both hurricanes and the telephone company, which used to nail the telegraph wires into them.

㉜ Basse-Terre. Because Pointe-à-Pitre is so much bigger, few people suspect that this little town of 15,000 inhabitants is the capital and administrative center of Guadeloupe. But if you have any doubts, walk up the hill to the state-of-the-art **Théâtre Nationale**, where some of France's finest theater and opera companies perform. Paid for by the French government, it's a symbol of the new Basse-Terre. The town has had a lot to overcome. Founded in 1640, it has endured not only foreign attacks and hurricanes but sputtering threats from La Soufrière as well. The last major eruption was in the 16th century, though the volcano seemed active enough to warrant evacuating more than 70,000 people in 1975.

Start exploring the city at the imposing 17th-century **Fort Louis Delgrès**. The fort's small museum gives a good outline of Basse-Terre's history. The **Cathedral of Our Lady of Guadeloupe**, to the north across the Rivière aux Herbes, is also worth a look. On boulevard Félix Eboué you can see the impressive colonial buildings housing the **government offices**. Two main squares, both with gardens, **Jardin Pichon** and **Champ d'Arbaud,** give you a feel for how the city used to be.Not far away from Champ d'Arbaud are the **botanical gardens.**

For shopping, walk down **rue Dr. Cabre,** with its brightly painted Creole houses and imposing church, Ste-Marie de Guadeloupe. The other main street is **rue St-François.** For a guided tour, climb aboard the *Pom, Pom* (☎ 590/81–24–83), a miniature train that does a circuit of the major historic sites. The ride costs 40F and lasts 2½ hours.

㉗ Bouillante. The name, literally translated, means "boiling," and so it's no surprise that the main attraction here is the hot springs. At the Source de Thomas, a few minutes' walk up the old Thomas Road, you can loll around in a hot, smelly, natural bathing spa.

㉓ Cascade aux Ecrevisses. Part of the ☞ Parc National de la Guadeloupe, Crayfish Falls is one of the loveliest (and most popular) spots on the island. There's a marked trail (walk carefully—the rocks along it can be slippery) leading to this splendid waterfall that dashes down into the Corossol River—a good place for a dip; go early, though, otherwise you probably won't have it to yourself.

㉟ Chutes du Carbet. You can reach three of the Carbet Falls (one drops from 65 ft, the second from 360 ft, the third from 410 ft) via a long steep path from the village of Habituée. On the way up, you'll pass the **Grand Etang** (Great Pond), a volcanic lake surrounded by interesting plant life. For horror fans there is also the curiously named **Etang Zombi.**

㉛ Etang As de Pique. Hiking to this 5-acre lake, 2,454 ft above the town of Gourbeyre, is a challenge, but you can also drive to it in an hour via paved Palmetto Road. The lake, formed by a lava flow, is named after its shape—French for "ace of spades."

㉑ Les Mamelles. Two mountains—Mamelle de Petit-Bourg at 2,350 ft and Mamelle de Pigeon at 2,500 ft—rise in the ☞ Parc National de la Guadeloupe. *Mamelle* means "breast," and when you see the mountains you'll understand why they are so named. Trails ranging from easy to arduous lace up into the surrounding mountains. There's a glorious view from the lookout point 1,969 ft up Mamelle de Pigeon. If you're a climber, plan to spend several hours exploring this area.

㉙ Matouba. This village was settled by East Indians whose descendants still practice ancient rites, including animal sacrifice. If you have an idle 10 hours or so, take off from Matouba for a 19-mi hike on a marked trail through the Monts Caraïbes to the east coast.

㉞ Parc Archéologique des Roches Gravées. In the town of Trois-Rivières, this site contains rocks engraved and carved by the Arawaks. The park, which is set in a lovely botanical garden full of moss-covered boulders, stairways cut into the rock, and lush plants, is a haven of tranquillity. ✉ *Bord de la Mer, Trois-Rivières,* ☎ *590/92–91–88.* ☎ *4F.* ☉ *Daily 9–5.*

⑲ Parc National de la Guadeloupe. This 74,100-acre park has been recognized by UNESCO as a Biosphere Reserve, of which there are only 325 worldwide. Before going, pick up a *Guide to the National Park* from the tourist office (☞ Visitor Information *in* Guadeloupe A to Z, *below*), which rates the hiking trails according to difficulty. (Note: The majority of mountain trails are in the southern half of the park.) The park is bisected by the **Route de la Traversée,** a 16-mi paved road lined with masses of tree ferns, shrubs, flowers, tall trees, and green plantains. It's the ideal point of entry to the park. Wear rubber-sole shoes and take along a swimsuit, a sweater, and perhaps food for a picnic. Try to get an early start to stay ahead of the hordes of cruise-ship passengers who are making a day of it. ⊠ *Administrative Headquarters, Basse-Terre,* ☎ *590/80–24–25.*

㉒ Parc Tropical de Bras-David. This part of the ☞ **Parc National de la Guadeloupe** is where you can park and explore various nature trails. The **Maison de la Forêt** has a variety of displays that describe (in French) the flora, fauna, and topography of the national park. It's open daily 9–5; admission is free. There are three marked botanical trails and picnic tables.

㉕ Petit-Bourg. The highlight of this town is the **Domaine de Valombreuse**, a floral park not far from the town. Three hundred species of flowers, spice gardens, and numerous bird species make this a pleasant place for a stroll. There is also a restaurant in the gardens. ⊠ *Petit-Bourg,* ☎ *590/95–50–50.* 🎫 *38F.* ☉ *Daily 9–5.*

㉖ Pigeon Island. This tiny, rocky island, a few hundred yards off the coast, is the site of the Jacques Cousteau Marine Reserve, the best scuba and snorkeling site on Guadeloupe (☞ Outdoor Activities and Sports, *above*). Les Heures Saines and Chez Guy et Christian, both on the attractive Malendure Beach, conduct diving trips, and the glass-bottom *Aquarium* and *Nautilus* make daily trips to this spectacular site.

⑱ Pointe-Noire. This town has two small museums devoted to local products. **La Maison du Bois** offers a glimpse into the traditional use of wood on the island. Superbly crafted musical instruments and furnishings are on sale. Just across the road is **La Maison du Cacao,** a working cocoa plantation. Pointe-Noire is a good jumping-off point to explore the little-visited **northwest coast** of Basse-Terre. A road skirts magnificent cliffs and tiny coves, dances in and out of thick stands of mahogany and gommier trees, and weaves through unspoiled fishing villages with boats and ramshackle houses as brightly colored as a child's finger painting. One of the most attractive villages is Deshaies. ☎ *590/98–17–09 (La Maison du Bois).* 🎫 *5F.* ☉ *Tues.–Sun. 9:30–5:30.* ☎ *590/98–21–23 (La Maison du Cacao).* 🎫 *25F.* ☉ *Daily 9–5.*

⑯ Ravine Chaude. It's not Vichy, but this modest spa is a good place to soak after tackling the trails. It draws upon the area's healthful geothermal waters and caters almost entirely to locals, though efforts are being made to upgrade it for an international clientele. Massage, sauna, algae masks, and hydrotherapy are some of the available treatments. The surrounding landscape, in the foothills of Grosse Montagne, with its cane fields, country lanes, and colorful little villages, is very pleasant. ⊠ *Lamentin,* ☎ *590/25–75–92.* 🎫 *20F.* ☉ *Daily 8–8.*

㉚ St-Claude. This village lies on the western slopes of La Soufrière, with good views of the volcano. You can get a closer look at it by driving up to the Savane à Mulets. Leave your car and hike (with an experienced guide) the strenuous two-hour climb to the summit at 4,813 ft, the highest point in the Lesser Antilles. The sulfurous fumaroles and solidified lava flows are impressive. When you get back down, head for **La Maison du Volcan** (☎ 596/78–15–16), a museum that will tell you everything you need to know about volcanoes. The museum is open daily 9–5, and admission is 15F.

⑰ Ste-Rose. As well as a sulfur bath, there are two good beaches, Amandiers and Clugny, and several interesting, small museums in Ste-Rose. **Le Domaine de Séverin** is a historic rum distillery with a working paddlewheel; the restaurant in a colonial house is well-known for its accras and colombos. The nearby **Musée du Rhum** is a bit of a tourist trap. It features the usual exhibits on the history of rum distillation and a collection of insects from the grotesque to the luminous. ☎ *590/*

28–91–86 (Le Domaine de Séverin). 🎫 Free. ⏲ Daily 8:30–12:30. ☎ 590/28–70–04 (Musée du Rhum). 🎫 40F. ⏲ Mon.–Sat. 9–1.

24 **Vernou.** Many of the old mansions in this area remain in the hands of the original aristocratic families, the Bekés ("whites" in Creole), who can trace their lineage to before the French Revolution. Traipsing along a path that leads beyond the village through the lush forest, you'll come to the waterfall at **Saut de la Lézarde** (Lizard's Leap).

33 **Vieux Fort.** In 1980, 40 local lace makers united to preserve—and display—the ancient tradition of lace making. At the **Centre de Broderie** (☞ Shopping, *above*) you can always see one of them at work. There are handkerchiefs, tablecloths, doilies, and even negligees for sale.

28 **Vieux-Habitants.** Good beaches, a restored coffee plantation, and the oldest church on the island (1650) make this village well worth a stop.

20 **Zoological Park and Botanical Gardens.** Titi the Raccoon is the mascot of this privately owned zoo in the ☞ **Parc National de la Guadeloupe.** The cramped cages are a sorrowful sight, and the 45F entrance fee is entirely too steep, but the views on the way here are stunning.

Iles des Saintes

The eight-island archipelago of Iles des Saintes, usually referred to as Les Saintes, dots the waters off the south coast of Guadeloupe. The islands are Terre-de-Haut, Terre-de-Bas, Ilet à Cabrit, Grand Ilet, La Redonde, La Coche, Le Pâté, and Les Augustins. Columbus discovered them on November 4, 1493, and christened them Los Santos in honor of All Saints' Day.

Only Terre-de-Haut and Terre-de-Bas are inhabited, with a combined population of 3,260. Many of les Saintois, as the islanders are called, are fair-haired, blue-eyed descendants of Breton and Norman sailors. Fishing is their main source of income, and the shores are lined with their boats and *filets bleus* (blue nets dotted with burnt-orange buoys). The fishermen wear hats called salakos, which look like inverted saucers. They're patterned after a hat said to have been brought here by a seafarer from China or Indonesia.

37 **Terre-de-Haut.** With 5 square mi and a population of about 1,500, Terre-de-Haut is the largest and most developed of Les Saintes. Its "big city" is Bourg, which has one street and a few bistros, cafés, and shops. Clutching the hillside are trim white houses with bright red or blue doors, balconies, and gingerbread frills.

Terre-de-Haut's ragged coastline is scalloped with lovely coves and beaches, including the semi-nudist beach at Anse Crawen. The beautiful bay, complete with a "sugarloaf" mountain, has been called a mini Rio. To get around, it's a good idea to rent a motorbike (☞ Getting Around *in* Guadeloupe A to Z, *below*). Although Terre-de-Haut is tiny, it's also very hilly. Take your time on these rutted roads because around nearly every bend you're apt to find a herd of goats chomping on a fallen palm frond. This island makes a great day trip, but you'll really get a feel for Les Saintes if you stay over.

Fort Napoléon. Nobody ever fired a shot at or from this imposing fort, but it makes a fine museum. Galleries hold a collection of 250 modern paintings, heavily influenced by cubism and surrealism. But the thing to come for is the exhaustive exhibit on one of the greatest sea battles ever fought, the Battle of Les Saintes, during which French admiral de Grasse proved no match for the firepower of the Royal Navy (history buffs may recall de Grasse from the American Revolution). You can also visit the well-preserved barracks and prison cells and admire the botanical gardens, which specialize in cacti of all sizes and descriptions. From the fort you can see Ft. Josephine across the channel on the Ilet à Cabrit. ⊠ *Bourg,* ☎ *590/37–99–59.* 🖭 *20F.* ☉ *Daily 9–12:30.*

❸❽ Marie-Galante

Columbus sighted this flat, 60-square-mi island on November 3, 1493, the day before he landed at Ste-Marie on Basse-Terre. He named it for his flagship, the *Maria Galanda,* and sailed on. It's dotted with ruined 19th-century sugar mills, and sugar is still one of its major products (the others are cotton and rum). One of the last refuges of the Carib Indians when they were driven from the mainland by the French, the island is now a favorite retreat of Guadeloupeans, who come on weekends to enjoy the beach at Petite-Anse. You'll find dramatic coastal scenery, with soaring cliffs—such as the Gueule Grand Gouffre (Mouth of the Giant Chasm) and Les Galeries (where the sea has sculpted a natural arcade)—and enormous sun-dappled grottoes, like Le Trou à Diable, whose underground river can be explored with a guide.

The **Château Murat** (⊠ Grand-Bourg, ☎ 590/97–94–41) is a restored 17th-century sugar plantation and rum distillery housing exhibits on the history of rum making and sugarcane production and an admirable *ecomusée,* whose displays celebrate local crafts and customs. The château is open daily 9:15–5; admission is 10F. You should also make it a point to see the distilleries, especially **Père Labat** (⊠ Heritiers E. Rameau, Marie Galante, ☎ 590/97–03–44), whose rum is considered one of the finest in the Caribbean and whose atelier turns out lovely pottery; it's open daily 9–5.

An entertainment complex in Grand Bourg, called El Rancho, has a 400-seat movie theater, a restaurant, a terrace grill, a snack bar, a disco, and a few double rooms. The new Marie-Galante tourism office (☎ 590/97–56–51) in Grand Bourg can provide additional information about the island.

❸❾ La Désirade

According to legend, this is the "desired land" of Columbus's second voyage. Like Marie-Galante, he spotted it on November 3, 1493. The 8-square-mi island, 5 mi east of St-François, was for many years a leper colony. Most of today's 1,600 inhabitants are fishermen. The main settlement is Grande-Anse, which has a pretty church and a couple of lodgings. There are good beaches here, notably Souffleur and Baie Mahault, and there's little to do but loll around on them. The island is virtually unspoiled by tourism.

Guadeloupe A to Z

Arriving and Departing

BY AIRPLANE

American Airlines (☎ 800/433–7300) is usually the most convenient, with year-round daily flights from more than 100 U.S. cities direct to San Juan, Puerto Rico, with direct connections to Guadeloupe's Aéroport Pole Caribe (☎ 590/82–11–81 or 590/90–34–34) on American Eagle. **Air France** (☎ 800/237–2747) flies nonstop from Paris to Guadeloupe and to Fort-de-France on Martinique and has direct service from Miami and San Juan. **Air Guadeloupe** (☎ 590/82–47–47 or 590/82–47–00) flies daily to to Guadeloupe's Le Raizet International Airport (☎ 590/21–14–32) from San Juan, St. Martin/St. Maarten, and St. Barts. **LIAT** (☎ 590/82–00–84) flies from St. Croix, Antigua, and St. Maarten in the north and is your best bet from Dominica, Martinique, St. Lucia, Grenada, Barbados, and Trinidad.

From the Airport: Cabs meet flights at Le Raizet Airport, which is 2½ mi from Pointe-à-Pitre. The metered fare is about 60F to Pointe-à-Pitre, 90F to Gosier, and 200F to St-François. Fares go up 40% on Sunday and holidays and from 9 PM to 7 AM nightly. For 5F, you can take a bus from the airport to downtown Pointe-à-Pitre.

BY BOAT

Major cruise lines call regularly, docking at berths in downtown Pointe-à-Pitre on Grande-Terre about a block from the shopping district. The **Caribbean Express** (☎ 590/83–04–43) has service to Dominica and Martinique from Pointe-à-Pitre. The fare to Dominica is 450F, and the ride takes 2½ hours; the fare to Martinique is 450F and takes four hours. The ferry departs at 8 AM four days a week; check the schedules because they frequently change.

Electricity
Electricity is 220 volts (though some hotels have 110 volts), so if you're visiting from North America you'll need to pack an adapter and a converter to use any appliances you bring with you.

Emergencies
Fire: On Grande-Terre (☎ 590/83–04–76); in Basse-Terre (☎ 590/81–19–22). **Hospitals:** There's a 24-hour emergency room at the main hospital, Centre Hôpitalier de Pointe-à-Pitre (✉ Abymes, ☎ 590/89–10–10). There are 23 clinics and five hospitals around the island. **Pharmacies:** Pharmacies alternate in staying open around the clock. The tourist offices (☞ Visitor Information, *below*) or your hotel can help you locate the one that's on duty and find an English-speaking doctor. **Police:** On Grande-Terre (☎ 590/82–13–17); on Basse-Terre (☎ 590/81–11–55). **SOS Taxi ambulance:** (☎ 590/82–89–33) or **SAMU** (☎ 590/89–11–00).

Festivals and Seasonal Events
Carnival starts in early January and continues until Lent, finishing with a parade of floats and costumes on Mardi Gras (Fat Tuesday) and a huge bash on Ash Wednesday. On a Sunday in early August, Point-à-Pitre on Grande-Terre holds the **Fête des Cuisinières,** which celebrates the masters of Creole cuisine with a five-hour banquet that's open to the public. The festival was started in 1916 by a guild of women cooks who wanted to honor the patron saint of cooks, St. Laurent. August also sees the **Tour Cycliste de la Guadeloupe** a highly competitive bike race that begins in Point-à-Pitre and covers more than 800 mi on both Grande-Terre and Basse-Terre.

Getting Around
AIRPLANES

Air Guadeloupe (☞ Arriving and Departing, *above*) has flights from Grand-Terre to landing strips on Terre-de-Haut, Marie-Galante, and La Désirade.

BICYCLES, MOPEDS, AND MOTORBIKES

If you opt to tour Guadeloupe by bike, you won't be alone. Biking is a major sport here (☞ Outdoor Activities and Sports, *above*).

You can rent a Vespa (motorbike) at **Vespa Sun** (✉ Locations in Pointe-à-Pitre, Grande-Terre, ☎ 590/91–30–36) and **Equator Moto** (✉ Gosier, Grande-Terre, ☎ 590/90–36–77). A motorbike generally costs 200F per day, including insurance. You'll need to put down a 1,000F deposit. On Terre-de-Haut simple-to-use mopeds start at about 120 francs a day. There are numerous vendors by the ferry dock; shop around for the best price. On Marie-Galante try **Loca Sol** (✉ Rue du Fort, Grand-Bourg, ☎ 590/97–76–58).

BUSES

Modern public buses on Grande-Terre and Basse-Terre run from 5 AM to 6 PM. There are stops and shelters marked ARRÊT-BUS, but you can also flag one down along its route. Three or four minibuses meet the flights and ferries in La Désirade, and you can negotiate with one for an island tour. The same is true of Terre-de-Haut and Marie-Galante, though on these islands, you're probably better of renting a moped.

CAR RENTALS

Your valid driver's license will suffice for up to 20 days, after which you'll need an international driver's permit. Guadeloupe has 1,225 mi of excellent roads (marked as in Europe), and driving around Grande-Terre is relatively easy. On Basse-Terre it will take more effort to navigate the hairpin bends on the mountains and around the eastern shore. Guadeloupeans are skillful (and fast) drivers.

There are rental offices at Aéroport Pole Caribe and the major resorts. Count on spending about $60 a day for a small car. Gas is expensive at about 6F per liter (roughly $4 per gallon). Note: Allow yourself an extra 30 minutes to drop off your car at the end of your stay—the rental return sites are still at the old airport in Raizet, 2 mi away.

Agencies on Guadeloupe include **Avis** (☎ 590/82–33–47), **Budget** (☎ 590/82–95–58), **Hertz** (☎ 590/82–00–14), **Thrifty** (☎ 590/91–42–17), and **Europcar** (☎ 590/21–13–52).

FERRIES

Trans Antilles Express (☎ 590/83–12–45) and **Transport Maritime Brudey Frères** (☎ 590/90–04–48) provide ferry service to Les Saintes and Marie-Galante. Schedules often change, especially on the weekends, so check them at the tourist offices (☞ Visitor Information, *below*) or the harbor offices.

It's a choppy 45-minute crossing to Terre-de-Haut from Trois-Rivières on Basse-Terre; ferries leave at about 8:30 AM (7:30 AM on Sunday) and return about 3 PM. From Pointe-à-Pitre on Grande-Terre, it's a 60-minute ride. The usual departure time is 8 AM, with return at 4 PM. The round-trip fare from either point is 170F.

The ferry to Grand Bourg on Marie-Galante departs from Pointe-à-Pitre at 8 AM, 2 PM, and 5 PM with returns at 6 AM, 9 AM, and 3:45 PM. The trip takes one hour, and the fare is 170F round-trip. The *Socimade* (☎ 590/88–48–63) runs between La Désirade and St-François on Grande-Terre, departing daily at 8 AM and 4 PM. Return ferries depart daily at 3:30 PM.

TAXIS

Taxis are metered and fairly pricey. During the day you'll pay about 60F from the airport to Pointe-à-Pitre, about 90F to Gosier, and about 200F to St-François. On Sundays, holidays, and between 9 PM and 7 AM, fares increase by 40%. If your French is in working order, you can contact radio cabs at ☎ 590/82–00–00, 590/83–09–55, and 590/20–74–74. On Basse-Terre call 590/81–79–70.

Guided Tours

Taxi tours have set fares to various points on the islands. Tourist offices (☞ Visitor Information, *below*) or your hotel can arrange for an English-speaking taxi driver and even organize a small group for you to share the cost of the tour.

Guides de Montagne de la Caraïbe (✉ Maison Forestière, Matouba, Basse-Terre, ☎ 590/80–05–79) provides guides for hiking tours in the mountains. A new, private venture, **Emeraude Guadeloupe** (☎ 590/81–

98–28), offers everything from hikes up the volcano to botanical tours and visits to Creole homes. Guides are certified by the state, but you will probably need some French to understand them. For those who really want a challenge, **Parfum d'Aventure** (☞ Outdoor Activities and Sports, *above*) offers adventure trips on Basse-Terre, including canoeing on the Lézarde, sea kayaking, four-wheel driving, and hiking. **Sport D'AV** (☏ 590/32–58–41) can set you up with adventures on Basse-Terre, including mountain climbing, sea kayaking, hiking, and diving.

Language

The official language is French. Everyone also speaks a Creole patois, which you won't be able to understand even if you're fluent in French. In the major hotels, most of the staff knows some English, but communicating may be more difficult in the countryside and in stores. Some taxi drivers speak a little English. Arm yourself with a phrase book, a dictionary, patience, and a sense of humor.

Money Matters

CURRENCY

Legal tender is the French franc, equal to 100 centimes. At press time the exchange rate was US$1 to 5.65F, but currencies fluctuate daily. Some places accept U.S. dollars, but it's best to change your money into the local currency. Credit cards are accepted in most major hotels, restaurants, and shops, less so in smaller places and in the countryside. There are ATMs that accept Visa and MasterCard at Aéroport Pole Caribe and at some banks (though they don't always work). Prices are quoted here in U.S. dollars unless otherwise noted.

SERVICE CHARGES, TAXES, AND TIPPING

The *taxe de séjour* (room tax) varies from hotel to hotel but never exceeds $1.50 per person, per day. Most hotel prices include a 10%–15% service charge; if not, it will be added to your bill. Restaurants are legally required to include a 15% gratuity in the menu price, and no additional gratuity is necessary. Tip skycaps and porters about 5F. Many cab drivers own their own cabs and don't expect a tip. You won't have any trouble ascertaining if a 10% tip is expected.

Opening and Closing Times

Banks and **post offices** are open weekdays 8–noon and 2–4. Crédit Agricole, Banque Populaire, and Société Générale de Banque aux Antilles have branches that are open Saturday. During the summer most banks are open 8–3. Banks close at noon the day before a legal holiday that falls during the week. As a rule, **shops** are open weekdays 8 or 8:30–noon and 2:30–6.

HOLIDAYS

New Year's Day, Ash Wednesday (Feb. 17), Good Friday (Apr. 2), Labor Day (May 1), Bastille Day (July 14), All Saints' Day (Nov. 1), Armistice Day (Nov. 11), and Christmas.

Passports

U.S. and Canadian citizens need only proof of citizenship. A passport is best (even one that expired up to five years ago). Other acceptable documents are a notarized birth certificate with a raised seal (not a photocopy) or a voter registration card, both accompanied by a government-authorized photo ID. A free temporary visa, good only for your stay in Guadeloupe, will be issued to you upon your arrival at the airport. British citizens need a national ID card or a valid passport, but no visa. In addition, all visitors must hold an ongoing or return ticket.

Precautions

Put your valuables in the hotel safe. Don't leave them unattended in your room or on the beach. Keep an eye out for motorcyclists riding double, as they sometimes veer close to the sidewalk and snatch shoulder bags. It isn't a good idea to walk around Pointe-à-Pitre at night, because it's almost deserted after dark. If you rent a car, always lock it with luggage and valuables stashed out of sight.

Ask permission before taking a picture of an islander, and don't be surprised if the answer is a firm "No." Guadeloupeans are also deeply religious and traditional. Don't offend them by wearing short shorts or swimwear off the beach.

Telephones and Mail

To call from the United States, dial 011–590, then the local number. (To call person-to-person, dial 01–590.) You can't place collect or credit-card calls to the United States from Guadeloupe. Coin-operated phones are rare. If you need to make many calls outside of your hotel, purchase a *télécarte* at the post office or other outlets marked TÉLÉCARTE EN VENTE ICI. Télécartes look like credit cards and are used in special booths labeled TÉLÉCOM. Local and international calls made with these cards are cheaper than operator-assisted calls.

To call the United States from Guadeloupe, dial 19 + 1 + the area code and phone number. To dial locally in Guadeloupe, simply dial the six-digit phone number.

Postcards to the United States and Canada cost 3.70F; letters up to 20 grams, 4.60F. Postcards and letters to the United Kingdom cost 3.60F. Stamps can be purchased at post offices, *café-tabacs,* (café–tobacco shops), hotel newsstands, and souvenir shops. When writing to Guadeloupe, be sure to include the name of the specific island in the archipelago (i.e., Grande-Terre, Basse-Terre, etc.) as well as the postal code, Guadeloupe, and the French West Indies.

Visitor Information

For further information, contact the U.S. representatives **Alexander & Richardson** (✉ 161 Washington Valley Rd., Warren, NJ 07059-7121). You may write to the U.S. branches of the **French Government Tourist Office** (✉ 444 Madison Ave., New York, NY 10022, ☎ 202/659–7779, for all information in the United States, www.fgtousa.org; ✉ 9454 Wilshire Blvd., Beverly Hills, CA 90212; ✉ 645 N. Michigan Ave., Chicago, IL 60611). There are also branches in Canada and the United Kingdom (✉ 1981 McGill College Ave., Suite 490, Montréal, Québec, H3A 2W9, ☎ 514/847–0211; ✉ 30 St. Patrick St., Suite 700, Toronto, Ontario, M5T 3A3, ☎ 416/593–6427; ✉ 178 Piccadilly, London, W1V 0AL, ☎ 0171/499–6911).

On Grande-Terre, the **Office Départemental du Tourisme** has an office in Pointe-à-Pitre (✉ 5 square de la Banque (Box 1099), 97181, ☎ 590/82–09–30), open weekdays 8–5, Saturday 8–noon. There's also a booth at Aéroport Pole Caribe and a tourist office in St-François (✉ Avenue de l'Europe 97118), ☎ 590/88–48–74). On Marie-Galante, you can try the tourism office (☎ 590/97–56–51) in Grand Bourg.

14 Jamaica

Updated by
Paris Permenter
and John
Bigley

Around one bend of the winding North Coast Highway lies a palatial home; around another, a shanty without doors or windows. The towns are frenetic centers of activity, filled with pedestrians, street vendors, and neighbors taking time to visit. Roads are crammed with vehicles and full of honking—not a chorus of hostility but notes of greeting or of friendly caution and just for the heck of it. Drivers wait patiently for groups of uniformed schoolchildren and housewives bearing loads on their heads to cross, and a spirit of cooperation prevails among chaos.

The cultural life of Jamaica is a wealthy one; its music, art, and cuisine have a spirit that's easy to sense but as hard to describe as the rhythms of reggae or an outburst of streetwise patois. The third largest island in the Caribbean (after Cuba and Hispaniola), this English-speaking nation enjoys a considerable self-sufficiency based on tourism, agriculture, and mining. Its physical attractions include jungle mountaintops, clear waterfalls, and unforgettable beaches, yet the country's greatest resource may be its people. Although 95% of the population traces its bloodlines to Africa, Jamaica is a stockpot of cultures, including those of other Caribbean islands, Great Britain, the Middle East, India, China, Germany, Portugal, and South America.

In addition to its north-coast pleasure capitals—Montego Bay and Ocho Rios—Jamaica has a real capital in Kingston. For all its congestion and for all the disparity between city life and the bikinis and parasails to the north, Kingston is the true heart and head of the island. This is where politics, literature, music, and art wrestle for acceptance in the largest (800,000 people) English-speaking city south of Miami.

The first group known to have reached Jamaica were the Arawaks, Indians who paddled their canoes from the Orinoco region of South America in about AD 1000. In 1494 Christopher Columbus stepped ashore at what is now called Discovery Bay. Having spent four centuries on the island, the Arawaks had little notion that his feet on their sand would mean their extinction within 50 years. What is now St. Ann's Bay was established as New Seville in 1509 and served as the Spanish capital until the local government crossed the island to Santiago de la Vega (now Spanish Town). The Spaniards were never impressed with Jamaica; they found no precious metals, and they let the island fester in poverty for 161 years. When 5,000 British soldiers and sailors appeared in Kingston Harbor in 1655, the Spaniards didn't put up a fight.

The arrival of the English, and the three centuries of rule that followed, provided Jamaica with both the genteel underpinnings of its present life—and a period of history enlivened by a rousing pirate tradition that was fueled by rum. The British buccaneer Henry Morgan counted Jamaica's governor as one of his closest friends and enjoyed the protection of His Majesty's government no matter what he chose to plunder. Port Royal, once said to be the "wickedest city of Christendom," grew up on a spit of land across from present-day Kingston precisely because it served so many interests. Morgan and his brigands were delighted to have such a haven, and the people of Jamaica profited by being able to buy pirate booty at terrific bargains.

Morgan enjoyed a prosperous life; he was knighted and made lieutenant governor of Jamaica before the age of 30, and, like every other good bureaucrat, he died in bed and was given a state funeral. Port Royal fared less well. On June 7, 1692, an earthquake tilted two-thirds of the city into the sea, the tidal wave that followed the last tremors washed away millions in pirate treasure, and Port Royal simply disappeared. In recent years divers have turned up some of the treasure, but most of it still lies in the depths, adding an exotic quality to the water sports pursued along Kingston's reefs.

The very British 18th century was a time of prosperity in Jamaica. This was the age of the sugar baron, who ruled his plantation great house and made the island the largest sugar-producing colony in the world. Because sugar fortunes were built on slave labor, however, production became less profitable when the Jamaican slave trade was abolished in 1807 and slavery was ended in 1838.

As was often the case in colonies, a national identity came to supplant allegiance to the British in the hearts and minds of Jamaicans. This new identity was given official recognition on August 6, 1962, when Jamaica became an independent nation with loose ties to the Commonwealth. The island today has a democratic government led by a prime minister and a cabinet of fellow ministers.

Lodging

Jamaica was the birthplace of the Caribbean all-inclusive resort, a concept that took the Club Med idea and gave it an excess-in-the-tropics spin. The all-inclusive is the most popular vacation option in Jamaica, offering incredible values with rates from $145 to $350 per person per night. Prices include airport transfers; accommodations; three meals a day plus snacks; all bar drinks, often including premium liquors; wine, beer, and soft drinks; a plethora of sports, including golf, tennis, aerobics, basketball, boccie, croquet, horseshoes, lawn chess, Ping-Pong, shuffleboard, volleyball, scuba diving, and nonmotorized water sports (instruction and equipment); an array of entertainment options (game rooms with billiards, darts, and/or slot machines; nightclubs; classes in local crafts, cooking, language, and dance; and a showroom or central theater with nightly entertainment); and all gratuities and taxes. The only surcharges are usually for such luxuries as massages, tours, and weddings or vow-renewal ceremonies (though these are often included at high-end all-inclusives). The all-inclusives have branched out, some of them courting families, others going after an upper crust that wouldn't even have picked up a brochure a few years ago. Most require a three-night minimum stay.

If you like to get out and explore, you may prefer an EP property. Many places offer MAP or FAP packages that include such extras as airport transfers and tours. Even if you don't want to be tied down to a meal plan, it pays to inquire, because the savings can be considerable. Rooms at most hotels are equipped with cable or satellite TV, air-conditioning, direct-dial phone, clock radio, and, in many cases, a safe. Larger properties usually have no-smoking rooms and rooms accessible to travelers with disabilities, as well as room service, laundry service, meeting rooms and business services, shops, a beauty parlor, a tour desk, and car rentals.

Jamaica's resorts and hotels have varying policies about children; some don't accept children under 16 or 18 years old, but those that do often allow up to two to stay free in their parents' room. Others allow kids to stay free in the off-season, or offer discounted meal plans. Baby-sitting is readily available at properties that accept children. If you plan to bring the kids, ask lots of questions before making a reservation, or have your travel agent find the best deal.

Please note that the price categories listed below are based on winter rates. As a rule, rates are reduced anywhere from 10% to 30% from April 30 to December 15. All price categories are assigned based on standard double rooms at the most comprehensive (and most expensive) meal-plan rate. Opting for a less comprehensive plan (if it's available in winter) can save you 20%–40%. The **Jamaica reservations service** (☎ 800/526–2422 in the U.S. and Canada) can book resorts, hotels, villas, and guest houses throughout the country.

CATEGORY	COST EP/CP*	COST MAP**	COST AI***
$$$$	over $245	over $250	over $275
$$$	$175–$245	$190–$250	$225–$275
$$	$105–$175	$130–$190	$175–$225
$	under $105	under $130	under $175

*EP prices are for a standard double room for two in winter, excluding 10% tax and any service charge. Many hotels either include breakfast in the tariff or offer a CP price, which includes breakfast as their minimum plan.
**MAP prices include daily breakfast and dinner for two in winter. Often MAP packages come with use of nonmotorized water sports and other benefits.
***All-inclusive (AI) winter prices are per person, double occupancy, and include tax, service, gratuities, all meals, drinks, facilities, lessons, and airport transfers. Motorized water sports and scuba are sometimes included; if it's important to you, ask.

Kingston

Some of the island's finest business hotels are in Kingston, and those high towers are filled with rooftop restaurants, English pubs, serious theater and pantomime, dance presentations, art museums and galleries, jazz clubs, upscale supper clubs, and disco dives.

$$$$ ☒ **Strawberry Hill.** One of many island properties owned by Chris
★ Blackwell, formerly the head of Island Records (the late Bob Marley's label), this Blue Mountains retreat 45 minutes north of Kingston offers refined luxury and absolute peace. Authors, musicians, and screenwriters come here for extended periods to relax, rejuvenate the creative

juices, and work. The food is top notch, as are the staff and the accommodations—elegant Georgian-style villas with mahogany furnishings and roomy balconies that have grand vistas. There's no air-conditioning here, simply because it's not needed at 3,100 ft above sea level. Sunday brunch, with an enormous Jamaican buffet, is an affair to remember, but reserve a spot early—it's a favored event among Kingston's movers and shakers. The resort recently added an Aveda spa with a full line of treatments. ⊠ *New Castle Rd., Irishtown, St. Andrew,* ☎ *876/944–8400 or 800/688–7678 (reservations service),* FAX *876/944–8408. 12 1-, 2-, and 3-bedroom villas. Restaurant, bar, refrigerators, room service, sauna, spa, croquet, airport shuttle. AE, MC, V. CP.*

$$$ 🏨 **Crowne Plaza Kingston.** This ochre-color high-rise sits on a hill in Constant Spring, a classy Kingston suburb. Sophisticated public areas are adorned with potted plants, overstuffed furniture, and intriguing Jamaican art. Decor varies from floor to floor; some of the amenity-laden rooms are blue-on-white, while others feature burgundy, yellow, and green color schemes and a mix of florals and plaids. There are business-class rooms that have in-room faxes and modems among their extra amenities. Request a room on the southwest side for grand sunset views, or time your dinner at Isabella's, the hotel's fine dining room, to catch the dwindling rays. ⊠ *211A Constant Spring Rd.,* ☎ *876/925–7676 or 800/618–6534 (reservations service),* FAX *876/925–5757. 115 rooms, 40 suites. Restaurant, 2 bars, grill, in-room safes, kitchenettes, minibars, refrigerators, room service, pool, massage, sauna, tennis court, exercise room, jogging, squash, concierge. AE, DC, MC, V. EP.*

$$$ 🏨 **Le Méridien Pegasus.** This 17-story complex near downtown has an efficient and accommodating staff, Old World decor, and a newly renovated lobby. Other features here include an excellent business center, duty-free shops, and 24-hour room service. Guests on the business floors can check out complimentary cellular phones for use during their stay. At press time, only three floors (9–11) of rooms—all with balcony, coffee/tea setups, and voice mail—had received desperately needed face-lifts. ⊠ *81 Knutsford Blvd. (Box 333),* ☎ *876/926–3690 or 800/225–5843 (reservations service),* FAX *876/929–5855. 325 rooms, 16 suites. 2 restaurants, 2 bars, coffee shop, in-room safes, minibars, room service, pool, wading pool, beauty salon, 2 tennis courts, basketball, exercise room, jogging, shops, playground, concierge, business services. AE, DC, MC, V. EP, MAP.*

$$–$$$ 🏨 **Wyndham New Kingston.** This high-rise Wyndham is the best of Kingston's business hotels. The expansive marble lobby leads to attractive, well-appointed guest rooms. The concierge floors include complimentary cocktails, hors d'oeuvres, and Continental breakfast. There are lots of extras throughout: secured-access elevators, an American Airlines service desk, and in-room coffee/tea setups. Rates include admission to Jonkanoo, the hotel's hot nightclub (☞ Nightlife, *below*); there's also an art gallery. A meal in the Continental ☞ **Palm Court** restaurant, will surely make your day (or night). ⊠ *75 Knutsford Blvd. (Box 112),* ☎ *876/926–5430 or 800/526–2422 (reservations service),* FAX *876/929–7439. 284 rooms, 13 suites, 6 1- and 2-bedroom units. 2 restaurants, 3 bars, in-room modem lines, in-room safes, pool, massage, sauna, 2 tennis courts, health club, shops, recreation room, concierge. AE, DC, MC, V. EP, MAP.*

$$ 🏨 **Morgan's Harbour Hotel, Beach Club, and Yacht Marina.** A favorite of the sail-into-Jamaica set, this small property has 22 acres of beachfront at the very entrance to the old pirate's town. Done in light tropical prints, the rooms are very basic, but many have a balcony and a mini-refrigerator; the suites with loft bedrooms are the nicest. Ask for one in the newer wing. Because the hotel is so close to the airport, passengers on delayed or canceled flights are often bused here to wait. ⊠

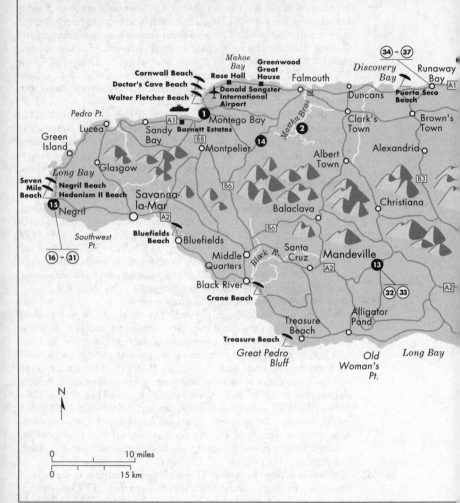

Exploring
Blue Mountains, **9**
Cockpit Country, **14**
Crystal Springs, **5**
Firefly, **4**
Kingston, **10**
Mandeville, **13**
Martha Brae River, **2**
Montego Bay, **1**
Negril, **15**
Ocho Rios, **3**
Port Antonio, **7**
Port Royal, **11**

Rio Grande, **8**
Somerset Falls, **6**
Spanish Town, **12**

Dining
Almond Tree, **42**
Blue Mountain
Inn, **57**
Cosmo's Seafood
Restaurant
and Bar, **24**
Evita's, **43**
Hot Pot, **59**
Ivor Guest House, **64**

Jade Garden, **62**
Kuyaba on
the Beach, **30**
Little Pub, **52**
Margueritaville, **17**
Ocho Rios Village
Jerk Centre, **40**
Palm Court, **60**
Peppers, **58**
Rick's Cafe, **16**
Sweet Spice, **19**
Tan-ya's, **22**

Lodging
Astra Country Inn &
Restaurant, **32**
Bonnie View
Plantation Hotel, **70**
Boscobel Beach, **48**
Breezes Golf & Beach
Resort, **35**
Charela Inn, **21**
Ciboney, Ocho
Rios, **45**
Club Caribbean, **36**
Club Jamaica
Beach Resort, **46**

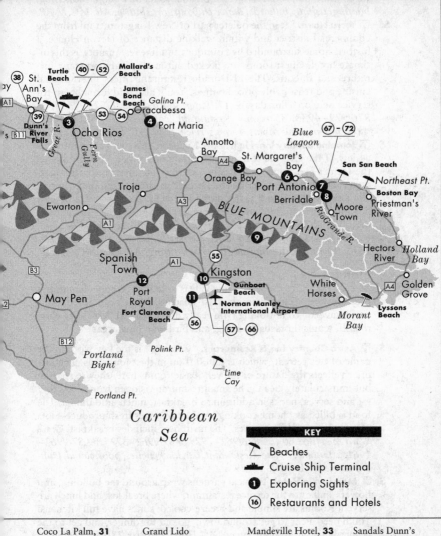

Turtle Beach
Mallard's Beach
James Bond Beach
St. Ann's Bay **38**
Dunn's River Falls **39**
Ocho Rios **3**
40 – **52**
53
54
Galina Pt.
Oracabessa
Port Maria **4**
Annotto Bay
St. Margaret's Bay
Orange Bay
A4
5
6
67 – **72**
Blue Lagoon
San San Beach
Northeast Pt.
Port Antonio **7**
Berridale **8**
Boston Bay
Priestman's River
Moore Town
Great R.
Fern Gully
Troja
Ewarton
BLUE MOUNTAINS
Rio Grande R.
Hectors River
Holland Bay
9
Spanish Town
A1
A3
Kingston
55
10
Gunboat Beach
White Horses
Golden Grove
A4
Port Royal **12**
B3
May Pen
Fort Clarence Beach **11**
Norman Manley International Airport
56
Lyssons Beach
Morant Bay
57 – **66**
B12
Polink Pt.
Portland Bight
Lime Cay
Portland Pt.
B11
A1
A1

Caribbean Sea

KEY

⚓ Beaches
🚢 Cruise Ship Terminal
1 Exploring Sights
16 Restaurants and Hotels

Coco La Palm, **31**
Comfort Suites, **49**
Couples, **47**
Crowne Plaza Kingston, **61**
Dragon Bay, **69**
Enchanted Garden, **41**
FDR, Franklyn D. Resort, **37**
Goblin Hill, **68**
Grand Lido Braco Village Resort, **34**

Grand Lido Negril, **26**
Grand Lido San Souci, **53**
Hedonism II, **25**
Hibiscus Lodge, **50**
High Hope Estate, **38**
Hotel Mocking Bird Hill, **67**
Jamaica Inn, **54**
Jamaica Palace, **72**
Jonreine Country Inn, **66**

Mandeville Hotel, **33**
Le Méridien Pegasus, **65**
Morgan's Harbour Hotel, Beach Club, and Yacht Marina, **56**
Negril Cabins Resort, **28**
Negril Gardens, **20**
Plantation Inn, **51**
Point Village, **29**
Renaissance Jamaica Grande, **44**
Rockhouse, **18**

Sandals Dunn's River Golf Resort and Spa, **39**
Sandals Negril, **27**
Strawberry Hill, **55**
Swept Away, **23**
Terra Nova, **63**
Trident Villas and Hotel, **71**
Wyndham New Kingston, **60**

Port Royal, ☎ *876/967–8040,* FAX *876/967–8073. 44 rooms, 6 suites. Restaurant, bar, room service, pool, volleyball, dive shop, snorkeling, boating, fishing, billiards, dance club, airport shuttle. AE, MC, V. EP.*

$$ ⌂ **Terra Nova.** Set in the quieter part of New Kingston, 1 mi from the commercial district and within walking distance of Devon House, a historic home surrounded by boutiques and fine restaurants, is this intimate hotel. Guest rooms are decked out in classical mahogany furniture and fine art. The El Dorado restaurant offers international cuisine and reasonably priced buffets. You'll also find formal high-tea service here on Thursday. ⊠ *17 Waterloo Rd.,* ☎ *876/926–9334,* FAX *876/929–4933. 35 rooms. Restaurant, coffee shop, grill, in-room safes, no-smoking rooms, room service, pool. AE, DC, MC, V. EP.*

$ ⌂ **Jonreine Country Inn.** High above Kingston, this small inn commands a view of the city, the sea, and the mountains. Once a private home, the former bedrooms have been converted into spacious guest quarters, each with private bath. The Forbidden Heights restaurant serves Chinese specialties and seafood and is a top place to see and be seen in Kingston. In the late hours, the owners take guests out for Kingston nightlife. ⊠ *7 West Kirkland Heights, Forest Hills,* ☎ *876/944–3340, 876/944–3513, or 800/526–2422 (reservations service);* FAX *876/944–3513. 14 rooms. Restaurant, bar, baby-sitting. AE, DC, MC, V. CP.*

Mandeville

At 2,000 ft above the sea, Mandeville is noted for its cool climate and proximity to secluded south-coast beaches. Most accommodations don't have air-conditioning (you really don't need it). Many are close to golf, tennis, horseback riding, and bird-watching areas.

$ ⌂ **Astra Country Inn & Restaurant.** "Country" is the key word in the name of this retreat, which is 2,000 ft up in the mountains. The low price reflects the nature of the very basic rooms here: they're spartan but immaculately clean. The small restaurant is open from 7 AM to 9 PM and serves snacks in addition to breakfast, lunch, and dinner. The food is billed as "home cooking" and emphasizes fresh produce—lots of vegetables and fruit juices. The tariff here includes breakfast. ⊠ *62 Ward Ave. (Box 60),* ☎ *876/962–7979 or 876/962–3725,* FAX *876/962–1461. 20 rooms, 1 suite. Restaurant, bar, kitchenettes, pool, sauna, laundry service. AE, MC, V. CP.*

$ ⌂ **Mandeville Hotel.** Tropical gardens wrap around the building, and flowers spill onto the terrace restaurant, where breakfast and lunch are served. Rooms are simple and breeze-cooled; suites have full kitchens. You'll need a car to get around town, go out for dinner, and get to the beach, which is an hour away. ⊠ *4 Hotel St. (Box 78),* ☎ *876/962–2460,* FAX *876/962–0700. 46 rooms, 17 1-, 2-, and 3-bedroom suites. Restaurant, bar, coffee shop, refrigerators, pool, golf privileges, baby-sitting, laundry service, meeting room, travel services. AE, MC, V. EP.*

Montego Bay

MoBay (as it's affectionately called) has miles of hotels, villas, apartments, and duty-free shops. Although lacking much in the way of cultural stimuli, it presents a comfortable island backdrop for the many conventions it hosts.

$$$$ ⌂ **Half Moon Golf, Tennis, and Beach Club.** For more than 40 years
★ this 400-acre resort has been a destination unto itself, with a reputation for doing the little things right. Although it has mushroomed from 30 to more than 400 units, it has maintained an intimate, luxurious feel. The rooms, suites, and villas—whether done in a modern or a Queen Anne style—are exquisitely decorated with such flourishes as Asian rugs and antique radios. Several villas (which come with a

cook, a butler, a housekeeper, and a rental car or g... vate pools, and the mile-long stretch of beach is ju... every room. On the grounds there's an upscale sh... as a nature reserve and a hospital. The ☞ **Sugar Mill** re... to serve something that will please you. ⊠ *7 mi east of MoBay* ... *80),* ☎ *876/953–2211 or 800/237–3237 (reservations service),* FAX *876/ 953–2731. 417 units. 7 restaurants, 3 bars, 2 pools, outdoor hot tub, sauna, spa, 18-hole golf course, 13 tennis courts, aerobics, badminton, croquet, exercise room, horseback riding, Ping-Pong, squash, beach, dive shop, snorkeling, windsuring, bicycles, shops, theater, library, children's programs, playground, convention center. AE, DC, MC, V. All-inclusive, EP, FAP, MAP.*

$$$$ ⊡ **Round Hill Hotel and Villas.** The Hollywood set frequents this peace-
★ ful resort, 8 mi west of town on a hilly peninsula. Twenty-seven villas with 74 suites are set on 98 acres, and there are 36 hotel rooms in Pineapple House, a building that overlooks the sea. Rooms are done in a refined Ralph Lauren style, with mahogany furnishings and terra-cotta floors. The villas are leased back to the resort by private owners and vary in decor, but jungle motifs are a favorite. All come with a personal maid and a cook (for an extra charge) to make your breakfast, and several have private pools. The restaurant's good food and elegant presentation make a meal in the dining room, or better yet on the seaside terrace, memorable. ⊠ *8 mi west of Montego Bay on North Coast Hwy. (Box 64),* ☎ *876/956–7050 or 800/237–3237 (reservations service),* FAX *876/956–7505. 36 rooms, 27 villas. Restaurant, room service, pool, beauty salon, massage, 5 tennis courts, aerobics, exercise room, jogging, beach, dive shop, snorkeling, windsurfing, shops, concierge, helipad. AE, DC, MC, V. All-inclusive, EP, FAP, MAP.*

$$$$ ⊡ **Tryall Golf, Tennis, and Beach Club.** Part of a posh residential development 15 mi west of MoBay, Tryall clings to a hilltop that overlooks a golf course and the Caribbean. Here you'll stay in one of the numerous villas—each with its own pool, full staff (butler, cook, maid, and gardener), and golf cart—that dot the 2,200-acre island plantation. All accommodations are individually and plushly decorated. The fine dining room in the great house is elegant and serves Continental and Jamaican cuisine. The beautiful seaside golf course is one of this resort's more memorable features. It's also reputed to be one of the meanest courses in the world, and, as such, hosts big-money tournaments. ⊠ *15 mi west of MoBay on North Coast Hwy. (Box 1206),* ☎ *876/956–5660, 876/956–5667, or 800/238–5290 (reservations service);* FAX *876/956–5658. 57 villas. Restaurant, 4 bars, refrigerators, pool, massage, driving range, 18-hole golf course, 9 tennis courts, jogging, beach, dive shop, snorkeling, windsurfing. AE, DC, MC, V. EP.*

$$$–$$$$ ⊡ **Coyaba Beach Resort and Club.** Owners Joanne and Kevin Robert-
★ son live on the property, interacting with guests daily and giving this oceanfront retreat the feel of an intimate and inviting country inn. Coyaba is also very family friendly. The plantation-style great house, just east of Montego Bay, successfully blends modern amenities with Old World grace. Rooms are decorated with lovely colonial prints and handcarved mahogany furniture, and sunshine pours through the tall windows and over terra-cotta floors and potted plants. Part of the package is a basket with bottled springwater and freshly baked banana bread greeting you upon check-in; weekly afternoon tea and evening cocktail parties; and tennis, scuba diving, and massage. ⊠ *Mahoe Bay, Little River,* ☎ *876/953–9150 or 800/237–3237 (reservations service),* FAX *876/953–2244. 50 rooms. 2 restaurants, 3 bars, pool, outdoor hot tub, massage, tennis court, exercise room, volleyball, beach, dive shop, snorkeling, windsurfing, library, recreation room, playground. AE, MC, V. All-inclusive, EP, MAP.*

...let, **14**

...O
...ntation
...estaurant, **5**

Julia's Italian
Restaurant, **13**

Margueritaville
Caribbean Bar
and Grill, **9**

Marguerites, **10**

The Native, **8**

Norma at the
Wharf House, **3**

Pier 1, **7**

Sugar Mill, **18**

Town House, **6**

Lodging

Atrium at
Ironshore, **17**

Coyaba Beach
Resort and
Club, **22**

Half Moon
Golf, Tennis,
and Beach
Club, **18**

Holiday Inn
Sunspree
Resort, **19**

Lethe Estate, **4**

Richmond Hill
Inn, **12**

Round Hill
Hotel and
Villas, **1**

Sandals Inn, **15**

Sandals
Montego
Bay, **16**

Sandals Royal
Jamaican, **21**

Tryall Golf,
Tennis, and
Beach Club, **1**

Verney's
Tropical
Resort, **11**

Wyndham
Rose Hall, **20**

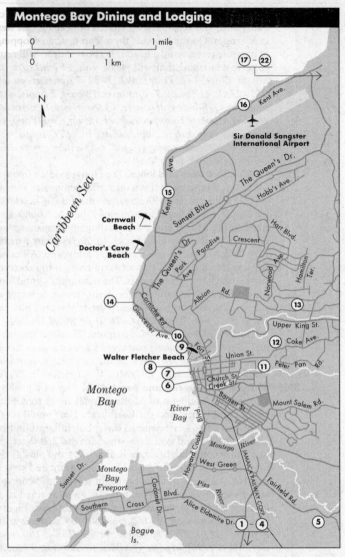

Montego Bay Dining and Lodging

$$$–$$$$ 🗺 **Sandals Montego Bay.** The largest private beach in MoBay is the spark that lights this Sandals—one of the most popular couples resorts in the Caribbean. Its all-inclusive rate and nonstop activities (not to mention its rooms overlooking the bay) make it a bit like a cruise ship that remains in port. The atmosphere here is one of a great big party, despite the planes that zoom overhead (the airport is nearby). Even staff members seem happy as they hum or sing their way through the work-day. Rooms are basic but comfortable enough, and you're seldom in them because there's so much to do. The Oleandor Restaurant is probably the best fine-dining establishment in the Sandals chain. ⊠ *Kent Ave. (Box 100),* ☎ *876/952–5510 or 800/726–3257 (reservations service),* FAX *876/952–0816. 246 rooms. 4 restaurants, 4 bars, snack bar, in-room safes, 4 pools, 3 outdoor hot tubs, sauna, 3 tennis courts, racquetball, beach, dive shop, dock, snorkeling, windsurfing, boating, library, concierge. 2-night minimum stay. AE, MC, V. All-inclusive.*

$$$–$$$$
★ 🏨 **Sandals Royal Jamaican.** Another all-inclusive resort for couples only, this Sandals establishment is distinguished by Jamaican-style buildings that are arranged in a semicircle around attractive gardens. Although there are plenty of activities here, this resort is quieter and more genteel than ☞ **Sandals Montego Bay** and draws something of an international crowd. Deluxe rooms have mahogany four-poster beds and mauve carpeting and bedspreads; bathrooms are small. Oceanfront rooms and suites are more elegant and inviting, with mahogany four-poster beds and floral-print fabrics. A colorful "dragon boat" transports you to Sandals's private island for meals at the Indonesian restaurant. ⊠ *4 mi east of airport on North Coast Hwy. (Box 167),* ☎ *876/953–2231 or 800/726–3257 (reservations service),* ℻ *876/953–2788. 190 rooms. 4 restaurants, 4 bars, in-room safes, 4 pools, beauty salon, 5 outdoor hot tubs, sauna, 3 tennis courts, aerobics, beach, dive shop, snorkeling, windsurfing, concierge. 3-night minimum stay. AE, MC, V. All-inclusive.*

$$$
🏨 **Lethe Estate.** This quiet mountainside inn is a far cry from the bustling beach resorts for which MoBay is known. Tucked on the banks of the Great River near the village of Lethe, interruptions at this small property come not from reggae music or dance contests, but from the sounds of birds. You don't have the sea nearby, but you can take a dip in the river (or float down it on a bamboo raft), take a jitney through the nearby Lethe Estate plantation, or fish in freshwater ponds. ⊠ *Reading Rd., 20 mins west of MoBay (Box 23),* ☎ *876/956–4920,* ℻ *876/956–4927. 15 rooms. Restaurant, pool, tennis court, horseback riding, fishing, airport shuttle. AE, MC, V. CP.*

$$–$$$
🏨 **Wyndham Rose Hall.** This self-contained resort, on the 400-acre Rose Hall Plantation, is a bustling business hotel (popular with large groups) with all the usual amenities: tennis courts, golf course, three interconnected pools, a nightclub, a water sports center, and a shopping arcade. Rooms, which were renovated in 1997, are done in tropical florals in shades of deep peach and are comfortable, though somewhat sterile. The waters off the thin crescent beach are good for sailing and snorkeling. ⊠ *4 mi east of airport on North Coast Hwy. (Box 999),* ☎ *876/953–2650 or 800/996–3426 (reservations service),* ℻ *876/953–2617. 470 rooms, 19 suites. 4 restaurants, 3 bars, in-room safes, room service, 3 pools, massage, 6 tennis courts, 18-hole golf course, aerobics, basketball, exercise room, volleyball, beach, dive shop, snorkeling, windsurfing, nightclub, children's program, playground, convention center. AE, DC, MC, V. All-inclusive, EP, MAP.*

$$
🏨 **Sandals Inn.** If you can forego a private beach (there's a public one across the street), you can stay here for much less than at other couples-only Sandals operations. Managed more as a small hotel than a large resort, this establishment is intimate and relatively quiet. The charming rooms are compact; most have balconies that face the pool. Dark carpet contrasts with white lacquered furniture and tropical-print fabrics. There's plenty to do here, and you can get in on the action at the other two MoBay Sandals by hopping on the free hourly shuttle. The in-town location puts you close to shops and sights. ⊠ *Gloucester Ave. (Box 412),* ☎ *876/952–4140 or 800/726–3257 (reservations service),* ℻ *876/952–6913. 52 rooms. 2 restaurants, 2 bars, in-room safes, pool, beauty salon, outdoor hot tub, tennis court, concierge, airport shuttle. 3-night minimum stay. AE, MC, V. All-inclusive.*

$–$$
🏨 **Atrium at Ironshore.** Fifteen moderately priced, fully furnished apartments make up this small complex. Decor varies, but each unit has pastel floral and plaid prints, cool white-tile floors, rattan furniture, a patio or a balcony, and a private housekeeper-cook on call. Large saltwater tanks full of tropical fish brighten the alfresco dining terrace near the waterfall-fed pool, and you'll often find lively games of darts

or skittles under way in the English-style pub. A shopping mall with a supermarket, a cinema, and several boutiques is within walking distance, but you'll have to take a shuttle to the beach. ⊠ *1084 Morgan Rd. (Box 604),* ☎ *876/953–2605,* FAX *876/953–3683. 15 1½-, 2-, and 3-bedroom suites. Restaurant, pub, kitchenettes, refrigerators, pool, meeting room. AE, DC, MC, V. EP.*

$ 🏨 **Holiday Inn Sunspree Resort.** At this family-oriented resort, you'll find activities day and night. Although the rooms—spread out in seven buildings—are cheerful enough, the hotel is big and noisy (rooms farthest from the pool and central dining-entertainment area are the quietest). Room service is available for breakfast. The beach is just a palm-shaded sliver. ⊠ *6 mi east of airport on North Coast Hwy. (Box 480),* ☎ *876/953–2485 or 800/352–0731 (reservations service),* FAX *876/ 953–2840. 496 rooms, 24 suites. 2 restaurants, 4 bars, 2 snack bars, in-room safes, no-smoking rooms, room service, pool, 4 tennis courts, beach, dive shop, snorkeling, windsurfing, children's program, playground, concierge, airport shuttle. AE, DC, MC, V. All-inclusive, EP.*

$ 🏨 **Richmond Hill Inn.** This hilltop inn—a quaint, 200-year-old great house originally owned by the Dewars clan—has spectacular views of the Caribbean and a great deal of peace. Decor tends toward the dainty: frilly lace curtains and doilies, lots of lavenders and mauves, and crushed-velvet furniture here and there. A free shuttle will take you to shops and beaches, about 10–15 minutes away. ⊠ *Union St. (Box 362),* ☎ *876/952–3859 or 800/423–4095 (reservations service). 15 rooms, 5 suites. Bar, coffee shop, dining room, pool, laundry service. AE, MC, V. EP, FAP, MAP.*

$ 🏨 **Verney's Tropical Resort.** Here you'll find a terrific view of MoBay and the sea as well as a warm atmosphere. Owners Kathleen and Earnest Sterling greet you like family (they have many repeat guests). Rooms are simple but clean. You can take the free weekday shuttle down to Doctor's Cave Beach or stay on the property for a dip in the hillside pool followed by a genuine Jamaican-style meal. Tennis courts and in-town shopping areas are within walking distance. ⊠ *3 Leader Ave.,* ☎ *876/952–2875 or 876/952–8628,* FAX *876/979–2944. 27 rooms. Restaurant, bar, pool, baby-sitting. AE, MC, V. CP.*

Negril

Some 50 mi west of Montego Bay, Negril was long a sleepy bohemian retreat. In the last decade the town has blossomed and added a number of classy all-inclusive resorts, with several more on the drawing board for Bloody Bay (northeast of Seven Mile Beach). Negril itself is only a small village with little of historic significance. But such sights are not what draws the sybaritic singles and couples. The young, hip crowd here comes for sun, sand, and sea.

$$$$ 🏨 **Grand Lido Negril.** The dramatic entrance of marble floors and
★ columns, filled with Jamaican artwork, sets an elegant tone at this SuperClubs all-inclusive property. It's geared to folks with some money in their pockets, and it attracts mature, settled couples and singles. The well-appointed, split-level oceanfront and garden rooms are spacious and stylish. For some guests, the pièce de résistance is a sunset cruise on the resort's 147-ft yacht, *Zien,* which was a wedding gift from Aristotle Onassis to Prince Rainier and Princess Grace of Monaco. The Piacere restaurant is superb. (Note that weddings at this resort are complimentary.) ⊠ *Norman Manley Blvd. (Box 88),* ☎ *876/957–5011 or 800/467–8737 (reservations service),* FAX *876/957–5517. 216 rooms, 16 suites. 3 restaurants, 9 bars, in-room safes, room service, 2 pools, 2 outdoor hot tubs, massage, 4 tennis courts, beach, dive shop, snorkeling, windsurfing, library, concierge, laundry service. 3-night minimum stay. AE, DC, MC, V. All-inclusive.*

$$$–$$$$ ⛱ **Sandals Negril.** Couples looking for an upscale, sports-oriented getaway and a casual atmosphere (you can wear dressy shorts to dinner) flock to this resort on one of the best (and longest stretches) of Negril's 7-mi beach. Water sports, particularly scuba diving, are emphasized; the capable staff is happy to work with neophytes (one pool is designated for scuba training) as well as certified veterans. There's a nearby island, a huge swim-up pool bar, and a range of spacious accommodations. Both rooms and staff are sunny and appealing. ⊠ *Norman Manley Blvd. (Box 12),* ☎ *876/957–5216 or 800/726–3257 (reservations service),* ℻ *876/957–5338. 215 rooms. 4 restaurants, 4 bars, in-room safes, 3 pools, 2 outdoor hot tubs, saunas, 4 tennis courts, racquetball, squash, beach, dive shop, snorkeling, windsurfing, concierge. 3-night minimum stay. AE, MC, V. All-inclusive.*

$$$–$$$$ ⛱ **Swept Away.** With its emphasis on sports and healthful cuisine, it's
★ no wonder that this resort attracts fitness-minded couples. The suites are in 26 cottages—each with a private garden atrium—that are spread out along a ½-mi stretch of gorgeous beach. There's an outstanding 10-acre sports complex across the road. At the Feathers Continental restaurant (open to nonguests), the chefs prepare dishes designed to keep you fit and trim with lots of fish, white meat, and fresh fruits and vegetables. Complimentary weddings are part of the all-inclusive package. ⊠ *Norman Manley Blvd., Long Bay,* ☎ *876/957–4061 or 800/ 545–7937 (reservations service),* ℻ *876/957–4060. 134 suites. 2 restaurants, 4 bars, in-room safes, pool, 2 outdoor hot tubs, massage, spa, 2 steam rooms, 2 saunas, 10 tennis courts, aerobics, health club, jogging, racquetball, squash, dive shop, beach, dive shop, snorkeling, windsurfing. 3-night minimum stay. AE, DC, MC, V. All-inclusive.*

$$$ ⛱ **Point Village.** This moderately priced resort is family friendly. Rooms have tile floors and basic furnishings, and each is decorated according to its owner's taste. Highly popular with tour groups, this sprawling property has two small crescent beaches, rocky grottoes to explore, fine snorkeling just offshore, and a petting zoo. If you don't opt for the all-inclusive plan, the one- and two-bedroom housekeeping suites with kitchens are a good choice. ⊠ *Norman Manley Blvd. (Box 105),* ☎ *876/957–5170 or 800/752–6824 (reservations service),* ℻ *876/957– 5351. 177 units. Restaurant, 3 bars, 2 grills, grocery, fresh- and salt-water pools, outdoor hot tub, massage, tennis court, aerobics, beach, snorkeling, windsurfing, children's programs, playground. AE, MC, V. All-inclusive, EP, FAP, MAP.*

$$–$$$ ⛱ **Negril Cabins Resort.** These elevated, timber cottages are nestled amid lush vegetation and towering royal palms. Rooms are open and airy, with floral bedspreads, gauzy curtains, natural wood floors, and high ceilings. The most popular rooms have TVs and air-conditioning; others have no TV and are cooled by ceiling fans and breezes that come through slatted windows. The gleaming beach across the road is filled with sunbathers and water sports enthusiasts; for shopping, you can take the shuttle into town. A most convivial place, this property is popular with young Europeans. Reasonably priced dive packages are available, and children under 12 stay free in their parents' room. ⊠ *Norman Manley Blvd. (Box 118),* ☎ *876/957–5350 or 800/382–3444 (reservations service),* ℻ *876/957–5381. 80 rooms, 2 suites. 3 restaurants, 3 bars, in-room safes, room service, pool, outdoor hot tub, tennis court, exercise room, beach, dive shop, snorkeling, recreation room, baby-sitting, playground. AE, MC, V. EP, MAP.*

$–$$$ ⛱ **Hedonism II.** Hedonism appeals mostly to single (60% of guests are), uninhibited vacationers age 18 and over who like a robust mix of physical activities. (You can try everything from scuba diving to a trampoline clinic.) Public areas are filled with potted plants and scantily clad guests. Handsome guest rooms have modern blond-wood furniture and mirrored ceilings above king-size or twin beds. There's no TV, but phones were added in 1997, as were a skinny-dipping pool and hot tub. Wooden floors in the open-air halls tend to amplify the noise. Solo guests pay a hefty supplement or are assigned a roommate of the same sex. With both "nude" and "prude" beaches, the atmosphere here is lively around the clock. Most guests prefer the nude beach, with its new pool and swim-up bar. Scheduled activities include nude body painting, volleyball—even shuffleboard in the buff. ⊠ *Norman Manley Blvd. (Box 25),* ☎ *876/957–5200 or 800/859–7873 (reservations service),* FAX *876/957–5289. 280 rooms. 2 restaurants, 6 bars, 2 grills, in-room safes, 2 pools, 2 outdoor hot tubs, 6 tennis courts, squash, beach, dive shop, snorkeling, windsurfing, boating. 3-night minimum stay. AE, DC, MC, V. All-inclusive.*

$–$$$ 🔟 **Negril Gardens.** Towering palms and well-tended gardens surround the pink and white buildings of this hotel. Half the rooms are on the beach, half (across the street) overlook the pool; all are attractive, with tile floors and rattan furniture. Water sports are available at the beach. On-site you'll find an ice cream parlor and a jerk center (for takeout). ⊠ *Norman Manley Blvd. (Box 58),* ☎ *876/957–4408 or 800/752–6824 (reservations service),* FAX *876/957–4374. 66 rooms. 2 restaurants, ice cream parlor, 2 bars, in-room safes, pool, tennis court, exercise room, beach, snorkeling. AE, MC, V. All-inclusive, CP, EP, FAP, MAP.*

$$ 🔟 **Charela Inn.** Each quiet, elegantly appointed room here has a private balcony or a covered patio. The owners' French-Jamaican roots find daily expression in La Vendome restaurant, where you can dine on local produce and seafood dressed up with French sauces; there's also an excellent selection of wines. The small beach is part of the glorious 7-mi Negril crescent. On Saturday night, many guests staying at other resorts come here to watch a folkloric show. ⊠ *Norman Manley Blvd. (Box 33),* ☎ *876/957–4277,* FAX *876/957–4414. 49 rooms. Restaurant, bar, pool, beach, windsurfing, boating, laundry service. 5-night minimum stay in high season, 3-night minimum stay in summer. MC, V. EP, MAP.*

$$ 🔟 **Coco La Palm.** This quiet seaside hotel features oversize rooms (junior suites average 525 square ft) in octagonal buildings set in a U-shape around the pool. Amenities include mini-refrigerators, coffeemakers, air-conditioning, ceiling fans, and private patios or terraces—most overlooking gardens (only seven rooms have ocean views). Centered on Negril Beach, the sandy shoreline of Coco La Palm is dotted with palm trees. The beachside restaurant is open-air and casual. ⊠ *Norman Manley Blvd.,* ☎ *876/957–4227 or 800/896–0987 (reservations service),* FAX *876/957–3460. 41 rooms. Restaurant, bar, grill, air-conditioning, fans, refrigerators, pool, outdoor hot tub, beach. AE, DC, MC, V. EP, MAP.*

$–$$ 🔟 **Rockhouse.** You're side by side with nature at this stylish resort on Negril's rugged cliffs. Accommodations are built from rough-hewn timber, thatch, and stone and are filled with furniture that echoes the nature theme. All rooms have private, indoor baths, but even these seem rustic; villa rooms have private, enclosed, outdoor showers. There's a thatched-roof Jamaican restaurant and a cliff-top pool and bar. At press time, the resort was adding eight studio units to its west side. Owing to the steep cliffs, parents traveling with children under 12 are well-advised to rule out a stay here. ⊠ *West End Rd. (Box 24),* ☎ *876/957–4373,* FAX *876/957–4373. 20 rooms. Restaurant, 2 bars, in-room safes, minibars, pool, snorkeling. AE, MC, V. EP.*

Ocho Rios

On the northeast coast halfway between Port Antonio and Montego Bay, Ocho Rios is hilly and lush. Its resorts (many all-inclusive), hotels, and villas are all a short drive from a bustling crafts market; boutiques and duty-free shops; restaurants; and several scenic attractions.

$$$$
★ **Boscobel Beach.** Families are made to feel very welcome at this all-inclusive resort. Everybody is kept busy all week for a single package price, and everyone leaves happy. The cheery day-care centers group children by age and offer an array of entertaining and educational activities. Thoughtfully, there's an adults-only section of the resort (for when the kids want to get away—perhaps to the petting zoo). Bedspreads in bright sea-life motifs or soothing pastel florals spice up the white tile floors and creamy walls of the rooms and suites. Like other members of the SuperClubs family, this resort offers free weddings. ⊠ *Boscobel, St. Mary (Box 63),* ☎ *876/975–7330 or 800/467–8737 (reservations service),* FAX *876/975–7370. 64 rooms, 152 junior suites. 5 restaurants, 5 bars, in-room safes, refrigerators, 2 pools, wading pool, 2 outdoor hot tubs, massage, 4 tennis courts, beach, children's programs, nursery, playground. 3-night minimum stay. AE, DC, MC, V. All-inclusive.*

$$$$ **Ciboney, Ocho Rios.** This stately plantation property has 56 rooms in its great house and 226 spacious one-, two-, and three-bedroom villa suites on 45 lush hillside acres. It's run by Radisson as an upscale, all-inclusive for singles and couples. Outstanding features are the European-style spa (you receive a complimentary massage, manicure, and pedicure) and four signature restaurants, including the Orchids, whose menu was developed by the Culinary Institute of America. Every villa has an attendant and a pool, for the ultimate in privacy and pampering. The decor is casual and contemporary—light-color rattan furnishings, tile floors, and pastel fabrics. If there are drawbacks here, it's how busy the place is and the fact that the private beach is a shuttle ride away. ⊠ *104 Main St. (Box 728),* ☎ *876/974–1027 or 800/ 333–3333 (reservations service),* FAX *876/974–7148. 226 1-, 2-, and 3-bedroom suites, 56 rooms. 4 restaurants, 6 bars, in-room safes, kitchenettes, minibars, refrigerators, in-room VCRs, 2 pools, 1 indoor and 5 outdoor hot tubs, 2 saunas, spa, 2 steam rooms, 6 tennis courts, aerobics, basketball, croquet, squash, beach, dive shop, snorkeling, windsurfing, dance club, concierge. AE, DC, MC, V. All-inclusive.*

$$$$
★ **Grand Lido Sans Souci.** This pastel-pink cliff-side resort looks and feels like a fantasy. A stay here is a wonderfully luxurious experience. Romantic oceanfront suites are equipped with oversize whirlpool tubs. Blond-wood furniture, cool tile floors, and sheer curtains are accented by pastel watercolors and Jamaican prints on the walls. A highlight is the pampering you receive at Charlie's Spa in the form of a massage, body scrub, reflexology session, facial, manicure, and and even a complimentary manicure and pedicure (book treatments as soon as you arrive, if not before). Complimentary weddings are part of the all-inclusive package. ⊠ *2 mi east of Ocho Rios (Box 103),* ☎ *876/974–2353 or 800/467–8737 (reservations service),* FAX *876/974–2544. 13 rooms, 98 suites. 3 restaurants, 4 bars, grill, in-room safes, minibars, 2 pools, hot tub, massage, spa, 4 tennis courts, beach, library, laundry service, concierge. 3-night minimum stay. AE, D, DC, MC, V. All-inclusive.*

$$$$ **Jamaica Inn.** A combination of class and quiet attracts a discerning crowd to this vintage property. Each room has its own veranda (larger than most hotel rooms) on the private cove's powdery champagne-color beach. The colonial decor is on the dark side, with Jamaican antique furniture, terrazzo floors, and walls hung with oil paintings (there are no TVs or radios). Jacket and tie are de rigueur after 7 PM during high season (December–April). ⊠ *East of Ocho Rios on North Coast Hwy. (Box 1),* ☎ *876/974–2514 or 800/837–4670 (reservations service),* FAX *876/974–2449. 44 rooms, 1 suite with private pool. Restaurant, 2* *bars, room service, pool, croquet, exercise room, beach, snorkeling, boating, library. AE, MC, V. FAP (summer only), MAP.*

$$$$ ⊞ **Sandals Dunn's River Golf Resort and Spa.** Twenty-five acres of man-★ icured gardens surround this luxury, couples-only all-inclusive. The pillared masterpiece, set on a wide sugary beach, is the finest of Sandals's Jamaican resorts. The rooms are larger than at other Sandals establishments and are decorated in light pink, blue, turquoise, and cream. Most have a balcony or patio that overlooks the sea or the lush grounds. Oceanfront suites have four-poster mahogany beds. The resort draws a well-heeled crowd in their thirties and forties and prides itself on catering to every guest's every whim. ⊠ *2 mi east of Ocho Rios on North Coast Hwy. (Box 51),* ☎ *876/972–1610 or 800/726–3257 (reservations service),* ℻ *876/972–1611. 256 rooms, 10 suites. 4 restaurants, 7 bars, in-room safes, 2 pools, 3 outdoor hot tubs, sauna, steam room, putting green, 2 tennis courts, racquetball, beach, concierge. 3-night minimum stay. AE, MC, V. All-inclusive.*

$$$–$$$$ ⊞ **Plantation Inn.** Looking so much like a Deep South plantation—à la *Gone With the Wind*—this inn conjures up an existence as soft as a southern drawl. All its big, breezy rooms have large private balconies with dramatic sea views. Corner rooms, which have mahogany half-canopy beds, are the most romantic. Afternoon tea is served, and you can dine by candlelight on Jamaican cuisine in the popular restaurant (where dancing is also an option). ⊠ *Main St. (Box 2),* ☎ *876/974–5601 or 800/752–6824 (reservations service),* ℻ *876/974–5912. 59 rooms, 17 suites. Restaurant, 2 bars, pool, massage, sauna, 2 tennis courts, croquet, exercise room, beach, snorkeling, windsurfing, library, children's programs. AE, MC, V. All-inclusive, EP, MAP.*

$$–$$$$ ⊞ **Couples.** The emphasis here is on romantic (and all-inclusive) ad-★ ventures for two. One-bedroom suites are designed for romance, with two-person hot tubs in the bathroom that peek through a window at the four-poster king-size bed. The newer wing has 40 rooms furnished in hand-carved mahogany. There's a lovely white beach for relaxation or water sports, and a private island where you can sunbathe in the buff. Weddings are included in the package. ⊠ *Tower Isle, St. Mary,* ☎ *876/975–4271 or 800/268–7537 (reservations service),* ℻ *876/975–4439. 201 rooms, 11 suites. 4 restaurants, 6 bars, in-room safes, room service, pool, 5 outdoor hot tubs, massage, sauna, 5 tennis courts, horseback riding, squash, beach, dive shop, snorkeling, windsurfing. 3-night minimum stay. AE, MC, V. All-inclusive.*

$$$ ⊞ **High Hope Estate.** The tranquillity here is undisturbed, the vista of Caribbean coast superb. Set on 40 acres in trade-wind-cooled hills 7 mi west of Ocho Rios, this 15th-century-style villa has Italian marble floors, graceful arches, mahogany trim, and spacious verandas. The staff is warm and attentive, and owner Dennis Rapaport is a charming host who's full of fascinating stories. There are no planned activities, no disco, no bustling beach (it's 10 minutes away by car); come to enjoy the peace, to explore the hibiscus- and orchid-dotted lawns, to listen to birdsong, and to watch for shooting stars. Families and groups can book the entire villa on an all-inclusive package, but rooms are also available on a bed-and-breakfast basis. ⊠ *St. Ann's Bay (Box 11),* ☎ *876/972–2277,* ℻ *876/972–1607. 6 rooms. Fans, pool, tennis court, library, laundry service. MC, V. All-inclusive, CP, EP.*

$$–$$$ ⊞ **Enchanted Garden.** The 20 acres of gardens here, filled with tropical plants and flowers and punctuated by streams and waterfalls, are enchanting. You'll also find an aviary and a seaquarium, where you can enjoy a deli lunch or tea surrounded by tanks of fish and hanging orchids. The futuristic cream-color villas (some with private plunge pools) seem somewhat out of place amid the natural splendor, but the rooms (on the small side) are comfortable, and you're never far from the soothing sound of rushing water. Don't miss the guided garden tour, just one of dozens of activities here. There's a free shuttle to the beach, several minutes away. ⊠ *Eden Bower Rd. (Box 284),* ☎ *876/974–1400 or 800/554–2008 (reservations service),* ℻ *876/974–5823. 113 units. 5 restaurants, 4 bars, 2 pools, outdoor hot tub, sauna, spa, Turkish bath, 2 tennis courts, croquet, beach, dive shop, snorkeling, windsurfing, airport shuttle. AE, DC, MC, V. All-inclusive.*

$$ 🏨 **Renaissance Jamaica Grande.** The largest conference hotel in Jamaica attracts all types of traveler: families, couples, singles (there are special singles activities, and no singles supplement fees), and conference attendees. Even though it's a beachfront resort, the focal point is definitely the tiered and winding pool, which has a waterfall, a swaying bridge, and a swim-up bar. Rooms in the south building are the largest, but those in the north building have slightly better views. Kids are kept busy in the daily Club Mongoose activity program (included in the rates). The hotel's disco, Jamaic'N Me Crazy (☞ Nightlife, *below*), is *very* popular. ⊠ *Main St. (Box 100),* ☎ *876/974–2201 or 800/468–3571 (reservations service),* ℻ *876/974–2289. 706 rooms, 14 suites. 5 restaurants, 9 bars, in-room safes, 3 pools, 2 outdoor hot tubs, massage, 4 tennis courts, beach, dive shop, snorkeling, windsurfing, boating, children's programs, nursery, playground, concierge, convention center. AE, DC, MC, V. All-inclusive, EP.*

$–$$ 🏨 **Club Jamaica Beach Resort.** At this intimate all-inclusive you get lots
★ of personal attention from the young, cheerful staff. Rooms are refreshing, with gleaming white-tile floors, modern furnishings, and gem-tone color schemes; more than half look out on the ocean. Guests, identified by their plastic, hospital-style bracelets, tend to be active middle-agers; most participate fully in the resort's daily activities (including nonmotorized water sports on the public beach). They also dance the night away to live music. The Ocho Rios crafts market is adjacent to the resort. ⊠ *Turtle Beach (Box 342),* ☎ *876/974–6632 or 800/818–2964 (reservations service),* ℻ *876/974–6644. 95 rooms. Restaurant, 3 bars, in-room safes, pool, outdoor hot tub, beach, dive shop, snorkeling, windsurfing, jet skiing. AE, MC, V. All-inclusive.*

$ 🏨 **Comfort Suites.** Families on a budget planning an extended stay should consider a suite here; the fully stocked kitchens can help keep the dining bills down. This is also one of the few places you'll find no-smoking rooms (if you want one, be sure to request it when booking). Each spacious, immaculate unit has white-tile floors, rattan furniture, and tropical floral prints. The two-bedroom suite has an open bathroom (it's divided from the main room by only a screen), as well as a whirlpool tub in its master-bedroom loft. This hotel is not on the beach (though it's close enough to walk to and a shuttle is provided), but suites in "A" block do have a partial ocean view. ⊠ *17 Da Costa Dr.,* ☎ *876/974–8050 or 800/221–2222 (reservations service),* ℻ *876/974–8070. 87 1- and 2-bedroom suites. Restaurant, bar, in-room safes, kitchenettes, no-smoking rooms, refrigerators, room service, outdoor hot tub, tennis court, airport shuttle. AE, DC, MC, V. EP, FAP, MAP.*

$ 🏨 **Hibiscus Lodge.** This gleaming white building with a blue awning sits amid beautifully manicured lawns, not too far from a tiny private beach. The impeccably neat, cozy rooms have just about everything you need (except phones), including TVs, air-conditioning, private (shower-only) baths, and terraces with partial sea views. The place is such a bargain that many of its guests return time and time again. There are two reefs just off the beach, so the snorkeling is great here. Breakfast is included in the room rate. ⊠ *83–87 Main St. (Box 52),* ☎ *876/974–2676 or 800/526–2422 (reservations service),* ℻ *876/974–1874. 26 rooms. Restaurant, bar, air-conditioning, pool, outdoor hot tub, tennis court. AE, DC, MC, V. CP.*

Port Antonio

Described by poet Ella Wheeler Wilcox as "the most exquisite port on earth," Port Antonio is a seaside town nestled at the foot of verdant hills toward the east end of the north coast. The area's must-do activities include rafting the Rio Grande, snorkeling or scuba diving in the Blue Lagoon, exploring Nonsuch Caves, and stopping at the classy Trident resort for lunch or a drink.

$$$$ ★ 🏨 **Trident Villas and Hotel.** The truly gracious living and white-gloved dining here will transport you back to the days of the Empire. Peacocks strut the manicured lawns, colonnaded walkways wind through whimsically sculpted topiaries that dot the 14 acres, and the pool—on a rocky bit of land that juts out into crashing surf—is a memory unto itself. The luxurious Laura Ashley–style rooms—many with turrets, bay windows, and balconies or verandas—are awash in mahogany and local art; they do not have TVs or clocks. ⊠ *Anchovy (Box 119),* ☎ *876/ 993–2602 or 800/428–4734 (reservations service),* 𝔽𝔸𝕏 *876/993–2590. 8 rooms, 12 suites, 14 villas. Restaurant, bar, in-room safes, minibars, pool, massage, 2 tennis courts, aerobics, croquet, beach, snorkeling, boating, library, concierge. AE, MC, V. CP, FAP, MAP.*

$$$ 🏨 **Goblin Hill.** This lush 12-acre estate is set atop a hill overlooking San San Bay. Each attractively appointed villa comes with its own dramatic view, plus a staff member to do the grocery shopping, cleaning, and cooking for you. The villas are not equipped with phones or TVs, but have ceiling fans and a tropical decor. The beach is a 10-minute walk away. Excellent villa and car-rental packages are available. ⊠ *San San (Box 26),* ☎ *876/925–8108 or 800/472–1148 (reservations service),* 𝔽𝔸𝕏 *876/925–6248. 28 villas. Bar, kitchenettes, pool, 2 tennis courts, beach, dive shop, library. AE, MC, V. EP.*

$$ 🏨 **Hotel Mocking Bird Hill.** With only 10 rooms overlooking the sea and the Blue Mountains, Mocking Bird Hill feels more like a cozy B&B than a hotel. Owners Barbara Walker and Shireen Aga run an extremely environmentally sensitive operation: You'll find bamboo, instead of hardwood, furniture; solar-heated water; ceiling fans instead of ozone-depleting air-conditioning systems; meals made with local produce in the Mille Fleurs dining terrace (which is open to the public); locally produced toiletries and stationery sets; and seven naturally landscaped acres. The tasteful blue and white rooms do not have phones or TVs, and most are designated no-smoking. There's also an array of eco-tour options. ⊠ *Box 254, Port Antonio,* ☎ *876/993–7267,* 𝔽𝔸𝕏 *876/993–7133. 10 rooms. Restaurant, bar, in-room safes, no-smoking rooms, room service, pool, massage. AE, MC, V. CP, EP, MAP.*

$$ 🏨 **Jamaica Palace.** Built to resemble a 17th-century Italian mansion, this imposing and somewhat impersonal white-columned property has black-lacquer and gilded oversize furniture throughout its common areas. Some rooms are more lavish than others, though each has a semicircular bed, European objets d'art, Asian rugs; none are equipped with TVs (you can, however, rent one). Although the hotel isn't on the beach, there's a 114-ft swimming pool that's shaped like Jamaica. ⊠ *Williamsfield (Box 227),* ☎ *876/993–2021 or 800/423–4095 (reservations service),* 𝔽𝔸𝕏 *876/ 993–3459. 24 rooms, 56 suites. 3 restaurants, 2 bars, in-room safes, room service, pool, laundry service. AE, MC, V. CP, EP, MAP.*

$–$$ 🏨 **Dragon Bay.** Set on a private cove, Dragon Bay is an idyllic grouping of individually decorated villas surrounded by tropical gardens. Villa 35 has a private pool, a large living room, and two bedrooms with separate sitting rooms that have sofa beds. This place is popular with German and Italian tour groups. ⊠ *Dragon Bay (Box 176),* ☎ *876/ 993–8751 or 800/633–3284,* 𝔽𝔸𝕏 *876/993–3284. 30 1-, 2-, and 3-bedroom villas. 2 restaurants, 3 bars, refrigerators, room service, pool, mas-*

sage, 2 tennis courts, aerobics, exercise room, volleyball, beach, dive shop, snorkeling. AE, MC, V. All-inclusive, EP, FAP, MAP.

$ ⊞ **Bonnie View Plantation Hotel.** Accommodations here are spartan, mattresses are a tad lumpy, and the furnishings a bit frayed. But sublime views and tranquil air, rather than rooms and amenities, are the draws here. The nicest rooms (more expensive) are those with private verandas. But in any room you can open your window for a burst of invigorating mountain air. The restaurant also has unparalleled water panoramas. Beachcombers take note: It's a 25-minute drive to the ocean. ⊠ *Bonnie View Rd. (Box 82),* ☎ *876/993–2752 or 800/423–4095,* FAX *876/993–2862. 20 rooms. Restaurant, pool. AE, MC, V. EP.*

Runaway Bay

The smallest of the resort areas, Runaway Bay has a handful of modern hotels, a few new all-inclusive resorts, and an 18-hole golf course.

$$$$ ⊞ **FDR, Franklyn D. Resort.** Jamaica's first all-inclusive, family resort is the answer to parents' prayers. Upscale yet unpretentious, the complex has spacious, well-thought-out one, two-, and three-bedroom suites in pink villas set in a horseshoe around a pool. Best of all, a staff member is assigned to each suite, filling the role of nanny, housekeeper, and cook. Children and teens are kept busy with supervised activities and sports. Parents can join in the activities or just lounge by the pool, golf, or scuba dive. ⊠ *St. Ann's Bay (Box 201),* ☎ *876/973–4591 or 800/654–1337 (reservations service),* FAX *876/973–3071. 76 suites. 2 restaurants, 3 bars, kitchenettes, pool, golf privileges, tennis court, beach, children's programs. AE, MC, V. All-inclusive.*

$$$$ ⊞ **Grand Lido Braco Village Resort.** Just a 15-minute drive west of Run-
★ away Bay, this all-inclusive, adults-only, gingerbread- and Georgian-style village (a member of the SuperClubs family) focuses on the culture, crafts, music, and food of Jamaica. Boutiques, an art shop, and several restaurants—including a jerk grill, a pastry shop, and a sidewalk café—fan out from a central fountain in the "town square." The meandering pool next to the white-sand beach is one of the largest in the country. Rooms, done in bright tropical colors, are generously sized, and all but a few (which have garden views) are steps from the 2,000-ft beach or have a great view of the ocean from a patio. ⊠ *Rio Bueno, Trelawny,* ☎ *876/954–0000 or 800/GO–SUPER (reservations service),* FAX *876/954–0020. 232 rooms. 4 restaurants, 3 bars, café, in-room safes, pool, 2 hot tubs, 9-hole golf course, 2 tennis courts, hiking, soccer, beach, fishing, shops, dance club, theater. 3-night minimum stay. AE, DC, MC, V. All-inclusive, EP, FAP, MAP.*

$$$–$$$$ ⊞ **Breezes Golf and Beach Resort.** This moderately priced SuperClubs
★ all-inclusive emphasizes an active, sports-oriented vacation—from golf (at the nearby 18-hole course), tennis, and horseback riding to an array of water sports. Expert instruction and top-rate equipment are part of the package. Rooms have white-tile floors, cozy love seats, TVs, carved wooden headboards, and big marble bathrooms. Guests—often Germans, Italians, and Japanese—flock here for the psychedelically colored reef just off the beach, as well as the superb golf school. ⊠ *North Coast Hwy. (Box 58),* ☎ *876/973–2436 or 800/859–7873 (reservations service),* FAX *876/973–2352. 238 rooms, 4 suites. 2 restaurants, 4 bars, grill, in-room safes, 2 pools, 3 outdoor hot tubs, 2 tennis courts, golf privileges, horseback riding, beach. 3-night minimum stay. AE, DC, MC, V. All-inclusive.*

$$–$$$ ⊞ **Club Caribbean.** Families, including many from Europe, are drawn to this all-inclusive complex of Caribbean cottages on a narrow beach. The rooms are simple and clean, with rattan furnishings and floral-print fabrics; some have kitchenettes. For more space, ask for a garden suite. Swings provide seating in the gazebo bar, a popular hangout around sunset. ✉ Box 65, ☎ 876/973–3507 or 800/223–9815 (reservations service), FAX 876/973–3509. 135 rooms, 19 suites. Restaurant, 3 bars, in-room safes, pool, massage, 2 tennis courts, beach, children's programs, playground. AE, MC, V. All-inclusive.

Dining

Although many cultures have contributed to Jamaica's cuisine, it has become a true cuisine in its own right—interesting, and ultimately rewarding. It would be a shame to travel to the heart of this complex culture without having at least one typical island meal.

Probably the most famous Jamaican dish is jerk pork—the ultimate island barbecue. The pork (purists cook a whole pig) is covered with a paste of Scotch bonnet peppers, pimento berries (also known as allspice), and other herbs and cooked slowly over a coal fire. Many aficionados believe that the best jerk comes from Boston Beach near Port Antonio. Jerked chicken and fish are also seen on many menus. The ever-so traditional rice and peas, also known as "coat of arms," is similar to the *moros y christianos* of Spanish-speaking islands: white rice cooked with red kidney beans, coconut milk, scallions, and seasonings.

The island's most famous soup—the fiery pepper pot—is a peppery (of course) mixture of salt pork, salt beef, okra, and the island green known as callaloo. Patties (spicy meat pies) elevate street food to new heights. Although they actually originated in Haiti, Jamaicans excel at making them. Curry goat is another island standout: young goat is cooked with spices and is more tender and has a gentler flavor than the lamb for which it was substituted by immigrants from India. Salted fish was once the best islanders could do between catches. Out of necessity, a breakfast staple (and the national dish of Jamaica) was invented. It joins seasonings with salt fish and ackee, a red fruit that grows on trees throughout the island. When cooked in this dish, ackee reminds most people of scrambled eggs.

Where restaurants are concerned, Kingston has the widest selection, with establishments that serve Italian, French, Cantonese, German, Thai, Indian, Korean, and Continental fare as well as Rasta natural foods. There are also fine restaurants in all the resort areas, many in the resorts themselves. Most restaurants outside the hotels in MoBay and Ocho Rios will provide complimentary transportation.

What to Wear

Dress is usually casual chic (or just casual at many local hangouts). There are a few exceptions in Kingston and at the top resorts, some of which require semiformal wear in the evening during high season. People tend to dress up for dinner—just because they feel like it—so men might be more comfortable in nice slacks, women in a sundress.

CATEGORY	COST*
$$$$	over $40
$$$	$30–$40
$$	$20–$30
$	Under $20

*per person, excluding drinks, service, and tip

Kingston

ASIAN

$–$$ ✕ **Jade Garden.** On the third floor of the Sovereign Centre shopping mall, this establishment, with its shiny black-lacquer chairs and views of the Blue Mountains, garners rave reviews for its Cantonese and Thai menu. Favorites include steamed fish in black-bean sauce, black mushrooms stuffed with shrimp, and shrimp with lychee. Dim sum is served every Sunday afternoon. ⊠ *106 Hope Rd.,* ☎ *876/978–3476 or 876/ 978–3479. AE, MC, V.*

CONTINENTAL

$$$–$$$$ ✕ **Blue Mountain Inn.** The elegant Blue Mountain Inn is a 30-minute taxi
★ ride from New Kingston and worth every penny of the fare. On a former coffee plantation, the antiques-laden inn complements its English colonial atmosphere with Continental cuisine. All the classic beef and seafood dishes are here, including chateaubriand béarnaise and lobster thermidor. ⊠ *Gordon Town Rd.,* ☎ *876/927–1700 or 876/927–2606. Reservations essential. Jacket required. AE, MC, V. Closed Sun. No lunch.*

$$$–$$$$ ✕ **Palm Court.** Nestled on the mezzanine floor of the ☞ **Wyndham New Kingston,** the elegant Palm Court is open for lunch and dinner. The menu is Continental; the rack of lamb, sautéed snapper almandine, and grilled salmon are very tasty. ⊠ *75 Knutsford Blvd.,* ☎ *876/926–5430. AE, DC, MC, V. No lunch weekends.*

ECLECTIC

$$$–$$$$ ✕ **Ivor Guest House.** This elegant yet cozy restaurant is in an 1870s home in the hills 2,000 ft above sea level. Go for dinner, when the view is dramatically caught between shimmering stars and the glittering lights of Kingston. International cuisine with Jamaican flare is served in prix-fixe four-course dinners that average $35 per person. Owner Helen Aitken is an animated and cordial hostess. Afternoon tea here is a treat. There are three antiques-furnished guest rooms for those who want more time in this tranquil spot. ⊠ *Jack's Hill,* ☎ *876/702–0510 or 876/702–0276. Reservations essential. AE, MC, V.*

JAMAICAN

$–$$ ✕ **Peppers.** This casual outdoor bar with picnic tables is the *in* spot in Kingston. It's slow during weekday afternoons but frenetic on Friday night and Saturday. Sample the grilled lobster or jerk pork and chicken with the local Red Stripe beer, sit back and enjoy the local reggae band that plays. ⊠ *31 Upper Waterloo Rd.,* ☎ *876/925–2219. MC, V. Closed Sun.*

$ ✕ **Hot Pot.** Jamaicans love the Hot Pot for breakfast, lunch, and din-
★ ner. Fricassee chicken is the specialty, along with other local dishes, such as mackerel run-down (salted mackerel cooked with coconut milk and spices) and ackee and salted cod. The restaurant's fresh juices "in season" are the best—tamarind, sorrel, coconut water, soursop, and cucumber. ⊠ *2 Altamont Terr.,* ☎ *876/929–3906. MC, V.*

Montego Bay
ECLECTIC

$$–$$$ ✕ **Day-O Plantation Restaurant.** Transport yourself back in time with a fine meal served on the garden terrace of this Georgian-style plantation house. Start with smoked marlin, then segue into seafood ragout, broiled rock lobster with lemon butter, or beef fillet with béarnaise sauce. Sweeten things up with one of the traditional Jamaican desserts (rum pudding, sweet cakes, or fruit salad). ⊠ *Beside Barnett Estate Plantation, Fairfield,* ☎ *876/952–1825. AE, MC, V. Closed Mon.*

$$–$$$ ✕ **Sugar Mill.** Seafood is served with flair at this terrace restaurant on
★ the golf course of the ☞ **Half Moon Golf, Tennis, and Beach Club.** Caribbean specialties, steak, and lobster are usually offered in a pungent sauce that blends Dijon mustard with Jamaica's own Pickapeppa sauce. Otherwise, choices are the daily à la carte specials and anything flamed. Live music and a well-stocked wine cellar round out the experience. ⊠ *7 mi east of MoBay,* ☎ *876/953–2228. Dinner reservations essential. AE, MC, V.*

$–$$ ✕ **Margueritaville Caribbean Bar and Grill.** This brightly painted bar-restaurant is tough to miss: just look for the slide that connects it with the water. You'll find plenty of casual dishes on the menu, including burgers, chicken sandwiches, tuna melts, pizza, and the like. ✉ *Glouces-ter Ave.,* ☎ *876/952–4777. AE, MC, V.*

$–$$ ✕ **The Native.** This open-air stone terrace, shaded by a large poinciana tree and overlooking Gloucester Avenue, serves Jamaican and inter-national dishes. To go native, start with smoked marlin, move on to the *boonoonoonoos* platter (a sampler of local dishes), and round out with coconut pie or *duckanoo* (a sweet dumpling of cornmeal, coconut, and banana wrapped in a banana leaf and steamed). Caesar salad, seafood linguine, and shrimp kabobs are fine alternatives. Live enter-tainment and candlelit tables make this a romantic choice for dinner on weekends. The popular afternoon buffets on Friday and Sunday are family affairs. ✉ *29 Gloucester Ave.,* ☎ *876/979–2769. Dinner reser-vations essential. AE, MC, V.*

$–$$ ✕ **Town House.** Most of the rich and famous who have visited Jamaica over the decades have eaten here. You'll find daily specials, delicious variations of standard dishes (red snapper *papillote* is a specialty, with lobster, cheese, and wine sauce), and many Jamaican favorites (curried chicken with breadfruit and ackee). The 18th-century Georgian house is adorned with original Jamaican and Haitian art. There's alfresco din-ing on the stone patio. ✉ *16 Church St.,* ☎ *876/952–2660. Dinner reservations essential. AE, DC, MC, V. No lunch Sun.*

$ ✕ **Le Chalet.** Don't let the French name fool you. This Denny's look-★ alike, set in a nondescript shopping mall, serves heaping helpings of some of the best Chinese and Jamaican food in MoBay. Tasty lobster Cantonese costs only $15. ✉ *32 Gloucester Ave.,* ☎ *876/952–5240. AE, MC, V. No lunch Sun.*

ITALIAN

$$$–$$$$ ✕ **Julia's Italian Restaurant.** Couples flock to this romantic Italian restau-rant in the hills overlooking MoBay. You can choose from an à la carte menu or order a five-course prix-fixe meal ($33–$45 per person) that includes homemade soups and pastas; entrées of fish, chicken, and veal; and scrumptious desserts. Don't expect the meal to equal the stupen-dous view, and you won't be disappointed. ✉ *Bogue Hill,* ☎ *876/952–1772. Reservations essential. AE, MC, V.*

JAMAICAN

$$–$$$ ✕ **Norma at the Wharf House.** This sister property to creative chef-entrepreneur Norma's successful Kingston restaurant has gathered rave reviews as a supper club. The setting is a converted 300-year-old, stone, sugar warehouse on the water, decorated in blue and white. In-novative Jamaican cuisine ranges from Caribbean lobster steamed in Red Stripe beer to jerk chicken with mangoes flambé. ✉ *10 mins west of MoBay in Reading,* ☎ *876/979–2745. Dinner reservations essen-tial. MC, V. Closed Mon. and May–Aug.*

SEAFOOD

$$$ ✕ **Marguerites.** This romantic pierside dining room specializes in seafood. Flambé is the operative word here: lobster, shrimp, fish, and several desserts are prepared in dancing flames as you sip on an exotic cocktail. The Cae-sar salad, prepared tableside, is also a treat. ✉ *Gloucester Ave.,* ☎ *876/952–4777. Reservations essential. AE, MC, V. No lunch.*

$$–$$$ ✕ **Pier 1.** After tropical drinks at the deck bar, you'll be ready to dig into the international variations on fresh seafood, the best of which are the grilled lobster and any preparation of island snapper. Several party cruises leave from the marina here, and on Friday night the restaurant is mobbed by locals who come to dance. ⊠ *Just off Howard Cooke Blvd.,* ☎ *876/952–2452. AE, MC, V.*

Negril

CARIBBEAN/CREOLE

$ ✕ **Sweet Spice.** This mom-and-pop diner run by the Whytes serves inexpensive, generous plates of conch, fried or curried chicken, freshly caught fish, oxtail in brown stew sauce, and other down-home specialties. The fresh juices are quite satisfying. Drop by for breakfast, lunch, or dinner. ⊠ *1 White Hall Rd.,* ☎ *876/957–4621. Reservations not accepted. MC, V.*

ECLECTIC

$$ ✕ **Margueritaville.** Set on a beautiful stretch of Seven Mile Beach, this
★ operation, a sibling of the wildly popular Margueritaville in MoBay, is a sports bar, a disco, a beach club, and a restaurant. There is also an art gallery, a gift shop, a five-star PADI dive shop, volleyball and basketball courts, and changing rooms so that you can slip out of your wet suit. Lobster is the house specialty. Far less expensive are the fish, chicken, and sandwich platters. There are also more than 50 margaritas from which to choose. ⊠ *Norman Manley Blvd.,* ☎ *876/957–4467. AE, MC, V.*

$$ ✕ **Tan-ya's.** This alfresco restaurant overlooks the pool and hot tub at Sea Splash Resort, an intimate, 15-suite property surrounded by palm trees on lovely Seven Mile Beach. Jamaican delicacies with an international flavor are served for breakfast, lunch, and dinner. Try the excellent deviled crab backs or the smoked marlin. ⊠ *Norman Manley Blvd.,* ☎ *876/957–4041. AE, DC, MC, V.*

$–$$ ✕ **Rick's Cafe.** Here it is, the local landmark complete with cliffs, cliff divers, and powerful sunsets, all perfectly choreographed. Most folks come for the drinks and the renowned sunset party, since the standard pub menu is overpriced. In the sunset ritual, the crowd toasts Mother Nature with rum drinks amid shouts, laughter, and ever-shifting meeting and greeting. When the sun slips below the horizon, there are more shouts, more cheers, and more rounds of rum. ⊠ *West End Rd.,* ☎ *876/957–0380. MC, V.*

$ ✕ **Kuyaba on the Beach.** This charming thatch-roof eatery features an international menu—including curried conch, kingfish steak, grilled lamb with sautéed mushrooms, and an array of pasta dishes—and a lively ambience, especially at the bar. There's a crafts shop on the premises, and chaise longues line the beach; come prepared to spend some time, and don't forget a towel and bathing suit. ⊠ *Norman Manley Blvd.,* ☎ *876/957–4318. AE, MC, V.*

SEAFOOD

$–$$ ✕ **Cosmo's Seafood Restaurant and Bar.** Owner Cosmo Brown has made
★ this seaside open-air bistro a pleasant place to spend the afternoon— and maybe stay on for dinner. Fish is the main attraction, and the conch soup—a house specialty—is a meal in itself. You'll also find lobster (grilled or curried), fish-and-chips, and a catch-of-the-morning. Customers often drop cover-ups to take a dip before coffee and dessert and return to lounge in chairs scattered under almond and seagrape trees. (There's a small entrance fee for the beach.) ⊠ *Norman Manley Blvd.,* ☎ *876/957–4330. Reservations not accepted. AE, MC, V.*

Ocho Rios

ECLECTIC

$$$–$$$$ ✕ **Almond Tree.** One of the most popular restaurants in Ocho Rios,
★ the Almond Tree has a menu of Jamaican and Continental favorites: pumpkin and pepper-pot soups, and many wonderful preparations of fresh fish, veal piccata, and fondue. The swinging rope chairs of the terrace bar and the tables perched above a lovely Caribbean cove are

great fun. ✉ *83 Main St.*, ☎ *876/974–2813. Dinner reservations essential. AE, DC, MC, V.*

$–$$ ✕ **Evita's.** The setting here is a hilltop 1860s gingerbread house. Large,
★   open windows open to cooling mountain breezes and stunning views
        of city and sea. More than 30 kinds of pasta are served, ranging from
        lasagna Rastafari (vegetarian) and fiery "jerk" spaghetti to *rotelle
        colombo* (crabmeat with white sauce and noodles). There are also excellent
        fish dishes—sautéed fillet of red snapper with orange sauce, scampi
        and lobster in basil cream sauce, red snapper stuffed with crabmeat—
        and several meat dishes, among them a tasty grilled sirloin with mushroom
        sauce. Kids under 12 eat for half price, and light eaters will
        appreciate half-portion orders. ✉ *Mantalent Inn, Eden Bower Rd.,* ☎
        876/974–2333. AE, MC, V.

$–$$ ✕ **Little Pub.** Alfresco dining in a village-square setting awaits you at
        this charming restaurant. It also has a bustling sports bar and an energetic
        Caribbean review several nights a week. Jamaican standards
        (jerk or curried chicken, baked crab, sautéed snapper) accompany surf
        and turf, lobster thermidor, pasta primavera, seafood stir-fry, crêpe
        suzette, and bananas flambé. Burgers and other standard pub fare are
        also available. ✉ *59 Main St.,* ☎ *876/974–2324. AE, MC, V.*

JAMAICAN

$ ✕ **Ocho Rios Village Jerk Centre.** This blue-canopied, open-air eatery
★   is a good place to park yourself for frosty Red Stripe beer and fiery
        jerk pork, chicken, or seafood. Milder barbecued meats, also sold by
        weight (typically ¼ or ½ pound make good servings), also turn up on
        the fresh daily chalkboard menu posted on the wall. It's lively at lunch,
        especially when passengers from cruise ships swamp the place. ✉ *DaCosta
        Dr.,* ☎ *876/974–2549. MC, V.*

Beaches

Jamaica has 200 mi of beaches, some of them relatively deserted. Generally,
the farther west you go, the lighter and finer the sand. The beaches
listed below are public (though there's usually a small admission
charge) and are among the best Jamaica has to offer. In addition,
nearly every resort has its own private beach, complete with towels and
water sports. Some of the larger resorts sell day passes to nonguests.

DISCOVERY BAY

Puerto Seco Beach is a stretch of sand that's frequented primarily by
locals. There's an admission charge of $5 for the beach, which is open
daily 9–5. You'll find plenty of water-sports activities and some concessions
that sell local foods.

KINGSTON AREA

As a rule, the beaches outside Kingston are not as beautiful as those
in the resort areas. **Fort Clarence,** in the Hellshire Hills area southwest
of the city, has changing facilities and entertainment. **Hellshire Beach,**
in Bridgeport, about a 20- to 30-minute drive from Kingston, is very
popular. You'll find food vendors, changing rooms, and plenty of
(recorded) music. You can reach **Lime Cay** by boat (which you can hire
at Morgan's Harbor Marina in Port Royal for a small fee). This island,
just beyond Kingston Harbor, is perfect for picnicking, sunning, and
swimming. **Lyssons Beach,** in Morant Bay, sometimes lures Kingstonians
32 mi east of the city to its lovely golden sand.

MONTEGO BAY

Cornwall Beach is a lively beach with lots of places that sell food and
drink as well as a water sports concession. The 5-mi **Doctor's Cave Beach**
has been spotlighted in so many travel articles and brochures that it

In case you want to be welcomed there.

We're here to see that you're always welcomed at establishments everywhere. That's why millions of people carry the American Express® Card – for peace of mind, confidence, and security, around the world or just around the corner.

do more

Cards

In case you're running low.

We're here to help with more than 118,000 Express Cash locations around the world. In order to enroll, just call American Express before you start your vacation.

do more

Express Cash

And just in case.

We're here with American Express® Travelers Cheques and Cheques *for Two.*® They're the safest way to carry money on your vacation and the surest way to get a refund, practically anywhere, anytime.

Another way we help you...

do more ®

Travelers Cheques

often resembles Fort Lauderdale during spring break. On the bright side, it has much to offer admirers beyond just sugary sand, including changing rooms, colorful if overly insistent vendors, and plenty of places to grab a snack. **Rose Hall Beach Club,** east of central MoBay near Rose Hall Great House, is a secluded area with changing rooms and showers, a water sports center, volleyball and other beach games, and a beach bar and grill. **Walter Fletcher Beach,** near the center of town, offers protection from the surf on a windy day and, therefore, unusually fine swimming; the calm waters make it a good bet for children.

NEGRIL

Not too long ago **Seven Mile Beach** was a beachcomber's Eden. Today much of its white sand is fronted by resorts, although some stretches along Bloody Bay remain relatively untouched. In sections where there are no hotels, there are some nude beach areas, such as one adjacent to Cosmo's (☞ Dining, *above*). A few resorts have built accommodations overlooking their nude beaches, thereby adding a new dimension to the traditional notion of "ocean view."

OCHO RIOS

Turtle Beach, stretching behind Renaissance Jamaica Grande and Club Jamaica, is the busiest beach in Ocho Rios (where the islanders go to swim). **James Bond Beach,** east of Ocho Rios in the quaint village of Oracabessa, was opened in 1997 and has become a favorite, owing to the live reggae performances on the bandstand here.

PORT ANTONIO

Boston Bay, approximately 11 mi east of Port Antonio, beyond the Blue Lagoon, is a small, intimate beach. It's a good place to buy the famous peppery delicacy, jerk pork, available at any of the shacks spewing scented smoke along the beach. **San San Beach,** about 5 mi east of Port Antonio, has beautiful blue waters and is used mainly by area villa or hotel owners and their guests.

THE SOUTH COAST

To find a beach off the main tourist routes, head for Jamaica's unexploited south coast. **Bluefields Beach,** near Savanna-La-Mar (or just Sav-La-Mar to locals), south of Negril, is nearest to "civilization." **Crane Beach,** at Black River, has retained its natural beauty and has—so far—remained undiscovered by most tourists. **Treasure Beach** has to be the best that the south shore has to offer. Set by a quaint fishing village, this undeveloped beach has coves that are ideal for snorkeling explorations. These isolated beaches are some of the island's safest because the population is sparse in this region and hasslers are practically nonexistent. You should, however, use common-sense precautions; never leave valuables unattended on the beach.

Outdoor Activities and Sports

The tourist board licenses all recreational activity operators and outfitters, which should ensure you of fair business practices as long as you deal with companies that display the decals.

BIRD-WATCHING

Many bird-watchers flock (excuse the pun) here for the chance to see the vervian hummingbird (the second smallest bird in the world, larger only than Cuba's bee hummingbird), the Jamaican tody (which nests underground), or another of the island's 27 endemic species. A great place to spot birds is the **Rocklands Feeding Station** (✉ Anchovy, south of Montego Bay, ☎ 876/952–2009). In Mandeville, tours of the bird sanctuary at **Marshall's Penn Great House** (☎ 876/963–8569) are by appointment only and are led by owner Robert Sutton, one of Jamaica's leading ornithologists.

FISHING

Port Antonio makes deep-sea fishing headlines with its annual Blue Marlin Tournament, and Montego Bay and Ocho Rios have devotees who exchange tales (tall and otherwise) about sailfish, yellowfin tuna, wahoo, dolphinfish, and bonito. Licenses aren't required, and you can arrange to charter a boat at your hotel. A boat (with captain, crew, and equipment) that accommodates four to six passengers costs about $400 for a half day.

GOLF

Golfers appreciate both the beauty and the challenges offered by Jamaica's courses. Caddies are mandatory throughout the island, and rates are $5–$15. Cart rentals are available at all courses except Constant Spring and Manchester Country Club; costs are $20–$35.

Some of the best courses are in Montego Bay at **Tryall** (⊠ 15 mi west of MoBay on North Coast Hwy., ☎ 876/956–5681), which has an 18-hole championship course on the site of a 19th-century sugar plantation (greens fees run $40–$60 for guests, $100–$125 for nonguests), **Half Moon** (⊠ 7 mi east of MoBay, ☎ 876/953–3105) the 18-holes course that's the home of the Red Stripe Pro Am and that was designed by Robert Trent Jones (the greens fee is $95), **Wyndham Rose Hall** (⊠ 4 mi east of airport on North Coast Hwy., ☎ 876/953–2650), which hosts several invitational tournaments (fees run $50–$60), and **Ironshore** (⊠ 3 mi east of airport, ☎ 876/953–2800), an 18-hole links-style course (the greens fee is $45).

Good Kingston courses include **Caymanas** (⊠ 6 mi west of Kingston, ☎ 876/997–8026), Jamaica's first major championship 18-hole course (greens fee is $53) and **Constant Spring** (⊠ A3, Constant Spring, ☎ 876/924–1610), a short 18-hole course designed in 1920 (greens fee is $53). In Runaway Bay try **Breezes Golf Club** (⊠ North Coast Hwy., ☎ 876/973–2561), an 18-hole course that has hosted many championship events (greens fees are $58 for nonguests) and **Grand Lido Braco Village Resort** (⊠ Trelawny, between Duncans and Rio Bueno, ☎ 876/954–0000, a 9-hole course with lush vegetation, (non guests should call for fee information). Ocho Rios has the **Sandals Golf and Country Club** (⊠ 2 mi east of Ocho Rios, ☎ 876/975–0119), an 18-hole course 700 ft above sea level (the greens fee is $70 for nonguests).

A 9-hole course in the hills of Mandeville, the **Manchester Club** (⊠ Caledonia Rd. and Ward Ave., ☎ 876/962–2403) is the Caribbean's oldest golf course, and has a greens fee of $14. Great golf, rolling hills, and a "liquor mobile" go hand in hand at the 18-hole **Negril Hills Golf Club** (⊠ East of Negril on Sheffield Rd., ☎ 876/957–4638); the greens fee is $58. **Prospect Plantation** (⊠ A3, 3 mi east of Ocho Rios, ☎ 876/994–1058) in Ocho Rios and the **Anancy Family Fun and Nature Park** (⊠ Norman Manley Blvd., ☎ 876/957–5100) in Negril have 18-hole minigolf courses.

HORSEBACK RIDING

Jamaica is fortunate to have an outstanding equestrian facility: **Chukka Cove** (☎ 876/972–2506) near Ocho Rios. This resort offers instruction in riding, polo, and jumping, as well as hour-long trail rides, three-hour beach rides, and six-hour rides to a restored great house. During in-season weekends this is the place for polo (and social) action. You can also saddle up at the **Rocky Point Riding Stables at Half Moon** (☎ 876/953–2286), which is just east of the Half Moon Club in Montego

Bay; the **Barnett Estate Great House** (☎ 876/952–2382) in Montego Bay; and the **Prospect Plantation** (☎ 876/994–1058) in Ocho Rios.

SCUBA DIVING AND SNORKELING

The major areas for scuba diving and snorkeling are Negril in the west and Port Antonio in the east. MoBay is also known for its wall dives. All the large resorts rent equipment, and the all-inclusive places have scuba diving on their lists of activities included in the rate.

To scuba dive you need to show a C-card; the following operators offer certification courses and dive trips as well as snorkel gear rentals and are licensed by the tourist board: **Dolphin Divers** (⊠ Norman Manley Blvd., Negril, ☎ 876/957–4944), **Garfield Diving Station** (⊠ Shop 13, Santa Maria, west of Renaissance Jamaica Grande, Ocho Rios, ☎ 876/974–5749), **Lady G'Diver** (⊠ San San Beach, Port Antonio, ☎ 876/993–3281), which also offers windsurfing, glass-bottom boating, and sailing (excursions start at $25 per person), **Negril Scuba Centre** (⊠ Negril Beach Club, Norman Manley Blvd., Negril, ☎ 876/957–4425), **North Coast Marine Sports** (⊠ Several locations in Montego Bay, ☎ 876/953–2211), **Resort Divers** (⊠ Gloucester Ave., Montego Bay, ☎ 876/952–4285; ⊠ 1 Carib Arcade, Ocho Rios, ☎ 876/974–5338; ⊠ Breezes Golf and Beach Resort, North Coast Hwy., Runaway Bay, ☎ 876/973–5750), and **Sandals Beach Resort Watersports** (⊠ Norman Manley Blvd., Negril, ☎ 876/957–5216).

TENNIS

Many hotels have tennis facilities that are free to their guests, but some will allow nonguests to play for a fee. In MoBay, the sport is a highlight at **Tryall** (⊠ 15 mi west of MoBay on North Coast Hwy., ☎ 876/956–5660), **Round Hill Hotel and Villas** (⊠ 8 mi west of MoBay on North Coast Hwy., ☎ 876/952–5150), **Sandals Montego Bay** (⊠ Kent Ave., ☎ 876/952–5510), with four courts lit for night play and a tennis pro, and **Half Moon Golf Club** (⊠ 7 mi east of MoBay, ☎ 876/953–2211) with 13 Laykold tennis courts (7 lit for night play) along with a pro and a pro shop. You'll find five hard courts and five clay courts, all lit for night play, at **Swept Away** (⊠ Norman Manley Blvd., ☎ 876/957–4040) in Negril. **Sandals Dunn's River** (⊠ North Coast Hwy., ☎ 876/972–1610), has four courts lit for night play as well as the services of a pro. **Grand Lido Sans Souci** also has four lighted courts and a pro (⊠ North Coast Hwy., 2 mi east of Ocho Rios, ☎ 876/974–2353). At **Ciboney, Ocho Rios** (⊠ 104 Main St., Ocho Rios, ☎ 876/974–1027) you'll find a pro and six lighted courts (three clay and three hard). **Breezes Golf and Beach Resort** (⊠ North Coast Hwy., ☎ 876/973–2436), in Runaway Bay, also has tennis facilities.

In Kingston, the **Crowne Plaza** (☎ 876/925–7676), the **Le Méridien Pegasus** (☎ 876/926–3690), and the **Wyndham New Kingston** (☎ 876/926–5430) all have courts for guest use.

Shopping

Shopping here goes two ways: things Jamaican and things imported. Jamaican crafts are made with style and skill and take the form of resort wear, hand-loomed fabrics, silk screens, wood carvings, paintings, and other fine arts. Jamaican rum is a great take-home gift. So is Tia Maria, Jamaica's world-famous coffee liqueur. The same goes for the island's prized Blue Mountain and High Mountain coffees and its jams, jellies, and marmalades. If you shop around, you'll find good deals on such duty-free luxury items as jewelry, cameras, china, Swiss watches, and Irish crystal. The top-selling French perfumes are sold alongside Jamaica's own fragrances.

Shopping Areas and Malls

A shopping tour of the **Kingston** area should begin at Constant Spring Road or King Street. No matter where you start, keep in mind that shopping malls have caught on here with a fever. The ever-growing roster includes Twin Gates Plaza, New Lane Plaza, the New Kingston Shopping Centre, Tropical Plaza, Manor Park Plaza, the Village, the Springs, and the newest (and some say nicest), Sovereign Shopping Centre. Devon House is the place to find old and new Jamaica. The great house is now a museum with antiques and furniture reproductions; boutiques and an ice cream shop—try one of the tropical flavors (mango, guava, pineapple, and passion fruit)—now fill what were once the stables.

In **MoBay,** you should visit the "crafts market" on Market Street; just be prepared for haggling over prices in the midst of pandemonium. If you want to spend serious money, head for City Centre Plaza; Half Moon Village; Holiday Inn Shopping Centre; St. James's Place; Westgate Plaza; and Montego Bay Shopping Center, a favorite with locals.

Unless there's a cruise ship in port, the crafts markets in **Ocho Rios** are less hectic than the one in MoBay. The area's shopping plazas are Pineapple Place, Ocean Village, the Taj Mahal, Coconut Grove, and Island Plaza. The crafts markets in **Port Antonio** and **Negril** are good fun: you'll find a plethora of T-shirts; straw hats, baskets, and place mats; carved wood statues; colorful Rasta berets; and cheap jewelry.

Specialty Items

CLOTHES

Vaz Enterprises, LTD. (⊠ 77 East St., Kingston, ☏ 876/922–9200), the manufacturing outlet of designer Sonia Vaz, sells teeny-weeny bikinis. They're also for sale at several resorts.

COFFEE

In Kingston, you'll find Blue Mountain coffee at **John R. Wong's Supermarket** (⊠ 1–5 Tobago Ave., ☏ 876/926–4811). **Magic Kitchen Ltd.** (⊠ Village Plaza, ☏ 876/926–8894) sells the magic beans. The **Sovereign Supermarket** (⊠ Sovereign Center, 106 Hope Rd., ☏ 876/978–1254) has a wide selection of coffee and other goods. In Negril, java lovers will find beans and ground coffee at **Hi-Lo Supermarket** (⊠ West End Rd., ☏ 876/957–4546). If the stores are out of Blue Mountain, you may have to settle for High Mountain coffee, the locals' second-preferred brand.

HANDICRAFTS

Caribatik (⊠ A–1, 2 mi east of Falmouth, ☏ 876/954–3314), the studio of the late Muriel Chandler, stocks silk batiks, by the yard or made into chic designs. Drawing on patterns in nature, Chandler translated the birds, seascapes, flora, and fauna into works of art.

Gallery of West Indian Art (⊠ 1 Orange La., Montego Bay, ☏ 876/956–7050, ext. 312; ⊠ Round Hill, ☏ 876/952–5150) is the place to find Jamaican and Haitian paintings. A corner of the gallery is devoted to hand-turned pottery (some painted) and beautifully carved and painted birds and animals.

Harmony Hall (⊠ 8-min drive east on A–1 from Ocho Rios, ☏ 876/975–4222), a restored great house, is where Annabella Proudlock sells her unique wooden boxes (their covers are decorated with reproductions of Jamaican paintings). Also on sale—and magnificently displayed—are larger reproductions of paintings, lithographs, and signed prints of Jamaican scenes and hand-carved, wooden combs. In addition, Harmony Hall is well-known for its art shows by local artists.

Ital-Craft (⊠ Upper Manor Park Shopping Plaza, 184C Spring Rd., Kingston, ☏ 876/931–0477) sells belts, bangles, and beads. Although Ital-Craft's handmade treasures are sold in boutiques throughout Jamaica, this, the factory location, has an outstanding selection of the belts, which are made of spectacular shells as well as leather, feathers, or fur. (The most ornate creations sell for about $75.) You'll also find some intriguing jewelry and purses here.

Magic Toys (☎ 875/990–6030) has a large studio in Mandeville, though the company's creations are seen in the resorts throughout the Caribbean. Gift items include jigsaw puzzles, mirrors, picture frames, and magnets—each item featuring a tropical design such as a parrotfish, a bird of paradise, or Jamaica's own doctor bird.

Things Jamaican (⊠ Devon House, 26 Hope Rd., Kingston, ☎ 876/929–6602; ⊠ 44 Fort St., Montego Bay, ☎ 876/952–5605) sells some of the best Jamaican crafts—from carved wooden bowls and trays to reproductions of silver and brass period pieces.

JEWELRY

L. A. Henriques (⊠ Shop 12, Upper Manor Park Plaza, Kingston, ☎ 876/931–0613) sells high-quality jewelry made to order.

LIQUOR AND TOBACCO

As a rule, only rum distilleries, such as Sangster's, have better deals than the airport stores. Best of all, if you buy your rum or Tia Maria at either the Kingston or the MoBay airport before you leave, you don't have to tote all those heavy, breakable bottles to your hotel and then home again. Fine handmade Macanudo cigars make great easy-to-pack gifts; why not pick some up at Montego Bay airport on your way home? If you get the urge to puff during your stay, call 876/925–1082 for outlet information.

RECORDS

In Negril, music buffs should check out **Countryside** (⊠ Hi-Lo Shopping Centre, Negril, ☎ 876/957–4538). If you like reggae by world-famous Jamaican artists—Bob Marley, Ziggy Marley, Peter Tosh, and Third World, to name a few—a pilgrimage to **Randy's Record Mart** (⊠ 17 N. Parade, Kingston, ☎ 876/922–4859) is a must.

Also worth checking out are **De Muzic Shop** (⊠ Island Plaza, Ocho Rios, ☎ 876/974–9500), **Record City** (⊠ 1 William St., Port Antonio, ☎ 876/993–2836), **Record Plaza** (⊠ Tropical Plaza, Kingston, ☎ 876/926–7645), and **Top Ranking Records** (⊠ Westgate Plaza, Montego Bay, ☎ 876/952–1216).

SHOES

Cheap sandals are good buys in shopping centers throughout Jamaica. Although workmanship and leathers don't rival the craftsmanship of those found in Italy or Spain, neither do the prices (about $20 a pair). In Kingston, **Jacaranda** (⊠ Devon House, ☎ 876/929–6602) is a good place to sandal shop as is **Lee's Fifth Avenue Shoes** (⊠ Tropical Plaza, ☎ 876/926–7486). In Ocho Rios, the **Pretty Feet Shoe Shop** (⊠ Ocean Village Shopping Centre, ☎ 876/974–5040) is a good bet. In Montego Bay, try **Westgate Plaza.**

Nightlife and the Arts

Nightlife

Jamaica—especially Kingston—supports a lively community of musicians. For starters there's reggae, popularized by the late Bob Marley and the Wailers and performed today by son Ziggy Marley, Jimmy Tosh (the late Peter Tosh's son), Gregory Isaacs, Third World, Jimmy Cliff, and many others. If your experience of Caribbean music has been limited to steel drums and Harry Belafonte, then the political, racial, and religious messages of reggae may set you on your ear; listen closely and you just might hear the heartbeat of the people.

Those who know and love reggae should visit in mid-July to August for the Reggae Sunsplash. This four-night concert—at the Bob Marley Performing Center (a field set up with a temporary stage) in the Freeport area of Montego Bay—showcases local talent and attracts such big-name performers as Rick James, Gladys Knight and the Pips, Steel Pulse, Third World, and Ziggy Marley and the Melody Makers.

DANCE AND MUSIC CLUBS

For the most part, the liveliest late-night happenings throughout Jamaica are in the major resort hotels. Some of the all-inclusives offer a dinner and disco pass from about $50. Pick up a copy of *The Daily Gleaner, The Jamaica Observer,* or *The Star,* (available at newsstands throughout the island) for listings on who's playing and when and where.

The most popular spots in Kingston are **Asylum** (⊠ 69 Knutsford Blvd., ☎ 876/929–5459), **Jonkanoo** (⊠ Wyndham New Kingston, 75 Knutsford Blvd., ☎ 876/929–3390), and the trendy disco **Mirage** (⊠ Sovereign Centre, ☎ 876/978–8557).

The hottest places in MoBay are **Walter's** (⊠ 39 Gloucester Ave., ☎ 876/ 952–9391), **Hurricanes Disco** (⊠ Breezes Montego Bay Resort, Gloucester Ave., ☎ 876/940–1150), and the **Rhythm Nightclub** (⊠ Holiday Inn Sunspree Resort, 6 mi east of airport on North Coast Hwy., ☎ 876/953– 2485). After 10 on Friday nights, the crowd gathers at **Pier 1** (⊠ Howard Cooke Blvd., ☎ 876/952–2452) opposite the straw market. Two very popular new sports bars, both on Gloucester Avenue, are the **Brewery** (☎ 876/940–2433) and **Margueritaville** (☎ 876/952–4777).

In Negril, you'll find the best music at **Alfred's Ocean Palace** (⊠ Norman Manley Blvd., ☎ 876/957–4735); **De Buss** (⊠ Norman Manley Blvd., ☎ 876/957–4405); the disco at **Hedonism II** (⊠ Norman Manley Blvd., ☎ 876/957–4200); and at the hot, hot spot **Kaiser's Cafe** (⊠ Lighthouse Rd., ☎ 876/957–4070).

The principal clubs in Ocho Rios are **Acropolis** (⊠ 70 Main St., ☎ 876/ 974–2633); **Jamaic'N Me Crazy** (⊠ Renaissance Jamaica Grande, Main St., ☎ 876/974–2201); **Silks** (⊠ Shaw Park Beach Hotel, Shaw Park Ridge Rd., 1½ mi south of Ocho Rios, ☎ 876/974–2552); and the **Little Pub** (⊠ Main St., ☎ 876/974–2324), which produces Caribbean revues several nights a week.

In Port Antonio, if you have but one night to dance, do it at the **Roof Club** (⊠ 11 West St., ☎ 876/993–3817). On weekends, from 11 on, this is where it's all happening. An alternative for Port Antonio nightlife is the dance scene at **Shadows** (⊠ 40 West St., ☎ 876/993–3823) or the live jazz performances on Saturday evenings at the **Blue Lagoon Restaurant** (⊠ San San Beach, ☎ 876/993–8491).

The Arts

Jamaican culture is most evident in the island's theatrical and dance shows. Although many resorts offer a "native night" with dances and limbo shows, for true Jamaican culture you should see a stage show in Kingston. Recommended are performances by the Jamaica Philharmonic, the National Chorale, the Jamaica Folk Singers, and the National Dance Theater Company. For schedules, check with the tourist board (☞ Visitor Information *in* Jamaica A to Z, *below*).

Exploring Jamaica

Touring Jamaica can be both thrilling and frustrating. Rugged (albeit beautiful) terrain and winding—often potholed—roads make for slow going. (In the rainy season from June through October, roads can be entirely washed out; *always* check conditions prior to heading out.) Primary roads that loop around and across the island are two lanes, signs are not prevalent, numbered addresses are seldom used outside of major townships, locals drive aggressively, and people and animals seem to have a knack for appearing out of nowhere before your vehicle. That said, Jamaica's scenery should not be missed. The solution? Stick to guided tours and licensed taxis—to be safe and to avoid frustration.

If you're staying in Kingston or Port Antonio, set aside at least one day for the capital city's highlights and another for a guided excursion to the Blue Mountains. If you have more time, head for Mandeville. You'll find at least three days' worth of activity right along MoBay's boundaries; you should also consider a trip to Cockpit Country or Ocho Rios. If you're based in Ocho Rios, be sure to visit Dunns' River Falls; you may also want to stop by Firefly or Port Antonio. If Negril is your hub, take in the south shore, including Y. S. Falls and the Black River.

Numbers in the margin correspond to points of interest on the Jamaica map.

SIGHTS TO SEE

❾ Blue Mountains. These lush mountains rise to the north of Kingston. If you admire Jamaica's coffee, be sure to visit **Pine Grove,** a working coffee farm that doubles as an inn. It also has a restaurant that serves owner Marcia Thwaites's Jamaican cuisine. Another place worth a visit is **Mavis Bank** and its Jablum coffee plant. This spot is surprisingly (and delightfully) primitive considering the retail price of the beans it processes. A half-hour guided tour is available for $5; inquire when you arrive at the main office. Stop in World's End for a free tour of **Dr. Sangster's Rum Factory** (☎ 876/926–8888; call ahead for tour reservations), open weekdays 8:30–4:30. The small factory produces wonderful liqueurs flavored with local coffee beans, oranges, coconuts, and other Jamaican produce; samples are part of the tour.

Unless you're traveling with a local, don't rent a car and go to the Blue Mountains on your own; the roads wind and dip, hand-lettered signs blow away, and you could easily get lost—not just for hours, but for days. It's best to hire a taxi (look for red PPV license plates to identify a licensed taxi) or to take a guided tour. Another way to see the Blue Mountains is on a downhill bicycle tour offered by **Blue Mountain Tours** (☞ Guided Tours *in* Jamaica A to Z, *below*).

⒕ Cockpit Country. Fifteen miles inland from MoBay is one of the most primitive areas in the West Indies: a terrain of pitfalls and potholes carved by nature in limestone. For nearly a century after 1655, it was known as the Land of Look Behind because British soldiers nervously rode their horses through here, always looking out for the savage freedom fighters known as Maroons. Fugitive slaves who refused to surrender to the invading English, the Maroons eventually won their independence. Today their descendents continue to live in this area, untaxed and virtually ungoverned by outside authorities. Most visitors stop in Accompong, a small community in St. Elizabeth Parish where you can stroll through town, take in a couple historic structures, and learn more about the Maroons—considered Jamaica's greatest herbalists.

❺ Crystal Springs. About 18 mi west of Port Antonio on a former sugarcane plantation, Crystal Springs has more than 15,000 orchid blooms. The hummingbirds that dart among the blossoms here will land on your outstretched hand. Hiking and camping are options here; to camp, be sure to call the Jamaican Tourist Board (☞ Visitor Information *in* Jamaica A to Z, *below*) to arrange a site. ✉ Buff Bay, ☎ 876/993–2609 or 876/996–1400. ☞ J$100. ☉ Daily 9–5.

❹ **Firefly.** About 20 mi east of Ocho Rios in Port Maria, Firefly was once Sir Noël Coward's vacation home and is now maintained by the Jamaican National Heritage Trust. Although the setting is Eden-like, the house is surprisingly spartan, considering that he often entertained jet-setters and royalty. He wrote *High Spirits, Quadrille,* and other plays here, and his simple grave is on the grounds next to a small stage where his works are occasionally performed. Recordings of Coward singing about mad dogs and Englishmen echo over the lawns. Tours include time in the photo gallery and a walk through the house and grounds, the viewing of a video on Coward, and a drink in the gift shop. ✉ *Port Maria,* ☎ *876/997–7201.* 💷 *$10.* 🕐 *Daily 8:30–5:30.*

❿ **Kingston.** The reaction of most newcomers to the capital is far from love at first sight. Yet the islanders themselves can't seem to let the city go. Everybody talks about it, about their homes or relatives there, about their childhood memories. Indeed, Kingston seems to reflect more of the true Jamaica—a wonderful cultural mix—than do the sunny havens of the north coast. As one Jamaican put it, "You don't really know Jamaica until you know Kingston." Parts of the city may be dirty, crowded, and raucous, yet it's still where international and local movers and shakers come to move and shake, where the arts flourish, and where the shopping is superb. It's also home to the University of the West Indies, which has departments devoted to Caribbean art and literature as well as to science.

Sprawling Kingston spills over into communities in every direction. To the west, coming in from Spanish Town, lie some of the city's worst slums in the neighborhoods of Six Miles and Riverton City. South along the waterfront, Spanish Town Road skirts through the downtown, a high-crime district that many Kingstonians avoid. In the heart of downtown, the pace is more peaceful, with a lovely waterfront walk and parks on Ocean Boulevard, near the world-class Jamaica Convention Centre, the home of the UN body that creates all laws for the world's seas. From the waterfront, you can look across Kingston Harbour to the Palisadoes Peninsula. This narrow strip is home to Norman Manley International Airport and, farther west, Port Royal, the island's former capital, which, was destroyed by an earthquake. (A few words of caution: Downtown Kingston is considered unsafe, particularly at night, when even true Kingstonians beat a quick path out.)

New Kingston, north of downtown is bordered by Old Hope Road on the east and Half Way Tree Road (which changes to Constant Spring Road) on the west. The area is sliced by Hope Road, a major thoroughfare that connects this region with the University of the West Indies, about 15 minutes east of New Kingston. You may feel the most comfortable in New Kingston, which glistens with hotels, office towers, apartments, and boutiques. But don't let your trip to the capital end here, though; away from the high-rises of the new city, Kingston's colonial past is very much alive.

North of New Kingston, the city gives way to steep hills and magnificent homes. East of here, the views are even grander as the road winds into the Blue Mountains. Hope Road, just after the University of the West Indies, becomes Gordon Town Road and starts twisting up through the mountains—it's a route that leaves no room for error.

Devon House, built in 1881 and bought and restored by the government in the 1960s, is filled with period furnishings, such as Venetian crystal chandeliers, and period reproductions. You can see the inside of the two-story mansion (built with a South American gold miner's fortune) only on a guided tour. On the grounds you'll find some of the best crafts shops on the island (☞ also Shopping, *above*) as well as one of the few mahogany trees to have survived Kingston's ambitious, but not always careful, development. ⊠ *26 Hope Rd.,* ☎ *876/929–7029.* ▣ *J$110 for house tour.* ☉ *Devon House Tues.–Sat. 9:30–5, shops Mon.–Sat. 10–6.*

The **Institute of Jamaica,** near the waterfront, is a natural history museum and library that traces the island's history from the Arawaks through to current events. The charts and almanacs here are often fascinating; the famed Shark Papers, for example, contain evidence of wrongdoing by a sea captain. (In an attempt to destroy this evidence, the guilty captain tossed it overboard his ship, but it was later recovered from the belly of a shark.) ⊠ *12 East St.,* ☎ *876/922–0620.* ▣ *Museum $2, library free.* ☉ *Mon.–Thurs. 9–5, Fri. 9–4.*

The artists represented at the **National Gallery** may not be household names in other nations, yet their paintings reveal a sensitivity that transcends academic training. You'll find works by such intuitive Jamaican masters as John Dunkley, David Miller Sr., and David Miller Jr. Among other highlights from the 1920s through the 1980s are works by intuitive artist Kapo. Reggae fans should look for Christopher Gonzalez's controversial statue of Bob Marley. ⊠ *12 Ocean Blvd. (Kingston Mall, near the waterfront),* ☎ *876/922–1561.* ▣ *J$40.* ☉ *Weekdays 11–4:30.*

At the height of his career, Bob Marley built a recording studio. Today this structure—which is painted in Rastafarian red, yellow, and green—houses the **Bob Marley Museum.** The guided tour takes you through the medicinal herb garden, his bedroom, and other rooms wallpapered with magazine and newspaper articles that chronicle his rise to stardom. The tour includes a 20-minute biographical film on him; there's also a reference library if you want to learn more. Certainly there's much here that will help you to understand Marley, reggae, and Jamaica itself. The Ethiopian flag is a reminder that Rastas consider the late Ethiopian emperor Haile Selassie, a descendant of King Solomon and the Queen of Sheba, to be the Messiah. A striking mural by Jah Bobby, *The Journey of Superstar Bob Marley,* depicts the hero's life from its beginnings in a womb shaped like a coconut to enshrinement in the hearts of the Jamaican people. ⊠ *56 Hope Rd.,* ☎ *876/927–9152.* ▣ *J$350.* ☉ *Mon.–Tues. and Thurs.–Fri. 9–5, Wed. and Sat. 12:30–6.*

Although no longer lovingly cared for, the **Royal Botanical Gardens at Hope** is a nice place to picnic or while away an afternoon. Donated to Jamaica by the Hope family following the abolition of slavery, the garden consists of 50 acres filled with tropical trees, plants, and flowers; most are clearly labeled. Free concerts are given here on the first Sunday of each month. ⊠ *Off Hope Rd.,* ☎ *876/927–1085.* ▣ *J$20.* ☉ *Weekdays 10–5, weekends 10–5:30.*

The **Rockfort Mineral Baths** are named for the stone fort that the British built above Kingston Harbour in 1694 and for the natural mineral spring that emerged after the devastating earthquake in 1907. Today, you can join the Kingstonians who come here to cool off in the public swimming pool that's filled with invigorating spring water or to unwind tense muscles in a private whirlpool tub. You can also visit the juice bar or the cafeteria before staking out a people-watching spot on the landscaped grounds. Baths must be booked in advance. ⊠ *On A–1, just east of town,* ☎ *876/938–5055.* ▣ *Pool J$70, private baths start at J$450.* ☉ *Weekdays 6:30–6, weekends 8–6.*

❸ **Mandeville.** At 2,000 ft above sea level, Mandeville is considerably cooler than the coastal areas 25 mi to the south. Its vegetation is also more lush, thanks to the mists that drift through the mountains. But climate and flora are not all that separates it from the steamy coast: Mandeville seems a hilly tribute to all that is genteel and admirable in the British character. The people here live their lives in tidy cottages with gardens around a village green; there's even a Georgian courthouse and a parish church. The entire scene could be set down in Devonshire, were it not for the occasional poinciana blossom or citrus grove.

The **Manchester Club** (☎ 876/962–2403) has tennis courts and a well-manicured 9-hole golf course, the first golf course in the Caribbean. Mrs. Stephenson conducts horticultural tours of her **gardens** (☎ 876/962–2328), which are filled with orchids and fruit trees.At the **Bird Sanctuary at Marshall's Penn Great House** (☎ 876/963–8569) you may spot some of the more than 25 species of birds indigenous to Jamaica. Tours (by appointment only) are led by owner Robert Sutton, one of the island's leading ornithologists. Other sights worth visiting are **Lover's Leap,** where legend has it that two slave lovers chose to jump off the 1,700-ft-high cliff rather than be recaptured by their owner, and the **High Mountain Coffee Plantation** (☎ 876/963–4211) in nearby Williamsfield, where free tours (by appointment only) show how coffee beans are turned into one of America's favorite morning drinks.

② **Martha Brae River.** The gentle waterway takes its name from an Arawak Indian who killed herself because she refused to reveal the whereabouts of a local gold mine to the Spanish. According to legend, she agreed to take them there and, on reaching the river, used magic to change its course, drowning herself and the greedy Spaniards. Her *duppy* (ghost) is said to guard the mine's entrance. Rafting on this river is a very popular activity, and **Martha Brae River Rafting** (☞ Guided Tours *in* Jamaica A to Z, *below*) arranges trips down river. The rafting company ticket office, gift shops, a bar-restaurant, and a swimming pool are at the top of the river.

① **Montego Bay.** Today many explorations of MoBay are conducted from a reclining chair—frothy drink in hand—on Doctor's Cave Beach. Believe it or not, the area had a history before all the resorts went up. If you can pull yourself away from the water's edge and brush the sand off your toes, you'll find some very interesting colonial sights.

The outstanding tour of **Barnett Estates** is led by a charming guide in period costume who recites period poetry and sings period songs. The Kerr-Jarrett family has held the land here for 11 generations, and they still grow coconut, mango, and sugarcane on 3,000 acres; you'll get samples during the optional plantation tour by horseback (one hour), which follows the tour of the great house. ✉ *Granville Main Rd.,* ☎ *876/952–2382,* ℻ *876/952–6342.* 🎟 *Great house tour $10, great house and plantation tour $45.* ☉ *Great house 9:30 AM–10 PM; tours daily at 10 and 2.*

In the 1700s **Rose Hall** may well have been the greatest of great houses in the West Indies. Today it's popular less for its architecture than for the legend surrounding its second mistress: Annie Palmer was credited with murdering three husbands and a *busha* (plantation overseer) who was her lover. The story is told in a novel that's sold everywhere in Jamaica: *The White Witch of Rose Hall.* There's a pub on-site. ✉ *East of Montego Bay, across highway from Rose Hall resorts,* ☎ *876/953–2323.* 🎟 *$15.* ☉ *Daily 9–6.*

Greenwood Great House has no spooky legend to titillate you, but it's much better than Rose Hall at evoking the atmosphere of life on a sugar plantation. The Barrett family, from which the English poet Elizabeth

Barrett Browning descended, once owned all the land from Rose Hall to Falmouth and built this and several other great houses on it. (The poet's father, Edward Moulton Barrett, "the Tyrant of Wimpole Street," was born at Cinnamon Hill, currently the estate of country singer Johnny Cash.) Highlights of Greenwood include oil paintings of the Barretts, china made for the family by Wedgwood, a library filled with rare books printed as early as 1697, fine antique furniture, and a collection of exotic musical instruments. There's a pub on-site as well. ✉ *15 mi east of Montego Bay,* ☎ *876/953–1077.* 🎟 *$10.* ⊙ *Daily 9–6.*

⑮ **Negril.** In the 18th century, this was where English ships assembled in convoys for dangerous ocean crossings. The infamous pirate Calico Jack and his crew were captured right here, while they guzzled rum. All but two of them were hanged on the spot; Mary Read and Anne Bonney were pregnant at the time, so their executions were delayed.

On the winding coast road 55 mi southwest of MoBay, Negril was once Jamaica's best-kept secret. Recently, however, it has begun to shed some of its bohemian, ramshackle atmosphere for the attractions and activities traditionally associated with Montego Bay. Applauding the sunset from Rick's Cafe may still be a highlight in Negril, yet, increasingly, the hours before and after are filled with conventional recreation. One thing that hasn't changed around this west coast center (whose only true claim to fame is a 7-mi beach) is the casual approach to life. As you wander from lunch in the sun to shopping in the sun to sports in the sun, you'll find that swimsuits are common attire. Want to dress for a special meal? Slip a caftan over your swimsuit.

Negril stretches along the coast south from the horseshoe-shape **Bloody Bay** (named during the period when it was a whale-processing center) along the calm waters of **Long Bay** to the Lighthouse (☞ *below*) section and the landmark **Rick's Cafe** (☞ Dining, *above*). Sunset at Rick's is a Negril tradition. Divers spiral downward off 50-ft-high cliffs into the deep green depths as the sun turns into a ball of fire and sets the clouds ablaze with color.

Even nonguests can romp at **Hedonism II** (☞ Lodging, *above*) for a day. The resort beach is divided into a "prude" and "nude" side but a quick look around the property reveals where most guests pull their chaise longue. Volleyball, body-painting contests, and shuffleboard—all done in the nude—keep daytime hours lively; at night most action occurs in the high-tech disco or in the nude hot tub. Your day (10:30–5) pass ($50) gets you a taste of the spirit as well as the food and drink—and participation in water sports, tennis, squash, and other activities. Night passes ($35) cover dinner, drinks, and entrance to the disco. Day or night, reservations are a must.

The **Anancy Family Fun & Nature Park** (✉ Norman Manley Blvd., ☎ 876/957–5100) is named after a mischievous spider character in Jamaican folktales. The 3-acre site has an 18-hole miniature golf course, go-cart rides, a minitrain, a fishing pond, a nature trail, and three small museums—one dedicated to crafts, another to conservation, and the third to heritage.

Around sunset **Norman Manley Boulevard,** which intersects with **West End Road,** Negril's main (and only) thoroughfare, comes to life with bustling bistros and ear-splitting discos. West End Road leads to the town's only building of historical significance, the **Lighthouse.** You can stop by the adjacent caretaker's cottage and, for the price of a tip, climb the spiral steps to the best view in town.

3 **Ocho Rios.** Although Ocho Rios is not near eight rivers as its name implies, it does have a seemingly endless series of cascades that sparkle from limestone rocks along the coast. (The name Ocho Rios came about because the English misunderstood the Spanish name "Las Chorreras" or "the waterfalls.")

For as long as anyone can remember, Ocho Rios has been the Jamaicans' favorite escape from the heat of Kingston. Indeed, they can fill the place by themselves, especially on a busy market day, when cars and buses from the countryside clog the coastal road that links Port Antonio with Montego Bay. Add a tour bus or three and the entire passenger list from a cruise ship, and you may find yourself mired in a major traffic jam.

Yet a visit to Ocho Rios is worthwhile, if only to enjoy its two chief attractions—Dunn's River Falls and Prospect Plantation. A few steps from the main road in Ocho Rios are some of the most charming inns and oceanfront restaurants in the Caribbean. Lying on the sand of what seems to be your very own cove or swinging gently in a hammock while sipping a tropical drink, you'll soon forget the traffic that's just a stroll away.

Dunn's River Falls is an eye-catching sight: 600 ft of cold, clear mountain water splashing over a series of stone steps to the warm Caribbean. The best way to enjoy the falls is to climb the slippery steps: don a swimsuit, take the hand of the person ahead of you, and trust that the chain of hands and bodies leads to an experienced guide. The leaders of the climbs are personable fellows who reel off bits of local lore while telling you where to step. ⊠ *Off A–1, between St. Ann's and Ocho Rios,* ☎ *876/974–2857.* ⊡ *$6.* ⊙ *Daily 8:30–4.*

To learn about Jamaica's former agricultural lifestyle, a trip to **Prospect Plantation** is a must. But it's not just a place for history lovers or farming aficionados; everyone seems to enjoy the views over the White River Gorge and the tour by jitney (a canopied open-air cart pulled by a tractor). The grounds are full of exotic fruits and tropical trees, some planted over the years by such celebrities as Winston Churchill and Charlie Chaplin. You can also go horseback riding on the plantation's 900 acres or play miniature golf, grab a drink in the bar, or buy souvenirs in the gift shop. If you want more time to really explore, you can rent one of the on-site villas. ⊠ *Hwy. A–1, just west of downtown Ocho Rios,* ☎ *876/994–1058.* ⊡ *$12.* ⊙ *Daily 8–5. Tours Mon.–Sat. at 10:30, 2, and 3:30; Sun. at 11, 1:30, and 3:30.*

The original "defenders" stationed at the **Old Fort,** which was built in 1777, spent much of their time sacking and plundering as far afield as St. Augustine, Florida, and sharing their bounty with the local plantation owners who financed their missions. Fifteen miles west is **Discovery Bay,** site of Columbus's landing, with a small museum of artifacts and Jamaican memorabilia.

Jamaica's national motto is "Out of Many, One People," and at the **Coyaba River Garden and Museum** you can see exhibits on the many cultural influences that have contributed to the creation of the one. The museum covers the island's history from the time of the Arawak Indians up to the modern day. A guided 45-minute tour through the lush 3-acre garden introduces you to the flora and fauna of the island. The complex includes a crafts and gift shop and a snack bar. ⊠ *Shaw Park Estate, Shaw Park Ridge Rd., 1½ mi south of Ocho Rios,* ☎ *876/974–6235.* ⊡ *$4.50.* ⊙ *Daily 8–5.*

Other excursions of note include Runaway Bay's **Green Grotto Caves** (and the boat ride on an underground lake); a ramble through the **Shaw**

Park Botanical Gardens; a visit to **Sun Valley**, a working plantation with banana, coconut, and citrus trees; and a drive through **Fern Gully**, a natural canopy of vegetation filtered by sunlight (Jamaica has the world's largest number of fern species, more than 570).

❼ **Port Antonio.** Early in the century the first tourists who arrived on the northeast coast were drawn by the exoticism of the island's banana trade and seeking a respite from the New York winters. The original posters of the shipping lines make Port Antonio appear as foreign as the moon, yet in time it became the tropical darling of a fast-moving crowd and counted J. P. Morgan, Rudyard Kipling, William Randolph Hearst, Clara Bow, Bette Davis, and Ginger Rogers among its admirers. Its most passionate devotee was the actor Errol Flynn, whose spirit still seems to haunt the docks, devouring raw dolphinfish and swigging gin at 10 AM. Although the action has moved elsewhere, the area can still weave a spell. Robin Moore wrote *The French Connection* here, and Broadway's tall and talented Tommy Tune found inspiration for the musical *Nine* while being pampered at Trident.

Port Antonio has also long been a center for some of the Caribbean's finest deep-sea fishing. Dolphins (the delectable fish, not the lovable mammal) are the likely catch here, along with tuna, kingfish, and wahoo. In October the weeklong Blue Marlin Tournament attracts anglers from around the world. By the time everyone has had their fill of beer, it's the fish stories—rather than the fish—that carry the day.

The town's best-known landmark is **Folly**, a Roman-style villa in ruins on the eastern edge of East Harbor. The creation of a Connecticut millionaire in 1905, the manse was made almost entirely of concrete. Unfortunately, the cement was mixed with seawater, and it began to crumble as it dried. According to local lore, the millionaire's bride took one look at her shattered dream, burst into tears, and fled forever. Little more than the marble floor remains today. (Note that Folly becomes something of a ganja—marijuana—hangout after sundown and should be avoided then.)

A good way to spend a day in Port Antonio is swimming in the deep azure water of the **Blue Lagoon**. Although there's not much beach to speak of, you will find a water sports center, changing rooms, and a soothing mineral pool. Yummy, inexpensive, Jamaican fare is served at a charming waterside terrace restaurant; it's open daily for lunch and dinner and has live jazz music on Saturday night. ⊠ *1 mi east of San San Beach,* ☎ *876/993–8491.*

Queen Street, in the residential Titchfield area, a couple miles north of downtown Port Antonio, has several fine examples of Georgian architecture. **DeMontevin Lodge** (⊠ 21 Fort George St., on Titchfield Hill, ☎ 876/993–2604), owned by the Mullings family (the late Gladys Mullings was Errol Flynn's cook, and you can still get great food here), and structures on the nearby **Musgrave Street** (the crafts market is here) are in a traditional seaside style that's reminiscent of architecture found in New England.

A short drive east from Port Antonio puts you at **Boston Bay**, which is popular with swimmers and has been enshrined by lovers of jerk pork. The spicy barbecue was originated by the Arawaks and perfected by runaway slaves called the Maroons. Eating almost nothing but wild hog preserved over smoking coals enabled them to survive years of fierce guerrilla warfare with the English.

Some 6 mi northeast of Port Antonio in the village of Nonsuch are the **Athenry Gardens**, a 3-acre tropical wonderland, and the **Nonsuch**

Caves, whose underground beauty has been made accessible by concrete walkways, railed stairways, and careful lighting. ✉ *Athenry/Nonsuch, first right after Dragon Bay east of Port Antonio,* ☎ *876/ 993–3740.* 🎫 *$5.* ⊙ *Daily 10–4:30.*

⓫ **Port Royal.** Just south of Kingston, Port Royal was called "the wickedest city in the world"—before an earthquake tumbled it into the sea in 1692. The spirits of Henry Morgan and other buccaneers add a great deal of energy to what remains. The proudest possession of St. Peter's Church, rebuilt in 1726 to replace Christ's Church, is a silver communion set said to have been donated by Morgan himself (who probably obtained it during a raid on Panama).

Port Royal is slated for a massive redevelopment project that will renovate existing historical sites and introduce new museums, shops, restaurants, and perhaps even a cruise-ship pier. However, funding for these ambitious plans was not yet in place at press time.

A ferry from the square in downtown Kingston goes to Port Royal at least twice a day, and the town is small enough to see on foot. If you drive out to Port Royal from Kingston, you'll pass several other sights, including remains of old forts virtually covered over by vegetation, an old naval cemetery (which has some intriguing headstones), and a monument commemorating Jamaica's first coconut tree, planted in 1863 (there's no tree there now, just plenty of cactus and scrub brush).

You can no longer down rum in Port Royal's legendary 40 taverns (well, two small pubs still remain in operation), but you can explore the impressive remains of **Ft. Charles**, once the area's major garrison. Built in 1662, this is the oldest surviving monument of the British occupation of Jamaica. On the grounds is a maritime museum and the old artillery storehouse, Giddy House, that gained its name after being tilted by the earthquake of 1907 (locals say its slant makes you giddy). In the graveyard of **St. Peter Church** is the tombstone of Lewis Galdy, who was swallowed up in the 1692 quake, spewed into the sea, rescued, and lived another two decades in "Great Reputation." Nearby is the tomb of three small children, victims of the earthquake, whose bodies were recovered by archaeologists from Texas A&M University. ☎ *876/967–8059 (church).* 🎫 *$4.* ⊙ *Daily 9–5.*

❽ **Rio Grande.** The Rio Grande (yes, Jamaica has a Rio Grande, too) is a granddaddy of river-rafting attractions: an 8-mi-long, swift, green waterway from Berrydale to Rafter's Rest (it flows into the Caribbean at St. Margaret's Bay). The trip of about three hours is made on bamboo rafts pushed along by a raftsman who is likely to be a character. You can pack a picnic lunch and eat it on the raft or along the riverbank; wherever you lunch, a vendor of Red Stripe beer will appear at your elbow. A restaurant, bar, and souvenir shops are at Rafter's Rest. The trip costs about $40 per two-person raft (☞ Guided Tours *in* Jamaica A to Z, *below*).

❻ **Somerset Falls.** At this sun-dappled spot crawling with flowering vines, you can climb the 400-ft falls with some assistance from a concrete staircase. A brief raft ride takes you part of the way. ✉ *North Coast Hwy.* 🎫 *J$35.* ⊙ *Daily 10–5.*

⓬ **Spanish Town.** Twelve miles west of Kingston on A–1, Spanish Town was the island's capital under Spanish rule. The town has the tiered Georgian **Antique Square**, the **Jamaican People's Museum of Crafts and Technology** (in the Old King's House stables), and **St. James**, the oldest cathedral in the Western Hemisphere. Spanish Town's original name was Santiago de la Vega, which the English corrupted to St. Jago de la Vega, meaning St. James of the Plains. Contact the Institute of Jamaica (☎ 876/922–0620) for further information on this heritage town.

Jamaica A to Z

Arriving and Departing

BY AIRPLANE

Donald Sangster International Airport (☎ 876/952–3124), in Montego Bay, is the most efficient point of entry for visitors destined for Montego Bay, Ocho Rios, Runaway Bay, and Negril. **Norman Manley International Airport** (☎ 876/924–8235), in Kingston, is best for visitors to the capital or Port Antonio.

Air Canada (☎ 876/952–5160 in Montego Bay, 876/942–8211 in Kingston) offers daily service from Toronto, Halifax, Winnipeg, and Montréal in conjunction with Air Jamaica. **Air Jamaica** (☎ 876/952–4100 in Montego Bay, 876/922–4661 in Kingston) provides the most frequent service from U.S. cities, including Atlanta, Baltimore, Chicago, Fort Lauderdale, Los Angeles, Miami, New York, Orlando, Philadelphia, and San Francisco. Flights are also available from London. **American Airlines** (☎ 876/952–5950 in Montego Bay, 876/924–8305 in Kingston) flies nonstop daily from New York, Miami, and San Juan, Puerto Rico. **British Airways** (☎ 876/952–3771 in Montego Bay, 876/929–9020 in Kingston) connects the island with London. **Continental** (☎ 876/952–4495) flies in four times a week from Newark. Panamanian carrier **Copa** (☎ 876/926–1762) offers service between Miami and Kingston. **Cubana** (☎ 876/978–3410) flies in from Havana. **Northwest Airlines** (☎ 876/952–9740) has daily direct service to Montego Bay from Minneapolis and Tampa. **US Airways** (☎ 876/929–9020) flies in from Baltimore and Charlotte.

Electricity

Like the electrical current in North America, the current in Jamaica is 110 volts/50 cycles with flat, two-prong American outlets. Some hotels provide 220-volt plugs as well as special shaver outlets.

Emergencies

Air rescue and police: ☎ 119. **Ambulance and fire department:** ☎ 110. **Hospitals:** Cornwall Regional Hospital (✉ Mt. Salem, Montego Bay, ☎ 876/952–5100), **Port Antonio General Hospital** (✉ Naylor's Hill, Port Antonio, ☎ 876/993–2646), **St. Ann's Bay Hospital** (✉ St. Ann's Bay, ☎ 876/972–0150), which has a hyperbaric chamber for scuba diving emergencies, and **University Hospital** (✉ Mona, Kingston, ☎ 876/927–1620). **Pharmacies:** Great House Pharmacy (✉ Brown's Plaza, Ocho Rios, ☎ 876/974–2352), Le Méridien Jamaica Pegasus Hotel (✉ 81 Knutsford Blvd., Kingston, ☎ 876/926–3690), and McKenzie's Drug Store (✉ 16 Strand St., Montego Bay, ☎ 876/952–2467).

Festivals and Seasonal Events

The biggest festival is **Carnival,** an event filled with lots of music and dancing in the streets. It's held in Kingston, Ocho Rios, and Montego Bay every April and in Negril every May. Music lovers also fill the island for the August **Reggae Sunsplash International Music Festival,** which is getting hotter every year, as the best, brightest, and newest of the reggae stars gather to perform in open-air concerts in Montego Bay. Anglers come to Port Antonio to compete in the annual **Blue Marlin Tournament,** which is usually held in October.

Getting Around

AIRPLANES

Air Jamaica Express (☎ 876/952–5401 in Montego Bay, 876/923–8680 in Kingston), a new subsidiary of Air Jamaica, provides shuttle services on the island. Be sure to reconfirm your departing flight a full 72 hours in advance. Shuttle service between Montego Bay, Ocho Rios, and Negril is now available from **Air SuperClub** (☎ 876/940–7746). **Tropical Airlines** (☎ 876/968–2473 in Kingston, 876/979–3565 in Montego Bay) offers service between Kingston and Montego Bay as well as Cuba.

BICYCLES, MOPEDS, AND MOTORCYCLES

The front desks of most major hotels can arrange the rental of bicycles, mopeds, and motorcycles. Daily rates run from about $45 for a moped to $70 for a Honda 550. Deposits of $100–$300 or more are required. However, we highly recommend that you *not* rent a moped or motorcycle. The strangeness of driving on the left, the less-than-cautious driving style that prevails on the island, the abundance of potholes, and the prevalence of vendors who will approach you at every traffic light are just a few reasons to skip cycles.

BUSES

Buses are the mode of transportation Jamaicans use most, and consequently they're *extremely* crowded and slow. They're also not air-conditioned and rather uncomfortable. Yet the service is fairly frequent between Kingston and Montego Bay and between other significant destinations. Schedule or route information is available at bus stops or from the bus driver.

CAR RENTALS

Traffic keeps to the left in Jamaica. Driving in Jamaica is a chore and can be extremely frustrating. You must constantly be on guard—for enormous potholes, people and animals darting out in the street, and aggressive drivers. Although Jamaica has dozens of car-rental companies (you'll find branches at the airports and the resorts among other places), rentals can be difficult to arrange once you've arrived. Make reservations and send a deposit before your trip. (Cars are scarce, and without either a confirmation number or a receipt, you may have to walk.) You must be at least 21 years old to rent a car (at least 25 years old at several agencies), have a valid driver's license (from any country), and have a valid credit card. You may be required to post a security of several hundred dollars before taking possession of your car; ask about it when you make the reservation. Rates average $65–$120 a day. Gas stations are open daily but accept cash only. Gas costs roughly $1–$1.10 a gallon.

Avis (☎ 800/331–1212 or 876/952–4543 in Montego Bay, 876/924–8013 in Kingston), **Budget** (☎ 876/952–3838 in Montego Bay, 876/924–8762 in Kingston), **Hertz** (☎ 800/654–3131 or 876/979–0438 in Montego Bay), **Island Car Rentals** (☎ 876/952–5771 in Montego Bay, 876/926–5991 in Kingston), **Jamaica Car Rental** (☎ 876/952–5586 in Montego Bay, 876/974–2505 in Ocho Rios), or **United Car Rentals** (☎ 876/952–3077).

TAXIS

Some but not all of Jamaica's taxis are metered. If you accept a driver's offer of his services as a tour guide, be sure to agree on a price before the vehicle is put into gear. All licensed taxis display red Public Passenger Vehicle (PPV) plates. Cabs can be summoned by telephone or flagged down on the street. Rates are per car, not per passenger, and 25% is added to the metered rate between midnight and 5 AM. Licensed minivans are also available and bear the red PPV plates. JUTA is the largest taxi franchise and has offices in all resort areas.

Guided Tours

Half-day tours are offered by a variety of operators in the important areas of Jamaica. The best great-house tours include Rose Hall, Greenwood, and Devon House. Plantations to tour are Prospect, Barnett Estates, and Sun Valley. The Appleton Estate Tour uses a bus to visit villages, plantations, and a rum distillery. The increasingly popular waterside folklore feasts are offered on the Dunn's, Great, and White rivers. The significant city tours are in Kingston, Montego Bay, and Ocho Rios. Quality tour operators include **Caribic Tours** (⊠ 1310 Providence Dr., MoBay, ☎ 876/953–9895), **CS Tours** (⊠ 66 Claude Clarke Ave., MoBay, ☎ 876/952–6260), **Glamour Tours** (⊠ Montego Freeport, MoBay, ☎ 876/979–8415), **Tourwise** (⊠ 103 Main St., Ocho Rios, ☎ 876/974–2323), and **SunHoliday Tours** (⊠ 57 S. James St. or Sangster International Airport, MoBay, ☎ 876/952–5629).

BOAT

An Evening on the Great River (⊠ 4 Sewell Ave., ☎ 876/952–5047 or 876/952–5097) includes a boat ride up the torch-lit river, a full Jamaican dinner, an open bar, a folklore show, and dancing to a reggae band. It costs around $60 per person with hotel pickup and return, less if you arrive via your own transport. Tours are offered Sunday–Thursday. **Calico Sailing** (⊠ North Coast Highway, ☎ 876/952–5860) offers snorkeling trips and sunset cruises on the waters of Montego Bay; costs are $35 and $25, respectively. **Martha Brae River Rafting** (⊠ Claude Clarke Ave., ☎ 876/952–0889) leads trips down the Martha Brae River, about 25 mi from most hotels in Montego Bay. The cost is just under $40 per raft (two per raft) for the 1½-hour river run. **Mountain Valley Rafting** (⊠ Lethe, ☎ 876/952–0527 or 876/952–6388) runs trips down the River Lethe, approximately 12 mi (about 50 minutes) southwest of Montego Bay. The hour-long trip is about $45 per raft (two per raft) and takes you through unspoiled hillside country. Bookings can also be made through hotel tour desks.

Rio Grande Attractions Ltd. (⊠ St. Margaret's Bay, ☎ 876/993–2778) guides raft trips down the Rio Grande (☞ Exploring, *above*). The cost is $40 per raft. **South Coast Safaris Ltd.** (⊠ 1 Crane Rd., Black River, ☎ 876/965–2513) has guided boat excursions up the Black River for some 10 mi (round-trip), into the mangroves and marshlands to see the alligators, birds, and plant life, aboard the 25-passenger *Safari Queen* and 25-passenger *Safari Princess*. The cost is around $15. **Undersea Tours MoBay** (⊠ Casa Blanca Hotel, Gloucester Ave., ☎ 876/922–1287) offers you a good look at MoBay's marine sanctuary without getting wet, by booking passage (around $40) on a semisubmersible craft.

HELICOPTER

Helitours Jamaica Ltd. (⊠ 1 mi west of Ocho Rios, North Coast Hwy., ☎ 876/974–2265 or 876/974–1108), in Ocho Rios, offers helicopter tours of Jamaica, ranging from 20 minutes to an hour at prices that vary accordingly ($65–$225).

SPECIAL-INTEREST

Blue Mountain Tours (⊠ Shop 15, Santa Maria Plaza, Ocho Rios, ☎ 876/974–7705, ℻ 876/974–0635) offers a daylong downhill bicycle tour of the mountains, which coasts 18 mi down from 5,060 ft through coffee plantations and rain forests. The cost is about $80 and includes lunch. **Countrystyle** (⊠ 62 Ward Ave., Mandeville, ☎ 876/962–3725 or 800/JAMAICA) offers unique, personalized tours of island communities. You're linked with community residents based on your interests; there are tours that include anything from bird-watching in Mandeville to nightlife in Kingston. **Maroon Attraction Tours Co.** (⊠ North Coast Hwy., ☎ 876/952–4546) leads full-day tours from Montego Bay to Maroon headquarters at Accompong, giving you a glimpse of the society of Maroons, descendants of fugitive slaves, who live in Cockpit Country. The cost is under $50 per person. **Touring Society of**

Jamaica (☎ 876/975–7158 in Ocho Rios, 876/967–1792 in Kingston), operated by American Lynda Lee Burke, offers several eco-tours, from birding in the Blue Mountains to exploring the natural history of Cockpit Country.

Language

The official language of Jamaica is English. Islanders usually speak a patois among themselves, a lyrical mixture of English, Spanish, and various African languages. Some examples of patois are *me diyah* (I'm here; pronounced "mee de-ya"), *nyam* (eat; pronounced "yam"), and, if someone asks how your vacation is going, just say "*irie*" (pronounced eye-ree), which means "great."

As you travel the island, you'll see Rastafarians, identified by their flowing dreadlocks (although some prefer to wear their hair beneath knitted mushroom caps, especially in work situations). Rastas smoke marijuana as part of their religious rites, do not eat salt or pork (many are vegetarians), and often sell crafts. Always ask for permission before taking a photograph; if you purchase an item from a vendor (no matter how small), many will allow a photo if asked politely.

Money Matters

CURRENCY

The official currency is the Jamaican dollar. At press time the exchange rate was about J\$35 to US\$1. U.S. money (currency only, no coins) is accepted at most establishments, although you'll often be given change in Jamaican money. Currency can be exchanged at airport bank counters, exchange bureaus, or commercial banks. ATM machines do not accept American bank cards, although cash advances can be made using credit cards. Note that prices quoted throughout this chapter are in U.S. dollars unless otherwise noted.

SERVICE CHARGES, TAXES, AND TIPPING

Most hotels and restaurants add a 10% service charge to your bill. Hotels collect a 10% government consumption tax on room occupancy. The departure tax is J\$750. When a service charge isn't included, a 10% to 20% tip is appreciated. Tips of 10% to 20% are customary for taxi drivers as well.

Opening and Closing Times

Normal business hours for **stores** are weekdays 8:30–4:30, Saturday 8–1. **Banks** are generally open Monday–Thursday 9–2, Friday 9–4. **Post offices** are open weekdays 9–5.

HOLIDAYS

New Year's Day, Ash Wednesday (Feb. 17), Good Friday (Apr. 2), Easter Monday (Apr. 5), Labor Day (May 23), Independence Day (first Mon. in Aug.), National Heroes Day (Oct. 21), Christmas, and Boxing Day (Dec. 26).

Passports

U.S. and Canadian citizens must have a passport (not expired beyond one year). Or, to prove citizenship, bring an original birth certificate (with a raised seal) or a naturalization certificate along with a government-issued photo ID (all documents must bear the same name). British visitors need passports. Each visitor must possess a return or ongoing ticket. Declaration forms are distributed in flight to keep customs formalities to a minimum.

Precautions

Do not let the beauty of Jamaica cause you to relax the caution and good sense you would use in any unfamiliar place. Never leave valuables in your room; use the safe-deposit boxes that most hotels make available. Carry your funds in traveler's checks and keep a record of the check numbers in a secure place. Never leave a rental car unlocked, and never leave valuables in a locked car. Finally, resist the call of the wild when it presents itself as a scruffy-looking local who offers to show you the "real" Jamaica. Jamaica on the beaten path is wonderful enough; don't take chances by wandering far from it. And ignore efforts, however persistent, to sell you ganja (marijuana). Independent travelers, especially those renting cars, need to take special precautions. Some travelers have been harassed by locals offering to "guard" cars and have experienced vandalism when requests for money were denied. Taxi travel, using the services of knowledgeable, certified taxi drivers, is highly recommended. Carry along insect repellent and a strong sunscreen to avoid natural hazards.

Telephones and Mail

To dial Jamaica from the US, just dial 1 + the area code 876 (recently changed from 809). Most hotels offer direct-dial telephone services; local businesses provide telegraph and fax services for a fee. Some U.S. telephone companies, such as MCI, will not permit credit card calls to be placed from Jamaica due to recent fraud cases. The best option is to purchase a phone card, which are sold in most stores across the island. While on the island, calls from town to town are long distance. Pay phones are available in most communities.

Postcards may be mailed anywhere in the world for 90¢ Jamaican; letters to the United States and Canada cost J$10; to Europe, J$12.50.

Visitor Information

Before you go, contact the **Jamaica Tourist Board** (⊠ 801 2nd Ave., 20th floor, New York, NY 10017, ☎ 212/856–9727 or 800/233–4582, www.jamaicatravel.com; ⊠ 500 N. Michigan Ave., Suite 1030, Chicago, IL 60611, ☎ 312/527–1296; ⊠ 1320 S. Dixie Hwy., Suite 1100, Coral Gables, FL 33146, ☎ 305/665–0557; ⊠ 3440 Wilshire Blvd., Suite 805, Los Angeles, CA 90010, ☎ 213/384–1123; ⊠ 1 Eglinton Ave. E, Suite 616, Toronto, Ontario M4P 3A1, ☎ 416/482–7850; ⊠ 1–2 Prince Consort Rd., London SW7 2BZ, ☎ 0171/224–0505).

In Jamaica, the main office of the **Jamaica Tourist Board** (JTB) is in Kingston (⊠ 2 St. Lucia Ave. (Box 360, Kingston 5), New Kingston, ☎ 876/929–9200). There are also JTB desks at both Montego Bay and Kingston airports and offices in Black River (⊠ Hendriks Bldg., 2 High St., ☎ 876/965–2074), Montego Bay (Cornwall Beach, ☎ 876/952–4425), Negril (Coral Seas Plaza, ☎ 876/957–4243), Ocho Rios (Ocean Village Shopping Centre, ☎ 876/974–2570), and Port Antonio (City Centre Plaza, ☎ 876/993–3051). While on island, Jamaica Tourist Board also offers a help line (☎ 888/995–9999).

If you'd like to delve into the heart of Jamaica rather than simply explore her sybaritic pleasures, the tourist board will arrange for you to spend time with a local host family through the **Meet the People** program. They'll try to match interests, vocations, ages, whatever, so you'll have common ground. There's no fee involved (other than for activities you and your hosts might select); this is the best way to come to know the warmth and companionship the island has to offer.

15 Martinique

Updated by
David H. Jones

On a hilltop at Leyritz Plantation, a brisk alizé rustles palm fronds. A vast banana plantation rolls out below and does more than suggest the Old World—it is the past. The Atlantic stretches beyond to the horizon. Reaching this vantage point requires travel up serpentine roads etched into Mont Pelée, an active volcano that earlier in this century erased St-Pierre, the former capital, leaving only one survivor: a prisoner locked in his underground cell. The breeze smells of earth and sea. From this singular spot, the New World—out there—is all but forgotten.

The Arawak Indians named Martinique Madinina (Island of Flowers). Exotic wild orchids, frangipani, anthurium, jade vines, flamingo flowers, and hundreds of vivid varieties of hibiscus still grow on the island. But, these days, the scent of flowers competes with those of Chanel No. 5 and espresso. Martinique is a tropical suburb of Paris: a rich, highly developed island with a six-lane highway, the biggest shopping malls, and some of the finest restaurants in the Caribbean.

Everything about Martinique, from the snappy new airport to the old plantation houses, has style. Even the women working at the rental-car desks look as if they're dressed for an evening at the opera. It's no surprise, then, that the island, along with Barbados, has one of the highest standards of living in the Caribbean. In their dealings with foreigners, Martinicans are courteous, polite, and self-assured—qualities anchored in the privileged position the island has enjoyed historically.

As Jamaica was the key to the British-ruled islands, so Martinique was the administrative, social, and cultural center of the French Antilles. Guadeloupe was an island of merchants and shopkeepers. Martinique was a rich, aristocratic island, famous for its beautiful women and gracious living, which gave birth to an empress and saw the full flowering of plantation-house society with its servants and soirées, wine cellars and snobbery.

This 425-square-mi island, the largest of the Windwards, has landscapes as varied as its culture and history. In the south, where most of the development and the best beaches are, there are rolling hills and sugarcane fields. In the north, look for lush, tropical vegetation; fields of bananas and pineapples; deep gorges; towering cliffs; and one of the Caribbean's most impressive volcanoes, Mont Pelée. Fort-de-France is the island's capital city as well as its cultural and commercial hub. Most of the other towns—such as Ste-Anne and Vauclin to the south and Carbet and Marigot to the north—are generally small resorts or fishing villages.

Britain and France squabbled over Martinique until 1815, when the island was ceded by treaty to Paris. Today, the French connection means excellent food and wine, grumpy waiters, superb roads, terrible pop music, high prices, and plenty of culture and arts (Martinique has one of the finest jazz festivals in the Caribbean, and in Patrick Chamoiseau it has a world-class novelist). You'll need some French to feel truly at home, though the locals are more forthcoming with English here than in other places in the French-speaking world. This island is not *like* France. It *is* France. Most everything shuts down at midday and reopens sometime after 2:30. Franglais is universal (*Les softs* is what you should look for if you want a soda), topless bathing is almost de rigueur, the driving is frenetic, and poodles are everywhere.

Lodging

Martinique's accommodations range from tiny inns called *relais Créoles* to splashy tourist resorts and luxurious plantation houses. The majority of hotels are clustered in Pointe du Bout and Anse-Mitan on Les Trois-Ilets peninsula across the bay from Fort-de-France, Le Diamant, and Ste-Anne. In recent years, the big resorts have worked at attracting a mass package-tour clientele. There are only four deluxe properties on the island; only one of them, Habitation Lagrange, would receive such a rating on any other island. Most hotels have the busy, slightly frenetic feel that the French seem to like. The major establishments usually include a large buffet breakfast of fresh fruit, croissants, baguettes, jam, and café au lait.

CATEGORY	COST*
$$$$	over $240
$$$	$150–$240
$$	$85–$150
$	under $85

All prices are for a standard double room, excluding $1.50-per-person, per-night, tax and 10% service charge.

Hotels
BASSE-POINTE

$$ ⊞ **Leyritz Plantation.** Sleeping on a former sugar plantation, in one of
★ the antiques-furnished rooms of the manor house, cottages, or renovated slave cabin is a novelty. The isolated Leyritz sits on 16 lush acres, with manicured lawns and stunning views of Mont Pelée. Nicest are the 10 cottage rooms, which have rough wood beams, mahogany four-poster beds, marble-top armoires, secretaries, and other antiques. The slightly larger former slave quarters have eaves, stone-and-stucco walls, more-contemporary furnishings, and madras linens. Ironically, it's the newer bungalows that are cramped and lacking individuality. Except for periodic invasions of cruise-ship passengers, it's very quiet here—

406

Exploring
Ajoupa-Bouillon, **12**
Balata, **4**
Basse-Pointe, **11**
Bellefontaine, **3**
Diamond Rock, **20**
Dubuc Castle, **15**
Forêt de Montravail, **21**
Fort-de-France, **1**
Le François, **16**
Lamentin, **17**
Macouba, **10**
Le Marin, **24**
Le Morne Rouge, **8**
Musée Gauguin, **6**
Pointe du Bout, **19**
Le Prêcheur, **9**
Presqu'île du
Caravelle, **14**
Ste-Anne, **23**
Ste-Luce, **22**
Ste-Marie, **13**
St-Pierre, **7**
Schoelcher, **2**
Les Trois-Ilets, **18**
La Vallée des
Papillons, **5**
Le Vauclin, **25**

Dining
Au Poisson d'Or, **49**
Aux Filets Bleus, **70**
Bidjoul, **58**
Chez Christiane, **65**
Le Colibri, **29**
Le Coq Hardi, **39**
Délices de la Mer, **73**
La Dunette, **71**
L'Ecrin Bleu, **60**
La Factorérie, **31**
La Fontane, **38**
Le Fromager, **30**
La Maison de l'Ilet
Oscar, **48**
Le Marie Sainte, **36**
La Marina, **50**
Les Passages du Vent, **57**
La Petite
Auberge, **66**
Poï et Virginie, **72**
Pointe-Nord, **26**
Relais Caraïbes, **64**
Le Ruisseau
Restaurant, **27**
Le Second Soufflé, **37**
Tamarin Plage
Restaurant, **59**
Le Verger, **44**
Le Vieux Galion, **32**
La Villa Creole, **53**

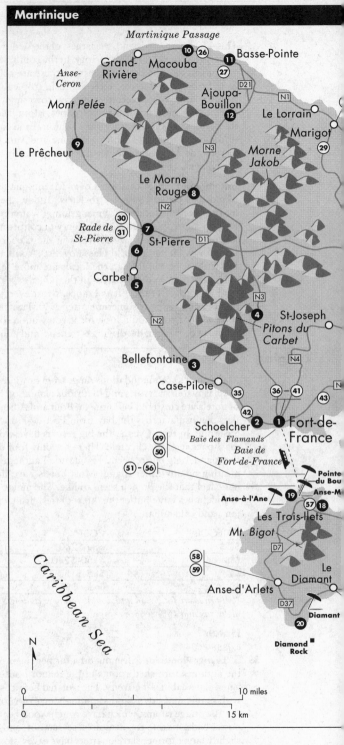

Martinique

KEY

🏖 Beaches

1 Exploring Sights

26 Restaurants and Hotels

ATLANTIC OCEAN

28 Habitation Lagrange

N1

13 Ste-Marie

Havre de la Trinité

Caravelle Peninsula

14

33 Tartane

15 Pointe Caracoli

32

La Trinité

D2

34

N4

Baie du Galion

Gros-Morne

Le Robert

Havre du Robert

N1

Pte. Larose

N1 **44**

45

46

17 Lamentin

16 Le François

47

48

Lamentin International Airport

Mt. Vauclin

N5

Ducos

N6

te out Mitan

D7

Le Vauclin

25

Rivière-Salée

N5

Rivière-Pilote

21

D17

D18

N6

Ste-Luce

22 **66**

D18A

Le Marin

24

D7

N5

nt

60–**65**

Pte. Figuier

67

Pointe Marin

Cul-de-Sac du Marin

D9

68 **72**

Cap Chevalier

23 Ste-Anne

La Savanne (Petrified Forest)

Les Salines

73

Grande Anse

Anse-Trabaud

Pte. des Salines

Pte. d'Enfer

St. Lucia Channel

Lodging

Anse Caritan, **68**

Baie du Galion, **33**

Le Bakoua, **55**

La Batelière Hotel, **35**

Carayou Novotel, **56**

Club Med/Buccaneer's Creek, **67**

Diamant Les Bains, **62**

Diamant-Novotel, **61**

Fregate Bleue, **47**

Habitation Lagrange, **28**

Hôtel L'Anse Colas, **42**

L'Impératrice, **40**

Le Lafayette, **41**

Leyritz Plantation, **27**

Manoir de Beauregard, **69**

Le Marine, **63**

Martinique Cottages, **45**

Le Méridien Trois-Ilets, **54**

La Pagerie, **51**

Relais Caraïbes, **64**

Rivage Hotel, **52**

La Riviera, **46**

Saint Aubin, **34**

Valmenière, **43**

a sharp contrast to the frenzied level of activity at the hotels in Pointe du Bout. You may not want to spend your entire vacation here, but it makes an interesting overnight stop on a tour of the northern part of the island. There's free transportation to the beach, about 30 minutes away. Recent renovations have rendered ☞ **Le Ruisseau Restaurant** and some lodging accessible to people with disabilities. ⌂ *Bourg 97218,* ☎ *596/78–53–92,* ℻ *596/78–92–44. 67 rooms. Restaurant, bar, air-conditioning, pool, tennis court. DC, MC. CP, MAP.*

LE DIAMANT

$$$–$$$$ ⊞ **Diamant-Novotel.** This self-contained resort is in an ideal windsurfing location. Just beyond the reception area, a footbridge spans a large pool on the way to the spacious guest rooms, each of which has a small balcony facing either the sea or the pool. Furnishings are cane and wicker painted in pastel peach and green. The dining room is large and unromantic, set up to accommodate groups, but there's a pleasant terrace bar where a local band plays. A smaller, more formal restaurant is open during peak season. The four beaches on the 5-acre property are small. The staff speaks English and maintains a surprising level of enthusiasm and efficiency, given the hotel's size and the number of tour groups that stay here. Children under 16 stay free with their parents. ⌂ *Pointe de la Chery 97223,* ☎ *596/76–42–42 or 800/322–2223,* ℻ *596/76–22–87. 180 rooms. 2 restaurants, 3 bars, air-conditioning, pool, beauty salon, 2 tennis courts, 4 beaches, dive shop, snorkeling, windsurfing, shops, car rental. AE, DC, MC, V. CP, MAP.*

$$$ ⊞ **Le Marine.** Mini-apartments—one room with a bed, kitchenette, and balcony—are in rows of pristine stucco buildings placed down the hillside to the beach. The rooms are painted in mint, aqua, and periwinkle and decorated with bright abstract prints. The main building, which contains the restaurant, front desk, boutique, and flower shop, is 100 ft above the beach, and a pool is at the bottom of the hill, just above the beach. If you stay at this hotel, you can use the water-sports equipment at ☞ **Diamant-Novotel** free of charge. The hotel caters to French families on tour packages, and the high turnover and large-group clientele contribute to the wear and tear on facilities, although management works hard at maintenance. ⌂ *Pointe de la Chery 97233,* ☎ *596/76–46–00 or 800/221–4542,* ℻ *596/76–25–99. 149 rooms. Restaurant, 2 bars, kitchenettes, 2 pools, 2 tennis courts, beach, dive shop, fishing, shops. AE, DC, MC, V. CP, MAP.*

$$–$$$ ⊞ **Relais Caraïbes.** Of all the hotels on Martinique, this one comes clos-
★   est to having the individuality of a country inn. A note of immediate chic is struck in the thatched public rooms, awash in interior gardens, white-wicker furnishings, and antiques ranging from bronze Indian elephants to African masks, culled from the world travels of owner Monsieur Senez. Decorated in a similar eclectic style and with views of the sea and Diamond Rock, the 12 bungalows are spread over the manicured grounds. Each has a bedroom, a small salon with a sofa bed, a kitchenette, and a bathroom. There are also three standard rooms in the main house, which have such unusual touches as hand-painted headboards. The pool is on the edge of a cliff that overlooks the sea. The hotel is a mile off the main road, and you need a car to get around. The beach, however, is a short walk away, there's on-site scuba instruction, and the French food is divine at the ☞ **Relais Caraïbes** restaurant. ⌂ *Pointe de la Chery 97223,* ☎ *596/76–44–65 or 800/ 223–9815,* ℻ *596/76–21–20. 3 rooms, 12 bungalows. Restaurant, bar, kitchenettes, pool, dive shop, boating. AE, MC, V. CP, MAP.*

$$ ⊞ **Diamant Les Bains.** For the last 30 years Hubert Andrieu and his
★   wife, Marie-Yvonne, have been doing everything they can to make people feel at home at this intimate, beachfront property. Their 22-year-

old son, Hervé, serves as the chef and turns out fine, Creole dishes for
the excellent, on-site restaurant. A few rooms are in the main house,
above the restaurant, but most are in pretty, whitewashed chalets surrounded by flowers and palm trees. The tile floors, cheerfully painted
furniture, white ceilings, and the light breeze that always plays off the
ocean give them the feeling of an old-fashioned, seaside hotel. The beach
is a few yards away, and there is a pool (small) in the center of the property. For those who just want to rest and relax, this quiet, pretty hotel
is the perfect spot—although you will need to speak some French to
feel truly at home. ⊠ *Le Diamant 97223,* ☎ *596/76–40–14;* 𝖥𝖠𝖷 *596/
76–27–00. 27 rooms. Restaurant, bar, air-conditioning, refrigerators,
pool, beach, snorkeling. MC, V. CP, MAP. Closed Sept.*

FORT-DE-FRANCE

$$–$$$ ⊡ **Valmenière.** If you have to fly in, have a meeting, and fly out, this
new property, part of the Best Western group, is ideal. With its blue-
tinted windows, high-tech elevator, and white tubular steel walkways,
it would not be out of place in La Défense, Paris's business district.
Perched on a hill between the airport and Fort-de-France, it is squeaky
clean, efficient, and wired for work. The beds are king-size, and the
imported French mattresses are a boon for anyone with a backache.
The suites are large, with a separate entrance to the living room, abundant cupboard space, and a desk. Three *chambres de bureau* (business
rooms) have beds that you can fold away, turning the room into a flexible office space. The hotel offers a full range of business services, from
fax machines to conference rooms and translation and secretarial assistance. There's also a good restaurant. A pool and sunroof are on
the top floor. Only the views—of an oil refinery, a landfill, and the island's main highway—remind you that the main purpose of the hotel
is not leisure. ⊠ *Av. des Arawaks 97200,* ☎ *596/75–75–75,* 𝖥𝖠𝖷 *596/
75–69–70. 113 rooms, 7 suites. Restaurant, bar, pool, exercise room,
business services, meeting rooms. AE, DC, MC, V. CP.*

$–$$ ⊡ **L'Impératrice.** A central location is the draw here: the rooms (slightly
musty) are in a 1950s five-story building that overlooks La Savane park
in the heart of the city. Those in front are either the best or the worst,
depending upon your sensibilities: they're noisy, but have great views
of all the hustle and bustle. All rooms have bright Creole prints, four-
poster beds, TVs, and private baths; 20 have balconies. Children under
eight stay free in a room with their parents, and children 8–15 stay at
a 50% discount. The hotel also has a popular sidewalk café. ⊠ *Rue
de la Liberté 97200,* ☎ *596/63–06–82; 800/223–9815; or 212/251–
1800 in NY and 800/468–0023 in Canada (reservations services);* 𝖥𝖠𝖷
596/72–66–30. 24 rooms. Café, bar, air-conditioning. AE, DC, V. CP.

$ ⊡ **Le Lafayette.** If you want cheap lodgings in the heart of town, this
is one of the few decent options. Owner Simone Broussillon is a mine
of information and a great help. Rooms are dark and old-fashioned—
heavy wood furnishings, teal linens, and floral curtains—but all have
TVs and phones. ⊠ *5 rue de la Liberté 97200,* ☎ *596/73–80–50 or
800/223–9815,* 𝖥𝖠𝖷 *596/60–97–75. 24 rooms. Bar. AE, DC, V. CP.*

LE FRANÇOIS

$$$ ⊡ **Fregate Bleue.** The owner of this distinctive inn, Madame Yveline
★ de Lucy de Fossarieu, left the management of Leyritz Plantation for
the quiet life. In 1991 she opened this bed-and-breakfast, which is a
member of the French association Les Relais du Silence, whose primary
criterion is that the hotel be quiet. The house is captivating—filled with
light, plants, trompe l'oeil paintings, and hand-carved parrots. The spa-
cious rooms are decorated with off-white furnishings, patterned car-
pets, and the occasional antique; most balconies overlook Les Ilets de
l'Impératrice. All rooms have a small kitchenette and a modern bath-

room with such niceties as bathrobes. Madame de Lucy serves *le petit déjeuner* (breakfast) on the upstairs veranda, and dinner, when requested. The nearest restaurants are a 10-minute drive away, and you must negotiate a rutted road to get to the highway. The on-site pool is small, but the beaches of Le François and Le Vauclin are only five minutes away. ⊠ *Quartier Frégate, 5 mi south of Le François on Vauclin Rd. (Le François) 97240,* ☎ *596/54–54–66 or 800/633–7411,* ℻ *596/54–78–48. 7 rooms. Kitchenettes, pool. AE, MC, V. BP.*

$$ 🏨 **La Riviera.** Three pretty whitewashed buildings with red tile roofs overlook Le François Bay and do, indeed, seem to have been transported straight from St-Tropez. All rooms have a balcony opening onto breathtaking water views. Decor is contemporary and fresh, mostly in floral patterns. Owner-manager Marie-Anne Prian and her husband, Jacques, speak English and are most helpful. The restaurant serves marvelous Continental-tinged Creole cuisine, and the long private pier makes La Riviera popular with yachties. ⊠ *Rte. du Club Nautique 97240,* ☎ *596/54–68–54,* ℻ *596/54–30–43. 14 rooms. Restaurant, bar, air-conditioning, minibars, boating. AE, MC, V. CP, MAP.*

LAMENTIN

$–$$ 🏨 **Martinique Cottages.** These garden bungalows set in the countryside have kitchenettes, terraces, cable TV, and phones. The beaches are a 15-minute drive away. The on-site restaurant, La Plantation, is a gathering spot for gourmets and specializes in *nouvelle cuisine Créole,* with such inventive delicacies as yellow banana and foie gras mille-feuille. The cottages are difficult to find; take advantage of the property's airport transfers. ⊠ *Jeanne d'Arc (Box 408) 97232,* ☎ *596/50–16–08 or 596/50–16–09,* ℻ *596/50–26–83. 8 rooms. Restaurant, kitchenettes, airport shuttle. AE, MC, V. EP.*

MARIGOT

$$$$ 🏨 **Habitation Lagrange.** Nowhere on the island do you feel the style,
★ romance, and elegance of the old plantation-house society more than in this 19th-century manor house, set in a fertile valley on the northeast coast. Everything—from the Staffordshire tableware in the dining room to the antique shaving mirrors and Hermès toiletries in the bathrooms—is done with impeccable taste. A huge entrance hall, hung with murals that depict Martinique's history, opens onto a bar and a small library where you can browse or play solitaire or backgammon. Rooms in the main building have four-poster beds, mahogany floors, beautiful linens, and tall French windows that open onto a wraparound veranda. The Ecurie, which once served as the stables, houses three more rooms. The original stone walls have been incorporated into the decor; parquet floors, huge windows, and canopy beds complete the picture. A pink-and-white Creole-style building houses another 12 rooms with gabled ceilings, mahogany armoires, wicker chaise longues, and chintz curtains. Superb gourmet food is served in the *ajouba,* a beautiful, wooden structure open to the night breeze. The wine list is one of the most extensive on the island. Giant ficus trees, a profusion of flowers, and a babbling brook make wandering the grounds a delight. ⊠ *Marigot 97225,* ☎ *596/53–60–60,* ℻ *596/53–50–58. 17 rooms, 1 suite. Bar, dining room, pool, tennis court, library. AE, DC, MC, V. BP, MAP. Closed Sept.–mid-Oct.*

STE-ANNE

$$$–$$$$ 🏨 **Anse Caritan.** This appealing property combines the amenities of a large hotel with the service and ambience of a more intimate one. It's nestled amid exquisite gardens fronting a ribbon of champagne-color sand. Management does its best to give the hotel an "island" feel. A large traditional fishing boat, or *gommier,* sits next to the pool; and rooms, though nothing exceptional, have unusual touches like hand-painted leaves and bamboo on the walls. All rooms are done in soft colors (periwinkle, mauve, and gray) and have phones, safes, hair dryers, and rough-wood terraces or balconies, most with a sea view. The restaurant is known for its innovative Creole fare, and there's live music nightly. The staff is remarkably friendly and diligent. The gardener, for example, will pick herbs to soothe your sunburn, and the managers actually encourage guests' comments. ⊠ *Pointe des Salines 97227,* ☎ *596/76–74–12 or 800/322–2223,* ℻ *596/76–72–59. 96 rooms. Restaurant, bar, snack bar, air-conditioning, in-room safes, pool, beach, dive shop, snorkeling, boating, fishing, dance club. AE, MC, V. CP, MAP.*

$$$–$$$$ 🏨 **Club Med/Buccaneer's Creek.** Occupying 48 landscaped acres, Club Med is an all-inclusive village with plazas, cafés, restaurants, a boutique, and a small marina. Air-conditioned pastel cottages contain twin beds and private shower. The only money you need to spend here is for bar drinks, personal expenses, and excursions. There's a white-sand beach, a plethora of water sports, and plenty of nightlife. ⊠ *Pointe du Marin 97227,* ☎ *596/76–72–72, 800/258–2633, or 212/750–1670 in NY;* ℻ *596/72–76–02. 300 rooms. 2 restaurants, 2 bars, air-conditioning, 7 tennis courts, exercise room, beach, dive shop, dock, snorkeling, boating, dance club, nightclub. AE, MC, V. All-inclusive.*

$$$ 🏨 **Manoir de Beauregard.** Built in the early 18th century, this impos-
★ ing plantation house was made into a hotel by the Saint-Cyr family in 1928. For more than 60 years it was one of the best small hotels in Martinique; then, tragically, in 1990, it was ravaged by fire. Now it has risen like the proverbial phoenix from the ashes. The main building, with its 2-ft-thick stone walls and mullioned windows, feels like a medieval abbey. Where the nave would be is a drawing room with bentwood rockers, chandeliers, and checkerboard marble floors. On either side of the drawing room are two "aisles" with sloping roofs; one serves as the bar, which leads out onto a sunny terrace and a small L-shape pool, while the other has been turned into a Creole dining room. The restaurant is across a small courtyard and serves such dishes as shrimp with green pepper sauce and other examples of *la nouvelle cuisine antillaise.* The three rooms upstairs in the main building have wood-beam ceilings, antique furniture, four-poster beds, and rich linens. Other rooms are in a modern annex at the other side of the property. Most are not very nice, but one is a gem: a circular tower room, with a four-poster bed, that was traditionally reserved for *les jeunes mariés* (honeymooners). All rooms have phones and TVs. ⊠ *Chemin des Salines 97227,* ☎ *596/76–73–40,* ℻ *596/76–93–24. 10 rooms. Restaurant, bar, air-conditioning, pool. AE, MC, V. CP.*

SCHOELCHER

$$$ 🏨 **La Batelière Hotel.** On a flower-filled, 5-acre property north of Fort-
★ de-France, this smart resort hotel has some of the island's largest rooms and by far its best tennis courts. Things here are extremely well run: service is prompt, security intimidating (a veritable army of uniformed guards hovers about the main gate). Many rooms overlook the sea, and all have contemporary furniture, a direct-dial phone, cable TV, a radio, and a private balcony or patio. The restaurant where breakfast is served is on an airy terrace with great ocean views. One level below is the semicircular pool and pool bar. Below that is a small beach sheltered from the waves by a breakwater. ⊠ *La Batelière 97233,* ☎ *596/61–49–49 or 800/223–6510,* ℻ *596/61–62–29. 192 rooms, 5 duplexes, 2 suites. 2 restaurants, 2 bars, air-conditioning, pool, 6 tennis courts, beach, snorkeling, boating, shops, casino, dance club, meeting rooms. AE, DC, MC, V. CP, MAP.*

$$ 🏨 **Hôtel L'Anse Colas.** Laid out like a fan overlooking the Caribbean,
★ all of Hôtel L'Anse Colas's rooms face the sea. Some have private gardens, and the 11 duplexes have mezzanines. The focal point of the hotel is its beautiful lagoon-shape pool, which mirrors the sea and is lined on one side by palm trees. The architectural motif of the hotel is based on the traveler's palm, a unique plant that only grows facing the east, is 90% water, and was used by travelers of the past for sustenance. This theme is carried through in absolutely everything from the mirrors to the small ornaments that adorn the bedposts. Dining is offered in the Pomme Canelle Restaurant, which serves three meals a day. Quaint, quiet, and personal, the hotel's only drawback is the scarcity of grounds for walking. It's about 2 mi north of Fort-de-France, so you'll need a car or taxi to get around. ⊠ *Rte. du Petit Tamarin 97233,* ☎ *596/61–28–18,* FAX *596/61–04–78. 43 rooms. Restaurant, bar, air-conditioning, in-room safes, refrigerators, pool. AE, MC, V. CP, MAP.*

LA TRINITÉ

$$–$$$ 🏨 **Baie du Galion.** A member of the Best Western chain, this new hotel is on the lovely, wild Presqu'île du Caravelle (Caravelle Peninsula). The medium-size rooms are furnished in a charming Creole style, with polished dark-wood furnishings and bright fabrics. All have TVs, phones, and balconies; 50 also have kitchenettes. Hiking is good in the adjacent nature reserve. The Atlantic beach is relatively good for swimming, and the enormous pool is a gathering place for guests. ⊠ *Anse Tartane 97220,* ☎ *596/58–65–30 or 800/223–9815,* FAX *596/58–25–76. 146 rooms. Restaurant, bar, air-conditioning, in-room safes, refrigerators, pool, tennis court, beach. AE, MC, V. BP, MAP.*

$$ 🏨 **Saint Aubin.** This restored, coral-color, colonial house—with pretty gables and intricate gingerbread trim—is in the countryside above the Atlantic coast. Each modern, if musty, room has wicker furnishings, a TV, phone, and private bath. Those on the top floor are larger and ideal for families; five second-floor rooms open onto a shared balcony with sweeping sea views. This is a peaceful retreat, and only 3 mi from La Trinité, 2 mi from the beaches on the Caravelle Peninsula. The inn's restaurant serves estimable Creole fare. Owner Guy Foret is an engaging host. ⊠ *La Trinité (Box 52) 97220,* ☎ *596/69–34–77, 800/223–9815; 212/840–6636 in NY, 800/468–0023 in Canada (reservations services);* FAX *596/69–41–14. 15 rooms. Restaurant, bar, air-conditioning, pool. AE, DC, MC, V. CP.*

LES TROIS-ILETS

$$$$ 🏨 **Le Bakoua.** It's a sure sign that a hotel is going downscale when it sells rooms at reduced rates to airline crews: Le Bakoua is full of flight attendants and pilots from Corsair, a private French airline. Accommodations are in three hillside buildings and a fourth on the man-made white-sand beach. The decor is cushy-cum-rustic, with polished hardwood furnishings, frilly floral linens, and white tile floors. All rooms have a balcony or patio; a bathroom with hand-painted tiles, a marble vanity, and a hair dryer; and the usual deluxe amenities. The beach is small and tends to get overrun with the ubiquitous *vendeuses de plage,* who try to sell you everything from skimpy bikinis to day trips on a catamaran. The pool is above the beach, and the water flows over one side, giving the impression that the pool is part of the ocean. Entertainment consists of live music and shows nightly, including dancing, limbo, and Friday-night performances of Les Grands Ballets de la Martinique (☞ Nightlife, *below).* ⊠ *Pointe du Bout 97229,* ☎ *596/66–02–02, 800/221–4542, or 0171/730–7144 in the U.K.;* FAX *596/66–00–41. 138 rooms, 2 1-bedroom suites. 2 restaurants, bar, air-conditioning, minibars, pool, beauty salon, 2 tennis courts, beach, snorkeling, boating, shop. AE, DC, MC, V. CP, MAP.*

$$$–$$$$ 🏨 **Carayou Novotel.** The three-story, apartment-style buildings here are not the most beautiful, but their white, blue, and yellow trim is snappy. Each room has white-tile floors, blue fabrics, and spacious bathrooms. The main restaurant, where you're served breakfast, is up a flight of steps on a terrace with views of Fort-de-France. The Café Créole, at the somewhat cramped beach, also serves light meals. For those seeking an action-packed vacation, the hotel offers a plethora of activities—from tennis (one rather poor court) to sailing to parasailing—though not all are included in the base rate. Up to two children (under age 16) can stay free, and for 150F per day the Club Ti-Pirate will take them off your hands. The service here is somewhat languid, the clientele mostly package-tour groups from France. ✉ *Pointe du Bout 97229,* ☎ *596/ 66–04–04 or 800/322–2223,* FAX *596/66–00–57. 200 rooms, 1 suite. Restaurant, bar, café, pool, tennis court, beach, windsurfing, boating, parasailing, waterskiing, shop, children's programs. AE, MC, V. CP.*

$$$–$$$$ 🏨 **Le Méridien Trois-Ilets.** There's a great deal of activity here, even in the low season, much of it revolving around the always-congested pool and man-made beach. Unfortunately, the hotel has aged. Despite sporadic redecorations, the boxy, oddly configured rooms—done in blond woods and floral fabrics—remain patchworked with repairs. They are, however, air-conditioned and have wall-to-wall carpeting, hair dryers, and TVs. Some have balconies with a splendid view of the bay and Fort-de-France. The beachfront restaurant, La Cocoteraie, offers a limited but competent menu. The staff speaks excellent English, the atmosphere is the island's most convivial, and there's live entertainment nightly. ✉ *Pointe du Bout 97229,* ☎ *596/66–00–00, 800/543– 4300, or 212/245–2920 in NY;* FAX *596/66–00–74. 295 rooms, 2 luxury suites, 4 1-bedroom suites. 2 restaurants, bar, air-conditioning, minibars, pool, 2 tennis courts, dive shop, snorkeling, boating, casino, car rental. AE, DC, MC, V. BP, MAP.*

$$$ 🏨 **La Pagerie.** La Pagerie looks as if it were plucked out of the Côte d'Azur and planted near the marina in Pointe du Bout. The hotel has small air-conditioned rooms and studios, all with a bath and a trim little balcony and some with a kitchenette. The decor is handsome throughout, with dark-wood furnishings, planters, and lace curtains, but in recent years the property has become slightly run-down. Although there's no beach or water sports, you're only a short stroll from resort hotels, restaurants, and many activities. Lunch and dinner are served alfresco by the pool. The lively, cheerful atmosphere has made the bar a favorite evening watering hole of local expatriates and the sailing crowd. ✉ *Pointe du Bout 97229,* ☎ *596/66–05–30; 800/221–4542 or 212/ 757–6500 in NY (reservations services);* FAX *596/66–00–99. 98 rooms. Restaurant, bar, air-conditioning, pool. AE, MC, V. EP, MAP.*

$ 🏨 **Rivage Hotel.** You get good value for your money at Maryelle and Jean Claude Riveti's small hotel. The place does have the air of a motor inn circa the Eisenhower years, but it's immaculately maintained, and for about a third of the cost, the studios are much larger than comparable rooms at neighboring hotels. Each garden-view unit has a private bath and either a kitchenette (not always as clean as the rest of the property) or a mini-refrigerator. Breakfast and light meals are served in the friendly, informal snack bar. You should have no trouble communicating: English, Spanish, and French are spoken. The beach is across the road. ✉ *Anse-Mitan 97229,* ☎ *596/66–00–53,* FAX *596/ 66–06–56. 17 rooms. Snack bar, air-conditioning, pool, beach, car rental. MC, V. EP.*

Villas

The **Villa Rental Service** (☎ 596/71–56–11, FAX 596/63–11–64) can help you find a home, a villa, or an apartment to rent. Most proper-

ties are in the south of the island near good beaches, and you can rent
for a week or a month.

Dining

Martinique's restaurants serve classic French, contemporary, and Creole cuisines, though its cellars are generally filled with fine French wines.
Hotel restaurants are predictably good, but some of the best places are
tucked away in the countryside. The farther you venture from tourist
hotels, the less likely you are to find English-speaking folk. But that
shouldn't stop you from savoring the food.

The local Creole specialties are *colombo* (curry), *accras* (cod or vegetable fritters), *crabes farcis* (stuffed land crab), *écrevisses* (freshwater
crayfish), *boudin* (Creole blood sausage), *lambi* (conch), *langouste*
(clawless Caribbean lobster), *soudons* (sweet clams), *blaff* (fish or
shellfish plunged into seasoned stock), and *oursin* (sea urchin). And,
if you like your *poisson* (fish) or any other dish with a little tang, try
the *chien* sauce, a slightly spicy concoction that smacks of something
vaguely Mexican. It literally means "dog" sauce but don't let that dis-
suade you. It's just made from onions, shallots, peppers, oil, and vinegar. Don't confuse chien sauce with the local pepper which is sometimes
served in oil and has an atomic kick. The favorite local libation is 'ti
punch, concocted of four parts white rum, one part sugarcane syrup
(some people like a little more syrup), and a squeeze of lime.

Most restaurants offer a prix-fixe menu, often with several choices of
entrées and wine. Finding a cheap, American-style bite at lunch is almost impossible. For additional savings, pick up a copy of the *Ti
Gourmet* booklet at the tourist office and larger hotels; most of the
restaurants listed offer a free drink or discount upon presentation.

What to Wear

For dinner, people dress in casual resort wear. Men don't wear jackets but do wear collared shirts. Women typically wear light cotton sundresses. Nice shorts are fine for lunch, but at dinnertime beach attire
is too casual for most restaurants.

CATEGORY	COST*
$$$	over $50
$$	$30–$50
$	under $30

per person for a three-course meal, excluding drinks and service

Anse-d'Arlets

SEAFOOD

$–$$ ✗ **Tamarin Plage Restaurant.** The lobster *vivier* (tank) in the middle
of the room gives you a clue to the specialty here, but there are other
recommendable offerings as well: fish soup and Creole boudin starters
and crayfish fricassee or octopus. The beachfront bar is a popular local
hangout. ⊠ *Grande Anse,* ☎ *596/68–71–30. MC, V.*

$ ✗ **Bidjoul.** Many modest restaurants line the small side street that is
actually Anse-d'Arlets's main drag. The street borders the water, and
fishermen sail right up to the eateries with their latest catch. Bidjoul
has a tiny dining room; opt for one of the tables set up under the canopy
on the beach across the road. The salads (try the smoked salmon, or
the *pêcheur,* with tuna, shrimp, crab, and rice) are huge, and the grilled
fish as fresh as can be. So, too, is the fish at the other restaurants, but
the owner's enthusiasm makes it stand out. It has become the popular gathering spot for watching the sun set into the Caribbean Sea. ⊠
Grande Anse, ☎ *596/68–65–28. Reservations not accepted. MC, V.*

Basse-Pointe

CARIBBEAN/CREOLE

$$–$$$ ✕ **Le Ruisseau Restaurant.** The restored 18th-century ☞ Leyritz Plan-
★ tation inn has exquisite stone walls and a dramatic view of Mont
Pelée. It is the pride of Martinique and *the* place that many cruise passengers head to as soon as they disembark (just remember that it will
take nearly the entire day to complete this trip). The restaurant here
serves mostly Creole fare—boudin, chicken with coconut, curried
dishes, and steaks. The wonderful alfresco atmosphere does much to
enhance the experience, and the waitstaff is very helpful. Recent improvements have made it accessible to people with disabilities. ⊠
Bourg, ☎ *596/78–53–92. Reservations essential. MC, V.*

Le Diamant

CARIBBEAN/CREOLE

$ ✕ **Chez Christiane.** Don't be deceived by the seedy front bar (which
★ rocks during pool tournaments and free Friday rum tastings). The
back dining room is delightful, with bamboo walls, fresh flowers, and
local artist Roland Brival's imaginative paintings of local fauna (he adds
texture with shards of green glass). The Creole cuisine is magnificent.
The prix-fixe (70F) menu might offer boudin, fried fish in caper sauce,
and a *coupe glacée* (sundae). Other top choices are a smoky callaloo
soup (here called *soupe verte aux crabes*) and braised ray with ginger.
⊠ *Rue Diamant,* ☎ *596/76–49–55. No credit cards.*

FRENCH

$$$ ✕ **Relais Caraïbes.** Although Parisian Jean Senez has been busy since
★ opening the ☞ Relais Caraïbes bungalow colony *avec* restaurant, he
still manages to spend enough time in Paris to gather original objets
d'art for decor and for sale. Lunch or dinner choices include spicy chicken
Antilloise, a half lobster in two sauces, fish fillet in a basil sauce, and
fricassee of country shrimp. The crisply decorated dining room, awash
in fresh flowers, commands a clear view of Diamond Rock. ⊠ *Pointe
de la Chery,* ☎ *596/76–44–65. AE, MC, V. Closed Mon.*

SEAFOOD

$$ ✕ **L'Ecrin Bleu.** The breathtaking views of the sea and St. Lucia would
be reason enough to visit this terrace eatery, but you hardly need more
incentive than the delectable, affordable seafood. Choose your own lobster or try the salmon tartare, sea bream in spiced beurre blanc, swordfish with saffron, or conch *en feuilleté* (in puff pastry). The gourmet
menu (260F) includes crayfish in ginger or saffron sauce, half a grilled
lobster, and John Dory in sweet pepper sauce. ⊠ *Rte. des Anse-d'Arlets,* ☎ *596/76–41–92. AE.*

Fort-de-France

CONTEMPORARY

$$$ ✕ **La Fontane.** Mango trees shade the wraparound veranda of this his-
★ toric house on the road to Balata, with distant views of Les Pitons de
Carbet, a chain of volcanic hills, and Balata's wedding-cake cathedral.
Inside you'll find Asian rugs, fresh flowers, and antiques that include
a gramophone and a grandfather clock. Try *le bambou de la Fontane,*
a salad of fish, tomato, corn, melon, and crayfish. Other options are
cream soup with crab, lobster stewed with basil, *noisettes d'agneau*
(medallions of lamb) with boletus mushrooms and mango, and the red
snapper with lemon-lime sauce. For dessert, the *nuage de sorbet,* a med-
ley of nine homemade ice creams, is a treat. There's an excellent wine
list, and the espresso is not to be missed. ⊠ *Km 4, rte. de Balata,* ☎
596/64–28–70. Reservations essential. AE. Closed Sun.–Mon.

ECLECTIC

$–$$ ✕ **Le Marie Sainte.** Warm wood paneling, exposed beams, colorfully
★   tiled tables, and bright napery create a homey ambience in this wildly
popular lunchtime spot. It's worth waiting on the occasional line for
the scrumptious *daube des poissons* (braised fish), crayfish, and banana beignets. The 75F prix-fixe menu gets you all that you need and
then some. ⊠ *160 rue Victor Hugo,* ☎ *596/70–00–30. AE, MC, V.
Closed Sun. No dinner.*

STEAK HOUSE

$$ ✕ **Le Coq Hardi.** You'll need a road map to reach this bistro, which is
at the bottom of a small one-way street. Once you are here, chef and
patron Alphonse Sint-Ive, a genial butcher-turned-restaurateur, and ex-
member of the French Foreign Legion, will help you choose your own
steak and regale you with stories of his experiences in Vietnam. A spe-
cialty is the *coutancie* steak, a French version of Japanese Kobe steak
(cattle are fed exclusively on grain, plants, and beer, and the meat is
flown in from Périgord). Tournedos Rossini (with artichoke hearts, foie
gras, truffles, and Madeira sauce), entrecôte bordelaise, prime rib, and
T-bone steaks are also on the menu. The decor (gruesome prints of cock-
fights) and red-blooded ambience make this an absolute no-no for an-
imal lovers and vegetarians. ⊠ *Km 0.6, rue Martin Luther King,* ☎
596/63–66–83. AE, MC, V. No lunch Wed. or Sat.

VEGETARIAN

$ ✕ **Le Second Soufflé.** This place is heaven for vegetarians. The chef uses
★   fresh produce to make soufflés ranging from *aubergine* (eggplant) to
filet de ti-nain (small green bananas) with chocolate sauce. He also whips
up such nonsoufflé items as eggplant ragout and okra quiche. The food
echoes the famous Voltaire line painted on the wall: TU NE POSSÈDES
RIEN SI TU NE DIGÈRES PAS BIEN ("You have nothing if you don't have
good digestion"). The decor pays tribute to the menu, with colorful
murals of fruits and vegetables. ⊠ *27 rue Blénac,* ☎ *596/63–44–11.
No credit cards. Closed weekends.*

Le François

SEAFOOD

$$$ ✕ **La Maison de l'Ilet Oscar.** To get to this Robinson Crusoe bistro under
the palms you have to be fetched by fishing boat (the trip is included
in the price of the two, fairly basic, seafood menus offered). The Creole house was won by the proprietor—who also owns the upscale ☞
Habitation Lagrange resort—in a poker game. Tables are laid out
under palm trees at the water's edge. Before lunch, you'll probably be
taken to La Beignoir de Joséphine, a gorgeous, shallow pool with
emerald-color water and white sand, where according to legend,
Napoléon's ill-fated wife would swim. After your dip, you'll be served
a glass of 'ti punch and some accras as you stand in the water. ⊠ *Baie
de François,* ☎ *596/53–60–60. Reservations essential. AE, MC, V.*

Lamentin

ECLECTIC

$$–$$$ ✕ **Le Verger.** An orchard is the setting for this green-and-white coun-
★   try house not far from the airport. But you don't come for the locale—
the food is the draw. Chef Bruno Hoang, who's also the owner's son,
has years of experience in Paris under his belt, plus an insider's knowledge of local Creole traditions. He creates an oursin blaff that's justly
renowned; to make it, you need 20 pounds of sea urchins (only the
eggs are used); a rich broth of onion, spices, parsley, and white wine;
and great patience. Pheasant, duck (try the perfect *magret* with green
peppercorns), and other game are on the extensive menu. Classic
French wines round out an excellent meal. Follow the signs for La Trinité;

BONUS MILES MAKE GREAT SOUVENIRS.

MCI Calling Card
123 456 7891 2345
J.D. SMITH
WorldPhone

Earn Miles With Your MCI Card.

Take the MCI Card along on this trip and start earning miles for the next one. You'll earn frequent flyer miles on all your calls and save with the low rates you've come to expect from MCI. Before you know it, you'll be on your way to some other international destination.

Sign up for MCI by calling 1-800-FLY-FREE

Earn Frequent Flyer Miles.

Is this a great time, or what? :-)

Easy To Call Home.

1. To use your MCI Card, just dial the WorldPhone access number of the country you're calling from.
2. Dial or give the operator your MCI Card number.
3. Dial or give the number you're calling.

American Samoa	633-2MCI (633-2624)
# Antigua	1-800-888-8000
(Available from public card phones only)	#2
# Argentina (CC)	0-800-5-1002
# Aruba ÷	800-888-8
# Bahamas	1-800-888-8000
# Barbados	1-800-888-8000
# Belize	557 from hotels
	815 from pay phones
# Bermuda ÷	1-800-888-8000
# Bolivia ♦(CC)	0-800-2222
# Brazil(CC)	000-8012
# British Virgin Islands ÷	1-800-888-8000
# Cayman Islands	1-800-888-8000
# Chile(CC)	
To call using CTC ■	800-207-300
To call using ENTEL ■	800-360-180
# Colombia(CC)♦	980-16-0001
Collect Access in Spanish	980-16-1000
# Costa Rica♦	0800-012-2222
# Dominica	1-800-888-8000
# Dominican Republic(CC)÷	1-800-888-8000
Collect Access in Spanish	1121
# Ecuador(CC) ÷	999-170
El Salvador	800-1767
# Grenada ÷	1-800-888-8000
Guatemala (CC)♦	9999-189
Guyana	177
# Haiti ÷ Collect Access	193
Collect Access in French/Creole	190
Honduras ÷	8000-122
# Jamaica ÷ Collect Access	1-800-888-8000
(From Special Hotels only)	873
From payphones	★2
# Mexico(CC)	
Avantel	01-800-021-8000
Telmex ▲	001-800-674-7000
Mexico Access in Spanish	01-800-021-1000
# Netherlands Antilles(CC)÷	001-800-888-8000
Nicaragua (CC)	166
(Outside of Managua, dial 02 first)	
Collect Access in Spanish from any public payphone	★2
# Panama	108
Military Bases	2810-108
# Paraguay ÷	00-812-800
# Peru	0-800-500-10
# Puerto Rico(CC)	1-800-888-8000
# St. Lucia ÷	1-800-888-8000
# Trinidad & Tobago ÷	1-800-888-8000
# Turks & Caicos ÷	1-800-888-8000
# Uruguay	000-412
# U.S. Virgin Islands (CC)	1-800-888-8000
# Venezuela(CC)÷♦	800-1114-0

You've read the book. Now book the trip.

For all the best deals on flights, hotels, rental cars, and vacation packages, book them online at www.previewtravel.com. Then click on our Destination Guides featuring content from Fodor's and more. You'll find hotels, restaurants, attractions, and things to do around the globe. There are even interactive maps, videos, and weather forecasts. You'll have everything you need to make your vacation exactly what you want it to be. All it takes is a trip online.

Travel on Your Terms™
www.previewtravel.com
aol keyword: previewtravel

preview travel SM

the restaurant's entrance is on the right immediately after an Esso station. ⊠ *Pl. d'Armes*, ☎ *596/51–43–02. AE, DC, MC, V. Closed Sun.*

Macouba

SEAFOOD

$–$$ ✕ **Pointe-Nord.** If you're driving around the northern end of the island, this is one of the few watering holes in the area (it's busy on the weekend, so be sure you make a reservation). Built among the ruins of the Perpigna rum distillery, with fine views of Dominica in the distance, it serves lunch seven days a week. Seafood is the specialty here; try the poached thazar, a local fish, marinated with red beans, onions, and tomatoes. ⊠ *On road to Grand' Rivière*, ☎ *596/78–56–56. MC, V.*

Morne-des-Esses

CONTEMPORARY

$$ ✕ **Le Colibri.** Jules Palladino, a gregarious man who clearly loves his
★ food, is continuing a family culinary tradition with this little spot in the island's northeastern reaches. Dishes—such as tarte aux lambis, a quiche made with conch paste, and *buisson* d'écrevisses, a pyramid of six giant freshwater crayfish decorated with flowers and accompanied by a tomato sauce seasoned with thyme, scallions, and tiny bits of crayfish—involve hours of work in the kitchen. Some of the traditional Creole dishes, like stuffed pigeon and *cochon au lait* (suckling pig), are also offered here. There's an excellent wine list. The view, across the ocean, is spectacular: If you're lucky, you'll see a rainbow. ⊠ *Morne-des-Esses*, ☎ *596/69–91–95. AE, MC, V. Closed Mon. off-season.*

Ste-Anne

ECLECTIC

$–$$ ✕ **Délices de la Mer.** At the southernmost tip of Les Salines beach, you'll find this small, open-air, beachfront restaurant that serves solid fare from land and sea. The prices are generally modest (although the langouste fricassee will run you about 200F) and the views of the Diamond Rock and the ocean are spectacular. During your meal, don't be surprised if hummingbirds dart in and out of sight. Reservations at this casual eatery are not required, although it can get awfully crowded during the high season. ⊠ *Pointe des Salines*, ☎ *596/74–85–39. AE, DC, MC, V. Closed Sun. No dinner Mon.–Tues.*

$–$$ ✕ **La Dunette.** Dinner at this restaurant, in the small Ste-Anne hotel of the same name, is served on a plant-hung terrace overlooking the sea. Wrought-iron chairs and tables and bright blue awnings add to the refreshing garden atmosphere. Your choices for lunch or dinner include fish soup, grilled fish or lobster, snapper stuffed with sea urchin, conch fricassee, and several colombos and tandooris. There's a piano bar in the evening, and waterskiing is offered after lunch for those who ignore digestion rules. ⊠ *Le Bourg*, ☎ *596/76–73–90. MC, V.*

$–$$ ✕ **Poï et Virginie.** Facing the jetty in the center of Ste-Anne is this popular restaurant with bamboo walls, bright art naïf, ceiling fans, and fresh-cut flowers. It's had the honor of winning the Clé d'Or Gault Millau culinary award. The menu is extensive—from meats to fish—but the specialty is the lobster and crab salad. Other noteworthy dishes are lemon chicken in coconut milk and crayfish in saffron. Lunchtime is busy, especially on weekends; get here soon after noon if you want a table with views of the bay and St. Lucia in the distance. ⊠ *Pl. de l'Eglise*, ☎ *596/76–72–22. AE, DC, MC, V. Closed Mon. No lunch Tues.*

SEAFOOD

$$$ ✕ **Aux Filets Bleus.** In addition to dining at this open-air, beachfront eatery, you can go for a swim and dance to live music on top of the underground lobster tank. The cheerful decor ripples in various shades of blue from azure to teal. Be sure to check out the astonishing, angry

mural outside the restaurant, all upraised fists and Picasso-esque profiles (à la *Guernica*). Fish soup, stuffed crab, and avocado vinaigrette are all good opening bids. In addition to an assortment of lobster entrées, you'll find grilled or steamed fish and octopus with red beans and rice. ⊠ *Pointe Marin,* ☎ *596/76–73–42. AE, MC.*

Ste-Luce
CONTEMPORARY

$$ ✕ **La Petite Auberge.** *Filet de poisson aux champignons* (fish cooked with mushrooms), conch flamed in aged rum, and magret *à la mangue* (with mango) are just some of the specialties here. Two viviers, one for lobster, the other for *z'habitants* (the local name for crayfish), ensure that these options are fresh. ⊠ *Plage du Gros Raisins,* ☎ *596/ 62–59–70. AE, MC, V.*

St-Pierre
ECLECTIC

$–$$ ✕ **La Factorérie.** The food is appealing and the views sweeping at this open-air restaurant alongside the ruins of the Eglise du Fort. Fresh vegetables from the nearby agricultural training school accompany grilled langouste, grilled chicken in a piquant Creole sauce, and the fresh catch of the day. This is a convenient spot to have lunch when visiting St-Pierre, though it's not worth a special trip. ⊠ *Quartier Fort,* ☎ *596/ 78–12–53. Reservations essential. AE, MC, V.*

$–$$ ✕ **Le Fromager.** This beautiful restaurant is perched high above St-Pierre, ★ with smashing views of the town's red roofs and the sea beyond from the breezy terrace. Dining inside is also pleasant, thanks to the gleaming ecru tile floors, white wicker, polished hardwood furnishings, lace tablecloths, old rum barrels, and potted plants. Superlative choices include crayfish colombo, marinated octopus, and duck fillet with pineapple. You may also opt for the 100F chef's choice menu, which might include avocado vinaigrette and sole *sauce pêcheur* (in a Creole sauce), as well as fruit or crème caramel. ⊠ *On road to Fond St-Denis,* ☎ *596/78–19–07. AE, DC, MC, V.*

La Trinité
SEAFOOD

$$ ✕ **Le Vieux Galion.** This seaside restaurant plays up the nautical theme, with a huge aquarium and murals of old sailing ships complementing fantastic Atlantic views. The crashing surf serenades you on the terrace. Owner Jean-Pierre Maur does wonders with seafood. Especially memorable are grouper rouged with peppers and conch *à l'armoricaine* (with tomato, garlic, crème fraîche, and cognac). ⊠ *Rte. du Tartane, Anse Bellune,* ☎ *596/58–20–58. AE, MC, V. Closed Wed.*

Les Trois-Ilets
CARIBBEAN/CREOLE

$–$$ ✕ **Au Poisson d'Or.** This typical Creole restaurant offers several excellent set menus. You might choose seafood callaloo, fried conch or sea urchin, or scallops sautéed in white wine. The decor is attractive: bamboo walls, straw thatching, madras napery, a veritable jungle of potted plants, and clever paintings of seafood. The only drawback is its position on the "wrong side" of the road, away from the beach. Choose a table in the front area of the terrace to benefit from any passing breezes. ⊠ *Anse Mitan,* ☎ *596/66–01–80. Reservations not accepted. AE, MC. Closed Mon.*

ECLECTIC

$$ ✕ **La Villa Creole.** The food at this fine bistro, now in its 17th year, is ★ superb; however, the real draw here is owner Guy Bruère-Dawson, a popular singer and guitarist who entertains during dinner. The setting is romantic, with tables laid out around two sides of a lush garden, and there's always an animated crowd. For starters, try the *salade de poisson cru mariné,* a Tahitian version of sushi, and for the main course, *le filet de St-Pierre et z'habitants,* a medley of local fish and crayfish. The café Creole, coffee laced with aged rum and chantilly cream, is delicious. ⊠ *Anse-Mitan,* ☎ *596/66–05–53. Reservations essential. AE, DC, V. Closed Sun. No lunch Mon.*

$ ✕ **La Marina.** Beckoning red-and-white awnings and colorful murals give this breezy terrace a cheerful atmosphere. Views are of the yachts cruising in and out of their berths. Top choices include seafood risotto and lambi fricassee. Tasty pizzas and salads are the best budget options. ⊠ *Pointe du Bout,* ☎ *596/66–02–32. AE, MC, V.*

$ ✕ **Les Passages du Vent.** In a pretty brick building on the main street, this bistro has art naïf, shuttered windows, and a wooden ceiling and floors that give it a warm character. There's a terrace for alfresco dining. The menu is simple—grills, chicken, pizza, and seafood—and the crowd is lively and young. There's jazz and blues on Saturday. ⊠ *27 rue de l'Impératrice Joséphine,* ☎ *596/68–42–11. MC, V. Closed Mon.*

Beaches

All of Martinique's beaches are open to the public, but hotels charge a fee for nonguests to use changing rooms and facilities. There are no official nudist beaches, but topless bathing is prevalent. Unless you're an expert swimmer, steer clear of the Atlantic waters, except in the area of Cap Chevalier and the Caravelle Peninsula. The soft, white-sand beaches are south of Fort-de-France; to the north, the beaches are hard-packed gray volcanic sand. Some of the most pleasant beaches are around Ste-Anne and Ste-Luce.

Anse-à-l'Ane beach has picnic tables and a nearby shell museum. Cool off in the bar of Le Calalou hotel. **Anse-Mitan** has golden sand and excellent snorkeling. Small, family-owned bistros are half hidden among palm trees nearby. **Anse-Trabaud** is on the Atlantic side, across the southern tip of the island from Ste-Anne. There's nothing here but white sand and the sea. **Diamant,** the island's longest beach (2½ mi), has a splendid view of Diamond Rock, but the waters are sometimes rough, and the currents are strong.

Les Salines is a 1½-mi cove of soft white sand lined with coconut palms. A short drive south of Ste-Anne, Les Salines is awash with families and children during holidays and on weekends but quiet and uncrowded during the week—even at the height of the winter season. This beach, especially the far end, is the most peaceful and beautiful. **Pointe du Bout** beaches are man-made and lined with luxury resorts, among them the Méridien and the Bakoua, but they tend to be rather small. **Pointe Marin** stretches north from Ste-Anne. A good windsurfing and waterskiing spot, it also has restaurants, campsites, sanitary facilities, and a 10F charge. Club Med occupies the northern edge.

Outdoor Activities and Sports

BICYCLING

Mountain biking is popular in mainland France, and now it has reached Martinique. You can rent a VTT (Vélo Tout Terrain), a bike specially designed with 18 speeds to handle all terrains, from **V.T. Tilt** (⊠ Les Trois-Ilets, ☎ 596/66–01–01), which also does some fun day tours that include lunch.

BOATING AND SAILING

Only people very familiar with handling marine craft should consider striking out on the rough Atlantic side. The Caribbean side is much calmer—more like a vast lagoon rather than an actual sea. If you're unsure of your nautical prowess, it might be prudent to let one of the following companies take you out. **Caraibes Evasion** (⊠ Pointe du Bout marina, ☎ 596/66–02–85), **Moorings Antilles Françaises** (⊠ Port de Plaisance du Marin, ☎ 596/74–75–39), **Stardust** (⊠ Port de Plaisance du Marin, ☎ 596/74–98–17, 909/678–2250, or 800/227–5317 in the U.S.), **Star Voyages** (⊠ Pointe du Bout marina, ☎ 596/68–16–75), or **Tropic Yachting** (⊠ Pointe du Bout marina, ☎ 596/66–03–85).

You can rent Hobie Cats, Sunfish, and Sailfish by the hour from hotel beach shacks. Also check with **Alphamar** (⊠ Les Trois-Ilets, ☎ 596/66–00–89), **Club Nautique du Marin** (⊠ Le François, ☎ 596/74–92–48), **Soleil et Voile** (⊠ Le François, ☎ 0596/66–09–14), and **Stardust** (☞ *above*).

FISHING

Fish cruising these waters include tuna, barracuda, dolphinfish, kingfish, and bonito. For a day's outing on the 37-ft *Egg Harbor,* with gear and breakfast included, contact **Bathy's Club** (⊠ Méridien, Pointe de Bout , ☎ 596/66–00–00). **Bleu Marine Evasion** (⊠ Le Diamant, ☎ 596/76–46–00) also offers excursions. Charters of up to five days can be arranged on Captain René Alaric's 37-ft *Rayon Vert* (⊠ Auberge du Vare, Case-Pilote, ☎ 596/78–80–56).

GOLF

At **Golf de l'Impératrice Joséphine** (⊠ Les Trois-Ilets, ☎ 596/68–32–81, FAX 596/68–38–97) there's a par-71, 18-hole Robert Trent Jones course with an English-speaking pro, a fully equipped pro shop, a bar, and a restaurant. A mile from the Pointe du Bout resort area and 18 mi from Fort-de-France, the club offers special greens fees to guests of some hotels and cruise-ship passengers. Normal greens fees are $40; an electric cart costs another $40.

HIKING

The island has 31 marked hiking trails. At the beginning of each, a notice is posted advising on the level of difficulty, the duration of a hike, and any interesting points of note. The **Parc Naturel Régional de la Martinique** (⊠ 9 bd. Général de Gaulle, Fort-de-France, ☎ 596/73–19–30) organizes inexpensive guided excursions year-round.

HORSEBACK RIDING

Excursions and lessons are available at the **Black Horse Ranch** (⊠ Near La Pagerie in Les Trois-Ilets, ☎ 596/68–37–80), **La Cavale** (⊠ Pointe de la Chery, near Le Diamant, ☎ 596/76–20–23), **Ranch Jack** (⊠ Near Anse-d'Arlets, ☎ 596/68–37–69), and **Ranch Val d'Or** (⊠ Ste-Anne, ☎ 596/66–03–46).

SCUBA DIVING

To explore the old shipwrecks, coral gardens, and other undersea sites, you must have a medical certificate and insurance papers. Among the island's dive operators are **Atout Plongee** (⊠ 46 Plateau Roy, Schoelcher, ☎ 596/70–29–33), **Le Marine Hotel** (⊠ Le Diamant, ☎ 596/76–46–00), **Méridien Plongée** (⊠ Hotel Méridien, Pointe du Bout, Les Trois-Ilets, ☎ 596/66–00–00), **Okeonos Club** (⊠ Le Diamant, ☎ 596/76–21–76), **Planete Bleue** (⊠ La Marina, Trois-Ilets, ☎ 596/66–08–79), and **Plongée Passion** (⊠ Anse-d'Arlets, ☎ 596/76–27–39).

The semisubmersible **Aquascope** (✉ Pointe du Bout marina, ☎ 596/68–36–09; ✉ Ste-Anne, ☎ 596/74–87–41) and the glass-bottom boat **Seaquarium** (✉ Les Trois-Ilets, ☎ 596/66–05–50) conduct 45- to 60-minute excursions. For details on sailing, swimming, snorkeling, and beach picnic trips, contact **Affaires Maritimes** (☎ 596/71–90–05).

The **Anse-Spoutourne** (☎ 596/73–19–30), on the Caravelle Peninsula, is an open-air sports and leisure center offering sailing, tennis, and other activities.

In addition to its links, the **Golf de l'Impératrice Joséphine** (✉ Les Trois-Ilets, ☎ 596/68–32–81) has three lighted tennis courts. There are also two courts at **Le Bakoua** (✉ Pointe du Bout, Les Trois Ilets, ☎ 596/66–02–02), six excellent courts at **La Batelière Hotel** (✉ La Batelière, Schoelcher, ☎ 596/61–64–52), seven courts (six lighted) at **Club Med/Buccaneer's Creek** (✉ Pointe du Marin, ☎ 596/76–74–52), two courts at **Diamant-Novotel** (✉ Pointe de la Chery, Le Diamant, ☎ 596/76–42–42), one court at the **Leyritz Plantation** (✉ Bourg, Basse-Pointe, ☎ 596/78–53–92), and two courts at **Le Méridien Trois-Ilets** (✉ Pointe du Bout, Les Trois-Ilets, ☎ 596/66–00–00).

Several other hotels have tennis courts that are available to nonguests when empty, including the **Anchorage Hotel** (✉ Domaine de Belfond, Ste-Anne), ☎ 596/76–92–32), **Le Marine** (✉ Pointe de la Chery, Le Diamant, ☎ 596/76–46–00), and **Primerêve Hotel** (✉ Ste-Marie, ☎ 596/69–40–40). For additional information about tennis on the island, contact **La Ligue Régionale de Tennis** (✉ Petit Manoir, Lamentin, ☎ 596/51–08–00), a tennis club where an hour's court time averages 50F for nonguests. There are also three squash courts at the modern, aptly named **Squash Hotel** (✉ 3 bd. de la Marine, ☎ 596/63–00–34), just outside Fort-de-France.

Shopping

French fragrances and designer scarves, fine china and crystal, leather goods, and liquors and liqueurs are all good buys in Fort-de-France. Purchases are further sweetened by the 20% discount on luxury items when paid for by traveler's checks or certain major credit cards. Among local items, look for Creole gold jewelry, such as loop earrings and heavy bead necklaces; white and dark rum; and handcrafted straw goods, pottery, and tapestries.

Areas and Malls

The area around the cathedral in Fort-de-France has a number of small shops that carry luxury items. Of particular note are the shops on **rue Victor Hugo, rue Moreau de Jones, rue Antoine Siger,** and **rue Lamartine.** The **Galleries Lafayette** department store in downtown Fort-de-France sells everything from perfume to crockery. On the outskirts of Fort-de-France, shopping malls include **Centre Commercial de Cluny, Centre Commercial de Dillon, Centre Commercial de Bellevue,** and more than 100 boutiques at **La Galleria** in Le Lamentin.

Specialty Items

Cadet Daniel (✉ 72 rue Antoine Siger, Fort-de-France, ☎ 596/71–41–48) sells Lalique, Limoges, and Baccarat. **Roger Albert** (✉ 7 rue Victor Hugo, Fort-de-France, ☎ 596/71–71–71) carries crystal from all the major designers.

HANDICRAFTS

Following the roadside signs advertising ATELIERS ARTISANALES (art studios) can yield unexpected treasures, many of them reasonably priced. **Art et Nature** (⊠ Ste-Luce, ☎ 596/62−59−19) features Joel Gilbert's unique wood paintings, daubed with 20−30 shades of earth and sand. **Atelier Céramique** (⊠ Just outside Le Diamant, ☎ 596/76−42−65) displays the ceramics, paintings, and miscellaneous souvenirs of owners and talented artists David and Jeannine England. They've lived in the Caribbean for more than a decade and are members of the island's small British expatriate community. **Centre des Métiers d'Art** (⊠ Rue Ernest Deproge, Fort-de-France, ☎ 596/70−25−01) exhibits authentic local arts and crafts. **Galerie Arti-Bijoux** (⊠ 89 rue Victor Hugo, Fort-de-France, ☎ 596/63−10−62) has some unusual and excellent Haitian art—paintings, sculptures, ceramics, and intricate jewelry cases—at reasonable prices.

Artisanat & Poterie des Trois-Ilets (⊠ Trois-Ilets, ☎ 596/68−18−01) allows you to watch the creation of Arawak- and Carib-style pots, vases, and jars. **L'Eclat de Verre** (⊠ Hwy. N4, outside Gros Morne, ☎ 596/58−34−03) specializes in all manner of glittering glasswork. **La Paille Caraibe** (⊠ Morne des Esses, ☎ 596/69−83−74) is where you can watch artisans weave straw baskets, mats, hats, and amphorae. **Victor Anicet** (⊠ Monésie, ☎ 596/68−25−42) fashions lovely ceramic masks and vases.

PERFUME

Airport minishops sell the most popular scents at in-town prices. **Roger Albert** (⊠ 7 rue Victor Hugo, Fort-de-France, ☎ 596/71−71−71) stocks such popular scents as those by Dior, Chanel, and Guerlain.

RUM

One of the best rums on the island is the *vieux rhum* from **JM distillery** (⊠ Macouba, ☎ 596/78−92−55). You can also get some great rum and tour the grounds of the bucolic 32-acre **Habitation Clément** (⊠ Le François, ☎ 596/54−62−07, FAX 596/54−63−50). Other distilleries include **Duquesnes** (⊠ Fort-de-France, ☎ 596/71−91−68), **St. James** (⊠ Ste-Marie, ☎ 596/69−30−02), and **Trois Rivières** (⊠ Ste-Luce, ☎ 596/62−51−78).

Nightlife

Although Martinique is dotted with lively discos and nightclubs, nightlife isn't confined to partying. Most leading hotels offer nightly entertainment in season, including the marvelous **Les Grands Ballets de Martinique,** one of the finest folkloric dance troupes in the Caribbean. Consisting of about 30 musicians and dancers dressed in traditional costume, the ballet brings alive the Martinique of yesteryear through dance rhythms such as the beguine or the *mazurka*. In addition, many restaurants offer live combos, usually on weekends.

CASINOS

The island's newest casino is in the **Casino Batelière Plaza** (⊠ Schoelcher, ☎ 596/61−91−51, FAX 596/61−99−04) on the outskirts of Fort-de-France. The casino is divided into two areas: to the left are more than 100 slot machines; to the right, you'll need 70F, a passport (you must be 21 to play), and the proper attire (jacket and tie for men, dresses for women) to play blackjack, roulette, or baccarat. Fine dining is offered in an area about the size of a boxing ring. The slots are open Monday−Saturday noon− 3 AM; for the other games, things start rolling at 8 PM and continue until 3 AM.

You must be at least 21 (with a picture ID) to enter the **Casino Trois-Ilets** and play American and French roulette or blackjack. Admission

to slot-machine room is free. ⊠ *Méridien*, ☎ *596/66–00–30*. ☜ *70F.*
🕐 *Mon.–Sat. 9 PM–3 AM.*

DISCOS

Your hotel or the tourist office can put you in touch with the current
"in" places. It's also wise to check on opening and closing times and cover
charges. For the most part, the discos draw a mixed crowd. Some of the
current hot spots are **L'Alibi** (⊠ Morne Tartenson, Fort-de-France, ☎
596/63–45–15), **Le Manikou** (⊠ Zac de Rivière Roche, Fort-de-France,
☎ 596/50–96–99), **Le Queen's** (⊠ La Batelière Hotel, ☎ 596/61–49–
49), **Le Top** (⊠ Zone Artisanale, La Trinité, ☎ 596/58–61–43), and **Zenith**
(⊠ 24 bd. Allègre, Fort-de-France, ☎ 596/60–20–22).

JAZZ AND ZOUK

Jazz musicians, like their music, tend to be informal and independent.
They rarely hold regular gigs. Zouk music mixes Caribbean rhythm
and an Occidental tempo with Creole words. Jacob Devarieux is the
leading exponent of this style and is occasionally on the island. You'll
hear zouk played by one of his followers at the hotels and clubs.

In season, you'll find one or two combos playing at clubs and hotels,
but it's only at **Cocoloco** (⊠ Bd. Alfassa, Fort-de-France, ☎ 596/63–
63–77), next to the tourist office, that there are regular jazz sessions.
The **Neptune** (⊠ Le Diamant, ☎ 596/76–25–47) is a hot spot for zouk.

OTHER MUSIC

L'Amphore (⊠ Behind Le Bakoua hotel, ☎ 596/66–03–09) is a late-
night hangout with a popular piano bar. **Las Tapas** (⊠ 7 rue Garnier
Pages, Fort-de-France, ☎ 596/63–71–23) presents flamenco or salsa
and merengue bands. **La Villa Creole** (⊠ Anse-Mitan, ☎ 596/66–05–
53) is a charming bistro whose owner, Guy Dawson, strums nightly on
the guitar—everything from Piaf to Sting, and some original ditties.

Exploring Martinique

The north of the island will appeal to nature lovers, hikers, and mountain climbers. The drive from Fort-de-France to St-Pierre is particularly
impressive, as is the one across the island, via Morne Rouge, from the
Caribbean to the Atlantic. This is Martinique's wild side—a place of
waterfalls, rain forest, and mountains. The highlight is Mont Pelée. The
south is the more developed half of the island, where the resorts and
restaurants are, as well as the casinos, shopping malls, and beaches.

Numbers in the margin correspond to points of interest on the Mar-
tinique map.

SIGHTS TO SEE

⑫ Ajoupa-Bouillon. This flower-filled, 17th-century village amid pineapple fields is the jumping-off point for several sights. The **Saut Babin** is
a 40-ft-high waterfall, half an hour's walk from Ajoupa-Bouillon.The
Gorges de la Falaise is a river gorge where you can swim. **Les Ombrages**
botanical gardens has marked trails through the rain forest. ☜ *20F.*
🕐 *Daily 9–5.*

❹ Balata. This quiet little town has two sights worth visiting. **Balata Church**
is an exact replica of Sacré-Coeur Basilica in Paris built in 1923 to commemorate those who died in World War I. The **Jardin de Balata** (Balata Gardens), created over 20 years by Jean-Philippe Thoze, a
professional landscaper and devoted horticulturist, has thousands of
varieties of tropical flowers and plants. There are shaded benches from
which to take in the panoramic views of the mountains. ⊠ *Rte. de Bal-*
ata, ☎ *596/72–58–82, 596/64–48–73*. ☜ *35F.* 🕐 *Daily 9–5.*

⑪ Basse-Pointe. On the route (and there's really only one) to this village on the Atlantic coast at the island's northern end, you pass many vast banana and pineapple plantations—agriculture for as far as the eye can see. Just south of Basse-Pointe is a **Hindu temple**, one of the relics of the East Indians who settled in this area in the 19th century. The view of the eastern slope of Mont Pelée is lovely from here. But the highlight of Basse-Pointe is the estimable **Leyritz Plantation**, which has been a hotel for several years. When tour groups from cruise ships aren't swarming the property, the rustic setting, complete with sugarcane factory and gardens, is delightful. Fans of the arcane can visit the plantation's Musée des Figurines Végétales. Local artisan Will Fenton has used bananas, *balisier* (a tall grass), and other local plants to make dolls of famous French women—from Marie Antoinette to Madame Curie—all in extravagant period costumes. ⊠ *Musée de des Figurines Végétales, Leyritz Plantation,* ☎ *596/78–53–92.* ⊑ *15F.* ☉ *Daily 10–7.*

❸ Bellefontaine. This colorful fishing village has pastel houses on the hillsides and beautifully painted gommiers (fishing boats made from the gum tree) bobbing in the water. Look for the house built in the shape of a boat.

⑳ Diamond Rock. A mile offshore from the small, friendly village of Le Diamant is this volcanic mound. In 1804, during the squabbles over possession of the island between the French and the English, the latter commandeered the rock, armed it with cannons, christened it HMS *Diamond Rock,* and proceeded to use it as a warship. For almost 1½ years, the British held the rock, attacking any French ships that came along. The French got wind of the fact that the British were getting cabin fever on their isolated ship-island and arranged a supply of barrels of rum for those on the rock. The French easily overpowered the inebriated sailors, ending one of the most curious engagements in naval history.

⑮ Dubuc Castle. At the eastern tip of the ☞ **Presqu'île du Caravelle** are the ruins of this castle, once the home of the Dubuc de Rivery family, who owned the Caravelle Peninsula in the 18th century. According to legend, young Aimée Dubuc de Rivery was captured by Barbary pirates, sold to the Ottoman Empire, became a favorite of the sultan, and gave birth to Mahmud II.

㉑ Forêt de Montravail. A few miles north of ☞ **Ste-Luce,** this tropical rain forest is one of the best places in the south of the island for a short hike. Look for the interesting group of Carib rock drawings.

❶ Fort-de-France. With its historic fort and superb setting beneath the towering Pitons du Carbet on the Baie des Flamands, Martinique's capital and home to about ⅓ of the island's 360,000 inhabitants, should be a grand place. It isn't. The most pleasant districts, such as Bellevue and Schoelcher, are on the hillside, and you need a car to reach them. Yet if you come here by car, you may find yourself trapped in gridlock in the warren of narrow streets that is the center of town. True, there are some good shops with Parisian wares (at Parisian prices) and lively street markets that sell, among other things, human hair for wigs (starting price, 200F). But the heat, exhaust fumes, and litter tend to make exploring here a chore. At night, the city feels dark and gloomy, with little street life except for the extravagantly dressed *femmes de nuit* who openly parade the streets from 10 PM.

The city's heart is **La Savane,** a 12½-acre landscaped park filled with trees, fountains, and benches. It's a popular gathering place and the scene of promenades, parades, and impromptu soccer matches. Along the east side, there are numerous snack wagons. A statue of Pierre Belain d'Esnambuc, leader of the island's first settlers, is unintentionally upstaged by Vital Dubray's vandalized white Carrara marble statue of the empress Joséphine, Napoléon's first wife. Sculpted in a high-waisted Empire gown, Joséphine used to gaze toward Les Trois-Ilets across the bay, where, in 1763, she was born Marie-Joseph Tascher de la Pagerie. But not any more. A couple of years ago, vandals decapitated the statue and cut off one hand. Then, adding a final gruesome touch, they poured a red, blood-like paint all around. So far, the government has refused to remove or restore the monument. The most imposing historic site is **Fort St-Louis,** which runs along the east side of La Savane. It is open Tuesday–Saturday 9–3 and admission is 25F. Near the harbor is a marketplace where local crafts and souvenirs are sold. Across from La Savane, you can catch the ferry *La Vedette* for the beaches at Anse-Mitan and Anse-à-l'Ane and for the 20-minute run across the bay to the resort hotels of Pointe du Bout. It's much faster than the journey round the bay by car and costs $5.

The **Bibliothèque Schoelcher** is the wildly elaborate Byzantine-Egyptian-Romanesque-style public library. It was named after Victor Schoelcher, who led the fight to free the slaves in the French West Indies in the 19th century. The eye-popping structure was built for the 1889 Paris Exposition, after which it was dismantled, shipped to Martinique, and reassembled piece by ornate piece. ⊠ *Corner of rue de la Liberté (runs along west side of La Savane) and rue Perrinon,* ☎ *596/ 70–26–67.* ⊙ *Mon. 1–5:30, Tues.–Thurs. 8:30–5:30, and Fri.–Sat. 8:30–noon.*

At the southern end of rue de la Liberté is the **Musée Départementale de Martinique,** with exhibits on the pre-Columbian Arawak and Carib periods, including pottery, beads, and part of a skeleton that turned up during excavations in 1972. One exhibit examines the history of slavery; costumes, documents, furniture, and handicrafts from the island's colonial period are on display. ⊠ *9 rue de la Liberté,* ☎ *596/ 71–57–05.* ⊠ *15F.* ⊙ *Weekdays 8:30–1 and 2:30–5, Sat. 9–noon.*

Rue Victor Schoelcher runs through the center of the capital's primary shopping district, a six-block area bounded by rue de la République, rue de la Liberté, rue de Victor Severe, and rue Victor Hugo. Stores feature Paris fashions (at Paris prices) and French perfume, china, crystal, and liqueurs, as well as local handicrafts. The Romanesque **St-Louis Cathedral** (⊠ Rue Schoelcher) was the sixth to be built on this site (the others were destroyed by fire, hurricane, or earthquake). It dates from 1878 and has lovely stained-glass windows. A number of Martinique's former governors are interred beneath the choir loft.

The Galerie de Biologie et de Géologie at the **Parc Floral et Culturel,** in the northeastern corner of the city center, will acquaint you with the island's exotic flora. There's also an aquarium. The park contains the island's official cultural center, where there are sometimes free evening concerts. Wandering about the grounds, you'll run into musicians and artists, who may give you an impromptu lesson on how to play a steel drum or work with driftwood. ⊠ *Pl. José-Marti, Sermac,* ☎ *596/71–66–25.* ⊠ *Grounds free, aquarium 35F, botanical and geological gallery 5F.* ⊙ *Park daily dawn–10 PM; aquarium daily 9–7; gallery Tues.–Fri. 9:30–12:30 and 3:30–5:30, Sat. 9–1 and 3–5.*

The **Rivière Madame** meanders through the park and joins the bay at Pointe Simon. The river divides the downtown area from the ritzy residential district of Didier in the hills. Fronting the river, on avenue Paul Nardal, are the vibrantly noisy, messy, smelly vegetable and fish markets. One of the best shows in town occurs around 4 PM, when fishermen return with their catch, effortlessly tossing 100-pound bundles of rainbow-hued fish.

🔟 **Le François.** With some 16,000 inhabitants, this is the main city on the Atlantic coast. Sadly, the old wooden buildings are being replaced by concrete structures. But the classic West Indian cemetery, with its black-and-white tiles, is still here. The **Habitation Clément** is Martinique's Williamsburg, complete with Creole ladies in traditional dresses moving about the grounds. It was built with the wealth generated by its rum distillery, and its 18th century splendor has been lovingly preserved, providing a glimpse into the elegance and privilege of plantation society. French President Jacques Chirac visited; President Bush and François Mitterrand had a summit meeting here; Barbara Hendricks, the opera singer, loved it. The rum distillery is operational and offers free tastings. The grounds contain a superb collection of ancient trees. ✉ *Domaine de l'Acajou,* ☎ *596/54–62–07.* 🎫 *40F.* ☼ *Daily 9–6.*

Le François is also noted for its snorkeling. Offshore are the privately owned **Les Ilets de l'Impératrice.** The islands received that name because, according to legend, this is where Empress Joséphine came to bathe in the shallow basins known as *fonds blancs* because of their white-sand bottoms. Group boat tours leave from the harbor ($30 per person includes lunch and drinks). You can also haggle with a fisherman to take you out for a while on his boat to indulge in the uniquely Martinican custom of standing waist-deep in warm water, sipping a 'ti punch, eating accras, and smoking. There's a fine bay 6 mi farther along the coast at **Le Robert,** though the town is somewhat lackluster.

🔟 **Lamentin.** There's nothing pretty about Lamentin. The multibillion-franc airport, which opened in 1995, is its most notable landmark. The rest of the town is a sprawling industrial and commercial zone. But you come here for shopping rather than sightseeing. Be sure to browse in the big, fancy shopping mall **Euromarché.** The brand-new **La Galleria,** a megamall of roughly 100 shops and boutiques, offers everything from pâté de foie gras and Camembert to CDs and sunglasses.

🔟 **Macouba.** Named after the Carib word for "fish," this village was a prosperous tobacco town in the 17th century. Today, its cliff-top location affords magnificent views of the sea, the mountains, and—on clear days—the neighboring island of Dominica. The **JM distillery** produces the best rhum vieux on the island here. A tour and samples are free. Macouba is also the starting point for a spectacular drive, the **6-mi route to Grand' Rivière** on the northernmost point. This is Martinique at its greenest; groves of giant bamboo, cliffs hung with curtains of vines, and 7-ft tree ferns that seem to grow as you watch them. At the end of the road is Grand' Rivière, a sprawling fishing village at the foot of high cliffs—the village is, literally, the end of the road. On weekends, it's a bustling place with plenty of snack bars and cafés as well as colorfully painted boats pulled up onto the beach. Hardy folk can trek 11 mi to the beach at Anse-Ceron on the northwest coast.

🔟 **Le Marin.** The yachting capital of Martinique is also known for its colorful August carnival and its Jesuit church, which was built in 1766 and is one of the oldest on the island. From Le Marin a small road leads to picturesque **Cap Chevalier** (Cape Knight), about 1 mi from town.

🔟 **Le Morne Rouge.** This town sits on the southern slopes of the volcano that destroyed it in 1902. Today it's a popular resort spot and offers hikers some fantastic mountain scenery. From Le Morne Rouge you can start the climb up the 4,600-ft **Mont Pelée** volcano. But don't try it without a guide unless you want to get buried alive under pumice stones. Instead, drive up to the Refuge de l'Aileron. From the parking lot it's a mile up a well-marked trail to the summit. Bring a sweatshirt, because there's often a mist that makes the air damp and chilly. From the summit, follow the Route de la Trace (Route N3), which winds south of Le Morne Rouge to St-Pierre. The route used to be one of the main footpaths across the northern half of the island. It's steep and winding, but that didn't stop the *porteuses* of old: Balancing a tray, these women would carry up to 100 pounds of provisions on their heads for the 15-hour trek to the Atlantic coast.

6 **Musée Gauguin.** Martinique was a brief station in Paul Gauguin's wanderings but a decisive moment in the evolution of his art. He arrived from Panama in 1887 with friend and fellow painter Charles Laval and, having pawned his watch at the docks, rented a wooden shack on a hill above the village of Carbet. He stayed only seven months, before sickness and poverty drove him back to Paris, but his stay here precipitated a change in his art. Indeed, he would later say that to understand him and his art, one had to understand his Martinique period. Dazzled by the tropical colors and vegetation, Gauguin developed a style that directly anticipated his Tahitian paintings. This modest museum is a labor of love on the part of local art historian Maiotte Dauphite and a group of other Martinicans. Though it has no originals (Gauguin's most famous Martinique painting, *Végétation Tropicale*, is in the Royal Scottish Museum in Edinburgh), it does have a set of reproductions. Indeed, this is the only place you can see all of Gauguin's Martinique work under one roof. There are also interesting exhibits of letters and documents relating to the painter, and an exhibition of local costumes. Another major artist also remembered here is the writer Lafcadio Hearn, who came to Martinique in the same year as Gauguin, on assignment for *Harper's* magazine. In his endearing book *Two Years in the West Indies,* he provides the most extensive description of the island before ☞ St-Pierre was buried in ash and lava. ⊠ *Anse-Turin, Carbet,* ☎ *596/78–22–66.* 🖅 *15F.* ☉ *Daily 9–5:30.*

19 **Pointe du Bout.** This area is filled with resort hotels, among them the Bakoua and the Méridien. The Pointe du Bout marina is a colorful spot where a whole slew of boats are tied up. The ferry to Fort-de-France leaves from here. More than anywhere else on Martinique, Pointe du Bout caters to the vacationer. A cluster of boutiques, ice cream parlors, and rental-car agencies forms the hub from which restaurants and hotels of varying caliber radiate. The beach at **Anse-Mitan** is one of the best on the island. At **Anse-à-l'Ane,** a little to the west of Pointe du Bout, there is a pretty white-sand beach complete with picnic tables. There are also numerous small restaurants and inexpensive guesthouse hotels here. Ten miles south is **Anse-d'Arlets,** a quiet backwater fishing village. You'll see fishermen's nets strung up on the beach to dry and pleasure boats on the water.

9 **Le Prêcheur.** This quaint town, the last on the northern Caribbean coast, is surrounded by volcanic hot springs. The village itself was the childhood home of Françoise d'Aubigné, who later became the Marquise de Maintenon and the second wife of Louis XIV. At her request, the Sun King donated a handsome bronze bell to the village, which you can see hanging outside the church. **The Tomb of the Carib Indians,** on the way from St-Pierre, commemorates a sadder event. The site is actually a formation of limestone cliffs from which the last of the Caribs are said to have flung themselves to avoid capture by the Marquise's forebears.

The **Maison de la Canne** (at Pointe Vatable, as you leave town) will teach you everything you ever wanted to know about sugarcane. Exhibits take you through three centuries of cane production, with displays of tools, scale models, engravings, and photographs. ⊠ *Les Trois-Ilets,* ☎ *596/68–32–04.* ⌷ *15F.* ⊙ *Tues.–Sun. 9–6.*

⓮ **Presqu'île du Caravelle.** Much of the Caravelle Peninsula, which juts 8 mi into the Atlantic Ocean, is under the auspices of the Regional Nature Reserve and offers places for trekking, swimming, and sailing. This is also the cite of Anse-Spoutourne (☞ Outdoor Activities and Sports, *above*), an open-air sports and leisure center operated by the reserve. Tartane has a popular beach with cool Atlantic breezes.

㉓ **Ste-Anne.** A lovely white-sand beach and a Roman Catholic church are the highlights of this town on the island's southern tip. To the south of Ste-Anne is Pointe des Salines, the southernmost tip of the island and site of Martinique's best beach, **Les Salines,** 1½ mi of soft white sand. It's definitely *the* place for beach bums, and there's a lively scene here on weekends; *le topless* is almost de rigueur. Near Ste-Anne is **La Savane des Pétrifications,** the Petrified Forest. This desertlike stretch was once swampland and is a veritable geological museum where a few specimens of petrified wood can still be found.

㉒ **Ste-Luce.** This quaint fishing village has a sleepy main street that's deserted at midday, and panoramic views across to the island of St. Lucia. Ste-Luce also has excellent beaches. To the east is **Pointe Figuier,** an excellent spot for scuba diving. On the way from Ste-Luce to Pointe Figuier, you'll find the **Ecomusée de Martinique,** which is more a historical than a natural history museum. Holdings include artifacts from Arawak and Carib settlements through the plantation years. ⊠ *Anse Figuier,* ☎ *596/62–79–14.* ⌷ *20F.* ⊙ *Tues.–Sun. 9–5.*

⓭ **Ste-Marie.** This town is home to about 20,000 Martinicans and is the commercial capital of the island's north. There's a lovely mid-19th-century church here, as well as the **Musée du Rhum,** operated by the St. James Rum Distillery. It's housed in a graceful, galleried, Creole house. Guided tours take in displays of the tools of the trade and include a visit to the distillery. And, yes, you may sample the product. ⊠ *Ste-Marie,* ☎ *596/69–30–02.* ⌷ *Free.* ⊙ *Weekdays 9–6, weekends 9–1, except during the harvest period, Feb.–June.*

Le Musée de la Banane. You probably won't find more cordial hosts than those at the Banana Museum in Ste-Marie. After navigating the extremely narrow road (beep your horn several times as you approach blind curves), you'll arrive at the well-maintained compound. Once on the grounds, four different stops tell the story of the banana (Martinique's primary export) as it makes its way from the fields to your table. Excellent graphics and beautiful prints aid immeasurably in the storytelling. ⊠ *Ste-Marie,* ☎ *596/69–45–01.* ⌷ *30F.* ⊙ *Daily 9–5.*

❼ **St-Pierre.** The rise and fall of St-Pierre is one of the most remarkable stories in the Caribbean. Martinique's modern history began here when Belain d'Esnambuc, a French adventurer, cast anchor in 1635. He and his men settled and built a fort. By the turn of this century, St-Pierre was a flourishing city of 30,000. It was known as the Paris of the West Indies: There were cabarets, cafés, and a cathedral; warehouses climbed the hills. As many as 30 ships at a time stood at anchor. By 1902 it was the most modern town in the Caribbean, with electricity, phones, and a tram. But in the spring of 1902, Mont Pelée began to rumble and spit out ash and steam. On May 2, it spewed out a river of lava that engulfed a factory, killing 25. City officials, however, ignored the warning, needing voters in town for an upcoming election. Shortly after 8 AM on May 8, 1902, two thunderous explosions rent the air. As it erupted, Mont Pelée split in half, belching forth a cloud of burning ash, poisonous gas, and lava that raced down the mountain at 250 mph. With temperatures of more than 3,600°F, St-Pierre was instantly vaporized. Thirty thousand people were killed in two minutes. The Paris of the West Indies had become its Pompeii. One man survived. Of all the inhabitants of St-Pierre, he was probably the last person anyone would have expected to live—and the last many would have wanted to. His name was Cyparis and he was a prisoner in the town's jail. Though he was scorched by the heat, the thick walls of his underground cell saved him. He was later pardoned and for some years afterward was a sideshow attraction in the Barnum & Bailey Circus.

For those interested in the eruption of 1902, the **Musée Vulcanologique** is a must. It was established in 1932 by American volcanologist Franck Perret. His collection includes photographs of the old town, documents, and a number of relics—some gruesome—excavated from the ruins, including molten glass, melted iron, and contorted clocks stopped at 8 AM. ⊠ *St-Pierre,* ☎ *596/78–15–16.* ⊡ *15F.* ⊙ *Daily 9–5.*

Today, St-Pierre is trying to reinvent itself. A snappy new Office du Tourisme has been built, as well as a seafront promenade. There are plenty of sidewalk cafés, some of which have live music, and you can also see the ruins of the island's first church (built in 1640), the theater, the toppled statues, and Cyparis's cell. The *Cyparis Express* is a small tourist train that runs through the city, hitting the important sights with a running narrative (in French). ⊠ *Train departs from pl. des Ruines du Figuier,* ☎ *596/55–50–92.* ⊡ *30F.* ⊙ *Runs every 45 mins, weekdays 9:30–1 and 2:30–5:30; call for exact times.*

❷ **Schoelcher.** Pronounced "shell-*share,*" this suburb of Fort-de-France is home of the University of the French West Indies and Guyana. La Batelière Hotel (☞ Lodging, *above*), noted for its sports facilities, is also here.

⑱ **Les Trois-Ilets.** Named after the three rocky islands nearby, this lovely little village (population 3,000) has unusual brick and wood buildings roofed with antique tiles. It's known for its pottery, straw, and woodwork, but above all as the birthplace of Napoléon's empress Joséphine. In the square, where there's also a market and a fine *mairie* (town hall), you can visit the simple church where she was baptized Marie-Joseph Tascher de la Pagerie. The Martinicans have always been enormously proud of Joséphine, even though she reintroduced slavery on the island and most historians consider her to have been a rather shallow woman. A stone building that held the kitchen of the estate where she grew up is home to the **Musée de la Pagerie.** (The main house blew down in the hurricane of 1766, when Joséphine was three.) It contains an assortment of memorabilia pertaining to Joséphine's life and rather unfortunate loves. At 16 she was wed (an arranged marriage) to Alexandre de Beauharnais. When he died, she married Napoléon, but he divorced her because she didn't produce any children. There are family portraits; documents, including a marriage certificate; a love letter written to her in 1796 by Napoléon; and various antique furnishings. ☎ *596/68–33–06.* ⊡ *20F.* ⊙ *Tues.–Fri. 9–5, weekends 9–1.*

❺ **La Vallée des Papillons.** Enter the dream world of flight as delicate butterflies dance on your shoulders. Situated among the ruins of one of the first 17th-century settlements on Martinique, the Valley of the Butterflies educates as it enchants. Their complete lifecycle is played out before your eyes in a luxuriant garden with a great assortment of flowers and trees as well as waterfalls. As a counterbalance, some rather grotesque and altogether imposing insects gathered from throughout the Caribbean are also on display but all of them are safely stick-pinned under glass. The grounds also contain a modest restaurant and gift shop.

✉ *Habitation Anse Latouche in Carbet (just around corner from Musée Gaugin)* , ☎ *596/78–19–19.* 🖼 *38F.* ⊙ *9:30–4:30.*

㉕ **Le Vauclin.** The return of the fishermen shortly before noon is the big event in this important fishing port on the Atlantic coast. There's also an 18th-century church here, the **Chapel of the Holy Virgin.** Nearby is the highest point in the south, **Mont Vauclin** (1,654 ft). A hike to the top will reward you with one of the best views on the island.

Martinique A to Z

Arriving and Departing

BY AIRPLANE

The most frequent flights from the United States are on **American Airlines** (☎ 596/42–19–19), which has year-round daily service from more than 100 U.S. cities to San Juan. From there, the airline's American Eagle flies on to Martinique with a stop first at Guadeloupe. **Air France** (☎ 596/55–33–33) flies direct from Miami and San Juan. **Air Canada** (☎ 800/776–3000) has service from Montréal and Toronto. **LIAT** (☎ 596/42–16–02), with its extensive coverage of the Antilles, flies in from Antigua, St. Maarten, Guadeloupe, Dominica, St. Lucia, Barbados, Grenada, and Trinidad and Tobago.

From the Airport: You'll arrive at the new **Lamentin International Airport** (☎ 596/42–16–00, 596/42–19–95, or 596/42–19–96), which is about a 15-minute taxi ride from Fort-de-France and about 40 minutes from Les Trois-Ilets peninsula, the first of many resort areas on the southern beaches and where most hotels are.

BY BOAT

The **Express des Isles** (☎ 596/63–12–11) offers scheduled interisland service aboard a 128-ft, 227-passenger motorized catamaran, linking Martinique with Dominica, Guadeloupe, Les Saintes, and St. Lucia. For those who don't get seasick, it's an enormously pleasurable way to travel, with great views of the islands. Fares run approximately 25% below economy airfares. Sailings are not every day of the week for all destinations; check the schedule.

Electricity

Most tourist locations on the island are equipped with 220-volt electrical outlets; if you're coming from North America and plan to use your own appliances, bring a converter kit with a variety of adaptors.

Emergencies

Ambulance: ☎ 70–36–48 or 71–59–48. **Fire:** ☎ 18. **Hospital:** There's a 24-hour emergency room at **Hôpital La Meynard** (✉ Châteauboeuf, just outside Fort-de-France, ☎ 596/55–20–00). **Pharmacies: Pharmacie de la Paix** (✉ Corner rue Victor Schoelcher and rue Perrinon, Fort-de-France, ☎ 596/71–94–83) and **Pharmacie Cypria** (✉ Bd. Général de Gaulle, Fort-de-France, ☎ 596/63–22–25). **Police:** ☎ 17.

Festivals and Seasonal Events

Martinique's **Carnival** begins in early January and runs through the first day of Lent. About 20 days into Lent, there's a mini-Carnival called **Mi-carême.** This one-day hiatus from what is traditionally 40 days of abstinence brings parties, dances, and the like; after it, however, everyone returns to the somber (and often sober) business of penance until Easter. Early August sees the **Tour des Yoles Rondes** point-to-point yawl race. In Early December, the island hosts the Caribbean's premier jazz festival, **Jazz à la Martinique.** In addition to showcasing the best musical talent of the islands, it has attracted such top American performers as Branford Marsalis, Dizzy Gillespie, and Eddie Daniels.

Getting Around
BICYCLES AND MOTORBIKES
Bikes, scooters, and motorbikes are all popular, and you can rent them from **Discount** (✉ Marina Pointe du Bout, Les Trois Ilets, ☎ 596/66–05–34), **Funny** (✉ 80 rue Ernest Deprage, Fort-de-France, ☎ 596/63–33–05), or **Grabin's Rental** (✉ Morne Calbasse, Fort-de-France, ☎ 596/71–51–61). In Ste-Anne try **Huet** (☎ 596/76–79–66); and in Ste-Luce check out **Vespa Marquis** (☎ 596/60–02–84).

BUSES
Public buses are crowded, and if you're at all timid, you probably won't like them. But eight-passenger minivans (license plates bear the letters TC) are an inexpensive—and fun—means of transportation. In Fort-de-France, the main terminal for the minivans is at Pointe Simon on the waterfront. There are frequent departures from early morning until 8 PM; fares range from $1 to $5.

CAR RENTALS
Unless you're at an all-inclusive resort, you'll definitely need a car. With about 175 mi of well-paved and well-marked roads (albeit with international signs), Martinique is a good place for driving. The Martinicans drive with aggressive abandon but are surprisingly courteous and will let you into the flow of traffic. Country roads are mountainous with hairpin curves. Watch out, too, for *dos d'ânes* (literally, donkey backs), speed bumps that are extremely hard to spot—particularly at night—though if you hit one you'll know about it. Streets in Fort-de-France are narrow and choked with traffic during the day. If you want a detailed map, the *Carte Routière et Touristique* is available at bookstores. A full tank of gas will get you all the way around the island with gallons to spare—a good thing because gas is costly (about 6F per liter or roughly $4 per gallon).

A valid U.S. driver's license is needed to rent a car for up to 20 days. After that, you'll need an International Driver's Permit. U.K. visitors can use their EU licenses. Rates are about $60 per day (unlimited mileage), but always question agents thoroughly about possible discounts. If you book from the United States at least 48 hours in advance, you can qualify for a hefty discount. Among the many agencies in Fort-de-France are **Avis** (☎ 596/70–11–60 or 800/331–1212), **Budget** (☎ 596/63–69–00 or 800/472–3325), and **Hertz** (☎ 596/60–64–64 or 800/654–3131).

FERRIES
Weather permitting, *vedettes* (ferries) operate daily between Fort-de-France and the Marina Méridien in Pointe du Bout as well as between Fort-de-France and Anse-Mitan and Anse-à-l'Ane (all trips take about 25 minutes). The Quai d'Esnambuc is the arrival and departure point in Fort-de-France. At press time, the one-way fare was 30F.

TAXIS
Taxis are expensive. From the airport to Fort-de-France is about 100F; from the airport to Pointe du Bout, about 225F. A 40% surcharge is in effect between 8 PM and 6 AM and on Sunday. This means that if you arrive at Lamentin at night, depending on where your hotel is, it may be cheaper to rent a car from the airport and keep it for 24 hours than to take a one-way taxi to your hotel. To request a cab, call ☎ 596/63–63–62 or 596/63–10–10.

Guided Tours
The folks at the tourist office (*see* Visitor Information, *below*) can help you arrange a personalized island tour with an English-speaking taxi

driver. There are set rates for tours to various points, and if you share the ride with two or three others, the price will be whittled down.

Madinina Tours (⌧ 111–113 rue Ernest Deproge, Fort-de-France, ☎ 596/70–65–25) offers half- and full-day jaunts, with lunch included in the all-day outings. Boat tours are also available, as are air excursions to the Grenadines and St. Lucia. Madinina has tour desks in most of the major hotels. **Parc Naturel Régional de la Martinique** (⌧ 9 bd. Général de Gaulle, Fort-de-France 97206, ☎ 596/73–19–30) organizes inexpensive guided hiking tours year-round. Descriptive folders are available at the tourist office (*see* Visitor Information, *below*).

Language

Many Martinicans speak Creole, a mixture of Spanish and French. Even if you do speak fluent French, you may have a problem understanding the accent. Try *sa ou fe* for "hello." In major tourist areas you'll find someone who speaks English, but using a few French words—even if it's only to say *"Parlez-vous anglais?"*—will be appreciated. Most menus are written in French, so a dictionary is helpful. But rest assured that the people of Martinique are extremely courteous and will work with you on your French—or lack of it.

Money Matters

CURRENCY

The currency is the French franc. At press time, the exchange rate was 6F to US$1. U.S. dollars are accepted in some hotels, but for convenience, it's better to convert your money into francs. Banks give a more favorable rate than hotels. A currency exchange service that also offers a favorable rate is **Change Caraibes** (☎ 596/51–57–91), in the arrivals building at Lamentin International Airport; it's open weekdays 7 AM–9 PM and Saturday 8:30–2. Another is in **Fort-de-France** (⌧ Rue Ernest Deproge, across from tourist office, ☎ 596/60–28–40) and is open weekdays 7:30–6 and Saturday 8–12:30. Prices quoted here are in U.S. dollars unless indicated otherwise.

Major credit cards are accepted in hotels and restaurants in Fort-de-France and the Pointe du Bout areas; few establishments in the countryside accept them. There are ATMs at the airport and at branches of the Crédit Agricole bank, which are on the Cirrus system and also accept Visa and MasterCard. There's a 20% discount on luxury items paid for with traveler's checks or with certain credit cards.

SERVICE CHARGES, TAXES, AND TIPPING

All restaurants include a 15% service charge in their menu prices. You can always add to this if you feel that service was exceptional. A resort tax varies from hotel to hotel; the maximum is $1.50 per person per day. Rates quoted by hotels usually include a 10% service charge; some hotels add 10% to your bill.

Opening and Closing Times

Stores that cater to tourists are generally open weekdays 8:30–6, Saturday 8:30–1. **Banks** are open weekdays 7:30–noon and 2:30–6.

HOLIDAYS

New Year's Day, Ash Wednesday (Feb. 17) Good Friday (Apr. 2), Labor Day (May 1), Bastille Day (July 14), All Saints' Day (Nov. 1), Armistice Day (Nov. 11), and Christmas.

Passports

U.S. and Canadian citizens must have a passport (one that expired no more than five years ago is acceptable) or proof of citizenship, such as an original (not photocopied) birth certificate or a voter registration card, both accompanied by a government-authorized photo identification. British citizens need a national ID or a passport. In addition, all visitors must have a return or ongoing ticket.

Precautions

Exercise the same safety precautions you would in a big city. Don't leave jewelry or money unattended on the beach. Except for the area around Cap Chevalier and the Tartane Peninsula, the Atlantic waters are rough and should be avoided by all but expert swimmers.

Beware of the *mancenillier* (manchineel) trees. These pretty trees with green fruits that look like apples are poisonous. Sap and even raindrops falling from the trees can cause painful, scarring blisters. The trees have red warning signs posted by the forestry commission. If you plan to ramble through the rain forest, be careful where you step. Fer-de-lances and other poisonous snakes exist on Martinique.

Telephones and Mail

To call Martinique station-to-station from the United States, dial 011 + 596 + the local six-digit number. You can't make collect calls from Martinique to the United States, but you can use a calling card. There are few coin phone booths, and those are usually in hotels and restaurants. Most public telephones now use a télécarte, which you can buy at post offices, *café-tabacs* (café-tobacco stores), and hotels.

To place an interisland call, dial the local six-digit number. To call the United States from Martinique, dial 19–1, area code, and the local number. For Great Britain, dial 19–44, the area code (without the first zero), and the number.

Airmail letters to the United States and Canada cost 4.60F for up to 20 grams; postcards, 3.70F. For Great Britain, the costs are 4.40F and 3.60F, respectively. Stamps may be purchased from post offices, café-tabacs, and hotel newsstands. Letters to Martinique should include the name of the business, street (if available), town, postal code, the island, and French West Indies. Be forewarned, however, that mail is extremely slow both coming and going.

Visitor Information

For information, contact the **French West Indies Tourist Board** (☎ 800/ 391–4909). You can also contact the **French Government Tourist Office, Martinique Promotion Bureau** (www.martinique.org; ✉ 444 Madison Ave., New York, NY 10022, ☎ 800/391–4909; ✉ 9454 Wilshire Blvd., Beverly Hills, CA 90212, ☎ 310/271–2358; ✉ 676 N. Michigan Ave., Chicago, IL 60611, ☎ 312/751–7800; ✉ 1981 McGill College Ave., Suite 490, Montréal, Québec H3A 2W9, ☎ 514/844–8566; ✉ 1 Dundas St. W, Suite 2405, Toronto, Ontario M5G 1Z3, ☎ 416/ 593–4723 or 800/361–9099; ✉ 178 Piccadilly, London, W1V 0AL, ☎ 0181/124–4123).

On Martinique, the **Martinique Tourist Office** (✉ Bd. Alfassa, Fort-de-France, ☎ 596/63–79–60) is open Monday–Thursday 8–5, Friday 7:30–5, Saturday 8–noon. The office's free maps and booklets, *Chouboulule* and *Martinique Info,* are useful. The information booth at the airport is open daily until the last flight has landed.

16 Puerto Rico

Updated by
Karl Luntta

T*he pigeons have made Old San Juan their own. They flutter through plazas, rushing for scraps dropped by office workers lunching on the run. Old men sit on shaded benches, enveloped by the scent of roasting coffee from a nearby kiosk, talking quietly about long lives, and holding crumbling paper bags of stale bread. The birds dance for that bread, their gray wings buffing arms and shoulders. It's an ancient, symbiotic moment—a gentle touch for morsels of food.*

Few cities in the Caribbean are as steeped in Spanish tradition as Puerto Rico's Old San Juan. Originally built as a fortress enclave, the old city has myriad attractions, including restored 16th-century buildings, museums, art galleries, bookstores, and 200-year-old houses with balustraded balconies of filigreed wrought iron overlooking narrow cobblestone streets. This Spanish tradition also spills over into the island's countryside, from its festivals celebrated in honor of various patron saints in the little towns to the *paradores*, inexpensive but accommodating inns whose concept originated in Spain.

Puerto Rico is ringed with hundreds of beaches offering every imaginable water sport and acres of golf courses and tennis courts. It has, in San Juan's sophisticated Condado and Isla Verde areas, glittering hotels; flashy, Las Vegas–style shows; casinos; and discos. It has the ambience of the Old World in the seven-square-block area of the old city and in its quiet colonial towns. Out in the countryside lie its natural attractions, including the extraordinary, 28,000-acre Caribbean National Forest, more familiarly known as the El Yunque rain forest, with 100-ft-high trees (more than 240 species of them) and dramatic mountain ranges. You can hike through forest reserves laced with trails, go spelunking in vast caves, and explore coffee plantations and sugar mills. Having seen every sight on the island, you can then do further exploring on the outlying islands of Culebra, Vieques, and Mona, where aquatic activities, such as snorkeling and scuba diving, prevail.

Puerto Rico, 110 mi long and 35 mi wide, was populated by several tribes of Indians when Columbus landed on the island on his second voyage in 1493. In 1508 Juan Ponce de León, the frustrated seeker of the Fountain of Youth, established a settlement on the island and became its first governor, and in 1521, he founded Old San Juan. For three centuries, the French, Dutch, and English tried unsuccessfully to wrest the island from Spain. In 1897 Spain granted the island dominion status. In 1899, as a result of the Spanish American War, Spain ceded the island to the United States, and in 1917, Puerto Ricans became U.S. citizens. In 1952 Puerto Rico became a semiautonomous commonwealth territory of the United States. There have been many referendums over the years where the island's political status has been put to a vote. The choices for Puerto Ricans have been independence, full statehood, or remaining a commonwealth. While strong opinions have been voiced on all sides, the vote has yet to produce statehood or independence.

If you're a U.S. citizen, you need neither passport nor visa when you land at Luis Muñoz Marín International Airport, outside San Juan. You don't have to clear customs, and you don't have to explain yourself to an immigration official. Though the official language is Spanish, English is widely spoken, particularly by those in the tourism industry.

Lodging

Accommodations come in all shapes and sizes. Self-contained luxury resorts cover hundreds of acres. San Juan's high-rise beachfront hotels likewise cater to the cruise-ship and casino crowd; several target business travelers. Outside San Juan, the government-sponsored paradores are modeled after Spain's successful parador system. Some are rural inns, some offer no-frills apartments, and some are large hotels. They must meet certain standards, such as proximity to an attraction or beach. Most have a small restaurant that serves local cuisine. Parador prices range from $50 to $125 for a double room. Reservations for all paradores can be made by writing Box 4435, Old San Juan, Puerto Rico 00902, or by calling 800/443–0266 in the United States, 787/721–2884 in San Juan, or 800/981–7575 elsewhere in Puerto Rico. They're great bargains but can get noisy on weekends, when local families descend for minivacations.

Most hotels in Puerto Rico operate on the European Plan (EP). In some larger hotels, however, packages are available that include several or all meals, while others offer all-inclusive deals. Also, beware when booking hotels outside of San Juan that rates most often do not include airport transfers. Be sure to ask if the hotel offers transportation, what the cost is, and if advance arrangements are necessary. Villa, condominium, or apartment rentals are becoming increasingly popular in Puerto Rico, particularly outside San Juan. If you are traveling with several people, these are often a very affordable option. Call the tourist information office in the area where you want to stay, or try the options below.

If you'd like to investigate rates at higher-end properties in San Juan's Isla Verde area, contact **Condo World** (⊠ 26645 W. Twelve Mile Rd., Southfield, MI 48034, ☎ 800/521–2980). For rentals out on the island, try **San Juan Vacations** (⊠ Marabella del Caribe Oeste S-5, Isla Verde 00979, ☎ 787/727–1591 or 800/266–3639 reservations service, FAX 787/268–3604). They represent some 200 properties in the Condado and Isla Verde areas, in the $ to $$$ range. **Island West Properties** (⊠ Rte. 413, Km 1.3, Box 700, Rincón 00677, ☎ 787/823–

2323, FAX 787/823–3254)has weekly and monthly vacation rentals in Rincón that fall into the $ to $$ range. For rentals on Vieques, the person to talk to is Jane Sabin at **Connections** (⊠ Box 358, Vieques 00765, ☎ 787/741–0023). Or try **Acacia Apartments** (⊠ 236 Calle Acacia, Esperanza, Vieques 00765, ☎ 787/741–1856).

CATEGORY	COST*
$$$$	over $225
$$$	$150–$225
$$	$75–$150
$	under $75

All prices are for a standard double room, excluding 9% tax (11% for hotels with casinos) and 10%–15% service charge.

Old San Juan

$$$$ ☆   🏨 **Hotel El Convento.** After a $15 million refurbishment, El Convento reopened in 1997 with a new luxury status. The 350-year-old, caramel-color building emerged with much of its original architecture intact, including an interior courtyard so popular in Spanish Colonial design. Shaded by a giant nispero tree, the courtyard's Café de Nispero has a popular Sunday brunch. The second floor El Picoteo Restaurant is fast becoming one of the old city's hottest eateries. Rooms now have a Spanish Deco look, with dark woods, wrought-iron lamps, and ornate furniture; walls are ocean blue or mustard yellow. Complimentary evening wine and hors d'oeuvres are served before dinner, and the third floor honor bar is open until 4 AM. The El Convento now hosts an intimate casino, a source of controversy during the hotel's refurbishment—the "convento" of the name refers to the structure's erstwhile life as a Carmelite convent. ⊠ *100 Calle Cristo (Box 1048) 00902, ☎ 787/723–9020 or 800/468–2779, FAX 787/721–2877. 53 rooms, 6 suites. 2 restaurants, 2 bars, air-conditioning, in-room safes, minibars, pool, exercise room, shops, casino, library, meeting room. AE, D, DC, MC, V. CP.*

$$$$ 🏨 **Wyndham Old San Juan Hotel & Casino.** In the pier area of Old San Juan, the gleaming, new, $45 million Wyndham hotel is a triangular structure subtly echoing the cruise ships docked nearby, while also following the old city's classic neo-Spanish Colonial lines. The lobby, adjacent to the casino, gleams with multihued tiles and mahogany. Each standard room—done in honey-color rugs, floral prints, and light woods—has a two-line phone, cable TV and VCR, a coffeemaker, and a hair dryer. Spacious suites feature sitting rooms, an extra TV, and a minibar. The second floor is the domain of executive chef Tony Cortes's Dársena restaurant, where the cuisine is a mix of Caribbean and Puerto Rican dishes tinged with spices from around the world. The ninth floor houses a small patio swimming pool and whirlpool bath, and a seventh floor concierge level provides hassle-free check-ins and Continental breakfasts for VIPs. Everyone receives complimentary pastries and bottled water with turn-down service and a copy of the *San Juan Star* in the morning. ⊠ *100 Calle Brumbaugh 00901, ☎ 787/721–5100 or 800–WYNDHAM (reservations service), FAX 787/721–1111. 200 rooms, 40 suites. Restaurant, 2 bars, in-room VCRs, pool, hot tub, exercise room, casino, concierge floor, business services, meeting rooms. AE, D, DC, MC, V. EP.*

$$–$$$$ ☆   🏨 **Gallery Inn.** Owners Jan D'Esopo and Manuco Gandia restored this rambling, classically Spanish house, one of the oldest private residences in the area, and turned it into an inn. It's full of quirky details—winding, uneven stairs; private balconies; a music room with a Steinway grand piano; lots of public rooms, areas, and decks to hide out with a book; and small interior gardens. The rooms are individually decorated and have telephones but no televisions; most are air-conditioned. Views from the rooftop deck are some of the best in the old city—a panorama of

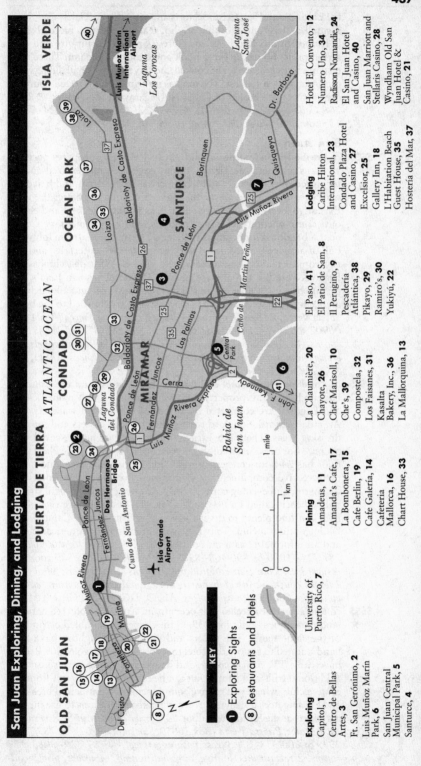

San Juan Exploring, Dining, and Lodging

OLD SAN JUAN

PUERTA DE TIERRA

ISLA VERDE

ATLANTIC OCEAN

CONDADO

OCEAN PARK

MIRAMAR

SANTURCE

Laguna del Condado

Bahía de San Juan

Caño de San Antonio

Isla Grande Airport

Caño de Martín Peña

Laguna San José

Laguna Los Corozas

Luis Muñoz Marín International Airport

Del Cristo
Fortaleza
Ponce de León
Fernández Juncos
Muñoz Rivera
Matina
Dos Hermanos Bridge
Cristo
Cerra
Las Palmas
Baldorioty de Castro Expreso
Ponce de León
Loíza
Luis Muñoz Rivera
Ponce de León
Martín Peña
Borínquen
Quisqueya
Dr. Barbosa
Luis Muñoz Rivera Expreso
John F. Kennedy
Central Park

KEY

1 Exploring Sights

8 Restaurants and Hotels

1 mile
1 km

Exploring
Capitol, **1**
Centro de Bellas Artes, **3**
Ft. San Gerónimo, **2**
Luis Muñoz Marín Park, **6**
San Juan Central Municipal Park, **5**
Santurce, **4**
University of Puerto Rico, **7**

Dining
Amadeus, **11**
Amanda's Cafe, **17**
La Bombonera, **15**
Cafe Berlin, **19**
Cafe Galería, **14**
Cafetería Mallorca, **16**
Chart House, **33**
La Chaumière, **20**
Chayote, **26**
Chef Marisoll, **10**
Che's, **39**
Compostela, **32**
Los Faisanes, **31**
Kasalta Bakery, Inc., **36**
La Mallorquina, **13**
El Paso, **41**
El Patio de Sam, **8**
Il Perugino, **9**
Pescadería Atlántica, **38**
Pikayo, **29**
Ramiro's, **30**
Yukiyú, **22**

Lodging
Caribe Hilton International, **23**
Condado Plaza Hotel and Casino, **27**
Excelsior, **25**
Gallery Inn, **18**
L'Habitation Beach Guest House, **35**
Hostería del Mar, **37**
Hotel El Convento, **12**
Numero Uno, **34**
Radisson Normandie, **24**
El San Juan Hotel and Casino, **40**
San Juan Marriott and Stellaris Casino, **28**
Wyndham Old San Juan Hotel & Casino, **21**

the El Morro and San Cristóbal forts and the Atlantic. Galería San Juan, a small gallery and working studio, features various pieces by Jan D'Esopo, Bruno Lucchesi, and Teresa Spinner—sculpture and silkscreen prints fill nearly every nook and cranny of the inn. There is no restaurant, but meals can be cooked and served in the small dining room for groups upon request. The inn has no sign in front, so tell your taxi driver it's on the corner of Calles Norzagaray and San Justo. ✉ *204– 206 Calle Norzagaray 00901,* ☎ *787/722–1808,* ℻ *787/724–7360. 13 rooms, 10 suites. Bar, dining room. AE, MC, V. CP.*

San Juan

$$$$ ⌂ **Caribe Hilton International.** Built in 1949, this property occupies 17 acres on Puerta de Tierra. Rooms have been modernized and refurbished over the years and have a crisp, pastel decor and balconies with ocean or lagoon views; the higher the floor, the better the view. Executive levels provide services such as private check-in and checkout, complimentary evening cocktails, and complimentary Continental breakfast for business travelers. The spacious atrium lobby—a hub of activity—is decorated with beige marble, waterfalls, and lavish tropical plants. Restaurants include El Café for deli choices and Peacock Paradise for Chinese cuisine. The hotel has San Juan's only private beach, complete with the Islita bar and grill and a boardwalk at its edge. Guests interested in water sports are shuttled to the beach at Isla Verde. ✉ *San Gerónimo Grounds, Puerta de Tierra (Box 1872) 00902,* ☎ *787/721–0303 or 800/468–8585,* ℻ *787/725–8849. 672 rooms. 4 restaurants, air-conditioning, 2 pools, 6 tennis courts, exercise room, racquetball, squash, beach, business services. AE, D, DC, MC, V. CP, EP, MAP.*

$$$$ ⌂ **Condado Plaza Hotel and Casino.** The Atlantic and the Condado Lagoon border this property. Two wings, appropriately named Ocean and Lagoon, are connected by an enclosed, elevated walkway over Avenida Ashford. Standard rooms have walk-in closets and separate dressing areas. There is a variety of suites, including spa suites with oversize hot tubs, and a fully equipped business center. The Plaza Club floor has 24-hour concierge service and a private lounge, and guests there receive complimentary Continental breakfast, afternoon hors d'oeuvres, and evening coffee. The Ocean wing sits on a small strip of public beach called La Playita la Condado, and there are two pools. Kids can find plenty to do at their own activity center, Camp Taino. Dining options include Tony Roma's (a branch of the American chain) and an informal restaurant poolside. ✉ *999 Av. Ashford 00902,* ☎ *787/721–1000 or 800/468–8588,* ℻ *787/722–7955. 589 rooms. 7 restaurants, 3 bars, air-conditioning, 3 pools (1 saltwater), 2 hot tubs, 2 tennis courts, health club, beach, dock, windsurfing, boating, casino, concierge floor, business services. AE, D, DC, MC, V. CP, EP, MAP.*

$$$$ ⌂ **Radisson Normandie.** This oceanfront, Art Deco hotel is a national
★   landmark. It was built in 1939, in the shape of the fabled ocean liner of the same name. The pillars and molding throughout have been hand-painted to restore the hotel to its original Deco splendor. Rooms have cable TV, coffeemakers, and hair dryers; some have sunrooms. Additional frills and pampering can be found at the seventh-floor executive club, where you receive complimentary Continental breakfast and evening hors d'oeuvres. You can make reservations to use the tennis courts at the Hilton next door. ✉ *Corner of Av. Muñoz Rivera and Av. Rosales, Puerta Tierra (Box 50059, San Juan 00902),* ☎ *787/729– 2929 or 800/333–3333 (reservations service),* ℻ *787/729–3083. 177 rooms. 2 restaurants, lounge, air-conditioning, minibars, pool, wading pool, exercise room, jogging, dive shop, snorkeling, boating, business services. AE, D, DC, MC, V. CP, EP, MAP.*

$$$$ ★ 🏨 **El San Juan Hotel and Casino.** An immense chandelier illuminates the hand-carved mahogany paneling, Italian rose marble, and French tapestries in the huge lobby of this 12-acre resort on the Isla Verde beach. You'll be hard pressed to decide if you want a suite in the main tower, with whirlpool bath and wet bar; a garden lanai room with patio and whirlpool bath; or a casita, with a sunken Roman bath. All rooms have a CD player, three phones, modem jack, TV with VCR (some rooms feature a TV in the bathroom), minibar, and walk-in closets with an iron and board. Dark rattan furnishings are complemented by rich carpets and tropical-print spreads and drapes. This luxurious hotel attracts a moneyed mix of international business and leisure travelers. Don't miss the informal rooftop Tequila Bar and Grill; watching the sunset from here is a splendid end to a day of sightseeing. Or, relax at the lobby's Cigar Bar and sample some of Puerto Rico's finest cigars, selected from one of 100 humidors. ⊠ *Av. Isla Verde (Box 2872) 00902,* ☎ *787/ 791–1000 or 800/468–2818 (reservations service),* FAX *787/791–0390. 389 rooms. 7 restaurants, 8 bars, air-conditioning, in-room modem lines, minibars, no-smoking rooms, in-room VCRs, 2 pools, wading pool, 3 hot tubs, 3 tennis courts, health club, beach, shops, casino, business services. AE, DC, MC, V. EP, MAP.*

$$$$ ★ 🏨 **San Juan Marriott and Stellaris Casino.** The red neon sign atop this hotel is a beacon to its excellent Condado location. Rooms have soothing pastel carpeting, flowered spreads, attractive tropical artwork on the walls, and balconies overlooking the ocean, the pool, or both. Restaurants include Tuscany, for northern Italian cuisine, and the more casual La Vista, open 24 hours and popular for dining alfresco. On weekends, there's live entertainment in the enormous lobby, which, combined with the persistent ringing of slot machines from the adjoining casino, makes the area quite noisy (rooms are soundproof). Gorgeous Condado beach is right outside, as is a large pool area. The hotel's spa-gym is the best of any resort in Puerto Rico. ⊠ *1309 Av. Ashford 00907,* ☎ *787/722–7000 or 800/228–9290 (reservations service),* FAX *787/722– 6800. 512 rooms, 13 suites. 3 restaurants, 2 lounges, air-conditioning, no-smoking rooms, pool, beauty salon, hot tub, sauna, 2 tennis courts, health club, beach, casino, children's programs, business services, meeting rooms. AE, D, DC, MC, V. EP, FAP, MAP.*

$$ 🏨 **Excelsior.** Across the Condado Lagoon in Miramar (a 15-minute walk or a two-minute shuttle to the beach), the family-run Excelsior is in a commercial area and has been popular with business travelers for 30 years. Room decor here is standard hotel fare, but the rates are a good value. Each room has a phone, fridge, cable TV with video game hookups, microwave oven, and a private bath with a hair dryer; some have kitchenettes. Fine carpets adorn the corridors, and sculptures decorate the glass-laden lobby. Augusto's, one of the hotel's restaurants, is highly respected for its international cuisine. Complimentary coffee, newspaper, and shoe shine are offered each morning. ⊠ *801 Av. Ponce de León 00907,* ☎ *787/721–7400 or 800/289–4274,* FAX *787/723– 0068. 140 rooms. 2 restaurants, bar, air-conditioning, refrigerators, pool, exercise room, free parking. AE, D, DC, MC, V. EP.*

$$ 🏨 **Hostería del Mar.** Right on the beach in Ocean Park, a residential neighborhood, this small, white inn–guest house is a wonderful alternative to the hustle and bustle of the Condado or Old San Juan— you have to go down to the beach and look west to see the high-rises of the Condado looming in the distance. Rooms here are attractive and simple, with tropical prints and rattan furniture, and many have ocean views. Four apartments have kitchenettes with microwaves and two-burner stoves. The staff is courteous and helpful. A vegetarian-oriented restaurant is on the ground floor facing the trade winds and offers fabulous views of the wide beach in front. ⊠ *1 Calle Tapia, Ocean Park*

00911, ☎ *787/727–3302,* 𝔽𝔸𝕏 *787/268–0772. 8 rooms, 4 apartments, 1 minisuite. Restaurant, air-conditioning, beach. AE, DC, MC, V. EP.*

$$ ▦ **Numero Uno.** Former New Yorker Esther Feliciano bought this
★ three-story, red-roof guest house on the beach, spruced it up, and turned it into a very pleasant accommodation. It's in a quiet residential neighborhood, right in the middle of the nicest beach in San Juan. The simple but clean rooms offer double, queen-, or king-size beds, and all are air-conditioned and have ceiling fans and phones. Three rooms offer ocean views. A walled-in patio provides privacy for sunning or hanging out by the small pool, the bar, and the restaurant, Pamela's. On the other side of the wall, a wide, sandy beach beckons: Beach chairs and towels are provided to guests. ⊠ *1 Calle Santa Ana, Ocean Park 00911,* ☎ *787/726–5010,* 𝔽𝔸𝕏 *787/727–5482. 12 rooms. Restaurant, bar, air-conditioning, fans, pool, beach. AE, MC, V. CP.*

$–$$ ▦ **L'Habitation Beach Guest House.** On the beach in Ocean Park is this gay-oriented guest house with a definite French atmosphere. Owner Alain Tasca is from Paris by way of Guadeloupe and Key West. He has established a very relaxed ambience in this 10-room accommodation. Rooms are simple and comfortable. A bar–snack bar sits in a corner of a palm-shaded patio between the guest house and the beach. Rooms 8 and 9 are the largest and have ocean views. Beach chairs and towels are provided: Pick one before you have one of Alain's margaritas—they'll knock your sandals off. ⊠ *1957 Calle Italia, Ocean Park 00911,* ☎ *787/727–2499,* 𝔽𝔸𝕏 *787/727–2599. 10 rooms. Bar, snack bar, air-conditioning, beach. AE, D, MC, V. CP.*

Western Puerto Rico

$$$$ ▦ **Horned Dorset Primavera.** The Spanish colonial–style resort is
★ tucked away amid lush landscaping overlooking the sea. The only sounds that you're likely to hear as you lounge on the long, secluded, narrow beach are the crash of the surf and an occasional squawk from Pompidou, the enormous *guacamayo* (parrot) in the lounge. Suites have balconies and are exquisitely furnished with antiques, including mahogany four-poster beds, dressers, and nightstands. Casa Escondida has eight rooms—four with their own plunge pool and hot tub—and is designed as a turn-of-the-century Puerto Rican hacienda, with tile or wood floors, mahogany furnishings, terraces, and black marble baths. There are no radios, TVs, or phones in any of the rooms. The ☞ **Horned Dorset Primavera** restaurant is popular with locals. (Parents take note: young children won't feel comfortable here.) ⊠ *Rte. 429, Km 3 (Box 1132) Rincón 00677,* ☎ *787/823–4030 or 787/823–4050,* 𝔽𝔸𝕏 *787/823–5580. 31 rooms. Restaurant, lounge, air-conditioning, fans, 2 pools, beach, library. AE, MC, V. EP, MAP.*

$$$ ▦ **Copamarina Beach Resort.** Sprawling across 18 acres between the
★ sea and the Guánica Dry Forest is this well-landscaped, recently renovated resort. The pool is surrounded by the open-air reception area, manicured lawns, the Las Palmas Cafe, and the building wings. The bay bottom on this section of beach is covered in seaweed, but secluded beaches with clear water can be found a few minutes' drive down the road. The spotless rooms have small terraces with water views and one queen-size or two double beds. Try the red snapper in the Wilo's Coastal Cuisine dining room, and stop in the Las Palmas bar for the bartender's straight-up margarita. There are scuba-diving packages available, or you can arrange a snorkeling excursion to Gilligan's Island (about $3), an offshore key. ⊠ *Rte. 333, Km 6.5, Caña Gorda (Box 805, Guánica 00653),* ☎ *787/821–0505 or 800/468–4553,* 𝔽𝔸𝕏 *787/821–0070. 106 rooms. 2 restaurants, 2 bars, air-conditioning, 2 pools, wading pool, 2 hot tubs, 2 tennis courts, volleyball, dive shop, bicycles, shop, meeting rooms. AE, D, MC, V. EP.*

$$$ ⊞ **Ponce Hilton and Casino.** By far the biggest resort on the south coast, this cream-and-turquoise hotel, nestled amid 80 acres of landscaped gardens, caters to a corporate clientele. Completely self-contained, it offers several restaurants (La Hacienda's antiques mimic an old coffee plantation; the romantic and elegant La Cava has a working wine cellar and can be reserved for a private dinner; the informal La Terraza serves breakfast and lunch buffets as well as lighter dinner fare), access to a public beach, casino, shopping arcade, pool, and a disco with pool tables and live music on weekends. Although the lobby has all the warmth of an airline terminal, the large guest rooms are attractive enough; they're decorated in sky blue, teal, and peach, with modern rattan, and they have balconies. A drawback is the hotel's location— a 10-minute cab ride from town. ⊠ *Rte. 14, 1150 Av. Caribe (Box 7419), Ponce 00732,* ☎ *787/259–7676 or 800/445–8667 (reservations service),* 𝔽𝔸𝕏 *787/259–7674. 145 rooms, 8 suites. 4 restaurants, 5 bars, in-room safes, minibars, pool, beauty salon, hot tub, driving range, 4 tennis courts, basketball, exercise room, Ping-Pong, volleyball, beach, shops, casino, dance club, baby-sitting, playground, business services, meeting rooms. AE, D, MC, V. EP.*

$$ ⊞ **Lemontree Waterfront Cottages.** These sparkling, large apartments
★ sit right on the beach, with staircases from their decks to the sand. There are four units, each with a full kitchen, a TV, and a deck with a wet bar and a grill. The owner-managers, Mary Jeanne and Paul Hellings, have put their touches on the apartments. Paul creates all the detailed woodwork, and Mary Jeanne designs the interiors. The bright tropical decor includes local artwork. There's one three-bedroom unit with two baths, one two-bedroom unit, and two one-bedroom units. The one-bedroom units have wooden cathedral ceilings and picture windows. There's weekly maid service and phones are available by request. The beach is small, but larger ones are close by. It's a 10-minute drive to downtown Rincón. ⊠ *Rte. 429 (Box 200, Rincón 00677),* ☎ *787/ 823–6452,* 𝔽𝔸𝕏 *787/823–5821. 4 units. Air-conditioning, kitchenettes, beach, laundry service. MC, V. EP.*

$$ ⊞ **Parador Villa Parguera.** This parador is a stylish hotel on Phosphorescent Bay. Large, colorfully decorated rooms all have a balcony or terrace. A spacious dining room, overlooking the small swimming pool and the bay beyond, serves excellent native and international dishes. Children under 10 stay free in their parents' room. Ask about honeymoon packages. ⊠ *Rte. 304 (Box 273), Lajas 00667,* ☎ *787/899– 7777 or 800/443–0266 (reservations service),* 𝔽𝔸𝕏 *787/899–6040. 62 rooms. Restaurant, lounge, air-conditioning, saltwater pool, dance club. AE, D, DC, MC, V. EP.*

$–$$ ⊞ **Hotel Meliá.** Set in the heart of Ponce and facing the Parque de Bombas and the Ponce Cathedral, this family-owned hotel provides a wonderful, low-key base for exploring the marvelous turn-of-the-century architecture, museums, and landmarks of downtown Ponce. The lobby has an Old World feel, with high ceilings, blue- and beige-tiled floors, and well-worn but charming decor. Rooms have standard, if somewhat dated, decor. Six of the rooms have balconies that overlook the park. Breakfast is served on the rooftop terrace, which offers pretty views of the city and mountains. A welcome addition is Mark's, the hotel restaurant owned by Mark French, former executive chef at the Ponce Hilton. The restaurant serves an eclectic menu, from teriyaki tuna to corn-crusted snapper to Long Island duck breast. ⊠ *2 Calle Cristina (Box 1431), Ponce 00733,* ☎ *787/842–0260,* 𝔽𝔸𝕏 *787/841–3602. 78 rooms. Restaurant, bar, air-conditioning. AE, MC, V. CP.*

$–$$ ⊞ **Parador Boquemar.** You can walk to the Boquerón public beach (one of the island's best) from this small parador. Rooms are comfortable, each decorated in the island uniform of tropical prints and rattan. Ask

Puerto Rico

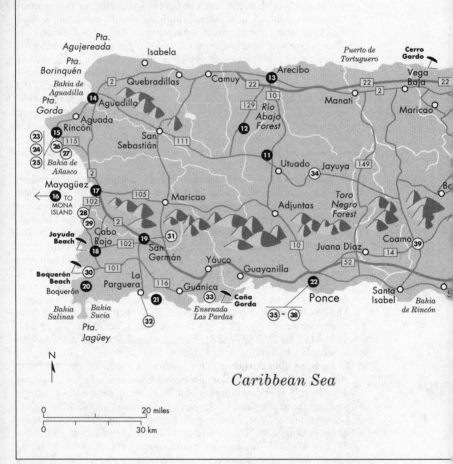

Pta.
Agujereada

Pta.
Borinquén

Isabela

Puerto de
Tortuguero

**Cerro
Gordo**

Quebradillas

Camuy

13 Arecibo

Vega
Baja

Bahia de
Aguadilla

2

22

22

2

Pta.
Gorda

14 Aguadilla

10

Manatí

Maricao

Aguada

129

Río
Abajo
Forest

15 Rincón

115

San
Sebastián

111

12

23
24
25

26
27

Bahia de
Añasco

2

11

Utuado

Jayuya

149

34

Mayagüez

17

105

Maricao

Adjuntas

Toro
Negro
Forest

Bo

16 TO
MONA
ISLAND

102

2

28
29

Cabo
Rojo

31

19

San
Germán

Yáuco

33

10

Juana Díaz

Coamo

39

14

**Joyuda
Beach**

18

102

Guayanilla

52

**Boquerón
Beach**

30

101

La
Parguera

116

Guánica

**Caña
Gorda**

22

Ponce

Santa
Isabel

Bahia
de Rincón

20 Boquerón

21

Ensenada
Las Pardas

35 – **38**

S

Bahia
Salinas

Bahia
Sucia

32

Pta.
Jagüey

N

Caribbean Sea

0   20 miles

0   30 km

Exploring
Aguadilla, **14**
Arecibo
Observatory, **13**
Bacardi Rum Plant, **3**
Barrilito Rum Plant, **2**
Bayamón, **4**
Boquerón, **20**
Las Cabezas de San
Juan Nature Reserve, **7**

Cabo Rojo, **18**
Caguana Indian
Ceremonial Park, **11**
Caparra Ruins, **1**
Caribbean National
Forest, **5**
Culebra, **9**
Fajardo, **8**
Luquillo Beach, **6**
Mayagüez, **17**

Mona Island, **16**
Phosphorescent
Bay, **21**
Ponce, **22**
Rincón, **15**
Río Camuy Cave
Park, **12**
San Germán, **19**
Vieques, **10**

Dining
Anchor's Inn, **44**
Black Eagle, **25**
El Bohio, **29**
La Casona de
Serafín, **28**
Horned Dorset
Primavera, **26**
Lazy Parrot, **24**
Lupita's, **35**

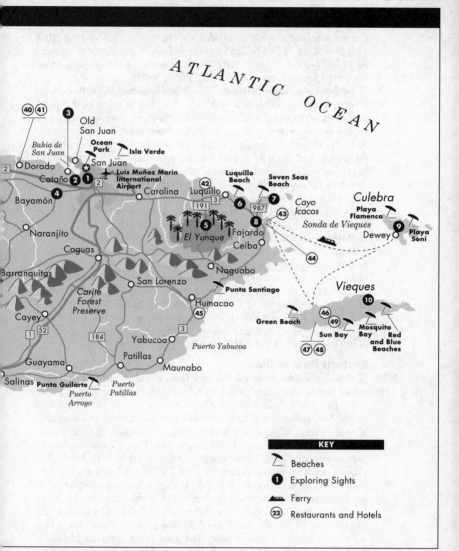

El Molino del Quijote Restaurante, **23**
Restaurant El Ancla, **37**

Lodging
Casa del Francés, **49**
El Conquistador Resort & Country Club, **43**

Copamarina Beach Resort, **33**
Crow's Nest, **46**
Hacienda Tamarindo, **48**
Horned Dorset Primavera, **26**
Hotel Meliá, **38**
Hyatt Dorado Beach, **41**

Hyatt Regency Cerromar Beach, **40**
Inn on the Blue Horizon, **47**
Lemontree Waterfront Cottages, **27**
Parador Baños de Coamo, **39**
Parador Boquemar, **30**
Parador Hacienda Gripiñas, **34**

Parador Oasis, **31**
Parador Villa Parguera, **32**
Ponce Hilton and Casino, **36**
Westin Rio Mar Beach Resort and Country Club, **42**
Wyndham Palmas del Mar, **45**

for a third-floor room with a balcony overlooking the water. La Cascada restaurant is well-known for its traditional Puerto Rican cuisine. On weekends the lounge is filled with live music. ⊠ *Boquerón (Box 133) 00622,* ☎ *787/851–2158 or 800/443–0266 (reservations service),* FAX *787/851–7600. 75 rooms. Restaurant, lounge, air-conditioning, minibars, refrigerators, pool. AE, D, DC, MC, V. EP.*

$ ⊞ **Parador Hacienda Gripiñas.** This white hacienda is for those who
★   want a romantic mountain hideaway (the sea is more than 30 mi away). Polished wood and beam ceilings warm the interior. Large, airy rooms are decorated with native crafts. Relaxation beckons at every turn: Rocking chairs nod in the spacious lounge, hammocks swing on the porch, and splendid gardens invite a leisurely stroll. Your morning coffee is grown on the adjacent working plantation, and its aroma seems to fill the grounds, as does the chirp of the ubiquitous coquís (tree frogs). ⊠ *Rte. 527, Km 2.5 (Box 387), Jayuya 00664,* ☎ *787/ 828–1717 or 800/443–0266 (reservations service),* FAX *787/828–1719. 19 rooms. Restaurant, lounge, pool, hiking. AE, MC, V. EP.*

$ ⊞ **Parador Oasis.** The Oasis, not far from the town's two plazas, was
★   a family mansion 200 years ago; the lobby retains a taste of the house's history, with peppermint-pink walls and white-wicker furniture. The older rooms are convenient—right off the lobby—but show their age. The newer rooms in the rear lack character but are functional, clean, and a little roomier. ⊠ *72 Calle Luna (Box 144), San Germán 00683,* ☎ *787/892–1100 or 800/443–0266 (reservations service),* FAX *787/892– 1175. 52 rooms. Restaurant, lounge, air-conditioning, pool, sauna, exercise room. AE, D, DC, MC, V. EP.*

Eastern Puerto Rico

$$$$ ⊞ **El Conquistador Resort & Country Club.** Divided into four self-con-
★   tained hotels, this complex is a world unto itself. It's perched dramatically atop a 300-ft bluff overlooking the ocean and the El Yunque rain forest. The architecture is a blend of Moorish and Spanish colonial: cobblestone streets, white stucco and terra-cotta buildings, open-air plazas with tinkling fountains, tiled benches, and gas lamps. Plants and caged parrots decorate many of the open spaces. One of the four hotels, Las Olas, is actually built into the cliff face. Each room has a seating area with couch, glass-top coffee table, desk, chairs, and entertainment center. Enormous bathrooms have sunken tubs, marble countertops, makeup mirrors, and walk-in closets. Extras include well-stocked minibars, CD players, and VCRs. The hotel's beach is the offshore Palomino Island, which you reach via shuttle boat. The pampering begins at LMM International Airport: The resort is one of the few on the island to provide deluxe motor-coach transfers (for $55 per person round-trip, $27.50 one way). The ride is a little over an hour. ⊠ *1000 Av. El Conquistador (Box 70001), Fajardo 00738,* ☎ *787/863–1000 or 800/ 468–5228,* FAX *787/863–6500. 918 units. 9 restaurants, 8 bars, air-conditioning, minibars, in-room VCRs, 7 pools, spa, 18-hole golf course, 4 tennis courts, health club, beach, dive shop, dock, snorkeling, windsurfing, boating, jet skiing, shops, casino, nightclub, children's program, business services, convention center, car rental. AE, D, DC, MC, V. EP, MAP.*

$$$$ ⊞ **Hyatt Dorado Beach.** The ambience is more subdued here than at
its sister, the ☞ **Hyatt Regency Cerromar Beach,** and you can take advantage of the facilities there. A variety of accommodations are in low-rise buildings on 1,000 landscaped acres. Most rooms have patios or balconies, and all have polished terra-cotta floors and marble baths. Upper-level rooms in the Oceanview Houses have a view of the two beaches. The only drawback to this resort is the service, which can be less than attentive. ⊠ *Rte. 693, Km 10.8 (Box 1351), Dorado 00646,*

☎ *787/796–1234 or 800/233–1234 (reservations service),* FAX *787/796–2022 or 787/796–6560. 298 rooms. 3 restaurants, 2 lounges, air-conditioning, 2 pools, wading pool, spa, 2 18-hole golf courses, 7 tennis courts, health club, hiking, jogging, beach, snorkeling, windsurfing, boating, bicycles, casino. AE, D, DC, MC, V. EP, MAP.*

$$$$ ⬚ **Hyatt Regency Cerromar Beach.** One of the best sports-oriented resorts in the Caribbean, the family-oriented Cerromar has two Robert Trent Jones golf courses, 14 tennis courts, a spa and health club, jogging and biking trails, a 900-ft river pool, a hot tub in a man-made cavern, a swim-up bar, and a three-story-high water slide. It's 22 mi west of San Juan, right on the Atlantic. The modern seven-story hotel is done up in tropical style. Rooms have tile floors, marble baths, and a king-size or two double beds. You'll find quieter rooms on the west side, away from the pool activity. Guests at the Cerromar and its sister facility, the ☞ **Hyatt Dorado Beach,** a mile down the road, have access to the facilities of both resorts, and colorful red trolleys make frequent runs between the two. Chi Chi's Steak House serves prime cuts of beef, and Medici's is a sophisticated northern Italian eatery. ✉ *Rte. 693, Km 11.8 (Box 1351), Dorado 00646,* ☎ *787/796–1234 or 800/233–1234 (reservations service),* FAX *787/796–4647. 506 rooms. 4 restaurants, 3 bars, air-conditioning, pool, hot tub, spa, 2 18-hole golf courses, 14 tennis courts, health club, hiking, jogging, beach, snorkeling, bicycles, casino, dance club. AE, D, DC, MC, V. EP, MAP.*

$$$$ ⬚ **Westin Rio Mar Beach Resort and Country Club.** This extensive re-
★ sort is on the grounds of a former country club. Set on 481 acres, the nouveau Spanish-Moorish resort has red-tile roofs and a massive lobby with ocher floor tiles, ornate stairways, potted plants, and shimmering chandeliers. The rooms and suites are uniformly new and spacious and feature lots of dark-grained wood and floral patterns, in-room video games, and a balcony; the suites also have large desks. Avoid suites 5099 and 5101—the balconies overlook the hotel's air-conditioning ducts. The resort has two 18-hole golf courses, and it's kid-friendly as well. In addition to the beach, kids have their own activities centers indoors and out, and a large pool with a winding slide. The resort is about an hour from San Juan, and El Yunque is just minutes away. ✉ *6000 Río Mar Blvd. (Box 6100), Río Grande 00745,* ☎ *787/888–6000 or 800/474–6627,* FAX *787/888–6600. 528 rooms, 72 suites. 10 restaurants, bar, lounge, air-conditioning, in-room safes, minibars, no-smoking rooms, 2 pools, beauty salon, spa, 2 18-hole golf courses, 13 tennis courts, health club, beach, dive shop, snorkeling, water slide, windsurfing, boating, jet skiing, parasailing, shops, casino, recreation room, children's programs, meeting rooms, car rental. AE, D, DC, MC, V. EP, MAP.*

$$$–$$$$ ⬚ **Wyndham Palmas del Mar.** This resort community is on 2,750 acres of a former coconut plantation on the southeast coast (about an hour's drive from San Juan). Two hotels, the 23-suite Palmas Inn and 102-room Wyndham Hotel, are the centerpieces of the complex. In the rustic yet elegant Wyndham, rooms are airy and spacious. The Palmas Inn suites, all with stunning sea or garden views, evoke luxurious Mediterranean villas, with pastel-pink connecting walkways, cobblestone plazas, and fountains adorned with hand-painted tile work. ✉ *Rte. 906 (Box 2020, Humacao) 00792,* ☎ *787/852–6000 or 800/468–3331,* FAX *787/852–6330. 100 rooms; 140 villas; 23 1-, 2-, and 3-bedroom suites. 14 restaurants, 14 bars, beach bar, air-conditioning, pool, 18-hole golf course, 20 tennis courts, exercise room, horseback riding, beach, dive shop, dock, boating, fishing, bicycles, casino. AE, DC, MC, V. EP, MAP.*

$$$ ⬚ **Inn on the Blue Horizon.** Known for its restaurant, Cafe Blu, and
★ its octagonal Blu bar, this small and popular hotel sits on 20 windswept acres fronting the Caribbean. Owners and former New Yorkers James Weis and Billy Knight added four more rooms in 1997. Two rooms

have air-conditioning and all have fans. Furnished with antiques, the rooms are sumptuous and lovely, as is the patio-lounge area. ⊠ *Rte. 996 (Box 1556), Vieques 00765,* ☎ *787/741–3318,* FAX *787/741– 0522. 9 rooms. Restaurant, bar, fans, pool. MC, V. CP.*

$$ ☜ **Casa del Francés.** Self-professed curmudgeon Irving Greenblatt, a ★ former Bostonian, runs this atmospheric if somewhat run-down guest house in a restored French sugar-plantation great house. Rooms are rather plain but enormous, with vaulted 17-ft ceilings. The food is good, the pool inviting, the guests an eclectic mix, and Irving a true character who will regale you with horror stories of running a Caribbean hotel. The sightseeing boat for the phosphorescent bay leaves from here. ⊠ *Rte. 996 (Box 458), Vieques 00765,* ☎ *787/741–3751,* FAX *787/741– 2330. 18 rooms. Restaurant, bar, fans, pool, snorkeling. AE, MC, V. EP, MAP. MAP compulsory in season.*

$$ ☜ **Hacienda Tamarindo.** Set on a windswept hill with sweeping views ★ of the Caribbean, the new Hacienda Tamarindo is the nicest place to stay on Vieques. Owners Burr and Linda Vail left Vermont to build this extraordinary hotel—with a huge tamarind tree right in the middle. Rooms are individually decorated but have such details as mahogany louvered doors and terra-cotta tile floors. Some rooms have terraces, and half of the rooms have air-conditioning; the rest face the trade winds. All have ceiling fans and are furnished with eclectic art and antiques shipped from Vermont. A full breakfast is served on the second-floor terrace. You can walk down the hill to the ☞ **Inn on the Blue Horizon** for dinner. Box lunches are available on request. (Children under 12 will not feel comfortable here; best to leave the kids at home.) ⊠ *Rte. 996 (Box 1569), Vieques 00765,* ☎ *787/741–8525,* FAX *787/741– 3215. 16 rooms. Bar, fans, pool. AE, MC, V. CP.*

$$ ☜ **Parador Baños de Coamo.** On Route 546, Km 1, northeast of Ponce, this mountain inn is at the hot sulfur springs that are said to be the Fountain of Youth of Ponce de León's dreams. Rooms open onto latticed wooden verandas and have a pleasing blend of contemporary and period furnishings. The parador can make arrangements for you to ride Puerto Rico's glorious, unique breed of show horse called *paso fino.* ⊠ *Coamo (Box 540) 00769,* ☎ *787/825–2186 or 800/443–0266 (reservations service),* FAX *787/825–4739. 48 rooms. Restaurant, lounge, air-conditioning, pool. AE, DC, MC, V. EP.*

$–$$ ☜ **Crow's Nest.** Owner Liz O'Dell has made her simple but comfort-★ able inn a very satisfying place to stay. A southerner by way of Massachusetts, Liz is a wealth of information and hospitality. She will arrange for you to do just about anything that's available on the island. Her 13-room lodging, set on 5 hilltop acres with pretty ocean views, is a great value. Rooms have either kitchenettes or full kitchens, and 11 are air-conditioned. Liz provides you with beach chairs and coolers— a thoughtful touch. There's a lounge with TV/VCR, and one of the island's best restaurants is on the premises. ⊠ *Rte. 201, Km 1.6 (Box 1521), Vieques 00765,* ☎ *787/741–0033,* FAX *787/741–1294. 13 rooms. Restaurant, bar, kitchenettes, pool, car rental. AE, MC, V. EP.*

Dining

In San Juan you'll find everything from Italian to Thai, as well as superb local eateries serving *comidas criollas* (traditional Caribbean-Creole meals). Many of San Juan's best restaurants are in small, lesser-known hotels. *Mesónes gastronómicos* are restaurants designated as such by the government for preserving island culinary traditions and maintaining high standards. There are more than 40 of these restaurants island-wide. Wherever you go, it is *always* a good idea to make reservations in the busy season, mid-November–April.

Puerto Rican cooking emphasizes local vegetables: Plantains are cooked a hundred different ways—*tostones* (fried green), *amarillos* (baked ripe), and chips. Rice and beans with tostones or amarillos are basic accompaniments to every dish. Locals cook white rice with *habichuelas* (red beans), *achiote* (annatto seeds), or saffron; brown rice with *gandules* (pigeon peas); and *morro* (black rice) with *frijoles negros* (black beans). Garbanzos and white beans are served in many daily specials. A wide assortment of yams is served baked, fried, stuffed, boiled, mashed, and whole. *Sofrito*—a garlic, onion, sweet pepper, coriander, oregano, and tomato puree—is used as a base for practically everything.

Beef, chicken, pork, and seafood are rubbed with *adobo,* a garlic-oregano marinade, before cooking. *Arroz con pollo* (chicken with rice), *sancocho* (beef and tuber soup), *asopao* (a soupy rice with chicken or seafood), and *encebollado* (steak smothered in onions) are all typical plates. Fritters are served in snack places along the highways as well as at cocktail parties. You may find *empanadillas* (stuffed fried turnovers), *surrullitos* (cheese-stuffed corn sticks), *alcapurias* (stuffed green banana croquettes), and *bacalaitos* (codfish fritters). Local *pan de agua* is an excellent French loaf bread, best hot out of the oven. It's also good toasted and should be tried in the *Cubano* sandwich (roast pork, ham, Swiss cheese, pickles, and mustard). Local desserts include flans, puddings, and fruit pastes served with native white cheese.

Homegrown mangoes and papayas are sweet, and *pan de azucar* (sugar bread) pineapples make the best juice on the market. Fresh *parcha* (passion fruit), *guarapo* (sugarcane), and *guanabana* (a fruit similar to papaya) juice are also sold cold from trucks along the highway. Puerto Rican coffee is excellent served espresso-black or generously cut *con leche* (with hot milk). Local legend has it that the birthplace of the piña colada is San Juan's Hotel El Convento. Rum can be mixed with cola (known as a *cuba libre*), soda, tonic, juices, water, served on the rocks, or even up. Puerto Rican rums range from light white mixers to dark, aged sipping liqueurs. Look for Bacardi, Don Q, Ron Rico, Palo Viejo, and Barrilito.

What to Wear

Dress codes vary greatly, though a restaurant's price category is a good indicator of its formality. For less expensive places, anything but beachwear is fine. Ritzier eateries will expect collared shirts for men and chic attire for women (jacket and tie requirements are rare). However, Puerto Ricans enjoy dressing up for dinner, so chances are you'll never feel overdressed.

CATEGORY	COST*
$$$$	over $45
$$$	$30–$45
$$	$15–$30
$	under $15

*per person for a three-course meal, excluding drinks and service

Old San Juan

ASIAN

$$–$$$ ✕ **Yukiyú.** The only Japanese restaurant in Old San Juan manages to
★ serve some of the best Japanese food in Puerto Rico under the supervision of chef Igarashi. Those craving a sushi bar should beeline for this establishment, as sushi is a specialty. ✉ *311 Recinto Sur,* ☎ *787/721–0653. AE, D, MC, V.*

CAFÉ

$–$$ ✕ **Cafe Berlin.** This casual café, bakery, and delicatessen has outdoor
★ seating overlooking the Plaza Colón. Tasty vegetarian fare prevails—

try one of the creative salads—but nonvegetarian dishes are also available. The café's pastries, desserts, fresh juices, and Puerto coffees are the perfect elixir to a day of touring Old San Juan. ⊠ *407 Calle San Francisco,* ☎ *787/722–5205. AE, MC, V.*

$ ✕ **Cafeteria Mallorca.** This small, neighborhood cafeteria features a staff
★   in crisp, green uniforms and funky caps. The specialty here is in its name—the *mallorca,* a sweet pastry that's buttered and grilled, then sprinkled with powdered sugar. Try the breakfast mallorca, with ham and cheese, washed down with one of the city's best cups of *café con leche.* ⊠ *300 Calle San Francisco,* ☎ *787/724–4607. MC, V. Closed Sun.*

$ ✕ **La Bombonera.** This landmark restaurant, with its ornate streetside facade, was established in 1903, and is known for its strong Puerto Rican coffee and excellent pastries. It opens every day from 7:30 AM until early evening, and full breakfasts are served until 11. It's a favorite Sunday-morning gathering place in Old San Juan. ⊠ *259 Calle San Francisco,* ☎ *787/722–0658. AE, MC, V.*

CONTEMPORARY

$$$–$$$$ ✕ **Chef Marisoll.** Set on two sides of a Venetianesque courtyard surrounded by ornate balconies (you can dine inside or out), this dark-wooded, high-ceilinged restaurant serves gourmet international cuisine. Start with a small duck Caesar salad or a cream of exotic wild mushroom soup. Then feast on a beef tenderloin or a fillet of salmon. For dessert, try chef Marisoll's specialty, a crème caramel. ⊠ *202 Calle Cristo,* ☎ *787/725–7454. AE, MC, V. Closed Mon. No lunch Sun.*

$$–$$$ ✕ **Amadeus.** In an atmosphere of gentrified Old San Juan, a trendy,
★   pretty crowd enjoys the nouvelle Caribbean menu here. The front dining room is attractive—whitewashed walls, dark wood, white tablecloths, ceiling fan—but go through the outside passage to the romantic back dining room with printed cloths, candles, and exposed brick. The roster of appetizers includes buffalo wings and plantain mousse with shrimp. Escargots, cheese ravioli with a goat-cheese-and-walnut sauce, and Cajun-grilled mahimahi are a few of the delectable entrées. ⊠ *106 Calle San Sebastián,* ☎ *787/722–8635. AE, MC, V. Closed Mon.*

ECLECTIC

$$–$$$ ✕ **Cafe Galería.** This stylish, airy restaurant, with marble floors, white walls, and dark wood accents, is centered on a skylit atrium. Chef Figueroa prepares Italian and international cuisine, including fresh pastas and sauces (you mix and match), risottos, and seafood dishes as well as delicious local desserts like flan, *arroz con dulce* (rice pudding), and kiwi tart. ⊠ *205 Calle San Justo,* ☎ *787/725–0478. AE, MC, V. Closed Sun.*

$$ ✕ **Amanda's Cafe.** This airy café, across from San Cristóbal on the north side of the city, offers seating inside or out with a view of the Atlantic and the old city wall. The cuisine is Mexican, French, and Caribbean, and the nachos, fruit frappés, and margaritas are the best in town. ⊠ *424 Calle Norzagaray,* ☎ *787/722–0187. AE, MC, V.*

$–$$ ✕ **El Patio de Sam.** A warm dark-wood and faux-brick interior and a wide selection of beers make Sam's a popular late-night spot. The menu is mostly steaks and seafood, with a few native dishes mixed in. Try the Samuel's Special pizza—mozzarella, tomato sauce, beef, pepperoni, and black olives: it feeds two or three. The flan melts in your mouth. There's live entertainment every evening but Sunday. ⊠ *102 Calle San Sebastián,* ☎ *787/723–1149. AE, D, DC, MC, V.*

FRENCH

$$$–$$$$ ✕ **La Chaumière.** Reminiscent of an inn in the French provinces, this intimate two-story restaurant with black-and-white tiled floors, heavy wood beams, and floral curtains serves onion soup, oysters Rockefeller,

rack of lamb, scallops Provençale, and veal Oscar (layered with lobster and asparagus in béarnaise sauce), in addition to daily specials. The restaurant, under the same management since 1969, is one of the older French eateries on the island and one of the better ones. All that experience makes the service quite smooth. ⊠ *367 Calle Tetuan,* ☎ *787/722–3330. AE, DC, MC, V. Closed Sun. No lunch.*

ITALIAN

$$$–$$$$ ✕ **Il Perugino.** The best Italian restaurant in Old San Juan, this small
★ and intimate eatery set in a 200-year-old building stresses attentive service and delicious Italian cuisine. Classic carpaccios; scallops with porcini mushrooms and other exotic salads; homemade pastas like black fettuccine with crayfish and baby eels; hearty main courses such as rack of lamb with red wine sauce and aromatic herbs; and desserts like a killer tiramisu make this a must for serious gourmets. A choice from the excellent wine cellar, housed in the former cistern, completes the experience. ⊠ *105 Calle Cristo,* ☎ *787/722–5481. AE, MC, V.*

LATIN

$$–$$$ ✕ **La Mallorquina.** The food here is basic Puerto Rican and Spanish fare, such as asopao and paella, but the atmosphere is what recommends this spot. Said to date from 1848, this is the oldest restaurant in Puerto Rico, with pale pink walls and whirring ceiling fans, and a nattily attired and friendly wait staff. ⊠ *207 Calle San Justo,* ☎ *787/ 722–3261. AE, MC, V. Closed Sun.*

San Juan

ARGENTINE

$$ ✕ **Che's.** Juicy *churrasco* (barbecued steaks), lemon chicken, and grilled sweetbreads are specialties at this casual Argentinean restaurant. The hamburgers are huge, and the french fries are fresh. The Chilean and Argentine wine list is also decent. ⊠ *35 Calle Caoba, Punta Las Marías,* ☎ *787/726–7202. AE, D, DC, MC, V.*

CAFÉ

$–$$ ✕ **Kasalta Bakery, Inc.** Make your selection from rows of display
★ cases offering a seemingly endless array of tempting treats. Walk up to the counter and order from an assortment of sandwiches (try the Cubano), meltingly tender octopus salad, savory *caldo gallego* (a soup jammed with fresh vegetables, sausage, and potatoes), cold drinks, strong café con leche, and luscious pastries. ⊠ *1966 Calle McLeary, Ocean Park,* ☎ *787/727–7340. AE, MC, V.*

CARIBBEAN/CREOLE

$–$$ ✕ **El Paso.** This family-run restaurant serves genuine Creole food seasoned for a local following. Specialties include asopao, pork chops, and breaded empanadas (meat pastries). There's always tripe on Saturday and arroz con pollo on Sunday. ⊠ *405 Av. De Diego, Puerto Nuevo,* ☎ *787/781–3399. AE, DC, MC, V.*

CONTEMPORARY

$$–$$$$ ✕ **Los Faisanes.** This Continental stunner is one of San Juan's most
★ distinguished eateries. Mahogany doorways, faux-Tiffany lamps, crisp white and ecru napery, and Bernadaud china set a refined tone, carried through by the equally elegant cuisine. Feast on roast duck with guava and cinnamon, veal chops with scallion and mushroom sauce, and wonderfully light soufflés. ⊠ *1108 Av. Magdalena, Condado,* ☎ *787/725–2801. AE, MC, V.*

ECLECTIC

$$$$ ✕ **Pikayo.** Chef Wilo Benet artfully fuses classic French, Caribbean Creole, and California nouvelle cuisine with definite Puerto Rican flair.
★

The beautifully presented dishes, which change regularly, are a feast for the eye as well as the palate. Your meal might consist of tostones stuffed with oven-dried tomatoes, followed by *monfongo* (spiced, mashed green plantains topped with saffron shrimp) or a hearty land-crab stew. More traditional and equally delicious dishes are also available. The decor is smartly contemporary, with lots of black-and-white accents and comfortable banquettes, and the service is very attentive. ⊠ *Tanama Princess Hotel, 1 Calle Joffre, Condado,* ☎ *787/721–6194. AE, MC, V. Closed Sun. No lunch Sat.*

$$–$$$$ ✕ **Chayote.** Slightly off the beaten path, this elegant and chic eatery
★ of earthen tones and contemporary Puerto Rican art is an "in" spot to eat. The chef blends haute international cuisine with tropical panache. Appetizers include *sopa del día* (soup of the day) made with local produce, chayote stuffed with prosciutto, and corn tamales with shrimp in coconut sauce. Half of the entrées on the menu are seafood dishes, including the excellent pan-seared tuna with Asian ginger sauce. The ginger flan and the almond floating island in rum custard sauce are musts for dessert. ⊠ *Hotel Olimpo Court, 603 Av. Miramar, Miramar,* ☎ *787/722–9385. AE, MC, V. Closed Sun. No lunch Sat.*

$$–$$$ ✕ **Chart House.** It's no secret that the graceful veranda of this restored Ashford mansion across from the Marriott is a perfect spot for cocktails, and a lively crowd gathers here in the evening. The upstairs open-air dining rooms are splashed with bright marine-theme artwork. The menu includes prime rib, steak, shrimp teriyaki, Hawaiian chicken, and the signature dessert: mud pie. ⊠ *1214 Av. Ashford, Condado,* ☎ *787/724–0110. AE, D, DC, MC, V. No lunch.*

SEAFOOD

$$ ✕ **Pescadería Atlántica.** This combination seafood restaurant and retail store has become popular over the years. The seafood is fresh and reasonably priced. Stop in for a cool drink at the bar and a side dish of *calamares,* lightly breaded squid in a hot spicy sauce. ⊠ *2475 Calle Loiza, Punta Las Marías,* ☎ *787/728–5444. AE, MC, V. Closed Sun.*

SPANISH

$$$$ ✕ **Compostela.** Contemporary Spanish food and a 10,000-bottle wine
★ cellar are the draws here. The restaurant, with its bright interior and many plants, is honored yearly in local competitions for specialties such as mushroom pâté and Port *pastelillo* (wild mushroom turnover), grouper fillet with scallops in salsa verde, rack of lamb, duck with orange and ginger sauce, and paella. ⊠ *106 Av. Condado, Santurce,* ☎ *787/724–6088. AE, DC, MC, V. Closed Sun.*

$$$–$$$$ ✕ **Ramiro's.** Step into a soft sea-green dining room for some imagi-
★ native Castillian cuisine. Chef-owner Jesus Ramiro is known for his artistic presentation: flower-shape peppers filled with fish mousse, a mix of seafood caught under a vegetable net, roast duckling with sugarcane honey, and, if you can stand more, a kiwi dessert sculpted to resemble twin palms. ⊠ *1106 Av. Magdalena, Condado,* ☎ *787/721–9049. AE, DC, MC, V. No lunch Sat.*

Eastern Puerto Rico

SEAFOOD

$–$$ ✕ **Anchor's Inn.** Under the direction of raffish owner Joe Cruz, this
★ mesón gastronómico is a perfect example that good things come in simple packages. The fisherman pull their boats into the nearby Fajardo Harbor, with flotillas of brightly colored yachts, and must head straight for the restaurant with their catch, for the seafood is as fresh and succulent as it gets. It shows up in such Puerto Rican dishes as surrullitos, asopao, and lobster *mofongo* (green plantains stuffed with seafood).

There are 13 guest rooms upstairs. ⊠ *Rte. 987, Km 2.4,* ☎ *787/863–7200. AE, MC, V. Closed Tues.*

Western Puerto Rico

CONTEMPORARY

$–$$ ✕ **Lazy Parrot.** Highly regarded for its fresh mahimahi, filet mignon, and homemade desserts, this little restaurant is also an art gallery and guest house. Perched in the hills, with mountain and ocean views, this is a great place to kick back and listen to the ever-present sound of the coquis. ⊠ *Rte. 413, Km 4.1, Barrio Puntas,* ☎ *787/823–5654. AE, D, MC, V. Closed Mon. in winter and weekdays in summer.*

FRENCH

$$$–$$$$ ✕ **Horned Dorset Primavera.** Tucked away on the west coast of the is-
★ land in the posh hotel ☞ Horned Dorset Primavera, this is the finest food you'll encounter outside of San Juan. Owners Harold Davies and Kingsley Wratten take their dining room very seriously. Although tropical accents appear here and there, the cuisine is heavily Cordon Bleu–influenced: filet mignon in a mushroom sauce, grilled squab in a black currant sauce, and grilled fish du jour are de rigueur here. A five-course, prix-fixe menu is available for $56 per person. ⊠ *Rte. 429, Km 3, Box 1132,* ☎ *787/823–4030 or 787/823–4050. AE, MC, V.*

LATIN

$$–$$$ ✕ **Restaurant El Ancla.** The seafood and Puerto Rican specialties of this mesón gastronómico are served with tostones, *papas fritas* (french fries), and garlic bread. The menu ranges from lobster and shrimp to chicken, beef, and asopao. The salmon fillet with capers is one of the most popular dishes, and the piña coladas, with or without rum, and the flan are especially good. ⊠ *Av. Hostos Final 9, Playa-Ponce,* ☎ *787/840–2450. AE, D, DC, MC, V.*

$$ ✕ **El Molino del Quijote Restaurante.** Amid beautifully landscaped gardens just off the beach, this festive, colorful restaurant with tile-topped tables and local artwork serves Spanish and Puerto Rican cuisine. Try the *bolas de pescado* (fish balls) appetizer and one of the paellas as an entrée, or combine several appetizers for a meal. The sangria is terrific. Two two-bedroom cabanas are available to rent. ⊠ *Rte. 429, Km 3.3,* ☎ *787/823–4010. AE, MC, V. Closed Mon.–Thurs.*

ECLECTIC

$$ ✕ **Black Eagle.** The inconsistent quality of the food here hasn't dimmed its status as a Rincón dining landmark. It's on the water's edge, and you dine on the veranda, listening to the lapping waves. The steak-and-seafood menu lists breaded conch fritters, a fresh fish of the day, lobster, and imported prime meats. ⊠ *Rte. 413, Km 1, Ensenada,* ☎ *787/823–3510. AE, DC, MC, V.*

$$ ✕ **La Casona de Serafín.** This informal, ocean-side bistro specializes in steaks, seafood, and Puerto Rican criolla (Creole) dishes. The indoor dining room has bleached walls and mahogany furniture. Try the tostones, asopao, and surrullitos, and follow up with the pumpkin-custard dessert. The somewhat dilapidated palm-fringed patio sits right on the beach, so you can listen to the waves lap the shore. ⊠ *Rte. 102, Km 9.7, Playa Joyuda,* ☎ *787/851–0066. AE, MC, V.*

SEAFOOD

$–$$$ ✕ **El Bohio.** A local favorite, this informal restaurant 15 minutes south of Mayagüez serves steak and a variety of seafood—all cooked just about any way you want it. You can dine on the large, enclosed wooden deck that juts out over the sea or in the dining room inside. ⊠ *Rte. 102, Km 13.9, Playa Joyuda,* ☎ *787/851–2755. AE, DC, MC, V.*

TEX-MEX

$–$$ ✕ Lupita's. A fine mariachi band patrols the mezzanine and courtyard
of this festive Mexican restaurant Thursday–Sunday nights. The handsome arched dining room has an Aztec decor, with ponchos and ser-
apes hung on the walls for added color. The food—Mexican-American
standards like nachos, tacos, and chicken mole—is quite good, the margaritas and shooters even better, and the ambience festive. ⊠ *Calle Isabel 60,* ☎ 787/848–8808. *AE, MC, V.*

Beaches

By law, all of Puerto Rico's beaches are open to the public (except for
the Caribe Hilton's man-made beach in San Juan). The government
runs 13 *balnearios* (public beaches), which have dressing rooms, lifeguards, parking, and in some cases picnic tables, playgrounds, and camping facilities. Admission is free, parking is $2. Most balnearios are open
9–5 daily in summer and Tuesday–Sunday the rest of the year. Listed
below are some major balnearios. You can also contact the Department of Recreation and Sports (☎ 787/722–1551 or 787/724–2500).

Boquerón Beach, on the southwest coast, is a broad beach of hard-packed
sand fringed with coconut palms. It has picnic tables, cabin rentals,
bike rentals, basketball court, minimarket, scuba diving, and snorkeling. **Isla Verde,** a white-sand beach bordered by huge resort hotels, has
picnic tables and good snorkeling, with equipment rentals nearby. Set
near San Juan, it's a lively beach popular with city folk. **Luquillo Beach**
is crescent-shape and comes complete with coconut palms, picnic tables, and tent sites. Coral reefs protect its crystal-clear lagoon from the
Atlantic waters, making it ideal for swimming. It's one of the largest
and best-known beaches on the island, and it gets crowded on weekends. **Ocean Park,** a residential neighborhood just east of the Condado,
is home to the prettiest beach in San Juan. Here you'll find a mile-long,
wide stretch of fine golden sand and often choppy but very swimmable
waters. Very popular on weekends with local college students, this is
also one of the cities' two beaches popular among gays (the other is in
front of the Atlantic Beach Hotel). **Playa Flamenco,** one of the most
beautiful beaches in the Caribbean, is on the north shore of Culebra.
The 3-mi-long crescent has shade trees, picnic tables, and rest rooms
and is popular on weekends with day-trippers from Fajardo. During
the winter, storms in the North Atlantic often create great waves for
bodysurfing. **Playa Soni,** on the eastern end of Culebra, is a wide
strand of sparkling white sand on a protected bay with calm waters.
Views of the islets of Culebrita, Cayo Norte, and St. Thomas are stunning. As there are no facilities and little shade, bring lots of water and
an umbrella. **Seven Seas Beach,** an elongated beach of hard-packed
sand east of Luquillo at Las Croabas, is always popular with bathers.
It has picnic tables and tent and trailer sites; snorkeling, scuba diving,
and boat rentals are nearby. **Sun Bay,** a white-sand beach on the island
of Vieques, has shade trees, picnic tables, and tent sites and offers snorkeling and scuba diving. Boat rentals are nearby.

Outdoor Activities and Sports

Participant Sports

BOATING AND SAILING

Virtually all the resort hotels on San Juan's Condado and Isla Verda
strips rent paddleboats, Sunfish, Windsurfers, kayaks, and the like. The
waves here can be strong, but the constant wind makes for good sailing. Contact **Caribe Hilton** (☎ 787/721–0303), **Condado Plaza Hotel
Watersports Center** (☎ 787/721–1000, ext. 1361), or the **El San Juan
Hotel Watersports Center** (☎ 787/791–1000).

Outside of San Juan, your hotel will be able either to provide rentals or recommend rental outfitters. **Iguana Water Sports** (⊠ Westin Río Mar, ☎ 787/888–6000) has a particularly good selection of small boats. Sailing instruction is offered by **Palmas Sailing Center** (⊠ Wyndham Palmas del Mar, Humacao, ☎ 787/852–6000, ext. 10310) and most of the large resort hotels. Day trips, party cruises, sunset cruises, and snorkeling excursions are all popular sailing activities. Trips are offered by **Caribe Aquatic Adventures** (⊠ San Juan Bay Marina, ☎ 787/729–2929, ext. 240) and **Castillo Watersports** (⊠ ESJ Towers, Isla Verde, ☎ 787/791–6195 or 787/725–7970).

CYCLING

In general, you'll want to stay away from the main highways and streets of San Juan and Old San Juan for biking—the traffic is too heavy and the automobile fumes will make you think twice about deep breathing. However, in the countryside, particularly along the south and southwest coasts, biking is easy and a great way to get around. The broad beach at Boquerón makes for easy wheeling.

You can rent bikes at **Boquerón Balnearios** (⊠ Rte. 101, Boquerón, Dept. of Recreation and Sports, ☎ 787/722–1551 or 787/722–1771). In the Dorado area on the north coast, bikes can be rented at the **Hyatt Dorado Beach** (☎ 787/796–1234) or the **Hyatt Regency Cerromar Beach** (☎ 787/796–1234). Bikes are for rent at many of the hotels out on the island, including the **Copamarina Beach Resort** (☎ 787/821–0505), **Ponce Hilton** (☎ 787/259–7676), and the **Westin Río Mar,** (☎ 787/888–6000, ext. 3484).

FISHING

Puerto Rico's waters are home to large game fish such as marlin, wahoo, dorado, tuna, and barracuda; as many as 30 world records for catches have been set off the island's shores. Half-day, full-day, split charters, and big- and small-game fishing can be arranged through **Benitez Deep-Sea Fishing** (⊠ Club Náutico de San Juan, Miramar, ☎ 787/723–2292), **Caribe Aquatic Adventures** (⊠ San Juan Bay Marina, ☎ 787/729–2929, ext. 240), and **Castillo Watersports** (⊠ ESJ Towers, Isla Verde, ☎ 787/791–6195 or 787/726–5752).

Out on the island, try **Dorado Marine Center** (⊠ 271 Méndez Vigo, ☎ 787/796–4645), **Parguera Fishing Charters** (⊠ La Parguera, Lajas, ☎ 787/899–4698 or 787/382–4698), and **Tropical Fishing Charters** (⊠ El Conquistador, Fajardo, ☎ 787/860–8551 or 787/759–1255).

GOLF

For aficionados worldwide, Puerto Rico is known as the birthplace of golf great and raconteur Chi Chi Rodriguez—and he had to hone his craft somewhere. Currently, you'll find 15 courses on the island, including 10 championship links. Be sure to call ahead when you plan to play; hours vary, and you should schedule a tee time (also several hotel courses allow only guests, or give preference to guests). Greens fees start at about $25. There are four beautiful Robert Trent Jones–designed 18-hole courses shared by the **Hyatt Dorado Beach** and the **Hyatt Regency Cerromar Beach** hotels (⊠ Dorado, ☎ 787/796–1234, ext. 3238 or 3016).

You'll also find 18-hole courses at the **Berwind Country Club** (⊠ Río Grande, ☎ 787/876–3056), **Punta Borinquén** (⊠ Aguadilla, ☎ 787/890–2987), **Westin Río Mar** (⊠ Río Grande, ☎ 787/888–6000), and **Wyndham Palmas del Mar Resort** (⊠ Humacao, ☎ 787/852–6000). The **Bahia Beach Plantation** (⊠ Río Grande, ☎ 787/256–5600) is one of Puerto Rico's newer courses. There are two 9-hole courses out on the island, one at the **Aguirre Golf Club** (⊠ Aguirre, ☎ 787/853–4052) and the other at the **Club Deportivo del Oeste** (⊠ Mayagüez, ☎ 787/851–8880). The **Ponce Hilton** (⊠ Ponce, ☎ 787/259–7676) has a driving range.

HIKING

Parts of Puerto Rico were meant to be explored on foot. Trails lace the rain forests of **El Yunque** (information: ⊠ El Portal Tropical Forest Center, Rte. 191, ☎ 787/888–1810 or 787/888–1880). You can also hit the trails in **Río Abajo Forest** (south of Arecibo) and **Toro Negro Forest** (east of Adjuntas). Each reserve has a ranger station.

HORSEBACK RIDING

Puerto Rico's famous and unique paso fino horses, with their distinct gait, are often used for riding. **Hacienda Carabalí** (⊠ Rte. 992, Km 4, Luquillo, ☎ 787/889–5820 or 787/889–4954) offers beach riding and rain-forest trail rides. Beach trail rides can be arranged at **Wyndham Palmas del Mar Equestrian Center** (⊠ Wyndham Palmas del Mar, Humacao, ☎ 787/852–6000).

SCUBA DIVING AND SNORKELING

There is excellent diving off Puerto Rico's coast. Some outfits offer package deals combining accommodations with daily diving trips. Escorted half-day dives range from $45 to $90 for one- and two-tank dives, including all equipment. Packages, which include lunch and other extras, start at $60. Night dives are often available at close to double the price. Snorkeling excursions, which include transportation (most often a sailboat filled with snorkelers), equipment rental, and sometimes lunch, start at $25. Snorkel equipment rents at beaches for about $5. (Caution: Coral-reef waters and mangrove areas can be dangerous to novices. Unless you're an expert or have an experienced guide, avoid unsupervised areas and stick to the water-sports centers of hotels.)

Snorkeling and scuba-diving instruction and equipment rentals are available at **Boquerón Dive Shop** (⊠ Main St., Boquerón, ☎ 787/851–2155); **Caribe Aquatic Adventures** (⊠ San Juan Bay Marina, ☎ 787/729–2929, ext. 240); **Caribbean School of Aquatics** (⊠ Taft No. 1, Suite 10F, San Juan, ☎ 787/728–6606); **Coral Head Divers** (⊠ Wyndham Palmas del Mar, Humacao, ☎ 787/852–6000 or 800/468–3331); **Dive Copamarina** (⊠ Copamarina Beach Resort, Rte. 333, Guánica, ☎ 787/821–6009), where hotel-dive packages are available; **Island Queen** (⊠ Rincón, ☎ 787/823–6301); **Parguera Divers Training Center** (⊠ La Parguera, ☎ 787/899–4171); and **Viking Puerto Rico** (⊠ Rincón, ☎ 787/823–7010).

SURFING

Surfing is best November–April. Aviones and La Concha beaches in San Juan and Casa de Pesca in Arecibo are summer surfing spots and have nearby surf shops. The best surfing beaches are along the Atlantic coastline from Borinquén Point south to Rincón, where there are several surf shops, including **West Coast Surf Shop** (⊠ 2 E. Muñoz Rivera St., ☎ 787/823–3935).

TENNIS

If you'd like to use the courts at a property where you are not a guest, call in advance for information about reservations and fees. Your best bet for playing tennis in the San Juan area are the 17 lighted courts at **San Juan Central Municipal Park** (⊠ Calle Cerra exit on Rte. 2, ☎ 787/722–1646). Fees run $3 per hour 8 AM–6 PM and $4 per hour 6–10 PM. There are six lighted courts at the **Caribe Hilton International** (⊠ Puerta de Tierra, ☎ 787/721–0303, ext. 1730); eight courts, four lighted, at **Carib Inn** (⊠ Isla Verde, ☎ 787/791–3535, ext. 6); and two lighted courts at the **Condado Plaza Hotel** (⊠ Condado, ☎ 787/721–

1000, ext. 1775). Fees for nonguests at these hotels range $10–$20 per hour.

Out on the island, there are seven courts, two lighted, at the **Hyatt Dorado Beach** (⊠ Dorado, ☎ 787/796–1234, ext. 3220); 14 courts, two lighted, at **Hyatt Regency Cerromar Beach** (⊠ Dorado, ☎ 787/796–1234, ext. 3040); four lighted courts at the **Ponce Hilton** (⊠ Ponce, ☎ 787/259–7676); four lighted courts at **Punta Borinquén** (⊠ Aguadilla, ☎ 787/891–8778); 13 lighted courts at the **Westin Río Mar** (⊠ Río Grande, ☎ 787/888–6000); and 20 courts, four lighted, at **Wyndham Palmas del Mar** (⊠ Humacao, ☎ 787/852–6000, ext. 51).

WINDSURFING

Many resort hotels rent Windsurfers to their guests, including **El Conquistador, El San Juan, Wyndham Palmas del Mar,** the **Hyatts,** and the **Condado Plaza.** If your hotel doesn't provide them, they can probably help you make arrangements with a local outfitter.

Spectator Sports

BASEBALL

Does the name Roberto Clemente ring a bell? The late, great star of the Pittsburgh Pirates, who died in a 1972 plane crash delivering supplies to Nicaraguan earthquake victims, was born near San Juan and got his start in the Puerto Rican pro leagues. The island's season runs October–February. Stadiums are in San Juan, Santurce, Ponce, Caguas, Arecibo, and Mayagüez; the teams also play once or twice in Aguadilla. Contact the tourist office for details or call **Professional Baseball of Puerto Rico** (☎ 787/765–6285).

HORSE RACING

Thoroughbred races are run year-round at **El Comandante Racetrack,** about 20 minutes east of San Juan. On race days—Wednesday, Friday, and Sunday—the dining rooms open at 12:30 PM. Post time is 2:30 PM. ⊠ *Rte. 3, Km 15.3, Canóvanas,* ☎ *787/724–6060.* ⊙ *Wed., Fri., and Sun. 12:30–6.*

Shopping

San Juan is not a free port, and you won't find bargains on electronics and perfumes. You can, however, find excellent prices on china, crystal, fashions, and jewelry. Shopping for local Caribbean crafts can be great fun. You'll run across a lot of tacky things you can live without, but you can also find some treasures, and in many cases you'll be able to watch the artisans at work. (For guidance, contact the Puerto Rico Tourism Company's Artisan Center (☎ 787/721–2400) or the Fomento Crafts Project (☎ 787/758–4747, ext. 2291).

Popular items include *santos* (small hand-carved figures of saints or religious scenes), hand-rolled cigars, handmade *mundillo* lace from Aguadilla, Carnival masks (papier-mâché from Ponce and fierce *veijigantes* made from coconut husks in Loiza, an African-American enclave near San Juan), and fancy men's shirts called *guayaberas*. Also, some folks swear that Puerto Rican rum is the best in the world.

Shopping Areas

Old San Juan is full of shops, especially on Cristo, Fortaleza, and San Francisco streets. The shops are all within walking distance of each other, and trolleys are at your beck and call. **Plaza Las Américas,** south of San Juan, is the largest shopping mall in the Caribbean, with 200 shops, restaurants, and movie theaters. Other malls out on the island include the **Carolina Mall** near San Juan, **Plaza del Caribe** in Ponce, **Plaza del Carmen** in Caguas, and the **Mayagüez Mall.**

Speciality Items

ART

Corinne Timsit International Galleries (⊠ 104 Calle San Jose, Old San Juan, ☎ 787/724–1039) features work by contemporary Latin American painters. **DMR Gallery** (⊠ 204 Calle Luna, Old San Juan, ☎ 787/722–4181) features handmade furniture by artist Nick Quijano. **Galería Botello** (⊠ 208 Calle Cristo, Old San Juan, ☎ 787/723–2879; ⊠ Plaza Las Américas, ☎ 787/754–7430) exhibits and sells antique santos (religious sculptures). **Galería Gotay** (⊠ 212 Calle San Francisco, Old San Juan, ☎ 787/722–5726) carries contemporary art. **Galería San Juan** (⊠ Gallery Inn, 204–206 Calle Norzagaray, Old San Juan, ☎ 787/722–1808), has the bronze sculptures of artist Jan D'Esopo.

CLOTHES

You can get discounts on Hathaway shirts and Christian Dior clothing at **Hathaway Factory Outlet** (⊠ 203 Calle Cristo, Old San Juan, ☎ 787/723–8946). Discounts on Ralph Lauren apparel are found at the **Polo/Ralph Lauren Factory Store** (⊠ 201 Calle Cristo, Old San Juan, ☎ 787/722–2136).

The **London Fog Factory Outlet** (⊠ 156 Calle Cristo, Old San Juan, ☎ 787/722–4334) offers reductions on men's, women's, and children's raincoats. The **Harley Davidson Boutique** (⊠ 313 Calle Fortaleza, ☎ 787/721–4202) sells Harley-themed T-shirts, jeans, sun glasses, and riding leathers. People line up to enter **Marshall's** (⊠ Plaza de Armas, Old San Juan, ☎ 787/722–0874) for basic clothing and department store items. Try the **Bikini Factory** (⊠ 3 Palmar Norte, Isla Verde, ☎ 787/726–0016) for stylish men's and women's swimwear.

HANDICRAFTS

For one-of-a-kind buys, head for **Puerto Rican Arts & Crafts** (⊠ 204 Calle Fortaleza, Old San Juan, ☎ 787/725–5596). More authentic Puerto Rican craft is also found at the **Instituto de Cultura Puertorriqueña** (⊠ 98 Calle Norzagaray, Old San Juan, ☎ 787/721–6866), situated in the Dominican Convent on the north side of the old city. Here you'll find baskets, masks, the famous *cuatro* guitars, santos, books and tapes, and Indian artifacts.

You should pay a visit to the **artisan markets** in Sixto Escobar Park (⊠ Puerta de Tierra, ☎ 787/722–0369) and Luis Muñoz Marín Park (⊠ Next to Las Américas Expressway west on Piñero Ave., Hato Rey, ☎ 787/763–0568). The **Haitian Gallery** (⊠ 367 Calle Fortaleza, Old San Juan, ☎ 787/725–0986) carries Puerto Rican crafts and a selection of folksy, often inexpensive paintings from around the Caribbean. In Ponce, consult the **Casa Paoli Center of Folkloric Investigations** (⊠ 14 Calle Mayor, ☎ 787/840–4115).

JEWELRY

There is gold, gold, and more gold at **Reinhold** (⊠ 201 Calle Cristo, Old San Juan, ☎ 787/725–6878). For brand-name watches visit the **Watch and Gem Palace** (⊠ 204 Calle San José, Old San Juan, ☎ 787/722–2136).

Nightlife and the Arts

Qué Pasa, the official visitor's guide, has current listings of events in San Juan and out on the island. Also, pick up a copy of the *San Juan Star, Quick City Guide,* or *Sunspots,* and check with the local tourist offices and the concierge at your hotel to find out what's doing.

Nightlife

Fridays and Saturdays are big nights in San Juan, so dress to party. Bars are usually always casual; however, if you try to go out in jeans, sneakers, and a T-shirt, you will probably be refused entry at most nightclubs or discos (except the gay ones), unless you look like a model.

BARS

Calle San Sebastián in Old San Juan is lined with trendy bars and restaurants; if you're in the mood for barhopping, head in that direction—it's pretty crazy on weekend nights.

Blue Dolphin (⊠ 2 Calle Amapola, Isla Verde, ☎ 787/791–3083) is a hangout where you can rub elbows with some offbeat locals and enjoy stunning sunset happy hours. While strolling along the Isla Verde beach, just look for the neon blue dolphin on the roof—you can't miss it. **Hard Rock Cafe** (⊠ 253 Recinto Sur, Old San Juan, ☎ 787/724–7625), almost as common as McDonald's these days, is in Old San Juan.

El Patio de Sam (⊠ 102 Calle San Sebastián, Old San Juan, ☎ 787/723–1149) is an Old San Juan institution whose clientele claims it serves the best burgers on the island. The dining room is awash in potted plants and strategically placed canopies that create the illusion of dining on an outdoor patio. **El Batey** (⊠ 101 Calle Cristo, Old San Juan, ☎ 787/725–1787) is a hole-in-the-wall run by crusty New Yorker Davydd Gwilym Jones III; it looks like a military bunker, complete with a pool table and graffiti covering the walls and ceiling (grab a marker and add you own message). But it has the best oldies juke box in the city and is wildly popular.

CASINOS

By law, all casinos are in hotels, primarily in San Juan. The government keeps a close eye on them. Dress for the larger casinos tends to be on the more formal side, and the atmosphere is refined. The law permits casinos to operate noon–4 AM, but individual casinos set their own hours.

Casinos are in the following San Juan hotels (☞ Lodging, *above*): **Condado Plaza Hotel, Caribe Hilton, El San Juan, Holiday Inn Crowne Plaza** (⊠ Rte. 187, Isla Verde), and **Radisson Ambassador** (⊠ 1369 Ashford Ave., Condado). Elsewhere on the island, there are casinos at **El Conquistador,** the **Hyatt Dorado Beach** and **Hyatt Regency Cerromar** hotels, the **Ponce Hilton,** the **Westin Río Mar** and the **Wyndham Palmas del Mar.**

DANCE AND MUSIC CLUBS

Out on the island, nightlife is hard to come by, but there are discos in the **Ponce Hilton.** Nightclubs have a short shelf life; they come and go with the whims of the hip crowd. Currently, everyone is heading to **Egipto** (⊠ Av. Robert Todd, Santurce, ☎ 787/725–4664 or 787/725–4675) for live music and dancing. Wednesdays are casual nights and Thursday–Saturday are dressy dancing nights.

Café Matisse (⊠ Av. Ashford, Condado, ☎ 787/723–7910) offers live jazz and blues on weekends. The **Casino Lounge** offers live jazz Wednesday–Saturday. **Club Hollywood** (⊠ Recinto Sur, Old San Juan) offers a mix of club music and reggae Thursday–Sunday. The Condado Plaza Hotel's **La Fiesta Lounge** sizzles with steamy Latin shows. **Houlihan's** (⊠ Av. Ashford, Condado, ☎ 787/723–8600) is a restaurant with an upstairs nightclub popular among the local party crowd. On weekends revelers line up on the sidewalk waiting to get in. **Krash** (⊠ 1257 Av. Ponce de León, Santurce, ☎ 787/722–1390) plays the best dance music on the island; gay crowds flock here. **Lazer Videoteque** (⊠ 251 Calle Cruz, ☎ 787/721–4479), with multilevels and a landscaped roof deck overlooking San Juan, attracts different crowds on different nights; Thursdays and Sundays are gay nights.

Arts

ISLAND CULTURE

LeLoLai is a year-round festival that celebrates Puerto Rico's Indian, Spanish, and African heritage. Performances take place each week, moving from hotel to hotel, showcasing the island's music, folklore, and culture. Because it is sponsored by the Puerto Rico Tourism Company and major San Juan hotels, passes to the festivities are included in some packages offered by participating hotels. You can also purchase tickets to a weekly series of events for $10. For information, contact ☎ 787/723–3135 weekdays, or 787/791–1014 on weekends and evenings. **La Tasca de Abel** (⊠ 351 Calle Fortaleza, ☎ 787/721–1689) is renowned for its tapas bar and the cabaret show (usually including flamenco guitar) performed by its engaging, talented staff.

Exploring Puerto Rico

Numbers in the margin correspond to points of interest on the Old San Juan Exploring map.

Old San Juan

Old San Juan, the original city founded in 1521, contains carefully preserved examples of 16th- and 17th-century Spanish colonial architecture. More than 400 buildings have been beautifully restored. Graceful wrought-iron balconies, with lush hanging plants, extend over narrow streets paved with *adequines* (blue-gray stones originally used as ballast for Spanish ships). The old city is partially enclosed by walls that date from 1633 and once completely surrounded it. Designated a U.S. National Historic Zone in 1950, Old San Juan is chockablock with shops, open-air cafés, private homes, tree-shaded squares, monuments, plaques, pigeons, and people. The traffic is awful. Get an overview of the inner city on a morning's stroll (bearing in mind that this "stroll" includes some steep climbs). However, if you plan to immerse yourself in history or to shop, you'll need two or three days. You may want to set aside extra time to see El Morro and Fort San Cristóbal, especially if you're an aficionado of military history. UNESCO has designated each fortress a World Heritage Site; each is also a National Historic Site. Both are administered by the National Park Service; you can take one of its tours or wander on your own.

SIGHTS TO SEE

❻ Casa Blanca. The original structure on this site, not far from the ramparts of El Morro, was a frame house built in 1521 as a home for Ponce de León. But Ponce de León died in Cuba, never having lived in it, and it was virtually destroyed by a hurricane in 1523, after which his son-in-law had the present masonry home built. His descendants occupied it for 250 years. From the end of the Spanish-American War in 1898 to 1966, it was the home of the U.S. Army commander in Puerto Rico. A museum devoted to archaeology is on the second floor. The lush surrounding gardens, cooled by spraying fountains, are a tranquil spot for a restorative pause. ⊠ 1 Calle San Sebastián, ☎ 787/724–4102. ⛝ $2. ☉ Tues.–Sat. 9–noon and 1–3:45.

⓫ Casa del Libro. This 18th-century building contains exhibits devoted to books and bookbinding. The museum's 5,000 books, sketches, and illustrations include some 200 rare volumes written before 1501. ⊠ 255 Calle Cristo, ☎ 787/723–0354. ⛝ Free. ☉ Tues.–Sat. 11–4:30.

⓯ City Hall. Called the *Alcaldía*, this structure was built between 1604 and 1789. In 1841 extensive renovations were done to make the Al-

Casa Blanca, **6**
Casa del Libro, **11**
City Hall, **15**
Cristo Chapel, **10**
Dominican Convent, **5**
La Fortaleza, **9**
Fuerte San Felipe del Morro, **1**
La Intendencia, **14**
Pablo Casals Museum, **4**
Paseo de la Princesa, **19**
Plaza de Armas, **13**
Plaza de Colón, **16**
Plazuela de la Rogativa, **8**
Popular Arts and Crafts Center, **12**
San Cristóbal, **17**
San José Church, **3**
San Juan Cathedral, **7**
San Juan Museum of Art and History, **2**
Tapia Theater, **18**

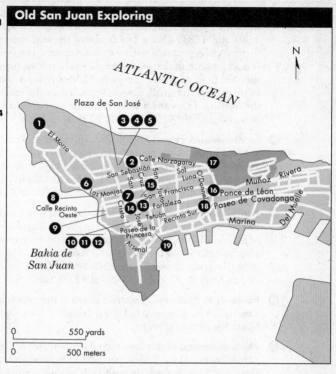

Old San Juan Exploring

caldía resemble Madrid's city hall, with arcades, towers, balconies, and a lovely inner courtyard. A tourist information center and an art gallery are on the first floor. ⊠ *North side of Plaza de Armas,* ☎ *787/724–7171, ext. 2391.* ⊙ *Weekdays 8–4.*

🔟 **Cristo Chapel.** According to legend, in 1753 a young horseman named Baltazar Montañez, carried away during festivities in honor of the patron saint, raced down the street and plunged over the steep precipice. A witness to the tragedy promised to build a chapel if the young man's life could be saved. Historical records maintain the man died, though legend contends that he lived. Inside is a small silver altar, dedicated to the Christ of Miracles. ⊠ *Calle Cristo.* ⊙ *Tues. 10–3:30.*

❺ Dominican Convent. Built by Dominican friars in 1523, the convent often served as a shelter during Carib Indian attacks and, more recently, as headquarters for the Antilles command of the U.S. Army. Now home to the Institute of Puerto Rican Culture, the beautifully restored building contains an ornate 18th-century altar, religious manuscripts, artifacts, and art. The institute also maintains a bookshop here, and occasionally classical concerts are held. The convent is the intended future home of the city's museum of fine arts. ⊠ *98 Calle Norzagaray,* ☎ *787/721–6866.* ⊡ *Free.* ⊙ *Mon.–Sat. 9–5.*

❾ La Fortaleza. Sitting on a hill overlooking the harbor, La Fortaleza, the Western Hemisphere's oldest executive mansion in continuous use and official residence of the present governor of Puerto Rico, was built as a fortress. The original primitive structure, built in 1540, has seen numerous changes over the past four centuries, resulting in the present collection of marble and mahogany, medieval towers, and stained-glass galleries. Guided tours are conducted every hour on the hour in English, on the half hour in Spanish. ⊠ *Calle Recinto Oeste,* ☎ *787/721–7000, ext. 2211 or 2358.* ⊡ *Free.* ⊙ *Weekdays 9–4.*

🖐 **①** **Fuerte San Felipe del Morro.** On a rocky promontory on the northwestern tip of the old city is El Morro, a fortress built by the Spaniards between 1540 and 1783. Rising 140 ft above the sea, the massive six-level fortress covers enough territory to accommodate a 9-hole golf course. It is a labyrinth of dungeons, ramps and barracks, turrets, towers, and tunnels. Built to protect the port, El Morro has a commanding view of the harbor. Its small, air-conditioned museum traces the history of the fortress. Tours and a video show are available in English. ⊠ *Calle Norzagaray,* ☏ *787/729–6960.* 🎟 *Free.* ⊙ *Daily 9–5.*

⑭ **La Intendencia.** From 1851 to 1898, this three-story neoclassical building was home to the Spanish Treasury; now it's the headquarters of Puerto Rico's State Department. ⊠ *Calle San José, at the corner of Calle San Francisco,* ☏ *787/722–2121, ext. 230.* 🎟 *Free.* ⊙ *Weekdays 8– noon and 1–4:30. Tours at 2 and 3 in Spanish, at 4 in English.*

④ **Pablo Casals Museum.** This museum contains memorabilia of the famed cellist, who made his home in Puerto Rico for the last 16 years of his life. Manuscripts, photographs, and his favorite cellos are on display, in addition to recordings and videotapes of Casals Festival concerts (the latter shown on request). ⊠ *101 Calle San Sebastián, Plaza de San José,* ☏ *787/723–9185.* 🎟 *$1.* ⊙ *Tues.–Sat. 9:30–5:30.*

⑲ **Paseo de la Princesa.** This street down at the port is spruced up with flowers, trees, benches, and street lamps. Take a seat and watch the boats zip across the water.

⑬ **Plaza de Armas.** This is the original main square of Old San Juan. The plaza, bordered by Calles San Francisco, Fortaleza, San José, and Cruz, has a lovely fountain with 19th-century statues representing the four seasons.

⑯ **Plaza de Colón.** This bustling square has a statue of Christopher Columbus atop a high pedestal. Originally called St. James Square, it was renamed in honor of Columbus on the 400th anniversary of the discovery of Puerto Rico. Bronze plaques in the base of the statue relate various episodes in the life of the great explorer. On the north side of the plaza is a terminal for buses to and from San Juan. ⊠ *On pedestrian mall of Calle Fortaleza.*

⑧ **Plazuela de la Rogativa.** In this little plaza, statues of a bishop and three women commemorate a legend, according to which the British, while laying siege to the city in 1797, mistook the flaming torches of a *rogativa* (religious procession) for Spanish reinforcements and beat a hasty retreat. The monument was donated to the city in 1971 on its 450th anniversary. ⊠ *Caleta de las Monjas.*

⑫ **Popular Arts and Crafts Center.** Run by the Institute of Puerto Rican Culture, the center is in a colonial building next door to the Casa del Libro (☞ *above*) and is a superb repository of island crafts work, some of which is for sale. ⊠ *253 Calle Cristo,* ☏ *787/722–0621.* 🎟 *Free.* ⊙ *Mon.–Sat. 9–5.*

🖐 **⑰** **San Cristóbal.** This 18th-century fortress guarded the city from land attacks. Even larger than El Morro, San Cristóbal, during the 17th and 18th centuries, was known as the Gibraltar of the West Indies. ⊠ *Norzagaray Blvd.,* ☏ *787/729–6960.* 🎟 *Free.* ⊙ *Daily 9–5.*

③ **San José Church.** With its vaulted ceilings, this is a splendid example of 16th-century Spanish Gothic architecture. The church, one of the oldest in the Western Hemisphere, was built in 1532 under the supervision of Dominican friars. The body of Ponce de León, the Spanish explorer who came to the New World seeking the Fountain of Youth, was buried here for almost three centuries before being removed in 1913 and placed in the San Juan Cathedral (☞ *below*). ✉ *Calle San Sebastián, Plaza de San José,* ☎ *787/725–7501.* 🎟 *Free.* ⊘ *Mon.–Sat. 8:30–4; mass Sun. at 12:15 PM.*

❼ San Juan Cathedral. The Catholic shrine of Puerto Rico had humble beginnings in the early 1520s as a thatch-topped wood structure. Hurricane winds tore off the thatch and destroyed the church. It was reconstructed in 1540, when the graceful circular staircase and vaulted Gothic ceilings were added, but most of the work was done in the 19th century. The remains of Ponce de León are in a marble tomb near the transept. ✉ *153 Calle Cristo,* ☎ *787/722–0861.* ⊘ *Weekdays 8:30–4; masses Sat. 7 PM, Sun. 9 and 11 AM, weekdays 12:15 PM.*

❷ San Juan Museum of Art and History. A bustling marketplace in 1855, this handsome building is now a modern cultural center that houses exhibits of Puerto Rican art. Multi-image audiovisual shows present the history of the island; concerts and other cultural events take place in the huge courtyard. ✉ *Calle Norzagaray, at the corner of Calle MacArthur,* ☎ *787/724–1875.* 🎟 *Free.* ⊘ *Tues.–Sun. 10–4.*

❶⑧ Tapia Theater. This theater was named after the Puerto Rican playwright Alejandro Tapia y Rivera. Built in 1832 and remodeled in 1949 and again in 1987, the municipal theater is the site of ballets, plays, and operettas. Stop by the box office to find out what's showing. ✉ *Calle Fortaleza at Plaza de Colón,* ☎ *787/722–0407.*

San Juan

You'll need to resort to taxis, buses, *públicos* (public cars), or a rental car to reach the points of interest in "new" San Juan. Avenida Muñoz Rivera, Avenida Ponce de León, and Avenida Fernández Juncos are the main thoroughfares that cross Puerta de Tierra, just east of Old San Juan, to the business and tourist districts of Santurce, Condado, and Isla Verde. Dos Hermanos Bridge connects Puerta de Tierra with Miramar, Condado, and Isla Grande. Isla Grande Airport, from which you can take short hops, is on the bay side of the bridge. On the other side of the bridge, the Condado Lagoon is bordered by Avenida Ashford, which threads past the high-rise Condado hotels and Avenida Baldorioty de Castro Expreso, which barrels east to the airport and beyond. Due south of the lagoon is Miramar, a residential area with fashionable turn-of-the-century homes and a few hotels and restaurants. South of Santurce is the "Golden Mile"—Hato Rey, the financial hub. Isla Verde, with its glittering beachfront hotels, casinos, discos, and public beach, is to the east, near the airport.

Numbers in the margin correspond to points of interest on the San Juan Exploring, Dining, and Lodging map.

SIGHTS TO SEE

❶ Capitol. In Puerta de Tierra is Puerto Rico's capitol, a white marble building that dates from the 1920s. The grand rotunda, with mosaics and friezes, was completed a few years ago. The seat of the island's bicameral legislature, the capitol contains Puerto Rico's constitution and is flanked by the modern buildings of the Senate and the House of Representatives. There are spectacular views from the observation plaza on the sea side of the capitol. Pick up a booklet about the building from the House Secretariat on the second floor. Guided tours are by appointment only. ✉ *Av. Ponce de León, Puerta de Tierra,* ☎ *787/721–6040, ext. 2458 or 3548.* 🎟 *Free.* ⊘ *Weekdays 8–4.*

❸ Centro de Bellas Artes. Internationally acclaimed performers appear at the Fine Arts Center. This completely modern facility, the largest of its kind in the Caribbean, has a full schedule of concerts, plays, and operas. ⊠ *Corner of Av. De Diego and Av. Ponce de León, Box 41287, Minillas Station, Santurce 00940,* ☎ *787/725–7353.*

❷ **Ft. San Gerónimo.** At the eastern tip of Puerta de Tierra, behind the splashy Caribe Hilton, this tiny fort is perched over the Atlantic like an afterthought. Added to San Juan's fortifications in the late 18th century, the structure barely survived the British attack of 1797. Restored in 1983 by the Institute of Puerto Rican Culture, it is now a military museum. At press time, however, the museum remained closed for repairs, and no reopening date had been announced, so visitors could only view the fort from the outside. ⊠ *Calle Rosales, Puerta de Tierra,* ☎ *787/724–5477.*

⟳ ❻ **Luis Muñoz Marín Park.** This idyllic, 90-acre tree-shaded spot is dotted with gardens, lakes, playgrounds, and picnic areas. An aerial gondola connects the park with the parking area and provides a 6½-minute tour of the park. An outdoor amphitheater is the venue for plays, concerts, and folk performances. ⊠ *Next to Las Américas Expressway, west on Av. Jesús Piñero, Hato Rey,* ☎ *787/751–3353.* ☞ *Free, parking $1 per vehicle.* ☉ *Tues.–Sun. 9–5.*

❺ **San Juan Central Municipal Park.** Southeast of Miramar, Avenida Muñoz Rivera skirts along the northern side of the mangrove-bordered Parque Central Municipo de San Juan, a convenient place for jogging, biking, and tennis. The park was built for the 1979 Pan-American Games. Inside you'll find a sports shop and cafeteria. ⊠ *Cerra St. exit on Rte. 2, Santurce,* ☎ *787/722–1646.* ☞ *75¢ per vehicle.* ☉ *Mon. 2–10, Tues.– Thurs. 6:30 AM–10 PM, Fri. 6:30 AM–9 PM, weekends 6:30 AM–6 PM.*

❹ **Santurce.** The area that lies between Miramar on the west and the Laguna San José on the east is a busy mixture of shops, markets, and offices. The classically designed **Sacred Heart University** is the home of the **Museum of Contemporary Puerto Rican Art** (⊠ Barat Bldg., ☎ 787/268–0049), which showcases the works of such modern masters as Rodon, Campeche, and Oller. The museum is free and is open weekdays 9–5.

❼ **University of Puerto Rico.** Río Piedras, a southern suburb, is home to the university, between Avenida Ponce de León and Avenida Barbosa. The campus is one of two sites for performances of the Puerto Rico Symphony Orchestra. Theatrical productions and other concerts are also scheduled here. The **University Museum** has archaeological and historical exhibits and occasionally mounts art displays. ⊠ *Next to main entrance on Av. Ponce de León, Río Piedras,* ☎ *787/764–0000, ext. 2452.* ☞ *Free.* ☉ *Mon.–Wed. and Fri. 9–4:30, Thurs. 9–9, Sat.–Sun. 9–3.*

The university's main attraction is the **Botanical Garden,** a lush forest of more than 200 species of tropical and subtropical vegetation. Footpaths lead to a graceful lotus lagoon, a bamboo promenade, an orchid garden, and a palm garden. ⊠ *Intersection of Rtes. 1 and 847 at entrance to Barrio Venezuela, Río Piedras,* ☎ *787/763–4408.* ☞ *Free.* ☉ *Daily 9–4:30.*

San Juan Environs

Numbers in the margin correspond to points of interest on the Puerto Rico map.

SIGHTS TO SEE

❸ **Bacardi Rum Plant.** Visitors can take a 45-minute tour of the bottling plant, museum, and distillery (called the Cathedral of Rum), which has the capacity to produce 100,000 gallons of rum a day. There is a gift shop. (Yes, you'll be offered a sample.) ⊠ *Rte. 888, Km 2.6, Cataño,*

☎ 787/788–1500. ☎ *Free.* ⊙ *Tours every 30 mins Mon.–Sat. 9–10:30 and noon–4.*

❷ Barrilito Rum Plant. On the grounds are a 200-year-old plantation home and a 150-year-old windmill, listed on the National Register of Historic Places. ⊠ *Rte. 5, Km 1.6, Bayamón,* ☎ *787/785–3490.* ☎ *Free.* ⊙ *Weekdays 8–11:30 and 1–4:30.*

❹ Bayamón. In the central park, across from Bayamón's city hall, there are some historical buildings and a 1934 sugarcane train that runs through the park (☎ 787/798–8191), open daily 8 AM–5 PM. On the plaza, in the city's historic district, stands the 18th-century Catholic church of Santa Cruz and the old neoclassic city hall, which now houses the **Francisco Oller Art and History Museum** (⊠ Calle Santiago Veve, ☎ 787/787–8620). The museum is free and is open Tuesday–Saturday 9–4.

❶ Caparra Ruins. In 1508 Ponce de León established the island's first settlement here. The ruins are that of an ancient fort. Its small **Museum of the Conquest and Colonization of Puerto Rico** contains historical documents, exhibits, and excavated artifacts. (You can see the museum's contents in less time than it takes to say the name.) ⊠ *Rte. 2, Km 6.6, Guaynabo,* ☎ *787/781–4795.* ☎ *Free.* ⊙ *Tues.–Sat. 8:30–4:30.*

Eastern Puerto Rico

Puerto Rico's 3,500 square mi is a lot of land to explore. While you can get from town to town via público, we don't recommend traveling that way unless your Spanish is good and you know exactly where you're going. The public cars stop in each town's main square, leaving you on your own to reach the beaches, restaurants, paradores, and attractions. You'll do much better if you rent a car. Most of the roads are excellent. However, there's a tangle of routes through the mountains, and they're not always well marked, so buy a good road map.

Numbers in the margin correspond to points of interest on the Puerto Rico map.

❼ Las Cabezas de San Juan Nature Reserve. The reserve contains mangrove swamps, coral reefs, beaches, and a dry forest—most of Puerto Rico's natural habitats rolled into a microcosmic 316 acres. The only habitat missing is a rain forest. Nineteenth-century El Faro, one of the island's oldest lighthouses, is restored and still functioning; its first floor contains a small nature center that has an aquarium and other exhibits. The reserve is open, by reservation only, to the public Friday–Sunday and to tour groups Wednesday–Thursday. Tours are given on request (in advance, by phone) four times a day–in Spanish at 9:30 AM, 10:30 AM, and 2 PM; in English at 2 PM. ⊠ *Rte. 987, Km 5.8,* ☎ *787/722–5882, 787/860–2560 on weekends.* ☎ *$5.*

❺ Caribbean National Forest. To take full advantage of the 28,000-acre El Yunque (as it's commonly known) rain forest, go with a tour. Dozens of trails lead through the thick jungle (it sheltered the Carib Indians for 200 years), and the tour guides take you to the best observation points, bathing spots, and waterfalls. Some of the trails are slippery, and there are occasional washouts. However, if you'd like to drive there yourself, take Route 3 east from San Juan and turn right (south) on Route 191, about 25 mi from the city. Stop in at the **El Portal Tropical Forest Center** (☎ 787/888–1810), on Route 191 at the entrance to the park. Nature talks, programs, and displays at the center are in Spanish and English. The center is open daily 9–5; admission is $3.

El Yunque, named after the good Indian spirit Yuquiyu, is in the Luquillo mountain range. The rain forest is verdant with feathery ferns, thick ropelike vines, white tuberoses and ginger, miniature orchids, and some 240 species of trees. More than 100 billion gallons of rainwater fall on it annually. Rain-battered, wind-ravaged dwarf vegetation clings to the top peaks. (El Toro, the highest peak in the forest, is 3,532 ft.) El Yunque is also a bird sanctuary and the base of the rare Puerto Rican parrot. Millions of inch-long coquis can be heard singing (or squawk-ing, depending on your sensibilities). The visitors centers at Palo Col-orado and Sierra Palm (☎ 787/888–1880) are open daily 8–5. Call in advance and take advantage of the park's "Rent-a-Ranger" program (you'll pay a fee) for guided tours. ⊠ *For further information, write Caribbean National Forest, Box B, Palmer, PR 00721, or call Catalina Field Office,* ☎ *787/887–2875 or 787/766–5335.*

9 Culebra. This island off the east coast of Puerto Rico has lovely white-sand beaches, coral reefs, and a wildlife refuge. In the sleepy town of Dewey (called "town" by everyone on the island), on Culebra's south-western side, check at the visitor information center at city hall (☎ 787/742–3291, FAX 787/742–0111) about boat, bike, or car rentals. Don't miss **Playa Flamenco,** 3 mi north of town, or **Playa Soni** on the eastern end of the island: they are two of the prettiest beaches in the Caribbean.

8 Fajardo. This is a major fishing and sailing center with thousands of boats tied and stacked in tiers at its three large marinas. Boats can be rented or chartered here, and the *East Wind,* a 53-ft catamaran, can take you out for a full day of snorkeling, swimming, and sunning for $55 per person. Fajardo is also the embarkation point for ferries to the islands of Culebra (a $2.25 fare) and Vieques ($2). ⊠ *Rte. 3.*

6 Luquillo Beach. One of the island's best and most popular beaches, Luquillo was once a flourishing coconut plantation. Coral reefs pro-tect its calm, pristine lagoon, making it an ideal place for a swim. You'll find lockers, showers, and changing rooms, as well as stands selling savory Puerto Rican delicacies. The beach gets crowded on weekends, when it seems as if the whole world heads for Luquillo. ⊠ *Rte. 3, Km 35.4.* 🖃 *$1 per car.*

10 Vieques. On this island off the east coast of Puerto Rico, is **Sun Bay public beach,** a gorgeous stretch of sand with picnic facilities and shade trees. **Red** and **Blue** beaches, on the U.S. Marine/Camp Garcia base (open to the public 6 AM–6 PM), are superb for snorkeling and privacy. **Mosquito Bay** is best experienced on moonless nights, thanks to the millions of bioluminescent organisms that glow when dis-turbed—it's like swimming in a cloud of fireflies. Seventy percent of Vieques is owned by the U.S. Navy, ensuring it will remain unspoiled. The deserted beaches—Green, Red, Blue, Navia, and Media Luna—are among the Caribbean's loveliest; you might see a wild paso fino horse galloping in the surf. The **visitor information center** (☎ 787/741–5000) is in the fishing village of Esperanza. Both Vieques and Culebra (☞ *above*), parched in contrast to the lush eastern end of Puerto Rico, are havens for colorful "expatriates" escaping the rat race stateside. This is pure old-time Caribbean: fun, funky, and unspoiled—the kind of getaway that is fast disappearing.

Western Puerto Rico

14 Aguadilla. In this area, somewhere between Aguadilla and Añasco, south of Rincón, Columbus dropped anchor on his second voyage in 1493. Both Aguadilla and **Aguada,** a few miles to the south, claim to be the spot where his foot first hit ground, and both towns have plaques to commemorate the occasion. ⊠ *Rte. 111.*

13 Arecibo Observatory. The town of Arecibo is home to one of the world's largest radar/radio telescopes. A 20-acre radar dish, with a 600-

ton suspended platform hovering over it, sits in a 565-ft-deep sinkhole (karst fields, an alien landscape of collapsed limestone sinkholes, are the prevalent geology throughout this part of the island). You can take a self-guided tour of the observatory, where groundbreaking work in astronomy, including SETI (the search for extraterrestrial intelligence), continues. This facility is part of the National Astronomy and Ionosphere Center of Cornell University. ⊠ *Rte. 625,* ☎ *787/878–2612.* 🎟 *$3.50.* ☉ *Wed.–Fri. noon–4, weekends 9–4..*

⑳ **Boquerón.** This tiny, funky, pastel village has sidewalk oyster vendors, bars, restaurants serving fresh seafood, and several of the standard T-shirt shops. There are also diving and snorkeling tours at the Boquerón Dive Shop on Main Street. Boquerón's balneario is one of the best beaches on the island. Parking is $2 per car, and two-room rustic cabins are for rent (☎ 787/724–2500, ext. 130 or 131). ⊠ *Rte. 101.*

⑱ **Cabo Rojo.** Once a pirates' hangout, this town is now a favorite resort area of Puerto Ricans. The area has long stretches of white-sand beaches on the clear, calm Caribbean Sea, as well as many seafood restaurants, bars, and hotels. There are also several paradores in the region. ⊠ *Rte. 102.*

⑪ **Caguana Indian Ceremonial Park.** This area was used 800 years ago by the Taíno tribes for recreation and worship. Mountains surround a 13-acre site planted with royal palms and guava. According to Spanish historians, the Taínos played a game similar to soccer, and in this park there are 10 courts (*bateyes*) bordered by cobbled walkways. There are also stone monoliths, some with colorful petroglyphs; a small museum; and a souvenir shop. ⊠ *Rte. 111, Km 12.3,* ☎ *787/894–7325.* 🎟 *Free.* ☉ *Daily 9–4:30.*

⑰ **Mayagüez.** Puerto Rico's fourth-largest city has a population approaching 100,000. Although bypassed by the mania for restoration that saw Ponce and Old San Juan spruced up for the Columbus quincentennial, Mayagüez is graced by some lovely turn-of-the-century architecture, such as the landmark Art Deco Teatro Yagüez and the Plaza de Colón.

North of town visit the ☺ **Mayagüez Zoo,** a 45-acre tropical compound that's home to exotic animals from around the world. The zoo's massive three-year renovation plan began in 1996, so some exhibits may be sporadically closed. ⊠ *Rte. 108 at Barrio Miradero,* ☎ *787/834–8110.* 🎟 *$3, parking $1.* ☉ *Wed.–Sun. 9–4.*

⑯ **Mona Island.** Fifty miles west of Mayagüez in the turbulent shark-infested Mona Passage, Mona Island is nicknamed the Galápagos of the Caribbean, thanks to the plethora of endangered and unique indigenous species that call it home. The variety of marine and bird life is especially breathtaking. The coastline is rimmed with imposing limestone cliffs up to 200 ft high pocked with caves that are said to contain buried treasure; the many perfectly preserved Taíno hieroglyphs and rock paintings there are of great archaeological value. Access to the island is only via private plane or boat. Very limited camping facilities are available on the pristine beaches. Call the Department of Natural Resources for information and camping reservations (☎ 787/723–1616 or 787/721–5495).

㉑ **Phosphorescent Bay.** The fishing village of **La Parguera,** an area of simple seafood restaurants, mangrove cays, and small islands, lies south of San Germán at the end of Route 304, off Route 116. This is an excellent scuba-diving area, but the main attraction is Phosphorescent Bay. Boats tour the bay, where microscopic dinoflagellates (marine plankton) light up like Christmas trees when disturbed by any kind of movement. The phenomenon can be seen only on moonless nights. Boats leave for the hour-long trip nightly from dusk until midnight, depending on demand, and the trip costs $5 per person. You can also rent or charter a small boat to explore the numerous cays.

② **Ponce.** From San Germán (☞ *below*), Route 2 traverses splendid peaks and valleys; pastel houses cling to the sides of steep green hills. The Cordillera Central mountains run parallel to Route 2 here and provide a stunning backdrop to the drive. East of Yauco, the road dips and sweeps right along the Caribbean and into Ponce.

Puerto Rico's second-largest city (population 300,000) underwent a massive restoration in preparation for its 300th anniversary, celebrated in 1996, of the city's first settlement. The town's 19th-century style has been recaptured with pink marble-bordered sidewalks, gas lamps, painted trolleys, and horse-drawn carriages. You have not seen a firehouse until you've seen the red-and-black-striped **Parque de Bombas,** a structure built in 1882 for an exposition and converted to a firehouse the following year. The city hired architect Pablo Ojeda O'Neill to restore it, and it is now a museum of Ponce's history, which, not surprisingly, has a display of Fire Brigade memorabilia. ⊠ *Plaza Las Delicias,* ☎ *787/284–4141, ext. 342.* ☞ *Free.* ☉ *Wed.–Mon. 9:30–6.*

Ponce's charm stems from a combination of neoclassic, Ponce Creole, and Art Deco styles. The tiny streets lined with wrought-iron balconies are reminiscent of New Orleans's French Quarter. Stop in and pick up information about this seaside city at the columned **Casa Armstrong-Poventud,** the home of the Institute of Puerto Rican Culture and a Tourism Information Office, open weekdays 8–noon and 1–4:30 (use the side entrance). Stroll around the **Plaza Las Delicias,** with its perfectly pruned India-laurel fig trees, graceful fountains, gardens, and park benches. View **Our Lady of Guadelupe Cathedral** (masses are held daily), and walk down Calles Isabel and Christina to see turn-of-the-century wooden houses with wrought-iron balconies.

Two superlative examples of early 20th-century architecture house the **Ponce History Museum** (Museo de la Historia de Ponce), where 10 rooms of exhibits vividly re-create Ponce's golden years, providing especially fascinating glimpses into the worlds of culture, high finance, and journalism during the 19th century. ⊠ *53 Calle Isabel,* ☎ *787/844–7071.* ☞ *$3.* ☉ *Mon. and Wed.–Fri. 10–5, weekends 10–6.*

Continue as far as Calles Mayor and Christina to the white stucco **La Perla Theater,** with its Corinthian columns. Be sure to allow time to visit the **Ponce Museum of Art** (Museo de Arte de Ponce). The architecture alone is worth seeing: The modern, two-story building designed by Edward Durell Stone (who designed New York's Museum of Modern Art) has seven interconnected hexagons, glass cupolas, and a pair of curved staircases. The collection includes late Renaissance and Baroque works from Italy, France, and Spain, as well as contemporary art by Puerto Ricans. ⊠ *Av. Las Américas,* ☎ *787/848–0505 or 787/ 848–0511.* ☞ *$4.* ☉ *Daily 10–5.*

Another fine museum is **Castillo Serrallés,** a splendid Spanish Revival mansion perched on El Vigía Hill, with smashing views of Ponce and the Caribbean. This former residence of the Serrallés family, owners of the Don Q rum distillery, has been restored with a mix of original furnishings and antiques that recall the era of the sugar barons, including a baronial dining room with heavy carved mahogany and wrought-iron doors. A short film details the history of the sugar and rum industries. The 100-ft-tall cross (La Cruceta del Vigía) behind the museum has a windowed elevator; you can ascend for panoramic views of Ponce and the coast. ⊠ *17 El Vigía Hill,* ☎ *787/259–1774.* 🎫 *$3.* ☉ *Tues.–Sun. 10–5.*

There are two intriguing historical sights just outside the city. **Hacienda Buena Vista** is a 19th-century coffee plantation, restored by the Conservation Trust of Puerto Rico, with much of the authentic machinery and furnishings intact. Reservations are required for the 90-minute tours; tours in English are given on request (in advance) once a day. ⊠ *Rte. 10, Km 16.8, north of Ponce,* ☎ *787/722–5882 weekdays, 787/848– 7020 weekends.* 🎫 *$5.* ☉ *Wed.–Fri. open to tour groups; Fri.–Sun. open to public.*

The **Tibes Indian Ceremonial Center** is the oldest cemetery in the Caribbean. It is a treasure trove of pre-Taíno ruins and burials, dating from AD 300 to AD 700. Some archaeologists, noting the symmetrical arrangement of stone pillars, surmise the cemetery may have been of great religious significance. The complex includes a detailed re-creation of a Taíno village and a museum. ⊠ *Rte. 503, Km 2.2,* ☎ *787/840– 2255 or 787/840–5685.* 🎫 *$2.* ☉ *Wed.–Sun. 9–4.*

⓯ **Rincón.** Located along Route 115, one of the island's most scenic areas of rolling hills dotted with pastel-color houses, Rincón is perched on a hill and overlooks its beach, the site of the World Surfing Championship in 1968. Skilled surfers flock to Rincón during the winter, when the water is rough and challenging. The town is also increasingly popular with divers. Locals boast that the best diving and snorkeling in Puerto Rico (and some even say the Caribbean) is off the Rincón coast, particularly around the island of Desecheo, a federal wildlife preserve. Whale-watching is another draw for this town; humpback whales winter off the coast December–February. ⊠ *Rte. 115.*

⓬ **Río Camuy Cave Park.** This 268-acre reserve contains one of the world's largest cave networks. Guided tours take you on a tram down through dense tropical vegetation to the entrance of the cave, where you continue on foot over underground trails, ramps, and bridges. The caves, sinkholes, and subterranean streams are all spectacular (the world's second-largest underground river runs through here), but this trip is not for the claustrophobic. Be sure to call ahead; the tours allow only a limited number of people, and hours change slightly in the off-season. ⊠ *Rte. 129, Km 18.9,* ☎ *787/898–3100 or 787/756–5555.* 🎫 *$10, parking $2.* ☉ *Tues.–Sun. 8–4. Last tour starts at 3:50.*

⓳ **San Germán.** This quiet and colorful Old World town is home to the oldest intact church under the U.S. flag. Built in 1606, **Porta Coeli** (Gates of Heaven) overlooks one of the town's two plazas (where the townspeople continue the Spanish tradition of promenading at night). The church is now a museum of religious art, housing 18th- and 19th-century paintings and wooden statues. ⊠ *Rte. 102,* ☎ *787/892–5845.* 🎫 *Free.* ☉ *Tues.–Sun. 9–noon and 1–4.*

Puerto Rico A to Z

Arriving and Departing

BY AIRPLANE

The **Luis Muñoz Marín International Airport** (☎ 787/462–3147), east of downtown San Juan, is one of the easiest and cheapest destinations to reach in the Caribbean. The airport is the Caribbean hub for **American Airlines** (☎ 787/749–1747 or 800/433–7300). American has nonstop flights from New York, Newark, Miami, Orlando, Tampa, Boston, Philadelphia, Chicago, Dallas-Fort Worth, Baltimore, Hartford, and Washington, D.C. **Continental** (☎ 800/231–0856) has daily nonstop service from Newark. **Delta** (☎ 787/754–3333 or 800/241–4141) operates nonstop service from Atlanta. **Northwest** (☎ 800/447–4747) has daily nonstop flights from Detroit. **TWA** (☎ 800/892–4141) flies nonstop from New York. **United** (☎ 800/241–6522) flies daily nonstop from Chicago, and has seasonal nonstop weekend flights from New York. **US Airways** (☎ 800/428–4322) offers nonstop flights from Pittsburgh, Philadelphia, and Charlotte. **Tower Air** (☎ 800/221–2500) flies nonstop from New York. **American Trans Air (ATA)** (☎ 800/382–5892) operates nonstop from New York, St. Petersburg, Orlando, Milwaukee, and Las Vegas.

Foreign carriers include **Air Canada** (☎ 800/776–3000), **Air France** (☎ 800/237–2747), **British Airways** (☎ 800/247–9297), **BWIA** (☎ 800/538–2942), **Iberia** (☎ 800/772–4642), **LACSA** (☎ 800/225–2272), and **Lufthansa** (☎ 800/645–3880).

Connections between Caribbean islands can be made through **American Eagle** (☎ 787/749–1747 or 800/433–7300), **Air Jamaica** (☎ 800/523–5585), **ANA** (☎ 800/693–0007), **Carib Air** (☎ 800/981–0212), **KLM** (☎ 800/826–7976), and **LIAT** (☎ 800/468–0482).

From the Airport: Taxi Turisticos (☞ Getting Around, *below*) charge set rates based on zones, so the fare depends on the destination. Uniformed and badged officials help you find a cab at the airport (look for the tourism company booth) and hand you a slip with your fare, which you can present to your driver. To Isla Verde, the fare is $8; to Condado, it's $12; to Old San Juan, it's $16. If you don't hail one of these cabs, you're at the mercy of the meter and the cabdriver.

Other options are the **Airport Limousine Service** (☎ 787/791–4745), which provides minibus service to hotels in the Isla Verde, Condado, and Old San Juan areas at basic fares of $2.50, $3.50, and $4.50, respectively; the fares do vary, depending on the time of day and number of passengers. Limousines of **Dorado Transport Co-op** (☎ 787/796–1214) serve hotels and villas in the Dorado area for $15 per person.

Electricity
Puerto Rico uses a 110-volt AC (60-cycle) electrical system as in the U.S. European guests who have traveling appliances that use other systems can call ahead to confirm that their hotel has adapters and converters.

Emergencies
Hospitals: Ashford Memorial Community Hospital (✉ 1451 Av. Ashford, Condado, San Juan, ☎ 787/721–2160); San Juan Health Centre (✉ 200 Av. De Diego, San Juan, ☎ 787/725–0202). **Pharmacies:** Puerto Rico Drug Company (✉ 157 Calle San Francisco, Old San Juan, ☎ 787/725–2202); Walgreens (✉ 1130 Av. Ashford, Condado, San Juan, ☎ 787/725–1510). Walgreens also operates more than 30 pharmacies on the island. **Police, fire, and medical emergencies:** ☎ 911.

Festivals and Seasonal Events
Puerto Rico's festivals are colorful and inclined toward lots of music and feasting. The towns and villages are particularly fond of their patron saints, and every year each of the island's 78 municipalities celebrate what is know as *fiestas patronales* (patron saints festivals). The festivities are religious in origin, and feature processions, sports events, folklore shows, feasts, music, and dance. The fiestas are about 10 days in length, with more activities on weekends than on weekdays. San Juan's fiesta patronale honors San Juan Bautista in late June; Ponce honors Nostra Señora de la Guadalupe in mid-December. For a full list of fiestas patronales, contact the **tourism company** (☞ Visitor Information, *below*).

Several towns and regions celebrate pre-Lenten **Carnivals,** complete with parades, folk music, local dishes, selection of Carnival Queen, and music competitions. All are in early-to-late February. Contact the **tourism company** (☞ Visitor Information, *below*) for a complete list.

In addition to the patron saints festivals, Old San Juan holds an annual **San Sebastián Street Festival** (☎ 787/724–7171); **Emancipation Day** on March 22 honors the abolition of slavery; mid-April's **Sugar Harvest Festival** (☎ 787/892–5574) in San Germán celebrates the crop with exhibitions, music, and feasts; the **Casals Festival** (☎ 787/ 721–7727), held at the Luis A. Ferré Performing Arts Center in San Juan in early June, honors the late, great cellist with 10 days of classical music; in mid-November you can find the annual **Festival of Puerto Rican Music** (☎ 787/724–0700) in San Juan and other venues, celebrating the vibrancy of Puerto Rico's *plena* and *bomba* folk music, highlighted by a contest featuring the *cuatro,* a traditional guitar; and during Christmas week you can join the residents of Hatillo for the **Hatillo Masks Festival** (☎ 787/898–3853) when they retell the biblical tale of King Herod and his attempt to find and kill the infant Jesus. Men in masks move about town all day, representing Herod's soldiers, and the town brings out music and crafts.

Getting Around

If you are staying in San Juan, you can get around by walking, bus, taxi, or hotel shuttle. However, if you venture out on the island, a rental car is your best transportation option. Roads in Puerto Rico are generally well marked (just keep in mind that distances are posted in kilometers while road speed signs are in miles per hour). A good road map, however, is helpful when traveling to more remote areas on the island. Some car-rental agencies distribute free maps of the island when you pick up your car. These maps lack detail and are usually out-of-date due to new construction. The simplest thing to do is head to the nearest gas station—most of them sell better maps. Good maps are also available at the **Cronopios** (✉ 255 Calle San José, Old San Juan, ☎ 787/724–1815).

AIRPLANES

From the Isla Grande Airport, you can take a **Vieques Air-Link** (☎ 787/ 722–3736) flight to Vieques ($35 one-way), or a **Flamenco Airways** (☎ 787/725–7707) flight to Culebra for $30 one-way.

BUSES

The **Metropolitan Bus Authority (AMA)** (☎ 787/250–6064) operates *guaguas* (buses) that thread through San Juan. The fare is 25¢, and the buses run in exclusive lanes, *against the traffic* on major thoroughfares, stopping at magenta, orange, and white signs marked PARADA or PARADA DE GUAGUAS. The main terminals are Covadunga parking lot and Plaza de Colón, in Old San Juan, and Capetillo Terminal in Río Piedras, next to the central business district.

CAR RENTALS

U.S. driver's licenses are valid in Puerto Rico for three months. Rental rates can start as low as $30 (plus insurance), with unlimited mileage. Discounts are offered for long-term rentals, and insurance can be waived for those who rent with American Express or certain gold credit cards (be sure to check with your credit-card company before renting). Some discounts are offered for AAA or 72-hour advance bookings. Most car rentals have shuttle service to or from the airport and the pickup point. If you plan to drive across the island, arm yourself with a good map and be aware that there are many unmarked roads up in the mountains. Many service stations in the central mountains do not take credit cards. Speed limits are posted in miles, distances in kilometers, and gas prices in liters.

All major U.S. car-rental agencies are represented on the island, including **Avis** (☎ 787/721–4499 or 800/874–3556), **Hertz** (☎ 787/791–0840 or 800/654–3131), **Budget** (☎ 787/791–3685 or 800/468–5822), **Thrifty** (☎ 787/253–2525 or 800/367–2277), and **National** (☎ 787/791–1805 or 800/568–3019). Local rental companies, sometimes less expensive, include **Charlie Car Rental** (☎ 787/728–2418 or 800/289–1227), **L & M Car Rental** (☎ 787/725–8416 or 800/666–0807), and **Target** (☎ 787/728–1447 or 800/934–6457).

FERRIES

The ferry between Old San Juan (Pier 2) and Cataño (☎ 787/788–1155) costs a mere 50¢ one-way. The ferry runs every half hour from 6 AM to 10 PM. The 400-passenger ferries of the **Fajardo Port Authority** (☎ 787/863–0852), which carry cargo as well as passengers, make the 90-minute trip between Fajardo and the island of Vieques twice on weekdays and three times on weekends ($2 one-way). They make the 90-minute run between Fajardo and the island of Culebra once a day Monday–Thursday and twice a day Friday–Sunday ($2.25 one-way).

LINÉAS

Linéas are private taxis you share with three to five other passengers. There are more than 20 companies, each usually specializing in a certain region. Most will arrange door-to-door service. Check local yellow-pages listings under Linéas de Carros. They're a cheaper method of transport and a great way to meet people, but be prepared to wait: they usually don't leave until they have a full load.

PÚBLICOS

Públicos (public cars), with yellow license plates ending in "P" or "PD," scoot to towns throughout the island, stopping in each town's main plaza. These 17-passenger vans operate primarily during the day, with routes and fares fixed by the Public Service Commission. In San Juan, the main terminals are at the airport and at Plaza Colón on the waterfront in Old San Juan.

TAXIS

The Puerto Rico Tourism Company has recently instituted a much-needed and well-organized taxi program for tourists. Taxis painted white and sporting the *garita* (sentry box) logo and **Taxi Turístico** label charge set rates depending on the destination; they run from the airport or the cruise-ship piers to Isla Verde, Condado/Ocean Park, and Old San Juan, with rates ranging from $6 to $16. Metered cabs authorized by the **Public Service Commission** (☎ 787/751–5050) start at $1 and charge 10¢ for every additional 10th of a mile, 50¢ for every suitcase, and $1 for home or business calls. Waiting time is 10¢ for each 45 seconds. The minimum charge is $3. Be sure the driver starts the meter. You can also call **Major Taxicabs** (☎ 787/723–2460) in San Juan and **Ponce Taxi** (☎ 787/840–0088).

TROLLEYS

If your feet fail you in Old San Juan, climb aboard the free open-air trolleys that rumble and roller-coast through the narrow streets. Departures are from La Puntilla and from the marina, but you can board anywhere along the route.

Guided Tours

Old San Juan can be seen either on the free trolley, on a self-guided walking tour, or using an excellent tour guide from **Colonial Adventure** (✉ 201 Recinto Sur, ☎ 787/729–0114) tours. The superb and small tour company offers a variety of informative walking tours of the old city, rates ranging $16–$25 per person.

To explore the rest of the city and the island, consider renting a car. (We do, however, recommend a guided tour of the vast El Yunque rain forest.) If you'd rather not do your own driving, there are several tour companies you can call. Most San Juan hotels have a tour desk that can make arrangements for you. The three standard half-day tours ($15–$30) are of Old and "new" San Juan; Old San Juan and the Bacardi Rum Plant; and Luquillo Beach and El Yunque rain forest. All-day tours ($25–$45) can include a trip to Ponce, a day at El Comandante Racetrack, or a combined tour of the city and El Yunque rain forest.

Leading tour operators include **Gray Line of Puerto Rico** (☎ 787/727–8080), **Normandie Tours, Inc.** (☎ 787/722–6308), **Rico Suntours** (☎ 787/722–2080 or 787/722–6090), **Tropix Wellness Tours** (☎ 787/268–2173), and **United Tour Guides** (☎ 787/725–7605 or 787/723–5578). **Cordero Caribbean Tours** (☎ 787/786–9114 or 787/780–2442 evenings) runs tours in air-conditioned limousines for an hourly rate.

Language

Puerto Rico's official language is Spanish, and although English is widely spoken, you will probably want to take a Spanish phrase book along if you rent a car to travel around the island.

Money Matters

CURRENCY

Puerto Rico, as a commonwealth of the United States, uses the U.S. dollar as its official currency.

SERVICE CHARGES, TAXES, AND TIPPING

Some hotels automatically add a 10%–15% service charge to your bill. Check ahead to confirm whether this charge is built into the room rate or will be tacked on at check-out. Some smaller hotels might charge extra (as much as $5 per day) for use of air-conditioning, called an "energy tax." The government tax on room charges is 9% (11% in hotels with casinos). Some hotels build the taxes into the quoted room rate; others do not. Call ahead to confirm. Tips are expected, and appreciated, by restaurant waitstaff (if a service charge isn't included), hotel porters ($1 per bag), maids ($1–$2 a day), and taxi drivers (10%–15%).

Opening and Closing Times

Street **shops** are open Monday–Saturday 9–6 (9–9 during Christmas holidays), while mall stores tend to stay open later, until 8 or 9 in most cases. **Banks** are open weekdays 8:30–2:30 and Saturday 9:45–noon. **Post offices** have hours Monday–Friday 7:30–4:30 and Saturday 8–noon.

HOLIDAYS

New Year's Day, Three Kings Day (Jan. 6), Dr. Martin Luther King Jr. Day (Jan. 18), President's Day (Feb. 15), Palm Sunday (Mar. 28), Good Friday (Apr. 2), Easter Sunday (Apr. 4), Independence Day (July 4), Luis Muñoz Rivera Day (July 15), José Celso Barbosa Day (July 27), Labor Day (Sept. 6), Columbus Day (Oct. 11), Veteran's Day (Nov. 11), Puerto Rico Discovery Day (Nov. 19), Thanksgiving Day (Nov. 25), and Christmas.

Passports

Puerto Rico is a commonwealth of the United States, and U.S. citizens do not need passports to visit the island. British citizens must have passports. Canadian citizens need proof of citizenship (preferably a valid passport; otherwise bring a birth certificate with a raised seal along with a government-issued photo ID).

Precautions

San Juan, like any other big city and major tourist destination, has its share of crime, so guard your wallet or purse on the city streets. Puerto Rico's beaches are open to the public, and muggings can occur at night even on the beaches of the posh Condado and Isla Verde tourist hotels. While you certainly can and should explore the city and its beaches, using common sense will make your stay more secure and enjoyable. Don't leave anything unattended on the beach. Leave your valuables in the hotel safe, and stick to the fenced-in beach areas of your hotel. Always lock your car and stash valuables and luggage out of sight. Avoid deserted beaches at night.

Telephones and Mail

Puerto Rico's area code is 787—for North Americans, dialing Puerto Rico is the same as dialing another state or Canadian province. The island uses U.S. postage stamps and has the same mail rates: 20¢ for a postcard, 32¢ for a first-class letter to the U.S.; 40¢ for a postcard and 46¢ for a letter to Canada; 50¢ for a postcard and 60¢ for a letter to the U.K. Post offices in major Puerto Rican cities offer Express Mail next-day service to the U.S. mainland and to Puerto Rican destinations.

Visitor Information

Before you go, contact the **Puerto Rico Tourism Company** (⊠ Box 902-3960, Old San Juan Station, San Juan, PR 00902-3960, ☎ 787/721–2400, FAX 787/721–4417; www.discoverpuertorico.com). From the States, you can call toll-free at ☎ 800/223–6530. Other branches: ⊠ 575 5th Ave., 23rd floor, New York, NY 10017, ☎ 212/599–6262, FAX 212/818–1866; ⊠ 3575 W. Cahuenga Blvd., Suite 560, Los Angeles, CA 90068, ☎ 213/874–5991, FAX 213/874–7257; ⊠ 901 Ponce de León Blvd., Suite 604, Coral Gables, FL 33134, ☎ 305/445–9112, FAX 305/445–9450.

On Puerto Rico, the **Puerto Rico Tourism Company** (⊠ Paseo de la Princesa, Old San Juan 00901, ☎ 787/721–2400) is an excellent source for maps and printed tourist materials. Be sure to pick up a free copy of *Qué Pasa,* the official visitors' guide. Government and tourism-company information offices are also found at **Luis Muñoz Marín International Airport** in Isla Verde (☎ 787/791–1014 or 787/791–2551), **La Casita** (☎ 787/722–1709), near Pier 1 in Old San Juan, and at **La Playita la Condado,** the small public beach at the Condado Plaza Hotel. Out on the island, information offices are located in **Ponce** (⊠ Fox Delicias Mall, 2nd floor, Plaza Las Delicias, ☎ 787/840–5695), **Aguadilla** (⊠ Rafael Hernández Airport, ☎ 787/890–3315), **Cabo Rojo** (⊠ Rte. 100, Km 13.7, ☎ 787/851–7070), and in many towns' city halls on the main plaza. Offices are usually open weekdays 8–noon and 1–4:30.

17 Saba

Updated by
Karl Luntta

Joe, a Saban, sits at a table with his hands wrapped around a mug. Surrounded by the accoutrements of his life—his simple bar and restaurant—his thirtyish face is relaxed. He was educated in the United States, and spent several years in major cities, working in industry. His accent is almost pure New England when he says, "See, my family had this land." What prompted him to give up a career and return? He gestures, palms up—as if to catch the sun—and smiles. Waves lick the shore, and the breeze smells of mountain palm. Well, of course . . .

Tiny Saba (pronounced *say*-ba) has some of the Caribbean's most dramatic scenery in its sweeping, steep mountainsides and sheer cliffs. The breeze is always pleasant, the 1,200 friendly Sabans more so. Everyone knows everyone—indeed, there are less than a dozen family names on the island, so everyone not only knows everyone, but many are also related—and unemployment and crime are virtually nonexistent. The island is a perfect hideaway, a challenge for hikers (Mt. Scenery rises to 2,855 ft), a haven for seasoned divers, and heaven on water. It's no wonder Sabans call their island the Unspoiled Queen.

Despite all its glories, however, this 5-square-mi fairy-tale isle isn't for everybody. If you want exciting nightlife or lots of shopping, forget Saba (or make it a one-day excursion from St. Maarten). There are only a handful of shops, even fewer inns and eateries, and the island's movie theater closed with the arrival of cable. Sun worshippers should also note that Saba is an essentially beachless volcanic island: steep cliffs ring the island and plummet sharply to the sea.

The capital of Saba is the Bottom, which sits at the bottom of an extinct volcano, hence the name. In Windwardside, the island's second-largest village, the streets have no names. On the Road (and there's really only one), meandering goats have right-of-way, though chickens cross at their own risk. In tiny, toylike villages, flower-draped walls and neat picket fences border narrow paths. Tidy houses with red roofs and gingerbread trim are planted on the mountainside among the bromeliads, palms, hibiscus, orchids, and Norwegian pines. Despite such modern additions as television sets (since 1965) and electricity (since 1970), this immaculate, picturesque island's uncomplicated lifestyle has persevered, giving it a make-believe air. Saban ladies still hand-embroider delicate lace—a genteel art that has flourished since the 1870s—and brew a potent rum-based liquor, Saba Spice, that's sweetened with secret herbs and spices. Families still follow the generations-old tradition of burying their dead in their neatly tended gardens.

Saba is part of the Netherlands Antilles Windward Islands and is 28 mi—a 15-minute flight with a hair-raising landing on a teeny airstrip (with a 100% safety record)—from St. Maarten. The island is a volcano that has been extinct for 5,000 years. Columbus spotted the little speck in 1493, but except for the Carib Indians who may have lived here around AD 800, Saba somehow remained uninhabited until the first Dutch settlers arrived from Statia in 1640. In the 17th, 18th, and early 19th centuries, the French, Dutch, English, and Spanish vied for control of the island, and Saba changed hands 12 times before permanently raising the Dutch flag in 1816. Today, the Kingdom of the Netherlands comprises three entities: Holland, the Netherlands Antilles (Saba, St. Maarten, St. Eustatius, Bonaire, and Curacao), and Aruba. Saba's local administration supervises internal affairs, and the island elects representatives and sends them to the capital of the Netherlands Antilles, Willemstad in Curacao, to attend to regional issues.

Sabans are a hardy lot. To get from Fort Bay to the Bottom, early settlers carved 900 steps out of the mountainside. Everything that arrived on the island, from a pin to a piano, had to be hauled up. Those rugged steps were the only way to travel until the Road was built by Josephus Lambert Hassell (a carpenter who took correspondence courses in engineering) in the 1940s. An extraordinary feat, the Road took 25 years to build. If you like roller coasters, you'll love the 9-mi, white-knuckle route, which begins at sea level in Fort Bay, zigs up to 1,968 ft, and zags down to 131 ft above sea level at the airport, constructed on the island's only flat point, called (what else?) Flat Point.

Lodging

Saba has experienced a (relative) boom in hotel development of late but is still very low-key compared to other islands. Accommodations are invariably neat and reasonably priced, though the selection is essentially limited to tiny hotels and guest houses tucked into tropical gardens. Because most restaurants are in lodging establishments, you would do well to take advantage of meal plans. In addition, dive packages are available with almost all accommodations, so be sure to ask.

CATEGORY	COST*
$$$$	over $200
$$$	$125–$200
$$	$75–$125
$	under $75

All prices are for a standard double room in high season, excluding 5% room tax and 3% "turnover" tax, and 10%–15% service charge.

Hotels

$$$$ **Willard's of Saba.** Set as it is 2,000 ft up the side of a cliff, this lux-
★   urious hotel has stunning views of the Caribbean as well as neighbor-

ing St. Kitts, Nevis, and St. Barts islands. It also has a large heated pool and a tennis court (the *only* court on the island). The three types of room—bungalow, luxury, and VIP—vary in size, decor, and bath (some have just a shower, others a tub and shower), but all have tile floors, white walls, ceiling fans, rattan furniture, and a balcony. Though you may find the location isolated and inconvenient to town, you'll certainly relish the privacy and the vistas. The on-site ☞ **Willard's of Saba** restaurant is quite good. (Note that owing to its precarious perch, this hotel is highly inappropriate for families with young children.) ⌂ *Windwardside (Box 515),* ☎ *599/4–62498 or 800/613–1511 (reservations service),* ℻ *599/4–62482. 7 rooms. Restaurant, bar, fans, pool, hot tub, tennis court. AE, D, MC, V. EP, MAP.*

$$$ 🏨 **Queens Garden Resort.** This fine resort—high on Troy Hill and, as
★ its name suggests, amid lush gardens—is proof that Saba has become a world-class destination. Four ornate buildings house 12 suites with authentic antique Dutch colonial and Indonesian furnishings; four-poster beds; TVs in dark-wood armoires; large, well-equipped kitchens; and hot tubs on hidden verandas that have breathtaking ocean views. Some suites have a sleeping loft. In the main building, the restaurant has seating inside or on a patio beside the island's largest pool and beneath towering mango trees. Don't miss the Friday night barbecue—the torches are lit, the music is soft, and the views are spectacular. ⌂ *1 Troy Hill Dr. (Box 4), Troy Hill,* ☎ *599/4–63494 or 800/599–9407 (reservations service),* ℻ *599/4–63495. 12 suites. Restaurant, bar, air-conditioning, fans, kitchenettes, pool, hot tubs. EP. AE, MC, V.*

$$–$$$ 🏨 **Juliana's.** Juliana and Franklin Johnson's comfortable, tidy studios
★ have tile floors, light-wood furnishings, and floral-print spreads. One has a queen-size bed; the others have doubles and twins. Through almost every window there's a fabulous view of the Caribbean. If you need more space, consider booking the 2½-room Aunt Flossie's Cottage, which has a kitchenette, a living-dining room, a bedroom, and a large porch that faces the sea. Across the street you'll find the pool, and the ☞ **Tropics** restaurant, where breakfast (included in the rates) is served. ⌂ *Windwardside,* ☎ *599/4–62269 or 800/328–5285 (reservations service),* ℻ *599/4–62389. 9 studios, 1 apartment, 1 2-bedroom cottage. Restaurant, pool, car rental. MC, V. BP.*

$$ 🏨 **Captain's Quarters.** These quarters consist of a three-bedroom cot-
★ tage and four other units set around a small pool on grounds graced with hibiscus, poinsettia, and papaya trees. All the spacious, airy rooms have ocean views and are furnished with Victorian antiques. Two choice bedrooms are in the small main house, which was built by a Saban sea captain in 1832. (Avoid the older rooms in the street-side building; they can be somewhat noisy due to neighbors' TV sets.) The long bungalow has four rooms, and Nos. 9 and 10 can easily sleep four. Two cliffside rooms beneath the ☞ **Captain's Quarters** restaurant, the bar, and the library have particularly spectacular sea views. ⌂ *Windwardside,* ☎ *599/4–62201 or 800/446–3010,* ℻ *599/4–62377. 12 rooms, 1 1-bedroom cottage, 1 3-bedroom cottage. Restaurant, bar, pool, library. AE, D, MC, V. BP.*

$$ 🏨 **Cottage Club.** Local brothers Dean and Mark Johnson run this property of 10 gingerbread bungalows tucked into rainbow-hued tropical gardens. All have balconies that overlook the water or the village of English Quarter; Bungalows 1, 2, and 6, however, have the best views. Interiors are large and breezy with gleaming tile floors; high, beamed ceilings; drapes and spreads in pastel shell prints; walls decked with local art; a dining area; a bath (shower only); a phone; cable TV; and a full kitchen, which Dean and Mark will stock for you if you give them a shopping list. The stone, colonial-style main house holds the reception area and is full of antiques, plants, and Saba-lace curtains. ⌂ *Wind-*

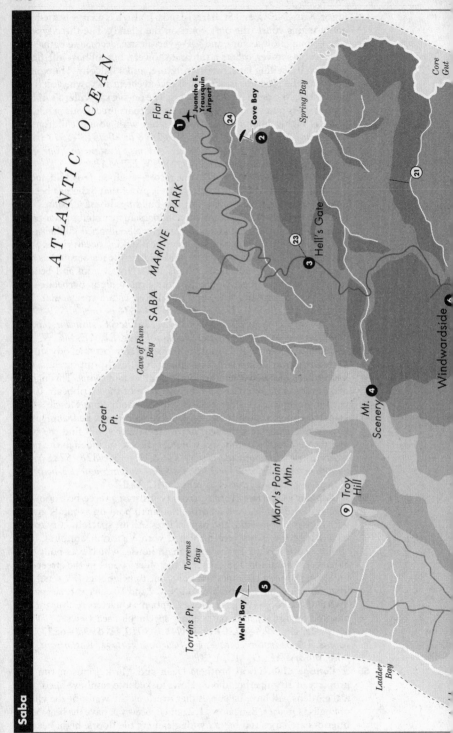

ATLANTIC OCEAN

Flat Pt.

Juancho E. Yrausquin Airport ✈ ①

Cove Bay ②
24

Spring Bay

Core Gut

SABA MARINE PARK

Cave of Rum Bay

Great Pt.

23

Hell's Gate ③

21

Windwardside

Mt. Scenery ④

Mary's Point Mtn.

Troy Hill ⑨

Torrens Bay

Torréns Pt.

Well's Bay ⑤

Ladder Bay

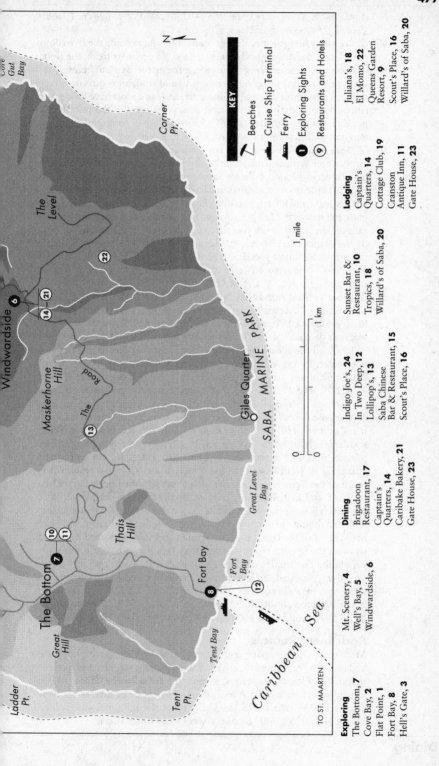

KEY

🏖 Beaches
⚓ Cruise Ship Terminal
⛴ Ferry
① Exploring Sights
⑨ Restaurants and Hotels

Lodging
Captain's
Quarters, **14**
Cottage Club, **19**
Cranston
Antique Inn, **11**
Gate House, **23**
Juliana's, **18**
El Momo, **22**
Queens Garden
Resort, **9**
Scout's Place, **16**
Willard's of Saba, **20**

Dining
Brigadoon
Restaurant, **17**
Captain's
Quarters, **14**
Caribake Bakery, **21**
Gate House, **23**
Indigo Joe's, **24**
In Two Deep, **12**
Lollipop's, **13**
Saba Chinese
Bar & Restaurant, **15**
Scout's Place, **16**
Sunset Bar &
Restaurant, **10**
Tropics, **18**
Willard's of Saba, **20**

Exploring
The Bottom, **7**
Cove Bay, **2**
Flat Point, **1**
Fort Bay, **8**
Hell's Gate, **3**
Mt. Scenery, **4**
Well's Bay, **5**
Windwardside, **6**

TO ST. MAARTEN

Caribbean Sea

SABA MARINE PARK

1 mile

1 km

wardside, ☎ *599/4–62486 or 599/4–62386,* FAX *599/4–62476. 10 units. Pool, kitchenettes. D, MC, V. EP.*

$$ 🏨 **Cranston Antique Inn.** Recent renovations have made the five rooms of this affordable inn good values, indeed. The paint is fresh, the floors have been redone (making them even more attractive than before), and the fabrics used throughout are new. In addition, all rooms now have private baths, cable TV, air-conditioning, and fans; most have four-poster beds. The pool bar is festive, and nonguests can use the pool for $5 per day. ✉ *The Bottom,* ☎ FAX *599/4–63203. 5 rooms. Restaurant, bar, air-conditioning, fans, pool. D, MC, V. EP.*

$$ 🏨 **Gate House.** This place is a true getaway. Its location—between the airport and Windwardside in the tiny village of Lower Hell's Gate— make it very secluded, even for Saba. Spacious rooms have whitewashed walls and tile floors and are decorated with crisp pinstripe and checked fabrics and colorful art; two units have kitchenettes. The pool is a great place to relax as the sun goes down. The six-table ☞ **Gate House** restaurant off the lobby overlooks the sea and has created an admiring buzz on the island. Chef Beverly changes the menu of local specialties daily; the prix-fixe dinner is $20. ✉ *Hell's Gate,* ☎ *599/4–62416 or 708/ 354–9641 (reservations service),* FAX *599/4–62529. 6 rooms. Restaurant, pool. D, MC, V. CP, MAP.*

$–$$ 🏨 **Scout's Place.** Accurately billed as "Bed 'n' Board, Cheap 'n' Cheerful," Scout's Place makes up in convenience and value what it lacks in luxury. Staying here puts you in the center of Windwardside, within walking distance of the Sea Saba dive center. Thanks to renovations in 1997, all the rooms now have private baths with cold *and* hot running water; 11 rooms have four-poster beds and balconies. The ☞ **Scout's Place** restaurant serves three meals daily. ✉ *Windwardside,* ☎ *599/ 4–62205,* FAX *599/4–62388. 14 rooms, 1 apartment. Restaurant, bar, pool, shop, car rental. D, MC, V. BP.*

$ 🏨 **El Momo.** This fun, funky inn is amid tropical gardens about 1,500 ft up Jimmy's Hill (at Booby Hill, roughly five minutes from Windwardside). Four of its five, clean, bright, gingerbread cottages have porches that take in the view. You can also watch the sun set over the village of St. John's from the hammock or a chair in the small sitting room of the main house (there's also a refrigerator/honor bar). Owners Gied and Els Mommers have made the cottages simple yet inviting—each is equipped with towels, soap, extra blankets, a reading lamp, and a flashlight for getting around (there are loads of steep stairways here). Four of the cottages share a toilet and solar-powered hot-water shower; the Iguana House cottage may lack a porch, but it has a private bath. The small pool has a foot bridge across it, the only bridge on Saba. Ask Gied, an amateur archaeologist and former teacher, to show you his collection of colonial artifacts found locally. Breakfast is available for about $6. ✉ *Jimmy's Hill (Box 519, Windwardside),* ☎ FAX *599/4–62265. 5 cottages. Snack bar, pool, shop. EP. D, MC, V.*

Apartment Rentals

More than a dozen apartments, cottages, and villas, all with hot water and modern conveniences, are available for daily, weekly, and monthly rental. For a list of properties, contact the **Saba Tourist Office** (☞ Visitor Information *in* Saba A to Z, *below*). **WIMCO** (✉ Box 1461, Newport, RI 02840 ☎ 800/932–3222) rents the fabulous and palatial Haiku House ($2,000–$4,500 a week) and other villas.

Dining

In most of Saba's restaurants—many of which are in hotels or guest houses—you pretty much have to take potluck, and it's tough to find gourmet cooking. But you won't go hungry. Several restaurants serve wonderfully fresh seafood and such Caribbean dishes as stuffed crabs, goat stew, and grilled lobster. Don't miss the poolside barbecues at Queen's Gardens or Captain's Quarters hotels, where grilled ribs and chicken are the order of the day, and where you're likely to eat to the sounds of a steel pan band. A decent selection of wines is available at the better restaurants, but try the local Saba Spice, an aromatic rum-based drink, as an aperitif. Reservations aren't necessary in most establishments, but it wouldn't hurt to call ahead to confirm opening times and, perhaps, get a ride to the restaurant.

What to Wear

Restaurants are informal. Shorts or a nice cover-up over your swimsuit are fine during the day. For dinner you may want to put on pants or a casual sundress, but you won't find any dress requirements. Just remember that nights in Windwardside can be cool due to the elevation.

CATEGORY	COST*
$$$	over $25
$$	$15–$25
$	under $15

per person for a three-course meal, excluding drinks and service

ASIAN

$–$$ ✕ **Saba Chinese Bar & Restaurant.** In this plain little house with plastic tablecloths you can get, among other things, sweet-and-sour pork or chicken, cashew chicken, and curried dishes. ⊠ *Windwardside,* ☎ *599/4–62268. No credit cards. Closed Mon.*

CAFÉ

$ ✕ **Caribake Bakery.** From 7 AM to 3 PM, this small bakery behind the tourist office serves coffee, cookies, cold drinks, pastries, sandwiches, and the island's freshest bread. There's a small sitting area if you need to take the load off your feet. ⊠ *Windwardside,* ☎ *599/4–62539. No credit cards. Closed Sun.*

CARIBBEAN/CREOLE

$–$$$ ✕ **Gate House.** Slightly out of the way, on the road to the airport, this restaurant in the ☞ **Gate House** hotel features Caribbean cuisine. The menu changes daily, making use of the freshest seafood, poultry, and meats, as well as local produce and herbs. There are only six tables here, and they're often filled by Sabans—making this one of the few places on the island where reservations are a good idea. ⊠ *Hell's Gate,* ☎ *599/4–62416. MC, V. Closed Wed. No lunch.*

$–$$ ✕ **Lollipop's.** Owner Carmen Caines was nicknamed Lollipop in honor
★ of her sweet disposition. She and her husband, Will, prepare land crab, goat, and fresh grilled fish. Meals are served on the tranquil outdoor terrace, with its stonework and charming aqua-and-white trellis. No reservations are necessary, but if you call, Lollipop will pick you up and drop you off at your hotel after dinner—a sweet touch, indeed. ⊠ *St. John's,* ☎ *599/4–63330. MC, V.*

$–$$ ✕ **Sunset Bar & Restaurant.** Artificial flowers and colorful place mats enliven this humble, homey place. Authentic Creole food—heavenly johnnycakes, bread tart pudding, and lip-smacking ribs—is served. ⊠ *The Bottom,* ☎ *599/4–63332. No credit cards.*

CONTEMPORARY

$$–$$$ ✕ **Captain's Quarters.** At this restaurant in the ☞ **Captain's Quarters** hotel, you can dine in comfort on a breezy terrace surrounded by flowers and mango trees. The chef artfully blends French and Creole cuisines. The fish (whatever is fresh that day) is prepared with a variety of sauces, including lime butter. On Saturday night the owner takes over the grill and barbecues steaks, chicken, and fish. The last dinner seating is at 8:30; service is pleasant but can be slow. ⊠ *Windwardside,* ☎ *599/4–62201. Reservations essential. AE, D, MC, V.*

$$–$$$ ✕ **Willard's of Saba.** Stunningly set on a cliff high above Windwardside, Saba's most expensive restaurant in the ☞ **Willard's of Saba** hotel has views of the sea a dizzying 2,000 ft below. The fusion menu of international and Asian cuisine includes such specialties as chicken adobo, Shanghai rolls, and fresh lobster. A unique touch is the restaurant's hot-lava stone grill, where you grill your seafood or meat as you like it and add the chef's sauces. Order one of the Bava wines from Italy; Willard's is the only restaurant in the Caribbean that offers them. Access to the restaurant is up a steep drive; only a few taxis will make the climb, but you can call the restaurant to arrange transport. ⊠ *Windwardside,* ☎ *599/4–62498. AE, D, MC, V.*

$–$$ ✕ **Tropics.** A black-and-white-checked tile floor, crisp black-and-white napery, and gleaming silver flatware create a chic, if not exactly tropical, atmosphere in this restaurant at ☞ **Juliana's** cottages. The entrées, a mix of Continental and West Indian dishes, can be on the bland side; stick with steak and simply prepared fresh seafood. Try the croquette appetizer: a spicy blend of meat lightly breaded and deep-fried. Tropics serves lunch weekdays and Saturday, and dinner Tuesday through Friday. ⊠ *Windwardside,* ☎ *599/4–62469. MC, V. Closed Sun. No dinner Mon. or Sat.*

ECLECTIC

$–$$ ✕ **Brigadoon Restaurant.** A local favorite, this open-front restaurant
★   on the first floor of a colonial building allows you to take in the passing action on the street—which may not mean a whole lot on Saba, but it's still a nice thought. Fresh fish grilled and served with a light Creole sauce is the specialty, but there are also chicken and steak dishes, lobster, and flavorful creations such as shrimp encrusted with salt and pepper. Monday night is Mexican night. ⊠ *Windwardside,* ☎ *599/4–62380. D, MC, V. No lunch.*

$–$$ ✕ **Indigo Joe's.** Owner Joe Johnson, recently returned from several years in the United States, built a small restaurant on this family property, and named it after an old indigo (the plant grows locally) boiling house that used to operate nearby. Popular with students from the local medical school, this place sits on the gray-sand Cove Bay near the airport—giving you one of the few opportunities to dine alfresco near the ocean on Saba. The fare is steaks, ribs, lobster, and sandwiches, and the setting is simple tables on a cement patio, with thundering waves just a walk away. ⊠ *Cove Bay,* ☎ *599/4–62292. No credit cards. Closed Sun. and off-season.*

$–$$ ✕ **In Two Deep.** The owners of Saba Deep run this delightful harborside spot, with its stained-glass window and mahogany bar. The soups, sandwiches (especially the Reuben), and smoothies (try the lemon pucker) are excellent, and the customers are usually high-spirited—most have just come from a dive. It's open daily 8 AM–4 PM. ⊠ *Fort Bay,* ☎ *599/4–63438. MC, V. No dinner.*

$–$$ ✕ **Scout's Place.** At this restaurant in the ☞ **Scout's Place** hotel, chef-manager Diana Medero cooks up braised steak with mushrooms, curried goat, and chicken cordon bleu. You can also opt for a simple sandwich—the crab is best. Tables covered with flowered plastic cloths are arranged on a porch with stunning views of the water. Wednesday breakfast serves as the unofficial town meeting for expatriates. ⊠ *Windwardside,* ☎ *599/4–62205. Reservations essential. MC, V.*

Outdoor Activities and Sports

FISHING

This island is not a big fishing destination, but a few Sabans will take you out on their boats. Keep in mind that these are not big, fancy vessels. If you want to arrange a fishing trip, contact the tourist office (☞ Visitor Information *in* Saba A to Z, *below*) or Saba Deep (☞ Scuba Diving and Snorkeling, *below*), or ask your hotel to arrange it for you.

HIKING

You can't avoid some hiking, even if you just go to mail a postcard. The big deal, of course, is Mt. Scenery, with 1,064 steps leading up to its top. Many of the trails, including the Mt. Scenery trail, have signs that describe the flora you encounter. For information about Saba's 18 recommended botanical hiking trails, check with the tourist office (☞ Visitor Information *in* Saba A to Z, *below*) or the **Saba Conservation Foundation** (⊠ Behind the tourist office, ☎ 599/4–62630), which maintains the trails. The foundation operates the small **Trail Shop**, which has trail information as well as gifts. Botanical tours are available upon request. A guided, strenuous full-day hike through the undeveloped back side of Mt. Scenery costs about $50.

SCUBA DIVING AND SNORKELING

Saba has long been recognized as one of the world's premier scuba diving destinations. Within ½ mi from shore, sea walls drop to depths of more than 1,000 ft; visibility is extraordinary and the dive sites administered by the Saba Marine Park (☞ Exploring, *below*) include shoals, reefs, and sea walls, all with a wide variety of corals and sea life. Divers have a pick of 26 sites—many with such intriguing names as Third Encounter, Man of War Shoals, and Ladder Labyrinth—where likely sightings include groupers, sea turtles, and sharks. Snorkelers need not feel left out: The marine park has marked several spots where reefs or rocks sit in shallow water. Among these sites are Torrens Point, at the northwest side of the island, and the new Edward S. Arnold Snorkel Trail—a self-guided underwater tour with 11 numbered and marked sites. Waterproof maps are available from the marine park, the Saba Conservation Foundation, or from any of the island's dive shops (where you can also make arrangements for snorkel gear and trips).

Saba Deep (⊠ Fort Bay, ☎ 599/4–63347), **Saba Reef Divers** (⊠ Windwardside, ☎ 599/4–62541), and **Sea Saba** (⊠ Windwardside, ☎ 599/4–62246) will take you to all of Saba's dive sites. All three offer rental equipment, SSI- (Scuba Schools International) and PADI-certified instructors, and dive packages that include accommodations anywhere on the island. Saba Reef Divers also has ANDI (American Nitrox Divers Institute) instruction, and nitrox diving facilities. For information on dive packages, call the dive shops directly, or contact **Dive Saba Travel** (⊠ 11703 40th Ave. NW, Gig Harbor, WA 98332, ☎ 713/789–1396 or 800/883–7222, FAX 713/461–6044) or **Dive Tours** (⊠ 18219 Strack Dr., Spring, TX 77379, ☎ 612/931–9101 or 800/328–5285, FAX 612/931–0209). **Unique Destinations** (⊠ 120 Elmdale Rd., North Scituate, RI 02857, ☎ FAX 401/934–3398) organizes diving and hiking tours and packages.

Shopping

Lace is one of the island's most popular purchases. The history of Saba lace (also called Spanish lace) goes back more than a century to Saban Gertrude Johnson, who attended a Caracas convent school where she learned the arts of drawing and tying threads to adorn fine linens. When she returned home in the 1870s, she taught lace making to other Saban ladies, and the art has endured ever since. Every weekday Saban ladies display and sell their creations at the community center in Hell's Gate. Many also sell their wares from their houses; just follow the signs. Collars, tea towels, napkins, and other small items are relatively inexpensive, but larger items, such as tablecloths, can be pricey. You should know that the fabric requires some care—it's not drip-dry.

Saba Spice is another island buy. Although it *sounds* as delicate as Saba lace, and the aroma is as sweet as can be, the base for this liqueur is 151-proof rum. All the rest is window dressing.

You'll find a variety of souvenirs and gifts in almost every shop. Look for the superlative book *Saban Cottages: A Book of Watercolors,* sold in several stores. In the Bottom, the **Saba Artisan Foundation** (☎ 599/4–63260) turns out hand-screened fabrics that you can buy by the yard or already made into resort clothing. It also sells T-shirts and spices.

While you're wandering around Windwardside, stop in at **Around the Bend** (☎ 599/4–62519), which carries island souvenirs and clothing as well as "gifts, oddments, and pretties." The **Breadfruit Gallery** (☎ 599/4–62509) showcases and sells local artists' work. **Jobean Designs** (☎ 599/4–62490) features intricate, handmade, glass-bead jewelry as well as sterling silver and gold pieces by artist and owner Jo Bean. The **Little Shop** (☎ 599/4–62519) features bags and handmade items by Frieda. **Saba Tropical Arts** (☎ 599/4–62373) has silk-screened T-shirts and souvenirs. **Sea Saba** (☎ 599/4–62246) carries T-shirts, diving equipment, and beach paraphernalia. The **Square Nickel** (☎ 599/4–62477) is Saba's five-and-dime.

Nightlife

On Friday and Saturday nights, Guido's Pizzeria is transformed into the **Mountain High Club** (✉ Windwardside, ☎ 599/4–62330)—there's even a mirrored disco ball suspended from the ceiling—and you can dance till 2 AM. Do the nightclub scene at the **Inner Circle** (✉ The Bottom, ☎ 599/4–62240), or just hang out at **Scout's Place** or the **Captain's Quarters** (☞ Dining, *above*). Consult the bulletin board in each village for a listing of the week's events.

Exploring Saba

Getting around the island means negotiating the narrow, twisting roadway that clings to the mountainside and rises from sea level to almost 2,000 ft. Although driving is not difficult, just be sure to go slowly and cautiously. If in doubt, leave the driving to an experienced cabbie so you can enjoy the scenery. You won't need long to tour the island by car—you can cover the entire circuitous length of the Road, without stopping, in the space of a morning. If you plan to stop for shopping, lunch, and sightseeing, plan on a full day.

Numbers in the margin correspond to points of interest on the Saba map.

SIGHTS TO SEE

❼ **The Bottom.** Sitting in a bowl-shape valley 820 ft above the sea, this town is the seat of government and the home of the lieutenant governor. The **gubernatorial mansion**, next to Wilhelmina Park, has fancy fretwork, a high-pitched roof, and wraparound double galleries. In 1993 Saba University opened a **medical school** in the Bottom, at which about 200 students are enrolled.

On the other side of town is the **Wesleyan Holiness Church,** a small stone building with white fretwork, dating from 1919. Stroll by the church, beyond a place called the Gap, to a lookout point where you can see the 400 rough-hewn steps leading down to **Ladder Bay**. Ladder Bay and Fort Bay were the two landing sites from which Saba's first settlers had to haul themselves and their possessions. Sabans sometimes walk down to Ladder Bay to picnic. Think long and hard before you do: It's 400 steps back *up* to the Road.

② **Cove Bay.** On the northeastern side of the island near the airport, a 20-ft-long strip of rocks and pebbles laced with gray sand is now the only place for sunning (and moonlit dips after a Saturday night out). The restaurant Indigo Joe's (☞ Dining, *above*) is here, and a small tidal pool encircled by rocks for children to swim in.

❶ **Flat Point.** It is the only place on the island where planes can land. The runway here is one of the world's smallest, measuring only 1,200 ft long. Only STOL (Short Takeoff and Landing) prop planes dare land here, as each end of the runway drops off more than 100 ft into the crashing surf below.

❽ **Fort Bay.** The end of the Road is also the jumping-off place for all of the island's dive operations and the location of the St. Maarten ferry dock. The island's only gas station is here as well as a 277-ft deep-water pier that accommodates the tenders from ships. On the quay is a decompression chamber, one of the few in the Caribbean, and Saba Deep's dive shop; its snack bar, In Two Deep (☞ Dining, *above*), is a good place to catch your breath while enjoying some refreshments and the view of the water.

❸ **Hell's Gate.** The Road makes 20 hairpin turns up over 1,000 vertical ft to Hell's Gate. **Holy Rosary Church,** on Hell's Gate's hill, is a stone church that looks medieval but was built in 1962. In the **community center** behind the church, village ladies sell blouses, handkerchiefs, tablecloths, and tea towels embellished with the delicate and unique Saba lace. The same ladies make the potent, rum-based Saba Spice, each according to her old family recipe. The truly intrepid can venture to Lower Hell's Gate, where the **Old Sulphur Mine Walk** leads to bat caves (with a sulfuric stench) that can—with caution—be explored.

❹ **Mt. Scenery.** Stone and concrete steps—1,064 of them—rise to the top of Mt. Scenery. En route to the mahogany grove at the summit, the steps pass giant elephant ears, ferns, begonias, mangoes, palms, and orchids; there are six identifiable ecosystems in all. Signs name the trees, plants, and shrubs, and the tourist office (☞ Visitor Information *in* Saba A to Z, *below*) can provide a field guide. Have your hotel pack a picnic lunch, wear nonslip shoes, take along a jacket and a canteen of water, and hike away. The round-trip excursion will take about three hours and is best begun in the early morning.

Saba Bank. This fertile fishing ground 3 mi southwest of Saba is an excellent diving spot because of its coral gardens and undersea mountains. As other islands become "dived out," Saba is dedicated to preserving its marine life, which attracts more than 3,000 divers each year.

Saba Marine Park. Established in 1987 to preserve and manage the island's marine resources, the park circles the entire island, dipping down to 200 ft, and is zoned for diving, swimming, fishing, boating, and anchorage. One of the unique features of Saba's diving is the submerged pinnacles of land at about the 70-ft depth mark. Here all forms of sea creatures rendezvous. The information center offers talks and slide shows for divers and snorkelers and provides literature on marine life. (Divers are requested to contribute $3 a dive to help maintain the park facilities.) Before you go, call first to see if anyone is around. ⊠ *Harbor Office, Fort Bay,* ☎ *599/4–63295.* ☉ *Weekdays 8–5.*

⑤ **Well's Bay.** Saba's famous, disappearing black-sand beach, on the northwestern coast, is usually around for a few months in the summer. (The sand is washed in and out by rough winter surf.)

⑥ **Windwardside.** The island's second-largest village, perched at an altitude of 1,968 ft, commands magnificent views of the Caribbean. Here, among the oleander bushes, you'll find rambling lanes and narrow alleyways winding through the hills and a cluster of tiny, neat houses and shops. At the northern end of the village is the **Church of St. Paul's Conversion,** a colonial building with a red-and-white steeple. Just down the road is the **Saba Tourist Office,** where you can pick up books about Saba. You may also want to browse through the town's shops.

Small signs mark the way to the **Saba Museum.** This 150-year-old house, which is surrounded by lemongrass and clover, has been set up to look much as it did when it was a sea captain's home. Period pieces on display include a handsome mahogany four-poster bed, an antique organ, and, in the kitchen, a rock oven. You can also look at old documents, such as a letter a Saban wrote after the hurricane of 1772, in which he sadly says, "We have lost our little all." The first Sunday of each month, the museum holds croquet matches on its grounds; all-white attire is requested at this formal but fun social event. ✉ *Windwardside,* ☎ *no phone.* 🎫 *$1 (suggested donation).* ⊙ *Weekdays 10–4.*

Saba A to Z

Arriving and Departing

BY AIRPLANE

Unless you parachute in, you'll arrive from St. Maarten via **Windward Islands Airways** (Winair) (☎ 599/4–62255 or 800/634–4907). The approach to Saba's tiny airstrip is the stuff of which nightmares are made. The strip is only ¼-mi long, but the STOL aircraft are built for it, and the pilot needs only half of it to land properly. Try not to panic; remember that the pilot knows what he's doing and wants to live just as much as you do. (If you're nervous, don't sit on the right. The wing just misses grazing the cliffside on the approach.) Once you've touched down on the airstrip, the pilot taxis an inch or two, turns, and deposits you just outside a little shoe box called the **Juancho E. Yrausquin Airport** (☎ 599/4–62255).

BY BOAT

The Edge (☎ 599/5–42640 in St. Maarten), a high-speed ferry, leaves St. Maarten's Pelican Marina in Simpson Bay for Saba on Wednesday, Friday, and Sunday at 9 AM and boards up for the return trip at about 4 PM. The trip to Saba's Fort Bay takes just over an hour, and the round-trip fare is $60, plus 5% if you pay by credit card. The trip over open ocean can be rough.

From the Airport and the Docks: Taxis meet planes and the ferry and take you to your destination. They charge a set rate for up to four people per taxi, with an additional cost for each person more than four. The fare from the airport to Hell's Gate is $6, to Windwardside is $8, to the Bottom is $12.50. The fare from the Fort Bay ferry docks to Windwardside is $9.50. A taxi from Windwardside to the Bottom is $6.50.

Electricity

Saba's current is 110 volts, 60 cycles, and visitors from North America should have no trouble using their travel appliances.

Emergencies

Hospital: The **A. M. Edwards Medical Center** (✉ The Bottom, ☎ 599/4–63288) is a 10-bed hospital with a full-time physician. **Police:**

In the Bottom, ☎ 599/4–63237; in Windwardside, ☎ 599/4–62221.
Pharmacy: The **Pharmacy** (⊠ The Bottom, ☎ 599/4–63289) is open
8–noon and 1–5.

Festivals and Seasonal Events

Saba's **Carnival** might not be as big as those of other Caribbean islands,
but it *is* energetic. This week-long celebration, which starts in late July
and runs till early August, features many special events, local and imported steel-pan bands, food booths, and parades (including the final
Grand Carnival Parade). And just so Sabans don't forget what fun it
was, they hold a **Winter Mini-Carnival** in early December—three days
of band contests, food tastings, and other events.

Getting Around

CAR RENTALS

The Road (Saba's one and only) is serpentine, with many a hairpin (read:
hair-raising) curve. However, if you dare to drive, you can rent a car
through **Scout's Place** (⊠ Windwardside, ☎ 599/4–62205) and **Johnson's Rent A Car** (⊠ Juliana's cottages, Windwardside, ☎ 599/4–62469).
A car rents for about $40 per day, with a full tank of gas and unlim-
ited mileage. If you run out of gas, call the island's only gas station (☎
599/4–63272), down at Fort Bay; note that it closes at noon. Gas costs
roughly NAf1.32 per liter ($3 per gallon).

HITCHHIKING

Carless Sabans get around the old-fashioned ways—walking and hitchhiking (very popular and safe). If you choose thumb rides, you'll need
to know the rules of the Road. To get a ride from the Bottom (which
actually is near the top of the island), sit on the wall opposite the Anglican church; to catch one in Fort Bay, sit on the wall opposite Saba
Deep dive center, where the road begins to twist upward.

Guided Tours

Saba Deep (☎ 599/4–63347, FAX 599/4–63397) occasionally conducts
one-hour, round-island cruises that include cocktails, hors d'oeuvres,
and a marvelous view of the sunset. The taxi drivers who meet the planes
at the airport or the ferries at Fort Bay conduct tours of the island. The
cost for a full-day tour is $40 for one to four passengers and $10 per
person for groups larger than four. If you're just in from St. Maarten
for a day trip, you can do a full morning of sightseeing, stop off for lunch
(have your driver make reservations before starting), complete the tour
afterward, and return to Yrausquin in time to make the last flight back
to St. Maarten. Guides are available for hiking; arrangements may be
made through the tourist office (☞ Visitor Information, *below*).

Language

Saba's official language is Dutch, but everyone on the island speaks
English.

Money Matters

CURRENCY

U.S. dollars are accepted everywhere, but Saba's official currency is the
Netherlands Antilles florin (NAf; also called the guilder). The exchange rate fluctuates slightly but was around NAf1.80 to US$1 at press
time. Prices quoted here are in U.S. dollars unless noted otherwise. **Barclays Bank** and **Antilles Bank** in Windwardside are the only banks on
the island. Barclays is open weekdays 8:30–2; Commercial, 8:30–4.

SERVICE CHARGES, TAXES, AND TIPPING

Several of the larger hotels will tack on a 10%–15% service charge,
others will build it into the rates. Call ahead to inquire about service
charges. Restaurants on Saba add service charges of 10%–15%.

Hotels add a 5% government tax plus a 3% "turnover" tax to the cost of a room (sometimes it's tacked on to your bill, other times it's built into the room rate). You must pay a $2 departure tax when leaving Saba by plane for either St. Maarten or St. Eustatius, or $10 when continuing on an international flight. There's no departure tax when you leave by ferry. Even if service charges have been added into your bill, it's customary to tip hotel personnel and restaurant waitstaff, and to tip taxi drivers. About 10%–15% should do it.

Opening and Closing Times

Businesses and **government offices** (including post offices) on Saba are open weekdays 8–5. Most **shops** are open weekdays and Saturday 8–5. The island's two **banks** are open 8:30–2 (Barclays) or 8:30–4 (Antillies).

HOLIDAYS

New Year's Day, Good Friday (Apr. 2), Easter Monday (Apr. 5), Coronation Day and the Queen's Birthday (Apr. 30, celebrating both the birthday and coronation of Holland's Queen Beatrix), Labor Day (May 1), Ascension Day (May 14), Christmas, and Boxing Day (Dec. 26).

Passports

U.S. and Canadian citizens need proof of citizenship. A valid passport is preferred, but a birth certificate with a raised seal along with a government-issued photo ID will do. British citizens must have a British passport. All visitors must have an ongoing or return ticket.

Precautions

Take along insect repellent, sunscreen, and sturdy, no-nonsense shoes that get a good grip on the ground.

Telephones and Mail

To call Saba from the United States, dial 011/599/4, followed by the five-digit number. Telephone communications are excellent on the island, and you can dial direct long-distance. You'll find public phone booths in the Bottom and Windwardside.

Airmailing a letter to North America and Europe costs NAf2.25; a postcard, NAf1.10. Book reservations through a travel agent or over the telephone; mail can take a week or two to reach the island. When writing to Saba, don't worry about addresses without post office box numbers or street locations—on an island this size, all mail finds its owner. However, do make sure to include "Netherlands Antilles" in the address. Airmail can take one to two weeks to reach the island.

Visitor Information

For help planning your trip, contact the **Saba Tourist Office** (⌧ Box 6322, Boca Raton, FL 33427, ☎ 561/394–8580 or 800/722–2394, FAX 561/488–4294, www.turq.com/saba).

On Saba, the amiable Glenn Holm and Wilma Hassell are at the helm of the **Saba Tourist Office** (⌧ Box 527, Windwardside, ☎ 599/4–62231 or 599/4–62322, FAX 599/4–62350). It's open weekdays and Sat. 8–noon and 1–5, Sunday 10–2.

18 St. Barthélemy

Updated by
David H. Jones

T he small plane banks hard, swoops in like a crop duster, and then touches down with a screech. Sun worshipers on a beach at the far end of the short runway casually lift their heads from towels and water floats to see if the plane will stop in time. It does—just barely—and then it taxis up to the nondescript terminal, where an old man in fatigues drowsily checks passports as people disembark. "Of course," he says "All your luggage will arrive later today." After such a carnival-ride landing, no one feels inclined to complain.

St. Barthélemy blends the essence of the Caribbean with the essence of France. You can spend the day on a deserted beach under a palm tree, then choose from more than 50 excellent restaurants for an elegant evening meal. When you tire of the sun, you can easily drive all over the island, taking in vistas and soft breezes, or you can shop for duty-free French perfumes and the latest in French fashion.

The island, a mere 8 square mi, has lots of hills and sheltered inlets. Gustavia, the only sizable town, wraps itself neatly around a lilliputian harbor. Red-roof bungalows dot the hillsides. Beaches that run the gamut from calm to "surfable," shell to fine white sand, and crowded to deserted encircle the island. The French cuisine here is tops in the Caribbean. A French *savoir vivre* pervades, and the island is definitely for the style conscious—casual but always chic.

Rothschild owns property and Rockefeller built an estate here, and for a long time the island, 15 mi from St. Martin in the French West Indies, was the haunt of the well-heeled and well-informed. Although the island still has cachet for the cash-flow set, the tourist base has expanded in the last decade. Last year, more than 200,000 people visited, including day-trippers from nearby islands and passengers from cruise ships (although island officials are currently attempting to stem the tide of cruise ships that come calling).

St. Barts is the most English-speaking of the French islands. You'll be understood here better than on either Guadeloupe or Martinique. The reason is quite simple: money talks. This is the *consummate* resort community, where the only export is a blissful state-of-mind. If you can afford it, you *will* forget all your worries and cares on this island.

Longtime visitors speak wistfully of the old, quiet St. Barts. Development has quickened the pace, but the island has not been overrun with prefab condos or glitzy resorts (although vacation villas are under construction everywhere). The largest hotel has fewer than 100 rooms, and the remaining rooms are scattered in about 40 small hotels around the island; no high-rises are allowed. The tiny airport accommodates nothing bigger than 19-passenger planes (and only during the day), and there aren't any flashy late-night attractions. Moreover, St. Barts is not a destination for the budget-minded: development has largely been in luxury lodgings and gourmet restaurants.

Christopher Columbus "discovered" the island in 1493 and named it after his brother, Bartholomeo. A small group of French colonists arrived from nearby St. Kitts in 1656 but were wiped out by the Carib Indians who dominated the area. A new group from Normandy and Brittany arrived in 1694. This time the settlers prospered—with the help of French buccaneers, who took advantage of the island's strategic location and protected harbor. In 1784 the French traded the island to King Gustav III of Sweden in exchange for port rights in Göteborg. He dubbed the capital Gustavia, laid out and paved streets, built three forts, and turned the community into a prosperous free port. The island thrived as a shipping and commercial center until the 19th century, when earthquakes, fire, and hurricanes brought financial ruin. Many residents fled for newer lands of opportunity, and in 1878 France agreed to repurchase its beleaguered former colony.

Today the island is still a free port and, as a dependency of Guadeloupe, is part of an overseas department of France. Dry, sunny, and rocky, St. Barts was never one of the Caribbean's "sugar islands" and thus never developed an extensive slave base. Most natives are descendants of those tough Norman and Breton settlers of three centuries ago. They are feisty, industrious, and friendly, but insular. However, you will find many new, young French arrivals—predominantly from northwestern France—who also speak English well.

Lodging

Expect to be shocked at the prices of accommodations. You pay for the privilege of staying on the island rather than for the hotel, and even at $500 a night, bedrooms tend to be small. Still, if you're flexible—in terms of timing and in your choice of lodgings—you can save a good deal of money.

The most expensive season falls during the holidays (mid-December to early January), and hotels are booked far in advance for this period. (Rates in listings below are for the second highest period, early January–April—still in season, but not the holiday peak.) Although more hotels and restaurants here have seasonal closings (from July or August to September or October) than on other islands, some places are still open in August. Most top hotels are on four northern beaches—Anse des Flamands, Anse des Cayes, Baie de St-Jean, and Grand Cul de Sac—and, fortunately, St. Barts's gorgeous beaches never close. If you're on a budget, look into an off-season stay, when rates can drop by as much as 50% below those in high season.

In the hills away from the beaches are a number of small hotels and bungalows—even some villas—that are surprisingly reasonable. On St. Barts, "villa" is used to describe anything from a small cottage to a truly luxurious house with a cook, a maid, and a pool. You get what you pay for. In-season rates range from $700 to $25,000 a week. If you get a group of friends together, you can rent a villa with several rooms and a pool for significantly less than it would cost for each person to stay in an expensive hotel. Peak periods are usually booked solid by the previous summer. Though cancellations do occur, it's best to *reserve a villa as far in advance as possible.* Regardless of the lodgings you choose, you will almost always need to rent a car, so be sure to factor that into your budget.

CATEGORY COST*

CATEGORY	COST*
$$$$	over $450
$$$	$325–$450
$$	$200–$325
$	under $200

All prices are for a standard double room, excluding a 10%–15% service charge; there is no government room tax.

Hotels

$$$$ **Carl Gustaf.** The red-tile-roof buildings of this small, very expensive,
★   luxury resort spill down a hill. Each one- and two-bedroom suite looks out across a deck (with a small private plunge pool) to lovely views of quaint Gustavia town, its harbor, and the island's coastline. Each suite has high ceilings and spacious, gleaming-white bedrooms and living rooms stylishly decorated with nautical and tropical prints; rough marble floors; marble baths; tiny but state-of-the-art kitchens; and such welcome extras as a fax machine, two TVs, and two stereos. The glittering nighttime view from the piano-bar lounge and the elegant open-air ☞ **Carl Gustaf** restaurant (known for its classic French cuisine) is spectacular. ⊠ *Rue des Normands (Box 700), Gustavia 97133,* ☎ *590/27– 82–83 or 800/932–3222 (reservations service),* FAX *590/27–82–37. 14 suites. Restaurant, air-conditioning, in-room VCRs, kitchenettes, minibars, refrigerators, pool, sauna, health club. AE, DC, MC, V. CP.*

$$$$ **Le Toiny.** Luxury awaits you at this exquisite little hillside hideaway.
★   The 12 spacious, green-roof villas—each with a patio and pool—were sited with privacy in mind. Each is elegantly appointed, with a massive four-poster mahogany bed and armoire, Chinese porcelain vases, Italian fabrics, and fine linens. There are phones, a fax, a stereo, and you can request either a stair-stepper or a stationary bike. The bathroom has a walk-in shower as well as a tub. The alfresco restaurant, ☞ **Le Gaiac,** overlooks the Italian-tiled communal pool and beyond to the ocean. A wonderful beach, Saline, is a 10-minute drive away. ⊠ *Anse de Toiny 97133,* ☎ *590/27–88–88 or 800/932–3222,* FAX *590/ 27–89–30. 13 villas. Restaurant, bar, air-conditioning, in-room safes, in-room VCRs, minibars, pool, laundry service. AE, DC, MC, V. CP.*

$$$–$$$$ **Eden Rock.** Set on a craggy bluff that splits St. Jean Beach is St. Barts's
★   first hotel—a fabulous, fun, slightly funky place that was opened in the '50s by Rémy de Haenen (he was the first to land a plane on the island and the first to establish a hotel). It has since been completely restored by the current British owners, Jane and David Matthews. Six original rooms cling to the rock; six newer ones are on the beach. All are painted in bold colors and have four-poster beds, tropical-print fabrics, mosquito netting, sparkling silver fixtures, terra-cotta floors, and stunning bay views. Whimsical, homey touches such as old-fashioned

St. Barthélemy

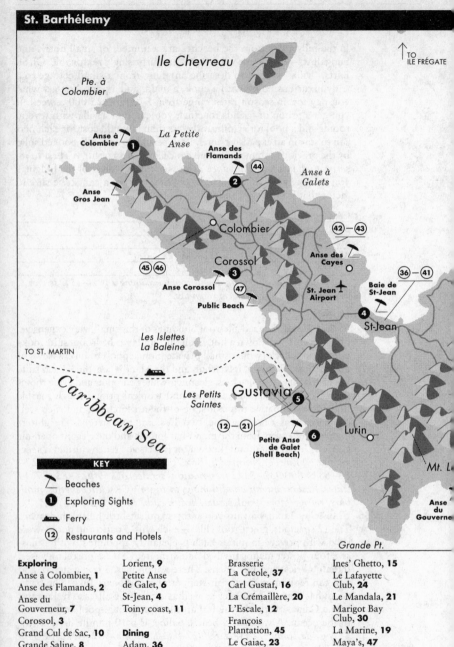

KEY

- Beaches
- **1** Exploring Sights
- Ferry
- **12** Restaurants and Hotels

Exploring
Anse à Colombier, **1**
Anse des Flamands, **2**
Anse du Gouverneur, **7**
Corossol, **3**
Grand Cul de Sac, **10**
Grande Saline, **8**
Gustavia, **5**

Lorient, **9**
Petite Anse de Galet, **6**
St-Jean, **4**
Toiny coast, **11**

Dining
Adam, **36**
Le Bambou, **27**

Brasserie
La Creole, **37**
Carl Gustaf, **16**
La Crémaillère, **20**
L'Escale, **12**
François
Plantation, **45**
Le Gaiac, **23**
Gloriette, **25**

Ines' Ghetto, **15**
Le Lafayette
Club, **24**
Le Mandala, **21**
Marigot Bay
Club, **30**
La Marine, **19**
Maya's, **47**
New Born, **42**

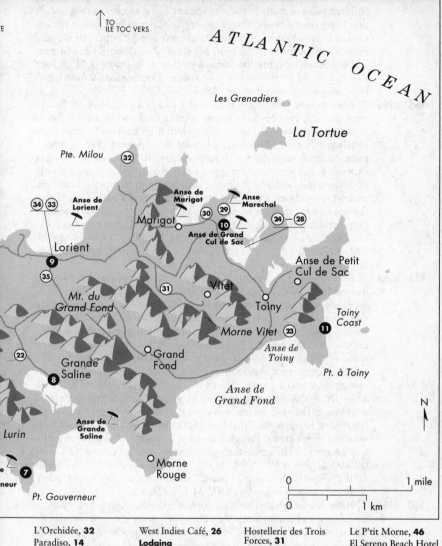

TO
ILE TOC VERS

ATLANTIC OCEAN

Les Grenadiers

La Tortue

Pte. Milou ③②

Anse de
Marigot

Anse de
Lorient ③④ ③③

Anse
Marechal

Marigot ③⓪ ②⑨ ②④ ②⑧

⑩

Anse de Grand
Cul de Sac

Lorient ⑨

③⑤

③①

Vitet

Anse de Petit
Cul de Sac

Mt. du
Grand Fond

Toiny

Toiny
Coast

Morne Vitet ②③ ⑪

②② Grand
Fond

Anse de
Toiny

Grande
Saline ⑧

Pt. à Toiny

Anse de
Grand Fond

Anse de
Grande
Saline

Lurin

N

Morne
Rouge

e ⑦
neur

Pt. Gouverneur

0   1 mile

0   1 km

L'Orchidée, **32**
Paradiso, **14**
Le Patio, **41**
Le Repaire, **13**
Le Rivage, **28**
Le Sapotillier, **17**
Le Tamarin, **22**
Wall House, **18**

West Indies Café, **26**
Lodging
Carl Gustaf, **16**
Club La Banane, **34**
Eden Rock, **38**
Filao Beach, **39**
François
Plantation, **45**
Guanahani, **29**

Hostellerie des Trois
Forces, **31**
Hôtel Christopher, **32**
Hôtel Manapany
Cottages, **42**
Hôtel Isle de France, **44**
Hôtel Yuana, **43**
Les Mouettes, **33**
La Normandie, **35**

Le P'tit Morne, **46**
El Sereno Beach Hotel
and Villas, **26**
Le Toiny, **23**
Tropical Hôtel, **40**
Village St-Jean
Hôtel, **41**

steamer trunks abound, and Jane anticipates incorporating still more heirlooms and antiques. In addition, she and the youngest of her three children painted many of the watercolors and gouaches of local scenes that hang on the walls. David has set up the new beachfront restaurant so that it doubles as a caviar and cigar bar. The open-air bar and French restaurant atop the bluff are great places to enjoy sea breezes and watch frigate birds dive for fish. ⊠ *Baie de St-Jean 97133,* ☎ *590/ 27–72–94,* FAX *590/27–88–37. 12 rooms. 3 restaurants, 2 bars, minibars, snorkeling, windsurfing. AE, MC, V. CP.*

$$$–$$$$ ⚓ **Filao Beach.** Excellent service and a location on one of St. Barts's most popular beaches keep guests coming back to this casual Relais & Châteaux resort. Rooms are in two-unit bungalows—many completely rebuilt after Hurricane Luis swept them away in 1995—set back from the beach amid gardens. (Quarters closer to the beach are the most expensive, but note that the more affordable garden rooms are only steps from the sand.) Each simple, smallish room has rattan furniture, pastel-print fabrics, a compact but tidy bath, and a patio. You'll find the restaurant (open for breakfast and lunch) on a raised wooden deck that surrounds the pool; the bartender is well-known for his killer cocktails. ⊠ *Baie de St-Jean (Box 667) 97099,* ☎ *590/27–64–84 or 800/ 742–4276,* FAX *590/27–62–24. 30 rooms. Restaurant, bar, air-conditioning, refrigerators, pool, beach. AE, MC, V. CP.*

$$$–$$$$ ⚓ **Guanahani.** This elegant 7-acre resort is between one beach that's
★ sheltered and one that's open to ocean waves. The lobby is a riot of color— deep greens, soothing blues, and rich plaids—and has a terrace where you can relax over a drink. Rooms and one-bedroom suites (some with private pools) are in tightly clustered bungalows. Most units are decorated with bright tropical fabrics and Georgian-style furniture, though some of the newer ones are done in a stunning contemporary style: wooden floors; dark wood furniture; colorful walls; funky art; a sunken seating area; and a partial, curved wall between the sleeping and bath areas. (Note that units vary in terms of privacy, view, and distance from activities; make your preferences known when reserving.) The poolside restaurant is open for breakfast and lunch. The more formal Bartolomeo serves classic French dinners in an indoor dining room and a tropical garden. The service throughout the resort is impeccable. ⊠ *Grand Cul de Sac (Box 609) 97098,* ☎ *590/27–66–60 or 800/223–6800,* FAX *590/27–70–70. 56 rooms, 21 suites. 2 restaurants, 2 pools, beauty salon, 2 tennis courts, windsurfing . AE, MC, V. CP.*

$$$–$$$$ ⚓ **Hôtel Christopher.** The Christopher, a Sofitel hotel, has oversize
★ rooms and a gracious, attentive staff, which make it one of the island's best deals. Four, two-story, colonial-style buildings house beautifully furnished suites, each with a balcony or terrace—from which you can see St. Martin and nearby islets—a sitting area, colonial reproduction furnishings, delightful island artwork and clever fabrics, and a contemporary marble bath. (Note that some baths have a little garden; if seeing a small lizard is the kind of thing that would ruin your vacation, ask for a bath sans greenhouse.) The hotel's 4,500-square-ft swimming pool has islands and footbridges. ☞ L'Orchidée restaurant serves French-Creole cuisine. In season, there's a complimentary shuttle to St. Jean Beach twice daily except Sunday. ⊠ *Pointe Milou 97133,* ☎ *590/27–63–63 or 800/221–4542 (reservations service),* FAX *590/ 27–92–92. 40 suites. 2 restaurants, air-conditioning, room service, pool, exercise room. AE, DC, MC, V. CP, EP, FAP, MAP.*

$$$–$$$$ ⚓ **Hôtel Isle de France.** Everything at this intimate resort has recently been whipped into tip-top shape, including the beachside pool and restaurant that were completely lost to Hurricane Luis. Enormous rooms and suites are either in a two-story beachfront clubhouse or across the street in bungalows that face gardens and a pool. All units have a patio or a balcony, mahogany furniture, authentic 19th-century island prints, and white cotton bedspreads; some garden bungalows have kitchenettes. The restaurant serves breakfast (in its dining area or in your room) and lunch. ⊠ *Baie des Flamands (Box 612) 97098,* ☎ *590/27–61–81,* FAX *590/27–86–83. 12 rooms, 18 bungalows, 3 junior suites. Restaurant, bar, refrigerators, 2 pools, tennis court, exercise room, squash. AE, MC, V. CP.*

$$$–$$$$ 🖼 **Hôtel Manapany Cottages.** A ramshackle road leads to this complex's eclectic collection of lodgings, which stretch back from a narrow (and not very swimmable) beach. Accommodations range from rather snug St. Barts–style cottages and suites on a hillside to much-in-demand beachfront digs with marble baths and four-poster beds. The atmosphere here is cosmopolitan, with a sophisticated clientele made up of many repeat guests. Bronzed bodies ring the small but attractive pool all day long, and outsiders drop in regularly to dine at the hotel's ☞ **New Born** restaurant. ⊠ *Anse des Cayes (Box 114) 97133,* ☎ *590/27–66–55 or 800/ 847–4249 (reservations service),* FAX *590/27–75–28. 32 units. 2 restaurants, 2 bars, pool, hot tub, tennis court, exercise room, beach, snorkeling, shop, airport shuttle. AE, D, DC, MC, V. CP.*

$$$–$$$$ 🖼 **El Sereno Beach Hotel and Villas.** The quiet, casual chic of this small resort attracts many repeat guests. Compact, simply furnished rooms have whitewashed walls, blue-painted beams, and either a sea view or a garden view and a patio. There are also nine comfortably furnished, one-bedroom, gingerbread-trimmed villas. The beach, with its exceptionally calm waters, is just steps away. The ☞ **West Indies Café** is now the locale for a dazzling Parisian-style revue once mounted by the late, lamented Jean-Marie Rivière of Club La Banane. ⊠ *Grand Cul de Sac (Box 19) 97133,* ☎ *590/27–64–80,* FAX *590/27–75–47. 20 rooms, 9 1-bedroom villas. 2 restaurants, bar, air-conditioning, refrigerators, pool, beach, snorkeling, boating, shop. AE, DC, MC, V. EP.*

$$–$$$ 🖼 **François Plantation.** A colonial-era graciousness pervades this hillside complex of West Indian–style cottages. It's owned and managed by longtime island habitués Françoise and François Beret. Monsieur Beret is a passionate gardener, and the grounds are an intense display of tropical flowers and greenery. The smallish rooms (four with garden views, eight with sea views) are dominated by queen-size, antique, mahogany, four-poster beds that are lightened by colorful fabrics. Two larger rooms can accommodate an extra bed. The pool is atop a very steep hill, with magnificent views of nearby islets. You'll need a car (some packages include one) to get down to the sand and out and about for lunch (the ☞ **François Plantation** restaurant is open only for breakfast and dinner). ⊠ *Colombier 97133,* ☎ *590/27–78–82, 800/932– 3222 in the U.S. (reservations service),* FAX *590/27–61–26. 12 rooms. Restaurant, air-conditioning, refrigerators, pool. AE, MC, V. CP.*

$$–$$$ 🖼 **Hôtel Yuana.** Here green-roof, West Indian–style cottages are strung along a flowery hillside. Appealing rooms have white-tile floors, colorful-tile baths, blue- or peach-painted wicker furniture, floral-print fabrics, a kitchenette, and a wide terrace that overlooks the ocean. You can rent the hotel's 30-ft boat. Package rates are available, and children under 12 stay free. ⊠ *Anse des Cayes 97133,* ☎ *590/27–80–84 or 800/645–6030 (reservations service),* FAX *590/27–78–45. 12 rooms. Bar, breakfast room, air-conditioning, fans, in-room VCRs, kitchenettes, pool, airport shuttle. AE, MC, V. EP.*

$$–$$$ 🖼 **Tropical Hôtel.** Straight up the hill from St. Jean Beach is a classic example of what the French affectionately call a *hôtel bourgeois:* a simple, stylish place that's also a good value. You'll find well-maintained rooms (those with lower numbers are the best) in a one-story, L-shape building. All open onto patios with views of either the ocean or thick tropical foliage and have pristine white walls, linens, and furnishings;

beam ceilings; and beds swaddled in mosquito netting. The main build-ing houses reception, a TV/game room, and an open-air bar-lounge, where the charming owner offers a sensational three-salad lunch spe-cial for only 70F. ⊠ *Baie de St-Jean (Box 147) 97133,* ☎ *590/27–64–87,* FAX *590/27–81–74. 21 rooms. Bar, snack bar, air-conditioning, refrigerators, pool, recreation room. AE, MC, V. CP.*

$$ 🏨 **Club La Banane.** For privacy, you can't beat this intimate hideaway. The nine unique rooms have sunken baths, four-poster beds, and all kinds of antiques. Though rooms face dense greenery, the lack of sun-light blazing through your window is offset by the cheer of houseplants, Haitian artwork, and unusual pottery. There are two small pools (one with a waterfall), and the beach is just a three-minute walk away. The restaurant is open only to hotel guests for breakfast and lunch; visi-tors come from around the island for an alfresco dinner by the lily-filled pool. ⊠ *Quartier Lorient 97133,* ☎ *590/27–68–25,* FAX *590/27–68–44. 9 rooms. Restaurant, bar, 2 pools. AE, MC, V. CP.*

$–$$ 🏨 **Village St-Jean Hôtel.** For two generations, the Charneau family has
★ seen to it that the quality of the service here remains high and the rates reasonable. The handsome stone-and-redwood cottages are spacious (though all but the two-bedroom units are sparsely furnished) and have open-air kitchenettes and patios. The six hotel-style rooms lack fully equipped kitchens but have refrigerators. All units are decorated with elegant natural fabrics and dark-wood (and some teak) pieces; some rooms have beam ceilings, and most have king-size beds. The views vary from full ocean to almost none, but who needs a great vista when you've got a convenient location? From here it's an easy three-minute walk down to St. Jean Beach and to stores and restaurants (though the walk back up is slightly more strenuous). The open-air restaurant, ☞ **Le Patio,** serves excellent Italian fare. ⊠ *Baie de St. Jean (Box 623) 97098,* ☎ *590/27–61–39 or 800/651–8366,* FAX *590/27–77–96. 6 rooms, 20 cottages. Restaurant, bar, grocery, air-conditioning, kitch-enettes, pool, hot tub, shop, library. AE, MC, V. EP.*

$ 🏨 **Hostellerie des Trois Forces.** This somewhat isolated mountaintop
★ inn is an idiosyncratic delight. Each of its tiny, gingerbread-trimmed, West Indian cottages is done in an astrological color scheme (Libra is soft blue; Leo, bright red; etc.), and the very personable owner and as-trologer, Hubert de la Motte (a Gemini), handcrafted furnishings to suit each sign. All the units have air-conditioning or a ceiling fan as well as a terrace with a breathtaking ocean view; most have four-poster beds. When Hubert isn't busy arranging readings, yoga classes, and even past-life-regression therapy sessions for his guests, he's putting his talents to work in the kitchen alongside chef Bernard Calci. The tinkle of chimes floats through the pleasant, rustic restaurant, whose slogan is "Food is love." Hubert was recently named a *chevalier* (knight) of the Marmite d'Or, a prestigious French culinary academy founded in 1557. ⊠ *Morne Vitet 97133,* ☎ *590/27–61–25,* FAX *590/27–81–38. 8 rooms. Restaurant, bar, minibars, pool. AE, MC, V. EP.*

$ 🏨 **Les Mouettes.** Here, six spacious, simply furnished bungalows open
★ onto the island's best surfing beach. Each has a bathroom with shower, a kitchenette, a patio, two double beds, and a twin bed or fold-out sofa, making it a good bet for families. ⊠ *Quartier Lorient 97133,* ☎ *590/27–60–74. 6 rooms. Kitchenettes, beach, shop, car rental. No credit cards. EP.*

$ 🏨 **La Normandie.** This cozy, family-run hotel offers modestly fur-nished rooms (some with a TV) for well under $100 a night, making it one of the best deals on St. Barts. There's a small pool here, and the beach is a five-minute walk away. ⊠ *Quartier Lorient 97133,* ☎ *590/27–61–66,* FAX *590/27–68–64. 8 rooms. Air-conditioning, pool. No credit cards. EP.*

$ ★ 🖼 **Le P'tit Morne.** Each of the modestly furnished mountainside studios here has a private balcony and panoramic views of the coastline. The small kitchenettes are adequate for creating picnic lunches and other light meals. The snack bar serves breakfast. It's relatively isolated here, however; the beach is a 10-minute drive away. ✉ *Colombier (Box 14) 97133,* ☎ *590/27–62–64,* FAX *590/27–84–63. 14 rooms. Snack bar, air-conditioning, kitchenettes, pool, library. AE, MC, V. CP.*

Villas

Based in Stowe, Vermont, **Country Village Rentals–St. Barths** (☎ 802/253–8777 or 800/320–8777, FAX 802/253–2144) represents more than 200 properties. Owner Doug Foregger and his friendly staff try to find the perfect villa for each customer. Prices range from $700 to $25,000 per week. St. Barts is the *only* island that **St. Barth Properties, Inc.** (☎ 508/528–7727 or 800/421–3396, FAX 508/528–7789) in Franklin, Massachusetts, represents. Owner Peg Walsh wouldn't have it any other way. Her company, in business since 1989, publishes a free four-color booklet with details on more than 60 villas. Weekly peak-season rates range from $1,400 to $32,000.

At **Sibarth** (☎ 590/27–62–38, FAX 590/27–60–52), Madame Lecour, the reigning queen of St. Barts's real estate, oversees more than 200 properties. **WIMCO** (☎ 800/932–3222, FAX 401/847–6290), based in Newport, Rhode Island, is Sibarth's U.S. representative, and its pleasant agents are very knowledgeable about the properties. Rents range from $1,000 to $2,000 per week for one-bedroom villas, $1,600 to $7,000 for two- and three-bedroom villas. Larger villas rent from $9,000 to $19,000 per week.

Dining

If you enjoy exquisitely prepared cuisine served at an enjoyable pace (and don't mind paying for it), then you've come to the right island. A la carte prices at the well-known French restaurants are very high, but many offer a more reasonable prix-fixe menu. Lunch is usually a less costly meal than dinner (with the exception of lunch at Le Lafayette), and Italian, Creole, and French-Creole restaurants tend to be less expensive day and night. Note that restaurants here typically charge for drinking water (a French custom), which comes by the bottle, both sparkling and flat, and costs about $4. *Accras* (salt cod fritters) with Creole sauce (minced hot peppers in oil), spiced christophene (a kind of squash), *boudin Créole* (a very spicy blood sausage), and a lusty *soupe de poissons* (fish soup) are some of the delicious and ubiquitous Creole dishes. Reservations are always recommended; on weekend nights in season, they're essential almost everywhere.

What to Wear

Jackets are rarely required and rarely worn, but this is a tony island, and people here are fashionably dressed. Jeans are de rigueur when worn with a hip collared shirt or T-shirt. Shorts at the dinner table will label you *américain*. Think casual chic and you'll be fine.

CATEGORY	COST*
$$$$	over $60
$$$	$45–$60
$$	$30–$45
$	under $30

*per person for a three-course meal, excluding drinks, service, and 4% sales tax

ASIAN

$$ ✕ **Le Bambou.** In the hills above Grand Cul du Sac is this small restaurant, serving creative Asian fare. A Laotian chef, Monsieur Thao, pre-

pares Vietnamese, Thai, and Chinese food. You can dine inside—all black lacquer with changing exhibits of art on the walls and impeccable floral arrangements throughout—but most guests opt for the breezy terrace (reservations for this area are a good idea) with a fine view of the countryside and the distant sea. ⊠ *Grand Cul de Sac,* ☎ *590/27–75–65. MC, V. Closed Mon. No lunch.*

CARIBBEAN/CREOLE

$$–$$$ ✕ **L'Orchidée.** This elegant French-Creole restaurant with coral stucco walls and mahogany archways is in the ☞ **Hôtel Christopher.** Have a seat in a casual captain's chair on the deck, amid the white napery and gleaming silver, and listen to the waves on the rocky shore. The staff is friendly and solicitous, the atmosphere romantic, and the food beautifully presented. Try roast lobster with mango and ginger, grilled mahimahi with lime, or chicken with curry-and-coconut sauce served with two kinds of mashed potatoes. A prix-fixe menu is available for about $45. ⊠ *Pointe Milou,* ☎ *590/27–63–63. AE, MC, V. No lunch.*

$$ ✕ **New Born.** For authentic Creole cuisine, head down the bumpy road that leads to the ☞ **Hôtel Manapany.** The sky-blue restaurant is somewhat devoid of decoration except for a large aquarium in the back. Ask for a table near it to watch sharks, turtles, and tropical fish swim while you eat such Creole specialties as accras, boudin, curried goat or shrimp, and salt-cod salad. The seafood served here is caught at the beach (just steps away) by owners Franky and David. For dessert try the coconut custard or bananas flambé. ⊠ *Anse des Cayes,* ☎ *590/27–67–07. AE, MC, V. Closed Sun. in off-season. No lunch.*

$–$$ ✕ **Gloriette.** This beachside spot serves delicious local Creole dishes, such as crunchy accras and cassoulet of local lobster, as well as light salads. ⊠ *Grand Cul de Sac,* ☎ *590/27–75–66. AE, MC, V.*

$–$$ ✕ **Le Rivage.** Bathing suits are acceptable attire at this popular Creole establishment on the beach at Grand Cul de Sac. Delicious lobster salad, sandwiches, and fresh grilled fish are served at indoor and outdoor tables. The relaxed atmosphere and surprisingly low prices can make for an enjoyable meal. ⊠ *St. Barth Beach Hôtel, Grand Cul de Sac,* ☎ *590/27–82–42. AE, MC, V.*

CONTEMPORARY

$$$–$$$$ ✕ **Carl Gustaf.** Not even the sweeping views of the harbor can deflect
★   attention from the sublime creations of Patrick Gateau at this restaurant in the ☞ **Carl Gustaf** hotel. Monsieur Gateau, who trained at the Crillon in Paris, deftly weaves tropical influences into his classical cuisine. Among his standouts are warm goat-cheese salad, lobster spring rolls, ravioli in shellfish cream sauce, and grilled swordfish steak with stewed aubergines, tomatoes, sweet peppers, and onions. You choose your dessert when you order your meal to allow time for it to be prepared. Look no further than the praline cake—with a center unexpectedly flooded with warm gooey chocolate. The large, breezy, white dining room has an open-air terrace that overlooks Gustavia harbor, as well as a piano bar. ⊠ *Rue des Normands, Gustavia,* ☎ *590/27–82–83. AE, MC, V. No lunch Sun. in summer.*

$$$–$$$$ ✕ **François Plantation.** Follow the lanterns down the arborway to this
★   elegant restaurant in the ☞ **François Plantation** complex. Inside, mahogany tables and chairs are surrounded by plants. Chef Philippe Ruiz's lighter version of classic French cuisine draws guests from all over the island; locals consistently rate it in their top three. Try his ravioli of goat cheese and foie gras, and move on to roasted sea bass spiced with vanilla or lamb fillet roasted in a light crust with basil and Gorgonzola cheese and served with sautéed fennel and tomato. You can also order the rare Coutancie beef (the cattle must drink 3 liters of beer and receive a 20-minute rubdown twice daily, among other strict guidelines,

to qualify). Dessert specials include a warm, dark-chocolate tart served with vanilla ice cream. ✉ *Colombier,* ☎ *590/27–78–82. Reservations essential. AE, D, MC, V. Closed Sept.–Oct. No lunch.*

$$$–$$$$ ✕ **Le Gaiac.** Cool breezes waft through this open-air restaurant at the elegant, out-of-the-way ☞ **Le Toiny** hotel. Pale blue napery and blue canvas chairs beautifully complement the blue bay view. Chef Maxime Des Champs hails from France and combines local ingredients with traditional French preparations. Lunch includes duck carpaccio with coffee-flavored vinaigrette, a delicious chilled spicy mango soup, club sandwiches, salads, and grilled seafood. The dinner menu features such dishes as roast rack of lamb in a clay shell with thyme and honey, yellowtail snapper with lightly curried lentils and squash, and pigeon layered with red cabbage and sweet potato and spiced with local herbs. Don't miss the fabulous buffet lunch on Sunday. ✉ *Anse de Toiny,* ☎ *590/27–88–88. AE, DC, MC, V. Closed Sept.–mid-Oct..*

$$$ ✕ **Le Sapotillier.** Dining inside this cozy boîte or in its courtyard under
★ a grand old sapodilla tree, you may feel like a guest in the owners' house—a loving re-creation of a typical St. Barts *case* (Creole for cottage), down to the brick walls, hand-painted wooden chairs, exquisite white linen tablecloths, and vivid Creole paintings. Yet the food is anything but down-home. This long-established French-Creole restaurant serves such delicacies as frogs' legs; fillet of baby turbot in potato crust; and snail lasagna with spinach, walnuts, and Roquefort sabayon. The sumptuous black-and-white-chocolate mousse is a house favorite. ✉ *Rue de Centenaire, Gustavia,* ☎ *590/27–60–28. Reservations essential. MC, V. Closed May–mid-Oct. No lunch.*

$$–$$$$ ✕ **West Indies Café.** This café at ☞ **El Sereno Beach Hotel and Villas** is on an outdoor pavilion that overlooks the bay. Chef Yvan, hailing from St. Tropez and Paris, prepares French cuisine à la Provence; he's best known for his innovative cooking with beer. Try the veal kidneys with basil and beer sauce and the crispy pineapple with caramelized juice. Weekend nights, the staff performs a rather racy Caribbean version of a Parisian floor show in tribute to the great Jean Marie Rivière, the cabaret impresario who ran Club La Banane for years. ✉ *Grand Cul de Sac,* ☎ *590/27–64–80. AE, DC, MC, V. Closed June–Aug.*

$$ ✕ **Adam.** Vincent Adam, a graduate of the Culinary Academy of France, opened this haute cuisine gem in the hills just off St. Jean Beach. Dinner is served in the Creole-style house or in the garden. While standards have lowered since Bernard Hinault supplanted Vincent as chef, Adam still offers splendid bargains with its more extensive à la carte menu (offered only in season) and a very reasonable prix-fixe menu (about $38). Offerings include lobster tabbouleh, salmon tartare with caviar and oysters, terrine of sweetbreads, and fillet of beef. ✉ *St-Jean, just outside of town,* ☎ *590/27–93–22. AE, MC, V. No lunch.*

$$ ✕ **Le Tamarin.** Always among the favorite restaurants of those who live
★ on St. Barts, this open-air eatery on the way to Saline Beach is famous for its French and Creole fusion cuisine and its resident noisy parrot, Cooky. Relax in a hammock under the tamarind tree with a *'ti punch* (pronounced tee poonch; a powerful concoction of rum, lime juice, and sugarcane syrup) and then savor some of the house specialties, including carpaccios of salmon, tuna, and beef; fresh grilled lobster; and the renowned lemon tart and chocolate cake. ✉ *Salines,* ☎ *590/27–72–12. AE, MC, V. Closed Mon. No dinner in summer.*

$$ ✕ **Wall House.** Consistently excellent French cuisine is the hallmark of this restaurant on the far end of the far side of Gustavia's harbor. The interior is glistening white—shiny white-wicker furniture, white tile floors, white tablecloths and walls—with pots of greenery here and there. Owner Gerard Began is unobtrusively present most evenings, and the staff is gracious and will make enthusiastic recommendations.

Start with marinated salmon with dill, gazpacho, grilled mahimahi over sliced cucumbers, foie gras, or cold eggplant mousse. For your main course, try fillet of shark in lobster sauce, duck in cassis sauce with sautéed potatoes, or beef with pepper sauce. Three prix-fixe menus offer excellent value. The lunch menu features lighter fare. ⊠ *Rue Jeanne d'Arc, Gustavia,* ☎ *590/27–71–83. AE, MC, V.*

ECLECTIC

$$$–$$$$ ✕ **Le Lafayette Club.** Despite outrageous prices, this lunch-only, beachside bistro is such an in-season in spot that reservations are necessary between noon and 2. Expect to pay about $18 for a green salad with bacon and croutons or goat cheese and sliced tomatoes, $30 and up for grilled local fish, fillet of duck, and shrimp with fresh pasta. The grilled lobster entrée is a whopping $70. ⊠ *Grand Cul de Sac,* ☎ *590/ 27–62–51. No credit cards. Closed May–mid-Nov. No dinner.*

$$ ✕ **Le Mandala.** The decor at this ultrahip spot ranges from fancy (wrought-iron chairs, a mahogany bar) to fanciful (huge painted ceramic frogs, enormous ashtrays shaped like a hand). The owners, Boubou and Christophe, and their food are equally witty. They offer a full menu (including a three-course buy at 170F) with such offerings as chicken breast in coconut milk. But this is the place to sample tapas, that wonderful Spanish tradition of small tasting platters; they go well with a potent rum punch whose colors match the setting sun, clearly visible across the harbor from the sweeping terrace. ⊠ *Rue Thiers, Gustavia,* ☎ *590/27–96–96. AE, MC, V. No lunch June and Sept.*

$$ ✕ **La Marine.** Mussels from France arrive on Thursday, and in-the-know islanders are there to eat them at the very popular dockside picnic tables. The lunch menu always includes fresh fish, hamburgers, and omelets; dinner sees more grilled meat and fish. ⊠ *Rue Jeanne d'Arc, Gustavia,* ☎ *590/27–70–13. AE, MC, V.*

$$ ✕ **Maya's.** Locals, visitors, and celebs keep returning to pack this in-
★   formal, open-air restaurant, just outside of Gustavia on the north end of Public Beach. Relax in a colorful deck chair and watch the boats in Gustavia's harbor as you contemplate the Creole, Vietnamese, and Thai menu. You choose from five selections for each of three courses. The menu changes nightly, but you might find christophene au gratin, several fresh salads, duck *à l'orange* (in orange sauce), salmon teriyaki, and shrimp curry. ⊠ *Public Beach,* ☎ *590/27–75–73. AE, D, MC, V. Closed Sun. and June–Oct. No lunch.*

$–$$ ✕ **Brasserie La Creole.** Right in the center of the St-Jean shopping arcade, this casual brasserie has indoor and outdoor seating, and a comfortable bar. Drop by any time after 7 AM for freshly baked croissants and great coffee (though there's also a full breakfast menu). At lunch try the *croque-monsieur* (a hot sandwich made with two slices of buttered bread, sans crusts, and thin slices of cheese and ham); from noon till midnight you can order sandwiches; salads; and beef, chicken, and fish entrées. ⊠ *St-Jean,* ☎ *590/27–68–09. AE.*

$–$$ ✕ **Ines' Ghetto.** The imaginatively prepared, modestly priced fare—bar-
★   becued ribs (a house specialty), crab salad, ragout of beef, crème caramel—wild decor (a virtual jungle of plants, bamboo furnishings, and metal garbage-can sculpture), and a disarmingly fun-loving atmosphere guarantee an interesting meal. The crowd is lively, and the wine list is impressive (but avoid the house white). ⊠ *Just off rue de Général de Gaulle, Gustavia.* ☎ *No phone. No credit cards.*

$–$$ ✕ **Paradisio.** Five kinds of homemade pasta and carpaccios are served each day at this friendly eatery in a historic apricot-and-white gingerbread Creole building. Specialties include fresh lobster medallions served on a bed of lentils, veal kidneys sautéed and served with a mustard sauce, and lamb filet mignon with rosemary. You can eat in the air-conditioned dining room, festively painted in canary yellow and teal, or on the breezy terrace. ⊠ *Rue du Roi, Gustavia,* ☎ *590/27–80–78. AE, MC, V. No lunch Sun.*

$–$$ ✕ **Le Repaire.** This busy brasserie overlooks Gustavia's harbor and is a popular spot from 6 AM to 1 AM. Grab a cappuccino, pull a captain's chair up to the front window, and watch cruise-ship passengers descend upon the town. The menu includes everything from cheeseburgers to foie gras and grilled fish and lobster. Stick to the simpler bistro and Creole favorites like the crab Creole salad. There's a billiards table, and on weekends you'll find live music. ⊠ *Quai de la République, Gustavia,* ☎ *590/27–72–48. MC, V. Closed Sun.*

FRENCH

$–$$ ✕ **La Crémaillère.** The setting in a 19th-century Swedish stone-wood-and-brick house is sublime. Several intimate, individually decorated rooms—with wood-beam ceilings, wrought-iron wall sconces, hurricane lamps, and peacock rattan chairs—surround a cool, dark, romantic courtyard. The food is solidly traditional, but rather than having a standard, if fine, veal in mushroom cream sauce or pork *dijonnaise* (in a mustard-flavored, mayonaisse-type sauce), try one of the outstanding fondues—especially the more unusual ones, such as *forestière* (wild mushrooms) or *cabrette* (goat cheese). The real treat here are *les pierrades,* beef or seafood grilled on hot stones. ⊠ *Rue de Général de Gaulle, Gustavia,* ☎ *590/27–82–95. AE, MC, V. No lunch Sun.*

ITALIAN

$$ ✕ **Le Patio.** Classic Italian food is served à la Créole at this pleasant
★ restaurant in the ☞ **Village St-Jean Hôtel.** Dine inside by candlelight, where it's romantic and intimate, or on the terrace, with nice views of the bay. Entrées change weekly, but you may find snapper in parchment with herbs and peppers, or grouper medallions with a light ginger and lime sauce, in addition to pastas and pizzas. The antipasto here is renowned. Service is unhurried, despite the remarkably reasonable prices: witness the $36 prix-fixe menu. ⊠ *St-Jean Hill,* ☎ *590/27–61–39. MC, V. Closed Wed. and June. No lunch.*

$–$$ ✕ **L'Escale.** Great food, ambience, and views draw locals and visitors
★ alike to this open-air restaurant at the water's edge on the far side of Gustavia's harbor. The varied menu includes a wide range of pasta (lasagna, tortellini, ravioli, and spaghetti with marinara, Bolognese, and other sauces), as well as fresh local fish, veal scallopini in an assortment of sauces, steak tartare, chicken, and 12 kinds of pizza. Many dishes are cooked in a wood-burning oven. ⊠ *Rue Jeanne d'Arc, Gustavia,* ☎ *590/27–81–06. Reservations essential. MC, V. No lunch.*

SEAFOOD

$$ ✕ **Marigot Bay Club.** Have a seat at the dark-wood bar or at a table on the covered patio, and take in the views of the colorful sailboats moored in the bay. The owner of this casual spot loves to fish and often reels in the catch of the day himself. It might be grouper, tuna, red snapper, or yellowtail—all of which are frequently served with a Creole sauce. Other specials here include lobster ravioli, conch sausages, codfish fritters, and steamed shark in a red pepper and butter sauce. Lunch is served in-season, except on Monday. ⊠ *Marigot,* ☎ *590/27–75–45. Reservations essential. AE, MC, V. No lunch Mon. or off-season.*

Beaches

There are many *anses* (coves) with nearly 20 *plages* (beaches) scattered around the island, each with a distinctive personality and each open to the general public. Even in season, you can find a nearly empty beach.

Topless sunbathing is common, but nudism is forbidden—although both Saline and Gouverneur are de facto nude beaches.

The beach at **Anse à Colombier** is the least accessible but the most private; to reach it you must take either a rocky footpath from Petite Anse or brave the 30-minute climb down a cactus-bordered trail from the top of the mountain behind the beach. A lot of boaters favor this beach and cove for its calm anchorage. **Anse Corossol** is a top boat- and sunset-watching spot. **Anse du Gouverneur** is secluded—hence the nude sunbathing—and truly beautiful, with good snorkeling and views of St. Kitts, Saba, and St. Eustatius. Next to the Guanahani Hotel, is tiny **Anse Marechal**, which offers some of the island's best snorkeling. **Baie de St-Jean** is like a mini Côte d'Azur—beachside bistros, bungalow hotels, bronzed bodies, windsurfing, and lots of day-trippers. The reef-protected strip is divided by Eden Rock promontory, and there's good snorkeling west of the rock.

Flamands is the most beautiful of the hotel beaches—a roomy strip of silken sand, now even wider due to Hurricane Luis. Shallow, reef-protected **Grand Cul de Sac** is especially nice for small children and windsurfers; it has excellent lunch spots and lots of pelicans. Secluded **Grande Saline,** with its sandy ocean bottom, is just about everyone's favorite beach and is great for swimmers. Despite the law, young and old alike go nude. It can get windy here, so go on a calm day.

Lorient is popular with St. Barts families and surfers, who like its rolling waves. **Marigot** is a tiny, calm beach with good snorkeling along the rocky far end. A five-minute walk from Gustavia is **Petite Anse de Galet** (Shell Beach), named after the tiny shells on its shore. **Public Beach** is an excellent place to watch the boats or a sunset.

Outdoor Activities and Sports

BOATING AND SAILING

St. Barts is a popular yachting and sailing center thanks to its location midway between Antigua and St. Thomas. Gustavia's harbor, 13 to 16 ft deep, has mooring and docking facilities for 40 yachts. There are also good anchorages available at Public, Corossol, and Colombier.

Loulou's Marine (⊠ Gustavia, ☎ 590/27–62–74), a ship chandlery, is the place for yachting information and supplies. **Marine Service** (⊠ Gustavia, ☎ 590/27–70–34) offers full-day outings on a 40-ft catamaran to the uninhabited Ile Fourchue for swimming, snorkeling, cocktails, and lunch; the cost is $96 per person. Marine Service also arranges deep-sea-fishing trips, with a full-day charter of a 30-ft crewed cabin cruiser running $800; an unskippered motor rental runs about $260 a day. Marine Service can also arrange an hour's cruise ($32) on the glass-bottom boat *L'Aquascope.* **OcéanMust Marina** (☎ 590/27–62–25), in Gustavia, offers all kinds of boat charters. **St. Barth Caraibes Yachting** (☎ 590/27–52–48), in Gustavia, can charter any type of boat you require. **Nautica** (⊠ Gustavia , ☎ 590/27–56–50) specializes in day sails and charters.

FISHING

Most of the fishing is done in the waters north of Lorient, Flamandes and Corossol. Popular catches are tuna, marlin, wahoo, and barracuda. Deep-sea fishing can be arranged through **Marine Service, St. Barth Caraibes Yachting,** or **OcéanMust Marina** (☞ Boating, *above*).

HORSEBACK RIDING

Laure Nicolas leads two-hour excursions in the morning and the afternoon for $35 per person from **Ranch des Flamands** (⊠ Anse des Flamands, ☎ 590/27–80–72).

SCUBA DIVING

Marine Service (☞ Boating and Sailing, *above*) also operates a PADI-certified diving center and offers scuba-diving trips for about $50–$80 per person, gear included. The CMAS-certified **Club La Bulle** (☎ 590/27–62–25), **Odysee Caraibe** (☎ 590/27–55–94), and PADI-certified **St. Barth Plongée** (☎ 590/27–54–44), all in Gustavia, are other scuba options.

TENNIS

If you wish to play tennis at a hotel at which you are not a guest, be sure to call ahead to inquire about fees and reservations. There are two lighted tennis courts each at the **Guanahani** (⊠ Grand Cul de Sac, ☎ 590/27–66–60), **Le Flamboyant Tennis Club** (⊠ Anse de Toiny, ☎ 590/27–75–65), and the **Sports Center of Colombier** (⊠ Colombier, ☎ 590/27–61–07).

There's one lighted court each at **Hôtel Manapany Cottages** (⊠ Anse de Cayes, ☎ 590/27–66–55), **Taiwana** (⊠ Baie des Flamands, ☎ 590/27–65–01), and **Hôtel Isle de France** (⊠ Baie des Flamands, ☎ 590/27–61–81), which also has the island's only squash court.

WINDSURFING

Windsurfing fever has definitely caught on here. You can rent boards for about $20 an hour at water-sports centers along Baie de St-Jean and Grand Cul de Sac beaches. Lessons are offered for about $40 an hour at **St. Barth Wind School** (⊠ Baie de St-Jean, ☎ 590/27–71–22), **Le Centre Nautique** (⊠ Eden Rock at Baie de St.-Jean, ☎ 590/27–72–94), and **Wind Wave Power** (⊠ St. Barths Beach Hotel at Grand Cul de Sac, ☎ 590/27–60–70).

Shopping

St. Barts is a duty-free port, and there are especially good bargains in jewelry; porcelain; imported liquors; and French perfumes, cosmetics, and designer resort wear. Note that stores often close from noon to 2, so plan your shopping day accordingly.

Areas and Malls

In **Gustavia,** small stores along rue du Roi Oscar II, rue de la France, rue du Bord de Mer, and rue de Général de Gaulle sell French perfume, clothing, and many luxury items. Shops are also clustered in **La Savane Commercial Center** (across from the airport) and **La Villa Créole** in St-Jean. It's worth working your way from one end to the other at both of these shopping complexes—just to see or maybe be seen. A number of boutiques in all three areas carry the latest in French and Italian sportswear and haute-couture items. The prices may astound you (even after you convert the francs to dollars you may still be in high three figures), but they're actually well below European prices—real bargains to some people. Shops to look for include Stéphane&Bernard, Libertine, Hermès, Gucci, Cartier, Gianni Versace, Tommy Hilfiger, Giorgio Armani, and Black Swan, all of which are in Gustavia and have branches either across from the airport, in St-Jean, or both.

Specialty Items

CLOTHES

In Gustavia and St-Jean you'll find many clothing shops (usually clustered together), including **Mirage** (⊠ Les Hauts du Carré d'Or, Gustavia, ☎ 590/27–97-11), **Libertine** (⊠ 3 Rue de la France, Gustavia, ☎ 590/27–61–56), and **Samaly** (⊠ La Village Créole, St-Jean , ☎ 590/27–54–91).

FOODSTUFFS

A gourmet supermarket, **Match,** is across from the airport, as is **Unic Plus,** another supermarket with a good selection of fruits, vegetables, and meats. Two other supermarkets worth checking out are **Sodexa** in La Villa Créole and **MonoShop** in Marigot. For exotic groceries or picnic fixings, stop by one of St. Barts's fabulous gourmet delis; **La Rotisserie** (☎ 590/27–63–13) is a good bet on rue du Roi Oscar II (there are also branches in St-Jean and Pointe Milou).

HANDICRAFTS

Stop in Corossol to pick up some of the intricate straw work—wide-brim beach hats, mobiles, handbags—that the ladies of Corossol create by hand.

Gustavia has a market, **Le 'Ti Marché,** dedicated to arts and crafts handmade on the island. It's open every day except Sunday and is on the corner of rue du Roi Oscar II near the city hall. The much-sought-after Belou's P line of aromatic oils is available here. For details call ☎ 590/27–83–72 or the tourist office (☞ Visitor Information *in* St. Barthélemy A to Z, *below*), which can also provide information about the studios of such island artists as Robert Danet, Marion Vinot, Patricia Guyot, Nathalie Daniel, Rose Lemen, Christian Bretoneiche, and Eliane Lefèvre.

Fabienne Miot displays her utterly unique gold jewelry at **L'Atelier de Fabienne** (⊠ Rue de la République, Gustavia, ☎ 590/27–63–31). **La Boutique Roots** (☎ 590/27–53–53) fashions marvelous sandals, sunbonnets, and handbags from straw. Superb local skin-care products are available at **Ligne de St. Barth** (⊠ Rte. de Saline, Lorient, ☎ 590/27–82–63) in Lorient. **M'Bolo** (⊠ Les Hauts du Carré d'Or, Gustavia, ☎ 590/27–90–54) is a fragrant grab bag of local spices; flavored rums; *pareos* (sarong-like beach wraps); and hand-painted blouses, T-shirts, bags, and bikinis. In Gustavia, look for hand-turned pottery at **St. Barts Pottery** (☎ 590/27–62–74).

LIQUOR AND TOBACCO

Wine lovers will enjoy **La Cave** (⊠ Rue de Général de Gaulle, Gustavia, ☎ 590/27–63–21), where an excellent collection of French vintages is stored in temperature-controlled cellars. **Le Comptoir du Cigare** (⊠ Rue de Général de Gaulle, Gustavia, ☎ 590/27–50–62) is one of the finest purveyors of cigars (and accessories) in the Caribbean, with a comprehensive selection from Davidoff to Dunhill, including the oh-so-tempting Cubanos.

Nightlife

For such a petite island, St. Barts offers a surprising number of things to do at night, notably on weekends. There are many special places to go for cocktail hour, and some of the hotels and restaurants provide late-night fun.

American Bar (⊠ Rue du Roi Oscar II, Gustavia, ☎ 590/27–86–07) is an after-dinner hangout for the retro-hip; there's a 1968 Cadillac Eldorado outside and lots of neon inside. **Bar de l'Oubli** (⊠ Rue du Roi Oscar II, Gustavia, ☎ 590/27–70–06), where the young French who work on the island gather for drinks, gets hopping late at night. **Carl Gustaf** (⊠ Rue des Normands, Gustavia, ☎ 590/27–82–83) lures those in search of quiet conversation and some gentle piano music at the day's end. It's also Gustavia's best sunset-watching spot. **Feeling** (☎ 590/27–88–67) is one of the island's hot spots for dancing. An indoor dance floor and spacious outdoor bar-patio make this a fun place to hang out. The disco is in the hills above Gustavia. **Guanahani** (⊠ Grand Cul de Sac, ☎ 590/27–66–60) has a piano bar, as well as *spectacle* (nightclub revue-style) shows and theme evenings (Latin dancing night is particularly wild) a couple of times a week in season at its poolside L'Indigo restaurant.

Jungle Cafe (⊠ 6 rue Jeanne d'Arc, ☎ 590/27–67–29), an upstairs eatery overlooking the harbor in Gustavia, jumps and jives at happy hour, with knockout drink specials and fairly priced Asian snack fare. **La Licorne** (☎ 590/27–83–94), in Lorient, is very hot with a local crowd and open only on Saturday night. **Le Petit Club** (☎ 590/27–66–33), in Gustavia, is the place to head for real late-night dancing. **Le Repaire** (⊠ Rue de la République, ☎ 590/27–72–48), in Gustavia, lures a crowd for cocktail hour. **Le Select** (☎ 590/27–86–87), in Gustavia, is St. Barts's original hangout and has a boisterous garden where the barefoot boating set gathers for a brew. **Manapany** (☎ 590/27–66–55), in Anse des Cayes, has a piano bar.

Exploring St. Barthélemy

Except for some steep, curvy, haphazardly paved roads in the farthest reaches, most of St. Barts's routes are excellent. Though they're usually well marked, it can't hurt to buy a map before setting out on a tour. The main road completely encircles the island; smaller arteries off it head inland. You can rent a four-wheel-drive vehicle or a minimoke (a small open-air vehicle with a bumper-car feel) at the airport and see all of this small, hilly, very picturesque island in half a day.

Numbers in the margin correspond to points of interest on the St. Barthélemy map.

SIGHTS TO SEE

❶ Anse à Colombier. At the end of Flamands Road, a 25-minute hike around a rocky footpath leads to a pretty beach and cove, popular with boaters.

❷ Anse des Flamands. This wide beach has small hotels, including the Hôtel Isle de France, and many rental villas. From here you can take a brisk hike to the top of the now-extinct volcano believed to have given birth to St. Barts. From the peak are gorgeous views of the islands.

❼ Anse du Gouverneur. Legend has it that pirates' treasure is buried at this, one of St. Barts's most beautiful beaches. The road here from Gustavia supplies some spectacular vistas. If the weather is clear, you'll be able to see the islands of Saba, St. Eustatius, and St. Kitts from the beach.

❸ Corossol. The island's French provincial origins are most evident in this two-street fishing village with a little rocky beach. Residents speak an old Norman dialect, and some of the older women still wear traditional garb—ankle-length dresses, bare feet, and starched white sunbonnets called *quichenottes* (kiss-me-not hats). The women don't like to be photographed, but they aren't shy about selling you some of their handmade straw work—handbags, baskets, broad-brim hats, and delicate strings of birds—made from lantana palms. The palms were introduced to the island 100 years ago by foresighted Father Morvan, who planted a grove in Corossol and Flamands, thus providing the country folk with a living that survives today. Here, too, is the **Inter Oceans Museum**, with more than 7,000 seashells from around the world. ☎ 590/27–62–97. ⊠ 20F. ☉ *Daily 9–5.*

❿ Grand Cul de Sac. A winding road passes through the mangroves, ponds, and beach of Grand Cul de Sac. Here there are plenty of water-sports concessions and excellent beachside restaurants, including the West Indies Café and the ultrachic Le Lafayette Club (☞ Dining, *above*).

⑧ Grande Saline. The big salt ponds of Grande Saline are no longer in use, and the place looks a little desolate. Still, you should climb the short hillock behind the ponds for a surprise—the long arc of **Anse de Grande Saline.**

⑤ Gustavia. With just a few streets on three sides of its tiny harbor, you can easily explore all of Gustavia during a two-hour stroll. As you walk about, you'll notice that plaques sometimes spell out names in both French and Swedish, a reminder of the days when the island was a Swedish colony. You'll find excellent shopping, many restaurants, and a museum. Remember that most shops close from noon to 2, so you might want to combine shopping with lunch, perhaps at a place that overlooks the harbor.

A good spot to park your car is rue de la République, where flashy catamarans, yachts, and sailboats are moored. If you haven't gotten a map or have some questions, head to the **tourist office** on the pier, where you can pick up an island map and a free copy of *St. Barth Magazine*, a monthly publication on island happenings.

If you feel like stopping for a café au lait, a croissant, or a drink, there are several **cafés** from which to choose. Settle in at either Bar de l'Oubli or Le Select, two cafés just a few steps from each other. The former tends to attract a more American crowd, the latter a youthful French bunch shrouded in a Gauloise haze. There are also two ultracasual hangouts on the quai that have become equally popular among the young, trendy, and relatively penniless, L'Entracte and Cantina. On the "unfashionable" side of the harbor, the vibrantly colored Bistrot des Arts attracts colorful yet tony types who enjoy gazing at the harbor; the powerful, almost disturbing Creole artwork; or each other, usually over a lobster selected from the enormous aquarium.

On the far side of the harbor known as Le Pointe is the charming **Municipal Museum**, where you will find watercolors, portraits, photographs, and historic documents detailing the island's history as well as displays of the island's flowers, plants, and marine life. ☎ *599/27–89–07.* 🖾 *10F.* ☯ *Mon.–Thurs. 8:30–12:30 and 2:30–6, Fri. 8:30–12:30 and 3–6, Sat. 9–11.*

⑨ Lorient. Site of the first French settlement, Lorient is one of the island's two parishes, and a restored church, historic headstones, a school, post office, and gas station mark the spot. Lorient Beach has royal palms and rolling waves. One of St. Barthélemy's treasured secrets, **Le Manoir,** a 1610 Norman manor, was painstakingly shipped from France and reconstructed here in 1984 by the charming Jeanne Audy Rowland in tribute to the island's Viking forebears. The tranquil surrounding courtyard and garden contain a waterfall and a lily-strewn pool. Madame Rowland is no longer on the island, but the Savoyard family, who purchased the property, graciously welcomes visitors. Cramped cottages surrounding the manor are available at a very reasonable daily or weekly rate (☎ *590/27–79–27*). It helps if you speak some French.

⑥ Petite Anse de Galet. Just south of Gustavia, this quiet little plage is also known as Shell Beach because of the tiny shells heaped ankle-deep in some places.

④ St-Jean. Brimming with bungalows, bistros, and sunbathers, the ½-mi crescent of sand at St-Jean is the island's most popular beach. Windsurfers skim along the water here, catching the strong trade winds. If you walk as far west as possible, you can get a close look at the little planes taking off from the airport. For respite from the sun, cross the street near Eden Rock Hotel, and you'll find branches of Gustavia boutiques and several restaurants.

❶ Toiny coast. Over the hills beyond Grand Cul de Sac is this much-photographed coastline. Stone fences crisscross the steep slopes of Morne Vitet, one of many small mountains on St. Barts, along a rocky shore that resembles the rugged coast of Normandy.

St. Barthélemy A to Z

Arriving and Departing

BY AIRPLANE

The principal gateway from North America is St. Maarten's Juliana International Airport. Although it's only 10 minutes by air to St. Barts, the last two may take your breath away. Don't worry when you see those treetops out your window. You're just clearing a hill before dropping down to the runway of Aéroport de St-Jean (St-Jean Airport, ☏ 590/27–65–41). Flights leave at least once an hour between 7:30 AM and 5:30 PM on either **Windward Islands Airways** (☏ 590/27–61–01) or **Air St. Barthélemy** (☏ 590/27–71–90).

Air Guadeloupe (☏ 590/27–61–90) offers daily service from Espérance Airport in St. Martin as well as direct flights to St. Barts from Guadeloupe and Puerto Rico. **Air St. Thomas** (☏ 590/27–71–76) has daily flights to St. Barts from both St. Thomas and Puerto Rico.

You must reconfirm your return interisland flight, even during off-peak seasons, or you may very well lose your reservation. Be prepared to fly at a more convenient time for the airlines if they don't have enough passengers to justify a previously scheduled flight.

From the Airport: Taxis will cost anywhere from $5 for rides to nearby hotels up to $20 to hotels farthest from the airport. Since cabs are unmetered, you may be charged more if you make stops on the way. Drivers set a fare before setting out, and it's usually not negotiable. Cabs meet some flights, and a taxi dispatcher (☏ 590/27–66–31) is there sometimes, but if you plan to rent a car, which most people do, it's really easiest to do it at the airport. Many hotels offer free airport shuttles.

BY BOAT

Catamarans leave Philipsburg in St. Maarten at 9 AM daily, arriving in Gustavia's harbor around 11 AM. These are one-day, round-trip excursions (about $50, including open bar), with departures from St. Barts at 3:30 PM. If there's room, one-way passengers ($25) are often taken as well. The seas can be choppy, and seasickness is not uncommon.

Contact **Bobby's Marina** in Philipsburg (☏ 599/52–31–70) for reservations. The **St. Barth Express** (☏ 590/27–77–24) sails from Gustavia at 7:30 AM for the trip to Philipsburg (Bobby's Marina), and Marigot (Port la Royale); it leaves Marigot at 3:30 PM for the return trip (stopping at Philipsburg). **Voyageur** (☏ 590/27–77–24) offers ferry service several times between St. Barts and Marigot on weekends for 310F round-trip, 220F one-way. **White Octopus** (☏ 599/52–40–96) makes the run from Philipsburg to Gustavia at 9 AM Tuesday and Thursday–Saturday, returning at 4 PM for the same fares as for Voyageur.

Emergencies

Hospital: Gustavia Clinic (☏ 590/27–60–35 or 590/27–76–03 for the doctor on call) is on the corner of rue Jean Bart and rue Sadi Carnot. **Pharmacies:** There's a pharmacy in Gustavia on quai de la République (☏ 590/27–61–82) and one in St-Jean at the **La Savane Commercial Center** (☏ 590/27–66–61).

Festivals and Seasonal Events

In January St. Barts hosts an international collection of musicians as part of the **St. Barts Music Festival.** February brings a flood of events (feasting, dancing, music, and parades) during **Carnival** season. In late April, a weeklong **gastronomic festival** spotlights not only local cuisine, but also different regional fare and the wines of France. On July 14, **Bastille Day** is celebrated with a parade, a regatta, parties, and a fireworks display. The **Route du Rosé,** a transatlantic regatta of tall ships that sails from St-Tropez in early November is welcomed to St. Barts in December with a round of festivities.

Getting Around

CAR RENTALS

Though renting a four-wheel-drive vehicle is definitely an option, the most common—and by far the most fun—rental car is the minimoke, a small open-air vehicle with a bumper-car feel. Regardless of what type of car you rent, be sure to check its brakes before you head out. St. Barts's drivers seem to be in some kind of unending grand prix and keep their minimokes maxed out at all times. They pause for no one. Prepare yourself for cars charging every which way, making sudden changes in direction while honking wildly and backing up at astonishingly high speeds.

You'll find major rental agencies at the airport, and all accept credit cards. Check with several counters for the best price. You must have a valid driver's license to rent, and in high season there may be a three-day minimum. During peak periods, such as Christmas week and February, be sure to arrange for your car rental ahead of time. Your choices will most likely be limited to stick-shift minimokes, Suzuki Jeeps, and open-sided Gurgels (VW four-wheel-drive vehicles), which rent in season for about $50 a day (unlimited mileage and limited collision insurance). If your hotel has its own fleet of cars (and a few of them do), make arrangements to rent when you make your room reservations. Though the choice of vehicles may be limited, many hotels offer 24-hour emergency road service—something most rental companies don't offer. There are only two gas stations on the island, one near the airport and one in Lorient. They aren't open after 5 PM or on Sunday, but you can use the one near the airport with a credit card at any time. A full tank of gas will cost $13–$15.

Among the agencies at the airport are **Avis** (☎ 590/27–71–43), **Budget** (☎ 590/27–83–94), **Europcar** (☎ 590/27–73–33), and **Hertz** (☎ 590/27–71–14).

HITCHHIKING

Hitching rides is a popular, safe, legal, and interesting way to get around. It's widely practiced in the more heavily trafficked areas on the island.

MOTORBIKES

Several companies rent motorbikes, scooters, mopeds, and mountain bikes. Motorbikes go for about $30 per day and require a $100 deposit. Call **Rent Some Fun** (☎ 590/27–70–59 or 590/27–83–05) or **St. Barth Motobike** (☎ 590/27–67–89).

TAXIS

Taxis are expensive and not particularly easy to arrange, especially in the evening. There's a taxi station at the airport and another in Gustavia; from elsewhere you must contact a dispatcher (☎ 590/27–66–31 or 590/27–75–81). There's a flat rate of 25F for rides up to five minutes long. Each additional three minutes is 20F. Usually, however, cabbies name a fixed rate—and will not budge. Fares are 50% higher from 8 PM to 6 AM and on Sunday and holidays.

Guided Tours

You can arrange tours by minibus or car at hotel desks, through the tourist office, or through any of the island's taxi operators (☎ 590/27–66–31 in Gustavia; 590/27–75–81 at the airport). If you don't speak French, be sure to request a driver whose English is good; Stephane Brin (☎ 590/27–75–21) is highly recommended. A private five-hour island tour costs about $100 per vehicle (three to four people); an hour-long tour costs about $40 for up to three people and $50 for up to eight people. Itineraries are negotiable. The tourist office's three tours (about 45 minutes, 1 hour, or 1½ hours long) are less expensive (about $10 per person for the shortest one).

St. Barth's Services (☎ 590/27–56–26, FAX 590/27–56–81) can arrange customized tours as well as take care of virtually any other needs you may have, including airline ticketing, maid service, private parties, etc. Helicopter tours are offered by **Trans Helico Caraibes** (☎ 590/27–40–68) for about $65 per person.

Language

Though French is the official language (it can't hurt to pack a phrase book and/or a French dictionary), you may hear some old-timers speak the Norman patois of their ancestors (or see the older women dressed in the traditional garb of provincial France). Most hotel and restaurant employees speak some English—at least enough to help you find what you need.

Money Matters

CURRENCY

The French franc is legal tender, but U.S. dollars are accepted in most establishments (though you may receive change in francs). Figure about 5F to the U.S. dollar. Credit cards are accepted at most shops, hotels, and restaurants. Note: Prices quoted here are in U.S. dollars unless indicated otherwise.

SERVICE CHARGES, TAXES, AND TIPPING

Some hotels add a 10%–15% service charge to bills; others include it in their tariffs. Many restaurants include a 15% service charge in their published prices. It is important to remember this when your credit-card receipt is presented to be signed with the tip space blank (just draw a line through it), or you could end up paying a 30% service charge. Be sure to ask whether service is included. Most taxi drivers own their vehicles and don't expect a tip. A 10F departure tax is charged when your next stop is another French island, 16F if you're off to anywhere else.

Opening and Closing Times

Banks are generally open weekdays 8–noon and 2–3:30. The main post office, on rue du Roi Oscar II in Gustavia, is open Monday–Tuesday and Thursday–Friday 8–3, Wednesday and Saturday 8–noon. The branch in Lorient is open weekdays 7 AM–11AM and Saturday 8 AM–10 AM. The post office in St-Jean has hours Monday–Tuesday 8–2 and Wednesday and Saturday 8–noon. Stores are generally open weekdays 8:30–noon and 2–5, and Saturday 8:30–noon. Some of the shops across from the airport and in St-Jean stay open on Saturday afternoon and until 7 PM on weekdays.

HOLIDAYS

New Years Day, Easter weekend (Apr. 2–4), Labor Day (May 1), Pentecost (May 23), Bastille Day (July 14), Pitea Day (commemorates the joining of St. Barts with Pitea in Sweden; Aug. 15), All Saints' Day (Nov. 1), Armistice Day (Nov. 11), and Christmas.

Passports

U.S. and Canadian citizens need either a passport (one that expired no more than five years ago will suffice) or a notarized birth certificate with a raised seal accompanied by photo identification. A valid passport is required for stays of more than three months. British and other EU citizens need a national identity card. All visitors need a return or ongoing ticket.

Precautions

Roads are sometimes unmarked, so be sure to get a map. Instead of road signs, look for signs pointing to a destination. These will be nailed to posts at all crossroads. Roads are narrow and sometimes very steep, so check the brakes and gears of your rental car before you drive away. Some hillside restaurants and hotels have steep entranceways and difficult steps that require a bit of climbing or negotiating. If this could be a problem for you, ask about accessibility ahead of time.

Telephones and Mail

To phone St. Barts from the United States, dial 011–590 and the local six-digit number. To call the United States from St. Barts, dial 19–1, the area code, and the local number. For St. Martin, dial just the six-digit number; for St. Maarten, dial 3 plus the five-digit number. For local information, dial 12. Public telephones do not accept coins; they accept *télécartes,* a prepaid calling card that you can buy at the gas station next to the airport and at post offices in Lorient, St-Jean, and Gustavia. Making an international call using a télécarte is less expensive than making it through your hotel.

Mail is slow. It can take up to three weeks for correspondence between the United States and the island. Post offices are in Gustavia, St-Jean, and Lorient. It costs 3.10F to mail a postcard to the United States, 3.90F to mail a letter. When writing to an establishment on St. Barts, be sure to include "French West Indies" at the end of the address.

Visitor Information

You can get information by contacting the **French West Indies Tourist Board** (⊠ 610 5th Ave., New York, NY 10020, www.fgtousa.org) or by calling **France-on-Call** (☎ 900/990–0040; 50¢ per minute). Also try the **French Government Tourist Office** (⊠ 444 Madison Ave., 16th floor, New York, NY 10022; ⊠ 9454 Wilshire Blvd., Suite 303, Beverly Hills, CA 90212, ☎ 213/272–2661; ⊠ 645 N. Michigan Ave., Suite 3360, Chicago, IL 60611, ☎ 312/337–6301; ⊠ 1981 McGill College Ave., Suite 490, Montréal, Québec, H3A 2W9, ☎ 514/288–4264; ⊠ 30 St. Patrick St., Suite 700, Toronto, Ontario, M5T 3A3, ☎ 416/593–4723; ⊠ 178 Piccadilly, London W1V OAL, ☎ 0171/629–9376).

The **Office du Tourisme** (☎ 590/27–87–27, ℻ 590/27–74–47) is in a white-and-blue building on the Gustavia pier; the people who work there are eager to please and can help you out weekdays 8:30–6 and Saturday 9–noon.

19 St. Eustatius

Updated by
Karl Luntta

The old man with thick gray brows over slightly moist eyes tells his story: A few years back, an American visitor waded into the waters at Zeelandia Bay and was overwhelmed by the strong undertow. The man, then in his 70s, jumped in and pulled her out. Later that year he received a letter, on crisp White House stationery, from the president of the United States. It thanked him for his courageous act. He carries that letter with him today and every day. With calloused hands and an almost reluctant smile, he proffers it like the icon it is—an understated metaphor for his life.

The tiny Dutch island of St. Eustatius, commonly called Statia (pronounced *stay*-sha), in the Netherlands Antilles, is ideal for those with a penchant for quiet times and strolls through history. It was once one of the most powerful merchant centers in the Caribbean; today it's home to remnants of those times—forts, narrow cobblestone streets, and historic buildings. Statians themselves, a very welcoming people, are reason enough to visit. So is the landing approach: in the distance looms the Quill, an extinct volcano with a primeval rain forest in its crater.

This 12-square-mi island, past which Columbus sailed in 1493, prospered from the day the Dutch Zeelanders colonized it in 1636. In the 1700s, a double row of warehouses crammed with goods stretched 1 mi along the bay, and there were sometimes as many as 200 ships tied up at the duty-free port. The island was called the "Emporium of the Western World" and "Golden Rock." There were almost 8,000 Statians in the 1790s (today the population is about 2,100). Holland, England, and France fought over the island, which changed hands 22 times. It has been a Dutch possession, however, since 1816.

During the American War of Independence, when the British blockaded the North American coast, food, arms, and other supplies for the revolutionaries were diverted to the West Indies, notably to neutral Statia. (Benjamin Franklin had his mail routed through the island to ensure its safe arrival in Europe.) On November 16, 1776, the brig-of-war *Andrew Doria,* commanded by Captain Isaiah Robinson of the Continental Navy, sailed into Statia's port flying the Stars and Stripes. The ship fired a 13-gun salute to the Royal Netherlands standard, and Governor Johannes de Graaff ordered the cannons of Fort Oranje to return the salute. That first official acknowledgment of the new American flag by a foreign power earned Statia the nickname America's Childhood Friend. In retaliation, British admiral George Rodney attacked and destroyed much of the island in 1781. Statia has yet to recover its prosperity, which, ironically, ended partly because of the American Revolution's success: The island was no longer needed as a trans-shipment port, and its bustling economy gradually came to a stop.

Statia is in the Dutch Windward Triangle, 178 mi east of Puerto Rico and 35 mi south of St. Maarten. Oranjestad, the capital and only "city" (note quotes), is on the western side facing the calm Caribbean. On the eastern side are the oft-rough waters of the expansive Atlantic. The island is anchored at the north and the south by extinct volcanoes, like the Quill, that are separated by a central, dry plain. The higher elevations are alive with untended greenery and abloom with flowers—bougainvillea, oleander, and hibiscus.

Statia is a playground for divers and hikers. Colorful coral reefs and myriad ships rest on the ocean floor alongside 18th-century warehouses that were slowly absorbed by the sea. On land, much of the activity involves archaeology and restoration; students from William and Mary's College of Archaeology converge here each summer, the University of Leiden in the Netherlands has a pre-Columbian program, and the island's historical foundation is actively engaged in restoring local landmarks. Statia is also a way station for oil, with a 16-million-barrel storage bunker encased in the Boven, an extinct volcano on the northern end of the island. On any given day, there will be several oil tankers at anchor waiting to give or receive the liquid gold.

Most visitors will be content with a day visit from nearby St. Maarten, exploring some of the historical sights and maybe enjoying a meal. Those who stay longer tend to be collectors of unspoiled islands with a need to relax and a taste for history. Statia is mindful of the potential gold mine of tourism and is making the necessary investments to restore its many historical buildings and forts, expand its pier facilities, and improve its infrastructure. But it may be the locals who make coming here such a pleasure. Folks in these parts still say hello to strangers, and drivers wave or beep to other drivers—such a warm, friendly environment is sure to make you feel at home.

Lodging

There are no luxury accommodations on Statia; as a rule, cheerful, tidy, and homey are the best you can expect. Most of the properties include breakfast, making them quite affordable. All the hotels, and there are only four as of this writing, have 20 units or less; room decor and furnishing are eclectic but comfortable. If there's a philosophy to owning and running a hostelry on Statia, it's "do what you can with what you have." For the most part, the hotels have done well.

CATEGORY	COST*
$$$	$100–$125
$$	$75–$100
$	under $75

All prices are for a standard double room, excluding 7% room tax and 3% "turnover" tax, and 10%–15% service charge.

Hotels

$$$ 🏨 **La Maison sur la Plage.** A stay here puts you in an isolated area on the wild Atlantic whose waters slap a 2-mi gray-sand crescent. (Though the undertow for much of this strip is dangerous, a safer area is a short walk down the beach.) The cozy lobby has well-worn rattan furnishings and shelves filled with weathered books. There's a stone-and-wood bar and ☞ **La Maison sur la Plage** restaurant, which is bordered by a trellis and greenery. Owners Therese and Michel Viali are slowly redecorating the five peach-color stucco cottages with pastel-print fabrics, natural wood furnishings, and ceiling fans. Continental breakfast is served on the porch of the main building, overlooking the water. ✉ *Zeelandia Rd. (Box 157), Zeelandia,* ☎ *599/3–82256,* FAX *599/3–82831. 10 rooms. Restaurant, bar, fans, pool. D, MC, V. CP.*

$$–$$$ 🏨 **Talk of the Town.** Here five tidy cottages with red roofs and coral
★ trim surround a medium-size pool. They contain simple but bright rooms decorated with locally handcrafted furnishings, dark carpeting, wood-beam ceilings, floral spreads, and local art. All rooms have air-conditioning, gleaming white baths (shower only), cable TV, and direct-dial phones. There's a poolside deck with lounge chairs, and the on-site **Talk of the Town** restaurant serves great seafood. The hotel is on the road between the airport and town, an excellent choice for those who don't need a water view. Children under 12 stay free. ✉ *L.E. Saddlerweg, near Upper Town, Oranjestad,* ☎ *599/3–82236 or 800/223–9815 (reservations service),* FAX *599/3–82640. 17 rooms, 3 efficiencies. Restaurant, bar, air-conditioning, pool. AE, D, MC, V. EP.*

$$ 🏨 **Golden Era Hotel.** Although this harbor-front hotel is in need of some sprucing up, its rooms are air-conditioned and motel-modern, with mini-refrigerators; TVs; phones; and simple, well-worn furniture. All have little terraces, but only half have full or partial sea views; the rest look out over concrete or down onto the roof of the restaurant. The hotel's lack of aesthetic appeal is offset by its central (and waterside) location. It also attracts a cheerful clientele and has an accommodating and friendly staff. The ☞ **Golden Era Hotel** restaurant serves great Creole food. ✉ *Bay Rd., Lower Town (Box 109), Oranjestad,* ☎ *599/3–82345 or 800/ 223–9815 (reservations service),* FAX *599/3–82445. 19 rooms, 1 suite. Restaurant, bar, air-conditioning, refrigerators, saltwater pool. AE, D, MC, V. EP, MAP.*

$–$$ 🏨 **King's Well Hotel.** Perched on the cliffs between Upper Town and
★ Lower Town, this small hotel offers nine rooms, two of which are efficiencies. All guest quarters are pleasant (though sparsely furnished) and have balconies, mini-refrigerators, TVs, mosquito netting, and private baths (shower only). The four back rooms are more spacious and face the water. They also have ceiling fans and queen-size waterbeds. The owners, Win and Laura Piechutzki, an expatriate couple, hope to attract a sailing clientele; they will lease their yacht-charter license and arrange sailing lessons. They also plan to open a small health spa, with massage and skin treatments. The ☞ **King's Well Restaurant** serves breakfast (complimentary for guests), lunch, and dinner. ✉ *Bay Rd., Lower Town, Oranjestad,* ☎ FAX *599/3–82538. 9 rooms. Restaurant, bar, refrigerators. D, MC, V. BP.*

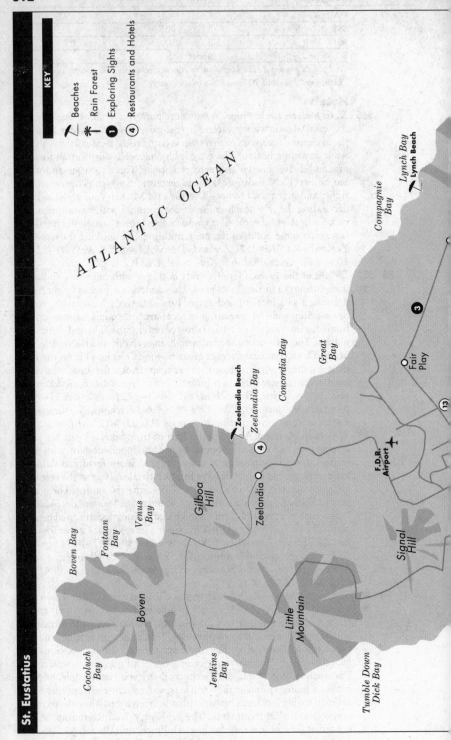

St. Eustatius

KEY

- Beaches
- Rain Forest
- ① Exploring Sights
- ④ Restaurants and Hotels

ATLANTIC OCEAN

Boven Bay

Cocoluch Bay

Fontaan Bay

Boven

Venus Bay

Jenkins Bay

Gilboa Hill

Zeelandia

Little Mountain

Tumble Down Dick Bay

Signal Hill

Zeelandia Beach

④

Zeelandia Bay

Concordia Bay

Great Bay

F.D.R. Airport

Fair Play

Compagnie Bay

Lynch Bay

Lynch Beach

③

⑬

513

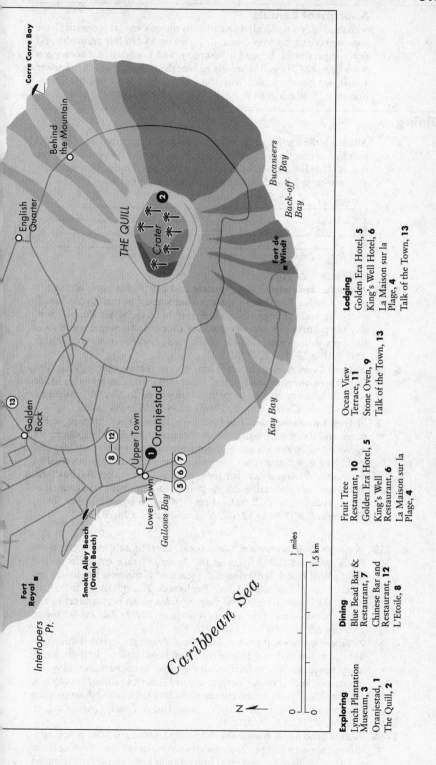

Exploring
Lynch Plantation
Museum, **3**
Oranjestad, **1**
The Quill, **2**

Dining
Blue Bead Bar &
Restaurant, **7**
Chinese Bar and
Restaurant, **12**
L'Etoile, **8**

Fruit Tree
Restaurant, **10**
Golden Era Hotel, **5**
King's Well
Restaurant, **6**
La Maison sur la
Plage, **4**

Ocean View
Terrace, **11**
Stone Oven, **9**
Talk of the Town, **13**

Lodging
Golden Era Hotel, **5**
King's Well Hotel, **6**
La Maison sur la
Plage, **4**
Talk of the Town, **13**

Apartment Rentals

Statia has only a handful of apartments, though several properties have gone up recently to meet demand. Figure on $50 or less per night, and don't expect much beyond a bathroom and kitchenette. **Country Inn** (☎ 599/3–82484), in Biesheuvelweg near the airport, is one of the newer apartment houses. Check with the tourist office (☞ Visitor Information *in* St. Eustatia A to Z, *below*) for more options.

Dining

Although the variety of cuisine available may surprise you, don't expect fine cuisine or fancy restaurants. Your best bet is to eat local-style, that is, West Indian, and keep your expectations simple. All restaurants are very casual, but do cover up your beachwear.

CATEGORY	COST*
$$$	over $25
$$	$15–$25
$	under $15

per person for a three-course meal, excluding drinks and service

CARIBBEAN/CREOLE

$–$$ ✕ **Golden Era Hotel.** The restaurant and bar of this establishment in the ☞ **Golden Era Hotel** are somewhat stark, but the Creole food is excellent, and the large dining room is right on the water. Popular Sunday-night buffets are served outside by the pool and ocean, with a local band providing entertainment. ⊠ *Bay Rd., Lower Town, Oranjestad,* ☎ *599/3–82345. AE, D, MC, V.*

$–$$ ✕ **Stone Oven.** A Spanish couple runs this cozy eatery, offering such West Indian specialties as "goat water" (goat stew). You can eat either inside the little house or outside on the palm-fringed patio. ⊠ *16A Feaschweg, Upper Town, Oranjestad,* ☎ *599/3–82543. No credit cards.*

$ ✕ **Fruit Tree Restaurant.** The Fruit Tree, named after the papaya, ba-
★ nana, and soursop trees that grow on its grounds, serves heaping plates of West Indian specialties: bullfoot soup (a stew with vegetables and beef), goat water (goat stew), *fungi* (a cornmeal resembling grainy mashed potatoes), oxtail and rice. Top it all off with johnnycakes and bush tea. There are only four tables on the patio, but you won't wait long, if at all. Next door is a small crafts shop. ⊠ *484 Prinseweg, Upper Town, Oranjestad,* ☎ *599/3–82584. No credit cards. Closed Sat.*

ECLECTIC

$$–$$$ ✕ **King's Well Restaurant.** GOOD FOOD, COLD DRINKS AND EASY PRICES reads the hand-painted sign at this breezy terrace eatery in the ☞ **King's Well Hotel.** It overlooks the sea, and is run by a fun-loving expatriate couple, Win and Laura Piechutzki. The steaks are from Colorado, the lobster is fresh, and the *rostbraten* (roast beef) and schnitzels are authentic—one of the owners is German. ⊠ *Bay Rd., Lower Town, Oranjestad,* ☎ *599/3–82538. MC, V.*

$$ ✕ **Talk of the Town.** Breakfast, lunch, and dinner are served at this pleasant restaurant in the ☞ **Talk of the Town** hotel. Pink tablecloths, hanging plants, and softly seductive calypso music in the background weave a romantic spell. Local, Continental, and American dishes are offered, with seafood (predictably) the standout. Try the curried shrimp or the filet mignon. ⊠ *L.E. Saddlerweg, near Upper Town, Oranjestad,* ☎ *599/3–82236. AE, D, MC, V.*

$–$$ ✕ **Blue Bead Bar & Restaurant.** A friendly Dutch expatriate couple runs
★ this restaurant with spectacular water views—don't miss a sunset cocktail here. Meals are served on a cheery, bright blue- and yellow-trimmed veranda decked with potted plants; the fare runs the gamut of influences: West Indian, Indonesian, Dutch, Mexican, and American. The

daily specials are recommended, as is anything made with chef-owner Phil Engeldorp's own *saté* sauce—a spicy, peanutty heaven. A steel band plays here on Saturday night; the bar swings long after the kitchen closes. ⊠ *Bay Rd., Lower Town, Oranjestad,* ☎ *599/3–82873. MC, V.*

$–$$ ✕ **Chinese Bar and Restaurant.** Owner Kim Cheng serves up tasty Asian and Caribbean dishes—*bamigoreng* (Indonesian chow mein), pork chops Creole—in hearty portions at his unpretentious establishment. Dining indoors can be claustrophobic; just ask your waitress if you may tote your Formica-top table out onto the terrace. She'll probably be happy to lend a hand and then serve you under the stars. ⊠ *Prinsesweg, Upper Town, Oranjestad,* ☎ *599/3–82389. No credit cards.*

$–$$ ✕ **L'Etoile.** West Indian dishes, such as spicy stuffed land crab and goat meat, are served at this simple snack bar–restaurant. You can also order hot dogs, hamburgers, and spare ribs. ⊠ *Heiligerweg, Upper Town, Oranjestad,* ☎ *599/3–82299. No credit cards.*

$–$$ ✕ **Ocean View Terrace.** This patio spot in the courtyard next to the tourist office serves sandwiches and burgers at lunch, and local cuisine—baked snapper with shrimp sauce, spicy chicken, tenderloin steak—at dinner (you can also get breakfast here). The courtyard is surrounded by the beautiful old stone fort and government buildings. ⊠ *Oranjestraat, Upper Town, Oranjestad,* ☎ *599/3–82733. No credit cards. No lunch Sun.*

FRENCH

$$–$$$ ✕ **La Maison sur la Plage.** The three top attractions here, in the restaurant of the ☞ **La Maison sur la Plage** hotel, are the view of the Atlantic; the French fare; and Therese, the grande dame of the place, who's ★ a kick. The chef, Michel, prepares some of the finest cuisine on the island. For dinner, start with the escargots and move on to the veal terrine with mushrooms, an herb sauce, and a pastry top, or try the lamb medallions broiled with Roquefort cheese. ⊠ *Zeelandia Rd., Zeelandia,* ☎ *599/3–82256. D, MC, V.*

Beaches

Beachcombing is for the intrepid: Statia's beaches are pristine but tiny, unmaintained, and occasionally rocky. Sand is mainly volcanic black (actually varying shades of gray). The nicest strands are on the Atlantic side, but the surf is generally too rough for swimming. You can (though it's not recommended) hike around the coast at low tide; but driving is the best way to reach remote Atlantic stretches. A big deal on the beaches here is searching for Statia's famed blue-glass beads. Manufactured in the 17th century by the Dutch West Indies Company, these beads were traded for rum, slaves, cotton, and tobacco. They were also awarded to faithful slaves or included as a part of the groom's settlement by the bride's father. Although they are found only on Statia, some researchers believe that it was beads like these that were traded for Manhattan. They're best unearthed after a heavy rain, but as the locals chuckle, "If you find one, it's a miracle, man."

A 30-minute hike down an easy, marked trail behind the Mountain Road will bring you to **Corre Corre Bay** and its gold-sand cove. Two bends north of Corre Corre Bay, **Lynch Bay** is somewhat protected from the wild swells. On the Atlantic side, especially around Concordia Bay, the surf is rough, and there's sometimes a dangerous undertow, making beaches in this area better for sunning than swimming. **Smoke Alley Beach** (also called Oranje Beach) is the nicest and most accessible. The beige-and-black-sand beach is on the Caribbean, off Lower Town, and is relatively deserted until late afternoon, when the locals arrive. **Zeelandia Beach** is a 2-mi strip of black sand on the Atlantic side. A dangerous undertow runs here, but a small section is considered okay for swimming. Plans are being made to construct a breakwater to make the area safer for swimming. As is, it's a lovely and deserted stretch for sunning, walking, and wading.

Outdoor Activities and Sports

Participant Sports

FISHING

By and large, deep-sea fishing is not a major activity off Statia's shores. But it's nice to be out on the water. **Golden Rock Dive Center** (⊠ Bay Rd., Lower Town, Oranjestad, ☎ FAX 599/3−82964) offers full- and half-day trips for $500 and $350, respectively, including gear and bait.

HIKING

Trails range from the easy to the "Watch out!" The big thrill here is the Quill, the 1,968-ft extinct volcano with its crater full of rain forest. Give yourself two to three hours to make the climb and the return. The tourist office has a list of 12 marked trails and can put you in touch with a guide (whose fee will be about $20). Wear layers: It can be cool on the summit and steamy in the interior. It's rumored that monkeys have taken up residence in the rain forest.

SCUBA DIVING AND SNORKELING

Statia has more than 30 dive sites, including **Barracuda Reef,** where barracudas swim around colorful coral walls, and **Double Wreck,** where coral has taken on the shape of the two disintegrated ships. The government is also establishing a national marine park, protected waters that will encircle the island and help preserve coral and other sea life. Park authorities will install mooring buoys, some 40 in all, for diving boats. At press time, some 14 buoys were completed. For snorkelers, **Crooks Castle** has several stands of pillar coral, giant yellow sea fans, and sea whips. **Jenkins Bay** and **Venus Bay** are other favorites. You can rent snorkeling gear for about $20 a day.

Dive Statia (⊠ Bay Rd., Lower Town, Oranjestad, ☎ 599/3−82435 or 800/883−7222 in the U.S., FAX 599/3−82539), a fully equipped and PADI-certified dive shop offering certification courses, is operated by Rudy and Rinda Hees out of a warehouse just down the road from the Old Gin House. Several hotels offer dive packages with Dive Statia. Courses are also available in underwater photography, night diving, and multilevel diving. The company also rents snorkeling gear. Statia's other dive shops are the **Golden Rock Dive Center** (⊠ Bay Rd., Lower Town, Oranjestad, ☎ FAX 599/3−82964) and **Scubaqua** (⊠ Golden Era Hotel, Bay Rd., Lower Town, Oranjestad, ☎ 599/3−82345, FAX 599/3−82160), which also rents snorkeling equipment; both are PADI facilities.

TENNIS

There are two lighted tennis courts at the **community center** (⊠ Rosemary Laan, Upper Town, Oranjestad, ☎ 599/3−82249); the center has changing rooms, but you'll have to bring your own rackets and balls. The cost is $2 per hour. Check with the tourist office (☞ Visitor Information *in* St. Eustatius A to Z, *below*) for more information. (Volleyball and basketball are also played here.)

WATERSKIING

Scubaqua (☞ Scuba Diving and Snorkeling, *above*) will take you waterskiing for $90 per hour.

Spectator Sports

Cricket and soccer matches are played at the sports complex in Upper Town. Statia hosts teams from other Caribbean islands on weekends;

admission is free. Call the office of the sports coordinator (☏ 599/3–82209) for schedules.

Shopping

Though shopping on Statia is duty-free, it is also somewhat limited. A handful of shops in Oranjestad does offer unusual items, however. Check out the **Fun Shop** (⊠ Van Tonningenweg, Upper Town, ☏ 599/3–82253) for toys and souvenirs. **Mazinga Gift Shop** on Fort Oranjestraat in Upper Town (☏ 599/3–82245) is a small department store of sorts. It has duty-free jewelry, cosmetics, and liquor, in addition to beachwear, sports gear, stationery, film, books, and magazines. The **Paper Corner** (⊠ Van Tonningenweg, Upper Town, ☏ 599/3–82208) sells magazines, a few books, and stationery supplies.

Nightlife

Nightlife on Statia is far from brisk. Local bands play around the island on weekends, and the hotels are good places to have a few quiet drinks. Sometimes the **community center** (⊠ Rosemary Laan, Upper Town, Oranjestad, ☏ 599/3–82249) holds a dance. **Cool Corner** (☏ 599/3–82523), a tiny corner bar in the heart of town, across from the St. Eustatius Historical Foundation Museum, is a lively after-work and weekend hangout. The **Exit Disco** (☏ 599/3–82543), at the Stone Oven restaurant (☞ Dining, *above*), has dancing on weekends and occasionally hosts live bands. **Talk of the Town** hotel (☏ 599/3–82236; ☞ also Lodging, *above*) is the place to be for live music on Sunday night.

Exploring St. Eustatius

Statia is an arid island consisting of a valley between two mountain peaks. Most sights lie in the valley, making touring the island easy. From the airport, you can rent a car or take a taxi and be in historic Oranjestad in minutes; to hike the Quill, Statia's highest peak, you can drive to the trailhead in less than 15 minutes from just about anywhere.

Numbers in the margin correspond to points of interest on the St. Eustatius map.

SIGHTS TO SEE

❸ **Lynch Plantation Museum.** Also known as the Berkel Family Plantation, this museum consists of two one-room buildings, set up as they were almost 100 years ago. A remarkable collection preserves this family's history—pictures, Bibles, spectacles, original furniture, and farming and fishing implements give a detailed perspective of life in Statia. Ismael Berkel guides tours of the houses, and if you ask, he may proudly show you his two medals of honor from the Dutch royal families for his conservation efforts. Be sure to sign the guest register. You'll need either a taxi or a car to visit, and it's well worth the trouble. ⊠ *Lynch Bay,* ☏ *599/3–82209 to arrange tour.* ☑ *Free (donations accepted).*

❶ **Oranjestad.** Statia's capital and only town sits on the western coast facing the Caribbean. Both Upper Town and Lower Town are easily explored on foot. History buffs will enjoy poking around the Dutch colonial buildings, which are being restored by the historical foundation. At the **tourist office**, right at the entrance to Fort Oranje, you can pick up maps, brochures, friendly advice, and a listing of 12 marked hiking trails. You can also arrange for guides and tours.

With its three bastions, **Fort Oranje** has clutched these cliffs since 1636. In 1976 Statia participated in the U.S. bicentennial celebration by restoring the old fort, and now the black cannons point out over the ramparts. In the parade grounds a plaque, presented in 1939 by Franklin D. Roosevelt, reads, HERE THE SOVEREIGNTY OF THE UNITED STATES OF AMERICA WAS FIRST FORMALLY ACKNOWLEDGED TO A NATIONAL VESSEL BY A FOREIGN OFFICIAL. The post office used to be in the fort but burned in 1991. There are plans under way to rebuild the structure to house boutiques and restaurants.

In the center of Upper Town is the award-winning **St. Eustatius Historical Foundation Museum.** It's set in the Doncker house, a lovely building with slim columns and a high gallery. British admiral Rodney set up his headquarters here during the American Revolution, while he was stealing everything from gunpowder to port in retaliation for Statia's gallant support of the fledgling country. The house, acquired by the foundation in 1983 and completely restored, is Statia's most important intact 18th-century dwelling. Exhibits trace the island's history from the 6th century to the present. The basement exhibit details Statia's pre-Columbian history with the results of archaeological digs. Statia is the only island thus far where ruins and artifacts of the Saladoid, a newly discovered tribe, have been excavated. ⊠ *3 Wilhelminaweg,* ☎ *599/3–82288.* 🖾 *$2.* ☉ *Weekdays 9–5, weekends 9–noon.*

The **Dutch Reformed church,** on Kerkweg (Church Way), was built in 1775. It has been partially restored and has lovely stone arches facing the sea. Ancient tales can be read on the gravestones in the adjacent 18th-century cemetery. On Synagogepad (Synagogue Path), off Kerkweg, is **Honen Dalim** ("She Who Is Charitable to the Poor"), one of the Caribbean's oldest synagogues. Dating from 1738, it is now in ruins but is slated for restoration.

Lower Town sits below Fort Oranjestraat (Fort Orange Street) and some steep cliffs and is reached from Upper Town on foot via the zigzagging, cobblestone Fort Road or by car via Van Tonningenweg. Warehouses and shops that, in the 18th century, were piled high with European imports are now either abandoned or simply used to store local fishermen's equipment and house Dive Statia. The **Old Gin House,** a restored 18th-century cotton mill, on the land side of Bay Road, was the best hotel on Statia but is now closed and at press time was slated to reopen under new management in the near future. The palms, flowering shrubs, and park benches along the water's edge are the work of the historical foundation members. All along the beach are the crumbling ruins of 18th-century buildings, dating from Statia's period of prosperity. The sea, which has slowly advanced since then, now surrounds many of the ruins, making for fascinating snorkeling.

❷ **The Quill.** This 1,968-ft-high extinct volcano has a primeval rain forest in its crater. Hikers will want to head here to see giant elephant ears, ferns, flowers, wild orchids, fruit trees, wildlife, and birds hiding in the trees. The volcanic cone rises 3 mi south of Oranjestad on the main road. Local boys go up to the Quill by torchlight to catch delectable sand crabs. You can join them and ask your hotel to prepare your catch for dinner. The tourist board (☞ Visitor Information *in* St. Eustatius A to Z, *below*) will make arrangements.

St. Eustatius A to Z

Arriving and Departing
BY AIRPLANE
Windward Islands Airways (☎ 599/3–82362) makes the 20-minute flight from St. Maarten to Statia's **Franklin Delano Roosevelt Airport** (☎ 599/3–82362) several times a day, the 10-minute flight from Saba

daily, and the 15-minute flight from St. Kitts twice a week. Be sure to confirm your flight a day or two ahead; schedules change abruptly.

From the Airport: Taxis meet all flights and charge about $3.50 for the drive into town. There's an Avis outlet at the airport (☞ Getting Around, *below*), should you decide to rent a car.

Electricity
Statia, like the other islands of the Netherlands Antilles, uses a 110 volt–120-volt system, the same as in North America.

Emergencies
Hospital: Queen Beatrix Medical Center (✉ 25 Prinsesweg, ☎ 599/3–82211 or 599/3–82371) has a full-time licensed physician on duty. **Police:** ☎ 599/3–82333.

Festivals and Seasonal Events
Statia celebrates **Carnival** for a week in July, and the events include parades (culminating in the Grand Carnival Parade), street parties called "jump-ups," local and imported steel-pan bands, sports activities, and food tastings. Occasionally, international music stars, such as the indomitable calypso king Mighty Sparrow from Trinidad, show up for the festivities.

Getting Around
Statia's roads are pocked with potholes, and the going is slow and bumpy. To explore the island (and there isn't very much), car rentals are available through the **Avis** (☎ 599/3–82421) outlet at the airport. **Rainbow Car Rental** (☎ 599/3–82811) has several Hyundais for rent. **Brown's** (☎ 599/3–82266) and **Walter's** (☎ 599/3–82719) rent cars and Jeeps.

Guided Tours
All 10 of Statia's taxis are available for island tours. A two- to three-hour outing costs $40 per vehicle of four (extra persons are $5 each), usually including airport transfer. One of the better taxi tour operators is driver/historian **Josser Daniel** (☎ 599/3–82358); ask him to show you his citation from President Clinton for rescuing an American tourist from drowning. You can also call **Rainbow Taxis** (☎ 599/3–82811).

The **St. Eustatius Historical Foundation Museum** (☞ Exploring, *above*) sells a sightseeing package, which includes a guided walking tour, a booklet detailing the tour sights, and museum admission. The tour begins in Lower Town at the marina and ends at the museum. You can take it on your own with the book (there are corresponding numbered blue signs on most of the sights), but a guide may prove more illuminating.

Language
Statia's official language is Dutch (it's used on government documents), but everyone speaks English. Dutch is taught as the primary language in the schools, and street signs are in both Dutch and English. Statians tend to emphasize social niceties, and everyone seems to have time for a "Good morning," or "Hello." Do the same, and you'll find it opens doors and hearts.

Money Matters
CURRENCY
U.S. dollars are accepted everywhere, but legal tender is the Netherlands Antilles florin (NAf), also referred to as the guilder, and you shouldn't be surprised to receive change in them. The exchange rate fluctuates slightly but was about NAf1.80 to US$1 at press time. Prices quoted throughout this chapter are in U.S. dollars unless noted otherwise. **Wind-**

ward Islands Bank and **Barclays Bank** are the island's two main banks; both are in Upper Town.

Hotels collect a 10%–15% service charge, which may or may not be included in the quoted rate. Most restaurants add a 10%–15% service charge. Hotels collect a 7% government tax and 3% "turnover tax." The departure tax is $5 for flights to other islands of the Netherlands Antilles and $10 to foreign destinations. In addition, you'll probably be asked to contribute your leftover guilders to the latest cause. Although your hotel or restaurant might add a 10%–15% service charge, it's customary to tip maids, waitstaff, and other service personnel, including taxi drivers. About 10% for taxi drivers should do it. Tip service workers about a dollar or two per day for hotel maids, and an extra 5%–10% for waitstaff.

Opening and Closing Times

Most **offices** (including post offices) are open weekdays 8–noon and 1–4 or 5. **Stores** are open 8–6, and grocery markets often stay open until 7. **Banks** have varying hours: Barclays Bank is open Monday–Thursday 8:30–3:30, Friday 8:30–12:30 and 2–4:30; Windward Islands Bank is open weekdays 8–noon, with extra hours on Friday, 2–4:30.

New Year's Day, Good Friday (Apr. 2), Easter Monday (Apr. 5), Coronation Day and the Queen's Birthday (April 30, celebrating both the birthday and the coronation of Holland's Queen Beatrix), Labor Day (May 1), Ascension Day (May 14), Statia–America Day (Nov. 16, commemorating the events of 1776, when Statia became the first foreign government to salute the American flag), Christmas, and Boxing Day (Dec. 26).

Passports

U.S. and Canadian visitors must have proof of citizenship. A valid passport is best, but a birth certificate with a raised seal along with a photo government-authorized photo ID will do. British citizens need a valid passport. All visitors need a return or ongoing ticket.

Precautions

Statia is relatively crime free, but common sense should prevail. Lock your rental car when leaving it, store valuables in the hotel safe, and lock your hotel room door behind you. When driving, particularly at night, be on the lookout for goats and other animals that have wandered onto the road.

Telephones and Mail

Statia has microwave telephone service to all parts of the world. To call Statia from the United States, dial 011–599/3 and the local number, which always begins with 8. Direct dial is available. There are two pay phones on the island, one near the airport and one in Landsradio. Airmail letters to North America and Europe are NAf2.25; postcards, NAf1.10.

Visitor Information

Before leaving home, you can contact the **Statia Tourist Office** (✉ Box 6322, Boca Raton, FL 33427-6322, ☎ 561/394–8580 or 800/722–2394, FAX 561/488–4294, www.turq.com/statia), which is very willing to advise you on any aspect of planning a trip to Statia.

Once on the island, the **tourist office** (✉ Fort Oranjestraat, Oranjestad, ☎ 599/3–82213, ☎ FAX 599/3–82433), at the entrance to Fort Oranje, can provide you with a map and help arrange guided tours. Office hours are Monday–Thursday 8–noon and 1–5; on Friday the office closes at 4:30.

20 St. Kitts and Nevis

Updated by
Jordan Simon

*S*everal couples—men in blazers and slacks, women in flowing cotton dresses—sip cocktails on the patio of a magnificently restored, 18th-century plantation great house. A mountain carpeted in lush rain forest towers over the building; a flawlessly green croquet lawn sweeps down to the sea. Some people sit quietly; others jabber into cell phones, checking on stocks or tots back home. It's an incongruous, anachronistic, utterly delightful scene: a Gatsbyesque party transplanted to the '90s Caribbean.

The sister islands of St. Kitts and Nevis (pronounced *nee*-vis) have developed a sibling rivalry. They're competing for increasingly upscale visitors, and it's a tight race: Both islands have uncrowded beaches; lush rain forests; historic ruins; charming, if slightly dilapidated, capitals in Basseterre (St. Kitts) and Charlestown (Nevis); and restored 18th-century plantation inns. And yet, despite their rivalry, both blissful islands have remained mellow. Though many of their guests are the well-heeled types who enjoy playing dress-up, others prefer the comfort of sandals—whatever the type, they're a self-sufficient lot. They know how to amuse themselves, and they genuinely seem to enjoy experiencing local culture. Smaller accommodations with an air of history appeal more than large modern resorts. Indeed, St. Kitts's Frigate Bay is the only area with big new hotels and condominiums; Nevis didn't even have a resort till 1991, when the Four Seasons opened.

Mountainous St. Kitts, the first English settlement in the Leeward Islands, crams some stunning scenery into its 65 square mi. (Its shape has been compared to a whale, a cricket bat, and a guitar; suffice to say it's roughly oval with a narrow peninsula trailing off toward Nevis, 2 mi southeast across the strait.) Vast, brilliant-green fields of sugarcane run to the shore. The fertile, lush island has some fascinating natural and historical attractions: a rain forest, replete with waterfalls, thick vines, and secret trails; a central mountain range, dominated by the 3,792-ft Mt. Liamuiga, whose crater has long been dormant; and Brimstone Hill, the Caribbean's most impressive fortress—known in the 17th century as the Gibraltar of the West Indies.

St. Kitts is known as the mother colony of the West Indies because it was from here that English settlers sailed to Antigua, Barbuda, Tortola, and Montserrat and French settlers dispatched colonizing parties to Martinique, Guadeloupe, St. Martin, and St. Barts. The French, who inexplicably brought a bunch of green vervet monkeys—an African species—with them as pets (the creatures now outnumber the 35,000 residents), arrived on St. Kitts a few years after the British. As rich in history as it is fertile and lush with tropical flora, St. Kitts is just beginning to develop its tourism industry. It now hosts some 60,000 overnight visitors annually—no doubt drawn by the island's rare combination of natural and historic attractions and fine sailing, island hopping, and water sports opportunities.

In 1493 when Columbus spied a cloud-crowned volcanic isle during his second voyage to the New World, he named it Nieves—the Spanish word for "snows"—because it reminded him of the snowcapped peaks of the Pyrénées. Nevis rises from the water in an almost perfect cone, the tip of its 3,232-ft central mountain smothered in clouds. Even less developed than St. Kitts, Nevis is known for its long beaches with white and black sand, for its lush greenery, for its half-dozen mineral-spa baths, and for its restored sugar plantations that now house charming inns. In 1628 settlers from St. Kitts sailed across the 2-mi channel that separates the two islands. At first they grew tobacco, cotton, ginger, and indigo, but with the introduction of sugarcane in 1640, Nevis became the island equivalent of a boomtown. As the mineral baths were drawing crowds, the island was producing an abundance of sugar. Slaves were brought from Africa to work on the magnificent estates, many of them nestled high in the mountains amid lavish tropical gardens.

Restored plantation homes that now operate as inns are true sybaritic lures. Though there's plenty of activity for the energetic—mountain climbing, swimming, tennis, horseback riding, snorkeling—the going is easy here, with hammocks for snoozing, lobster bakes on palm-lined beaches, and candlelit dinners in stately dining rooms and on romantic verandas. Each inn, run by British or American expatriates, has its own ambience, thanks to the delightful, often eccentric owners.

St. Kitts and Nevis, along with Anguilla, achieved self-government as an Associated State of Great Britain in 1967. In 1983 St. Kitts and Nevis became an independent nation. Nevis papers sometimes run fiery articles advocating independence, and the sister islands may separate someday. However, it's not likely not likely that a shot will be fired: Any war will probably be waged through ad campaigns.

ST. KITTS

Lodging

St. Kitts has an appealing variety of places to stay—beautifully restored plantation inns, full-service hotels, simple beachfront cottages, and one all-inclusive resort. There are also a number of guest houses and a few self-catering condos. Fans and breezes keep things cool, so air-conditioning in rooms is rare; of all the plantation inns, only Ottley's has air-conditioning. Also, don't expect to find much more than the basic amenities (and reasonable prices) at the hotels. The only modern chain hotel—a 200-room Hyatt in South Friar's Bay with a casino, a water sports complex, and a health club—won't be open until 2000.

CATEGORY	COST*
$$$$	over $350
$$$	$250–$350
$$	$150–$250
$	under $150

All prices are for a standard double room, excluding 7% tax and 10% service charge.

$$$$ ★ 🏨 **Golden Lemon.** Arthur Leaman, a former decorating editor for *House and Garden* magazine, created and runs this world-renowned retreat on the isolated north end. The eight rooms in the restored 17th-century great house are each impeccably decorated. There are canopied, wrought-iron and four-poster beds swaddled in mosquito netting; armoires; chaise longues; rocking chairs; and a variety of fabrics in delectable shades from mango to raspberry. You can also stay in a one- or two-bedroom town house with a wraparound terrace and kitchenette (some have a private pool). These are decorated with an eclectic yet harmonious blend of West Indian crafts, antiques, and artwork culled from Leaman's world travels. The cool, dark, well-appointed bar-lounge is a haven from the bright sun, and the ☞ **Golden Lemon** restaurant, which serves Continental cuisine with West Indian flourishes, is one of the best on the island. A gray-sand beach, guarded by rusty cannonballs and shaded by spindly, elegant palms, has views of St. Martin. (Note that this is a serene place for couples; children under 18 won't feel comfortable.) ⊠ *Dieppe Bay (Box 17),* ☎ *869/465–7260 or 800/633–7441,* ℻ *869/465–4019. 10 rooms, 22 suites. Restaurant, fans, pool, tennis court, beach, shop. AE, MC, V. MAP.*

$$$$ ★ 🏨 **Ottley's Plantation Inn.** At the foot of Mt. Liamuiga, on 35 manicured acres that border a rain forest, this former sugar plantation has views of the wild Atlantic. The 18th-century, English colonial–style great house and stone cottages hold 19 spacious guest rooms—many with high ceilings and white wood floors—decorated with white wicker, antiques, and floral-print fabrics. The cottages, with exquisite old tile and stonework and English country house decor, are honeymoon heavens. Four deluxe units, with private plunge pools or oversize hot tubs, imported Laura Ashley–style fabrics, and exquisite reproductions of colonial mahogany furniture, were added in 1997; a gradual expansion, perhaps including a tennis court and a spa, is planned over the next few years, but the property is sufficiently vast and the owners so scrupulous in their planning that the inn's intimacy—and unimpeded ocean views—will be preserved. The 65-ft spring-fed pool stretches from the remaining walls of the sugar factory and has an open-air bar at one end and the alfresco ☞ **Royal Palm** restaurant to one side. Take a stroll on the property's rain-forest trail, one of whose forks leads to a sprawling banyan tree with roots like playground slides. The engaging owners or their (grown) kids will treat you like family. There's a shuttle to the beach or town. ⊠ *Just southwest of Nicola Town (Box 345),* ☎ *869/465–7234 or 800/772–3039,* ℻ *869/465–4760. 19 rooms. Restaurant, bar, air-conditioning, in-room safes, pool. AE, MC, V. MAP.*

$$$$ ★ 🏨 **Rawlins Plantation.** On the island's northern end you'll find yet another of St. Kitts's sugar plantation inns. On 20 isolated acres at the end of a notoriously bumpy dirt access road, the views from here are spectacular: On one side, lush greenery climbs up Mt. Liamuiga; on the other side, the Caribbean Sea stretches out to the island of Statia. Ten rooms, each with a bath, are inside restored estate buildings (including the original sugar mill) throughout the lavishly landscaped grounds. Hammocks are slung between pear or almond trees, and the

524

Exploring
Basseterre, **1**
Black Rocks, **8**
Bloody Point, **2**
Brimstone Hill, **6**
Middle Island, **5**
Old Road Town, **3**
Romney Manor, **4**
Sandy Point Town, **7**

Dining
Arlecchino, **28**
Ballahoo, **24**
Chef's Place, **26**
Fisherman's Wharf, **25**
Georgian House, **29**
Golden Lemon, **10**
Mango's, **29**
Manhattan Gardens, **32**
PJ's Pizza, **16**
Patio Restaurant, **20**
Rawlins Plantation, **9**
Royal Palm, **11**
Sprat Net, **33**
Turtle Beach Bar and Grill, **17**
White House, **13**

Lodging
Bird Rock Beach Resort, **23**
Coconut Beach Club, **21**
Fairview Inn, **31**
Fort Thomas Hotel, **27**
Frigate Bay Beach Hotel, **19**
Golden Lemon, **10**
Horizons Villas Resort, **22**
Jack Tar Village Royal St. Kitts Hotel and Casino, **14**
Morgan Heights Condo Resort, **12**
Ocean Terrace Inn, **25**
Ottley's Plantation Inn, **11**
Palms Hotel, **30**
Rawlins Plantation, **9**
Rock Haven Bed and Breakfast, **18**
Sun 'n' Sand Beach Village, **15**
White House, **13**

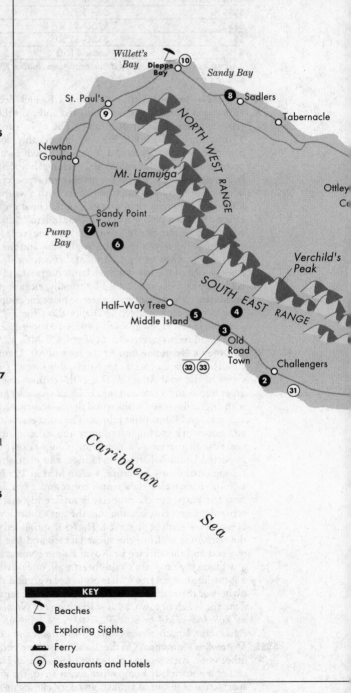

St. Kitts

KEY

⟋ Beaches
❶ Exploring Sights
⛴ Ferry
⑨ Restaurants and Hotels

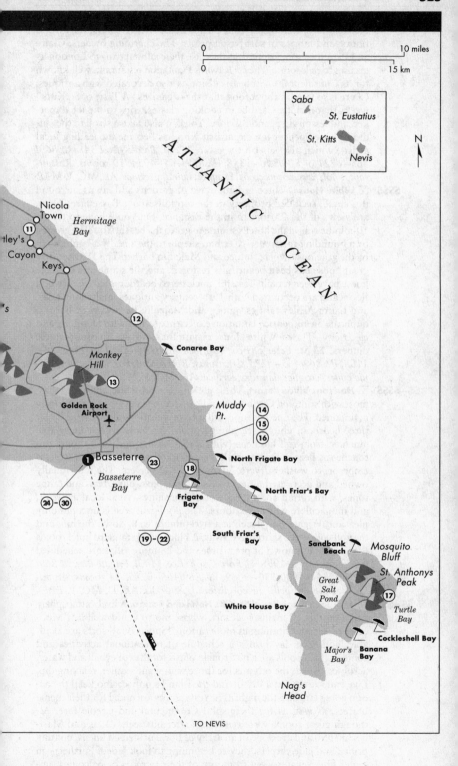

0 | 10 miles
0 | 15 km

Saba

St. Eustatius

St. Kitts

Nevis

N

A T L A N T I C   O C E A N

Nicola Town

Hermitage Bay

(11) tley's

Cayon

Keys

(12)

Conaree Bay

Monkey Hill

(13)

Muddy Pt. (14)

(15)

(16)

Golden Rock Airport

(1) Basseterre   (23)

(18)

North Frigate Bay

Basseterre Bay

Frigate Bay

North Friar's Bay

(24)-(30)

(19)-(22)

South Friar's Bay

Sandbank Beach

Mosquito Bluff

St. Anthonys Peak

(17)

Great Salt Pond

Turtle Bay

White House Bay

Cockleshell Bay

Major's Bay   **Banana Bay**

Nag's Head

TO NEVIS

plantation's original copper syrup vats pop up hither and yon. Guest quarters have mahogany four-poster beds, wicker chairs, hardwood floors, and fabrics in soft pastel prints. The charming owners, Claire and Paul Rawson, admit that they use their annual trips to London as excuses to redecorate. The ☞ **Rawlins Plantation** restaurant, well-known for its Continental-Caribbean cuisine, is also decorated with antiques. Claire is so fanatic about food that she organizes "A Taste of St. Kitts" weeks that include Caribbean cooking classes, trips to the local market, and lessons in island folklore. You can also take a stroll to the studio of Kate Spencer (an expat Brit who has become the leading local artist), which also sits on the estate. ⊠ *St. Paul's (Box 34),* ☎ *869/ 465–6221 or 800/346–5358,* ℻ *869/465–4954. 10 rooms. Restaurant, pool, fans, tennis court, croquet, laundry service. AE, MC, V. MAP.*

$$$$ 🏨 **White House.** Three radiant acres of gardens and lawns surround this small, secluded property in the foothills above Basseterre. There are views of the Caribbean in the distance, but you'll have to take a 10-minute ride in the hotel's shuttle to get to the beach. You'll be greeted by a bounding rottweiler–German shepherd (he's really a lamb), then by the gracious owners, Janice and Malcolm Barber. The 18th-century great house has been beautifully restored, and the stable and carriage house have been rebuilt. Tasteful, uncluttered bedrooms have hardwood floors and are decorated with 19th-century antiques, mahogany beds, and Laura Ashley fabrics. Janice and Malcolm have worked hard to duplicate an authentic plantation experience (albeit with plumbing and electricity). The ☞ **White House** restaurant serves creative four-course dinners. ⊠ *St. Peter's (Box 436),* ☎ *869/465–8162 or 800/223– 1108,* ℻ *869/465–8275. 10 rooms. Restaurant, bar, fans, pool, tennis court, croquet, laundry service. AE, MC, V. MAP.*

$$–$$$$ 🏨 **Horizons Villas Resort.** These gleaming coral-white-and-jade villas, most with stunning Caribbean and/or Atlantic views, are meticulously maintained. The one-bedroom villas have enormous terraces; the larger three-bedroom units have plunge pools. All have every conceivable amenity, from full kitchens (with a dishwasher and such thoughtful touches as beer mugs left in the freezer); to bathtubs fit for a Roman emperor; to washer-dryers, VCRs, and CD players. The individually owned and decorated units favor soothing pink, olive, teal, and taupe tones, with rattan and blond-wood furnishings, vivid local artwork, and immaculate white-tile floors. The pool-grill area is uncommonly pleasant, Frigate Bay Beach is a two-minute walk down the hill, and the golf course is a short drive away. A block of 24 standard hotel rooms (decor was unknown at press time) and 28 more villas are scheduled for completion in 1998. ⊠ *Fort Tyson (Box 1143), Frigate Bay,* ☎ *869/ 465–0584 or 800/830–9069,* ℻ *869/465–0785. 24 rooms, 46 villas. Restaurant, grill, air-conditioning, 2 pools. AE, D, MC, V. EP.*

$$–$$$ 🏨 **Jack Tar Village Royal St. Kitts Hotel and Casino.** A lively atmosphere pervades this all-inclusive resort, whose motto could well be "Moderate prices, but nothing in moderation." Sports of all sorts are available, and each day brings a schedule of recreational activities and contests. Two pools are a nice touch: one is for the volleyball and water-aerobics crowd, the other is for those who want a quiet, relaxing dip. Live entertainment, a disco, and the island's only casino keep the action going late into the night. The restaurants are noted for their theme buffets, as well as for their solid Continental and Creole fare. Although guest rooms were renovated after hurricanes Luis and Marilyn in 1996 and are done in an array of floral or striped linens, boating prints, and jade carpets, they're beginning to look faded. Further, you won't find a water view from any of their terraces or balconies (unless you count water hazards on the golf course or slivers of ocean from some top-floor quarters). Still, if all you want is an occasionally rowdy, hassle-free week in the sun, the bill for billeting and bill-of-fare here will be low indeed. ✉ *Frigate Bay (Box 406)*, ☎ *869/465–8651 or 800/858–2258 (reservations service)*, ℻ *869/465–1031. 240 rooms, 2 suites. 2 restaurants, 3 bars, air-conditioning, in-room safes, 2 pools, beauty salon, massage, spa, 18-hole golf course, 4 tennis courts, aerobics, basketball, health club, Ping-Pong, shuffleboard, volleyball, dive shop, snorkeling, windsurfing, boating, waterskiing, shops, casino, nightclub, baby-sitting, car rental. AE, D, DC, MC, V. All-inclusive.*

$$ ▦ **Bird Rock Beach Resort.** On a bluff above its own poky beach, a few miles from the airport and downtown, this rather plain resort consists of several two-story buildings. Though ordinary and somewhat worn, the rooms are still satisfactory with tile-floors, rattan and wicker furniture, floral fabrics, and paintings of birds. All have balconies and ocean views; suites also have kitchenettes and sofa beds. An informal, alfresco dining room turns out Continental favorites with local ingredients. Golf and the larger Frigate Bay beaches are just five minutes away (there's a shuttle), but there are exceptional snorkeling and diving opportunities in the waters off the resort's recently expanded golden-sand cove. The staff is hospitable, and the mix of young Europeans on a budget and divers from around the world gives Bird Rock an international flavor. ✉ *Basseterre Bay (Box 227, Basseterre)*, ☎ *869/ 465–8914 or 800/621–1270 (reservations service)*, ℻ *869/465–1675. 38 units. Restaurant, 2 bars, grill, air-conditioning, fans, 2 pools, tennis court, beach, dive shop, shop. AE, DC, MC, V. EP, MAP.*

$$ ▦ **Sun 'n' Sand Beach Village.** Families are drawn to this simple complex on an Atlantic beach. Studios in two-story buildings and two-bedroom units in Antillean-style wood-and-stucco cottages stretch back from the shore. In 1997 guest quarters were given fresh coats of paint and new fabrics. Decor is simple: rattan furnishings, island prints and batiks, and beige-tile floors. Studios have twin or queen-size beds, a bath (with a shower), a kitchenette, and a terrace. Cottages have ceiling fans and sofa beds in their living rooms, full kitchens, and air-conditioners in their bedrooms. In early 1998, 16 oceanfront rooms were added; each is striking with white tile floors, rattan furnishings, and green color schemes. Other additions include a new reception area; a conference room; and a handsome restaurant with cedar shingles, cathedral ceilings, and trellises that crawl with bougainvillea. ✉ *Frigate Bay (Box 341)*, ☎ *869/465–8037 or 800/223–6510*, ℻ *869/465–6745. 16 rooms, 32 studios, 18 2-bedroom cottages. Restaurant, bar, grocery, air-conditioning, pool, wading pool, 2 tennis courts, beach, shop, meeting room. AE, D, MC, V. CP, MAP.*

$–$$ ▦ **Coconut Beach Club.** The management is attentive and friendly at this casual hotel. Simple beige-stucco buildings hold comfortable, adequately furnished rooms and suites. Larger units have kitchens and multiple bedrooms. Opt to stay in one of the original buildings; they're right on the beach and are larger and airier and have better views than recent additions. New owners promise major redecorations, but since the units are time-share condos, this may take time. Still, a few cosmetic changes have gone a long way toward sprucing things up: You'll now find fashionable canary-yellow facades, blue-stripe awnings reminiscent of St. Tropez, lush landscaping, and a renovated beachfront restaurant. You can choose from a variety of sports activities here, and fees for the nearby golf course are included in the rates. ✉ *Frigate Bay (Box 1158)*, ☎ *869/465–8597 or 800/777–1700 (reservations service)*, ℻ *869/465– 7085. 60 rooms. Restaurant, bar, air-conditioning, pool, golf privileges, beach, snorkeling, windsurfing, boating, shop. AE, MC, V. EP.*

$–$$ ▦ **Fort Thomas Hotel.** This hotel, popular with business travelers and tour groups, is on the site of an old fort. Unfortunately, the cannons anchoring the driveway and a few ramparts near the pool are the only reminders of its storied past. The building resembles an antiseptic motel, though this look is somewhat softened by such "colonial" touches as gingerbread trim and arched picture windows. The spacious rooms are done in seashell colors and have wicker furnishings. There are terrific views of Basseterre and/or the coast from the second-floor rooms, the pool area, the porch swings, and the gingerbread gazebos. Service is friendly but lackadaisical. There's a free shuttle bus to the Frigate Bay beaches, and the town and the stores at Pelican Mall are within walking distance. ⊠ *Basseterre (Box 407) ,* ☎ *869/465–2695,* FAX *869/465–7518. 64 rooms. Restaurant, bar, pizzeria, air-conditioning, pool, shop, recreation room. AE, D, MC, V. EP, MAP.*

$–$$ ⊡ **Frigate Bay Beach Hotel.** The third fairway of the island's golf course adjoins this property (a stay here gets you discounts on greens fees), and you can reach the two nearby beaches—Caribbean and Atlantic—by complimentary shuttle buses (you can also take a path from the far end of the pool to the Caribbean beach). The whitewashed buildings house standard rooms as well as condos with full kitchens. There are hillside and poolside units; the latter have nicer views and fresher ambience but tend to be noisier. All accommodations have ceiling fans, beige- or navy-tile floors, floral linens, sailing prints, and sliding glass doors that open onto a terrace or balcony; older rooms are more appealing and slightly larger. There's a pool with a swim-up bar; a restaurant overlooks the pool area and is the site of raucous buffet theme nights with live music and decent Caribbean/Continental food. ⊠ *Frigate Bay (Box 137, Basseterre),* ☎ *869/465–8935 or 800/468–3750 (reservations service),* FAX *869/465–7050. 64 rooms. Restaurant, bar, fans, pool. AE, D, MC, V. EP, MAP.*

$–$$ ⊡ **Ocean Terrace Inn.** OTI, as the locals call it, is a stylish, intimate
★ hotel with many amenities for business travelers—a rarity on St. Kitts. The main building—which has several rooms, a fancy restaurant, and a pool with a swim-up bar—is atop a hill overlooking the ocean and amid lovingly tended gardens. One- and two-bedroom condos farther down the hill also have water views. Down on the waterfront, ☞ **Fisherman's Wharf** is a casual seafood restaurant. All rooms are handsomely decorated in rattan and bright fabrics. To create a more upscale image, new owners began to renovate and expand in 1997. Some touches are thoughtful: hair dryers in all the rooms, a concierge, and turndown service in some rooms. Other changes threaten the hotel's cozy appeal: formerly distinctive bar areas with murals of cavorting dancers and drummers have been replaced by yo-ho-hum nautical themes and screeching parrots. There's now a free-form pool (with a waterfall), a business center, a third restaurant, and a dizzying array of new guest rooms. Work continues on 23 luxury junior suites (slated for completion in 1998), which have maple paneling, beige-tile floors, and yellow and blue fabrics. The on-site marina has a fleet of boats for rent or charter, and there's a shuttle to nearby beaches. ⊠ *Bay Rd. (Box 65, Basseterre),* ☎ *869/465–2754 or 800/524–0512,* FAX *869/465–1057. 73 units. 3 restaurants, 2 bars, air-conditioning, 3 pools, outdoor hot tub, dock, windsurfing, boating, waterskiing, shops. AE, D, MC, V. EP, MAP.*

$ ⊡ **Fairview Inn.** The main building of this quiet, simple inn is an 18th-century great house, with graceful white verandas and Asian rugs on hardwood floors. The cottages lack ocean views, but Mt. Liamuiga towers in the distance. The owner's son, Adrian Lamb, has taken over management and completely renovated the rooms. Though they lack period flair, they're comfortable. Each has a wood ceiling, white-tile floors, wicker furnishings, and light pastel or floral fabrics. Some, like Room 11, are built into original foundations and have partial fieldstone walls and a little more atmosphere. Yellow allemanda climbs the trellises surrounding the pool, where tables face the the mountain or the sea. The dining room serves authentic island fare—marvelous baked chicken in Creole sauce, curries, and such specials as goat stew or *rotis* (sort of an East Indian burrito). ⊠ *Off Old Town Rd., 7 mi northwest of Basseterre (Box 212, Basseterre),* ☎ *869/465–2472 or 800/223–9815,* FAX *869/465–1056. 15 rooms. Restaurant, bar, air-conditioning, fans, refrigerators, pool. AE, D, MC, V. EP, MAP.*

$ ⚇ **Morgan Heights Condo Resort.** There's a laid-back atmosphere at this complex along the Atlantic (it's a shuttle ride to the beach) and 10 minutes from Basseterre, that makes the "resort" recently added to its name seem a bit of a stretch. Rooms are clean and comfortable, with simple, contemporary white-wicker furniture; ceramic tile floors; and covered patios with water views. The buildings are along a main highway and can be somewhat noisy during the day. The Atlantic Club serves excellent local cuisine and piña coladas with a punch. ⊠ *On coastal rd. just northwest of Conaree Bay Beach (Box 536, Basseterre),* ☎ *869/465–8633,* FAX *869/465–9272. 15 units. Restaurant, air-conditioning, kitchenettes, pool. AE, D, MC, V. EP.*

$ ⚇ **Palms Hotel.** This all-suites hotel has a prime location right in the Palms Arcade in Basseterre. Units have coral and teal color schemes, bright throw rugs, pastel floral linens, and art deco–style fixtures. In-room amenities include cable TVs, refrigerators, coffeemakers, and phones. Drawbacks? The hotel hasn't been renovated since its construction in 1990 (the rooms, although still pleasant, are beginning to fray at the edges), the nearest beach is a 10-minute drive, and the central location means it can be rather noisy (don't stay here during Carnival or other major festivals if you crave peace). ⊠ *The Circus (Box 64, Basseterre),* ☎ *869/465–0800,* FAX *869/465–5889. 10 units. Bar, air-conditioning, refrigerators, shops. AE, MC, V. EP, MAP.*

$ ⚇ **Rock Haven Bed and Breakfast.** Judith and Keith Blake have converted their stylish gingerbread house, just 2 minutes' drive from Frigate Bay beaches, into a relaxing, homey B&B. The stunning living and dining rooms have carved mahogany doors, crystal chandeliers, English rugs, straw mats, and hardwood floors. There are two units, both with cable TV, ceiling fans, and iron beds draped with mosquito netting. The larger one is more basic, but has a full kitchen, a private patio, and a separate entrance. The vast, breezy terrace is lovely, with a terra-cotta floor, white-wicker chaise longues, and majestic sea views. Judith prepares sumptuous breakfasts of banana pancakes, Spanish omelets, fried plantains, and pumpkin fritters. Islander's also cherish her homemade ice cream, which she purveys to the supermarkets. ⊠ *Frigate Bay (Box 821),* ☎ FAX *869/465–5503. 2 units. Fans, laundry service. No credit cards. BP.*

Dining

St. Kitts restaurants range from funky beachfront bistros to elegant plantation dining rooms; there's a variety of cuisine to sample, most tinged with the flavors of the Caribbean. Many restaurants offer West Indian specialties such as curried mutton, pepper pot (a stew of vegetables, tubers, and meats), and Arawak chicken (seasoned and served with rice and almonds on breadfruit leaf).

What to Wear

Throughout the island dress is casual at lunch (but no bathing suits). Dinner, although not necessarily formal, definitely calls for long pants and sundresses.

CATEGORY	COST*
$$$$	over $40
$$$	$30–$40
$$	$20–$30
$	under $20

per person for a three-course meal, excluding drinks and service; excluding sales tax on Nevis; there's no sales tax on St. Kitts

CARIBBEAN/CREOLE

$ ✕ **Chef's Place.** Two things seem to be the draw at this restaurant in a charmingly dilapidated 19th-century house: inexpensive West Indian meals and eavesdropping opportunities (the clientele runs toward local cops, cabbies, and middle-level government workers). Try the St. Kitts version of jerk chicken (moister than usual) or the goat stew. The best seats are outside on the wide, white veranda. ⊠ *Upper Church St., Basseterre,* ☎ *869/465–6176. No credit cards. Closed Sun.*

$ ✕ **Manhattan Gardens.** Even the gingerbread exterior of this 17th-century Creole house looks appetizing, painted as it is in tangerine, teal, and peach. Inside is homey, with batik hangings, lace tablecloths, and wood carvings. The garden in back overlooks the sea and comes alive for Saturday's Caribbean Food Fest and Sunday's brunch and barbecue. The regular menu includes such island fare as lobster in lemon butter and wahoo in Creole sauce; specials might consist of goat water (goat stew), souse (pickled pigs' trotters), jerk, and salt fish. ⊠ *Old Road Town,* ☎ *869/465–9121. No credit cards. No dinner Sun.*

$ ✕ **Sprat Net.** This simple cluster of picnic tables, sheltered by a brilliant turquoise, corrugated-tin roof and decorated with driftwood and fish nets, is on a strip of sand that just barely qualifies as a beach. Nonetheless, it is one of the hottest spots on St. Kitts. There's nothing fancy on the menu: just grilled fish, lobster, and meats—served with mountains of cole slaw and peas and rice. But the fish is amazingly fresh: The fishermen-owners heap their catches on a center table, where you choose your own dinner, just as if you were at market, and then watch it grilled to your specification. ⊠ *Old Road Town,* ☎ *no phone. No credit cards. Closed Sun. No lunch.*

$ ✕ **Turtle Beach Bar and Grill.** Simple but scrumptious cuisine has made this a popular daytime watering hole. Treats include honey-mustard ribs, coconut-shrimp salad, and grilled lobster. Business cards and pennants from around the world plaster the bar, and the room is decorated with colorful crusted bottles dredged from the deep; ships' lanterns; conch shells; and painted wooden fish, lobsters, and toucans. You can snorkel here; spot monkeys and hawksbill turtles; schedule a deep-sea fishing trip, or rent a kayak, Windsurfer, or mountain bike. On Sunday night, locals come for dinner, dancing, and volleyball. ⊠ *Turtle Beach (south end of South East Peninsula Rd.; look for signs),* ☎ *869/469–9086. AE, MC, V. No dinner Mon.–Sat.*

CONTEMPORARY

$$$$ ✕ **Golden Lemon.** Arthur Leaman creates the recipes for the West In-
★ dian, Continental, and American dishes served in the restaurant of his ☞ **Golden Lemon** hotel. The evening begins with cocktails and hors d'oeuvres on the flagstone patio amid bougainvillea and ferns and beneath a turquoise-and-yellow-stripe awning. Afterward, a set, three-course dinner is served in a tasteful room with crystal chandeliers, white rattan furnishings, antiques, and arched doorways that welcome the breezes. Longtime Kittitian chef Trevor Browne might tempt you with a breadfruit puff in a peanut sauce, grilled snapper with eggplant and sweet-pepper relish, or baked chicken in an orange and white wine sauce. The patio is a popular spot for Sunday brunch with such offerings as

banana pancakes, and beef stew made with rum. ✉ *Dieppe Bay,* ☎ *869/465–7260. Reservations essential. AE, MC, V.*

$$$$ ✕ **Rawlins Plantation.** The lovely dining room of the ☞ **Rawlins Plan-**
★ tation inn has fieldstone walls and high-vaulted ceilings. The fixed-price, four-course dinner ($45 per person) changes nightly but always emphasizes local ingredients. Dishes may include christophene or pumpkin-and-coconut soup, smoked snapper and watercress salad, shrimp ceviche with coriander and sour oranges, or lobster in puff pastry with tarragon sauce. The guava and lime parfaits and chocolate terrine with passion-fruit sauce are delicious. The bountiful lunch buffet ($25) offers such items as breadfruit salad, flying-fish fritters, and *bobote* (ground beef, eggplant, spices, curry, and homemade chutney). ✉ *St. Paul's,* ☎ *869/465–6221. Reservations essential. AE, MC, V.*

$$$$ ✕ **Royal Palm.** Set beside the pool at ☞ **Ottley's Plantation Inn,** this
★ is a restaurant to experience at night, under the latticed roof, gazing across manicured lawns to the lights of the elegant great house. The menu is an eclectic mix of American regional fare with a French gloss and Caribbean ingredients. You might start your four-course feast with egg rolls with coconut and mango relish or butternut-squash soup perfumed with cumin, then segue into shrimp in phyllo with sun-dried tomato and rosemary cream; Brie-crusted filet mignon in sauce *marchand du vin* (a reduction); or seared tuna with creamy garlic leek sauce. For dessert, try banana fritters *l'antillaise* (spiced and fried in rum) or mango mousse with raspberry sauce. This is the island's merriest dining spot, in no small part due to co-owners Art and Ruth Keusch; their daughters Karen and Nancy; and Nancy's husband, Marty. Art serenades diners with a twinkle in his eye while Ruth comically rolls her eyes. The combination of superb food, artful presentation, and warm bonhomie is unbeatable. ✉ *Just southwest of Nicola Town,* ☎ *869/ 465–7234. Reservations essential. AE, D, MC, V.*

$$$$ ✕ **White House.** At the ☞ **White House** inn, you can enjoy lunch on the garden terrace or a romantic dinner, complete with candlelight and crystal, in the elegant, antiques-filled dining room. Each night the chef prepares a four-course dinner that may include pumpkin or crab soup, Cornish game hen with banana stuffing, or fresh broiled local seafood. Many of the ultrafresh ingredients are cultivated in owner Janice Barber's gardens. Afternoon tea is also served. ✉ *St. Peter's,* ☎ *869/ 465–8162. Reservations essential. AE, MC, V.*

$$$ ✕ **Patio Restaurant.** In their flower-filled home, sixth-generation Kittitians Joan and Peter Mallalieu and their staff (dressed in colorful Creole madras frocks) prepare a full à la carte menu with complimentary wine and liqueur. Try the superlative Black Angus steak, New Zealand rack of lamb in mango mint glaze, or lobster tail stuffed with crab and mushrooms. Piña colada *gâteau* (cake), chocolate mousse pie, homemade tropical-fruit ice creams (guava, soursop, ginger), and passion fruit sorbet make tempting desserts. ✉ *Frigate Bay Beach,* ☎ *869/465– 8666. Reservations essential. MC, V. Closed May–Oct.*

$–$$$ ✕ **Georgian House.** Janice and Malcolm Barber, owners of the ☞
★ **White House** inn and restaurant, took over and reinvigorated this once-tired institution. Inside this brick-and-fieldstone town house (circa 1750), everything is "just so"—gorgeous parquet floors, Bernadaud and Wedgwood china, crisp white tablecloths, candles in glass vases, huge floral arrangements, high-back mahogany chairs. The fare is equally elegant; the menu changes weekly, but among the signature dishes are conch scallopini, a near perfect rack of lamb, and snapper in a shrimp and sesame sauce. The prices aren't stratospheric, given the quality and refined atmosphere; even the wine list is carefully considered and reasonably priced. The courtyard ☞ **Mango's** restaurant—serving more

casual fare—has a bar. ✉ *S. Independence Sq., Basseterre,* ☎ *869/465–4049. AE, MC, V. Closed Sun. No lunch.*

ECLECTIC

$–$$ ✗ **Ballahoo.** This second-floor terrace restaurant, in the heart of downtown, draws a crowd for breakfast, lunch, and dinner. Lilting calypso and reggae on the sound system, whirring ceiling fans, potted palms, and colorful island prints create the appropriate tropical ambience. Specialties include conch simmered in garlic butter, madras beef curry, lobster and shrimp in a light creamy sauce, and (it's true) a rum-and-banana toasted sandwich. Go at lunchtime when you can watch the bustle of the Circus and the prices for many dishes are slashed nearly in half. ✉ *Fort St., Basseterre,* ☎ *869/465–4197. AE, MC, V. Closed Sun.*

$–$$ ✗ **Mango's.** Set in the tranquil stone courtyard of the ☞ **Georgian House** restaurant and seemingly part of the luxuriant garden, is this cheery eatery. The menu runs the gastronomic gamut from enchiladas and burgers to focaccia and Thai shrimp coconut curry. By all means, try the definitive conch fritters and goat cheese in phyllo parcels. Even the island's chefs repair here for a drink at the hopping bar. ✉ *Independence Sq., Basseterre,* ☎ *869/465–4049. AE, MC, V. Closed Sun.*

ITALIAN

$ ✗ **Arlecchino.** Whether it's afternoon or evening, bypass the nondescript interior and head straight for the shaded, breezy courtyard of this trattoria. Enjoy the fantastic minestrone, fresh pastas (try the spaghetti in conch sauce), creative pizzas (the picante is as hot as its name promises; the tropical, with pineapples, refreshing), veal parmigiana, or swordfish *pizzaiola* (with tomato, basil, and mozzarella); top off the meal with the best cappuccino and cannoli on St. Kitts. ✉ *Cayon St., Basseterre,* ☎ *869/465–9927. AE, MC, V. Closed Sun.*

$ ✗ **PJ's Pizza.** "Garbage pizza" may not sound appetizing, but this pie—topped with everything but the kitchen sink—is a favorite. You can also choose from 10 other pizzas or create your own. Sandwiches and Italian standards are also served (lasagna is a specialty). Finish your meal with delicious, moist rum cake. This casual spot, bordering the golf course and open to cooling breezes, is always boisterous. ✉ *Frigate Bay,* ☎ *869/465–8373. AE, MC, V. Closed Mon. and Sept.*

SEAFOOD

$–$$ ✗ **Fisherman's Wharf.** Part of the **Ocean Terrace Inn** (head straight rather than up the hill to the hotel's main building), this extremely casual waterfront eatery is decorated in swaggering nautical style, with rustic wood beams, rusty anchors, cannons, and buoys. Try the excellent conch chowder, followed by fresh grilled lobster or other shipshape seafood, and finish off your meal with a slice of the memorable banana cheesecake. The tables are long, wooden affairs, and it's generally lively, especially on weekend nights. ✉ *Fortlands, Basseterre,* ☎ *869/465–6623. AE, MC, V. No lunch.*

Beaches

The powdery white-sand beaches, free and open to the public (even those occupied by hotels), are in the Frigate Bay area or on the lower peninsula. Two of the island's best are the twin beaches of **Banana Bay** and **Cockleshell Bay,** which cover more than 2 mi at the southeastern tip of the island. Several large hotels, including the Banana Bay and Casablanca, were abandoned in the early stages of development—their skeletal structures marring an otherwise idyllic scene.

Conaree Bay on the Atlantic side is a narrow strip of gray-black sand where the water is good for body surfing. Snorkeling and windsurfing are good at **Dieppe Bay,** a black-sand beach on the north coast, home of the Golden Lemon hotel.

Locals consider the Caribbean (southern) side of **Friar's Bay** the island's finest beach, although construction of the new Hyatt through 1999 will spoil its idyllic tranquillity. You can haggle with fishermen here to take you snorkeling off the eastern point. The waters on the Atlantic (northern) side are rougher, but the beach has a wild, desolate beauty. **Frigate Bay,** on the Caribbean, has talcum-powder-fine sand, while on the Atlantic side, its 4-mi-wide stretch is a favorite with horseback riders.

A tiny dirt road, virtually impassable after heavy rains, leads to **Sandbank Beach,** a long, taupe crescent on the Atlantic. The shallow coves are protected here, making it ideal for families, and it's usually deserted. **White House Bay** is rocky, but the snorkeling, taking in several reefs surrounding a sunken tugboat, is superb.

Outdoor Activities and Sports

BOATING

Most operators are on Frigate Bay, which is known for its gentle currents. Turtle Bay offers stronger winds and stunning views of Nevis. **Tropical Surf (a.k.a. Turtle Tours)** (✉ Turtle Bay, ☎ 869/469–9086) rents Sunfish, Hobie Cats, surfboards, kayaks, and boogie boards. **Mr. X Watersports** (✉ Frigate Bay, ☎ 869/465–4995) rents a variety of small craft, including motorboats.

FISHING

The waters surrounding St. Kitts aren't renowned for their big gamefish. Still, you can angle for yellowtail snapper, wahoo, mackerel, tuna, dolphinfish, shark, and barracuda with **Turtle Tours** (☞ Boating, *above*) and **Captain Redbeard Boat Charters** (☎ 869/465–0482).

GOLF

The **Royal St. Kitts Golf Club** (✉ Frigate Bay, ☎ 869/465–8339) is an 18-hole, par 72, 6,918-yard championship course. Greens fees are $35 for 18 holes, $25 for 9; cart rentals are $30 for 9 holes, $40 for 18. Despite some attractive palm-lined fairways and a few strategically placed water hazards and sand traps, avid golfers may be disappointed by the course. It's rarely challenging and has surprisingly undramatic water views, and greens that aren't as immaculate as they should be.

HIKING

Trails in the central mountains vary from easy to don't-try-it-by-yourself. Monkey Hill and Verchild's Peak aren't difficult, although the Verchild's climb will take the better part of a day. Don't attempt Mt. Liamuiga without a guide. You'll start at Belmont Estates on horseback, then proceed on foot to the lip of the crater, at 2,600 ft. You can go down into the crater, clinging to vines and roots. Tour rates range from $35 for a rain forest walk to $60 for a volcano expedition.

Addy of **Addy's Nature Tours** (☎ 869/465–8069) offers picnic lunch and cold drinks during treks through the rain forest; she also discusses the history and folklore surrounding native plants. **Greg Pereira** (☎ 869/465–4121), whose family has lived on St. Kitts for well over a century, takes groups on half-day trips into the rain forest and on full-day hikes up the volcano and through the grounds of a private 250-year-old great house, followed by excursions down canyons and past petroglyphs. He and his staff relate fascinating historical, folkloric, and botanical insights and serve refreshing fruit juices (with CSR [Cane Spirit Rothschild], the local firewater). **Kriss Tours** (☎ 869/465–4042) takes small groups into the crater, through the rain forest, and to Dos d'Anse

Pond on Verchild's Mountain. **Oliver Spencer's Off the Beaten Track**
(☎ 869/465–6314) leads treks to ruins of an abandoned coffee plantation taken over by sprawling banyan trees.

HORSEBACK RIDING

Wild North Frigate Bay and desolate Conaree Beach are great for riding. Guides from **Trinity Stable** (☎ 869/465–3226) will lead you into
the hills at a leisurely gait. **Royal Stables** (☎ 869/465–2222) offers sunset beach rides and trips into the rain forest.

SCUBA DIVING AND SNORKELING

St. Kitts has more than a dozen excellent dive sites. Coconut Tree Reef,
one of the largest in the area, includes sea fans, sponges, and anemones.
Black Coral Reef features the rare black coral tree. Brassball Wreck is
a shallow-water wreck, good for snorkeling and photography. The extensive reef at Redonda Bank is just beginning to be explored. At shallow Tug Boat snorkelers will spot everything from gliding rays to
darting grunts and jacks. Bloody Bay Reef is noted for its network of
underwater grottoes daubed with purple anemones, sienna bristle
worms, and canary-yellow sea fans that seem to wave you in.

Kenneth Samuel of Kenneth's Dive Centre (☎ 869/465–7043 or 869/
466–5320) is a PADI-certified dive master who takes small groups of
divers with C-cards to nearby reefs. Rates average $40 for single tank
dives, $60–$65 for double tank dives. **Auston MacLeod**, a PADI-certified dive master–instructor and owner of Pro-Divers (☎ 869/465–
3223), offers resort and certification courses. **Mr. X Watersports** (✉
Frigate Bay, next to Monkey Bar, ☎ 869/465–0673) arranges various
snorkeling trips ($35 per person), as well as waterskiing and sailing.
With **St. Kitts Scuba** (✉ Bird Rock Hotel, 2 mi east of Basseterre, ☎
465–1189) single tank dives run $40, double tank $60.

TENNIS

There are four lighted courts at **Jack Tar Village Royal St. Kitts Hotel
and Casino** (✉ Frigate Bay, ☎ 869/465–8651), two lighted courts at
Sun 'n' Sand Beach Village (✉ Frigate Bay, ☎ 869/465–8037), as well
as one court each (unlighted) at **Bird Rock Beach Resort** (✉ Basseterre
Bay, just east of Basseterre, ☎ 869/465–8914), the **Golden Lemon** (✉
Dieppe Bay, ☎ 869/465–7260), and **Rawlins Plantation** (✉ St. Paul's,
☎ 869/465–6221).

WINDSURFING

Winds are usually calm on the Caribbean side, meaning beginners
won't get into deep waters. Turtle Bay, where the prime outfitter is, is
particularly well-protected. **Turtle Tours** (☞ Boating, *above*) rents
Windsurfers and offers lessons; it also rents surfboards, kayaks, and
boogie boards.

Shopping

St. Kitts has limited shopping, but there are a few duty-free shops with
good deals on jewelry, perfume, china, and crystal. Several galleries sell
excellent paintings and sculptures. The batik fabrics, scarves, caftans,
and wall hangings of Caribelle Batik are well known. British expat Kate
Spencer is an artist who has lived on the islands for years, reproduc-
ing its vibrant colors in everything from silk *pareos* (beach wraps) to
notecards to place mats. Other good island buys include jams, jellies,
and herbal teas as well as crafts of local shell, straw, and coconut. Don't
forget to pick up some CSR, a "new cane spirit drink" that's distilled
from fresh sugarcane right on St. Kitts.

Areas and Malls

Most shopping plazas are in downtown Basseterre. **Palms Arcade** is on Fort Street, near the Circus. The **Pelican Mall**—a shopping arcade designed to look like a traditional Caribbean street—has 26 stores, a restaurant, tourism offices, and a bandstand. **Shoreline Plaza** is next to the Treasury Building, right on Basseterre's waterfront. **TDC Mall** is just off the Circus in downtown.

Specialty Items

ART AND ANTIQUES

Rosemary Lane Antiques (⊠ 7 Rosemary La., Basseterre, ☎ 869/465–5450) occupies a beautifully restored 18th-century town house and is crammed with superlative, affordable antiques and objets d'art from throughout the Caribbean. The staff will gladly ship any purchases. **Spencer Cameron Art Gallery** (⊠ N. Independence Sq., Basseterre, ☎ 869/465–1617) has historical reproductions of Caribbean island charts and prints, in addition to owner Rosey Cameron's popular Carnevale clown prints and a wide selection of exceptional artwork by Caribbean artists. They will mail anywhere.

CLOTHES

Splash (⊠ TDC Plaza, Fort St., Basseterre, ☎ 869/465–9279) carries colorful beachwear by local designers.

DUTY-FREE GOODS

Slice of the Lemon (⊠ Palms Arcade, Basseterre, ☎ 869/465–2889) stocks fine perfumes but is better known for elegant jewelry.

HANDICRAFTS

Caribelle Batik (⊠ Romney Manor, ☎ 869/465–6253) sells batik wraps, T-shirts, dresses, wall hangings, and the like. **Glass Island** (⊠ Corner of Princes and Fort Sts., Basseterre, ☎ no phone) features frames, earrings, and rough-blown glass. **Island Hopper** (⊠ The Circus, Basseterre, ☎ 869/465–2905) is a good place for island crafts, especially wood carvings, pottery, and textiles, as well as humorous T-shirts and trinkets. **Kate Designs** (⊠ Bank St., Basseterre, ☎ 869/465–5265) showcases the enchanting silk pareos, jewelry, prints, and papier-mâché works of Kate Spencer (who also has a studio just outside the Rawlins Plantation), and the fanciful, striking hats of Dale Isaacs. **Palm Crafts** (⊠ Palms Arcade, Basseterre, ☎ 869/465–2599) sells a variety of goodies, including savory Caribbean jams and jellies, resort wear by noted island designer John Warden, and hand-painted ceramics.

MUSIC

Music World (⊠ The Circus, Basseterre, ☎ 869/465–1998) offers a vast selection of island rhythms—lilting *soca* (a mix of soul and calypso) and *zouk,* (a bopping beguine from in Martinique and Guadeloupe) pulsating salsa and merengue, wicked hip-hop, and mellow reggae and calypso.

Nightlife

Most nightlife revolves around the hotels, which host folkloric shows and calypso and steel bands of the usual limbo-rum-and-reggae variety. Check with your hotel or the tourist board (☞ Visitor Information *in* St. Kitts and Nevis A to Z, *below*) for schedules.

BARS

Bayembi Cultural Entertainment Bar and Cafe (⊠ Just off the Circus, Basseterre, ☎ 869/466–5280) looks like a U.N. garage sale, and the ambience is definitely Peace Corps hip, with jazz guitar sets Wednesdays, karaoke Saturdays, joyous happy hours daily, and even poetry readings. It also sells light snacks and local artwork. A favorite happy-hour watering hole is the **Circus Grill** (⊠ Bay Rd., Basseterre, ☎ 869/465–0143), a second-floor eatery whose veranda offers views of the harbor and the activity on the Circus. The hot spot for happy hour is **Stonewalls** (⊠ Princes St., Basseterre, ☎ 869/465–5248), a courtyard bar with live music (sometimes), free eats—including luscious coconut shrimp if you're lucky—and congenial Canadian owners.

CASINOS

The only game in town is at the **Jack Tar Village Beach Resort and Casino** (☞ Lodging, *above*), where you'll find blackjack tables, roulette wheels, craps tables, and one-armed bandits. Dress is casual, and play continues till the last player leaves. You don't need to purchase Jack Tar passes to play, even though the casino entrance is in the hotel lobby.

DANCE AND MUSIC CLUBS

The **Cotton House Club** (⊠ Canada Estate, outside Basseterre, ☎ no phone), open weekends from 10 PM, is considered to have the best sound system and dance mixes. **Doo-Wop Days** (⊠ Memory La., Frigate Bay, ☎ 869/465–1960) is the color of raspberry sorbet and painted with musical notes. The engaging American owners, Linda and Joe Pozzuolo, seem to be living out a 50s rock-and-roll fantasy and have decked the place out accordingly: old 45s, photos—some autographed, like those of Sinatra and Chuck Berry—velvet Elvis paintings, guitar-shape pillows, hula hoops, and *Look* magazine covers. Joe serves up some fair Italian fare at reasonable prices. There's live music some nights, notably Ronn and the Rascals (a doo-wop group, of course). Drinks with such suggestive names as Body Shot and "Lick, Shoot, and Bite Contests" (better not to ask) put you in the mood for karaoke on Saturday.

Locals disco down at **Henry's Night Spot** (⊠ Dunn's Cottage, Lower Cayon St., Basseterre, ☎ 869/465–3508). Weekends, **Kool Runnins** (⊠ Morris Paul Dr., Pond Industrial Site, ☎ 869/466–5665) serves up jerk chicken, rotis, and goat-water stew, to the accompaniment of live local bands in an open-air gazebo. On Saturday night head for the **Turtle Beach Bar and Grill** (⊠ Turtle Bay, ☎ 869/469–9086), where you can play volleyball and then dance on the beach under the stars.

Exploring St. Kitts

You can see the sights of Basseterre, the capital city, in a half hour or so; allow three to four hours for an island tour. Main Road traces the northwestern perimeter through seas of sugarcane and past breadfruit trees and stone walls. Although villages with tiny pastel-color houses of stone and weathered wood are scattered throughout the island, the drive back to Basseterre around the island's other side passes through several of them. This road is slowly being repaved through 1998.

The most spectacular stretch of scenery is on the splendid Dr. Kennedy Simmonds Highway to the tip of the South East Peninsula. Reminiscent of California's famed Highway 1, this ultrasleek modern road twists and turns through the undeveloped grassy hills that rise between the calm Caribbean and the windswept Atlantic, past the shimmering pink Great Salt Pond, a volcanic crater, and seductive beaches.

Numbers in the margin correspond to points of interest on the St. Kitts map.

SIGHTS TO SEE

❶ Basseterre. In the south of the island, St. Kitts's capital is a walkable town. It's graced with tall palms, and although many of the buildings appear run-down and in need of paint, there are interesting shops, excellent art galleries, and some beautifully maintained houses.

The octagonal **Circus,** built in the style of London's famous Piccadilly Circus, has duty-free shops along the streets and courtyards off from it. There are lovely gardens on the site of a former slave market at **Independence Square** (⊠ Off Bank St.). The square is surrounded on three sides by 18th-century Georgian buildings. **St. George's Anglican Church** (⊠ Cayon St.) is a handsome stone building with a crenellated tower originally built by the French in 1670 and called Nôtre Dame. The British burned it down in 1706 and rebuilt it four years later, naming it after the patron saint of England. Since then, it has suffered fire, earthquake, and hurricanes and was once again rebuilt in 1859.

❽ Black Rocks. This series of lava deposits was spat into the sea ages ago when the island's volcano erupted. It has since been molded into fanciful shapes by centuries of pounding surf. ⊠ *On Atlantic coast, just outside town of Sadlers, in Sandy Bay.*

❷ Bloody Point. French and British soldiers joined forces here in 1629 to repel a mass Carib attack. ⊠ *Outside village of Challengers.*

❻ Brimstone Hill. The well-restored 38-acre fortress atop this hill is St. Kitts's most important historic site. From the parking area it's a steep walk up, but it's well worth it if military history and/or spectacular views interest you. After routing the French in 1690, the English erected a battery here, and by 1736 there were 49 guns in the fortress. In 1782, 8,000 French troops laid siege to the fortress, which was defended by 350 militia and 600 regular troops of the Royal Scots and East Yorkshires. A plaque in the old stone wall marks the place where the fort was breached. When the English finally surrendered, the French allowed them to march from the fort in full formation out of respect for their bravery. (The English afforded the French the same honor when they surrendered the fort a mere year later.) A hurricane damaged the fortress extensively in 1834, and in 1852 it was evacuated and dismantled. The beautiful stones were carted away to build houses.

The citadel has been partially reconstructed and its guns remounted. A seven-minute orientation film recounts the fort's history and restoration. You can see what remains of the officers' quarters, the redoubts, the barracks, the ordinance store, and the cemetery. Its museums display, among other things, pre-Columbian artifacts, a collection of objects pertaining to the African heritage of the island's slaves (masks, ceremonial tools, etc.), weaponry, uniforms, photographs, and old newspapers. In 1985 Queen Elizabeth visited Brimstone Hill and officially opened it as part of a national park. There's a splendid view from here that includes Montserrat and Nevis to the southeast, Saba and Statia to the northwest, and St. Barts and St. Maarten to the north. Nature trails snake through the tangle of surrounding hardwood forest and savannah (a fine spot to catch the green vervet monkeys skittering about). ⊠ *Main Rd., Brimstone Hill.* ☜ *$5.* ☉ *Daily 9:30–5:30.*

❺ Middle Island. Thomas Warner, the "gentleman of London" who brought the first settlers to St. Kitts, died here in 1648 and is buried beneath a green gazebo in the churchyard of St. Thomas Church.

❸ Old Road Town. This site marks the first permanent English settlement in the West Indies, founded in 1624 by Thomas Warner. Take the side road toward the interior to find some **Carib petroglyphs,** testimony of even earlier habitation. ⊠ *Main Rd., west of Challengers.*

❹ Romney Manor. The ruins of this somewhat restored house (destroyed by fire in 1996) house and surrounding cottages that duplicate the old chattel-house style are set in 6 acres of gardens, with exotic flowers, an old bell tower, and a 350-year-old saman tree (sometimes called a rain tree). Inside, at **Caribelle Batik** (☞ Shopping, *above*), you can watch artisans hand-printing fabrics by a 2,500-year-old Indonesian process known as batik. Look for signs indicating a turnoff for Romney Manor near Old Road Town.

❼ Sandy Point Town. This quaint village contains West Indian–style raised cottages and features a Roman Catholic church with lovely stained-glass windows.

NEVIS

Lodging

Most lodgings are in restored manor or plantation houses scattered throughout the island's five parishes (counties). The owners often live in these inns with their families, and they receive you warmly. It's easy to begin thinking you've been personally invited down for a visit. Before dinner, you may find yourself in the drawing room having a cocktail and conversing with the family, other guests, and visitors who have come for a meal in the restaurant. Most inns operate on MAP and offer a free shuttle service to their private stretch on Pinney's Beach. For price categories, *see* the chart *under* Lodging *in* St. Kitts.

$$$$ 🏨 Four Seasons Resort Nevis. There's no denying that the Four Sea-
★ sons is run flawlessly and combines world-class elegance with West Indian ambience and hospitality. On Pinney's Beach, the hotel offers a complete range of water activities (nonmotorized sports included in the rate); clay and all-weather tennis courts; a free-form pool; an 18-hole Robert Trent Jones Jr.–designed golf course; and a health club. It even has its own American Airlines pavilion where you can pay departure tax and check luggage. Spacious rooms are furnished with mahogany armoires and headboards and cushioned rattan sofas and chairs in bold colors. Each room has large seating areas—indoors and on a veranda—where you can enjoy a private meal. In 1996, 20 villas, Nevis Resort Estates, were added near the golf course, with more to come by 2000. Each offers a cedar cathedral ceiling, tile floors, an open kitchen, a masterful master bedroom, an enormous veranda, and as much pampering as you can handle. At the outstanding ☞ **Four Seasons Resort** restaurant, dining is fairly formal. Activities for children are scheduled regularly, and there are good-value packages available, even in high season. ⊠ *Pinney's Beach, 2½-mi north of Charlestown (Box 565, Charlestown),* ☎ *869/469–1111; 800/332–3442 in the U.S., 800/268–6282 in Canada (reservations services);* ☏ *869/469–1112. 196 rooms, 20 villas. 2 restaurants, pub, air-conditioning, fans, pool, 18-hole golf course, 10 tennis courts, aerobics, health club, beach, dive shop, snorkeling, windsurfing, boating, shops, baby-sitting, children's programs, coin laundry, laundry service, car rental. AE, D, MC, V. EP, FAP, MAP.*

$$$$ 🏨 Nisbet Plantation Beach Club. From the manor house of this 18th-
★ century plantation you can see the blinding white-sand beach; from one of its bars you look out over an old sugar mill covered with hibiscus, cassia, frangipani, and flamboyants. Accommodations range from plantation-style cottages to suites. All are well-maintained and simply but tastefully appointed with patios, vaulted ceilings, gleaming tile floors, whitewashed wicker and rattan, grass mats and baskets, soothing seafoam and peach fabrics, and tropical prints. Among the in-room amenities are such touches as coffeemakers and hair dryers. All the units are along an avenue lined with coconut palms that leads to the beach, where a new deck and bar have been built. Be sure to stop by to enjoy

a drink, a sunset, or maybe a barbecue. The ☞ **Nisbet Plantation Beach Club** great house restaurant has varied five-course menus. ✉ *Newcastle Beach,* ☎ *869/469–9325 or 800/742–6008,* FAX *869/469–9864. 38 rooms. 2 restaurants, 2 bars, fans, in-room safes, refrigerators, pool, tennis court, croquet, beach, snorkeling, shop, laundry service. AE, MC, V. EP, MAP.*

$$$–$$$$
★
🏨 **Hermitage Plantation Inn.** A 250-year-old great house—said to be the oldest wooden house on the island—is the heart of this hillside complex. The vivacious owners Maureen and Richard "Loopy" Lupinacci add to the charm and will no doubt introduce you to everyone who's anyone on Nevis. Guest quarters are in rooms or duplex cottages (the Blue Cottage and the Yellow Room are knockouts) that are furnished with antiques—including four-poster canopy beds (mostly king-size)—and have patios or balconies; some units also have full kitchens and lovely views of the distant ocean. If you need more space, there's a two-bedroom replica of a manor house with a private pool. You can spend your days, as many guests do, relaxing in a hammock or lounging by the peaceful pool. The beach is 15 minutes away; don't worry if you don't have a car, as transportation will be arranged. In the great house, you can feast on contemporary cuisine in the ☞ **Hermitage Plantation Inn**'s restaurant. ✉ *St. John's, Fig Tree Parish,* ☎ *869/469–3477,* FAX *869/469–2481. 12 units. Restaurant, bar, fans, refrigerators, pool, tennis court, horseback riding. AE, MC, V. BP, MAP.*

$–$$$$
🏨 **Hurricane Cove Bungalows.** Don't be deceived by the ramshackle exteriors of these cottages that cling precariously to a hill above lovely Tamarind Bay. The plain wood-paneled interiors are charmingly rustic with hand-carved wood furnishings, batik wall hangings, local artwork, rough-textured ceramics, and gleaming tile floors. All have full kitchens and enclosed patios with breathtaking ocean views (save for one cottage, far in the back). Several have private pools, and one three-building complex has its own grill. The postage-stamp-size pool is in the foundation of a 250-year-old fort. The beach is a three-minute walk away. The only drawback is that these glorified tree houses can be stifling on still days. ✉ *Oualie Bay,* ☎ FAX *869/469–9462. 11 1-, 2-, and 3-bedroom bungalows. Fans, kitchenettes, pool. MC, V. EP.*

$$$
★
🏨 **Montpelier Plantation Inn.** Iron gates provide a majestic entrance to this intimate inn on 100 beautiful acres. Reception, evening cocktails, and dinner take place at the great house—an imposing fieldstone structure furnished with antiques. Accommodations are in spare but sparkling hillside cottages. Each has one or two rooms, two patios, Italian-ceramic tile floors, and large bathrooms with exquisite tracery; most rooms have four-poster or rattan beds and delicate floral spreads that contrast with vivid yellow-and-white striped curtains. A gorgeous mural decorates one of the walls around the large pool area; if you need saltwater and sand to enjoy the sun, you can take the free shuttle to Pinney's Beach, where the estate has a private 3-acre stretch and a pavilion. Guests come not so much for the amenities as for the incomparable quiet and unpretentious elegance. Owners James and Celia Gaskell downplay their royal connections; James prefers to talk about his organic gardens or engage in droll debates. The Gaskells' gracious presence, particularly at dinner in the ☞ **Montpelier Plantation Inn** restaurant, makes this a civilized place, indeed. ✉ *Pond Hill (Box 474, Charlestown),* ☎ *869/469–3462 or 800/223–9832 (reservations service),* FAX *869/469–2932. 17 rooms. Restaurant, bar, fans, pool, tennis court, beach. AE, MC, V. BP, MAP. Closed late Aug.–early Oct.*

$$–$$$
★
🏨 **Oualie Beach Hotel.** This cozy, congenial resort consists of white-and-hunter-green, West Indian–style cottages with gingerbread trim—all on a beautiful tawny beach and all with views of St. Kitts. Bright, airy rooms are tastefully furnished: Deluxe rooms have mahogany

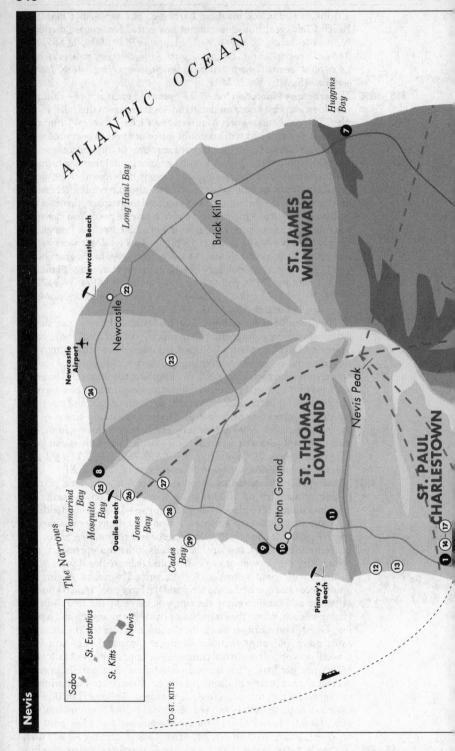

Nevis

ATLANTIC OCEAN

Huggins Bay

ST. JAMES WINDWARD

Brick Kiln

Long Haul Bay

Newcastle Beach

Newcastle

Newcastle Airport

Nevis Peak

ST. THOMAS LOWLAND

Cotton Ground

ST. PAUL CHARLESTOWN

Tamarind Bay

Mosquito Bay

Oualie Beach

Jones Bay

Cades Bay

The Narrows

Pinney's Beach

Saba

St. Eustatius

St. Kitts

Nevis

TO ST. KITTS

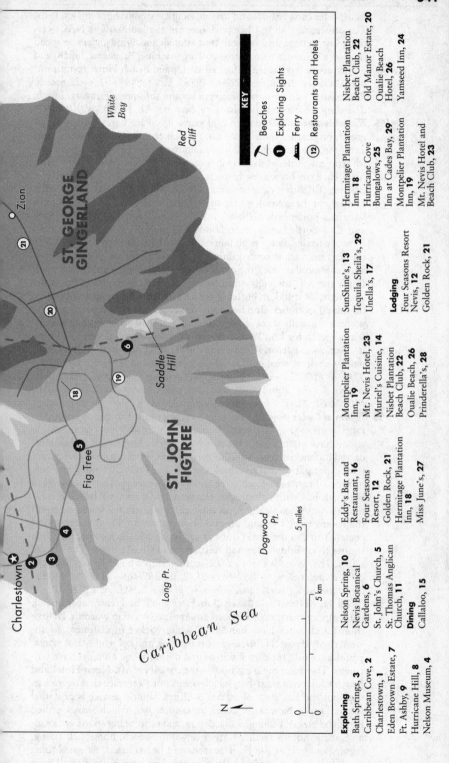

KEY

〰 Beaches
● Exploring Sights
⛴ Ferry
⑫ Restaurants and Hotels

Exploring
Bath Springs, **3**
Caribbean Cove, **2**
Charlestown, **1**
Eden Brown Estate, **7**
Ft. Ashby, **9**
Hurricane Hill, **8**
Nelson Museum, **4**

Nelson Spring, **10**
Nevis Botanical
Gardens, **6**
St. John's Church, **5**
St. Thomas Anglican
Church, **11**

Dining
Callaloo, **15**

Eddy's Bar and
Restaurant, **16**
Four Seasons
Resort, **12**
Golden Rock, **21**
Hermitage Plantation
Inn, **18**
Miss June's, **27**

Montpelier Plantation
Inn, **19**
Mt. Nevis Hotel, **23**
Muriel's Cuisine, **14**
Nisbet Plantation
Beach Club, **22**
Oualie Beach, **26**
Prinderella's, **28**

SunShine's, **13**
Tequila Sheila's, **29**
Unella's, **17**

Lodging
Four Seasons Resort
Nevis, **12**
Golden Rock, **21**

Hermitage Plantation
Inn, **18**
Hurricane Cove
Bungalows, **25**
Inn at Cades Bay, **29**
Montpelier Plantation
Inn, **19**
Mt. Nevis Hotel and
Beach Club, **23**

Nisbet Plantation
Beach Club, **22**
Old Manor Estate, **20**
Oualie Beach
Hotel, **26**
Yamseed Inn, **24**

four-poster canopy beds and marble vanities; studios have full kitchens. The on-site dive shop (dive packages are available) offers NAUI-certified instruction, and you can rent Sunfish and Windsurfers or spend time on a Skimmer waterborne rowing machine. Breakfast, lunch, and dinner are served at the informal ☞ **Oualie Beach Hotel** restaurant-bar. ⊠ *Oualie Beach,* ☎ *869/469–9735,* FAX *869/469–9176. 22 rooms. Restaurant, bar, air-conditioning, in-room safes, refrigerators, beach, dive shop, snorkeling, windsurfing, boating. AE, D, MC, V. EP, MAP.*

$$ 🏨 **Golden Rock.** More than 200 years ago, Pam Barry's great-great-great-grandfather built this estate, which she now co-owns and runs as an inn. It's set amid 150 mountainous acres (25 of them have lavish tropical gardens) that are crisscrossed by trails. (An avid horticulturalist, Pam organizes historical and nature hikes—just bring a machete!) Rusting cannons and old church pews placed strategically throughout the grounds add to the historic ambience. The 16 guest units have four-poster beds of mahogany or bamboo, native grass mats, straw and glass-bottle lamps, porcelain vases, rocking chairs, hand-painted shower curtains, floral-print fabrics, private baths, and patios. The sugar mill has been transformed into a bilevel suite (with a glorious wood-and-bamboo staircase), the old cistern into a spring-fed swimming pool. Enjoy the Atlantic view and cooling breeze from the bar. The Saturday night West Indian buffet in the ☞ **Golden Rock** restaurant is very popular December–June. Green vervet monkeys skitter about the premises (usually showing up punctually at 4 PM), and anyone is a potential perch for Lou Rau, a gloriously colored (and doesn't he know it?) Amazona parrot. Pam swears she doesn't know how he learned to wolf-whistle at women. . . . ⊠ *Gingerland (Box 493),* ☎ *869/469–3346 or 800/223–9815 (reservations service),* FAX *869/469–2113. 16 rooms, 1 suite. Restaurant, bar, fans, pool, tennis court, hiking. AE, MC, V. EP, MAP. Closed Sept.–early Oct.*

$$ 🏨 **Inn at Cades Bay.** At this complex, each of the tidy peach-color cottages with sage-green, gabled roofs has its own tiny lawn. Sizable rooms have high ceilings; bleached-wood paneling; rattan beds; hand-carved Indonesian teak furnishings; smart, abstract Spanish fabrics; and terra-cotta patios that overlook the sea. The lovingly tended grounds include 10 varieties of palm tree and a cactus garden. The beach is lined with gazebos with hammocks; the activity on Pinney's Beach is a bit of a hike, but doable. At press time, plans were in the works to equip the rooms with TVs and air-conditioning and to add a water sports center. You can dine next door at ☞ **Tequila Sheila's** or take the free shuttle to ☞ **Eddy's Bar and Restaurant** in Charlestown. The on-site alfresco bar is made from a once-scuttled ship whose top has been cut off. ⊠ *Cades Bay,* ☎ *869/469–8139,* FAX *869/469–8129. 16 rooms. 2 restaurants, 3 bars, fans, minibars, pool. AE, MC, V. EP, MAP.*

$$ 🏨 **Mt. Nevis Hotel and Beach Club.** Here you'll find reasonably priced, contemporary accommodations and typical Nevisian warmth. Deluxe rooms and suites have handsome white wicker furnishings, Southwestern-style pastel fabrics, glass-top tables, and colorful island prints. Suites have full, modern kitchens and dining areas; all units have balconies. The main building houses the casual ☞ **Mt. Nevis Hotel and Beach Club** restaurant-bar, which opens onto a terrace that overlooks the pool and has view of distant St. Kitts. Shuttle service is provided to the hotel's Newcastle Beach restaurant-bar, which serves grilled items and pizzas. Fishing, scuba diving, and other water sports are available at the hotel's facility farther down the beach; horseback riding, tennis, and golf at the Four Seasons can be arranged. At press time, two of six fully equipped hillside houses had been built; all will have two or three bedrooms, handsome individual decor, and spacious sea-

view patios. ⊠ *Shaw's Rd. (Box 494, Newcastle),* ☎ *869/469–9373 collect,* FAX *869/469–9375. 28 units, 2 houses. 2 restaurants, bar, air-conditioning , fans, refrigerators, in-room VCRs, pool, golf privileges, windsurfing, boating, waterskiing. AE, D, MC, V. EP, MAP.*

$$ ⌐ **Old Manor Estate.** Vast tropical gardens surround this former sugar plantation set in the shadow of Mt. Nevis. The smokehouse, the jail, and other outbuildings have been imaginatively restored as public spaces used for barbecues, musical performances, and banquets; the old cistern is now the pool. New owners have brightened the once-dour exteriors with fresh coats of peach and forest-green paint; they're also gradually redecorating the interiors. Throughout there's a striking blend of old and new. Many of the enormous guest rooms have high ceilings, exposed wood beams, gorgeous stone or tile floors, marble vanities, king-size four-poster beds, antique wardrobes, and colonial reproductions. Some rooms, however, are still a bit gloomy with dowdy madras settees and soiled carpets. There's a pleasant game room–library where you can mingle with other guests or catch up on the latest scores on the satellite TV. The terrace of the manor house's respected Cooperage restaurant has splendid views of the sea and the unfortunate island of Montserrat. There's transportation to and from the beach. (Parents take note: This hotel isn't recommended for children under 12.) ⊠ *Charlestown (Box 70),* ☎ *869/469–3445 or 800/892–7093 (reservations service),* FAX *869/469–3388. 14 rooms. 2 restaurants, 2 bars, fans, pool, library. AE, MC, V. EP, MAP.*

$ ⌐ **Yamseed Inn.** At the end of a very rough access road and away from other inns, friendly innkeeper Sybil Siegfried receives guests (note that there's a three-night minimum) at her pale-yellow house. Chirping hummingbirds on the B&B's beautiful grounds (Sybil is an avid gardener) welcome you to the stylish reception area. Each of the four guest rooms has a private bath and is handsomely appointed with a mahogany bed, wood-paneled ceiling, throw rugs, white-tile floors, and antiques. Breakfast includes homemade muffins and grated-coconut muesli. The B&B has a view of St. Kitts and its own patch of white sand. The only flaw in this paradise is its location in the flight path of the nearby airport (fortunately, air traffic isn't busy). ⊠ *Newcastle Beach,* ☎ *869/ 469–9361. 4 rooms. Beach. No credit cards. CP.*

Dining

Dinner options include the elegance of the dining room at the Four Seasons Resort, intimate dinners at plantation guest houses (where the menu is often set), and a variety of casual eateries. Seafood is ubiquitous, and there are many places in which to sample West Indian fare.

What to Wear

Dress is casual at lunch, although beach attire is unacceptable. Dress pants or a sundress is apropos for dinner; men may even want to put on a jacket in season at some inns and at the Four Seasons Resort. For price categories, *see* the chart *under* Dining *in* St. Kitts.

CARIBBEAN/CREOLE

$$$ ✕ **Golden Rock.** Tables are draped in pink and arranged in a romantic, dimly lit room whose fieldstone walls date from when the ☞ **Golden Rock** inn was a plantation house. Enchanting Eva Wilkin originals grace the walls (be sure to peek at the mural behind the bamboo bar). Local Nevisian cuisine is the specialty here; velvety pumpkin soup, chicken in a raisin curry, grilled local snapper with *tania* (a type of tuber) fritters, and green papaya pie are house favorites. ⊠ *Gingerland,* ☎ *869/469–3346. Reservations essential. AE, MC, V. Closed Sun.*

$ ✕ **Callaloo.** This simple but stylish eatery—run by genial Abdul Hill, who learned to cook with French-Creole flair on St. Martin—is another local standout. Delicious rotis make a quick, cheap lunch. Or opt for the yummy grilled kingfish in lemon butter, conch Creole, curried goat, or ribs—all served with generous side portions of rice, beans, and salad. ✉ *Government Rd. and Main St., Charlestown,* ☎ *869/469– 5389. AE, D, MC, V. Closed Sun.*

$ ✕ **Eddy's Bar and Restaurant.** Here you can dine with a view of all
★ the activity (well, lounging) in Charlestown's central Memorial Square. The enclosed front room is comfortable, but ask to be seated in the back terrace: a local artist designed the bright wall hangings and tablecloths and hand-painted all the tables. You can order fine stir-fries and such West Indian specialties as cream of cauliflower soup and tender, crispy conch fritters with just the right amount of sass in the sauce (it's made by Eddy's mom, Eulalie). At happy hour on Wednesday, drinks are half price, and snacks are free. ✉ *Main St., Charlestown,* ☎ *869/ 469–5958. AE, MC, V. Closed Thurs., Sun., and Sept.*

$ ✕ **Muriel's Cuisine.** Hanging plants, local still lifes, and table vases dress
★ up this eatery. Three meals are served daily, except Sunday. Bountiful entrées come with mounds of rice and peas as well as fresh vegetables, a side salad, and garlic bread. The subtly spiced jerk chicken would pass muster in many a Jamaican kitchen, and the goat-water and beef stews are fabulous: full-bodied and fragrant with garlic and coriander. Muriel St. Jean is the gracious hostess. Her restaurant attracts a very local clientele—women in hair curlers and young men who come to flirt shyly with the waitresses. ✉ *Upper Happy Hill Dr., Charlestown,* ☎ *869/469–5920. AE, D, MC, V. Closed Sun.*

$ ✕ **SunShine's.** Everything about this palm-thatched beach shack is colorful and larger-than-life, including the Rasta man SunShine himself. Flags from around the world drape the lean-to and complement the international clientele who wander over from the adjacent Four Seasons. Picnic tables are splashed with bright Rasta sunrise-to-sunset colors; nothing has been left unpainted, including the palm trees. Fishermen cruise up to the grill with their catch; you might savor lobster rolls, conch fritters, or snapper Creole. Try the lethal house specialty, the Killer Bee rum punch; as SunShine boasts, "One and you're stung, two you're stunned, three it's a knockout." SunShine is a character; he means well, but has a hard time committing to dinner plans. "Six of you tonight? Well come at six, maybe I'll be here." He probably won't. ✉ *Pinney's Beach,* ☎ *869/469–5817. No credit cards. No dinner.*

$ ✕ **Unella's.** The atmosphere is nothing fancy—just tables on a second-floor porch overlooking Charlestown's waterfront—but the fare is good West Indian. Stop here for exceptional lobster (more expensive than the rest of the menu), curried lamb, island-style spareribs, and steamed conch, all served with local vegetables, rice, and peas. Unella opens shop around 9 AM, when locals and boaters appear waiting for their breakfast, and stays open all day. ✉ *Waterfront, Charlestown,* ☎ *869/469–5574. No credit cards.*

CONTEMPORARY

$$$$ ✕ **Hermitage Plantation Inn.** After cocktails in the antiques-filled parlor, dinner is served at one long table on the outside veranda of the ☞ **Hermitage Plantation Inn.** The four-course preset menu might include carrot and tarragon soup, red snapper in ginger sauce, fried conch steak, and a rum soufflé, all lovingly prepared by the local chef, Lovey. The conversation is always lively, thanks to witty, gregarious owners Maureen and Richard Lupinacci. ✉ *St. John's, Fig Tree Parish,* ☎ *869/469– 3477. Reservations essential. AE, MC, V.*

$$$$ ✕ **Montpelier Plantation Inn.** Genial owners James and Celia Gaskell
★ preside over an elegant evening. Cocktails and hors d'oeuvres are
served amid the antiques-filled parlor of the ☞ **Montpelier Plantation
Inn** great house. Note the detail of the embroidered upholstery, all done
by local ladies, and look for the circa 1880 portrait of James's relative, Lady Catherine Gaskell. Dinner is served by candlelight on the
white terrace. Cream of avocado and coconut soup, lobster, red snapper, chicken calypso, sirloin steak bordelaise, and roast beef and York-
shire pudding are some of the choices on chef Neil Savage's sterling
menu. Many of the ingredients are homegrown in the extensive gardens. Lunches are served on the refreshing patio, and are much simpler affairs than dinner; you'll find quiches and such creative experiments
as tuna, wahoo, and mushroom flan. ✉ *Pond Hill,* ☎ *869/469–3462.
Reservations essential. AE, MC, V. Closed late Aug.–early Oct.*

$$$$ ✕ **Nisbet Plantation Beach Club.** The dining room in the great house
★ of the ☞ **Nisbet Plantation Beach Club** inn—an oasis of polished
hardwood floors, mahogany and cherrywood furnishings, straw mats,
wicker furnishings, and stone walls—has long been a popular place for
lunch and dinner. There are also tables on the screened-in veranda, where
there's a view down the palm-tree-lined fairway to the sea. The five-
course menu offers dishes that combine Continental and Caribbean
cuisines and local ingredients. Sumptuous choices include seared yellowfin tuna in mixed peppercorn crust with champagne beurre blanc,
a rendezvous of beef and lamb in sage sauce, bacon-wrapped monkfish on spicy tania fritters with dill and mustard dressing, and chocolate truffle torte. Lighter fare (sandwiches, salads, hamburgers) is
served at lunch at the beach restaurant, Coconuts. ✉ *Newcastle Beach,*
☎ *869/469–9325. Reservations essential. AE, MC, V.*

$$–$$$ ✕ **Mt. Nevis Hotel.** White-wicker tables are set with coral tablecloths,
flickering candles, china, and silver in the airy dining room of the ☞
Mt. Nevis Hotel and Beach Club. It opens onto the terrace and pool,
and there's a splendid view of St. Kitts in the distance. The creative
menu deftly blends local ingredients with classic haute-cuisine preparations. Starters include lobster and conch cakes with scallions, ginger, and lime jalapeño mayonnaise, or crispy duck spring roll with
marinated beet salad; excellent entrées include prosciutto-wrapped
chicken breast in sun-dried tomato sauce or sautéed scallops and stir-
fried fettuccine with ginger-soy glaze. The service is endearing, the setting sublime, and the food perfectly pitched to the climate: elegant yet
light. ✉ *Shaws Rd.,* ☎ *869/469–9373. AE, D, MC, V.*

$–$$$ ✕ **Four Seasons Resort.** This elegant dining room at the ☞ **Four Sea-
sons Resort** is paneled in imported South American hardwood and has
graceful, 12-ft-high doors that open to the sea breezes and views. The
nouvelle cuisine has a Caribbean flair—curry and Scotch bonnet broth;
Antiguan wahoo baked in a banana leaf with coconut milk; and pan-
seared local red snapper with mango salsa and bitter orange sauce.
There's a weekly Caribbean buffet with a full steel band. ✉ *Pinney's
Beach, 2½-mi north of Charlestown,* ☎ *869/469–1111. Reservations
essential. AE, D, MC, V.*

ECLECTIC

$$$$ ✕ **Miss June's.** Dinner with Miss June Mestier, a lady from Trinidad,
★ could never be called ordinary. While she prepares the fare, her son
serves drinks—from Miss June's secret rum punch to a very proper mar-
tini—to guests (limited to 20) on the veranda. Promptly at 8:30 every-
one heads to the dining room, where tables are set with mismatched
fine china and crystal. The first course is a soup, usually something
spicy; the second course, fresh fish prepared in some exotic local style,
followed by salad. "Now that you've had your dinner," Miss June an-

nounces, "it's time to have fun!" You and other guests will be directed
to a buffet table laden with at least 18 dishes. Selections change nightly
but always include curries; local vegetable dishes; seafood and such meats
as leg of lamb in champagne orange sauce, chicken simmered in coconut milk, or ribs in *mauby* (a bark distillation) and pineapple—all
adapted from Trinidadian recipes. Wine flows freely. Later, Miss June
will join you for coffee and brandy; she won't kick you out, but she
may ask you to turn the lights out when you leave. ⊠ *Jones Bay,* ☏
869/469–5330. Reservations essential. MC, V.

$ ✕ **Oualie Beach.** At the low-key restaurant-bar in the ☞ **Oualie Beach
Hotel** you'll find authentic Nevisian fare with a French flair. Try the
delicious homemade soups, including ground-nut or breadfruit vichyssoise. Then move on to Creole conch stew, lobster crepes, or chicken
breast stuffed with spinach. The decor alone is luscious: partial fieldstone walls, local murals, straw lamps, and fish netting. The atmosphere
is rollicking on weekends, with live music and local crowds. ⊠ *Oualie
Beach,* ☏ *869/469–9735. AE, D, MC, V.*

$ ✕ **Prinderella's.** This casual open-air restaurant-bar enjoys a stunning
setting on Tamarind Bay, with views across the channel to St. Kitts.
Seafood is the obvious specialty, although the English owners, Ian and
Charlie Mintrim, do a proper shepherd's pie and roast beef with York-
shire pudding. Friday brings a boisterous happy hour, with snacks such
as salmon mousse, hummus, and chicken wings. At Sunday brunch the
eggs Benedict or Florentine are delicious. Yachties buzz around the bar
at any time during the week, and there's wonderful snorkeling right
around the point. Ask Charlie to tell you the story behind the restaurant's name; it features Prinderella, a cince, and a gairy frogmother.
You'll want a bouble dourbon when she's finished. ⊠ *Jones Bridge,*
☏ *869/469–1291. AE, MC, V. Closed Mon. June–Sept.; Mon.–Wed.
Oct.–Nov.; and Apr. 15–May.*

$ ✕ **Tequila Sheila's.** Right next door to the ☞ **Inn at Cades Bay,** this
shack of corrugated-tin and wood sits right on a beach (there are even
chaise longues). It has been gussied up with plant-filled baskets and
colorful billowing windsocks, but the laid-back air remains. A new chef
has introduced Pacific Rim–California cuisine (with lighter fare and
sauces and local ingredients) that includes everything from blackened
wahoo to fish quesadillas to chicken in mango or coconut sauce. The
Sunday Beach Party Brunch and the Saturday Night Fever discos draw
locals and tourists alike (though management plans to tone things
down a bit for the sake of neighboring hotel guests). ⊠ *Cades Bay,* ☏
869/469–1633. MC, V. Closed Mon. No lunch Tues.

Beaches

All the beaches are free to the public and there are no changing facilities, so wear a swimsuit under your clothes. **Newcastle Beach,** by Nisbet Plantation (☞ Lodging, *above*), is popular among snorkelers. This
broad swath of soft, ecru sand, shaded by coconut palms, sits at the
northernmost tip of the island, on the channel between St. Kitts and
Nevis. **Oualie Beach,** just south of Mosquito Bay and north of Cades
and Jones Bays, is a beige-sand beach where the folks at Oualie Beach
Hotel (☞ Lodging, *above*) can mix you a drink and fix you up with
water-sports equipment. The island's showpiece beach, **Pinney's Beach**
has almost 4 mi of soft, golden sand, on the calm Caribbean Sea, lined
with a magnificent grove of palm trees. The palm-shaded lagoon is a
scene right out of South Pacific. The Four Seasons Resort is here, as
are the private cabanas and pavilions of several mountain inns.

Outdoor Activities and Sports

Participant Sports

BOATING

The seas are usually uncommonly calm, with light breezes. The north-west side of Nevis is particularly delightful, thanks to the sterling views of St. Kitts. **Newcastle Bay Marina** (⊠ Newcastle, ☎ 869/469–9395) rents Phantom sailboats, a 23-ft KenCraft powerboat, and sev-eral inflatables with outboards. You can rent Hobie Cats and Sunfish from **Oualie Beach Club** (⊠ Oualie Beach, ☎ 869/469–9518).

FISHING

The game here is kingfish, wahoo, grouper, tuna, and yellowtail snap-per, but nothing as thrilling as marlin. If you want local expertise, call **Captain Valentine Glasgow** (☎ 869/469–1989), who has a 31-ft Ocean Master, *Lady James,* to take you in search of the big ones. **Jans Travel Agency** (☎ 869/469–5578) and **Mt. Nevis Hotel and Beach Club** (☎ 869/469–9373) arrange deep-sea fishing trips.

GOLF

Duffers doff their hats to the beautiful, impeccably maintained Robert Trent Jones Jr.–designed 18-hole, par 72, 6,766-yard championship course at the Four Seasons (☎ 869/469–1111). The signature hole is the 15th, a 660-yard monster that encompasses a deep ravine. Greens fees are $75 per person for 9 holes; $125 for 18.

HIKING

The center of the island is Nevis Peak, which soars up to 3,232 ft, flanked by Hurricane Hill on the north and Saddle Hill on the south. If you plan to scale Nevis Peak, a daylong affair, it is highly recommended that you go with a guide. Your hotel can arrange it for you; you can also ask the hotel to pack a picnic lunch.

Eco-Tours Nevis (☎ 869/469–2091), headed by David Rollinson, ram-bles through 18th-century estates and explores what remains of Nevis's last working sugar factory as well as archaeological evidence of pre-Colombian settlements. David also offers treks up Mountravers, a spectacular great-house ruin, and historical walks through Charlestown. **Michael Herbert** (☎ 869/469–2856) leads four-hour nature hikes up to his 1,500-ft-high property, Herbert Heights, where he offers fresh local juices as you drink in the views of Montserrat; his powerful tele-scope makes you feel as if you're staring right into that island's sim-mering volcano. **Top to Bottom** (☎ 869/469–9080), run by Jim and Nikki Johnston, offer eco-rambles (slower tours) and hikes that em-phasize Nevis's volcanic and horticultural heritage. The Johnstons are also keen bird-watchers. Three-hour rambles or hikes are $20 per per-son; it's $30 for a more strenuous climb up Mt. Nevis.

HORSEBACK RIDING

You can take leisurely beach rides or tackle more demanding trail rides through the lush hills. You can arrange for both types of ride ($45 per person) and lessons ($20 per hour) through **Nevis Equestrian Cen-tre** (⊠ Pinney's Beach near Cottonground, ☎ 869/469–8118).

SCUBA DIVING AND SNORKELING

The village of Jamestown was washed into the sea around Fort Ashby, just south of Cades Bay, making the area a popular spot for snorkeling and diving. Reef-protected Pinney's Beach offers especially good snorkel-ing. The Caves are a series of grottoes where divers can navigate tun-nels and view lobsters, sea fans, sponges, squirrel fish, and many others. Single-tank dives are usually $45, two-tank dives $70–$80. Try **Dive Nevis** (⊠ Pinney's Beach, ☎ 869/469–9373), **Nevis Water Sports** (⊠ Oualie

Beach, ☎ 869/469–9690), or **Scuba Safaris** (⊠ Oualie Beach, ☎ 869/469–9518), for everything from a resort course to full certification.

TENNIS

There are 10 lighted tennis courts at the **Four Seasons Resort** (⊠ Pinney's Beach, ☎ 869/469–1111), two at **Pinney's Beach Hotel** (⊠ Pinney's Beach, just outside Charlestown, ☎ 869/469–5207), and one court each at **Golden Rock** (⊠ Gingerland, ☎ 869/469–3346), **Nisbet** (⊠ Newcastle Beach, ☎ 869/469–9325), and **Montpelier Plantation** (⊠ Pond Hill, ☎ 869/469–3462).

WINDSURFING

Waters are generally calm and winds steady yet gentle, making Nevis an excellent spot for beginners and intermediates. **Windsurfing Nevis** (⊠ Oualie Beach Hotel, ☎ 869/469–9682) also offers top-notch instructors and equipment for $25 per half hour.

Spectator Sports

One of the Caribbean's most unusual events is the occasional "Day at the Races," sponsored by the **Nevis Turf and Jockey Club** (☎ 869/469–3477). The races, which attract a "pan-Caribbean field" (as the club likes to boast), are held on a windswept course called Indian Castle, overlooking the "white horses" of the Atlantic. Last-minute changes and scratches are common; a party atmosphere prevails.

Shopping

Nevis is certainly not the place for a shopping spree, but there are some unique and wonderful surprises, notably the island's stamps and batik and hand-embroidered clothing. Beekeeping is a buzzing biz, and you'll find beeswax candles (which burn longer than those made of regular wax) and the fragrant, tropically flavored honey at many stores. Nevis also had an artist of some international repute, the late Dame Eva Wilkins, who for more than 50 years painted island people, flowers, and landscapes in an evocative art-naïf style. (An Eva Wilkins mural hangs over the bar at the Golden Rock; (☞ Dining, *above*). Her originals sell for $100 and up, and prints are available in some local shops.

Shopping Areas

Other than a few hotel boutiques and isolated galleries, virtually all the shopping is concentrated on or just off **Main Street** in Charlestown. A small mall on the Charlestown waterfront, called the **Cotton Ginnery Complex,** was restored in 1997. The lovely old stonework and wood floors make an appropriate setting for stalls of local artisans.

Specialty Items

ART

The **Eva Wilkin Gallery** (⊠ Clay Ghaut, Gingerland, ☎ 869/469–2673) occupies her former light-filled atelier; the terraces afford understandably inspiring ocean views. If the paintings, drawings, and prints are out of your price range, consider buying the lovely note cards based on her designs. Kate Spencer's lovely island paintings and silk scarves and pareos are on sale at **Kate Designs** (⊠ Main St., Charlestown, ☎ 869/469–5694). **Robert Humphreys** sells his paintings, flowing bronze sculptures of pirouetting marlins, and clay renderings of local fauna from his studio (⊠ Palm Hill, Brazier Estate, ☎ 869/469–2421).

CLOTHING

Beach Works (⊠ Pinney's Beach, inside Beachcomber restaurant, ☎ 869/469–0620) has become the island's classiest boutique, with an excellent selection of everything from bathing suits to Balinese batik and puppets. The adjoining restaurant also exhibits works by island artists on its walls. You'll find batik caftans, scarves, shorts, blouses, caps, and T-shirts—as well as wall hangings and fabric—in the Nevis branch of **Caribelle Batik** (⊠ Arcade, Charlestown, ☎ 869/469–1491).

HANDICRAFTS

Caribco Gifts (⊠ Main St., Charlestown, ☎ 869/469–1432) sells affordable T-shirts, candles, and pottery emblazoned with Nevis logos. **Knick Knacks** (⊠ Between Waterfront and Main Sts., Charlestown, ☎ 869/469–5784) showcases top local artisans, including Marvin Chapman (stone and wood carvings) and Jeannie Rigby (exquisite dolls). It also sells whimsical hats, beach wraps, and pottery. The **Nevis Handicraft Co-op Society** (☎ 869/469–1746), next to the tourist office, offers work by local artisans (clothing, ceramic ware, woven goods) and locally produced honey and jellies. Stamp collectors should head for the **Philatelic Bureau** (☎ 869/469–0617), just off Main Street opposite the tourist office. St. Kitts and Nevis are famous for their decorative, and sometimes lucrative, stamps. An early Kittitian stamp recently brought in $7,000. For dolls and baskets handcrafted in Nevis, visit the **Sandbox Tree** (⊠ Evelyn's Villa, Charlestown, ☎ 869/469–5662). Among other items here are hand-painted chests.

Nightlife

In season, it is usually easy to find a local calypso singer or a steel or string band performing at one of the hotels on weekends. Such performances are usually in tandem with a special buffet dinner.

BARS

A new and improved **Beachcomber** (⊠ Pinney's Beach, ☎ 869/469–1192) offers huge barbecues, happy hours, and occasional live bands in addition to a simple menu of burgers and grilled items. At the **Sunset Terrace at Cliff Dwellers** (⊠ Tamarind Bay, ☎ 869/469–0262)—which is only open in high season (mid-December–April)—you can take a tram ride up the side of a sheer cliff that's even more dramatic than the sunset views. Call ahead: The tram is notoriously temperamental.

DANCE AND MUSIC CLUBS

Apart from the hotel scene, there are a few places where young locals go for late-night calypso, reggae, and other island music. **Club Trenim** (⊠ Government Rd., Charlestown, ☎ no phone) has disco dancing starting at 8:30 every night except Tuesday. **Dick's Bar** (⊠ Brickiln, ☎ no phone) has live music or a DJ on Friday and Saturday evenings.

THEME NIGHTS

Eddy's Bar and Restaurant (⊠ Main St., Charlestown, ☎ 869/469–5958) holds raucous West Indian nights with a buffet and a live string band Friday and Saturday. You can count on entertainment at the **Four Seasons Resort** (⊠ Pinney's Beach, ☎ 869/469–1111) on Friday and Saturday. The **Golden Rock** (⊠ Gingerland, ☎ 869/469–3346) brings in David Freeman's Honeybees String Band to jazz things up for the Saturday buffet. On Friday the Shell All-Stars steel band entertains in the gardens of the **Old Manor Estate** (⊠ , ☎ 869/469–3445). **Oualie Beach Hotel** (⊠ Oualie Beach, ☎ 869/469–9735) throws a popular Saturday buffet with live string band and masquerade troupe. You can have dinner and a dance on Wednesday at **Pinney's Beach Hotel** (⊠ Pinney's Beach, ☎ 869/469–5207). **Tequila Sheila's** (⊠ Cades Bay, ☎ 869/469–1633) is legendary for its wild (for Nevis) Saturday Night Fever disco, when locals trot out their best polyester, and Sunday Beach Party Brunches, which often continue past dark.

Exploring Nevis

Nevis's main road makes a 20-mi circuit through the five parishes; various offshoots of the road wind into the mountains. You can tour Charlestown, the capital, in a half hour or so, but you'll need three to four hours to explore the entire island.

Numbers in the margin correspond to points of interest on the Nevis map.

SIGHTS TO SEE

❸ **Bath Springs.** The springs and the ruins of the **Bath Hotel,** built by John Huggins in 1778, sustained recent hurricane damage, and reopening has been delayed while the government lobbies the private sector to create a modernized spa (well, that's the official story, anyway; the full story is a complex web of Caribbean politics). The springs, with temperatures of 104–108°F, emanate from the hillside. Huggins's 50-room hotel, the first hotel in the Caribbean, was adjacent to the waters. Eighteenth-century accounts reported that a few days of imbibing and immersing in these waters resulted in miraculous cures. It would take a minor miracle to restore the decayed hotel to anything like grandeur—it closed down in the late 19th century—but the spring house has been partially restored, and locals still swear some of the springs are still as hot and restorative as ever. Although locals still romp in the waters, you might want to think twice about it. Still, this is a fascinating sight. ☉ *Weekdays 8–noon and 1–3:30, Sat. 8–noon.*

❷ **Caribbean Cove.** This lavish (by Caribbean standards) amusement park seems incongruous on peaceful, rather posh Nevis. Yet locals flock here to play miniature golf, ride in bumper boats, shop in stores full of T-shirts and stuffed animals, and eat at the pizzeria–ice cream parlor. As these things go, it's been tastefully done, with faux grottoes, a winding lagoon spanned by rickety suspension bridges, and splashing fountains everywhere. The miniature golf course has been cleverly devised to teach kids about Nevisian history. Holes include a rain forest, a Carib encampment, a fort, a Spanish galleon, and a treasure-filled cave. The sound effects when you hole your ball are cute. ⊠ *Stoney Grove,* ☎ *869/469–1286.* 🎟 *$4.* ☉ *Daily 10–10*

❶ **Charlestown.** About 1,200 of the island's 9,300 inhabitants live in the capital of Nevis. The town faces the Caribbean, about 12½ mi south of Basseterre in St. Kitts. If you arrive by ferry, as most people do, you'll walk smack onto Main Street from the pier. Although it's true that tiny Charlestown, founded in 1660, has seen better times, it's easy to imagine how it must have looked in its heyday. The weathered buildings still have their fanciful galleries, elaborate gingerbread, wood shutters, and hanging plants. The stonework building with the clock tower houses the **courthouse** and the second floor **library,** open Monday–Saturday 9–6. A fire in 1873 damaged the building and destroyed valuable records; the current building dates from the turn of the century. You're welcome to poke around the library, one of the coolest places on the island. The little park opposite is **Memorial Square,** dedicated to the fallen of World Wars I and II.

The Alexander Hamilton Birthplace, which contains the **Museum of Nevis History,** is on the waterfront, covered in bougainvillea and hibiscus. This Georgian-style house is a reconstruction of the statesman's original home, built in 1680 and thought to have been destroyed during an earthquake in the mid-19th century. Hamilton was born here in 1755. He left for the American colonies 17 years later to continue his education; he became secretary to George Washington and died in a duel with political rival Aaron Burr. The **Nevis House of Assembly** sits on the second floor of this building, and the museum downstairs contains Hamilton memorabilia; documents pertaining to the island's history; and displays on island geology, politics, and cuisine. ☒ *Low St.,* ☎ *869/469–5786.* ☒ *$2.* ☉ *Weekdays 8–4, Sat. 10–1.*

❼ **Eden Brown Estate.** This government-owned mansion, built around 1740, is known as Nevis's haunted house or, rather, haunted ruins. In 1822, apparently, a Miss Julia Huggins was to marry a fellow named Maynard. However, on the day of the wedding, the groom and his best man had a duel and killed each other. The bride-to-be became a recluse, and the mansion was closed down. Local residents claim they can feel the presence of "someone" whenever they go near the eerie old house with its shroud of weeds and wildflowers. You're welcome to drop by; it's always open, and it's free.

❾ **Ft. Ashby.** Overgrown with tropical vegetation, this site overlooks the place where the settlement of Jamestown fell into the sea after a tidal wave hit the coast in 1680. Needless to say, this is a beloved scuba diving site. ☒ *1½ mi southwest of Hurricane Hill, on Main Rd.*

❽ **Hurricane Hill.** Many people take the drive up here to see the splendid view of St. Kitts. ☒ *West of Newcastle Airport.*

❹ **Nelson Museum.** This collection merits a visit for its memorabilia of Lord Nelson, including letters, documents, paintings, and even furniture from his flagship. Nelson was based in Antigua but came to Nevis often to court, and eventually to marry, Frances Nisbet, who lived on a 64-acre plantation here. ☒ *Bath Rd.,* ☎ *869/469–0408.* ☒ *$2 ($1 if admission already paid to affiliated Museum of Nevis History).* ☉ *Weekdays 9–4, Sat. 10–1.*

❿ **Nelson Spring.** The spring's waters have considerably decreased since the 1780s, when young Captain Horatio Nelson periodically filled his ships with fresh water here.

❻ **Nevis Botanical Gardens.** In addition to terraced gardens and arbors, this remarkable 7.8 acre site (begun in 1997) has natural lagoons, streams, and waterfalls. You'll find a proper rose garden; sections devoted to orchids and bromeliads, cacti, and flowering trees and shrubs; and even a bamboo garden. The entrance to the Rain Forest Conservatory—which attempts to include every conceivable Caribbean ecosystem and then some—duplicates an imposing Mayan temple. A splendid re-creation of a plantation-style great house contains a tearoom with sweeping sea views and a souvenir shop that sells teas, teapots, jams, Caribbean cookbooks, and the like. ☒ *Montpelier Estate,* ☎ *no phone.* ☒ *$8.* ☉ *Daily 10–6.*

❺ **St. John's Church.** Among the records of this church built in 1680 is a tattered, prominently displayed marriage certificate that reads: "Horatio Nelson, Esquire, to Frances Nisbet, Widow, on March 11, 1787." ☒ *Fig Tree Parish.*

⓫ **St. Thomas Anglican Church.** The island's oldest church was built in 1643 and has been altered many times over the years. The gravestones in the old churchyard have stories to tell, and the church itself contains memorials to the early settlers of Nevis.

ST. KITTS AND NEVIS A TO Z

Arriving and Departing

BY AIRPLANE

American (☎ 869/465–0500) and **Delta** (☎ 800/221–1212) fly from the United States to Antigua, St. Croix, St. Thomas, St. Maarten, and

San Juan, Puerto Rico, where connections to St. Kitts (and, to a lesser extent, to Nevis) can be made on **American Eagle** (☎ 869/465–0500), **LIAT** (☎ 869/465–8613), and **Windward Island Airways** (☎ 869/465–8010). **British Airways** (☎ 800/247–9297) flies from London to Antigua; **Air Canada** (☎ 800/776–3000) from Toronto to Antigua.

From the Airport: Taxis meet every flight at Robert L. Bradshaw Golden Rock Airport on St. Kitts (☎ no phone) and Newcastle Airport on Nevis (☎ no phone). The taxis are unmetered, but fixed rates, in E.C. dollars, are posted at the airport and at the jetty. On St. Kitts the fare from the airport to the closest hotel in Basseterre is EC$16; to the farthest point, EC$56. On Nevis it costs EC$40 from the ferry slip to Nisbet Plantation (EC$20 from the airport) and EC$30 to Golden Rock (EC$45 from the airport). Before setting off in a cab, be sure to clarify whether the rate quoted is in E.C. or U.S. dollars. There's a 50% surcharge for trips made between 10 PM and 6 AM.

Electricity
St. Kitts and Nevis function on 100 volts, 60 cycles, making all North American appliances safe to use.

Emergencies
Hospital: Joseph N. France General Hospital (✉ Cayon St., Basseterre, St. Kitts, ☎ 869/465–2551); **Alexandra Hospital** (✉ Government Rd., Charlestown, Nevis ☎ 869/469–5473). **Pharmacies:** On St. Kitts, **Parris Pharmacy** (✉ Central St., Basseterre, ☎ 869/465–8569) is open Monday–Wednesday 8–5, Thursday 8–1, Friday 8–5:30, and Saturday 8–6; **City Drug** (✉ Fort St., Basseterre, ☎ 869/465–2156) has hours Monday–Wednesday and Friday–Saturday 8–7, Thursday 8–5, Sunday 8–10 AM; the branch at the Sun 'n' Sand Beach Resort (✉ Frigate Bay, ☎ 869/465–1803) is open Monday–Saturday 8:30–8, Sunday 8:30–10:30 and 4–6. On Nevis, **Evelyn's Drugstore** (✉ Main St., Charlestown, ☎ 869/469–5278) is open weekdays 8–5, Saturday 8–7:30, and Sunday 7 AM–8 PM; the **Claxton Medical Centre** (✉ Main St., Charlestown, ☎ 869/469–5357) has hours Monday–Wednesday and Friday 8–6, Thursday 8–4, Saturday 7:30–7, and Sunday 6 PM–8 PM. **Police:** ☎ 911.

Festivals and Seasonal Events
Carnival (☎ 869/465–4151 for information) is held for 10 days immediately following Boxing Day (December 26) and is the usual riot of color and noise, with steel band and Calypso Monarch competitions, and flamboyant parades of the various troupes. On Nevis, a special **Tourism Week** (☎ 869/469–1042) is usually held in mid-February and includes horse races, bartender competitions, and jump-ups. The annual **Nevis Lions Club Sailing Regatta** (☎ 869/469–5324) in mid-June features fishing boat and Sunfish races, volleyball and domino competitions, a "best beach legs" contest, and a Saturday evening dance. The **St. Kitts Music Festival** (☎ 869/465–9787), held the last week of June, celebrates everything from R&B to reggae. Among the top international acts to perform have been Chaka Khan, Earl Klugh, and Peabo Bryson. Mid-September's **Heritage Week** (☎ 869/469–1992) includes celebrations of local culture, from food fairs to craft exhibitions.

Getting Around
AIRPLANES
LIAT (☞ Arriving and Departing By Airplane, *above*) has two flights daily between St. Kitts and Nevis. **Air St. Kitts–Nevis** (☎ 869/469–9064 in St. Kitts, 869/465–8571 in Nevis), **Carib Aviation** (☎ 869/469–9295 in St. Kitts, 869/465–3055 in Nevis), and **Nevis Express** (☎ 869/

469–9755) are reliable charter operations providing service between St. Kitts and Nevis and to other islands.

BOATS

The 150-passenger government-operated ferry M/V *Caribe Queen* makes the 45-minute crossing from Nevis to St. Kitts twice daily except Thursday and Sunday. The schedule is erratic, so confirm departure times with the tourist office. Round-trip fare is $8. An air-conditioned, 110-passenger ferry, M/V *Spirit of Mount Nevis,* makes the run twice daily Thursday and Sunday. The fare is $12 round-trip. Call **Nevis Cruise Lines** (☎ 869/469–9373) for information and reservations.

Sea-taxi service between the two islands is operated by Kenneth Samuel (☎ 869/465–2670) and Auston MacLeod of **Pro-Divers** (☎ 869/465–3223) for $20 one-way in summer, $25 in winter; discounts can be negotiated for small groups.

BUSES

A privately owned minibus circles St. Kitts. Check with the tourist office (☞ Visitor Information, *below*) about schedules and fares.

CAR RENTALS AND SCOOTERS

You'll need a local driver's license, which you can get by presenting yourself, your valid driver's license, and $12 at the police station on Cayon Street in Basseterre. (On Nevis, the car-rental agency will help you obtain a local license at the police station.) The license is valid for one year. Car rentals start at about $35 per day for a compact; expect to pay a few extra bucks for air-conditioning. Most agencies offer substantial discounts when you rent by the week. At press time, the price of gas was $2.50 per gallon. Driving is on the left.

St. Kitts agencies include **Avis** (✉ Golden Rock Airport, ☎ 869/465–6507), which has the best selection of Suzuki and Daihatsu four-wheel-drive vehicles, **Budget** (✉ Golden Rock Airport, ☎ 869/466–5585), **Delise Walwyn** (☎ 869/465–8449), and **Sunshine** (✉ Cayon St., Basseterre; Golden Rock Airport, ☎ 869/465–2193). **TDC Rentals** (✉ W. Independence Sq., Basseterre, ☎ 869/465–2991) has a wide selection of vehicles and outstanding service.

You may not want to drive in Nevis. The island's roads are pocked with crater-size potholes; driving is on the left, and, to make it more difficult, you may be given a right-drive vehicle. Pigs, goats, and cattle amble along the road, and if you deviate from Main Street in Charlestown, you're likely to have trouble finding your way. But if you can't resist, try renting from **TDC Rentals** (✉ Bay Rd., Charlestown, ☎ 869/469–5690), which is known for its exceptional service and wide range of vehicles; it has offices on St. Kitts and offers a three-day rental that includes a car on both islands. **Avis** (✉ Stoney Grove, ☎ 869/469–1240) provides Suzuki Jeeps and Nissan cars. **Nisbett Rentals** (✉ Newcastle Airport, ☎ 869/469–9211) rents cars, *minimokes* (essentially covered, glorified golf carts), and Jeeps.

TAXIS

Taxi rates are government-regulated and are posted at the airport, the dock, and in the free visitor tourist guide. There are fixed rates to and from all the hotels and to and from major points of interest. In St. Kitts, you can call the **St. Kitts Taxi Association** (☎ 869/465–8487; 869/465–7818 after hrs). In Nevis, taxi service (☎ 869/469–5621; 869/469–5515 after dark) is available at the airport, by the dock in Charlestown, and through arrangements made at your hotel.

Guided Tours

The taxi driver who picks you up will probably offer to act as your guide to the island. Each driver is knowledgeable and does a three-hour tour for $60. He can also make a lunch reservation at one of the plantation restaurants, and you can incorporate this into your tour.

BOAT

On St. Kitts, **Leeward Island Charters** (☎ 869/465–7474) offers day and overnight charters on two catamarans—the 47-ft *Caona* and the 70-ft *Spirit of St. Kitts*. Day sails are from 9:30 to 4:30 and include a barbecue, an open bar, and use of snorkeling equipment. **Tropical Tours** (☎ 869/465–4167) offers moonlight cruises on the 52-ft catamaran *Cileca III* as well as glass-bottom-boat tours. **Jazzie II** (☎ 869/465–3529) is another glass-bottom boat that cruises the southeastern coast. The catamaran **Tropical Dreamer** (☎ 869/465–8224) is available for day and sunset cruises. On Nevis, **Sea Nevis Charters** (⊠ Cades Bay, ☎ 869/469–9239) offers its 44-ft *Sea Dreamer* for snorkeling and island sunset cruises.

ORIENTATION

Tropical Tours (⊠ Cayon St., Basseterre, ☎ 869/465–4167) can run you around St. Kitts and take you to the rain forest, for $45 per person. Also try **Kantours** (☎ 869/465–2098) for general island tours. On Nevis, **Fitzroy "Teach" Williams** (⊠ Main St., Charlestown, ☎ 869/469–1140) is recommended: He's former president of the taxi association—even older cabbies call him "the Dean." **All Seasons Streamline Tours** (☎ 869/469–1138) has a fleet of air-conditioned, 14-seat vans—operated by uniformed drivers—to take you around the island at a cost of $75 for three hours. **Jan's Travel Agency** (⊠ Arcade, Charlestown, ☎ 869/469–5578) arranges half- and full-day tours of the island. You can also stop by the Nevis Tourist Office (☞ Visitor Information, *below*) for the historical society's self-guided island tour.

SPECIAL-INTEREST

Addy's Nature Tours (☎ 869/465–8069), **Kriss Tours** (☎ 869/465–4042), and **Greg's Safari** (☎ 869/465–4121) specialize in rain-forest and volcano tours on St. Kitts. David Rollinson of **Eco-Tours Nevis** (☎ 869/469–2091) and **Top to Bottom** (☎ 869/469–5371) organizes hiking adventures on Nevis. For more information, *See* Hiking sections *in* Outdoor Activities and Sports, *above*.

Money Matters

CURRENCY

Legal tender is the Eastern Caribbean (EC) dollar. At press time, the rate of exchange was EC$2.70 to US$1. U.S. dollars are accepted practically everywhere, but you'll usually get change in EC currency. Most large hotels, restaurants, and shops accept major credit cards, but small inns and shops often do not. Prices quoted throughout this chapter are in U.S. dollars unless noted otherwise.

SERVICE CHARGES, TAXES, AND TIPPING

Hotels add a 10% service charge to your bill. Restaurants occasionally do the same; to be on the safe side, ask, if it is isn't printed on the menu. Hotels collect a 7% government tax. In restaurants, where there's no service charge included in the bill, a tip of 15% is appropriate. The departure tax is $10. There's no departure tax when you depart from St. Kitts to Nevis, or vice-versa. There is no sales tax on either St. Kitts or Nevis. Taxi drivers typically receive a 10% tip, porters and bellmen $1 per bag; if you feel the service was exemplary, leave $3–$4 per night for the housekeeping staff.

Language

English with a strong West Indian lilt is spoken here.

Opening and Closing Times

Although **shops** used to close for lunch from noon to 1, more and more establishments are remaining open Monday–Saturday 8–4. Some shops close earlier on Thursday. Hours vary somewhat for **banks** but are typically Monday–Thursday 8–3 and Friday 8–5. St. Kitts & Nevis National Bank is also open Saturday 8:30–11 AM. **Post offices** are open Monday–Wednesday and Friday 8–3, Thursday and Saturday 8–noon.

HOLIDAYS

New Year's Day, Ash Wednesday (Feb. 17), Easter Monday (Apr. 5), Independence Day (Sept. 19), Labour Day (May 4), Whit Monday (May 24), Christmas, and Boxing Day (Dec. 26).

Passports

U.S. and Canadian citizens need a valid passport or must prove citizenship with a birth certificate (with a raised seal) accompanied by a government-issued photo ID. British citizens must have a passport. A return or ongoing ticket is mandatory.

Precautions

Visitors, especially women, should not jog on long, lonely roads.

Telephones and Mail

To call St. Kitts and Nevis from the United States, dial the area code 869, then access code 465, 466, 468, or 469 and the local four-digit number. Phone cards, which you can buy in denominations of $5, $10, and $20, are handy for making local phone calls, calling other islands, and accessing USA Direct lines. To make an intraisland call, dial the seven-digit number. Warning for both islands: Many private lines and hotels charge access rates if you use your ATT, Sprint, or MCI calling card; there's no regularity, so phoning can be frustrating. Avoid using the widely advertised Skantel, which ostensibly allows you to make credit-card calls; rates are usurious, and they freeze an outrageous amount for up to a week on your credit card until they put through the exact bill.

Airmail letters to the United States and Canada cost EC80¢ per half ounce; postcards require EC50¢; to the United Kingdom letters cost EC1.20, postcards EC.60¢. Mail takes at least 7–10 days to reach the United States. St. Kitts and Nevis issue separate stamps, but each honors the other's. The beautiful stamps are collector's items, and you may have a hard time pasting them on postcards. As usual in the Caribbean, you needn't worry about a postal code, or even a street address (though sometimes there's a postal box number): the business's/person's name, the town, and the island name will usually suffice.

Visitor Information

Before leaving home, contact the **St. Kitts & Nevis Tourist Board** (✉ 414 E. 75th St., New York, NY 10021, ☎ 212/535–1234 or 800/582–6208, www.stkitts-nevis.com; ✉ 365 Bay St., Suite 806, Toronto, Ontario M5H 2V1, ☎ 416/368–6707; ✉ 10 Kensington Ct., London W8 5DL, ☎ 0171/376–0881).

On St. Kitts, contact **St. Kitts/Nevis Department of Tourism** (✉ Pelican Mall, Bay Rd. Box 132,Basseterre, ☎ 869/465–2620 or 869/465–4040) and the **St. Kitts–Nevis Hotel Association** (✉ Box 438, Basseterre, ☎ 869/465–5304). The **Nevis Tourist Office** (☎ 869/469–1042) is on Main Street in Charlestown. The office is open Monday–Tuesday 8–4:30 and Wednesday–Friday 8–4.

21 St. Lucia

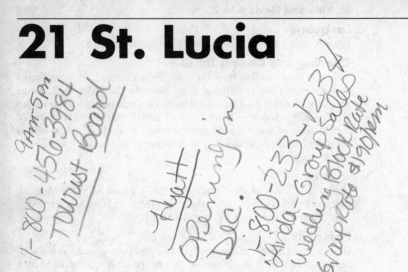

Updated by
Jane E. Zarem

Watching the festivities from the porch of the corner bar, the woman seems disappointed with the Friday night street party. The beat sounds more disco than Caribbean. "Where's the reggae, the calypso?" she wonders aloud. "It's down there, miss," offers a wiry young man with a broad smile and smooth moves. "You have to be dancing, near the speakers. Come on." Taking her hand, he leads her to the middle of the street, where the melody is loud and clear; the rhythm, definitely Caribbean. To enjoy the Gros Islet "jump up," you have to jump in.

Contrary to local legend, which claims Columbus "discovered" St. Lucia on December 13, 1502, historians now feel certain that the intrepid explorer never set foot on the island. Until a few years ago, neither had most Americans. Over the last decade, a combination of inviting resorts, fine beaches, plenty of water sports activities, fascinating natural beauty, and a welcoming environment—including friendly folks who like to make sure that you enjoy yourself—have drawn more and more visitors to this lush, tropical paradise.

St. Lucia is a 238-square-mi (2,714 mi at its widest) island in the Windward chain, between Martinique and St. Vincent, and 100 mi due west of Barbados. Because of its natural beauty, St. Lucia has been dubbed "the Helen of the West Indies." The capital city of Castries and surrounding villages in the north are home to 40% of the population; this is also the destination of most vacationers, who stay at posh beach resorts and play on honey-color beaches. The central part of the island is covered with thick jungle, dense rain forest, and vast banana plantations. From the populous north to the gorgeous south, a torturously winding road passes through fertile valleys, forests, and small villages on secluded bays. Marigot Bay, whose claim to fame is having been the filming location for the 1967 movie *Doctor Doolittle,* on the west coast just south of Castries, is one of the Caribbean's prettiest anchorages.

The south is dominated by striking natural attractions and vistas, breathtaking from land or sea. The area around the old capital of Soufrière is the focus of most sightseeing trips. The town itself is a charming and refreshingly authentic West Indian hamlet, with many examples of original French Colonial architecture. Bubbling sulfur springs gurgle at the mouth of a low-lying volcano that erupted thousands of years ago and still produces highly acclaimed curative waters. The Pitons (Petit and Gros), the island's unusual twin peaks, rise from the sea to more than 2,400 ft. They're familiar to sailors as navigational landmarks, and nearby reefs are well-known by divers.

Historians are convinced that the first European sighting of St. Lucia was in 1499 (not 1502) by Juan de la Cosa, Columbus's navigator on his first and second voyages, but the Arawaks were the island's first inhabitants. They paddled up from South America sometime before AD 200. The much more aggressive Caribs followed and conquered the Arawaks around AD 800. The Caribs called the island *Hewanorra* (Land Where the Iguana Is Found), and were still resident on the island when Europeans attempted to establish a settlement.

François Le Clerc, a pirate nicknamed Jambe de Bois (Wooden Leg) for obvious reasons, was actually the first European to settle on St. Lucia. During the late 16th century, he holed up on Pigeon Island, at the northernmost point of the island, and attacked passing ships. In 1605, 67 English settlers bound for Guiana aboard a vessel called the *Olive Branch* were blown off course and landed near Vieux Fort. Within a few weeks, the Caribs had killed all but 19, who escaped in a canoe. Another group of English settlers came by 30 years later and were met with a similar lack of hospitality. The French arrived in 1651 after the French West India Company bought the island and took control.

Thus began a 150-year period of battles between the French and the English that saw a dizzying 14 changes in power before the British took possession in 1814. During those battle-filled years, Europeans colonized the island. They developed sugar plantations, using slaves from West Africa to work the fields. By 1838, when slaves were emancipated, more than 90% of the population consisted of African descendants. This is also largely the case for today's 150,000 St. Lucians.

On February 22, 1979 St. Lucia became an independent state within the British Commonwealth of Nations, with a resident governor-general appointed by the queen. Still, there are many relics of French occupation, notably in the island patois that's spoken (in addition to English), the cuisine, the place names, and the people's surnames.

St. Lucia developed a coal industry beginning in 1863, which flourished until about 1920. Castries was a leading coal port in the West Indies. Indentured Indian laborers arrived in 1882 to help bail out the dying sugar industry, which had been huge until slavery was abolished. Sugar all but died in the 1960s, when bananas became the major money crop. Today, tourism is running neck and neck with bananas, particularly since the banana-growing countries of the Eastern Caribbean are competing for a share of the European market. The importance of tourism pleases the savvy St. Lucians, but they are also working hard to avoid ruining their island with overbuilding. They are also diversifying their agriculture base to strengthen their economy further by reducing imports. Consequently, there's a tangible solidity to St. Lucia, an optimism that's reflected in general friendliness as well as in a startling number of delightful small hotels and spectacular resorts.

Lodging

St. Lucia rivals Jamaica in the number of all-inclusive resorts it has. Additionally, several small, inexpensive hotels and inns offer bright, clean, modern accommodations at reasonable prices. You won't find high-rise hotels; instead, resorts are tucked into lush surroundings to preserve the island's visual beauty. Virtually all lodgings are located along the calm Caribbean coast, either around Soufrière to the south or, more commonly, between Castries and Cap Estate in the north.

Resorts and hotels run the gamut as to price range and style. Some are large and lavish; others, little and laid-back. Many properties listed under the highest price category are all-inclusive; your room rate includes three meals a day, snacks, all beverages, sports and nonmotorized water sports (including instruction), airport transfers (an otherwise significant expense), taxes, and gratuities. Some properties offer a choice of MAP or EP meal plans, and most offer wedding packages: St. Lucian law requires residency for only three days to acquire a marriage license, so weddings and renewal-of-vows ceremonies have become a big attraction. Just about every resort has friendly, accommodating service and is either in a fairly secluded cove or along an unspoiled beach.

A group of 31 small hotels and inns are represented by a central reservations service. Establishments range in size from 3 to 62 rooms and are located near prime resort areas or in more remote surroundings, with prices that start as low as $15 per room. Contact: **Inns of St. Lucia** (⌧ 20 Bridge St., Castries, St. Lucia, ☎ 758/452–4599, ℻ 758/452–5428). For villa rentals, contact **Tropical Villas** (⌧ Box 189, Castries, St. Lucia, ☎ 758/452–8240, ℻ 758/450–8089).

CATEGORY	COST*
$$$$	over $350
$$$	$200–$350
$$	$150–$200
$	under $150

*All prices are for a standard double room, excluding 8% tax and 10% service charge.

Castries and the North

$$$$ 🏨 **East Winds Inn.** On a private beach 10 minutes north of Castries, the inn's 26 Caribbean gingerbread-style bungalows are set amid 8 acres of tropical gardens. Rooms have patios or terraces; deluxe rooms have TVs and VCRs and private indoor/outdoor showers. Guests mingle at the clubhouse, in the free-form pool with swim-up bar, on the sundeck, and on the beach—where kayaks, aqua boards, aqua trikes, and snorkeling equipment are provided. The international and Creole creations of a French chef are served in the inn's open-air, thatched-roof restaurant (vegetarian selections are always included). ⌧ *Labrelotte Bay, Gros Islet (Box 193, Castries),* ☎ *758/452–8212,* ℻ *758/452–9941. 26 rooms. Restaurant, 2 bars, fans, refrigerators, pool, beach, snorkeling, boating, shop. AE, MC, V. All-inclusive.*

$$$$ 🏨 **LeSPORT.** Though crowned by the Oasis—a temple to well-being that ★   was built to resemble the Alhambra in Spain—LeSPORT is not exactly a spa. It's an attractive resort that hugs Cariblue Beach at the very northern tip of St. Lucia, with daily (if you wish) spa treatments included in the rates. Guests laze around in white robes awaiting thalassotherapy—seawater beauty treatments—before throwing themselves into one of the dozens of things to do (archery, tai chi, fencing, waterskiing, scuba diving, tennis, volleyball, yoga classes, etc.). Rooms are spacious and decorated in soft, muted pastel colors with ceramic tile floors and king-size four-poster or twin beds. Bathrooms are marble-tiled and modern but rather small. Each room has a balcony or terrace; deluxe rooms are oceanfront or have an ocean view. Two one-bedroom suites (expandable to two bedrooms) have a hand-stenciled gingerbread motif on the walls, cool blue-and-white fabrics, white marble floors throughout, huge double balconies, and a stocked wet bar. A separate plantation house, called "Mandalay," can be rented with or without the all-inclusive features of the resort. It's all new construction but replicates a typical great house—filled with antiques and all the comforts of home (if you live like the lord of the manse!). ⊠ *Cariblue Beach, Cap Estate (Box 437, Castries),* ☎ *758/450–8551 or 800/544–2883 (reservations service),* FAX *758/450–0368. 100 rooms, 2 suites, 1 plantation house. Restaurant, 2 bars, piano bar, air-conditioning, refrigerators, 3 pools, beauty salon, hot tub, sauna, spa, golf privileges, tennis court, aerobics, archery, croquet, exercise rooms, hiking, Ping-Pong, volleyball, beach, dive shop, snorkeling, windsurfing, boating, waterskiing, bicycles, shop, laundry service, airport shuttle. AE, DC, MC, V. All-inclusive.*

✓**$$$$** ⚏ **Rex Papillon.** Spun off from neighboring Rex St. Lucian, this 10-acre property on Reduit Beach is an all-inclusive resort. Rooms are furnished with one king-size or two twin beds. Deluxe and superior rooms are air-conditioned with full baths; standard rooms have ceiling fans and shower only. Deluxe rooms also have cable TV, sitting area, minibar, and a guaranteed ocean view. All rooms are decorated with rattan furniture and tropical-print fabrics (blues and peaches), with tile floors. Some rooms are designed especially for guests with disabilities. Meals are served at Monarch, the main restaurant, or Clipper, the informal beachside snack bar. Evening entertainment is presented at Tropigala lounge. In keeping with its name, the resort's pool is in the shape of a butterfly. ⊠ *Reduit Beach, Rodney Bay (Box 512, Castries),* ☎ *758/452–0984; 800/255–5859 or 800/223–9868 (reservations services);* FAX *758/452–9332. 140 rooms. Restaurant, bar, snack bar, pool, 2 tennis courts, beach, snorkeling, windsurfing, boating, babysitting, children's program. AE, DC, MC, V. All-inclusive.*

✓**$$$$** ⚏ **Royal St. Lucian.** This classy resort, facing beautiful Reduit Beach,
★ caters to your every whim. The colonnaded reception area is stunning—an Italian palazzo with vaulted atrium, cool marble walls, a gurgling fountain, and a sweeping grand staircase. The russet-roofed white buildings form a "U" in the pristine landscaped grounds. The large, rambling pool has Japanese-style bridges, a natural rock waterfall, and a swim-up bar. The split-level suites are sumptuous, with a separate sitting area, luxurious bathroom, large patio or balcony, soothing pastel color scheme, background music system, cable TV, three phones, and jet shower. Massages, hydrotherapy and other spa treatments can be arranged at the Royal Spa, a small, intimate facility that's also open to nonguests. Food and service are stellar. Guests may use the tennis and water-sports facilities at the adjacent sister property, the ☞ **Rex St. Lucian.** ⊠ *Reduit Beach, Rodney Bay (Box 977, Castries),* ☎ *758/452–9999; 800/255–5859 or 800/223–9868 (reservations services);* FAX *758/452–9639. 96 suites. 2 restaurants, 2 bars, air-conditioning, in-room safes, minibars, pool, massage, spa, health club, tennis court, beach, snorkeling, meeting rooms. AE, DC, MC, V. EP, MAP.*

$$$$ ⚏ **Sandals Halcyon St. Lucia.** This couples-only Sandals resort is at Choc Bay, 10 minutes north of Castries. More low-key than its sister resort, there's still a lot of activity and enthusiasm on the part of both guests and staff. All rooms are surrounded by gardens and are attractively decorated with mahogany furniture, king-size four-poster beds with bright-print spreads, and white tile floors. Rooms each have cable TV. The sea here is generally calm, and guests enjoy a wide range of water sports and other activities—exercise equipment, nightly entertainment,

Exploring

Anse-la-Raye and Canaries, **5**

Barre de l'Isle Forest Reserve, **18**

Castries, **1**

Choiseul, **12**

Diamond Botanical Gardens, **7**

Errard Plantation, **17**

Fort Charlotte, **2**

Fregate Island Nature Reserve, **16**

Gros Islet, **20**

Laborie, **13**

Maria Islands Nature Reserve, **15**

Marigot Bay, **4**

Marquis Estate, **19**

Morne Coubaril Estate, **9**

Morne Fortune, **3**

Pigeon Island, **22**

The Pitons, **8**

Rodney Bay, **21**

St. Lucia National Rain Forest, **10**

Soufrière, **6**

La Soufrière Drive-in Volcano, **11**

Vieux Fort, **14**

Dining

Bang...between the Pitons, **54**

Beach Restaurant and Bar, **49**

Camilla's, **50**

Capone's, **27**

Dasheene Restaurant and Bar, **55**

Great House, **23**

Green Parrot, **45**

J.J.'s, **48**

Jimmie's, **42**

Key Largo, **26**

Lifeline Bar & Restaurant, **51**

The Lime, **28**

Piton Restaurant and Bar, **49**

San Antoine, **46**

The Still, **52**

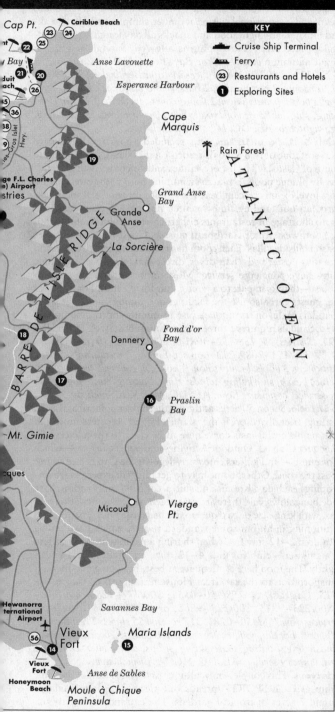

Lodging

Anse Chastanet Beach Hotel, **49**

Auberge Seraphine, **41**

Bay Gardens, **33**

Candyo Inn, **32**

Club St. Lucia, **25**

East Winds Inn, **37**

Green Parrot, **45**

Harmony Marina Suites, **29**

Hummingbird Beach Resort, **51**

Jalousie Hilton Resort & Spa, **53** *

Ladera Resort, **55**

LeSPORT, **24**

Marigot Beach Club, **47**

Orange Grove Hotel, **36**

Rendezvous, **40**

Rex Papillon, **34**

Rex St. Lucian, **30**

Royal St. Lucian, **31**

Sandals Halcyon St. Lucia, **39**

Sandals St. Lucia at La Toc, **43**

Skyway Inn, **56**

Still Plantation & Beach Resort, **52**

Tuxedo Villas, **44**

Windjammer Landing Villa Beach Resort, **35**

Wyndham Morgan Bay Resort, **38**

KEY

⚓ Cruise Ship Terminal

⛴ Ferry

㉓ Restaurants and Hotels

❶ Exploring Sites

Cap Pt.

Cariblue Beach

Anse Lavouette

Esperance Harbour

Cape Marquis

Rain Forest

ATLANTIC OCEAN

Grand Anse Bay

Grande Anse

La Sorcière

BARRE DE L'ISLE RIDGE

Fond d'or Bay

Dennery

Praslin Bay

Mt. Gimie

Micoud

Vierge Pt.

Hewanorra International Airport

Savannes Bay

Vieux Fort

Maria Islands

Vieux Fort

Anse de Sables

Honeymoon Beach

Moule à Chique Peninsula

Odyssy Orange Grove Hotel 758-452-0021

and more. A shuttle runs hourly between the two Sandals resorts, so guests can "stay at one, play at two." Three restaurants serve Italian, Caribbean, and international cuisine at dinner, sumptuous buffet breakfasts and lunches, and light food and snacks all day long. Seaside weddings take place often. No tipping is allowed. Sandals requires a three-night minimum stay. ⊠ *Choc Bay (Box GM 910, Castries),* ☎ *758/453–0222 or 800/223–6510 (reservations service),* ℻ *758/451–8435. 170 rooms. 3 restaurants, 2 bars, piano bar, snack bar, air-conditioning, 3 pools, beauty salon, 2 tennis courts, basketball, health club, Ping-Pong, shuffleboard, volleyball, beach, snorkeling, windsurfing, boating, nightclub. AE, DC, MC, V. All-inclusive.*

$$$$
★
Sandals St. Lucia at La Toc. This secluded 155-acre all-inclusive couples resort, one of two Sandals resorts on the island, is a 10-minute drive south of Castries. The list of facilities and amenities is almost endless: private plunge pools, a ¼-acre swimming pool with waterfall and bridges, a lovely ½-mi crescent beach, a 9-hole golf course, floodlit tennis courts, an outstanding fitness center, nightly entertainment, etc. There's no shortage of restaurants either; choose Asian, Continental, French, Southwestern, or Caribbean cuisine. Guest rooms and suites are in pastel hillside villas. Each room has rich mahogany furniture and king-size four-poster beds, hair dryer, direct-dial telephone, and cable TV. Suites have concierge service. Most important, guests seem to have a blast—thanks in part to a young, fun-loving staff. For a change of scene, guests can also use the facilities and dining choices at sister resort Sandals Halcyon (☞ *above*), just 15 minutes north. No tipping is allowed. Sandals requires a three-night minimum stay. ⊠ *La Toc Rd. (Box 399, Castries),* ☎ *758/452–3081 or 800/223–6510 (reservations service),* ℻ *758/453–7089. 213 rooms, 60 suites. 5 restaurants, 5 bars, air-conditioning, 3 pools, beauty salon, 9-hole golf course, 5 tennis courts, health club, beach, snorkeling, windsurfing, boating, shop, nightclub, laundry service, concierge floor. AE, DC, MC, V. All-inclusive.*

✓**$$$–$$$$**
Club St. Lucia. Set on 50 acres at the northernmost point of St. Lucia, this bustling, friendly resort is the island's largest. It caters mostly to Brits, but tennis enthusiasts come here to be close to the adjacent St. Lucia Racquet Club (☞ *Outdoor Activities and Sports, below*)—which is free for guests—and golfers enjoy privileges at the Cap Estate course just across the road. Others come here to get hitched; expect to see several weddings each day. Rooms and suites, called "family rooms," are in hillside bungalows, and there are two beaches. Accommodations are spacious, with king-size or two queen-size beds, tile floors, patios, and air-conditioning in all but some standard rooms, which have ceiling fans. Children 2–12 stay free when sharing a room with parents, and there's a children's club for kids 4–12. Live entertainment is scheduled nightly. The food here is adequate at best, but you get a discount and transportation to the ☞ **Great House** restaurant. ⊠ *Cap Estate (Box 915, Castries),* ☎ *758/450–0551; 800/777–1250, 800/742–4276, 800/223–9815, 800/223–9868, or 800/223–6510 (reservations services);* ℻ *758/450–0281. 317 rooms, 55 suites. 2 restaurants, 3 bars, 3 pools, hot tub, golf privileges, 2 tennis courts, 2 beaches, snorkeling, windsurfing, boating, waterskiing, shops, dance club, children's program, laundry service. AE, DC, MC, V. All-inclusive.*

$$$–$$$$
★
Rendezvous. This couples-only, all-inclusive resort (under the same ownership as ☞ **LeSPORT**) spreads out along 2-mi-long Malabar Beach amid 7 acres of tropical gardens. The entrance is directly opposite the end of Vigie Airport runway, so planes taking off can be a distraction. Since the airport only accommodates small prop aircraft, however, the effect seems almost charming—in a retro, B-movie kind of way. Days and nights at Rendezvous tend to be quite active, with volleyball in the pool and on the beach, aerobics and exercise classes,

scuba instruction, and an array of water-sports activities. The activities desk will arrange practically anything for you, including a complimentary wedding or renewal of vows. Accommodations have ginger-color marble floors, king-size four-poster beds, large marble bathrooms, and a balcony or terrace—but no TVs (anywhere on the resort property, in fact). There's nightly entertainment, music for dancing, and a piano bar that's open until the last couple goes to bed. Food and drinks are available virtually every waking hour. Two chefs (one French, one American) turn out very tasty meals (not always the case at all-inclusive properties), encompassing a range of cuisines and with many choices at every meal. Meals are served buffet-style at the beachfront terrace restaurant. There's also an air-conditioned dining room, The Trysting Place, where the elegant atmosphere has food, wine, and service to match. ⊠ *Malabar Beach (Box 190, Castries),* ☎ *758/452–4211 or 800/544–2883 (reservations service),* FAX *758/452–7419. 84 rooms, 8 suites, 8 cottages. 2 restaurants, 2 bars, piano bar, air-conditioning, fans, 2 pools, 2 hot tubs, sauna, 2 tennis courts, aerobics, archery, exercise room, volleyball, beach, dive shop, boating, waterskiing, bicycles, shop, airport shuttle. AE, MC, V. All-inclusive.*

$$$–$$$$ ▥ **Windjammer Landing Villa Beach Resort.** This sun-kissed resort, with sweeping views of one of St. Lucia's prettiest bays, fulfills anyone's beachcombing fantasies. White stucco villas crowned with tile climb a hillside; a porticoed reception area and thatched-hut public rooms stretch along the beachfront. Villas are huge and tastefully decorated in island pastels and wicker furnishings; two- and three-bedroom villas have plunge pools. You can self-cater, eat at the Mango Tree restaurant, or arrange to have dinner prepared and served in your villa. The ambience is rustic simplicity with painted natural wood timbers, tile floors, wicker chairs, and straw mats. A people-mover transports guests up the steep hill to their villas from the main building and shops. A waterfall connects two bilevel pools. ⊠ *Labrelotte Bay (Box 1504, Castries),* ☎ *758/452–0913; 800/613–7193, 800/742–4276, or 800/223–9868 (reservations services);* FAX *758/452–9454. 131 1-, 2-, 3-, and 4-bedroom villas. 3 restaurants, 3 bars, air-conditioning, kitchenettes, 2 pools, beauty salon, 2 lighted tennis courts, beach, dive shop, snorkeling, windsurfing, boating, waterskiing, shops, children's program, laundry service, car rental. AE, MC, V. EP, MAP.*

$$$ ▥ **Rex St. Lucian.** The broad, white, informal lobby, with potted plants and upholstered sofas, leads to the gardens, pool area, and beautiful Reduit Beach. Rooms are attractively decorated in rattan and tropical prints and have two double beds, TVs, and patios or balconies. Deluxe rooms have minibars, hair dryers, and a guaranteed ocean view. Guests can enjoy fine dining at either the Oriental or Mariners open-air restaurant—or stroll to several restaurants and nightspots in the Rodney Bay Marina area. ⊠ *Reduit Beach, Rodney Bay (Box 512, Castries),* ☎ *758/452–8351; 800/255–5859 or 800/223–9868 (reservations services);* FAX *758/452–8331. 120 rooms. 2 restaurants, 2 bars, ice cream parlor, air-conditioning, pool, 2 tennis courts, beach, dive shop, snorkeling, windsurfing, boating, waterskiing, shops, baby-sitting, children's program, car rental. AE, DC, MC, V. EP, MAP.*

$$$ ▥ **Wyndham Morgan Bay Resort.** Eight three-story buildings fan out from a central pool-restaurant area at this all-inclusive resort on Choc Bay. Rooms are decorated in tropical pastel florals and peach wicker and are furnished with comfortable king-size beds. Each has a color television, radio, coffeemaker, hair dryer, and small veranda with either a garden or partial sea view. Drinks, activities, and entertainment flow freely—from early morning aerobics to midnight pizza at the beachside Palm Grill—to the delight of a largely European crowd. ⊠ *Choc Bay, Gros Islet (Box 2167, Castries),* ☎ *758/450–2511 or 800/WYN-*

DHAM (reservations service), ℻ *758/450–1050. 238 rooms. 2 restaurants, 2 bars, air-conditioning, pool, hot tub, sauna, 4 tennis courts, aerobics, archery, exercise room, Ping-Pong, beach, snorkeling, boating, waterskiing, shop, recreation room, children's programs, meeting room, airport shuttle. AE, D, MC, V. All-inclusive.*

$–$$ 🏨 **Marigot Beach Club.** On beautiful Marigot Bay, this quiet spot 9 mi south of Castries is not too far from the mountains and sights around Soufrière. "Firefly suites" climb the steep hillside that forms a backdrop for the resort, and a tram transports guests up and down. Studios and one-bedroom apartments have kitchenettes, pickled-wood furniture, and private patios that overlook the water. Marigot Bay is a favorite of yachtspeople, so the boating activity adds atmosphere. The resort has an excellent water-sports center, where you can arrange diving and snorkeling, windsurfing, kayaking, waterskiing, or sailing. The lovely beach, shaded by coconut palms, looks like one you'd see in the South Seas. Club Paradis, the open-air waterfront bar and restaurant, offers a wide selection of Caribbean and Continental fare. ⊠ *Marigot Bay (Box 101, Castries),* ☎ *758/451–4974 or 800/223– 9815 (reservations service),* ℻ *758/451–4973. 44 units. Restaurant, bar, kitchenettes, pool, beauty salon, exercise room, beach, dive shop, snorkeling, windsurfing, boating, shops. MC, V. EP, MAP.*

$–$$ 🏨 **Tuxedo Villas.** This pristine-white complex set around a tiny pool in a peaceful corner of Rodney Bay, close to Reduit Beach, is good value. Each of the small but comfortable villas has a living room with cable TV, dining room, and kitchenettes. There are six two-bedroom, two-bath units and four one-bedroom, one-bath units. Larger villas have kitchens equipped with full-size refrigerators, glass-top bamboo tables and breakfast bars, and patios. There's nothing exciting here, but everything works, everything is spotless, and the staff is friendly. ⊠ *Rodney Bay (Box 419, Castries),* ☎ *758/452–8553; 800/223–6510 or 800/223– 9815 (reservations services);* ℻ *758/452–8577. 10 apartments. Restaurant, bar, air-conditioning, kitchenettes, pool. AE, MC, V. EP.*

$ 🏨 **Auberge Seraphine.** This impressive small hotel overlooks Vigie Cove and is minutes from Vigie Airport, Pointe Seraphine, and downtown Castries. Accommodations are spacious, cheerful, and bright, and most have a view of the cove and Vigie Yacht Marina. All have cable TV and direct-dial telephones. A broad clay-tiled sundeck—the center of activity—surrounds a small pool. A shuttle service transports guests to and from a nearby beach. The popular restaurant offers fine Caribbean, French, and Continental cuisine; the management is proud of its well-stocked wine cellar. One child (age 2–12) stays free when sharing a room with two adults. ⊠ *Vigie Cove (Box 390, Castries),* ☎ *758/453–2073,* ℻ *758/451–7001. 22 rooms. Restaurant, bar, air-conditioning, pool, shop, meeting rooms. AE, MC, V. EP, MAP.*

$ 🏨 **Bay Gardens.** Conveniently located on the south side of Rodney Bay
★   and 7 mi north of Castries, this compact resort is an easy walk to beautiful Reduit Beach, several popular restaurants and nightclubs, and the marina. Shuttle service to the beach is free. Bay Gardens is modern and colorful—the lime-green building is studded with flower gardens. Guest rooms surround a courtyard with a double serpentine pool and Jacuzzi. Rooms are furnished with white wicker furniture and colorful print spreads in tropical colors, and each has cable TV and a balcony or patio. Executive rooms also have a trouser press and whirlpool bath. Eight self-contained apartments with kitchenettes and separate sitting rooms cater especially to families. Spices restaurant offers a varied menu, along with a weekly barbecue, Caribbean buffet, and Sunday brunch. One child (age 2–12) stays free when sharing a room with two adults. ⊠ *Rodney Bay (Box 1892, Castries),* ☎ *758/452–8060 or 800/223–9815 (reservations service),* ℻ *758/452–8059. 45 rooms,*

8 apartments. Restaurant, bar, ice cream parlor, air-conditioning, re-frigerators, 2 pools, beauty salon, hot tub, shops, recreation room, li-brary, meeting rooms. AE, MC, V. EP, MAP.

$ ⊞ **Candyo Inn.** This small pink hotel, in the heart of Rodney Bay, is one of the best buys in the Caribbean. It's a five-minute walk to beaches and several good restaurants. The inn has a small pool and lanai area. An outdoor bar near the pool serves drinks and snacks. The two-story building and its lush grounds are carefully looked after and spotless. All rooms have cable TV, veranda, white-tile floors, and white contemporary furniture with floral upholstery. The eight suites have kitchenettes, sitting rooms, and tubs; they're worth the extra $15 a night. ⊠ *Rodney Bay (Box 386, Castries),* ☎ *758/452–0712 or 800/223–9815 (reservations service),* FAX *758/452–0774. 4 rooms, 8 suites. Bar, air-conditioning, pool. AE, MC, V. EP.*

$ ⊞ **Green Parrot.** The hillside setting is the draw at this small hotel on Morne Fortune, set high above Castries and the harbor. The motel-like rooms have telephone, cable TV, and patios. A free bus scoots you to town and the beach; the hotel also arranges excursions to Anse Jam-bette, a private beach, for swimming and snorkeling. The ☞ **Green Par-rot** restaurant, open to the public, is internationally acclaimed for its cuisine. ⊠ *Morne Fortune (Castries, Box 648),* ☎ *758/452–3399,* FAX *758/453–2272. 55 rooms. Restaurant, bar, air-conditioning, pool, shop, billiards, cabaret. AE, MC, V. EP, MAP.*

$ ⊞ **Harmony Marina Suites.** Your suite may have a view of the pool or Rodney Bay Marina, but Reduit Beach is only 200 yards away. The two-story, colonial-style hotel is surrounded by gardens. Its 22 one-bedroom suites are done in pastel colors, with rattan furniture. Each has a large bathroom with hair dryer, a red-clay-tile balcony or ter-race, cable TV, kitchenettes, and wet bar. Eight VIP suites have dou-ble hot tubs and four-poster beds. The property also has its own waterfront restaurant, Mortar & Pestle, which serves Caribbean cui-sine. The adjacent, well-stocked minimarket makes the suites ideal for long-term stays. ⊠ *Rodney Bay (Box 155, Castries),* ☎ *758/452–8756; 800/742–4276 or 800/223–9815 (reservations services);* FAX *758/452–8677. 30 suites. Restaurant, bar, air-conditioning, kitchenettes, mini-bars, pool, beauty salon, massage, windsurfing, boating, fishing, shops, baby-sitting, laundry service. MC, V. EP, MAP.*

$ ⊞ **Orange Grove Hotel.** Up a long hill, off the road to Windjammer Landing, you'll find this small hotel on a French colonial plantation. The rooms—large, light, and clean—are packed with the conveniences you'd expect at a larger resort. Standard rooms have showers; supe-rior rooms and suites have bath and shower. Each has tropical-print decor, Caribbean-style rattan furniture and king-size bed, tile floor, TV, phone, and hair dryer, as well as a separate sitting area and balcony or patio overlooking the hill. And although you're away from the beach, you are welcome to use the facilities at ☞ **Club St. Lucia,** 15 minutes away; free transportation is available. Café Clementine serves West Indian and International cuisine. Children 2-11 stay free when sharing with adults. ⊠ *Bois d'Orange, Gros Islet (Box GM 702, Cas-tries),* ☎ *758/452–0021; 800/223–6510 or 800/223–9815 (reserva-tions services);* FAX *758/452–8094. 51 rooms, 11 suites. Restaurant, bar, air-conditioning, pool, shop. AE, MC, V. EP, MAP.*

Soufrière

$$$$ ⊞ **Anse Chastanet Beach Hotel.** If you invest in one of the premium or
★ deluxe rooms (Numbers 7 and 14) here, you're in for a slice of heaven. Nick Troubetzkoy, the Canadian owner-architect, designed them to meld into the tropical mountainside, with louvered wooden walls that open to stunning Piton and Caribbean vistas or to the deep green for-

est. Each has a balcony, terra-cotta-tile floor, madras cotton fabrics, chunky handmade wood furniture, and truly covetable artwork. Rooms are typically 900–1,600 square ft, and most have an irresistible quirk: a tree growing in the bathroom or a shower completely open to the panorama of the Pitons. Standard rooms are mostly octagonal gazebos, with the same decor but far less drama. Rooms do not have a phone or TV, but each has a hair dryer, refrigerator, and coffeemaker. This is a magical setting, as long as you're fit to climb the 100 steps from the gray-sand beach up to the ☞ **Piton Restaurant and Bar** and then another steep climb to your room. Great diving is one of the attractions: Divers come from the earth's four corners to peep at the nearby reefs. They often take a break at the ☞ **Beach Restaurant and Bar.** ⊠ *Anse Chastanet (Box 7000),* ☎ *758/459–7000 or 800/223–1108 (reservations service),* FAX *758/459–7700. 48 rooms. 2 restaurants, 2 bars, fans, refrigerators, tennis court, exercise room, 2 beaches, dive shop, snorkeling, windsurfing, boating, shops, airport shuttle. AE, DC, MC, V. EP, MAP.*

$$$$　　🏨 **Jalousie Hilton Resort & Spa.** Reopened under new management in
🖈 ★　　December 1997, this spectacular 325-acre property has a dramatic location. Dozens of wooden cottages tumble down the mountainside directly between the Pitons. The foliage is so lush that villas are all but hidden from view. Paved pathways connect them, and an electric-powered shuttle bus passes every few minutes to take you down to the beach, restaurants, spa, and central buildings. Villas have elegant furnishings, king-size beds, stocked refrigerators, cable TV, huge bathrooms, clay-tile floors, and plenty of closet space. Villa suites have separate sitting rooms with sofas, coffee tables, and soft lighting. Each villa has its own plunge pool, so you can take a romantic dip amid the breathtaking scenery. Meals range from fine dining to beach buffet at four on-site restaurants (or 24-hour room service). A full-service spa offers massage, aromatherapy, and beauty treatments; the fitness center has aerobics, weight-training sessions, and exercise classes. There's an executive 3-hole par-3 golf course, horses to ride, tennis, and all kinds of water sports. The black-sand beach has been transformed, thanks to the importation of tons of powdery white sand. ⊠ *Anse des Pitons, 2 mi south of town (Box 251),* ☎ *758/459–7666; 800/445–8667 or 800/223–9868 (reservations services);* FAX *758/459–7667. 114 rooms. 4 restaurants, 4 bars, air-conditioning, fans, minibars, no-smoking rooms, refrigerators, room service, pool, beauty salon, massage, spa, 3-hole golf course, 4 tennis courts, aerobics, basketball, health club, horseback riding, racquetball, squash, beach, dive shop, dock, snorkeling, windsurfing, boating, waterskiing, shop, dance club, children's programs, business services, airport shuttle, helipad. AE, D, DC, MC, V. All-inclusive.*

$$$–$$$$　🏨 **Ladera Resort.** This quiet, elegantly rustic hideaway is nestled in lush
🖈 ★　　botanical gardens, high in the mountains, overlooking the Pitons and the Caribbean Sea. It is one of the most sophisticated and unusual small resorts in the Caribbean—a home away from home for rock stars, TV celebs, corporate VIPs, and honeymooners. Many people also stay here for the last night or two of a vacation spent at a larger resort up north. Each villa or suite is stylishly furnished with a harmonious blend of French colonial antiques and local crafts and has a completely open west wall that provides a dazzling view of the Pitons. Six deluxe villas have private pools fed by waterfalls; eight suites have smaller plunge pools. Daily shuttle service to Soufrière and Anse Chastanet Beach is provided. ☞ **Dasheene Restaurant and Bar** is considered the best on the island. Certainly the view is! Rates include breakfast, and transfers to Hewanorra are complimentary for guests staying at least three nights. Children 8–15 stay free when sharing a room with an adult. The resort's location on a mountainside 1,100 ft above sea level, with open-walled guest rooms and individual pools, isn't appropriate for

young children. ⊠ *Above the Pitons, 2 mi south of town (Box 225),* ☎ *758/459–7323; 800/223–9868 or 800/738–4752 (reservations services);* FAX *758/459–5156. 6 villas, 13 suites. Restaurant, bar, pool, shop, library, airport shuttle. AE, MC, V. EP, MAP.*

$–$$$ ⚜ **Hummingbird Beach Resort.** This charming little resort is on the bay
★ at the northern edge of Soufrière. Rooms are in small seaside cabins joined by a maze of wooden decking. Most have breathtaking views of the Pitons. The decor is attractive but simple; a primitive motif is emphasized by African sculptures. Two rooms each have a dark mahogany four-poster bed hung with a sheer mosquito-net drape; the cool trade winds will lull you to sleep and keep away annoying bugs. Most rooms have private modern baths; two rooms and a suite share a bathroom. The two-bedroom country cottage—with sitting room, kitchenettes, and a spectacular Piton view—is suitable for a family or two couples vacationing together. The ☞ Lifeline Bar & Restaurant is a favorite hangout of locals and expatriates. ⊠ *On the bayfront, north of wharf (Box 280),* ☎ *758/459–7232 or 800/223–9815 (reservations service),* FAX *758/459–7033. 9 rooms, 1 suite, 1 2-bedroom cottage. Restaurant, bar, pool, beach, shop. D, MC, V. EP, MAP.*

$ ⚜ **Still Plantation & Beach Resort.** At the Still Plantation, about a five-minute walk inland from Soufrière, there are one- and two-bedroom modern self-catering apartments with sitting rooms and kitchenettes, as well as studios with no kitchens. The ☞ The Still restaurant here is well-known for its excellent Caribbean cuisine. There's a swimming pool and boutique. The Still Beach Resort, at the northern end of Soufrière Bay, has just three one-bedroom apartments and two studios that are right on the black-sand beach with a commanding view of the Pitons. There's a restaurant at the beach resort, as well, but most units have a kitchenette and all have a beachfront patio where you can dine alfresco. If hiking and nature walks are more important than a beach, the Plantation is the better choice. If you prefer sand and sea to pool and gardens, choose the Beach Resort. Guests at one can use the facilities of the other. Rates are the same year-round. ⊠ *½ mi from downtown (Box 246),* ☎ *758/459–7261 or 800/223–9815 (reservations service),* FAX *758/459–7301. 13 apartments, 6 studios. 2 restaurants, 2 bars, pool, beach, shops, laundry service. MC, V. EP.*

Vieux Fort

$ ⚜ **Skyway Inn.** If you're staying in the north but have an early morning flight to catch from Hewanorra—or if you're an avid windsurfer but don't need the trappings and luxuries that come with a resort—this inn is ideal. It's just 100 yards from the airport and minutes from Vieux Fort, Lonely Tree Beach, and the Windsurfing Centre. The inn is clean and comfortable, rooms are spacious and have TVs. There's a rooftop restaurant-bar and a pool down below. A free shuttle runs to both the beach and the airport. ⊠ *Beanfield, Vieux Fort (Box 353),* ☎ *758/454–7111 or 800/223–9815 (reservations service),* FAX *758/454–7116. 43 rooms. Restaurant, bar, air-conditioning, pool, windsurfing, shop, meeting room, airport shuttle. AE, MC, V. EP*

Dining

Mangoes, plantains, breadfruit, avocados, limes, pumpkins, cucumbers, papaya (pawpaw), yams, christophenes (a squashlike vegetable), and coconuts are among the fruits and vegetables that appear on menus. Every menu also lists fresh-caught fish along with the ever-popular lobster. And you may see the national dish—salt fish and green fig—a stew of dried, salted codfish and boiled green banana, which is definitely an acquired taste. Caribbean standards include callaloo, stuffed crab back, pepper pot stew, curried chicken or goat, and *lambi* (conch). On

St. Lucia, soups and stews are traditionally prepared in a coal pot, a heavy rustic, clay casserole on a matching stand that holds the hot coals. Chicken, pork, and barbecues are also popular here. Most of the meats are imported—beef from Argentina and Iowa, lamb from New Zealand. Piton is the local brew, and Bounty is the local rum. The French influence is strong, and most chefs cook with a Creole flair.

What to Wear

Dress on St. Lucia is casual but conservative. Shorts are usually fine during the day, but bathing suits and immodest clothing are frowned upon anywhere but at the beach. In the evening, the mood is casually elegant, but even the fanciest places generally expect only a collared shirt for men and a cotton sundress or pants for women.

CATEGORY	COST*
$$$$	over $40
$$$	$25–$40
$$	$15–$25
$	under $15

per person for a three-course meal, excluding drinks, 8% government tax, and 10% service charge

Castries and the North

CARIBBEAN/CREOLE

$–$$ ✕ **J. J.'s.** Not only are the prices right here, but the food is among the best local cuisine on the island. Superbly grilled fish with fresh vegetables gets top honors. The welcome is friendly and the atmosphere is casual; tables are set on a terrace overlooking the road to Marigot Bay. Wednesday night is Seafood Night, where owner-chef J. J. prepares an enormous selection of local fish and shellfish. On Friday nights the music blares, and the locals come to hang out, eat barbecue, and dance in the street or on the disco dance floor. ⊠ *Marigot Bay Rd. (3 mi before the bay), Marigot,* ☎ *758/451–4076. No credit cards.*

CONTINENTAL

$$$–$$$$ ✕ **San Antoine.** High on the Morne, with splendid views of Castries
★   below and Martinique in the distance, this restored plantation house was originally the historic San Antoine Hotel—built in the late 1800s, destroyed by fire in 1970, and rebuilt soon after. The hotel once hosted literary luminary Somerset Maugham. Now San Antoine is one of the most elegantly appointed restaurants on the island, the cuisine is arguably the best, and the wine list is impressive. Try the grilled fish or the caramelized *filet de boeuf Robert* (beef tenderloin with a sauce seasoned with white wine and a dash of mustard); all entrées are served with fresh vegetables. You may dine à la carte or opt for the five-course prix-fixe dinner. Complimentary taxi service is available for parties of four or more. ⊠ *Old Morne Rd., Morne Fortune (south of Castries),* ☎ *758/452–4660. AE, MC, V. Closed Sun.*

ECLECTIC

$$$–$$$$ ✕ **Great House.** From this romantic plantation house you can enjoy views of the water and of Martinique in the distance. The restaurant is operated by the owners of ☞ **Club St. Lucia**, and resort guests are given a discount and free transportation. Traditional French dishes have Creole overtones, as in the appetizer of pumpkin and potato soup and entrées like lime-grilled dorado fillet, Antillean shrimp sautéed in a Creole sauce, and broiled sirloin with thyme butter and sweet-potato chips. The menu changes nightly and always includes vegetarian dishes. The Derek Walcott Theatre is next door. ⊠ *Cap Estate,* ☎ *758/450–0450 or 758/450–0211. AE, DC, MC, V. No lunch.*

$$$ ✕ **Green Parrot.** Part of the ☞ **Green Parrot** hotel, this restaurant comes
★ complete with sommelier and crisp napery. The menu of West Indian,
Creole, and international dishes, prepared by chef Harry Edwards
(who was trained at London's prestigious Claridge's hotel), always in-
cludes a lot of seafood. There's lively entertainment—a floor show with
belly dancer on Wednesday night and limbo dancing on Saturday—
but the real reason to dine here is the view over Castries and the har-
bor. The best deal of all is on Monday (Ladies Night): If a lady wears
a flower in her hair and is accompanied by a "well-dressed" gentle-
man, the lady receives a free dinner! This is St. Lucia's most-famous
restaurant and a hot spot for locals and tourists alike. ☒ *Morne For-
tune (south of Castries),* ☎ *758/452–3399. Reservations essential. Jacket
required. AE, MC, V.*

$$ ✕ **The Lime.** A casual bistro with lime-color gingham curtains, straw
★ hats decorating the ceiling, and hanging plants, the Lime offers a three-
course lunch and a buffet of local dishes. Starters may include homemade pâté or stuffed crab back. Entrée choices may be medallions of
pork with the chef's special orange-and-ginger sauce, stewed lamb, or
fish poached in white wine and mushroom sauce. The prices are reasonable, which is perhaps why expatriates and locals gather here in
the evenings. Next door is Late Lime's (☞ *Nightlife, below*), the nightclub where the crowd gathers as evening turns to morning. ☒ *Rodney
Bay,* ☎ *758/452–0761. MC, V. Closed Tues.*

ITALIAN

$$–$$$ ✕ **Capone's.** The tropics meet the Jazz Age in this two-in-one restau-
rant. In a setting of black-and-white tile floors, a polished wood bar,
and a player piano, waiters dressed like gangsters serve rum drinks called
"Valentine's Day Massacre" and "Mafia Mai Tai." Your check is delivered in a violin case. The pasta is fresh, and the meat dishes include
osso buco and chicken rotisserie. The open-air pizzeria, open 11 AM–
midnight, turns out burgers and sandwiches, as well as pizza. ☒ *Rodney Bay, across from Rex St. Lucian hotel,* ☎ *758/452–0284. AE, MC,
V. Closed Mon. No lunch.*

$–$$ ✕ **Key Largo.** Brick-oven gourmet pizzas are the specialty at this ca-
sual eatery at Rodney Bay Marina, across the lagoon from Rodney Bay's
many hotels. You're welcome simply to stop in for an espresso or cappuccino, but the popular Pizza Key Largo—topped with shrimp, artichokes, and what seems like a few pounds of mozzarella—is tough to
pass up. ☒ *Rodney Bay,* ☎ *758/452–0282. MC, V.*

SEAFOOD

$$–$$$ ✕ **Jimmie's.** This popular, open-air mom-and-pop restaurant and bar
perched above the bay makes a relaxing daytime stop and becomes a
romantic dinner spot when the harbor lights twinkle below. Appetizers on the seafood-dominated menu include a great Creole stuffed
crab, while a wise choice of entrée is the special seafood platter with
samplings from every part of the day's catch. If you want to try the
national dish—salt fish and green fig—it's the lunch special on Friday
and Saturday. All entrées come with several local vegetables—pumpkin, black beans, christophenes, greens—plus garlic bread. Dessert
lovers had better be in a banana mood, since the menu lists about 10
options—from warm fritters to ice cream. ☒ *Vigie Cove Marina, Castries,* ☎ *758/452–5142. Reservations not accepted. AE, MC, V.*

Soufrière

CARIBBEAN/CREOLE

$$ ✕ **Lifeline Bar & Restaurant.** On the north side of town, within walk-
ing distance of the wharf, the award-winning chef at this cheerful wa-
terfront bar and restaurant at the ☞ **Hummingbird Beach Resort**

serves delicious French Creole cuisine, using fresh seafood or chicken flavored with local herbs. Sandwiches and salads are also available for a lighter lunch. After lunch, be sure to stop in at the proprietors' batik studio. ⊠ *Hummingbird Beach Resort, on waterfront just north of the wharf,* ☏ *758/459–7232. AE, D, MC, V.*

$$ ✕ **The Still.** For visitors to Diamond Falls, lunching at The Still is a good option. The two dining rooms of the ☞ **Still Plantation & Beach Resort** seat up to 400 people, so it is a popular stop for tour groups and cruise passengers. The emphasis is on Creole cuisine using local vegetables—christophenes, breadfruits, yams, callaloo—and seafood, but there are also pork chops and beef dishes. All fruits and vegetables used in the restaurant are produced organically on the estate, a working plantation. ⊠ *Bay St.,* ☏ *758/459–7224 or 758/459–7060. MC, V.*

$–$$ ✕ **Bang . . . between the Pitons.** The eccentric Brit Colin Tennant (a.k.a. Lord Glenconner), developer of the glamorous hideaway island of Mustique, came to St. Lucia to open his dream resort between the Pitons, over which he eventually lost control (it's a long story). But Tennant stayed on to open this cute spoof on a Jamaican jerk pit and rum shop, with ice-cream-color paint, assorted wooden chairs and cushion-strewn booths, a cerise velvet-draped stage for music, and a buzz like that of the early days of Mustique—when Jagger was young. Besides the atmosphere, of course, great barbecued chicken is the reason you come here. The best way to arrive is by boat. But beware, the place closes on a whim. ⊠ *Anse des Pitons, 2 mi south of town,* ☏ *758/459–7864. DC, MC, V.*

$–$$ ✕ **Beach Restaurant and Bar.** This open-air lunch spot at the ☞ **Anse Chastanet Beach Hotel** is the perfect place to take a break from a day of diving, boating, or sunbathing. The West Indian cuisine is delicious, and many specialties are grilled prepared right before your eyes. The *rotis* (turnovers filled with curried meat and/or vegetables) here are the best on the island, served with homemade mango chutney you could eat by the jar. Also try the pepper pot—pork, beef, or lamb simmered for hours with local veggies and spices; or have a good old tuna melt in case you're homesick. Dessert always features an unusual flavor of ice cream. There's a young and lively crowd here, and although the restaurant caters mostly to the resort's guests, everyone is welcome. Lunch is served daily; dinner—a very popular beach barbecue and Creole buffet—is available Tuesday and Friday only. ⊠ *Anse Chastanet, 1 mi north of town,* ☏ *758/459–7000. AE, DC, MC, V.*

$–$$ ✕ **Camilla's.** Tiny, second-floor Camilla's is pretty in pink, somewhat under-ventilated on a hot night (apart from the two balcony tables) but friendly as anything. The menu is simple and local—you can have today's catch curried, Creole-style, or grilled with lemon sauce; there's barbecued chicken with garlic sauce and fries, or lobster salad. Vegetarian specials are available as well. The list of tropical cocktails is almost bigger than the restaurant. ⊠ *7 Bridge St.,* ☏ *758/459–5379. AE.*

CONTEMPORARY

$$$–$$$$ ✕ **Dasheene Restaurant and Bar.** Part of the striking ☞ **Ladera Re-**
★ **sort,** this small, casual terrace restaurant has breathtaking views of the Pitons and the sea between them. This is some of the best food in St. Lucia—Caribbean specialties with new American and Continental accents. Appetizers on the changing menu may include smoked kingfish crepes and spicy seafood gazpacho. Typical entrées are tuna steak with coconut-avocado cream sauce and chicken breast with a mango or a pecan-and-peanut sauce. For dessert, the chocolate crème brûlée flambée takes five minutes to cool but is worth the wait. There's live entertainment many nights, and soft, jazzy background music otherwise. This is a favorite spot for those celebrating an anniversary or other spe-

cial event—try to arrive in time to watch the sunset. ⊠ *Ladera Resort, 2 mi south of town,* ☎ *758/459–7323. AE, DC, MC, V.*

$$$ ✕ **Piton Restaurant and Bar.** On two terraces—one magically sus-
★ pended among the trees, the other a spacious rooftop—at the moun-
tainside ☞ **Anse Chastanet Beach Hotel,** French chef Jacky Rioux works
with a St. Lucian maestro to invent sublime variations on local dishes.
The menu might include a creamed conch soup *en croute* (with a lat-
ticed puff-pastry lid), dolphinfish poached in coconut milk with a lime
sauce, and—the best local food joke you'll ever taste—"St. Lucian apple
pie," made not with apples but with candied christophenes and served
with passion-fruit ice cream. Between them, these chefs cater to every
culinary fantasy. Be prepared to hike up many steps to get here. ⊠ *Anse
Chastanet, 1 mi north of town,* ☎ *758/459–7000. AE, DC, MC, V.*

Beaches

Beaches are all public, and many are flanked by hotels, where you can
rent water sports equipment and have a rum punch. On the other hand,
some are difficult to reach because they are surrounded by resort prop-
erty. A few secluded beaches are only accessible by water; hotels can
arrange boat trips. Don't swim along the windward (east) coast; the
Atlantic waters are rough and sometimes dangerous.

In front of the resort of the same name, just north of Soufrière, **Anse
Chastanet** is a palm-studded, dark-sand beach with a backdrop of
green hills, brightly painted fishing skiffs bobbing at anchor, and the
island's best reefs for snorkeling and diving. The hotel's wooden gaze-
bos are nestled among the palms; its dive shop, restaurant, and bar are
on the beach (☞ Lodging, *above*). On an uncrowded cove south of
Anse-la-Raye, **Anse Cochon** is a remote, black-sand beach accessible
by boat. The waters and adjacent reef are superb for swimming, div-
ing, and snorkeling. South of Soufrière, between the Pitons on Jalousie
Bay, **Anse des Pitons** is a crescent of white sand, which was imported
by Jalousie Hilton Resort (☞ Lodging, *above*) and spread over the orig-
inal black-sand beach. It's accessible through the resort or by boat and
offers great snorkeling and diving in deep cobalt-blue water.

Just west of Vieux Fort, **Honeymoon Beach** is a sandy escape near the
airport. **Malabar Beach** is a 2-mi stretch of white sand that runs par-
allel to the Vigie Airport runway, in Castries, and continues on to be-
come the beachfront for Rendezvous Resort (☞ Lodging, *above*). The
finger of sand studded with palm trees on **Marigot Bay** is a postcard-
pretty scene; dive trips can be arranged nearby, and cool drinks and
meals are available at adjacent restaurants. **Pigeon Point,** part of the
Pigeon Island National Historic Park, is a small beach; there's a restau-
rant, but it's a perfect spot for picnicking. **Reduit Beach** is a long
stretch of beige sand next to Rodney Bay. The Rex St. Lucian Hotel
(☞ Lodging, *above*), which faces the beach, has a water sports center.
Many feel Reduit (pronounced red-wee) is the finest beach on the is-
land. At the southernmost tip of St. Lucia, **Vieux Fort** has miles of se-
cluded white sand and clear waters protected by reefs.

Outdoor Activities and Sports

Participant Sports

BOATING AND SAILING

Rodney Bay and Marigot Bay are centers for bareboat or crewed yacht
charters. Their marinas offer safe anchorage, shower facilities, restau-
rants, groceries, and maintenance for yachts sailing the waters of the
eastern Caribbean and the Grenadines. **Destination St. Lucia Ltd.** (⊠
Rodney Bay, ☎ 758/453–8531) offers bareboat yacht charters rang-

ing in length from 38 ft to 51 ft. **Moorings Yacht Charter** (⊠ Marigot Bay, ☎ 758/451–4357 or 800/535–7289) charters bareboat or crewed yachts ranging from a 39-ft Beneteau to a 60-ft Morgan. **Sunsail Stevens** (⊠ Rodney Bay, ☎ 758/452–8648) is one of the oldest charter companies in the Caribbean and offers a variety of crewed or bareboat charters.

CAMPING

St. Lucia's first campsite opened in 1997 at the **Environmental Educational Centre** at Anse La Liberté, on the west coast near the village of Canaries. Rough campsites and platformed tent huts are available, along with communal toilets and showers, a cooking center, a beautiful beach, and hiking trails. Outdoor cooking and charcoal production are part of the experience. The campsite is administered by the St. Lucia National Trust (☎ 758/452–5005).

FISHING

Among the deep-sea creatures you'll find in St. Lucia's waters are dolphinfish, Spanish mackerel, barracuda, kingfish, sailfish, and white marlin. Sport fishing is done on a catch-and-release basis. Neither spearfishing nor collecting live fish in coastal waters is permitted. Half- or full-day deep-sea fishing excursions can be arranged at Vigie Cove or Rodney Bay Marina. **Captain Mike's** (⊠ Vigie Cove, ☎ 758/452–1216 or 758/452–7044) has five Bertram fishing boats (up to 38 ft) that accommodate up to eight passengers; all equipment and cold drinks are supplied. **Mako Watersports** (⊠ Rodney Bay Marina, ☎ 758/452–0412 or 758/452–0778) has the well-equipped, six-passenger *Annie Baby*.

FITNESS CENTERS

If your hotel lacks the kind of equipment you'd like to use, a commercial alternative may suit your needs. **St. Lucia Racquet Club** (⊠ Club St. Lucia, Cap Estate, ☎ 758/450–0551) has Nautilus equipment, exercise machines, and aerobics and step classes. **Body Inc.** (⊠ Gablewoods Mall, ☎ 758/451–9744) is a well-equipped gym and aerobics studio. Day passes are available to **LeSPORT** (⊠ Cap Estate, ☎ 758/450–8551), which has spa treatments and a complete fitness facility.

GOLF

Courses on St. Lucia are scenic and good fun, but they're not championship quality. **Sandals St. Lucia at La Toc** (⊠ La Toc Rd., Castries, ☎ 758/452–3081) has a 9-hole course for Sandals guests only. **St. Lucia Golf and Country Club** (⊠ Cap Estate, ☎ 758/452–8523) is the island's only public course. It's a beautiful course at the northern tip of the island, with panoramic views of both the Atlantic and Caribbean. Its 9 holes can be played as 18, although an additional 9 holes are on the drawing board. The clubhouse has a bar, and there's a pro shop where you can rent clubs and arrange lessons. A $49.50 package includes 18 holes, cart, and clubs. Reservations are essential.

HIKING

The island is laced with trails, but you should not attempt the challenging peaks on your own. The **Forest and Land Department** (☎ 758/450–2231 or 758/450–2078) has trails throughout the rain forest and can provide a guide. The **St. Lucia National Trust** (☎ 758/452–5005) maintains two trails: one at Anse La Liberté, near Canaries on the Caribbean coast; the other is in the southwest, on the Atlantic coast, from Mandélé to the Fregate Islands Nature Reserve. Full-day excursions, with lunch, cost about $40 per person and can be arranged through hotels or tour operators.

HORSEBACK RIDING

Riding is popular on St. Lucia. Creole horses, an indigenous breed, are fairly small, fast, sturdy, and even-tempered animals suitable for beginners. Established stables suit all skill levels and offer countryside trail rides, beach rides with picnic lunches, plantation tours, carriage rides, and lengthy treks. Prices run about $35 for one hour, $45 for two hours, and $55 for a three-hour beach ride with picnic. Transportation is usually provided between the stables and nearby hotels. Local people sometimes appear on beaches with their steeds and offer 30-minute rides for $10; ride at your own risk!

Country Saddles (⊠ Marquis Estate, 45 mins east of Castries, ☎ 758/450–1231) provides horses for visitors to the plantation to explore the estate, traverse a river, and canter through banana fields. **International Riding Stables** (⊠ Beauséjour Estate, Gros Islet, ☎ 758/452–8139) offers either English or Western style. Their beach picnic ride includes time for a swim—with or without your horse. The stable is fully insured. **Trim's National Riding Stable** (⊠ Cas-en-Bas, Gros Islet, ☎ 758/452–8273), the island's oldest riding establishment, offers four riding sessions per day, plus beach tours, trail rides, and carriage tours to Pigeon Island. In Soufrière, **Trekkers** (⊠ Morne Coubaril Estate, ☎ 758/459–7340) provides rides through the plantation and to area attractions. Overnight treks can also be arranged.

PARASAILING

For a spectacular view of the northwest coast from high above Rodney Bay, parasailing may be just the ticket. For information, contact the water-sports facility at **Rex St. Lucian** hotel (⊠ Rodney Bay, ☎ 758/452–8351).

SCUBA DIVING AND SNORKELING

The coral reefs at Anse Cochon and Anse Chastanet, on the southwest coast, are popular dive sites. There are also two sunken freighters near Anse Cochon—Waiwinette, a large freighter in 90 ft of water and Lesleen M, a 165-ft freighter in 60 ft of water—that have created artificial reefs. Divers can view a variety of marine life: huge gorgonians, black coral trees, gigantic barrel sponges, and lace corals; schooling fish, angel fish, sea horses, spotted eels, stingrays, nurse sharks, and sea turtles. Anse La Raye, midway up the west coast, is one of St. Lucia's finest wall and drift dives and a great place for snorkeling. Other interesting dive sites are at the base of the Pitons, where strong currents ensure good visibility, and around Pigeon Island.

Dolphin Divers (⊠ Rodney Bay Marina, ☎ 758/452–9485) offers wall, wreck, reef, and deep dives; resort courses and open-water certification with advanced and specialty courses are taught by PADI-certified instructors. **Frogs** (⊠ Windjammer Landing, Castries, ☎ 758/452–0913) provides resort courses and open-water certification. Two-tank and night dives are offered, and rental equipment is available. **Rosamond's Trench Divers** (⊠ Marigot Bay, ☎ 758/451–4761) offers PADI training, wreck dives, night dives, and special dive packages for yachties. **Scuba St. Lucia** (⊠ Soufrière and Rodney Bay, ☎ 758/459–7355 or 800/223–1108) is a PADI five-star training facility, with a dive shop at Anse Chastanet and at the Rex St. Lucian hotel. Daily beach and boat dives, resort courses, underwater photography, and day trips are offered.

SEA EXCURSIONS

Several yachts take passengers on day sails to Soufrière and the Pitons for about $70 per person. From Vigie Cove, Castries, sail on the 140-ft **Brig Unicorn** (☎ 758/452–6811), used in the filming of the TV miniseries *Roots*; the 56-ft catamarans **Endless Summer I** and **Endless**

Summer II (☎ 758/450–8651); *Surf Queen* (☎ 758/452–8232), a trimaran; and *Calypso Queen* (☎ 758/452–8232), a motor yacht. From Pigeon Island, Rodney Bay, sail on a 56-ft luxury cruiser, the **MV Vigie** (☎ 758/452–8232). Sea and snorkeling excursions can be arranged through **Mako Watersports** (☎ 758/452–0412), **Captain Mike's** (☎ 758/452–0216 or 758/452–7044), or through your hotel.

TENNIS AND SQUASH

All large resorts have their own courts, most of which are floodlit for night play, and often have pros who offer lessons. Anyone staying at a smaller hotel without courts or who wants to play squash can try the following: The **Rex St. Lucian** hotel (⊠ Rodney Bay, ☎ 758/452–8351) has two tennis courts available to the public. **St. Lucia Racquet Club** (⊠ Club St. Lucia, ☎ 758/450–0551) is one of the top tennis facilities in the Caribbean—probably the best in the Lesser Antilles. Its nine floodlit courts are in perfect shape, the pro shop is extensive, and the staff is knowledgeable. The club also has a squash court and a pro; the court is not air-conditioned. **St. Lucia Yacht Club** (⊠ Rodney Bay, ☎ 758/452–8350), at the north end of the island, has two air-conditioned, wooden-floored, glass-backed squash courts open to the public; rackets can be rented.

WATERSKIING

The calm Caribbean waters on the northwest coast of the island are perfect for waterskiing. Most resorts in that vicinity offer that activity to guests. If your hotel doesn't offer waterskiing, contact **Waves** (⊠ Choc Beach, Castries, ☎ 758/451–3000).

WINDSURFING

Major resorts generally offer Windsurfers and instruction; some will accommodate nonguests for a fee. Cas-en-Bas on the northeast coast and Vieux Fort on the southeast, the two areas with the best wind, are most popular with advanced and intermediate windsurfers. Reduit Beach, near Rodney Bay, and elsewhere along the calmer west coast are the best areas for beginners. From August to October, the wind loses strength island-wide. **Island Windsurfing Ltd.** (⊠ Anse de Sables Beach, Vieux Fort, ☎ 758/454–7400) offers board rentals and instruction; it's open daily from 10 AM until dusk. The **Rex St. Lucian** hotel (⊠ Reduit Beach, Rodney Bay, ☎ 758/452–8351) is the local agent for Mistral Windsurfers. **Waves** (⊠ Choc Beach, Castries, ☎ 758/451–3000) has a windsurfing center attached to the restaurant of the same name.

Spectator Sports

CRICKET AND SOCCER

Cricket and soccer, the two national pastimes, are played at Mindoo Philip Park in Marchand, 2 mi east of Castries. Contact the tourist board (☞ Visitor Information *in* St. Lucia A to Z, *below*) for specific information regarding schedules and tickets.

TENNIS

The **St. Lucia Racquet Club** (☎ 758/450–0551), which hosted the Davis Cup in 1994, is the site of regional tennis events, the most important being the St. Lucia Open in early December.

Shopping

The island's best-known products are unique clothing, artwork, and household items made from batik and silk-screened fabrics that are designed and printed in island workshops. You can also take home native-made wooden boxes and carvings, pottery, straw hats and baskets, and locally grown cocoa, coffee, spices, and tropical bouquets.

Areas and Malls

In Castries, there are several markets on the harborside, under bright orange roofs. They're open from 6 AM to 5 PM daily (except Sunday); Saturday morning is the busiest and most colorful time. At the **Castries Market,** farmers' wives have gathered for more than a century to sell produce, which, alas, you can't import to the United States. But you can bring home the spices, such as cocoa, turmeric, cloves, bay leaves, ginger, peppercorns, cinnamon sticks, nutmeg, mace, and vanilla essence. You can buy a variety of bottled hot pepper sauces for a fraction of what you'd spend back home. The **Craft Market,** which backs up to the produce market, has aisles and aisles of baskets and other handmade straw items, rustic brooms made from palm fronds, wood carvings and leather work, clay pottery, and souvenirs—all at inexpensive prices. The **Vendor's Arcade,** across the street, is a maze of stalls and booths where you'll find handmade wood carvings and other handicrafts among the T-shirts and costume jewelry.

Gablewoods Mall on the Gros Islet Highway just a couple of miles north of downtown Castries, has about 35 shops that sell groceries, wines and spirits, jewelry, clothing, local crafts, books and foreign newspapers, music, souvenirs, household goods, and snacks. At the grocery or liquor store at Gablewoods, you might pick up a bottle of Bounty Rum, the local firewater made at a distillery in Roseau, just south of Castries. Die-hard shoppers will want to visit **Pointe Seraphine,** an attractive Spanish-style complex on Castries Harbour with more than two dozen boutiques that sell duty-free goods and local crafts. **La Place Carenage,** on the opposite side of the harbor, is another duty-free complex with many of the same stores as at Pointe Seraphine. **William Peter Boulevard,** the capital's main shopping street is lined with places where the local people shop for household goods.

Most shops in **Soufrière** provide goods and services for local consumption; the few that might be of interest to visitors are just steps from the boat jetty. The market is in a building that faces the town square. A small craft center, where local women sell sticks of fresh cocoa and handmade crafts such as dolls and doilies, is right on the waterfront.

Specialty Items

ART

Artsibit Gallery (⊠ Corner of Brazil and Mongiraud Sts., Castries, ☎ 758/452–7865) exhibits and sells moderately priced artwork by St. Lucian artists and sculptors. **Modern Art Gallery** (⊠ Gros Islet Highway, Bois d'Orange, ☎ 758/452–9079) sells contemporary and avant-garde Caribbean art. **Snooty Agouti** (⊠ Rodney Bay, ☎ 758/452–0321) sells Caribbean artwork, prints, and maps. **St. Lucia Fine Art** (⊠ Pointe Seraphine, Castries, ☎ 758/459–0891) has original fine artwork by world-renowned artists, including local painter Llewellyn Xavier.

BOOKS AND MAGAZINES

Sunshine Bookshop (⊠ Gablewoods Mall, Castries, ☎ 758/452–3222) has novels and titles of regional interest, including books by Caribbean authors, among them the work of St. Lucia's Nobel Laureate Derek Walcott. You'll also find current newspapers and magazines.

CLOTHING AND TEXTILES

Bagshaw Studios (⊠ La Toc Rd., La Toc Bay, Castries, ☎ 758/452–2139 or 758/451–9249) sells clothing and table linens in colorful tropical designs; the fabric is designed and silk-screened by hand in the adjacent workroom. Bagshaw boutiques are located at Pointe Seraphine, La Place Carenage, and Rodney Bay; Bagshaw items are also sold at gift shops in the airport. **Caribelle Batik** (⊠ 37 Old Victoria Rd., the

Morne, Castries, ☎ 758/452–3785) creates batik clothing and wall hangings in their studios; visitors are welcome to watch the craftspeople at work and purchase items in the shop. **Sea Island Cotton Co.** (✉ Bridge St., Castries, ☎ 758/452–3674; ✉ Gablewoods Mall, ☎ 758/451–6946) sells quality T-shirts, Caribelle Batik clothing, and other resort wear, as well as colorful souvenir items.

DUTY-FREE GOODS

Pointe Seraphine and La Place Carenage in Castries, the arcade at Rex St. Lucian Hotel in Rodney Bay, and Hewanorra International Airport are the only places where duty-free goods are sold. You must present your passport and airline ticket to get the duty-free price. If you can forget for a moment that you're in the tropics, try on beautiful wool sweaters at **Benetton** (✉ Pointe Seraphine, ☎ 752/452–7685). **Colombian Emeralds** (✉ Pointe Seraphine, La Place Carenage, and the airport, ☎ 758/452–7233) has fine quality emeralds and other gems fashioned into beautiful jewelry. **Images** (✉ Pointe Seraphine, La Place Carenage, Rodney Bay, and the airport, ☎ 758/452–6883) sells designer fragrances; they also stock watches, cameras, sunglasses, electronics, and gifts. **Little Switzerland** (✉ Pointe Seraphine and La Place Carenage, ☎ 758/452–7587 or 758/451–6785) specializes in imported china and crystal, jewelry, and leather goods.

GIFTS AND SOUVENIRS

Caribbean Perfumes (✉ Green Parrot, Morne Fortune, Castries, ☎ 758/453–7249) blends a half dozen lovely scents for women and two aftershaves for men from exotic flowers, fruits, tropical woods, and spices. Fragrances are reasonably priced and available at the perfumery and at many hotel gift shops. **Noah's Arkade** (✉ Jeremie St., Castries, ☎ 758/452–2523; ✉ Pointe Seraphine, ☎ 758/452–7488) has hammocks, wood carvings, straw mats, T-shirts, books, and other regional gift items. Take home a cassette recording or CD by a local band, which you can find at **Jeremie's** (✉ 83 Brazil St., Castries, ☎ 758/452–5079). **Sights 'n Sounds** (✉ 46 Micoud St., Castries, ☎ 758/451–9600; ✉ Gablewoods Mall, Castries, ☎ 758/451–7300) also sells CDs and cassettes—reggae, zouk, soca, steel band. The **St. Lucia Philatelic Bureau,** at the General Post Office (✉ Bridge St., Castries, ☎ 758/452–3774), supplies collectors and stamp dealers throughout the world with beautiful St. Lucian commemoratives.

HANDICRAFTS

Batik Studio (✉ Hummingbird Beach Resort, ☎ 758/459–7232) offers superb batik sarongs, scarves, and wall panels designed and created on site by Joan Alexander. **Choiseul Art & Craft Centre** (✉ La Fargue, Choiseul, ☎ 758/454–3226) stands among the remnants of the last Carib presence in St. Lucia. The center, on the southwest coast, about a 30-minute drive from Soufrière, has a huge selection of handmade Amerindian basketware, place mats, chairs, clay coal pots and other pottery, as well as sculpture and bas-reliefs carved from local woods. The quality is excellent, and prices are reasonable.

Eudovic Art Studio (✉ Morne Fortune, Castries, ☎ 758/452–2747) is a workshop and studio where trays, masks, and figures sculpted from local mahogany, red cedar, and eucalyptus wood are created, displayed, and sold. **Made in St. Lucia** (✉ Gablewoods Mall, Castries, ☎ 758/453–2788) sells only items that are made on the island of St. Lucia. You'll find sandals, shirts, dolls, sauces and jams, costume jewelry, carved wooden objects, steel drums, coal pots for cooking, original art, and other quality items at fair prices.

Nightlife and the Arts

Nightlife

The large, all-inclusive resort hotels feature nightly entertainment—island music, calypso singers, and steel-band jump-ups, as well as disco, karaoke, and even talent shows and toga parties. Many offer entertainment packages, including dinner, to nonguests.

BARS

Banana Split (✉ St. George's St., Castries, ☎ 758/450–8125) offers entertainment in a perpetual spring-break atmosphere. The **Captain's Cellar** (✉ Pigeon Island, ☎ 758/450–0253) is a cozy Old English pub that features live jazz on weekends. **Shamrocks Pub** (✉ Rodney Bay, ☎ 758/452–8725) is an Irish-style pub with live entertainment on weekends. **Waves** (✉ Choc Bay, Castries, ☎ 758/451–3000) is a popular hangout day and night, with daily happy hours, weekly karaoke nights, and live music some nights.

DANCE CLUBS

Most dance clubs with live bands have a cover charge of EC$15–$20. **Indies** (✉ Rodney Bay, ☎ 758/452–0727) is a disco where you can dance to the hottest Caribbean and international rhythms Wednesday, Friday, and Saturday nights from 11 PM on; dress is casual, though smart—no hats or sandals, no shorts or sleeveless shirts for men. There's shuttle bus service from most major hotels. **The Late Lime** (✉ Reduit Beach, Rodney Bay, ☎ 758/452–0761) is a particular favorite of St. Lucians; it's air-conditioned and intimate, with DJ dance music or local entertainment every night but Tuesday.

THEME NIGHTS

Green Parrot (✉ Morne Fortune, ☎ 758/452–3399) is in a class all by itself. On Wednesday and Saturday, chef Harry Edwards hosts the floor show, singing and dancing—and shimmying under the limbo pole—himself. Dress semiformally for these evenings of frolic. The **Gros Islet Jump Up** is legendary. Every Friday night, this sleepy fishing village a mile or so north of Rodney Bay becomes a huge street party starting at about 9 PM. A mammoth sound system facing the central intersection beats out the pulsating rhythms, vendors sell local foods and beverages, and everyone lets their hair down and dances until about 1 AM. It's very crowded and can get rowdy, so it's best to travel in a group, and don't carry a purse. **J. J.'s** (✉ Marigot Bay, ☎ 758/451–4076) has Seafood Night every Wednesday. Local crab, lobster, fish, shrimp, conch, and crayfish are prepared using expert chef J. J.'s secret recipes (reservations essential). Afterward, diners can work off their meal by dancing in the street to live music. At J. J.'s **Friday Night Street Jam,** island music is supplied by a live band, and the popular fare is curried goat.

Arts

GALLERIES

Artsibit Gallery (✉ Corner of Brazil and Mongiraud Sts., ☎ 758/452–7865) exhibits works by St. Lucian artists and sculptors. **Modern Art Gallery** (✉ Gros Islet Hwy., Bois d'Orange, ☎ 758/452–9079) exhibits contemporary and avant-garde Caribbean art. **Snooty Agouti** (✉ Rodney Bay, ☎ 758/452–0321) has Caribbean artwork, prints, and maps **St. Lucia Fine Art** (✉ Pointe Seraphine, ☎ 758/459–0891) exhibits and sells original artwork by renowned artists, including local painter Llewellyn Xavier. **Llewellyn Xavier** (☎ 758/450–9155) exhibits his paintings at his own studio in Cap Estate; call to arrange a visit.

THEATER

Derek Walcott Center Theatre. This small, open-air theater, built on the foundation of an 18th-century Cap Estate plantation house, seats just

200 people for monthly productions of music, dance, and drama, as well as Sunday brunch programs. The Trinidad Theatre Workshop also presents an annual performance here. For schedule and ticket information, contact the Great House Restaurant (⊠ Cap Estate, ☎ 758/450–0551 or 758/450–0450, 𝕱𝕬𝕏 758/450–0451).

Exploring St. Lucia

One main route encircles all of St. Lucia, except for a small portion in the extreme northeast. The road snakes along the coastline, cuts across mountains, makes hairpin turns, takes sheer drops, and reaches dizzying elevations. It takes about three hours to drive the whole loop. Even under ideal conditions, it's a tiring drive; so plan to stop along the way.

The new West Coast Road from Castries to Soufrière was completed in 1995. It still has steep hills and sharp turns, but it's well-marked and incredibly scenic. South of Castries, the road climbs Morne Fortune, cuts through a huge banana plantation (more than 127 varieties of bananas, called "figs" in this part of the Caribbean, are grown on the island), and passes by fishing villages. The area north of Soufrière is the island's "fruit basket," where most of the mangoes, breadfruit, tomatoes, limes, and oranges are grown. In the mountainous region, you'll see Mt. Parasol and Mt. Gimie (pronounced Jimmy), St. Lucia's highest peak, which rises to 3,117 ft. As you approach Soufrière, you'll have several opportunities for spectacular views of the Pitons.

The landscape changes dramatically between the Pitons and Vieux Fort, on the southeast tip of the island. The terrain starts as steep mountainside with dense vegetation, progresses to undulating hills that form a backdrop for tiny coastal fishing villages, and finally becomes rather flat. Anyone arriving at Hewanorra International Airport and staying at a resort near Soufrière will travel along this South Coast Road, a journey of about an hour. From Vieux Fort to Castries, the East Coast Road passes through the villages of Micoud and Dennery, twists and turns through other tiny villages, winds up, down, and around mountains, crosses Barre de l'Isle Ridge, and slices through the rain forest. The scenery is breathtaking: The Atlantic Ocean pounds against rocky cliffs, and dense vegetation—mostly acres and acres of bananas and coconut palms—covers the hillsides. Visitors who arrive at Hewanorra and stay at a resort near Castries travel along the East Coast Road.

Numbers in the margin correspond to points of interest on the St. Lucia map.

Castries and the North

Castries, St. Lucia's capital, and the area north of the city is the most developed part of the island. The roads are straight, flat, and easy to navigate. This area features some of the best beaches, numerous resorts, and busy Rodney Bay Marina. One of the island's important historical sites, Pigeon Island, is at the northwestern tip.

SIGHTS TO SEE

⑱ Barre de l'Isle Forest Reserve. Barre de l'Isle Ridge divides the eastern and western halves of St. Lucia. A mile-long trail cuts through the Forest Reserve; four lookout points provide panoramic views of the island. Visible in the distance are Mount Gimie, both the Caribbean Sea and the Atlantic coast, immense green valleys, and tiny coastal communities. The reserve is about a half hour from Castries. It takes about an hour to walk the trail and another hour to climb Mt. La Combe ridge. Permission of the Forest and Lands Department (☎ 758/450–2231 or 758/450–2078) is required to access the trail; a naturalist or forest officer guide will accompany you.

❶ Castries. On the northwest coast, the capital is a busy commercial city of about 65,000 people that wraps around a sheltered bay. Morne Fortune rises sharply to the south of town, creating a dramatic green backdrop. Castries's charm lies entirely in its liveliness, since practically all the colorful old colonial buildings were razed by four devastating fires that occurred between 1796 and 1948. Freighters (exporting bananas, coconut, cocoa, mace, nutmeg, and citrus fruits) and cruise ships come and go daily, making **Castries Harbour** one of the busiest ports in the Caribbean.

Spanish-style **Pointe Seraphine** is a duty-free shopping complex on the north side of the harbor, about a 20-minute walk or two-minute cab ride from the city center; a launch shuttles passengers across the harbor when ships are in port. More than 20 upscale duty-free shops, a tourist information kiosk, a taxi stand, and car-rental agencies surround a Spanish-style courtyard. The St. Lucia Tourist Board has its main office on the upper level.

Derek Walcott Square is a green oasis bordered by Brazil, Laborie, Micoud, and Bourbon streets. Formerly Columbus Square, it was renamed in 1993 to honor the hometown poet who won the 1992 Nobel Prize in Literature—one of two Nobel laureates from St. Lucia. (The late Sir W. Arthur Lewis won the 1979 Nobel Prize in Economics.) Some of the 19th-century buildings that managed to survive fire, winds, and rains can be seen on Brazil Street, the southern border of the square. On the Laborie Street side, there is a 400-year-old *samaan* tree. A local story tells of the English botanist who came to St. Lucia many years ago to catalog the flora. Awestruck by this huge old tree, she asked a passerby what it was. "Massav," he replied, and she dutifully jotted that down in her notebook, unaware that "massav" is patois for "I don't know!" Directly across Laborie Street is the Roman Catholic **Cathedral of the Immaculate Conception**, which was built in 1897. Though rather somber on the outside, the interior walls are decorated with colorful murals painted by St. Lucian artist Dunstan St. Omer and reworked in 1985, just prior to the Pope's visit. This church has an active parish and is open daily for both public viewing and religious services.

☺ At the corner of Jeremie and Peynier streets, spreading beyond its brilliant orange roof, is the **Castries Market.** Full of excitement and bustle, the market is open every day but is most lively on Saturday mornings, when farmers bring their fresh produce and spices to town, as they have for more than a century. Next door is the **Craft Market**, where you can buy pottery, wood carvings, and handwoven straw items. Across Peynier Street at the **Vendor's Arcade,** you'll find more handicrafts and souvenirs.

Just 2 mi south of downtown, **Bagshaw Studios** gives you the opportunity to see how Stanley Bagshaw's original tropical designs are turned into colorful silk-screened fabrics and then shop for fashions and household items created on site. ⊠ *La Toc Rd., La Toc Bay,* ☎ *758/452–7570.* ▱ *Free.* ☺ *Weekdays 8:30–5, Sat. 8:30–4, Sun. 10–1; weekend hrs extended if cruise ship is in port.*

⓱ Errard Plantation. Near the village of Dennery, on the east coast, this family-operated cocoa plantation provides an excellent opportunity to see how cocoa beans are processed on a working agricultural estate. Tours end with a Creole lunch, accompanied by fresh fruit juices. For arrangements, call ☎ 758/453–1260.

❷ Fort Charlotte. Begun in 1764 by the French as the Citadelle du Morne Fortune, Fort Charlotte was completed after 20 years of battling and changing hands. Its old barracks and batteries have now been converted to government buildings and local educational facilities, but you can drive around and look at the remains, including redoubts, a guardroom, stables, and cells. You can also walk up to the Inniskilling Monument, a tribute to the battle fought in 1796, when the 27th Foot Royal Inniskilling Fusiliers wrested the Morne from the French. At the Military Cemetery, which was first used in 1782, faint inscriptions on the tombstones tell the tales of French and English soldiers who died here. Six former governors of the island are buried here, as well. From this vantage point on the top of Morne Fortune, you'll see Martinique to the north and the twin peaks of the Pitons to the south.

㉔ Gros Islet. North of the lagoon at Rodney Bay, Gros Islet (pronounced grow zee-*lay*) is a quiet little fishing village. But on Friday nights, Gros Islet springs to life with a wild and raucous street festival ("jump-up") to which everyone is invited (☞ Nightlife, *above*).

❹ Marigot Bay. A few miles south of Castries, this is one of the most beautiful natural harbors in the Caribbean. In 1778 British admiral Samuel Barrington sailed into this secluded bay-within-a-bay and covered his ships with palm fronds to hide them from the French. Today, this resort community—where parts of the movie *Doctor Doolittle* were filmed more than 30 years ago—is a favorite anchorage. You can charter a yacht, swim, snorkel, or mingle with the yachting crowd at one of the bars. There are several inns, resorts, and restaurants here. A 24-hour ferry connects the bay's two sides.

㉑ Marquis Estate. If you want a close-up view of a working plantation and are willing to get a little wet and muddy in the process, you can tour the island's largest one. The 600-acre Marquis Estate (☎ 758/452–3762) is at Marquis Bay, on the north Atlantic coast. The estate began as a sugar plantation. Now it produces bananas and copra (dried coconut processed for oil) for export, as well as a number of other tropical fruits and vegetables for local consumption. St. Lucia Representative Services Ltd. (☞ Guided Tours *in* St. Lucia A to Z, *below*) conducts the tour and will pick you up at your hotel in an air-conditioned bus. You may tour the estate by bus or on horseback, and a river ride to the coast and lunch at the plantation house are included. Self-drive or private taxi tours are not permitted. Wear your most casual clothes, and be prepared to rough it.

❸ Morne Fortune. Just to the south of Castries, Morne Fortune forms a striking backdrop for the capital. With a name that translates to "Hill of Good Luck," this mountain has, ironically, seen more than its share of bad luck over the years—including devastating hurricanes and those four fires that leveled Castries. The drive to Morne Fortune from Castries will take you past **Government House,** on Government House Road, the official residence of the governor-general of St. Lucia and one of the island's few remaining examples of Victorian architecture.

㉒ Pigeon Island. Jutting out of the northwest coast, Pigeon Island is connected to the mainland by a causeway that was built several years ago. Tales are told of the pirate Jambe de Bois (Wooden Leg), who used to hide out here. This 44-acre hilltop islet, a strategic point during the struggles for control of St. Lucia, is now a national landmark. It's also a venue for concerts, festivals, and family gatherings. There are two small beaches with calm waters for swimming and snorkeling, a restaurant, and picnic areas. Scattered around the grounds are ruins of barracks, batteries, and garrisons dating from 18th-century French and English battles. In the Museum and Interpretative Centre, housed in the restored British officers' mess, a multimedia display unfolds the ecological and historical significance of this island. ✉ *Pigeon Island, St.*

Lucia National Trust, ☎ *758/450–8167 or 758/452–5005,* FAX *758/453–2791.* 🖅 *EC$10.* ☉ *Daily 9–5.*

㉑ **Rodney Bay.** About 15 minutes north of Castries, the body of water named for Admiral Rodney is an 80-acre, man-made lagoon surrounded by hotels and many popular restaurants. Rodney Bay Marina is one of the Caribbean's premier water-sports centers and the destination of the Atlantic Rally for Cruisers (trans-Atlantic yacht crossing) each December. Yacht charters and sightseeing day trips can be arranged at the marina. The Rodney Bay Ferry makes the trip between the marina and the shopping complex daily on the hour from 9 to 4 for $4 round-trip.

Soufrière and the South

The southwest coast is the destination of most sightseeing trips. This is where you'll find the landmark Pitons and the French colonial town of Soufrière, with its drive-in volcano, botanical gardens, working plantations, and countless other examples of the natural beauty for which St. Lucia is famous.

SIGHTS TO SEE

❺ **Anse-la-Raye and Canaries.** These two small West Coast fishing villages on the road between Marigot Bay and Soufrière are quaint and colorful. Along their beachfronts, fishing nets hang on poles to dry and brightly painted fishing boats bob in the water. The fishermen of Anse-la-Raye still make canoes the old-fashioned way—by burning out the center of a log.

⑫ **Choiseul.** This small village on the southwest coast is the island's wood-carving and pottery center. At the turn of the road past the Anglican Church, built in 1846, a bridge crosses the River Dorée, so named because the riverbed is blanketed with fool's gold. In La Fargue, just to the south, the **Choiseul Art & Craft Centre** (☎ 758/459–3226) displays and sells superb traditional Carib handicrafts, including pottery, wickerwork, and braided grass mats and baskets that local artisans have created.

🖐 ❼ **Diamond Botanical Gardens.** These splendid gardens are a portion of Soufrière Estate, a 2,000-acre land grant made in 1713 by Louis XIII to three Devaux brothers from Normandy in recognition of their services to France. The estate is still owned by their descendants; the gardens are maintained by Mrs. Joan Du Bouley Devaux. Bushes and shrubs laden with brilliant tropical flowers grow beneath towering trees and line pathways that lead to a natural gorge. Vapor steaming up from La Soufrière volcano and water bubbling up from sulfur springs stream downhill in rivulets to become **Diamond Waterfall,** deep in the botanical gardens. Over the centuries, the rocks over which the cascade spills have become encrusted with minerals and tinted yellow, green, and purple. Adjacent to the falls, curative **mineral baths** are fed by underground sulfur springs. For $2.50, you can slip into your swimsuit and bathe for 30 minutes in one of the outside pools; a private bath costs $3.75. King Louis XVI of France provided funds in 1784 for the construction of a building with a dozen large stone baths to fortify his troops against the St. Lucian climate. It is claimed that Josephine Bonaparte bathed here as a young girl while visiting her father's plantation nearby. During the Brigand's War, just after the French Revolution, the bath house was destroyed. In 1930, the site was excavated by André Du Boulay, owner of Soufrière Estate, and two of the baths were restored for his own use. The outside baths were added later. ⊠ *Soufrière Estate, Soufrière,* ☎ *758/452–4759 or 758/454–7565.* 🖅 *$2.75 (EC$7).* ☉ *Mon.–Sat. 10–5, Sun. and holidays 10–3.*

16 **Fregate Island Nature Reserve.** A mile-long trail encircles the preserve, which you reach from the East Coast Road near the fishing village of Praslin. A natural promontory provides a lookout where you can view the two small islets, Fregate Major and Fregate Minor, and—with luck—the frigate birds that nest here in summer. Guided tours, which include a ride in an Amerindian-style canoe to a tiny island for a picnic lunch and swim, are arranged through the St. Lucia National Trust (⊠ Box 595, Castries, ☎ 758/453–7656 or 758/452–8735, 𝔽𝔸𝕏 758/453–2791). All visitors must be accompanied by a guide.

13 **Laborie.** Located on the south coast, this is the prototypical St. Lucian fishing village, little changed over the centuries. You can stop to buy some local bread and fresh fish. Above the village is Morne Le Blanc, which offers a panoramic view of the entire southern plain of St. Lucia. The crest, with picnic facilities and viewing platform, can be reached by trail (a 45-minute hike) or by road.

15 **Maria Islands Nature Reserve.** Two tiny islands in the Atlantic, off the southeast coast, compose the reserve, which has its own interpretive center. The 25-acre Maria Major and 4-acre Maria Minor, its little sister, are inhabited by two rare species of reptiles (the colorful Maria Island ground lizard and the harmless grass snake) that share their home with frigate birds, terns, doves, and other wildlife. There's a small private beach for swimming and snorkeling, an undisturbed forest, a vertical cliff covered in cacti, and a coral reef for diving. Boat trips are arranged by the St. Lucia National Trust; bring a picnic lunch. ⊠ *Moule à Chique*, ☎ *758/453–7656 or 758/452–8735.* ▣ *EC$3 Wed.–Sat., EC50¢ Sun.* ☼ *Wed.–Sun. 9:30–5; closed mid-May–July.*

9 **Morne Coubaril Estate.** This 250-acre coconut and cocoa plantation in Soufrière, the first major estate established in St. Lucia, has a rich French history that dates from 1713, when Crown land was granted to three St. Lucian brothers by King Louis IV. Authentic 18th-century plantation life is explained, as a guide escorts you along an original mule-carriage pathway and through a typical reconstructed "village." You'll see how cocoa, copra, and manioc were processed in the days before mechanization. This is a fascinating 90-minute eco-tour. The foliage is thick and green; the tropical flowers, beautiful. The plantation house has been renovated and furnished according to the original plans. You can purchase freshly made cocoa, straw items, and hand-carved wooden pieces. If you wish to have lunch, a Creole buffet is available by reservation for EC$25 per person. ⊠ *Soufrière,* ☎ *758/459–7340.* ▣ *EC$15.* ☼ *Daily 9–5.*

8 **The Pitons.** These incredible mountains have become the symbol of St. Lucia. The road south out of Soufrière offers a magnificent view of the twin peaks, which rise precipitously out of the cobalt-blue Caribbean. The two pyramidal cones, covered with thick tropical vegetation, were formed by lava from a volcanic eruption 30 to 40 million years ago. They are not identical twins since—confusingly—Petit Piton (2,619 ft) is taller than Gros Piton (2,461 ft), though Gros is, as the word translates, broader. Gros Piton is currently the only one where climbing is permitted, though the trail up even this shorter Piton is one very tough trek and requires the permission of the Forest and Lands Department (☎ 758/450–2231 or 758/450–2078) and a knowledgeable guide.

10 **St. Lucia National Rain Forest.** Dense tropical rain forest stretches from one side of the island to the other, sprawling over 19,000 acres of mountains and valleys. It's home to a multitude of exotic flowers and plants, as well as rare birds—including the brightly feathered Jacquot parrot. The **Edmund Forest Reserve**, on the western side of the island, is most easily accessible from just east of Soufrière, on the road to Fond St.

Jacques. A trek through the lush landscape, with spectacular views of mountains, valleys, and the sea beyond, can take a full day. It takes an hour or so just to reach the preserve from the north end of the island. You'll also need plenty of stamina and strong hiking shoes. The permission of the Forest and Lands Department (☎ 758/450–2231 or 758/450–2078) is required to access the trails, and the department provides a naturalist or forest officer guide.

⑥ Soufrière. The oldest town in St. Lucia, the picturesque fishing village of Soufrière was founded by the French in 1746 and named for the nearby volcano. The former French colonial capital currently has a population of about 9,000. Its harbor is the deepest on the island, accommodating smaller cruise ships that tie up at the wharf or at moorings in the bay. On a nearby jetty, there's a small crafts center. French colonial influences can be noticed in the architecture of the wooden buildings around the market square, with their second-story verandas and gingerbread trim. The market building is decorated with colorful murals. The **Soufrière Tourist Information Centre** (⊠ Bay St., ☎ 758/459–7200) provides information about area attractions.

☾ ⑪ La Soufrière Drive-in Volcano. Your nose will pick up the strong scent of the sulfur springs—more than 20 belching pools of muddy water, multicolor sulfur deposits, and assorted other minerals baking and steaming on the surface. Actually, you don't drive in. You walk behind your guide—whose service is included in admission—around a fault in the substratum rock, which provides a fascinating 20-minute experience that can be stinky on a hot day. ⊠ *Bay St., Soufrière,* ☎ *758/459–5500.* ☜ *EC$3.* ☉ *Daily 9–5.*

⑭ Vieux Fort. St. Lucia's second-largest city and port is the location of Hewanorra International Airport. From the **Moule à Chique Peninsula,** the island's southernmost tip, you can see all of St. Lucia to the north and the island of St. Vincent 21 mi south. This is where the clear Caribbean waters blend with those of the deeper blue Atlantic.

St. Lucia A to Z

Arriving and Departing

BY AIRPLANE

There are two airports on St. Lucia. Hewanorra International Airport (☎ 758/454–6249), on the southern tip of the island, is a modern airport with a long runway capable of handling wide-body jets. George F. L. Charles (Vigie) Airport (☎ 758/452–2596), in Castries, is a short airstrip that accommodates small, propeller-driven aircraft used for interisland and charter flights.

American Airlines (☎ 758/454–6777 or 758/453–2970) has daily service to Hewanorra through San Juan from New York and most other major U.S. cities. **American Eagle** (☎ 758/452–1820) flies daily from San Juan to Vigie Airport. **Air Canada** (☎ 758/454–6038 or 758/452–3051) has direct weekend service from Toronto and Montréal. **Air Jamaica** (☎ 758/454–8869) flies nonstop to Hewanorra from New York four times weekly. **British Airways** (☎ 758/452–3951 or 758/454–6172) has direct service from London. **BWIA** (☎ 758/452–3778 or 758/452–3950) has direct service from Miami, New York, and London.

Regional airlines also serve St. Lucia. **Air Martinique** (☎ 758/452–2463) flies into Vigie from Martinique. **Helenair** (☎ 758/452–7196) flies into Vigie from Grenada, St. Vincent, and other eastern Caribbean islands. **LIAT** (☎ 758/452–3051, 758/452–2348, or 758/454–6341) operates at both Hewanorra and Vigie and links St. Lucia with Barbados, Trinidad, Antigua, Martinique, Dominica, Guadeloupe, and other islands.

From the Airport: The drive from Hewanorra to Castries takes about 1¼ hours; to Soufrière, about one hour. Although both are long rides, either route follows a picturesque coastline and traverses lush rain forest. Vigie Airport is only 10–20 minutes from resorts in or near Castries; it's about 30 minutes to Marigot and 1½ hours from Soufrière.

Many resorts include airport transfers in their rates. Taxis are always available at the airports. If you take one, be sure to agree on the fare (and in which currency it's being quoted) before you get in. Between Hewanorra and Castries, expect to pay about $50; between Vigie and nearby resorts, $10–$20.

Electricity

Electric voltage is 220 volts, 50 cycles, with a square three-pin plug. Most hotels have 110-volt (U.S. standard current) outlets for shavers. To use American appliances, though, you'll need a transformer to convert voltage and a plug adapter; dual-voltage computers or appliances will still need a plug adapter. Hotels will sometimes lend you an adapter for use during your stay.

Emergencies

Ambulance/fire/police: ☎ 999. **Hospitals:** Victoria Hospital (✉ Hospital Rd., Castries, ☎ 758/452–2421 or 758/453–7059); **St. Jude's Hospital** (✉ Vieux Fort, ☎ 758/454–7671 or 758/454–6041); **Soufrière Hospital** (✉ Soufrière, ☎ 758/459–7258); and **Dennery Hospital** (✉ Dennery, ☎ 758/453–3310). **Pharmacies:** Clarke's Drugstore (✉ Bridge St., Castries, ☎ 758/452–2727); **M & C Drugstore** (✉ Bridge St., Castries, ☎ 758/452–2811 or ✉ Gablewoods Mall, Gros Islet Hwy., north of Castries, ☎ 758/451–7808); **Williams Pharmacy** (✉ Bridge St., Castries, ☎ 758/452–2797). **Sea/Air Rescue:** (☎ 758/452–2894, 758/452–1182, or 758/453–6664).

Festivals and Seasonal Events

St. Lucia's **Carnival,** the most extravagant festival of the year, is held in February on the Monday and Tuesday before Ash Wednesday. A costume parade winds through Castries, prizes are awarded for the best band, the calypso king and queen are crowned, and there's endless music and dancing in the streets. In April, the **Festival of Comedy** is the St. Lucia National Trust's annual fundraiser; two nights of adult comedy are presented at the Cultural Centre in Castries, and there's a day of family entertainment at Pigeon Island. For four days each May (since 1992), the **St. Lucia Jazz Festival** is the premier jazz festival in the Caribbean; international jazz musicians entertain at outdoor venues on Pigeon Island and at various hotels, and free concerts are held at Derek Walcott Square in downtown Castries. **Heritage Sundays** are Carnival-like outdoor events held on Sunday throughout the summer months either at Pigeon Island or at the old sugar mill in Anse La Raye village (on the West Coast); there's steel-band music and dancing, and local foods are served buffet style. The **St. Lucia Billfishing Tournament,** held the first week in October, attracts anglers from all over the Caribbean; prizes are awarded for the biggest fish and the largest catch. Traditional dishes and cultural presentations from around the world are the main attraction at the **International Food Fair,** an annual event sponsored by the tourist board; it takes place at Pointe Seraphine in November. The annual **Atlantic Rally for Cruisers,** the world's largest ocean-crossing race, starts in Las Palmas, Canary Islands, and ends in early December in Rodney Bay; the event is marked by a week of festivities and parties.

Getting Around

BUSES

Privately owned and operated minivans constitute St. Lucia's bus system, an inexpensive and efficient means of transportation used primarily by local people. Minivan routes cover the entire island and run from early morning until approximately 10 PM. Visitors will find this method of getting around most useful for short distances, between Castries and the Rodney Bay area for example; longer hauls would be uncomfortable. The fare between Castries and Gablewoods Mall is EC$1; Castries and Rodney Bay, EC$1.50; Castries and Vieux Fort (a very long trip that takes more than two hours), EC$7. Minivans follow designated routes (displayed on the front window); ask at your hotel for the appropriate route number for your destination. Wait at a marked bus stop or hail a passing minivan from the roadside; you can also catch one in Castries, at the corner of Micoud and Bridge streets.

CAR RENTALS

St. Lucia has about 500 mi of roads, but only about half (281 mi) are paved. All towns and villages are connected to major roads. The highways on both coasts are in good shape, although they are often winding and steep. Driving in St. Lucia is on the left, British-style.

To rent a car, you must be 25 years or older and hold a valid driver's license and a credit card. If you don't have an International Driver's License, you must buy a temporary St. Lucian driving permit available through car-rental firms, the Immigration Office at either airport, or at the Gros Islet police station. The permit costs $12 and is valid for three months. Car-rental rates range from $55–$75 per day or $295–$390 per week, depending on the car. Gasoline is expensive: $2.25 per gallon.

Car-rental agencies generally include free pick-up at your hotel and unlimited mileage. U.S. car-rental firms operating in St. Lucia are: **Avis** (✉ Pointe Seraphine, ☎ 758/452–2700; ✉ Hewanorra, ☎ 758/454–6325; ✉ Vigie, ☎ 758/452–2046), **Budget** (✉ Castries, ☎ 758/452–0233; ✉ Hewanorra, ☎ 758/454–5311), **Hertz** (✉ Castries, ☎ 758/452–0679; ✉ Hewanorra, ☎ 758/454–9636; ✉ Vigie, ☎ 758/451–7351), and **National** (✉ Castries, ☎ 758/450–8721; ✉ Pointe Seraphine, ☎ 758/453–0085; ✉ Hewanorra, ☎ 758/454–6699; ✉ Vigie, ☎ 758/452–3050).

Local agencies include: **C.T.L. Rent-a-Car** (✉ Rodney Bay Marina, ☎ 758/452–0732), **Cool Breeze Jeep/Car Rental** (✉ Soufrière, ☎ 758/459–7729), **Courtesy Car Rental** (✉ Bois D'Orange, Gros Islet, ☎ 758/452–8140), **Gibin Rent A Car** (✉ Rodney Bay Marina, ☎ 758/452–9528), **S.L.Y.S. Car Rentals** (✉ Castries, ☎ 758/452–5057), **St. Lucia Car Rentals Services** (✉ Castries, ☎ 758/450–8721), and **Trevor's Rent-a-Car** (✉ Auberge Seraphine, Castries, ☎ 758/459–0015).

FERRIES

The **Rodney Bay Ferry** (✉ Box 672, Castries, ☎ 758/452–0087, FAX 758/452–8816) has ferry service twice daily from Rodney Bay (right by The Lime restaurant) to Pigeon Island. The round-trip fare is $40 and includes the entrance fee to Pigeon Island and lunch. Snorkel equipment can be rented for $12.

HELICOPTERS

Some visitors to St. Lucia opt for helicopter transportation—a more expensive mode but much quicker. The cost for the 15-minute flight from Hewanorra to Castries is $100 per person, including luggage; for the 10-minute flight to Soufrière, $85 per person. There are helipads at Pointe Seraphine, Windjammer Landing, Jalousie Hilton, and Rodney Bay. Contact **St. Lucia Helicopters** (✉ Pointe Seraphine, ☎ 758/

453–6950, ⨳ 758/452–1553) or **Eastern Caribbean Helicopter Service** (✉ Pointe Seraphine, ☎ 758/452–6952).

TAXIS

Taxis are always available at the airport, the harbor, and in front of major hotels. They are expensive and unmetered, although nearly all drivers belong to a taxi cooperative and adhere to standard fares. Sample fares for up to four people: Castries to Rodney Bay, $12; Castries to Cap Estate, $20; Castries to Marigot Bay, $20. Always ask the driver to quote the price *before* you get in, and be sure that you both understand whether it's in E.C. or U.S. dollars. Drivers are knowledgeable and courteous.

Guided Tours

A variety of guided half- and full-day land and/or sea tours depart from the Castries area (Vigie Cove) or Rodney Bay and head north to Pigeon Island or south along the picturesque west coast to the Pitons and the sights in and around Soufrière. Half-day tours range in price from $35–$40 per person; full-day tours, $70–$100; sunset cruises, $35–$40; children, half price.

BOAT

Board the 140-ft **Brig Unicorn** (✉ Vigie Cove, Castries, ☎ 758/452–8811) for a full-day sail to Soufrière or a sunset cruise under full sail, accompanied by champagne, snacks, and live music. **Carnival Sailing** (✉ Castries, ☎ 758/452–5586) offers full-day sailing tours to the Pitons aboard their two catamarans, 65-ft *Carnival Sailing I* and 55-ft *Carnival Sailing II*. **Endless Summer Cruises** (Cats Inc., ✉ Rodney Bay, ☎ 758/450–8651) offers full-day tours and champagne sunset cruises aboard one of their huge catamaran party boats, 58-ft *Endless Summer I* or 46-ft *Endless Summer II*. The 56-ft Motor Cruiser **Vigie** (✉ Rodney Bay Marina, ☎ 758/452–9423 or 758/452–8232) takes passengers for half-day cruises to Pigeon Island or full-day tours to the Pitons and the sights around Soufrière, with lunch, swimming, and snorkeling at Anse Cochon included.

HELICOPTER

Helicopter sightseeing tours are fascinating ways to get a bird's-eye view of the island. A 10-minute North Island Tour ($45 per person) leaves from Pointe Seraphine, in Castries, continues up the west coast to Pigeon Island, then flies along the rugged Atlantic coastline before returning inland over Castries. The 20-minute South Island Tour ($80 per person) starts at Pointe Seraphine and follows the western coastline, circling picturesque Marigot Bay, Soufrière, and the majestic Pitons before returning inland over the volcanic hot springs and tropical rain forest. To arrange a helicopter sightseeing trip, contact **St. Lucia Helicopters** (☞ Getting Around, *above*).

ORIENTATION

Taxi drivers are well-informed and can give you a full tour—and often an excellent one, since government-sponsored training programs were introduced in 1994. Full-day island tours or sightseeing trips to Soufrière (from the Castries area) cost $120 for up to 4 people. If you plan your own day, expect to pay the driver $20 per hour plus tip.

Barnard's Travel (✉ Micoud St., Castries, ☎ 758/452–2214) offers a full range of half- and full-day island tours, as well as excursions to Dominica, Martinique, St. Vincent, and the Grenadines. **Explorer Adventure** (✉ Castries, ☎ 758/450–8356) specializes in Jeep safaris, where you spend a day exploring the rain forest, enjoying a barbecue lunch, and swimming and snorkeling at a west coast beach. **St. Lucia Representative Services Ltd.** (☎ 758/452–3762) has half- and full-day island tours, as well as excursions to a number of neighboring islands. **Sun-link International** (☎ 758/452–8232) offers dozens of land, sea, and combination sightseeing tours, as well as shopping tours, plantation and rain forest adventures, deep-sea fishing excursions, and day trips to other islands. With **Trailblazers Adventure Tours** (✉ Castries, ☎ 758/450–0998), you take a catamaran down the west coast to Soufrière, then travel into the island's interior in an open-top 4 × 4 Land Rover.

Language
English is the official language and is spoken everywhere, but you'll often hear local people speaking a French Creole patois among themselves. If you're interested in learning some patois words and phrases, pick up a copy of *A Visitor's Guide to St. Lucia Patois,* a small paperback book sold in local bookstores for $4.

As in many of the Caribbean islands, to "hang out" is to *lime* and a *jump-up* is a big party with lots of dance music (often in the street, as in the village of Gros Islet every Friday night). Don't be surprised if people in St. Lucia call you *darling* instead of "ma'am" or "sir"—they're being friendly, not forward.

Money Matters
CURRENCY
The official currency is the Eastern Caribbean dollar (EC$). It's linked to the U.S. dollar at EC$2.67, but stores and hotels often exchange at EC$2.50 or EC$2.60. U.S. currency is readily accepted, but you'll often get change in E.C. dollars. Major credit cards and traveler's checks are widely accepted. Prices quoted in this chapter are in U.S. dollars unless otherwise indicated.

SERVICE CHARGES, TAXES, AND TIPPING
Some hotels and restaurants add a 10% service charge to your bill in lieu of tipping. A government tax of 8% is added to all hotel and restaurant bills. There is no sales tax on items purchased in shops. The departure tax for all persons leaving the island of St. Lucia is $11 (EC$27).

Taxi drivers appreciate a 10%–12% tip. If no service charge has been added to your restaurant bill, a 10%–12% tip is appropriate for good service. Tip porters and bellhops 75¢ per bag, although many of the all-inclusive resorts have a no-tipping policy.

Opening and Closing Times
Most **stores** are open weekdays 8:30–12:30 and 1:30–4:30, Saturday 8–12:30; Gablewoods Mall shops are open Monday–Saturday 9–7; Pointe Seraphine shops are open weekdays 9–5, Saturday 9–2. **Banks** are open Monday–Thursday 8–3, Friday 8–5, and, at a few branches in Rodney Bay, Saturday 9–noon.

HOLIDAYS
New Year's Day, Carnival (Feb. 15–16), Independence Day (Feb. 22), Good Friday (Apr. 2), Easter Monday (Apr. 5), Labour Day (May 1), Whit Monday (May 24), Corpus Christi (June 3), Emancipation Day (1st Mon. in Aug.), Thanksgiving Day (Oct. 25), National Day (Dec. 13), Christmas, and Boxing Day (Dec. 26).

Passports
U.S., Canadian, and British citizens whose stay does not exceed six months must have a valid passport (or one not expired by more than five years) or prove citizenship with a birth certificate (with a raised seal) and a government-issued photo ID. All visitors must have a return or ongoing ticket.

Precautions

Coastal waters surrounding the island of St. Lucia are protected areas. Spearfishing and collecting live fish are prohibited. Crime is not a significant problem, but don't take unnecessary risks—lock your door, secure your valuables, and don't carry too much money or flaunt expensive jewelry on the street. Insects can be a problem during the rainy season (July–November), particularly in the rain forest; bring along repellent to ward off mosquitoes and sand flies. Be aware that sea urchins live among the rocks on the coastline; should one's long black spines lodge under your skin, don't try to pull them out. Apply an ammonia-based liquid and the spine will retreat, allowing you to ease it out.

Manchineel trees have poisonous fruit and leaves that can cause skin blisters on contact. Even raindrops falling off the trees can cause blisters, so don't stand under one of these trees to get out of the rain. Manchineels are usually marked when on hotel property. If you wish to take photographs of local people or their property, be sure to ask permission first and offer a small gratuity in appreciation. Swimming on the rough Atlantic side of the island is dangerous. Souvenir vendors can be persistent, particularly outside some of the popular attractions in and around Soufrière. Be polite but firm if you're not interested. Tap water is perfectly safe to drink throughout the island.

Telephones and Mail

The area code for St. Lucia is 758. You can make direct-dial overseas and interisland calls from St. Lucia, and the connections are excellent. To charge an overseas call to a major credit card, dial 811; there is no surcharge. There's a public fax bureau at the Cable & Wireless office, Bridge Street, Castries.

The General Post Office is on Bridge Street, Castries, open weekdays 8:30–4:30. All towns and villages have sub-offices, and there's also one at Gablewoods Mall. Postage for airmail letters to the United States, Canada, and Great Britain is EC95¢ for up to 1 ounce. Postcards are EC75¢ to the United States and Canada, EC85¢ to Great Britain.

Visitor Information

Before you go, contact the **St. Lucia Tourist Board** (⊠ 820 2nd Ave., 9th floor, New York, NY 10017, ☎ 212/867–2950, 800/456–3984, or 888/4–STLUCIA, ℻ 212/867–2795 in the U.S. or Canada; ⊠ 421A Finchley Rd., London NW3 6HJ, ☎ 0171/431–3675, ℻ 0171/437–7920 in the U.K.). For information about St. Lucia on the **Internet**: www.st-lucia.com.

On St. Lucia, the **St. Lucia Tourist Board** is based at Pointe Seraphine on Castries Harbor (⊠ Box 221, Castries, ☎ 758/452–4094 or 758/452–5968, ℻ 758/453–1121). The office is open weekdays 8–4:30. There are also information offices in downtown Castries (⊠ Jeremie St., ☎ 758/452–2479), Soufrière (⊠ Bay St., ☎ 758/459–7200), at Vigie Airport (☎ 758/452–2596), and at Hewanorra International Airport (☎ 758/454–6644).

22 St. Martin/ St. Maarten

Updated by
Karl Luntta

Baby won't see the long side of 50 again, but the name fits. She has an easy laugh and relaxed manner even though she's a taxi driver caught in a traffic jam that would make most cabbies cry. "Sure, it's a hard job," she says. "But business is good, and a woman's got to do what a woman's got to do." The cars ahead suddenly lurch; backups here are like dieting—frequent but short-lived. Baby's off to find her next fare, maybe at a posh restaurant or hotel or a sun-drenched beach—the pattern varies only with the faces in her rearview mirror.

There are several advantages to visiting St. Martin/St. Maarten. Planes fly in nonstop all the time from the United States, so you don't have to spend half your vacation getting here. The 37-square-mi island is home to two sovereign nations, St. Maarten (Dutch) and St. Martin (French), so you can experience two cultures for the price of one. And the island is ideal if you like to have lots of things to do.

Whatever can be done in or on the water—snorkeling, windsurfing, waterskiing—is available here; there is golf and tennis as well. Serious diners will find a different top class restaurant each night. The duty-free shopping is as good as anywhere else in the Caribbean. There's an active nightlife, with discos and casinos. Day trips can be taken by ship or plane to the nearby islands of Anguilla, Saba, St. Eustatius, and St. Barthélemy. There are hotels for every taste and budget—from motel-type units for the package tour trade to some of the most exclusive resorts in the Caribbean. The standard of living is one of the highest in the Caribbean, so the islanders can afford to be honest and to treat visitors as welcome guests. If you wander even slightly off the beaten track, you'll find friendly and opinionated locals willing and eager to share their insider knowledge. Corruption and crime, which had been on the rise, have decreased dramatically in the '90s, thanks to an exemplary cooperative effort between the two governments.

On the negative side, St. Martin/St. Maarten has been thoroughly discovered and exploited; unless you stay in an exclusive resort, you will often find yourself sharing beachfronts with tour groups or conventioneers (the exception being some of the beaches in Terres Basses on the French side). Yes, there is gambling, but the table limits are so low that hard-core gamblers will have a better time gamboling on the beach. As is often the case in the Caribbean, the island infrastructure has not kept pace with development. There are plans to expand marina, airport, and road services, but meanwhile, you will probably run into congestion at the airport and seemingly endless traffic.

Lodging

Until recently, the Dutch side commanded all the big, splashy resorts. The casinos are still to be found exclusively on the Dutch side—gambling is illegal on the French side. However, St. Martin is having a building boom, especially around Nettlé and Orient bays. All hotels on the French side have an English-speaking staff. There are also small inns and Mediterranean-style facilities on both sides. Many hotels offer enticing packages and you'll save substantially if you travel off-season, although some hotels and restaurants are closed. In general, the French resorts are more intimate, but what the Dutch properties lack in ambience, they compensate for in clean comfortable rooms with all the "extras." Most of the larger Dutch resorts feature time-share annexes; the units are often available for rental for those who prefer the condo lifestyle at comparable rates. Most properties are EP or CP (the latter usually only in season), though meal plans are sometimes available.

CATEGORY	COST*
$$$$	over $310
$$$	$235–$310
$$	$160–$235
$	under $160

All prices are for a standard double room in high season, excluding 5% room tax and 3% "turnover" tax (Dutch side), a taxe de séjour (set by individual hotels on the French side), and a 10%–15% service charge.

Hotels

DUTCH SIDE

$$$–$$$$ **Maho Beach Hotel & Casino.** This pink-and-white megaresort is almost an institution on St. Maarten. The spacious rooms have cathedral ceilings and light pastel and deep ocean-color decor, plus sea or garden views from their balconies. The trick is to get a room far enough from the airport's landing strip (those behind the main lobby are the quietest). Dining options include Italian fare at Cafe Toscano, burgers and live music at Cheri's Café, and beachside American fare at Harbor Point. The hotel is home to the island's largest casino, the Casino Royal (☞ Nightlife and the Arts, *below*), and its largest pool. Unfortunately, the service can't keep up with the sprawl; you may be neglected as the staff struggles to meet guest needs. ✉ *Maho Bay,* ☎ *599/5–52115 or 800/223–0757 (reservations service),* FAX *599/5–53180. 586 rooms, 29 suites. 10 restaurants, 3 bars, air-conditioning, 3 pools, hot tub, spa, 4 tennis courts, health club, beach, dive shop, dock, snorkeling, jet skiing, waterskiing, shops, casino, dance club, babysitting, business services, car rental. AE, D, MC, V. EP, MAP.*

$$$–$$$$ **Royal Palm Beach Club.** A complex of suites and shops sitting on Kimsha Beach, the Royal Palm is in an excellent location for exploring Simpson Bay and the rest of the island. Each room comes with a full kitchen, including a full-size refrigerator. The rooms all face the sea and are decorated in standard floral patterns and lots of rattan furniture. Rooms can accommodate as many as six and come equipped with two full baths and a TV and VCR. The small beachfront restaurant and bar is okay for the daytime, but hit other restaurants at night. The pool has a small swim-up bar. ⊠ *Airport Rd., Simpson Bay,* ☎ *599/5–43732,* FAX *599/5–43727. 140 suites. Restaurant, bar, air-conditioning, in-room VCRs, pool, beach, boating, jet skiing, waterskiing, shops, baby-sitting, laundry service. AE, D, MC, V. EP.*

$–$$$$ 🏨 **Pelican Resort & Casino.** An assortment of white stucco buildings houses the resort's apartments, suites, and deluxe studios, all of which have sweeping views of the Caribbean. This centrally located resort has 1,400 ft of beach (though it's not great for swimming because of the seaweed). Walk into the reception area and you're greeted by gaming tables. On the lower level is a sales office enticing you to buy into this hotel-condo complex. Sadly, the resort has not kept up with the pace of refurbishment that swept most of the island after 1995's Hurricane Luis, and the grumpy staff seems more interested in selling time-share units than attending to guests. A new management company, the Royal Resorts Group, took over in late 1997, so there may be hope. ⊠ *Simpson Bay,* ☎ *599/5–42503 or 800/550–7088 (reservations service),* FAX *599/5–42133. 210 suites, 132 studios. 2 restaurants, 4 bars, grocery, kitchenettes, 5 pools, spa, 4 tennis courts, beach, dive shop, dock, snorkeling, windsurfing, boating, jet skiing, waterskiing, casino, playground, car rental. AE, D, DC, MC, V. EP.*

$$–$$$ 🏨 **Oyster Bay Beach Resort.** The refined elegance of this hotel is quite
★ out of character with the rest of St. Maarten. Two towers with Moorish arches and stone walls surround a courtyard. There are split-level suites and standard rooms, all with terra-cotta floors, a balcony or terrace, and pastel French cottons. A newer building has larger rooms whose balconies face the sea. The hotel is a one-minute walk from Dawn Beach, which is excellent for snorkeling, sunbathing, and swimming. The outstanding ☞ **Oyster Bay Beach Resort** restaurant opens onto the Atlantic Ocean, and the pool is perched right at the water's edge. ⊠ *Oyster Pond (Box 239, Philipsburg),* ☎ *599/5–36040 or 800/231–8331 (reservations service);* FAX *599/5–36695. 40 units. Restaurant, bar, air-conditioning, fans, pool, car rental. AE, D, MC, V. BP, EP.*

$$ 🏨 **Divi Little Bay Beach Resort.** Hurricane Luis in 1995 gave the Divi a chance to spend millions refurbishing the entire resort. It will eventually host 256 rooms and suites, but you shouldn't be adversely affected by any ongoing construction. The hotel, in a light blue and cream, Dutch Colonial motif, sits on Little Bay at the south end of Great Bay, on a beach that is clean but rocky in places. The large rooms feature wide balconies with sea views, king-size beds, and small but adequate kitchens. Bathrooms have a luxurious whirlpool baths and separate showers. The poolside Sea Breeze Bar hosts weekly barbecues and live music. ⊠ *Little Bay Rd. (Box 961, Philipsburg),* ☎ *599/5–22333 or 800/367–3484 (reservations service),* FAX *599/5–25410. 49 rooms. Restaurant, bar, grocery, refrigerators, 3 pools, 3 tennis courts, beach, snorkeling, boating, coin laundry. AE, DC, MC, V. EP, FAP, MAP.*

$$ 🏨 **Great Bay Beach Hotel & Casino.** One of the island's few properties operating as an all-inclusive as well as with a room-only rate, this resort, a 10-minute walk from the center of Philipsburg, has its own stretch of beach and terrific views of the bay. The bustling open-air lobby, with striped awnings overlooking the sea, is more striking than the rooms, furnished in typical muted pastels. You do get a private balcony or terrace with an ocean or mountain view. A list of activities is posted each morning, and the hotel staff can arrange virtually any type of island excursion or sport. ⊠ *Philipsburg (Box 910) ,* ☎ *599/5–22446*

Exploring

French Cul de Sac, **5**
Friar's Beach, **7**
Grand Case, **6**
Guana Bay Point, **2**
Marigot, **8**
Orléans, **4**
Oyster Pond, **3**
Philipsburg, **1**
St. Martin
Museum, **9**

Dining

Alizéa, **13**
Antoine, **51**
Le Bec Fin, **55**
Bistrot Nu, **25**
Chesterfield's, **52**
Chez Martine, **17**
L'Escargot, **53**
Indiana Beach, **46**
Kangaroo Court
Caffé, **54**
Maison sur le Port, **30**
Le Marocain, **32**
Mary's Boon, **38**
Mini-Club, **26**
Oyster Bay Beach
Resort, **62**
Le Perroquet, **41**
La Plaisance, **33**
Le Poisson d'Or, **29**
Le Pressoir, **16**
Rainbow Café, **19**
Ric's Place, **61**
Le Santal, **34**
Saratoga, **47**
Shiv Sagar, **56**
Spartaco, **48**
Le Tastevin, **18**
Turtle Pier Bar &
Restaurant, **42**
La Vie En Rose, **28**
Wajang Doll, **57**
Yvette's, **64**

Lodging

Alizéa, **13**
Anse Margot, **37**
Captain Oliver's, **63**
Divi Little Bay Beach
Resort, **49**
Esmeralda Resort, **12**
Grand Case Beach
Club, **20**
Great Bay Beach Hotel
& Casino, **50**
Green Cay Village, **10**
Hévéa, **21**
Holland House
Beach Hotel, **58**

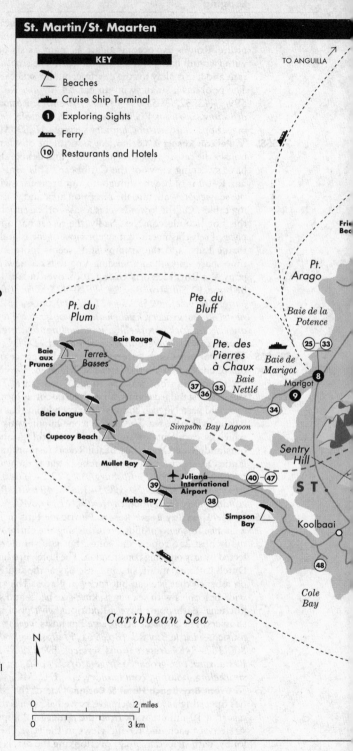

St. Martin/St. Maarten

KEY

Beaches
Cruise Ship Terminal
Exploring Sights
Ferry
Restaurants and Hotels

TO ANGUILLA

Caribbean Sea

Horny Toad
Guesthouse, **43**

Hôtel l'Atlantide, **23**

Hôtel L'Esplanade
Caraïbes, **24**

Hôtel Mont
Vernon, **11**

Maho Beach Hotel &
Casino, **39**

Mary's Boon Beach
Plantation, **38**

Mercure Simson Beach
Coralia, **36**

Le Méridien, **15**

Nettlé Bay Beach
Club, **35**

Oyster Bay
Beach Resort, **62**

Pasanggrahan Royal
Inn, **59**

Pavillon Beach
Hotel, **22**

Pelican Resort &
Casino, **44**

Le Privilege Resort
& Spa, **14**

La Résidence, **27**

Royal Palm Beach
Club, **40**

Le Royale
Louisiana, **31**

Sea View Hotel &
Casino, **60**

La Vista, **45**

or 800/223–0757 (reservations service), FAX *599/5–23859. 275 rooms, 10 1-bedroom suites. 2 restaurants, 3 bars, 2 pools, beauty salon, tennis court, exercise room, beach, snorkeling, boating, shop, casino, nightclub, car rental. AE, DC, MC, V. All-inclusive, EP.*

$–$$ 🏨 **Holland House Beach Hotel.** This is a centrally situated hotel, with the shops of Front Street at its doorstep and mile-long Great Bay Beach as its backyard. Each room has muted-pastel spreads and drapes and a balcony; most have kitchenettes. Ask for a beach view. The delightful open-air restaurant overlooking the water serves reasonably priced dinners, and the indoor-outdoor patio lounge is a popular spot to watch the sunset. ⊠ *43-A Front St. (Box 393), Philipsburg,* ☎ *599/ 5–22572 or 800/223–9815 (reservations service),* FAX *599/5–24673. 45 rooms, 6 suites. Restaurant, lounge, air-conditioning, meeting room. AE, D, DC, MC, V. EP.*

$–$$ 🏨 **Horny Toad Guesthouse.** This is one of the most charming properties
★ on the island, thanks to the caring touch of owners Betty and Earle Vaughan, who keep things immaculate. The eight apartments on the beach, some with air-conditioning, are individually decorated, and the blue-and-white sun terrace duplicates the patterns of delftware . There is a barbecue area for guests, but no restaurant. ⊠ *Simpson Bay (Box 3029),* ☎ *599/5–54323 or 800/417–9361, ext. 3013,* FAX *599/5–53316. 2 studios, 6 1-bedroom apartments. Fans, library. D, MC, V. EP.*

$–$$ 🏨 **La Vista.** On this intimate property, Antillean buildings are connected by brick walkways lined with riotous hibiscus and bougainvillea. All accommodations are suites with a small stove, cable TV, mini-refrigerator, and private balcony. Guests have the use of the pool, tennis courts, and spa facilities at the adjacent Pelican Resort. The views from the wood-decked pool are fabulous. ⊠ *Pelican Key (Box 2086),* ☎ *599/ 5–43005 or 599/5–43008,* FAX *599/5–43010. 32 suites. Restaurant, air-conditioning, refrigerators. AE, MC, V. EP.*

$–$$ 🏨 **Mary's Boon Beach Plantation.** When new owners Mark and Chris Cleveland took over this landmark Simpson Bay guest house in 1996, they quickly made it their own. Gingerbread fretwork adorns the roofline and the lobby (with bookshelves and a large aquarium) opens out to the windswept dining room and bar with views of the ocean. The rooms are studios designed in a plantation motif, with raised four-poster beds, reproduction antique mahogany furniture, wooden beam roofs, and detailed molding. All feature small kitchenettes with coffeemaker, microwave, cable TV, phones, and private bath. All except one unit sit on the beach, and a long verandah stretches across the back of the rooms. The grounds feature exotic flora, and at press time plans were underway to construct a swimming pool with a wet and dry bar. ☞ **Mary's Boon** restaurant is well worth a visit. (Note that you're right next to the airport here; parents should note that the hotel is not the best place for preteens during high season.) ⊠ *117 Simpson Bay Rd.,* ☎ *599/5–54235,* FAX *599/5–53403. 16 studios. Restaurant, kitchenettes, minibars. D, MC, V. EP.*

$ 🏨 **Pasanggrahan Royal Inn.** It's entirely appropriate that the bar here
★ is named Sidney Greenstreet. This is the island's oldest inn, refurbished and given additional suites following after hurricane damage, and it looks like a set for an old Bogie-Greenstreet film. The green-and-white building was once Queen Wilhelmina's residence. Wicker peacock chairs, balconies shaded by tropical greenery, and a broad tile veranda are some of its hallmarks. There are no TVs or phones in the rooms. ⊠ *15 Front St. (Box 151), Philipsburg,* ☎ *599/5–23588, 599/ 5–22743, or 800/223–9815 (reservations service),* FAX *599/5–22885. 22 rooms, 6 suites. Restaurant, bar. AE, MC, V. EP.*

$ 🏨 **Sea View Hotel & Casino.** Behind a black-marble facade, you'll find one of the good buys on Front Street and Great Bay Beach. The air-conditioned, twin-bed rooms are modest, cheerful, and clean. Ten rooms look out on the courtyard, where breakfast is sometimes served; four rooms face the sea. Children under 12 stay free. ⊠ *67 Front St. (Box 965), Philipsburg,* ☎ *599/5–22323;* FAX *599/5–24356. 46 rooms. Breakfast room, air-conditioning, casino. AE, D, MC, V. EP.*

FRENCH SIDE

$$$–$$$$ 🏨 **Esmeralda Resort.** The green roofs and stacked configuration make this villa complex look like a Sun Belt development, but the interiors are tastefully decorated. The 65 rooms and suites in 18 villas can be combined any way you like, from studios to five-bedroom palatial digs. Each villa has a private pool, and all rooms have terraces. The restaurant, L'Astrolabe, serves excellent French cuisine. Five other restaurants on the nearby beach let you charge meals to your room. ⊠ *Baie Orientale (Box 5141) 97064,* ☎ *590/87–36–36 or 800/622–7836 (reservations service),* FAX *590/87–35–18. 18 villas. 6 restaurants, kitchenettes, 17 pools, 2 tennis courts, shop. AE, MC, V. EP.*

$$$–$$$$ 🏨 **Grand Case Beach Club.** This informal condo complex is on a crescent beach (another "secret" strand of sand is a short walk away). The club has undergone a complete restoration, including new furnishings and new decor. Studios and one- and two-bedroom apartments have balconies or patios; the 62 oceanfront units are in demand. The aptly named Sunset Café sits over the beach, facing west. ⊠ *Grand Case (Box 339) 97150,* ☎ *590/87–51–87 or 800/223–1588 (reservations service),* FAX *590/87–59–93. 71 units. Restaurant, lounge, air-conditioning, kitchenettes, tennis court, beach, car rental. AE, D, MC, V. CP.*

$$$–$$$$ 🏨 **Green Cay Village.** Set high above Orient Beach facing the trade winds,
★ this complex is a great choice for small groups or families. Green Cay offers 48 rooms in spacious one-, two-, and three-bedroom villas, each with its own pool, large deck, full kitchen, and outdoor dining patio. Daily maid service is included. Although all villas have plenty of privacy, those highest on the hill enjoy the most seclusion, as well as the most stunning views. A reasonably priced breakfast is served by the pool, and at Orient Bay Resort, you have charge privileges at all the restaurants and bars and access to tennis and water sport facilities. ⊠ *Parc Baie Orientale (Box 3006) 97064,* ☎ *590/87–38–63 or 800/932–3222 (reservations service),* FAX *590/87–39–27. 16 villas. Kitchenettes, room service, in-room VCRs, 16 pools. AE, MC, V. EP.*

$$$–$$$$ 🏨 **Nettlé Bay Beach Club.** The 240 units of this large resort, about five minutes from Marigot, are spread across the sands of striking Baie Nettlé. Four sets of villa suites and one set of garden bungalows, each set with its own pool, face the waterfront and, across the bay, Dutch St. Maarten. The rooms and suites are furnished simply but comfortably and come with kitchens, TVs, and patios or balconies. On the grounds are two restaurants, including the South American–influenced La Parilla and the French La Fayette, as well as the beach bar Le Grand Bleu. This is an excellent location for exploring Marigot and the south side of the island. ⊠ *Sandy Ground Rd. (Box 4081), Marigot 97064,* ☎ *590/87–68–68 or 800/999–3543 (reservations service),* FAX *590/87–21–51. 240 units. 2 restaurants, 5 pools, air-conditioning, kitchenettes, 3 tennis courts, beach, snorkeling, jet skiing, shop. AE, MC, V. EP.*

$$$–$$$$ 🏨 **Le Privilege Resort & Spa.** So heavy was the damage from Hurricane Luis, that this resort, all of three years old, had to be virtually rebuilt. The result is a sparkling new Le Privilege, perched above Anse Marcel and ☞ **Le Méridien.** Those into the spa life can take advantage of all kinds of treatments, from massage to lymphatic drainage. Rooms and suites are spacious and comfortably furnished, with tile floors, marble baths, and such touches as CD players and in-room safes. There's a free shuttle to the beach and the resort's marina. ⊠ *Anse Mar-*

cel 97150, ☎ *590/87–38–38 or 800/874–8541 (reservations service),* ℻ *590/87–44–12. 16 rooms, 18 suites. 2 restaurants, bar, in-room safes, in-room VCRs, 3 pools, beauty salon, spa, 6 tennis courts, health club, racquetball, squash, dive shop, dock, windsurfing, boating, fishing, nightclub. AE, MC, V. CP.*

$$–$$$$ 🏨 **Le Méridien.** This bustling resort, comprising two smaller complexes called L'Habitation and Le Domaine, is wildly popular with tour groups and families. There are 1,600 ft of white-sand beach and a slew of sports facilities; nonmotorized water sports are included in the room rates. The service is polite and the setting pleasant—at the end of a white-knuckle road, amid beautifully landscaped gardens on enchanting but windless Marcel Cove. All the rooms and suites have balconies (only the top floors, about half the rooms, have ocean views), and suites on the marina have fully equipped kitchens and private patios. Guests have free access to the facilities of ☞ **Le Privilege Resort & Spa.** La Belle France is a typically solid and *très cher* gourmet restaurant. ✉ *Anse Marcel (Box 581) 97150,* ☎ *590/87–67–00 or 800/543–4300 (reservations service),* ℻ *590/87–30–38. 314 rooms, 82 suites. 4 restaurants, 4 bars, air-conditioning, refrigerators, 2 pools, miniature golf, 6 tennis courts, aerobics, exercise room, racquetball, squash, beach, dive shop, dock, snorkeling, boating, jet skiing, waterskiing, shops, dance club, car rental. AE, MC, V. EP.*

$$$ 🏨 **Hôtel L'Esplanade Caraïbes.** This complex, built on a hillside over-
★ looking Grand Case Bay, is a three-minute walk from the beach. Two curved stone staircases with inlaid tile and brick lead up from the bougainvillea beds to the open-air reception area. Standard suites are large, with balconies and gleaming wood ceilings; some have an office alcove (but hopefully you've left your work at home). Duplexes have cathedral ceilings and mahogany staircases, as well as an extra half bath and a loft bedroom; upholstery throughout is striped with muted pinks and corals. There is no restaurant at the hotel, but Grand Case's roster of gourmet spots is just a short walk away. ✉ *Grand Case (Box 5007) 97150,* ☎ *590/87–06–55,* ℻ *590/87–29–15. 23 units. Pool, wading pool, car rental. AE, MC, V. EP.*

$$–$$$ 🏨 **Hôtel Mont Vernon.** Gingerbread work decorates this rambling hotel, which sits on a bluff over Orient Bay, but its multicolor veneer makes it an eyesore when seen from the beach. Looking out is another story: Rooms in the buildings on the crest facing the ocean have the best views and are slightly larger than the others. Other choice rooms are in the buildings by the pool and beach. All rooms have a private balcony. This is a big resort that lures package-tour groups and business seminars. ✉ *Baie Orientale (Box 1174) 97062,* ☎ *590/87–62–00,* ℻ *590/87–37–27. 394 suites. 2 restaurants, 2 bars, pool, 2 tennis courts, exercise room, beach, snorkeling, windsurfing, shops, children's program, car rental. AE, DC, MC, V. CP, MAP.*

$$–$$$ 🏨 **Pavillon Beach Hotel.** Every room and suite here faces the sea and has a balcony. The spacious studios and one-bedroom suites are done in warm pastel colors and have tile floors and elegant rattan furniture. Bathrooms come with a hair dryer and shower but no tub. From ground-level rooms, you can walk onto the beach through sliding wooden shutters. ✉ *Plage de Grand Case, RN 7, Grand Case 97150,* ☎ *590/87–96–46 or 800/223–9815 (reservations service),* ℻ *590/ 87–71–04. 16 units. Kitchenettes, beach. AE, MC, V. EP.*

$$ 🏨 **Alizéa.** The view of Orient Bay from this Mont Vernon hill setting is stunning. An open-air feeling pervades the hotel, from its terrace restaurant—the food is superb—to the 26 guest apartments done up with contemporary light-wood furnishings. Rooms vary in style and design, but all are tasteful and each has a kitchenette and a large private balcony. There is a path to the beach (a 10-minute walk) and the ☞ **Al-**

izéa restaurant is excellent. ⊠ *Mont Vernon 25 97150,* ☎ *590/87–33–42,* 𝔽𝔸𝕏 *590/87–41–15. 8 1-bedroom bungalows, 18 studios. Restaurant, bar, kitchenettes, pool. AE, D, MC, V. CP.*

$$ 🏨 **Anse Margot.** This quiet, thoroughly French property is one of the many hotels that line the stretch of land between the sea and Simpson Bay Lagoon, known as Baie Nettlé. The rooms here are in eight three-story town house buildings. All units have a private balcony with either a garden or beach view. Upholstery, drapes, and spreads are a brown-and-coral geometric print. There is a stretch of beach along the Lagoon that's good for sunbathing but not swimming; you may prefer the Nettlé beach across the street. A complimentary breakfast buffet is served in the open-air Entre Deux Mers, one of the better hotel restaurants. It's about a five-minute drive to Marigot. ⊠ *Baie Nettlé (Box 979) 97150,* ☎ *590/87–92–01 or 800/742–4276 (reservations service),* 𝔽𝔸𝕏 *590/87–92–13. 96 units. Restaurant, bar, 2 pools, hot tub, beach, snorkeling, boating, jet skiing, waterskiing, shop, business services, meeting room. AE, D, DC, MC, V. BP.*

$$ 🏨 **Captain Oliver's.** This property straddles the St. Maarten–St. Mar-
★ tin border: Stay in France, and dine in the Netherlands. The bungalows are a good bargain and a good way to avoid the hustle and bustle of St. Maarten. The small hotel faces a beautiful horseshoe-shape bay; bungalows have a view of the marina or garden. The exceptionally clean, fresh rooms have a patio/deck; sail-and-stay packages can be arranged by the friendly and helpful staff. ⊠ *Oyster Pond 97150,* ☎ *590/87–40–26,* 𝔽𝔸𝕏 *590/87–40–84. 50 rooms. Restaurant, snack bar, air-conditioning, kitchenettes, minibars, pool. AE, DC, MC, V. CP.*

$–$$ 🏨 **Hôtel l'Atlantide.** This small hotel has 10 sun-drenched units, ranging in size from a studio to a two-bedroom suite. Private balconies overlook Grand Case Bay and the beach. The decor is airy, with gleaming white-tile floors and crisp pastel-striped or floral upholstery. There's no restaurant or bar, but the village of Grand Case is known for its lively restaurant scene. ⊠ *Grand Case (Box 5140) 97150,* ☎ *590/87–09–80,* 𝔽𝔸𝕏 *590/87–12–36. 9 apartments, 1 suite. Beach. MC, V. EP.*

$–$$ 🏨 **Mercure Simson Beach Coralia.** This complex, formerly the Marine
★ Hotel, may be the best bargain on the Nettlé Bay hotel strip. Rooms and suites are cheerfully decorated; most have water views, and all have a kitchenette and balcony. Budget-conscious Europeans love this place because of such extras as a huge breakfast buffet and nightly local entertainment. There are shuttles (not free) to Marigot, Philipsburg, and beaches. ⊠ *Baie Nettlé (Box 172) 97150,* ☎ *590/87–54–54,* 𝔽𝔸𝕏 *590/87–92–11. 130 studios, 45 1-bedroom duplexes. Restaurant, bar, grocery, kitchenettes, pool, tennis court, beach, dive shop, snorkeling, windsurfing, boating, jet skiing, waterskiing. bicycles, shop, coin laundry, car rental. AE, DC, MC, V. CP.*

$ 🏨 **Hévéa.** This small white guest house with smart striped awnings is
★ across the street from the beach in the heart of Grand Case. The rooms are dollhouse small but will appeal to romantics. There are beam ceilings, washstands, and carved-wood beds with lovely white coverlets and mosquito nets. The five rooms, studios, and apartment are on the terrace level; two studios and one apartment are on the garden level. Hotel guests can get a special "house" dinner at the delightful gourmet restaurant for $30. ⊠ *163 bd. de Grand Case, Grand Case 97150,* ☎ *590/87–56–85 or 800/423–4433 (reservations service),* 𝔽𝔸𝕏 *590/87–83–88. 8 units. Restaurant. MC, V. EP.*

$ 🏨 **La Résidence.** The downtown location and soundproof rooms of this
★ Marigot hotel make it a popular place for business travelers. All the accommodations have a phone, a TV, a balcony, dark rattan furniture, and tile floors. You have a choice among single or double rooms, some with loft beds. The intimate restaurant offers a good $28 three-course

menu. You'll have to take a cab or drive to the beach. ⊠ *Rue du Général de Gaulle, Marigot 97150,* ☎ *590/87–70–37 or 800/223–9815 (reservations service),* FAX *590/87–90–44. 22 rooms. Restaurant, lounge, minibars, shop. AE, D, MC, V. CP, MAP.*

$ ⊡ **Le Royale Louisiana.** In downtown Marigot in the boutique shopping area, this upstairs hotel has white and pale green galleries that overlook the flower-filled courtyard. There's a selection of twin, double, and triple duplexes. You can reach the nearest beach by a 20-minute walk or by taxi. ⊠ *Rue du Général de Gaulle (Box 476), Marigot 97055,* ☎ *590/87–86–51,* FAX *590/87–96–49. 58 rooms. Restaurant, snack bar, air-conditioning, beauty salon. AE, D, MC, V. CP.*

Villas

Both sides of the island offer a wide variety of homes, villas, condominiums, and housekeeping apartments. Information in the United States can be obtained through **WIMCO** (⊠ Box 1461, Newport, RI 02840, ☎ 401/849–8012 or 800/932–3222), **Caribbean Vacation Villas** (⊠ 35 Pleasant St., Concord, NH 03301, ☎ 603/783–3339 or 800/530–2212) or **Villas of Distinction** (⊠ Box 55, Armonk, NY 10504, ☎ 914/273–3331 or 800/289–0900). On the island, contact **Carimo** (⊠ Box 220, rue du Général de Gaulle, Marigot 97150, ☎ 590/87–57–58), which has some truly fabulous villas for rent in the tony and desirable Terres Basses section of the island, or **St. Martin Rentals** (⊠ Beacon Hill, Sint Maarten, Netherlands Antilles, or Box 10300, Bedford, NH 03110, ☎ 599/5–54330 or 800/308–8455 for reservations service).

Dining

It may seem that this island has no monuments, but they're here—all are dedicated to gastronomy. You'll scarcely find a touch of Dutch; the major influences are French and Italian. This season's "in" eatery may be next season's remembrance of things past, as things do have a way of changing rapidly. The steep prices reflect both the island's high culinary reputation and the difficulty of obtaining fresh ingredients. The hotel restaurants on the French side are usually more sophisticated, but sometimes at budget-breaking prices. In high season, *make reservations,* and call to cancel if you can't make it. Many restaurants close completely or just for lunch during August, September, and into October; in the off-season, call ahead to check hours.

What to Wear

Appropriate dining attire on this island ranges from swimsuits to sport jackets. For men, a jacket and khakis or jeans take you anywhere; for women, dressy pants, a skirt, or even fancy shorts are usually acceptable. Jeans are de rigueur in the less formal and more trendy eateries. In the listings below, dress is casual (and chic) unless otherwise noted, but ask when making reservations if you're unsure.

CATEGORY	COST*
$$$$	over $50
$$$	$35–$50
$$	$25–$35
$	under $25

**per person for a three-course meal, excluding drinks and service*

Dutch Side

AMERICAN

$–$$ ✕ **Turtle Pier Bar & Restaurant.** Monkeys and parrots greet you at the
★   entrance to this classic Caribbean hangout, teetering over the lagoon and festooned with creeping vines. There are 200 animals in this informal zoo, but that's nothing compared to the menagerie hanging out

at the bar during happy hour. The genial owner, Sid Wathey, whose family is one of the island's oldest, and his American wife, Lorraine, have fashioned one of the funkiest, most endearing places in the Caribbean, with cheap draft beer, huge American breakfasts, all-you-can-eat rib dinners, and live music several nights a week. ⊠ *114 Airport Rd., Simpson Bay,* ☎ *599/5–52562. No credit cards.*

AMERICAN/CASUAL

$–$$ ✕ **Ric's Place.** This Front Street sports bar is popular with Americans who need a dose of home, and with just about anyone who wants to drool over one of the biggest burgers in town. College and pro sports banners and caps hang all over the place, and seating is indoors at the bar or over the water of Great Bay. The fare is American and Tex-Mex; try the nachos *grande* with a couple of friends. ⊠ *69 Front St., Philipsburg,* ☎ *599/5–26050. No credit cards.*

ASIAN

$–$$ ✕ **Wajang Doll.** Indonesian dishes are served in the garden of this West Indian–style house. *Nasi goreng* (fried rice) and red snapper in a sweet soy glaze are standouts, as is rijsttafel, a traditional Indonesian meal of rice accompanied by 15 to 20 dishes. A wajang doll is used in Indonesian shadow plays, a traditional art form. ⊠ *167 Front St., Philipsburg,* ☎ *599/5–22687. AE, MC, V. Closed Sun. No lunch.*

CAFÉ

$ ✕ **Kangaroo Court Caffé.** The Kangaroo might have the best cup of coffee on St. Martin/St. Maarten. Festooned with potted plants and colorful tiles and umbrellas, it's located in an old salt weighing station off Front Street. The fare is salads, pastas, and sandwiches, but the draw here is the fresh pastries and wide array of coffee, including cappuccinos, mocha lattes, caramel lattes, and espressos. Also, their selection of ice cream is among the island's best. The restaurant is open for three meals per day. ⊠ *6 Hendrickstraat, Philipsburg,* ☎ *599/5–24278. No credit cards.*

CONTEMPORARY

$$$–$$$$ ✕ **Le Perroquet.** A cool green-and-white West Indian–style house overlooking a lagoon is the peaceful—and romantic—setting for this restaurant. Chef Pierre Castagna prepares exotic specialties, such as grilled breast of ostrich in a bordelaise sauce, as well as savory dishes featuring duck, veal, beef, and more. ⊠ *Airport Rd., Simpson Bay,* ☎ *599/5–54339. AE, MC, V. Closed Mon., June, and Sept. No lunch.*

CONTINENTAL

$$ ✕ **Mary's Boon.** At this eatery in ☞ Mary's Boon Beach Plantation the deal is simple; you've got one seating each evening at 8, and one choice for an entrée. You might find beef tenderloin, veal Dijonnaise, shrimp Provençale, or perhaps lobster Creole. Dinners are served "family" style (although, oddly, this is really not a place where young children will feel welcome), meaning you take your helpings from a serving plate. They come with an appetizer, choice of vegetable, dessert, and coffee. Seconds are on the house. It's a great feed and, with the dining room overlooking the bay, a great location. It's also a St. Martin/St. Maarten institution, so reservations are essential. ⊠ *117 Simpson Bay Rd.,* ☎ *599/5–54235. D, MC, V. Closed Sun. off-season.*

$ ✕ **Chesterfield's.** Casual lunches of burgers and salads and more elaborate Continental dinners are served at this informal, nautically themed restaurant at the marina. The dinner menu includes French onion soup, roast duckling with fresh pineapple and banana sauce, and several different preparations of shrimp. The Mermaid Bar is a popular spot with yachties. ⊠ *Great Bay Marina, Philipsburg,* ☎ *599/5–23484. No credit cards.*

ECLECTIC

$$–$$$ ✕ **Saratoga.** The handsome mahogany-outfitted dining room in the
★ Yacht Club's stucco and red-tile building has views of the Simpson Bay Marina. The menu changes daily, borrowing from various influences, including Asian and southwestern. You might start with Malpeque oysters with balsamic-horseradish sauce or seven-seaweed salad with sea beans, daikon, and sesame, then segue into crispy fried roundhead snapper in fermented black bean sauce or grilled chicken breast in a cumin-Gouda crust. The wine list is admirably balanced and reasonably priced, with 10–12 wines offered by the glass. ⊠ *Simpson Bay Yacht Club, Airport Rd.,* ☎ *599/5–42421. Reservations essential. AE, MC, V. Closed Sun. No lunch.*

$$ ✕ **Indiana Beach.** This quirky restaurant-bar is fronted by Kimsha Beach at Simpson Bay. The motif is pure adventure and jungle exotic. Terracotta walls and tables are decorated with painted Indian petroglyphs, and you'll find caged monkeys, snakes, parrots, and Wally the alligator on the lush grounds. You can swim at Kimsha or at the restaurant's own pool, and, although the fare is mainly sandwiches, steaks, and seafood, don't be surprised to find wild boar or alligator ribs on the menu. ⊠ *Pelican Key,* ☎ *599/5–42797. AE, MC, V.*

FRENCH

$$–$$$$ ✕ **Antoine.** Antoine moved his restaurant a few doors down on Front Street recently, but the setting is still romantic at this elegant spot overlooking Great Bay. Candles glow on tables set with crisp blue-and-white tablecloths and gleaming silver, and the sound of the surf drifts up from the beach. You might start your meal with French onion soup or lobster bisque, then move on to steak au poivre, duck in brandy sauce with cherries, or lobster thermidor. Pastas and Creole specials are also available. For dessert, try the sublime Grand Marnier soufflé. ⊠ *103 Front St., Philipsburg,* ☎ *599/5–22964. Reservations essential. AE, MC, V. Closed Sun. off-season.*

$$–$$$ ✕ **Le Bec Fin.** You stroll through a flowery courtyard to reach this well-known upstairs restaurant. The rotation of chefs has unfortunately led to inconsistency in the quality of the classical French cuisine, but it's pleasant for its ambience and views of Great Bay. Starters include vol-au-vent (pastry) bursting with escargots in fennel cream sauce and tagliatelle with shrimp in ginger. Fish, such as red snapper fillet in rum butter sauce, is your best bet for a main course. The meringue swan with mint ice cream is delightful to the eye and the palate. The breezy downstairs café serves breakfast and lunch with great crepes (try the seafood) and salads. ⊠ *141 Front St., Philipsburg,* ☎ *599/5–22976. AE, MC, V.*

$$–$$$ ✕ **Oyster Bay Beach Resort.** A more genteel evening on St. Maarten
★ is hard to find than at this restaurant in the ☞ Oyster Bay Beach Resort. A delightful terrace with wonderful sea views is decked with linens, china, and fresh flowers. Lobster medallions dancing in a truffle, tomato, and basil sauce; fillet of red snapper in sauce piquant; and sweet, billowy dessert soufflés are specialties. The hotel's guests have priority in this romantic dining room, so you should reserve well in advance. ⊠ *Oyster Pond,* ☎ *599/5–22206 or 599/5–23206. Reservations essential. AE, MC, V.*

$–$$ ✕ **L'Escargot.** A 19th-century house wrapped in verandas is home to one of St. Maarten's oldest French restaurants. Starters include frogs' legs in garlic sauce and crepes filled with caviar and sour cream. There is also, of course, a variety of snail dishes. For an entrée, try grilled red snapper with red wine and shallot sauce or *canard de l'escargot* (duck in pineapple and banana sauce). There's a cabaret Wednesday night;

you don't have to pay the cover charge if you come for dinner. ⊠ *84 Front St., Philipsburg,* ☏ *599/5–22483. AE, MC, V.*

INDIAN

$ **✕ Shiv Sagar.** Authentic East Indian cuisine, emphasizing Kashmiri and
★ Mogul specialties, is served in this small mirrored room fragrant with
cumin and coriander. Marvelous tandooris and curries are offered, but
try one of the less-familiar preparations like *madrasi machi* (red snapper with hot spices). A large selection of vegetarian dishes is also offered. There's a friendly open-air bar out front. ⊠ *20 Front St.,
Philipsburg,* ☏ *599/5–22299. AE, D, DC, MC, V. Closed Sun.*

ITALIAN

$$–$$$ **✕ Spartaco.** Every element of the northern Italian cuisine served in this
200-year-old stone plantation house is either homemade or imported
from Italy. Some of the specialties are black angel-hair pasta with
shrimp and garlic; swordfish baked with pink peppercorns and rosemary, served over linguine; and veal Vesuviana, with mozzarella,
oregano, and tomato sauce. ⊠ *Almond Grove, Cole Bay,* ☏ *599/5–
45379. AE, MC, V. Closed Mon., and May. No lunch.*

French Side

CAFÉ

$–$$ **✕ Bistrot Nu.** For simple, unadorned fare at a reasonable price, this
★ may be the best spot on the islands. Traditional brasserie-style food—
coq au vin, fish soup, snails, pizza, and seafood—is served in a friendly
atmosphere. The place is enormously popular; its tables are packed until
it closes at 2 AM. ⊠ *Rue de Hollande, Marigot,* ☏ *590/87–97–09.
MC, V. Closed Sun.*

CARIBBEAN/CREOLE

$–$$$ **✕ Mini-Club.** This brightly decorated upstairs restaurant on the harbor
★ in Marigot serves some of the island's best Creole and French cuisine.
The chairs and madras tablecloths are a mélange of sun-yellow and orange,
and the whole place is built (tree house–like) around the trunks of co-
conut trees. It's the place to be for Wednesday and Saturday's lunch buf-
fet ($40), featuring roast pig, lobster, and roast beef. ⊠ *Front de Mer,
Marigot,* ☏ *590/87–50–69. AE, MC, V. No lunch Sun.*

$–$$ **✕ Yvette's.** The attempts at romance couldn't be more endearing:
★ classical music plays softly, and the tiny, eight-table room is a symphony
in Valentine red, from the curtains, tablecloths, and roses to the hot
pepper sauce. Yvette herself couldn't be more down-home, nor her food
more delicious. Plates are piled high with lip-smacking Creole specialties,
such as *accras* (spicy fish fritters), stewed chicken with rice and beans,
and conch and dumplings. ⊠ *Orléans,* ☏ *590/87–32–03. AE.*

CONTEMPORARY

$$$–$$$$ **✕ Le Tastevin.** A chic pavilion, with tropical plants, ceiling fans, and
water views, provides an elegant dining setting. Owner Daniel Passeri,
a native of Burgundy, also founded the homey Auberge Gourmande
across the street. The menu here is more ambitious, including foie gras
in Armagnac sauce, duck breast in banana-lime sauce, and red snap-
per fillet with curry and wild-mushroom sauce. ⊠ *86 bd. de Grand
Case, Grand Case,* ☏ *590/87–55–45. Reservations essential. AE,
DC, MC, V. No credit cards at lunch.*

ECLECTIC

$$$–$$$$ **✕ Rainbow Café.** In a town of splendid seaside boîtes, this is one of
★ the best. The cobalt-blue-and-white decor of the split-level dining
room is strikingly simple, and the atmosphere, created by lapping
waves and murmuring guests, is highly romantic. Fleur and David are
the stylish, energetic hosts, and chef Mario Tardif is from one of the

world's gastronomic capitals, Québec City. Try his shrimp and scallop fricassee with Caribbean chutney, duck *maigret* (breast meat served with its skin), grilled swordfish, or sautéed veal scallopini with capers, garlic, and chives. Dishes are dressed with fanciful touches like red cabbage crisps. ⊠ *176 bd. de Grand Case, Grand Case,* ☏ *590/87–55–80. AE, MC, V. Closed Sun.*

$$–$$$ ✕ **Maison sur le Port.** Watching the sunset from the palm-fringed terrace is not the least of the pleasures in this old West Indian house surrounded by romantically lit garden fountains. Try the sautéed duck fillet in passion-fruit sauce or red snapper with beurre blanc. Chef Jean-Paul Fahrner's imaginative salads are lunchtime treats. There is a children's menu with burgers and chicken sandwiches. ⊠ *On the port, Marigot,* ☏ *590/87–56–38. AE, D, MC, V. Closed Sun., and June and Sept.*

$$–$$$ ✕ **Le Pressoir.** Many say that presentation is everything. Combine that
    ★   with excellent food in a charming West Indies house, where the bill won't break the bank, and you have a great restaurant. French and Creole fusion cuisine reigns; go for the fresh local fish prepared with tropical fruit glazes and sauces. The crème brûlée is superb. ⊠ *30 bd. de Grand Case, Grand Case,* ☏ *590/87–76–62. AE, MC, V. Closed Sun. No lunch.*

FRENCH

$$$–$$$$ ✕ **Chez Martine.** A charming, globe-trotting French couple, Eliane
    ★   and Jean-Pierre Bertheau, have made this small hotel into a personable hostelry with an excellent French restaurant. Dine by the water's edge in an intimate room with polished silverware, blue glassware, and white napkins. You might begin with superb velvety seafood consommé, then segue into roast lamb on a bed of eggplant and spinach in corn sauce or lobster in puff pastry; the homemade duck-liver pâté also claims a loyal following. The wine list has several very drinkable wines for under $20. ⊠ *140 bd. de Grand Case, Grand Case,* ☏ *590/87–51–59. DC, MC, V. No lunch off-season.*

$$$–$$$$ ✕ **Le Santal.** The approach to this dazzler, through a working-class sub-
    ★   urb of Marigot, is forbidding. The exterior appears ramshackle, but the interior is transformed by soft lighting, china, and crystal. Specialties of the house include lobster soufflé on a bed of spinach and eggplant, foie gras sautéed in cassis, and lacquered duck. The owners also run the excellent Jean Dupont and Asia, but this is their showplace. Reservations are not required, but they're highly recommended if you want to eat at one of the five tables by the water. ⊠ *Sandy Ground,* ☏ *590/87–53–48. AE, MC, V. No lunch.*

$$–$$$$ ✕ **Le Poisson d'Or.** Feast in this posh, popular place on a constantly
    ★   changing menu of dishes such as sautéed foie gras with pear and walnut cream sauce or smoked lobster in champagne sauce. Piano classics provide a backdrop for the setting, a restored stone house with a huge veranda holding 20 tables. The space doubles as a gallery with works by top-notch Caribbean artists. ⊠ *14 rue d'Anguille, Marigot,* ☏ *590/87–72–45. AE, MC, V. Closed Sept.–early Oct. No lunch.*

$$–$$$$ ✕ **La Vie En Rose.** This bustling restaurant is right off the pier, about a 30-second stroll from the tourist office. The menu is classic French with an occasional Caribbean twist—fillet of swordfish sautéed in a passion-fruit butter sauce, freshwater crayfish in puff pastry. Appetizers include a warm smoked salmon with potatoes and chives and lobster salad spiced with a touch of ginger. Save room for chocolate mousse cake topped with vanilla sauce. The ground-floor tearoom and pastry shop serve an excellent luncheon with wine for $20. In season, you may make dinner reservations up to one month in advance. ⊠ *Rue de la République and bd. de France, Marigot,* ☏ *590/87–54–42. Reservations essential in season. AE, D, DC, MC, V. No lunch Sun.*

$$–$$$ ✕ **Alizéa.** Many claim that this elegant terrace restaurant at the ☞ Al-
★ izéa hotel offers the best cuisine on the island. French chef Laurent Guyon
trained with Roger Verge from the famous Moulin de Mougins. Sample the homemade foie gras with red wine jelly or roasted sea scallop
appetizers. Entrées include mahimahi with fennel and sweet potatoes,
and beef tenderloin with stewed shallots in red wine sauce. There are
several vegetarian selections. You won't go wrong with the crème
brûlée with honey and vanilla for dessert. ✉ *Hotel Alizéa, Mont Vernon,* ☏ *590/87–41–20. AE, DC, MC, V.*

MOROCCAN

$$ ✕ **Le Marocain.** This exotic oasis in the middle of Marigot resembles
a pasha's posh digs, with lush potted plants, intricate mosaics, hand-
painted tiles, and wood carvings. The food is as colorful and enticing
as the decor, with wonderfully perfumed *tajines* (casseroles of chicken
or meat) and *pastillas* (fragrant pastries filled with spices, raisins, and
meat or chicken) among the standouts. ✉ *147 rue de Hollande,
Marigot,* ☏ *590/87–83–11. AE, MC, V.*

SEAFOOD

$–$$ ✕ **La Plaisance.** Cool strains of jazz waft through this lively open-air
brasserie as you sample terrific salads (try the Niçoise or *landaine*—duck,
smoked ham, croutons, and fried egg), pizzas (wonderful lobster), pastas (garlic and basil pistou), and grilled seafood at unbeatable prices.
This is one of several ultracasual eateries at Port La Royale, all offering simple, appetizing food; fixed-price menus; and happy hours. ✉ *La
Marina Port la Royale, Marigot,* ☏ *590/87–85–00. AE, MC, V.*

Beaches

The island's 10 mi of beaches are all open to the public. Beaches occupied by resorts may charge a fee (about $3) for changing facilities.
You cannot, however, enter the beach via the hotel unless you are a
paying guest or will be renting water sports equipment there. Some of
the 37 beaches are secluded, and some are in the thick of things, but
on several vendors rent beach umbrellas and chairs for $5 each per day.
Topless bathing is virtually de rigueur on the French side, where the
beaches are generally better than on the Dutch side. If you take a cab
to a remote beach, be sure to arrange a specific time for your driver
to pick you up. Don't leave valuables unattended on the beach or in
your rental car, even in the trunk.

Baie Longue (Long Bay) is one of the best beaches on the island. It's a
beautiful, mile-long curve of white sand on the westernmost tip of the
island. This is a good place for snorkeling and swimming, but beware
of a strong undertow when the waters are rough. You can sunbathe
in the buff, though only a few do. There are no facilities. Beyond Baie
Longue is **Baie aux Prunes** (Plum Bay), where the oft-rocky beach arcs
between two headlands and the occasional sunbather discloses all. **Baie
Rouge** (Red Bay) is right off the main road past Baie aux Prunes. Some
rate it the prettiest beach on the island. The waves here can be rough.
You'll find refreshments and beach chair and umbrella rentals.

Cupecoy Beach is a small shifting arc of white sand fringed with eroded
limestone cliffs, just south of Baie Longue on the western side of the
island, near the Dutch-French border. At one time the beach was split
between "suits" and clothing-optional sections, but these days the
entire strip seems to have gone clothing-optional. The beach also attracts the island's gay crowd. On the beach you'll find vendors who
sell cold sodas and beers and rent chairs and umbrellas. There are
two parking spots for the beach, one near the Cupecoy and Sapphire

beach clubs, and the other just a few yards west, where you can park
for about $2.

You have to approach the **Dawn Beach–Oyster Pond** area through the
grounds of the Dawn Beach Hotel. The long white-sand beach is partly
protected by reefs (good for snorkeling), but the water is not always
calm. When the waves come rolling in, this is the best spot on the island for bodysurfing. **Ilet Pinel** is a little speck off the northeast coast
with about 500 yards of beach where you can have picnics and privacy. There are no facilities. Putt putts (small boats) are available to
take you from French Cul de Sac and Orient Beach. Ecru-color sand,
palm and sea-grape trees, calm waters, and the roar of jets lowering
to nearby Juliana International Airport distinguish the beach at **Maho
Bay.** Concession stand, beach chairs, and facilities are available. At **Mullet Bay,** the powdery white-sand beach is crowded, even though the
Mullet Bay Resort was still closed at press time.

Hurricane Luis made **Orient Beach** much wider and sandier, the silver
lining of such a devastating storm. This is the island's best-known clothing-optional beach—on the agenda for voyeurs from cruise ships. You
can enter from the parking area. The nude section is to the right on
the southern end of the beach. Farther down toward the middle of the
beach is the Orient Bay Resort, with several restaurants, bars, and chaises
(with food and beverage service) for rent. This is windsurfing heaven,
with a couple of rental shops on the beach to take advantage of the
steady onshore trade winds. **Simpson Bay** is a long half moon of white
sand near Simpson Bay Village, one of the last undiscovered hamlets
on the island. In this small fishing village you'll find refreshments, a
dive shop, and neat little ultra-Caribbean town homes.

Outdoor Activities and Sports

BOATING AND SAILING

The island's combination of water and winds make it ideal for exploring
or relaxing by boat. Motorboats, speedboats, and sailboats can be rented
at **Caribbean Watersports** (⊠ Nettlé Bay, ☎ 590/87–58–66), and
Caraïbes Sport Boats (⊠ Marina Port la Royale, ☎ 590/87–89–38).

Sun Yacht-Charters (☎ 590/87–30–49 or 800/772–3500), based in
Oyster Pond, has a fleet of 50 Centurion sailboats for hire. The cost
of a week's bareboat charter for a 36-ft Centurion with four berths is
$3,066 in peak winter season. Also in Oyster Pond, the **Moorings** (☎
590/87–32–55 or 800/535–7289 for reservations service) has a fleet
of Beneteau yachts, and bareboat and crewed catamarans. For the best
full-service yacht and water-sports rentals on the French side, contact
Marine Time (☎ 590/87–20–28, FAX 590/87–20–78), behind the
tourist office on the port in Marigot.

FISHING

Angle for yellowtail, snapper, grouper, marlin, tuna, and wahoo on half-
or full-day deep-sea excursions, from $300 (four people) for the half-
day to $600 for the full-day trip. Prices usually include bait and tackle,
instruction for novices, and an open bar. Contact **Bobby's Marina** (⊠
Philipsburg, ☎ 599/5–22366, FAX 599/5–25442), **Lee Deepsea Fishing** (⊠ Philipsburg, ☎ 599/5–44233, 599/5–44234, or 599/5–70747),
Rudy's Fishing (⊠ Simpson Bay, ☎ 599/5–52177), or **Sailfish Caraïbes**
(⊠ Port Lonvilliers, ☎ 590/87–31–94 or 590/27–40–90).

FITNESS CENTERS

L'Aqualigne (☎ 599/5–42426), on the Dutch side at the Pelican Resort, is a health spa with gym, sauna, and beauty treatments, including manicures, facials, and massages. **Fitness Caraïbes** (☎ 590/

87–35–81) is a toning center at Nettlé Bay. **Future Fitness Center** (☎ 590/87–90–27), in Marigot, has decent free-weight equipment as well as machines and aerobics. **Le Privilège** (☎ 590/87–37–37), a sports complex at Anse Marcel above Le Méridien's L'Habitation, has a full range of exercise equipment and the island's best spa.

GOLF

Mullet Bay Resort (☎ 599/5–52801) has an 18-hole championship course—the *only* course on the island. Greens fees are $105 ($25 club rental) for 18 holes, $60 ($20 club rental) for 9 holes. The course remains open, even though the resort was closed at press time.

HORSEBACK RIDING

Rides can be arranged through your hotel, or you can contact **Bayside Riding Club** (⊠ Orient Bay, ☎ 590/87–36–64), **Caid & Isa** (⊠ Anse Marcel, ☎ 590/87–45–70), **Crazy Acres Riding Center** (⊠ Wathey Estate, Cole Bay, ☎ 599/5–42793), or **O.K. Corral** (⊠ Oyster Pond, ☎ 590/87–40–72). All the outfits offer beach rides and can accommodate different skill levels; cost starts at $50 for a two-hour ride.

PARASAILING

On the French side, **Orient Bay Watersports** (☎ 590/87–40–75) offers parasailing rides on Orient Bay.

SCUBA DIVING AND SNORKELING

The water temperature here is rarely below 70°F, and visibility is usually excellent. There are many diving attractions, both right around the island and around numerous nearby islands. On the Dutch side is Proselyte Reef, named for the British frigate HMS *Proselyte,* which sank south of Great Bay in 1801. In addition to wreck dives, reef, night, and cave dives are popular. Off the northeast coast of the French side, dive sites include Ilet Pinel, for good shallow diving; Green Key, with its vibrant barrier reef; and Tintamarre, for sheltered coves and underwater geologic faults.

On the Dutch side, SSI- (Scuba Schools International) and PADI-certified dive centers include **Leeward Island Divers** (⊠ Simpson Bay, ☎ 599/5–42268), **Ocean Explorers Dive Shop** (⊠ Simpson Bay, ☎ 599/5–45252), **Pelican Dive Adventures** (⊠ Pelican Resort Marina, ☎ 599/5–42503, ext. 1553), **St. Maarten Divers** (⊠ Philipsburg, ☎ 599/5–22446), and **Trade Winds Dive Center** (⊠ Bobby's Marina, ☎ 599/5–75176).

On the French side, **Blue Ocean** (⊠ Marigot, ☎ 590/87–89–73) is PADI- and CMAS-certified. **Lou Scuba** (⊠ Mercure Simson Beach Coralia, Nettlé Bay, ☎ 590/87–16–61) is a PADI-certified dive center. **Octoplus** (⊠ Bd. de Grand Case, ☎ 590/87–20–62) is a complete dive center. In general, one-tank dives start at $45; two-tank dives start at $80; and certification courses start at $325. Coral reefs around the island teem with marine life, and clear water allows visibility of up to 200 ft.

Some of the best snorkeling on the Dutch side can be found around the rocks below Fort Amsterdam off Little Bay Beach, in the west end of Maho Bay, off Pelican Key, and around the reefs off Dawn Beach and Oyster Pond. On the French side, the area around Orient Bay, Green Key, Ilet Pinel, and Flat Island (or Tintamarre) is especially lovely and should soon be officially classified a regional underwater nature reserve. Arrange rentals and trips through **Kontiki Watersports** (☎ 590/87–28–75, **Ocean Explorers** (☎ 599/5–45252), and **Orient Bay Watersports** (☎ 590/87–40–75).

SEA EXCURSIONS

The 50-ft catamaran **Bluebeard II** (☎ 599/5-52898), moored in Simpson Bay, sails around Anguilla's south and northwest coasts to Prickly Pear, where there are excellent coral reefs for snorkeling and powdery white sands for sunning. The average range for these excursions is $45–$65 per person. You can take a daylong picnic sail to nearby islands or secluded coves aboard the 45-ft ketch **Gabrielle** (☎ 599/5-23170), or the sleek 76-ft catamaran **Golden Eagle** (☎ 599/5-30068). The **Laura Rose** (☎ 599/5-70710) offers a variety of half- and full-day sails, ranging $25–$65 per person. The 91-ft **Lady Mary** (☎ 599/5-53892) sails around the island each evening from La Palapa Center on Simpson Bay; the fare, about $65 per person, includes dinner, open bar, and live calypso music. It's tremendous fun.

The luxurious 75-ft motor catamaran **White Octopus** (☎ 599/5-24096 or 599/5-23170) makes the run to St. Barts, departing at 9 AM from Bobby's Marina or Captain Oliver's Marina and returning at 5 PM. Cost is $50 per person, $25 for children 12 and under, which includes an open bar, snacks, and snorkel equipment.

In St. Martin, sailing, snorkeling, and picnic excursions to nearby islands can be arranged through **Kontiki Watersports** (☎ 590/87-28-75), **Le Méridien's L'Habitation** (☎ 590/87-33-33), and **Orient Bay Watersports** (✉ Club Orient, ☎ 590/87-40-75).

TENNIS

If you want to play tennis at a hotel at which you are not a guest, be sure to call ahead to find out whether it allows visitors. You'll probably need to make reservations, and there's usually an hourly fee. There are three lighted courts at the **Pelican Resort** (☎ 599/5-42503); three lighted courts at the **Divi Little Bay Beach Resort** (☎ 599/5-22333); three lighted courts at the **Maho Beach Hotel** (☎ 599/5-52115); six lighted courts at **Le Privilège** (✉ Anse Marcel, ☎ 590/87-38-38), which also has four squash and two racquetball courts; two lighted courts at the **Mont Vernon Hotel** (☎ 590/87-62-00); one lighted court at the **Mecure Simson Beach Coralia** (☎ 590/87-54-54); and nine lighted courts each at the **Grand Case Beach Club** (☎ 590/87-51-87) and the **Coralita Beach Hotel** (☎ 590/87-31-81).

WATERSKIING

On the Dutch side, rent waterskiing and jet skiing equipment through the **Divi Little Bay Resort**'s water-sports activity center (☎ 599/5-22333); at Simpson Bay's Kimsha Beach, contact **Westport Watersports** (☎ 599/5-42557). On the French side, try **Orient Bay Watersports** (☎ 590/87-40-75), **Kontiki Watersports** (☎ 590/87-28-75), and **Laguna Watersports** (☎ 590/87-91-75) at Nettlé Bay.

WINDSURFING

Rental and instruction are available at **Orient Bay Watersports** (☎ 590/87-40-75). The **Nathalie Simon Windsurfing Club** (☎ 590/87-48-16) offers rentals and lessons in Orient Bay.

Shopping

About 180 cruise ships call at St. Maarten each year, and they do so for about 500 reasons. That's roughly the number of duty-free shops on the island. Prices can be 25%–50% below those in the United States and Canada on French perfumes, liquor, cognac and fine liqueurs, cigarettes and cigars, Swedish crystal, Finnish stoneware, Irish linen, Italian leather, German cameras, European designer fashions, Swiss watches, plus thousands of other things you never knew you wanted. But check prices before you leave home, especially if you live in the

New York City area—Manhattan's prices (including mail order) for cameras and electronics equipment are hard to beat. If you're shopping for electronics in Philipsburg, try negotiating for a lower price. Competition is fierce, and some stores will bargain if you pay cash. You'll find more fashion on the French side in Marigot, although stalwarts like Polo Ralph Lauren and Benetton have Philipsburg outlets. You will also find Marigot to be a much more pleasant place to shop and stroll.

In general, those looking for local crafts will be disappointed. You will find carvings, painting, basketry, and some jewelry that has been produced locally and on other islands mixed in with the T-shirts at the crafts stalls on the Marigot harbor, but these tend to be of the cheesy type. St. Maarten's best-known local product is its guavaberry liqueur, made from rum and the wild local berries (not to be confused with guavas) that grow only on this island's central mountains.

Prices are quoted in florins, francs, and dollars; shops take credit cards and traveler's checks. Most shopkeepers, especially on the Dutch side, speak English. (If more than one cruise ship is in port, avoid Front Street. It's so crowded you won't be able to move.) Although most merchants are reputable, there are occasional reports of inferior or fake merchandise passed off as the real thing. As a rule of thumb, if you can bargain excessively, it's probably not worth it.

Areas

Front Street, Philipsburg, is one long strip lined with sleek boutiques and colorful shops, including, oddly, a Harley-Davidson outlet. **Old Street,** near the end of Front Street, has 22 stores, boutiques, and open-air cafés. There is a slew of boutiques in the **Mullet** (closed at press time) and **Maho** shopping plazas, as well as at the **Plaza del Lago,** at the Simpson Bay Yacht Club complex. Wrought-iron balconies, colorful awnings, and gingerbread trim decorate Marigot's smart shops, tiny boutiques, and bistros in the **Marina Port La Royale** complex and on the main streets, **rue de la Liberté** and **rue de la République.**

Specialty Items

DUTY-FREE GOODS

Carat (✉ Marigot, ☎ 590/87–73–40; ✉ Philipsburg, ☎ 599/5–22180) sells china and jewelry. **La Cave du Savour Club** (✉ Marigot, ☎ 590/87–58–51) is the place to pick up a bottle of wine for your picnic. **H. Stern** (✉ Philipsburg, ☎ 599/5–23328) specializes in colorful jewelry and elegant watches. **Havane** (✉ Marigot, ☎ 590/87–70–39) sells designer fashions. **Lil' Shoppe** (✉ Philipsburg, ☎ 599/5–22177) carries eel-skin wallets, handbags, perfumes, and a large selection of swimwear. **Lipstick** (✉ Marina Port la Royale, ☎ 590/87–73–24; ✉ Marigot, ☎ 590/87–53–92; ✉ Philipsburg, ☎ 599/5–26051) carries an enormous selection of perfume and cosmetics (including sunscreen).

Little Europe (✉ Philipsburg, ☎ 599/5–24371) sells fine jewelry, along with crystal and china. **Little Switzerland** (✉ Marigot, ☎ 590/87–50–03; ✉ Philipsburg, ☎ 599/5–23530) sells fine crystal, china, perfume, and jewelry. **New Amsterdam Store** (✉ Philipsburg, ☎ 599/5–22787) handles designer fashions, fine linens, and porcelain. **Oro de Sol** (✉ Marigot, ☎ 590/87–56–51) carries jewelry and watches, as well as perfume, cosmetics, and Cuban cigars. **La Romana** (✉ Front St., Philipsburg, ☎ 599/5–22181) stocks designer fashions. **Yellow House** (✉ Philipsburg, ☎ 599/5–23438) carries perfumes, cosmetics, and gifts.

HANDICRAFTS

ABC Art Gallery (⊠ Marigot, ☎ 590/87–96–00) exhibits the work of local artists. **Galerie Lynn** (⊠ 83 bd. de Grand Case, ☎ 590/87–77–24) sells stunning paintings and sculptures. **Gingerbread Galerie** (⊠ Port La Royale, ☎ 590/87–73–21) specializes in Haitian art. **Greenwith Galleries** (⊠ Front St., Philipsburg, ☎ 599/5–23842) specializes in Caribbean art.

Minguet (⊠ Rambaud Hill, ☎ 590/87–76–06) carries pictures by the artist Minguet depicting island life. **Shipwreck Shop** (⊠ Front St., Philipsburg, ☎ 599/5–22962; ⊠ Port La Royale, ☎ 590/87–27–37) stocks Caribelle batiks, hammocks, handmade jewelry, the local guavaberry liqueur, and herbs and spices. The **Guavaberry Shop** (⊠ Front St., Philipsburg, ☎ 599/5–22965) is the small factory where the famous guavaberry liqueur is made by the Sint Maarten Guavaberry Company; on sale are myriad versions of the liqueur (including one made with jalapeño peppers), as well as spices and batiks.

Nightlife and the Arts

To find out what's doing on the island, pick up any of the following publications: "St. Maarten Nights," "What to Do in St. Maarten," "St. Maarten Events," "Focus St. Maarten/St. Martin," or *St. Maarten Holiday*—all distributed free in the tourist office (☞ Visitor Information *in* St. Martin/St. Maarten A to Z, *below*) and hotels. *Discover St. Martin/St. Maarten,* also free, is a glossy magazine that includes articles about the island's history and the latest on shops, discos, restaurants, and even archaeological digs.

Most of the resort hotels have a Caribbean spectacular one night a week, replete with limbo and fire dancers and steel bands. Casinos are the main focus on the Dutch side, but there are discos that usually start late and keep on till the fat lady sings.

BARS

Bamboo Cocktail Bar (⊠ Rue de la Liberté, Marigot, ☎ 590/29–01–00) is the place for karaoke fans. **Le Bar de la Mer** (⊠ Market Square, Marigot, ☎ 590/87–81–79) on the harbor is a popular gathering spot in the evening (it's open until 2). **Cheri's Café** (⊠ Across from Maho Beach Hotel & Casino, Airport Rd., Simpson Bay, ☎ 599/5–53361) is a local institution, with cheap food and great live bands.

News Café (⊠ Airport Rd., Simpson Bay, ☎ 599/5–42236) is a friendly spot where you can order food into the wee hours. **Peace and Love Disco** (⊠ La Savanne, ☎ 590/87–58–34) features local bands, calypso, and dancing. **Surf Club South** (⊠ just east of Grand Case Town, ☎ 590/87–50–40) is American-owned and comes complete with road signs from the Garden State Parkway posted at the entrance. **Turtle Pier Bar & Restaurant** (⊠ Airport Rd., Simpson Bay, ☎ 599/5–52230) always hops with a lively crowd.

CASINOS

All the casinos have craps, blackjack, roulette, and slot machines. You must be 18 years or older to gamble. Many of the casinos are in hotels such as Great Bay Beach Hotel, Pelican Resort, Sea View Hotel, and Casino Royal at Maho Beach (which produces the splashy Paris Revue Show). You'll also find the independent casinos **Coliseum** (⊠ Front St., Philipsburg, ☎ 599/5–32101), the **Neptune Casino** (⊠ Front St., Philpsburg, ☎ 599/5–32721), and the **Lightning Casino** (⊠ Cole Bay, 599/5–43290).

Amnesia (⊠ Maho Beach Hotel & Casino, ☎ 599/5–22962) is Maho's disco, popular with young people. Like the Amnesia in Ibiza, Spain, it sometimes features "foam" dancing. **Greenhouse** (⊠ Front St., Philipsburg, ☎ 599/5–22941), next to Bobby's Marina, features canned DJ music and a two-for-one happy hour that lasts all night Tuesday. **Zenith Club–L'Atmo 2000** (⊠ Marina Royale, Marigot, ☎ 590/87–98–41) is where French nationals and locals flock for salsa and soca on Friday. It's open every night but Monday.

Exploring St. Martin/St. Maarten

St. Martin/St. Maarten's roads are in very good condition and are generally well marked. With the exception of some annoying traffic congestion, especially in and around Philipsburg and Marigot, the island is easily traversed (it's best to rent a car, motorcycle, or scooter), and there's much to see in its historic forts, museums, beaches, and countryside.

Numbers in the margin correspond to points of interest on the St. Martin/St. Maarten map.

SIGHTS TO SEE

⑤ **French Cul de Sac.** Just north of Orient Beach, you'll find the French colonial mansion of St. Martin's mayor nestled in the hills. Little red-roof houses look like open umbrellas tumbling down the green hillside. The scenery here is glorious, and the area is great for hiking. There is a lot of construction, however, as the surroundings are slowly being developed, including the hideous eyesore of the Mont Vernon Hotel, which looks like a hospital. From the beach here, shuttle boats make the five-minute trip to **Ilet Pinel,** an uninhabited island that's fine for picnicking, sunning, and swimming.

⑦ **Friar's Beach.** This small, picturesque cove between Marigot and Grand Case attracts a casual crowd of locals. A small snack bar, **Kali's,** owned by a welcoming gentleman wearing dreadlocks, serves refreshments. A bumpy, tree-canopied road leads inland to **Pic du Paradis,** at 1,278 ft the island's highest point, affording breathtaking Caribbean vistas.

⑥ **Grand Case.** The most picturesque town on the island is set in the heart of the French side on the beach at the foot of green hills and pastures. Though it has only one mile-long main street, it's known as the "Restaurant Capital of the Caribbean": More than 20 restaurants serve French, Italian, Indonesian, and Vietnamese fare. The budget-minded love the half dozen "lolos"—kiosks at the far end of town selling savory barbecue and seafood. Grand Case Beach Club is at the end of this road and has two beaches where you can take a dip.

② **Guana Bay Point.** North of Philipsburg off Sucker Garden Road, Guana Bay Point offers a splendid view of the island's east coast, tiny deserted islands, and petite St. Barts, which is anything but deserted.

⑧ **Marigot.** This town is a wonderful place to tarry awhile if you are a shopper, a gourmet, or just a Francophile. Marina Port La Royale is the shopping complex at the port, but rue de la République and rue de la Liberté, which border the bay, are also filled with duty-free shops, boutiques, and bistros. The harbor area has a new crafts pavilion selling everything from handmade crafts to fish so fresh they're still mad. You are likely to find more creative and fashionable buys in Marigot than in Philipsburg. There is less bustle here, and the open-air cafés are tempting places in which to stop for a rest. Marigot does not die at night, so you might wish to stay into the evening. In the main parking lot of the harbor you'll find the kiosk for the Anguilla ferry as well as several crafts stalls. Across the parking lot, near the small traffic rotary, is the helpful **French tourist office,** where you can pick up the usual assortment of free maps and brochures. Just north of town there is a shopping complex on the inland side of the main road. At the back of it is **Match** (☎ 590/87–92–36), the largest supermarket on the French side, carrying a broad selection of tempting picnic makings—from country pâté to foie gras—and a vast selection of wines.

❹ Orléans. North of Oyster Pond and the Etang aux Poissons (Fish Lake) is the oldest settlement on the island, also known as the French Quarter. Noted local artist Roland Richardson makes his home here. He opens his **studio** to the public on Thursday from 10 to 6, or by appointment (☎ 590/87–32–24). He's a proud islander ready to share his wealth of knowledge about the island's cultural history.

❸ Oyster Pond. Just north of Dawn Beach on Sucker Garden Road is the point where two early settlers, a Frenchman and a Dutchman, allegedly began to pace in opposite directions around the island to divide it between their respective countries. Local legend maintains that the obese, sweaty Hollander stopped frequently to refresh himself with gin—the reason that the French side is nearly twice the size of the Dutch. (The official boundary marker is on the other side of the island.)

❶ Philipsburg. The Dutch capital of St. Maarten stretches about a mile along an isthmus between Great Bay and the Salt Pond and has three more or less parallel streets: Front Street, Back Street, and Pondfill. Front Street has been recobbled, cars are discouraged from using it, and the pedestrian area has been widened. Shops, restaurants, and casinos vie for the hordes coming off the cruise boats. Little lanes called *steegjes* connect Front Street with Back Street, considerably less congested because it has fewer shops.

Wathey Square (pronounced watty) is in the middle of the isthmus on which Philipsburg sits. The square bustles with vendors, souvenir shops, and tourists. Directly across the street from the square is a striking white building with a cupola. It was built in 1793 and has since served as the commander's home, a fire station, and a jail. It now serves as the town hall, courthouse, and the post office and was beautifully restored in 1995. The streets surrounding the square are lined with hotels, duty-free shops, fine restaurants, and cafés, most of them in pastel-color West Indian cottages gussied up with gingerbread trim. Narrow alleyways lead to arcades and flower-filled courtyards where there are yet more boutiques and eateries. The **Capt. Hodge Pier** just off the square is a good spot to view Great Bay and the beach that stretches alongside it for about a mile.

The **Sint Maarten Museum** hosts rotating cultural exhibits and a permanent historical display entitled "Forts of St. Maarten/St. Martin," featuring artifacts ranging from Arawak pottery shards to articles salvaged from the wreck of HMS *Proselyte.* ✉ *7 Front St., Philipsburg,* ☎ *599/5–24917.* 🔳 *$1.* 🕐 *Mon.–Sat. 10–4.*

❾ St. Martin Museum. The Musée de Saint-Martin, subtitled "On the Trail of the Arawaks," is a small and ambitious museum presenting artifacts from the island's pre-Columbian days. Included are pottery displays, rock carvings, and petroglyphs, as well as displays from the colonial and sugar plantation days. Upstairs is a small art gallery, featuring locally produced art, lithographs, and posters. ✉ *Sandy Ground Rd., Marigot,* ☎ *590/29–22–84.* 🔳 *$5.* 🕐 *Mon.–Sat. 9–1 and 3–7.*

Sucker Garden Road. This road runs north of Philipsburg through spectacular scenery—soaring mountains, turquoise waters, quaint West Indian houses, and wonderful views of St. Barts. The paved roller-coaster road eventually leads down to **Dawn Beach,** one of the island's best snorkeling beaches.

Terres Basses. This area of the island incorporates the coastline from Sandy Ground, just south of Marigot, to Cupecoy Beach, a small but beautiful beach of sandstone cliffs and coves, on the Dutch side. Some of the island's nicest beaches are found in this region: **Baie Rouge, Baie aux Prunes,** and **Baie Longue** cling to its westernmost point. They are all accessible down bumpy but short dirt roads and are perfect for swimming and picnicking. Also found here is **Baie Nettlé,** with its many reasonably priced hotels.

St. Martin/St. Maarten A to Z

Arriving and Departing

BY AIRPLANE

There are two airports on the island. **L'Espérance** (☎ 590/87–53–03) on the French side is small and handles only island-hoppers. Jumbo jets fly into **Princess Juliana International Airport** (☎ 599/5–54211) on the Dutch side. The most convenient carrier from the United States is **American Airlines** (☎ 599/5–52040), with daily nonstop flights from New York and Miami, as well as connections from more than 100 U.S. cities via its San Juan hub. **Air Guadeloupe** (☎ 599/5–53651 or 590/87–53–74) has several flights daily to St. Barts and Guadeloupe from both sides of the island. **Air Martinique** (☎ 596/51–08–09 or 599/5–54212) connects the island with Martinique twice a week. **Air St. Barthélemy** (☎ 590/87–73–46 or 599/5–53651) has frequent service between Juliana and St. Barts.

ALM (☎ 599/5–54240) has daily service from Aruba, Bonaire, and Curaçao, and from Fort Lauderdale via Curaçao Thursday and Sunday. **BWIA** (☎ 599/5–54344) offers service from Trinidad, Jamaica, and Antigua. **Continental Airlines** (☎ 599/5–53444) has several nonstop flights a week from Newark. **LIAT** (☎ 599/5–54203) has daily service from San Juan and several Caribbean islands, including Antigua, the USVI, the BVI, and St. Kitts. **US Airways** ☎ 599/5–54344 has nonstop service from Baltimore on Saturday and Sunday, and from Charlotte on Sunday. **Windward Islands Airways** (Winair, ☎ 599/5–54230), which is based on St. Maarten, has daily scheduled service to Saba, St. Barts, St. Eustatius, and St. Kitts/Nevis, and several weekly flights to Anguilla, Dominica, and Tortola. The company also offers tour and charter services. You can also arrange tours and charters through **St. Martin Helicopters** (☎ 599/5–54287, Dutch side).

BY BOAT

Motorboats zip several times a day from Anguilla and St. Barts to the French side at Marigot, and three times a week from St. Barts. Catamaran service is available daily from the Dutch side to St. Barts on the **White Octopus** (☎ 599/5–24096 or 599/5–23170). Cost is $50 per person, $25 for children 12 and under, including an open bar, snacks, and snorkel equipment. The high-speed ferry **Edge** (☎ 599/5–42640) motors from Simpson Bay's Pelican Marina to Saba on Sunday, Monday, and Friday (90 minutes, $60 round-trip) and to St. Barts on Tuesday, Thursday, and Saturday (45 minutes, $50 round-trip). The trips depart at 9 and return by 5 the same day. Note that there is a 5% surcharge when paying by credit card.

A ferry makes the 20-minute trip between the Marigot piers and Blowing Point on Anguilla on a daily basis, departing and returning every half hour from 8 AM until 7 PM. The fare is $10 one way, half price for children under 12. Departure tax at the ferry is $2 on the French side and $2 on the Anguilla side.

Electricity

The Dutch side operates mostly on 110 volts AC (60-cycle), the same as North America, and the plug outlets are for flat prongs, also the same as North America. The French side operates on 220 volts AC (60-cycle), with round-prong plugs. You'll need an adapter. There are exceptions on both sides; some Dutch-side hotels are 220 volts, and some French hotels are 110 volts. Call ahead to confirm. The larger hotels stock adapters for guest use.

Emergencies

Ambulance: (☎ 599/5–22111 Dutch side; 590/87–50–25 French side). **Hospital:** St. Maarten Medical Center (✉ Cay Hill, ☎ 599/5–31111) is a fully equipped hospital. **Pharmacies:** Central Drug Store (✉ Philipsburg, ☎ 599/5–22321) and Pharmacie du Port (✉ Marigot, ☎ 590/87–50–79) are open Monday–Saturday 7–5. **Police:** (☎ 599/5–22222 Dutch side; 590/87–50–06 French side).

Festivals and Seasonal Events

Given the dual nature of the island's cultures, St. Maarten and St. Martin have dozens of seasonal festivals; all the more choice for you. The French side's **Carnival** is a pre-Lenten bash of costume parades, music competitions, and feasts. On the Dutch side, Carnival takes place after Easter, usually in early May.

Other yearly events on the French side include a **Calypso Festival** in early July, and the annual **Caribbean Quest Musical Awards,** a huge festival of regional music with guests from around the islands, held in early August. On the Dutch side, the **Sualougia Festival,** from an Amerindian name for the island meaning "Land of Salt," is held every Friday in Philipsburg. The festival celebrates local cuisine, crafts, and music with displays and shows.

Getting Around

BUSES

One of the island's best bargains at 80¢ to $2, depending on your destination, buses operate frequently between 6 AM and midnight and run from Philipsburg through Cole Bay to Marigot and on to Grand Case. There are no official stops: You just stand by the side of the road and flag the bus down. Exact change is preferred though not required, and drivers don't accept bills over $5.

CAR RENTALS

You can book a car at Juliana International Airport, where all major rental companies have booths. If you don't have a reservation and aren't exactly sure whom to rent from, be prepared for an onslaught of hawkers, most of whom represent local companies, shouting that they have newer cars with more features and better prices. The upside of this is that prices tend to go down the longer your wait. Depending on demand, you can get a car for as low as $25 a day. There are also rentals at every hotel area. Rental cars, in general, are inexpensive—approximately $35–$45 a day for a subcompact car. All foreign driver's licenses are honored, and major credit cards are accepted. If you opt for collision coverage, most policies still require a $500 or more deductible. Check with your credit card company about coverage. **Avis** (☎ 800/331–1084), **Budget** (☎ 800/472–3325), **Dollar** (☎ 800/800–4000),

Hertz (☎ 800/654–3131), and **National (Eurocar)** (☎ 800/328–4567) all have offices on the island.

MOTORCYCLES AND SCOOTERS

The roads are crowded and there are some spots where people drive too fast, but a motorbike might just be what you're looking for to get around the island. Parking is easy, the gas costs are reduced, and you've got that sea breeze in your hair. Scooters rent for $20–$30 a day at **Eugene Moto** (⊠ Sandy Ground Rd., ☎ 590/87–13–97). If you're in the mood for a more substantial bike, contact the **Harley-Davidson** dealer (⊠ Cole Bay, ☎ 599/5–26565), where you can rent a big hog for $90 a day.

TAXIS

Taxi rates are government regulated, and authorized taxis display stickers of the St. Maarten Taxi Association. There is a taxi service at the Marigot port near the Tourist Information Bureau. Fixed fares apply from Juliana International Airport and the Marigot ferry to the various hotels around the island. Fares are 25% higher between 10 PM and midnight, 50% higher between midnight and 6 AM.

Guided Tours

BOAT

A cross between a submarine and a glass-bottom boat, the 34-passenger *Seaworld Explorer* (⊠ Grand Case, ☎ 599/5–24078) crawls along the water's surface while passengers in the submerged lower chamber view marine life and coral through large windows. Kids will love it as divers jump off the boat and circle among and feed the fish and eels. The cost is $30, and, for an extra $10, they'll provide transport to and from your hotel.

ORIENTATION

A 2½-hour taxi tour of the island costs $30 for one or two people, $10 for each additional person. Your hotel or the tourist office can arrange it for you. Best bets are **St. Maarten Sightseeing Tours** (⊠ Philipsburg, ☎ 599/5–22753) and **Calypso Tours** (⊠ Philipsburg, ☎ 599/5–42858), which offer, among other options, a three-hour island tour for $17 per person. You can tour in deluxe comfort with **St. Maarten Limousine Service** (☎ 599/5–24698) for $40–$50 per hour; there's a three-hour minimum. Fully equipped Lincoln Continentals accommodate up to six people and are furnished with stereo, fully stocked bar, and air-conditioning. The limo service also offers transportation to and from Juliana Airport at rates ranging from $30 to $65 one-way. (This includes one hour of waiting time free of charge for late arrivals.) On the French side, **R&J Tours** (⊠ Colombier, ☎ 590/87–56–20) will show you the island; prices vary with the number of people and the itinerary; a three-hour tour for one person is $15.

Language

Dutch is the official language of St. Maarten, and French is the official language of St. Martin, but almost everyone speaks English. If you hear a language you can't quite place, it's Papiamento, a Spanish-based Creole of the Netherlands Antilles.

Money Matters

CURRENCY

Legal tender on the Dutch side is the Netherlands Antilles florin (guilder), written NAf; on the French side, the French franc (F). The exchange rate fluctuates, but in general, it is about NAf1.80 to US$1 and 5F to US$1. On the Dutch side, prices are usually given in both NAf and U.S. dollars, which are accepted all over the island, as are credit cards. Note: Prices quoted here are in U.S. dollars unless otherwise noted.

SERVICE CHARGES, TAXES, AND TIPPING

In lieu of tipping, service charges are added to hotel and restaurant bills all over the island and are often included in all menu prices on the French side. On the Dutch side, most restaurants add 10%–15% to the bill. Hotels on the Dutch side add a 15% service/energy charge to the bill. Hotels on the French side add 10%–15% for service.

On the Dutch side, a 5% government tax and a 3% "turnover" tax is added to hotel bills. On the French side, a *taxe de séjour* (visitor's tax) is tacked on to hotel bills (the amount differs from hotel to hotel, but the maximum is $3 per day, per person). Departure tax from Juliana Airport is $5 to destinations within the Netherlands Antilles and $16 to all other destinations. It will cost you 15F to depart by plane from l'Espérance Airport, and $2 by ferry to Anguilla from Marigot's pier.

Tip as you might at home; taxi drivers, porters, chambermaids, and restaurant waitstaff all expect a tip, even though, in the cases of hotels and restaurants, a service charge might have been added to the bill. Think about 10%–15% for waitstaff, a couple dollars for cabbies.

Opening and Closing Times

Shops on the Dutch side are open Monday–Saturday 8–noon and 2–6; on the French side, Monday–Saturday 9–noon or 12:30 and 2–6. Some of the larger shops on both sides of the island open Sunday and holidays when the cruise ships are in port. Some of the small Dutch and French shops set their own capricious hours. **Banks** on the Dutch side are open Monday–Thursday 8:30–3:30 and Friday 8:30–4:40. French banks are open weekdays 8:30–12:30 and 2:30–4 and close afternoons preceding holidays.

HOLIDAYS

Both sides of the island celebrate specific holidays related to their government and culture, and some, such as New Year's, the Easter holidays (Apr. 2–5), Labor Day (May 1), Christmas, and Boxing Day (Dec. 26) are celebrated together.

Other French-side holidays are: Ascension Day (May 14), Bastille Day (July 14), Schoelcher Day, (July 21), All Saints' Day (Nov. 1), and the Feast of St. Martin (Nov. 11). Dutch-side holidays are: Antillian Day (Oct. 21) and St. Maarten Day (Nov. 11; coincides with Feast of St. Martin on the French side).

Passports

U.S. and Canadian citizens need proof of citizenship. A passport (valid or not expired more than five years) is preferred. An original birth certificate with raised seal (or a photocopy with notary seal) or a voter registration card are also acceptable. All visitors must have a confirmed room reservation and an ongoing or return ticket. British citizens need a valid passport or a national ID card.

Telephones and Mail

To call the Dutch side from the United States, dial 011–599 + local number; for the French side, 011–590 + local number. To phone from the Dutch side to the French, dial 00–590 + local number; from the French side to the Dutch, 00–5995 + local number. Keep in mind that a call from one side to the other is an overseas call, not a local call.

At the Landsradio in Philipsburg, there are facilities for overseas calls and an AT&T USADirect telephone, where you are directly in touch with an AT&T operator who will accept collect or credit-card calls. On the French side, you can't make collect calls to the United States, and there are no coin phones. If you need to use public phones, go to the special desk at Marigot's post office and buy a Telecarte, which gives you 40 units (it takes 120 units to cover a five-minute call to the United States) for around 31F or 120 units for 93F. There's a public phone at tourist office in Marigot where you can make credit-card calls: The operator takes your card number (any major card) and assigns you a PIN (Personal Identification Number), which you then use to charge calls to your card.

Letters from the Dutch side to North America and Europe cost NAf2.25; postcards, NAf1.10. From the French side, letters up to 20 grams and postcards are 3.80F. When writing to Dutch St. Maarten, call it "Sint Maarten" and make sure to add "Netherlands Antilles" to the address. When writing to the French side, the proper spelling is "Saint-Martin," and you add "French West Indies" to the address.

Visitor Information

For information about the Dutch side, contact the **tourist office** on the island directly (☎ 599/5−22337), or, in New York, contact the **St. Maarten Tourist Office** (✉ 675 3rd Ave., Suite 1806, New York, NY 10017, ☎ 800/786−2278 or 212/953−2084). In Canada, contact **St. Maarten Tourist Information** (✉ 243 Ellerslie Ave., Willowdale, Toronto, Ontario M2N 1Y5, ☎ 416/223−3501). Information about French St. Martin can be obtained by writing the **St. Martin Office of Tourism** (✉ 10 E. 21st St., Suite 600, New York, NY 10010, ☎ 212/529−8484, www.st-martin.org) or by calling France-on-Call at ☎ 900/990−0040 (50¢ per minute).

You can also write to or visit the U.S. branches of the **French Government Tourist Office** (✉ 444 Madison Ave., 16th floor, New York, NY 10022; ✉ 9454 Wilshire Blvd., Suite 715, Beverly Hills, CA 90212, ☎ 310/271−6665; ✉ 676 N. Michigan Ave., Suite 3360, Chicago, IL 60611, ☎ 312/751−7800), and write, visit, or call the Canadian and U.K. offices (✉ 1981 McGill College Ave., Suite 490, Montréal, Québec H3A 2W9, ☎ 514/288−4264; ✉ 30 St. Patrick St., Suite 700, Toronto, Ontario M5T 3A3, ☎ 416/593−6427; ✉ 178 Piccadilly, London W1V OAL, ☎ 0171/629−9376).

On the Dutch side, a **tourist information bureau** is on Cyrus Wathey Square in the heart of Philipsburg, at the pier where the cruise ships send their tenders. The administrative office is at Walter Nisbeth Road 23 (Imperial Building) on the third floor. ☎ 599/5−22337. ☉ Weekdays 8−noon and 1−5.

On the French side, there is the very helpful **tourist information office** on the Marigot pier. ☎ 590/87−57−21. ☉ Weekdays 8:30−1 and 2:30−5:30, Sat. 8−noon.

23 St. Vincent and the Grenadines

Updated by
Jane E. Zarem

*S**tanding on Dorcestershire Hill, above Kingstown, the wily old guide points to an island just offshore. On it is a large white cross that glimmers in the sun. "Know what that's about?" he asks. The grin on his weathered face fades to a wry smile as, without pause, he tells the tale. A local land developer, it seems, bought the island and put up the cross. When he died his body was placed upright inside it so that, in death, he could face his life's work. "Well," continues the guide with a shrug, "to some this is extreme. But Vincentians love their country with a passion."*

The island of St. Vincent and the string of 32 islands and cays in the Grenadines compose a single nation—one that's loved passionately by its inhabitants as much for its interesting history as for its natural beauty. SVG is in the southern Windward chain (only Grenada and Trinidad and Tobago are farther south). Mountainous St. Vincent, only 18 mi long and 11 mi wide, is just over 13° north of the equator; its Grenadines extend in a 45-mi arc southwest to Grenada. Each island is, in its own way, a refuge for demanding escapists. You will be hard put to find glitzy resorts, discos, or duty-free shopping malls. Rather, these islands dazzle you with their lush mountains, fertile valleys, quiet villages, secluded beaches, and fine sailing waters.

St. Vincent's major export is bananas, and these plants, along with coconut palms and breadfruit trees, crowd more of the island than the 100,000-person population (another 10,000 live on the Grenadines). This has obvious charm for nature lovers, who can spend days walking or hiking St. Vincent's well-defined trails, perhaps sighting the rare St. Vincent parrot in the Vermont Valley, or climbing La Soufrière, an active volcano that last erupted in 1979. Below sea level, snorkeling and scuba landscapes are similarly exciting.

Despite the island's beauty, most people simply stop off en route to their preferred Grenadine, whose beaches will no doubt be crescents of powdery white sand (those on St. Vincent tend to be narrow stretches of dark coarse sand). But St. Vincent deserves more than a pass-through. It has spectacular scenery, cascading waterfalls, a rugged coastline, and a fascinating history. Tourist facilities are varied and reasonably priced, and Vincentians are welcoming.

Historians believe that the Ciboney Indians were the first to journey from South America to St. Vincent, which they called Hairoun (Land of the Blessed). The Ciboney ultimately made their way to Cuba and Haiti, leaving St. Vincent to agrarian Arawak tribes, who had more recently journeyed from coastal South America to islands throughout the Lesser Antilles. Not long before Columbus sailed by in 1492, the Arawaks succumbed to the powerful Carib Indians, who paddled their way north from South America, conquering one island after another.

St. Vincent's mountains and forests served as defenses that thwarted European settlement. As colonization advanced elsewhere in the Caribbean, many Caribs fled to St. Vincent—making it even more of a Carib stronghold. In 1626 the French managed to settle on the island, but this success was short-lived; England took over a year later. Though "possession" of the island seesawed between France and England for years, the Caribs continued to make complete European colonization impossible. Ironically it was a rift in the Carib community itself that enabled the Europeans to gain a greater foothold.

In 1675 African slaves who had survived a Dutch shipwreck were welcomed into the Carib community. Over time, the Carib nation became, for all intents and purposes, two nations—one of the so-called Yellow Caribs, the other of the so-called Black Caribs. Relations between the two groups were often rivalrous. In 1719 tensions rose to a point where the Yellow Caribs united with the French (who were the colonizers that year) against the Black Caribs in what is known as the First Carib War. Ultimately, the Black Caribs retreated to the hills, but they continued to resist the Europeans.

The French went on to establish plantations, importing slaves to work the fertile land. In 1763 the British claimed the island yet again, and a wave of Scottish slave masters and indentured servants from India arrived. (Descendents of the Scots live in a community near Dorsetshire Hill.) In 1779 the French surprised the British and retrieved the island without a struggle. Four years later, by the Treaty of Versailles, St. Vincent was back in the British grip. The French weren't content with that; in 1795 they backed the Black Caribs against the British in the Second Carib War (also known as the Brigands War). British plantations were ravaged and burned on the island's windward coast, and Black Carib Chief Chatoyer pushed British troops down the leeward coast to Kingstown. On Dorsetshire Hill, high above the town, Chatoyer lost a duel with a British officer. Members of his tribe were rounded up and shipped off to Honduras and present-day Belize, where descendents still remain. A monument to Chatoyer's has been erected on Dorcestershire Hill, where there's a magnificent view over Kingstown and the Caribbean Sea toward Central America.

The Grenadines were as free from war and politics as their beaches today are free from debris and crowds. Just south of St. Vincent is Bequia, the largest of the islands. Its Admiralty Bay is one of the most popular anchorages in the Caribbean. With superb views, snorkeling, hiking, and swimming, the island has much to offer the international mix of backpackers and luxury-yacht owners who frequent its shores.

On the exclusive, private island of Mustique, just south of Bequia, posh villas are tucked into lush hillsides. Mustique does not encourage wholesale tourism, least of all those hoping for a glimpse of the rich and famous (Princess Margaret, Mick Jagger, Tommy Hilfiger, for example) who own villas here. The appeal of Mustique is its seclusion.

Boot-shape Canouan, just over 3 square mi, is an unspoiled island where you can relax on the beach, snorkel, or hike. Its 1,000 residents earn their livings by farming and fishing. Tiny Mayreau has less than 200 residents and one of the area's most beautiful beaches: the Caribbean Sea is often mirror-calm; yet, just yards away, on the southern end of this narrow island, is the rolling Atlantic surf.

John Caldwell spent more than 20 years turning a 100-acre, mosquito-infested, mangrove swamp called Prune Island into a small paradise called Palm Island. Today, the Caldwell family also hosts day-tripping cruise passengers who like to lounge on one or another of the island's five palm-fringed, white-sand beaches. Union Island isn't really a place for landlubbers: it caters to French sailors, who prefer to keep to themselves. Surface transport is limited, and to see the island you really need a car. Petit St. Vincent is another private luxury-resort island, reclaimed from the jungle by owner-manager Hazen K. Richardson II. The resort's stone houses are so far apart, that you can spend your entire vacation here without ever seeing another human being.

You can charter yachts and catamarans for day sails from any of the Grenadines to the four tiny, uninhabited Tobago Cays. Avid snorkelers claim that these cays, which have been declared a wildlife preserve, have some of the best hard and soft coral formations found outside the Pacific Ocean. The beaches here are perfect for secluded picnics.

Although SVG has its share of the poor and unemployed, the super-fertile soil allows everyone to grow enough food to eat and trade for necessities. Villages are busy and clean; concrete-block homes are painted in tropical colors; and brilliant flowers and bright-green foliage grow in profusion everywhere. The issue of possession of St. Vincent has long since been resolved. It fully belongs to a diverse, culturally rich people now known only as Vincentians. And they truly have cause to passionately love their homeland.

ST. VINCENT

Lodging

Luxury resorts may require advance booking, but most St. Vincent hotels can squeeze you in on short notice. There's a lull in January—after Christmas week and before the February rush—when rooms are sometimes available with little advance notification. Most hotels offer MAP; at resorts in the rather isolated Grenadines, FAP is common.

CATEGORY	COST*
$$$$	over $250
$$$	$150–$250
$$	$100–$150
$	under $100

*All prices are for a standard double room, excluding 7% tax and 10% service charge.

Kingstown

$$$–$$$$ ⊞ **Camelot Inn.** In the hills of Kingstown Park, just five minutes from
★   downtown and 10 minutes from the airport, this inn is on the site of the island's oldest guest house (1781), formerly the residence of St. Vin-

cent's first French governor. The atmosphere is stylish and elegant; the service is impeccable; and the location offers magnificent views of the capital, the hills, and the sea. Owner Audrey Ballantyne decorated each guest room in a soothing white and deep-green color scheme, with gray-green wicker furniture, antique mirrors and prints, and parquet floors. Each spacious room has a patio, a hair dryer, a TV, a bathroom scale, robes and slippers. Bathrooms have porcelain sinks imported from France. The ☞ **King Arthur Dining Room** is excellent; there's an outdoor dining terrace (with entertainment in season), and afternoon tea is served in the garden. As a guest here, you'll receive complimentary airport pickup, a city tour, and one massage as well as access to Young Island Resort's beach and water-sports facilities (transportation included). ✉ *Kingstown Park (Box 787),* ☎ *809/456–2100 or 800/223–6510 (reservations service),* FAX *809/456–2233. 20 rooms, 2 suites. Restaurant, bar, air-conditioning, fans, in-room safes, pool, beauty salon, massage, sauna, tennis court, exercise room, library, laundry service, meeting room. AE, DC, MC, V. MAP. Closed Sept.–Oct.*

$ ▥ **Cobblestone Inn.** On the waterfront in "the city," as Vincentians call Kingstown, this former sugar and arrowroot warehouse, built in 1814 of local stone, has been renovated to expose its original Georgian architecture, sunny interior courtyard, and cobblestone walkways and arches. All rooms have exposed-stone walls, rattan furniture, and small, private bathrooms. Number 5, at the front, is lighter and bigger than most of the other rooms but noisier, too. A popular rooftop bar-restaurant serves breakfast and soup-salad-burger lunches. Downstairs, you'll find ☞ **Basil's Bar and Restaurant** and an array of shops that sell local crafts and fashions. Rates are year-round. ✉ *Upper Bay St. (Box 867),* ☎ *809/456–1937,* FAX *809/456–1938. 19 rooms. Restaurant, bar, air-conditioning, shops. AE, D, MC, V. EP.*

$ ▥ **Heron Hotel.** Just steps from the Grenadines wharf, above a Georgian warehouse that now contains shops but once housed plantation bosses, this inn caters mostly to vacationing island-hoppers and interisland business travelers. Its atmosphere is old fashioned, and its rooms are simple, with thin carpets, billowing floral drapes, single beds, bentwood chairs, and tiny bathrooms. Rooms fan out from a palm-filled courtyard. On the veranda, tables are available for breakfast and light lunches; West Indian dinners are served by reservation only. A corner TV lounge is rather austere, with black floorboards, two giant ficus plants, and rows of wooden armchairs. Rates are year-round. ✉ *Upper Bay St. (Box 226),* ☎ *809/457–1631,* FAX *809/457–1189. 14 rooms. Dining room, lounge, air-conditioning. MC, V. CP.*

Villa Beach Area

$$$$ ▥ **Young Island Resort.** St. Vincent's premier resort has its own 35-
★   acre island 200 yards off Villa Beach. A hotel launch takes you across the channel (a five-minute ride) to the island, where you're first handed a rum punch crowned with a hibiscus blossom and then are escorted to one of 30 small hillside cottages. Rooms are done in natural colors (ecru, ochre, and green) and have bamboo and rattan furniture, walls of stone and glass, a sitting area, a patio, and a bathroom with a private open-air shower. Two luxury beachfront cottages have their own plunge pools. All accommodations have ocean views despite being hidden in fragrant tropical vegetation. Superior cottages are nearest the beach; deluxe are higher on the hillside. Watch hummingbirds flutter among the flowers as you enjoy breakfast on your terrace; sip a cool drink at the swim-up bar, anchored several feet off the white-sand beach; laze away the day in a hammock; or dine in one of the private thatched-roof gazebos adjacent to the ☞ **Young Island** dining room. Sailaway packages include five nights at the hotel and two nights touring the

St. Vincent

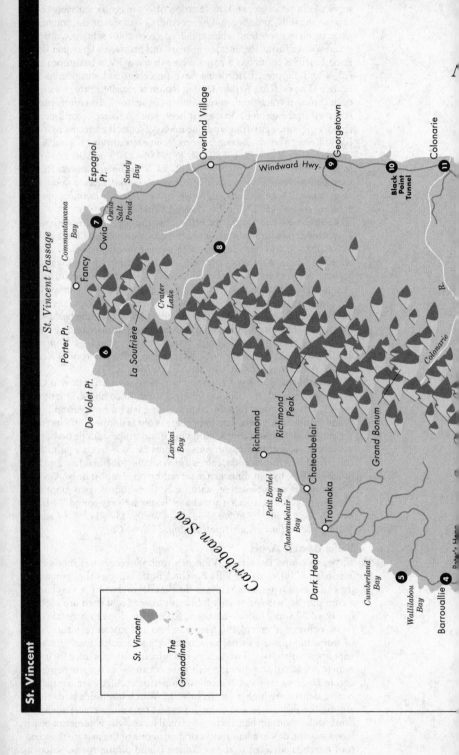

St. Vincent Passage

Commantawana Bay

Porter Pt.

Espagnol Pt.

Sandy Bay

Owia Salt Pond

Overland Village

Windward Hwy.

Georgetown

Colonarie

Black Point Tunnel

Fancy

Owia

De Volet Pt.

La Soufrière

Crater Lake

Larikai Bay

Richmond

Richmond Peak

Chateaubelair

Colonarie

Grand Bonum

Colonarie R.

Petit Bordel Bay

Chateaubelair Bay

Troumaka

Caribbean Sea

Dark Head

Cumberland Bay

Wallilabou Bay

Barrouallie

Point's Hope

St. Vincent

The Grenadines

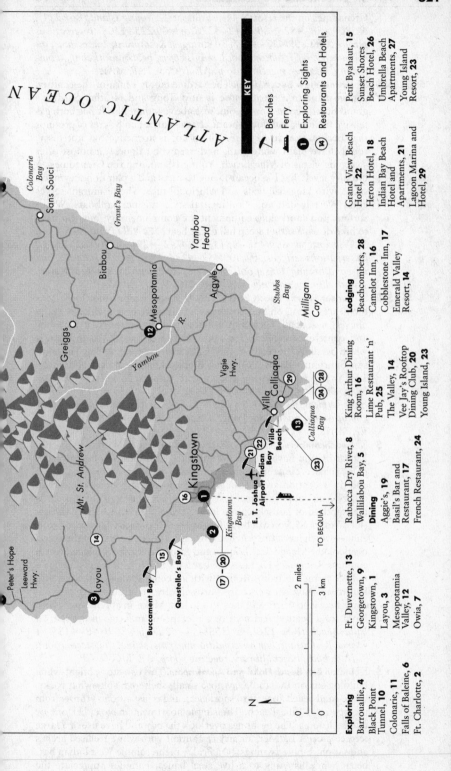

ATLANTIC OCEAN

Colonarie Bay
Sans Souci
Grant's Bay
Biabou
Yambou Head
Greiggs
Mesopotamia **12**
Yambou R.
Stubbs Bay
Milligan Cay
Argyle
Vigie Hwy.
Peter's Hope
Mt. St. Andrew
Leeward Hwy.
Layou **14**
Calliaqua
Villa **22**
Villa Beach **21**
Kingstown **1** **16**
Questelle's Bay **15**
Buccament Bay
Kingstown Bay
E. T. Joshua Airport Indian Bay
2
17 – **20**
23
24 / **28**
29
13
TO BEQUIA

N

0 ___ 2 miles
0 ___ 3 km

KEY

⌐ Beaches
⛴ Ferry
1 Exploring Sights
14 Restaurants and Hotels

Exploring
Barrouallie, **4**
Black Point Tunnel, **10**
Colonarie, **11**
Falls of Baleine, **6**
Ft. Charlotte, **2**
Ft. Duvernette, **13**
Georgetown, **9**
Kingstown, **3**
Layou, **1**
Mesopotamia Valley, **12**
Owia, **7**
Rabacca Dry River, **8**
Wallilabou Bay, **5**

Dining
Aggie's, **19**
Basil's Bar and Restaurant, **17**
French Restaurant, **24**
King Arthur Dining Room, **16**
Lime Restaurant 'n' Pub, **25**
The Valley, **14**
Vee Jay's Rooftop Dining Club, **20**
Young Island, **23**

Lodging
Beachcombers, **28**
Camelot Inn, **16**
Cobblestone Inn, **17**
Emerald Valley Resort, **14**
Grand View Beach Hotel, **22**
Heron Hotel, **18**
Indian Bay Beach Hotel and Apartments, **21**
Lagoon Marina and Hotel, **29**
Petit Byahaut, **15**
Sunset Shores Beach Hotel, **26**
Umbrella Beach Apartments, **27**
Young Island Resort, **23**

Grenadines on the resort's 44-ft sailboat. ⊠ *Young Island (Box 211)*, ☎ *809/458–4826; 800/742–4276 or 800/223–1108 (reservations services)*, FAX *809/457–4567. 30 cottages. Restaurant, 2 bars, fans, in-room safes, refrigerators, pool, tennis court, beach, snorkeling, wind-surfing, boating, meeting room. AE, MC, V. FAP, MAP.*

$$$–$$$$ 🏨 **Grand View Beach Hotel.** The Sardine family's turn-of-the-century,
★ cotton-plantation great house is now Tony and Heather Sardine's grand hotel, perched on a point just above Indian Bay. It has both extensive facilities and down-home charm—all set on 8 acres of grounds that beckon you to explore. The decor is attractive but not fussy; rooms have plain white walls and hardwood floors, and most offer sweeping vistas of Villa Beach, Young Island, and the Grenadines. A "luxury level" has big ocean-facing terraces and a pair of honeymoon suites with king-size beds and whirlpool tubs. The restaurant serves good West Indian and Continental-style cuisine. Sailboats, Wind-surfers, and snorkeling equipment are complimentary, but you have to hike down a rather steep hill to the beach. ⊠ *Villa Point (Box 173), St. Vincent,* ☎ *809/458–4811; 800/742–4276 or 800/223–6510 (reservations services),* FAX *809/457–4174. 19 rooms. Restaurant, bar, air-conditioning, fans, pool, massage, sauna, tennis court, health club, squash, library, meeting room. AE, MC, V. CP, EP, MAP.*

$$–$$$ 🏨 **Sunset Shores Beach Hotel.** This U-shape, lemon-color low-rise is the nearest thing on St. Vincent to a corporate hotel, which is really not very near at all. There's a Caribbean news update board in the lobby and conference facilities for 100. All rooms have TVs, and patios which overlook the center of the "U," which faces Indian Bay. The pool-side Sunrunner Bar is nicely placed opposite the sunset. Children 2–12 stay free when sharing a room with parents. ⊠ *Villa Beach (Box 849),* ☎ *809/458–4411; 800/742–4276 or 800/223–6510 (reservations service),* FAX *809/457–4800. 32 rooms. Restaurant, 2 bars, air-conditioning, pool, Ping-Pong, beach, meeting room. AE, D, MC, V. EP, MAP.*

$ 🏨 **Beachcombers.** At Villa Beach, next to Sunset Shores, Flora and Richard Gunn have built a darling village on their sloping lawns. A pair of chalets contain the guest rooms, an open-terrace bar-restaurant, and the reception area. Though some rooms are better located than others, you could eat breakfast off the floor of any of them, such is the standard of housekeeping. In one chalet, Rooms 1–3 face the sea (for an extra $5, you can book Room 1—in top-to-toe dark-wood paneling—which has a tiny kitchen); Rooms 4–6 are in back of these and overlook the Mango Tree Lounge and garden. The other building, which contains Rooms 7–12, faces the garden's frenzy of flowers and has a red-tile terrace in front. Rooms with air-conditioning cost extra, and bathrooms have showers only—insignificant privations when the welcome here is so warm and the rates so low. Make an appointment with Flora for a beauty treatment or a therapeutic massage in the spa. ⊠ *Villa Beach (Box 126),* ☎ *809/458–4283,* FAX *809/458–4385.14 rooms. Restaurant, bar, air-conditioning, fans, sauna, spa, steam room, Turkish bath, beach, library, meeting room. AE, MC, V. CP.*

$ 🏨 **Indian Bay Beach Hotel and Apartments.** This two-story, bright-white building sits on Indian Bay, whose small, sheltered, somewhat rocky, white-sand beach appeals to snorkelers, and is just a stone's throw from the action at Villa Beach. The simple apartments have either one or two bedrooms. The best ones overlook the bay and have use of a large terrace atop A La Mer, an airy restaurant with white-trellised arches and sapphire-blue awnings. (On Friday night, sample West Indian barbecue while listening to a live steel band.) Families appreciate the weekly rates and the baby-sitting services. ⊠ *Indian Bay Beach (Box 538),* ☎ *809/458–4001 or 800/742–4276 (reservations service),* FAX

809/457–4777. *14 apartments. Restaurant, bar, air-conditioning, kitchenettes, beach, baby-sitting. AE, D, MC, V. CP, EP, MAP.*

$ ⊞ **Umbrella Beach Apartments.** If you don't mind sacrificing gorgeous bedroom decor for the sake of your pocketbook, but still want to be well located, this very simple cluster of small rooms may fit the bill. All are clean but have shower-only bathrooms and are rather plain with white walls, marble-chip floors with rush mats, and plastic chairs at a small Formica table. However, only steps away are Villa Beach, the ferry to Young Island, and waterfront restaurants where you can spend all the cash you saved on the room. ⊠ *Villa Beach (Box 530),* ☎ *809/ 458–4651,* FAX *809/457–4930. 9 rooms. Fans, kitchenettes. MC, V. EP.*

Elsewhere on St. Vincent

$$$ ⊞ **Petit Byahaut.** For those with Swiss Family Robinson fantasies, this 50-acre retreat 7 mi (20 minutes by boat) north of Kingstown, accommodates you in 10 × 13-ft tents, complete with wood floors, private decks, queen-size beds, and solar-heated alfresco showers. This adult camp is accessible only by a boat that you catch in Kingstown (a complimentary trip if you stay for three or more nights). Once you've settled in, you'll find a selection of other boats with which to play as well as scuba and snorkeling equipment; a 600-ft, private, black-sand beach; hammocks; a boutique; and some interesting Carib Indian finds. If you tire of the seclusion, excursions are easily arranged. Weekly rates are available. ⊠ *Petit Byahaut Bay,* ☎ FAX *809/457–7008. 7 tents. Restaurant, bar, hiking, beach, dive shop, snorkeling, boating. MC, V. FAP. Closed July–Oct.*

$$ ⊞ **Lagoon Marina and Hotel.** The only hotel overlooking sheltered Blue
★   Lagoon Bay may well be the island's friendliest hotel. Thanks to its marina, there are usually seafaring types liming (hanging out) in the terrace bar and plenty of yacht traffic to watch from one of two couches on your big balcony. Sliding patio doors lead onto these perches from the wood-ceilinged, carpeted rooms. You can practically dive into the sea from Rooms 1–9, which hang over the wooden quay; Rooms 10–20 overlook the narrow, curved, black-sand beach. Basic wooden furniture, twin beds, rather dim lighting, tiled bathrooms, and ceiling fans provide an adequate level of comfort; about half the rooms have air-conditioning (for a few extra bucks), but don't expect luxury. Sloping garden grounds contain a secluded two-level pool, and there's a pretty terrace restaurant. ⊠ *Blue Lagoon, Ratho Mill (Box 133),* ☎ *809/458–4308 or 800/742–4246 (reservations service),* FAX *809/457–4716. 19 rooms. Restaurant, bar, air-conditioning, fans, pool, beach, dock, snorkeling, windsurfing, boating, meeting room. AE, V. EP.*

$ ⊞ **Emerald Valley Resort.** The rural, rain-forested Penniston Valley, a ½-hour drive north of Kingstown, is the unlikely setting for SVG's only casino, which is, equally improbably, attached to this family-friendly 5-acre resort. Two pairs of Brits toiled for two years to bring a run-down property up to very high standards; the 12 chalets now have stone terraces, kitchenettes (but no stoves), and king-size or twin beds that were made locally. On the grounds are an outdoor bar, a two-level pool bisected by a wooden bridge and diving platform, a stage (local bands play here on weekends), two tennis courts (pro lessons available), and ☞ **The Valley** restaurant. What you don't get, of course, is a beach, and the nearest grocery stores are in Kingstown. On the plus side, the Vermont Nature Trail is 2½ mi away, and you can gamble until the wee hours if you choose. ⊠ *Penniston Valley (Box 1081),* ☎ *809/456–7140 or 800/742–4276 (reservations service),* FAX *809/456–7145. 12 chalets. Restaurant, 2 bars, air-conditioning, fans, kitchenettes, in-room VCRs, pool, 2 tennis courts, croquet, volleyball, casino. AE, MC, V. EP.*

Dining

You'll enjoy interesting local fare that is reasonably priced at all but the most expensive hotels. Dishes include callaloo (spinachlike) soup, curry goat, *rotis* (turnovers filled with curried meat or vegetables, seasonal seafood (lobster, kingfish, snapper, and dolphinfish), local vegetables and roots (yams, christophenes, breadfruit, dasheen, and *eddoes*), and tropical fruit (from sugar apples and soursop to mangoes and papaya). Fried or baked chicken is available everywhere, and you can get burgers at some restaurants. The local lager, Hairoun, is brewed according to a German recipe at Camden Park, just north of Kingstown.

What to Wear

Restaurants are casual. You may want to dress up a little but none of the places listed below require gentlemen to wear a jacket or tie. On the Grenadines, ultracasual is fine everywhere. Beachwear, however, should always be reserved for the beach.

CATEGORY	COST*
$$$	over $30
$$	$20–$30
$	under $20

per person for a three-course meal, excluding drinks and 7% sales tax

Kingstown

CARIBBEAN/CREOLE

$–$$ ✕ **Aggie's.** Opposite the Sardine Bakery (that's a family name, not the fish), in downtown Kingstown, this casual second-floor bar and family restaurant has a swimming-pool-blue ceiling and trellis arches. It serves such local seafood dishes as conch souse and kingfish steak as well as pumpkin or callaloo soup, rotis, baked chicken leg, rice 'n' peas, and salads. Service continues right up until midnight, and takeout is also available. There's also a Friday happy hour from 4 to 6. ⊠ *Grenville St.,* ☎ *809/456–2110. No credit cards.*

$–$$ ✕ **Basil's Bar and Restaurant.** This air-conditioned restaurant, downstairs at the ☞ **Cobblestone Inn,** is owned by the famous Basil of Mustique but has little else in common with that laid-back glitterati hangout in the Grenadines. This is the Kingstown power-lunch venue, where local businesspeople gather for the daily buffet. Dinner entrées of pasta, local seafood, and chicken (try it poached in fresh ginger and coconut milk) are served at candlelit tables. There's a Chinese buffet on Friday, and takeout is available that night only. The bar gets lively in the evenings. ⊠ *Upper Bay St.,* ☎ *809/457–2713. AE, MC, V.*

$–$$ ✕ **Vee Jay's Rooftop Dining Club.** This eatery above Roger's Photo Studios (have your pix developed while you eat) and opposite the Cobblestone Inn, offers downtown Kingstown's best harbor view from beneath a green, corrugated-plastic roof. Among the "authentic Vincy cuisine" specials chalked on the blackboard are mutton or fish stew, chicken or vegetable rotis, curried goat, souse, *buljol* (sautéed codfish, breadfruit, and vegetables); not-so-Vincy sandwiches and burgers can be authentically washed down with *mauby,* a bittersweet drink made from tree bark (an acquired taste); linseed, peanut or sorrel punch; beer; or a cocktail. Lunch is buffet-style. ⊠ *Upper Bay St.,* ☎ *809/457–2845. Dinner reservations essential. AE, MC, V. Closed Sun.*

CONTINENTAL

$$–$$$ ✕ **King Arthur Dining Room.** Expect fine cuisine and elegant service when supping at this intimate dining room downstairs in the ☞ **Camelot Inn.** The chef's table d'hôte menu offers you a choice of two to three starters and entrées, which change daily. Cuisine is international (beef fillet, grilled fish with herb sauces, chicken sautéed in white wine) and is served with local vegetables. The homemade callaloo soup is memorable, and so is the rum-raisin ice cream. There's entertainment in season and a weekly barbecue on the breezy Guinevere Terrace, which overlooks the harbor. ⊠ *Kingstown Park,* ☎ *809/456–2100. Reservations essential. AE, D, MC, V.*

Villa Beach Area
CONTINENTAL

$$$ ✕ **Young Island.** Even if you're not a guest of ☞ **Young Island Resort,**
★ you can take a ferry over to the island for a very special evening. Stone paths lead through lush foliage to thatched huts with individual candlelit tables; the water laps upon the shore and a warm breeze rustles the leaves—it doesn't get any more romantic than this. Five-course table d'hôte, prix-fixe dinners of grilled seafood, roast pork, beef tenderloin, and sautéed chicken are accompanied by local vegetables; a board of wonderful fresh breads are cut to order at your table. Two or three choices are offered for each course. Day-trippers can partake of the daily luncheon—served buffet- or barbecue-style on the beachfront terrace.⊠ *Young Island,* ☎ *809/458–4826. Dinner reservations essential. AE, MC, V.*

ECLECTIC

$$–$$$ ✕ **Lime Restaurant 'n' Pub.** Although this sprawling, waterfront, restaurant-bar is named after the *pursuit* of liming, its decor also features a great deal of green. An eclectic all-day menu caters to beachgoers and boaters, who drop by for a roti and a bottle of Hairoun; burgers, curries, sandwiches, soups, and salads appear on the snack menu. Dinner choices include fresh seafood, volcano chicken (with a Creole sauce that's as spicy as lava is hot), curried goat, and pepper steak. Casual and congenial during the day, the mood is all candlelight and romance at night—enhanced by the twinkling lights of boats at anchor and waves quietly breaking against the seawall. Stay late and dance on weekends, when the atmosphere is more like that of a singles bar. Happy hour is 9–10 PM.⊠ *Young Island Channel,* ☎ *809/ 458–4227. AE, MC, V.*

FRENCH

$$–$$$ ✕ **French Restaurant.** Referred to as "The French," this popular wa-
★ terfront bistro facing Young Island is where people go when they're in a lobster mood. There's a lobster pool on the terrace, where you can watch the staff fish for your supper. As befits a bistro run by a couple from Orléans, most dishes are the Gallic version of local cuisine. Stuffed crab back, for instance, comes in a shell of pastry, not crab; steak—au poivre, with garlic butter, or with béarnaise—is imported; onion soup and lemon tart are done the way they should be; and the warm, fresh bread is a real baguette. At the inside bar, frothy cocktails and Martinique-style punch are served to yachties who hang out here in winter. ⊠ *Young Island Channel,* ☎ *809/458–4972. AE, V.*

Elsewhere on St. Vincent
CONTINENTAL

$$–$$$ ✕ **The Valley.** This pretty poolside dining terrace hung with fishnets is part of the ☞ **Emerald Valley Resort**—which includes the only casino on SVG. The menu is table d'hôte, and selections are a local–international mix. The pride of the kitchen is lobster, retrieved from the nearby Vermont River. Other choices include tomato, mozzarella, and basil salad; baked red snapper with coconut stuffing; and broiled *poussin* (young chicken) with local herbs. If it's Saturday (also some Fridays), a local band will serenade you. Get directions if you're driving, and call first—the restaurant's hours are unpredictable. ⊠ *Penniston Valley,* ☎ *809/456–7140. AE, MC, V.*

Beaches

St. Vincent is of volcanic origin, so the sand on its beaches ranges in color from golden brown to black. Young Island has the only truly white-sand beach, but it's reserved for hotel guests. On the windward coast, dramatic swaths of broad black sand are strewn with huge black boulders, but the water is rough and unpredictable. Swimming is only recommended on the leeward coast. No beach has lifeguards, so even experienced swimmers are taking a risk.

Buccament Bay, which is good for swimming, is a tiny black-sand beach 20 minutes north of Kingstown. **Indian Bay** has golden sand but is slightly rocky—a good location for snorkeling. **Questelle's Bay** (pronounced keet-*ells*), on the leeward side just north of Kingstown and next to Camden Park, has a black-sand beach. **Villa Beach,** 10 minutes south of Kingstown, is the island's main beach (although it's hardly big enough to merit such a title). This narrow strip of golden sand faces Young Island and offers safe swimming. Boats bob at anchor in the channel; dive shops and restaurants line the shore.

Outdoor Activities and Sports

BOATING AND SAILING

From St. Vincent, you can charter a sailboat or catamaran (bare or complete with captain, crew, and cook) to weave you around the Grenadines for a day or a week. Boats of all sizes and degrees of luxury are available. **Barefoot Yacht Charters** (⊠ Blue Lagoon, ☎ 809/456–9526) has a fleet of yachts for charter, with or without crew. **Blue Water Charters** (⊠ Wharfside at the Aquatic Club, Villa Beach, ☎ 809/456–1232) will take you on full-day, half-day, or overnight fishing or sightseeing excursions on its modern, 55-ft sportfishing boat. **Lagoon Marina and Yacht Charters** (⊠ Blue Lagoon, ☎ 809/458–4308) has 44-ft crewed sloops from $200 per day; 7- or 10-day packages are also available. **TMM St. Vincent Ltd.** (⊠ Blue Lagoon, ☎ 809/456–960) charters catamarans and monohulls for weeklong cruises.

HIKING

Lush, mountainous St. Vincent offers hikers and trekkers a choice of experiences: easy, picturesque walks near Kingstown; moderate-effort nature trails in the central valleys; and exhilarating climbs through a rain forest to the rim of an active volcano. Bring a hat, long pants, and insect repellent if you plan to hike in the bush.

Vermont Trails are two well-marked and maintained hiking trails in the Buccament River Valley, 5 mi north of Kingstown. A network of 1.5 mi loops pass through stands of bamboo, evergreen forest, and rain forest. In the late afternoon, you may be lucky enough to see the rare St. Vincent parrot, *Amazona guidingii,*. A hike up **Dorsetshire Hill,** about 3 mi from Kingstown, rewards you with a sweeping view of city and harbor. You can also see picturesque Queen's Drive, which passes through residential areas and is the route taken by Queen Elizabeth II when she tours the island. **La Soufrière,** the queen of climbs, is St. Vincent's active volcano (which last erupted, appropriately enough, on Friday the 13th, 1979). Approachable from either the windward or leeward coast, this is *not* a casual excursion for inexperienced walkers—the massive mountain covers nearly the entire northern third of the island. Climbs are all-day excursions. You'll need stamina and sturdy shoes to reach the top and peep into the mile-wide crater at just over 4,000 ft. Be sure to check the weather before you leave; hikers have been sorely disappointed to find, after their climb, the view completely obscured by enveloping clouds. A guide ($25–$30) can be arranged through your hotel, the SVG Department of Tourism (☎ 809/457–1502), or tour operators (☞ Guided Tours *in* St. Vincent and the Grenadines A to Z, *below*). Approaching from the west, the climb is longer and rougher but more scenic; the eastern approach is more popular. In a four-wheel-drive vehicle, you pass through Rabacca Dry River, north of Georgetown, and then the Bamboo Forest. Then, it's a 2-hour, 3 ½-mi hike to the summit. You can return the same way you came; but if you want to go down the other side of the mountain, arrangements will be made in advance to pick you up in the Châteaubelair area. **Mt. St. Andrew,** on the outskirts of Kingstown, is a pleasant climb on a well-marked trail through a rain forest. **Trinity Falls,** in the north, requires a trip by four-wheel-drive vehicle from Richmond to the interior, then a steep two-hour climb beneath a thick canopy of tropical vegetation. The trail leads to a crystal-clear river and three waterfalls, one of which forms a whirlpool where you can take a refreshing swim.

SCUBA DIVING AND SNORKELING

Diving experiences are top quality, with brilliant sponges, huge deep-water coral trees, and shallow reefs teeming with colorful fish. Many sites are still virtually unexplored.

You'll find dive shops on St. Vincent as well as Bequia, Mustique, Canouan, Petit St. Vincent, Union, and Palm islands (☞ Scuba Diving and Snorkeling, *for individual islands, below*). Generally modest operations, they are, nevertheless, competent and professional. Most offer three-hour beginner "resort" courses, full certification courses, and excursions to nearby reefs, walls, and wrecks.

Most dive shops also rent snorkel gear. At Tobago Cays, you'll experience some of the best snorkeling in the world. Young Island is also good; if you're not a resort guest, phone for permission to take the ferry over and rent snorkeling equipment from the resort's water-sports center (☞ Lodging, *above*).

Dive St. Vincent (☒ Young Island Dock, Villa Beach, ☎ 809/457–4714) is where NAUI and PADI-certified instructor Bill Tewes and his staff offer beginner and certification courses and trips to the Falls of Baleine. A single-tank dive is about $50; 2-tank, $95; 10-dive package, $400. All prices include equipment.

Shopping

The 12 blocks that hug the waterfront in downtown Kingstown comprise St. Vincent's main shopping district. Among the simple shops that sell goods to fulfill household needs are a few that sell local crafts, gifts, and souvenirs. Bargaining is not expected nor appreciated. At Villa Beach, there are a few boutiques that sell swimsuits, batik beachwear, beach toys, water-sports equipment, and souvenirs.

DUTY-FREE GOODS

St. Vincent isn't a duty-free port, but a few shops sell luxury goods at duty-free prices. You'll find small selection of Swiss watches, jewelry, leather goods, and perfume at **Voyager** (☒ Halifax St., ☎ 809/456–1686). **Y De Lima** (☒ Bay St. at Egmont St., ☎ 809/457–1681) is a large department store with a some duty-free jewelry and watches. At **Carsyl Duty-Free Liquor** (☒ Airport, ☎ 809/457–2706) departing passengers can purchase duty-free liquor at discounts of up to 40%.

HANDICRAFTS

In Kingstown's central shopping area, street vendors sell handmade jewelry, leather goods, wood carvings, and sundry items. In the shops, the best local crafts are handwoven grass floor mats (from scatter rug to full-room size) and place mats, batik and screen-printed clothing, straw baskets, costumed dolls, and hand-carved wood sculptures.

Artisans Craft Shop (⊠ Upstairs in Bonadie's Bldg., Bay St., Kingstown, ☎ 809/458–4436) sells local crafts, such as straw art, macrame, and hand-painted and tie-dyed clothing. **Noah's Arkade** (⊠ Bay St., Kingstown, ☎ 809/457–1513) sells appealing crafts and gifts from all over the Caribbean, as well as T-shirts and a good selection of books on local customs and history. **St. Vincent Craftsmen's Center** (⊠ James St., Kingstown, ☎ 809/457–1288), 3 blocks from the wharf, sells locally made grass floor mats, place mats, and other straw items, as well as batik cloth, handmade dolls, hand-painted calabashes, and framed artwork. The large grass rugs can be rolled for easy transport home.

SOUVENIRS

St. Vincent is known worldwide for its particularly beautiful and colorful commemorative stamps, which are illustrated with tropical flowers, undersea creatures, and local architecture. (Oddly enough, a recent stamp honored Elvis Presley.) You can view and purchase stamps at the **Philatelic Bureau,** (⊠ Bay St. at Egmont St., ☎ 809/457–1911). When you're mailing your postcards at the **Kingstown Post Office,** (⊠ Halifax St., east of Egmont St., ☎ 809/456–1111), you can also buy sheets of commemorative stamps. To bring back sounds of the islands, stop by **Music World** (⊠ Egmont St., ☎ 809/547–1884), where you can find the latest reggae, soca, and calypso music on CD or tape.

Nightlife

Nightlife here consists mostly of once-a-week hotel barbecue buffets and jump-ups, so called because the lively steel-band and calypso music makes listeners jump up and dance. At nightspots in Kingstown and at Villa Beach, you can join Vincentians for late-night dancing to live or recorded reggae, hip-hop, and *soca* music. Soca, which is also called soul calypso, is an up-tempo calypso beat that the legendary Lord Kitchener and The Mighty Sparrow began in Trinidad more than 30 years ago. It's played and danced to throughout the Caribbean and, along with the more traditional calypso, is typical Carnival music.

CASINO

Emerald Valley Casino (⊠ Penniston Valley, ☎ 809/456–7140) combines the homey atmosphere of an English pub with the gaming of Vegas; you'll find roulette (the only single-zero roulette tables in the Caribbean), blackjack, Caribbean stud poker, craps, slots and video slots here. It's generally open Wednesday–Monday 9 PM–3 AM, until 4 AM on Saturday. Call to make sure, though.

DANCE AND MUSIC CLUBS

At the **Aquatic Club** (⊠ Villa Beach, ☎ 809/458–4205), the rhythmic sounds of soca and reggae bounce off the water on Friday and Saturday nights as locals, visitors, and boaters dance to live music. **Touch Entertainment Centre** (⊠ Grenville St., Kingstown, ☎ 809/457–1825) is a dance hall with disco music on Friday and live music on Saturday. It attracts a local crowd of mostly young people. Dance clubs generally charge a small cover of about $3.75 (EC$10), slightly more for headliners.

The **Attic** (⊠ 1 Melville St., above Kentucky Fried Chicken, Kingstown, ☎ 809/457–2558), features international jazz and blues artists on Thursday nights; weekends, party time begins at 10 PM. There's a small cover charge; call ahead for hours and performers. Other popular nightspots in Kingstown are **Level 3** (⊠ Grenville St., ☎ 809/456–2015) and **Cafe Echelon** (⊠ Bay St., ☎ 809/456–2126).

On Wednesday and Friday evenings, at **Vee Jay's Rooftop Dining Club** (⌧ Bay St., Kingstown, ☎ 809/457–2845), karaoke accompanies dinner, drinks, and the open-air harbor view. **Young Island Resort** (⌧ Young Island, ☎ 809/458–4826) hosts **sunset cocktail parties** with hors d'oeuvres every Friday evening at adjacent Ft. Duvernette, the island fortress immediately behind Young Island. Hotel guests and nonguests (with reservations) are ferried from Young Island Resort to the tiny island, where the 100 steps up the hill are lit by flaming torches. **The National String Band** plays infectious music on guitars and instruments made of bamboo, bottles, and gourds. The band performs at various hotels in addition to Young Island Resort's weekly parties.

Exploring St. Vincent

Kingstown's shopping and business district, its historic churches and cathedrals, and its other points of interest can easily be seen in a half day, with another half day for the Botanical Gardens. A drive along the windward coast or a boat trip to the Falls of Baleine each require a full day; exploring La Soufrière and the Vermont Trail are major undertakings, requiring a very early start and a full day's strenuous hiking. The coastal roads of St. Vincent offer panoramic vistas and views of the island way of life. The Leeward Highway follows the scenic Caribbean coastline; the Windward Highway follows the more dramatic Atlantic coast. Island maps are in the "Discover SVG" booklet, available everywhere on the island.

Numbers in the margin correspond to points of interest on the St. Vincent map.

SIGHTS TO SEE

4 Barrouallie. This was once an important whaling village; now, however, the fishermen of Barrouallie (pronounced *bar*-relly) earn their livelihoods trawling for blackfish, a kind of small whale. The one-hour drive north from Kingstown, on Leeward Highway, takes you along ridges that drop to the sea, through small villages and lush valleys, and beside picturesque bays with black-sand beaches and safe bathing.

10 Black Point Tunnel. In 1815, under the supervision of British colonel Thomas Browne, Carib and African slaves drilled this 300-ft-long tunnel through solid volcanic rock to facilitate the transportation of sugar from estates in the north to the port in Kingstown. The tunnel, an engineering marvel for the times, links Grand Sable with Byera Bay, just north of Colonarie (pronounced con-a-*ree*; *see below*).

11 Colonarie. In the hills behind the village of Colonarie, about half way up St. Vincent's east coast, are hiking trails. Signs on the trails are limited, but the local residents are helpful with directions. To get to Colonarie, drive from Kingstown through scenic Mesopotamia, then follow Windward Highway.

6 Falls of Baleine. They're impossible to reach by car, so book an escorted, all-day boat trip from Villa Beach or the Lagoon Marina (☞ Guided Tours, *below*). The boat ride up the coast to the falls offers scenic island views. When you arrive, be prepared to get wet. You have to wade through shallow water to get to the beach. Local guides help you make the easy five-minute trek to the 60-ft falls and its rock-enclosed freshwater pool—be sure to take a dip.

2 Ft . Charlotte. Started by the French in 1786 and completed by the British in 1806, the fort sits on a dramatic promontory 636 ft above sea level. From here there's a stunning view of Kingstown and the Grenadines.

Interestingly, cannons face inward—the fear of attack by native peoples was far greater than any threat approaching from the sea though, truth be told, the fort saw no action. Nowadays, it serves as a signal station for ships; the ancient cells house a series of paintings depicting early island history. What was once a leper's colony, adjacent to the fort, is now the women's prison.

⑬ Ft. Duvernette. The fort was built around 1800, on a massive rock island behind Young Island, to defend the bay. Views from the 195-ft summit are terrific, but you'll have to climb about 100 steps carved into the mountain to get here. Two complete batteries of rusting armaments remain near the top. Arrange your visit at the Young Island Resort (☞ Lodging, *above*)—their little ferry will transport you to the fort and bring you back at a prearranged time.

⑨ Georgetown. St. Vincent's second-largest city, halfway up the island's east coast, is surrounded by acres and acres of coconut groves. This is also the site of long-defunct Mount Bentinck sugar factory. The town is interesting because it is an authentic, busy West Indian town—with a few streets, small shops, and modest homes—that has been truly untainted by tourism. It's also a convenient place (one of the very few places, in fact) to stop for a cool drink or snack or other essential shopping while traveling along the west coast.

① Kingstown. The capital city of St. Vincent and the Grenadines is on the island's southwestern coast. The town of 25,000 residents, about of the nation's population, wraps around Kingstown Bay; a ring of green hills and ridges, studded with homes, forms a backdrop for the city. This is very much a working city, with a busy harbor, and with few concessions made to tourists.

In fact, **Kingstown Harbour,** the only deep-water port on the island, is far more likely to host a freighter than a passenger ship, but that should change when a new, long-promised cruise-ship facility is built.

What few gift shops there are can be found on and around **Bay Street,** near the harbor. Upper Bay Street, which stretches along the bayfront, bustles with daytime activity—businesspeople going about their business and housewives doing their shopping. Many of Kingstown's downtown buildings are built of stone or brick brought to the island in the holds of 18th-century ships as ballast (and replaced with rum for the return trip to Europe). Originally warehouses, the Georgian-style stone arches and second-floor overhangs create shelter from midday sun and the brief, cooling showers common to the tropics.

The **Administrative Centre,** an attractive, modern office building built in 1992 and the tallest structure on Bay Street, is where you'll find the tourist office. **Grenadines Wharf,** at the south end of Bay Street, is busy with schooners loading supplies and ferries loading people bound for the Grenadines. Several of the 19th-century buildings nearby were built of bricks used as ballast in ships that returned to Europe with holds filled with sugar and molasses.

An interesting thing to do in Kingstown is to browse among the infinite varieties of produce at the **Kingstown Market,** in the center of town along Bedford Street. (At the other end of the block, across from the court house, a new, two-story, enclosed marketplace is expected to open by late 1999.) The market is open daily, except Sunday, but the busiest times are Friday and Saturday mornings.

At **Little Tokyo,** so-called because funding for the project was a gift from Japan, there's a bustling indoor fish market and dozens of stalls where you can buy inexpensive homemade meals, drinks, ice cream, bread and cookies, clothing, trinkets, and even get a haircut. The bus terminal is also in this area.

St. George's Cathedral, on Grenville Street, is a pristine, lemon-color Anglican church built in 1820. The dignified Georgian architecture includes simple wooden pews, an ornate chandelier, and stained-glass windows. The markers in the cathedral's graveyard recount the history of the island.Across the street is **St. Mary's Cathedral of the Assumption** (Roman Catholic), built in stages beginning in 1828, is a strangely appealing blend of Moorish, Georgian, and Romanesque styles applied to black brick. Nearby, freed slaves built the **Kingstown Methodist Church** in 1841. The exterior is brick, simply decorated with quoins (solid blocks that form the corners), and the roof is held together by metal straps, bolts, and wood pins; not a single nail was used. **Scot's Kirk** (1839–80) was built by and for Scottish settlers but became a Seventh Day Adventist church in 1952.

A few minutes north of downtown by taxi is St. Vincent's famous **Botanical Garden.** Founded in 1765, it is the oldest botanical garden in the Western Hemisphere. Captain Bligh—of *Bounty* fame—brought the first breadfruit tree to this island to feed the slaves. You can see a direct descendant of this tree among the specimen mahogany, rubber, and teak trees in the gardens. Several rare St. Vincent parrots live in the small aviary. Christian Daniel, who is a font of knowledge, and other guides offer their services for about US$3 per person per hour. ⊠ *Off the Leeward Hwy., Montrose,* ☎ *809/457–1003.* 🎟 *Free.* ☉ *Daily 6–6.*

The **National Museum** houses a series of maps that trace the migrations of the Ciboney, the very first Vincentians, who arrived on the island around 4000 BC. The pre-Columbian Indian clay pottery on exhibit was unearthed by Dr. Earle Kirby, resident archaeologist and the museum's director. Dr. Kirby's historical knowledge is as entertaining as it is extensive, and a visit here is much enhanced by his annotations. ⊠ *Botanical Gardens, Montrose,* ☎ *809/456–1787.* 🎟 *$1.* ☉ *Wed. 9–noon, Sat. 2–6.*

❸ **Layou.** Just beyond this small fishing village, about 45 minutes north of Kingstown, are petroglyphs (rock carvings) left by the Caribs 13 centuries ago. If you're seriously interested in archaeological mysteries, you'll want to arrange a visit (through the Tourist Board) with Victor Hendrickson, who owns the land. For $2, Hendrickson or his wife will meet you and escort you to the site.

⑫ **Mesopotamia Valley.** The rugged, ocean-lashed scenery along St. Vincent's windward coast is the perfect counterpoint to the lush, calm west coast. The Mesopotamia Valley offers a breathtaking panoramic view that is unsurpassed in this part of the Caribbean; you'll see dense forests, streams, and endless banana plantations. Blue plastic bags cover the fruit—particularly important for export—to protect it from wind and insects. Coconut, breadfruit, sweet corn, peanuts, and arrowroot also grow in the rich soil here, which is why the area is nicknamed the Breadbasket of St. Vincent. The valley is surrounded by mountain ridges, including 3,181-ft Grand Bonhomme Mountain.

❼ **Owia.** The Carib village of Owia, on the island's far northeast coast about two hours from Kingstown, is the home of many descendents of the Carib people of St. Vincent. It is also the location of the Owia Arrowroot Processing Factory. Used for generations to thicken sauces and flavor cookies, arrowroot is now in demand as a finish for computer paper. Close to the village is the Owia Salt Pond, where you can take a dip before the long ride back to Kingstown.

❽ Rabacca Dry River. Looking every bit like a moonscape, this rocky gulch just beyond the village of Georgetown was carved out of the earth by the lava flow from the 1902 eruption of **La Soufrière** volcano. This volcano, which last erupted in 1979, is so huge that it covers virtually the northern third of the island. The eastern trail to the rim of the crater, a two-hour ascent, begins at Rabacca Dry River. An alternate, more difficult trail begins on the leeward coast (☞ Hiking *in* Outdoor Activities and Sports, *above*).

❺ Wallilabou Bay. You can sunbathe, swim, and picnic at Wallilabou (pronounced wally-la-*boo*) Anchorage, on the bay. This is a favorite stop for landlubbers exploring the leeward coast, boat trips returning from the Falls of Baleine (☞ Outdoor Activities and Sports, *above*), and boaters anchoring for the evening. Nearby, there's a river with a small waterfall where you can take a fresh water plunge.

THE GRENADINES

The Grenadine Islands offer fine diving and snorkeling opportunities, good beaches, and unlimited chances to laze on the beach with a picnic, watching boats, and waiting for the sun to set. If you're seeking peace and quiet or active water sports and informal socializing, then you'll be happy on a Grenadine, though which one you choose may take some trial and error—each island has a different appeal.

Bequia

Just 9 mi south of St. Vincent's southwestern shore, Bequia (pronounced *beck*-way) is the largest of the Grenadines. Boatbuilding, sailing, whaling, and fishing have been industries here for generations.

Hilly and green, with several sandy beaches, Bequia's picturesque Admiralty Bay is a favorite anchorage for those on private or chartered yachts. Having an airport and regular, frequent ferry service from St. Vincent makes the island a favorite for day trips. The ferry docks in Port Elizabeth, a tiny town with waterfront bars, restaurants, and shops where you can buy handmade souvenirs and watch artisans build the model boats for which Bequia is famous. A range of lodging possibilities and congenial nightlife attracts visitors who can stay awhile.

Lodging

For price categories, *see* the chart *under* Lodging *in* St. Vincent, *above*.

$$$$ 🏨 **Plantation House.** The peach-color Plantation House, a former
★   colonial residence, is set on 20 manicured acres of grass and gardens on Admiralty Bay. The property is punctuated by swaying palms, alabaster statuary, and strategically placed hammocks and lounge chairs. Standard rooms are in 17 garden cabanas; each has a dressing room, twin beds, and veranda. Five deluxe rooms are in the second floor of the main building; two have verandas that overlook the bay. Five suites are in two beachfront cottages. Rooms are furnished with bamboo furniture and rich-textured fabrics in soft pastels and floral prints. Each room has a TV and a hair dryer. Buffet breakfast and candlelight dinners are served at the Verandah restaurant in the main house. The informal, beachfront Green Flash bar-restaurant serves lunch and is also a convivial gathering place in the evening. (For more details on both restaurants, ☞ **Plantation House** *in* Dining, *below*). Taxi-boat service to Princess Margaret Beach (a three-minute ride) is complimentary. ✉ *Admiralty Bay (Box 16),* ☎ *809/458–3425,* 🖷 *809/458–3612. 5 rooms, 5 suites, 17 cabanas. 2 restaurants, bar, air-conditioning, fans,*

in-room safes, minibars, room service, pool, tennis court, beach, dive shop, snorkeling, windsurfing, boating, waterskiing, shop, piano, baby-sitting, laundry service. AE, MC, V. MAP.

$$$ ⊞ **Friendship Bay Beach Resort.** This attractive, casual complex hugs a curve of white-sand beach and includes a sprawling white house on a hillside (with sweeping bay views) and a group of coral-stone accommodations on plant-filled grounds. Rooms are done in bright colors and have terraces with ocean views. The open-air ☞ **Spicy 'n' Herby** restaurant serves mainly seafood and Creole cuisine. On Saturday night, the beach bar hosts an extremely lively barbecue and jump-up; the bar's swing seats keep you upright even after a couple of those potent rum punches. If sailing is your pleasure, you can book a trip on the 160-ft, three-mast schooner, *Lady Ellen.* ⊠ *Friendship Bay (Box 9),* ☎ *809/458–3222,* ☎ *809/458–3840. 27 rooms, 1 suite. Restaurant, 2 bars, fans, room service, tennis court, volleyball, beach, dive shop, snorkeling, windsurfing, boating, waterskiing, shop, baby-sitting, laundry service, meeting room. AE, MC, V. CP, MAP.*

$$$ ⊞ **Old Fort Country Inn.** This secluded inn—a stone, castlelike estate house that was built by the French 200 years ago—has a stunning setting on a seaside cliff. Rooms have panoramic Grenadine vistas—you can see as far as Grenada on a clear day—as well as cooling trade-wind breezes (no need for air-conditioning here). There are only six units, all with kitchen facilities; the decor of chunky hardwoods and exposed stone is a cross between Captain Bligh's cabin and a Provençal farmhouse. Because the nearest beach, Ravine, is nearly 450 ft below and is too rough for swimming, the inn is better for getaway purists than for those who want a lazy vacation base. The ☞ **Old Fort** restaurant is well worth the 10-minute trek into town by car. ⊠ *Mt. Pleasant,* ☎ *809/458–3440,* ☎ *809/457–3340. 6 rooms. Restaurant, bar, kitchenettes, pool, hiking. MC, V. CP, EP, MAP.*

$$–$$$ ⊞ **Spring on Bequia.** Serenity and seclusion reign at Spring on Bequia. It's nestled on the 20 acres of green hills that belong to the 200-year-old Spring Plantation, about 1 mi north of Port Elizabeth. (It's a pretty walk into town, but you may want to take a taxi back uphill.) The 10 large guest rooms are attractively designed in wood and stone; three of the rooms have been built on the foundation of the plantation's original great house. In the garden, there's an open-air bar and restaurant. Stroll down to the beach, and you'll pass the ruins of a sugar mill (now overgrown with colorful flowers), groves of tall palms, and grazing goats. The beach is shallow and occasionally seaweedy, but it's still refreshing. ⊠ *Spring Bay,* ☎ *809/458–3414,* ☎ *809/457–3305.* ⊠ *U.S. agent: Spring on Bequia (Box 19251), Minneapolis, MN 55419,* ☎ *612/823–1202. 10 rooms. Restaurant, bar, pool, tennis court. No credit cards. EP, MAP. Closed mid-June–Oct..*

$–$$ ⊞ **Frangipani Hotel.** The venerable Frangipani is an institution—partly
★ because its owner, Honorable James Mitchell, is long-time prime minister of SVG, and partly because its waterfront bar and its excellent ☞ **Frangipani** restaurant are favorites of the yachting crowd. The five, simple, inexpensive rooms in the original, shingle-sided sea captain's home are decorated in old West Indian style, with painted-wood walls and floors, grass rugs, simple furniture, and no air-conditioning; all but one share a bath. The more luxurious garden units are built of local stone and hardwoods and rise on a gentle slope that has flowering trees and bushes. Rooms in these units have tile floors with grass mats, louvered windows and doors, spacious modern baths and dressing rooms, and private verandas with spectacular sunset views of the yacht basin. In season, string bands appear on Monday night and folksingers on Friday night; the Thursday evening Frangi barbecue and steel-band jump-up is a must. You can arrange a day's sail aboard the hotel's 44-ft yacht,

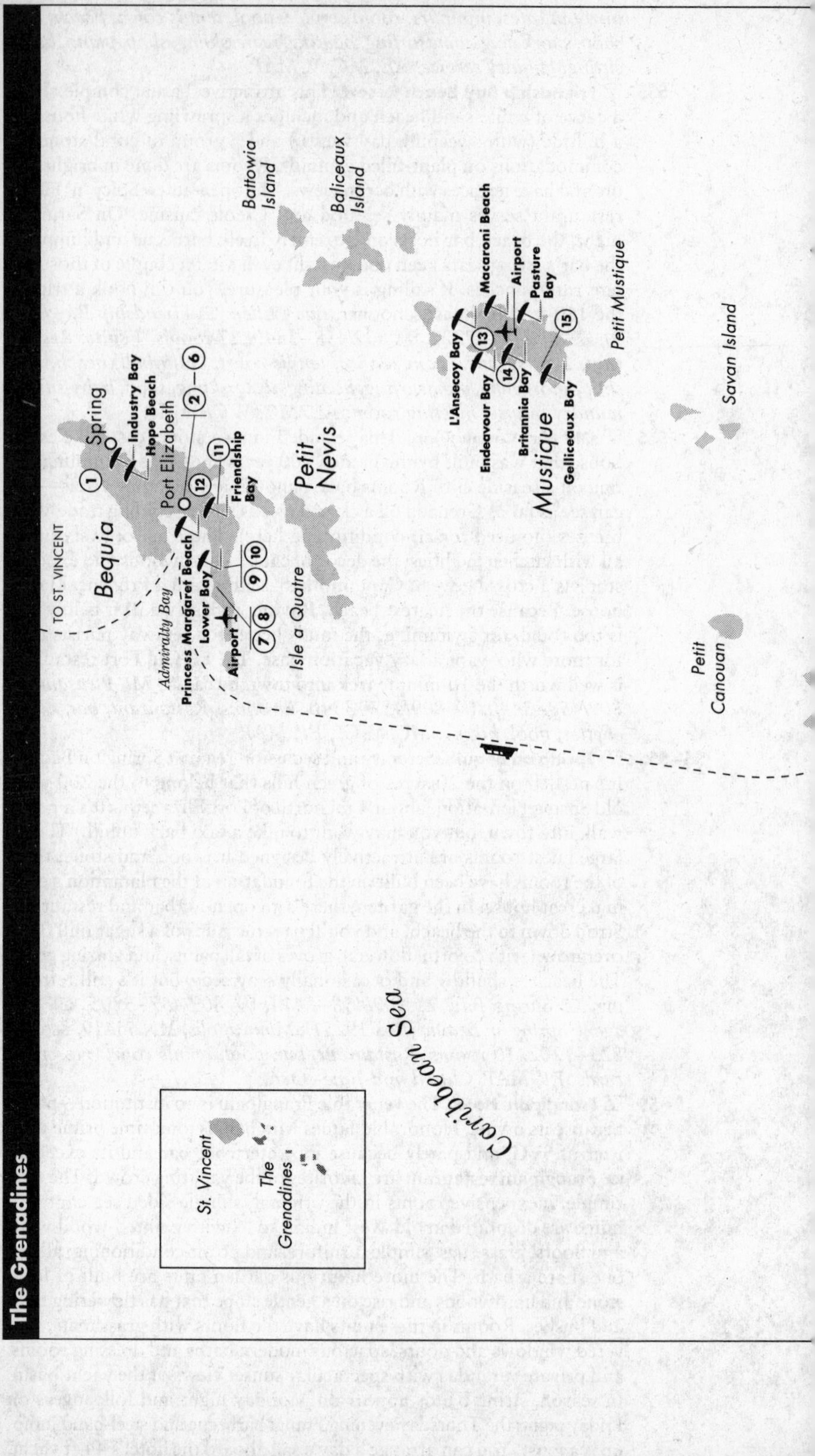

The Grenadines

TO ST. VINCENT

Spring ①

Bequia

Industry Bay
Hope Beach
Port Elizabeth
Admiralty Bay
Princess Margaret Beach
Lower Bay
Airport

② ⑥
⑫ ⑪
Friendship Bay
⑦ ⑧ ⑨ ⑩

Battowia Island

Baliceaux Island

Isle a Quatre

Petit Nevis

Macaroni Beach
Airport
Pasture Bay
L'Ansecoy Bay
Endeavour Bay
Britannia Bay
Gelliceaux Bay
⑬ ⑭ ⑮

Mustique

Petit Mustique

Savan Island

Petit Canouan

Caribbean Sea

St. Vincent

The Grenadines

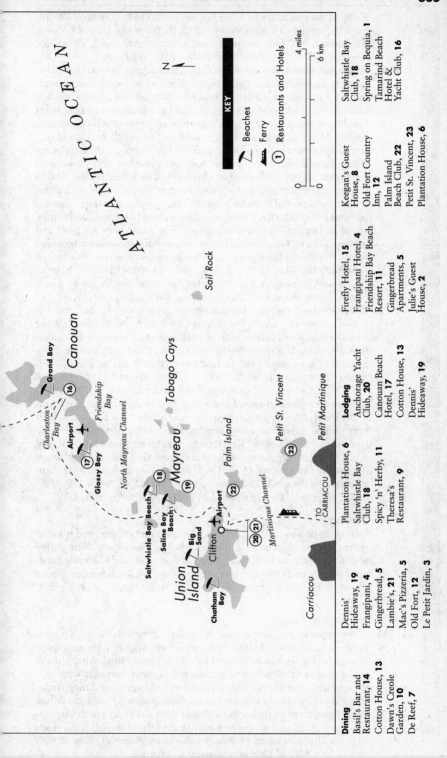

KEY

⚓ Beaches

⛴ Ferry

① Restaurants and Hotels

0 ——— 4 miles
0 ——— 6 km

Dining

Basil's Bar and
Restaurant, **14**
Cotton House, **13**
Dawn's Creole
Garden, **10**
De Reef, **7**
Dennis'
Hideaway, **19**
Frangipani, **4**
Gingerbread, **5**
Lambie's, **21**
Mac's Pizzeria, **5**
Old Fort, **12**
Le Petit Jardin, **3**

Plantation House, **6**
Saltwhistle Bay
Club, **18**
Spicy 'n' Herby, **11**
Theresa's
Restaurant, **9**

Lodging

Anchorage Yacht
Club, **20**
Canouan Beach
Hotel, **17**
Cotton House, **13**
Dennis'
Hideaway, **19**

Firefly Hotel, **15**
Frangipani Hotel, **4**
Friendship Bay Beach
Resort, **11**
Gingerbread
Apartments, **5**
Julie's Guest
House, **2**

Keegan's Guest
House, **8**
Old Fort Country
Inn, **12**
Palm Island
Beach Club, **22**
Petit St. Vincent, **23**
Plantation House, **6**

Saltwhistle Bay
Club, **18**
Spring on Bequia, **1**
Tamarind Beach
Hotel &
Yacht Club, **16**

Pelangi; the cost is about $200 per day for up to four people. ⊠ *Admiralty Bay (Box 1),* ☎ *809/458–3255,* ⨳ *809/458–3824. 15 rooms. Restaurant, bar, fans, room service, tennis court, beach, dive shop, snorkeling, boating, shop, baby-sitting. MC, V. EP.*

$–$$ 🏠 **Gingerbread Apartments.** The Gingerbread complex—so-named be-
★ cause of the West Indian gingerbread details on its facade—sits on Admiralty Bay's busy waterfront. Owner Pat Mitchell has added a building with six luxurious suites to the three original apartments in her main building. These newer units are large, modern, and stylishly decorated, with bedroom alcoves, adjoining salons, and full kitchens. Downstairs rooms have twin beds and large porches that overlook the bay; upper rooms have king-size four-poster beds and verandas with views of all the harbor activity. Each suite has a built-in bed for a third person. Rooms are decorated and furnished in a sophisticated tropical style, with terra-cotta tiles imported from Italy on the floors; blue-and-white, geometric-print bed quilts; sheer mosquito netting gathered over beds; and natural wood and rattan furniture throughout. The bathrooms are large and modern. The ☞ Gingerbread restaurant, upstairs in the main building, serves full meals; for snacks, head to the café at the water's edge. ⊠ *Admiralty Bay (Box 1),* ☎ *809/458–3800,* ⨳ *809/458–3907. 9 suites. Restaurant, bar, café, ice cream parlor, fans, kitchenettes, tennis court, beach, 2 dive shops, snorkeling, boating, baby-sitting. MC, V. EP.*

$ 🏠 **Julie's Guest House.** This unpretentious pink-stucco guest house is a block from the water. Furnishings are spare and simple, but the rooms are airy and bright, with private baths and bay-view balconies. If you're content with simply having a clean, comfortable room, foregoing the trappings of a full-fledged resort, then this is the place. ⊠ *Admiralty Bay (Box 12),* ☎ *809/458–3304 or 809/458–3323;* ⨳ *809/457–3812. 20 rooms. Restaurant, bar, laundry service. D, MC, V. EP.*

$ 🏠 **Keegan's Guest House.** Here you'll find budget accommodations and a quiet, friendly atmosphere—all just yards from the beach. This *very* simple guest house has comfortable single, double, and triple rooms, and family-style West Indian breakfasts and dinners if you wish. The least-expensive rooms share a bath that only has cold water (you really can get used to it). There's also a two-bedroom apartment available by the week. ⊠ *Lower Bay,* ☎ *809/458–3254 or 809/458–3530. 11 rooms. Dining room, bar, beach. No credit cards. EP.*

Dining

Dining on Bequia ranges from casual to gourmet cuisine, and it's consistently good. Barbecues at Bequia's hotels mean spicy West Indian seafood, chicken, or beef, plus a buffet of side salads and vegetable dishes and sweet desserts. Restaurants are occasionally closed Sunday; phone ahead. For price categories, *see* the chart *under* Dining *in* St. Vincent, *above.*

CARIBBEAN/CREOLE

$$–$$$ ✗ **Frangipani.** Just before sunset, sailors come ashore from yachts
★ bobbing in Admiralty Bay to relax and dine at, arguably, the most popular gathering spot in Bequia—the ☞ **Frangipani Hotel.** After a drink and a chat at the beachfront bar, the mood turns romantic with candlelight and excellent Caribbean cuisine in the open-air dining room. The à la carte menu is extensive but emphasizes seafood and local dishes. Each night, there's a three-course dinner special. Frangi's barbecue buffet (about $25) and jump-up, with live steel-band music, is the place to be on Thursday night. ⊠ *Belmont Walkway, Admiralty Bay,* ☎ *809/458–3255. MC, V. Dinner reservations essential.*

$$–$$$ ✗ **Old Fort.** Otmar and Sonja Schaedle, owners of the ☞ **Old Fort Country Inn,** restored this mid-1700s estate to its current bougainvillea-shaded, stone-arched, candlelit beauty and continue to serve food good enough to attract nonhotel guests to the castlelike atmosphere with one of the best views—and coolest breezes—on the island. At lunch take in the view while feasting on pumpkin or callaloo soup, omelets, crepes, sandwiches, salads, or pasta. At dinner, cool breezes complement the French Creole cuisine, which includes such dishes as spring lamb, tuna steak, langouste Grenadines, or char-grilled whole snapper, accompanied by fresh, homemade bread and a curry of pigeon peas. ⊠ *Old Fort Country Inn, Mt. Pleasant,* ☎ *809/458–3440. Reservations essential. MC, V.*

$–$$ ✕ **Dawn's Creole Garden.** The walk uphill to the Creole Garden Hotel is worth it for the delicious West Indian food and the view. For lunch there's fresh mutton, "goat water" (a savory soup, with bits of goat meat and spices), and fresh fish and conch dishes; the five-course Creole dinners feature the christophene and breadfruit accompaniments for which Dawn's is known. Barbecue is always available on request. There's live guitar music most Saturday nights. ⊠ *Lower Bay,* ☎ *809/ 458–3154. Dinner reservations essential. AE, MC, V.*

$–$$ ✕ **De Reef.** This café-restaurant on Lower Bay is the primary feeding station for long, lazy beach days. When the café closes at dusk, the restaurant takes over—if you've made reservations, that is. For breakfast (from 7 AM) or light lunch, the café bakes its own breads, croissants, coconut cake, and cookies—and blends fresh juices to accompany them. For a full lunch or dinner, conch, lobster, whelks, and shrimp are treated the West Indian way, and the mutton curry is famous. Every other Saturday in season, there's a seafood buffet dinner accompanied by live music. Sunday lunch is always popular. ⊠ *Lower Bay,* ☎ *809/458–3484. Dinner reservations essential. No credit cards.*

$ ✕ **Theresa's Restaurant.** Just steps from the beach, this simple local restaurant is full of color and character. Take a break during the day, sit outside under the grass roof, and enjoy a snack, sandwich, or burger. On Monday night, owners Theresa and John Bennett offer a rotating Greek, Indian, Mexican, or Italian buffet—regardless of the cuisine, the spread is enormous and the food is tasty. West Indian dishes are served at lunch and dinner the rest of the week. Vegetarian dishes are a specialty and are always available. ⊠ *Lower Bay,* ☎ *809/ 458–3802. Dinner reservations essential. No credit cards.*

CONTINENTAL

$$$–$$$$ ✕ **Plantation House.** At the posh ☞ Plantation House hotel, dinner is served nightly (except Saturday) at the Verandah restaurant, where menu selections reflect international cuisine presented with a local flair. Specialties include fresh seafood and regional vegetables. On Saturday evening, check out the barbecue buffet at the Green Flash waterfront restaurant. This feast includes a variety of barbecued meats and fish, side salads, vegetable dishes, and an excellent array of pastries. A pianist plays during dinner hours at the Verandah, and a local band provides entertainment at the Saturday barbecues. ⊠ *Plantation House Hotel, Admiralty Bay,* ☎ *809/458–3425. AE, MC, V.*

ECLECTIC

$$ ✕ **Gingerbread.** This airy, upstairs dining room at the ☞ Gingerbread Apartments overlooks Admiralty Bay and all the waterfront activity. The lunch crowd can enjoy barbecued beef or chicken kebabs with fried potatoes or onions, grilled fish, homemade soups, salads and sandwiches. In the evening, steaks, seafood, and curries are specialties of the house. Save some room for homemade desserts; including, of course, warm, fresh gingerbread—served here with lemon sauce. In season, dinner is often accompanied by music. ⊠ *Belmont Walkway, Admiralty Bay,* ☎ *809/458–3800. MC, V. Dinner reservations essential.*

$$ ✕ **Spicy 'n' Herby.** The open-air restaurant at ☞ Friendship Bay Beach Resort is smack against the beach and is perfect for lunch (sandwiches and bar snacks are always available) or dinner. Evening specials appear on a blackboard next to the busy bar and might include grilled fish with rice, jerk chicken with fries, or rack of lamb with a baked potato. The menu emphasizes fresh seafood, often prepared with an Asian or Swedish twist (the owners and the chef are Swedish). ✉ *Friendship Bay,* ☎ *809/458–3222. AE, MC, V.*

FRENCH

$$–$$$ ✕ **Le Petit Jardin.** The chef-proprietor at this chalet-style restaurant pre-
★   pares gourmet lobster and fish dishes using West Indian ingredients and following French methods and recipes. If you're missing your ration of prime beef, the house specialty is steak imported from the United States, which you can wash down with a bottle of wine from the longer-than-average list. Classical music enhances the ambience. ✉ *Port Elizabeth,* ☎ *809/458–3318. Reservations essential. AE, D, MC, V.*

PIZZA

$–$$ ✕ **Mac's Pizzeria.** Overheard at the dock in Mustique: "We're sailing
★   over to Bequia for pizza." The two-hour sunset sail to Admiralty Bay is worth the trip for Mac's pizza. Choose from 14 mouthwatering toppings (including lobster); or select quiche, pita sandwiches, lasagna, or soups and salads. Mac's home-baked cookies and muffins are great for dessert or a snack. The outdoor terrace offers fuchsia bougainvillea and water views. ✉ *Belmont Walkway, Admiralty Bay, Port Elizabeth,* ☎ *809/458–3474. Dinner reservations essential. No credit cards.*

Beaches

Bequia offers some beautiful, clean, uncrowded, white-sand beaches. Some are within a short walk of the jetty at Port Elizabeth; others require transportation.

Friendship Bay can be reached by land taxi. At Friendship Bay Resort, on the beach, you can rent windsurfing and snorkeling equipment and grab a bite to eat or a cool drink. **Hope Beach,** on the Atlantic side, is accessible by a long taxi ride (about $7.50—every driver knows how to get there) and a mile-long walk downhill on a semipaved path. Your reward is a magnificent crescent of white sand, total seclusion, and— if you prefer—nude bathing. Be sure to ask your taxi driver to return at a prearranged time. Bring your own lunch and drinks; there are no facilities. Even though the surf is fairly shallow, swimming can be dangerous because of the undertow. **Industry Bay** boasts towering palm groves, a nearly secluded beach. This is a good beach for snorkelers, but there could be a strong undertow. Industry Bay is on the northeast side of the island and requires transportation from Port Elizabeth. Bring a picnic; the nearest facilities are at Spring on Bequia resort, a 10- to 15-minute walk from the beach. **Lower Bay,** a wide, palm-fringed beach that can be reached by taxi or hiking beyond Princess Margaret Beach, is an excellent location for swimming and snorkeling. There are facilities to rent water-sports equipment here, as well as De Reef restaurant. **Princess Margaret Beach,** which is quiet and wide and has a natural stone arch at one end, is a ½ hour walk over rocky bluffs from the Plantation House Hotel on Admiralty Bay. Though it has no facilities, it's a popular spot for swimming, snorkeling, or simply relaxing under palm and sea-grape trees.

Outdoor Activities and Sports

BOATING AND SAILING

With regular trade winds, visibility for 30 mi, and generally calm seas, Bequia is a center for some of the best blue-water sailing opportunities you'll find anywhere in the world. There are all kinds of options: day sails or weekly charters, bareboat or fully crewed, single hulls or catamarans—whatever your pleasure.

The 60-ft catamaran **Passion** (⊠ Belmont, ☎ 809/458–3884), custombuilt for day sailing, offers all-inclusive, daylong trips from Bequia to Mustique, the Tobago Cays, and St. Vincent's Falls of Baleine. It's also available for private charter. **Meteor** can be chartered through Bequia Yacht Charter, at the Friendship Bay Hotel (☎ 809/458–3222). **S. Y. Pelangi,** a 44-ft cutter, is available for day sails or longer charters through the Frangipani Hotel (☎ 809/458–3255); four guests can be accommodated comfortably, and the cost is $200 per day.

SCUBA DIVING AND SNORKELING

About 35 dive sites around Bequia and nearby islands are accessible within 15 minutes by boat. The leeward side of the 7-mi reef that fringes Bequia has been designated a marine park. The best dive sites are: Devil's Table, a shallow dive that's rich in fish and coral and has a sailboat wreck nearby at 90 ft; the Wall, a 90-ft drop off West Cay; the Bullet, off Bequia's north point, good for spotting rays, barracuda, and the occasional nurse shark; the Boulders for soft corals, tunnel-like rock formations, and thousands of fish; and Moonhole, shallow enough in places for snorkelers to enjoy. For snorkeling on your own, take a water taxi to the bay at Moonhole and arrange a pickup time.

Dive Bequia (⊠ Belmont Walkway, Admiralty Bay, ☎ 809/458–3504) at the Gingerbread complex in Port Elizabeth, offers dive and snorkel tours, night dives, and full equipment rental. Resort and certification courses are available. **Sunsports** (⊠ Belmont Walkway, Admiralty Bay, ☎ 809/458–3577), also at the Gingerbread complex in Port Elizabeth, is a full-service PADI facility, offering dives three times a day, instruction, equipment rental, and snorkeling trips. **Dive Paradise,** (⊠ Friendship Bay Beach Hotel, Friendship Bay, ☎ 809/458–3563) has two modern dive boats and offers dive packages and certified instruction for beginners and advanced divers, equipment rental, night and wreck dives, and snorkeling packages (but it doesn't take credit cards).

TENNIS

You'll find tennis courts at four island hotels: **Frangipani Hotel** (⊠ Admiralty Bay, ☎ 809/458–3255); **Friendship Bay Beach Resort** (⊠ Friendship Bay, ☎ 809/458–3222); **Plantation House** (⊠ Belmont Beach, ☎ 809/458–3425); and **Spring on Bequia** (⊠ Spring Bay, ☎ 809/458–3414). There are also **public tennis courts** adjacent to the Bequia airport.

Shopping

All Bequia's shops are on Front Street and its waterfront extension, Belmont Walkway, just steps away from the jetty where the ferry arrives in Port Elizabeth. On the north side, there's an open-air market. Farther along the road are the model boatbuilders' shops. Just opposite the jetty, at Bayshore Mall, a dozen or so shops sell ice cream, baked goods, stationery, gifts, and clothing; there's a liquor store, pharmacy, travel agent, and bank. On Belmont Walkway, to the south, there are interesting shops and workshops where you can buy gifts and handmade items. Shops are open weekdays 9–6, Saturday 8–noon.

HANDICRAFTS

Long renowned for their boatbuilding skills, Bequians have translated that craftsmanship to model boatbuilding. In their workshops in Port Elizabeth, you can watch as hair-thin lines are attached to delicate sails or individual strips of wood are glued together for decking. Other Bequian artisans work with fabric, designing or hand-painting it first and then creating clothing and gift items for sale.

Crab Hole (☎ 809/458–3290) sells hand-printed and batik fabric, clothing, and household items. You can see the fabrics being created (and even request your own designs) in the workshop behind the boutique. **Local Color** (☎ 809/458–3202), above The Porthole restaurant, has an excellent and unusual selection of handmade jewelry, wood carvings, and resort clothing. **Mauvin's Model Boat Shop** (☎ no phone) is where you can purchase handmade model boats (you can even special-order a replica of your own yacht) for which Bequia is known. They're incredibly detailed and quite expensive—from a few hundred to several thousand dollars. The simplest ones take about a week to make. **Melinda's by Hand** (☎ 809/458–3409) sells hand-painted cotton and silk clothing and accessories. **Sargeant Brothers Model Boat Shop,** is another location where you can buy a handmade model boat or commission one to be built for you. The shop is on Front St., a short walk from the jetty.

SOUVENIRS

Bequia Bookshop (☎ 809/458–3905) has an exhaustive selection of Caribbean literature, plus cruising guides and charts, Caribbean flags, beach novels, souvenir maps, and exquisite scrimshaw and whalebone penknives hand-carved by Bequian scrimshander Sam McDowell. **Noah's Arkade** (☎ 809/458–3424), has gifts, souvenirs, and contemporary arts and crafts from all over the Caribbean. **Solana's** (☎ 809/458–3554) offers attractive beachwear, *pareos* (sarong-like beach cover-ups), and handy plastic beach shoes.

Nightlife

Along the Admiralty Bay waterfront in **Port Elizabeth,** friendly land-lubbers and yachties gather around the bars at the **Frangipani** and **Gingerbread** hotels (☞ Lodging, *above*). There's usually a barbecue night, a weekly jump-up, and local string- or steel-band music.

Coco's Place (✉ Lower Bay, ☎ 809/458–3463) has live calypso on Sunday and a string band on Tuesday. **De Reef** (✉ Lower Bay, ☎ 809/458–3484) has a weekly jump-up.

Exploring Bequia

To see the views, villages, beaches, and boatbuilding sites around Bequia, hire a taxi at the jetty in Port Elizabeth. There are usually several lined up to meet the ferry from St. Vincent. Negotiate the fare in advance; the established rate is $15 per hour.

Charlie Leslie, a native of Bequia whose Scottish ancestors emigrated to the island several hundred years ago to manage sugar plantations, operates **Doc Taxi** (☎ 809/458–3382). In a couple of hours, he'll show you all the island sights, point out a good place for lunch, and drop you (if you wish) at a great beach for swimming and snorkeling.

Water taxis are available for transportation between the jetty in Port Elizabeth and the beaches. The cost is only a couple of dollars per person each way, but keep in mind that most of these operators are not insured. You ride at your own risk.

SIGHTS TO SEE

Admiralty Bay. This huge, sheltered bay, on the leeward side of Bequia, is a favorite anchorage of yachtsmen. Throughout the year, it's filled with boats; in season, they're moored, literally, cheek by jowl. It's the perfect spot for watching the sun dip over the horizon each evening—either from your boat or from the terrace bar of one of Port Elizabeth's bayfront hotels.

Belmont Walkway. This walkway meanders down the bayfront from the center of Port Elizabeth south to the Plantation House. Along the way are shops, cafés, restaurants, bars, and hotels. This is where you'll find the action.

Hamilton Battery. Just north of Port Elizabeth, high above Admiralty Bay, the battery was built to protect the harbor from 18th-century marauders. Today, it's a place to enjoy a magnificent view. **Mt. Pleasant.** Bequia's highest point (881 ft) is a reasonable goal for a hiking trek. It's also a pleasant drive. The reward is a stunning view of the island and surrounding Grenadines. **Port Elizabeth.** Bequia's capital is at the north end of Admiralty Bay. The ferry from St. Vincent docks at the jetty, in the center of the tiny town that's only a few blocks long and a couple of blocks deep. Walk north along Front Street, which faces the water, to the open-air market, where you can buy local fruits and vegetables and some handicrafts; farther along, you'll find the model boatbuilders' workshops (☞ Shopping, *above*) for which Bequia's is renowned.

Spring Plantation. The mile-long, uphill hike (or drive) to this plantation north of Port Elizabeth has its rewards. The ruins of its 19th-century sugar mill, along the roadside near the Spring on Bequia hotel, is a photo opportunity. There's also a beach here where you can take a refreshing swim before the walk back to town.

Whaling Museum. For a $2 admission, Athneal Olivierre, the old whaler himself, will show you around his one-room museum. His collection of whaling artifacts represent the lifetime career of this "last of Bequia's harpooners." Olivierre will tell you that even in this, his ninth decade, he still hunts for whales from a sailboat with a hand-held harpoon gun. Although a mainstay of the island economy in centuries past, whaling on Bequia is now more of a ritual. The Whaling Museum is in a tiny white and blue house on the waterfront in Paget Farm, on Bequia's south coast.

Whaling Station. From the front door of the Whaling Museum, you can see the whaling station on Petit Nevis, a small island just off the shore of Bequia. This is where the kill is slaughtered, packed up, and shipped out. A limit of three whales per year can be caught in Bequia's waters, but catching them is rare nowadays.

Canouan

Goat-herding is still a career possibility here. Half-way down the Grenadines chain, this tiny, boot-shape island—just 3½ mi long and 1¼ mi wide—has only about 1,000 residents; but it does have a modern airstrip with night-landing facilities. Canouan also claims some of the finest, most pristine, white-sand beaches in the Caribbean. Walk, loaf, swim, dive, or snorkel—these are your options. Roads are scarce, and taxis are rare; boats and shoe leather are the usual modes of transportation. So pack light.

Dining and Lodging

For price categories, *see* the chart *under* Lodging *in* St. Vincent, *above*.

$$$$ ✕▥ **Canouan Beach Hotel.** Perched on a beach that sticks out of the southwest end of the island, this hotel attracts French tourists most of the year. Simple white cottages with pastel roofs and trim have patios; most have ocean views. Catamaran day sails from the on-site marina are included in the rates. Twice a week, there's live music and dancing. ⊠ *S. Glossy Bay (Box 520)*, ☎ *809/458–8888*, ☒ *809/458–8875. 32 rooms. Restaurant, bar, air-conditioning, driving range, tennis*

court, volleyball, beach, dive shop, snorkeling, windsurfing, boating, shop. AE, MC, V. FAP.

$$$$ ✕🏨 **Tamarind Beach Hotel & Yacht Club.** Thatched-roofs are a trademark of this attractive hostelry on reef-protected Grand Bay Sandy Beach. Accommodations are in three large two-story buildings that face the beach. Rooms have natural wood walls and are decorated with rattan furniture; louvered wooden doors open onto a spacious veranda with lounge chairs and a beautiful Caribbean vista. Ceiling fans join with the trade winds to keep you cool. The alfresco Restaurant Palapa features fascinating Caribbean specialties, grilled meat or fish, pizzas and pasta, and international cuisine prepared by a European chef. Barbecues and themed dinners (Italian, French, and Caribbean menus) rotate throughout the week. Live Caribbean music is featured fairly regularly at the Pirate Cove bar. The resort's Frangipani Championship Golf Course, under construction at press time, adds an entirely new dimension to the Canouan sports scene. Tamarind Beach Hotel also has a 55-ft catamaran available for day sails. ⊠ *Charlestown,* ☎ *809/458–8044; 800/961–5006, or 800/223–1108 (reservations service),* 𝖥𝖠𝖷 *809/458–8851.42 rooms. Restaurant, 2 bars, ice cream parlor, fans, golf course, beach, dive shop, snorkeling, windsurfing, boating, fishing, shop, baby-sitting, meeting room. No credit cards. MAP.*

Beaches

Glossy Bay and other beaches along the southwest (windward) coast of Canouan are absolutely spectacular. To reach them, you cross a narrow ridge that runs the length of the island. **Grand Bay,** in the center of the leeward side, is the main beach and site of the jetty where the ferries dock.

Outdoor Activities and Sports

SCUBA DIVING AND SNORKELING

The mile-long reef and waters surrounding Canouan offer excellent snorkeling opportunities as well as spectacular dives for both novice and experienced divers. Gibraltar, a giant stone almost to 30 ft in depth, is a popular site; plenty of colorful fish and corals are visible. Tony Alongi, the owner-operator of **Dive Canouan** (⊠ Tamarind Beach Hotel, ☎ 809/458–8044 or 809/458–8234), offers dive and snorkel packages that include tours to the Tobago Cays. This full-service dive facility offers resort or certification courses.

Nightlife

Surprise: There's a bar with a disco on weekends at **Villa Le Bijou** (☎ 809/458–8025), a small guest house atop a hill 10 minutes (on foot) from Friendship Bay and 15 minutes from the airstrip.

Mayreau

Privately owned Mayreau (pronounced my-*row*) is minuscule—just 1½ square mi. Farm animals outnumber the 200 or so residents, and there are no proper roads. Except for water sports and hiking, there's not much to do, and visitors like it that way. To get to Mayreau, take a boat from Union Island.

Dining and Lodging

For price categories, *see* the chart *under* Lodging *in* St. Vincent, *above.*

$$$$ ✕🏨 **Saltwhistle Bay Club.** This small resort is so cleverly hidden within its 22 acres of manicured grounds that sailors need binoculars to be sure it's there at all. Gorgeous Saltwhistle Bay is a half-moon of crystal-clear water rimmed by ¾ mi of sparkling white, sandy beach—a favorite anchorage of touring yachtsmen. Each roomy stone cottage has a name such as Oleander or Ivora, and is decked out with wooden shut-

ters, ceiling fans, batiks on the walls, a selection of books, and a stone, circular shower that looks like a large, medieval telephone booth. You can dry your hair on the breezy, second-story veranda atop each two-room building. The outdoor dining area has stone tables—protected from sun and the occasional raindrop by thatched roofs—where you can enjoy turtle steak, duckling, lobster, and à la carte lunches. ⊠ *Saltwhistle Bay,* ☎ *809/458–8444,* FAX *809/458–8944. 10 cottages. Restaurant, bar, fans, Ping-Pong, volleyball, beach, dive shop, snorkeling, windsurfing, boating, baby-sitting. MC, V. FAP. Closed Oct.*

$ ✕🔲 **Dennis' Hideaway.** Dennis (who plays guitar two nights a week) is a charmer, the seafood is great, the drinks are strong, and the view is heaven. The rooms in the guest house are clean but very simple: a bed, a nightstand, a chair, a private bath, and a place to hang some clothes. ⊠ *Saline Bay,* ☎ FAX *809/458–8944. 7 rooms. Restaurant, bar, air-conditioning. No credit cards. EP.*

Beaches

Saline Bay Beach is beautiful, but there are no facilities. The dock here is where the tender from the mail boat from St. Vincent (☞ Ferries, *below*) ties up. **Saltwhistle Bay Beach** takes top honors—it's an exquisite half-moon of powdery white sand, shaded by perfectly spaced palms and flowering bushes.

Outdoor Activities and Sports

HIKING

Hike 25 minutes over Mayreau's only hill (wear sturdy shoes; bare feet or flip-flops are a big mistake) to a good photo opportunity at the stone church in the hilltop village and stunning views of the Tobago Cays. Then have a drink at Dennis' Hideaway and enjoy a swim at Saline Bay Beach.

SCUBA DIVING AND SNORKELING

Saltwhistle Bay Club (☎ 809/458–8444) will arrange day trips by charter yachts to the cays or nearby islands for swimming, scuba diving, and snorkeling.

Mustique

Trendsetter Princess Margaret put this small, lush island, a former copra, cotton, and sugarcane estate, on the map after owner Colin Tennant (now Lord Glenconner) presented her with a plot of land in 1960 as a wedding gift. The Mustique Company, which Tennant formed in 1968 to develop the island into the glamorous hideaway it has become, now has 80 privately owned villas, housing for all island employees, and a house rentals department. Arrangements must be made about a year in advance to rent the royal holiday home or another of the luxury villas that pepper the northern half of the island. Mick Jagger and designer Tommy Hilfiger are among the glitterati who own villas here.

Sooner or later, star-gawkers will get to see whoever's "on island" at Basil's Bar, the island's social center. Basil also runs a boutique crammed with clothes and accessories specially commissioned from all over the world. A few steps away, in a pair of candy-color buildings that don't quite qualify as a village, there's a gift shop and clothing boutique. There's also a cornucopian delicatessen/grocery to stock yachts and feed residents fresh Brie and Moët and an antiques shop stocked with fabulous pieces for those fabulous houses.

Lodging

For price categories, *see* the chart *under* Lodging *in* St. Vincent, *above*.

HOTELS

$$$$ ⊞ **Cotton House.** The Mustique Company's world-class resort has been
★ built around the island's 18th-century plantation house and stone sugar
mill (now the boutique), which are the oldest structures on Mustique.
The main house's wraparound terrace functions as the lounge, bar, tea
room, ☞ **Cotton House** restaurant, and social center. A fantastic oceanfront suite and four oceanfront rooms ooze charm. Walkways from private terraces lead to the beach. A quartet of spacious, deluxe oceanview
suites have sunken baths, king-size beds with mosquito nets, and individual terraces with beautiful views. Three charming private cottages,
next to the pool, have balcony views of L'Ansecoy Bay. The remainder
are deluxe terrace rooms with sweeping views of hillside and ocean. Stone
walkways lead to the main house, which is decorated with original artwork and furnishings. The decor is sophisticated yet reflects Caribbean
simplicity and light—white walls and ceiling fans, antiques, and rattan
furniture. Rooms have dressing areas, French doors and windows, desks
with a selection of books, bathrooms with marble fittings, a choice of
bed pillows, and perfect peace. Airport transfers and an island tour are
included, as are water sports, tennis, and a driver who will chauffeur
you to ☞ **Basil's** restaurant or the beach. ⊠ *Endeavour Bay (Box 349),*
☎ *809/456–4777 or 800/223–1108 (reservations service),* FAX *809/
456–5887. 12 rooms, 5 suites, 3 cottages. Restaurant, 2 bars, air-conditioning, fans, in-room safes, minibars, pool, 2 tennis courts, horseback
riding, 2 beaches, dive shop, snorkeling, windsurfing, boating, shop, library, baby-sitting, meeting room, airport shuttle. AE, D, MC, V. FAP.*

$$$–$$$$ ⊞ **Firefly Hotel.** Tiny and charming with just four guest rooms, this
exclusive, reclusive aerie is wedged into the thick foliage on a hillside
above Britannia Bay. The views out to sea are panoramic. Rooms are
attractively appointed and have private baths. The restaurant serves
Caribbean cuisine, along with gourmet pizza and pasta dishes, in an
intimate, candlelit atmosphere. Swim in two pools connected by a wa-
terfall or pack a picnic and spend a day at the beach, just down the
(rather steep) garden path. Picnic equipment is provided in each room.
Arrangements can be made for scuba diving trips and other water sports
or to play tennis or horseback ride nearby. ⊠ *Britannia Bay (Box 349),*
☎ *809/458–3414,* FAX *809/456–4499. 4 rooms. Restaurant, bar, re-
frigerators, 2 pools. No credit cards. CP.*

VILLAS

$$$$ **Villa rentals** on Mustique are arranged solely through The Mustique
Company's House Rentals Department, even though the villas are pri-
vately owned. Renting one of these magnificent homes is not as ex-
pensive as you may think, since rates are per villa, not per person—and
they include a full staff (with a cook but without groceries), laundry
service, and a vehicle or two. Houses range from simple rusticity (if
you can call en-suite bathrooms for every bedroom, at least one phone
line, probably a pool, cable TV, VCR, CD player, and even fax, rus-
tic) to extravagant, expansive, faux-Palladian follies with resident but-
ler. All are designer-elegant and immaculately maintained. Villas
accommodate up to 12 guests. Rental rates start at $2,800 a week for
the two-bedroom Pelican Beach off-season and soar to $16,000 a
week for the palatial five-bedroom, five-person-staff, two-Jeep, one-
Jacuzzi Blackstone during winter. Princess Margaret's seven-bedroom
place is a mere $7,000 a week in summer. ⊠ *House Rentals Dept.,
The Mustique Co. Ltd., Box 349, St. Vincent and the Grenadines,* ☎
809/458–4621, FAX *809/456–4565. 43 villas. AE, DC, MC, V. FAP.*

Dining

For price categories, *see* the chart *under* Dining *in* St. Vincent, *above.*

SEAFOOD

$$$ ✕ **Cotton House.** Expect a world-class dining experience on the terrace
★ of the Great Room of the fine ☞ **Cotton House** resort. Executive Chef
Daniel Pochron and his staff whip up memorable dishes, pairing fresh
island ingredients with excellent wines. Each evening, a three-course
menu du jour is offered (priced at $40) or you can select from the mouth-
watering choices on the à la carte menu. Appetizers of conch Napoléon
with potato crisps and cucumber or tuna carpaccio with cucumber slaw
and candied ginger vinaigrette are every bit as tempting as the entrées—
which might include grilled barracuda with thyme-braised potatoes or
curry-rubbed chicken breast with coconut rice. A grilled vegetable
plate is always available. Homemade ice cream or sorbet may be
enough for dessert, if you can blink when the warm chocolate cake
with lava center is offered. Lunch is served on the terrace, by the pool
bar, or packed for you in a picnic basket. Pastas, sandwiches and light
fare are offered—the curried chicken salad in a whole wheat pita is
both elegant and filling. ⊠ *Endeavour Bay,* ☎ *809/456–4777. Reser-
vations essential. AE, D, MC, V.*

$–$$$ ✕ **Basil's Bar and Restaurant.** Basil's is *the* place to be, and only partly
★ because it is the *only* place to be aside from hotel restaurants. This rus-
tic eatery has a wooden deck built over the waves, a thatched roof, a
congenial bar, and a dance floor that's open to the stars—in every sense.
There's something about the atmosphere that hints at happenings.
You never know what recognizable face may show up at the next table.
The food is simple and good—mostly fish hauled from the water a hundred yards away, homemade ice cream, burgers and salads, great
French toast, the usual cocktails, and unusual wines. It's great to enjoy
a quiet breakfast or brunch watching the morning sunshine dance on
the water. Wednesday is barbecue and party night; on Monday, there's
live music. ⊠ *Britannia Bay,* ☎ *809/458–4621. AE, MC, V.*

Beaches

Macaroni Beach is Mustique's most famous stretch of fine white
sand— offering "surfy" swimming (no lifeguards) in water that's several shades of blue—with a few palm huts and picnic tables in a shady
grove of trees. **L'Ansecoy Bay,** at the island's very northern tip, is a
crescent of white sand with brilliant turquoise water. **Endeavour Bay,**
on the northwest coast, is where the Cotton House is located. There's
a dive shop and water-sports equipment rental available. **Britannia Bay**
is best for day-trippers, since it's next to the jetty, and Basil's Bar is
convenient for lunch. **Gelliceaux Bay,** on the southwest coast, is a good
beach for snorkelers. Swimming is dangerous at **Pasture Beach,** on the
Atlantic side.

Outdoor Activities and Sports

Water-sports facilities are available at the Cotton House, and most villas have equipment of various sorts. Four communal flood-lit tennis
courts are near the airport for those whose villa lacks its own, a cricket
ground for the Brits, and motorbikes or "mules" (beach buggies) to
ride around the bumpy roads, rent for $45 per day.

HORSEBACK RIDING

Mustique is one of the few islands where you can rent a fine horse.
Daily excursions leave from the **Equestrian Centre** (⊠ 1 block from the
airport, ☎ 809/458–4316). Rates are $50 per hour for an island trek,
$60 per hour for a surf ride, and $45 per hour for lessons. All rides
are accompanied, and children over 5 years are allowed to ride.

SCUBA DIVING AND SNORKELING

Basil's Bar (☎ 809/458–4621) arranges scuba diving and snorkeling
trips and rents equipment. You can also arrange scuba diving excur-

sions, instruction, and certification through **Mustique Watersports** (⊠ Cotton House, ☎ 809/456–4777). Rates are $60 for a one-tank dive, with multidive packages available.

Palm Island

A private speck of land, Palm Island has wide, white-sand beaches and a very casual resort. Access is through Union Island, 1 mi to the west; you're picked up by the resort launch for the 10-minute boat ride.

Dining and Lodging

For price categories, *see* the chart *under* Lodging *in* St. Vincent, *above.*

$$$$ 🏨 **Palm Island Beach Club.** An intrepid American sailor, his Australian-born wife, and his two sons sailed the world's oceans for 15 years until they settled on swamp-ridden, mosquito-infested Prune Island in the Grenadines. The family toiled for more than 25 years, planting palm trees and transforming the island into Palm Island Beach Club. You can read all about it over tea, delivered at 4 PM to your cabana terrace. Some cabanas offer a private sunset view over Casuarina Beach through room-width patio doors. Bathrooms aren't the greatest, with dribbly yet scenic outdoor showers in the newer cabanas, but balanced against that is the staff's genuine warmth. Food is important when you're a captive audience; the island buffets and full-service dinners are just fine, and the pastry chef makes breakfast worth getting up for. Adjacent to the hotel is a separate yacht club, the only change of scene apart from a jog on what's amusingly referred to here as Highway 90 (1¼ mi around) or a day sail to the Tobago Cays. Windsurfers, Sunfish, and floats are complimentary. Leave your fancy clothes at home—this is a really casual place—and plan on busy, active days. Nightlife is practically nil but for Wednesday and Saturday barbecues with calypso music—in season. ⊠ *Palm Island,* ☎ *809/ 458–8824 or 800/999–7256 (reservations service),* 🅵🅰🆇 *809/458– 8804. 24 cottages. Restaurant, bar, grocery, tennis court, jogging, beach, dive shop, snorkeling, windsurfing, boating, fishing, recreation room, baby-sitting. AE, MC, V. FAP.*

Petit St. Vincent

The southernmost of St. Vincent's Grenadines, tiny PSV could also be dubbed "Private" St. Vincent. It's ringed with white-sand beaches and covered with beautiful tropical foliage. Guests are treated royally at the one classy, secluded resort. To get here, you fly into Union Island, where the resort's motor launch meets you for the 30-minute trip.

Dining and Lodging

For price categories, *see* the chart *under* Lodging *in* St. Vincent, *above.*

$$$$ ✕🏨 **Petit St. Vincent.** On this very special 113-acre private island, you can indulge in shipwreck fantasies without foregoing the frozen mango daiquiri at sunset, room-service breakfast, the skills of a great chef, and so on. Each of the 22 U-shape cottages has a bedroom, a sitting room, and one or two bathrooms—all around a big, partly covered wooden deck. Floors are tiled with grass mats. Walls are stone and—on two sides—glass, with patio doors that slide away entirely, giving you trade winds for a lullaby. Despite their rustic appearance, with copra matting vanities and cobblestone shower stalls, bathrooms conceal fabulous toiletries, robes, beach bags, towels, and an iron—and they have American-style 110-volt, two-prong outlets, so you don't need transformers. No house is more than a five-minute walk from dinner, yet each is completely private, with a system of signal flags to convey whims to the staff (who outnumber guests two to one). Hoist your red flag, and nobody *dreams* of approaching; hoist the yellow, and you can have lunch or dinner, tea or drinks, a ride to the jetty, or a picnic for a day on the "West End" promptly delivered. Some prefer the houses that fringe the windward beach, others like the distant trio high up on the bluff, and still others swear by the three perched above the Atlantic surf, with stone steps to the beach. ⊠ *PSV, Box 12506, Cincinnati, OH 45212,* ☎ *809/458–8801; 513/242–1333 or 800/654–9326 (reservations service) ,* FAX *809/458– 8428. 22 cottages. Dining room, beach, tennis, snorkeling, boating. AE, MC, V. FAP. Closed Sept.–Oct.*

Union Island

Gorgeous from a distance, the jagged peaks of Union Island's Mt. Parnassus soar 900 ft. Although Union is a popular stopping-off point for yachtspeople and others heading to the smaller islands just minutes away by speedboat, it doesn't offer the charm of other Grenadines. The main town, Clifton, is small and commercial, with a bustling harbor, three simple beachfront inns, a few restaurants, and shops that cater to yachts. The airstrip is also in Clifton, right behind the Anchorage Yacht Club. Taxis and minibuses are available.

Lodging

For price categories, *see* the chart *under* Lodging *in* St. Vincent, *above.*

$$ 🏨 **Anchorage Yacht Club.** Between the airstrip and a small beach are comfortably furnished seaside rooms and beach bungalows with concealed outdoor showers and terraces that offer great bay views. Grounds are attractive, with flower gardens, palm trees, and a large fish pool. You'll find water-sports and yacht-chartering opportunities galore. The full-service marina creates a cosmopolitan buzz throughout the resort. Rates include breakfast at Les Pieds dans l'Eau, the adjoining restaurant, which also serves a barbecue lunch and French and Creole cuisine at dinner. There's a pizza and sandwich counter as well. Each night, guests and stranded sailors are serenaded by steel-band, reggae, or piano music in the bar. ⊠ *Clifton,* ☎ *809/458–8221,* FAX *809/458– 8365. 10 rooms, 6 bungalows. Restaurant, bar, air-conditioning, beach, dock, snorkeling, boating, fishing, shop. MC, V. CP, MAP, FAP.*

Dining

For price categories, *see* the chart *under* Dining *in* St. Vincent, *above.*

CARIBBEAN/CREOLE

$–$$ ✕ **Lambie's.** On the waterfront in Clifton, enjoy Lambie's specialty— delicious conch Creole. Lambie means conch in Creole patois, and the restaurant's walls are even constructed from conch shells. The menu also offers other local seafood as well as grilled meats. Upstairs dining is slightly more formal; downstairs, it's strictly casual. There's steel-band music every night in season. ⊠ *Clifton,* ☎ *809/458–8549. No credit cards.*

Beaches

Union has relatively few good beaches, but the trek to **Big Sand,** on the north shore, is worth the effort. The beach around **Clifton Harbour** is narrow, unattractive, rocky, and shadeless. The desolate but lovely **Chatham Bay** offers good swimming.

Outdoor Activities and Sports

BOATING AND SAILING

Union considers itself the center of the southern Grenadines and is a good base for yacht charters and sailing trips. At **Anchorage Yacht Club** (⊠ Clifton, ☎ 809/458–8647), you can arrange crewed yacht or sailboat charters for day sails to the Tobago Cays, or longer trips around the Grenadines. The marina is also a good place to stock up on fresh-baked bread and croissants, ice, water, food, and other boat supplies.

SCUBA DIVING AND SNORKELING

Grenadines Dive (⊠ Sunny Grenadines Hotel, Clifton, ☎ 809/458–8138), run by NAUI instructor Glenroy Adams, offers Tobago Cays snorkeling trips and wreck dives at the *Purina,* a sunken World War I English gunship.

ST. VINCENT AND THE GRENADINES A TO Z

Arriving and Departing

BY AIRPLANE

Most U.S. visitors fly via **American Airlines** (☎ 809/456–5000) into San Juan, Puerto Rico, then fly **American Eagle** (☎ 809/456–5000) nonstop to St. Vincent's E. T. Joshua Airport. Alternate connections can be made through Barbados, St. Lucia, or Grenada. Other airlines with connections to St. Vincent are: **BWIA** (☎ 809/627–2942); **British Airways** (☎ 809/952–3124) from Jamaica; **Air Canada** (☎ 246/428–5077) from Barbados; and **Air France** (☎ 05/90–826–000 in Guadeloupe; 05/96–553–333 in Martinique).

Regional carriers fly between St. Vincent and Bequia, Mustique, Canouan, or Union, which each have an airstrip. Other destinations in the Grenadines require a boat ride on either a scheduled ferry, a chartered boat, or a hotel launch.

Interisland air carriers are: **Air Martinique** (☎ 809/458–4528); **HelenAir** (☎ 809/458–4528); **LIAT** (Leeward Islands Air Transport, ☎ 809/457–1821 or 809/458–4841; 212/251–1717 in the U.S.); **Mustique Airways** (☎ 809/458–4380), which operates the twice-daily **Bequia Shuttle,** serving St. Vincent, Bequia, and Canouan; and **SVG AIR** (☎ 809/456–5610, 809/456–4942, or 809/457–2364). Delays are common on interisland flights but usually not outrageous.

From the Airport: Taxis and buses are readily available at St. Vincent's E. T. Joshua Airport. A taxi from the airport to hotels in either Kingstown or the Villa Beach area costs about $5.50–$7.50 (EC$15–EC$20); bus fare is less than 50¢ (EC$1). If you have a lot of luggage, take a taxi—buses (actually minivans) are usually full with passengers. Taxis and buses are available, but rarer, on those Grenadine islands with airstrips.

Electricity

Electricity is generally 220/240 volts, 50 cycles. Some resorts also have 110-volt current (U.S. standard); most have 110-volt shaver outlets. Dual-voltage computers or small appliances will still require a plug adapter. Some hotels will let you borrow transformers to convert voltage and plug adapters during your stay.

Emergencies

ST. VINCENT

Ambulance/fire/police: ☎ 999. **Coast Guard:** ☎ 809/457–4578. **Hospital:** Kingstown General Hospital (☎ 809/456–1185). **Pharmacies:** Davis Drugmart (⊠ Tyrrell and McCory Sts., Kingstown, ☎ 809/456–1174). Deane's (⊠ Halifax St., Kingstown, ☎ 809/457–2056). Medix Pharmacy (⊠ Grenville St., Kingstown, ☎ 809/456–2989), or People's Pharmacy (⊠ Bedford St., Kingstown, ☎ 809/456–1170).

THE GRENADINES

Ambulance/fire/police: ☎ 999 on Bequia, ☎ 809/458–8227 on Union Island. **Hospitals:** Bequia Casualty Hospital (✉ Port Elizabeth, ☎ 809/458–3294).Canouan Clinic (☎ 809/458–8305). Mustique Co. Island Clinic (☎ 809/458–4621, ext. 353), and Union Island Health Centre (☎ 809/458–8339). **Pharmacy:** Imperial Pharmacy (✉ Back St., Port Elizabeth, ☎ 809/458–3373).

Festivals and Seasonal Events

In St. Vincent, the **National Music Festival** is held at Kingstown's Memorial Hall during late February and early March. The best in Vincentian music and song is presented—folk songs and calypso, solos and duets, choirs and group ensembles. **Fisherman's Day** (Labour Day, which falls on the first Monday in May), marks the end of a week's activities honoring the fisherman's contribution to the economy. All kinds of fishing competitions take place. **Vincy Mas,** St. Vincent's Carnival, is the biggest festival of the year, with street parades, costumes, calypso, steel bands, food and drink, and the crowning of Miss Carnival and the Soca Monarch. It begins in late June, builds in intensity through the first two weeks in July, and culminates in a calypso competition on the final Sunday (Dimanche Gras) and a huge street party (Jouvert) on the final Monday. The **National Dance Festival** is held in September each year at Kingstown's Memorial Hall, with presentations of traditional, folk, ballroom, ballet, and tap dancing. Arts and crafts exhibitions, caroling, and street parties with music and dancing mark the **Nine Mornings Festival,** which occurs during the nine days immediately before Christmas.

On Bequia, the **Easter Regatta** is held during the four-day Easter weekend. Revelers gather to watch boat races and celebrate Bequia's seafaring traditions with food, music, dancing, and competitive games. The **Bequia Carnival,** with calypso music and revelry, is a four-day celebration held in late June, just prior to St. Vincent's Carnival. On Canouan, the **Canouan Yacht Races** are held in August. Besides competitive boat races and sailing events, there are fishing contests, calypso competitions, donkey and crab races, and a beauty pageant. On Union, **Easterval** occurs during the Easter weekend. Festivities include boat races, sports and games, a calypso competition, a beauty pageant, and a cultural show featuring the Big Drum Dance (derived from French and African traditions). Union is one of the few islands (along with Grenada's Carriacou) that perpetuates this festive dance.

Getting Around

BUSES

Public buses are really privately owned, brightly painted minivans with names like *Easy Na, Irie,* and *Who to Blame.* Bus fares run 37¢– $2.25 on St. Vincent; for the 10-minute ride from Kingstown to Villa Beach, for example, the fare is 58¢. Buses operate from early morning until about midnight, and routes are indicated on a sign on the windshield. Just wave from the road, and the driver will stop. When you want to get out, signal by knocking twice on a window. A conductor usually rides along to open the door and collect fares; have the correct change in EC coins, if possible. In Kingstown, the bus terminal is near Market Square. Buses serve the entire island, although trips to remote villages are infrequent.

Bequia, Mustique, Canouan, Union, and some of the smaller Grenadine islands have taxi service. Bequia also has vans and small trucks with benches in back and canvas covers.

About 300 mi of paved road winds around St. Vincent, except for a significant section in the far north with no road at all, precluding a circle tour of the island. A handful of roads jut into the interior a few miles, and only one road (through the Mesopotamia Valley) bisects the island. It's virtually impossible to get lost. Be sure to drive on the left, and honk your horn before you enter blind curves out in the countryside—you'll encounter plenty of steep hills and hairpin turns. Roads are narrow in the countryside, often not wide enough for two cars to pass, and people (including school children), dogs, goats, and chickens often occupy such routes. Although major improvements are being made, roads are not always well marked or maintained. Outside populated areas, they can be bumpy and potholed; be sure your rental car has proper tire-changing equipment and a spare in the trunk.

Rental cars cost about $50–$55 per day or $300 a week, with some free miles. Gasoline costs $2.50 per (Imperial) gallon. Unless you already have an international driver's license, you'll need to buy a temporary local license for $15. You'll also need to present your valid driver's license. Temporary licenses are valid for six months, and you can get one at the airport, the police station on Bay Street, or the Licensing Authority on Halifax Street.

Car rental firms are all local operations. Among the firms on St. Vincent are: **Ben's Auto Rental** (⊠ Sharpe St., Kingstown, ☏ 809/456–2907), **David's Auto Clinic** (⊠ Sion Hill, just south of Kingstown, ☏ 809/456–4026), **Kim's Rentals** (⊠ Grenville St., Kingstown, ☏ 809/456–1884), **Star Garage** (⊠ Grenville St., Kingstown, ☏ 809/456–1743), and **UNICO Auto Rentals,** (⊠ Airport, ☏ 809/456–5744). On Bequia: **Phil's Car Rental** (⊠ Port Elizabeth, ☏ 809/458–3304) or **Sunset View Rental,** (⊠ Road Hamilton, ☏ 809/458–3558).

All scheduled ferries leave St. Vincent from Grenadines Wharf in Kingstown. The *Discover St. Vincent and the Grenadines* booklet, available in hotels and at the airport, includes current interisland schedules and fares. Schedules are subject to change, so be sure to recheck times upon your arrival.

MV Admiral I and **MV Admiral II** (☏ FAX 809/458–3348) make four round-trips between Bequia and Kingstown each weekday, beginning at 7:30 AM in Bequia or 9 AM in St. Vincent; the latest departure each day is at 5 PM from Bequia or 7 PM from Kingstown. On Saturday, there are departures from Bequia at 6:30 AM or 5 PM; from Kingstown at 12:30 PM or 7 PM. The one-way trip takes 60 minutes and costs $4 ($4.75 on weekends and holidays).

MV Barracuda (☏ 809/456–5180) leaves St. Vincent on Monday and Thursday mornings, stopping in Bequia, Canouan, Mayreau, and Union Island. It makes the return trip Tuesday and Friday. On Saturday, it does the round-trip from St. Vincent to each island and return in a day. Including stopover time, the trip takes 3¼ hours from St. Vincent to Canouan ($5), 4½ hours to Mayreau ($6), and 5¼ hours to Union Island ($7.50).

MV Bequia Eagle (☏ 809/458–3212) makes two runs daily (except Sunday) between Kingstown and Bequia. **MV Bequia Express** (☏ 809/458–3472) travels between Kingstown and Bequia, making two or three trips daily, including holidays.

TAXIS

Fares are set by the government. Between Kingstown and the hotels and restaurants at Villa Beach, the one-way fare is about $7.50. To hire a taxi by the hour, the rate throughout St. Vincent and the Grenadines is about $15.

On some islands, most notably Bequia, water taxis can take you to and from the beaches for a couple of dollars each way. Keep in mind that these taxi operators are not insured. You travel at your own risk.

Guided Tours

Several operators offer sightseeing tours on land or by sea. Per-person prices range from $20 for a two-hour tour to St. Vincent's Botanical Gardens to $140 for a day sail to the Grenadines.

You can arrange informal land tours through taxi drivers, who double as knowledgeable guides. Your hotel or the tourism board can recommend someone. Always settle the fare first, in either U.S. or EC dollars. Expect to pay $15 per hour.

You can also arrange speedboat and sailing tours on both St. Vincent (at Villa Beach) and Bequia (at Port Elizabeth).

Baleine Tours (⌧ Villa Beach, St. Vincent, ☎ 809/457–4089) offers scenic coastal trips to the Falls of Baleine as well as charters to Bequia and Mustique, deep-sea fishing trips, and snorkeling excursions to the Tobago Cays. **Dive St. Vincent** (⌧ Young Island Dock, Villa Beach, St. Vincent, ☎ 809/457–4714) offers a day trip to the Falls of Baleine that includes a scenic voyage along the coast, snorkeling, and swimming at a black-sand beach. **Fantasea Tours** (⌧ Villa Beach, ☎ 809/457–4477) will take you by speedboat to Falls of Baleine, Bequia and Mustique, or to the Tobago Cays for snorkeling. **Grenadine Travel Co.** (⌧ Arnos Vale, St. Vincent, ☎ 809/458–4818) arranges air, sea, and land excursions throughout the islands. **Sam's Taxi Tours** (⌧ Cane Garden, ☎ 809/456–4338) offers half- or full-day tours of St. Vincent, as well as hiking tours to La Soufrière and scenic walks along the Vermont Nature Trails. Sam's also operates on Bequia, where a sightseeing tour includes snorkeling at Friendship Bay. **SVG Tours** (⌧ Kingstown, ☎ 809/457–4322) has several hiking itineraries on St. Vincent and sailing day-trips to the Grenadines.

Language

English is spoken throughout St. Vincent and the Grenadines. Although there's certainly a Caribbean lilt, you won't hear the Creole patois common on other islands that have a historical French presence. One term to listen for is "jump-up," in which case you can expect a party with plenty of music and dancing.

Money Matters

CURRENCY

Although U.S. dollars are accepted nearly everywhere, Eastern Caribbean currency (EC$) is preferred. The exchange rate at banks is approximately EC$2.70 to US$1; hotels and shops generally give a rate of EC$2.60 to US$1. Price quotes in shops are often given in both currencies. When you negotiate taxi fares, be sure you know which type of dollar you're agreeing on. Note: Prices quoted throughout this chapter are in U.S. dollars unless otherwise noted.

SERVICE CHARGES, TAXES, AND TIPPING

Hotels and restaurants generally add a 10-percent service charge to all bills. A government tax of 7% is added to all hotel and restaurant bills. If the 10-percent service charge has not been added to your hotel or restaurant bill, a gratuity at that rate is appropriate. Otherwise, tipping is expected only for special service. The departure tax from St. Vincent and the Grenadines is $7.50; children under 12 are exempt.

Opening and Closing Times

Banks are open weekdays 8–1, 2, or 3, Friday until 5. The branch of National Commercial Bank of St. Vincent at the airport is open Monday–Saturday 7–5. Bank branches on Bequia, Canouan, and Union are open Monday–Thursday 8–1 and Friday 8–5. Stores in Kingstown are open weekdays 8–4. Many close for lunch noon–1; Saturday hours are 8–noon.

HOLIDAYS

Banks, offices, and most shops close on the following public holidays in 1999: New Year's Day, St. Vincent and the Grenadines Day (Jan. 22), Good Friday (Apr. 2), Easter Monday (Apr. 5), Labour Day (first Monday in May), Whit Monday (May 24), August Monday (first Monday in August), Independence Day (Oct. 27), Christmas, and Boxing Day (Dec. 26).

Passports

U.S., Canadian, and U.K. travelers need a valid passport or a birth certificate with a raised seal along with a government-issued photo ID. All visitors must hold return or ongoing tickets.

Precautions

There's relatively little crime here, but don't tempt fate by leaving your valuables lying around or your room or your rental car unlocked. Also, be alert and mindful of your belongings around the wharf area in Kingstown; it's congested when passengers are disembarking from ferries. When taking photos of market vendors, private citizens, or homes, be polite enough to ask permission first and offer a gratuity for the favor. Water is safe to drink from the tap, and bottled water is generally available. Fresh fruits and vegetables from the market are safe to eat, but (as at home) you should wash them first. Cooked food purchased at the market, in small shops, or at village snackettes is wholesome and safe to eat.

Insects can be a minor problem on the beach during the day. When hiking and sitting outdoors in the evening, though, you'll be glad to have industrial-strength mosquito repellent. Sea urchins are spiny black sea creatures that sit on sand in shallow water. If you step on one, you can put away your dancing shoes. It's painful! Rubbing a little lime or an ammonia-based liquid on the wound may help. Beware of certain flora. The manchineel tree has little green apples that look tempting but are toxic. Even touching the sap of the leaves will cause an uncomfortable rash, and you should not take shelter beneath one during a rainstorm. Most manchineels on hotel grounds are marked with signs; on more remote islands, the bark may be painted with a red stripe. Hikers should watch for brazilwood trees and bushes, which look and act similar to poison ivy.

Telephones and Mail

The area code for St. Vincent and the Grenadines is expected to change from 809 to 784. Either area code may be used for one year following the changeover date, which had not been determined at press time. When you dial a local number, you can drop the 45 prefix; for local information, dial 118. International direct dialing is available throughout St. Vincent and the Grenadines; for international information, dial 115. Pay phones are best operated with a prepaid phone card, available from stores and usable on several Caribbean islands.

The General Post Office, on Halifax Street in Kingstown, is open daily 8:30–3; Saturdays 8:30–11:30. Airmail between St. Vincent and the United States may take about 10 days. Airmail postcards cost EC90¢; airmail letters cost EC$1.80 an ounce. When writing to a location in the Grenadines, the address on the envelope should always indicate the particular island name followed by "St. Vincent and the Grenadines." ZIP codes are not used.

Visitor Information

Before you go, contact the **St. Vincent and the Grenadines Tourist Office** (⊠ 801 2nd Ave., 21st floor, New York, NY 10017, ☎ 212/687–4981 or 800/729–1726, 𝖥𝖠𝖷 212/949–5946; ⊠ 6505 Cove Creek Pl., Dallas, TX 75240, ☎ 214/239–6451 or 800/235–3029, 𝖥𝖠𝖷 214/239–1002; ⊠ 32 Park Rd., Toronto, Ontario N4W 2N4, ☎ 416/924–5796, 𝖥𝖠𝖷 416/924–5844; ⊠ 10 Kensington Court, London W8 5DL, ☎ 0171/937–6570, 𝖥𝖠𝖷 0171/937–3611). Ask for a visitor's guide, which is filled with useful, up-to-date information. For tourist information about St. Vincent and the Grenadines on the Internet: www.vincy.com.

On St. Vincent, the **St. Vincent and the Grenadines Board of Tourism** (⊠ Box 834, Upper Bay St., Kingstown, ☎ 809/457–1502, 𝖥𝖠𝖷 809/456–2610) is in the Administrative Centre, close to the port. It's open weekdays 8–noon and 1–4:30. Satellite offices are on Bequia (⊠ At the wharf in Port Elizabeth, ☎ 809/458–3286), open daily 9–12:30 and 1:30–4 (except Sat. afternoon) and on Union (⊠ at the airstrip in Clifton, ☎ 809/458–8350), open daily 8–noon and 1–4. There's a tourist information desk with folders and brochures in the arrivals area of St. Vincent's E.T. Joshua Airport (☎ 809/458–4685) and one at the Grantley Adams International Airport on Barbados (☎ 246/428–0961).

24 Trinidad and Tobago

Updated by
JoAnn
Milivojevic

A mist rises from the valley below the veranda of Trinidad's Asa Wright Nature Preserve—the perfect perch from which to view the rain forest. Greenery grows on still more greenery; everything drips with life. A ranger spreads sliced bananas and pineapple on a table. In moments, small multicolored birds flock in, including one with a purple body and yellow feet. A pair of cackling parrots fly over head; nearby, iridescent hummingbirds beat their wings fervently—a momentary purr in a jungle of tweets and whistles.

From the beat of calypso and *soca* to the steady tapping of raindrops accompanied by birdsong, Trinidad and Tobago offer cultural and natural diversions that are refreshing, vivid, and alive. This two-island republic—T&T, as it's commonly called—is the southernmost link in the Antillean island chain, lying some 9 mi off the coast of Venezuela and safely outside the path of all those devastating Caribbean hurricanes. Both Trinidad and Tobago are more geologically akin to continental South America than they are to other Caribbean islands: Tobago's Main Ridge and Trinidad's Northern Range are believed to represent the farthest reaches of the Andes Mountains. But although the two islands are linked geographically and politically, in some ways they could not be more dissimilar.

Trinidad's growth arose out of oil prosperity—it remains one of the largest petroleum producers in the western hemisphere—which made it a prime destination for business travelers. They enjoyed the sophisticated shopping, restaurants, and hotels in the republic's lively capital, Port-of-Spain, partying late into the night to the syncopated steel-band sounds that originated in Trinidad.

In the mid-1980s the economy slumped along with oil prices, but Trinidad is now recovering with an influx of small businesses. Port-of-Spain is still one of the most active commercial cities in the West Indies. The cultural scene is as vital as ever, especially during the country's riotous Carnival—a period of festivities, concerts, and shows that begins after Christmas and culminates in a two-day street parade that ends on Ash Wednesday. The capital is home to around 51,000 of Trinidad's 1.3 million residents—Africans, Indians, Americans, Europeans, and Asians, each with their own language and customs (the official language is English, however). About a quarter of the population is Hindu, which is why there's an abundance of India festivals, religious celebrations, and delicious East Indian food. Outside Port-of-Spain you'll find good beaches and many other natural attractions, though there are currently few hotels that offer more than bare-bones comfort.

On Tobago, 22 mi away, the pace of life is slower, and seclusion is easier to find. Though a variety of seaside lodgings beckon, you can still lazily explore unspoiled rain forests, coral reefs, and a largely undeveloped coastline—for now, anyway. Tourism is a growing industry; plans include a 40% increase in the number of rooms by the year 2000. If this goes unchecked, Tobago could lose its idyllic quality.

Columbus reached these islands on his third voyage, in 1498. Three prominent peaks around the southern bay of Trinidad prompted him to name the land La Trinidad, after the Holy Trinity. Trinidad was captured by British forces in 1797, ending 300 years of Spanish rule. Tobago's history is more complicated. It was "discovered" by the British in 1508. The Spanish, Dutch, French, and British all fought for it until it was ceded to England under the Treaty of Paris in 1814. In 1962 both islands gained their independence within the British Commonwealth, finally becoming a republic in 1976.

TRINIDAD

Lodging

Trinidad accommodations range from charming guest houses to large business hotels; most of the acceptable establishments, however, are within the vicinity of Port-of-Spain, far from any beach. Most places offer breakfast and dinner for an additional flat rate (MAP). Port-of-Spain has a small downtown core—with a main shopping area along Frederick Street—and is surrounded by inner and outer suburbs. The inner areas include: Belmont, Woodbrook, Newtown, St. Clair's, St. Ann's, and Cascade. The number of private homes in Trinidad that offer bed-and-breakfast accommodations is growing each year. Contact the **Trinidad and Tobago Bed and Breakfast Co-operative Society** (✉ Box 3231, Diego Martin, ☎ FAX 868/627–2337). Regardless of the type of accommodation, be prepared to book far in advance (and to pay a good deal more) for stays during the Christmas and Carnival seasons.

CATEGORY	COST*
$$$$	over $175
$$$	$100–$175
$$	$60–$100
$	under $60

All prices are for a standard double room, excluding 15% tax and 10% service charge.

$$$–$$$$ 🏨 **Trinidad Hilton and Conference Center.** Beautifully landscaped
★ grounds and a singular setting are among the draws here. The complex stretches across the top and along the side of a hill above the Gulf

Trinidad

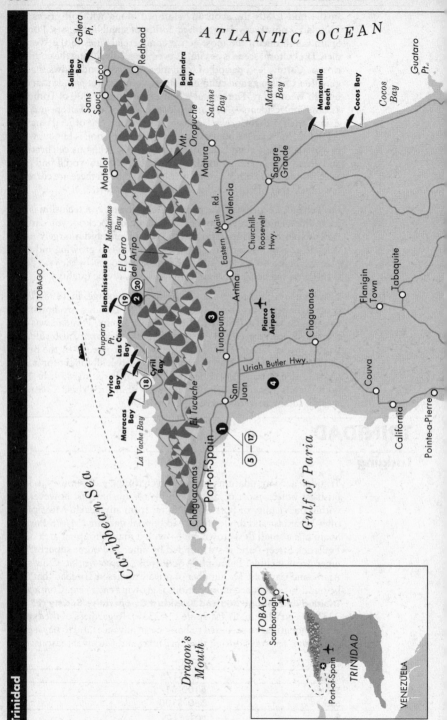

ATLANTIC OCEAN

Galera Pt.

Salibea Bay

Redhead

Balandra Bay

Saline Bay

Matura Bay

Manzanilla Beach

Cocos Bay

Cocos Bay

Guataro Pt.

Sans Souci

Toco

Matelot

Mt. Oropuche

Matura

Sangre Grande

Madamas Bay

Blanchisseuse Bay

El Cerro del Aripo

Valencia

Eastern Main Rd.

Churchill-Roosevelt Hwy.

19 **2** **20**

3

Arima

Piarco Airport

Flanigin Town

Tabaquite

Chupara Pt.

Las Cuevas Bay

Cyril Bay

Tunapuna

Chaguanas

Tyrico Bay

18

El Tucuche

Uriah Butler Hwy.

4

Couva

Maracas Bay

La Vache Bay

San Juan

California

Pointe-a-Pierre

TO TOBAGO

1 **17**

5 **17**

Port-of-Spain

Gulf of Paria

Chaguaramas

Caribbean Sea

Dragon's Mouth

TOBAGO

Scarborough

TRINIDAD

Port-of-Spain

VENEZUELA

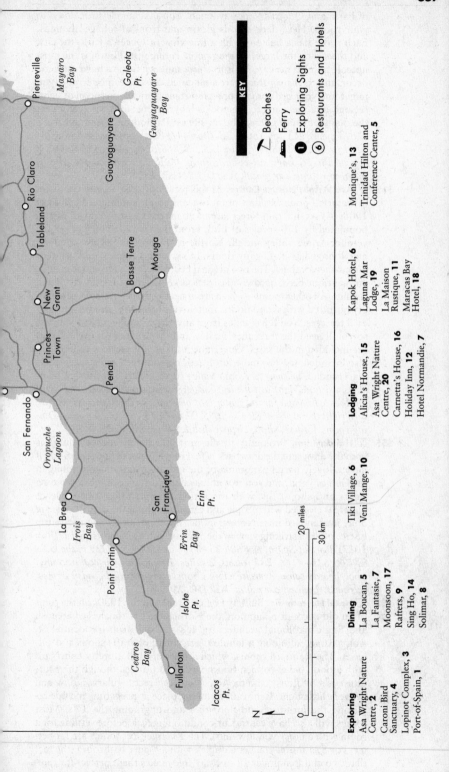

KEY

⌇ Beaches

➤ Ferry

❶ Exploring Sights

⑥ Restaurants and Hotels

Exploring
Asa Wright Nature
Centre, **2**
Caroni Bird
Sanctuary, **4**
Lopinot Complex, **3**
Port-of-Spain, **1**

Dining
La Boucan, **5**
La Fantasie, **7**
Moonsoon, **17**
Rafters, **9**
Sing Ho, **14**
Solimar, **8**

Tiki Village, **6**
Veni Mange, **10**

Lodging
Alicia's House, **15**
Asa Wright Nature
Centre, **20**
Carnetta's House, **16**
Holiday Inn, **12**
Hotel Normandie, **7**

Kapok Hotel, **6**
Laguna Mar
Lodge, **19**
La Maison
Rustique, **11**
Maracas Bay
Hotel, **18**

Monique's, **13**
Trinidad Hilton and
Conference Center, **5**

of Paria and Queen's Park Savannah. You take an elevator *down* to your room. Here dark woods gleam and tropical foliage abounds. Each room has a balcony with a fine view of Queen's Park, the city, and the sea or the large, inviting pool. Though the Hilton is the most upscale hotel in the city, it has its shortcomings: Rooms have a generic decor, and their furnishings are a bit dated. Service can be erratic (you might find your bed unmade upon returning from an afternoon of sightseeing), and the route to the pool is labyrinthine. Still, you can't beat the many amenities here. The on-site ☞ **La Boucan** restaurant has a varied menu. ✉ *Lady Young Rd. (Box 442) Port-of-Spain,* ☎ *868/624–3211 or 800/445–8667 in the U.S.,* FAX *868/624–4485. 394 rooms. 2 restaurants, 3 bars, air-conditioning, pool, 2 tennis courts, shops, meeting rooms, car rental. AE, DC, MC, V. EP.*

$$$ 🖼 **Asa Wright Nature Centre.** At this piece of paradise, you can swim
★   in waterfall pools beside vibrant toucans and hummingbirds. Built in 1908, it's set in a rain forest (about 90 minutes east of Port-of-Spain) populated by 170 species of bird. From the veranda you can see the verdant Arima Valley and the Northern Range. The elegant, comfortable lounge has mahogany floors, bookcases, antiques, and ornithological memorabilia. The two original bedrooms are large and romantic, with antique beds, hardwood closets, and fans that turn slowly on tall ceilings. All other rooms—which are in nearby modern lodges—are simply outfitted with wood floors, motel-style furniture, and private covered terraces. You'll feel miles from anywhere, and, actually, you are, so you'll need the three meals a day and the evening rum punch that are included in the rates. Government taxes and services charges are also included. (☞ For more information about the center, *see* Exploring Trinidad, *below*.) ✉ *Arima Valley (Box 4710), ½ hr outside Blanchisseus; take right at fork in road (signposted to Arima), and drive another ½ hr. (sign for the center is at milepost 7¾ on Blanchisseus Rd.; turn right there),* ☎ *868/667–4655,* FAX *868/273–6370. 24 rooms. Dining room, lounge, shop, airport shuttle. No credit cards. FAP.*

$$$ 🖼 **Holiday Inn.** Proximity to the port and Independence Square is both the draw and the drawback here. From any upper floor room you'll have a lovely pastel panorama of the old town and of ships idling in the Gulf of Paria, and you're within walking distance of the downtown sights and shops. But with the action comes traffic: Independence Square is clogged with people and cars throughout the day. Rooms are done in standard international mode. La Ronde, a revolving rooftop bistro, offers a striking view of the city at night. ✉ *Wrightson Rd. (Box 1017), Port-of-Spain,* ☎ *868/625–3366 or 800/465–4329 in the U.S.,* FAX *868/625–4166. 235 rooms, 2 suites. Restaurant, air-conditioning, pool, beauty salon, exercise room, shops, baby-sitting, laundry service, business services, car rental. AE, DC, MC, V.*

$$ 🖼 **Hotel Normandie.** Built by French Creoles in the 1930s on the ruins
★   of an old coconut plantation, the Normandie has touches of Spanish and English colonial architecture. It's set back from residential St. Ann's Road, adjoining a fabulous artsy mall of crafts shops and galleries. The standard rooms, which are set around a pretty courtyard with a pool, have wooden floorboards and fittings, though their furniture is a bit flimsy, and they have only one rectangular window and get very little light. Renovations taking place at press time include replacing the furniture and floor tiles and upgrading the TVs. Most rooms will also have central air-conditioning (ask before settling for a room with a noisy window unit). The 13 larger loft rooms are far better: For $25 more, you get a duplex with a bigger bathroom (the fact that two children under 12 can stay free makes them perfect for families). Service is friendly and efficient, and ☞ **La Fantasie** restaurant provides room service until 11 PM. ✉ *10 Nook Ave. (Box 851), St. Ann's,*

Port-of-Spain, ☎ FAX *868/624–1181. 53 rooms. Restaurant, bar, café, air-conditioning, pool, shops, meeting rooms, car rental. AE, DC, MC, V. EP, MAP.*

$$ ⊞ **Kapok Hotel.** Leave it to business travelers to find a well-run hotel that's a good-value for the money. Even if you've left work behind (and your laptop at home), it's nice to know that each spacious room is equipped with voice mail (just in case) and data ports. Sunlight (front rooms have views of the Savannah) complements the pastel color schemes and rattan furniture. If you're in to cooking for yourself, the studios have kitchenettes. A new wing with 24 additional rooms was being added at press time (winter 1998). The ☞ **Tiki Village** restaurant has terrific views of the city and is popular with locals. ✉ *16–18 Cotton Hill, St. Clair, Port-of-Spain,* ☎ *868/622–6441 or 800/344–1212 (reservations service),* FAX *868/622–9677. 56 rooms, 6 suites, 9 studios. Restaurant, air-conditioning, pool, exercise room, beauty salon, shops, coin laundry, business services. AE, DC, MC, V. EP.*

$$ ⊞ **Laguna Mar Lodge.** Economics (a reasonable price) and ecology (a
★ setting with both ocean and rain forest) are the key words here. You can hike to waterfalls and linger in their inviting natural pools; there's also a friendly fishing village nearby. A wide, golden-sand beach, fringed with coconut palms and wild almond trees, is a two-minute walk away. The rooms are simple and clean, with private tile showers, locally made teak furnishings, nets over the beds (don't forget the bug spray), oscillating table fans, and wide-open balconies. The owner is German and so are many of the guests. The dining room serves local dishes, often made with fruit—bananas, oranges, mangos, and bread-fruit—grown on the property and fresh fish. ✉ *Mile Marker 65, Paria Main Rd.,Blanchisseuse,* ☎ *868/628–3731 or 868/628–8267,* FAX *868/628–3737. 6 rooms. Bar, dining room. MC, V.*

$$ ⊞ **La Maison Rustique.** You'll find plenty to charm you at this B&B, with its gingerbread detail, its setting amid other wonderful Victorian homes, and its proximity to Queen's Park Savannah. Rooms in the garden cottage are the nicest, but all are clean and presentable. Some have air-conditioning, and a few have private baths. The proprietor, Maureen Chin-Asiong, is a hotel school graduate, who studied at the Wilton School of Cake Decorating in Chicago, among other places. She not only serves good breakfasts—popovers, croissants, quiche—but also whips up afternoon tea, snacks, and picnic baskets. There's a five-night Carnival package for $500. ✉ *16 Rust St., St. Clair, Port-of-Spain,* ☎ FAX *868/622–1512. 7 rooms, 3 with bath. No credit cards. EP.*

$$ ⊞ **Maracas Bay Hotel.** This is the only beachside hotel in Trinidad. It
★ sits on a popular stretch of sand strewn with palm trees about ½ hour outside Port-of-Spain. Rooms are simple and clean, with bright, white-painted wood walls; firm double beds; and cool maroon tile floors. All have spectacular bay views. In-house meals are well prepared and usually feature a local catch brought in from a nearby fishing village. Watercolors depicting Hindu festivals adorn the walls of the popular bar-lounge, where you can relax after a hard day at the beach. There are some good rain-forest hikes nearby; the hotel staff can arrange for a guide. ✉ *Maracas Bay,* ☎ *868/669–1914,* FAX *868/623–1444. 40 rooms. Dining room, lounge, air-conditioning. MC, V. EP, MAP.*

$ ⊞ **Alicia's House.** When the Govias converted their home into a guest house, they kept the family atmosphere. All here is welcoming and re-assuring. The enormous, breezy lounge has squashy sofas, round tables, cane chairs, a piano, and a fish tank. Rooms vary greatly in size and amenities; the large Admiral Rooney offers a garden-view deck and a giant bathtub, while the little Back Room has a private spiral staircase to the pool. Some furnishings, bed coverings, and curtains have seen better days, but rates are very reasonable and include such amenities as a phone and a bath in every room and a hot tub. Alicia's House is a 10-minute walk from the Savannah. ⌧ *7 Coblentz Gardens, St. Ann's, Port-of-Spain,* ☎ *868/623–2802 or 868/624–8651,* ℻ *868/ 622–8560. 17 rooms. Dining room, lounge, air-conditioning, pool, hot tub, laundry service. AE, MC, V. CP, EP, MAP.*

$ ⊞ **Carnetta's House.** When Winston Borrell retired as director of tourism for T&T, he and his wife, Carnetta, opened up their suburban two-story house to guests. One guest room is on the upper floor, the same level as the lounge and terrace dining room. The other four are on the ground floor, with the choice room, Le Flamboyant, opening onto the garden patio. All rooms have a bath (with shower), phone, radio, and TV. And, although there is air-conditioning, cool breezes usually do the trick. (Unfortunately, the doors need to be shuttered at night for security reasons.) Carnetta uses her garden-grown herbs in her cooking and prepares excellent dinners. Carnetta and Winston know what's happening in Trinidad and can help you to organize your evenings. ⌧ *28 Scotland Terr., Andalusia, Maraval,* ☎ *868/628–2732,* ℻ *868/628–7717. 5 rooms. Dining room, lounge, air-conditioning, laundry service, airport shuttle, car rental. AE, DC, MC, V. EP, MAP.*

$ ⊞ **Monique's.** Mike and Monique Charbonné really *like* having guests,
★ as they have been proving for more than a decade. Rooms here are sizable and spotless, with beautiful solid-teak floors and furniture. Numbers 25 and 26 can sleep up to six; they're darker than the other rooms, but each has a little sunken red-stone patio where you can soak up some sun. Breakfast and dinner are available in the parlorlike dining room. The airy, marble-floor lounge (with a TV) is a great place to hang out—with the hosts as often as not. Mike sometimes organizes a picnic to the couple's 100-acre plantation near Blanchisseuse. ⌧ *114 Saddle Rd., Maraval,* ☎ *868/628–3334 or 868/628–2351,* ℻ *868/ 622–3232. 26 rooms. Dining room, air-conditioning. AE. EP, MAP.*

Dining

The food on T&T is a delight to the senses and has a distinctively Creole touch, though everyone has a different idea about what Creole seasoning is (just ask around, and you'll see). Bountiful herbs and spices include bay, rosemary, *chadon beni* (similar to cilantro), nutmeg, saffron, and a variety of peppers. The cooking also uses a lot of guava, plantain, and local fish and meat. If there's fresh juice on the menu, be sure to try it. You'll taste Asian, Indian, African, French, and Spanish influences, among others, often in a single meal. Indian food is a favorite: *rotis* (East Indian sandwiches of soft dough with an inside filling, similar to a burrito) are served as a fast food; a mélange of curried meat or fish and vegetables frequently makes an appearance as do *pelau*—a slow stewed chicken with peas and brown rice—and a wide selection of *vindaloos* (spicy hot meat, vegetable, and seafood dishes). Crab lovers will find large blue-backs curried, peppered, or served with tomatoes or in callaloo soup (with green dasheen leaves, okra, and coconut milk). Shark-and-bake (lightly seasoned, fried shark meat) is the sandwich of choice.

No Trinibagan dining experience is complete without a rum punch with fresh fruit and the legendary Angostura Bitters, made by the same local company that produces the excellent Old Oak rum, but watch out for the fiendish sugar content. Light, refreshing Carib beer is the local lager; dark-beer aficionados can try Royal Extra Stout (R.E.). Local chocolate, found in supermarkets, is made in squares and often flavored with bay leaf and nutmeg.

What to Wear

Restaurants are informal: You won't find any jacket-and-tie requirements. Beachwear, however, is a little too casual for most places. A nice pair of shorts is apropos for lunch; for dinner, you'll probably feel most comfortable in a pair of slacks or a casual sundress.

CATEGORY	COST*
$$$	over $25
$$	$15–$25
$	under $15

per person for a three-course meal, excluding drinks, service, and 15% tax

ASIAN

$$ ✕ **Tiki Village.** Cosmopolitan Port-of-Spainers are passionate about their Asian cuisine. Everyone touts their favorite, but this capacious eatery, a serious (nonkitsch) version of Trader Vic's, is one of the better ones. It's high under the rafters atop the ☞ **Kapok Hotel,** sunlit during the day and affording good views of an electrified Trinidad at night. The table lamps are pretty, but the smell of kerosene can be unpleasant. The dim sum—with tasting-size portions of such dishes as pepper squid and tofu-stuffed fish—is very popular. ⊠ *Kapok Hotel, 16–18 Cotton Hill, St. Clair, Port-of-Spain,* ☎ *868/622–6441. AE, DC, MC, V.*

$–$$ ✕ **Sing Ho.** The food and the prices at this authentic Chinese restaurant will make you smile. The main room has red carpeting, white-linen tablecloths, and fish tanks filled with large, lazy goldfish; the walls are adorned with gold-gilded Chinese art. There are several private rooms where a screen separates you from an otherwise noisy atmosphere. Besides the typical selections of egg rolls, wonton soup, sesame chicken, and shrimp foo young, there are also some island-inspired dishes, such as shark-fin soup and shredded seafood with bean cake. ⊠ *Long Circular Mall, Level 3, Port-of-Spain,* ☎ *868/628–2077. MC, V.*

CONTEMPORARY

$$–$$$ ✕ **La Fantasie.** The ☞ Hotel Normandie's restaurant is done up in lovely Caribbean art deco, the clean lines of the design complemented by deep peach, mauve, and other vibrant island colors. La Fantasie pioneered *cuisine nouvelle Créole,* and many of the dishes are lighter versions of local fare made with a French flair. Seafood is the best bet—grilled snapper stuffed with shrimp in tart tomato sauce, perhaps. The air-conditioning is blissfully glacial, but on cooler nights it's nice to dine outside on the terrace, gazing at the moon through the palms. ⊠ *Hotel Normandie, 10 Nook Ave., St. Ann's, Port-of-Spain,* ☎ *868/624–1181. AE, DC, MC, V.*

CREOLE

$$ ✕ **Veni Mange.** The best lunches in town are served upstairs in a tra-
★ ditional West Indian house that has been renovated for dining. Colorful paintings by local artists hang on the walls, and simple wood furniture is painted in bright primary colors. The waitstaff wears flowing white, gauzy attire that completes the artsy effect. Credit Allyson Hennessy—a Cordon Bleu–trained cook who has become a celebrity of sorts because of a TV talk show she hosts—and her friendly, flamboyant sister-partner, Rosemary Hezekiah. The creative Creole menu changes daily; starters might include callaloo soup, and for a main course you could find stewed oxtail with banana fritters and stewed lentils or boneless baby red snapper with tamarind sauce—simply divine. There's always a vegetarian entrée, too. Leave room to indulge in the delightful homemade desserts. This place is popular, and reservations are advised; dinner is served only on Wednesday. ⊠ *64A Ariapita Ave., Woodbrook, Port-of-Spain,* ☎ *868/624–4597. AE, MC, V. Sat. & Sun.*

ECLECTIC

$$$ ✕ **La Boucan.** Trinidadian dancer Geoffrey Holder painted the large
mural of a social idyll in the Savannah that dominates one wall of this
room at the ☞ **Trinidad Hilton.** A more leisurely Trinidad is also re-
flected in the old-fashioned charm of silver service, uniformed wait-
ers, soft lighting, pink tablecloths, and the serenade of a grand piano.
The menu is international, including steaks, seafood grills, and other
simple preparations, but you can also find such local specialties as callaloo
soup, shrimp Creole, and West Indian chicken curry (these dishes are
served mild unless you tell your waiter you want them spicy). After-
noon tea, served Wednesday–Friday 4–6, is a treat. ✉ *Trinidad Hilton,
Lady Young Rd., Port-of-Spain,* ☎ *868/624–3211. AE, DC, MC, V.*

$$–$$$ ✕ **Solimar.** In a series of dimly lit, plant-filled eating areas, chef Joe
Brown offers a menu that tries to travel the world in one meal: You
might enjoy shrimp tempura, Irish smoked salmon, Hawaiian barbe-
cued mahimahi, Greek salad, or Zwiebel schnitzel, all the while listening
to a guitarist gently strumming 1970s classics. Best bets are the day's
specials—seafood mixed grill, perhaps, followed by a light and fluffy
hot chocolate soufflé with mango ice cream. Solimar is popular with
expat types and tends toward careful casualness. ✉ *6 Nook Ave., St.
Ann's, Port-of-Spain,* ☎ *868/624–6267. AE, DC, MC, V.*

$–$$ ✕ **Rafters.** Behind a stone facade with a green-tin awning and wooden
doors stands a pub that has become an urban institution. Once it was
a rum shop; currently it's a bar and a restaurant divided by a small
hallway. The pub is the center of activity, especially Friday night. In
late afternoons the place swells with Port-of-Spainers ordering burgers and burritos. The cool, dimly lit dining room is a welcome respite
from the hot sun. Lunch is a buffet with a tasty assortment that might
include lobster crepes, roast beef, curries, freshly steamed vegetables,
and an array of cold salads. Desserts include homemade ice creams.
Dinner is served on Saturday night only. ✉ *6A Warner St., Port-of-
Spain,* ☎ *868/628–9258. AE, MC, V. Sun.*

INDIAN

$ ✕ **Moonsoon.** This take-out place has some of the best roti in town.
You can choose from fillings that include goat, conch, chicken, and
delicious curries made with pumpkin, potato, and beans. This East Indian sandwich is the perfect snack to take to the beach or on a tour of
the island. The price is right, too. ✉ *Corner of Tragarete Rd. and Pic-
ton St., Newtown, Port-of-Spain,* ☎ *868/628–7684. No credit cards.*

Beaches

Although Trinidad is not the beach destination Tobago is, it has its share
of fine shoreline along the North Coast Road within an hour's drive
of Port-of-Spain. To reach the east coast beaches, you must drive several hours and take the detour road to Arima. But "goin' behind God's
back," as the Trinis say, rewards the persistent traveler with gorgeous
vistas and secluded stretches of sand.

Balandra Bay, on the northeast coast, is sheltered by a rocky outcropping
and is popular with bodysurfers.

Blanchisseuse Bay, on the North Coast Road, is a narrow, palm-fringed
beach. Facilities are nonexistent, but the beach is ideal for a romantic
picnic. You can haggle with local fishermen to take you out in their
boats to explore the coast.

Las Cuevas Bay, also on the North Coast Road, is a narrow, picturesque strip named for the series of partially submerged and explorable
caves that ring the beach. A food stand offers tasty snacks, and vendors hawk fresh fruit across the road. There are basic changing and

toilet facilities. It's less crowded here than at nearby Maracas Bay (☞ *below*), and seemingly serene, although, as at Maracas, the current can be treacherous.

Manzanilla Beach has picnic facilities and a pretty view of the Atlantic, though its water is occasionally muddied by the Orinoco River, which flows in from South America. The road here, nicknamed the Cocal, is lined with stately palms whose fronds vault like the arches at Chartres. This is where many well-heeled Trinis have vacation homes.

Maracas Bay is a long stretch of sand with a cove and a fishing village at one end. It's *the* local favorite, so it can get crowded on weekends. Watch out for the *very* strong current. Parking sites are ample, and there are snack bars and rest rooms. Try a shark-and-bake at one of the huts (Patsy's is considered the best) along the road. Wash it down with grenadillo (like a giant passion fruit) juice, if it's available, from the stand on Patsy's right.

Salibea Bay, just past Galera Point, which juts toward Tobago, is a gentle beach with shallows and plenty of shade—perfect for swimming. Snack vendors abound in the vicinity.

Tyrico Bay is a small beach made lively by the surfers who flock here. The strong undertow may be too much for some swimmers.

Outdoor Activities and Sports

BIRD-WATCHING

Trinidad and Tobago ranks among the top 10 countries in the world in terms of the number of species of birds per square mile—more than 600 altogether, many living within pristine rain forests, lowlands and savannahs, and fresh- and saltwater swamps. If you're lucky, you might spot the collared trogon, blue-backed manakin, or rare white-tailed Sabrewing hummingbird. Restaurants often hang feeders outside their porches, as much to keep the birds away from your food as to provide a chance for observation.

You can fill up your books with notes on the variety of species to be found in Trinidad at the **Asa Wright Nature Centre** and the **Caroni Bird Sanctuary** (☞ Exploring Trinidad, *below*), as well as the **Pointe-à-Pierre Wild Fowl Trust** (⊠ 42 Sandown Rd., Point Cumana, ☎ 868/637–5145), on 26 acres within the unlikely confines of a petrochemical complex; you must call in advance for a reservation at Pointe-à-Pierre. **Winston Nanan** (☎ 868/645–1305) runs highly regarded bird-watching tours to nearby Guayana and Venezuela.

FISHING

The islands off the northwest coast of Trinidad offer excellent waters for deep-sea fishing, where you'll find wahoo, king fish, and marlin, to name a few. The ocean here was a favorite angling spot of Franklin D. Roosevelt's. Members of the **Trinidad and Tobago Yacht Club** (⊠ Bayshore, ☎ 868/637–4260) may be willing to arrange a tour.

GOLF

The best course in Trinidad is the 18-hole **St. Andrew's Golf Club** (⊠ Moka, Maraval, ☎ 868/629–2314), just outside Port-of-Spain.

TENNIS

The following private tennis courts allow nonmembers or nonresidents to play: the **Trinidad Hilton** (⊠ Lady Young Rd., Port-of-Spain, ☎ 868/624–3211), the **Trinidad Country Club** (⊠ Long Circular Rd., Maraval, ☎ 868/622–3470), and the **Tranquility Square Lawn Tennis Club** (⊠ Victoria Ave., Port-of-Spain, ☎ 868/625–4182).

Shopping

Good buys on the islands include such duty-free items as Angostura Bitters and Old Oak or Vat 19 rum, all widely available throughout the country.

Areas and Malls

Downtown Port-of-Spain, specifically **Frederick, Queen** and **Henry** streets are full of fabrics and shoes. **Ellerslie Plaza** (⊠ Cotton Hill, behind Kapok Hotel in St. Clair, Port-of-Spain, ☎ no phone) is an attractive outdoor mall well worth browsing through. You can drop by for a snack at the Patisserie or lunch at the stylish Gourmet Club. **Excellent City Centre** (⊠ Off Brian Lara Promenade, Port-of-Spain, ☎ 868/623–6503) is set in an old-style oasis under the lantern roofs of three of downtown's oldest commercial buildings. Look for cleverly designed keepsakes, trendy cotton garments, and original artwork. The upstairs food court overlooks bustling Frederick Street. **Long Circular Mall** (⊠ Long Circular Rd., St. James, ☎ 868/622–4925) has upscale boutiques that will keep you occupied window-shopping. **The Market** (⊠ Nook Ave., adjoining Hotel Normandie, St. Ann's, Port-of-Spain, ☎ 868/624–1181) is a collection of shops that specialize in indigenous fashions, crafts, jewelry, basketwork, and ceramics.

Specialty Items

CLOTHING

Bonga! (⊠ Ellerslie Plaza, ☎ 868/624–8819) stocks smart T-shirts, carryalls, shorts, and bathing suits. A fine designer clothing shop, **Meiling** (⊠ Ellerslie Plaza, ☎ 868/628–6205), features cottons in ecru or white and smart little girls' dresses with shirred tops.

DUTY-FREE GOODS

Stecher's (⊠ Trinidad Hilton, Lady Young Rd., Port-of-Spain, ☎ 868/624–3322; ⊠ Long Circular Mall, ☎ 868/622–0017) is a familiar name for those seeking to avoid taxes on fine perfumes, electronics, and jewelry; you can arrange to have your purchases delivered to the airport the day of your departure. **Y. de Lima** (⊠ High St., Port-of-Spain, ☎ 868/655–8872; ⊠ West Mall, Western Main Rd., St. James, ☎ 868/622–7050) sells traditional, luxury, duty-free items.

HANDICRAFTS

The tourism office can provide a list of local artisans who specialize in everything from straw and cane work to miniature steel pans. **The Batique** (⊠ 43 Syndeham Avenue, St. Ann's, Port-of-Spain, ☎ 868/624–3274) carries batik silks created by artist Althea Bastien, who makes some of the finest fabric art around. Works include table runners, napkins, and screens, all done in a maze of color and elegant swirls. For painted plates, ceramics, aromatic candles, wind chimes, and carved wood pieces and instruments, check out **Cockey** (⊠ Level 3, Long Circular Mall, ☎ 868/628–6546). **Craft Boutique** (⊠ Corner of Adam Smith Sq. S and Murray St., Woodbrook, Port-of-Spain, ☎ 868/627–2736) is in Monica Monceaux's house, a delight in gingerbread wood tracery. Almost every inch of the house is utilized by Monica and her craftspeople, who make Carnival and folk dolls, Christmas ornaments (even those for the Hilton tree), crocheted picture frames, preserves, and dozens of other items in merry disarray. The **Craft Shop** (⊠ The Market, ☎ 868/623–0377) carries goods more imaginative than its name, including beautiful metallic wall sconces and mirrors. **Gallery 1,2,3,4** (⊠ The Market, ☎ 868/625–8732) features local artists from a variety of disciplines, including batik and fine art painting; shows change every two weeks. **Poui Boutique** (⊠ Ellerslie Plaza, ☎ 868/622–5597) has stylish hand-done wax batik clothing and Ajoupa ware, an attractive, local terra-cotta pottery.

Check out the jewelry at the **Signature Collection** (⊠ Long Circular Mall, ☎ 868/622–9945), with its pricey but one-of-a-kind pieces.

MUSIC

Just CDs and Accessories (⊠ Level 1, Long Circular Mall, ☎ 868/622–7516) has a good selection of popular local musicians as well as other genres of music. **Rhyner's Record Shop** (⊠ 54 Prince St., ☎ 868/623–5673; ⊠ Piarco International Airport, ☎ 868/669–3064) has a decent selection of calypso and *soca* (a blend of Caribbean soul and calypso) music—it's duty free, but if you're a music maven in search of particular artists, you're better off in Port-of-Spain's local shops.

TEXTILES

Thanks in large part to Carnival costumery, there's no shortage of fabric shops on the islands. The best bargains for Asian and East Indian silks and cottons can be found in downtown Port-of-Spain, on **Frederick Street** and around **Independence Square.**

Nightlife and the Arts

Nightlife

There's no lack of nightlife in Port-of-Spain, and spontaneity plays a big role—look for the handwritten signs announcing the PAN YARD where the next informal gathering of steel drum bands is going to be.

Blue Iguana (⊠ Main St., Chaguanas, ☎ no phone) is the place to go for lively late-night action. It's about 20 minutes west of Port-of-Spain, so get a party together from your hotel and hire a cab. It opens at 10 PM, Wednesday–Sunday. **Cricket Wicket** (⊠ 149 Tragarete Rd., Port-of-Spain, ☎ 868/622–1808), a popular watering hole, with a cupola-shape bar in the center, is a fine place to hear top bands, dance, or just sit and enjoy the nocturnal scenery. **Mas Camp Pub** (⊠ Corner of Ariapata Ave. and French St., Woodbrook, Port-of-Spain, ☎ 868/623–3745) is Port-of-Spain's most comfortable and dependable nightspot. Along with a bar and a large stage where a DJ or live band reigns, there's an open-air patio. The kitchen dishes up hearty, reasonably priced Creole lunches, and if one of the live bands strikes your fancy, chances are you can buy a cassette of its music here. **Moon over Bourbon Street** (⊠ Southern Landing, Westmall, Westmoorings, ☎ 868/637–3448) has comedy or music most nights, plus long, long happy hours. **Pelican** (⊠ 2–4 Coblentz Ave., St. Ann's, Port-of-Spain, ☎ 868/627–7486), an English-style pub, gets increasingly frenetic as the week closes, with a singles-bar atmosphere. **Smokey & Bunty** (⊠ Western Main Rd. and Dengue St., St. James, ☎ no phone) is where you can collect gossip over a beer. It calls itself a sports bar but is really just a liming (relaxing, hanging out) spot.

The Arts

Trinidad always seems to be either anticipating, celebrating, or recovering from a festival. Visitors are welcome to these events, and they're a great way to explore the rich cultural traditions.

CARNIVAL

Trinidad's version of the pre-Lenten bacchanal is reputedly the oldest in the Western Hemisphere; there are festivities all over the country, but the most lavish are in Port-of-Spain. Not as overwhelming as its rival in Rio or as debauched as Mardi Gras in New Orleans, Trinidad's Carnival has the warmth and character of a massive family reunion.

The season begins right Christmas, and the parties, called fêtes, don't stop till Ash Wednesday. Listen to a radio station for five minutes, and you'll find out where the action is. The Carnival event itself officially lasts only two days, from *J'ouvert* (sunrise) on Monday to midnight the following day, Carnival Tuesday. It's best to arrive in Trinidad a week or two early, to enjoy the preliminary events. (Hotels fill up quickly, so be sure to make reservations months in advance.)

Carnival is about extravagant costumes. Colorfully attired *mas* (troupes), whose membership sometimes numbers in the thousands, march to the beat set by steel bands. You can visit the various mas "camps" around Port-of-Spain where these elaborate getups are put together—the addresses are listed in the newspapers—and perhaps join one that strikes your fancy. Fees run anywhere from $35 to $100; you get to keep the costume. Children can also parade in a kiddie carnival that takes place on the Saturday morning before the official events.

Carnival is also a showcase for performers of calypso, music that mixes dance rhythms with social commentary, sung by characters with such evocative names as Shadow, the Mighty Sparrow, and Black Stalin. As Carnival approaches, many of these singers perform nightly in calypso tents around the city. Many hotels also have special concerts by popular local musicians. You can also visit the city's panyards, where steel orchestras, such as the Renegades, Desperadoes, Catelli All-Stars, Invaders, and Phase II rehearse their calypso arrangements. (Note that most can also be heard during the fall and winter seasons.)

For several nights before Carnival, costume makers display their work, and the steel bands and calypso singers perform in competitions in the grandstands of the old racetrack in Queen's Park. Here the Calypso Monarch was crowned until 1993, when the final festivities moved to the National Stadium in the Cruise Ship Complex. The city starts filling with metal-frame carts carrying steel bands, trucks hauling sound systems, and revelers who squeeze into the narrow streets. At midnight on "Mas Tuesday," Port-of-Spain's exhausted merrymakers go to bed. The next day feet are sore, but spirits have been refreshed. Lent (and theoretical sobriety) takes over for a while.

MUSIC

Trinidadian culture doesn't end with music, but it definitely begins with it. Although both calypso and steel bands are best displayed during Carnival, steel bands play at clubs, dances, and fêtes throughout the year. A type of folk music that's popular now is *sweet parang*, a mixture of Spanish patois and calypso sung to tunes played on a string instrument much like a mandolin. (☞ *see* Lopinot Complex *in* Exploring *below*.)

THEATER

When Nobel prize–winning poet Derek Walcott returns home to Trinidad, he often gives readings or gets involved in one of the productions of the thriving local theater. There are several excellent theaters in Port-of-Spain. Consult local newspapers for listings.

Exploring Trinidad

The intensely urban atmosphere of Port-of-Spain belies the tropical beauty of the countryside surrounding it. You'll need a car, and three to eight hours to see all there is to see. Begin by circling the Queen's Park Savannah to Saddle Road, in the residential district of Maraval. After a few miles the road begins to narrow and curve sharply as it climbs into the Northern Range and its undulating hills of dense foliage. Stop at the lookout on North Coast Road, and have Keith Davis sing you a hilarious calypso, complete with any biographical details you give him. (He's not allowed to ask, but a few T&T dollars are appreciated—and deserved.) From the town of Blanchisseuse en route to the Asa Wright Nature Centre, the road winds through canyons of towering palms, mossy grottoes, and "big bamboo"—so large that a calypso song was written about them. In this rain forest, keep an eye out for vultures, parakeets, hummingbirds, toucans, and, if you're lucky, maybe red-bellied, yellow-and-blue macaws.

Numbers in the margin correspond to points of interest on the Trinidad map.

❶ Port-of-Spain

Most tours begin at the port. If you're planning to explore on foot, which will take two to four hours, start early in the day; by midday the port area can be hot and as packed as Calcutta. You'll want to end up on a bench in the Queen's Park Savannah, sipping a cool coconut water bought from one of the vendors operating out of a flatbed truck. For about 50¢, he'll lop the top off a green coconut with a deft swing of the machete and, when you've finished drinking, lop again, making a bowl and spoon of coconut shell for you to eat the young pulp. As in most cities, take extra care at night; women should not walk alone.

Emperor Valley Zoo and the Botanical Gardens. The cultivated expanse of parkland just north of the Savannah is the site of the president's and prime minister's official residences. A meticulous lattice of walkways and local flora, the parkland was first laid out in 1820 for Governor Woodford and is a model of what a tropical garden should be. In the midst of this serene wonderland is the 8-acre zoo, which features primarily birds and animals of the region—from the brilliantly plumed scarlet ibis to slithering anacondas and pythons; you'll also see (and hear) the wild parrots that breed in the surrounding foliage. The zoo draws a quarter of a million visitors a year, and more than half of them are children, so admission is priced accordingly—a mere TT$2 for folks under 12. ✉ *Botanical Gardens,* ☎ 868/622–3530. ☜ *TT$4.* ☉ *Daily 9:30–6.*

Frederick Street. Port-of-Spain's main shopping drag, starting north from the midpoint of Independence Square, is a market street of scents—corn roasting and Indian spices—and crowded shops.

Independence Square. Across Wrightson Road from the south side of King's Wharf (☞ *below*), this is not a square at all: It's a wide, dusty thoroughfare crammed with pedestrians, car traffic, taxi stands, and peddlers of everything from shoes to coconuts—not a pleasant walk for lone females. Flanked by government buildings and the familiar twin towers of the Financial Complex (familiar because it adorns one side of all T&T dollar bills), the square is gloriously chaotic, loud, and confusing. On its south side, the Cruise Ship Complex, full of duty-free shops, forms an enclave of international anonymity with the Holiday Inn. On the eastern end of the square is the Cathedral of the Immaculate Conception; it was by the sea when it was built in 1832, but subsequent landfill around the port gave it an inland location. The imposing Roman Catholic structure is made of stone from nearby Laventille.

King's Wharf. Though it is no longer as frenetic as it was during the oil boom of the 1970s, the town's main dock entertains a steady parade of cruise and cargo ships, a reminder that the city started from this strategic harbor. It's on Wrightson Road, the main street along the water on the southwest side of town.

Magnificent Seven. A series of astonishing buildings constructed in a variety of 19th-century styles flanks the western side of the Savannah. Notable are Killarney, patterned (loosely) after Balmoral Castle in Scotland, with an Italian-marble gallery surrounding the ground floor;

Whitehall, constructed in the style of a Venetian palace by a cacao-plantation magnate and currently the office of the prime minister; Roomor, a flamboyantly Baroque colonial house with a preponderance of towers, pinnacles, and wrought-iron trim that suggests an elaborate French pastry; and the Queen's Royal College, in German Renaissance style, with a prominent tower clock that chimes on the hour.

National Museum and Art Gallery. Head over to the southeast corner of the Savannah, to see the Carnival exhibits, the Amerindian collection and historical re-creations, and the fine 19th-century paintings of Trinidadian artist Cazabon. ✉ *117 Upper Frederick St.,* ☎ *868/623–5941 or 868/623–5941.* ▨ *Free.* ☉ *Tues.–Sat. 10–6.*

Queen's Park Savannah. If the downtown port area is the pulse of Port-of-Spain, the great green expanse roughly bounded by Maraval Road, Queen's Park West, Charlotte Street, and Saddle Road is the city's soul. Its 2-mi circumference is a popular jogger's track. On the west side of the Savannah, you'll see a garden of architectural delights: the elegant lantern-roof George Brown House, what remains of the Old Queen's Park Hotel, and the Magnificent Seven (☞ *above*). The racetrack at the south end is no longer a venue for horse racing, but it's still the setting for music and costume competitions during Carnival and, when not jammed with calypso performers, tends toward quietude. The northern end of the Savannah is devoted to plants. A rock garden, known as the Hollow, and a fishpond add to the rusticity.

Water Park. The water park at the Valley Vue Hotel is open to nonguests and has the biggest, wettest slides in the West Indies—three 400-ft chutes leading to a shallow pool. ✉ *Ariapita Rd., St. Ann's,* ☎ *868/624–0940.* ▨ *TT$20.* ☉ *Daily 10–6.*

Woodford Square. At Prince and Frederick streets, the square has served as the site of political meetings, speeches, public protests, and occasional violence. It's dominated by the magnificent Red House, a Renaissance-style building that takes up an entire city block. Trinidad's House of Parliament takes its name from a paint job done in anticipation of Queen Victoria's Diamond Jubilee in 1897. The original Red House was burned to the ground in a 1903 riot, and the present structure was built four years later. The chambers are open to the public.

The view of the south side of the square is framed by the Gothic spires of Trinity, the city's Anglican cathedral, consecrated in 1823; its mahogany-beam roof is modeled after that of Westminster Hall in London. On the north is the impressive public library building, the Hall of Justice and City Hall.

Out on the Island

❷ **Asa Wright Nature Centre.** Its nearly 500 acres are covered with plants, trees, and multihued flowers, and the surrounding acreage is atwitter with more than 170 species of birds, from the gorgeous blue-green motmot to the rare, nocturnal oilbird. If you stay at the center's inn for two nights or more (☞ Lodging, *above*), the oilbirds' breeding grounds in Dunston Cave are included in the center's guided hikes. Those who don't want to hike can relax on the inn's veranda and watch birds swoop about the porch feeders—an armchair bird-watcher's nirvana. This stunning plantation house looks out to the lush, untouched Arima Valley. Even if you're not staying over, book ahead for lunch (TT$37.50) Monday–Saturday or for a noontime Sunday buffet (TT$62.50). ✉ *Arima Valley (Box 4710), ½ hr outside Blanchisseus; take right at fork in road (signposted to Arima), and drive another ½ hr. (sign for the center is at milepost 7¼ on Blanchisseus Rd.; turn right there),* ☎ *868/667–4655.* ▨ *$6.* ☉ *Daily 9–5. Guided tours at 10:30 and 1:30; reservations essential.*

❹ Caroni Bird Sanctuary. This large swamp with mazelike waterways is bordered by mangrove trees, some plumed with huge termite nests. In the middle of the sanctuary are several islets that are home to Trinidad's national bird, the scarlet ibis. Just before sunset the ibis arrive by the thousands, their richly colored feathers brilliant in the gathering dusk, and, as more flocks alight, they turn their little tufts of land into bright Christmas trees. Bring a sweater and insect repellent.

Across from the sanctuary's parking lot sits a sleepy canal with several boats and guides for hire; the smaller boats are best. The fee is usually about $6–$15. The only official tour operator is Winston Nanan (☞ Guided Tours *in* Trinidad and Tobago A to Z, *below*); phone or write him in advance for reservations. ⊠ *½ hr from Port-of-Spain; take Churchill Roosevelt Hwy. east to Uriah Butler south; turn right and in about 2 mins, after passing Caroni River Bridge, follow sign for sanctuary,* ☎ *868/645–1305.* ⊠ *Free.*

❸ Lopinot Complex. It's said that the ghost of the French count Charles Joseph de Lopinot prowls his former home on stormy nights. Lopinot came to Trinidad in 1800 and chose this magnificent site to plant cocoa. His restored estate house has been turned into a museum; a guide is available from 10 to 6. This is one of the centers for parang, a beautiful string-based folk music. ⊠ *Take Eastern Main Rd. from Port-of-Spain to Arouca; look for sign that points north,* ☎ *no phone.* ⊠ *Free.* ☉ *Daily 6–6.*

TOBAGO

Lodging

On Tobago, there are a few modest lodgings in the towns, but the trend is toward seaside resorts, many of them appealingly low-key. If you're staying on the east side of Tobago, accommodations with meal plans are almost essential because of the dearth of restaurants.

For information on B&Bs, contact the **Trinidad and Tobago Bed and Breakfast Co-operative Society** (☞ Lodging *under* Trinidad, *above*) or the **Tobago Bed and Breakfast Association** (⊠ Federal Villa, 1–3 Crooks River, Scarborough, ☎ 868/639–3926, FAX 868/639–3566). ☞ For price categories, *see* the chart *under* Lodging *in* Trinidad, *above*.

$$$$ 🏨 **Coco Reef Resort.** Service and luxury are the twin pillars of this swank resort. And, with its concierge, social director, fine ☞ **Tamara's** restaurant, water sports options, and arcade with tony boutiques, this place attracts an active international set that's used to being pampered. Elements of Caribbean, colonial, and Mediterranean architecture blend in an abundance of arches, tiles, and fretwork flourishes; harsh angles have been eliminated to create a soothing space. Rooms have cool, calming tiles; pretty wall stencils; and handcrafted wicker furniture. If you want to venture off Coco Bay, the resort's small beach, Pigeon Point and Store Bay are both nearby. ⊠ *Pigeon Point (Box 434), Scarborough,* ☎ *868/639–8571 or 800/221–1294,* FAX *868/639–8574 or 800-221–1294 (reservations service). 96 rooms, 39 suites. 2 restaurants, 2 bars, air-conditioning, pool, beauty salon, spa, 2 tennis courts, health club, baby-sitting, car rental, dive shop, snorkeling, windsurfing. AE, D, DC, MC, V. CP, MAP.*

$$$$ 🏨 **Grafton Beach Resort.** If any hotel has the action on Tobago, it's
★ the Grafton. Yet it's stretched out languidly along the shore under the tall palms, and so it's possible, with sea-view rooms, to feel away from it all. This sparkling complex has the most international ambience of any Tobago hotel, from the huge lobby-bar-restaurant-pool area

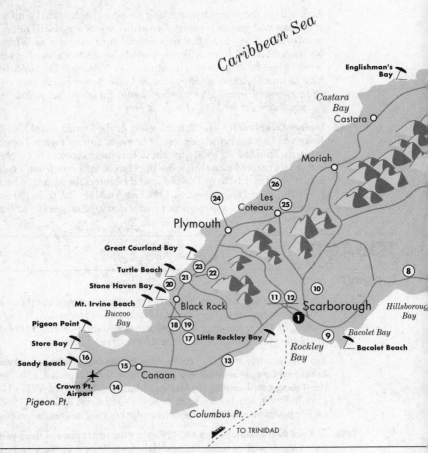

Caribbean Sea

Englishman's Bay

Castara Bay
Castara

Moriah

26
24
Les Coteaux
25

Plymouth

Great Courland Bay
23
22
Turtle Beach
21
20
Stone Haven Bay
8
10
Mt. Irvine Beach
11 12
Buccoo Bay
Black Rock
Scarborough
Hillsborough Bay
Pigeon Point
18 19
1
Store Bay
17 **Little Rockley Bay**
9
Bacolet Bay
Bacolet Beach
Sandy Beach
16
Rockley Bay
15
13
Canaan
Crown Pt. Airport
14
Pigeon Pt.

Columbus Pt.

TO TRINIDAD

Exploring
Charlotteville, **5**
Flagstaff Hill, **4**
Ft. King George, **2**
Scarborough, **1**
Speyside, **3**

Dining
Arnos Vale
Waterwheel, **25**
Blue Crab, **11**
Cocrico Inn, **24**
Dillon's, **15**
First Historical
Cafe/Bar, **8**

Kariwak Village, **14**
Ocean View, **19**
Old Donkey Cart, **9**
Papillon, **20**
Rouselle's, **12**
Tamara's, **16**

Lodging
Arnos Vale Hotel, **26**
Blue Horizon
Resort, **17**
Blue Waters Inn, **6**
Coco Reef Resort, **16**
Grafton Beach
Resort, **19**

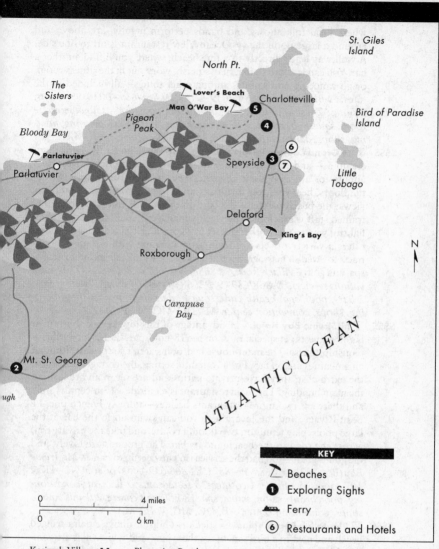

St. Giles
Island

North Pt.

The
Sisters

Bloody Bay

Lover's Beach
Charlotteville
Man O'War Bay
5
4

Bird of Paradise
Island

Pigeon
Peak

Parlatuvier
Parlatuvier

Speyside **3**
6
7

Little
Tobago

Delaford

King's Bay

Roxborough

Carapuse
Bay

2 Mt. St. George

ATLANTIC OCEAN

N

ugh

0   4 miles

0   6 km

KEY

Beaches

1 Exploring Sights

Ferry

6 Restaurants and Hotels

Kariwak Village, **14**
Le Grande Courlan
Resort and Spa, **22**
Manta Lodge, **7**
Mt. Irvine Bay
Hotel, **18**
Ocean Point, **13**
Old Donkey Cart
House, **9**

Plantation Beach
Villas, **23**
Rex Turtle Beach
Hotel, **21**
Richmond Great
House, **10**

to the top-class in-room amenities and decor (solid, teak furniture and terra-cotta-tile floors). The Neptune seafood restaurant and the bar, where local folk shows and bands perform nightly, are above and around a large pool; the ☞ **Ocean View** restaurant is off to one side. A walkway leads directly to a fine beach, where you'll find another a bar. You can learn to scuba, play squash, work out in the fitness room, or go canoeing and sailing, among other things—all included in the rates. ✉ *Black Rock,* ☎ *868/639–0191,* FAX *868/639–0030. 99 rooms, 2 suites. 2 restaurants, 3 bars, air-conditioning, pool, sauna, exercise room, squash, beach, dive shop, snorkeling, surfing, windsurfing, boating, shops, dance club. AE, DC, MC, V. All-inclusive, EP, MAP.*

$$$$ 🏨 **Le Grand Courlan Resort and Spa.** This hotel, under the same ownership as—and right next door to—the ☞ **Grafton Beach Resort**, is aiming for a *very* upscale clientele. The spacious rooms have white-tile floors, heavy wicker furniture, and large balconies with fantastic views; the beach is one of the best on the island; and the impeccably trained staff is gracious. The weekly manager's cocktail party is a delightful way to meet other guests in a cordial, elegant setting. The spa offers a variety of services from aromatherapy with essential oil extracts to Swedish massage. Several packages are available including scuba, spa, and golf. ✉ *Black Rock,* ☎ *868/639–9667 or 800/468–3750 (reservations service),* FAX *868/639–9292. 68 rooms, 10 suites. 2 restaurants, 2 bars, pool, spa, health club, squash, dive shop, windsurfing, boating, shops, convention center. AE, DC, MC, V. EP, MAP.*

$$$$ 🏨 **Mt. Irvine Bay Hotel.** The advantage of this low-key establishment is golf—guests get special rates on the 18-hole, par-72, 127-acre, championship course. The main-house bedrooms aren't so special, although all amenities are on tap. For a romantic setting, the cottages are worth the extra cost; they have private patios and are set in an arc around the main building. The main restaurant is set inside a 17th-century mill, and there are two more restaurants besides—a dressy French one, Le Beau Rivage, and the Jacaranda. You can swim up to the bar at the large pools, play tennis on two floodlit courts, and take the private trail across the road to the beach and its bar. The grounds are lovely, and the golf is great—too bad the service isn't always up to par. ✉ *Mt. Irvine Bay (Box 222),* ☎ *868/639–8871,* FAX *868/639–8800 or 800/742–4276. 107 rooms, 5 suites, 51 cottages. 3 restaurants, 2 bars, air-conditioning, pool, beauty salon, sauna, spa, 18-hole golf course, 2 tennis courts, shops, convention center. AE, DC, MC, V. EP, MAP.*

$$$$ 🏨 **Plantation Beach Villas.** Nestled on a hillside above a palm-fringed beach and next to a bird sanctuary, these pink-and-white villas are comfortably furnished in plantation style—four-poster beds, rocking chairs, louver doors, and lots of West Indian fretwork. The accommodations (and the price) are perfect for large families or other groups: each two-story villa has three bedrooms (one air-conditioned, two with ceiling fans), three baths, and a teak veranda with a view of the sea. Cleaning service and linens are included, a cook can be provided on request, and baby-sitting is available. ✉ *Stone Haven Bay, Black Rock (write to Box 1020, Port-of-Spain, Trinidad),* ☎ FAX *868/639–0455 or 800/ 742–4276 (reservations service). 6 villas. Bar, air-conditioning, kitchenettes, pool, laundry service. MC, V.*

$$$$ 🏨 **Rex Turtle Beach Hotel.** At this sprawling, well-maintained, beach-
★   front property you'll find a relaxed atmosphere, evening entertainment, an array of complimentary water sports, and lovely grounds. Rooms are attractive, with typical Tobagonian teak ceilings, wooden louver doors, and brightly colored bedspreads; all have garden and ocean views. Parents take note: There are baby-sitting services and many children's activities. The family annex room is an especially good deal: for just $21 more you get a small extra bedroom. As the name suggests, tur-

tles use this beach to lay their eggs February–June; you can request a wake-up call (perhaps at 2 AM or 3 AM) if you want to watch. Unfortunately, the pool is small—two strokes and you've made it to the other side. The stretch of beach, however, is lovely. ⊠ *Great Courland Bay (write to Box 201, Scarborough),* ☎ *868/639–2851 or 305/471–6170 for U.S. reservations,* FAX *868/639–1495. 125 rooms. Restaurant, 2 bars, coffee shop, pool, 2 tennis courts, volleyball, dive shop, snorkeling, bicycles, shop. AE, DC, MC, V. EP, MAP.*

$$$ 🏨 **Arnos Vale Hotel.** Romance isn't hard to find at this Mediterranean-style complex on 400 lush acres. Rooms are in white-stucco cottages on a hill; from your quarters, you can take a winding path down to a secluded beach, a pool, and a bar. Some of the rooms have had bathroom renovations that include new tile and vanities. The hilltop restaurant—with antique pieces, iron-lattice tables, a chandelier, and a hand-painted piano—has a crescent-shape patio with a sweeping sea view. While you feast on Italian cuisine, birds flit about the veranda, occasionally touching down to feast on crumbs. ⊠ *Arnos Vale (Box 208), Scarborough,* ☎ *868/639–2881,* FAX *868/639–4629. 35 rooms, 3 suites. Restaurant, bar, air-conditioning, pool, 2 tennis courts, beach, dive shop, snorkeling, shop, dance club. AE, DC, MC, V. EP, MAP.*

$$$ 🏨 **Blue Waters Inn.** A 90-minute drive from Scarborough and trek up
★ a bumpy driveway brings you to this beach hotel and its villas. They're set amid 46 acres of greenery on the northeast Atlantic coast (Little Tobago and Bird of Paradise islands are just across the bay). So lush is the location that the massive gnarled beach trees here seem to hold up the entire complex. Although rooms are beach-motel standard, they're pleasant, and you're guaranteed the sounds of waves all night. The bungalows have one or two bedrooms, a living room, and a kitchen. There are only small stores in the area; if you don't want to shop in Scarborough before you set out, you can fax in an order for provisions and have the staff stock your room. The restaurant serves the freshest of fish, and the lively bar serves an array of exotic drinks. ⊠ *Bateaux Bay, Speyside,* ☎ *868/660–4341 or 800/742–4276 (reservations service),* FAX *868/660–5195. 31 rooms, 4 apartments, 3 bungalows. Restaurant, bar, tennis court, beach, dive shop, snorkeling, windsurfing, boating, car rental. AE, MC, V. CP, EP, FAP, MAP.*

$$$ 🏨 **Kariwak Village.** There are many return guests to Allan and Cyn-
★ thia Clovis's charming, reasonably priced cabana village. Perhaps folks find the peaceful atmosphere appealing; or maybe they're drawn by the all-natural cuisine (vegetarians love this place) and the weekly yoga classes in the open-air conference area (nothing like a good stretch under a thatched roof and on a gleaming teak floor). A bamboo pavilion houses the highly respected ☞ **Kariwak Village** restaurant. You can stroll through Cynthia's herb-and-vegetable garden, drink terrific rum punches and maybe listen to local bands in the lobby-bar area (all done up in bamboo, raw teak, and coral stone), or make the 10-minute walk to the beach. The complex is also near the airport, Store Bay, and Pigeon Point. ⊠ *Crown Point (write to Box 27, Scarborough),* ☎ *868/ 639–8442,* FAX *868/639–8441. 24 rooms. Restaurant, bar, air-conditioning, pool. AE, DC, MC, V. EP, MAP.*

$$–$$$ 🏨 **Manta Lodge.** Rooms in this comfortable lodge are named for such fish and fowl as the green moray, the tarpon, and the toucan. Rooms farthest from the dining room are the most private. All have wooden walls accented with brilliant blues or reds, white-tile floors, wicker furniture, and views of the ocean and the beach across the street. Though island breezes should keep you cool, some rooms have air-conditioning. Food in the on-site restaurant can be inconsistent in quality, but Jemma's restaurant, a lovely wooden house nestled inside a giant almond tree at the edge of the sea, serves lunch and dinner (there is no alcohol served) and is a five-minute walk into the small town of Speyside. Scuba diving is the main attraction here, and there's a fully equipped dive shop with certification classes and dive packages. ⊠ *Speyside (Box 433), Scarborough,* ☎ *868/660–5268 or 800/544–7631,* FAX *868/660–5030. 20 rooms, 2 lofts. Restaurant, bar, air-conditioning, pool, dive shop. AE, DC, MC, V. FAP, MAP.*

$$–$$$ 🏨 **Old Donkey Cart House.** The apartment-style accommodations here have beautiful ocean views (the vista from the ultraprivate penthouse is especially panoramic). Rooms have rattan chaise lounges; jalousied doors that allow breezes to sweep through; ceiling fans, and mosquito netting over four-poster, king-size beds. Continental breakfast is included, and all rooms have refrigerators (but no kitchen facilities). The ☞ **Old Donkey Cart** restaurant serves both local and international dishes. It's a 5-minute walk to a quiet beach and a 15-minute walk to town. ⊠ *73 Bacolet St., Scarborough,* ☎ *868/639–3551,* FAX *868/639–6124. 2 garden apartments, 4 studios, 2 superiors, 1 penthouse. Restaurant, fans, refrigerators, pool. AE, MC, V.*

$$–$$$ 🏨 **Richmond Great House.** A stay here will give you a taste of Caribbean estate life. Owned by a Tobago-born professor of African history, the Great House dates from the late 18th century. Its guest rooms have mahogany floors and are furnished with antiques; throughout you'll find plantation-period items and African art. Though panoramic views of rain forest and sea are all around, the view of sunset from the Rain Forest Suite is particularly noteworthy. There are also several rooms (20th-century additions) just under the original house; what they lack in ambience, they make up for in privacy. The kitchen serves delicious island food, and meal plans are available and necessary—you really are off the beaten path here. ⊠ *Belle Garden,* ☎ FAX *868/660–4467. 3 suites, 7 double rooms. Restaurant, bar, pool. MC, V. MAP.*

$$ 🏨 **Ocean Point.** This friendly complex has studios beneath split-level loft accommodations—all tucked tidily into a setting that includes a tiny kitsch fountain, a quartet of parakeets and Raj the macaw, a barbecue pit, and a palm-thatched East Indian restaurant-bar beside a child-size, kidney-shape pool. Guest quarters are all sparkly white with pine fittings and terra-cotta floors, a big shower in the bathroom, and an inviting hammock on a balcony or porch. Lofts have views of the sunrise over the ocean; studios face the pool area, which can be hectic and noisy during the day (the nearby Little Rockley beach is narrow and rocky—not the best for sunbathing). A 10-minute drive takes you to Store Bay. A free shuttle to the airport and supermarket is provided. Dive packages are available. ⊠ *Milford Rd., Lowlands,* ☎ FAX *868/639–0973. 5 studios, 5 apartments. Restaurant, bar, air-conditioning, kitchenettes, pool, airport shuttle. AE, DC, MC, V. EP.*

$–$$ 🏨 **Blue Horizon Resort.** To call the Blue Horizon a "resort" is a stretch—the only amenities you get here are a small pool, a barbecue pit, and an understocked food shop. What you *do* get are reasonably priced, quiet, spacious rooms—some with a view, all with a kitchen and a bathroom. Parents will appreciate the room size and the fact that they can observe their children in the pool from each unit. Deluxe apartments have spiral staircases leading to galleried lofts that children adore (though little ones could easily fall from them). The one "luxury" apartment has an extra bedroom and tons of space. ⊠ *Jacamar Dr., Mt. Irvine,* ☎ *868/639–0433,* FAX *305/592–4935. 13 apartments. Pool, shop, airport shuttle. AE, MC, V. EP.*

Dining

Macaroni pie and chicken is Tobago's Sunday dinner favorite, perhaps with fried plantain or potatoes. Oil Down—a local dish—tastes better than it sounds: It's a gently seasoned mixture of boiled breadfruit and salt beef or pork flavored with coconut milk. Mango ice cream or a sweetly sour tamarind ball makes a tasty finish. You may want to take home some hot pepper sauce or chutney to a spice-loving friend or relative. For price categories, *see* the chart *under* Dining *in* Trinidad, *above.*

CARIBBEAN/CREOLE

$$ ✕ **Kariwak Village.** Recorded steel-band music plays gently in the
★ background at this romantic candlelit spot in the ☞ **Kariwak Village** complex. In a bamboo pavilion created to resemble an Amerindian round hut, Cynthia Clovis orchestrates a very original four-course menu. Changing daily, the choices may include christophene (a squash-like fruit) soup, curried green figs, kingfish with shrimp sauce, and coconut cake. Whatever the dish, it will be full of herbs and vegetables picked from Cynthia's own organic garden (she really knows how to honor squash and green beans). The nonalcoholic drinks are wonderful, especially the iced coffee, which is more like a frozen coconut cappuccino. Saturday buffets, with live jazz or calypso, are a Tobagonian highlight. ⊠ *Crown Point,* ☎ *868/639–8442. AE, DC, MC, V.*

$–$$ ✕ **Blue Crab.** Alison Sardinha is Tobago's most ebullient and kindly
★ hostess, and her husband, Ken, one of its best chefs. He cooks "like our mothers cooked," serving local cuisine (though he occasionally adds a Portuguese or Asian touch). What's on the menu depends upon what's fresh and available, and anyone on the waitstaff will gladly explain the daily selection. There might be kingfish, *katchowrie* (spiced split pea patties, a little like falafel), curried chicken, or suckling pig. You'll always find callaloo, rotis, and *cou-cou* (a cornmeal dish); sometimes you'll find a "cookup"—pelau-type rice with *everything* in it. The place is officially open only on Wednesday and Friday nights, but Miss Alison will open up on other evenings and for weekend lunches (even for one table), if you call in the morning. The setting, on a wide, shady terrace overlooking the bay, is just about perfect. ⊠ *Robinson St. at Main St., Scarborough,* ☎ *868/639–2737. AE, MC, V.*

$–$$ ✕ **Cocrico Inn.** This café-bar offers delectable home cooking. The chefs use fruits and vegetables grown in the neighborhood. They zealously guard their recipes, including a marvelous cou-cou and breaded, subtly spiced grouper. There's nothing fancy here, just warm, delicious food and cool air-conditioning. The fresh juices are delicious. A sign over the bar reads, SMILE, IT'S THE SECOND BEST THING YOU CAN DO WITH YOUR LIPS. Eating here just might be the first. ⊠ *Corner of North and Commissioner Sts., Plymouth,* ☎ *868/639–2661. AE, V.*

$ ✕ **First Historical Café/Bar.** This funky little roadside eatery is housed in a traditional West Indian building. The back-porch dining area has a crushed-rock-and-coral floor; brightly painted yellow, green, and red bamboo walls; and a thatched roof. The main attractions are the time-line posters that present historical tidbits of Tobago. Do you want to know the definition of the Tobago Jig, the Tobago Reel, or the Tobago Bongo? This is the place to find out. The food is simple but good, featuring such island delights as fruit plates and fish sandwiches. ⊠ *Mile Marker 8, Windward Main Rd. in Studley Park area en route to Charlotteville,* ☎ *no phone. No credit cards.*

CONTEMPORARY

$$$ ✕ **Tamara's.** Here, at the elegant ☞ **Coco Reef Resort,** you dine on
★ contemporary cuisine with an island twist while musicians stroll around you playing upbeat island songs on stringed instruments. The peach decor and whitewashed wooden ceiling give the place a light feel, and island breezes waft through the palm-tree-lined terrace. You might start with the homemade chicken liver pâté with pear chutney and char-grilled

brioche, followed by the grilled barracuda set on a bed of black olive purée and dressed with pepper sauce. If you have room for dessert, the cherry yogurt parfait is very good. A full tropical buffet breakfast is served daily; dinner is served nightly. ✉ *Pigeon Point Scarborough,* ☎ *868/639–8571. AE, MC, V.*

$$–$$$ ✕ **Arnos Vale Waterwheel.** You'll find this popular eatery is on landscaped grounds in a rain-forest nature park, where gleaming hardwood walkways take you past remnants of an old sugar mill. There's a roof overhead, but otherwise you're completely outdoors (bug spray is a good idea). The decor is naturally elegant with evergreen wrought-iron tables and chairs and lights fashioned in the shape of large pineapples. The menu changes but has an Italian flair with choices like shaved pear and Parmesan salad, focaccia with grilled goat cheese, seviche of kingfish, or caramelized breast of chicken on moist polenta with a callaloo sauce. There's no admission cost to the park; let them know that you intend to dine as you enter. ✉ *Arnos Vale Estate, Franklyn Rd.,* ☎ *868/660–0815. MC, V.*

ECLECTIC

$$–$$$ ✕ **Ocean View.** The ☞ **Grafton Beach Resort**'s main restaurant is a large open terrace that overlooks the Caribbean but has a better view of the hotel pool, the bar, and the evening's entertainment than of the waves. Four times a week, you can enjoy an all-you-can-eat dinner buffet, which might include char-grilled chicken, steak, pork, Creole dolphinfish, curried blue crab, any number of root vegetables, spaghetti, *pelau* (rice and peas), cauliflower with cheese, a salad bar, and an array of desserts. If they have an Indian buffet, do what you must to dine here; it's nothing short of incredible. ✉ *Black Rock,* ☎ *868/639–0191. AE, DC, MC, V.*

$$–$$$ ✕ **Rouselle's.** An enchanting terrace high above Scarborough Bay with
★ a big, congenial bar, Rouselle's was just a liming spot until friends and regulars demanded proper food. But they didn't expect food this good. The menu dons different accessories rather than changing completely, so you may find grouper, broiled and served with a fresh Creole sauce and several vegetables (garlicky green beans, carrots with ginger, a raw bok choy salad, and potato croquette with spices and celery); dolphinfish with white wine sauce; or lobster, which is very hard to procure, steamed just so. Whatever there is, you can trust that it will be delicious. An appetizer, hot garlic bread, and dessert (save room for pineapple pie or homemade ice cream) are included in the entrée price. Don't forego the Rouselle's punch: the recipe is a secret, but the lovely, welcoming co-owners, Bobbie and Charlene, will probably let you in on it. ✉ *Old Windward Rd., Bacolet,* ☎ *868/639–4738. Lunch reservations essential. AE, MC, V.*

$–$$$ ✕ **Old Donkey Cart.** Dine in the outdoor tropical palm garden or inside the 100-year-old, French Colonial–style ☞ **Old Donkey Cart House.** Friendly cats wind their way around your legs and welcome the occasional pat on the head. The menu has both international and local cuisine; the callaloo soup is wonderful, as are the conch fritters. Spicy pasta, grilled lobster, and crayfish with coconut sauce round out the main courses. There's an extensive wine list, and you should try the specialty drink made fresh from hibiscus (with or without rum)— a thirst-quenching way to get your vitamin C. ✉ *73 Bacolet St., Scarborough,* ☎ *868/639–3551. MC, V.*

SEAFOOD

$$–$$$ ✕ **Dillon's.** Stanley Dillon's other career as a fishing-charter operator
★ guarantees the freshest catch at his seafood restaurant by the airport. White walls hung with local art, red plaid tablecloths, and a silver-service waitstaff create an atmosphere that's halfway between homey and posh. The menu mixes traditional favorites, such as shrimp cocktail,

French onion soup, lobster thermidor, and surf and turf with callaloo, stuffed kingfish, chunky fish broth, and other Creole dishes. Get here early on weekends, before the line stretches to the runway. ⊠ *Airport Rd. near Crown Point,* ☎ *868/639–8765. AE, MC, V.*

$–$$$ ✕ **Papillon.** Named after one of the proprietor's favorite books, this seafood restaurant consists of a homey room with an adjoining patio. Lobster Buccoo Bay is marinated in sherry and broiled with herbs. Seafood casserole au gratin means chunks of lobster, shrimp, fish, and cream—all seasoned in ginger wine. Baby shark is marinated in rum and lime. Papillon is one good reason for staying at the modest Old Grange Inn next door, owned by the same Trinidadian family. ⊠ *Buccoo Bay Rd., Mt. Irvine,* ☎ *868/639–0275. AE, DC, MC, V.*

Beaches

You'll not find manicured, country-club sand here. But those who enjoy feeling as though they've landed on a desert island will relish the untouched quality of these shores.

Bacolet Beach is a dark-sand beach that was the setting for the films *Swiss Family Robinson* and *Heaven Knows, Mr. Allison.*

Englishman's Bay is a charming beach; what's more, it's completely deserted.

Great Courland Bay, near Fort Bennett, has clear, tranquil waters. Its sandy beach—one of Tobago's longest—is home to several glitzy hotels. A marina attracts the yachting crowd.

King's Bay, surrounded by steep green hills, is the most visually satisfying of the swimming sites off the road from Scarborough to Speyside—the bay hooks around so severely that you feel as if you're in a lake. The crescent-shape beach is easy to find because it's marked by a sign about halfway between Roxborough and Speyside. Just before you reach the bay, there's a bridge with an unmarked turnoff that leads to a gravel parking lot; beyond that, a landscaped path leads to a waterfall with a rocky pool. You may meet locals who'll offer to guide you to the top of the falls, a climb that you may find not worth the effort.

Little Rockley Bay is just west of Scarborough (take Milford Road off the main highway). The beach is craggy and not much good for swimming or sunbathing, but it's quiet and offers a pleasing view of Tobago's capital across the water.

Lover's Beach is so called because of its pink sand and because of its seclusion: You have to hire a local to bring you here by boat.

Man O' War Bay is in the pretty little fishing village of Charlotteville (just northwest of Speyside). You can lounge on the sand and purchase the day's catch for your dinner.

Mt. Irvine Beach, across the street from the Mt. Irvine Bay Hotel, is an unremarkable setting, but it has great surfing in July and August; the snorkeling is excellent, too. It's also ideal for windsurfing in January and April. There are picnic tables surrounded by painted concrete pagodas and a snack bar.

Parlatuvier, on the north side of the island, is best approached via the road from Roxborough. The beach here is a classic Caribbean crescent, a scene peopled by villagers and fishermen.

Pigeon Point is the stunning locale displayed on Tobago travel brochures. Although the beach is public, it abuts part of what was once a large coconut estate, and you must pay a token admission (about TT$10) to enter the grounds and use the facilities. The beach is lined with towering royal palms, and there's a food stand, a few gift shops, a diving concession, and paddleboats for rent. The waters are calm.

Sandy Beach, along Crown Point, is abutted by several hotels. You won't lack for amenities around here.

Stone Haven Bay is a gorgeous stretch of sand that's across the street from the luxurious Grafton Beach Resort.

Store Bay, where boats depart for Buccoo Reef, is a very convivial setting. The beach is little more than a small sandy cove between two rocky breakwaters, but, ah, the food stands here: six shacks licensed by the tourist board to local ladies, who sell roti, pelau, and the world's messiest dish—crab and dumplings. Miss Jean's (☎ 868/639–0563) is the most popular; you should try Miss Esmie's crab, though.

Turtle Beach is named for the turtles that lay their eggs here at night between February and June. (If you're very quiet, you can watch; the turtles don't seem to mind.) It's set on Great Courland Bay (☞ *above*).

Outdoor Activities and Sports

BIRD-WATCHING

Some 200 hundred varieties of birds have been documented here: Look for the yellow oriole, scarlet ibis, and the comical mot-mot—the male of the species clears sticks and stones from an area and then does a dance complete with snapping sounds to attract a mate. The flora is as vivid as the birds. Purple and yellow poui trees and spectacular orange immortelles splash color over the country side, and something is blooming virtually every season. The naturalist **David Rooks** (☎ 868/639–4276) offers walks inland and trips to offshore bird colonies. Call Pat Turpin (☎ 868/660–4327) or Renson Jack (☎ 868/660–5175) at **Pioneer Journeys** for information about their 6½-hour bird-watching tours of Bloody Bay rain forest.

BOATING

Through **Bayshore Charters** (✉ Bayshore, ☎ 868/637–8711) you can fish for an afternoon or hire a boat for a weekend; the *Melissa Ann* is fully equipped for comfortable cruising, sleeps six, and has an air-conditioned cabin, refrigerator, cooking facilities, and, of course, fishing equipment. Captain Sa Gomes is one of the most experienced charter captains on the islands. **Kalina Kats** (✉ Scarborough, ☎ 868/639–6304) has a 50-ft catamaran on which you can sail around the Tobago coastline with stops for snorkeling and exploring the rain forest. The romantic sunset cruise with cocktails is a great way to end the day.

FISHING

Dillon's Fishing Charter (✉ Pigeon Point, ☎ 868/639–8765) is excellent for full- and half-day trips for kingfish, barracuda, wahoo, dolphinfish, blue marlin, etc. Trips start at $165 for four hours, including equipment.

GOLF

The 18-hole course at the **Mt. Irvine Golf Club** (✉ Mt. Irvine Bay Hotel, ☎ 868/639–8871) has been ranked among the top five in the Caribbean. Green fees are $25 for 9-holes; $40 for 18-holes. (Note that these rates are subject to 15% VAT tax.)

HIKING

Eco-consciousness is strong on both islands and especially on Tobago, where the rain forests of the Main Ridge were set aside for protection in 1764, creating the first such preserve in the Western Hemisphere. Natural areas include Little Tobago and St. Giles islands, both major seabird sanctuaries. In addition, the endangered leatherback turtles maintain breeding grounds on some of Tobago's leeward beaches.

Arnos Vale Waterwheel. They groomed some of the rain forest here to insert a series of shiny wooden walkways that take you past the remnants of an old sugar factory. The walkways allow you to see much of the ruins without disturbing nature. There's also a small museum, an excellent restaurant (☞ Dining, *above*), and several hiking trails around the property, including a 2½-mi loop. The remnants of the Buckra Estate house is on a hilltop that has spectacular views of Tobago. There are also two Amerindian sights, a slave village, and a tomb. Guides are available and can make your nature-history walk truly come alive. There's a TT$10 admission charge unless you're dining at the restaurant, so let the attendants know if you are going to take in a meal as well. ⊠ *Arnos Vale Estate, Franklyn Rd.,* ☎ *868/660–0815. MC, V.*

SCUBA DIVING

An abundance of fish and coral thrive on the nutrients of South America's Orinoco River, which are brought to Tobago by the Guayana current. There are many good spots to submerge, including Crown Point, St. Giles Islands, and off the west coast, but it's the waters off Speyside that draw scuba-diving aficionados. There are an abundance of French and queen angel fish, some as large as a dinner plate. Most of the diving is drifting diving in the mostly gentle current.

You can get information, supplies, and instruction at **AquaMarine Dive Ltd.** (⊠ Blue Waters Inn, Batteaux Bay, Speyside, ☎ 868/660–4341), **Dive Tobago** (⊠ Pigeon Point, Scarborough, ☎ 868/639–0202), **Man Friday Diving** (⊠ Charlotteville, ☎ 868/660–4676), **Tobago Dive Experience** (⊠ Crown Point, ☎ 868/639–7034), and **Tobago Dive Masters** (⊠ Speyside, ☎ 868/639–4697).

SNORKELING

Tobago offers many wonderful spots for snorkeling. Although the reefs around Speyside are becoming better known, **Buccoo Reef** is still the most popular—perhaps too popular. Over the years the reef has been damaged by the ceaseless boat traffic and by the thoughtless visitors who take pieces of coral for souvenirs. Still, it's worth experiencing, particularly if you have children. Daily 2½-hour tours by flat, glass-bottom boats let you snorkel at the reef, swim in a lagoon, and gaze at Coral Gardens—where fish and coral are yet untouched. The trip costs about $8, and masks, snorkeling equipment, and reef shoes are provided. Departure is at 11 AM from Pigeon Point. Most dive companies also arrange snorkeling tours. There is also good snorkeling near the **Arnos Vale Hotel** and the **Mt. Irvine Bay Hotel.**

TENNIS

Rex Turtle Beach (⊠ Courland Bay, Black Rock,, ☎ 868/639–2851), **Mt. Irvine** (☎ 868/639–8871), and the **Blue Waters Inn** (⊠ Batteaux Bay, Speyside, ☎ 868/660–4341) allow nonmembers and nonresidents to play.

Shopping

The souvenir-bound will do better in Trinidad than they will in Tobago, but determined shoppers should manage to ferret out some things to take home: Scarborough has the largest collection of shops, and Burnett Street, which slopes sharply from the port to St. James Park, is a good place to browse.

FOODSTUFFS

Forro's (⊠ Wilson Rd., across from Scarborough market, Scarborough, ☎ 868/639–2979; ⊠ Crown Point Airport, ☎ no phone) sells its own fine line of homemade tamarind chutney, lemon or lime marmalade, hot sauce, and guava or golden apple jelly. Mrs. Eileen Forrester, wife of the Anglican priest at St. David's in Plymouth, supervises a kitchen full of good cooks who boil and bottle the condiments and pack them in little straw baskets. Most jars are small, east to carry, and very inexpensive.

HANDICRAFTS

Cotton House (✉ Bacolet St., Scarborough, ☎ 868/639–2727) is a good bet for jewelry and imaginative batik work. Paula Young runs her shop like an art school. You can visit the upstairs studio; if it's not too busy, you can even make a batik square at no charge. **Souvenir and Gift Shop** (✉ Port Mall, Scarborough, ☎ 868/639–5632) stocks straw baskets and other crafts.

Nightlife and the Arts

People will tell you there's no nightlife on Tobago. Don't believe them. Whatever you do the rest of the week, don't miss the huge impromptu party, affectionately dubbed Sunday School, that gears up after midnight on all the street corners of Buccoo and breaks up around dawn. Pick your band, hang out for a while, then move on. In downtown Scarborough on weekend nights, you can also expect to find competing sound systems blaring at informal parties that welcome extra guests. In addition, "blockos" (spontaneous block parties) spring up all over the island; look for the hand-painted signs. Tobago also has Harvest parties on Sunday throughout the year, when a particular village opens its doors to visitors for hospitality.

Bonkers (✉ Store Bay local road, Crown Point, ☎ 868/639–7173), a hot bar and disco with a castaway theme (watch out—the DJ may make you walk the plank into the pool) draws a young crowd. The music ranges from jazz and reggae to soca. More sedentary types might consider coming on games night, when chess and domino players take the floor. **Grafton Beach Resort** (✉ Black Rock, ☎ 868/639–0191) has some kind of organized cabaret-style event every night. Even if you hate that touristy stuff, check out Les Couteaux Cultural Group, who do a high-octane dance version of Tobagonian history. **Kariwak Village** (✉ Crown Point, ☎ 868/639–8442) has hip hotel entertainment and is frequented as much by locals as visitors on Friday and Saturday nights—one of the better local jazz-calypso bands almost always plays. **Rex Turtle Beach Hotel** (✉ Great Courland Bay, ☎ 868/639–2851) hosts Les Couteaux Cultural Group and other similar performers on Wednesday and Sunday. **Starting Gate** (✉ Shirvan Rd., Mt. Irvine, ☎ 868/639–0225), a casual indoor-outdoor pub, is the venue for disco parties.

Exploring Tobago

A driving tour of Tobago, from Scarborough to Charlotteville and back, can be done in about four hours, but you'd never want to undertake this spectacular, and very hilly, ride in that time. The switchbacks can make you wish for some motion sickness pills, if you're prone; it's best to take some along because it's curvy, indeed. Plan to spend at least one night at the Speyside end of the island, and give yourself a chance to enjoy this largely untouched country and seaside at leisure. The Blue Waters Inn (☞ Lodging, *above*) is open for meals and for overnighting; it's about as close to the sea as you can get without swimming.

Numbers in the margin correspond to points of interest on the Tobago map.

SIGHTS TO SEE

❺ Charlotteville. This delightful fishing village is enfolded in a series of steep hills. Fishermen here announce the day's catch by sounding their conch shells. A view of Man O' War Bay with Pigeon Peak, Tobago's highest mountain, behind it at sunset is an exquisite treat for the eye. The underwater cliffs and canyons at the nearby **St. Giles Islands** draw divers to this spot where the Atlantic meets the Caribbean. ⊠ *Take Windward Rd. inland across mountains from Speyside.*

❹ **Flagstaff Hill.** One of the highest points of the island sits at the northern tip of Tobago. Surrounded by ocean on three sides and with a view of other hills, Charlotteville, and St. Giles Island, this was the site of an American military lookout and radio tower during World War II. It's an ideal spot for a sunset picnic.

❷ **Ft. King George.** On Mt. St. George, a few miles east of Scarborough, Tobago's best-preserved historic monument clings to a cliff high above the ocean. Ft. King George was built in the 1770s and operated until 1854. It's hard to imagine that this lovely, tranquil spot commanding sweeping views of the bay and landscaped with lush tropical foliage was ever the site of any military action, but the prison, officer's mess, and several stabilized cannons attest otherwise. Just to the left of the tall wooden figures dancing a traditional Tobagonian jig is the former barrack guardhouse, now home to the small **Tobago Museum.** Exhibits include a variety of weapons along with pre-Columbian artifacts found in the area; the fertility figures are especially interesting. Upstairs are maps and photographs of Tobago past. Be sure to check out the gift display cases for the perversely fascinating jewelry made from embalmed and painted lizards and sea creatures; you might find it hard to resist a pair of bright yellow shrimp earrings. ⊠ *84 Fort St., Scarborough,* ☎ *868/639–3970.* ▨ *TT$5.* ☉ *Weekdays 9–5.*

The **Fine Arts Centre** at the foot of the fort complex features the work of local artists.

❶ **Scarborough.** Around Rockley Bay on the island's leeward hilly side, this town is near the airport and is a popular cruise-ship port, but it conveys the feeling that not much has changed here since the area was settled two centuries ago. It may not be one of the pastel-color, delightful cities of the Caribbean, but Scarborough does have its charms, including an array of interesting little shops. Note the red-and-yellow Methodist church on the hill, one of Tobago's oldest churches.

❸ **Speyside.** At the far reach of the windward coast of Tobago, this small fishing village has a few lodgings and restaurants. Glass-bottom boats operate between Speyside and **Little Tobago Island,** one of the most important seabird sanctuaries in the Caribbean. Divers are drawn to the unspoiled reefs in the area and to the strong possibility of spotting giant manta rays. The approach to Speyside from the south affords one of the most spectacular vistas of the island.

TRINIDAD AND TOBAGO A TO Z

Arriving and Departing

BY AIRPLANE

American (☎ 868/664–4661) offers direct flights from Miami to Trinidad; **American Eagle** also offers daily round-trip flights between San Juan and Tobago—making an overnight in Trinidad a thing of the past. There are daily direct flights to Trinidad's Piarco Airport (☎ 868/669–5196), about 30 minutes east of Port-of-Spain, from New York and Miami, and frequent direct flights from Toronto and London on **BWIA** (☎ 868/625–1010 or 868/664–4268), Trinidad and Tobago's national airline. BWIA flies direct to Tobago's Crown Point Airport (☎ 868/639–0509) from New York's JFK and from Miami International. BWIA also offers flights to Port-of-Spain from other cities in the Caribbean.

Air Canada (☎ 868/664–4065) flies nonstop to Trinidad from Toronto. There are numerous flights to Port-of-Spain from other Caribbean cities on **LIAT** (☎ 868/627–2942 or 868/623–1838). LIAT also has service from the eastern Caribbean islands to Tobago.

From the Airport: Taxis are readily available at Piarco Airport. The fare to Port-of-Spain is set at $20 ($30 after 10 PM), to the Hilton at $24. By car, take Golden Grove Road north to Arouca, and then follow Eastern Main Road west for about 10 mi to Port-of-Spain. In Tobago, the fare from Crown Point Airport to Scarborough is fixed at $8, to Speyside at $36.

Electricity
Electric current can be either 110 volts or 220 volts, so bring an adapter and a converter.

Emergencies
Ambulance and Fire: ☎ 990. **Hospitals:** Port-of-Spain General Hospital (✉ 169 Charlotte St., ☎ 868/623–2951), Tobago County Hospital (✉ Fort St., Scarborough, ☎ 868/639–2551). **Pharmacies:** Bhaggan's (☎ 868/627–4657) is at Charlotte and Oxford streets near the Port-of-Spain General Hospital; **Ross Drugs** (☎ 868/639–2658) is in Scarborough. For a complete list of other pharmacies, check the T&T Yellow Pages. **Police:** ☎ 999.

Festivals and Seasonal Events
In addition to the incomparable Trinidad Carnival (☞ Nightlife and the Arts *in* Trinidad, *above*), there are a number of celebrations throughout the year. During the **Tobago Heritage Festival** (July 16–August 1) villages throughout the island have events and activities that portray one aspect (music, dance, drama, cooking, costuming) of island arts or culture. October's **Divali**, known as the festival of lights, is the climax of long spiritual preparation in the Hindu community. Small lamps beautifully illuminate the night, and there are events involving music, dancing, gift exchanges, and much hospitality. **Pan Jazz Festival**, November 11–13, as the name implies, brings together jazz and steel pan and attracts such big-name jazzers as Wynton Marsalis.

Getting Around
AIRPLANES
Air Caribbean (☎ 868/623–2500) has 15-minute flights from Trinidad to Tobago that depart several times a day. **BWIA** (☞ By Airplane *in* Arriving and Departing, *above*) also flies from Trinidad to Tobago six to 10 times a day.

CAR RENTALS
It's not worth renting a car if you are staying in Port-of-Spain, where the streets are often jammed with drivers who routinely play chicken with one another; taxis are your best bet. If you're planning to tour Trinidad, however, get some wheels. As befits one of the world's largest exporters of asphalt, Trinidad's roads are generally good, although you may encounter roadwork in progress as major resurfacing is done. In the outback, roads are often narrow, twisting, and prone to washouts in the rainy season (July–September). Inquire about conditions before you take off, particularly if you're heading to the north coast. Never drive into downtown Port-of-Spain during afternoon rush hour.

In Tobago you're better off renting a four-wheel-drive vehicle than relying on expensive taxi service. Many roads, particularly in the interior, or on the coast near Speyside and Charlotteville, are bumpy, pitted, winding, and/or steep (though the main highways are smooth and fast). Driving is on the left, so always look to your right when pulling out into traffic. Gas runs about TT$2.45 per liter. Don't let your tank get low; there aren't many gas stations on the island.

All agencies require a credit-card deposit, and in peak season you must make reservations well in advance of your arrival. Figure on paying $40–$60 per day. Trinidad has a **Thrifty** (✉ Piarco International Airport, ☎ 868/669–0602) office. Reliable local companies include **Auto Rentals** (✉ Piarco International Airport, ☎ 868/669–2277), with many other locations; **Econo-Car Rentals** (✉ Piarco International Airport, ☎ 868/669–2342); and **Southern Sales Car Rentals** (✉ Piarco International Airport and other locations, ☎ 868/669–2424 or dial 269 from a courtesy phone in airport baggage area).

In Tobago, **Thrifty** is represented at the Rex Turtle Beach Hotel (✉ Courland Bay, Black Rock, ☎ 868/639–8507). Other options are **Rattan's Car Rentals** (✉ Crown Point Airport, ☎ 868/639–8271) and **Singh's Auto Rentals** (✉ Grafton Beach Resort, ☎ 868/639–0191, ext. 53).

FERRIES

The Port Authority maintains ferry service every day except Saturday between Trinidad and Tobago, although flying is preferable, because the sea can be very rough. The ferry leaves once a day (from the dock on Dock Road in Port-of-Spain and from the cruise ship complex at Rockly Bay in Scarborough), and the trip takes about five hours. Round-trip fare is TT$60. Cabins, when available, run TT$160 (one-way, double occupancy). Tickets are sold at offices in Port-of-Spain in Trinidad (☎ 868/625–3055) and at Scarborough in Tobago (☎ 868/639–2417).

TAXIS

Taxis in Trinidad are easily identified by their license plates, which begin with the letter H. Passenger vans, called Maxi Taxis, pick up and drop off passengers as they travel and are color-coded according to which of the six areas they cover. (Yellow is for Port-of-Spain, red for eastern Trinidad, green for south Trinidad, and black for Princes Town. Brown operates from San Fernando to the southeast—Erin, Penal, Point Fortin. The only color for Tobago is blue.) They are easily hailed day or night along most of the main roads near Port-of-Spain. For longer trips you will need to hire a private taxi. Taxis are not metered; many routes have fixed rates, though they are not always observed, particularly at Carnival. Pick up a rate sheet from the tourism office. On the whole, the drivers are honest, friendly, and informative, and the experience of riding in a Maxi Taxi with a souped-up sound system during Carnival is worth whatever fare you pay.

Guided Tours

Almost any taxi driver in Port-of-Spain will take you around town and to beaches on the north coast. It costs around $70 for up to four people to go Maracas Bay beach, plus $20 per hour extra if you decide to go farther; you may be able to haggle for a cheaper rate. For a complete list of tour operators and sea cruises, contact the tourism office (☞ Visitor Information, *below*).

Frank's Glass Bottom Boat and Birdwatching Tours (✉ Speyside, Tobago, ☎ FAX 868/660-5438) offers glass-bottom-boat and snorkeling tours off the shores of Speyside. Frank also offers guided tours of the rain forest and Little Tobago. As a native of Speyside, he's extremely knowledgeable about the flora, fauna, and folklore of the island. **Tobago Travel** (✉ Scarborough, ☎ 868/639–8778, FAX 868/639–8786), the most experienced tour operator on Tobago, offers a wide array of services. **Travel Centre** (✉ 44–58 Edward St., Port-of-Spain, ☎ 868/623–5096, FAX 868/623–5101) is one of Trinidad's best tour operators. Its office is also American Express's card-member service office, for check-cashing and other matters. **Winston Nanan** (⊠ Nanan Bird Sanctuary Tours, 38 Bamboo Grove No. 1, Uriah Butler Hwy., Valsayn, ☎ 868/645–1305) is the only official tour operator at the Caroni Bird Sanctuary (☞ Exploring Trinidad, *above*); phone or write him in advance for reservations. **Rooks Nature Tours** (⊠ 462 Moses Hill, Lambeau, ☎ 868/639–4276) offers a variety of tours, including rain-forest hikes and bird-watching expeditions, with ornithologist David Rooks.

Language

The official language is English, although there's no end of idiomatic expressions used by the loquacious locals. If the sun shines while it rains, folks here say that the devil and his wife are fighting over a ham bone. If someone invites you for a "lime," by all means go—you're being invited to a party; "limin'" means relaxing and having a good time. To "beat pan" is to play the steel drum; "wine" is a sexy dance style done by rotating the hips. You'll also hear smatterings of French, Spanish, Chinese, and Hindi. (Trinidad's population is about ¼ Indian)

Money Matters

CURRENCY

The Trinidadian dollar (TT$) has been devalued twice in recent years. The current exchange rate is about TT$5.50 to US$1. The major hotels in Port-of-Spain have exchange facilities whose rates are comparable to official bank rates. Trinidad's best rate is found at the Hilton. Most businesses on the island will accept U.S. currency if you're in a pinch. Note: Prices quoted in this chapter are in U.S. dollars unless indicated otherwise.

SERVICE CHARGES, TAXES, AND TIPPING

Almost all hotels will add a 10%–15% service charge to your bill. All hotels will add a 15% government tax to your bill. Restaurants charge a 15% VAT tax. Departure tax, payable at the airport, is TT$75. Most restaurants include a 10% service charge, which is considered standard on these islands. If it isn't on the bill, tip according to service: 10–15% is fine. Cabbies expect a token tip of around 10%.

Opening and Closing Times

Most **shops** are open Monday–Friday 8–4:30, Saturday 8–noon; malls stay open later during the week and operate all day Saturday. **Banks** are open Monday–Thursday 8–2 and Friday 8–noon and 3–5.

HOLIDAYS

New Year's Day, Good Friday (Apr. 2), Easter Monday (Apr. 5), Arrival Day (May 10), Labor Day (June 19), Emancipation Day (Aug. 1), Independence Day (Aug. 31), Republic Day (Sept. 24), Christmas, and Boxing Day (Dec. 26).

Passports

Citizens of the United States, the United Kingdom, and Canada who expect to stay for less than six weeks may enter the country with a valid passport.

Precautions

Insect repellent is a must during the rainy season (June–December) and is worth having around anytime. Trinidad is only 11 degrees north of the equator, and the sun here can be intense; bring a strong sunblock. Petty theft does occur, so don't leave cash in bags that you check in at the airport. It would also be wise to use hotel safes for valuables. If you have a sensitive stomach, you'd be best to drink bottled water, though water at major hotels is fine to drink.

Telephones and Mail

The area code for both islands is 868. Postage for first-class letters to the United States is TT$2.25; for postcards, TT$2. There are no zip codes on the islands. To write to an establishment on the islands, you simply need its address, town, and "Trinidad and Tobago."

Visitor Information

For advance information, it's best to call Trinidad and Tobago's **Tourism Hotline** (☎ 888-595–4TNT). You can also contact the **Trinidad and Tobago Tourism Office** (✉ 350 5th Ave., Suite 6316, New York, NY 10118, ☎ 800/748–4224; ✉ International House, 47 Chase Side, Enfield, Middlesex, EN2 6NB2, ☎ 0181/367–3752 or ☎ 0800/960–057 after 3 PM, FAX 0181/367–9949; ✉ Taurus House, 512 Duplex Ave., Toronto, Ontario M4R 2E3, ☎ 800/267–7600, or ☎ 416/485–7827, FAX 416/485–8256).

In Trinidad, information is available from **TIDCO** (✉ 10–14 Phillips St., Port-of-Spain, ☎ 868/623–1932, FAX 868/623–3848; ✉ Piarco Airport, ☎ 868/669–5196). For Tobago, contact the **Tobago Division of Tourism** (✉ N.I.B. Mall, Level 3, Scarborough, ☎ 868/639–2125, FAX 868/639–3566), or drop in at its information booth at Crown Point Airport (☎ 868/639–0509).

25 Turks and Caicos Islands

Updated
by JoAnn
Milivojevic

Descending into the warm sea, the diver is supported like a balloon suspended in space. Weightless and floating free, she sways with the whim of gentle currents. Beneath her, a turquoise parrot fish pecks at a coral wall that's painted with muted indigos, lavenders, yellows, and pinks. The diver delicately places her pinky finger on a pink-tipped sea anemone; it clings playfully, not wanting to let go. She gently pulls her hand away and then swims off to explore more of this world of grace and color.

Scuba divers and beach aficionados have long known about the Turks and Caicos (pronounced *kay*-kos). To them, this British Crown colony of more than 40 islands and small cays (only eight of which are inhabited) is a gem that offers priceless stretches of sand and offshore reefs that are rich in marine life. Situated in an archipelago that lies 575 mi southeast of Miami and about 90 mi north of Haiti, the total landmass of these two groups of islands is 193 square mi; the total population is some 12,350.

The Turks Islands include Grand Turk, which is the capital and seat of government, and Salt Cay, with a population of about 200. It is claimed that Columbus's first landfall was on Grand Turk. Legend also has it that these islands were named by early settlers who thought the scarlet blossoms on the local cactus resembled the Turkish fez.

Approximately 22 mi west of Grand Turk, across the 7,000-ft-deep Christopher Columbus Passage, is the Caicos group: South, East, West, Middle, and North Caicos and Providenciales (nicknamed Provo). South Caicos, Middle Caicos, North Caicos, and Provo are the only inhabited islands in this group; Pine Cay and Parrot Cay are the only inhabited cays. "Caicos" is derived from *cayos,* the Spanish word for cay, and is believed to mean, appropriately, "string of islands."

Around 1678, Bermudians began to rake salt from the flats on these islands, returning to Bermuda to sell their crop. Despite French and Spanish attacks and pirate raids, the Bermudians persisted and established a
trade that became the bedrock of the Bermudian economy. In 1766 Andrew Symmers settled here to hold the islands for England. Later, loy-
alists from Georgia obtained land grants in the Caicos Islands, imported
slaves, and continued the lifestyle of the pre–Civil War American South.

Today, the Turks and Caicos are known for their booming banking and
insurance institutions, which lure investors from the United States and
beyond. The government has also devised a long-term plan to promote
tourism. Provo, in particular, is well on its way to becoming a Caribbean
destination as well as an offshore financial center. Mass tourism, however, is not in the cards; government guidelines promote a "quality, not
quantity" policy, including conservation awareness and firm restrictions on building heights and casino construction. And, without a
port for cruise ships, the islands remain uncrowded and peaceful.

THE TURKS

Grand Turk

Bermudian colonial architecture abounds on this string bean of an island (just 6 mi long and 1 mi wide). Buildings have walled-in courtyards to keep wandering donkeys from nibbling on the foliage. The
island caters to divers, and it's no wonder, the Wall, a perpendicular
slice of vertical coral mountain, is a quick swim out from many lodges.
In fact, divers will usually spend their surface interval time comfortably on shore rather than confined to a boat.

Lodging

Throughout the islands, accommodations range from small (sometimes
non-air-conditioned) inns to splashy resorts to the ultimate-in-luxury
hotels. Most of the medium and large hotels offer a choice of EP and
MAP. People who don't rent a car or scooter tend to eat at their hotels, making MAP a better option.

Another option that's popular, particularly with families, is renting a
self-contained villa or private home; contact the **Ministry of Tourism**
(☎ 649/946–2321) three to six months in advance for more information.
Please note that the government hotel tax does not apply to guest houses
with fewer than four rooms. Because of the popularity of scuba diving on all the islands, virtually all the hotels offer dive packages. Dive
packagers offering air-hotel-dive packages include **Dive Provo** (☎ 800/
234–7768) and **Undersea Adventures** (☎ 800/234–7768).

CATEGORY	COST*
$$$$	over $250
$$$	$170–$250
$$	$110–$170
$	under $110

*All prices are for a standard double room in winter, excluding 8% tax and
10%–15% service charge.*

$$ 🖼 **Arawak Inn and Beach Club.** These yellow, condo-style accommo-
dations have private bedrooms, tiled baths, kitchens, and living rooms
with sofa beds. With so much space, you and your children (those under
12 stay free) will probably love it here. The complex is steps away from
a fabulous white-sand beach, and the management offers free shuttle
service into town daily. Don't feel like cooking? The restaurant serves
up delicious Caribbean meals. The hotel offers dive packages through

a shop just a two-minute walk down the main street. ⊠ *Near White Sands Beach (Box 190), Cockburn Town,* ☎ *649/946–2277 or 888/ 332–3113 (reservations service),* ⅢX *649/946–2279. 15 units. Restaurant, bar, air-conditioning, pool, horseback riding. MC, V.*

$$ Guanahani Beach Hotel. Sun worshipers take note: This hotel owns one of Grand Turk's finest stretches. The palm-tree-lined property is also popular with honeymooners, so you may find an air of romance. The rooms all have ocean views, pale ceramic tile floors, full baths, two double beds, and primary-color Caribbean-print spreads and curtains. You can rent a crewed 35-ft yacht for day trips or moonlight rides, and dive packages are available through a dive shop, just steps away. ⊠ *Cockburn Town (Box 178),* ☎ *649/946–2135 or 800/725–2822,* ⅢX *649/946–1460. 16 rooms. Restaurant, 2 bars, pool. MC, V.*

$$ Salt Raker Inn. Across the street from the beach, this galleried house was the home of a Bermudian shipwright 180 years ago. What the guest quarters lack in elegance they make up for in cleanliness and comfort. Each has tile floors, air-conditioning, and a mini-refrigerator. Ask for one of the three garden rooms, which have screened porches, or opt for a suite and an ocean view. (Note that dive packages are available.) The fare at the ☞ **Secret Garden** restaurant is straightforward; you can even get a piece of apple pie. ⊠ *Duke St. (Box 1) Cockburn Town,* ☎ *649/946–2260,* ⅢX *649/946–2817.* ⊠ *U.K. reservations: 44 Birchington Rd., London NW6 4LJ,* ☎ *0171/328–6474. 10 rooms, 2 suites. Restaurant, bar, air-conditioning, bicycles. AE, D, MC, V. EP.*

$$ Sitting Pretty Hotel. Cockburn Town's main drag halves this hotel.
★ On one side, comfortable, lodge-style rooms and balconied suites with kitchens run along a white-sand beach. Beachfront rooms have bamboo furniture, colorful Haitian art, and tidy baths. On the other side of the street are rooms that ooze island charm, as well as a pool, and a garden. The ☞ **Sandpiper** restaurant is a good place for a steak or lobster dinner. ⊠ *Duke St. (Box 42) Cockburn Town,* ☎ *649/946– 2232,* ⅢX *649/946–2877. 40 rooms, 2 suites. 2 restaurants, 2 bars, air-conditioning, room service, pool, dive shop, windsurfing, boating, bicycles, shop, baby-sitting, travel services. AE, MC, V. EP, MAP.*

$$ Turk's Head Inn. Built in 1850 by a prosperous salt miner, this building has served as the American consulate and as the governor's guest house (Queen Elizabeth reportedly took a room here on her last visit). Under new ownership as of 1997, many renovations are promised including restoring antique bedroom furniture. Rooms are currently done in peaches or limes and have mini-refrigerators and coffeemakers. An assortment of expats have made this place their stomping ground (the ☞ **Turk's Head Inn** bar and restaurant bustle at night). In the front courtyard, an oversize hammock is the perfect place from which to admire the well-tended garden. The beach is only a few strides away, and dive packages are available. ⊠ *Duke St. (Box 58) Cockburn Town,* ☎ *649/946–2466,* ⅢX *649/946–2825. 7 rooms, 1 apartment. Restaurant, bar, air-conditioning. AE, MC, V.*

$–$$ Coral Reef Beach Club. One- and two-bedroom units here have full kitchens, air-conditioning, and contemporary furnishings. A stay here puts you just a short drive from town and just steps from the beach. ⊠ *Near The Ridge (Box 10),* ☎ *649/946–2055,* ⅢX *649/946–2911. 18 units. Restaurant, bar, air-conditioning, pool, hot tub, tennis court, health club, shop. AE, MC, V. EP, MAP.*

Dining

Like everything else on these islands, dining out is a very laid-back affair, which is not to say that it's cheap. Because of the high cost of importing all edibles, the price of a meal is usually higher than in the United States. Reservations are generally not required, and dress is casual.

CATEGORY	COST*
$$$	over $25
$$	$15–$25
$	under $15

per person for a three-course meal, excluding drinks, service, and 7% sales tax

AMERICAN

$$ ✕ Sandpiper. Candles flicker on the Sandpiper's terrace, which is set beside a flower-filled courtyard at the ☞ **Sitting Pretty Hotel.** The leisurely pace here creates a relaxing setting to experience such blackboard specialties as lobster, filet mignon, seafood platter, or pork chops with applesauce. ✉ *Duke St., Cockburn Town,* ☎ *649/946–2232. AE, D, MC, V.*

$$ ✕ Secret Garden. Menu highlights at the ☞ **Salt Raker Inn's** restaurant, include a seafood platter, grilled lobster tail, pork chops, and roast leg of lamb. For dessert, try the tasty apple pie. The Sunday dinner and sing-along are popular. The outdoor garden is beautifully landscaped with hibiscus, bougainvillea, palms, and other tropical plants; sea nets, glass balls and local paintings round out the decor. ✉ *Duke St., Cockburn Town,* ☎ *649/946–2260. AE, D, MC, V.*

CARIBBEAN

$ ✕ Pepper Pot Beachside on Front Street is a little blue shack where Peanuts Butterfield makes her famous spicy conch fritters. ✉ *Front St., Cockburn Town,* ☎ *No phone. No credit cards.*

ECLECTIC

$–$$$ ✕ Turk's Head Inn. The menu changes daily at the lively restaurant in the ☞ **Turk's Head Inn,** touted by many residents as the best on the island. Some staples include escargots, pâté, and a handful of other delectables, including local grouper fingers perfectly fried for fish-and-chips. Look for lobster, quiche, steaks, and homemade soups on the blackboard menu. You may not want to leave after your meal—come nightfall, the inn's bar is abuzz with local gossip and mirthful chatter. ✉ *Duke St., Cockburn Town,* ☎ *649/946–2466. AE, MC, V.*

SEAFOOD

$ ✕ Regal Begal. Drop by this popular local eatery for local specialties such as cracked conch, minced lobster, and fish-and-chips. The atmosphere is casual and the decor unmemorable, but the portions are large and the prices easy on your wallet. ✉ *Hospital Rd., Cockburn Town,* ☎ *649/946–2274. No credit cards.*

$ ✕ Water's Edge. Relaxed waterfront dining awaits you at this pleasantly rustic eatery. The limited menu covers the basics with a twist—from barbecued grouper to a fresh seafood crepe. A kids' menu is also available. The food is authentic and filling, and the view at sunset breathtaking, but the irresistible homemade pies are enough to justify a visit. ✉ *Duke St., Cockburn Town,* ☎ *649/946–1680. MC, V. Closed Mon.*

Beaches

There are more than 230 mi of beaches in the Turks and Caicos Islands, ranging from secluded coves to miles-long stretches. Most beaches are soft coralline sand. Tiny cays offer complete isolation for nude sunbathing and skinny-dipping. Many are accessible only by boat. **Governor's Beach,** a long white strip on the west coast of Grand Turk, is one of the nicest beaches on this island; it's very long and wide, offering you plenty of sparkling, powder-soft sand on which to stroll.

Outdoor Activities and Sports

BICYCLING

The island's flat terrain isn't very taxing, and most roads have hard surfaces. On Duke Street in Cockburn Town, you can wheel past the

Turks and Caicos Islands

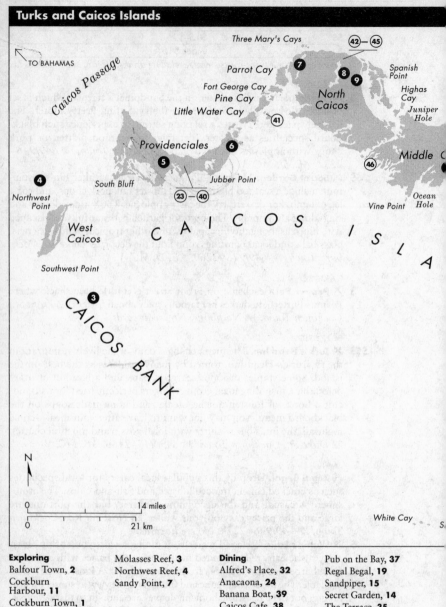

Exploring
Balfour Town, **2**
Cockburn
Harbour, **11**
Cockburn Town, **1**
Conch Bar Caves, **10**
Downtown Provo, **5**
Flamingo Pond, **8**
Island Sea Center, **6**
Kew, **9**

Molasses Reef, **3**
Northwest Reef, **4**
Sandy Point, **7**

Dining
Alfred's Place, **32**
Anacaona, **24**
Banana Boat, **39**
Caicos Cafe, **38**
Dora's, **33**
Fast Eddie's, **36**
Gecko Grille, **27**
Hey, José, **40**
Pepper Pot, **18**

Pub on the Bay, **37**
Regal Begal, **19**
Sandpiper, **15**
Secret Garden, **14**
The Terrace, **35**
Top O' the Cove
Gourmet
Delicatessen, **34**
Turk's Head Inn, **16**
Water's Edge, **20**

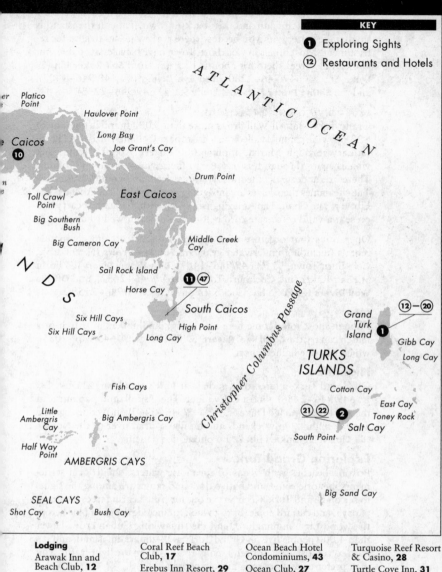

Lodging

Arawak Inn and Beach Club, **12**

Beaches, **23**

Blue Horizons Resort, **46**

Club Caribe Beach & Harbour Hotel, **47**

Club Med Turkoise, **25**

Club Vacanze Prospect of Whitby Hotel, **42**

Coral Reef Beach Club, **17**

Erebus Inn Resort, **29**

Grace Bay Club, **24**

Guanahani Beach Hotel, **13**

JoAnne's B&B, **45**

Le Deck Hotel & Beach Club, **26**

Meridian Club, **41**

Mount Pleasant Guest House, **22**

Ocean Beach Hotel Condominiums, **43**

Ocean Club, **27**

Pelican Beach Hotel, **44**

Salt Raker Inn, **14**

Sitting Pretty Hotel, **15**

Treasure Beach Villas, **30**

Turk's Head Inn, **16**

Turquoise Reef Resort & Casino, **28**

Turtle Cove Inn, **31**

Windmills Plantation, **21**

beautiful Bermudian buildings. Weave your way to the lighthouse on the island's northernmost point. Follow the western road past the Coral Reef Beach Club and then back to town. Though the island is small, take water with you because there are few places to stop for refreshment. Most hotels in Cockburn Town have bicycles available, but you can also rent them for about $10 a day from **Salt Raker Inn** (✉ Duke St., ☎ 649/946–2260), **Sea Eye Diving** (☎ 649/946–1407), and the **Sitting Pretty Hotel** (✉ Duke St., ☎ 649/946–2232).

SCUBA DIVING AND SNORKELING

Grand Turk's famed Wall drops more than 7,000 ft and is one side of a 22-mi-wide channel called the Christopher Columbus Passage. From January through March, about 6,000 eastern Atlantic humpback whales swim through this passage to their winter breeding grounds. There are undersea cathedrals, coral gardens, and countless tunnels. The site names themselves are intriguing: Rolling Hill, The Anchor, The Library, The Chair, The Amazing Abyss. Note that you must carry and present a valid certificate card before you'll be allowed to dive.

Operations that organize trips and provide instruction, equipment rentals (including underwater gear) are **Sea Eye Divers** (✉ Duke St., Cockburn Town, ☎ FAX 649/946–1407), **Blue Water Divers** (✉ Front St., Salt Raker Inn, Cockburn Town, ☎ 649/946–2432), and **Off the Wall Divers** (✉ Pond St., Cockburn Town, ☎ 649/946–2159).

TENNIS

Though most folks come here for diving, landlubbers in search of a match can try the **Coral Reef Resort** (✉ The Ridge, ☎ 649/946–2055), which has one lighted court.

Nightlife

On Grand Turk, a fun crowd gathers at **Turk's Head Inn** (✉ Duke St., ☎ 649/946–2466) almost every night. There's folk and pop music at the **Salt Raker Inn** (✉ Duke St., ☎ 649/946–2260) on Wednesday and Sunday nights. On weekends and holidays, head over to the **Nookie Hill Club** (✉ Nookie Hill, ☎ no phone) for dancing.

Exploring Grand Turk

Pristine beaches with vistas of turquoise waters, small local settlements, historic ruins, and native flora and fauna are among the sights to see on Grand Turk. Keep an eye out for fruit-bearing trees like lime, papaya, and custard apple. Birds to look for include the great blue heron, the woodstar hummingbird, and the squawking Cuban crow. Fewer than 4,000 people live on Grand Turk, a 7½-square-mi island, and it's hard to get lost as there aren't many roads. Given the light traffic, you may prefer to explore on a motor scooter.

Numbers in the margin correspond to points of interest on the Turks and Caicos Islands map.

❶ **Cockburn Town.** The buildings in this, the colony's capital and seat of government, reflect the 19th-century Bermudian style of architecture. The narrow streets are lined with low stone walls and old street lamps, now powered by electricity. Horses and cattle wander around as if they own the place, and the occasional donkey cart clatters by, carrying a load of water or freight. In one of the oldest stone buildings in the Turks and Caicos, the **Turks & Caicos National Museum** houses the Molasses Reef wreck of 1513, the earliest shipwreck discovered in the Americas. The natural-history exhibits include artifacts left by Taino, African, North American, Bermudian, French, and Latin American settlers. An impressive addition to the museum is the coral reef and sea-life exhibit, faithfully modeled on a popular dive site just off the island. ✉ *Duke*

St.,Cockburn Town, ☎ 649/946–2160. 🖾 $5. ⊘ Mon.–Tues. and Thurs.–Fri. 9–4, Wed. 9–6, Sat. 10–1.

Salt Cay

Only 200 people live on this 2½-square-mi dot of land. There's not much in the way of development, but there are splendid beaches on the north coast. As on the other Turks and Caicos islands, the land is arid, with mostly cactus and scrub brush growth. The most spectacular sites are beneath the waves: 10 dive sites are just minutes from shore.

Lodging

☞ For general information *and* price categories, *see* Lodging *under* Grand Turk, *above.*

$$$$ 🏨 **Windmills Plantation.** The attraction here is the lack of distraction:
★ no nightlife, no cruise ships, and no shopping. Owner-manager-architect Guy Lovelace and his interior designer wife, Patricia, built the hotel as their version of a colonial-era plantation. The great house has four suites, each with a sitting area, a four-poster bed, ceiling fans, and a veranda or balcony with a sea view. All are furnished in a mix of antique English and wicker furniture. Four other rooms are housed in two adjacent buildings. Rates for two people include snorkeling gear, three meals, and unlimited bar drinks, wine, and beer. ⊠ *North Beach Rd.,* ☎ *649/946–6962 or 800/822–7715 (reservations service),* FAX *649/946–6930. 4 rooms, 4 suites. Restaurant, bar, pool, hiking, horseback riding, beach, snorkeling, fishing, library. AE, MC, V. EP.*

$ 🏨 **Mount Pleasant Guest House.** This simple, somewhat rustic hotel offers guests inexpensive lodging at a remote location. Not all rooms have private baths. ⊠ *Balfour Town,* ☎ *649/946–6927 or 800/821–6670. 7 rooms, 1 with bath. Restaurant, bar, horseback riding, scuba diving, bicycles, library. MC, V.*

Beaches

There are superb beaches on the north coast of **Salt Cay. Big Sand Cay,** 7 mi to the south of Salt Cay, is also known for its excellent beaches.

Outdoor Activities and Sports

SCUBA DIVING AND SNORKELING

Scuba divers can explore the *Endymion,* a recently discovered, 140-ft, wooden-hull British warship that sank in 1790. It's just off the southern point of Salt Cay. **Porpoise Divers** (⊠ Salt Cay, ☎ 649/946–6927) rents all the necessary equipment.

Exploring Salt Cay

Salt sheds and salt ponds are silent reminders of the days when the island was a leading producer of salt. From February through March, whales pass by on the way to their winter breeding grounds.

❷ Balfour Town. What little development there is on Salt Cay is found in this town. It's home to the Windmills Plantation hotel, the Mount Pleasant Guest House, and a few stores that sell tourist items like handwoven baskets, T-shirts, convenience foods and beach items.

THE CAICOS

West Caicos

Accessible only by boat, this island is uninhabited and untamed, and there are no facilities whatsoever. A glorious white beach stretches for 1 mi along the northwest point, and the offshore diving here is among the most exotic in the islands. A wall inhabited by countless species of large marine life begins ¼ mi out. If you do tour West Caicos, take along several vats of insect repellent. It won't help much with the sharks, but it should fend off the mosquitoes and sand flies. Be advised, too, that the interior is overgrown with dense shrubs, including manchineel, whose green fruit is poisonous. Sap and even raindrops falling from the trees onto your skin can cause painful blisters.

Exploring West Caicos

③ Molasses Reef. It is rumored to be the final resting place of the *Pinta*, which is thought to have been wrecked here in the early 1500s. Over the past few centuries numerous wrecks have occurred in the area between West Caicos and Provo, and author Peter Benchley is among the treasure seekers who have been lured to this island.

④ Northwest Reef. The site offers great stands of elkhorn coral and acres of staghorn brambles. But it's only for experienced divers. The wall starts deep, the currents are strong, and there are sharks.

Providenciales

In the mid-18th century, so the story goes, a French ship was wrecked near here, and the survivors were washed ashore on an island they gratefully christened La Providentielle. Under the Spanish, the name was changed to Providenciales. Today, about 6,000 people live on Provo (as everybody calls it), a considerable number of whom are expatriate U.S. and Canadian businesspeople and retirees. The island's 44 square mi are by far the most developed in the Turks and Caicos.

Lodging

With its rolling ridges and 12-mi beach, the island is a prime target for developers. More than two decades ago a group of U.S. investors, including the DuPonts, Ludingtons, and Roosevelts, opened up this island for visitors and those seeking homesites in the Caribbean. In 1990 the island's first luxury resort, the Turquoise Reef Resort & Casino, opened as did luxurious Ocean Club, a condominium resort at Grace Bay. These were followed by the upscale Grace Bay Club resort in 1992. Competition created by the new resorts has spurred many older hotels to undertake renovations. ☞ For further information *and* price categories, *see* Lodging *under* Grand Turk, *above*.

$$$$ 🏨 **Beaches.** At this new member of the Sandals chain, couples are certainly still a part of the scene, but Beaches is geared toward families as well. Luxurious accommodations combined with a full range of water sports and bar service that extends to the beach make this all-inclusive resort an indulgent experience (though housekeeping can be inconsistent). The tropical landscaping is lovely and lush, as are the two large free-form lap pools (one has a swim-up bar). For even more pampering, head for the spa, which offers such services as body wraps, massages, and facials. ⊠ *Lower Bight Rd., Grace Bay,* ☎ *649/946–8000 or 800/726–3257,* ℻ *649/946–8001. 200 rooms. 3 restaurants, pool, hot tub, spa, 2 tennis courts, health club, dive shop, snorkeling, surfing, windsurfing. AE, MC, V. All-inclusive.*

$$$$ 🏨 **Grace Bay Club.** Staying at this Swiss-owned, Mediterranean-style,
★ all-suites resort is a little like being the guest of honor of a very gracious host with unbeatable taste. Guest quarters, which have breathtaking views of stunning Grace Bay, are furnished with rattan and pickled wood and have such appointments as Mexican-tile floors with elegant throw rugs from Turkey and India. Although there are plenty of activities here (from diving to golf to catered picnics on surrounding islands), just letting yourself relax amid the natural beauty of this peaceful yet invigorating getaway is a major activity itself. Pamper your-

self further with a French meal in the ☞ **Anacaona** restaurant. ⊠ *Grace Bay (Box 128),* ☎ *649/946–5757 or 800/946–5757,* ℻ *649/946–5758. 22 suites. Restaurant, bar, pool, hot tub, 2 tennis courts, beach, video games, library. AE, MC, V. EP, MAP.*

$$$–$$$$ 🏨 **Ocean Club.** This luxury resort is on a 12-mi stretch of pristine beach, a short walk from Provo's only golf course. The all-suite accommodations range from efficiency studios to deluxe quarters with an ocean view, a screened balcony, a kitchen, a dining room, and a living room. Third-floor rooms have striking cathedral ceilings, and all but efficiency units have a washer and dryer. The on-site ☞ **Gecko Grille** restaurant serves creative island dishes. ⊠ *Grace Bay (Box 240),* ☎ *649/946– 5880 or 800/457–8787,* ℻ *649/946–5845. 86 suites. 2 restaurants, bar, 2 pools, 18-hole golf course, tennis court, exercise room, dive shop, shops, car rental. AE, MC, V. EP.*

$$$ 🏨 **Club Med Turkoise.** This lavish resort is one of the most sumptuous of all Club Med's villages. One-, two-, and three-story bungalows line a 1-mi beach, and all the usual sybaritic pleasures are here. This club is geared toward couples, singles aged 28 and over, and divers. The package includes all the water sports and daytime activities you can handle, plus nightly entertainment. ⊠ *Grace Bay,* ☎ *649/946–5500 or 800/258– 2633; 212/750–1684 or 212/750–1687 in NY;* ℻ *649/946–5501. 298 rooms. 3 restaurants, bar, snack bar, pool, 8 tennis courts, exercise room, beach, dive shop, water sports, fishing, bicycles, shop, dance club, video games, library. AE, MC, V. All-inclusive (except drinks).*

$$$ 🏨 **Le Deck Hotel & Beach Club.** This pink hostelry was built in classic
★ Bermudian style around a tropical courtyard. Its rooms and suites are clean (right down to the tile floors) and have a few basic comforts, such as color TVs and air-conditioning. Most of the folk who stay here are divers, and the atmosphere is informal and lively. ⊠ *Grace Bay (Box 144),* ☎ *649/946–5547 or 800/528–1905,* ℻ *649/946–5770. 25 rooms, 2 suites. Restaurant, bar, air-conditioning, pool, beach, snorkeling, windsurfing. AE, D, MC, V. AP, CP, EP, MAP.*

$$$ 🏨 **Turquoise Reef Resort & Casino.** Oversize oceanfront rooms have
★ rattan furniture and a rich Caribbean color scheme. All rooms have a king or two double beds, a TV, and a terrace or patio. The island's only casino is here, and there's live nightly entertainment. You can also partake in daily activities that include pool volleyball and children's treasure hunts. ⊠ *Grace Bay (Box 205),* ☎ *649/946–5555 or 800/ 992–2015,* ℻ *649/946–5522. 228 rooms. 3 restaurants, 3 bars, air-conditioning, fans, room service, pool, hot tub, 2 tennis courts, exercise room, beach, dive shop, water sports, shops, casino, dance club, baby-sitting, travel services. AE, MC, V. EP, MAP.*

$$ 🏨 **Erebus Inn Resort.** The views are fabulous from this cliffside setting
★ overlooking Turtle Cove. All units have two double beds, wicker furnishings, and original island artwork, including some unique Haitian wall hangings. The higher priced cottages are atop the cliff and are more private than the rooms in the hotel proper. The lively restaurant and bar has a menu of French and Caribbean cuisine. Five affordable restaurants are within walking distance, as are snorkeling sites, a shopping center, and several dive operations. Frequent shuttles take you to a nearby beach. ⊠ *Turtle Cove (Box 238),* ☎ *649/946–4240 or 800/ 323–5655 (reservations service),* ℻ *649/946–4704. 30 rooms. Restaurant, bar, air-conditioning, 2 pools (1 saltwater), 2 tennis courts, aerobics, exercise room, baby-sitting. AE, MC, V. EP, MAP.*

$$ 🏨 **Treasure Beach Villas.** These one- and two-bedroom, modern, apartments have fully equipped kitchens and ceiling fans. You may want a car or bike (Treasure Beach has rentals) to reach the grocery store or restaurants; bus service is limited. Provo's 12 mi of white sandy beach is just outside your door, and the hotel can organize fishing, snorkeling, and scuba expeditions. ⊠ *The Bight,* ☎ *649/946–4325,* 𝖥𝖠𝖷 *649/ 946–4108; or* ⊠ *Box 8409, Hialeah, FL 33012. 8 single rooms, 10 double rooms. Pool, tennis court. AE, D, MC, V. EP.*

$ 🏨 **Turtle Cove Inn.** A marina, a free-form pool (set in a lushly landscaped area), a dive shop with equipment rentals and instruction, and lighted tennis courts attract the sporting crowd to this affordable, well-run hotel. Rooms are simple, clean, and comfortable (all have a TV, a phone, and air-conditioning; eight have mini-refrigerators). There's a free boat shuttle to the nearby beach and snorkeling reef, and dive packages are available. Turtle Cove is also within walking distance of a handful of good restaurants. ⊠ *The Bight (Box 131),* ☎ *649/946– 4203 or 800/887–0477 (reservations service),* 𝖥𝖠𝖷 *649/946–4141. 30 rooms, 1 suite. 2 restaurants, 2 bars, air-conditioning, pool, 2 tennis courts, dive shop, bicycles. AE, MC, V. EP.*

Dining

☞ For general information *and* price categories, *see* Dining *under* Grand Turk, *above.*

AMERICAN

$$–$$$ ✕ **Alfred's Place.** Austrian owner Alfred Holzfeind caters to an Amer-
★ ican palate with an extensive menu that has everything from prime rib to chicken salad. The alfresco lounge is a popular watering hole for locals and tourists alike. ⊠ *Turtle Cove,* ☎ *649/946–4679. AE, D, MC, V. Closed Mon. July–Oct. No lunch weekends.*

CARIBBEAN

$–$$ ✕ **Dora's.** This popular local eatery serves island fare—turtle, shredded lobster, spicy conch chowder—7 days a week, from 7 AM until the last person leaves the bar. Plastic print and lace tablecloths, hanging plants, and Haitian art add to the island ambience. Soups come with homemade bread; entrées such as fish-and-chips, conch Creole, and grilled pork chops come with a vegetable. Be sure to come early for the packed Monday- and Thursday-night all-you-can-eat $20 seafood buffets. The price includes transportation to and from your hotel. ⊠ *Leeward Hwy.,* ☎ *649/946–4558. No credit cards.*

DELI

$ ✕ **Top O' the Cove Gourmet Delicatessen.** You can walk to this tiny café on Leeward Highway from the Turtle Cove and Erebus inns (don't be put off by the location in the Napa Auto Parts plaza). Order breakfast, deli sandwiches, salads, and cool soft-swirl frozen yogurt. Top O' the Cove is open every day but Christmas and New Year's from 7 AM to 3:30 PM. ⊠ *Leeward Hwy.,* ☎ *649/946–4694. No credit cards.*

ECLECTIC

$$$ ✕ **The Terrace.** The cuisine here has a Euro-Caribbean flair, and the menu changes according to the freshest ingredients available. You can make a meal from such delicious starters as freshly baked tomato-and-goat-cheese tarts, lobster bisque, and simmered mussels. Main courses include roast rack of lamb, and fresh conch encrusted with pecans. Top it all off with a classic crème brûlée. ⊠ *Turtle Cove,* ☎ *649/946–4763. AE, MC, V. Closed Sun.*

$$–$$$ ✕ **Gecko Grille.** At this ☞ Ocean Club resort restaurant, you can eat indoors amid tropical murals or on the garden patio. Creative fare includes almond-cracked conch with a lime *rémoulade* (a cold, mayonnaise-based sauce), and grilled pork chops marinated in papaya juice. Portions are large, so either share or bring a hearty appetite. ⊠ *Grace Bay,* ☎ *649/946–5880. AE, MC, V.*

$–$$ ✕ **Fast Eddie's.** Plants festoon this cheerful restaurant, which is across from the airport. Broiled turtle steak, fried grouper fingers, and other island specialties are joined on the menu by old American standbys such as cheeseburgers and cherry pie. Wednesday evening there's a $20 ($10 for children) all-you-can-eat seafood buffet. Friday is prime rib and live music night. Free transportation to and from your hotel is provided. ⊠ *Airport Rd.,* ☎ *649/941–3175. MC, V.*

$–$$ ✕ **Pub on the Bay.** If beachfront dining is what you're after, it doesn't get much better than this. Located in the Blue Hill residential district, a five-minute drive from downtown Provo, this restaurant serves fried or steamed fish, oxtail stew, barbecue ribs, chicken, various sandwiches, and even turtle steak. There's no air-conditioning, so you may as well cross the street to one of three thatch-roof "huts," which stand on the beach. ⊠ *Blue Hill Rd.,* ☎ *649/941–5309. AE, MC, V.*

$ ✕ **Caicos Café.** There's a pervasive air of celebration in the uncovered outdoor dining area of this popular eatery. Choose from a selection of local and American cuisine, including lobster sandwiches, hamburgers, and a variety of excellent salads. ⊠ *Across from Turquoise Reef, Grace Bay,* ☎ *649/946–5278. AE, MC, V. No lunch Sun.*

FRENCH

$$–$$$ ✕ **Anacaona.** At the impressive ☞ **Grace Bay Club,** this exquisitely
★ designed restaurant offers a truly fine dining experience minus the tie, the air-conditioning, and the attitude. Start with a bottle of fine wine from the extensive cellar, and then enjoy a three- or four-course meal of the chef's light but flavorful cooking, which combines traditional French recipes with fresh seafood and Caribbean fruits, vegetables, and spices. Oil lamps on the tables, gently circulating ceiling fans, and the natural sounds of the breeze, ocean, birds, and tree frogs all add to the Eden-like environment. ⊠ *Grace Bay,* ☎ *649/946–5050. AE, MC, V.*

SEAFOOD

$$ ✕ **Banana Boat.** Buoys and other sea relics deck the walls of this brightly painted, casual restaurant on the wharf. Grilled grouper, lobster-salad sandwiches, conch fritters, and a refreshing conch salad are among the menu options. Excellent tropical drinks include the house specialty, the rum-filled Banana Breeze. ⊠ *Turtle Cove,* ☎ *649/941–5706. AE, MC, V.*

TEX-MEX

$–$$ ✕ **Hey, José.** Frequented by locals, this restaurant claims to serve the
★ island's best margaritas. Customers also return for the tasty Tex-Mex treats: tacos, tostados, nachos, burritos, fajitas, and José's special-recipe hot chicken wings. Creative types can build their own pizzas. ⊠ *Central Sq.,* ☎ *649/946–4812, V. Closed Sun.*

Beaches

A fine white-sand beach stretches 12 mi along the northeast coast of **Providenciales,** where most of the hotels are. There are also good beaches at **Sapodilla Bay.**

Outdoor Activities and Sports

BICYCLING

Provo has a few steep grades to conquer, but they're short, and there's little traffic. You can rent bikes at the **Island Princess** hotel (☎ 649/946–4260) at the Bight for $10 a day, through **Turtle Inn Divers** (⊠ Turtle Cove Inn, ☎ 649/941–5389) for $12 a day and $60 a week, or at the **Turquoise Reef Resort & Casino** (⊠ Grace Bay, ☎ 649/946–5555) for $14 a day.

BOATING AND SAILING

Dive Provo (⊠ Turquoise Reef Resort, Grace Bay, ☎ 649/946–5040) rents small sailboats for $20 per hour and offers beginning instruction

($40 for up to two hours). Sailing not your bent? Try ocean kayaking ($10 per hour for one and $15 per hour for two).

FISHING

You can rent a boat with a captain for a half or full day of sportfishing through **J&B Tours** (⊠ Leward Marina, ☎ 649/946–5047) for about $300 a day. **Silver Deep** (⊠ Turtle Cove Marina, ☎ 649/941–5595) will take you out for half- or full-day bonefishing or bottom-fishing, bait and tackle included. The same outfit will arrange half- or full-day deep-sea fishing trips in search of shark, marlin, kingfish, sawfish, wahoo, and tuna—with all equipment furnished. Deep-sea, bone-, and bottom fishing are also available aboard the **Sakitumi** (☎ 649/946–4065).

GOLF

Provo Golf Club (☎ 649/946–5991) has a par-72, 18-hole, championship course that was designed by Karl Litten. It has narrow "target areas" and sandy waste areas—a formidable challenge to anyone playing from the championship tees. Fees are $90, which includes a shared electric cart. A pro shop, driving ranges, and a restaurant–bar round out the facilities.

PARASAILING

A 15-minute flight over Grace Bay is available for $45 at either **Dive Provo** (⊠ Turquoise Reef Resort, Grace Bay, ☎ 649/946–5040 or 800/234–7768) or **J&B Tours** (⊠ Leward Marina, ☎ 649/946–5047).

SCUBA DIVING AND SNORKELING

For excellent close-to-shore snorkeling there's a reef near the White House off Penn's Road. Diving options include any of the spectacular walls, and visibility can often exceed 100 ft. The waters are generally quite warm, though you may want a wet suit to avoid a chill on the second or third dive of the day. Dive operators include: **Aquanaut** (⊠ Turtle Cove, ☎ 649/946–4048), **Art Pickering's Provo Turtle Divers** (⊠ Turtle Cove Marina, ☎ 649/946–4232), **Caicos Adventures** (⊠ Turtle Cove Marina, ☎ 649/946–3346), **Dive Provo** (⊠ Turquoise Reef Resort, Grace Bay, ☎ 649/946–5040 or 800/234–7768), **Flamingo Divers** (⊠ Turtle Cove, ☎ 649/946–4193), **J&B Tours** (⊠ Leward Marina, ☎ 649/946–5047).

SEA EXCURSIONS

The **Ocean Outback** (☎ 649/946–4080), a 70-ft motor cruiser, has barbecue-and-snorkel cruises to uninhabited islands. Both the 37-ft catamaran **Beluga** (☎ 649/941–5196), $39 per half day, and the 56-ft trimaran **Tao** (☎ 649/946–5040) run sunset cruises, as well as sailing and snorkeling outings. A full-day outing on the **Tao** is $59 per person, including snorkel rental and lunch.

For $20 per person, **Dive Provo** (⊠ Turquoise Reef Resort, Grace Bay, ☎ 649/946–5040 or 800/234–7768) gives two-hour glass-bottom-boat tours of the spectacular reefs. **Turtle Inn Divers** (⊠ Turtle Cove Inn, ☎ 649/941–5389) offers full-day Sunday excursions for divers for $64.50 per person ($25 per person for nondivers and snorkelers). The **Turks and Caicos Aggressor** (⊠ Turtle Cove Marina, ☎ 504/385–2416, FAX 504/384–0817) offers luxury six-day dive cruises.

TENNIS

Several hotels have courts. There are two lighted courts at **Turtle Cove Inn** (☎ 649/946–4203), eight courts (four lighted) at **Club Med Turkoise** (☎ 649/946–5500), two lighted courts at the **Turquoise Reef Resort** (☎ 649/946–5555), two lighted courts at the **Erebus Inn** (☎ 649/946–4240), one unlighted court at **Treasure Beach Villas** (☎ 649/946–4211), and two lighted courts at **Grace Bay Club** (☎ 649/946–5050).

WATERSKIING

Waterskiers will find the calm turquoise water ideal for long-distance runs. **Dive Provo** (⊠ Turquoise Reef Resort, Grace Bay, ☎ 649/946–5040 or 800/234–7768) charges $35 for a 15-minute run.

WINDSURFING

Rental and instruction are available at **Dive Provo** (⊠ Turquoise Reef Resort, Grace Bay, ☎ 649/946–5040 or 800/234–7768).

Shopping

New shops open every month. You'll find most stores in the five main shopping complexes: Market Place, Central Square, and Caribbean Place, all on Leeward Highway; Turtle Cove Landing, in Turtle Cove; and the newest complex, Ports of Call, in Grace Bay. Delicate baskets woven from the local top grasses and small metalworks are the only crafts native to the Turks and Caicos, and they are sold in many places.

The **Bamboo Gallery** (⊠ Market Place, ☎ 649/946–4748) sells Caribbean art, from vivid Haitian paintings to wood carvings and local metal sculptures. **Greensleeves** (⊠ Central Square, ☎ 649/946–4147) offers paintings by local artists, island-made rag rugs, baskets, jewelry, and sisal mats and bags. **Mama's Gifts** (⊠ Ports of Call, ☎ 649/941–3338) sells handwoven and embroidered straw baskets, handbags, hats, and shell and wood jewelry. **Maison Creole** (⊠ Grace Bay, ☎ no phone) has unique Caribbean arts and crafts: painted metal sculptures, furniture, carved wood masks, canes, and bowls. **Paradise Gifts/Arts** (⊠ Central Square, ☎ 649/946–4637) has an on-site ceramics studio; you also find jewelry, T-shirts, and paintings by local artists.

At **Pelican's Pouch/Designer I** (⊠ Turtle Cove Landing, ☎ 649/946–4343) you'll find resort wear, sandals, T-shirts, perfumes, and gold jewelry on the ground floor; head upstairs for basketry, sculpture, and watercolors. **Royal Jewels** (⊠ Leeward Hwy., ☎ 649/946–4885; ⊠ Turquoise Reef Resort, Provo, ☎ 649/946–5311; ⊠ Airport, Provo, ☎ 649/946–5311) sells gold and jewelry, designer watches, and perfumes—all duty-free.

Nightlife

Casablanca (⊠ Next to Club Med, ☎ 649/946–5449) is a Monte Carlo–style nightclub with a decked-out crowd. **Disco Elite** (⊠ Airport Rd., ☎ 649/946–4592) has strobe lights and an elevated dance floor. A band plays native, reggae, and contemporary music on Thursday night at the **Erebus Inn** (⊠ Turtle Cove, ☎ 649/946–4240).

Le Deck (⊠ Grace Bay, ☎ 649/946–5547) offers one-armed bandits every night. The **Turquoise Reef Resort** (⊠ Grace Bay, ☎ 649/946–5555) has a lively lounge, where a musician plays to the mostly tourist crowd, and the island's only gambling casino, **Port Royale** (☎ 649/946–5508).

Exploring Providenciales

⑤ Downtown Provo. Near Providenciales International Airport, the downtown is really a strip mall that houses car-rental agencies, law offices, boutiques, banks, and other businesses.

⑥ Island Sea Center. On the northeast coast, this is the place to learn about the sea and its inhabitants. Here you'll find the **Caicos Conch Farm,** a major mariculture operation where the mollusks are farmed commercially (there are more than 2.5 million conchs in the inventory here). The farm's facilities also include a video show, a boutique, and a hands-on tank with conchs in various stages of growth. Established by the PRIDE Foundation (Protection of Reefs and Islands from Degradation and Exploitation), the **JoJo Dolphin Project** is named after a 7-ft-long male bottlenose dolphin who cruises these waters and enjoys playing with local divers. You can watch a video about JoJo and learn how to interact with him safely if you see him on one of your dives. ⊠ *Island Sea Center,* ☎ *649/946–5330;* ⊠ *Caicos Conch Farm,* ☎ *649/946–5849.* ☞ *$6.* ⊙ *Mon.–Sat. 9–5.*

Little Water Cay

The small uninhabited cay is a protected area under the National Trust of the Turks and Caicos. On these 150 acres are two trails, a couple of small lakes, red mangrove, and an abundance of plants and trees. Boardwalks protect the ground and interpretive signs explain the habitat. The cay is home for about 2,000 rare, endangered rock iguanas. They say the iguanas are shy, but these creatures actually seem rather curious. They waddle right up to you, posing as if ready for a photo opportunity; you can usually get within a foot of them before they move.

Pine Cay

One of a chain of small cays linking North Caicos and Provo, 800-acre Pine Cay is privately owned and under development as a planned community. It's home to the Meridian Club resort—playground of jetsetters—and its 2½-mi beach is the most beautiful in the archipelago. The island has a 3,800-ft airstrip and electric carts for getting around.

Lodging
☞ For general information *and* price categories, *see* Lodging *under* Grand Turk, *above.*

$$$$ ⊞ **Meridian Club.** High rollers vacation in high style on this privately
★ owned 800-acre island. Club guests enjoy an unspoiled cay with 2½ mi of soft white sand and a 500-acre nature reserve with tropical landscaping, freshwater ponds, and nature trails that lure bird-watchers and botanists. A stay here is truly getting away from it all, as there are no air-conditioners, phones, or TVs. The accommodations range from spacious rooms with king-size beds (or twin beds on request) and patios to one- to four-bedroom cottage homes that range in decor and amenities from rustic to well appointed. There's also a "round room" cottage and two ocean-view atrium units that are separated by a lovely interior garden. Rooms in the main complex run $675 a night in high season and include all meals. Cottage homes start at $3,000 a week. ⊠ *Pine Cay (write to Resorts Management, 201 1/2 E 29th St, New York, NY 10016),* ☎ *800/331–9154,* ℻ *649/946–5128. 12 rooms, 13 cottage homes. Restaurant, bar, pool, tennis court, windsurfing, boating, bicycles. No credit cards. EP, FAP.*

North Caicos

Thanks to abundant rainfall, this 41-square-mi island is the garden center of the Turks and Caicos. Bird lovers will see a large flock of flamingos here, and fisherman will find creeks full of bonefish and tarpon. Bring all your own gear; this quiet island has no water-sports shops.

Lodging
☞ For general information *and* price categories, *see* Lodging *under* Grand Turk, *above.*

$$ ⊞ **Club Vacanze Prospect of Whitby Hotel.** This secluded retreat is run
★ by an Italian resort chain, Club Vacanze. Miles of beach are yours for sunbathing, windsurfing, or snorkeling. Spacious guest rooms have elegant Tuscan floor tiles, pastel pink paneling (some have fragrant cedar paneling), and white stucco walls decorated with bright paintings from Santo Domingo, Dominican Republic; in true getaway fash-

ion, rooms lack TVs and radios. The restaurant here is excellent (its cappuccino machine is a blessing for coffee lovers). ⊠ *Whitby,* ☎ *649/ 946–7119,* FAX *649/946–7114. 28 rooms, 4 suites. Restaurant, bar, pool, air-conditioning, tennis court, dive shop, windsurfing, baby-sitting, travel services. AE, MC, V. EP, MAP.*

$$ 🏨 **Ocean Beach Hotel Condominiums.** This unpretentious place provides family-style accommodations on a 10-mi stretch of sheltered beach. The spacious units, each with a kitchenette, face the ocean. (Who needs air-conditioning when there are constant trade winds passing through large sliding glass doors?) The hotel offers an intimate lifestyle away from the fray. ⊠ *Whitby,* ☎ *649/946–7113, 800/710–5204, or 905/336–2876 in Canada;* FAX *649/946–7386. 10 units. Restaurant, bar, fishing, bicycles, car rental. MC, V. MAP.*

$$ 🏨 **Pelican Beach Hotel.** This hotel has large rooms done in pastels and dark wood trim. Ask to stay on the second floor, where rooms have high wood ceilings and fabulous ocean views. Ceiling fans and constant sea breezes keep you cool. ⊠ *Whitby,* ☎ *649/946–7112,* FAX *649/ 946–7139. 14 rooms, 2 suites. Restaurant, bar, fishing. MC, V.*

$ 🏨 **JoAnne's B&B.** This no-frills, charming bed-and-breakfast on the beach is the perfect spot for those seeking peace and quiet. Rooms are light and airy with cool, white tile floors. Two friendly dogs escort you to the sea and trot along with you as you search for shells and sunbathe on a very private stretch of beach. The owner, a former Peace Corps worker, also runs Papa Grunts, an excellent restaurant nearby. Her island stories entertain and delight. Faxing is the best way to make reservations. ⊠ *Whitby,* ☎ FAX *649/946–7301. 3 rooms. MC, V.*

Beaches

The beaches of North Caicos are superb for shelling and lolling, and the waters offshore present excellent opportunities for snorkeling, bonefishing, and scuba diving (there are no outfitters on the island, so you'll have to make arrangements with shops on Provo). **Three Mary's Cays** has excellent snorkeling with a friendly ancient barracuda named Old Man.

Exploring North Caicos

❽ Flamingo Pond. This is a regular nesting place for the beautiful pink birds. They tend to wander out in the middle of the pond, so bring binoculars.

❾ Kew. This settlement has a small post office, a school, a church and ruins of old plantations—all set among lush tropical trees bearing limes, papayas, and custard apples. To visit Kew is to gain a better understanding of what life is like for many native islanders.

❼ Sandy Point. Getting to this settlement is half the fun, as you rattle along dirt and stone-filled roads. You'll pass salt flats where you'll very likely see flamingos standing around in the shallow waters. The secluded cove here is an excellent place to snorkel.

Middle Caicos

This is the largest (48 square mi) and least developed of the inhabited Turks and Caicos. Since phones are rare, the boats that dock here and the planes that land on the little airstrip provide the island's 275 residents with their connections to the outside world. **J&B Tours** offers boat trips from Provo to the mysterious Conch Bar Caves (☞ *below*).

Lodging

☞ For general information *and* price categories, *see* Lodging *under* Grand Turk, *above.*

$$–$$$$ 🏨 **Blue Horizon Resort.** This place offers sweet seclusion in condo-style accommodations. Units have screened-in porches, off-white tile floors, bleached wood furniture, comfortable beds, ceiling fans, and full kitchens. The slated windows open up to let in the nearly constant hillside breeze. Situated as it is on a spectacular cliff with a beach just down a short path, you'll feel like you're staying in your very own paradise. Fax a grocery list ahead of time, and the management will be happy to stock your refrigerator. Maid service is included in the room rate. Take a break from preparing your meals by making reservations at the café (open only January–March). Activities by request include cave exploring, fishing, and snorkeling. ⊠ *Mudjin Harbor,* ☎ *649/946–6141,* 🆊 *649/946–6139. 5 cottages. Fans, kitchenettes, refrigeratorsAE, MC, V.*

Exploring Middle Caicos

❿ **Conch Bar Caves.** These limestone caves have eerie underground lakes and milky-white stalactites and stalagmites. Archaeologists have discovered Arawak and Lucayan Indian artifacts in the caves and the surrounding area. It's an easy walk through the main part of the cave, but wear sturdy shoes to avoid slipping. You'll hear and see (and smell) some bats, but don't be afraid; they won't bother you.

South Caicos

This 8½-square-mi island was once an important salt producer; today it's the heart of the fishing industry. The beaches are small and unremarkable, but the vibrant reef makes it popular with divers.

Lodging

☞ For general information *and* price categories, *see* Lodging *under* Grand Turk, *above.*

$–$$$ 🏨 **Club Caribe Beach & Harbour Hotel.** Cockburn Harbour, the only natural harbor in Turks and Caicos, is the perfect setting for this hotel. In the 16 beachfront villas here you'll find studios and one-, two-, or three-bedroom apartments; they have cool tile floors and kitchenettes equipped with a mini-refrigerator and a microwave. Half the rooms don't have air-conditioning, but they get a nice breeze around the clock. The 22 harbor rooms are smaller than the others but have air-conditioning. There's a dive shop with a full-time instructor. ⊠ *Cockburn Harbour (Box 1),* ☎ *649/946–3444 or 800/722–2582,* 🆊 *649/ 946–3446. 38 rooms. Restaurant, bar, dive shop, windsurfing, bicycles. AE, D, MC, V. EP, MAP.*

Beaches

Due south is **Big Ambergris Cay,** an uninhabited cay about 14 mi beyond the Fish Cays, with a magnificent beach at Long Bay. To the north, **East Caicos** is an uninhabited island with a beautiful 17-mi-long beach on its north coast. The island was once a cattle range and the site of a major sisal-growing industry. Both these cays are accessible only by boat.

Exploring South Caicos

Spiny lobster and queen conch are found in the shallow Caicos bank to the west and are harvested for export by local processing plants. The bonefishing here is some of the best in the West Indies. At the northern end of the island are fine, white-sand beaches; the south coast is great for scuba diving along the drop-off; and there's excellent snorkeling off the windward (east) coast, where large stands of elkhorn and staghorn coral shelter a variety of small tropical fish.

⓫ **Cockburn Harbour.** The best natural harbor in the Caicos chain is home to the South Caicos Regatta, held each year in May.

TURKS AND CAICOS ISLANDS A TO Z

Arriving and Departing

BY AIRPLANE

American Airlines (☎ 800/433–7300; 649/941–5700 in Turks and Caicos) flies daily between Miami and Provo. **Turks & Caicos Islands Airlines** (☎ 649/946–4255) is the only regularly scheduled carrier that flies between Provo, Grand Turk, and other outer Turks and Caicos islands. Many air charter services also connect the islands (☞ Guided Tours, *below*).

From the Airport: Taxis are available at the airports; expect to share a ride. Rates are fixed. A trip between Provo's airport and most major hotels runs about $15. On Grand Turk, a trip from the airport to Cockburn Town is about $5; from the airport to hotels outside town, $6–$11.

BY BOAT

Because of the superb diving, three live-aboard dive boats call regularly. Contact the **Aquanaut** (⊠ c/o See & Sea, ☎ 800/348–9778), the **Sea Dancer** (⊠ c/o Peter Hughes Diving, ☎ 800/932–6237), or the **Turks and Caicos Aggressor** (⊠ c/o Aggressor Fleet, ☎ 504/385–2628 or 800/348–2628, ℻ 504/384–0817).

Electricity

Electricity is fairly stable throughout the islands, and the current is the same as in the United States (110 volts).

Emergencies

Police: Grand Turk, ☎ 649/946–2299; North Caicos, ☎ 649/946–7116; Providenciales, ☎ 649/946–4259; South Caicos, ☎ 649/946–3299.

Hospitals: There is a 24-hour emergency room at **Grand Turk Hospital** (⊠ Hospital Rd., ☎ 649/946–2333) and at **Providenciales Health-Medical Center** (⊠ Leeward Hwy., ☎ 649/946–4201).

Pharmacies: Prescriptions can be filled at the **Government Clinic** (⊠ Grand Turk Hospital, ☎ 649/946–2040) and at the **Providenciales Health-Medical Center** in Provo (⊠ Leeward Hwy., ☎ 649/946–4201).

Scuba-Diving Accidents: A modern hyperbaric/decompression chamber is on Provo in the **Menzies Medical Centre** (⊠ Leeward Hwy., ☎ 649/946–4242).

Getting Around

BUSES

A new public bus system on Grand Turk charges 50¢ one-way to any scheduled stop.

On Provo, shuttle buses operated by **Executive Tours** (☎ 649/946–4524) run from the hotels into town every hour, Monday–Saturday 9–6. Fares are $2 each way.

CAR RENTALS

Driving here is on the left side of the road; when pulling out into traffic, remember to look to your right. Rates average $40 to $65 per day, plus a $10-per-rental-agreement government tax.

On Grand Turk, try **Dutchie's Car Rental** (☎ 649/946–2244). Local rental agencies on Provo are **Turks & Caicos National** (☎ 649/946–4701), **Provo Rent-a-Car** (☎ 649/946–4404), **Rent a Buggy** (☎ 649/946–4158), and **Turquoise Jeep Rentals** (☎ 649/946–4910). To rent cars on South Caicos, check with your hotel manager for rates and information.

FERRIES

Ferries are available between some islands; check with local marinas. The only government ferry (☏ no phone) runs between Grand Turk and Salt Cay.

SCOOTERS

You can scoot around Provo by contacting **Scooter Bob's** (☏ 649/946–4684) or the **Honda Shop** (☏ 649/946–4397). On North Caicos, contact **North Caicos Scooter Rentals** (☏ 649/946–7301). Rates generally start at $25 per day for a one-seater and $40 a day for a two-seater, plus a onetime $5 government tax and gas expenses.

TAXIS

Taxis are unmetered, and rates, posted in the taxis, are regulated by the government. In Provo, call the Provo Taxi Association (☏ 649/946–5481) for more information.

Guided Tours

A **taxi** tour of the islands costs between $25 and $30 for the first hour and $25 for each additional hour. On Provo, contact **Paradise Taxi Company** (☏ 649/941–3555). **Turtle Tours** (☏ 649/946–5585) offers a variety of bus and small-plane tours, including flights to Middle Caicos, the largest of the islands, for a visit to its mysterious caves, or to North Caicos to see the ruins of a plantation.

If you want to island-hop on your own schedule, air charters are available through **Blue Hills Aviation** (☏ 649/941–5290), **Flamingo Air Services** (☏ 649/946–2109 or 649/946–4933), and **SkyKing** (☏ 649/941–5464), all based in Provo.

Language

The official language of the Turks and Caicos is English.

Money Matters

CURRENCY

The unit of currency is the U.S. dollar.

SERVICE CHARGES, TAXES, AND TIPPING

Hotels add from 10%–15% to your bill for service and restaurants and hotels both add a 7% government tax. You'll be charged a $15 departure tax at the airport. At restaurants tip according to service; 10%–18% is common. Taxis also expect a token tip, about 10% of your fare.

Opening and Closing Times

Most offices and shops are open weekdays from 8 or 8:30 till 4 or 4:30. Banks are open Monday–Thursday 8:30–2:30, Friday 8:30–12:30 and 2:30–4:30.

HOLIDAYS

New Year's Day, Commonwealth Day (Mar. 10), Good Friday (Apr. 2), Easter and Easter Monday (Apr. 4–5), National Heroes Day (May 26), Queen's Birthday (June 14), National Youth Day (Sept. 26), Columbus Day (Oct. 13), International Human Rights Day (Oct. 24), Christmas, and Boxing Day (Dec. 26).

Passports

U.S. and Canadian citizens need some proof of citizenship, such as a birth certificate (original or certified copy), plus a photo ID or a current passport. British subjects must have a current passport. All visitors must have an ongoing or return ticket.

Precautions

Petty crime does occur here, and you're advised to leave your valuables in the hotel safe-deposit box. Bring along a can of insect repellent: The mosquitoes and no-see-ums can be vicious. If you plan to explore the uninhabited island of West Caicos, be advised that the interior is overgrown with dense shrubs that include manchineel, which has a milky, poisonous sap that can cause painful, scarring blisters.

In some hotels on Grand Turk, Salt Cay, and South Caicos, there are signs that read PLEASE HELP US CONSERVE OUR PRECIOUS WATER. These islands have no water supply other than rainwater collected in cisterns, and rainfall is scant. Drink only from the decanter of fresh water your hotel provides; tap water is safe for brushing your teeth or other hygiene uses.

Telephones and Mail

The area code for the Turks and Caicos is 649 (recently changed from 809). To make calls from Turks and Caicos, dial 0 + 1 + area code + the number. You can call anywhere, anytime, through the cable and wireless system and local operators. To make local calls, dial the seven-digit number. To place credit-card calls, simply dial the 800 number of your provider. Note that calls from the islands are very expensive, and many hotels add steep surcharges for long-distance calls. Talk fast.

When sending letters to the Turks and Caicos Islands be sure to include the specific island as well as "Turks and Caicos, BWI" (British West Indies).

Visitor Information

For tourist information, contact the **Turks and Caicos Islands Tourist Board** (☎ 800/241–0824, tci.tourism@caribsurf.com). The **Caribbean Tourism Organization** (✉ 20 E. 46th St., New York, NY 10017, ☎ 212/682–0435) is another source of information. In the United Kingdom, contact **Morris-Kevan International Ltd.** (✉ International House, 47 Chase Side, Enfield Middlesex EN2 6NB, ☎ 0181/367–5175).

The **Government Tourist Office** (✉ Front St., Cockburn Town, Grand Turk, ☎ 649/946–2321; ✉ Turtle Cove Landing, Provo, ☎ 649/946–4970) is open Monday–Thursday 8–4:30 and Friday 8–5.

26 United States Virgin Islands

Updated
by Carol
Bareuther and
Lynda Lohr

Mornings at the Squirrel Cage coffee shop on St. Thomas aren't much different from those in coffee shops back home. A cop stops by to joke with the waitress and collect his first cup of coffee; a high-heeled secretary runs in for the paper and some toast; a store clerk lingers over a cup of tea to discuss politics with the cook. But is the coffee shop back home in a bright pink hole-in-the-wall of a 19th-century building, steps from a park abloom with frangipani—in January? Are bush tea and johnnycake served alongside oatmeal and omelets?

It is the combination of the familiar and the exotic found in St. Thomas, St. Croix, and St. John—the United States Virgin Islands (USVI)—that defines this "American Paradise" and explains much of its appeal. The effort to be all things to all people—while remaining true to the best of itself—has created a sometimes paradoxical blend of island serenity and American practicality in this U.S. territory 1,000 mi from the southern tip of the U.S. mainland.

The images you'd expect from a tropical paradise are here: Stretches of beach arc into the distance, and white sails skim across water so blue and clear it stuns the senses. Red-roof houses color the green hillsides as do the orange of the flamboyant tree, the red of the hibiscus, the magenta of the bougainvillea, and the blue stone ruins of old sugar mills. Towns of pastel-tone European-style villas, decorated by filigree wrought-iron terraces, line narrow streets that climb from the harbor. Amid all the images, you can find moments—sometimes whole days—of exquisite tranquillity: an egret standing in a pond at dawn, palm trees backlit by a full moon, sunrises and sunsets that can send your spirit soaring with the frigate bird flying overhead.

The other part of the equation are all those things that make it so easy and appealing to visit this cluster of islands. The official language is English, the dollar is the currency, and the U.S. government runs things. As a visitor, you can delve into a "foreign" culture while anchored by familiar language and landmarks. Surely not everything will suit your fancy, but chances are that among the three islands you'll find your own idea of paradise. Check into a beachfront condo on the East End of St. Thomas, eat burgers, and watch football at a beachfront bar and grill. Or stay at an 18th-century plantation great house on St. Croix, dine on Danish delicacies, and go horseback riding at sunrise. Rent a tent or a cottage in the pristine national park on St. John, take a hike, kayak off the coast, read a book, or just listen to the sounds of the forest at night. Or dive deep into "island time" and learn the art of "limin' " (hanging out, Caribbean-style) on all three islands.

Still, these idyllic bits of volcanic rock in the middle of the Caribbean Sea have not escaped the modern-day worries of overdevelopment, trash, crime, and traffic. The isolation and limited space of the islands have, in fact, accentuated these problems. What, for example, do you do with 76 million cans and bottles imported annually when the nearest recycling plant is across 1,000 mi of ocean? Despite dilemmas such as this, wildlife has found refuge here. The brown pelican is on the endangered list worldwide but is a common sight in the USVI. The endangered native tree boa is protected, as is the hawksbill turtle, whose females lumber onto the beaches to lay their eggs.

Preserving its own culture while progressing as an Americanized tourist destination is another problem. The islands have been inhabited in turn by Taino and Carib Indians; Danish settlers and Spanish pirates; traders and invaders from all the European powers; Africans brought in as slaves; migrants from other Caribbean islands; and, finally, Americans, first as administrators, then as businesspeople and tourists. All these influences are creating a more homogeneous culture, and with each passing year the USVI lose more of their rich, spicy, Caribbean personality.

Sailing into the Caribbean on his second voyage in 1493, Christopher Columbus came upon St. Croix before the group of islands including St. Thomas, St. John, and the British Virgin Islands (BVI). He named St. Croix "Santa Cruz" (called Ay Ay by the Carib Indians already living there) but moved on quickly after he encountered the fierce residents. As he approached St. Thomas and St. John, he was impressed enough with the shapely silhouettes of the numerous islands and cays (including the BVI) to name them after Ursula and her 11,000 virgins, but he found the islands barren and moved on to explore Puerto Rico.

Over the next century, as it became clear that Spain could not defend the entire Caribbean, other European powers began to settle the islands. During the 1600s the French were joined by the Dutch and the English on St. Croix, and St. Thomas had a mixture of European residents in the early 1700s. By 1695 St. Croix was under the control of the French, but the colonists had moved on to what is today Haiti. The island lay virtually dormant until 1733, when the Danish government bought it—along with St. Thomas and St. John—from the Danish West India Company. At that time settlers from St. Thomas and St. John moved to St. Croix to cultivate the island's gentler terrain. St. Croix grew into a plantation economy, but St. Thomas's soil and terrain were ill suited to agriculture. There the harbor became an internationally known seaport because of its size and ease of entry; it's still hailed as one of the most beautiful harbors in the world.

United States Virgin Islands

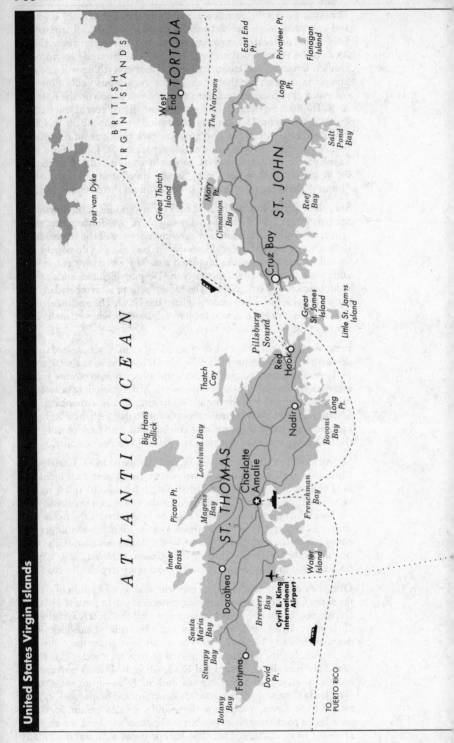

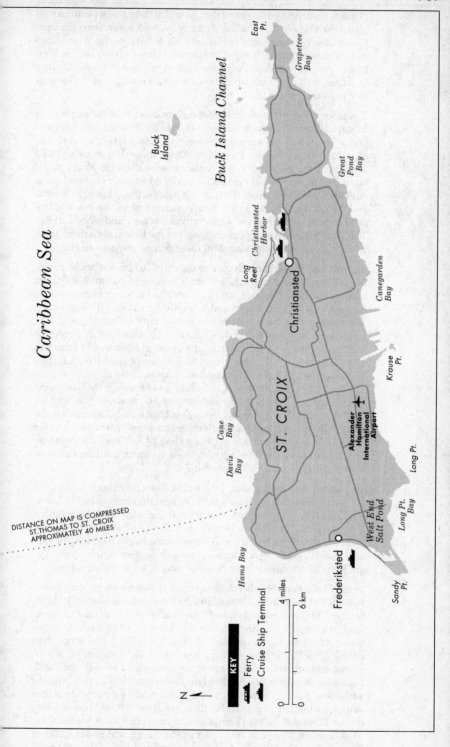

Caribbean Sea

Buck Island Channel

East Pt.

Grapetree Bay

Buck Island

Great Pond Bay

Christiansted Harbor

Long Reef

Canegarden Bay

Christiansted

ST. CROIX

Krause Pt.

Alexander Hamilton International Airport

Cane Bay

Davis Bay

Long Pt.

DISTANCE ON MAP IS COMPRESSED
ST.THOMAS TO ST. CROIX
APPROXIMATELY 40 MILES

West End Salt Pond

Long Pt. Bay

Long Pt.

Hams Bay

Frederiksted

Sandy Pt.

N

KEY
Ferry
Cruise Ship Terminal

4 miles
6 km

Plantations depended on slave labor, of which there was a plentiful supply in the Danish West Indies. As early as 1665 agreements between Brandenburger Company (which needed a base in the West Indies from which to ship the slaves it had imported from Africa) and the West India Company (which needed the kind of quick cash it could collect in duties, fees, and rents from the slave trade) established St. Thomas as a primary slave market.

It is from the slaves who worked the plantations that the majority of Virgin Islanders are descended. More than likely the sales clerk who sells you a watch and the waitress serving your rum punch trace their lineage back to ancestors captured in Africa some 300 years ago and brought to the West Indies, where they were sold on the block, priced according to their comeliness and strength. Most were captured along Africa's Gold Coast, from the tribes of Asante, Ibo, Mandika, Amina, and Woloff. They brought with them African rhythms in music and language, herbal medicine, and such crafts as basketry and wood carving. The West Indian–African culture comes to full bloom at Carnival time, when playing *mas* (with abandon) takes precedence over all else.

Yet you can still see the influence of the early Danish settlers here, too. It's reflected in the language and architecture; in common surnames such as Petersen, Jeppesen, and Lawaetz; and in street names such as Kongen's Gade (King Street) and Kronprindsen's Gade (Prince Street). The town of Charlotte Amalie was named after a Danish queen. The Lutheran Church is the state church of Denmark, and; Frederick Lutheran Church on St. Thomas, the oldest predominately Lutheran Church in the world, dates from 1666. Other peoples have left their marks on the USVI as well. Jewish settlers came to the territory as early as 1665; they were shipowners, chandlers, and brokers in the slave trade. Today their descendants coexist with nearly 1,500 Arabs—95% of whom are Palestinian. You'll also find many East Indians, who are active members of the business community. Immigrants from Puerto Rico and the Dominican Republic make up close to half of St. Croix's population. Transplants from Caribbean countries to the south continue to arrive, seeking better economic opportunities.

St. Thomas, St. Croix, and St. John were known collectively as the Danish West Indies until the United States bought the territory in 1917, during World War I, prompted by fears that Germany would establish a U-boat base in the Western Hemisphere. The name was changed to the United States Virgin Islands, and, almost immediately thereafter, British-held Tortola and Virgin Gorda—previously known simply as the Virgin Islands—hastily inserted "British" on the front of their name.

In the 1960s Pineapple Beach Resort (today Renaissance Grand Beach Resort) was built on St. Thomas and the Caneel Bay Resort on St. John, built in 1956, was expanded; and with direct flights from the U.S. mainland, the islands' tourism industry was born. In 1960 the total population of all three islands was 32,000. By 1970 it had more than doubled, to 75,000, as workers from the BVI, Antigua, St. Kitts–Nevis, and other Caribbean countries immigrated to man the building boom. When the boom waned the down-islanders stayed, bringing additional diversity to the territory but also putting a tremendous burden on its infrastructure. Today there are about 50,000 people living on the 32-square-mi St. Thomas (about the same size as Manhattan), 51,000 on the 84 square mi of pastoral St. Croix, and about 5,000 on 20-square-mi St. John, ⅔ of which is a national park. The per capita income in the USVI is the highest in the West Indies. Just over ¼ of the total labor force is employed by the government, and about 10% work in tourism or tourism-related jobs.

Agriculture has not been a major economic factor since the last sugarcane plantation on St. Croix ceased operating in the 1960s, but a few farmers in St. Croix and St. Thomas still produce some of the mangos, pineapples, and herbs you'll find on your plate. The cuisine of the islands reflects a dependency on a land that gives grudgingly of its bounty. Root vegetables such as sweet potato, hardy vegetables such as okra, and stick-to-your-ribs breads and stuffings were staples 200 years ago, and their influence is still evident in the *fungi* (cornmeal and okra), johnnycake, and sweet-potato stuffings that are ever-present on menus today. The fruits are sweet (slaves got energy to cut sugarcane from a sugar-water drink made from sugar apples). Beverages include not only rum but coconut water, fruit juices, and *maubi*, made from tree bark and reputedly a virility enhancer.

The backbone of the economy is tourism, but at the heart of the islands is an independent, separate being: a rollicking hodgepodge of West Indian culture with a sense of humor that puts sex and politics in almost every conversation. Lacking a major-league sports team, Virgin Islanders follow the activities and antics of their 15 elected senators with the rabidity of Washingtonians following their Redskins. Loyalty to country and faith in God are the rule in the USVI, not the exception. Prayer is a way of life, and ROTC is one of the most popular high-school extracurricular activities.

The struggle to preserve the predominantly black Caribbean–influenced culture is heating up in America's paradise. Native Virgin Islanders say they want access to more than just the beach when big money brings in big development. Senators in early 1996 agreed that majority ownership of two of the casino hotels to be built in St. Croix will be reserved for natives. But the three islands are far from united as to exactly how they will balance continued economic growth and the protection of their number-one resource—scenic beauty. The ongoing conflict between progress and preservation here is no mere philosophical exercise, and attempts at resolutions display yet another aspect of the islands' unique blend of character.

ST. THOMAS

Updated by
Carol
Bareuther

If you fly to the 32-square-mi island of St. Thomas, you'll land at the western end of the island; if you arrive by cruise ship, you'll come into one of the world's most beautiful harbors. Either way, one of your first sights of the island will be the town of Charlotte Amalie. From the harbor, you see an idyllic-looking village that spreads into the lower hills. If you were expecting a quiet village, its inhabitants hanging out under palm trees, you've missed that era by about 300 years. While other islands in the USVI developed plantation economies, St. Thomas cultivated its harbor, and it became a thriving commercial seaport soon after it was settled by the Danish in the 1600s.

The success of the naturally perfect harbor was enhanced by the fact that the Danes—who ruled St. Thomas (with only a couple of short interruptions) from 1666 to 1917—avoided involvement in some 100 years' worth of European wars. Denmark was the only European country with colonies in the Caribbean to stay neutral during the war of the Spanish succession in the early 1700s. Thus, products of the Dutch, English, and French islands—sugar, cotton, and indigo—were traded through Charlotte Amalie, along with the regular shipments of slaves. When the Spanish wars ended, trade fell off, but by the end of the 1700s, Europe was at war again, Denmark again remained neutral, and St. Thomas continued to prosper. Even into the 1800s, while the economies of St. Croix and St. John foundered with the market for sugarcane, St. Thomas's economy remained strong. This prosperity led to the development of shipyards for repairing boats, a well-organized banking system, and a large merchant class. In 1845 Charlotte Amalie had 101 large importing houses owned by Englishmen, Frenchmen, Germans, Haitians, Spaniards, Americans, Sephardim, and Danes.

Charlotte Amalie is still one of the most active cruise-ship ports in the world. On almost any day at least one and sometimes as many as eight cruise ships are tied to the dock or anchored outside the harbor. Gently rocking in the shadows of these giant floating hotels are just about every other kind of vessel imaginable: sleek sailing mono- and multi-hulls that will take you on a sunset cruise complete with rum punch and a Jimmy Buffett soundtrack; private megayachts that spirit busy execs away; and the 39-ft *Stars & Stripes*, which was sailed by Dennis Conner in the 1992 America's Cup Defender series and has been resurrected as the V.I. Challenge's first training vessel for the Cup 2000 in New Zealand. Huge container ships pull up in Sub Base, just west of the harbor, bringing in everything from cornflakes to tires. Anchored right along the waterfront are the picturesque down-island sloops of the type that has plied the waters between the Greater Antilles and the Leeward Islands for hundreds of years. The sloops still deliver fruits and vegetables, but today they also return down-island with refrigerators, VCRs, and disposable diapers.

The waterfront road through Charlotte Amalie was once part of the harbor. Before it was filled to build the highway, the beach came right up to the back door of the warehouses that now line the thoroughfare. Two hundred years ago, those warehouses contained indigo, tobacco, and cotton. Today the stone buildings house silk, crystal, linens, and leather. Exotic fragrances are still traded, but by island beauty queens in air-conditioned perfume palaces instead of through open market stalls.

Pirates of old used St. Thomas as a base from which to raid merchant ships of any and every nation, though they were particularly fond of the gold- and silver-laden treasure ships heading from Mexico, Cuba, and Puerto Rico to Spain. There are still pirates around, but today's version use St. Thomas as a drop-off for their contraband: illegal immigrants and drugs.

The western end of the island is the least developed: with the exception of some private homes, it's still relatively wild. If you're staying on the quiet north side, you'll go up the mountain along roads lined with giant ferns and philodendron, banana trees, and flamboyant trees that thrive in the cooler and wetter climate. The lush vegetation muffles the sound of all but the birds, and it's here you'll find many of the island's private villas for rent. In the drier areas to the south and east, the roads are lined with colossal cacti and succulents, punctuated by the bright colors of the hardy bougainvillea and hibiscus. The southeastern and far eastern ends of the island are flat, and this is where you'll find the beachfront hotels and condominiums. At the eastern tip is Red Hook, a friendly little village anchored by the marine community nestled at Red Hook harbor.

Lodging

Of the USVI, St. Thomas has the most rooms and the greatest variety of accommodations. You can let yourself be pampered at a world-class luxury resort—albeit at a price of $300 to more than $900 per night, not including meals. If your means are more modest, you will find fine hotels (often with rooms that have a kitchen and a living area) in lovely settings throughout the island. There are also guest houses and inns with great views (if not a beach at your door) and great service at about half the cost of the beachfront pleasure palaces. Many of these are in the hills above the historic district of Charlotte Amalie—ideal if you plan to get out and mingle with the locals. There are also inexpensive lodgings (most right in town) that are perfect if you just want a clean room to return to after a day of exploring or beach-bumming.

Families often stay at an East End condominium complex. Although condos are somewhat pricey (winter rates average $240 per night for a two-bedroom unit, which usually sleeps six), they have full kitchens, and you can definitely save money by cooking for yourself—especially if you bring your own nonperishable foodstuffs. (Virtually everything on St. Thomas is imported, and restaurants and shops pass shipping costs on to you.) Though you may spend some time laboring in the kitchen, many condos ease your burden with daily maid service and on-site restaurants; quite a few also have resort amenities, including pools and tennis courts. The East End is convenient to St. John, is home to the boating crowd, and has a fair number of good restaurants.

The prices below reflect rates during high season, which generally runs from December 15 to April 15. Rates are 25% to 50% lower the rest of the year.

CATEGORY	COST*
$$$$	over $200
$$$	$150–$200
$$	$100–$150
$	under $100

All prices are for a standard double room, excluding 8% tax.

Hotels

CHARLOTTE AMALIE

$$$–$$$$ 🏨 **Best Western Emerald Beach Resort.** On a white-sand beach, just across from the airport, this miniresort has the feel of its much larger cousins on the East End. Each room in the four pink three-story buildings has its own terrace or balcony, palms, and colorful flowers that frame a view of the ocean. The rooms are decorated in modern tropical prints and rattan. A plus: The resort is popular with businesspeople, so the pool and beach are rarely crowded. A minus: The noise from nearby jets taking off and landing can be heard intermittently over a three-hour period each afternoon. ⊠ *Lindbergh Bay (Box 340) 00804,* ☎ *340/777–8800 or 800/233–4936,* 📠 *340/776–3426. 90 rooms. Restaurant, air-conditioning, pool, beach. AE, D, MC, V. EP.*

$$$–$$$$ 🏨 **Bluebeard Castle.** Though not exactly a castle, this large red-roof complex offers kingly modern comforts on a steep hill overlooking the town. All rooms are air-conditioned and have terraces. The hotel is a short ride away from the shops of Charlotte Amalie and Havensight Mall—there's free transportation to Magens Bay Beach and to town. ⊠ *Bluebeard's Hill (Box 7480) 00801,* ☎ *340/774–1600 or 800/524–6599 (reservations service),* 📠 *340/774–5134. 170 rooms. 3 restaurants, bar, air-conditioning, pool, 2 tennis courts, exercise room. AE, D, DC, MC, V. EP.*

$$–$$$ 🏨 **Blackbeard's Castle.** This small and very popular hillside inn is laid out around a tower from which, it's said, Blackbeard kept watch for invaders on the horizon. It's an elegantly informal kind of place, where guests while away Sunday morning with the *New York Times*. You'll find stunning views (especially at sunset) of the harbor and Charlotte Amalie from the gourmet restaurant ☞ **Café LuLu**, the large freshwater pool, and the outdoor terraces (where locals come for cocktails). Char-

Outer
Brass

Picara
Pt.

Inner
Brass

Tropaco
Pt.

Vluck
Pt.

Santa
Maria
Bay

Hull Bay **38**

Magens
Bay

Stumpy
Pt.

40

37

Mag

Stumpy
Bay

Crown Mt.

79

36

35

Bordeaux
Bay

Dorthea

Signal
Hill

40

Target
Pt.

318

33

78

West Cay

Botany
Bay

33

30

Fortuna
Hill

30

81

85

1

Fortuna

Brewer's
Beach

Contant

Perseverance
Bay

39

41

Barents
Bay

Brewers
Bay

Cyril E. King
International
Airport

Frenchtown

Fortuna
Bay

David
Pt.

Altona

Lindbergh Bay
Beach

Hassel
Island

80

Red Pt.

Caribbean Sea

Water
Island

Para

Limestone
Bay

TO PUERTO RICO

TO
ST. CROIX

Exploring
Brewer's Beach, **39**
Coki Point, **33**
Compass Point
Marina, **29**
Coral World Marine
Park, **32**
Drake's Seat, **35**
Estate St. Peter
Greathouse Botanical
Gardens, **37**
Frenchtown, **41**

Hull Bay, **38**
Magens Bay
Beach, **36**
Mountain Top, **40**
Paradise Point
Tramway, **28**
Red Hook, **31**
Tillett Gardens, **34**
Virgin Islands
National Park
Headquarters, **30**

Dining
Agave Terrace, **73**
Alexander's Café, **84**
Beni Iguana's, **51**
Café LuLu, **45**
The Chart House, **83**
Craig & Sally's, **85**
Duffy's Love
Shack, **65**

Eunice's Terrace, **75**
Ferrari's, **79**
Gladys' Cafe, **49**
Greenhouse Bar and
Restaurant, **47**
Hard Rock Cafe, **48**
Hervé, **53**
Hotel 1829, **43**
Mim's Seaside
Bistro, **59**
Polli's, **77**
Raffles, **60**

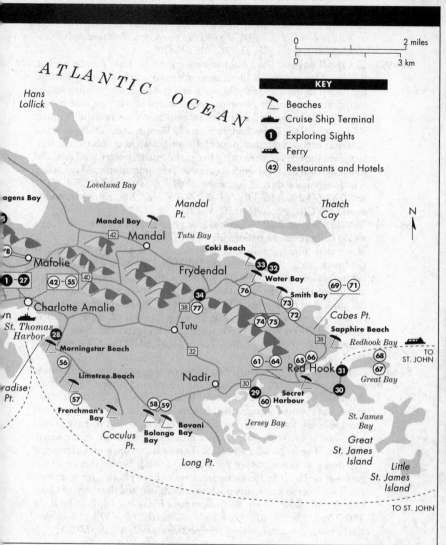

KEY

⤙	Beaches
⛴	Cruise Ship Terminal
❶	Exploring Sights
⛴	Ferry
㊷	Restaurants and Hotels

ATLANTIC OCEAN

Hans Lollick

Lovelund Bay

Mandal Bay

Mandal Pt.

Thatch Cay

Tutu Bay

Coki Beach

Frydendal

Water Bay

Smith Bay

Cabes Pt.

Sapphire Beach

Redhook Bay

TO ST. JOHN

Mafolie

Charlotte Amalie

St. Thomas Harbor

Morningstar Beach

Tutu

Nadir

Red Hook

Great Bay

Limetree Beach

Secret Harbour

Frenchman's Bay

Coculus Pt.

Bolongo Bay

Bovoni Bay

Jersey Bay

St. James Bay

Great St. James Island

Little St. James Island

Long Pt.

TO ST. JOHN

Randy's Bistro, **50**
Romanos, **74**
Seagrape, **69**
Sib's Mountain Bar and Restaurant, **78**
Tickles Dockside Pub, **66**
Victor's New Hide-Out, **81**
Virgilio's, **46**
Zorba's Sagapo, **52**

Lodging
Admiral's Inn, **82**
The Anchorage, **63**
Best Western Emerald Beach Resort, **80**
Blackbeard's Castle, **45**
Blazing Villas, **76**
Bluebeard Beach Villas, **57**
Bluebeard Castle, **42**
Bolongo Bay Beach Club & Villas, **58**

Crystal Cove at Sapphire Bay West, **71**
Danish Chalet Inn, **54**
Elysian Beach Resort, **67**
Hotel 1829, **43**
L'Hotel Boynes, **44**
Marriott Frenchman's Reef and Morning Star Beach Resorts, **56**
Renaissance Grand Beach Resort, **76**

Ritz-Carlton, St. Thomas, **68**
Sapphire Beach Resort & Marina, **69**
Sapphire Village, **70**
Sea Horse Cottages, **64**
Secret Harbour Beach Resort, **61**
Secret Harbourview Villas, **62**
Villa Santana, **55**
Wyndham Sugar Bay Beach Club & Resort, **72**

lotte Amalie is a short walk down the hill, and beaches are a short taxi ride away. ⊠ *Blackbeard's Hill (Box 6041)00804,* ☎ *340/776–1234 or 800/344–5771,* 𝖥𝖠𝖷 *340/776–4321. 16 rooms. Restaurant, bar, air-conditioning, pool. AE, D, DC, MC, V. CP.*

$$–$$$ 🖬 **L'Hotel Boynes.** On a hill just above the Charlotte Amalie harbor, this intimate inn stands like a monument to a time gone by. Each of the rooms in the 200-year-old stone and ballast-brick building has its own character—ranging from the sophisticated Red Room, with its mahogany four-poster bed and Persian carpets, to the fanciful Whimsy Room, where the bed is built into an old Danish oven. On Friday and Saturday nights, you can sip cocktails while watching spectacular sunsets from the terrace, then enjoy live piano music, poetry readings, and mingling with the local working crowd. Transportation to Magens Bay is included in the rate. ⊠ *Blackbeard's Hill, 00802,* ☎ *340/774–5511 or 800/377–2905,* 𝖥𝖠𝖷 *340/774–8509. 8 rooms. Bar, air-conditioning, in-room VCRs, pool. AE, MC, V. CP.*

$$–$$$ 🖬 **Villa Santana.** Built by General Santa Anna of Mexico, the villa (circa ★ 1857) still provides a panoramic view of the Charlotte Amalie harbor, along with plenty of age-old West Indian charm. This St. Thomas landmark, close to town, has six villa-style rooms. Dark wicker furniture, plaster and stone walls, shuttered windows, cathedral ceilings, and interesting nooks contribute to the feeling of romance and history. All units have full kitchens, TVs, and either four-poster or cradle beds; ceiling fans and natural trade winds keep things cool. Villas La Torre and La Mansion are split-level quarters with spiral staircases. ⊠ *2D Denmark Hill, 00802,* ☎ *340/776–1311,* 𝖥𝖠𝖷 *340/776–1311. 6 rooms. Pool, croquet. AE. EP.*

$–$$$$ 🖬 **Hotel 1829.** This historic Spanish-style inn is popular with visiting ★ government officials and people with business at Government House down the street. Rooms, on several levels (no elevator), range from elegant and roomy to quite small but are priced accordingly, so there's one for every budget. Author Graham Greene is said to have stayed here, and it's easy to imagine him musing over a drink in the small, dark bar. The second-floor botanical gardens and open-air champagne bar make a romantic spot for sunset viewing before dinner in the gourmet ☞ **Hotel 1829** restaurant. Rooms have phones, refrigerators, and TVs. There's a tiny, tiny pool for cooling off, and the shops of Charlotte Amalie are close by. ⊠ *Government Hill (Box 1567, 00804),* ☎ *340/776–1829 or 800/524–2002,* 𝖥𝖠𝖷 *340/776–4313. 14 rooms. Restaurant, air-conditioning, refrigerators, pool. AE, D, MC, V.*

EAST END

$$$$ 🖬 **Elysian Beach Resort.** At this East End property, coral-color villas are stepped down the hillside to the edge of Cowpet Bay. Rooms are decorated in muted tropical floral prints. Activity centers on a kidney-shape pool with a waterfall and thatch-roof pool bar. The Palm Court restaurant has gained a strong local following for the Sunday buffet brunch. All rooms have terraces, TVs, and phones; some have full kitchens. ⊠ *Estate Nazareth (Box 51) Red Hook 00802,* ☎ *340/775–1000 or 800/753–2554 (reservations service),* 𝖥𝖠𝖷 *340/776–0910. 175 rooms. 2 restaurants, 2 bars, air-conditioning, fans, pool, tennis court, health club, beach. AE, MC, V. CP.*

$$$$ 🖬 **Renaissance Grand Beach Resort.** This resort's zigzag architectural ★ angles spell luxury, from the marble atrium lobby to the one-bedroom suites with private whirlpool baths. The beach is excellent, and there's a fitness center with Nautilus machines. The lobby is often populated by those lucky business types whose companies favor the resort as a convention-and-conference center. Daily organized activities for children include iguana hunts, T-shirt painting, and sand-castle building.

This tends to be a very busy hotel, with lots of people in the restaurants and on the beach. ⊠ *Smith Bay Rd. (Box 8267) 00801,* ☎ *340/ 775–1510 or 800/468–3571,* ℻ *340/775–3757. 204 rooms, 86 suites. 2 restaurants, snack bar, air-conditioning, 2 pools, 6 tennis courts, beach, children's programs. AE, D, DC, MC, V. EP, MAP.*

$$$$ 🏨 **Ritz-Carlton, St. Thomas.** This premier luxury resort resembles a villa
★   in Venice and offers stunning ocean views through the lobby's glass doors. Guest rooms, in six buildings that fan out from the main villa, are spacious and tropically furnished—they just might tempt you to stay inside. When you do venture out, you'll find elegance everywhere, from the beautiful pool to the gourmet restaurant and the casual alfresco lunch area. A multilingual staff and 24-hour room service enhance the sophisticated atmosphere. ⊠ *6900 Great Bay Estate 00802,* ☎ *340/775–3333 or 800/241–3333,* ℻ *340/775–4444. 152 rooms. 3 restaurants, 3 bars, air-conditioning, room service, pool, 3 tennis courts, health club, beach. AE, D, DC, MC, V. EP.*

$$$$ 🏨 **Sapphire Beach Resort & Marina.** On a clear day the lush green mountains of the neighboring BVI seem close enough to touch from this resort on one of St. Thomas's prettiest beaches. There's excellent snorkeling on the reefs to each side of the beach. This is a quiet retreat where you can nap while swinging in one of the hammocks strung between the palm trees in your front yard; but on Sunday the place rocks with a beach party. All units have fully equipped kitchens, telephones, and satellite TV. Children may join the Kids Klub, where 4- to 12-year-olds can enjoy such supervised activities as sandcastle building, arts and crafts, and sing-alongs. Children under 12 sleep in their parents' accommodations at no extra charge and eat free (when dining with their parents) at the ☞ **Seagrape** restaurant. ⊠ *Sapphire Bay (Box 8088) 00801,* ☎ *340/775–6100 or 800/524–2090,* ℻ *340/775–2403. 155 suites. 4 restaurants, 2 bars, air-conditioning, 4 tennis courts, beach, children's programs. AE, MC, V. EP, MAP.*

$$$$ 🏨 **Secret Harbour Beach Resort.** The beige buildings, containing low-rise studios and suites, are nestled around an inviting, perfectly framed sandy cove on Nazareth Bay, where you can watch the marvelous sunsets. From early April to the end of December, children under age 12 stay free, making this a family-friendly resort all summer. ⊠ *6280 Estate Nazareth 00802-1104,* ☎ *340/775–6550 or 800/524–2250,* ℻ *340/775–1501. 60 suites, 7 studios. 2 restaurants, bar, 2 tennis courts, beach. AE, MC, V. CP.*

✗ $$$$ 🏨 **Wyndham Sugar Bay Beach Club & Resort.** From afar, this large cluster of bulky white buildings looks overwhelming, but the hotel has a lot to offer. Most rooms overlook water; some have views of the BVI. All units have balconies and are spacious and comfortable, and all come with such amenities as hair dryers and coffeemakers. The beach is small, but there's a giant pool with waterfalls. The rates cover meals and beverages; use of the fitness center, tennis courts, and beach facilities; and a daily activities program. ⊠ *6500 Estate Smith Bay 00802,* ☎ *340/ 777–7100 or 800/927–7100,* ℻ *340/777–7200. 300 rooms. Restaurant, bar, air-conditioning, 3 pools, 2 tennis courts, health club, beach, snorkeling, windsurfing. AE, D, DC, MC, V. All-inclusive.*

FRENCHTOWN

$–$$ 🏨 **Admiral's Inn.** This charming inn stretches down a hillside on the
★   point of land known as Frenchtown, just west of Charlotte Amalie. All rooms have wonderful views of either the town and the harbor or the ocean; the four ocean-view rooms have private balconies and refrigerators. All units have rattan furniture; cream- or teal-color bedspreads; vertical blinds; coral, teal, and cream carpeting; and large, tiled vanity areas. The rocky shoreline is perfect for snorkeling. The inn's

freshwater pool (there's bar service here) is surrounded by a large wooden deck that's ideal for sunning. ⌂ *Villa Olga 00802,* ☎ *340/774–1376 or 800/544–0493 (reservations service),* ℻ *340/774–8010. 12 rooms. Restaurant, bar, pool. AE, D, MC, V. CP.*

SOUTH SHORE

$$$$ ⊞ **Bolongo Bay Beach Club & Villas.** This 75-room beachfront resort also includes the 20-room Bolongo Villas next door and the six-room Bolongo Bayside Inn across the street. All resort rooms—which include minisuites and one- and two-bedroom units—have efficiency kitchens and balconies and are just steps from a strand of white beach. The resort offers a choice of all-inclusive or semi-inclusive plans, which means you can pay less if you opt for fewer activities. The all-inclusive rate covers all meals and drinks, the use of tennis courts, and many water-sports activities—including an all-day sail and half-day snorkel trip on one of the resort's yachts. There's a three-night minimum for the all-inclusive plan, and over holiday periods. ⌂ *50 Estate Bolongo 00802,* ☎ *340/775–1800 or 800/524–4746,* ℻ *340/775–3208. 101 units. 2 restaurants, air-conditioning, 3 pools, 2 tennis courts, health club, volleyball, beach, dive shop, dock, snorkeling, windsurfing, boating, jet skiing. AE, D, DC, MC, V. All-inclusive.*

$$$$ ⊞ **Marriott Frenchman's Reef and Morning Star Beach Resorts.** Sprawl-
★ ing, luxurious, and on a prime harbor promontory east of Charlotte Amalie, these two resorts are St. Thomas's full-service superhotels. Both properties were extensively renovated in 1997, and Frenchman's Reef was given 128 suites—each with glorious ocean and harbor views. Morning Star rooms are the more elegant, in buildings tucked among the foliage that stretches along the fine white sand of Morning Star Beach; the sound of the surf can lull you to sleep. In addition to enjoying various snack and sandwich stops and a raw bar, you can dine alfresco on American or gourmet Caribbean fare, or oceanfront on the Tavern on the Beach; there's also a lavish buffet served, overlooking the sparkling lights of Charlotte Amalie and the harbor. Live entertainment and disco, scheduled activities for all ages, and a shuttle boat to town make having fun easy. ⌂ *Estate Bakkeroe (Box 7100) 00801,* ☎ *340/776–8500 or 800/524–2000,* ℻ *340/776–3054. 373 rooms, 128 suites. 6 restaurants, 6 bars, snack bar, air-conditioning, 2 pools, 4 tennis courts, beach. AE, D, DC, MC, V. EP.*

$$$ ⊞ **Bluebeard Beach Villas.** This secluded sibling resort of the in-town Bluebeard's Castle hotel is set on 24 tropical acres bordering crescent-shape Limetree beach. The pastel-color, rattan-furnished rooms are steps from a full-service water-sports center that rents snorkel gear, Windsurfers, Sunfish sailboats, and kayaks. The biggest thrill is the resident population of iguanas, who love to be hand-fed bright red hibiscus blooms. ⌂ *100 Frenchman's Bay 00802,* ☎ *340/776–4770 or 800/524–6599 (reservations service),* ℻ *340/693–2648. 84 rooms. Restaurant, bar, air-conditioning, in-room safes, pool, 2 tennis courts, beach, snorkeling, windsurfing, boating. AE, D, DC, MC, V. CP.*

Guest House

CHARLOTTE AMALIE

$ ⊞ **Danish Chalet Inn.** Quaint and cozy, this bed-and-breakfast offers economy and hospitality within walking distance of Charlotte Amalie's shopping district. The late actor Alan Hale Jr.—who played the Skipper on the 1960s TV show *Gilligan's Island*—was a regular guest. On the wraparound porch, the perfect place to enjoy your Continental breakfast, there's a constant breeze and a lovely view of the harbor. Rooms have phones, ceiling fans, TVs, and private baths. ⌂ *Estate Solberg (Box 4319) 00803,* ☎ *340/774–5764 or 800/635–1531,* ℻ *340/777–4886. 12 rooms. Fans, pool. MC, V. CP.*

Villas and Condominiums

EAST END

$$$$ 🏨 **Secret Harbourview Villas.** These units rest on a gentle hill just behind Secret Harbour Resort and the beach and share all the resort's facilities. All units have air-conditioning and maid service. ⊠ *Estate Nazareth (Ocean Property Management, office in Bldg. No. 5 (Box 8529) 00801, ☎ 340/775–2600 or 800/874–7897, FAX 340/775–5901. 27 units. 2 restaurants, air-conditioning, pool, 3 tennis courts, exercise room. AE, D, DC, MC, V.*

$$$–$$$$ 🏨 **The Anchorage.** Next to the St. Thomas Yacht Club and facing Cowpet Bay, these two- and three-bedroom villas are right on the beach. They have washing machines and dryers, and the complex has two lighted tennis courts, a freshwater pool, and an informal dining room. ⊠ *Estate Nazareth (Ocean Property Management, Box 8529) 00801, ☎ 340/775–2600 or 800/874–7897, FAX 340/775–5901. 30 rooms. Dining room, ai-conditioning, pool, 2 tennis courts. AE, D, MC, V.*

$$$–$$$$ 🏨 **Sapphire Village.** A stay in these high-rise units may take you back to the swinging-singles days of apartment-house living, since many of the units are rented out long-term to refugees from northern winters. The best units overlook the marina and St. John; the beach is in sight and just a short walk down the hill. ⊠ *Sapphire Bay (Ocean Property Management, Box 852) 00801, ☎ 340/775–2600 or 800/874–7897, FAX 340/775–5901. 35 units. Restaurant, air-conditioning, pub, 2 pools. AE, D, MC, V.*

$$$ 🏨 **Crystal Cove at Sapphire Bay West.** One of the older condominium complexes on the island, Crystal Cove was built as part of a Harvard University–sponsored architectural competition. The unassuming buildings blend into the Sapphire Beach setting so well that egrets and ducks are right at home in the pond in the center of the property. There are studio, one-, and two-bedroom units, each with a porch or balcony. There's also good snorkeling. ⊠ *Sapphire Bay (Ocean Property Management, Box 8529) 00801, ☎ 340/775–2600 or 800/874–7897, FAX 340/775–5901. 56 units. Air-conditioning, pond, pool, 2 tennis courts, beach, snorkeling. AE, D, DC, MC, V.*

$$–$$$$ 🏨 **Blazing Villas.** On the Renaissance Grand Beach Resort property, ★ these cool pastel yellow, pink, green, and blue villas have their own private garden patio and can be combined with other villas to create a four-bedroom, four-bath unit. All rooms have a refrigerator, microwave, and phone. You can use all the adjoining resort's facilities. ⊠ *Smith Bay Rd. (Box 502697) 00805, ☎ 340/776–0760 or 800/382–2002, FAX 340/776–3603. 19 rooms. 2 restaurants, snack bar, air-conditioning, refrigerators, 2 pools, 6 tennis courts, beach. AE, MC, V.*

$ 🏨 **Sea Horse Cottages.** These simple cottages, at the eastern end of the island on Nazareth Bay, look across to St. Croix, 40 mi south. Although there's no beach, steps go directly into the sea from a swimming platform. All rooms have kitchens and ceiling fans. ⊠ *Estate Nazareth (Box 302312) 00803, ☎ 340/775–9231. 11 units, from studios to 2-bedrooms. Fans, pool. No credit cards.*

Private Homes

You can arrange private-home rentals through various agents, including **McLaughlin-Anderson Vacations** (⊠ 100 Blackbeard's Hill, Suite 3, 00802, ☎ 340/776–0635 or 800/537–6246) and **Calypso Realty** (⊠ Box 12178, 00801, ☎ 340/774–1620 or 800/747–4858). Both specialize in luxury-end villas; write for brochures with photos of the properties they represent. Some residences are suitable for travelers with disabilities.

Dining

The beauty of St. Thomas and its sister islands have attracted a cadre of professionally trained chefs who know their way around fresh fish and local fruits. And locals are beginning to realize how attractive their cuisine is to tourists. You can now dine on everything from terrific, cheap local dishes such as goat water and johnnycake, to imports such as hot pastrami sandwiches and raspberries in crème fraîche.

In a large hotel you will pay prices similar to those in New York City or Paris. Fancy restaurants may have a token chicken dish under $20, but otherwise, main courses are pricey. You can, however, find good inexpensive Caribbean restaurants. To snack on some local fare, order a johnnycake or a thick slice of dumb bread and cheese from any of the mobile food vans parked all over the island. Familiar fast-food franchises also abound. You'll find Kentucky Fried Chicken at four locations—Buccaneer Mall, Sub Base, Ft. Mylner, and Tutu Park Mall. McDonald's is open at Wheatley Center, in Frenchtown, and near Tutu Park Mall, where there's a playground. Pizza Hut is on the Charlotte Amalie waterfront.

If your accommodations have a kitchen and you plan to cook, you'll find good variety in St. Thomas's mainland-style supermarkets. Note, however, that grocery prices are about 20% higher than those on the mainland. As for drinking, outside the hotels, a beer in a bar will cost between $2 and $3 and a piña colada $4 or more.

What to Wear

Dining on St. Thomas is relaxed and informal. Few restaurants require a jacket and tie. Still, at dinner in the snazzier places, shorts and T-shirts are highly inappropriate, and you would do well to wear slacks and a shirt with buttons. Dress codes on St. Thomas rarely call for women to wear skirts, but you'll never go wrong with something flowing.

CATEGORY	COST*
$$$$	over $35
$$$	$25–$35
$$	$15–$25
$	under $15

average cost of a three-course dinner, per person, excluding drinks and service; there is no sales tax in the USVI

Charlotte Amalie

AMERICAN

$$–$$$ ✕ **Greenhouse Bar and Restaurant.** Watch the waterfront wake up at this large, bustling, open-air restaurant, whose waitstaff looks like a bunch of all-American college kids on spring break. Breakfast and lunch (burgers, salads, and sandwiches) are good values. Dinner specials include peel-'n'-eat shrimp, Maine lobster, and prime rib. You can work it all off dancing to the Wednesday night band, which plays until the crowd clears. ✉ *Waterfront Hwy. at Storetvaer Gade,* ☎ *340/774–7998. AE, D, MC, V.*

$–$$$ ✕ **Hard Rock Cafe.** A hot spot from the day it opened, this waterfront restaurant is pretty much like its namesakes around the world. Rock-and-roll memorabilia abound, and the menu offers hamburgers, sandwiches, salads, and great desserts. Doors are open from 11 AM until 2 AM; there's always a wait for a table during prime meal times. ✉ *International Plaza on the Waterfront,* ☎ *340/777–5555. AE, MC, V.*

ASIAN

$–$$ ✕ **Beni Iguana's.** Sushi is served as "edible art" in a charming Danish courtyard setting. Among the offerings are cucumber and avocado or scallop with scallion rolls, specialty big rolls like the Kung Fooee (shiitake, cucumber, daikon, and flying fish roe), and tuna or salmon sashimi. A pictorial menu board makes ordering by the piece, plate, or combination platter much easier. ⊠ *Grand Hotel Court,* ☎ *340/ 777–8744. No credit cards. Closed Sun.*

CARIBBEAN/CREOLE

$$–$$$
★ ✕ **Gladys' Cafe.** Even if the local specialties—conch in butter sauce, salt fish and dumplings, hearty red bean soup—didn't make this a recommended café, it would be worth going for Gladys's smile. While you're here, pick up some of her special hot sauce for $6 per bottle. ⊠ *Royal Dane Mall,* ☎ *340/774–6604. AE. Closed Sun. No dinner.*

CONTINENTAL

$$$–$$$$
★ ✕ **Hotel 1829.** You'll dine by candlelight flickering over stone walls and pink table linens at this restaurant on the terrace of the ☞ **Hotel 1829.** The menu and award-winning wine list (325 varieties to choose from; 15 available by the glass) are extensive, from Caribbean rock lobster to rack of lamb. Many items, including a warm spinach salad, are prepared table-side; and the restaurant is justly famous for its dessert soufflés—chocolate, Grand Marnier, raspberry, or coconut, to name a few. ⊠ *Government Hill near Main St.,* ☎ *809/776–1829. Reservations essential. AE, D, MC, V. Closed Sun.*

ECLECTIC

$$$–$$$$ ✕ **Hervé** French-trained Hervé Chassin's long experience in the St. Thomas restaurant industry has led to a menu that offers a delightful mix of Caribbean and Continental cuisine. You can start off with crispy conch fritters served with a spicy-sweet mango chutney, and then choose from such entrées as fresh tuna encrusted with sesame seeds, or succulent roast duck with a ginger and tamarind sauce. The raspberry cheesecake is to die for. ⊠ *Government Hill,* ☎ *340/777–9703. AE, MC, V. Closed Sun.*

$$–$$$$ ✕ **Café LuLu.** From the heights of ☞ **Blackbeard's Castle,** you can enjoy a 180-degree sweeping harbor view while sampling dishes that combine the essence of Caribbean, Asian, and Mediterranean cuisines. Crispy plantain-coated sea bass and a fork-tender filet mignon filled with goat cheese may be two of the selections on the monthly changing menu. For Sunday brunch, the orange-mango mimosas and wasabi-spiced Bloody Marys are musts. ⊠ *Blackbeard's Hill,* ☎ *340/714–1641. Reservations essential. AE, D, MC, V. No lunch.*

$$–$$$$ ✕ **Randy's Bistro.** Find an A to Z of sandwich fixings at this New York–style deli with a twist. In the sit-down restaurant, the signature dish Bistro Salad—a mix of romaine, plum tomatoes, red onions, Roman, imported salami, and house dressing—is served with freshly baked herb bread and virgin olive oil for dipping. Vegetarian selections are numerous, including homemade pastas, a roasted vegetable *timbale* (a savory baked custard with bell peppers, eggplant, and mushrooms), and tofu mango cheesecake. ⊠ *Waterfront, between Royal Dane Mall and Palm Passage,* ☎ *340/777–3199. AE, MC, V.*

GREEK

$$–$$$
★ ✕ **Zorba's Sagapo.** Tired of shopping? Summon up a little more energy and head up Government Hill to Zorba's. President Clinton and his family did on a New Year's 1997 visit to St. Thomas. Sit and have a cold beer or bracing iced tea in the 19th-century courtyard surrounded by banana trees. Greek salads and appetizers, moussaka, and an excellent vegetarian plate top the menu. ⊠ *Government Hill,* ☎ *340/776–0444. Dinner reservations essential. AE, MC, V.*

ITALIAN

$$$–$$$$ ✕ **Virgilio's.** For the best northern Italian cuisine on the island, don't
★   miss this intimate, elegant hideaway whose two dining rooms face each
other across a quiet side street. Eclectic art covers the two-story-high
brick walls. Come here for more than 40 homemade pastas comple-
mented by superb sauces—*cappellini* (very thin spaghetti) with fresh
tomatoes and garlic or spaghetti peasant-style (in a rich tomato sauce
with mushrooms and prosciutto), for example. Try Virgilio's own
mango flambé with crepes or a steaming cup of cappuccino for dessert.
Maître d' Matthew Richardson is on hand day and night, welcoming
customers and helping the gracious staff. ⊠ *16 and 18 Main St.,* ☎
340/776–4920. Reservations essential. AE, MC, V. Closed Sun.

East End

AMERICAN

$–$$ ✕ **Tickles Dockside Pub.** Both the Crown Bay and East End locations
of this casual, alfresco restaurant have a devout following of locals who
live and work on the boats docked nearby. Enjoy sandwiches, ribs, and
chicken (served with sweet potato French fries) while you watch the
iguanas beg for table scraps—and bring your camera. ⊠ *American Yacht
Harbor, Red Hook, Bldg. D,* ☎ *340/775–9425. MC, V.*

CARIBBEAN/CREOLE

$–$$ ✕ **Eunice's Terrace.** Eunice is an excellent West Indian cook, who is
justly famous for introducing President Clinton to native-style cuisine.
Her roomy, two-story restaurant has a bar and a menu of native dishes,
including callaloo (a spicy stew thick with spinach-like greens and
seafood), conch fritters, fried fish, local sweet potato, *fungi* (a polenta-
like cornmeal dish with okra), and green banana. Be sure to pick up
one of Eunice's gift-wrapped rum cakes to go for $4 apiece. ⊠ *Rte.
38 near Renaissance Grand Beach Resort and Coral World, Smith Bay,*
☎ *340/775–3975. AE, MC, V.*

ECLECTIC

$$–$$$ ✕ **Mim's Seaside Bistro.** Walk straight from Bolongo Beach into this
open-air eatery, where you can sip a Beach Bar Bomber while listening to the lapping waves. Try a ham and baked Brie open-face sandwich for lunch; for dinner, indulge in fish—served grilled, sautéed,
blackened, broiled, or island-style. Thursday is all-you-can-eat shrimp
night; Saturday nights feature a prime rib special. ⊠ *Watergate Villas,*
☎ *340/775–2081. AE, MC, V. Closed Sun.*

$–$$$ ✕ **Duffy's Love Shack.** If the floating bubbles don't attract you to this
zany eatery, the lime green shutters, loud rock music, and fun-loving
waitstaff sure will. Billed as the "ultimate tropical drink shack," bar-
tenders shake up such exotic concoctions as the Love Shack Volcano—
a 50-ounce flaming extravaganza. Dining selections are just as trendy.
Try the tequilla-lime shrimp or jerk chicken Caesar. Thursday nights
feature theme parties complete with prizes and giveaways. ⊠ *Red
Hook Plaza parking lot,* ☎ *340/775–4122. No credit cards.*

$–$$$ ✕ **Raffles.** In a homelike dining room, set in a quaint marina, owner-
★   chef Sandra Englesburger puts on a one-woman culinary show. Her
from-scratch creations include an English shepherd's pie, mahimahi in
a rich lobster sauce, and a two-day Peking duck. Entrées on the prix-
fixe ($10), three-course menu change nightly. For dessert, try Peter's
Paradise—a dark chocolate sphere filled with white chocolate mousse
and fruit. Raffles is definitely a find. ⊠ *41-6-1 Compass Point Marina,* ☎ *809/775–6004. AE, MC, V. Closed Mon. No lunch.*

ITALIAN

$$$–$$$$ ✕ **Romanos.** Inside this huge, old, stucco house in Smith Bay is a de-
★   lightful surprise: a spare, elegant setting and superb northern Italian

cuisine. Owner Tony hasn't advertised since the restaurant opened in 1988, and it's always packed. Try the pastas, either with a classic sauce or one of Tony's unique creations, such as a cream sauce with mushrooms, prosciutto, pine nuts, and Parmesan. ⊠ *97 Smith Bay,* ☎ *340/775–0045. Reservations essential. MC, V. Closed Sun. No lunch.*

SEAFOOD

$$$–$$$$ ✕ **Agave Terrace.** At this dimly lit, open-air pavilion restaurant, fresh fish is served as steaks or fillets, and the catch of the day is listed on the blackboard nightly. Come early and have a drink at the Lookout Lounge, which has breathtaking views of the BVI. The food enjoys as good a reputation as the view. ⊠ *Colony Point Pleasant Resort at Smith Bay,* ☎ *340/775–4142. AE, MC, V. No lunch.*

$$–$$$$ ✕ **Seagrape.** This restaurant at the ☞ Sapphire Beach Resort has an all-star location right on the beach. The menu emphasizes fresh fish (including mahimahi, wahoo, and tuna prepared in numerous ways, though with a Continental flare) caught daily by the charter fleet of the adjoining marina. The food is well prepared, the setting is lovely, and the staff is attentive and friendly. Some nights a band plays at the adjoining outdoor cocktail lounge. ⊠ *Sapphire Beach Resort & Marina,* ☎ *340/775–6100. AE, MC, V.*

TEX-MEX

$–$$$ ✕ **Polli's.** You feel as if your sitting deep within a tropical jungle at this open-air restaurant where a live parrot squawks a greeting to incoming diners. The menu is Tex-Mex complete with jalapeño poppers (deep-fried cheese-stuffed hot peppers), chicken- or seafood-stuffed fajitas and margarita pie for dessert. All entrées come vegetarian-style upon request, with soy replacing the meat. ⊠ *Tillett Gardens,* ☎ *340/775–4550. AE, MC, V.*

Frenchtown

AUSTRIAN

$$$ ✕ **Alexander's Café.** This restaurant is a favorite with the people in ★ the restaurant business on St. Thomas—always a sign of quality. Alexander is Austrian, and the schnitzels are delicious and reasonably priced; pasta specials are fresh and tasty. Save room for strudel. Next door is Alexander's Bar & Grill, serving food from the same kitchen but in a more casual setting and at lower prices. ⊠ *24A Honduras,* ☎ *340/776–4211. Reservations essential. AE, D, MC, V. Closed Sun.*

CARIBBEAN/CREOLE

$$–$$$ ✕ **Victor's New Hide-Out.** This landmark restaurant is a little hard to find—it's up the hill between the Nisky Shopping Center and the airport—but the search is worth it. Native food—steamed fish, marinated pork chops, and local lobster—and native music are offered in a casual, friendly, West Indian atmosphere. ⊠ *Sub Base,* ☎ *340/776–9379. AE, MC, V.*

ECLECTIC

$$–$$$$ ✕ **The Chart House.** In an old great house on the tip of the Frenchtown peninsula, this restaurant offers superb views along with fresh fish and teriyaki dishes, lobster, Hawaiian chicken, and a large salad bar. ⊠ *Villa Olga,* ☎ *340/774–4262. AE, D, DC, MC, V.*

$$–$$$ ✕ **Craig & Sally's.** In the heart of Frenchtown, Sally Darash whips up ★ such eclectic starters as grilled shrimp and melon kabobs and entrées such as polenta-crusted yellowtail snapper with artichoke and olive sauce. Save room for dessert—the white-chocolate cheesecake is truly special. Husband Craig makes sure more than a dozen wines are available by the glass and many more by the bottle. ⊠ *22 Honduras,* ☎ *340/777–9949. AE, MC, V. Closed Mon.–Tues. No lunch Sat.–Sun.*

Northside

AMERICAN

$$–$$$ ✕ **Sib's Mountain Bar and Restaurant.** Here you'll find live music, football, burgers, barbecued ribs and chicken, and beers. This friendly two-fisted drinking bar, with a restaurant on the back porch, is a good place for a casual dinner after a day at the beach. Kids of all ages can doodle on the paper tablecloths with the colorful crayons left on every table. ✉ *Mafolie Hill,* ☎ *340/774–8967. AE, MC, V.*

ITALIAN

$$–$$$$ ✕ **Ferrari's.** St. Thomas residents have consistently voted this the "best ★ value" restaurant in the *USVI Daily News* poll. The menu has such staples as antipasto, veal marsala, lasagna, pizzas, and garlic bread. Sit at a table or have a seat at the bar from 4:30 until 11. ✉ *33 Crown Mountain Rd.,* ☎ *340/774–6800. AE, MC, V. No lunch.*

Beaches

All beaches on St. Thomas are open to the public, but often you have to walk through a resort to reach them. Resort guests frequently have access to lounge chairs and floats that are off-limits to nonguests; for this reason, you may feel more comfortable at one of the beaches not associated with a resort, such as Magens or Coki. Whichever one you choose, remember to remove your valuables from the car, and keep them out of sight when you go swimming.

Coki Beach, next to Coral World, is a popular snorkeling spot for cruise-ship passengers; it's common to find a group of them among the reefs on the east and west ends of the beach.

Hull Bay's beach, on the north shore, faces Inner and Outer Brass cays and attracts fishermen and beachcombers. It's open to rough Atlantic waves, making it the only place to surf on the island.

Magens Bay is usually lively because of its spectacular crescent of white sand, more than ½-mi long, and its calm waters, which are protected by two peninsulas. The bottom is flat and sandy, so this is a place for sunning and swimming rather than snorkeling. You'll find food, changing facilities, and rest rooms here.

Morning Star Beach, close to Charlotte Amalie, is where many young locals show up for body surfing or volleyball. The pretty curve of beach fronts the Morning Star section of Marriott's Frenchman's Reef Hotel. Snorkeling is good near the rocks when the current doesn't affect visibility.

Sapphire Beach. From here there's a fine view of St. John and other islands. Snorkeling is excellent at the reef to the right or east, near Pettyklip Point. Sapphire Beach Resort rents water-sports gear.

Secret Harbour. The condo resort here doesn't at all detract from the attractiveness of this covelike East End beach. Not only is it pretty, it is also superb for snorkeling—go out to the left, near the rocks.

Outdoor Activities and Sports

BOATING AND SAILING

Calm seas, crystal clear waters, and close-by islands (perfect for picnicking, snorkeling, and exploring) make St. Thomas a favorite jumping-off spot for a weeklong sailing or power boat adventure. With well over 100 vessels to choose from, St. Thomas is the charter-boat mecca of the USVI. You can go through a broker to book a private sailing vessel with crew or contact a charter company directly.

Blue Water Cruises (✉ Box 1345, Camden, ME 04843, ☎ 800/524–2020) is a brokerage with an excellent worldwide reputation. Charter-boat companies on St. Thomas include **Island Yachts** (✉ 6100 Red Hook Quarter, Suite 4, ☎ 340/775–6666 or 800/524–2019) in Red Hook, **Regency Yacht Vacations** (✉ 5200 Long Bay Rd., ☎ 340/776–5950 or 800/524–7676) at the Yacht Haven Marina, and **VIP Yacht Charters** (✉ 6118 Estate Frydenhoj 58, ☎ 340/776–1510 or 800/524–2015), near Red Hook. **Nauti Nymph** (✉ 6501 Red Hook Plaza, Suite 201, ☎ FAX 340/775–5066 or 800/734–7345) has a large selection of powerboats for rent. Rates range from $215 to $350 a day and include snorkel gear.

CYCLING

Hills are steep and roads don't have shoulders, but you'll never ride too far from a beautiful beach and cool swim. **St. Thomas Mountain Bike Adventure** (✉ Box 7037, 00801, ☎ 340/776–1727) takes you on a 1½-hour cycle out past Magens Bay to Peterborg Point, using Trek 830 21-speed mountain bikes. There are lots of photo opportunities: flora, fauna, and a lesser-seen side of Magens's picturesque half-moon beach. Helmets, water, and a guide are provided, and the cost is $35.

FISHING

Fishing from St. Thomas is synonymous with blue marlin angling—especially from June through October. Four 1,000-pound plus blues, including three world records, have been caught on the famous North Drop, about 20 mi north of St. Thomas. If you're not into marlin fishing, try hooking up sailfish in the winter, dolphinfish come spring, and wahoo in the fall.

To book a boat, call the **American Yacht Harbor** (✉ 6100 Red Hook Plaza, ☎ 340/775–6454), **Charter Boat Center** (✉ 6300 Red Hook Plaza, ☎ 340/775–7990 or 800/866–5714), or **Sapphire Beach Marina** (✉ Sapphire Bay, ☎ 340/775–6100). Or, to find the trip that will best suit you, walk down the docks at either American Yacht Harbor or Sapphire Beach Marina and chat with the captains.

GOLF

The **Mahogany Run Golf Course** (✉ Rte. 42, ☎ 340/777–5000) is open daily and often hosts informal tournaments on weekends. A spectacular view of the neighboring BVI and challenging 3-hole "Devil's Triangle" attracts avid golfers—like President Clinton who played in 1997—to this Tom Fazio–designed, par-70, 18-hole course.

HORSE RACING

The **Clinton Phipps Racetrack** (✉ Rte.30 at Nadir 42, ☎ 340/775–4555) schedules races—especially on local holidays—with sanctioned betting. Be prepared for large crowds; this is a popular sport.

PARASAILING

The Caribbean waters are so clear here that the outline of submarine coral reefs are visible from high in the sky. Parasailers sit in a harness attached to a parachute that lifts off from the boat deck until they're sailing up in the air. **Caribbean Parasail and Watersports** (✉ 6501 Red Hook Plaza, ☎ 340/775–9360) makes parasailing pick-ups from every beachfront resort on St. Thomas. They also rent water toys like jet skis, kayaks, and floating battery-powered chairs.

SCUBA DIVING AND SNORKELING

Descend into a whimsical world where what look like rocks are really living sea creatures, where schools of fish come dressed in rainbow-color uniforms, and where a variety of other sea life plays hide-and-seek amid beautiful underwater flowers. The reefs here are perfect places to explore, whether you're a beginner or an expert diver.

Aqua Action (✉ 6501 Red Hook Plaza, ☎ 340/775–6285) is a full-service, PADI, five-star shop offering all levels of instruction. Vice president

Al Gore took a dive trip with **Chris Sawyer Diving Center** (⊠ 6300 Red Hook Plaza, Suite 29; other locations at Compass Point, American Yacht Harbor, and the Renaissance Grand Beach Resort; ☎ 340/775–7320 or 800/882–2965). This PADI five-star outfit specializes in dives to the 310-ft-long RMS *Rhone*. They also have a NAUI certification center offering instruction up to dive master. **Seahorse Dive Boats** (⊠ Crown Bay Marina, Suite 505, ☎ 340/774–2001) is another PADI five-star facility that does both day and night dives to wrecks and reefs.

SEA EXCURSIONS

Landlubbers and seafarers alike will enjoy the wind in their hair and salt spray in the air while exploring the waters surrounding St. Thomas. Several businesses can effortlessly book you on a half-day, inshore light-tackle fishing trip; a snorkel-and-sail to a deserted cay; or an excursion over to the BVI. Contact the **Adventure Center** (⊠ Marriott Frenchman's Reef Hotel, ☎ 340/774–2990), **Charter Boat Center** (☞ Fishing, *above*), or **Limnos Charters** (⊠ 6100 Red Hook Plaza, ☎ 340/775–3203).

SEA KAYAKING

Fish dart, birds sing, and iguanas lounge on the limbs of dense mangroves deep within a marine sanctuary on St. Thomas's south-east shore. **Virgin Islands Ecotours** (⊠ 2 Estate Nadir, on Rte. 32, ☎ 340/779–2155) offers 2½-hour, guided trips on two-man sit-atop ocean kayaks; there are stops for swimming and snorkeling. Many of the resorts in St. Thomas's eastern end have kayaks, too.

STARGAZING

Without the light pollution so prevalent in more densely populated areas, the heavens appear supernaturally bright. On a **Star Charters Astronomy Adventure** (⊠ Nisky Mail Center #693, 00802, ☎ 340/774–9211), peer into the Caribbean's largest optical telescope—an 18-inch Newtonian Reflector—and learn both the science and lore of the stars through a well-informed celestial guide.

SUBMARINING

Dive 90 ft under the sea to one of St. Thomas's most beautiful reefs without getting wet. **Atlantis Submarines** (⊠ Havensight Shopping Mall, Bldg VI, ☎ 340/776–5650) are 46-passenger, air-conditioned conduits to a watery world teeming with brightly colored fish, vibrant sea fans, and an occasional shark. A guide narrates the two-hour journey, while a diver makes a mid-tour appearance for a fish-feeding show. The cost is $75. No children under 36 inches tall are allowed.

TENNIS

The Caribbean sun is hot, so be sure to hit the courts before 10 AM or after 5 PM (many of the courts are lighted). You can indulge in a set or two even if you're staying in a guest house without courts, since most hotels rent time to nonguests. For reservations, call **Bluebeard's Castle Hotel** (☎ 340/774–1600, ext. 196), **Sapphire Beach Resort** (☎ 340/775–6100, ext. 2131), **Frenchman's Reef Tennis Courts** (☎ 340/776–8500, ext. 444), **Mahogany Run Tennis Club** (☎ 340/775–5000), **Marriott Renaissance Grand Beach Resort** (☎ 340/775–1510), **Ritz-Carlton, St. Thomas** (☎ 340/775–3333), or **Wyndham Sugar Bay** (☎ 340/777–7100). There are two public courts at **Sub Base** (next to the Water and Power Authority), open on a first-come, first-served basis. The lights are on here until 8 PM.

WINDSURFING

Expect some spills, anticipate the thrills, and try your luck clipping through the seas on a surfboard with a sail. Most beachfront hotel-resorts rent Windsurfers and offer 1-hour lessons for about $50. One of the best known independent outfits on the island is **West Indies Wind-**

surfing (⊠ Vessup Beach, #9 Nazareth, ☎ 340/775–6530)—which helped organize the U.S. Windsurfing Association National Championships on St. Thomas in 1997.

Shopping

Most people would agree that St. Thomas lives up to its self-described billing as a shopper's paradise. Even if shopping isn't your idea of how to spend a vacation, you still may want to slip in on a quiet day (check the cruise-ship listings—Monday and Saturday are usually the least crowded) to browse. Among the best buys are liquor, linens, imported china, crystal (most stores ship), and jewelry. The sheer volume of jewelry available makes this one of the few items for which comparison shopping is worth the effort.

Local crafts run the gamut from shell jewelry and carved calabash bowls to straw brooms and woven baskets. Dolls are a big hit. Creations by local doll maker Gwendolyn Harley—like her costumed West Indian market woman—have been goodwill ambassadors bought by visitors from as far away as Asia. Spice mixes, hot sauces, and tropical jams and jellies are other native products worth purchasing.

There's no sales tax in the USVI, and shoppers can take advantage of the $1,200 duty-free allowance per family member (remember to save your receipts). If you buy a plant, be sure to stop at the Department of Agriculture (⊠ Rte. 40) to get the roots sprayed for diseases and to pick up a certificate to present to U.S. customs when you leave the territory. Although you'll find the occasional salesclerk who will make a deal, bartering is not the norm here.

Areas and Malls

The prime shopping area in **Charlotte Amalie** is between Post Office and Market squares; it consists of three parallel streets that run east–west (Waterfront Highway, Main Street, and Back Street) and the alleyways that connect them. Particularly attractive are the historic **Royal Dane Mall** and **A. H. Riise Alley**, and pastel-painted **International Plaza**, quaint alleys between Main Street and the Waterfront.

Vendors Plaza, on the waterfront side of Emancipation Gardens, is a central location for outdoor vendors who sell handmade earrings, necklaces, and bracelets; straw baskets and handbags; T-shirts; fabrics; African artifacts; local foods; and fresh tropical fruit smoothies.

West of town, the pink-stucco **Nisky Center,** on Harwood Highway about ½-mi east of the airport, is more of a hometown shopping center than a tourist area, but there's a bank, a pharmacy, clothing stores, a record shop, and a Radio Shack.

Havensight Mall, next to the cruise-ship dock, may not be as charming as Charlotte Amalie, but it does have more than 60 shops. You'll find an excellent bookstore, a bank, a pharmacy, a gourmet grocery, and smaller branches of many downtown stores. Just steps away from the Havensight Mall, the dozen-plus **Port of $ale** shops offer factory-outlet prices on brand-name clothing and accessories.

East of town, **Tillett Gardens** (⊠ Estate Tutu, ☎ 340/775–1405) is an oasis of artistic endeavor on the highway across from the Tutu Park Shopping Center (☞ *below*). The late Jim Tillett and then-wife Rhoda converted this old Danish farm into an artist's retreat in 1959. Today you can watch craftspeople and artisans produce silk-screen fabrics, pottery, candles, watercolors, gold jewelry, stained glass, and other handicrafts. There's usually something special happening in the gardens as well: the Classics in the Gardens program is a classical music series presented under the stars, and Arts Alive is a visual arts and crafts festival held four times yearly.

Tutu Park Shopping Center, across from Tillet Gardens, is the island's one and only enclosed mall. The 47 stores and food court are anchored by a Kmart and a grocery store. Archaeologists have discovered evidence that ancient Arawak Indians once lived near the mall grounds. Red Hook now has **American Yacht Harbor,** a waterfront shopping area with a dive shop, tackle store, art gallery, bar, and a few restaurants.

Don't forget **St. John** (☞ Shopping *in* St. John, *below*). A ferry ride (an hour from Charlotte Amalie or 20 minutes from Red Hook) will take you to the charming shops of **Mongoose Junction** and **Wharfside Village,** which specialize in unique, often island-made items.

Specialty Items

ART

A. H. Riise Caribbean Print Gallery. Haitian and Virgin Islands art is displayed and sold here, along with art books, exquisite botanical prints, and historic-photo note cards. ⊠ *37 Main St., at Riise's Alley,* ☎ *340/776–2303.*

The Gallery. Inside the waterfront branch of Down Island Traders (and owned by the same people), the Gallery carries Haitian art along with works by a number of Virgin Islands artists. Items on display include metal sculpture, wood carvings, painted screens and boxes, figures carved from stone, and oversize papier-mâché figures. Prices range from $50 to $5,000. ⊠ *Waterfront Hwy. at Post Office Alley,* ☎ *340/776–4641.*

Camille Pissarro Art Gallery. This second-floor gallery, in the birthplace of St. Thomas's famous artist, offers a fine collection of original paintings and prints by local and regional artists. ⊠ *14 Main Street,* ☎ *340/775–5511.*

BOOKS AND MAGAZINES

Dockside Bookshop. This place is packed with books for children, travelers, cooks, and historians, as well as a good selection of paperback mysteries, best-sellers, art books, calendars, and art prints. It also carries a selection of books written in and about the Caribbean and the Virgin Islands. ⊠ *Havensight Mall,* ☎ *340/775–5511.*

Education Station Books. The emphasis at this full-service bookstore is on Caribbean literature and African-American and African history. There's also a large cookbook selection, a music section featuring jazz and world beat tapes from Africa, and prints by local artists. In addition, you can buy and sell used books of all types here. Visit Education Station Ltd., just next door, for children's books. ⊠ *Wheatley Center, intersection of Rtes. 35 and 38,* ☎ *340/776–3008.*

Island Newsstand. This place has the largest selection of magazines and stateside newspapers on St. Thomas. Expect to pay about 20% above stateside prices. ⊠ *Grand Hotel Court, Charlotte Amalie,* ☎ *340/774–0043;* ⊠ *Fort Mylner Shopping Center near Tillett Gardens,* ☎ *340/775–3430.*

CAMERAS AND ELECTRONICS

Boolchand's. A variety of brand-name cameras, audio and video equipment, and binoculars is sold here. ⊠ *31 Main St.,* ☎ *340/776–0794; and* ⊠ *Havensight Mall,* ☎ *340/776–0302.*

Royal Caribbean. Shop here for cameras, camcorders, stereos, watches, and clocks. ⊠ *33 Main St.,* ☎ *340/776–8166; and* ⊠ *Havensight Mall,* ☎ *340/776–8890.*

CHINA AND CRYSTAL

A. H. Riise Gift Shops. A. H. Riise carries Waterford, Royal Crown, and Royal Doulton at good prices. A five-piece place setting of Royal Crown Derby's Old Imari goes for less than $500. The branch at Riise's Alley also sells jewelry, pearls, perfumes, and watches. ✉ *37 Main St., at Riise's Alley,* ☎ *340/776–2303; and* ✉ *Havensight Mall,* ☎ *340/776–2303.*

The English Shop. This store offers figurines, cutlery, and china and crystal from major European and Japanese manufacturers, including Spode, Limoges, Royal Doulton, Portmeirion, Noritaki, and Wedgwood. You can choose what you like from the catalogs here, and shopkeepers will order and factory-ship it for you. (Be sure to keep your receipts in case something goes awry.) ✉ *Havensight Mall,* ☎ *340/776–3776.*

Island Galleria. This second-floor store displays china and crystal glasses, decanters, bowls, and vases in several patterns. Famous names here are Swarovski, Wedgwood, Royal Doulton, and Balleek. You don't have to carry purchases; they ship. ✉ *3B Main St.,* ☎ *340/777–5892.*

Little Switzerland. All of this establishment's shops carry crystal from Baccarat, Waterford, Orrefors, and Riedel; china from Villeroy & Boch and Wedgwood, among others; and fine Swiss watches, including an outstanding Rolex selection (they're the sole Rolex distributor for the USVI). There's also an assortment of cut-crystal animals, china and porcelain figurines, and many other affordable collectibles. They also do a booming mail-order business; ask for a catalog. ✉ *Tolbod Gade, across from Emancipation Garden; 5 Main Street, inside the A. H. Riise Gift Mart; dockside at Havensight Mall,* ☎ *340/776–2010.*

CLOTHES

The Beach House at Dilly D'Alley. Downstairs is the place for fancy T-shirts, sundresses, linen pants, and accessories; upstairs you'll find a giant selection of swimwear. ✉ *Trompeter Gade,* ☎ *340/776–5006.*

Cosmopolitan. At this sophisticated menswear emporium, look for such top lines as Paul and Shark, Bally, Timberland, Sperry Topsider, Testoni, Burma Bibas, Givenchy, Nautica, Fila, Hom, Lachco, and Gottex. ✉ *Drake's Passage at the Waterfront,* ☎ *340/776–2040.*

G'Day. Everything in this tiny shop is drenched in the bright colors of Australian artist Ken Done, Scandinavian artist Sigrid Olsen, and items by Cotton Fields—swimwear, resort wear, accessories, and umbrellas. ✉ *Waterfront Hwy. at Royal Dane Mall,* ☎ *340/774–8855.*

Janine's Boutique. Here you'll find women's and men's dressy and casual apparel from European designers and manufacturers, including the Louis Feraud collection, and select finds from Valentino, Christian Dior, YSL, and Pierre Cardin. ✉ *A–2 Palm Passage,* ☎ *340/774–8243.*

Java Wraps. Now you, too, can wear the snazzy Indonesian batik creations that the USVI's female athletes modeled at the opening ceremonies of the 1996 Summer Olympic Games in Atlanta. Snazzy swimwear; unisex floral-print shirts; cover-ups; and leisure attire for men, women, and children are the attractions at this shop. ✉ *Waterfront Hwy. at Royal Dane Mall,* ☎ *340/774–3700.*

Local Color. Here St. John artist Sloop Jones exhibits colorful, hand-painted island designs on cool dresses, T-shirts, and sweaters. You'll also find wearable art by other local artists; unique jewelry; sundresses, shorts, and shirts in bright prints; and big-brim straw hats dipped in fuchsia, turquoise, and other tropical colors. ✉ *Hibiscus Alley,* ☎ *340/774–3727.*

Lover's Lane. With the motto "Couples that play together, stay together," this romantic second-floor shop sells sensuous lingerie, sexy menswear, and provocative swimwear. ✉ *Waterfront Hwy. at Raadets Gade,* ☎ *340/777–9616.*

V.I. America's Cup Challenge. Support the VI's bid to win the 2000 Cup from New Zealand by wearing official team clothing—T-shirts, polo shirts, hats, caps, visors, and more. ✉ *Hibiscus Alley,* ☎ *340/774–9090.*

FOODSTUFFS

A Chew Or Two. Everything at this confectionery tastes as good as it smells. A wide assortment of Godiva chocolates shares space with Caribbean rum balls, tropical-flavor saltwater taffy, colorful jelly beans, homemade fudge, oversize chocolate chip cookies and Trinidadian coffees. ✉ *Trompeter Gade,* ☎ *340/774–6675.*

Cost-U-Less. This store sells everything from soup to nuts, but in giant sizes and case lots. The fresh meat and seafood department, however, offers smaller family-size portions. ✉ *Estate Tutu, off Route 38, 1-mi west of Tutu Park Shopping Center,* ☎ *340/777–3588.*

Fruit Bowl. For fruits and vegetables, this is the place. ✉ *Wheatley Center,* ☎ *340/774–8565.*

Gourmet Gallery. Visiting millionaires buy their caviar here. There's also an excellent and reasonably priced wine selection, as well as condiments, cheeses, and specialty ingredients for everything from tacos to curries to chow mein. ✉ *Crown Bay Marina,* ☎ *340/776–8555.*

Havensight Market. A full-time French chef makes a mouthwatering assortment of salads and freshly baked breads. There are also specialty produce, ethnic ingredients, and a full complement of wines. ✉ *Havensight Mall,* ☎ *340/774–4948.*

Marina Market. You won't find a better fresh meat and seafood department in any other place on the island. ✉ *Across from Red Hook ferry,* ☎ *340/779–2411.*

Plaza Extra. This mainland-type supermarket has a large selection of Middle Eastern foods. ✉ *Tutu Park Mall,* ☎ *340/775–5646.*

Pueblo Supermarket (✉ *Four Winds Plaza, across from Tillett Gardens,* ☎ *340/775–4655;* ✉ *Sub Base, ½-mi east of Nisky Center on Harwood Highway,* ☎ *340/774–4200;* and ✉ *Estate Thomas, 1 mi north of Havensight Mall,* ☎ *340/774–2695)* sells stateside brands but at higher prices because of the cost of shipping.

HANDICRAFTS

Caribbean Marketplace. This is a great place to buy handicrafts from the Caribbean and elsewhere. Also look for Sunny Caribee spices, soaps, coffee and teas from Tortola, and coffee from Trinidad. ✉ *Havensight Mall,* ☎ *340/776–5400.*

Down Island Traders. These traders deal in hand-painted calabash bowls; finely printed Caribbean note cards; jams, jellies, spices, hot sauces and herbs; herbal teas made of lemongrass, passion fruit, and mango; high-mountain coffee from Jamaica; and a variety of handicrafts from throughout the Caribbean. ✉ *Waterfront Hwy. at Post Office Alley,* ☎ *340/776–4641.*

Native Arts and Crafts Cooperative. More than 40 local artists—including school children, senior citizens, and people with disabilities—create an ever-changing array of handcrafted items: African-style jewelry, quilts, calabash bowls, dolls, carved-wood figures, woven baskets, straw brooms, note cards, and cookbooks. ✉ *Tolbod Gade, across from Emancipation Garden and next to the visitor center,* ☎ *340/777–1153.*

Parrot's Nest & Wrap Shak. Here you'll find handcrafted cloth dolls; wooden figurines; African artwork; shell art; and jewelry from the Far East, South America, and the Caribbean. The cool cotton wraps sold here make great resort wear. (✉ *Royal Dane Mall,* ☎ *340/774–9211).*

JEWELRY

Amsterdam Sauer. Many fine one-of-a-kind designs are displayed and sold here. ⊠ *14 Main St.,* ☎ *340/774–2222;* ⊠ *Havensight Mall,* ☎ *340/776–3828.*

Blue Carib Gems. At family-owned and -run Blue Carib Gems, watch Alan O'Hara Sr. polish Caribbean amber and larimar (blue-hued Caribbean gemstone), agate, and other gems and fashion them into gold and silver settings. Visit Alan Jr. at the Wharfside Village branch on St. John. ⊠ *2–3 Back St.,* ☎ *340/774–8525.*

Cardow's (⊠ 33 Main St., ☎ 340/776–1140; ⊠ Havensight Mall, ☎ 340/774–0530 or 340/774–5905) offers an enormous "chain bar" more than 100 ft long, where you're guaranteed 30%–50% savings off U.S. retail prices or your money will be refunded within 30 days of purchase.

Cartier. In addition to the fantastically beautiful and fantastically priced items, there are a surprising number of affordable ones, including Cartier silk scarves, which are cheaper than Hermès, and quite lush. ⊠ *31 Main St.,* ☎ *340/774–1590.*

Colombian Emeralds. Well-known in the Caribbean, this store offers set and unset emeralds as well as gems of every description. There are additional locations on the waterfront and at Havensight Mall. *(*⊠ *30 Main St.,* ☎ *340/774–3400).*

Diamonds International. Choose a diamond, emerald, or tanzanite gem and a mounting, and you'll have your dream ring set in an hour. Famous for having the largest inventory of diamonds on the island, this shop welcomes trade-ins, has a U.S. service center, and offers free diamond earrings with every purchase. ⊠ *31 Main St.,* ☎ *340/774–3707;* ⊠ *3 Drakes Passage,* ☎ *340/775–2010; and* ⊠ *7AB Drakes Passage,* ☎ *340/777–4787.*

H. Stern (⊠ 12 Main St., ☎ 340/776–1939; ⊠ 32AB Main St., ☎ 340/776–1146; and ⊠ Havensight Mall, ☎ 340/776–1223) is one of the most respected names in gems.

LEATHER GOODS

Coach Boutique. A whole wall of high-fashioned handbags leads deeper into the store where lightweight Tumi luggage of nylon or leather is so strong you can sit on it. There are also sporty canvas Kipling bags, all under $100. ⊠ *34 Main St.,* ☎ *340/777–1469.*

Fendi. This chic boutique carries the signature Fendi bags from Italy in understated colors like olive on black. The pale-lemon luggage trimmed in black patent is stunning. ⊠ *23 Main St.,* ☎ *340/777–5708.*

Leather Shop. You'll find mostly big names at big prices here (Fendi and Bottega Veneta are prevalent), but if you look hard enough you'll find some reasonably priced, high-quality purses, wallets, and briefcases. ⊠ *24 Main St.,* ☎ *340/776–3995;* ⊠ *Havensight Mall,* ☎ *340/776–0040.*

Zora's. Fine leather sandals made to order are the specialty here, as well as a selection of made-only-in-the-Virgin-Islands backpacks, purses, and briefcases in durable, brightly colored canvas. ⊠ *Norre Gade across from Roosevelt Park,* ☎ *340/774–2559.*

LINENS

Fabric In Motion. Fine Italian linens share space with Liberty of London silky cottons, colorful batiks, cotton prints, ribbons, and accessories at this small shop. There are also paintings, quilts, and dolls made by local craftspeople. ⊠ *Storetvaer Gade,* ☎ *340/774–2006.*

Mr. Tablecloth. The friendly staff here will help you choose among the floor-to-ceiling array of linens, from Tuscany lace tablecloths to Irish linen pillowcases. The prices will please you. ⊠ *6–7 Main St.,* ☎ *340/774–4343.*

LIQUOR AND TOBACCO

A. H. Riise Liquors. This Riise venture offers a large selection of tobacco (including imported cigars), as well as cordials, wines, and other liquors (rare vintage cognacs, Armagnacs, ports, and Madeiras). It also stocks fruits in brandy and barware from England. ⊠ *37 Main St., at Riise's Alley,* ☎ *340/776–2303;* ⊠ *Havensight Mall,* ☎ *340/776–7713.*

Al Cohen's Discount Liquor. The wine selection at this warehouse-style store is very large. ⊠ *Across from Havensight Mall, Long Bay Rd.,* ☎ *340/774–3690.*

Gourmet Gallery. This aromatic grocery store (there's a bakery in the back) caters to the yachting crowd by offering one of the best wine selections on St. Thomas. ⊠ *Crown Bay Marina,* ☎ *340/776–8555.*

MUSIC

Modern Music. Shop for the latest stateside and Caribbean CD and cassette releases, plus oldies, classical, and New Age music. ⊠ *Across from Havensight Mall,* ☎ *340/774–3100;* ⊠ *Nisky Center,* ☎ *340/777–8787.*

Parrot Fish Records and Tapes. A stock of standard stateside tapes and CDs, plus a good selection of Caribbean artists, including local groups, can be found here. For a catalog of calypso, *soca* (up-tempo calypso music), steel band, and reggae music, write to Parrot Fish, Box 9206, St. Thomas 00801. ⊠ *Back St.,* ☎ *340/776–4514.*

PERFUMES

Sparky's. Spiffy enough to match its neighbor, Cartier, Sparky's has a wide range of perfumes and cosmetics. The impeccably turned out salesclerks can also give you a facial and makeup lesson. ⊠ *30 Main St.,* ☎ *340/776–7510.*

Tropicana Perfume Shoppes. Tropicana has the largest selection of fragrances for men and women in all of the VI. ⊠ *2 Main St.,* ☎ *340/774–0010.*

SOUVENIRS

Pampered Pirate. This busy store carries island-made dolls, Christmas ornaments, prints, and paintings along with its other gift items. ⊠ *4 Norre Gade,* ☎ *340/775–5450.*

SUNGLASSES

Davante. Find an enormous eyewear collection tucked into this glittering, glamorous store. Filling prescriptions is no problem. ⊠ *A. H. Riise Mall,* ☎ *340/714–1220.*

Fashion Eyewear. Tucked into a tiny building is this even tinier sunglasses shop. ⊠ *20A Garden St.,* ☎ *809/776–9075.*

Sun Glass Hut. Take your pick from among such name-brand eyewear as Biagiotti, Serengetti, Carrera, and others. ⊠ *15 Main St.,* ☎ *340/777–5585;* ⊠ *37 Main St.,* ☎ *340/774–9030;* ⊠ *Havensight Mall,* ☎ *340/777–7563.*

TOYS

Mini Mouse House. Birds sing, dogs bark, and fish swim in this animated toyland. Adults have as much fun trying out the wares as do kids. ⊠ *3A Trompeter Gade,* ☎ *340/776–4242.*

Nightlife and the Arts

On any given night, especially in season, you'll find steel-pan orchestras, rock-and-roll bands, piano music, jazz, broken-bottle dancing (dancing atop broken glass), disco, and karaoke. Pick up a copy of the free, bright-yellow *St. Thomas This Week* magazine when you arrive (you'll see it at the airport, in stores, and in hotel lobbies); the back pages list who's playing where. The *Daily News* Thursday edition carries complete listings for the upcoming weekend.

Nightlife

BARS

Athena's. Dance to latin, jazz, R&B, and contemporary tunes against a backdrop mural that depicts the Greek Acropolis and Mt. Olympus. Side up to the bar and mingle with island business and political celebrities. The action runs from 5 PM until the wee hours, Thursday–Sunday. ⊠ *32 Raadets Gade,* ☎ *340/714–1909.*

The Greenhouse. This place is slowly making a transition from a waterfront bar to something like the Caribbean equivalent of the T.G.I. Friday's chain in the United States. It strives to meet all tastes, starting with a breakfast that's popular with locals; burgers and taco salad for lunch; and then prime rib and lobster specials for dinner. Once the Greenhouse puts away the salt-and-pepper shakers at 10 PM, it becomes a rock-and-roll club with a DJ or live reggae bands rousting the weary to their feet six days a week. ⊠ *Waterfront Hwy. at Storetvaer Gade,* ☎ *340/774–7998.*

Iggies. Sing along karaoke style to the sounds of the surf or the latest hits at this beachside lounge. There's often a DJ on weekends, when a buffet barbecue precedes the 9 PM music fest. Dance inside, or kick up your heels under the stars. ⊠ *50 Estate Bolongo,* ☎ *340/775–1800.*

Stixx On The Water. Old friends from anchorages around the world rendezvous at this Yacht Haven Marina bar and restaurant, and there's always room for a new friend or two. Stixx features rock, country, and reggae music nightly. There's a dance floor. ⊠ *Yacht Haven Marina,* ☎ *340/774–4480.*

You'll find a piano bar nightly at **Andiamo at the Martini Cafe** (⊠ Frenchtown, ☎ 340/776–7916) and on weekends at **L'Hotel Boynes** (⊠ Blackbeard's Hill, ☎ 340/774–5511). **Cafe LuLu** (⊠ Blackbeard's Hill, ☎ 340/714–1641) features guitar and jazz on Friday and Saturday nights, respectively. **Zorba's Sagapo** (⊠ Government Hill, ☎ 340/776–0444) fills in with guitar tunes on Saturday and Sunday.

The Arts

MUSEUMS

The Virgin Islands Museum. In Ft. Christian, the VI's oldest standing structure, see exhibits on USVI history, natural history, and turn-of-the-century furnishings. Local artists display their works monthly in the gallery. A gift shop sells local crafts, books, and other souvenir items. ⊠ *Waterfront Hwy. just east of shopping district,* ☎ *340/776–4566.* ⬛ *Free.* ☉ *Weekdays 9–4, Sun. 10–3.*

Weibel Museum. In this museum next to the synagogue (☞ Exploring, *below*), Jewish history (300 years of it) on St. Thomas is showcased. The small gift shop sells a commemorative coin in gold or silver celebrating the anniversary of the Hebrew Congregation's establishment on St. Thomas in 1796. ⊠ *15 Crystal Gade,* ☎ *340/774–4312.* ⬛ *Free.* ☉ *Weekdays 9–4.*

THEATER

Reichhold Center for the Arts. This open-air amphitheater has its more expensive seats covered by a roof. Schedules vary, so check the local paper to see what's on when you're in town. Throughout the year, there's an entertaining mix of local plays, dance exhibitions, and music of all types. The Boston Pops Traveling Ensemble entertained New Year's 1997. ⊠ *Rte. 30 across from Brewers Beach,* ☎ *340/693–1559.*

Exploring St. Thomas

St. Thomas is only 13 mi long and less than 4 mi wide, but it's an extremely hilly island, and even an 8- or 10-mi trip could take several hours. Don't let that discourage you, though, because the ridge of mountains that runs from east to west through the middle, and separates the Caribbean and Atlantic sides of the island, has spectacular vistas and is a lot of fun to explore.

Charlotte Amalie

When exploring Charlotte Amalie, look beyond the pricey shops, T-shirt vendors, and bustling crowds for a glimpse of the island's history. The city served as the capital of Denmark's outpost in the Caribbean until 1917, an aspect of the island often lost in the glitter and glitz of the shopping district. If you're driving, park in the public lot next to Ft. Christian.

Emancipation Gardens, right next to the fort, is a good place to start a walking tour. Tackle the hilly part of town first: head north up Government Hill to the historic buildings that house government offices and have incredible views. Several regal churches line the route that runs west back to the town proper and the old-time market. Virtually all the alleyways that intersect Main Street lead to eateries that serve frosty tropical drinks, sandwiches and burgers, and West Indian fare. You'll find public rest rooms in this area, too. Allow an hour for a quick view of the sights, two hours if you plan to tour Government House.

A note about the street names: In deference to the island's heritage, the streets downtown are labeled by their Danish names. Locals will use both the Danish name and the English name (such as Dronningens Gade and Norre Gade for Main Street), but most people refer to things by where they're located ("a block toward the Waterfront off Main Street," or "next to the Little Switzerland Shop"). It's best to ask for directions by shop names or landmarks.

Numbers in the margin correspond to points of interest on the Charlotte Amalie map.

SIGHTS TO SEE

⑰ All Saints Anglican Church. Built in 1848 from stone quarried on the island, the church has thick, arched window frames lined with the yellow brick that came to the islands as ballast aboard merchant ships. The merchants left the brick on the waterfront when they filled their boats with molasses, sugar, mahogany, and rum for the return voyage. The church was built in celebration of the end of slavery in the USVI. ✉ *Domini Gade,* ☎ *340/774–0217.* ☉ *Mon.–Sat. 6–3.*

㉓ Cathedral of St. Peter and St. Paul. This building was consecrated as a parish church in 1848 and serves as the seat of the territory's Roman Catholic diocese. The ceiling and walls are covered with murals painted in 1899 by two Belgian artists, Father Leo Servais and Brother Ildephonsus. The San Juan–marble altar and side walls were added in the 1960s. ✉ *Lower Main St.,* ☎ *340/774–0201.* ☉ *Mon.–Sat. 8–5.*

⑲ Danish Consulate Building. Built in 1830, this structure housed the Danish Consulate until the Danish West India Company sold its properties to the local government in 1992. It now serves as home to the territory's governor. ✉ *Take stairs north at corner of Bjerge Gade and Crystal Gade to Denmark Hill.*

⑯ Dutch Reformed Church. This church has an austere loveliness that's amazing considering all it has been through—founded in 1744, it burned down in 1804, and was rebuilt in 1844; it was then blown down by Hurricane Marilyn in 1995 and rebuilt in 1997. The unembellished cream-color hall gives you a sense of peace—albeit monochromatically. The only other color is the forest green of the shutters and the carpet. ✉ *Nye Gade and Crystal Gade,* ☎ *340/776–8255.* ☉ *Weekdays 9–5. Call ahead; doors are sometimes locked.*

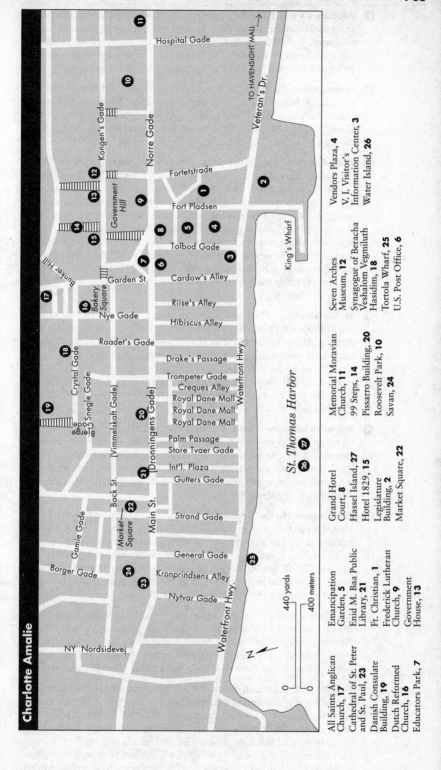

Charlotte Amalie

St. Thomas Harbor

All Saints Anglican Church, **17**
Cathedral of St. Peter and St. Paul, **23**
Danish Consulate Building, **19**
Dutch Reformed Church, **16**
Educators Park, **7**

Emancipation Garden, **5**
Enid M. Baa Public Library, **21**
Ft. Christian, **1**
Frederick Lutheran Church, **9**
Government House, **13**

Grand Hotel Court, **8**
Hassel Island, **27**
Hotel 1829, **15**
Legislature Building, **2**
Market Square, **22**

Memorial Moravian Church, **11**
99 Steps, **14**
Pissarro Building, **20**
Roosevelt Park, **10**
Savan, **24**

Seven Arches Museum, **12**
Synagogue of Beracha Veshalom Vegmiluth Hasidim, **18**
Tortola Wharf, **25**
U.S. Post Office, **6**

Vendors Plaza, **4**
V. I. Visitor's Information Center, **3**
Water Island, **26**

❼ Educators Park. A peaceful place amid the town's hustle and bustle, the park has memorials to three famous Virgin Islanders: educator Edith Williams, J. Antonio Jarvis (a founder of the *Daily News*), and educator and author Rothschild Francis. The latter gave many speeches from this location. ⊠ *Main St. across from U.S. Post Office.*

❺ Emancipation Garden. Built to honor the freeing of slaves in 1848, today the gazebo here is used for official ceremonies. There are two monuments here that show the island's Danish-American tie—a bust of Danish King Christian and a scaled-down model of the U.S. Liberty Bell. ⊠ *Between Tolbod Gade and Ft. Christian.*

㉑ Enid M. Baa Public Library. Like so many structures on the north side of Main Street, this large pink building is a typical 18th-century town house. Merchants built their houses (stores downstairs, living quarters above) across from the brick warehouses on the south side of the street. The library was once the home of merchant and landowner Baron von Bretton. It's the first recorded fireproof building, meaning that it was built of ballast brick instead of wood. Its interior (high ceilings and cool stone floors) is the perfect refuge from the afternoon sun. You can browse through historic papers or just sit in the breeze by an open window reading the paper. ⊠ *Main St.,* ☎ *340/774–0630.* ☽ *Weekdays 9–5, Sat. 9–3.*

☙ ❶ Ft. Christian. St. Thomas's oldest standing structure, this monument anchors the shopping district. It was built 1672–80, and now has U.S. national landmark status. The clock tower was added in the 19th century. This remarkable redoubt has, over time, been used as a jail, governor's residence, town hall, courthouse, and church. It now houses a museum, a gift shop, and art exhibits that change monthly. ⊠ *Waterfront Hwy. just east of shopping district,* ☎ *340/776–4566.* ▧ *Free.* ☽ *Weekdays 9–4.*

❾ Frederick Lutheran Church. This historic church has a massive mahogany altar, and its pews—each with its own door—were once rented to families of the congregation. Lutheranism is the state religion of Denmark, and, when the territory was without a minister, the governor—who had his own elevated pew—filled in. ⊠ *Norre Gade,* ☎ *340/776–1315.* ☽ *Mon.–Sat. 9–4.*

⓭ Government House. Built as an elegant residence in 1867, today Government House serves as the governor's office with the first floor open to the public. The staircases are of native mahogany, as are the plaques hand-lettered in gold with the names of the governors appointed and, since 1970, elected. Brochures detailing the history of the building are available, but you may have to search for them. (Look behind or under the guest book to the left of the entrance.)

The three murals at the back of the lobby were painted by Pepino Mangravatti in the 1930s as part of the U.S. government's Works Projects Administration. The murals depict Columbus's landing on St. Croix during his second voyage in 1493; the transfer of the islands from Denmark to the United States in 1917; and a sugar plantation on St. John.

A deputy administrator can take you on a tour of the second floor. You can call ahead for an appointment, or you can take a chance that an official will be in. It's worth the extra effort, if for no other reason than the terrace view. Imagine colonial affairs of state being conducted in the grandeur of the high-ceiling, chandeliered ballroom. In the reception room are four small paintings by Camille Pissarro, but unfortunately they are hard to appreciate because they're enclosed in frosted-glass cases. More interesting, and visible, is the large painting by an unknown artist that was found in Denmark; it depicts a romanticized version of St. Croix; the painting was purchased by former governor Ralph M. Paiewonsky, who then gave it to Government House. ⊠ *Government Hill,* ☎ *809/774–0001.* ⊞ *Free.* ⊘ *Weekdays 8–5.*

⑧ Grand Hotel Court. This imposing building stands at the head of Main Street. Once the island's premier hotel, it has been converted into offices and shops. ⊠ *Tolbod Gade at Norre Gade.*

㉗ Hassel Island. East of ☞ **Water Island** in Charlotte Amalie harbor, Hassle Island is part of the Virgin Islands National Park, due in part to the fact that it has the ruins of a British military garrison (built during a brief British occupation of the USVI during the 1800s) and the remains of a marine railway (where ships were hoisted into drydock for repairs). Also on Hassel Island is the shell of the hotel that writer Herman Wouk's fictitious character Norman Paperman tried to turn into his own paradise in the book *Don't Stop the Carnival.* There's a small ferry that runs from the Crown Bay Marina to the island; departure times are posted at Tickles Dockside Pub, and the fare is $3.

⑮ Hotel 1829. As its name implies, it was built in 1829, albeit as a residence of a prominent merchant named Lavalette rather than as a hotel. The building's bright coral-color exterior walls are accented with fancy black wrought iron, and the interior is paneled in a dark wood, which makes it feel delightfully cool. From the dining terrace, where gourmet food is served, there's an exquisite view of the harbor framed by tangerine-color bougainvillea. ⊠ *Government Hill,* ☎ *340/776–1829.*

❷ Legislature Building. Its pastoral-looking lime-green exterior conceals the vociferous political wrangling of the Virgin Islands Senate going on inside. Built originally by the Danish as a police barracks, the building was later used to billet U.S. Marines, and much later it housed a public school. You're welcome to sit in on sessions in the upstairs chambers. ⊠ *Waterfront Hwy. across from Ft. Christian,* ☎ *340/774–0880.* ⊘ *Daily 8–5.*

㉒ Market Square. Formally called Rothschild Francis Square, this is a good place to stop for a snack. A cadre of old-timers sell papaya, tannia roots, fresh-squeezed juices, and herbs; sidewalk vendors offer a variety of African fabrics and artifacts and tie-dyed cotton clothes at good prices. ⊠ *North side of Main St. at Strand Gade.*

⑪ Memorial Moravian Church. Built in 1884, it was named to commemorate the 150th anniversary of the Moravian Church in the VI. ⊠ *17 Norre Gade,* ☎ *340/776–0066.* ⊘ *Weekdays 8–5.*

☾ ⑭ 99 Steps. This staircase "street," built by the Danes in the 1700s, leads to the residential area above Charlotte Amalie and Blackbeard's Castle. The castle's tower, built in 1679, was once used by the notorious pirate Edward Teach. Today, this lookout is at the center of a small hotel. If you count the stairs as you go up, you'll discover, as have thousands before you, that there are more than 99. ⊠ *Look for steps heading north from Government Hill.*

⑳ Pissarro Building. Home to several shops and an art gallery, this was the birthplace and childhood home of Camille Pissarro, who later moved to France and became an acclaimed impressionist painter. In the art gallery, you'll find three original pages from Pissarro's sketchbook and two pastels by Pissarro's grandson, Claude. ⊠ *38 Main St.*

☾ ⑩ Roosevelt Park. A good spot to people-watch, you'll see members of the local legal community head to the nearby court buildings while you rest on a bench. The small monument on the park's south side is ded-

icated to USVI war veterans. Kids enjoy the wood-and-tire playground.
✉ *Norre Gade.*

㉔ **Savan.** A neighborhood of small streets and small houses, it was first
laid out in the 1700s as the residential area for a growing community
of middle-class black artisans, clerks, and shopkeepers. You'll find a
row of Rastafarian shops along the first block and a restaurant that
sells pâté and a delicious turnover-type pastry stuffed with meat or vegetables. ✉ *Turn north off lower Main St. onto General Gade.*

⑫ **Seven Arches Museum.** This restored 18th-century home is a striking
example of classic Danish West Indian architecture. There seem to be
arches everywhere—seven to be exact—all supporting a "welcoming
arms" staircase that leads to the second floor and the flower-framed
front doorway. The Danish kitchen is a highlight: It's housed in a separate building just off the main house, as were all cooking facilities in
the early days (in case of fire). Inside the house, you'll find historic furnishings, cannon balls, and gas lamps. Tall, cool glasses of *bush*—the
local lingo for herb—tea are served in a charming courtyard. Behind
the house is a quaint West Indian cottage. ✉ *Government Hill, 3
buildings east of Government House,* ☎ *340/774–9295.* ᐧ *$5 (sug-
gested donation).* ☉ *Tues.–Sun. 10–3 or by appointment.*

⑱ **Synagogue of Beracha Veshalom Vegmiluth Hasidim.** The synagogue's
Hebrew name translates to the Congregation of Blessing, Peace, and
Loving Deeds. The small building's white pillars contrast with rough
stone walls, as does the rich mahogany of the pews and altar. The sand
on the floor symbolizes the exodus from Egypt. Since the synagogue
first opened its doors in 1833, it has held a weekly Sabbath service,
making it the oldest synagogue building in continuous use under the
American flag and the second oldest (after the one on Curaçao) in the
Western Hemisphere. Next door, the **Weibel Museum** (☞ also Museums *in* The Arts, *above*) showcases Jewish history on St. Thomas. ✉
15 Crystal Gade, ☎ *340/774–4312.* ☉ *Weekdays 9–4.*

㉕ **Tortola Wharf.** Catch the *Native Son* and other ferries to the BVI from
here. There's an upstairs restaurant where you can watch the Charlotte Amalie harbor traffic as you enjoy an iced tea. ✉ *Waterfront Hwy.*

⑥ **U.S. Post Office.** While you buy your postcard stamps, contemplate the
murals of waterfront scenes by *Saturday Evening Post* artist Stephen
Dohanos. His art was commissioned as part of the WPA in the 1930s.
✉ *Tolbod Gade and Main St.*

④ **Vendors Plaza.** Here merchants sell everything from T-shirts to African
attire to leather goods. Look for local art among the ever-changing selections at this busy market. ✉ *West of Ft. Christian at the waterfront,*
☎ *800/372–8784.* ☉ *Weekdays 8–6, Sun. 9–1.*

③ **V.I. Visitor's Information Center.** This hospitality lounge comes complete with bathrooms and a place to stash your luggage if you want to
shop on your way to the airport. ✉ *Tolbod Gade across from Emancipation Garden,* ☎ *800/372–8784.* ☉ *Weekdays 8–6, Sun. 9–1.*

㉖ **Water Island.** This island, about ¼ mi out in Charlotte Amalie harbor,
was once a peninsula of St. Thomas, but a channel was cut through
so U.S. submarines could get to their base in a bay just to the west,
known as Sub Base. On December 12, 1996, the U.S. Department of
the Interior transferred 50 acres of the island, which included beaches
and roads, to the territorial government, making it the fourth largest
of the USVI. A ferry goes between Crown Bay Marina and the island
several times daily at a cost of $3.

Around the Island

To explore outside of Charlotte Amalie, you'll need to rent a car or hire a taxi. Your rental car should come with a good map; if not, pick up the "Island Map of St. Thomas" at a tourist information center. The roads are marked with route numbers, but they're confusing and seem to switch numbers suddenly. If you stop to ask for directions, it's best to have your map in hand because the locals probably know the road you're looking for by another name. Allow yourself a full day to explore St. Thomas by car, especially if you want to stop for picture taking or to enjoy a light bite or refreshing swim. Most of the gas stations are on the more populated eastern end of the island, so fill up before heading to the north side. And remember to drive on the left.

Although the eastern end has many major resorts and spectacular beaches, don't be surprised if a cow or a herd of goats crosses your path as you drive through the relatively flat dry terrain. The north side of the island is more lush and hush—fewer houses and less traffic. Here you'll find roller-coaster routes (made all the more scary because the roads have no shoulders) and be rewarded with incredible flora. Plan to spend a day on a driving tour, leaving time in the afternoon for a swim at the beach. Pick up some sandwiches from delis in the Red Hook Area for a picnic lunch or enjoy a slice of pizza at Magens Bay. A day in the country will reveal the tropical pleasures that have enticed more than one visitor to become a resident.

Numbers in the margin correspond to points of interest on the St. Thomas map.

SIGHTS TO SEE

39 **Brewer's Beach.** If you're hungry, trucks selling lunch, snacks, and drinks often park along the road bordering this long strand of powdery white beach. ⊠ *Rte. 30 near the airport.*

33 **Coki Point.** Snorkel the reefs at its eastern and western ends. You may want to dash in for a swim or just do some people-watching while nibbling on a meat pâté snack (a fried meat- or conch-filled pie), which you can buy from one of the vendors. Don't leave valuables unattended in your car or on the beach at Coki Point. ⊠ *Turn north off Rte. 38.*

29 **Compass Point Marina.** It's fun to park your car and walk around this marina. The boaters—many of whom have sailed here from points around the globe—are easy to engage in conversation. ⊠ *Turn south off Red Hook Rd. at well-marked entrance road just east of Independent Boat Yard.*

32 **Coral World Marine Park.** Reopened in late 1997 after extensive renovation, Coral World is home to a three-level underwater observatory (call ahead for shark-feeding times), the world's largest reef tank, and an aquarium with more than 20 TV-size tanks providing capsulated views of life in the waters of the VI. Coral World's staff will answer your questions about the turtles, iguanas, parrots, and flamingos that inhabit the park, and there's a restaurant, souvenir shop, and the world's only underwater mailbox, from which you can send postcards. ⊠ *Coki Point, turn north off Smith Bay Rd. at sign,* ☎ *340/775–1555.* ⊠ *$17.* ☉ *Daily 9–5:30*

35 **Drake's Seat.** Sir Francis Drake was supposed to have kept watch over his fleet and looked for enemy ships of the Spanish fleet from this vantage point. The panoramic vista is especially breathtaking (and romantic) at dusk, and if you arrive late in the day you'll miss the hordes of day-trippers on taxi tours who stop at Drake's Seat to take a picture and buy a T-shirt from one of the many vendors. By afternoon the crowd thins and most of the vendors are gone. ⊠ *Rte. 40.*

③⑦ Estate St. Peter Greathouse Botanical Gardens. Perched on a mountainside 1,000 ft above sea level, with views of more than 20 other islands and islets, is this unusual spot. You can wander through a gallery displaying local art, sip a complimentary rum or virgin punch while looking out at the view, or follow a nature trail that leads through nearly 200 varieties of tropical trees and plants, including an orchid jungle. ⊠ *Rte. 40, St. Peter Mountain Rd.,* ☎ *340/774–4999.* ☞ *$8.* ☉ *Mon.–Sat. 9–4:30.*

④① Frenchtown. Popular with tourists for its several bars and restaurants, Frenchtown also serves as home to the descendants of immigrants from St. Barthélemy (St. Barts). You can watch them pull up their boats and display their catch of the day along the waterfront. Frenchtown's harbor has an abundance of yellowtail, parrot fish, and oldwife nearly as colorful as the fishing boats. If you want to get a feel for the residential district of Frenchtown, walk west to some of the town's winding streets, where the tiny wood houses have been passed down from generation to generation. ⊠ *Turn south off Waterfront Hwy. at the U.S. Post Office.*

③⑧ Hull Bay. You may come across the fishing boats and homes of the descendants of settlers from the French West Indies who fled to St. Thomas more than 200 years ago. If you have the opportunity to engage them in conversation, you will hear speech patterns slightly different from those of other St. Thomians. Hull Bay, with its rougher Atlantic surf and relative isolation, is one of the best surfing spots on the island. Take a break from the rigors of sightseeing at the Hull Bay Hideaway, a laid-back beach bar where a local band plays rock and roll on Sunday afternoons. ⊠ *Rte. 37.*

③⑥ Magens Bay Beach. Popular with tourists and locals, it is the island's busiest beach. It's often listed among the world's most beautiful beaches, and on weekends and holidays it hops with groups partying under the sheds. There's also an outdoor bar, bathhouses, a nature trail, and a snack bar. Driving east from the beach, do as the locals do and stop at the Udder Delight, a one-room shop of the St. Thomas Dairies that serves a USVI tradition—a milk shake enlivened with a splash of Cruzan rum. Kids can enjoy virgin shakes, with a touch of soursop, mango, or banana flavoring. ⊠ *Rte. 35.* ☞ *$1.*

④⓪ Mountain Top. Don't forget to stop here for a banana daiquiri and spectacular views from the observation deck more than 1,500 ft above sea level. There are also a number of shops that sell everything from Caribbean art to nautical antiques, ship models, and T-shirts. Kids will like talking to the tropical parrots—and hearing them answer back. ⊠ *Head north off Rte. 33; look for signs.*

②⑧ Paradise Point Tramway. Fly skyward in a gondola straight up the hill to Paradise Point, a scenic overlook with breathtaking views of Charlotte Amalie and the harbor. There are several shops, a bar, and a restaurant. ⊠ *Rte. 30 at Havensight,* ☎ *340/774–9809.* ☞ *$10.* ☉ *Daily 7:30–4:30.*

③① Red Hook. This busy shopping village is the nautical mecca of St. Thomas, where you'll find fishing and sailing charter boats, dive shops, and power-boat rental agencies at the American Yacht Harbor marina. There are also several bars and restaurants, including Tickles Dockside Pub, Duffy's Love Shack, Mackenzie's steak house, and the seafood-oriented Blue Marlin and East Coast Bar and Grill. Two grocery stores (including the Marina Market), two delis, and a candy shop offer picnic fixings ranging from sliced meats and cheeses to rotisserie-cooked chickens, gourmet salads, and fresh baked breads.

㉞ Tillett Gardens. Clustered in a booming local shopping area, you'll find a colony where local artisans craft stained glass, pottery, gold jewelry, and ceramics. Tillett's paintings and silk-screened fabrics are also on display and for sale. The gardens encircle a shaded courtyard with fountains and Polli's Mexican restaurant. ✉ *Rte. 38 across from Tutu Park Shopping Center* ☎ *340/775–1929*

㉚ Virgin Islands National Park Headquarters. This park facility consists of a dock, a small grassy area with picnic tables, and a visitor center where maps and brochures are available. Iguanas are common here. If you see one, hold out a hibiscus flower, which is this prehistoric-looking creature's favorite food. ✉ *Turn east off Rte. 32 at sign,* ☎ *340/775–6238.* ☉ *Weekdays 8–5.*

ST. CROIX

Updated by
Lynda Lohr

St. Croix, the largest of the three USVI with 84 square mi, lies 40 mi to the south of St. Thomas. But unlike the bustling island-city of St. Thomas, its harbor teeming with cruise ships and its shopping district crowded with bargain hunters, St. Croix has a slower pace and a more diverse economy, mixing tourism with light and heavy industry on rolling land that was once covered with waving carpets of sugarcane.

St. Croix's population has grown dramatically over the last 30 years, and its diversity reflects the island's varied history. The cultivation of sugarcane was more important here than on St. Thomas or St. John and continued as an economic force into the 1960s. After the end of slavery in 1848, the need for workers brought waves of immigrants from other Caribbean islands, particularly nearby Puerto Rico. St. Croix was divided into plantation estates, and the ruins of great houses and more than 100 sugar mills that dot the island's landscape are evidence of an era when St. Croix rivaled Barbados as the greatest producer of sugar in the West Indies.

Tourism began and boomed in the 1960s, bringing visitors—as well as migrants—from the mainland United States (referred to by locals as Continentals). In the late 1960s and early 1970s industrial development brought St. Croix yet another wave of immigrants. This time they came mostly from Trinidad and St. Lucia, to seek work at the Hess oil refinery or at the aluminum-processing plants on the south shore.

St. Croix is a study of contrasting beauty. The island is not as hilly as St. Thomas or St. John. A lush rain forest envelops the northwest, the eastern end is dry, and palm-lined beaches with startlingly clear aquamarine water ring the island. The island's capital, Christiansted, is a restored Danish port on a coral-bound bay on the northeastern shore. The tin-roof, 18th-century buildings in both Christiansted and Frederiksted, on the western end of the island, are either pale yellow, pink, or ocher, resplendent with bright blazes of bougainvillea and hibiscus. The prosperous Danes built well (and more than once—both towns were devastated by fire in the 19th century), using imported bricks or blocks cut from coral, fashioning covered sidewalks (called galleries here) and stately colonnades, and leaving an enduring cosmopolitan air as their legacy.

Lodging

From plush resorts to simple beachfront digs, St. Croix's variety of accommodations is bound to suit every type of traveler. The island is home

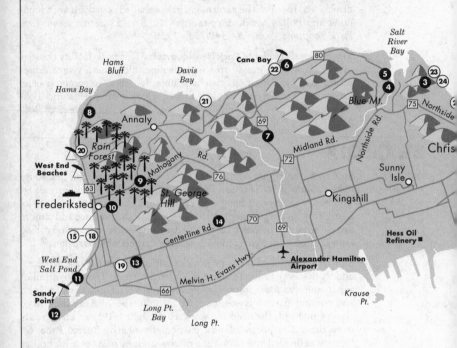

Exploring
Cane Bay, **6**
Cramer's Park, **2**
Estate Mount
Washington
Plantation, **8**
Estate Whim
Plantation
Museum, **13**
Judith's Fancy, **3**
Karl and Marie
Lawaetz Museum, **10**
Mt. Eagle, **7**

Point Udall, **1**
St. Croix Leap, **9**
St. George Village
Botanical
Gardens, **14**
Salt River Bay
National Historical
Park and Ecological
Preserve, **5**
Salt River Marina, **4**
Sandy Point Beach, **12**
West End
Salt Pond, **11**

Dining
Antoine's, **32**
Blue Moon, **16**
Bombay Club, **28**
Café du Soleil, **17**
The Galleon, **45**

Great House at Villa
Madeleine, **47**
Harvey's, **33**
Indies, **34**
Java Mon, **30**
Kendricks, **41**

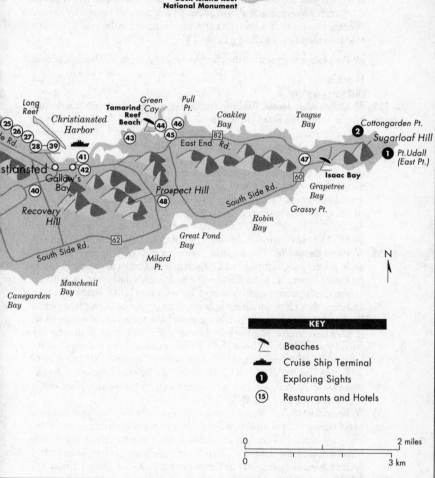

Buck Island

Buck Island Reef
National Monument

Long
Reef

Christiansted
Harbor

Green
Cay

Tamarind
Reef
Beach

Pull
Pt.

Coakley
Bay

Teague
Bay

Cottongarden Pt.

Sugarloaf Hill

Pt. Udall
(East Pt.)

le Rd.

25 26 27
28 39

41
42

40

Gallow's
Bay

Recovery
Hill

43

44 46
45

East End Rd.

82

Prospect Hill

48

South Side Rd.

Robin
Bay

47

60

Isaac Bay

Grapetree
Bay

Grassy Pt.

stiansted

South Side Rd.

62

Great Pond
Bay

Milord
Pt.

Canegarden
Bay

Manchenil
Bay

N

KEY

Beaches

Cruise Ship Terminal

1 Exploring Sights

15 Restaurants and Hotels

0   2 miles

0   3 km

Paradise Cafe, **29**
Le St. Tropez, **18**
South Shore Cafe, **48**
Tivoli Gardens **35**
Top Hat, **36**
Tutto Bene, **37**
Villa Morales, **19**

Lodging
Breakfast Club, **31**
Buccaneer, **43**
Chenay Bay Beach
Resort, **46**
Club St. Croix, **27**
Colony Cove, **25**
Cormorant Beach
Club and Villas, **24**

The Frederiksted, **15**
Hibiscus Beach
Hotel, **23**
Hilty House, **40**
Hotel Caravelle, **38**
King's Alley
Hotel, **39**

Schooner Bay, **42**
Sprat Hall, **20**
Sugar Beach, **26**
Tamarind
Reef Hotel, **44**
Villa Madeleine, **47**
Waves at Cane
Bay, **22**
Westin Carambola
Beach Resort, **21**

to several small-but-special properties that offer personalized service. If you're the type who enjoys all the comforts of home while you travel, you may prefer to stay in a condominium or villa. Room rates on St. Croix are competitive with those on other islands, and if you travel off-season, you'll find substantially reduced prices. Many properties offer honeymoon and dive packages that are also big money savers. Whether you stay in a hotel, a condominium, or a villa, you'll find up-to-date amenities, including cable TV.

☞ For price categories, *see* the chart *under* Lodging *in* St. Thomas, *above.*

Hotels

CHRISTIANSTED

$–$$$ 🖫 **King's Alley Hotel.** Right in the center of Christiansted's hustle and
★   bustle, this small hotel (which is part of the King's Alley shopping and restaurant complex) mixes convenience with charm. The 12 premium rooms in the section across the courtyard have mahogany four-poster beds, Mexican tile floors, and Indonesian print fabrics. French doors open onto balconies with a view of the waterfront and the shopping arcade below. The 23 standard rooms in the hotel's older section are a tad less interesting but still attractive. The staff can arrange all sorts of activities: water sports, tours, golf, and tennis. ⊠ *57 King St. (Box 4120), 00822,* ☎ *340/773–0103 or 800/843–3574,* 𝙵𝙰𝙓 *340/773–4431. 35 rooms. Air-conditioning, pool. AE, D, DC, MC, V. EP.*

$–$$ 🖫 **Hotel Caravelle.** The fetching, three-story Caravelle offers moderately priced lodgings right in Christiansted. Rooms are done in tasteful dusky blues and have floral-print bedspreads and curtains, vaulted ceilings, refrigerators, phones, and TV with free HBO. Baths are clean and new, though the unique tile in the showers is a holdover from when the hotel was built in 1968. Most rooms have some sort of ocean view; the best overlook the harbor. Owners Sid and Amy Kalmans are friendly and helpful. The Wahoo Willie, a casual terrace eatery, serves local and Continental cuisine. ⊠ *44A Queen Cross St., 00820,* ☎ *340/ 773–0687 or 800/524–0410,* 𝙵𝙰𝙓 *340/778–7004. 43 rooms, 1 2-bedroom suite. Restaurant, bar, air-conditioning, refrigerators, pool, meeting room. AE, D, DC, MC, V. EP.*

$ 🖫 **Breakfast Club.** This fetching guest house is within walking distance of downtown Christiansted. Rooms of various sizes and decors are clean, and each has a full kitchen and bath. Guests like to gather at the cluttered bar, and owner Toby Chapin includes gourmet breakfasts (they feature banana pancakes) in the room rates. ⊠ *18 Queen Cross St., 00820,* ☎ *340/773–7383,* 𝙵𝙰𝙓 *340/773–8642. 9 rooms. Air-conditioning, hot tub. AE, V. CP.*

$ 🖫 **Hilty House.** For an alternative to beach and in-town lodgings, try this tranquil hilltop bed-and-breakfast. Built on the ruins of an 18th-century rum factory, it has the feel of a Florentine villa. You can escape to a patio and while away an afternoon in sun or shade, or mingle with others in the immense great room, where a prix-fixe dinner is served on Monday to guests and locals (reservations essential). Unless you want to spend your entire vacation reading or sunning at the large tiled pool, however, you'll need a rental car to venture forth from here. ⊠ *Queste Verde Rd. (Box 26077) Gallows Bay 00824,* ☎ 𝙵𝙰𝙓 *340/773–2594. 4 rooms, 3 cottages. Dining room, pool. No credit cards. CP.*

EAST END

$$$$ 🖫 **The Buccaneer.** On the grounds of an old 300-acre sugar plantation, this complex has it all: sandy beaches, swimming pools, golf, and a vast array of activities. A palm tree–lined main drive leads to the large, pink, main hotel building atop a hill; shops, restaurants, and other guest quarters are scattered about rolling, manicured lawns. The ambience and decor are Mediterranean, with tile floors, four-poster beds, massive wardrobes of pale wood, pastel fabrics, spacious marble bathrooms, and local works of art. All rooms have such modern conveniences as hair dryers, refrigerators, and cable TV. ⊠ *Rte. 82 (Box 25207) Gallows Bay 00824,* ☎ *340/773–2100 or 800/225–3881,* 𝖥𝖠𝖷 *340/778–8215. 150 rooms. 4 restaurants, air-conditioning, in-room safes, refrigerators, 2 pools, spa, 8 tennis courts, jogging, beach, shops. AE, D, DC, MC, V. CP.*

$$$$ ⊞ **Villa Madeleine.** A West Indian plantation great house is the cen-
★ terpiece of this exquisite hotel. Richly upholstered furniture, Asian rugs, teal walls, and whimsically painted driftwood set the mood in the billiards room, the library, and the sitting room. The great house sits on a hill, and there are villas on both sides of it. Each has a full kitchen and a private pool. The decor is modern tropical: rattan furniture with plush cushions, rocking chairs, and in many villas, bamboo four-poster beds. Special touches include pink-marble showers and hand-painted floral wall borders. Enjoy fine dining on the terrace at the ☞ **Great House at Villa Madeleine** or steak at the Turf Club. ⊠ *Off Rte. 82 at Teague Bay (Box 26160) Gallow's Bay 00824,* ☎ *340/778–8782 or 800/496–7379,* 𝖥𝖠𝖷 *340/773–2150. 43 villas. 2 restaurants, bar, air-conditioning, tennis court, library, concierge. AE, D, MC, V. EP.*

$$$–$$$$ ⊞ **Chenay Bay Beach Resort.** The beachfront location and complimentary tennis and water-sports equipment (including kayaks) make this resort a real find. Rooms are basic with ceramic-tile floors, bright-peach or yellow walls, rattan furnishings, kitchenettes, and front porches. Gravel paths connect the terraced gray-and-white wood cottages with the shore, where you'll find a large L-shape pool, a protected beach, a picnic area, and a casual restaurant. The all-you-can-eat pasta night is a bargain. In summer the hotel offers a free morning camp for children 3–12. In spring and fall, parents get two free hours of baby-sitting per day. ⊠ *Rte. 82 (Box 24600), Christiansted 00824,* ☎ *340/773–2918 or 800/548–4457,* 𝖥𝖠𝖷 *340/773–6665. 50 rooms. Restaurant, bar, picnic area, air-conditioning, kitchenettes, pool, 2 tennis courts, baby-sitting. AE, MC, V. EP.*

$$$ ⊞ **Tamarind Reef Hotel.** At this casual, motel-like, seaside place, you can sunbathe at the large pool and sandy beach or snorkel in the reef, which comes right to the shore (serious swimming here is difficult). The spacious, modern rooms have rattan furniture, tropical-print drapes and bedspreads, and either a terrace or a deck with views of the water and St. Croix's sister islands to the north. Many rooms have basic kitchenettes—handy for preparing light meals—and three rooms have facilities for guests with disabilities. There's a snack bar just off the beach and a restaurant at the adjacent Green Cay Marina. ⊠ *Off Rte. 82, 5001 Tamarind Reef 00820,* ☎ *340/773–4455,* 𝖥𝖠𝖷 *340/773–3989 or 800/619–0014. 46 rooms. Snack bar, air-conditioning, kitchenettes, pool. AE, MC, V. EP.*

FREDERIKSTED

$–$$ ⊞ **The Frederiksted.** Don't be put off by the unprepossessing exterior. This modern four-story inn is your best bet for lodging in Frederiksted. In the inviting, tile courtyard, the glass tables and yellow chairs of the bar and restaurant crowd around a small freshwater swimming pool. Yellow-striped awnings and tropical greenery add still more cheer to the atmosphere. Guest rooms have light-color rattan furniture, print bedspreads, mini-refrigerators, and microwaves. Bathrooms are on the small side but are bright and clean. The nicest quarters have an ocean view and a bathroom with a tub instead of just a shower. ⊠ *442 Strand St., 00840,* ☎ *340/772–0500 or 800/595–9519,* 𝖥𝖠𝖷 *340/772–0500, ext. 147. 40 rooms. Restaurant, bar, air-conditioning, pool. AE, D, DC, MC, V. EP.*

$$$$ ⚓ **Cormorant Beach Club and Villas.** At these connected, Moorish-style villas, the open-air public spaces are filled with tropical plants and comfy wicker furniture in cool peach and mint green. Ceiling fans and tile floors keep things cool. Beachfront rooms have dark-wicker furniture, pale-peach walls, white-tile floors, and floral-print spreads and curtains; all rooms have a patio or balcony and a phone, cable TV, and electronic safes. The hotel offers partial and all-inclusive meal plans that include all drinks. ⊠ *Off Rte. 752 4126 La Grande Princesse, Christiansted 00820,* ☎ *340/778–8920 or 800/548–4460,* FAX *340/778– 9218. 34 rooms, 4 suites, 14 2- and 3-bedroom villas. Restaurant, bar, air-conditioning, in-room safes, pool, 2 tennis courts, beach, snorkeling. AE, D, DC, MC, V. EP.*

$$$$ ⚓ **Westin Carambola Beach Resort.** The 26 quaint, two-story red-
★ roof villas, including one that's wheelchair-accessible, are connected by lovely, lush arcades. The rooms are identical except for the view— ocean or garden. The decor is English country with a touch of Caribbean: terra-cotta floors, ceramic lamps, mahogany ceilings and furnishings, and rocking chairs and sofas upholstered in soothing floral fabrics. Each room has a patio and a huge bath (shower only). The two-bedroom suite, with its 3-ft-thick plantation walls and large patio, is the perfect Caribbean family dwelling—it has its own exquisite ecru beach and lots of secluded nooks. ⊠ *Rte. 80 (Box 3031), Kingshill 00851,* ☎ *340/ 937–8461 or 800/228–3000 (reservations service),* FAX *340/778–1682. 150 rooms, 1 2-bedroom cottage. 2 restaurants, deli, air-conditioning, pool, 4 tennis courts, library. AE, D, DC, MC, V. EP.*

$$$ ⚓ **Hibiscus Beach Hotel.** Guest rooms here are in five, two-story, pink buildings—each named for a tropical flower. Most rooms have views of the oceanfront, but those in the Hibiscus building are closest to the water. All rooms have such welcome amenities as a roomy balcony, cable TV, a safe, and a minibar, and all are tastefully decorated with white-tile floors, white walls, pink-stripe curtains, floral spreads, and fresh-cut hibiscus blossoms. Bathrooms are clean but nondescript— both the shower stalls and the vanity mirrors are on the small side. ⊠ *Off Rte. 752, 4131 Estate La Grande Princesse, Christiansted 00820- 4441),* ☎ *340/773–4042 or 800/442–0121,* FAX *340/773–7668. 37 rooms. Restaurant, air-conditioning, in-room safes, minibars, pool, snorkeling. AE, D, MC, V. EP.*

$–$$$ ⚓ **Waves at Cane Bay.** Lapping waves lull you to sleep at this isolated inn. Although the beach here is rocky, Cane Bay Beach is next door, and the world-famous Cane Bay Reef is just 100 yards offshore (divers take note). You can also sunbathe on a small patch of sand beside the very unusual pool: It's carved from the coral along the shore, and waves crash dramatically over its side, creating a foamy whirlpool on blustery days. Two peach and mint-green buildings house enormous, balconied guest rooms (all have kitchens or kitchenettes, but not all have air-conditioning) that are done in cream and soft pastel prints. ⊠ *Rte. 80 (Box 1749) Kingshill 00851,* ☎ *340/778–1805 or 800/545–0603,* FAX *340/778–4945. 12 rooms, 1 suite. Restaurant, bar, in-room safes, kitchenettes, pool, snorkeling. AE, MC, V. EP.*

WEST END

$–$$$$ ⚓ **Sprat Hall.** This 20-acre seaside property appeals to guests who enjoy the vagaries of a visit to someone's home. Joyce Hurd presides over the slightly ramshackle antiques-filled plantation where she was born. Some of the guest rooms in the cluttered great house have four-poster beds and planter's chairs. More-modern rooms and cottages are spread out all over the estate. A glorious strand of beach sits a good hike down a gentle hill. Joyce prepares dinner for guests and nonguests, but you have to make your menu selection when she delivers your complimentary Continental breakfast. To explore the island from here, you need to rent a car. Those who prefer the reins to the wheel can take advantage of the Hurd family's horseback riding facilities. ⊠ *Rte. 63 (Box 695), Frederiksted 00841,* ☎ *340/772–0305 or 800/843–3584. 9 rooms, 8 suites, 1 1-bedroom cottage, 2 2-bedroom cottages. Restaurant, horseback riding, beach. No credit cards. CP.*

Cottages and Condominiums

$$$–$$$$ 🏨 **Colony Cove.** Next door to Sugar Beach, this condo-style resort has sunny, tropical apartments done up with pastel prints, white tile, and rattan furnishings. Each unit has two bedrooms, two baths, a balcony, a washer and dryer, and a kitchen so complete that it even has lasagna pans. You'll find a large pool, a water-sports center, and tennis courts on the grounds, and you can walk along the beach to the restaurant next door. ⊠ *Rte. 752, 3221 Golden Rock, Christiansted 00820,* ☎ *340/773–1965 or 800/828–0746,* FAX *340/773–5397. 60 apartments. Snack bar, air-conditioning, pool, 2 tennis courts. AE, MC, V. EP.*

$$–$$$$ 🏨 **Club St. Croix.** Popular with honeymooners, this complex's studio, one-, and two-bedroom apartments are spacious and bright. Indian-print throw rugs and cushions complement the bamboo furniture and rough, white-tile floors; glass-top tables and mirrored closet doors are lovely modern touches. Penthouses have loft bedrooms atop spiral staircases; studios have Murphy beds in their sitting rooms. All units have full kitchens and sundecks with waterfront views of Christiansted and Buck Island. On the beach you'll find a poolside restaurant, a bar, and a dock. ⊠ *Rte. 752, 3230 Estate Golden Rock, Christiansted 00820,* ☎ *340/773–4800 or 800/524–2025,* FAX *340/778–4009. 54 suites. Restaurant, bar, air-conditioning, pool, 3 tennis courts, beach, dock. AE, D, MC, V. EP.*

$–$$$$ 🏨 **Schooner Bay.** This red-roof condo village climbs a hill above Gallows Bay and just outside Christiansted. Each modern two- or three-bedroom apartment has a balcony, ceiling fans, air-conditioning, a washer and dryer, and a full kitchen with a dishwasher and a microwave. Rattan furnishings are set on beige-tile floors; floral-print fabrics add splashes of color. Three-bedroom units have spiral staircases. Sun worshipers might be disappointed that the nearest beach is east, at the Buccaneer, but those with a yen to explore historic Christiansted will find the location ideal—within walking distance of downtown, yet away from its bustle. ⊠ *5002 Gallows Bay, Christiansted 00820,* ☎ *340/773–9150 or 800/524–2025,* FAX *340/778–4009. 40 apartments. Air-conditioning, fans, 2 pools, tennis court. AE, D, MC, V. EP.*

$–$$$ 🏨 **Sugar Beach.** A stay here puts you on the beach at the north side of the island and just five minutes outside Christiansted. The apartments, which range from studios to units with four bedrooms, are immaculate and breezy. Each has a full kitchen and a large patio or balcony with an ocean view; larger units have washers and dryers. Though the exteriors of these condos are ordinary beige stucco, the interiors are lovely (white with tropical furnishings). The pool is amid the ruins of a 250-year-old sugar mill. ⊠ *Rte. 752, 3245 Estate Golden Rock, Christiansted 00820,* ☎ *340/773–5345 or 800/524–2049,* FAX *340/773–1359. 46 apartments. Air-conditioning, pool, 2 tennis courts, beach, meeting room. AE, D, MC, V. EP.*

Private Homes and Villas

Renting a private house gives you the convenience of home as well as top-notch amenities. Many houses have private pools, hot tubs, and deluxe furnishings. Most companies meet you at the airport, arrange for a rental car, and provide useful information to make your vacation more interesting. Call **The Collection** (☎ 609/751–2413), **Island Villas** (☎ 340/773–8821), **Petan Corp./Rent A Villa** (☎ 800/533–6863), **Richards & Ayer** (☎ 340/772–0420), or **Teague Bay Properties** (☎ 340/773–4850).

Dining

Seven flags have flown over St. Croix, and each has left its legacy in the island's cuisine. You can feast on Italian, French, Danish, and American dishes; there are even Chinese and Mexican restaurants in Christiansted. Fresh local seafood is plentiful and always good; wahoo, mahimahi, and conch are popular. Island chefs often add Caribbean twists to familiar dishes. For a true island experience, stop at a local restaurant for goat stew, curry chicken, or fried pork chops. Regardless of where you eat, your meal will be an informal affair. But be forewarned, prices are a lot higher than you'd pay on the mainland.☞ For price categories, *see* the chart *under* Dining *in* St. Thomas, *above.*

Christiansted

CARIBBEAN/CREOLE

$$$–$$$$ ✕ **Indies.** Tables (covered with handmade floral-print cloths) in a his-
★ toric courtyard with green columns is the setting for a wonderful dining experience. Owner-chef Catherine Plav-Drigger prepares island-inspired dishes, and the menu changes each day to take advantage of the island's freshest bounties. Indulge in the crab cakes or the spicy Caribbean spring rolls to start, then the spice-rubbed chicken (every bite reveals a new, subtle flavor) or dolphinfish baked in coconut milk, ginger, tomato, and spicy peppers. Enjoy live jazz Saturday evening. ⊠ *55–56 Company St.,* ☎ *340/692–9440. AE, D, MC, V. No lunch weekends.*

$–$$$ ✕ **Harvey's.** The plain, even dowdy, dining room has just 12 tables, and plastic, flowered tablecloths constitute the sole attempt at decor. But who cares? The food is some of the island's most delicious. Daily specials, such as mouthwatering goat stew and tender whelks in butter, served with heaping helpings of rice, fungi, and vegetables, are listed on the blackboard. Genial owner Sarah Harvey takes great pride in her kitchen, bustling out from behind the stove to chat and urge you to eat up. ⊠ *11B Company St.,* ☎ *340/773–3433. No credit cards. Closed Sun. No dinner Mon.–Wed.*

CONTEMPORARY

$$$–$$$$ ✕ **Kendricks.** The chef at this open-air restaurant—a longtime favorite
★ with locals—conjures up creative, tasty cuisine. Try the lobster spring rolls with warm ginger and soy butter to start, or the warm *chipotle* pepper with garlic and onion soup. Move on to the house specialty: pecan-crusted roast pork loin with ginger mayonnaise. ⊠ *52 Company St.,* ☎ *340/773–9199. AE, MC, V.*

CONTINENTAL

$$$–$$$$ ✕ **Top Hat.** Owned by a delightful Danish couple, this restaurant has
★ been serving international cuisine (with Danish specialties, of course) since 1970. Dishes include roast duck stuffed with apples and prunes, *frikadeller* (savory meatballs in a tangy cocktail sauce), fried Camembert with lingonberries, and smoked eel. The salad bar has such fine Danish offerings as herring in sour cream and duck liver pâté. The signature dessert is a rum-ice-cream-filled chocolate windmill with blades

that turn. ✉ *52 Company St.,* ☎ *340/773–2346. AE, D, MC, V. Closed May–Aug. No lunch.*

\$\$–\$\$\$\$ ✕ **Tivoli Gardens.** Fresh breezes and bowers of hanging plants virtu-
★ ally transform this restaurant in the heart of Christiansted into a garden. The Continental menu features steak, lobster, and more lobster.
To make it easy to eat, the chef takes all the succulent meat from a whole
lobster, puts it into half the lobster's shell, and drips butter over the
top. For dessert, try the bittersweet chocolate velvet—a chocoholic's
dream that's closer to candy than cake. ✉ *39 Strand St.,* ☎ *340/773–
6782. AE, MC, V. No lunch weekends.*

\$\$–\$\$\$ ✕ **Antoine's.** Watch the seaplanes to St. Thomas take off and land while
you dine in this open-air restaurant above the Anchor Inn. Chef An-
toine Doos, a Swiss native, whips up international, Austrian, and German dishes. If you like sauerbraten, knockwurst, or bratwurst, this is
the place. Seafood lovers will enjoy the selection: snapper, tuna, dolphinfish, and shrimp. ✉ *58 King St.,* ☎ *340/773–0263. AE, MC, V.*

ECLECTIC

\$\$–\$\$\$ ✕ **Bombay Club.** This dimly lit spot—made cheerier with bright local
artwork—is in a historic pub. The bar, with its cool, exposed stone walls,
is a favorite expat hangout. The typical pub grub includes fine salads,
nachos, scrumptious buffalo wings, pastas, and simple chicken and steak
dishes. Don't pass up the heavenly stuffed crabs with roast garlic herb
sauce. ✉ *5A King St.,* ☎ *340/773–1838. MC, V. No lunch weekends.*

\$–\$\$\$ ✕ **Paradise Cafe.** The exposed brick walls of this tiny, lively spot are
splashed with colorful island prints. Stop in for lunch or a light supper: sandwiches and burgers are the big draw, though the daily seafood
special, often wahoo or mahimahi, is also popular. ✉ *Company and
Queen Cross Sts.,* ☎ *340/773–2985. No credit cards.*

\$ ✕ **Java Mon.** Java Mon has a 1950s decor that mimics the Norman
★ Rockwell magazine covers on its walls. As soon as owner Todd Phillips
opened this hole-in-the-wall on the Christiansted waterfront in July 1996,
it attracted a varied following of folks looking for takeout or eat-in
dreadlox and bagels, roast-pork Cubano sandwiches, black-cherry
cheesecake, and cups of espresso and cappuccino. Sun-dried-tomato
cream cheese is an interesting addition to a pedestrian bagel. ✉ *59 Kings
Wharf,* ☎ *340/773–2285. No credit cards. No dinner.*

ITALIAN

\$\$–\$\$\$\$ ✕ **Tutto Bene.** Its yellow walls, brightly striped cushions, and painted
trompe l'oeil tables make Tutto Bene look more like a sophisticated Mexican cantina than an Italian cucina. One bite of the food, however, will
clear up any confusion. Written on hanging mirrors is the daily menu,
which includes such fare as veal chop with sun-dried tomatoes and *zuppa
di mare* (clams, shrimp, and mussels poached in white wine and served
over cappellini). Desserts are prepared by one of the island's finest pastry chefs. ✉ *2 Company St.,* ☎ *340/773–5229. AE, D, MC, V.*

East End

CONTEMPORARY

\$\$\$–\$\$\$\$ ✕ **Great House at Villa Madeleine.** The elegant restaurant at the ☞
Villa Madeleine resort serves such diverse cuisine as penne pasta
sautéed with grilled chicken breast and served with roasted pepper *coulis*
(a puree of peppers and spices) or swordfish medallions sautéed with
green tomato and asparagus; there are also a number of fine beef
dishes. The wine list is extensive. ✉ *19A Teague Bay, take Rte. 82 out
of Christiansted, turn right at Reef Condominiums,* ☎ *340/778–7377.
AE, D, DC, MC, V.*

ECLECTIC

$$$–$$$$ ✕ **The Galleon.** Popular with both locals and visitors, this dockside restaurant has something for everyone. Start with the Caesar salad or gravlax (fresh salmon with dill and pepper). Pasta lovers should sample the eggplant ravioli (the homemade pasta is filled not only with grilled eggplant but also with Parmesan, ricotta, and mozzarella cheeses). The osso buco and rack of lamb are legendary. ✉ *Teague Bay, take Rte. 82 out of Christiansted, turn left at sign for Green Cay Marina,* ☎ *340/773–9949. AE, V. No lunch.*

$$–$$$ ✕ **South Shore Cafe.** This casual bistro sits near the Great Salt Pond on the island's south shore. Popular with locals for its good food and cozy ambience, the restaurant features dishes drawn from a variety of cuisines. Meat lovers and vegetarians can find common ground with a menu that features prime rib and eggplant lasagna. The selection isn't extensive, but the chef puts together a blackboard full of specials every day. ✉ *Junction of Rtes. 62 and 624,* ☎ *340/773–9311. V. Closed Mon.–Wed. No lunch.*

Frederiksted

CARIBBEAN/CREOLE

$–$$$ ✕ **Villa Morales.** Locals come to this family-run spot for the food and the dancing (in the cavernous back room). The kitchen turns out such well-prepared Cruzan and Spanish dishes as goat stew and baked chicken, all served with heaping helpings of fungi, rice, and vegetables. ✉ *Plot 82C, off Rte. 70, Estate Whim,* ☎ *340/772–0556. Reservations essential. AE, MC, V. Closed Sun.–Mon. No dinner Tues. or Wed.*

CONTEMPORARY

$$$–$$$$ ✕ **Café du Soleil.** This upstairs terrace eatery bills itself as "the perfect place to watch the sun set," and it's no exaggeration. Even the mauve walls and maroon and salmon napery cleverly duplicate the sun's pyrotechnics. The food understandably takes a back seat to the main event, but you won't go wrong with the stuffed Portobello mushrooms. For dinner, try the fresh fish and accompanying sauce, which vary with the catch of the day. ✉ *625 Strand St.,* ☎ *340/772–5400. AE, D, MC, V. Closed Mon.–Tues. No lunch.*

ECLECTIC

$$$–$$$$ ✕ **Le St. Tropez.** A ceramic-tile bar and soft lighting add to the Mediterranean atmosphere at this pleasant bistro, tucked into a courtyard off Frederiksted's main thoroughfare. Seated either inside or on the adjoining patio, you can enjoy French fare such as grilled meats in delicate sauces. The menu changes daily, often taking advantage of fresh local seafood. The fresh basil, tomato, and mozzarella salad is heavenly. ✉ *67 King St.,* ☎ *340/772–3000. AE, MC, V. Closed Sun.*

$$$ ✕ **Blue Moon.** This terrific little bistro, popular for its live jazz on Friday night, has an often-changing menu that draws heavily on Asian, Cajun, and local flavors. Try the seafood chowder or *luna* pie (veggies and cheese baked in phyllo dough) as an appetizer; the roasted vegetables and shrimp over linguine as an entrée; and the rum bread pudding for dessert. ✉ *17 Strand St.,* ☎ *340/772–2222. AE. Closed Mon. and Aug.–Sept.*

Beaches

Buck Island. A visit to this island, part of the U.S. National Park system, is a must on any trip to St. Croix. The beach is beautiful, but its finest treasures are those you can see when you plop off the boat and adjust your mask, snorkel, and flippers. To get here, you'll have to charter a boat (☞ Sailing *in* Outdoor Activities and Sports, *below*).

Cane Bay. The waters are not always gentle at this breezy north shore beach, but there are never many people around and the scuba diving and snorkeling are wondrous. You'll see elkhorn and brain corals, and less than 200 yards out is the drop-off or so-called Cane Bay Wall.

Isaac Bay. This East End beach is almost impossible to reach without a four-wheel-drive vehicle, but it's worth the effort. You'll find secluded sands for sunbathing, calm waters for swimming, and a barrier reef for snorkeling. You can also get here via footpaths from Jacks Bay.

Tamarind Reef Beach. Small but attractive Tamarind Reef Beach is east of Christiansted. Both Green Cay and Buck Island seem smack in front of you—an arresting view. The snorkeling is good.

West End Beaches. There are several unnamed beaches along the coast road north of Frederiksted. Just pull over at whatever piece of powdery sand catches your fancy. The beach at the Rainbow Beach Club has a bar, casual restaurant, water sports, and volleyball.

Outdoor Activities and Sports

CYCLING

Pedal through paradise. A bike tour to some of the island's top sites adds a new dimension to your vacation and helps you stay in shape. **St. Croix Bike and Tours** (⊠ Pier 69 Courtyard, Frederiksted, ☎ 340/772–2343 or 340/772–5004) offers two tours (both cost $40). One heads through historic Frederiksted before cycling on a fairly flat road to Hamm's Bluff. The second, for more hearty folks, takes you up and through the rain forest.

FISHING

In the past quarter-century, some 20 world records—many for blue marlin—have been set in these waters. Sailfish, skipjack, bonito, tuna (allison, blackfin, and yellowfin), and wahoo are abundant.

Ruffian Enterprises (⊠ St. Croix Marina, Gallows Bay, ☎ 340/773–6011) will take you out on a 42-ft powerboat, *Shenanigans*. Half- or full-day charters are also available on **Cruzan Diver's** *Afternoon Delight* (⊠ 330 Strand St., Frederiksted, ☎ 340/772–3701).

GOLF

St. Croix's courses welcome you with spectacular vistas and well-kept greens. Check with your hotel or the tourist board to determine when major celebrity tournaments will be held. There's often an opportunity to play with the pros. **The Buccaneer**'s (⊠ Off Rte. 82 at Teague Bay, ☎ 340/773–2100) 18-hole course is conveniently close to (east of) Christiansted. **The Reef Golf Course** (☎ 340/773–8844), in the northeastern part of the island, has 9 holes. The spectacular course at **Westin Carambola Beach Resort** (⊠ Rte. 80, ☎ 340/778–5638), in the northwest valley, was designed by Robert Trent Jones.

HIKING

Although you can set off by yourself on a hike through a rain forest or along a shore, a guide will point out what's important and tell you why. The nonprofit **St. Croix Environmental Association** (⊠ Arawak Bldg., Suite 3, Gallows Bay, 00820, ☎ 340/773–1989) offers hikes through several of the island's ecological treasures, including Estate Mt. Washington, Butler Bay, Estate Caledonia in the rain forests, and Salt River.

HORSEBACK RIDING

A horseback ride is a wonderful way to enjoy the island's spectacular scenery. Well-kept roads and expert guides make it a pleasurable experience, indeed. At Sprat Hall, near Frederiksted, Jill Hurd runs **Paul and Jill's Equestrian Stables** (⊠ Rte. 58, ☎ 340/772–2880 or 340/772–2627) and will take you clip-clopping through the rain forest (explaining the flora, fauna, and ruins along the way), along the coast, or on moonlit rides. Costs range from $50 to $75 for three-hour rides.

SAILING

Day sail to Buck Island aboard one of the island's charter boats. Most leave from the Christiansted waterfront or from Green Cay Marina. They stop for a snorkel at the eastern end of the island before dropping anchor off a gorgeous sandy beach for a swim, a hike, and lunch.

Big Beard's Adventure Tours (☎ 340/773–4482) takes you on a catamaran, *Renegade,* from the Christiansted Waterfront to Buck Island for snorkeling before dropping anchor at a private beach for a barbecue lunch. **Buck Island Charters**'s (☎ 340/773–3161) trimaran *Teroro II* leaves Green Cay Marina for full- or half-day sails. Bring your own lunch. **Mile Mark Charters** (☎ 340/773–2628 or 800/523–3483) departs from the Christiansted waterfront for half- and full-day sails on a variety of boats.

SCUBA DIVING AND SNORKELING

St. Croix's north shore wall is famous for its gorgeous drop-off. The island's dive shops take you out for one or two-tank dives. **Anchor Dive Center** (✉ Salt River Marina, Rte. 801, ☎ 340/778–1522 or 800/532–3483) explores the wall at Salt River Canyon from its base at Salt River Marina. It provides PADI certification up to dive master level. **Dive Experience** (☎ 340/773–3307), on Strand Street in Christiansted, is a five-star PADI training facility providing a range of activities from introductory dives to certification. It takes divers to the north shore walls and reefs. **Dive St. Croix** (☎ 340/773–3434 or 800/523–3483) takes divers to 35 different sites from its base on the Christiansted Wharf. It's the only operation that runs dives to Buck Island. **V.I. Divers Ltd.** (☎ 340/773–6045 or 800/544–5911) is near the water in the Pan Am Pavilion. It's a PADI five-star training facility and takes divers to their choice of 28 sites.

TENNIS

The public courts in Frederiksted and out east at Cramer Park are in questionable shape. It's better to pay a fee and play at one of the island's many hotel courts. There's a pro, a full tennis pro shop, and eight courts (two lighted) at the **Buccaneer Hotel** (✉ Rte. 82, ☎ 340/773–2100); two courts (no lights) at the **Chenay Bay Beach Resort** (✉ Rte. 82, ☎ 340/773–2918); three lighted courts at **Club St. Croix** (✉ Rte. 752, ☎ 340/773–4800); and four courts (two lighted) at the **Westin Carambola Beach Resort** (✉ Rte. 80, ☎ 340/778–3800).

WINDSURFING

St. Croix's trade winds make windsurfing a breeze. Most hotels rent Windsurfers and other water-sports equipment to nonguests.

Tradewindsurfing Inc. (✉ Hotel on the Cay, ☎ 340/773–7060) offers Windsurfer rentals, sales, and rides; parasailing; and a wide range of water-sports equipment, such as Jet Skis and kayaks.

Shopping

Areas and Malls

Although St. Croix doesn't offer as many shopping opportunities as St. Thomas, the island does have an array of small stores with unique merchandise. In Christiansted, the best shopping areas are the **Pan Am Pavilion** and **Caravelle Arcade** off Strand Street, **Kings Alley Walk,** and along **King** and **Company streets.** These streets give way to arcades filled with boutiques. **Gallow's Bay** has a blossoming shopping area in a quiet neighborhood. Stores are often closed on Sunday.

The best shopping in Frederiksted is along **Strand Street** and in the side streets and alleyways that connect it with **King Street.** Most stores close Sunday except when a cruise ship is in port.

Specialty Items

ART

The Gallery at the Pentheny. Even if you don't want to send home any of the pricey art works sold at this interesting cooperative gallery, it's worth a browse. Housed in the lobby of an old hotel, the thick, white-washed stone walls are the perfect backdrops for works by a changing group of St. Croix artists. Look for Sylvia Maratoba's pieces; she creates exquisite baskets and wire sculptures out of discards she finds around the island. ⊠ *1138 King St., Christiansted,* ☎ FAX *340/773–2781.*

BOOKS

The Bookie. This shop carries paperback novels as well as stationery, newspapers, and greeting cards. Stop in for the latest gossip and to find out about upcoming events. ⊠ *1111 Strand St., Christiansted,* ☎ *340/ 773–2592.*

Trader Bob's Dockside Book Store. If you're looking for Caribbean books or the latest good read, try this bookstore across from the post office in the Gallows Bay shopping area. ⊠ *5030 Anchor Way,* ☎ *340/ 773–6001.*

CHINA AND CRYSTAL

Little Switzerland. The St. Croix branch of this VI institution sells a variety of Rosenthal flatware, Lladro figurines, Waterford and Baccarat crystal, Lalique figurines, and Wedgwood and Royal Doulton china.⊠ *Hamilton House, 1108 King St., Christiansted,* ☎ *340/773–1976*

CLOTHES

Caribbean Clothing Company. This fashionable store features contemporary sportswear for men and women by top American designers. ⊠ *41 Queen Cross St., Christiansted,* ☎ *340/773–5012.*

From the Gecko. Come here for the hippest clothes on St. Croix, from superb batik sarongs to hand-painted silk scarves. ⊠ *1233 Queen Cross St., Christiansted,* ☎ *340/778–9433.*

Skirt Tails. Look for hand-painted batik and washable silk clothing in a rainbow of colors, perfect for vacations in the tropics. The store carries swimwear, sarongs, pant and short sets, and flowing dresses. ⊠ *Pan Am Pavilion, Christiansted,* ☎ *340/773–1991.*

Urban Threadz. Urban island wear by No Fear and many other lines for men and women are available here. Check the **Urban Kidz** store three doors down for Guess, Calvin Klein, Boss, Nautica, and Fila children's clothes. ⊠ *52C Company St., Christiansted,* ☎ *340/773–2883.*

The White House. This contemporary store sells clothes in all-white and natural colors. Look for exquisite lingerie, elegant evening wear, and unusual casual outfits. ⊠ *8B Kings Alley Walk, Christiansted,* ☎ *340/ 773–9222.*

FOODSTUFFS

If you've rented a condominium or a villa, St. Croix offers excellent shopping at its stateside-style supermarkets. Fresh vegetables, fruits, and meats arrive frequently. Try the open-air stands strung out along Route 70 for island produce. For supermarkets, try **Pueblo** (⊠ Orange Grove Shopping Center, Rte. 75, ☎ 340/773–9368); ⊠ Sunny Isle Shopping Center, Rte. 70, ☎ 340/778–5005; ⊠ Villa La Reine Shopping Center, Rte. 75, ☎ 340/778–1272). **Plaza Extra 9** (⊠ Rte. 70, ☎ 340/ 778–6240), at the United Shopping Plaza, and **Sunshine Supermarket** (⊠ Rte. 70, ☎ 340/692–2720), at the Sunshine Mall, are also good choices. **Cost-U-Less** (✉ Rte. 70, ☎ 340/692–2220) is a warehouse-style store (no membership fee) across from the Sunshine Mall.

Island Webe. The coffees, jams, and spices—produced locally or elsewhere in the Caribbean—here will tempt your taste buds. Small *mocko jumbie* dolls depict an African tradition transported to the islands during slave days (they represent the souls of the ancestors of African slaves). The fabric dolls wearing Caribbean costumes will delight kids of all ages. Turn the double dolls upside down to see a white face on one side and a black on on the other. Owner Diane Kershner also sells her own works (watercolors and acrylics in tropical pastels). ✉ *210 Strand St., Frederiksted,* ☎ *340/772–2555.*

The Royal Poinciana. You'll find island seasonings and hot sauces, West Indian crafts, bath gels, and herbal teas at this attractively designed shop. ✉ *1111 Strand St., Christiansted,* ☎ *340/773–9892.*

Trade Winds Shop. This shop seems to carry whatever has recently blown in from the four corners of the earth. Look for the exquisite model wooden sailboats (perfect for your coffee table); dishes the color of the sea and shaped like fish; attractive stationery with seashore motifs; and fashionable tropical clothing. ✉ *Kings Alley Walk, Christiansted,,* ☎ *340/713–9200,*

Folk Art Traders. Owners Patty and Charles Eitzen travel to Guyana as well as Haiti, Jamaica, and elsewhere in the Caribbean to find treasures for their shop. The baskets, ceramic masks, pottery, jewelry, and sculpture they find are unique examples of folk-art traditions. *(✉ 1B Queen Cross St., at Strand St., Christiansted,* ☎ *340/773–1900.*

Colombian Emeralds. Specializing—of course—in emeralds, this store also carries diamonds, rubies, sapphires, and gold. A branch store, **Jewelers' Warehouse** (✉ 1 Queen Cross St., Christiansted, ☎ 340/773–5590), is across the street. The chain, the Caribbean's largest jeweler, offers certified appraisal and international guarantees. ✉ *43 Queen Cross St., Christiansted,* ☎ *340/773–1928 or 340/773–9189.*

Crucian Gold. This store, in a small courtyard of a West Indian–style cottage, carries the unique gold creations of St. Croix native Brian Bishop. His trademark piece is the Turk's Head ring (a knot of interwoven gold strands). ✉ *59 King St., Christiansted,* ☎ *340/773–5241.*

Karavan West Indies. The owner here designs her own jewelry and also sells an assortment of tchotchkes, including handmade Christmas ornaments and magical beads, from amber to amethyst. ✉ *5030 Anchor Way, Gallows Bay,* ☎ *340/773–9999.*

Sonya's. Sonya Hough opened this store in 1964 to showcase her own jewelry creations; now she runs it with her daughter, Diana. Hough invented the hook bracelet, popular among locals. Hurricane Marilyn's visit to the island in 1995 inspired a "hurricane" bracelet. Its unique clasp features a gold strand shaped like the storm's swirling winds as they hit St. Croix, St. John, and St. Thomas. ✉ *1 Company St., Christiansted,* ☎ *340/778–8605.*

Kicks. This upscale shop carries a good, if small, selection of shoes and leather goods. ✉ *57 Company St., Christiansted,* ☎ *340/773–7801.*

Cruzan Rum Distillery. A tour of the company's rebuilt factory culminates in a tasting of its products, all sold here at bargain prices. ✉ *West Airport Rd.,* ☎ *340/692–2280.*

Harborside Market and Spirits. A good selection of liquor at duty-free prices is available at this conveniently located shop. ⊠ *59 Kings Wharf, Christiansted,* ☎ *340/773–8899.*

Kmart. This department store carries a huge line of discount, duty-free liquor. ⊠ *Sunshine Mall, Centerline Rd., Frederiksted,* ☎ *340/692–5848.*

PERFUMES

Violette Boutique. Perfume, skin-care, and makeup products are the draws here. ⊠ *Caravelle Arcade, 38 Strand St., Christiansted,* ☎ *340/773–2148.*

Nightlife and the Arts

The island's nightlife is ever-changing, and its arts scene is eclectic— ranging from Christmastime performances of the *Nutcracker* to whatever local group got organized enough to put on a show. Folk-art traditions, such as the island's quadrille dancers, are making a comeback. To find out what's happening, pick up the local newspapers— *V.I. Daily News* and *St. Croix Avis*–which are available at newsstands.

Nightlife

Christiansted has a lively and eminently casual club scene near the waterfront. On Thursday night, the **Cormorant** (⊠ 4126 La Grande Princesse, ☎ 340/778–8920) dishes up a West Indian buffet. Easy jazz flows from the courtyard bar at **Indies** (⊠ 55–56 Company St., ☎ 340/ 692–9440) Saturday evening. **Hotel on the Cay** (⊠ Protestant Cay, ☎ 340/773–2035) has a West Indian buffet on Tuesday night that features a broken-bottle dancer (a dancer who braves a carpet of broken bottles) and mocko jumbie characters. The **2 Plus 2 Disco** (⊠ 17 La Grande Princesse, ☎ 340/773–3710) spins a great mix of calypso, soul, disco, and reggae; there's live music on weekends. To party under the stars in a very, very informal setting, head to the **Wreck Bar** (☎ 340/ 773–6092), on Hospital Street, for crab races as well as rock and roll.

Although less hopping than Christiansted, Frederiksted has a couple of restaurants and clubs with a variety of weekend entertainment. **Blue Moon** (⊠ 17 Strand St., ☎ 340/772–2222), a waterfront restaurant, is the place to be for live jazz on Friday 9 PM–1 AM. **Pier 69** (⊠ 69 King St., ☎ 340/772–0069) has blues, jazz, and reggae every Friday and Saturday at 9:30 PM.

The Arts

The **Island Center for the Performing Arts** (⊠ Rte. 79, ☎ 340/778– 5272) hosts St. Croix's major concerts, plays, and performances by visiting entertainers.

Exploring St. Croix

Though there are things to see and do in St. Croix's two towns, Christiansted and Frederiksted (both named after Danish kings), there are lots of interesting spots in between them and to the east of Christiansted. Just be sure you have a map in hand (pick one up at rental-car agencies, or stop by tourist office for an excellent free one). Many secondary roads remain unmarked; if you get confused, ask for help.

Numbers in the margin correspond to points of interest on the St. Croix map.

Christiansted

Christiansted is a historic, Danish-style town that always served as St. Croix's commercial center. Trade here in the 1700s and 1800s was in sugar, rum, and molasses. Today the town is home to law offices, tourist shops, and restaurants, but many of the buildings, built from the harbor up into the gentle hillsides, date from the 18th century. You can't get lost. All streets lead gently downhill to the water.

Your best bet is to spend the morning, when it's still cool, exploring the historic sites. This two-hour endeavor won't tax your walking shoes and will leave you with energy to poke around the town's eclectic shops. Break for lunch at an open-air restaurant before spending as much time as you like shopping.

SIGHTS TO SEE

Ⓒ **Buck Island Reef National Monument.** This island off the northeast coast has pristine beaches that are just right for sunbathing, but there's enough shade for those who don't want to fry. The spectacular snorkeling trail set in the reef allows close-up study of coral formations and tropical fish. After your arrival by charter boat, crew members give special attention to novice snorkelers and children. There's an easy hiking trail to the island's highest point, where you'll be rewarded for your efforts by spectacular views of the reef below and St. John to the north. Charter boat trips leave daily from the Christiansted waterfront or from Green Cay Marina, about 2 mi east of Christiansted. Check with your hotel for recommendations. ⊠ *Northshore,* ☎ *340/773–1460 (national park headquarters).*

Danish Customs House. Built in 1830 on foundations that date from 1734, this building originally served as a customs house and a post office (second floor). In 1926 it became the Christiansted Library, and it has been the National Park Service headquarters since 1972. ⊠ *King St.* ☉ *Weekdays 8–5.*

D. Hamilton Jackson Park. When you're tired of sightseeing, stop here for a rest. It's named for a famed labor leader, judge, and journalist who started the first newspaper not under the thumb of the Danish crown. ⊠ *Between Ft. Christiansvaern and the Danish Customs House.*

Ft. Christiansvaern. This large yellow structure dominates the waterfront. In 1749 the Danish built the fort to protect the harbor, but the structure was repeatedly damaged by hurricane-force winds and was partially rebuilt in 1771. It's now a national historic site and the best preserved of the five remaining Danish-built forts in the VI. ⊠ *Hospital St.,* ☎ *340/773–1460.* ⊟ *$2 (includes admission to Steeple Building, ☞ below).* ☉ *Weekdays 8–5, weekends and holidays 9–5.*

Government House. One of the town's most elegant buildings, it was built as a home for a Danish merchant in 1747. Today it houses USVI government offices. If the building is open, slip into the peaceful inner courtyard to admire the still pools and gardens. A sweeping staircase leads you to a second-story ballroom, still the site of official government functions. ⊠ *King St.,* ☎ *340/773–1404. Closed for renovations at press time.*

The Market. Built in 1735 as a slave market, this wood-and-galvanized-aluminum structure is where today's farmers and others sell their goods every Wednesday and Saturday from 8 to 5. ⊠ *Company St.*

Post Office Building. Built in 1749, it once housed the Danish West India & Guinea Company warehouse. ⊠ *Church St.*

Ⓒ **St. Croix Aquarium.** The tanks contain an ever-changing variety of local sea creatures. Children are invited to explore the discovery room, with its microscopes, interactive displays, and educational videos. They'll especially enjoy the petting tank, where they can feel starfish relax to their touch. ⊠ *Caravelle Arcade,* ☎ *340/773–8995.* ⊡ *$4.50.* ☉ *Tues.–Sat. 11–4.*

Scale House. Closed for renovation at press time (winter 1998), it should open under National Park Service authority by 1999. The building, which was constructed in 1856, once was the spot where goods passing through the port were weighed and inspected. ⊠ *King St.*

Steeple Building. Built by the Danes in 1753, this was the first Danish Lutheran church on St. Croix. It's now a national parks museum and contains exhibits that document the island's Indian habitation. There are also archaeological artifacts; displays on plantation life; and exhibits on the architectural development of Christiansted, the early history of the church, and Alexander Hamilton, the first secretary of the U.S. Treasury, who grew up in St. Croix. ⊠ *Church St.,* ☎ *340/773–1460.* ⊡ *$2 (includes admission to Ft. Christiansvaern ☞ above.* ☉ *When staffing permits. Check at Ft. Christiansvaern.*

Visitor's Center. You'll find maps, brochures, and friendly advice here. ⊠ *41A and B Queen Cross St.,* ☎ *340/773–0495.* ☉ *Weekdays 8–5.*

Outside Christiansted and Points East

An easy drive (roads are flat and well marked) to the eastern end takes you through some choice real estate. Ruins of old sugar estates dot the landscape. You can make the entire loop in about an hour, a good way to end the day. If you want to spend an entire day exploring, you'll find some nice beaches and easy walks, with places to stop for lunch.

SIGHTS TO SEE

❷ **Cramer's Park.** This USVI territorial beach on the northeast coast is very popular with locals. It's a good spot for beach picnics and camping. Because of its isolation, though, it's not a good place to linger if you're traveling solo. ⊠ *Rte. 82.*

❶ **Point Udall.** This rocky promontory, the easternmost point in the United States, juts into the Caribbean Sea. The climb, via a rutted dirt road, may be slow, but you'll be rewarded with great views at the top. On the way down, look for The Castle, an enormous mansion that can only be described as a cross between a Moorish mosque and the Taj Mahal. It was built by an extravagant recluse known only as the Contessa. The point is in an isolated area, so be sure to make the walk to it in the company of others. ⊠ *Rte. 82.*

Between Christiansted and Frederiksted

A drive through St. Croix's countryside will take you past ruins of old plantations, many bearing whimsical names—Morningstar, Solitude, Upper Love—bestowed by early owners. The traffic moves quickly—by island standards—on the main roads, but you can pause and poke around if you head down some side lanes. It's easy to find your way west, but driving from north to south requires good navigation. Don't leave your hotel without a map. Allow an entire day for this trip so you'll have enough time for a swim at a north shore beach. Although you'll find lots of casual eateries on the main roads, pick up a picnic lunch if you plan to head off the beaten path.

SIGHTS TO SEE

❻ **Cane Bay.** This is one of St. Croix's best launches for scuba diving. Near the small stone jetty you may see a few wet-suited, tank-backed figures making their way out to the drop-off (a bit farther out there's a steeper drop-off of 12,000 ft). ⊠ *Rte. 80.*

❽ **Estate Mount Washington Plantation.** Several years ago, while surveying the property, the owners discovered the ruins of a sugar plantation beneath the rain-forest brush. The grounds have since been cleared and opened to the public. You can take a self-guided walking tour of the mill, the rum factory, and other ruins, and there's an antiques shop in what were once the stables. ✉ *Rte. 63 (watch for antiques shop sign),* ☎ *340/772–1026.* ⊙ *Ruins open daily; antiques shop, Sat. 10–4.*

❸ Judith's Fancy. In this upscale neighborhood you'll find the ruins of an old great house and tower of the same name, both remnants of a circa 1750 Danish sugar plantation. The "Judith" comes from the first name of a woman buried on the property. From the guard house at the neighborhood entrance, follow Hamilton Drive past some of St. Croix's loveliest homes. At the end of Hamilton Drive, the road overlooks Salt River Bay, where Christopher Columbus anchored in 1493. A skirmish between members of Columbus's crew and a group of Carib Indians resulted in the first bloody encounter between Europeans and West Indians. The peninsula on the east side of the bay is named for the event: Cabo de las Flechas (Cape of the Arrows). On the way back, make a detour left off Hamilton Drive onto Caribe Road, for a close look at the ruins. ✉ *Turn north onto Rte. 751 off Rte. 75.*

❼ Mt. Eagle. This is St. Croix's highest peak (1,165 ft). Leaving Cane Bay and passing North Star Beach, follow the beautiful coastal road that dips briefly into a forest, then turn left on Rte. 69. Just after you make the turn, the pavement is marked with the words THE BEAST and a set of giant paw prints. The hill you're about to climb is the location of the famous Beast of the America's Paradise Triathlon, an annual event in which participants must bike this intimidating slope. ✉ *Rte. 69.*

❾ St. Croix Leap. In the heart of the rain forest, sits this workshop where you can buy a wide range of articles, including mirrors, tables, bread boards, and mahogany jewelry boxes crafted by local artisans. ✉ *Rte. 76,* ☎ *340/772–0421.*

❺ Salt River Bay National Historical Park and Ecological Preserve. This joint national and local park was dedicated in November 1993. In addition to sites with cultural significance, it encompasses a bio-diverse coastal estuary with the largest remaining mangrove forest in the USVI, a submarine canyon, and several endangered species, including the hawksbill turtle and roseate tern. Plans are afoot to create a museum, interpretive walking trails, and a replica of a Carib village. A ceremonial ball court was discovered at the spot where the taxis park. Take a short hike up the dirt road to the ruins of an old earthen fort and great views of Salt River Bay and the surrounding countryside. ✉ *Rte. 75 to Rte. 80.*

❹ Salt River Marina. This lush lagoon is home to the Anchor Dive Shop, a shipbuilding company, and a casual eatery catering to yachties. The road that veers to the left behind the marina leads to the beach where Columbus landed. ✉ *Tradewinds Rd. at Rte. 80,* ☎ *340/778–9650.*

Frederiksted and Environs

Frederiksted, St. Croix's second largest town, was founded in 1751. It's noted less for its Danish than for its Victorian architecture, which dates from after the slave uprising and the great fire of 1878. One long cruise-ship pier juts into the sparkling sea. A stroll around the town's historic sights will take you no more than an hour. Allow a little more time if you want to browse in the few small shops.

SIGHTS TO SEE

Apothecary Hall. Built in 1839, this is a good example of 19th-century architecture; it's facade has both Gothic and Greek Revival elements. ✉ *King Cross St.*

Ft. Frederik. On July 3, 1848, 8,000 slaves marched on this redbrick fort to demand their freedom. Danish Governor Peter von Scholten, fearing they would burn the town to the ground, stood up in his carriage parked in front of the fort and granted them their freedom. The fort, completed in 1760, houses a number of interesting historical exhibits as well as an art gallery. ✉ *Waterfront,* ☎ *340/772–2021.* 🎫 *Free.* ⊙ *Weekdays 8:30–4:30.*

❿ Karl and Marie Lawaetz Museum. For a trip back in time, tour this circa 1750 farm. Owned by the prominent Lawaetz family since 1899, just after Karl arrived from Denmark, the lovely two-story house is nestled in a valley at La Grange. A Lawaetz family member shows you the four-poster mahogany bed Karl and Marie shared, the china Marie painted, the family portraits, and the fruit trees that fed the family for several generations. Initially a sugar plantation, it was subsequently used to raise cattle and produce. ✉ *Estate Little La Grange, Rte. 76, Mahogany Rd.,* ☎ *340/772–1539.* 🎫 *$5.* ⊙ *Tues.–Sat. 10–4.*

The Market. Stop here for fresh fruits and vegetables (be sure to wash or peel this produce before eating it) sold each morning, just as they have been for more than 200 years. ✉ *Queen St.*

St. Patrick's Church. This Roman Catholic church, complete with three turrets, was built in 1843 of coral. Wander inside and you'll find woodwork handcrafted by Frederiksted artisans. The churchyard is filled with 18th-century gravestones. ✉ *Prince St.*

St. Paul's Anglican Church. Built in 1812, this church is a mix of Georgian and Gothic revival architecture. The bell tower of exposed sandstone was added later. The simple interior has gleaming woodwork and a tray ceiling (it looks like an upside-down tray) popular in Caribbean architecture. It has survived several hurricanes. ✉ *Prince St.*

Visitor's Center. Right on the pier, this structure was built in the late 1700s; the two-story gallery was added in the 1800s. The building once served as the customs house; today you can stop in and pick up brochures or view the exhibits on St. Croix. ✉ *Waterfront,* ☎ *340/772–0357.* ⊙ *Weekdays 8–5.*

Frederiksted to Christiansted—the Southern Route

This trip takes you from the ends of the earth at Sandy Point to shopping center row. It's a good way to see both sides of this rapidly developing island. Make sure you have a map for finding out-of-the-way places.

SIGHTS TO SEE

⓭ Estate Whim Plantation Museum. The lovingly restored estate, with a windmill, cook house, and other buildings, will give you a sense of what life was like on St. Croix's sugar plantations in the 1800s. The oval-shape great house has high ceilings and antique furniture, decor, and utensils. Notice its fresh, airy atmosphere—the waterless stone moat around the great house was used not for defense but for gathering cooling air. The apothecary exhibit is the largest in all the West Indies. If you have kids, the spacious grounds are the perfect place for them to stretch their legs, perhaps while you browse in the museum gift shop. ✉ *Rte. 70, Frederiksted,* ☎ *340/772–0598.* 🎫 *$5.* ⊙ *Mon.–Sat. 10–4.*

⓮ St. George Village Botanical Gardens. At this 17-acre estate you'll find lush, fragrant flora amid the ruins of a 19th-century sugarcane plantation village. There are miniature versions of each ecosystem on St. Croix, from a semiarid cactus grove to a verdant rain forest. ✉ *Turn north off Rte. 70 at sign, Kingshill,* ☎ *340/692–2874.* 🎫 *$5.* ⊙ *Daily 9–5. Closed holidays.*

⑫ **Sandy Point Beach.** A ritual that began millions of years ago is played out here each spring: the majestic leatherback turtles come ashore to lay their eggs. These creatures, which can weigh up to 800 pounds and are of a species that's older than the dinosaurs, are oblivious to onlookers. With only the moonlight to guide them, Earthwatch volunteers patrol the beach nightly during the turtles' nesting season to protect the eggs from predators and poachers. The beach is a federal wildlife preserve; it's best to visit with a group rather than alone. ✉ *Rte. 66, west on unpaved road,* ☎ *340/773–1989.* ☉ *Spring turtle-watching, days and hrs vary.*

⑪ **West End Salt Pond.** A bird-watcher's delight, this salt pond attracts a vast variety of winged creatures, including flamingos. ✉ *Veteran's Shore Dr.*

ST. JOHN

Updated by
Lynda Lohr

Beautiful and largely undisturbed St. John is 3 mi east of St. Thomas across the Pillsbury Sound (a 20-minute ferry ride from Red Hook). In 1956 Laurance Rockefeller, who founded the Caneel Bay Resort, donated ⅔ of St. John's 20 square mi to the United States as a national park. Because of this, the island comes close to realizing that travel-brochure dream of "an unspoiled tropical paradise." It's covered with tropical vegetation, including a bay-tree forest that once supplied St. Thomas with the raw material for its fragrant bay rum. Along St. John's north shore, clean, gleaming, white-sand beaches fringe bay after bay, each full of iridescent water that's perfect for swimming, fishing, snorkeling, diving, and underwater photography.

In 1675 Jorgen Iverson claimed the unsettled island for Denmark. The British residents of nearby Tortola, however, considered St. John theirs, and when a small party of Danes from St. Thomas moved onto the uninhabited island, the British "invited" them to leave (which they did). Despite this, in 1717 a group of Danish planters founded the first permanent settlement at Coral Bay. The question of who owned St. John wasn't settled until 1762, when Britain decided that maintaining good relations with Denmark was more important than keeping St. John.

By 1728 St. John had 87 plantations and a population of 123 whites and 677 blacks. By 1733, there were more than 1,000 slaves working more than 100 plantations. In that year, the island was hit by a drought, hurricanes, and a plague of insects that destroyed the summer crops. Everyone felt the threat of famine, particularly the slaves, whose living and working conditions were already unusually harsh. Sensing the growing desperation, the landowners enacted even more severe measures in a misguided attempt to keep control. On November 23 the slaves revolted. With great military prowess, they captured the fort at Coral Bay, took control of the island, and held on to it for six months. During this time nearly a quarter of the island's population—black and white—was killed. The rebellion was eventually put down by 100 Danish militia and 220 Creole troops that were brought in from Martinique. Slavery continued until 1848, when slaves in St. Croix marched on Frederiksted to demand their freedom from the Danish government. After emancipation, St. John fell into decline, with its inhabitants eeking out a living on small farms. Life continued in much the same way until the national park was established and tourism became an industry.

Today St. John may well be the most racially integrated of the three USVI. Its 5,000 residents, black and white, have a strong sense of community that seems rooted in a desire to protect the island's natural beauty. Cruz Bay, the administrative capital, is home to the Virgin Islands National Park Visitor's Center and a few small shopping centers. It's more a small West Indian village (calm except when cruise ships arrive) than a major urban hub, and its residents want to keep it that way. When the government tried to install the island's first traffic light here, the citizens successfully opposed it, claiming it would change the character of the island and do little to help traffic. The consensus that the island's natural resources are sacrosanct may be curbing excesses on private land as well. Though Coral Bay and the East End are feeling some of the pressures of development, most of St. John—even areas outside the national park—still has a natural, undeveloped feel to it. Here you can truly escape the pressures of 20th-century life for a day, a week—perhaps, forever.

Lodging

St. John doesn't have many beachfront hotels, but that's a very small price to pay for all the pristine beaches. However, the island's two luxury hotels—Caneel Bay Resort and the Westin Resort, St. John—are world-class, and their rates (which some may consider expensive) include most water sports and endless privacy.

If you're looking for West Indian–village charm, there are a few inns in Cruz Bay. Just know that when bands play at any of the town's bars (some of which stay open till the wee hours), the noise can be a problem. Your choice of accommodations also includes condominium complexes and cottages near town; two campgrounds, both at the edges of beautiful beaches (bring bug repellent); eco-resorts; and luxurious villas, often with a pool, a stunning view, or both.

If your lodging comes with a fully equipped kitchen, you'll be happy to know that St. John's handful of grocery stores have improved their stock in recent years. You can now buy everything from the basics to sun-dried tomatoes and green chilies—though the prices will take your breath away. If you're on a budget, consider bringing some staples (pasta, canned goods, paper products) from home. ☞ For price categories, *see* the chart *under* Lodging *in* St. Thomas, *above*.

Hotels and Inns

$$$$ ★ ⊞ **Caneel Bay Resort.** Set on 170 lush peninsular acres—originally part of the Danish West India Company's Durloo plantation—Caneel Bay Resort mixes a good bit of peace and quiet into its luxurious air. You won't find crowds or glitz; your room won't have air-conditioning, a TV, or even a phone (though management will loan you a cellular). Instead, you'll discover spacious, restful rooms that are open to the breezes and are tastefully decorated with tropical furnishings; seven beaches, each more gorgeous than the next; and an attentive staff that will fill your every need. ⊠ *Rte. 20 (Box 720), Cruz Bay 00830,* ☎ *340/776–6111 or 800/928–8889. 166 rooms. 3 restaurants, 11 tennis courts, beaches, dive shop, dock, snorkeling, windsurfing, boating, children's program, meeting rooms. AE, MC, V. EP, FAP, MAP.*

$$$$ ⊞ **Gallow's Point Suite Resort.** These soft-gray buildings with peaked roofs and shuttered windows are clustered on a peninsula south of the Cruz Bay ferry dock. The garden apartments have kitchens and skylighted, plant-filled showers that are big enough to frolic in. The upper-level apartments have loft bedrooms and better views. There's air-conditioning only in the first-floor units; the harborside villas get better trade winds, but they're also noisier. The entranceway is bridged by ☞ **Ellington's** restaurant, which serves delicious contemporary cuisine. ⊠ *Gallow's Point (Box 58), Cruz Bay 00831,* ☎ *340/776–6434 or 800/323–7229,* ℻ *340/776–6520. 60 rooms. Restaurant, pool, beach, snorkeling. AE, DC, MC, V. EP.*

St. John

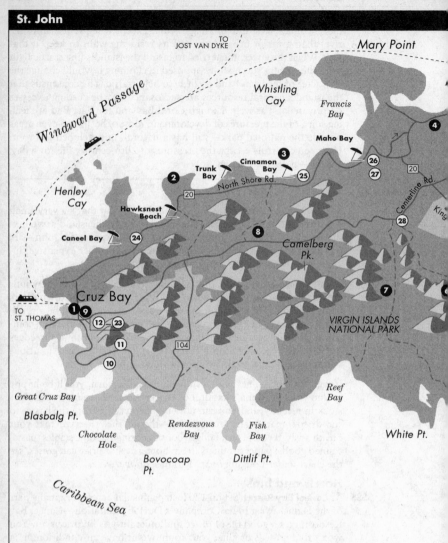

Exploring
Annaberg Plantation, **4**
Bordeaux Mountain, **6**
Catherineberg Ruins, **8**
Cinnamon Bay Beach, **3**
Coral Bay, **5**
Cruz Bay, **1**
Elaine Ione Sprauve Library and Museum, **9**
Peace Hill, **2**
Reef Bay Trail, **7**

Dining
Asolare, **14**
Cafe Roma, **12**
Ellington's, **13**
Fish Trap, **15**
Global Village Cuisine at Lattitude 18, **18**
La Tapa, **21**
Le Chateau Bordeaux, **28**
Lime Inn, **16**
Luscious Licks, **17**

Paradiso, **19**
Pusser's, **20**
Serafina Seaside Bistro, **30**
Shipwreck Landing, **32**
Skinny Legs Bar and Restaurant, **31**
Sun Dog Cafe, **22**

Lodging
Caneel Bay Resort, **24**
Cinnamon Bay Campground, **25**
Estate Concordia, **33**
Estate Zootenvaal, **29**
Gallows Point Suite Resort, **11**

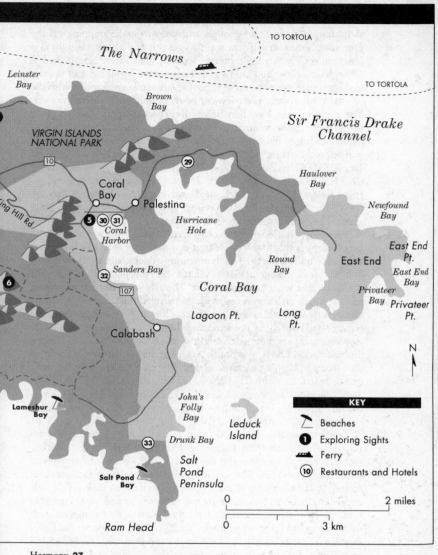

Harmony, **27**
Inn at Tamarind
Court, **23**
Maho Bay Camps, **26**
Serendip, **11**
Westin Resort, St.
John, **10**

$$$$ 🏨 **Westin Resort, St. John.** Spread out over 47 acres adjacent to Great Cruz Bay, the Westin has lushly planted gardens, a pool, a beach (the swimming is good), and enough amenities to make stepping off the grounds unnecessary. If you want to get out and about, though, taxi jaunts into Cruz Bay are a breeze. Rooms, which were refurbished in 1997, have yellow and blue bedspreads, rattan furniture, and phones and computer ports for those who just *have* to keep in touch with the world. Many rooms have views of boats bobbing in the turquoise sea. You can keep very busy here, if you like; perhaps play some tennis in the morning, go windsurfing in the afternoon, and then get a massage before heading to dinner in one of the on-site restaurants. Younger guests will appreciate the children's program. ⊠ *Rte. 104 (Box 8310), Cruz Bay 00831,* ☎ *340/693–8000 or 800/937–8461 (reservations service),* ℻ *340/693–8888. 285 rooms. 3 restaurants, air-conditioning, in-room modem lines, minibars, pool, massage, 6 tennis courts, exercise room, beach, dive shop, snorkeling, windsurfing, boating, fishing, shops, children's program, meeting room. AE, D, DC, MC, V. EP.*

$$–$$$ 🏨 **Harmony.** Nestled in the tree-covered hills adjacent to the ☞ **Maho Bay Camps** is this Stanley Selengut eco-tourism resort. The spacious two-story units have the usual amenities—decks, sliding glass doors, living-dining areas, great views. What makes this place unusual are the materials that were used to build it. Though you can't tell when you look at them, the carpets are made of recycled milk cartons, the pristine white walls of old newspapers. Energy for the low-wattage appliances is generated entirely by the wind and the sun, and each unit has a laptop computer programmed to monitor energy consumption. Tile floors, undyed cotton linens, and South American handicrafts create a decor that seems in keeping with the ideals. There's a water-sports outfitter on the beach. ⊠ *Maho Bay (Box 310), Cruz Bay 00830,* ☎ *340/693–5696 (direct to campground), 212/472–9453 or 800/392–9004 (reservations services);* ℻ *212/861–6210. 12 units. Restaurant, beach, snorkeling, windsurfing. MC, V. EP.*

$–$$$ 🏨 **Estate Concordia.** The latest brainchild of Stanley Selengut, the developer of ☞ **Maho Bay Camps** and ☞ **Harmony,** these "environmentally correct" studios and duplexes are on 51 oceanfront acres of remote Salt Pond Bay. The spacious units are constructed of recycled materials, and energy for all the appliances (even the ice makers) is wind- and solar-generated. Next door are five eco-tents, upscale camping structures made of environmentally friendly materials and equipped with solar power and composting toilets. ⊠ *20–27 Estate Concordia, Coral Bay 00830,* ☎ *340/693–5855 (direct to campground), 212/472–9453 or 800/392–9004 (reservations services);* ℻ *212/861–6210. 14 units. Kitchenettes, pool, beach. MC, V. EP*

$ 🏨 **Inn at Tamarind Court.** Within walking distance of Cruz Bay's shops and restaurants, this inn offers not only a convenient location but also affordable accommodations with a touch of charm. Though the rooms are plain, the courtyard is attractive: mature trees, plants, and umbrellas provide plenty of shade in which to enjoy your pasta in its open-air restaurant. Locals tend to gather in the small bar, which seems particularly hoppin' on Friday night. ⊠ *Rte. 104 (Box 350), Cruz Bay 00831,* ☎ *340/776–6378 or 800/221–1637,* ℻ *340/776–6722. 20 units. Restaurant, air-conditioning. MC, V. EP*

Villas, Condominiums, and Cottages

Tucked here and there between Cruz Bay and Coral Bay are about 350 villas, condominiums, and cottages (prices range from $ to $$$$). Villas often have pools and/or hot tubs; a few have private beaches. Condo complexes have pools and many modern amenities. Cottages tend to be more modest. Most condos are within walking distance of

Cruz Bay; if you rent a villa or a cottage, you'll need a car to get around. Many on-island managers pick you up at the ferry dock and answer any questions you have upon arrival as well as during your stay.

For luxury villas, try **Caribbean Villas and Resorts** (✉ Box 458, 00831, ☎ 340/776–6152 or 800/338–0987, FAX 340/779–4044), which also handles condo rentals for Cruz Views, Cruz Bay Villas, and Pastory Estates; **Catered To, Inc.** (✉ Box 704, 00830, ☎ 340/776–6641, FAX 340/693–8191); **Destination St. John** (✉ Box 8306, 00831, ☎ FAX 340/776–6969 or ☎ 800/562–1901), which also handles Lavender Hill condos; **Private Homes for Private Vacations** (✉ Mamey Peak, 00830, ☎ 340/776–6876); **Star Villa** (✉ Box 599, 00830, ☎ 340/776–6704, FAX 340/776–6183); **Vacation Homes** (✉ Box 272, 00831, ☎ 340/776–6094, FAX 340/693–8455); **Vacation Vistas** (✉ Box 476, 00831, ☎ FAX 340/776–6462); or **Windspree** (✉ 6-2-1A Estate Carolina, 00830, ☎ FAX 340/693–5423).

For condominiums, call **Coconut Coast** (✉ Box 618, 00831, ☎ 340/693–9100 or 800/858–7989, FAX 340/779–4157), which has on-the-water units; **Park Isle Villas** (✉ Box 1263, 00831, ☎ FAX 340/693–8261 or ☎ 800/416–1205), which manages Battery Hill and Villa Caribe; or the **Westin Vacation Club** (✉ Box 37, 00831, ☎ 340/693–8856 or 888/982–2582, FAX 340/693–8878), whose condo units are across the road from the Westin Resort, St. John, and whose guests have access to all the hotel's facilities.

Serendip (✉ Box 273, Cruz Bay 00831, ☎ FAX 340/776–6646, ☎ 888/800–6445) offers modest units on lush grounds with lovely views; but you need a rental car if you stay here, though; it's about 1 mi up a killer hill out of Cruz Bay. **Estate Zootenvaal** (✉ Hurricane Hole, 00830, ☎ FAX 340/776–6321), at the far reaches of the island in an area called Hurricane Hole, has basic cottages and a small private beach.

Campgrounds

$ ⚠ **Cinnamon Bay Campground.** Camping here puts you in the national park, surrounded by jungle and at the edge of Cinnamon Bay Beach. The unlockable, concrete "cottages" have electric lights, and the tents have propane lanterns; both come with propane camping stoves, coolers, cooking gear, and linens. Bring your own tent and supplies for the bare sites (a steal at $17 a night), which, like the cottages and tents, have a grill and a picnic table. The showers (on the cool side) and flush toilets, as well as a restaurant and a small store, are a trek down the hill. Hiking, snorkeling, swimming, and evening environmental or history programs are free and at your doorstep. Spaces for the winter months fill up far in advance (by as much as a year), so call for reservations. ✉ *Rte. 20 (Box 720), Cruz Bay 00830-0720, ☎ 340/776–6330 or 800/539–9998, FAX 340/776–6458. 44 tents, 38 cottages, 26 bare sites. Restaurant, hiking, beach, snorkeling, windsurfing. AE, MC, V. EP, FAP, MAP.*

$ ⚠ **Maho Bay Camps.** Eight miles from Cruz Bay, this eco-camp is a lush hillside community of rustic structures. The 16 × 16-ft tents (wooden platforms protected from the elements by canvas and screening) are linked by wooden stairs, ramps, and walkways—some of them elevated—so that you can trek around camp and down to the beach without disturbing the terrain. The tents sleep as many as four people and have beds, tables and chairs, electric lamps, propane stoves, coolers, and kitchenware and cutlery. Though all the units are surrounded by tropical greenery, some have spectacular views of the Caribbean. The camp has the chummy feel of a retreat, making it very popular; book well in advance. ✉ *Maho Bay (Box 310), Cruz Bay 00830, ☎ 340/693–5696 (direct to camp), 212/472–9453 or 800/392–9004 (reservations* *services);* 🖷 *212/861–6210. 113 shelters. Restaurant, beach, snorkeling, windsurfing. MC, V. EP.*

Dining

There was a time when food on St. John wasn't anything to write home about. Nowadays, though, the cuisine is surprisingly good, with many dishes featuring fresh herbs grown on St. John. There's also variety here, with restaurants to suit every taste and budget—from the elegant establishments at Caneel Bay Resort (where men may be required to wear a jacket at dinner) to the casual in-town eateries of Cruz Bay. For quick lunches, try the West Indian food stands in Cruz Bay Park and across from the post office. The cooks prepare fried chicken legs, *pates* (meat and fish-filled pastries), and callaloo.

Bordeaux Mountain

CONTEMPORARY

$$$–$$$$ ✕ **Le Chateau Bordeaux.** Whether you eat on the terrace or in the air-
★ conditioned dining room, the view is terrific. This rustic restaurant is practically a tree house, albeit one that's made very elegant and romantic by wrought-iron chandeliers, lace tablecloths, and antiques. The innovative preparations appeal equally to eye and palate. You might start with the velvety carrot soup with roasted chilies. Segue into rosemary-perfumed rack of lamb with a honey-Dijon-nut crust in a shallot-and-port-wine sauce, or salmon with mustard and maple glaze served on a bed of pasta. Don't miss the whelks, which are done to perfection. The comprehensive, moderately priced wine list is predictably strong on Bordeaux reds. ✉ *Rte. 10,* ☎ *340/776–6611. AE, MC, V.*

Coral Bay and Environs

AMERICAN

$ ✕ **Skinny Legs Bar and Restaurant.** Sailors who live aboard boats an-
★ chored just off shore and an eclectic coterie of residents gather for lunch and dinner at this funky, inexpensive spot. If owners Doug Sica and Mo Chabuz are around, take a gander at their gams; you'll see where the restaurant got its name. It's a great place for burgers, fish sandwiches, and watching whatever sports event is on cable TV. ✉ *Rte. 107 near the Coral Bay dinghy dock,* ☎ *340/779–4982. No credit cards.*

CONTEMPORARY

$$$–$$$$ ✕ **Serafina Seaside Bistro.** This cozy restaurant on the water's edge has a menu that's interesting, indeed. Many dishes are unique twists on old favorites such as New York strip steak—here it's marinated in Guinness stout and coated with pink, green, black, and white peppercorns. The midnight and saffron bow-tie pasta transports you to the Mediterranean with its sauce of grilled shrimp, tomatoes, scallions, garlic, basil, lime, and white wine. Look for fresh fish in parchment paper, chicken quesadilla, and salad made with local produce. ✉ *Rte. 107,* ☎ *340/693–5630. MC, V.*

ECLECTIC

$–$$$ ✕ **Shipwreck Landing.** Start with one of the house drinks, perhaps a fresh-squeezed concoction of lime, coconut, and rum, then move on to hearty taco salads, fried shrimp, teriyaki chicken, and conch fritters. The birds keep up a lively chatter in the bougainvillea that surrounds you at this open-air restaurant, and there's live music on Sunday night in season. ✉ *Rte. 107,* ☎ *340/693–5640. MC, V.*

Cruz Bay

ASIAN

$$$–$$$$ ✕ **Asolare.** Contemporary Asian cuisine dominates the menu at this elegant open-air eatery in an old St. John house. Come early and relax

over drinks while you enjoy the sunset over the harbor. Start with an appetizer, say, crayfish summer roll (a variation on the spring roll theme) with tamarind peanut sauce. Entrées include such delights as *pad thai,* a spicy dish of rice noodles, shrimp, chicken, and chilies. If you still have room for dessert, try the chocolate pyramid, a luscious cake with homemade ice cream. ⊠ *Caneel Hill,* ☎ *340/779–4747. AE, MC, V. No lunch.*

CONTEMPORARY

$$$–$$$$ ✕ **Ellington's.** This peaceful, appealing spot extends out onto the second-story veranda of the ☞ **Gallows Point Suite Resort**'s central building. The outside tables are particularly quiet and romantic. The menu has chicken, fish, and steak dishes. You might start with the jumbo shrimp cooked in sweet coconut and served with mango sauce or the seafood chowder. Entrées include sea scallops and pesto, swordfish scampi, filet mignon, and fresh lobster. For dessert, the banana–chocolate chip cake or the white-chocolate brownie are good bets. ⊠ *Gallow's Point, a 5-min walk from Cruz Bay,* ☎ *340/693–8490. AE, MC, V. No lunch.*

$$$ ✕ **Lime Inn.** This busy open-air restaurant has an ornamental garden and beach furniture. There are shrimp and steak dishes and such specials as sautéed chicken with artichoke hearts in lemon sauce. On Wednesday night there's an all-you-can-eat shrimp feast, and prime rib is the specialty every Saturday night. ⊠ *Downtown, east of Chase Manhattan Bank,* ☎ *340/776–6425. AE, MC, V. Closed Sun.*

ECLECTIC

$$–$$$$ ✕ **Fish Trap.** The rooms and terraces here all open to the breezes and buzz with a mix of locals and visitors. Chef Aaron Willis conjures up such tasty appetizers as conch fritters and Fish Trap chowder (a creamy soup of snapper, white wine, paprika, and some secret spices). The menu also includes an interesting pasta of the day, steak and chicken dishes, and hamburgers. ⊠ *Downtown, next to Our Lady of Mount Carmel Church,* ☎ *340/693–9994. AE, D, MC, V. Closed Mon.*

$$–$$$$ ✕ **La Tapa.** Locals congregate here to feast on tapas and sip sangria. Although street-side tables let you watch the world go by, they're a little noisy; head inside for a quiet, cozy, bistro-like atmosphere. Owner Alex Ewald dishes up a changing menu of delicious soups, tapas as lighter fare or dinner, and yummy desserts. The buffalo mozzarella served with tomatoes and basil is made in her own tiny kitchen. ⊠ *Across from Scotia Bank on unnamed street that heads inland from ferry dock,* ☎ *340/693–7755. AE, MC, V. Closed Sun.*

$$–$$$$ ✕ **Paradiso.** This popular spot is on the upper level of the island's largest
★ shopping complex. The menu is a mix of everything from Caribbean jerk chicken over vegetable linguine with spicy adobo sauce to grilled New York strip steak to rock lobster tail. You can dine indoors, in the comfort of air-conditioning, or outdoors on a small terrace that overlooks the street. ⊠ *Mongoose Junction shopping center,* ☎ *340/693–8899. AE, MC, V. No lunch.*

$$–$$$$ ✕ **Pusser's.** Its dark paneling and brass rails make you feel as if you just stepped into an old British pub. But this feeling will only be fleeting: tropical temperatures, lazily rotating ceiling fans, and menu items with a Caribbean twist are reminders that this is Cruz Bay, not Cambridge. Step outside the bar to the covered deck, have a seat, take in the view, and order up some terrific conch chowder or a lobster club sandwich. The rum Painkillers pack a punch. ⊠ *Wharfside Village,* ☎ *340/693–8489. AE, MC, V.*

$$–$$$ ✕ **Global Village Cuisine at Latitude 18.** Open to the breezes, this popular restaurant attracts an eclectic local crowd that tends to drop by for lunch at the bar. They aren't the only ones: tiny yellow birds peck at the wine glasses of sugar that are used as feeders. For lunch, there are ham-

burgers, sandwiches, and salads; for dinner, grilled local tuna, wahoo, or other fresh fish; grilled sirloin steak; and daily pasta specials. ⊠ *Mongoose Junction shopping center,* ☎ *340/693–8687. AE, MC, V.*

$–$$ ✕ **Sun Dog Cafe.** You'll find an unusual assortment of dishes at this charming restaurant tucked into a courtyard in the upper reaches of the Mongoose Junction shopping center. Kudos to the interesting combination of flavors and textures in the French country pie—a puff pastry shell stuffed with sliced chicken, Swiss cheese, artichoke hearts, and roasted red pepper. The Jamaican jerk chicken sub or the three-cheese quesadilla are also good choices. ⊠ *Mongoose Junction shopping center,* ☎ *340/693–8340. No credit cards.*

ITALIAN

$$–$$$ ✕ **Cafe Roma.** This casual, second-floor restaurant in the heart of Cruz Bay is *the* place for traditional Italian cuisine: lasagna, spaghetti and meatballs, manicotti, chicken Parmesan. There are also a variety of excellent pizzas. Polenta cake with raspberry sauce is a dessert specialty. ⊠ *Downtown on Vesta Gade,* ☎ *340/776–6524. MC, V. No lunch.*

VEGETARIAN

$ ✕ **Luscious Licks.** This funky hole-in-the-wall serves up mostly health food—all-natural fruit smoothies, veggie pita sandwiches, and homemade muffins. Try the barbecue tofu in sweet-and-sour sauce, the spinach and olive fettuccine, or the local's platter (a bit of this and that; really whatever owner Bonny Corbeil feels like whipping up on any given day). You can also get Ben & Jerry's ice cream and specialty coffees here. ⊠ *Across from V.I. National Park Visitor's Center,* ☎ *340/693–8400. No credit cards. Closed Sun.*

Beaches

St. John is blessed with so many beaches, and all of them fall into the good, great, and don't-tell-anyone-else-about-this-place categories. The beaches along the north shore are all within the national park. Some are more developed than others—and all are crowded on weekends, holidays, and in high season—but by and large they're still pristine. Beaches along the south and eastern shores are still quiet and isolated.

Caneel Bay. Caneel Bay is actually a catch-all name for seven white-sand north shore beaches, six of which can be reached only by water if you aren't a guest at the Caneel Bay Resort. (Access to beaches is a civil right in the USVI, but access to land that leads to the beaches is not.) The seventh, **Caneel Beach,** is open to the public and is easy to reach from the main entrance of the resort; just ask for directions at the gatehouse. Nonguests can also dine at the hotel's two restaurants and browse in its gift shop.

Cinnamon Bay. This long, sandy beach faces beautiful cays and abuts the national park campground. The facilities are open to the public and include showers, toilets, a commissary, a restaurant, a gift shop, and a small museum (☞ Exploring St. John, *below*). You can also rent watersports equipment here—a good thing, because there's excellent snorkeling off the point to the right—look for the big angelfish and large schools of purple triggerfish. Afternoons on Cinnamon Bay can be windy, so arrive early to beat the gusts. The Cinnamon Bay hiking trail begins across the road from the beach parking lot; the ruins of a sugar mill mark the trailhead. There are actually two paths here: a nature trail (signs along it identify the flora) that loops through the woods on level terrain and a steep trail that heads straight up to Centerline Road.

Hawksnest Beach. Sea-grape trees line this narrow beach, and there are rest rooms, cooking grills, and a covered shed for picnicking. It's the closest beach to town, so it's often crowded.

Lameshur Bay. This nifty beach is toward the end of a very long dirt road on the southeast coast. It offers solitude, good snorkeling, and a chance to spy on some pelicans. The ruins of the old plantation are a five-minute walk down the road past the beach.

Maho Bay. This popular beach is below the Maho Bay Camps—a wonderful hillside enclave of tents. The campground offers informal talks and slide and film presentations on nature, environmentally friendly living, and whatever else crosses the manager's mind. In spring, jazz and jungle harmonize when Maho sponsors a music series in its outdoor pavilion. Maho Bay is also the site of Harmony (☞ Lodging, *above*), an eco-resort.

Salt Pond Bay. If you're adventurous, this somewhat rocky beach on the scenic southeastern coast—next to Coral Bay and rugged Drunk Bay—is worth exploring. It's a short hike down a hill from the parking lot, and the only facilities are an outhouse and a few picnic tables scattered about. There are interesting tidal pools, and the snorkeling is good. Take special care to leave nothing valuable in your car; reports of thefts are common.

Trunk Bay. St. John's most-photographed beach is also the preferred spot for beginning snorkelers, because of its underwater trail. (Cruise-ship passengers interested in snorkeling for a day on St. John come here, so if you're looking for seclusion, check cruise-ship schedules in *St. Thomas This Week* before heading here.) Crowded or not, this stunning beach is sure to please. There are changing rooms, a snack bar, picnic tables, a gift shop, telephones, lockers, and snorkeling-equipment rentals.

Outdoor Activities and Sports

BOATING AND SAILING

For a speedy trip to offshore cays and remote beaches, a power boat is a necessity. More leisurely day sails to islands not far offshore or longer sails to points east are also possibilities. If you're boatless, book with one of the island's agents. Most day sails include lunch, beverages, and at least one stop to snorkel.

Connections (⊠ Cruz Bay, a block up from the ferry dock and cater-corner from Chase Manhattan Bank, ☎ 340/776–6922) pairs you up with the sailboat that suits you. Have simple tastes? The smiling staff can help. If luxury is more your style, they can book that, too. **Ocean Runner** (☎ 340/693–8809), on the waterfront in Cruz Bay, rents one and two-engine boats for fast trips around the island's seas. **Proper Yachts** (☎ 340/776–6956) books day sails and longer charters on its fleet of luxury yachts that depart from Caneel Bay Resort.

FISHING

Well-kept charter boats head out to the north and south drops or troll along the inshore reefs. The captains usually provide bait, drinks, and lunch, but you'll need your hat and sunscreen. **American Yacht Harbor** (☎ 340/775–6454) offers sportfishing trips, and though they're in Red Hook on St. Thomas, they'll come and pick you up on St. John. The **Charterboat Center** (☎ 340/775–7990), in Red Hook on St. Thomas, arranges fishing trips for folks in St. John. **Gone Ketchin'** (☎ 340/693–8657) in St. John arranges trips with old salt Wally Leopold. **St. John World Class Anglers** (☎ 340/779–4281) offers light-tackle shore and offshore half- and full-day trips.

HIKING

Although it's fun to go hiking with a Virgin Islands National Park guide, don't be afraid to strike out on your own. To find a hike that suits your ability, stop by the park's visitors center in Cruz Bay and pick up the free trail guide; it details points of interest, dangers, trail lengths, and estimated hiking times. Although the park staff recommends pants to protect against thorns and insects, most people hike in shorts because pants are too hot. Wear sturdy shoes or hiking boots even if you're hiking to the beach. Don't forget to bring water and insect repellant.

The **Virgin Islands National Park** (☎ 340/776–6201) maintains more than 20 trails on the north and south shores and offers guided hikes along popular routes. A full-day trip to Reef Bay is a must; it's an easy hike through lush and dry forest, past the ruins of an old plantation, and to a sugar factory adjacent to the beach. The park provides transportation to the trailhead, a ranger to point out trail highlights, and a boat trip back to Cruz Bay for $14.50. The schedule changes from season to season; call for times and reservations, which are essential.

HORSEBACK RIDING

Clip-clop along the island's byways for a slower-pace tour of St. John. **Carolina Corral** (☎ 340/693–5778) offers horseback, donkey-back, and donkey-cart rides as well as riding lessons. Look for Dana Romo and her animals along the road in Coral Bay.

SCUBA DIVING AND SNORKELING

To reach less accessible spots, head out with a professional dive operator. Most companies offer both dive and snorkel trips. On dive trips, you can choose to make several stops. **Cruz Bay Watersports** (☎ 340/776–6234 or 800/835–7730) has three locations. You'll find them in Cruz Bay, at the Westin Resort, and in the adjacent Palm Plaza Shopping Center. Owners Marcus and Patty Johnston offer regular reef, wreck, and night dives aboard their custom dive boats. **Low Key Watersports** (☎ 340/776–8999) at Wharfside Village offers PADI certification and resort courses, one- and two-tank dives, and specialty courses. **St. John Watersports** (☎ 340/776–6256) is a five-star PADI dive center in the Mongoose Junction shopping center.

SEA KAYAKING

Poke around crystal bays and explore undersea life from a sea kayak. **Arawak Expeditions**'s (☎ 340/693–8312 or 800/238–8687) professional guides use traditional kayaks to ply coastal waters. Prices start at $40 for a half-day trip.

TENNIS

With hot weather the norm, tennis players take to the courts in the morning or late afternoon. **Caneel Bay Resort** (✉ Rte. 20, ☎ 340/776–6111) has 11 courts (none lighted) for guests only and a pro shop. The **Westin Resort, St. John** (✉ Rte. 104, ☎ 340/693–8000) has six lighted courts. Nonguests are welcome to play here for a fee of $15 an hour. The **public courts,** near the fire station in Cruz Bay, are lighted until 10 PM and are available on a first-come, first-served basis.

WINDSURFING

Steady breezes and expert instruction make learning to windsurf a snap. Try **Cinnamon Bay Campground** (✉ Rte. 20, ☎ 340/776–6330), where rentals are available for $12–$15 per day. Lessons are available right at the waterfront; just look for the Windsurfers stacked up on the beach. The cost for an 1-hour lesson is about $40.

Shopping

Areas and Malls

You'll find luxury items and handicrafts on St. John. Most shops carry a little of this and a bit of that, so it pays to poke around. The Cruz Bay shopping district runs from **Wharfside Village,** just around the corner from the ferry dock, through the streets of town to North Shore Road and **Mongoose Junction,** an inviting shopping center with stonework walls. (Its name is a holdover from a time when those furry island creatures gathered at a garbage bin that was here.) Steps connect the two sections of the center, which has unique, upscale shops. Out on Route 104, stop in at **Palm Plaza** to explore its handful of gift and crafts shops. At the island's other end, you'll find a few stores—selling clothes, jewelry, and artwork—here and there from the village of **Coral Bay** to the small complex at **Shipwreck Landing.**

Specialty Items

ART

Coconut Coast Studios. This waterside shop, a five-minute walk from Cruz Bay, showcases the work of Elaine Estern and her daughter-in-law, Lucinda Schutt. Estern specializes in underseas scenes and Schutt in attractive pastels. ⊠ *Frank Bay,* ☎ *340/776–6944.*

Bajo el Sol. A cooperative gallery, Bajo el Sol features Aimee Trayser's expressionistic Caribbean scenes, Les Anderson's island scenes in oil, Kat Sowa's watercolors, and works by a handful of other artists. ⊠ *Mongoose Junction,* ☎ *340/693–7070.*

BOOKS

MAPes MONDe. Here you'll find a huge selection of books on the Caribbean, including the exquisite-looking publications that are the hallmark of Virgin Islands publisher MAPes MONDe. You'll also find many reproductions of old maps as well as contemporary prints and greeting cards. ⊠ *Mongoose Junction,* ☎ *340/779–4545.*

National Park Headquarters. The headquarters sells several good histories of St. John, including *St. John Back Time,* by Ruth Hull Low and Rafael Valls, and for linguists, Lito Valls's *What a Pistarckle!*— an explanation of the colloquialisms that make up the local version of English (*pistarckle* is a Dutch Creole word that means "noise" or "din," which pretty much sums up the language here). ⊠ *At the Creek,* ☎ *340/776–6201.*

St. John Books. This is the place to come for current newspapers and magazines, a variety of books, and a good cup of coffee. ⊠ *Wharfside Village,* ☎ *340/779–4260.*

CLOTHING

Big Planet Adventure Outfitters. You knew when you arrived that some place on St. John would sell Birkenstock sandals. Well, this outdoor-clothing store is where you'll find them along with colorful and durable cotton clothing and accessories by Patagonia, the North Face, Sierra Designs, and others. The adjacent **Little Planet** sells children's clothes, often made from such unlikely materials as recycled plastic bottles. ⊠ *Mongoose Junction,* ☎ *340/776–6638 or 800/238–8687.*

Bougainvillea Boutique If you want to look like you stepped out of the pages of the resort wear spread in an upscale travel magazine, try this store. Owner Susan Stair carries *very* chic men's and women's resort wear, straw hats, leather handbags, and fine gift items. ⊠ *Mongoose Junction,* ☎ *340/693–7190.*

The Clothing Studio. Several talented artists hand-paint original designs on clothing for all members of the family. You'll find T-shirts, beach cover-ups, pants, shorts, and even bathing suits with beautiful hand-painted creations. ⊠ *Mongoose Junction,* ☎ *340/776–6585.*

Pusser's Company Store. Pusser's stores originated in the BVI, and this branch carries all the items these stores are famous for: nautical memorabilia, casual sportswear, books, and, of course, famous Pusser's Rum. ⊠ *Wharfside Village, Cruz Bay,* ☎ *340/693–8489.*

FOODSTUFFS

If you're renting a villa, condo, or cottage and doing your own cooking, there are several good places to shop for food; just be aware that prices are much higher that those at home. **Starfish Market** (☎ 340/779–4949) is in the Boulon Center, **Marina Market** (☎ 340/779–4401) is on Route 104, and **Tropicale** (☎ 340/693–7474) is also on Route 104 in Palm Plaza.

GIFTS

Bamboula. Owner Jo Sterling travels the Caribbean and the world to find unusual housewares, rugs, bedspreads, accessories, shoes, and men's and women's clothes for this multicultural boutique. ⊠ *Mongoose Junction,* ☎ *340/693–8699.*

The Canvas Factory. If you're a true shopper who needs an extra bag to carry all your treasures home, this store offers every kind of tote and carrier imaginable—from simple bags to suitcases with numerous zippered compartments—all made of canvas, naturally. It also sells great canvas hats in assorted styles and colors. ⊠ *Mongoose Junction,* ☎ *340/776–6196.*

Donald Schnell Pottery. In addition to pottery, this place sells unique hand-blown glass, wind chimes, kaleidoscopes, fanciful water fountains, and more. Your purchases can be shipped worldwide. ⊠ *Mongoose Junction,* ☎ *340/776–6420.*

Fabric Mill. Shop here for handmade dolls, place mats, napkins, cookbooks, and batik wraps. Or take home a bolt of tropical brights from the upholstery-fabric selection. ⊠ *Mongoose Junction,* ☎ *340/776–6194.*

Isola. An eclectic array of handicrafts, gifts, and clothing from around the world fill this interesting store. You'll also find pottery and jewelry by local artists, CDs of Caribbean music, and whatever else owner Lorena Sitka has picked up in her travels. ⊠ *Wharfside Village,* ☎ *340/779–4212.*

Pink Papaya. This store is the home of St. Croix native M. L. Etre's well-known artwork plus a huge collection of one-of-a-kind gift items, including bright tablecloths, unusual trays, dinnerware, and unique tropical jewelry. ⊠ *Lemon Tree Mall, Cruz Bay,* ☎ *340/693–8535.*

JEWELRY

Blue Carib Gems. Here you'll find custom-made jewelry, loose gemstones, and old coins as well as a small art gallery. ⊠ *Wharfside Village,* ☎ *340/693–8299.*

Caravan Gallery. Owner Radha Speer creates much of the unusual jewelry you'll find here. And the more you look, the more you see—folk art, tribal art, and masks for sale cover the walls and tables, making this a great place to browse. ⊠ *Mongoose Junction,* ☎ *340/693–8550.*

Colombian Emeralds (⊠ Mongoose Junction, ☎ 340/776–6007) has high-quality emeralds, and also sells rubies, diamonds, and other jewels set in attractive gold and silver settings. This is also the only place on St. John that sells the latest perfumes. You can find still more jewels at Columbian Emeralds' sister store, **Jeweler's Warehouse** (⊠ Wharfside Village, ☎ 340/693–7490).

Free Bird Creations. Head here for the unique handcrafted jewelry—earrings, bracelets, pendants, chains—as well as the good selection of waterproof watches great for your excursions to the beach. ⊠ *Wharfside Village,* ☎ *340/693–8625.*

Heads Up. This tiny store carries the unique St. John watch for men and women. There's also a fine selection of hats and top-drawer sunglasses at lower-than-mainland prices. ⊠ *Veste Gade, Cruz Bay,* ☎ *340/693–8840.*

R&I Patton Goldsmiths. Rudy and Irene Patton design most of the unique silver and gold jewelry in this shop. The rest comes from various jeweler friends of theirs. Sea fans (those large, lacy plants that sway with the ocean's currents) in filigreed silver, lapis set in long drops of gold, starfish and hibiscus pendants in silver or gold, and gold sand dollar–shape charms and earrings are tempting choices. ⊠ *Mongoose Junction,* ☎ 340/776–6548.

Nightlife

St. John is not the place to go for glitter and all-night partying. Still, after-hours Cruz Bay can be a lively little village in which to dine, drink, dance, chat, or flirt. Notices posted on the bulletin board outside the **Connections** telephone center—up the street from the ferry dock in Cruz Bay—or listings in the island's two small newspapers (the *St. John Times* and *Tradewinds*) will keep you apprised of special events, comedy nights, movies, and the like.

After a sunset drink at **Ellington's** (⊠ Gallows Point Suite Resort, ☎ 340/693–8490), up the hill from Cruz Bay, you can stroll here and there in town (much is clustered around the small waterfront park). Many of the young people from the U.S. mainland who live and work on St. John will be out sipping and socializing, too.

You'll find friendly hubbub at the rough-and-ready **Backyard** (⊠ Cruz Bay, ☎ 340/776–8886), which is *the* place for sports-watching as well as grooving to Bonnie Raitt, et al. Outside of town, **Caneel Bay Resort** (⊠ Rte. 20, ☎ 340/776–6111) usually has entertainment (generally, of the quiet calypso variety) several nights a week in season. There's calypso and reggae on Wednesday and Friday at **Fred's** (⊠ Cruz Bay, ☎ 340/776–6363). The **Inn at Tamarind Court** (⊠ Rte. 104, ☎ 340/776–6378) serves up country rock on Friday and reggae on Saturday. At Coral Bay, on the far side of the island, check out the action at **Skinny Legs Bar and Restaurant** (☎ 340/779–4982). Young folks like to gather at **Woody's** (⊠ Cruz Bay, ☎ 340/779–4625). Its sidewalk tables provide a close-up view of Cruz Bay's action.

Exploring St. John

St. John is an easy place to explore. One road runs along the north shore, another across the center of the mountains. There are a few roads that branch off here and there, but it's hard to get lost. Pick up a map at the visitor center before you start out, and you'll have no problems. Few residents remember the route numbers, so have your map in hand if you stop to ask for directions. Bring along a swimsuit for stops at some of the most beautiful beaches in the world. You can spend all day or just a couple of hours exploring, but be advised that the roads are narrow and wind up and down steep hills, so don't expect to get anywhere in a hurry. There are lunch spots at Cinnamon Bay and in Coral Bay, or you can do what the locals do—picnic. The grocery stores in Cruz Bay even sell Styrofoam coolers just for this purpose.

If you plan to do a lot of touring, renting a car will be cheaper and will give you much more freedom than relying on taxis, which are reluctant to go anywhere until they have a full load of passengers. Although you may be tempted by an open-air Suzuki or Jeep, a conventional car can get you just about everywhere on the paved roads, and you'll be able to lock up your valuables. You may be able to share a van or open-air vehicle (called a safari bus) with other passengers on a tour of scenic mountain trails, secret coves, and eerie bush-covered ruins of old forts and palatial plantation houses.

SIGHTS TO SEE

❹ **Annaberg Plantation.** In the 18th century, sugar plantations dotted the steep hills of the USVI. Slaves and free Danes and Dutchmen toiled to harvest the cane that was used to create sugar, molasses, and rum for export. Built in the 1780s, the partially restored plantation at Leinster Bay was once an important sugar mill. Though there are no official visiting hours, the National Park Service has regular tours, and some well-informed taxi drivers will show you around. Occasionally you'll find a living-history demonstration—someone making johnnycake or weaving baskets. For information on tours and cultural demonstrations, contact the St. John National Park Service Visitor's Center. ⊠ *Leinster Bay Rd.,* ☎ *340/776–6201 (park service visitors center).* 🎟 *Free.*

❻ **Bordeaux Mountain.** St. John's highest peak rises to 1,277 ft. Centerline Road passes near enough to the top to offer breathtaking views before its plunges down to Coral Bay. Drive nearly to the end of the dirt road for spectacular views at Picture Point, and for the trailhead of the hike downhill to Lameshur. Get a trail map from the park service before you start. ⊠ *Centerline Rd.*

❽ **Catherineberg Ruins.** At this fine example of an 18th-century sugar and rum factory there's a storage vault beneath the windmill. Across the road, look for the round mill, which was later used to hold water. In the 1733 slave revolt, Catherineberg served as headquarters for Amina warriors, a tribe of Africans captured into slavery. It's now part of the Virgin Island National Park. ⊠ *Centerline Rd.*

❸ **Cinnamon Bay Beach.** The national park campground and more than 20 mi of hiking trails within the park are here. Two good trails begin at Cinnamon Bay, across the road from the beach. The ruins of a sugar mill mark the trailhead to an easy, level nature trail through the woods and past an old Danish cemetery. The other trail, which starts where the road bends past the ruins, heads all the way up to Centerline Road. If you prefer underwater pursuits to those on land, Cinnamon Bay also has terrific snorkeling, although watch out if the waves are up.

History buffs will enjoy the little, self-guided **Cinnamon Bay Museum.** It has some old pictures as well as a few items dating from the time when sugar ruled. ⊠ *North Shore Rd..* 🎟 *Free.* ☉ *Hrs. vary.*

❺ **Coral Bay.** This laid-back community at the dry, eastern end of the island is named for its shape rather than for its underwater life—the word *coral* comes from *krawl,* Danish for *corral.* It's a small, quiet, neighborhoody settlement; a place to get away from it all. You'll need a Jeep if you plan to stay at this end of the island, as some of the rental houses are up unpaved roads that wind around the mountain. If you come just for lunch, a regular car will be fine. ⊠ *Rte. 10.*

❶ **Cruz Bay.** St. John's main town may be compact (it consists only of several blocks), but it's definitely a hub: the ferries from St. Thomas and the BVI pull in here, and it's where you can get a taxis or rent a car to travel around the island. There are plenty of shops in which to browse, a number of watering holes where you can stop for a breather, many restaurants, and a grassy square with benches where you can sit back and take everything in. Look for the current edition of the handy, amusing "St. John Map" featuring Max the Mongoose.

To pick up a handy guide to St. John's hiking trails, see various large maps of the island, and find out about current park service programs, including guided walks and cultural demonstrations, stop by the **V.I. National Park Visitor's Center.** ⊠ *Cruz Bay, 00831,* ☎ *340/776–6201.* 🎟 *Free.* ☉ *Daily 8–4:30.*

⑨ Elaine Ione Sprauve Library and Museum. On the hill just above Cruz Bay is the **Enighed Estate Great House,** built in 1757. *Enighed* is the Danish word for "concord," meaning unity or peace. The great house and its outbuildings (a sugar-production factory and horse-driven mill) were destroyed by fire and hurricanes, and the house sat in ruins until 1982. Today it is home to a library and museum, and contains a small collection of Indian pottery, colonial artifacts, and contemporary crafts by local artisans. The library hosts occasional crafts demonstrations and classes. ⊠ *Rte. 104, make a right past Texaco station,* ☎ *340/776–6359.* ▨ *Free.* ⊙ *Weekdays 9–5.*

❷ Peace Hill. It's worth stopping at this unmarked spot just past the Hawksnest Bay overlook for breathtaking views of St. John, St. Thomas, and the BVI. The flat promontory features an old sugar mill. The pile of white stones you'll see is what remains of *Christ of the Caribbean,* a statue honoring world peace erected in 1953 by Col. Julius Wadsworth. The statue fell to Hurricane Marilyn's winds in 1995, and the park service decided not to restore it. From the parking lot, the statue is about 100 yards up a rocky path. ⊠ *Off North Shore Rd.*

❼ Reef Bay Trail. Although one of the most interesting hikes on St. John, unless you are a rugged individualist who wants a physical challenge (and that describes a lot of people who stay on St. John), you'll probably get the most out of the trip if you join a hike led by a park service ranger, who can identify the trees and plants on the hike down, fill you in on the history of the Reef Bay Plantation, and tell you about the petroglyphs you'll find in the rocks at the bottom of the trail. The park service provides bus transportation from Cruz Bay and a return trip by boat ($14.50), saving you the uphill return climb.

The **Reef Bay Plantation,** according to architectural historian Frederik C. Gjessing, is the most architecturally ambitious plantation structure on St. John. The great house is largely intact, though gutted, and its classical beauty is still visible from what remains. You'll also see the remnants of a cook house, servants' quarters, stable, and outhouse. Reef Bay was the last working plantation on St. John when it stopped production in 1920. ⊠ *Rte. 10 between Cruz Bay and Coral Bay; parking area is on the left, trail is to the right.*

U.S. VIRGIN ISLANDS A TO Z

Arriving and Departing

BY AIRPLANE

One advantage of visiting the USVI is the abundance of nonstop and connecting flights that can have you at the beach in three to four hours from most eastern United States departures. You may fly direct to St. Thomas's Cyril E. King Airport (☎ 340/774–5100) on **American** (☎ 340/774–6464 or 340/778–1140) from Miami and New York, **Delta** (☎ 340/777–4177) from Atlanta and **US Airways** (☎ 340/774–7885) from Philadelphia. Another option is to pick up a local flight from San Juan on **American Eagle** (☎ 340/776–2560 or 340/778–2000).

From the Airport: Most hotels on **St. Thomas** don't have airport shuttles, but taxi vans at the airport are plentiful. From the airport, fees (set by the VI Taxi Commission) for two or more people sharing a cab are: $12 to the Ritz-Carlton, $9 to Point Pleasant, $7.50 to Marriotts Frenchman's Reef, and $5 to Bluebeard's Castle. Expect to be charged 50¢ per bag and to pay a higher fee if you're riding alone. During rush hour the trip to East End resorts can take up to 40 minutes, but ½ hour is typical. Driving time from the airport to Charlotte Amalie is 15 minutes. Getting from the airport to **St. Croix** hotels by taxi costs about $10–$13.

Visitors to **St. John** fly into St. Thomas, take a taxi to either Charlotte Amalie or Red Hook, where they catch a ferry to Cruz Bay, St. John. The ferry from Charlotte Amalie makes the 45-minute trip several times a day and costs $7 a person. From Red Hook, the ferry leaves on the hour; the 20-minute trip costs $3 a person.

Virtually every type of ship and major cruise line calls at St. Thomas; only a few call at St. Croix. One or both of these ports is usually included as part of a ship's eastern Caribbean itinerary. Many of the ships that call at St. Thomas also call in St. John or offer an excursion to that island.

From the Docks: On **St. Thomas** taxi vans line up along Havensight and Crown Bay docks when a cruise ship pulls in. If you booked a shore tour, the operator will lead you to a designated vehicle. Otherwise, there are plenty of air-conditioned vans and open-air safari buses to take you to Charlotte Amalie or the beach. The cab fare from Havensight to Charlotte Amalie is $2.50 per person; you can, however, walk to town in about 30 minutes (1½ mi) along the beautiful waterfront. From Crown Bay to town the taxi fare is $3pp or $2.50 if you share; it's a 1-mi walk, but the route passes along a busy highway. Transportation from Havensight to Magens Bay for swimming is $6.50 per person ($4 if you share).

In **St. Croix,** taxis greet arriving cruise ships at the Frederiksted pier. All the shops are just a short walk away, and you can swim off the beach in Frederksted. Most ship passengers visit Christiansted on a tour. A taxi will cost $20 for one to two people.

Some cruise ships stop at **St. John** to let passengers disembark for a day. The main town of Cruz Bay is near the ship terminal. If you want to swim, the famous Trunk Bay is a $7.50 taxi ride (for two) from town.

Electricity

The USVI use the same current as the U.S. mainland—110 volts. Since power fluctuations occasionally occur, bring a heavy-duty surge protector (available at hardware stores) if you plan to use your computer.

Emergencies

Ambulance, Fire, and Police: ☎ 911. **Air Ambulance:** Air Ambulance Network (☎ 800/327–1966) serves the USVI area from Florida. **Bohlke International Airways** (☎ 340/778–9177) serves both St. Thomas and St. Croix, though it's based on St. Croix. **Medical Air Services** (☎ 340/777–8580 or 800/966–6272) has its Caribbean headquarters in St. Thomas. If you're on St. John, you'll have to go by ambulance boat to St. Thomas and by ambulance to St. Thomas airport.

Coast Guard: For emergencies, call the **Marine Safety Detachment** (☎ 340/776–3497 for St. Thomas and St. John or 340/772–5557 for St. Croix) from 7 to 3:30 weekdays. If there's no answer at either number, call the **Rescue Coordination Center** (☎ 787/729–6800, ext. 140) in San Juan, Puerto Rico; it's open 24 hours a day. **Scuba-Diving Accidents:** The only **decompression chamber** (☎ 340/776–2686) in the territory is at St. Thomas's Roy L. Schneider Hospital & Community Health Center (☞ *below*).

St. Thomas: The emergency room of the **Roy L. Schneider Hospital & Community Health Center** (⊠ Sugar Estate, 1 mi east of Charlotte Amalie, ☎ 340/776–8311) is open 24 hours a day.

St. Croix: Outside Christiansted there's the **Gov. Juan F. Luis Hospital and Health Center** (⊠ 6 Diamond Ruby, north of Sunny Isle Shopping Center, on Rte. 79, ☎ 340/778–6311). You can also try the **Frederiksted Health Center** (⊠ 516 Strand St., ☎ 340/772–1992).

St. John: For medical emergencies, visit the **Myrah Keating Smith Community Health Center** (⊠ Rte. 10 about 7 min east of Cruz Bay, ☎ 340/693–8900).

PHARMACIES

St. Thomas: **Havensight Pharmacy** (☎ 340/776–1235), in the Havensight Mall, is open daily 9–9. **Kmart** (☎ 340/777–3854) operates a pharmacy inside its Tutu Park Mall. **Sunrise Pharmacy** (☎ 340/775–6600), in Red Hook, is open daily 9–7.

St. Croix: Although most drugstores are open daily 8–8, off-season hours may vary; call ahead to confirm times. **People's Drug Store, Inc.** has two branches: on the Christiansted Wharf (☎ 340/778–7355) and at the Sunny Isle Shopping Center (☎ 340/778–5537), just a few miles west of Christiansted on Centerline Road. In Frederiksted, try **D&D Apothecary Hall** (⊠ 501 Queen St., ☎ 340/772–1890).

St. John: The **St. John Drug Center** (☎ 340/776–6353) is in the Boulon shopping center, up Centerline Road in Cruz Bay. It's open Monday–Saturday 9–5.

Festivals and Seasonal Events

ST. THOMAS

January–April sees **Classics In The Garden** (☎ 340/775–1405), a chamber music series at Tillett Gardens, where young musicians from all over the world perform. Tillett Gardens also hosts annual **Arts Alive** (☎ 340/775–1405) festivals in November, March, and August. In April, St. Thomas Yacht Club hosts the **Rolex Cup Regatta** (☎ 340/775–6320), which is part of the three-race Caribbean Ocean Racing Triangle (CORT) that pulls in yachties and their pals from all over. **Carnival** (☎ 340/776–3112) is a weeklong, major-league blowout of parades, parties, and island-wide events. The dates change from year to year, following the Easter calendar. Marlin mania begins in May and so do the **sportfishing tournaments.** There are also several locally sponsored fishing events throughout summer and fall.

The St. Thomas Gamefishing Club hosts its **July Open Tournament** (☎ 340/775–9144) over the Fourth of July weekend. There are categories for serious marlin anglers, just-for-fun fishermen, and even kids who want to try their luck from docks and rocks. The mid-July celebration of **Bastille Day**—which commemorates the French Revolution—is marked by a mini-carnival in Frenchtown. August's **Texas Society Chili Cook-Off** (☎ 340/776–3595) is a party on Sapphire Beach—you'll find country music performances, dancing, games, and, of course, chili tasting. During full moon in August, anglers from around the world compete for big-money prizes in the **USVI Open/Atlantic Blue Marlin Tournament.** (☎ 340/775–9500)In November the **St. Thomas–St. John Agricultural Fair** (☎ 340/693–1080) showcases fresh produce, home-grown herbs, and local dishes, such as callaloo, salt fish and dumplings, and fresh fish simmered with green banana, pumpkin, and potato-like tannia.

ST. CROIX

The island celebrates Carnival with its **Crucian Christmas Festival,** which starts in late December. After weeks of beauty pageants, food fairs, and concerts, the festival wraps up with a parade in early January. During the **St. Croix Blues and Heritage Festival** (☎ 800/260–2603), in late January, blues artists from the national and local scene play at various locations. In February and March, the **St. Croix Landmarks Society House Tours** (☎ 340/772–0598) visit some of the island's most exclusive or historic homes, and give you a chance to peek inside places you can usually view only from the road.

Serious swimmers should join island residents in early November for the **Coral Reef Swim** (☎ 800/524–2026). Participants swim about 5 mi from Buck Island to Christiansted. The event also includes an awards dinner. **The Mumm's Cup Regatta** (☎ 340/773–9531) sets sail on Veteran's Day weekend at the St. Croix Yacht Club. Sailors converge on Teague Bay for three days of sailing and parties.

ST. JOHN
The island dishes up its own version of Carnival with the **July 4th Festival.** Weeks of festivities—including beauty pageants and a food fair—culminate in a parade through the streets of Cruz Bay on July 4.

On the two days after Thanksgiving, an eclectic group of sailors take to the waters of Coral Bay for the annual **Coral Bay Thanksgiving Regatta.** Some boats are "live-aboards," whose owners only pull up anchor for this one event; other boats belong to Sunday sailors; and a very few are owned by hot-shot racers. If you'd like to crew, stop by Skinny Legs Bar and Restaurant (☞ Dining *in* St. John, *above*) to see who needs help.

Getting Around

AIRPLANES
American Eagle (☞ Arriving and Departing by Airplane, *above*) offers frequent flights daily from St. Thomas to St. Croix's Henry E. Rohlsen Airport (☎ 340/778–0589). **Seaborne Seaplane** (☎ 340/773–5991) also flies between St. Thomas and St. Croix several times daily as well as to Beef Island Airport on Tortola, British Virgin Islands. **LIAT** (☎ 340/774–2313) has service from St. Thomas and St. Croix to Caribbean islands to the south.

BUSES
St. Thomas: The island's 20, deluxe, mainland-size buses make public transportation a very comfortable—though slow—way to get from east and west to Charlotte Amalie and back (service to the north is limited). Buses run about every 30 minutes from stops that are clearly marked with VITRAN signs. Fares are $1 between outlying areas and town and 75¢ in town.

St. Croix: Privately owned **taxi vans** crisscross St. Croix regularly, providing reliable service between Frederiksted and Christiansted along Centerline Road. This inexpensive ($1.50 one-way) mode of transportation is favored by locals, and though the many stops on the 20-mi drive between the two main towns make the ride slow, it's never dull. The new **Vitran** buses are not the quickest way to get around the island, but they're comfortable and affordable. The fare is $1 between Christiansted to Frederiksted or to places in between.

St. John: Modern **Vitran** buses run from the Cruz Bay ferry dock through Coral Bay to the far eastern end of the island at Salt Pond, making numerous stops in between. The fare is $1 to any point.

CAR RENTALS
Any U.S. driver's license is good for 90 days on the USVI; the minimum age for drivers is 18, although many agencies won't rent to anyone under the age of 25.

Driving is on the left side of the road (although your steering wheel will be on the left side of the car). The law requires *everyone* in a car to wear seat belts: Many of the roads are narrow, and the islands are dotted with hills, so there's ample reason to put safety first. Even at a sedate speed of 20 mph, driving can be an adventure—for example, you may find yourself in a stick-shift Jeep slogging behind a slow tourist-packed safari bus at a steep hairpin turn. Give a little beep at blind turns. Note that the general speed limit on these islands is only 25–35 mph, which will seem fast enough for you on most roads. If you don't think you'll need to lock up your valuables, a Jeep or open-air Suzuki with four-wheel-drive will make it easier to navigate pot-holed dirt side roads and to get up slick hills when it rains. All main roads are paved. Gas is pricey: about $1.50 per gallon on St. Thomas, $1.70 on St. Croix, and $1.30 on St. John.

St. Thomas. Traffic can get pretty bad, especially in Charlotte Amalie at rush hour (7–9 AM and 4:30–6 PM). Cars often line up bumper to bumper along the waterfront. If you need to get from an East End re-sort to the airport during these times, find the alternate route (start-ing from the East End, Route 38 to 42 to 40 to 33) that goes up and over the mountain and then drops you back onto Veteran's Highway.

If you plan to explore by car, be sure to get one of the new maps that include the route number *and* the name of the road that's used by lo-cals. The standard USVI map does a pretty good job, but the "Island Map of St. Thomas" (⊠ Earle Publishing, Box 1859, 00801, ☎ 340/777–6557) gives even more detailed names as well as landmarks. It's available anywhere you find maps and guidebooks.

You can rent a car from **ABC Rentals** (☎ 340/776–1222 or 800/524–2080), **Anchorage E-Z Car** (☎ 340/775–6255 or 800/524–2027), **Avis** (☎ 340/774–1468 or 800/331–1084), **Budget** (☎ 340/776–5774 or 800/527–0700), **Cowpet Rent-a-Car** (☎ 340/775–7376 or 800/524–2072), **Dependable Car Rental** (☎ 340/774–2253 or 800/522–3076), **Discount** (☎ 340/776–4858), **Hertz** (☎ 340/774–1879 or 800/654–3131), or **Thrifty** (☎ 340/775–7282).

St. Croix. Unlike St. Thomas and St. John, where narrow roads wind through hillsides, St. Croix is relatively flat, and it even has a four-lane highway. The speed limit on the Melvin H. Evans Highway is 55 mph and ranges from 35 to 40 mph elsewhere. Roads are often unmarked, so be patient; sometimes, getting lost is half the fun.

Occasionally, all the rental companies run out of cars at once. To avoid disappointment, make your reservations early. Call **Atlas** (☎ 340/773–2886 or 800/426–6009), **Avis** (☎ 340/778–9355 or 800/331–1084), **Budget** (☎ 340/778–9636 or 800/527–0700), **Caribbean Jeep & Car** (☎ 340/773–7227), **Midwest** (☎ 340/772–0438), **Olympic** (☎ 340/773–2208 or 888/878–4227), and **Thrifty** (☎ 340/773–7200 or 800/367–2277).

St. John. Use caution on St. John. The terrain is very hilly, the roads winding, and the blind curves numerous. You may suddenly come upon a huge safari bus careening around a corner, or a couple of hikers strolling along the side of the road. Major roads are well paved, but once you get off a specific route, dirt roads filled with potholes are common. For such driving, a four-wheel-drive vehicle is your best bet.

At the height of the winter season, it may be tough to find a car; re-serve well in advance to ensure you get the vehicle of your choice. Call **Avis** (☎ 340/776–6374 or 800/331–1084), **Best** (☎ 340/693–8177), **Cool Breeze** (☎ 340/776–6588), **Delbert Hill Taxi Rental Service** (☎ 340/776–6637), **Denzil Clyne** (☎ 340/776–6715), **O'Connor Jeep** (☎

340/776–6343), **St. John Car Rental** (☎ 340/776–6103), or **Spencer's Jeep** (☎ 340/693–8784 or 888/776–6628).

Ferries are a great way to travel around the islands; there's service between St. Thomas and St. John and their neighbors, the BVI. A hydrofoil also runs the 40-mi route between St. Thomas and St. Croix. There's something special about spending a day on St. John and then joining your fellow passengers—a mix of tourists, local families, and restaurant staffers en route to work—for a peaceful, sundown ride back to St. Thomas.

Ferries to Cruz Bay St. John leave St. Thomas from either the Charlotte Amalie waterfront west of the U.S. Coast Guard dock or from Red Hook. From Charlotte Amalie, ferries depart at 9 and 11 AM and 1, 3, 4, and 5:30 PM. To Charlotte Amalie from Cruz Bay, they leave at 7:15, 9:15, and 11:15 AM and at 1:15, 2:15, and 3:45 PM. The one-way fare for the 45-minute ride is $7 for adults, $3 for children, and $5 for senior citizens with identification. From Red Hook, the ferries to Cruz Bay leave at 6:30 and 7:30 AM. Starting at 8 AM, they leave hourly until midnight. Returning from Cruz Bay, they leave hourly starting at 6 AM until 10 PM. The last ferry heads back to Red Hook at 11:15 PM. The 15- to 20-minute ferry ride is $3 one-way for adults, $1 for children under 12, and $1.25 for senior citizens with identification.

Reefer (☎ 340/776–8500, ext. 445) is the name of both brightly colored 26-passenger skiffs that run between the Charlotte Amalie waterfront and Marriott's Frenchman's Reef hotel daily every hour from 9 to 4, returning from the Reef from 9:30 until 4:30. It's a good way to beat the traffic (and is about the same price as a taxi) to Morning Star Beach, which adjoins the Reef. And you get a great view of the harbor as you bob along in the shadow of the giant cruise ships anchored in the harbor. The captain of the *Reefer* may also be persuaded to drop you at Yacht Haven, but check first. The fare is $4 one-way, and the trip takes about 15 minutes.

The hydrofoil **Katrun II** (☎ 340/776–7417) leaves daily from Charlotte Amalie in St. Thomas at 7:15 AM and 3:15 PM and from Gallows Bay outside Christiansted, St. Croix, at 9:15 AM and 5 PM. The 1¼-hour trip costs $37 one-way and $70 round-trip.

The regular ferry service makes day or overnight trips to the BVI easy. It's a beautiful ride, especially if you arrive early enough to get to a topside seat. Don't be surprised when seagulls ride along with you. You'll need to present proof of citizenship upon entering the BVI; a passport is best, but a birth certificate or voter's registration card will suffice.

There's daily service between either Charlotte Amalie or Red Hook on St. Thomas, and West End or Road Town, Tortola, BVI, by either **Smiths Ferry** (☎ 340/775–7292) or **Native Son, Inc.** (☎ 340/774–8685), and to Virgin Gorda, BVI, by Smiths Ferry. The times and days the ferries run change, so it's best to call for schedules once you're in the islands. The fare is $19 one-way or $35 round-trip, and the trip from Charlotte Amalie takes 45 minutes to an hour to West End, up to 1½ hours to Road Town; from Red Hook, the trip is only a half:hour. The twice-weekly, 2¼-hour trip from Charlotte Amalie to Virgin Gorda costs $28 one-way and $40 round-trip. There's also daily service between Cruz Bay, St. John, and West End, Tortola, aboard the **Sundance** (☎ 340/776–6597). The half-hour one-way trip is $18.

USVI taxis do not have meters, but you need not worry about fare-gouging if you check a list of standard rates to popular destinations (required by law to be carried by each driver and often posted in hotel and airport lobbies and printed in free tourist periodicals, such as *St. Thomas This Week* and *St. Croix This Week,* and settle on the fare before you start out. Fares are per person, not per destination, but drivers taking multiple fares (which often happens, especially from the airport) will charge you a lower rate than if you're in the cab alone.

St. Thomas. Taxis of all shapes and sizes are available at various ferry, shopping, resort, and airport areas, and they also respond quickly to calls. Try **Islander Taxi** (☎ 340/774–4077), the **VI Taxi Association** (☎ 340/774–4550), or **East End Taxi** (☎ 340/775–6974). There are taxi stands in Charlotte Amalie across from Emancipation Garden (in front of Little Switzerland, behind the post office) and along the waterfront. But you probably won't have to look for a stand, as taxis are plentiful and routinely cruise the streets. Walking down Main Street, you'll be asked "Back to ship?" often enough to make you never want to carry another shopping bag.

St. Croix. Taxis, generally station wagons or minivans, are a phone call away from most hotels and are available in downtown Christiansted, at the Alexander Hamilton Airport, and at the Frederiksted pier during cruise-ship arrivals. Try the **St. Croix Taxi Association** (☎ 340/778–1088) at the airport and **Antilles Taxi Service** (☎ 340/773–5020) or **Cruzan Taxi and Tours** (☎ 340/773–6388) in Christiansted.

St. John. Taxis meet ferries arriving in Cruz Bay. Most drivers use vans or open-air safari buses. You'll find them congregated at the dock and at hotel parking lots. You can also hail them anywhere on the road. You're likely to travel with other tourists en route to their destinations. It's very difficult to get taxis to respond to a phone call. If you need one to pick you up at your rental villa, ask the villa manager for suggestions on who to call or arrange a ride in advance.

Guided Tours

BOAT

St. Thomas's **Kon Tiki** party boat (✉ Gregorie Channel East dock, ☎ 340/775–5055) is a kick. Put your sophistication aside, climb on this big palm-thatch raft, and dip into bottomless barrels of rum punch along with a couple hundred of your soon-to-be closest friends. Dance to the steel-drum band, sun on the roof (watch out; you'll fry), and join the limbo dancing on the way home from an afternoon of swimming and beachcombing at Honeymoon Beach on Water Island. This popular three-hour afternoon excursion costs $29 for adults, $15 for children under 13 (although few come to this party).

HELICOPTER AND AIRPLANE

Air Center Helicopters (☎ 340/775–7335), on the Charlotte Amalie waterfront (next to Tortola Wharf) on St. Thomas, has 15-minute island tours priced at $100 per trip. You can also arrange longer flights that loop over to the neighboring BVI, as well as photography tours. **Seaborne Seaplane Adventures** (✉ 5305 Long Bay Rd., ☎ 340/777–4491) offers narrated "flightseeing" tours of the USVI and the BVI from it's Havensight base on St. Thomas. Large windows give exceptional views. The 40-minute "Round-the-Island" tour is $89 per person.

ORIENTATION

V.I. Taxi Association St. Thomas City-Island Tour (☎ 340/774–4550) gives a two-hour $20 tour for two people in an open-air safari bus or enclosed van; aimed at cruise-ship passengers, this tour includes stops at Drake's Seat and Mountain Top. For just a bit more money (about $30 for two) you can hire a taxi and ask the driver to take the opposite route so you'll avoid the crowds. But do see Mountain Top: the view is wonderful.

Tropic Tours (☎ 340/774–1855 or 800/524–4334) offers half-day shopping and sightseeing tours of St. Thomas by bus six days a week ($20 per person). The company also offers a full-day tour (by ferry) to St. John that includes snorkeling and lunch. The cost is $60 per person.

Van tours of St. Croix are offered by **St. Croix Safari Tours** (☎ 340/773–6700) and **St. Croix Transit** (☎ 340/772–3333). The tours, which depart from Christiansted and last about three hours, cost from $25 per person.

St. John taxi drivers provide tours of the island, making stops at various sites including Trunk Bay and Annaberg Plantation. Prices run around $15 a person.

WALKING

The **St. Thomas–St. John Vacation Handbook,** available free at hotels and tourist centers (☞ Visitor Information, *below*), has an excellent self-guided walking tour of Charlotte Amalie on St. Thomas.

Possible nature tours include bird-watching, whale-watching, and waiting hidden on a beach while the magnificent hawksbill turtles come ashore to lay their eggs. Contact the **St. Croix Environmental Association** (✉ Arawak Bldg. #3, Gallows Bay, St. Croix 00820, ☎ 340/773–1989) or **EAST** (✉ Environmental Association of St. Thomas–St. John, Box 12379, St. Thomas 00801, ☎ 340/776–1976) for more information on hikes and special programs, or check the community calendar in the *Daily News* for up-to-date information. **St. Croix Heritage Tours** (✉ Box 7937, Sunny Isle, 00823, ☎ 340/778–6997) leads walks through the historic towns of Christiansted and Frederiksted, detailing the history of the people and the buildings. Custom tours that cover the island are also available.

Along with providing trail maps and brochures about St. John National Park, the park service also gives a variety of guided tours on- and offshore. Note that some of the tours are only offered at certain times of the year, schedules for them vary, and some of them require reservations. For more information or to arrange a tour, contact the **V.I. National Park Visitor's Center** (✉ Cruz Bay, ☎ 340/776–6201; ✉ Cinnamon Bay, ☎ 340/776–6330).

Annaberg Ruins Tour. During the free tour of this fascinating plantation, park rangers discuss how slaves converted sugarcane to sugar and molasses, and tell you about how the red bricks came from Denmark and the yellow from Holland. They also point out the jail where slaves who were thought to be misbehaving were sent to await their fate.

Around-the-Island Snorkel Tour. A motorboat makes a six-hour trip around the island with three stops for snorkeling. You provide your own snorkeling gear and lunch; the cost of the tour is $40.

Bird Walks. Birders are bused to Francis Bay for a two-hour trail walk with a park-ranger guide. The $10 fee covers the cost of round-trip bus transportation.

Cinnamon Bay. Two to three evenings a week rangers hold informal talks on park history, marine research, and other topics. Confirm times, because schedules change often.

Reef Bay Hike. A bus (it costs $4.50 for the ride) takes you from the visitor center to the trailhead, where you begin a vigorous hike that visits petroglyph carvings and an old sugar-mill factory. You'll need serious walking shoes and your own food and drink. An optional return trip by boat ($10) saves you a hike back up the hill (making this a walk of only average difficulty) and will have you back in Cruz Bay by 3:30 PM.

Snorkel Trips. Easy, 1½-hour, free trips start at the Trunk Bay Beach. Bring your own gear and a T-shirt for protection from the sun.

Water's Edge Walk. This free, one-hour walk along the coral flats and mangrove lagoon starts at the shoreline below the Annaberg Plantation parking lot. You'll need wading shoes.

Language

English is the official language, though island residents often speak it with a lilting Creole accent, so you might not recognize certain words at first. If you have trouble understanding someone, ask them to speak slowly. A smile and a "good day" greeting will start any encounter off on the right foot.

Money Matters

The American dollar is used throughout the territory, as well as in the neighboring BVI. All major credit cards and traveler's checks are generally accepted. On St. Thomas, the branch of **First Bank** (☎ 340/776–9494) near Market Square and the waterfront locations of **Banco Popular** (☎ 340/693–2777) and **Chase Manhattan Bank** (☎ 340/775–7777) have automatic teller machines. On St. Croix, contact **Chase Manhattan Bank** (☎ 340/775–7777) or **Banco Popular** (☎ 340/693–2777) for information on branch and ATM locations. On St. John, contact **Chase Manhattan Bank** (☎ 340/775–7777) for branch information, including ATM locations.

SERVICE CHARGES, TAXES, AND TIPPING

Many hotels add a 10% to 15% service charge to cover the room maid and other staff. However, some hotels may use part of that money to fund their operations, passing on only a portion of it to the staff. Check with your maid or bell-boy to determine the hotel's policy. If you discover you need to tip, give bellmen and porters 50¢ to $1 per bag and maids $1 or $2 per day. Special errands or requests of hotel staff always require an additional tip. At restaurants, bartenders and waiters expect a 10% to 15% tip, but always check your tab to see whether or not service has already been included. Taxi drivers get a 15% tip.

There's no sales tax, but there is an 8% hotel-room tax. Departure taxes ($10 for those leaving by air, $5 for those leaving by sea) are generally written into your ticket. The St. John Accommodations Council members ask that hotel and villa guests voluntarily pay a $1-a-day surcharge to help fund school and community projects and other good works.

Opening and Closing Times

BANKS

Bank hours are generally Monday–Thursday 9–3 and Friday 9–5; a handful have Saturday hours (9–noon). Walk-up windows open at 8:30 on weekdays.

SHOPS

In **St. Thomas,** stores on Main Street in Charlotte Amalie are open weekdays and Saturday 9–5. Havensight Mall shops' (next to the cruise-ships dock) hours are the same, though some sometimes stay open until 9 on Friday, depending on how many cruise ships are at the dock. You may also find some shops open on Sunday if a lot of cruise ships are in port. At the American Yacht Harbor in Red Hook, shops are generally open Monday–Saturday 9–6. Hotel shops are usually open evenings, as well.

St. Croix shop hours are usually weekdays 9–5, but you will definitely find some shops in Christiansted open in the evening. Many stores are closed on Sunday.

On **St. John,** store hours run from 9 or 10 to 5 or 6. Wharfside Village and Mongoose Junction shops in Cruz Bay are often open into the evening.

HOLIDAYS

Although the government closes down for 28 days a year, most of these holidays have no affect on shopping hours. Unless there's a cruise ship arrival, expect most stores to close for Christmas and a few other holidays in the slower summer months.

In addition to the U.S. federal holidays, the USVI celebrate: Three Kings Day (Jan. 6); Transfer Day (commemorates Denmark's 1917 sale of the territory to the United States, Mar. 31); Holy Thursday and Good Friday (Apr. 1–2); Organic Act Day (the 1936 date when the U.S. Congress granted home rule and suffrage to the islands, June 16); Emancipation Day (when slavery was abolished in the Danish West Indies in 1848, July 3); Supplication Day (3rd Mon. in July, a day for prayer and protection from storms); Columbus Day and USVI–Puerto Rico Friendship Day (Oct. 11); Hurricane Thanksgiving Day (3rd Mon. in Oct., for the end of storm season); and Liberty Day (honoring Judge David Hamilton Jackson who secured freedom of the press and assembly from King Christian X of Denmark, Nov. 1).

Passports

If you're a U.S. or Canadian citizen, you can prove citizenship with a current or expired (but not by more than five years) passport or with a birth certificate (with a raised seal) along with a government-issued photo ID. U.K. citizens need a passport.

Precautions

Vacationers tend to assume that normal precautions aren't necessary in paradise. They are. Though there isn't quite as much crime here as in large U.S. mainland cities, it does exist. To be safe, stick to well-lighted streets at night, and use the same kind of street sense (don't wander the back alleys of Charlotte Amalie after five rum punches, for example) that you would in any unfamiliar territory. If you plan to carry things around, rent a car—not a Jeep—and lock possessions in the trunk. Keep your rental car locked wherever you park. Don't leave cameras, purses, and other valuables lying on the beach while you snorkel for an hour (or even for a minute), whether you're on the deserted beaches of St. John or the more crowded Magens and Coki beaches on St. Thomas. St. Croix has several remote beaches outside of Frederiksted and on the East End; it's best to visit them with a group rather than on your own. You should always wash produce before eating it. Also note that ciguatera, a toxin found in some reef fish (particularly kingfish), can be a problem at local restaurants.

Telephones and Mail

The area code for all of the USVI is 340, and you can dial direct to and from the mainland. Local calls from a public phone cost 25¢ for each five minutes.

On St. Thomas **Islander Services** (☎ 340/774–8128) at 5302 Store Tvaer Gade, behind the Greenhouse Restaurant in Charlotte Amalie, and **East End Secretarial Services** (☎ 340/775–5262, FAX 340/775–3590), upstairs at the Red Hook Plaza, offer long-distance dialing, copying, and fax services. **AT&T** (☎ 340/777–9201) has a state-of-the-art telecommunications center (it's across from the Havensight Mall) with 15 desk

booths, fax and copy services, video phone, and TDD equipment (
people with hearing impairments), across from the Havensight Ma

On St. Croix, visit **AnswerPLUS** (✉ 5005B Chandler's Wharf, Gallows
Bay, ☎ 340/773–4444) for copying and fax services, mail boxes, and
long-distance dialing. On St. John, the place to go for telephone or message needs is **Connections** (Cruz Bay, ☎ 340/776–6922; Coral Bay, ☎
340/779–4994).

The main **U.S. Post Office** on St. Thomas is near the hospital, with
branches in Charlotte Amalie, Frenchtown, and Tutu Mall; there's a
post office at Christiansted, Frederiksted, Gallows Bay, and Sunny Isle
on St. Croix, and at Cruz Bay on St. John. The postal service offers
Express Mail, one-day service to major cities if you mail before noon;
outlying areas may take two days. Standard postal rates are the same
as elsewhere in the United States.

For overnight **Federal Express** (☎ 340/774–3393) service, you must
get your package to the office at the Havensight Mall (☎ 340/777–
4140) in Charlotte Amalie on St. Thomas before 5 PM or to the St. Croix
office in the Villa La Reine Shopping Center (☎ 340/778–8180) before 4 PM. On St. John, **Sprint Courier Service** (☎ 340/693–8130) connects to all major couriers.

Visitor Information

ST. THOMAS

The **U.S.V.I. Division of Tourism** has an office in Charlotte Amalie (✉
Box 6400, 00804, ☎ 340/774–8784 or 800/372–8784). You'll also
find a visitor center in downtown Charlotte Amalie (☞ see Exploring
St. Thomas, above) and a cruise-ship welcome center at Havensight
Mall. The **National Park Service** has a visitor center across the harbor
from the ferry dock at Red Hook.

ST. CROIX

The **U.S.V.I. Division of Tourism** has offices at 41A and B Queen Cross
Street in Christiansted (✉ Box 4538, 00822, ☎ 340/773–0495) and
on the pier in Frederiksted (✉ Strand St., 00840, ☎ 340/772–0357).

ST. JOHN

There's a branch of the **U.S.V.I. Government Tourist Office** (✉ Box 200,
00830, ☎ 340/776–6450) in the compound between Sparky's and
the U.S. Post Office in Cruz Bay. The **National Park Service** (✉ Box
710, 00831, ☎ 340/776–6201) also has a visitor center at the Creek
in Cruz Bay.

WORLDWIDE

You can get information from the **U.S.V.I. Government Tourist Office**
Web site (www.usvi.net) or from the following locations: ✉ 225
Peachtree St., Suite 760, Atlanta, GA 30303, ☎ 404/688–0906; ✉ 500
N. Michigan Ave., Suite 2030, Chicago, IL 60611, ☎ 312/670–8784;
✉ 3460 Wilshire Blvd., Suite 412, Los Angeles, CA 90010, ☎ 213/
739–0138; ✉ 2655 Le Jeune Rd., Suite 907, Coral Gables, FL 33134,
☎ 305/442–7200; ✉ 1270 Ave. of the Americas, Room 2108, New
York, NY 10020, ☎ 212/332–2222; ✉ 900 17th Ave. NW, Suite 500,
Washington, DC 20006, ☎ 202/293–3707; ✉ 1300 Ashford Ave., Condado, Santurce, Puerto Rico 00907, ☎ 340/724–3816; ✉ 3300 Bloor
St., Suite 3120, Center Tower, Toronto, Ontario, Canada M8X 2X3,
☎ 416/233–1414; and ✉ 2 Cinnamon Row, Plantation Wharf, York
Place, London SW11 3TW, ☎ 0171/978–5262.

A

Acuario National (aquarium), *288*
Administrative Centre, (St. Vincent), *630*
Admiral's House Museum, *55*
Admiralty Bay, *640*
Adventure tours, *xxx*
Ajoupa-Bouillon, Martinique, *423*
Alcazar de Colón (castle), *288*
All Saints Anglican Church, *734*
Allée du Manoir, *353*
Alto Vista Chapel, *82*
Altos de Chavón (16th-century village and art colony), *292–293*
Amber Coast, Dominican Republic, *267, 270–271, 281–282, 294–295*
Amerindian Mini-Museum, *29*
Anancy Family Fun & Nature Park, *395*
Andromeda Gardens, *116*
Anegada, British Virgin Islands, *181–182, 184–187*
Anglican Cathedral (Dominica), *259*
Anglican Cathedral of St. John the Divine (Antigua), *56*
Anguilla, *13–33*
beaches, 25–26
electricity, 31
emergencies, 31
festivals and seasonal events, 31
guided tours, 32
language, 32
lodging, 14–15, 18–21
money matters, 32
nightlife and the arts, 28–29
opening and closing times, 32
outdoor activities and sports, 26–27
passports, 32
precautions, 33
restaurants, 21–25
shopping, 27–28
sightseeing, 29–30
telephones and mail, 33
transportation, 30–32
visitor information, 33
Animal Flower Cave, *115*
Annaberg Plantation, *774*
Annandale Falls and Visitors Centrem, *321*
Anse à Colombier, St. Barthélemy, *503*
Anse-à-l'Ane, Martinique, *427*

Anse Bertrand, Guadeloupe, *351*
Anse-d'Arlets, Martinique, *414, 427*
Anse de Colombier, St. Barthélemy, *503*
Anse-la-Raye, St. Lucia, *581*
Anse-Mitan, Martinique, *427*
Antigua, *6, 7, 34–61*
beaches, 48–49
electricity, 58
emergencies, 58
festivals and seasonal events, 58
guided tours, 59–60
language, 60
lodging, 35, 38–44
money matters, 60
nightlife and the arts, 53–54
opening and closing times, 60
outdoor activities and sports, 49–50
passports, 60
precautions, 61
restaurants, 44–48, 57
shopping, 51–53, 56–57
sightseeing, 54–57
telephones and mail, 61
transportation, 57–59
visitor information, 61
Antigua's sailing week, *58*
Apothecary Hall, *758*
Aquariums, *233–234, 288, 351, 425, 756–757*
Archaeology Museum (Aruba), *83*
Art galleries. ☞ Museums and galleries
Arts. ☞ Nightlife and the arts
Aruba, *6, 62–88*
beaches, 74–75
electricity, 84
emergencies, 84
festivals, 84
guided tours, 86–87
lodging, 63, 66–70
nightlife and the arts, 79–81
opening and closing times, 87
outdoor activities and sports, 75–77
passports, 88
precautions, 88
restaurants, 70–74
shopping, 77–79
sightseeing, 81–84
telephones and mail, 88
transportation, 84, 85
visitor information, 88
Asa Wright Nature Center, *668*
Athenry Gardens, *397–398*
Australia, tips for travelers from, *xviii, xxviii*

B

Bacardi Rum Plant, *462–463*
Bagshaw Studios, *579*
Balashi Gold Smelter (ruins), *83*
Balata, Martinique, *423*
Balata Church, *423*
Balfour Town, Turks and Caicos, *693*
Barahona, Dominican Republic, *271, 293*
Barbados, *6, 7, 89–123*
children, attractions for, 113, 114, 115, 117, 118
electricity, 119
emergencies, 119
festivals and seasonal events, 110
guided tours, 120–121
language, 121–122
lodging, 90–91, 94–99
money matters, 122
nightlife and the arts, 111–113
opening and closing times, 122
outdoor activities and sports, 105–109
passports, 122
precautions, 122–123
restaurants, 99–105
shopping, 109–111
sightseeing, 113–118
telephones and mail, 123
transportation, 118–120
visitor information, 123
Barbados Museum, *113*
Barbados Synagogue, *113–114*
Barbados Wildlife Reserve, *115*
Barbuda, *49, 57*
Barcadera (cavern), *142*
Barclays Park, *116*
Barnett Estates, *394*
Barre de l'Isle Forest Reserve, *578*
Barrilito Rum Plant, *463*
Barrouallie, St. Vincent, *629*
Bas-du-Fort, Guadeloupe, *351*
Baseball, *227, 283–284, 293, 455*
Basketball, *163–164*
Basse-Pointe, Martinique, *405, 408, 415, 424*
Basse-Terre, Guadeloupe, *339–340, 344–345, 353–357*
Basseterre, St. Kitts, *536–537*
Bath Springs, *550*
The Baths (grotto), *177*
Bay Gardens, *321*
Bayamón, Puerto Rico, *463*
Bayfront, Dominica, *259–260*

Index

Beaches, *10*
Anguilla, 25–26
Antigua, 48–49
Aruba, 74–75
Barbados, 104–105
Barbuda, 57
Bonaire, 134–135
British Virgin Islands, 161–162, 174–175, 179, 180
Cayman Islands, 197–198, 206, 208
Curaçao, 224–225
Dominica, 251
Dominican Republic, 281–282
Grenada, 315
the Grenadines, 638, 642, 643, 645, 647
Guadeloupe, 346
Jamaica, 384–385
Martinique, 419
Nevis, 546
St. Barthélemy, 499–500
St. Eustatius, 515–516
St. Kitts, 532–533
St. Lucia, 571
St. Martin/St. Maarten, 603–604
St. Vincent, 626
Trinidad and Tobago, 662–663, 677–678
Turks and Caicos, 689, 693, 697, 701
U.S. Virgin Islands, 724, 750–751, 768–769
Bed-and-breakfasts, *655, 669*
Belair, Grenada, *325*
Bellefontaine, Martinique, *424*
Belmont Walkway, *641*
Bequia, the Grenadines, *632–633, 636–641*
Bethel Methodist Church, *29*
Better Business Bureau, *xvi*
Betty's Hope, Antigua, *54*
Biblioteca Nacional, *292*
Bibliothèque Schoelcher, *425*
Bicycling, *xiv*
Anguilla, 26
Antigua, 49
Aruba, 85
Bonaire, 135, 144–145
Cayman Islands, 210
Dominican Republic, 282
Grenada, 316
Guadeloupe, 346–347, 356
Jamaica, 400
Martinique, 419, 431
Puerto Rico, 453
Turks and Caicos, 689, 692, 697
U.S. Virgin Islands, 725, 751
Bird sanctuaries
Barbuda, 57
Bonaire, 141
Cayman Islands, 207
Grenada, 322, 323
Jamaica, 394
Trinidad, 669

Bird-watching, *208, 260, 385–386, 663, 678*
Black Point Tunnel, *629*
Black Rocks (lava deposits), *537*
Bloody Bay, Jamaica, *395*
Bloody Point, St. Kitts, *537*
Blow Holes, *203*
Blue Lagoon, Jamaica, *397*
Blue Mountains, Jamaica, *391*
Boat travel. ☞ Also Cruises
to Anguilla, 31
to Barbados, 119
to British Virgin Islands, 184, 186
to Guadeloupe, 358
to Nevis, 553
to Saba, 484
to St. Barthélemy, 505
to St. Kitts, 553
to St. Martin/St. Maarten, 611–612
to U.S. Virgin Islands, 776
Boating, *8.* ☞ Also Sailing
Anguilla, 26
Antigua, 49
Bonaire, 137, 145
British Virgin Islands, 163, 175
Curaçao, 225
Dominica, 251
Dominican Republic, 282
Grenada, 315–316
the Grenadines, 638–639, 647–648
Guadeloupe, 347
Martinique, 420
Nevis, 547
Puerto Rico, 452–453
St. Barthélemy, 500
St. Kitts, 533
St. Lucia, 571–572
St. Martin/St. Maarten, 604
St. Vincent, 626
Tobago, 678
Turks and Caicos, 697–698
U.S. Virgin Islands, 724–725, 769
Bob Marley Museum, *393*
Boca Chica, Dominican Republic, *266, 277*
Boca Tabla (grotto), *232*
Bodden Town, Cayman Islands, *203*
Boggy Peak, Antigua, *55*
Boiling Lake, *258*
Bonaire, *7, 124–147*
beaches, 134–135
children, attractions for, 141, 143
electricity, 144
emergencies, 144
festivals and seasonal events, 144
guided tours, 145–146
lodging, 125, 128–131
money matters, 146
nightlife and the arts, 139–140

opening and closing times, 146
outdoor activities and sports, 135–138
passports, 147
precautions, 147
restaurants, 131–134
shopping, 138–139
sightseeing, 140–144
telephones and mail, 147
transportation, 144–145
visitor information, 147
Bordeaux Mountain, *766, 774*
Boston Bay, Jamaica, *397*
Botanical Garden, Puerto Rico, *462*
Botanical Garden, St. Vincent, *631*
Botanical Gardens, Dominica, *259*
Botanical Gardens, Guadeloupe, *354, 356*
The Bottom, Saba, *482–483*
Bouillante, Guadeloupe, *354*
Bowling, *75*
Brewer's Beach, St. Thomas, *739*
Bridgetown, Barbados, *91, 100, 113–115*
Brimstone Hill (fortress), *537*
British Virgin Islands, *7, 148–187*
beaches, 161–162, 174–175, 179, 180
electricity, 184
emergencies, 184–185
festivals, 185
guided tours, 186
language, 186
lodging, 152–153, 156–158, 169, 172, 178, 180, 181, 182, 183
money matters, 186
nightlife and the arts, 166, 176–177
opening and closing times, 186–187
outdoor activities and sports, 162–164, 175
passports, 187
precautions, 187
restaurants, 158–161, 172–174, 178–179, 180, 181–182
shopping, 164–165, 175–176, 182
sightseeing, 167–169, 177–178, 179–180, 181, 182, 183
telephones and mail, 187
transportation, 184, 185–186
visitor information, 168, 187
Buck Island Reef National Monument, *756*
Bushiribana Gold Smelter (ruins), *83*

...onal Park, 255–

...s Conch Farm, 699–700
Caicos Islands. ☞ Turks and
  Caicos Islands
Calibishie, Dominica, 259
California Lighthouse, 82
Calle Las Damas (oldest
  street), 288
Cameras and computers,
  traveling with, xiv–xv
Campgrounds
British Virgin Islands, 158,
  178, 181
Grenada, 316
St. Lucia, 572
U.S. Virgin Islands, 765–766
Canadian travelers, xviii,
  xxvi, xxviii
Canaries, St. Lucia, 581
Cane Bay, 757
Cane Garden Bay, 167
Canouan, the Grenadines,
  641–642
Cap Chevalier, Martinique,
  426
Caparra Ruins, 463
Capilla de los Remedios
  (Chapel of Our Lady of
  Remedies), 288
Capitol building (Puerto
  Rico), 461
Careenage, Barbados, 113
Carenage, Grenada, 323
Carib Indian Territory, 256
Carib petroglyphs, 537, 631
Carib's Leap, 321
Caribbean Cove, 550
Caribbean National Forest,
  463–464
Caroni Bird Sanctuary, 669
Car rentals, xv
Carriacou, Grenada, 310–
  311, 314–315, 325
Casa Armstrong-Poventud
  (offices), 466
Casa Blanca (historic
  home), 458
Casa de Bastidas (historic
  home), 288
Casa de los Jesuitas
  (library), 288
Casa de Tostado (historic
  home), 290
Casa del Cordón (historic
  home), 288, 290
Casa del Libro (museum),
  458
Cascade aux Ecrevisses, 354
Casinos, 6
Antigua, 53
Aruba, 80
Bonaire, 140
Curaçao, 229
Dominican Republic, 286–287
Guadeloupe, 350
Martinique, 422–423
Puerto Rico, 457

St. Kitts, 536
St. Martin/St. Maarten, 608
St. Vincent, 628
Castillo Serrallés (museum),
  466–467
Castles
Barbados, 118
Cayman Islands, 204
Dominican Republic, 288
Martinique, 424
Castries, St. Lucia, 558–559,
  562–565, 578–583
Catedral de San Felipe, 295
Catedral Santa Mariá la
  Menor, 290
Cathédrale de St-Pierre et St-
  Paul, 352
Cathedral of Our Lady of
  Guadeloupe, 353
Cathedral of St. Peter and St.
  Paul, 734
Cathedral of the Immaculate
  Conception, 579
Catherineberg Ruins, 774
Caverns
Aruba, 82
Barbados, 115, 117
Bonaire, 142
Cayman Islands, 203, 207
Curaçao, 234
Dominican Republic, 293
Jamaica, 396–398
Puerto Rico, 467
Saba, 483
Cayman Brac, Cayman
  Islands, 204, 206–207,
  209–213
Cayman Brac Museum, 207
Cayman Islands, 3, 188–213
beaches, 197–198, 206, 208
electricity, 209
emergencies, 209
festivals, 209–210
guided tours, 210–211
language, 211–212
lodging, 189, 191–194, 204,
  206, 207–208
money matters, 212
nightlife, 201
opening and closing times, 212
outdoor activities and sports,
  198–200, 206–207, 208–
  209
passports, 212
precautions, 212
restaurants, 195–197
shopping, 200–201
sightseeing, 201–204, 207
telephones and mail, 213
transportation, 209, 210
visitor information, 213
Cayman Islands Legislative
  Assembly Building, 202
Cayman Islands National
  Museum, 202
Cayman Islands Turtle Farm,
  203
Cayman Maritime Treasure
  Museum, 202

Centre de Broderie, 356
Centro de Bellas Artes
  (Puerto Rico), 461–462
Champ d'Arbaud, 354
Chapel of Our Lady of
  Antigua, 290
Charlestown, Nevis, 550–
  551
Charlotte Amalie, St. Thomas,
  713, 716, 718, 720–723,
  734, 736–738
Charlotteville, Tobago, 680–
  681
Château Murat, 357
Chaud dwe, 259
Children, traveling with, xv–
  xvi
Choiseul, St. Lucia, 581
Christiansted, St. Croix, 744,
  748–749, 755–757, 759–
  760
Christoffel Park, 232–233
Church of St. Paul's
  Conversion, 484
Churches
Anguilla, 29
Antigua, 55, 56
Aruba, 82
Barbados, 114
Cayman Islands, 202
Dominica, 259
Dominican Republic, 288,
  290–291, 292, 294, 295
Grenada, 324
Guadeloupe, 352, 353
Jamaica, 398–399
Martinique, 423, 425, 428
Nevis, 551
Puerto Rico, 459, 460–461,
  466, 467
Saba, 482–483, 484
St. Eustatius, 518
St. Kitts, 537
St. Lucia, 579
St. Vincent, 631
U.S. Virgin Islands, 734, 736,
  737, 759
Chutes du Carbet (Carbet
  Falls), 354
Cibao Valley, Dominican
  Republic, 293–294
Cinnamon Bay Beach, 774
Circus, St. Kitt, 537
City Hall (Puerto Rico),
  438–439
Climate, xxxi–xxxii
Clothing for the trip, xxvii
Coastal islands, British Virgin
  Island, 177
Cockburn Town, Turks and
  Caicos, 692–693
Cockpit Country, Jamaica,
  391
Codrington, Barbuda, 57
Codrington Theological
  College, 116
Coffee, 391, 394, 467
Coki Point, St. Thomas, 739
Colonaire, St. Vincent, 629

Compass Point Marina, *739*
Concepción de la Vega, *294*
Concord Falls, *321*
Condominiums
Anguilla, *19–21*
Barbados, *99*
Cayman Islands, *193–194,
    206*
U.S. Virgin Islands, *719, 747,
    764–765*
Consumer protection, *xvi*
Convent of La Merced, *294*
Cooper Island, British Virgin
    Islands, *182, 184–187*
Copper Mine Point, *177*
Coral Bay, St. John, *766,
    774*
Coral World Marine Park,
    739
Corossol, St. Barthélemy, *503*
Country House Museum, *233*
Courthouse (Cayman
    Islands), *202*
Courthouse (Nevis), *550*
Cove Bay, Saba, *483*
Coyaba River Garden and
    Museum, *396*
Cramer's Park, *757*
Crater Lake, *322*
Credit and debit cards, *xvi,
    xxi, xxvi*
Cricket
Antigua, *50*
Barbados, *108*
British Virgin Islands, *164,
    175*
Cayman Islands, *200*
St. Eustatius, *516–517*
St. Lucia, *574*
Cristo Chapel, *459*
Crocus Hill Prison, *29*
Cruises, *xvi–xvii*
Cruz Bay, St. John, *766–768,
    774*
Crystal Springs, Jamaica,
    391
Cuisine, *6–7*
Curaçao, *6, 7, 214–238*
beaches, *224–225*
children, attractions for, *233–
    234*
electricity, *235*
emergencies, *235*
festivals and seasonal events,
    235–236
guided tours, *236–237*
language, *237*
lodging, *215–217, 220–221*
money matters, *237*
nightlife, *229–230*
opening and closing times, *238*
outdoor activities and sports,
    225–227
passports, *238*
precautions, *238*
restaurants, *221–224*
shopping, *227–229*
sightseeing, *230–235*
telephone and mail, *238*

transportation, *235, 236*
visitor information, *238*
Curaçao Museum, *230*
Curaçao Seaquarium, *233–
    234*
Curaçao Underwater Marine
    Park, *234*
Currency exchange, *xxvi*
Curtain Bluff, Antigua, *54–
    55*
Customs and duties, *xvii–xix*

D

D. Hamilton Jackson Park,
    756
Danish Consulate Building,
    734
Danish Customs House, *756*
D'Auchamps Gardens, *260*
de la Grenade Industries
    (spice processing plant),
    324
Devil's Bridge (natural
    formation), *55*
Devon House, *392–393*
Diamond Botanical Gardens,
    581
Diamond Rock, Martinique,
    424
Diamond Waterfall, *581*
Dining. ☞ Restaurants
Disabilities and accessibility,
    xix–xx
Discounts and deals, *xx–xxi*
Discovery Bay, Jamaica, *384,
    396*
Distilleries
Barbados, *115–116, 118*
Curaçao, *235*
Dominican Republic, *293*
Grenada, *323*
Guadeloupe, *355–356, 357*
Jamaica, *391*
Martinique, *426*
Puerto Rico, *462–463*
Diving. ☞ Scuba diving
Dog Islands, British Virgin
    Islands, *177*
Dr. Sangster's Rum Factory,
    391
Domaine de Valombreuse,
    355
Dominica, *7, 239–263*
beaches, *251*
electricity, *261*
emergencies, *261*
festivals and seasonal events,
    261
guided tours, *262*
language, *262*
lodging, *240–241, 244–248*
money matters, *262*
nightlife and the arts, *254–255*
opening and closing times, *262*
outdoor activities and sports,
    251–253
passports, *262*
precautions, *263*
restaurants, *248–251*

shopping, *253–254*
sightseeing, *255–260*
telephones and mail, *263*
transportation, *260–262*
visitor information, *263*
Dominica Museum, *259–260*
Dominican Convent, *459*
Dominican Republic, *3, 6, 7–
    8, 264–301*
beaches, *281–282*
children, attractions for, *288,
    290, 293*
electricity, *297*
emergencies, *297*
festivals and seasonal events,
    297
guided tours, *299–300*
language, *300*
lodging, *265–267, 270–276*
money matters, *300*
nightlife, *286–287*
opening and closing times,
    300
outdoor activities and sports,
    282–284
passports, *300*
precautions, *300–301*
restaurants, *276–281*
shopping, *284–285*
sightseeing, *287–288, 290–
    296*
telephones and mail, *301*
transportation, *296–299*
visitor information, *301*
Dougaldston Spice Estate,
    321–322
Dows Hill Interpretation
    Center, *57*
Drake's Seat (overlook),
    739–740
Dubuc Castle, *424*
Dunn's River Falls, *396*
Dutch Reformed Church (St.
    Eustatius), *518*
Dutch Reformed Church (St.
    Thomas), *734*

E

East End, Anguilla, *24–25*
East End, Cayman Islands,
    203
Ecotourism, *xxi*
Eden Brown Estate, *551*
Edgar-Clerc Archaeological
    Museum, *351*
Educator's Park, *736*
El Batey, Dominican Republic,
    296
El Faro a Colón (Columbus
    Memorial Lighthouse),
    290
El Malecón, *291*
Elaine Ione Sprauve Library
    and Museum, *775*
Electrical current, *xxi*
Emancipation Garden, *736*
Emancipation Memorial,
    116
Emerald Pool, *256*

Emergencies
Anguilla, 31
Antigua, 58
Aruba, 84
Barbados, 119
Bonaire, 144
British Virgin Islands, 184–185
Cayman Islands, 209
Curaçao, 235
Dominica, 261
Dominican Republic, 297
Grenada, 326
the Grenadines, 649
Guadeloupe, 358
Jamaica, 399
Martinique, 430
Nevis, 552
Puerto Rico, 468
Saba, 484–485
St. Barthélemy, 505
St. Eustatius, 519
St. Kitts, 552
St. Martin/St. Maarten, 612
St. Vincent, 648
Trinidad and Tobago, 682
U.S. Virgin Islands, 776–777
Emperor Valley Zoo and the Botanical Gardens, 667
English Harbour, Antigua, 55
Enid M. Baa Public Library, 736
Errard Plantation, 579
Estate Mount Washington Plantation, 757–758
Estate St. Peter Greathouse Botanical Gardens, 740
Estate Whim Plantation Museum, 759
Etang As de Pique, 354
Etang Zombi, 354

F

Fallen Jerusalem, British Virgin Islands, 177
Falls of Baleine, 629
Falmouth, Antigua, 55
Farley Hill, 115
Fig Tree Drive, Antigua, 55
Firefly (Coward home), 392
Fisherman's Museum, 322
Fishing
Anguilla, 26
Antigua, 49
Aruba, 75
Barbados, 105
Bonaire, 135
British Virgin Islands, 163, 175
Cayman Islands, 198, 208–209
Curaçao, 225
Dominican Republic, 282
Grenada, 316
Guadeloupe, 347
Jamaica, 386
Martinique, 420
Nevis, 547
Puerto Rico, 453

Saba, 481
St. Barthélemy, 500
St. Eustatius, 516
St. Kitts, 533
St. Martin/St. Maarten, 604
Trinidad and Tobago, 663, 678
Turks and Caicos, 698
U.S. Virgin Islands, 725, 751, 769
Fitness centers
Antigua, 49
Curaçao, 225–226
Martinique, 421
St. Martin/St. Maarten, 604–605
Flagstaff Hill, 681
Flamingos, 141, 701
Flat Point, Saba, 483
Floating Market, 230
Flower Forest, 116–117
Flying (sport), 347
Fodor's choice, 10–12
Folkestone Marine Park & Visitor Centre, 115
Folly (villa ruins), 397
Fontein (cave), 82
The Forest, Anguilla, 23–24
Forêt de Montravail, Martinique, 424
Fort Amsterdam, 230
Fort Ashby, 551
Fort Bay, Saba, 483
Fort Burt, 167
Ft. Charles (Jamaica), 398
Fort Charlotte (St. Lucia), 579–580
Fort Charlotte (St. Vincent), 629–630
Fort Christian, 736
Fort Christiansvaern, 756
Fort-de-France, Martinique, 409, 415–416, 424–426
Fort Duvernette, 630
Fort Fleur d'Epée, 351
Fort Frederick, 324
Fort Frederik, 759
Fort George (Antigua), 55
Fort George (Grenada), 324
Fort James, 55
Fort King George, 681
Fort Louis Delgrès, 353
Fort Napoléon, 356–357
Fort Oranje (Bonaire), 141
Fort Recovery, 167
Fort St-Louis, 425
Fort San Gerómino, 462
Fort Shirley, 255–256
Fort Zoutman, 83
Fortaleza de San Felipe, 295
Forts
Antigua, 55
Aruba, 83
Bonaire, 141
British Virgin Islands, 167, 177
Curaçao, 230
Dominica, 255–256

Dominican Republic, 290–291, 295
Grenada, 324
Guadeloupe, 351, 353, 356–357
Jamaica, 396, 398
Martinique, 425
Nevis, 551
Puerto Rico, 460, 462
St. Kitts, 537
St. Lucia, 579–580
St. Vincent, 629–630
Tobago, 681
U.S. Virgin Islands, 736, 756, 759
Francia Plantation House, 117
Francisco Oller Art and History Museum, 463
Frederik Lutheran Church, 736
Frederiksted, St. Croix, 745, 750, 758–760
Fregate Island Nature Reserve, 582
French Cul de Sac, St. Martin/St. Maarten, 609
Frenchman's Cay, 167
Frenchman's Pass, 82–83
Frenchtown, St. Thomas, 717–718, 740
Freshwater Lake, 258
Friar's Beach, 609
Fuerte San Felipe del Morro, 460
Further reading on the Caribbean, xxii

G

Gardens
Barbados, 116–117
British Virgin Islands, 167
Cayman Islands, 204
Curaçao, 232–233
Dominica, 259, 260
Dominican Republic, 291
Grenada, 321, 322
Guadeloupe, 353–354, 355, 356
Jamaica, 393, 396–398
Martinique, 423, 425
Nevis, 551
Puerto Rico, 462
St. Lucia, 581
St. Vincent, 631
Trinidad, 667, 668
U.S. Virgin Islands, 736, 740, 741, 759
Gay and lesbian travelers, hints for, xxii–xxiii
General Post Office (Cayman Islands), 202
George Hill, Anguilla, 23–24
George Town, Cayman Islands, 202
George Washington House, 117
Georgetown, St. Vincent, 630

Golf, 8
Antigua, 49
Aruba, 75–76
Barbados, 105–106
Cayman Islands, 198
Curaçao, 226
Dominican Republic, 282–283
Grenada, 316
Guadeloupe, 347
Jamaica, 386
Martinique, 420
Nevis, 547
Puerto Rico, 453–454
St. Kitts, 533
St. Martin/St. Maarten, 605
tours, xxx
Trinidad and Tobago, 663, 678
Turks and Caicos Islands, 698
U.S. Virgin Islands, 725, 751
Gorges de la Falaise, 423
Gosier, Guadeloupe, 351
Goto Meer (saltwater lagoon), 142
Gouyave Nutmeg Processing Cooperative, 322
Government House (St. Croix), 756
Government House (St. Lucia), 580
Government House (St. Thomas), 736–737
Grand Anse, Grenada, 322
Grand Case, St. Martin, 609
Grand Cayman, Cayman Islands, 189, 191–204, 209–213
Grand Cul de Sac, St. Barthélemy, 503
Grand Hotel Court, 737
Grande Saline, St. Barthélemy, 504
Grand Etang National Park, 322
Grand' Rivière, Martinique, 426
Grand Turk, the Turks, 687–689, 692–693
Grande-Terre, Guadeloupe, 333–335, 338–339, 342–344, 351–353
Greater Antilles, 6
Green Grotto Caves, Jamaica, 396–397
Greenwood Great House, 394–395
Grenada, 7, 302–331
beaches, 315
children, attractions for, 322
electricity, 326
emergencies, 326
festivals, 326–327
guided tours, 328–329
language, 329
lodging, 303–305, 308–311
money matters, 329
nightlife and the arts, 319–321
opening and closing times, 330

outdoor activities and sports, 315–317
passports, 330
precautions, 330
restaurants, 311–315
shopping, 318–319
sightseeing, 321–325
telephones and mail, 330
transportation, 325–326, 327–328
visitor information, 330–331
Grenada National Museum, 323
the Grenadines, 616–618, 632–633, 636–653
Grenadines Wharf, 630
Grenville, Grenada, 322
Grenville Cooperative Nutmeg Association, 322
Gros Islet, St. Lucia, 580
Guadeloupe, 6, 7, 332–361
beaches, 346
electricity, 358
emergencies, 358
festivals, 358
guided tours, 359–360
language, 360
lodging, 333–335, 338–341
money matters, 360
nightlife, 350
opening and closing times, 360
outdoor activities and sports, 346–348
passports, 360
precautions, 361
restaurants, 341–346
shopping, 348–350
sightseeing, 350–357
telephones and mail, 361
transportation, 357–359
visitor information, 361
Guadeloupe Aquarium, 351
Guadirikiri (cave), 82
Guana Bay Point, St. Martin/St. Maarten, 609
Guana Island, British Virgin Islands, 183, 184–187
Guest houses and lodges
Cayman Islands, 193
Dominica, 246–248
U.S. Virgin Islands, 718
Gun Hill Signal Station, Barbados, 117
Gustavia, St. Barthélemy, 504

H

Habitation Clément, 426
Hacienda Buena Vista (restored coffee plantation), 467
Hamilton Battery, 641
Harmony Hall, 55–56
Harrison's Cave, 117
Harry Bayley Observatory, Barbados, 114
Hassel Island, St. Thomas, 737

Hato Caves, 234
Health issues, xxiii. ☞ Also Precautions under specific islands
Hell, Cayman Islands, 203
Hell's Gate, Saba, 483
Heritage Collection, 29
Heritage Passport, 113
Heritage Quay, 56–57
High Mountain Coffee Plantation, 394
Hiking
Aruba, 76
Barbados, 106
Cayman Islands, 198
Dominica, 252
Dominican Republic, 283
Grenada, 316–317
the Grenadines, 643
Guadeloupe, 347
Martinique, 420
Nevis, 547
Puerto Rico, 454
Saba, 481
St. Eustatius, 516
St. Kitts, 533–534
St. Lucia, 572
St. Vincent, 626–627
Tobago, 678–679
U.S. Virgin Islands, 751, 769–770
Hindu temple, 424
Historic Homes
Barbados, 116, 117, 118
Bonaire, 142
Cayman Islands, 203
Curaçao, 234, 235
Dominica, 258
Dominican Republic, 288, 290
Grenada, 324
Jamaica, 392–393, 394–395, 397
Martinique, 426
Nevis, 551
Puerto Rico, 458
St. Kitts, 537–538
Trinidad and Tobago, 667–668, 669
U.S. Virgin Islands, 757, 758
Historical Museum (Grenada), 325
History of Caribbean, 7–8
Holy Rosary Church, 483
Home and apartment rentals, xxv
Bonaire, 125
British Virgin Islands, 157–158, 172
Grenada, 310
Puerto Rico, 435–436
Saba, 478
St. Eustatius, 514
U.S. Virgin Islands, 719, 748
Home exchanges, xxv
Honen Dalim (synagogue), 518
Hooiberg (Haystack Hill), 83

Horse racing
Barbados, 108
Dominican Republic, 284
Nevis, 548
Puerto Rico, 455
U.S. Virgin Islands, 725
Horseback riding
Anguilla, 26
Antigua, 49–50
Aruba, 76
Barbados, 106
Bonaire, 135
British Virgin Islands, 162–163
Curaçao, 226
Dominican Republic, 283
the Grenadines, 645
Guadeloupe, 347
Jamaica, 386–387
Martinique, 420
Nevis, 547
Puerto Rico, 454
St. Barthélemy, 500
St. Kitts, 534
St. Lucia, 573
St. Martin/St. Maarten, 605
U.S. Virgin Islands, 751–752, 770
Hostal Palacio Nicolás de Ovando (historic home), 290
Hosteling, xxv–xxvi
Hot springs
Dominica, 258
Guadeloupe, 354
Nevis, 550
St. Lucia, 581
Hotel 1829, 737
Hotels, xxiv–xxv, 10–11
Anguilla, 14–15, 18–19
Antigua, 35, 38–44
Aruba, 63, 66–70
Barbados, 90–91, 94–99
Bonaire, 125, 128–131
British Virgin Islands, 152–153, 156–157, 168–169, 172, 178, 180, 181, 182, 183
Cayman Islands, 189, 191–193, 204, 206, 207–208
children, accommodations for, xvi
Curaçao, 215–217, 220–221
disabilities and accessibility, xix
Dominica, 240–241, 244–246
Dominican Republic, 265–267, 270–276
Grenada, 303–305, 308–311
the Grenadines, 632–633, 636, 641–644, 646–647, 647
Guadeloupe, 333–335, 338–341
Jamaica, 363–365, 368–380
Martinique, 405, 408–413
Nevis, 538–539, 542–543
Puerto Rico, 435–436, 438–441, 445–446

Saba, 474–475, 478
St. Barthélemy, 488–489, 492–495
St. Eustatius, 510–511
St. Kitts, 522–523, 526–529
St. Lucia, 558–559, 562–567
St. Martin/St. Maarten, 590–591, 594–598
St. Vincent, 618–619, 622–623
Trinidad and Tobago, 655, 658–660, 669, 672–674
Turks and Caicos, 687–688, 693, 694–696, 700–701
U.S. Virgin Islands, 712–713, 716–718, 741, 744–747, 761, 764
Hull Bay, St. Thomas, 740
Hurricane Hill, 551

I

Iglesia St. Stanislaus, 293
Iglesia Santa Bárbara, 290–291
Iglesia y Convento Dominico, 290
Iles des Saintes, Guadeloupe, 340–341, 345–346, 356–357
Indian inscriptions, 143
Indian River, 256–257
Indian Town (national park), 56
Institute of Jamaica, 393
Insurance, xxiii–xxiv
car rental, xv
for travelers from the U.K., xxiv
Isla Saona (park), 293
Island Harbour, Anguilla, 30
Island Sea Center, 699–700

J

J. R. O'Neal Botanic Gardens, 167
J. W. Edwards Building, 259
Jamaica, 6, 7, 362–403
beaches, 384–385
electricity, 399
emergencies, 399
festivals and seasonal events, 399
guided tours, 400–402
language, 402
lodging, 363–365, 368–380
money matters, 402
nightlife and the arts, 389–390
opening and closing times, 402
outdoor activities and sports, 385–387
passports, 402
precautions, 402–403
restaurants, 380–384
shopping, 387–389
sightseeing, 390–399
telephones and mail, 403
transportation, 399–400
visitor information, 403

Jamaican People's Museum of Crafts and Technology, 398–399
Jarabacoa, Dominican Republic, 294
Jardin Botánico Nacional Dr. Rafael M. Moscoso, 291
Jardin de Balata, 423
Jardin Pichon, 353–354
Jewish Cultural Museum, 231
JM Distillery, 426
JoJo Dolphin Project, 699–700
Jost Van Dyke, British Virgin Islands, 178–179, 184–187
Juan Dolio, Dominican Republic, 266, 278, 293
Judith's Fancy (historic home), 758

K

Karl and Marie Lawaetz Museum, 759
Kew, Turks and Caicos, 701
Kingston, Jamaica, 364–365, 368, 380–381, 384, 392–393
Kingstown, St. Vincent, 618–619, 624–625, 630–631
Kingstown Methodist Church, 631
Kralendijk, Bonaire, 140–141

L

La Atarazana (Royal Mooring Docks), 288
La Désirade, Guadeloupe, 357
La Fortaleza (executive mansion), 459
La Intendencia (historical building), 460
La Maison du Bois (museum), 355
La Maison du Cacao (museum), 355
La Perla Theater, 466
La Pointe de la Grande Vigie, Guadeloupe, 351
La Romana, Dominican Republic, 271–272, 277
La Savane (park), 424–435
La Soufrière Drive-in Volcano, 583
La Soufrière Volcano, 3, 632
La Trinité, Martinique, 412, 418
La Vallée des Papillons, 429–430
La Vega Vieja (ruins), 294
Laborie, St. Lucia, 582
Ladder Bay, Saba, 483
Lago Enriquillo, 293
Laguana Grí-Grí (swampland), 295
Lamentin, Martinique, 410, 416–417, 426

Landhuis Brievengat (historic home), 234
Landhuis Jan Kok (historic home), 234
Landhuis Karpata (historic home), 142
Landhuis Knip (historic home), 235
Language, xxiv
Las Cabezas de San Juan Nature Reserve, 463
Las Terrenas, Dominican Republic, 295–296
Laura Herb and Spice Garden, 322
Layou, St. Vincent, 631
Layou River Valley, 257
Le Diamant, Martinique, 408–409, 415
Le Domaine de Séverin (distillery), 355–356
Le François, Martinique, 409–410, 416, 426
Le Marin, Martinique, 426
Le Morne Rouge, Martinique, 426–427
Le Moule, Guadeloupe, 351
Le Prêcheur, Martinique, 427–428
Le Robert, Martinique, 426
Le Vauclin, Martinique, 430
Learning tours, xxx
Leewards, 3
Legislature Building (St. Thomas), 737
Les Islets de l'Impératrice, 426
Les Mamelles (mountains), 354
Les Ombrages (botanical gardens), 423
Les Trois-Ilets, Martinique, 412–413, 418–419, 429
L'Escalier Tête Chien (lava staircase), 256
Lesser Antilles, 6
Levera National Park and Bird Sanctuary, 323
Leyritz Plantation, 424
Liberta, Antigua, 55
Libraries
 Cayman Islands, 202
 Dominica, 259
 Dominican Republic, 288, 292
 Jamaica, 393
 Martinique, 425
 Nevis, 550
 U.S. Virgin Islands, 736, 775
Lighthouses
 Aruba, 82
 Barbados, 117
 Bonaire, 142
 Dominican Republic, 290
 Jamaica, 395
Little Cayman, Cayman Islands, 207–213
Little Fort National Park, 177
Little Tokyo, St. Vincent, 630–631

Little Water Cay, 700
Lodging, xxiv–xxvi, 10–12. ☞ Also Bed-and-breakfasts; campgrounds; condominiums; home and apartment rentals; hotels; villa rentals; under specific islands
Londonderry Estate, 258
Long Bay, Jamaica, 395
Lopinot Complex, 669
Lorient, St. Barthélemy, 504
Los Charamicos, Dominican Republic, 296
Los Haitises National Park, 295
Lover's Leap, 394
Luggage, xxvi–xxvii
Luis Muñoz Marin Park, 462
Luxury resorts, 10–11

M

Macorís Rum distillery, 293
Macouba, Martinique, 417, 426
Magens Bay Beach, 740
Magnificent Seven (historic homes), 667–668
Maison de la Canne (sugar farm), 427–428
Maison de la Forêt, 355
Mandeville, Jamaica, 368, 393–394
Maria Islands Nature Reserve, 582
Marie-Galante, Guadeloupe, 341, 346, 357
Marigot, Dominica, 258
Marigot, Martinique, 410
Marigot, St. Martin/St. Maarten, 609–610
Marigot Bay, St. Lucia, 580
Marina Cay, British Virgin Islands, 183, 184–187
Marquis Estate, 580
Marryshow House, 324
Marshall's Penn Great House, 394
Martello Tower, 57
Martha Brae River, 394
Martinique, 6, 7, 404–433
 beaches, 419
 electricity, 430
 emergencies, 430
 festivals and seasonal events, 430
 guided tours, 431–432
 language, 432
 lodging, 405, 408–414
 money matters, 432
 nightlife, 422–423
 opening and closing times, 432
 outdoor activities and sports, 419–421
 passports, 432–433
 precautions, 433
 restaurants, 414–419
 shopping, 421–422

 sightseeing, 423–430
 telephones and mail, 433
 transportation, 430, 431
 visitor information, 433
Mastic Trail, Cayman Islands, 203
Matouba, Guadeloupe, 354
Mavis Bank (coffee farm), 391
Medical services, xxiii. ☞ Also Emergencies
Megaliths of Greencastle Hill, 56
Memorial Moravian Church, 737
Memorial United Church, 202
Mesopatamia Valley, St. Vincent, 631
Middle Caicos, 701
Middle Island, St. Kitts, 537
Middleham Falls, 258
Mikveh Israel-Emmanuel Synagogue, 231
Mineral Baths, 393, 581
Molasses Reef, 694
Monasterio de San Francisco (San Francisco Monastery), 291
Money, xxvi
Mont Pelée (volcano), 426–427
Montego Bay, Jamaica, 368–372, 381–382, 384–385, 394–395
Montesina (statue), 291
Montserrat, 3
Morne-à-l'Eau, Guadeloupe, 351
Morne Aux Diables, 257
Morne Coubaril Estate, 582
Morne-des-Esses, Martinique, 417
Morne Diablotin, 257
Morne Fortune, St. Lucia, 580
Morne Trois Pitons National Park, 257–258
Mt. Brandaris, 143
Mount Eagle, 758
Mount Gay Rum Visitors Centre, 115–116
Mt. Healthy National Park, 167
Mt. Isabel de Torres, 295
Mt. Pleasant, 641
Mt. Rodney Estate, 323
Mt. Scenery, 483
Mountain Top, 740
Musée de la Banane (Banana Museum), 428
Musée de la Pagerie, 429
Musée Départementale de Martinique, 425
Musée du Rhum, 355–356, 428
Musée Gauguin, 427
Musée St-John Perse, 352
Musée Schoelcher, 352
Musée Vulcanologique, 429

Museo de Ambar Dominicano
(Dominican Amber
Museum), 295
Museo de Arte Moderno
(Museum of Modern
Art), 292
Museo de Historia Natural
(Museum of Natural
History), 292
**Museo de la Familia
Dominicana**, 290
Museo de las Casas Reales,
291
**Museo del Hombre
Dominicano** (Museum of
Dominican Man), 292
**Museum of Antigua and
Barbuda**, 56
**Museum of Contemporary
Puerto Rican Art**, 462
Museum of Nevis History,
550–551
**Museum of the Conquest and
Colonization of Puerto
Rico**, 463
Museums and galleries
Anguilla, 29
Antigua, 55–56, 57
Barbados, 112, 113, 115, 118
British Virgin Islands, 167
Cayman Islands, 202, 207
Curaçao, 230, 231, 233
Dominica, 259–260
Dominican Republic, 288,
290, 291, 292, 295
Grenada, 322, 323, 325
the Grenadines, 641
Guadeloupe, 351, 352, 355–
356
Jamaica, 392–393, 395, 396,
398–399
Martinique, 425, 427–428,
429
Nevis, 550–551
Puerto Rico, 458, 460, 461,
462–463, 466–467
Saba, 484
St. Eustatius, 518
St. Martin/St. Maarten, 610
St. Vincent, 631
Trinidad, 668, 669
Turks and Caicos, 692–693
U.S. Virgin Islands, 738, 740,
759, 775
Music, 6

N

National Gallery (Jamaica),
393
National Museum (St.
Vincent), 631
**National Museum and Art
Gallery** (Trinidad), 668
Natural Bridge, 83
Nature reserves
Barbados, 115
Bonaire, 143
British Virgin Islands, 168,
177, 178

Cayman Islands, 204
Curaçao, 232–233
Dominica, 256–258, 260
Dominican Republic, 293, 295
Grenada, 322, 323
Guadeloupe, 354–355
Puerto Rico, 463–464
St. Lucia, 578, 582–583
Trinidad, 668
U.S. Virgin Islands, 758
**Necker Island, British Virgin
Islands**, 183, 184–187
Negril, Jamaica, 372–374,
383, 385, 395
Nelson Museum, 551
Nelson Spring, 551
Nelson's Dockyard, 55
Nevis, 7, 521–522, 538–
539, 542–555
Nevis Botanical Gardens,
551
Nevis House of Assembly,
550–551
**New Zealand, tips for
travelers from**, xviii,
xxviii
Nightlife and the arts, 6. ☞
Also under specific
islands
99 Steps (staircase street),
737
Nonsuch Caves, 397–398
North Caicos, 700–701
North Shore Shell Museum,
167
Northeast Coast, Dominica,
258–259
Northwest Reef, 694
Numismatic Museum, 83

O

Ocho Rios, Jamaica, 374–
377, 383–384, 385, 396–
397
Oistins, Barbados, 117
Old Factory, 30
Old Fort, 396
Old Gin House, 518
Old Homestead, 203
Old Market (Marche), 231
Old Road Town, St. Kitts, 537
Old San Juan, Puerto Rico,
436, 438, 447–450, 458–
461
Old Sulphur Mine Walk, 483
1,000 Steps (limestone
staircase), 142–143
Onima, Bonaire, 143
Oranjestad, Aruba, 83
**Orléans, St. Martin/St.
Maarten**, 610
**Our Lady of Guadelupe
Cathedral**, 466
Outdoor activities and sports,
8–9. ☞ Also under
specific islands
Owia, St. Vincent, 631
**Oyster Pond, St. Martin/St.
Maarten**, 610

P

Pablo Casals Museum, 460
Package deals, xxi, xxx
Packing for the Caribbean,
xxvi–xxvii
Palacio de Borgella, 271–
292
Palm Island, the Grenadines,
646
Pantheon Nacional, 291
Paradise Point Tramway, 740
Parasailing
Aruba, 76
Barbados, 106
Bonaire, 135
St. Lucia, 573
St. Martin/St. Maarten, 605
Turks and Caicos, 698
U.S. Virgin Islands, 725
**Parc Archeologique des
Roches Gravées**, 354
Parc Floral et Culturel, 425
**Parc National de la
Guadeloupe**, 354–355
Parc Tropical de Bras-David,
355
Parham, Antigua, 56
Parliament Buildings
(Barbados), 114
Parque Colón, 290, 291–292
Parque de Bombas
(museum), 466
Parque de los Tres Ojos, 293
Parque Independencia, 292,
295
Parque Zoológico Nacional,
291
Parrot Preserve, 207
Paseo de la Princesa, 460
Passports and visas, xxvii–
xxviii
Peace Hill, St. Croix, 775
Peace Memorial Building,
202
Pearls Airport, 322
Pedro's Castle, 204
Père Labat (distillery), 357
**Peter Island, British Virgin
Islands**, 179–180, 184–
187
Petit-Bourg, Guadeloupe,
355
**Petite Anse de Galet, St.
Barthélemy**, 504
**Philipsburg, St. Martin/St.
Maarten**, 610
Pic du Paradis, 609
Pigeon Island, Guadeloupe,
355
Pigeon Island, St. Lucia,
580–581
Pine Cay, 700
Pine Grove (coffee farm),
391
Pissarro Building, 737
Pitons (twin peaks), 582
Plane travel, xii–xiv, 3
to Anguilla, 30
to Antigua, 57–58

to Aruba, 84
to Barbados, 118–119
to Bonaire, 144
to British Virgin Islands, 184, 185
to Cayman Islands, 209, 211
with children, xv–xvi
to Curaçao, 235
to Dominica, 260–261
to Dominican Republic, 296–297
to Grenada, 325–326
to the Grenadines, 648
to Guadeloupe, 357–358
to Jamaica, 399–400
luggage restrictions, xxvi–xxvii
to Martinique, 430
to Nevis, 551–553
to Puerto Rico, 467–468, 469
to Saba, 484
to St. Barthélemy, 505
to St. Eustatius, 518–519
to St. Kitts, 551–553
to St. Lucia, 583–584
to St. Martin/St. Maarten, 611
to St. Vincent, 648
scuba diving, xxi
to Trinidad and Tobago, 681–682
from the U.K., xii
to U.S. Virgin Islands, 775–776, 778
Plantations
Anguilla, 30
Antigua, 54
Barbados, 117, 118
Bonaire, 142
Curaçao, 234, 235
Grenada, 321–322, 323
the Grenadines, 641
Guadeloupe, 357
Jamaica, 391, 394, 396, 398
Martinique, 424
Puerto Rico, 467
St. Lucia, 579, 580, 582
Turks and Caicos, 701
U.S. Virgin Islands, 757–758, 759, 774, 775
Plaza de Armas, 460
Plaza de Colón, 460
Plaza de la Cultura, 292
Plaza Piar, 231–232
Plazuela de la Rogativa, 460
Point Udall, St. Croix, 757
Pointe-à-Pitre, Guadeloupe, 352
Pointe des Châteaux, Guadeloupe, 352
Pointe du Bout, Martinique, 427
Pointe-Noire, Guadeloupe, 355
Polo
Barbados, 108
Dominican Republic, 284
Ponce, Puerto Rico, 466–467
Ponce History Museum, 466

Popular Arts and Crafts Center, 460
Port Antonio, Jamaica, 378–379, 385, 397–398
Port Elizabeth, 641
Port Louis, Guadeloupe, 353
Port-of-Spain, Trinidad, 667–668
Port Royal, Jamaica, 398
Porta Coeli (church), 467
Porte d'Enfer (Gate of Hell), 352
Portsmouth, Dominica, 259
Post Office Building, St. Croix, 756
Presqu'ile du Caravelle, Martinique, 424, 428
Prince Rupert Bay, Dominica, 259
Princess Royal Hospital, 325
Project Sisserou (protected site), 260
Prospect Plantation, 396
Providenciales, Turks and Caicos, 694–700
Puerta de la Misericordia (Gate of Mercy), 292
Puerto Plata, Dominican Republic, 295
Puerto Rico, 3, 6, 7, 8, 434–472
children, attractions for, 460, 462, 463–464
electricity, 468
emergencies, 468
festivals, 468–469
guided tours, 470–471
language, 471
lodging, 435–436, 438–441, 445–446
money matters, 471
nightlife and the arts, 456–458
opening and closing times, 471
passports, 471–472
precautions, 472
restaurants, 446–455
shopping, 455–456
sightseeing, 458–467
telephones and mail, 472
transportation, 467–468, 469–470
visitor information, 472
Punta Cana, Dominican Republic, 272–273
Pusser's Landing, 167

Q

Queen Elizabeth II Botanic Park, 204
Queen Emma Bridge, 232
Queen Juliana Bridge, 232
Queen's Park, 114
Queen's Park Savannah, 668
Queen's View, 204
The Quill (volcanic cone), 518

R

RMS Rhone, 167–168
Rabacca Dry River (gulch), 632
Ragged Point Lighthouse, 117
Ravine Chaude, Guadeloupe, 355
Red Hook, St. Thomas, 740–741
Redcliffe Quay, 57
Reef Bay Plantation, 775
Reef Bay Trail, 775
Rendezvous Bay, Anguilla, 22–23
Restaurants, 12
Anguilla, 21–25
Antigua, 44–48, 57
Aruba, 70–74
Barbados, 99–103
Bonaire, 131–134
British Virgin Islands, 158–161, 172–174, 178–179, 180, 181–182, 183
Cayman Islands, 195–197
Curaçao, 221–224
Dominica, 248–251
Dominican Republic, 276–281
Grenada, 311–315
the Grenadines, 636–638, 641–643, 644–645, 646–647
Guadeloupe, 341–346
Jamaica, 380–384
Martinique, 414–419
Nevis, 543–546
Puerto Rico, 446–452
Saba, 478–480
St. Barthélemy, 495–499
St. Eustatius, 514–515
St. Kitts, 529–532
St. Lucia, 567–571
St. Martin/St. Maarten, 598–603
St. Vincent, 624–625
Trinidad and Tobago, 660–662, 674–677
Turks and Caicos, 688–689, 696–697
U.S. Virgin Islands, 720–724, 748–750, 766–768
Rincon, Bonaire, 143
Rincón, Puerto Rico, 467
Río Camuy Cave Park, 467
Rio Grande, Jamaica, 398
River Antoine Rum Distillery, 323
Rivière Madame, 425–426
Road Town, British Virgin Islands, 152–153, 156–160, 168
Rock formations, Aruba, 83
Rockfort Mineral Baths, 393
Rodney Bay, St. Lucia, 581
Romney Manor, 537–538
Roosevelt Park, 737–738
Rose Hall (great house), 394
Roseau, Dominica, 259–260

Route de la Traversèe, *354–*
355

Royal Botanical Gardens at
Hope, Jamaica, *393*

Rugby
Barbados, 109
Cayman Islands, 200

Rum Factory and Heritage
Park, *118*

Runaway Bay, Jamaica, *379–*
380

Running
Cayman Islands, 200
Curaçao, 226
Grenada, 317

S

Saba, *7, 473–486*
electricity, 484
emergencies, 484–485
festivals and seasonal events,
485
guided tours, 485
language, 485
lodging, 474–475, 478
money matters, 485–486
nightlife, 482
opening and closing times, 486
outdoor activities and sports,
481
passports, 486
precautions, 486
restaurants, 478–480
shopping, 481–482
sightseeing, 482–484
telephones and mail, 486
transportation, 484, 485
visitor information, 486

Saba Bank (fishing
grounds), *483*

Saba Marine Park, *483*

Saba Museum, *484*

Sacred Heart University, *462*

Sage Mountain National
Park, *168*

Sailing, *8.* ☞ Also Boating
Anguilla, 26
Antigua, 58
British Virgin Islands, 163,
175
Curaçao, 225
Dominica, 251
Grenada, 315–316
the Grenadines, 638–639,
647–648
Guadeloupe, 347
Martinique, 420
Puerto Rico, 452–453
St. Barthélemy, 500
St. Lucia, 571–572
St. Martin/St. Maarten, 604
St. Vincent, 626
school tours, xxx
Turks and Caicos, 697–698
U.S. Virgin Islands, 724–725,
752, 769

Sailing Week, *58*

St. Andrew's Presbyterian
Church, *324*

St. Barthélemy, *7, 487–508*
beaches, 499–500
emergencies, 505
festivals, 506
guided tours, 507
language, 507
lodging, 488–489, 492–495
money matters, 507
nightlife, 502–503
opening and closing times,
507–508
outdoor activities and sports,
500–501
passports, 508
precautions, 508
restaurants, 495–499
shopping, 501–502
sightseeing, 503–505
telephones and mail, 508
transportation, 505, 506–507
visitor information, 508

St-Claude, Guadeloupe, *355*

St. Croix, *741, 744–760,*
775–785. ☞ U.S. Virgin
Islands

St. Croix Aquarium, *756–*
757

St. Croix Leap, *758*

St. Eustatius, *7, 509–520*
beaches, 515–516
electricity, 519
emergencies, 519
festivals and seasonal events,
519
guided tours, 519
language, 519
lodging, 510–511, 514
money matters, 519–520
opening and closing times, 520
outdoor activities and sports,
516–517
passports, 520
precautions, 520
restaurants, 514–515
sightseeing, 517–518
telephones and mail, 520
transportation, 518–519
visitor information, 520

St. Eustatius Historical
Foundation Museum, *518*

St-François, Guadeloupe,
353

St. George Village Botanical
Gardens, *759*

St. George's, Grenada, *323–*
325

St. George's Anglican Church
(Grenada), *324*

St. George's Anglican Church
(St. Kitts), *537*

St. George's Cathedral (St.
Vincent), *631*

St. George's Harbour, *323*

St. George's Methodist
Church (Grenada), *324*

St. George's Roman Catholic
Church (Grenada), *324*

St. George's University
Medical School, *322*

St. Giles Islands, Tobago,
680–681

St. James cathedral, Jamaica,
398–399

St-Jean, St. Barthélemy, *504–*
505

St. John, *760–785.* ☞ Also
U.S. Virgin Islands

St. John's, Antigua, *56–57*

St. John's Church (Nevis),
551

St. Kitts, *7, 521–523, 526–*
538, 551–555

St-Louis Cathedral, *425*

St. Lucia, *6, 7, 556–588*
beaches, 571
children, activities for, 579,
580–581, 582, 583
language, 587
lodging, 538–539, 562–567
money matters, 587
nightlife and the arts, 577–578
opening and closing times,
587
outdoor activities and sports,
571–574
passports, 587
precautions, 588
restaurants, 567–571
shopping, 574–576
sightseeing, 578–583
telephones and mail, 588
transportation, 583
visitor information, 588

St. Lucia National Rain
Forest, *582–583*

St. Martin/St. Maarten, *6, 7,*
588–615
beaches, 603–604
electricity, 612
emergencies, 612
festivals, 612
guided tours, 613
language, 613
lodging, 590–591, 594–598
money matters, 613–614
nightlife and the arts, 608–609
opening and closing times, 614
outdoor activities and sports,
604–606
passports, 614
restaurants, 598–603
sightseeing, 609–611
shopping, 606–608
telephones and mail, 614–615
transportation, 611–613
visitor information, 615

St. Martin Museum, *610*

St. Mary's Cathedral of the
Assumption, *631*

St. Michael's Cathedral, *114*

St. Nicholas Abbey (great
house), *116*

St. Patrick's Church, *759*

St. Paul's Church, *55*

St. Paul's Anglican Church,
759

St. Peter Church, *398*

St. Peter's Church, *56*

St-Pierre, Martinique, *418*,
428–429
St. Thomas, *711–741*, *775–
785*. ☞ Also U.S. Virgin
Islands
St. Thomas Anglican Church
(Nevis), *551*
St. Vincent, *616–619*, *622–
632*, *648–653*
Ste-Anne, Guadeloupe, *353*
Ste-Anne, Martinique, *410–
411*, *417–418*, *428*
Ste-Luce, Martinique, *418*
Ste-Marie, Martinique, *428*
Ste-Rose, Guadeloupe, *355–
356*
Salina Mathijs (salt pad),
143
Salt Cay, *693*
Salt flats, *141*
Salt River Bay National
Historical Park and
Ecological Preserve, *758*
Salt River Marina, *758*
Sam Lord's Castle, *118*
Samaná, Dominican Republic,
274–276, *278–279*, *295–
296*
San Cristóbal (fortress), *460*
San Germán, Puerto Rico,
467
San José Church, *460–461*
San Juan, Puerto Rico, *438–
440*, *461–462*
San Juan Cathedral, *461*
San Juan Central Municipal
Park, *462*
San Juan Museum of Art and
History, *461*
San Nicolas, Aruba, *83–84*
San Pedro de Macorís,
Dominican Republic, *293*
Sandy Ground, Anguilla, *22–
23*, *30*
Sandy Island, Anguilla, *30*
Sandy Island, Grenada, *325*
Sandy Point, Turks and
Caicos, *701*
Sandy Point Beach, St. Croix,
760
Sandy Point Town, St. Kitts,
538
Santiago de los Caballeros,
Dominican Republic, *294*
Santo Cerro (Holy Mount),
294
Santo Domingo, Dominican
Republic, *274–276*, *279–
281*, *287–288*, *290–292*
Santurce, Puerto Rico, *462*
Sari Sari Falls, *258*
Saut Babin (waterfall), *423*
Savan, St. Thomas, *738*
Scale House, *757*
Scarborough, Tobago, *681*
Scharloo, Curaçao, *232*
Schoelcher, Martinique, *411–
412*, *429*
Scot's Kirk, *631*

Scuba diving, *8–9*
Anguilla, *26*
Antigua, *50*
Aruba, *76–77*
Barbados, *106–107*
Bonaire, *135–137*
British Virgin Islands, *163*,
167–168, *175*
Cayman Islands, *198–199*,
206, *209*
Curaçao, *226*
Dominica, *252*
Dominican Republic, *283*
and flying, *xxi*
Grenada, *317*
the Grenadines, *639*, *642*,
643, *645–646*, *648*
Guadeloupe, *347–348*
Jamaica, *387*
Martinique, *420*
Nevis, *547–548*
Puerto Rico, *454*
Saba, *481*
St. Barthélemy, *500*
St. Eustatius, *516*
St. Kitts, *534*
St. Lucia, *573*
St. Martin/St. Maarten, *605*
St. Vincent, *627*
Tobago, *679*
tours, *xxx*
Turks and Caicos, *692*, *693*,
698
U.S. Virgin Islands, *725–726*,
752, *770*
Sea Excursions
Anguilla, *26–27*
Barbados, *107*
Guadeloupe, *348*
Martinique, *421*
St. Lucia, *573–574*
St. Martin/St. Maarten, *606*
Turks and Caicos, *698*
U.S. Virgin Islands, *726*
Sea kayaking, *137*, *726*,
770
Sendall Tunnel, *324*
Senior citizens, tips for,
xxviii
Senior Curaçao Liqueur
Distillery, *235*
Seroe Colorado, Aruba, *84*
Seroe Largu, Bonaire, *143*
Seven Arches Museum, *738*
Shaw Park Botanical
Gardens, *396–397*
Shipwrecks, *167–168*
Shirley Heights, Antigua, *57*
Shopping
Anguilla, *27–28*
Antigua, *51–53*, *56–57*
Aruba, *77–79*
Barbados, *109–111*
Bonaire, *138–139*
British Virgin Islands, *164–
165*, *175–176*, *182*
Cayman Islands, *200–201*
Curaçao, *227–229*
Dominica, *253–254*

Dominican Republic, *284–286*
Grenada, *318–319*
the Grenadines, *639–640*
Guadeloupe, *348–350*
Jamaica, *387–389*
Martinique, *421–422*
Nevis, *548–549*
Puerto Rico, *455–456*
Saba, *481–482*
St. Barthélemy, *501–502*
St. Kitts, *534–535*
St. Lucia, *574–576*
St. Martin/St. Maarten, *606–
608*
St. Vincent, *627–628*
Trinidad and Tobago, *664–
665*, *679–680*
Turks and Caicos, *699*
U.S. Virgin Islands, *727–732*,
752–755, *770–773*
Sint Maarten Museum, *610*
Six Men's Bay, Barbados,
116
Skyworld, *168*
Slave huts, *141*
Snorkeling, *9*
Aruba, *76–77*
Barbados, *106–107*
Bonaire, *137–138*
British Virgin Islands, *163*,
167–168, *175*
Cayman Islands, *198–199*,
206, *209*
Curaçao, *226*
Dominica, *252*
Grenada, *317*
the Grenadines, *639*, *642*,
643, *645–646*, *648*
Guadeloupe, *348*
Jamaica, *387*
Montserrat, *421*
Nevis, *547–548*
Puerto Rico, *454*
Saba, *481*
St. Eustatius, *516*
St. Kitts, *534*
St. Lucia, *573*
St. Martin/St. Maarten, *605*
St. Vincent, *627*
Tobago, *679*
Turks and Caicos, *692*, *693*,
698
U.S. Virgin Islands, *725–726*,
752, *770*
Soccer
Barbados, *109*
Cayman Islands, *200*
Curaçao, *227*
St. Eustatius, *516–517*
St. Lucia, *574*
Softball, *164*
Somerset Falls, *398*
Sosua, Dominican Republic,
296
Soufrière, Dominica, *260*
Soufrière, St. Lucia, *565–
567*, *581–583*
South Hill, Anguilla, *22*
Southern Caribbean, *6*

Spa tours, *xxx*
Spanish Town, British Virgin Islands, *177–178*
Spanish Town, Jamaica, *398–399*
Spelunking, *207*
Speyside, Tobago, *681*
Sports Centers, Martinique, *421*
Spring Plantation, *641*
Squash
Barbados, 107–108
Martinique, 421
St. Lucia, 574
Stargazing, *726*
Steeple Building, *757*
Student travel, *xxviii*
Submarine rides
Barbados, 107
Cayman Islands, 199
U.S. Virgin Islands, 726
Sucker Garden Road, *611*
Sulfur springs
Dominica, 258
St. Lucia, 581
Sun Valley (plantation), *397*
Sunbury Plantation House & Museum, *118*
Surfing
Barbados, 107
Puerto Rico, 454
Swimming, *253*
Synagogue of Beracha Veshalom Vegmiluth Hasidim, *738*
Synagogues
Barbados, 113
Curaçao, 231
St. Eustatius, 518
U.S. Virgin Islands, 738
Syndicate Nature Trail, *260*

T

Tapia Theater, *461*
Teatro Nacional, *292*
Telephones, *xxviii, 3*
Tennis
Anguilla, 27
Antigua, 50, 58
Aruba, 77
Barbados, 107–108
Bonaire, 138
British Virgin Islands, 163
Cayman Islands, 199
Curaçao, 227
Dominican Republic, 283
Grenada, 317
Guadeloupe, 348
Jamaica, 387
Martinique, 421
Nevis, 548
Puerto Rico, 450–451
St. Barthélemy, 501
St. Eustatius, 516
St. Kitts, 534
St. Lucia, 574
St. Martin/St. Maarten, 606
Trinidad and Tobago, 663, 679

Turks and Caicos, *692, 698*
U.S. Virgin Islands, 726, 752, 770
Terre-de-Haute, Guadeloupe, *356–357*
Terres Basses, St. Martin/ St. Maarten, *611*
Tetelo Vargas Stadium, *293*
Theater. ☞ Nightlife and the arts
Théâtre Nationale, *353*
Theme trips, *xxx–xxxi*
Tibes Indian Ceremonial Center (cemetery), *467*
Tillett Gardens, *741*
Time-shares. ☞ Condominiums
TiTrou Gorge, *258*
Tobago. ☞ Trinidad and Tobago
Toiny coast, *505*
Tomb of the Carib Islands, *427*
Torre del Homenaje (Tower of Homage), *292*
Tortola, *152–153, 156–168, 184–187.* ☞ Also British Virgin Islands
Tortola Wharf, *738*
Tour operators, *xxviii–xxxi*
disability and accessibility, xix–xx
for gay and lesbian travelers, xxii
for group tours, xvi, xxix– xxx
packages, xxx
theme trips, xxx–xxxi
Trafalgar Falls, *258*
Trafalgar Square, Barbados, *115*
Trans-World Radio, *141*
Travel agencies, *xxix*
disabilities and accessibility, xix–xx
for gay and lesbian travelers, xxii–xxiii
for students, xxviii
Travel gear, *xxxi*
Traveler's checks, *xxvi*
Trinidad and Tobago, *6, 7, 654–685*
beaches, 662–663, 677–678
electricity, 682
emergencies, 682
festivals and seasonal events, 682
guided tours, 683–684
language, 684
lodging, 655, 658–660, 669, 672–674
money matters, 684
nightlife and the arts, 665– 666, 680
opening and closing times, 684
outdoor activities and sports, 663, 678–679
passports, 684
precautions, 684

restaurants, 660–662, 674– 677
shopping, 664–665, 679–670
sightseeing, 666–669, 680– 681
telephones and mail, 685
transportation, 681–683
visitor information, 685
Tunnel of Love (Aruba), *82*
Turks and Caicos Islands, *6, 686–705*
beaches, 689, 693, 697, 701
lodging, 687–688, 693, 694– 696, 700–701, 705
nightlife, 692, 699
outdoor activities and sports, 689, 692, 693, 697–699
restaurants, 688–689, 696– 697
sightseeing, 692–693, 694, 699–700, 701
telephones and mail, 705
visitor information, 705
Turks & Caicos National Museum, *692–693*
Turtle Farm, *203*
Tyrol Cot Heritage Village, *118*
Tyrrel Bay, Grenada, *325*

U

Union Island, the Grenadines, *647–648*
U.K., tips for travelers from, *xviii, xxiv, xxvi, xxviii*
U.S. Government travel information, *xxxi*
U.S. Post Office (St. Thomas), *738*
U.S. Virgin Islands, *706–785*
beaches, 724, 750–751, 768– 769
children, attractions for, 736, 737–738, 739–740, 756– 757, 759
electricity, 776
emergencies, 776–777
festivals, 777–778
guided tours, 781–783
language, 783
lodging, 712–713, 716–719, 741, 744–748, 761, 764– 766
money matters, 783
nightlife and the arts, 732– 733, 755, 773
opening and closing times, 783–784
outdoor activities and sports, 724–727, 751–752, 769– 770
passports, 784
precautions, 784
restaurants, 720–724, 748– 750, 766–768
shopping, 727–732, 752–755, 770–773
sightseeing, 733–734, 736– 741, 755–760, 773–775